The tree diagram shows the structure:

- 1. Strategy
  - Introduction
  - Strate-gizing
  - Missioning and Visioning
- 2. Strategy Content
  - Business Level Strategy
  - Corporate Level Strategy
  - Network Level Strategy
- 3. Strategy Process
  - Strategy Formation
  - Strategic Change
  - Strategic Innovation
- 4. Strategy Context
  - Industry Context
  - Organizational Context
  - International Context

STRATEGY

AN INTERNATIONAL PERSPECTIVE

*To Pam and Liz
and
Leen and Anneke
Family matters*

STRATEGY

AN INTERNATIONAL PERSPECTIVE

The first four editions of *Strategy: Process, Content and Context* were co-authored by Bob de Wit and Ron Meyer. The fifth edition was adapted by Bob de Wit.

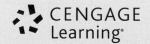

CENGAGE
Learning®

Australia • Brazil • Japan • Korea • Mexico • Singapore • Spain • United Kingdom • United States

**Strategy: An International Perspective,
5th Edition
Bob de Wit and Ron Meyer**

Publisher: Andrew Ashwin

Commissioning Editor: Annabel Ainscow

Senior Production Editor: Alison Burt

Senior Manufacturing Buyer: Eyvett Davis

Typesetter: MPS Limited

Cover design: Jeroen Brinkhuis

For product information and technology assistance,
contact: **emea.info@cengage.com**.
For permission to use material from this text or product,
and for permission queries,
email **emea.permissions@cengage.com**.

British Library Cataloguing-in-Publication Data
A catalogue record for this book is available from the British Library.

ISBN: 978-1-4080-8267-6

Cengage Learning EMEA
Cheriton House, North Way, Andover, Hampshire SP10 5BE
United Kingdom.

Cengage Learning products are represented in Canada by Nelson Education Ltd.

For your lifelong learning solutions, visit
www.cengage.co.uk.

Purchase your next print book, e-book or e-chapter at
www.cengagebrain.com.

Printed in Singapore by Seng Lee Press
1 2 3 4 5 6 7 8 9 10 – 16 15 14

BRIEF CONTENTS

CONTENTS

SECTION

ii

SECTION

V

CASES

LIST OF EXHIBITS

ACKNOWLEDGEMENTS

When coincidences pile up in this way, one cannot help being impressed by them – for the greater the number of terms in such a series, or the more unusual its character, the more improbable it becomes

Carl Jung (1875–1961) Swiss psychotherapist, psychiatrist and founder of analytical psychology

This book started in the early 1990s when I was a junior professor at the Rotterdam School of Management, Erasmus University in The Netherlands. Being unhappy with the available strategy texts, I developed a proposal for a new international and more academically rigorous educational book. I invited my 'academic buddy' Gep Eisenloeffel, with whom I successfully delivered a number of strategy courses, to become the co-author. Unfortunately for me, Gep had decided to build a sailing yacht and a few months later he departed for a two-year sailing trip around the world. Our lives took different directions.

As a member of a large strategy department with several young and brilliant colleagues, I was lucky to find another colleague to pick up the strategy text project: Ron Meyer. Although Ron and I had different personalities, we worked together for several years on the book. We shared the fruits of our successful book, and we started a strategy consulting firm: *Strategy Works*. Working together with Ron, a native English speaker as he partly grew up in Canada, has been a success. It was great to work with him, often until the deep of the night, and our differences in personality appeared to bring new insights and innovative ideas. Ron's work and commitment has therefore been a significant factor in the success of our book to date.

My old academic buddy, Gep Eisenloeffel, contacted me, inviting me to teach a strategy course in his *minor* 'International Strategy and Culture' at Leyden University. After returning from his sailing adventure, Gep had specialized in intercultural management and got an academic position at the Faculty of Humanity Studies of Leyden University in the Netherlands. His objective with the 'International Management and Intercultural Management' programme was to bridge the strategy field and intercultural management studies. The programme became the first phase of a renewed cooperation with Gep, and I invited him to contribute in developing the fifth edition. I am grateful that he accepted the invitation, and it was great to work with Gep again. His enormous knowledge on many scientific areas, including but not limited to international cultures, has been a great help. I appreciate his inputs, his commitment and our discussions.

Call it coincidence, luck or synchronicity – a term introduced by Carl Jung as 'an acausal connecting principle' – there was a seamless fit between Gep's areas of expertise and one of my objectives for the fifth edition. The international perspective has always been a major distinctive feature of the earlier editions, but I wanted to achieve the next level. With a fast changing economic and political power balance in the world from the North-West to the South-East, and an increased importance of countries such as China, India, Brazil, Russia, South Africa and Turkey, a major objective was to bridge Western and Eastern thinking on strategy. I wanted to go beyond exporting Western knowledge to other parts of the world. Interestingly and surprisingly, while doing research on Eastern thinking, I found that the main philosophy in the book was well recognized in the East.

Although the term paradox stems from ancient Greek philosophers, viewing strategy issues as paradoxes is not only applicable in the West. On the contrary, mainstream Eastern thinking appeared to be close to the philosophy of the book. I do accept that it is hard, if not impossible, to fully understand the rich pool of Eastern knowledge that had been developed over thousands of years, but I made a serious effort. I read everything I could find in either of the languages that I master, visited many countries to discuss the book with colleagues, and tested my ideas. This fifth edition reflects the new insights, and I hope that readers agree that this is the first truly international strategy text, bridging West and East, North and South, with readings, cases, quotes and insights from around the globe.

This fifth edition brings together the work of great people in the management field – chiefly from the field of strategy. I thank them for creating new knowledge and insights, for their inspiration and hard work, and for developing the management field to where it is today. Writing this book would not have been possible without the current academic knowledge base and the writers of many phenomenal papers. I also apologize for not including all excellent contributions in the book. As the architect of this edition I read many excellent papers, but since there is a limitation to a book's size I could select only a few. It was simply not possible to include all the great papers and, therefore, several tough and (sometimes) personal choices had to be made.

I would like to thank the professors who select the book as the basis of class discussions, to help students develop their strategic mind. As in each revised edition, many improvements in this fifth edition are based on the feedback of professors who have used previous editions in their classrooms. I am grateful for their valuable insights, and for sharing their experiences. Many thanks also to other academic colleagues: the anonymous reviewers of the manuscript and Paul Knott, who has been so kind to update his great Fonterra short case.

Developing the fifth edition has been an enormous effort of many people. I greatly appreciate the commitment to my mission of my *Strategy Works* team members, and particularly (in alphabetical order) Jeroen Brinkhuis, Marcel van Gils, Desiree Kradolfer and Roel Meijers. Jeroen especially deserves my gratitude, as he was not only supportive in several activities in the book development process, but also co-developed two short cases and illustrations, and helped develop the navigation tool *Tree of Strategy.* Many thanks also for my research associates Larissa Kalle, who has spent lots of time reading and pre-selecting the growing number of publications and cases in the strategy field, and Wester Wagenaar, Jasper de Vries, Jeremy Slingerland and Adriaan de Bruijn, as they have co-developed short cases and illustrations. Without their generosity this fifth edition would not have been possible. I am proud and grateful to be a member of this tremendous team.

Not only did I cooperate with my academic buddy of early years, new colleagues also contributed. After having accepted a position at Nyenrode Business University, the only private university in the Netherlands – residing on a 56 acres estate with modern facilities and a 13th century castle – I gradually realized I had made one of the best decisions in my academic career. The facilities are unique and picturesque, and the academic environment is stimulating. I would like to thank all of my colleagues, including management, support staff and faculty, and particularly my strategy department colleagues (in alphabetical order) Claudia Janssen, Richard Janssen, Fred Lachotski, Annemieke Roobeek and Jeroen van der Velden.

I would also like to thank the Cengage Learning team I worked with. Particularly, I thank Linden Harris and Andrew Ashwin for trusting me to develop the new editions and for creating the business context, and Annabel Ainscow for doing an incredible job in managing this great project. Also I do not forget the man who got us started twenty years ago, our first editor, David Godden. Thank you all.

Finally I would like to thank my family: my wife Pamela, my daughter Liz, my father Leen and his partner Anneke. Thank you so much.

AUTHOR BIOGRAPHY:

Bob de Wit is Professor of Strategic Leadership at Nyenrode Business University, The Netherlands. He is also founder and director of Strategy Works and Strategy Academy in Rotterdam. Bob is a member of the *Journal of Change Management* Advisory Board, and a reviewer for the Strategic Management Society conference. His mission is to combine academic rigour and practical relevance.

Bob holds a bachelor's degree in Psychology from Utrecht University, an MBA at the Interdisciplinary Institute Bedrijfskunde in Delft, and a PhD degree in Management Science from Erasmus University Rotterdam. After graduation he became a professor in strategic management at the Rotterdam School of Management, Erasmus University, teaching strategy in MSc programmes and the international MBA programme. In 1996 he started working at the Maastricht School of Management, a market leader in management education in non-Western countries. Since then, Bob has taught in over 40 countries on all continents. Bob has served as the Chairman of the Interest Group 'The Practice of Strategy' of the Strategic Management Society, and the Dutch Society for Strategic Decision Making (VSB), and has been a member of the Academic Council of the *Ecole Nationale des Ponts et Chaussees* in Paris.

Bob passionately loves his wife Pamela and daughter Liz.

Ron Meyer is Professor of Corporate Strategy at TiasNimbas Business School, Tilburg University in The Netherlands and Managing Director of the Center for Strategy and Leadership.

PREFACE

Not only is there an art in knowing a thing,
but also a certain art in teaching it.

Cicero (106–43 B.C.) Roman orator and statesman

What is a good strategy for teaching and learning about the topic of strategy? Judging by the similarity of the strategic management textbooks currently available, there seems to be a general consensus among business professors on the best approach to this task. It is not an exaggeration to say that strategic management education is dominated by a strong *industry recipe* (Spender, 1989). Almost all textbooks share the following characteristics:

■ *Few differing perspectives.* Only a limited number of perspectives and theories are presented, often as accepted knowledge, from which prescriptions can easily be derived;

■ *Step-by-step structure.* A step-by-step strategic planning approach is used as the books' basic structure, to decompose strategy-making into a number of simple sequential activities;

■ *No primary material.* The key academic articles and books on strategy are reworked into the textbook authors' own words to create consistent and easily digestible pieces of text;

■ *Domestic orientation.* Despite fancy subtitles referring to globalization, the choice of perspectives, theories, examples and cases are heavily biased towards the textbook authors' own domestic context.

It is interesting to speculate on the causes of this isomorphism in the 'strategic management education' industry. Institutionalists would probably point to the need for legitimacy, which leads textbook authors to conform to widely accepted practices and to avoid major innovations (e.g. Abrahamson, 1996; Powell and DiMaggio, 1991). Social psychologists would likely suggest that over the years shared cognitive structures have developed within the strategic management community, which makes the prevailing educational paradigm difficult to challenge (e.g. Smircich and Stubbart, 1985, Walsh, 1995). Theorists taking a new institutional economics perspective would probably interpret the uniformity of strategic management textbooks as a form of lock-in, caused by the large investments already made by publishers and business professors based on a shared educational 'standard' (e.g. Arthur, 1996; David, 1994). Whatever the reason, it is striking that the character of strategic management textbooks has not significantly changed since the founding of the field.

But what would strategy education look like if educational orthodoxy would be actively challenged and the industry rules were broken? How might strategy be taught if the current constraints were thrown aside and the teaching process was boldly reinvented? In short, what would happen if some strategic thinking were applied to the teaching of strategy?

During the last fifteen years, we have continuously asked ourselves these questions. Our conclusion is that all four of the above features of current strategic management textbooks greatly inhibit the development of independent strategic thinkers and therefore urgently need to be changed. It is for this reason that we decided to create a book ourselves, with the following characteristics:

■ *Multiple strategy perspectives.* A broad range of differing, and often opposite perspectives and theories, are presented, reflecting the richness of current debate among academics and practitioners in the field of strategic management;

■ *Issue-based structure.* An issue-based book structure is used, with each chapter focusing on a key strategic issue, which is discussed from a variety of angles, leaving readers to draw their own conclusions;

■ *Original readings.* A large number of original articles and book chapters are included, to offer readers a first hand account of the ideas and theories of influential strategy thinkers;

■ *International orientation.* A strong international orientation is at the core of this book, as reflected in the choice of topics, theories, readings, examples and cases.

In the following paragraphs the rationale behind the choice for these characteristics is explained. Following this discussion, the structure of the book and the ways in which it can be employed is further clarified.

USING MULTIPLE STRATEGY PERSPECTIVES

Learning without thought is labor lost; thought without learning is perilous

Confucius (551–479 BC) Chinese teacher, editor, politician and philosopher

What should students learn in a strategic management or business policy course? It seems an obvious question to start with, especially for professors who teach about objective setting. Yet, in practice, the large majority of strategic management textbooks do not make their teaching objectives explicit. These books implicitly assume that the type of teaching objectives and teaching methods needed for a strategic management course do not radically differ from any other subject – basically, strategy can be taught in the same way as accounting or baking cookies. Their approach is based on the following teaching objectives:

■ *Knowledge.* To get the student to clearly understand and memorize all of the major "ingredients";

■ *Skills.* To develop the student's ability to follow the detailed "recipes";

■ *Attitude.* To instill a disciplined frame of mind, whereby the student automatically attempts to approach all issues by following established procedures.

This is an important way of teaching – it is how all of us were taught to read and write, do arithmetic and drive a car. This type of teaching can be referred to as *instructional,* because students are told what to know and do. The instructor is the authority who has all of the necessary knowledge and skills, and it is his/her role to transfer these to the students. Thus, the educational emphasis is on communicating know-how and ensuring that students are able to repeat what they have heard. Students are not encouraged to question the knowledge they receive – on the contrary, it is the intention of instructional teaching to get students to absorb an accepted body of knowledge and to follow established recipes. The student should *accept, absorb* and *apply.*

However, while instructing students on a subject and programming their behaviour that might be useful in such areas as mathematics, cooking and karate, we believe it is not a very good way of teaching strategy. In our opinion, a strategic management professor should have a different set of teaching objectives:

- *Knowledge.* To encourage the understanding of the many, often conflicting, schools of thought and to facilitate developing insight into the assumptions, possibilities and limitations of each set of theories;
- *Skills.* To develop the student's ability to define strategic issues, to critically reflect on existing theories, to creatively combine or develop conceptual models where necessary and to flexibly employ theories where useful;
- *Attitude.* To instill a critical, analytical, flexible and creative mindset that challenges organizational, industry and national paradigms and problem-solving recipes.

In other words, strategy professors should want to achieve the opposite of instructors – not to instill recipes, but rather to encourage students to dissect and challenge recipes. Strategic thinking is in its very essence questioning, challenging, unconventional and innovative. These aspects of strategic thinking cannot be transferred through instruction. A critical, analytical, flexible and creative state of mind must be developed by practising these very qualities. Hence, a learning situation must encourage students to be critical, must challenge them to be analytical, must force them to be mentally flexible and must demand creativity and unconventional thinking. Students cannot be instructed to be strategists, but must learn the art of strategy by thinking and acting themselves – they must *discuss, deliberate* and *do*. The role of the professor is to create the circumstances for this learning. We therefore refer to this type of teaching as *facilitative*.

This teaching philosophy has led to a radical departure from traditional textbooks that focus on knowledge transfer and application skills, and that have often been written from the perspective of just one paradigm. In this book, the fundamental differences of opinion within strategic management are not ignored or smoothed over. On the contrary, an important objective of this book is to expose students to the many, often opposite, perspectives in the field of strategy. It is our experience that the challenge of comparing and reconciling rivalling strategy perspectives sharpens the mind of the 'apprentice' strategists. Throwing students into the midst of the central strategy debates, while simultaneously demanding that they apply their thinking to practical strategic problems, is the most likely way to enhance the qualities of creativity, flexibility, independence and analytical depth that students will need to become true strategic thinkers.

FOCUSING ON STRATEGY ISSUES

Some people are so good at learning the tricks of the trade that they never get to learn the trade.

Sam Levenson (1911–1980) American teacher and comedian

While it is the objective of this book to increase students' strategic thinking abilities by exposing them to a wide range of theories and perspectives, it is not the intention to confuse and disorient. Yet in a subject area like strategic management, in which there is a broad spectrum of different views, there is a realistic threat that students might go deaf listening to the cacophony of different opinions. The variety of ideas can easily become overwhelming and difficult to integrate.

For this reason, the many theories, models, approaches and perspectives have been clustered around eleven central strategy issues, each of which is discussed in a separate chapter. These eleven strategy issues represent the key questions with which strategists must deal in practice. Only the theorists whose ideas have a direct bearing on the issue at hand are discussed in each chapter.

The advantage of this issue-based book structure is that it is *decision-oriented* – each chapter is about a key type of strategic decision that needs to be made. Students are challenged to look at a strategic issue holistically, taking various aspects and perspectives into account, and to arrive at a proposed course of action. This type of decision-focus closely reflects what strategizing managers need to do in practice. Step-by-step books are much more *tool-oriented*, teaching students how to go through each phase of a strategic planning process and how to use each analysis framework – useful, especially for junior analysts, but unlikely to stimulate real strategic thinking and to provide insight into difficult strategic choices.

Within each chapter, the opposing perspectives on how the strategic issue should be approached are contrasted with one another by staging a virtual 'debate'. Two opposite perspectives are presented to kick off the debate and highlight areas of disagreement, after which the students (and their professors) are invited to further debate the issue and decide on the value and limitations of each point of view.

The advantage of this debate-based chapter structure is that it encourages the students' engagement and that it provokes critical thinking. As students need to determine the strengths and weaknesses of each strategy perspective, they also become more adept at combining different 'lenses' to gain a fuller understanding of a problem, while becoming more skilled at balancing and mixing prescriptions to find innovative solutions to these problems. Some students will feel ill at ease not being presented the 'right approach' or the 'best practice', as they are used to getting in many other books. This is all the more reason to avoid giving them one – as strategizing managers the security of one truth won't get them far, so it is preferable to learn to deal with (and benefit from) a variety of opinions as soon as possible.

While the intention is not to present the 'right answer' or provide a 'grand unifying theory', the chapter offers a third view on the issue that combines element of both perspectives. Not only leaders take elements of both perspectives into accounts to manage the issue at hand, increasingly also strategy theorists do. Recent works of thought leaders in the strategy field address a third way of dealing with the issue, not by choosing one of the opposite perspectives, but by providing possible routes on how to deal with opposites. This third view is meant to stimulate students' strategic thinking, to find innovative and creative resolutions to the problem, but still students must make up their own minds, depending on the context and based on the arguments placed before them.

TAKING AN INTERNATIONAL PERSPECTIVE

Be bent, and you will remain straight.
Be vacant, and you will remain full.
Be worn, and you will remain new.

Lao Tzu (6th century BC) – philosopher of ancient China

This book has been explicitly developed with an international audience in mind. For students, the international orientation of this book has a number of distinct advantages:

■ *Cross-cultural differences.* Although there has been relatively little cross-cultural research in the field of strategy, results so far indicate that there are significant differences in strategy styles between companies from different countries. This calls into question the habit among strategy researchers of presenting universal theories, without indicating the cultural assumptions on which their ideas have been based. It is not unlikely that strategy theories have a strong cultural bias and therefore cannot be simply transferred from one national setting to another. Much of the debate going on between strategy theorists might actually be based on such divergent cultural assumptions. In this book the issue of cross-cultural differences in strategy style is raised in each chapter, to discuss whether strategists need to adapt their theories, perspectives and approaches to the country in which they are operating.

- *International context.* Besides adapting to a specific country, many companies are operating in a variety of countries at the same time. In this international arena they are confronted with a distinct set of issues, ranging from global integration and co-ordination, to localization and transnationalization. This set of issues presented by the international context is debated in depth in Chapter 12.

- *International cases and illustrations.* To explore how the various strategy perspectives can be applied to different national contexts, it is imperative to have cases and illustrations from a wide variety of countries, spread around the world. In this book the 24 cases (12 long and 12 short cases) cover more than 20 countries and most of the cases have an international orientation. The 22 main illustrations have also been drawn from around the world. It must be noted, however, that we have had a bias towards well-known firms, as these examples are more recognizable to most audiences around the world.

USING ORIGINAL READINGS

Education is not filling a bucket but lighting a fire.

William Butler Yeats (1865–1939) Irish poet and dramatist

There are no better and livelier debates than when rivals put forward their own ideas as forcefully as they can. For this reason, we have chosen to structure the strategy debates by letting influential theorists speak for themselves. Instead of translating the important ideas of key writers into our own words, each chapter contains three original readings in which the theorists state their own case. These three readings can be viewed as the discussants in the debate, while our role is that of chairmen – we set the stage for the debate and introduce the various perspectives and 'speakers', but as conscientious chairmen we avoid taking a position in the debate ourselves.

The three readings in each chapter have been selected with a number of criteria in mind. As a starting point, we were looking for the articles or books that are widely judged to be classics in the field of strategy. However, to ensure the broad representation of different perspectives, we occasionally looked beyond established classics to find a challenging minority point of view. Finally, discussants are only as good as their ability to communicate to the non-initiated, and therefore we have sometimes excluded certain classics as too technical.

To keep the size of the book within acceptable limits, most readings have had to be reduced in length, while extensive footnotes and references have had to be dropped. At all times this editing has been guided by the principle that the author's key ideas and arguments must be preserved intact. To compensate for the loss of references in each article, a combined list of the most important references has been added to the end of each chapter.

CONTACT US

A stand can be made against invasion by an army; no stand can be made against invasion by an idea.

Victor Hugo (1802–1885) French poet, novelist and playwright

Books are old-fashioned, but based on a proven technology that is still the most appropriate under most circumstances. One drawback, however, is that a book is unidirectional, allowing us to send a message to you, but not capable of transmitting your comments, questions and suggestions back to us. This is unfortunate, as we are keen on communicating with our audience and enjoy hearing what works and doesn't work 'in the field'.

Therefore, we would like to encourage both students and professors to establish contact with us. You can do this by visiting our online support resources to check out the extra features we have for you and to leave your comments and suggestions. But you can also contact us directly by email at **b.dewit@strategy-academy.org**

REFERENCES

Abrahamson, E. (1996), Management Fashion, *Academy of Management Review,* Vol. 21, pp. 254–285.

Arthur, W.B. (1996), Increasing Returns and the New World of Business, *Harvard Business Review,* July/August, pp. 100–109.

David, P.A. (1994), Why are Institutions the 'Carriers of History'?: Path Dependence and the Evolution of Conventions, Organizations and Institutions, *Structural Change and Economic Dynamics,* pp. 205–220.

Powell, W.W. and DiMaggio, P.P. (Eds.) (1991), *The New Institutionalism in Organization Analysis,* Chicago: University of Chicago Press.

Smircich, L. and Stubbart, C. (1985), Strategic Management in an Enacted World, *Academy of Management Review,* Vol. 10, pp. 724–736.

Spender, J.C. (1989), *Industry Recipes: The Nature and Sources of Managerial Judgement,* Oxford: Basil Blackwell.

Walsh, J. (1995), Managerial and Organizational Cognition: Notes from a Trip Down Memory Lane, *Organization Science,* vol. 6, pp. 280–321.

DIGITAL SUPPORT RESOURCES

Dedicated Instructor Resources

To discover the dedicated instructor online support resources accompanying this textbook, instructors should register here for access:
http://login.cengage.com

Resources include:

- Instructor's Manual
- Testbank
- PowerPoint slides

Student resources

Students: to discover the dedicated student digital support resources accompanying this textbook, please search for *Strategy: An International Perspective Fifth Edition* on:
www.cengagebrain.co.uk

What kind of Strategist are you?

For the users of Bob de Wit's book we now offer an online assessment, the **Strategy Profiler**™. The **Strategy Profiler**™ is a validated tool that measures your strategy preferences on the dimensions in this book. The **Strategy Profiler**™ has been successfully used in leadership coaching, executive assessments and personal development for years, and is now available for you.

Do you want to know what kind of Strategist you are? Go to **www.strategy-works.com/cengage**, do the test and receive your personal **Strategy Profiler**™ report.

STRATEGY

INTRODUCTION

As conflict – difference – is here in the world, as we cannot avoid it, we should, I think, use it.

Mary Parker Follett (1868–1933), American social worker, management consultant and pioneer in organizational theory and organizational behaviour.

THE NATURE OF STRATEGY

In a book entitled *Strategy*, it seems reasonable to expect Chapter 1 to begin with a clear definition of strategy that would be employed with consistency in all subsequent chapters. An early and precise definition would help to avoid conflicting interpretations of what should be considered strategy and, by extension, what should be understood by the term 'strategic management'. However, any such sharp definition of strategy here would actually be misleading. It would suggest that there is widespread agreement among practitioners, researchers and theorists as to what strategy is. The impression would be given that the fundamental concepts in the area of strategy are generally accepted and hardly questioned. Yet, even a quick glance through current strategy literature indicates otherwise. There are strongly differing opinions on most of the key issues and the disagreements run so deep that even a common definition of the term 'strategy' is illusive.

This is bad news for those who prefer simplicity and certainty. It means that the topic of strategy cannot be explained as a set of straightforward definitions and rules to be memorized and applied. The strongly conflicting views mean that strategy cannot be summarized into broadly agreed-on definitions, rules, matrices and flow diagrams that one must simply absorb and learn to use. If the fundamental differences of opinion are not swept aside, the consequence is that a book on strategy cannot be like an instruction manual that takes you through the steps of how something should be done. On the contrary, a strategy book should acknowledge the disagreements and encourage thinking about the value of each of the different points of view. That is the intention of this book.

The philosophy embraced here is that an understanding of the topic of strategy can only be gained by grappling with the diversity of insights presented by so many prominent thinkers and by coming to terms with the fact that there is no simple answer to the question of what strategy is. Readers who prefer the certainty of reading only one opinion, as opposed to the intellectual stimulation of being confronted with a wide variety, should read no further – there are plenty of alternatives available. Those who wish to proceed should lay aside their 'opinions of habit', and open their minds to the many other opinions presented, for in these pages there is 'knowledge in the making'.

IDENTIFYING THE STRATEGY ISSUES

If the only tool you have is a hammer, you treat everything like a nail.
Abraham Maslow (1908–1970); American psychologist

The approach taken in this book is in line with the moral of Maslow's remark. To avoid hammering strategy issues with only one theory, a variety of ways of viewing strategic questions will be presented. But there are two different ways of presenting a broad spectrum of theoretical lenses. This point can be made clear by extending Maslow's hammer-and-nail analogy. To become a good carpenter, who wisely uses a variety of tools depending on what is being crafted, an apprentice carpenter will need to learn about these different instruments. One way is for the apprentice to study the characteristics and functioning of all tools individually and only then to apply each where appropriate. However, another possibility is for the apprentice to first learn about what must be crafted, getting a feel for the materials and the problems that must be solved, and only then to turn to the study of the necessary tools. The first approach to learning can be called 'tools-driven' – understanding each tool comes first, while combining them to solve real problems comes later. The second approach to learning can be termed 'problem-driven' – understanding problems comes first, while searching for the appropriate tools is based on the type of problem.

Both options can also be used for the apprentice strategist. In a tools-driven approach to learning about strategy, all major theories would first be understood separately, to be compared or combined later when using them in practice. A logical structure for a book aiming at this mode of learning would be to allot one chapter to each of the major theories or schools of thought. The advantage of such a theory-based book structure would be that each chapter would focus on giving the reader a clear and cohesive overview of one major theory within the field of strategy. For readers with an interest in grasping the essence of each theory individually, this would probably be the ideal book format. However, the principal disadvantage of a theory-by-theory summary of the field of strategy would be that the reader would not have a clear picture of how the various theories relate to one another. The apprentice strategist would be left with important questions such as: Where do the theories agree and where do they differ? Which strategy phenomena does each theory claim to explain and which phenomena are left unaccounted for? Can various theories be successfully combined or are they based on mutually exclusive assumptions? And which strategy is right, or at least most appropriate under particular circumstances? Not knowing the answers to these questions, how could the apprentice strategist try to apply these new theoretical tools to practice?

This book is based on the assumption that the reader wants to learn to actively resolve strategic problems. Understanding the broad spectrum of theories is not an end in itself, but a means for more effective strategizing. Therefore, the problem-driven approach to learning about strategy has been adopted. In this approach, key strategy issues are first identified and then each is looked at from the perspective of the most appropriate theories. This has resulted in an issue-based book structure, in which each chapter deals with a particular set of strategy issues. In each chapter, only the theories that shed some light on the issues under discussion are brought forward and compared to one another. Of course, some theories are relevant to more than one set of issues and therefore appear in various chapters.

In total, eleven sets of strategy issues have been identified that together largely cover the field of strategic management. These eleven will be the subjects of the remaining eleven chapters of this book. How the various strategy issues have been divided into these eleven sets are explained in the following paragraphs.

Strategizing, missioning and visioning

Section I of this book addresses two important inputs for strategy: the cognitive processes of individual strategists (strategizing) and purpose as the impetus for strategy activities (missioning and visioning).

It is widely presumed that strategists are rational actors who identify, determine, evaluate, choose, translate and carry out, based on rigorous logic and extensive knowledge of all important factors. This belief has been challenged, however. Many authors have criticized the strong emphasis on rationality in these traditional views of the strategizing process. Some writers have even argued that the true nature of strategic thinking is more intuitive and creative than rational. In their opinion, strategizing is about perceiving strengths and weaknesses, envisioning opportunities and threats and creating the future, for which imagination and judgment are more important than analysis and logic. This constitutes quite a fundamental disagreement about the cognitive processes of the strategizing manager. These issues surrounding the nature of strategic thinking will be discussed in Chapter 2 on strategizing.

Making strategy is not an end in itself, but a means for reaching particular objectives. Organizations exist to fulfil a purpose and strategies are employed to ensure that the organizational mission and vision are realized. Oddly enough, most authors write about missions and visions without any reference to the organizational purpose being pursued. It is generally assumed that all organizations exist for the same basic reasons, and that this purpose is self-evident. However, in reality, there is extensive disagreement about what the current purposes of organizations are, and especially about what their purpose should be. Some people argue that it is the business of business to make money. In their view, firms are owned by shareholders and therefore should pursue shareholders' interests. And it is the primary interest of shareholders to see the value of their stocks increase. On the other hand, others believe that companies exist to serve the interests of multiple stakeholders. In their opinion, having a financial stake in a firm should not give shareholders a dominant position vis-à-vis other groups that also have an interest in what the organization does. Other stakeholders usually include employees, customers, suppliers and bankers, but could also include the local community, the broader industry and even the natural environment. These issues on the organizational purpose will be discussed in Chapter 3 on missioning and visioning.

Strategy dimensions: Content, process and context

The most fundamental distinction made in this book is between strategy content, strategy process and strategy context (see Figure 1.1). These are the three dimensions of strategy that can be recognized in every real-life strategic problem situation. They can be generally defined as follows:

- Strategy content. The combined decisions and choices that lead a company into the future are referred to as the strategy content. Stated in terms of a question, strategy content is concerned with the *what* of strategy: what is, and should be, the strategy for the company and each of its constituent units?

- Strategy process. The manner in which strategies come about is referred to as the strategy process. Stated in terms of a number of questions, strategy process is concerned with the *how, who* and *when* of strategy: how is, and should, strategy be made, analysed, dreamt-up, formulated, implemented, changed and controlled; who is involved; and when do the necessary activities take place?

- Strategy context. The set of circumstances under which both the strategy content and the strategy process are determined is referred to as the strategy context. Stated in terms

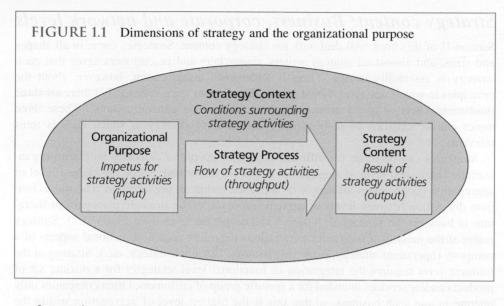

FIGURE 1.1   Dimensions of strategy and the organizational purpose

of a question, strategy context is concerned with the *where* of strategy: where (that is in which firm and which environment) are the strategy process and strategy content embedded?

It cannot be emphasized enough that strategy content, process and context are not different parts of strategy, but are distinguishable dimensions. Just as it is silly to speak of the length, width and height parts of a box, one cannot speak of the three parts of strategy either. Each strategic problem situation is by its nature three dimensional, possessing process, content and context characteristics, and only the understanding of all three dimensions will give the strategist real depth of comprehension. In particular, it must be acknowledged that the three dimensions interact (Pettigrew and Whipp, 1991; Ketchen, Thomas and McDaniel, 1996). For instance, the manner in which the strategy process is organized will have a significant impact on the resulting strategy content, while likewise, the content of the current strategy will strongly influence the way in which the strategy process will be conducted in future. If these linkages are ignored, the strategist will have a flat view instead of a three-dimensional view of strategy. A useful analytical distinction for temporarily unravelling a strategic problem situation will have turned into a permanent means for fragmenting reality.

However, it is possible to concentrate on one of the strategy dimensions if the other two are kept in mind. In fact, to have a focused discussion it is even necessary to look at one dimension at a time. The alternative is a debate in which all topics on all three dimensions would be discussed simultaneously: such a cacophony of opinions would be lively, but most likely less than fruitful. Therefore, the content–process–context distinction is cautiously used as the main structuring principle of this book, splitting the text into three major sections.

Most strategy research, by its very nature, is more atomistic than holistic, focusing on just a few variables at once. Consequently, most writings on strategy, including most of the theories discussed in this book, tend to favour just one, or at most two, strategy dimensions, which is usually complex enough given the need to remain comprehensible. In particular, the divide between strategy content and strategy process has been quite pronounced, to the extent of worrying some scholars about whether the connections between the two are being sufficiently recognized (Pettigrew, 1992). Although sharing this concern, use of the content–process–context–purpose distinction here reflects the reality of the current state of debate within the field of strategic management.

Strategy content: Business, corporate and network levels

Section II of this book will deal with the strategy content. Strategies come in all shapes and sizes, and almost all strategy writers, researchers and practitioners agree that each strategy is essentially unique. There is widespread disagreement, however, about the principles to which strategies should adhere. The debates are numerous, but there are three fundamental sets of issues around which most conflicts generally centre. These three topics can be clarified by distinguishing the level of strategy at which each is most relevant.

Strategies can be made for different groups of people or activities within an organization. The lowest level of aggregation is one person or task, while the highest level of aggregation encompasses all people or activities within an organization. The most common distinction between levels of aggregation made in the strategic management literature is between the functional, business and corporate levels (see Figure 1.2). Strategy issues at the *functional level* refer to questions regarding specific functional aspects of a company (operations strategy, marketing strategy, financial strategy, etc.). Strategy at the *business level* requires the integration of functional level strategies for a distinct set of products and/or services intended for a specific group of customers. Often companies only operate in one such business, so that this is the highest level of aggregation within the firm. However, there are also many companies that are in two or more businesses. In such companies, a multi-business or *corporate level* strategy is required, which aligns the various business level strategies.

A logical extension of the functional–business–corporate distinction is to explicitly recognize the level of aggregation higher than the individual organization. Firms often cluster together into groups of two or more collaborating organizations. This level is referred to as the multi-company or *network level*. Most multi-company groups consist of only a few parties, as is the case in strategic alliances, joint ventures and value-adding partnerships. However, networks can also have dozens, even hundreds, of participants. In some circumstances, the corporation as a whole might be a member of a group, while in other situations only a part of the firm joins forces with other organizations. In all cases, when a strategy is developed for a group of firms, this is called a network level strategy.

In line with the generally accepted boundaries of the strategic management field, this book focuses on the business, corporate and network levels of strategy, although this will often demand consideration of strategy issues at the functional level as well. In Section II, on the strategy content, the different strategy issues encountered at the different levels of strategy will be explored. And at each level of strategy, the focus will be on the fundamental differences of opinion that divide strategy theorists.

Chapter 4 deals with strategy issues at the business level. Here the fundamental debate surrounds whether firms are, and should be, primarily market-driven or resource-driven. Some authors argue that firms should be strongly externally oriented, engaged in a game of positioning vis-à-vis customers, competitors, suppliers and other parties in the environment, and should adapt the firm to the demands of the game. In other words, companies should think 'outside-in'. Yet, other authors strongly disagree, stressing the need for companies to exploit and expand their strengths. They recommend a more 'inside-out' view, whereby companies search for environments and positions that best fit with their resource base.

Chapter 5 is concerned with strategy issues at the corporate level. The fundamental debate in this chapter is whether corporations are, and should be, run as federations of autonomous business units or as highly integrated organizations. Some authors argue that corporate strategists should view themselves as investors, with financial stakes in a portfolio of business units. As a shrewd investor, the corporate centre should buy up cheap companies, divest underperforming business units, and invest its business units with the

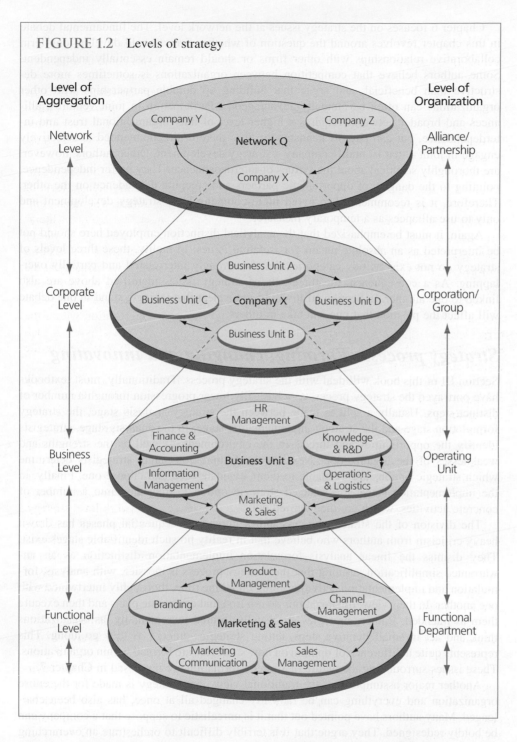

FIGURE 1.2 Levels of strategy

Level of
Aggregation

Network
Level

Corporate
Level

Business
Level

Functional
Level

Level of
Organization

Alliance/
Partnership

Corporation/
Group

Operating
Unit

Functional
Department

Network Q

Company Y

Company Z

Company X

Company X

Business Unit A

Business Unit C

Business Unit D

Business Unit B

Business Unit B

HR
Management

Finance &
Accounting

Knowledge
& R&D

Information
Management

Operations
& Logistics

Marketing
& Sales

Marketing & Sales

Product
Management

Branding

Channel
Management

Marketing
Communication

Sales
Management

highest profit potential, independent of what industry they are in. Each business unit should be judged on its merits and given a large measure of autonomy, to be optimally responsive to the specific conditions in its industry. However, other authors are at odds with this view, pointing to the enormous potential for synergy that is left untapped. They argue that corporations should be tightly knit groupings of closely related business units that share resources and align their strategies with one another. The ensuing synergies, it is expected, will provide an important source of competitive advantage.

Chapter 6 focuses on the strategy issues at the network level. The fundamental debate in this chapter revolves around the question of whether firms should develop long-term collaborative relationships with other firms or should remain essentially independent. Some authors believe that competition between organizations is sometimes more destructive than beneficial, and argue that building up durable partnerships with other organizations can often be mutually advantageous. Participation in joint ventures, alliances and broader networks requires a higher level of inter-organizational trust and interdependence, but can pay off handsomely. It is therefore recommended to selectively engage in joint – that is, multi-company – strategy development. Other authors, however, are thoroughly sceptical about the virtues of interdependence. They prefer independence, pointing to the dangers of opportunistic partners and creeping dependence on the other. Therefore, it is recommended to avoid multi-company level strategy development and only to use alliances as a temporary measure.

Again, it must be emphasized that the analytical distinction employed here should not be interpreted as an absolute means for isolating issues. In reality, these three levels of strategy do not exist as tidy categories, but are strongly interrelated and partially overlapping. As a consequence, the three sets of strategy issues identified above are also linked to one another. In Section III it will become clear that taking a stand in one debate will affect the position that one can take in others.

Strategy process: Forming, changing and innovating

Section III of this book will deal with the strategy process. Traditionally, most textbooks have portrayed the strategy process as a basically linear progression through a number of distinct steps. Usually a split is made between the strategy analysis stage, the strategy formulation stage and the strategy implementation stage. In the analysis stage, strategists identify the opportunities and threats in the environment, as well as the strengths and weaknesses of the organization. Next, in the formulation stage, strategists determine which strategic options are available to them, evaluate each and choose one. Finally, in the implementation stage, the selected strategic option is translated into a number of concrete activities, which are then carried out.

The division of the strategy process into a number of sequential phases has drawn heavy criticism from authors who believe that in reality no such identifiable stages exist. They dismiss the linear analysis–formulation–implementation distinction as an unwarranted simplification, arguing that the strategy process is messier, with analysis, formulation and implementation activities going on all the time, thoroughly intertwined with one another. In their view, organizations do not first make strategic plans and then execute them as intended. Rather, strategies are usually formed incrementally, as organizations think and act in small iterative steps, letting strategies emerge as they go along. This represents quite a difference of opinion on how strategies are formed within organizations. These issues surrounding the nature of strategy formation are discussed in Chapter 7.

Another major assumption of the traditional view, that strategy is made for the entire organization and everything can be radically changed all at once, has also been challenged. Many authors have pointed out that it is unrealistic to suppose that a company can be boldly redesigned. They argue that it is terribly difficult to orchestrate an overarching strategy for the entire organization that is a significant departure from the current course of action. It is virtually impossible to get various aspects of an organization all lined up to go through a change at the same time, certainly if a radical change is intended. In practice, different aspects of an organization will be under different pressures, on different timetables and have different abilities to change, leading to a differentiated approach to change. Moreover, the rate and direction of change will be seriously limited by the cultural, political and cognitive inheritance of the firm. Hence, it is argued, strategic change

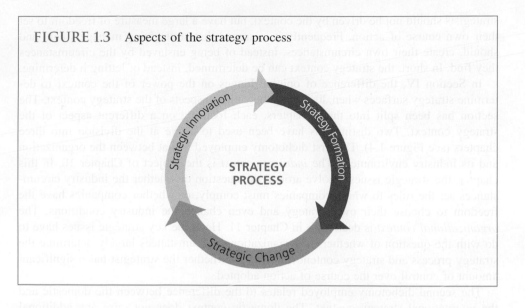

FIGURE 1.3   Aspects of the strategy process

is usually more gradual and fragmented than radical and coordinated. The issues surrounding this difference of opinion on the nature of strategic change will be discussed in Chapter 8.

The traditional focus on improving efficiency of current products, services and business models has also been challenged. Many authors argue that companies need constant renewal by developing new products, services and business models. Although improved efficiency of the present is important in organizational processes, enhancing effectiveness of innovation processes to secure the future is what managers should be focusing on. Exploring in uncharted waters may be costly and results are not guaranteed, but in order to be able to be efficient in the future, managers need to ensure the company has a future. The issues surrounding this difference of opinion on the nature of strategic innovation are discussed in Chapter 9.

These three chapter topics – strategy formation, strategic change and strategic innovation – do not constitute entirely separate subjects. Let it be clear that they are not phases, stages or elements of the strategy process that can be understood in isolation. Strategy formation, strategic change and strategic innovation are different aspects of the strategy process, which are strongly linked and partially overlapping (see Figure 1.3). They have been selected because they are sets of issues on which there is significant debate within the field of strategy. As will become clear, having a particular opinion on one of these aspects will have a consequence for views held on all other aspects as well.

Strategy context: Industry, organizational and international

Section IV in this book is devoted to the strategy context. Strategy researchers, writers and practitioners largely agree that every strategy context is unique. Moreover, they are almost unanimous that it is usually wise for managers to strive for a fit between the strategy process, strategy content and the specific circumstances prevalent in the strategy context. However, disagreement arises as soon as the discussion turns to the details of the alignments. Does the context determine what the strategizing manager must do, or can the manager actually shape the context? Some people argue or assume that the strategy context has a dynamic all on its own, which strategists can hardly influence, and therefore that the strategy context sets strict confines on the freedom to manoeuvre. The context is not malleable and hence the motto for the strategist is 'adapt or die'. Others believe that strategists should not be driven by the context, but have a large measure of freedom to set their own course of action. Frequently it is argued that strategizing managers can, and should, create their own circumstances, instead of being enslaved by the circumstances they find. In short, the strategy context can be determined, instead of letting it determine.

In Section IV, the difference of opinion hinges on the power of the context to determine strategy surfaces when discussing the various aspects of the strategy context. The section has been split into three chapters, each focusing on a different aspect of the strategy context. Two distinctions have been used to arrive at the division into three chapters (see Figure 1.4). The first dichotomy employed is that between the organization and its industry environment. The *industry context* is the subject of Chapter 10. In this chapter, the strategic issues revolve around the question of whether the industry circumstances set the rules to which companies must comply, or whether companies have the freedom to choose their own strategy and even change the industry conditions. The *organizational context* is dealt with in Chapter 11. Here, the key strategic issues have to do with the question of whether the organizational circumstances largely determine the strategy process and strategy content followed, or whether the strategist has a significant amount of control over the course of action adopted.

The second dichotomy employed relates to the difference between the domestic and the international strategy context. The domestic context does not raise any additional strategic issues, but the *international context* clearly does. Strategists must deal with the question of whether adaptation to the diversity of the international context is strictly required or whether companies have considerable freedom to choose their strategy process and content irrespective of the international context. The difference of opinion between writers on the international context actually goes one step further. Some authors predict that the diversity of the international context will decline over time and that companies can encourage this process. If global convergence takes place, it is argued, adaptation to the international context will become a non-issue. Other authors, however, disagree that international diversity is declining and therefore argue that the international context will remain an issue that strategists must attempt to deal with. This debate on the future of the international context is conducted in Chapter 12.

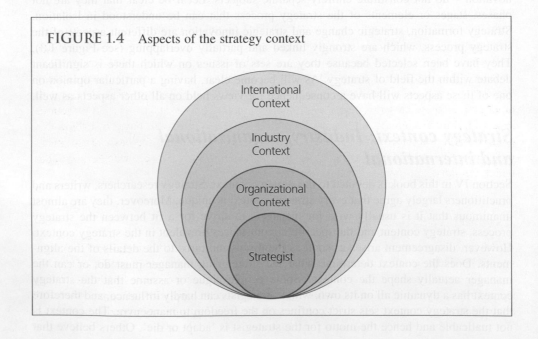

FIGURE 1.4   Aspects of the strategy context

STRUCTURING THE STRATEGY DEBATES

Where there is much desire to learn, there of necessity will be much arguing, much writing, many opinions; for opinion in good men is but knowledge in the making.

John Milton (1608–1674); English poet

Every real-life strategic problem is complex. Most of the strategic issues outlined earlier in this chapter are present in every strategic problem, making the prospect of a simple solution an illusion. Yet, even if each set of strategy issues is considered independently, it seems that strategy theorists cannot agree on the right way to approach them. On each of the topics, there is widespread disagreement, indicating that no simple solution can be expected here either.

Why is it that theorists cannot agree on how to solve strategic problems? Might it be that some theorists are right, while others are just plain wrong? In that case, it would be wise for problem-solvers to select the valid theory and discard the false ones. While this might be true in some cases, it seems unlikely that false theories would stay around long enough to keep a lively debate going. Eventually, the right (i.e. unfalsified) theory would prevail and disagreements would disappear. Yet, this does not seem to be happening in the field of strategic management.

Could it be that each theorist only emphasizes one aspect of an issue – only takes one cut of a multi-faceted reality? In that case, it would be wise for problem-solvers to combine the various theories that each approach the problem from a different angle. However, if this were true, one would expect the different theories to be largely complementary. Each theory would simply be a piece in the bigger puzzle of strategic management. Yet, this does not explain why there is so much disagreement, and even contradiction, within the field of strategy.

It could also be that strategy theorists start from divergent assumptions about the nature of each strategy issue and therefore logically arrive at a different perspective on how to solve strategic problems. In that case, it would be wise for problem-solvers to combine the various theories, in order to look at the problem from a number of different angles.

All three possibilities for explaining the existing theoretical disagreements should be kept open. However, entertaining the thought that divergent positions are rooted in fundamentally different assumptions about strategy issues is by far the most fruitful to the strategist confronted with complex problems. It is too simple to hope that one can deal with the contradictory opinions within the field of strategy by discovering which strategy theories are right and which are wrong. But it is also not particularly practical to accept all divergent theories as valid depictions of different aspects of reality – if two theories suggest a different approach to the same problem, the strategist will have to sort out this contradiction. Therefore, in this book the emphasis is on surfacing the basic assumptions underlying the major theoretical perspectives on strategy, and to debate whether, or under which circumstances, these assumptions are appropriate.

Assumptions about strategy tensions

At the heart of every set of strategic issues, a fundamental tension between apparent opposites can be identified. For instance, in Chapter 6 on network level strategy, the issues revolve around the fundamental tension between competition and cooperation. In Chapter 10 on the industry context, the fundamental tension between the opposites of compliance and choice lies at the centre of the subject (see Figure 1.5). Each pair of opposites creates a

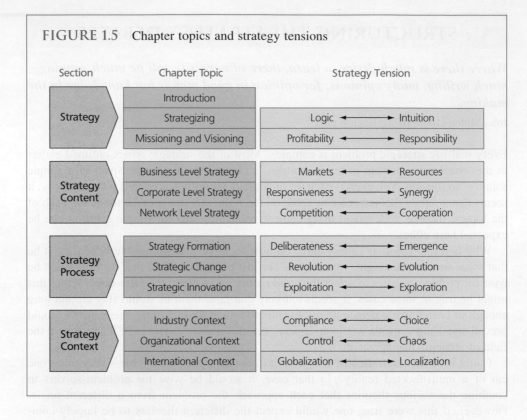

FIGURE 1.5   Chapter topics and strategy tensions

Section	Chapter Topic	Strategy Tension
Strategy	Introduction	
	Strategizing	Logic ⟷ Intuition
	Missioning and Visioning	Profitability ⟷ Responsibility
Strategy Content	Business Level Strategy	Markets ⟷ Resources
	Corporate Level Strategy	Responsiveness ⟷ Synergy
	Network Level Strategy	Competition ⟷ Cooperation
Strategy Process	Strategy Formation	Deliberateness ⟷ Emergence
	Strategic Change	Revolution ⟷ Evolution
	Strategic Innovation	Exploitation ⟷ Exploration
Strategy Context	Industry Context	Compliance ⟷ Choice
	Organizational Context	Control ⟷ Chaos
	International Context	Globalization ⟷ Localization

tension, as they seem to be inconsistent, or even incompatible, with one another; it seems as if both elements cannot be fully true at the same time. If firms are competing, they are not cooperating. If firms must comply with the industry context, they have no choice. Yet, although these opposites confront strategizing managers with conflicting pressures, somehow they must be dealt with simultaneously. Strategists are caught in a bind, trying to cope with contradictory forces at the same time.

The challenge of strategic management is to wrestle with these tricky strategy tensions. All strategy theories make assumptions, explicitly or implicitly, about the nature of these tensions and devise ways in which to deal with them. However, every theorist's assumptions differ, giving rise to a wide variety of positions. In fact, many of the major disagreements within the field of strategic management are rooted in the different assumptions made about coping with these strategy tensions. For this reason, the theoretical debate in each chapter will be centred around the different perspectives on dealing with a particular strategy tension.

Identifying strategy perspectives

The strategy issues in each chapter can be viewed from many perspectives. On each topic there are many different theories and hundreds of books and articles. While very interesting, a comparison or debate between all of these would probably be very chaotic, unfocused and incomprehensible. Therefore, in each chapter the debate has been condensed into its most powerful form – two diametrically opposed perspectives are confronted with one another. These two poles of each debate are not always the most widely held perspectives on the particular set of strategy issues, but they do expose the major points of contention within the topic area.

FIGURE 1.6   Strategy topics, paradoxes and perspectives

Strategy Topics	Strategy Paradoxes	Strategy Perspectives
Introduction		
Strategizing	Logic vs. Intuition	Analytic Reasoning vs. Holistic Reasoning
Missioning and Visioning	Profitability vs. Responsibility	Shareholder Value vs. Stakeholder Values
Business Level Strategy	Markets vs. Resources	Outside-in vs. Inside-out
Corporate Level Strategy	Responsiveness vs. Synergy	Portfolio Organization vs. Integrated Organization
Network Level Strategy	Competition vs. Cooperation	Discrete Organization vs. Embedded Organization
Strategy Formation	Deliberateness vs. Emergence	Strategic Planning vs. Strategic Incrementalism
Strategic Change	Revolution vs. Evolution	Discontinuous Renewal vs. Continuous Renewal
Strategic Innovation	Exploitation vs. Exploration	Strategic Improvement vs. Radical Rejuvenation
Industry Context	Compliance vs. Choice	Industry Dynamics vs. Industry Leadership
Organizational Context	Control vs. Chaos	Organizational Leadership vs. Organizational Dynamics
International Context	Globalization vs. Localization	Global Convergence vs. International Diversity

In every chapter, the two strategy perspectives selected for the debate each emphasize one side of a strategy tension over the other (see Figure 1.6). For instance, in Chapter 6 the discrete organization perspective stresses competition over cooperation, while the embedded organization perspective does the opposite. In Chapter 10, the industry dynamics perspective accentuates compliance over choice, while the industry leadership perspective does the opposite. In other words, the two perspectives represent the two extreme ways of dealing with a strategy tension, emphasizing one side or emphasizing the other.

In the first part of each chapter, the core strategic issue and the underlying strategy tension are explained. Also, the two strategy perspectives are outlined and compared. However, such a measured overview of the perspectives lacks colour, depth and vigour. Reading the summary of a debate does not do it justice – just like reading the summary of a sports match is nothing like watching a game live. Therefore, to give readers a first-hand impression of the debate, theorists representing both sides will be given an opportunity to state their own case by means of a reading. Readers will be part of a virtual debate in which the authors of the first and second readings will participate.

Strategy tensions as both/and problems

With both strategy perspectives emphasizing the importance of one side of a strategy tension over the other, how should strategists deal with these opposites? In general, there are two fundamentally different kinds of problems, 'either/or problems' and 'both/and problems', and each should be handled in different ways.

Either/or problems are for example:

■ Puzzles. A puzzle is a challenging problem with an optimal solution. Think of a crossword puzzle as an example. Puzzles can be quite complex and extremely difficult to analyse, but there is a best way of solving them. For example, when facing decreasing margins or market share, managers can solve the puzzle by testing several hypotheses on the root causes of the problem.

■ Dilemmas. A dilemma is a vexing problem with two possible solutions, neither of which is logically the best. Think of the famous prisoner's dilemma as an example. Dilemmas confront problem-solvers with difficult either/or choices, each with its own advantages and disadvantages, but neither clearly superior to the other. The uneasy feeling this gives the decision-maker is reflected in the often-used expression 'horns of a dilemma' – neither choice is particularly comfortable. The manager is forced to make a choice in favour of either one or the other. For instance, the manager must choose between forming an alliance with firm A or its main competitor firm B, each of which has clear advantages. Which of the two the strategist judges to be most appropriate will usually depend on the manager's preferences or the specific circumstances.

As opposed to either/or problems that can be solved by analysing and choosing, both/and problems can only be managed. Both/and problems are for example:

■ Trade-offs. A trade-off is a problem situation in which there are many possible solutions, each striking a different balance between two conflicting pressures. In a trade-off, many different combinations between the two opposites can be found, each with its own pros and cons, but none of the many solutions is inherently superior to the others. Think of the trade-off between work and leisure time as an example – more of one will necessarily mean less of the other. Of course a position on the trade-off line needs to be set, but when circumstances change the position may also change. In other words, the balance is unstable and temporal.

■ Paradoxes. A paradox is a situation in which two seemingly contradictory, or even mutually exclusive, factors appear to be true at the same time. A problem that is a paradox has no real solution, as there is no way to logically integrate the two opposites into an internally consistent understanding of the problem. Hence, a paradox presents the problem-solver with the difficult task of wrestling with the problem, without ever arriving at a definitive solution. For example, companies with more than one business unit need to create synergies between business units but also have to allow the businesses independence to act upon market circumstances. Comparable with trade-offs, the problem-solver can find a workable reconciliation to temporarily cope with the unsolvable paradox (see Figure 1.7).

MANAGING STRATEGY PARADOXES

Conflict is latent. Only by profound and meticulous ordering of aims, in advance, can it be prevented from emerging.
I Ching, *Book of Changes*, 3rd to 2nd millenium BC

Strategists need to understand the nature of problems, in order to select the appropriate way of dealing with them. A decreasing profit margin needs to be handled as an either/or problem, and paradoxes need to be managed as a both/and problem. Most people are used

FIGURE 1.7   Strategy tensions as puzzles, dilemmas, trade-offs and paradoxes

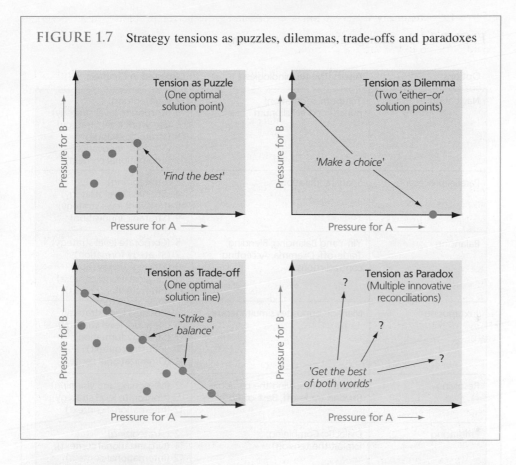

to solving either/or problems by solving puzzles and resolving dilemmas, and to making trade-offs in both/and problems. These ways of dealing with problems are common in daily life. They are based on the assumption that, by analysis, one or a number of logical solutions can be identified. It might require a sharp mind and considerable effort, but the answers can be found.

However, most people are not used to dealing with paradoxes. A paradox has no answer or set of answers – it can only be coped with as best as possible. Faced with a paradox, one can try to find novel ways of combining opposites, but one will know that none of these creative reconciliations will ever be *the* answer. Paradoxes will always remain surrounded by uncertainty and disagreements on how best to cope. A common misunderstanding of not arriving at the best answer is that all solutions will be equally good, that anything will do. In reality most answers will be suboptimal or just plain wrong, while only some reconciliations succeed.

Dealing with paradoxes

When faced with strategy paradoxes, managers have a range of options for dealing with the opposite elements of an issue. Several alternatives have been suggested in the management field, in some cases specifically related to the strategic issue at hand (e.g. scholars addressing tensions related to strategic innovation, such as Tushman and O'Reilly, 1996; Raisch *et al.*, 2009; Jay, 2012; and those in the resource-based paradigm discussing dynamic capabilities, such as Teece, 2007), but there is also a growing number of publications addressing how paradoxes may be dealt with in general (e.g. Poole and Van de Ven, 1989; Lewis, 2000; Smith, 2009; Smith and Lewis, 2011; Smith and

FIGURE 1.8 Managing paradoxes taxonomy

Options:	Alternative terminologies:	Discussed in Chapter:
Navigating	Temporal separation; punctuated equilibrium	2 (Strategizing) 5 (Corporate level strategy) 6 (Network level Strategy) 8 (Strategic change) 9 (Strategic innovation) 12 (International context)
Parallel processing	Spatial separation	2 (Strategizing) 4 (Business level strategy) 6 (Network level strategy) 9 (Strategic innovation)
Balancing	Yin Yang Balancing; Blending; Trade-off; Dilemma; Accepting contradictions	5 (Corporate level strategy) 7 (Strategy formation) 9 (Strategic innovation) 11 (Organizational context) 12 (International context)
Juxtaposing	Manage opposites simultaneously	4 (Business level strategy) 6 (Network level strategy) 7 (Strategy formation) 10 (Industry context) 11 (Organizational context)
Resolving	Synthesis; Resolving the paradox; Beyond trade-off; Best-of-Both	3 (Missioning and visioning) 5 (Corporate level strategy) 12 (International context)
Embracing	Dialectic; Combining; Exploit the tension	2 (Strategizing) 11 (Organizational context) 12 (International context)

Tushman, 2005, Reading 1.2). Taking all suggested options together, managers have six different options (see the taxonomy in Figure 1.8).

■ Navigating: The first option is to focus on one contrary element at a time. In this case the paradox is managed over time by a series of contrary initiatives, which leads to a development path comparable with a tacking sailing boat. Hence this option is called 'navigating' (Jay, 2013). In the literature, 'tacking' is often referred to as 'punctuating'; the phase of sustaining one route is called the state of 'equilibrium'; the combination is called 'punctuated equilibrium' (Burgelman, 2002; Tushman and O'Reilly, 1996). For example, in managing the paradox of multi-business synergy and business responsiveness a company may start a corporate initiative to capture synergies between businesses, which is then followed by improving responsiveness of the business units (discussed in Chapter 5 on corporate-level strategy).

■ Parallel processing: The second option, following Lawrence and Lorsch's (1967) seminal work, is to separate the contrary demands in different internal (departments or business units) or external (alliance partners) organizational units. Often, the differentiated demands are then integrated at a different – usually higher – organizational level. For example, a company may separate improving existing products and developing a new generation of products in different units, because the drivers such as processes, people and rewards differ (discussed in Chapter 9 on strategic innovation). In this case, managing the paradox of exploitation (improving) and exploration (rejuvenating) takes place at the next organizational level up. The company may also outsource one side of the paradox to alliance partners (discussed in Chapter 6 on network level strategy), and then import the products or outcomes into the organization (Rothermael, 2001). For example, a firm may outsource production while internally focusing on developing new products. The paradox is then dealt with at higher management levels. This option has also become known as 'spatial separation' (Duncan, 1976; Benner and Tushman, 2003).

■ Balancing: The third option – also referred to as Yin-Yang balancing – is to manage opposite demands by trading off elements of the opposing demands, and blending the most appropriate balance. The strategist is not searching for a synthesis, but instead chooses constituting elements of each demand to create a company-specific balance. For example, a manager may choose to comply with some industry rules while changing others (discussed in Chapter 10 on the industry context).

■ Juxtaposing: The fourth option is to simultaneously manage opposite demands on a permanent basis. The conflict between the two opposites is accepted, and the strategist will accommodate both factors at the same time. Juxtaposing requires dynamic capabilities (Teece, Pisano and Shuen, 1997) to manage the paradox on a daily or project basis. For example, companies may cooperate and compete in business networks at the same time, even with the same network partners (discussed in Chapter 6 on network-level strategy), or combine client-driven and resource-driven processes in the same units (discussed in Chapter 4 on business level strategy).

■ Resolving: The fifth option is to arrive at a higher level equilibrium, by developing a new synthesis between competing demands or by exploiting the tension. Developing a novel synthesis creates a new balance between contrary elements that will sustain for some time, but will eventually be replaced by a new one. For example, companies may adopt societal demands into their mission statement, and combine the need to create shareholder value with the need to create societal value to arrive at some statement of shared value (discussed in Chapter 3 on missioning and visioning).

■ Embracing: The sixth option is to embrace and actively use the tension as a source of creativity and opportunity (Beech et al., 2004). The conflict between two opposites is not only accepted, but actually exploited to benefit from the innovative power of tensions. For example, a firm may assign two opposite personalities in the leadership team to combine the messy entrepreneurial process with controlled execution (discussed in Chapter 11 on the organizational context).

As organizations are complex and dynamic systems in changing environments, the available and effective options depend on the specific context (contingencies) and timing. Strategic managers need to be able to master a variety of alternative options, actively manage strategy paradoxes and change route when needed. In other words, the list of available options as listed above is not a passive checklist of solutions for specific issues, but instead provides a menu of available strategizing options that can be dynamically applied. It should be kept in mind, however, that being able to effectively manage strategy paradoxes is not a *goal* in itself. For strategists, this capability is a necessary *means* to create an advantage over competitors. Ultimately, the desired outcome of managing paradoxes is to outperform competitors, by arriving in the synthesis area (see Figure 1.9).

Taking a dialectical approach

Throughout this book, the strategy tensions will be presented as strategy paradoxes. As stated earlier, the virtual debate in each chapter has been condensed into its most powerful form – two diametrically opposed perspectives are confronted with one another, each

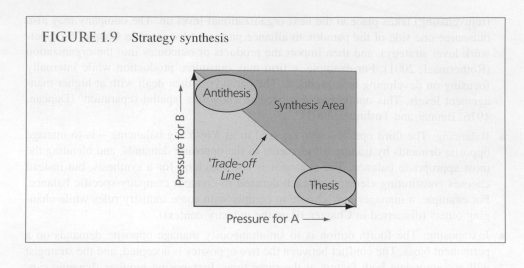

FIGURE 1.9   Strategy synthesis

emphasizing one pole of the paradox. These two opposite positions are in fact the thesis and the antithesis of the debate, challenging the reader to search for an appropriate option to manage the two tensions. This form of debate is called 'dialectical enquiry' – by using two opposite points of view, the problem-solver attempts to arrive at a better understanding of the issue and a 'higher level resolution' that integrates elements of both the thesis and the antithesis. This approach has a number of advantages:

■ Range of ideas. By presenting the two opposite poles in each debate, readers can quickly acquire an understanding of the full range of ideas on the strategy issue. While these two extreme positions do not represent the most widely held views, they do clarify for the reader how diverse the thinking actually is on each strategy issue. This is the *book-end function* of presenting the two opposite perspectives – they 'frame' the full set of views that exist on the topic.

■ Points of contention. Usually there is not across-the-board disagreement between the various approaches to each strategy issue, but opinions tend to diverge on a number of critical points. By presenting the two opposite poles in each debate, readers can rapidly gain insight into these major points of contention. This is the *contrast function* of presenting the two opposite perspectives – they bring the key points of contention into sharper focus.

■ Stimulus for bridging. As the two opposite poles in each debate are presented, readers will be struck by the fact that neither position can be easily dismissed. Both extreme strategy perspectives make a strong case for a particular approach and readers will experience difficulty in simply choosing one over the other. With each extreme position offering certain advantages, readers will feel challenged to incorporate aspects of both into a more sophisticated synthesis. This is the *integrative function* of presenting the two opposite perspectives – they stimulate readers to seek a way of getting the best of both worlds.

■ Stimulus for creativity. Nothing is more creativity-evoking than a challenging paradox whereby two opposites seem to be true at the same time. By presenting the two opposite poles of each debate, which both make a realistic claim to being valid, readers are challenged to creatively deal with this paradoxical situation. This is the *generative function* of presenting the two opposite perspectives – they stimulate readers to generate innovative ways of 'transcending' the strategic paradox.

Each chapter starts with the thesis, which is then contrasted with the opposite pole as the antithesis. The first two readings in each chapter will speak on behalf of the two-pole perspectives, while the third reading addresses the tension itself and means to manage the paradox. Although the intention of the third reading is not to give the "correct" outcome of the debate, it does suggest a route to deal with the paradox.

DEVELOPING AN INTERNATIONAL PERSPECTIVE

Every man takes the limits of his own field of vision for the limits of the world.
Arthur Schopenhauer (1788–1860); German philosopher

In a highly integrated world economy, in which many firms operate across national boundaries, strategy is by nature an international affair. Some theorists ignore the international arena as irrelevant, uninteresting or too complex, but most theorists, particularly those interested in strategy content, acknowledge the importance of the international context and write extensively on international competition and global strategy. In this book there has been a strong preference to include those authors who explicitly place their arguments within an international setting. Gaining an international perspective is greatly enhanced by reading works that do not take a domestic arena as their default assumption.

To further accentuate the international angle of this book, the international context has been singled out for a closer look in Chapter 12. In this chapter, the conflicting views about developments in the international context will be debated. This, too, should challenge readers to take an international perspective.

However, despite all this attention paid to the international competitive arena, internationalizing companies, cross-border strategies and global products, few authors in the strategy field explicitly question whether their own theories can be globally standardized. Most fail to wonder whether their theories are equally applicable in a variety of national settings. It is seldom asked whether they base themselves on universally valid assumptions, or if they have been severely limited by their domestic 'field of vision'. Yet, there is a very real danger that theories are based on local assumptions that are not true or appropriate in other nations – a threat that could be called 'think local, generalize global'.

Developing an international perspective requires strategists to guard against the indiscriminate export of domestically generated strategy theories across international borders. For international strategists it is important to question whether theories 'travel' as well as the companies they describe. Unfortunately, at the moment, strategizing managers have little to base themselves on. There has been only a modest amount of international comparative research carried out in the field of strategy. National differences in strategic management practices and preferences have occasionally been identified, but in general the topic has received little attention. In practice, the international validity of locally formulated strategy theories has gone largely unquestioned in international journals and forums.

Although there is still so little published material to go on, in this book readers will be encouraged to question the international limitations of strategy theories. Furthermore, they will be challenged to question whether certain strategy perspectives are more popular or appropriate in some countries than in others. To point readers in the right direction, in each chapter a subsection is presented that places the strategy topic being debated in an international perspective. In these subsections, it will be argued that the strategy paradoxes identified in this book are fundamentally the same around the world, but that there might be international differences in how each paradox is coped with. Strategy perspectives and theories might be more predominant in particular countries because they are based on certain assumptions about dealing with the strategy paradoxes that are more suitable to the national context. In each 'international perspective' subsection, a number of factors is discussed that might cause national differences in strategy styles.

Using the cases

An additional way of gaining an international perspective is by trying to employ the strategy perspectives in a variety of national settings. It is especially when trying to deal with concrete strategic problems on an international stage that the limitations of each theory will become more apparent. For this reason, a large number of cases have been included in this book, from many different countries. In each case, readers are encouraged to evaluate the specific national circumstances in which the problem situation is embedded, and to question whether the national context will have an influence on the validity or appropriateness of the various strategy theories and perspectives.

The cases have been selected to cover a wide variety of countries and industries. Furthermore, they have been chosen for their fit with a particular chapter. Each of the chapters in this book have two corresponding cases, in which the paradox under discussion is prominently present. One case per chapter is relatively lengthy, and has been included in Section V of this book. The short case for each chapter has been inserted as an exhibit into the main text. In each case readers will encounter the fact that grappling with strategy paradoxes in 'practice' is just as difficult as dealing with them in 'theory'.

EXHIBIT 1.1   SHORT CASE

DISNEY: IS MAGIC BACK IN THE MOUSE HOUSE?

It is little known that the world's most famous mouse, actually used to be a bunny. The main character in Walt Disney's first cartoon was a creature named 'Oswald the Lucky Rabbit', but after Disney was cheated out of his copyrights, he modified the ears and renamed him Mickey Mouse. What is more widely known is that Walt, together with his brother Roy, subsequently captured the attention of audiences around the world with Mickey as *Steamboat Willie* (1928), in the first cartoon with synchronized sound.

After some modest successes with such new characters as Goofy and Donald Duck, the business of Walt Disney Studios really started to accelerate when they moved into full-length animated films, releasing blockbusters like *Snow White and the Seven Dwarfs* (1937), *Pinocchio* (1940) and *Bambi* (1942). Soon Disney discovered the lucrative merchandising business, licensing the use of Disney characters for such things as clothing, pencils and soda-cans. On the basis of this success, Disney branched out into TV programmes, film music and live-action movie productions. In 1955, Walt's dream of creating a 'Magical Kingdom' was realized, when Disneyland was opened in Anaheim, California. After Walt's death in 1966, Roy carried on to build Disney World in Orlando, Florida, which was completed just before he passed away in 1971.

While the empire the brothers left behind carried on to entertain billions of children and adults all over the world, the creative pipeline dried up completely. After the release of Walt's last project, *Jungle Book* (1967), the Disney studios spent the 1970s looking for ways to emulate the founder's magic, but without clear results. By 1983, only 4 per cent of US moviegoers went to a Disney picture, and the 15-year drought of hit movies was being severely felt in the sales of Disney merchandise and licensing income. In the same year, the Disney Channel was launched in the US, but did not get off to a flying start. Making things worse, the hordes that initially swamped the theme parks were getting bored with Disney's dingy image and visitor numbers began to shrink, while at the same time Disney was incurring heavy costs to finish the Epcot Center at Disney World. To stem the tide, a new management team was hired in 1984, consisting of a brash young executive from Paramount Studios, Michael Eisner, who became CEO, and a level-headed operational man from Warner Brothers, Frank Wells, who became COO.

Together the two worked just like Walt and Roy, with the passionate and outspoken Eisner driving the creative process, and the stable and diplomatic

Wells getting things organized. At Paramount, Eisner had produced hit movies such as *Raiders of the Lost Ark* and *Grease*, as well as the successful television shows *Happy Days* and *Cheers*. He was known for his fanatical attention to detail, to the extent of getting involved in reading scripts and selecting costumes. At Disney, he did the same, getting deeply involved in rejuvenating the film business. On the live-action movie side, Eisner and Wells redirected Disney towards lower budget productions, using promising scripts from less established writers and recruiting actors that seemed at the end of their career. Through a new subsidiary, Touchstone Pictures, Disney also entered the attractive market for films for the teen and young adult audience. With hits such as *Good Morning Vietnam* and *Down and Out in Beverly Hills*, Disney reached a 19 per cent US box office share by 1988, causing Eisner to comment that 'nearly overnight, Disney went from nerdy outcast to leader of the popular crowd'. Later, Disney was responsible for successes such as *Pretty Woman* (1990) and *Pulp Fiction* (1994) – the latter made by Miramax, an avant-garde movie studio Disney had acquired a year before.

The animation part of the business was also revitalized, with major investments made in new animation technology and new people, in particular a new creative producer, Jeffrey Katzenberg. Eventually, this resulted in a series of very successful films: *The Little Mermaid* (1989), *Beauty and the Beast* (1991), *Aladdin* (1992) and *The Lion King* (1994). To get the new movies back in the limelight, alliances were formed with McDonald's and Coca-Cola to do promotional tie-ins. And to get spin-off merchandise flowing at greater volumes, Eisner moved beyond mere licensing, building up a global chain of Disney stores. Helped by a little luck, Disney also profited from the new home video trend that was sweeping the world. Not only could Disney release its new movies twice – first in the theatres and then on video – but it could also re-release a steady stream of classic pictures for home audiences.

In the theme park business, the major innovation spearheaded by Eisner and Wells was to make Disneyland and Disney World more appealing to adults. In 1989 the Disney-MGM Studios theme park was opened near Disney World, as well as the Pleasure Island nightlife complex. Based on the success of Tokyo Disneyland, which was opened in 1983, Disney also built a theme park outside of Paris, called Euro Disney in 1992. It turned out that while the Japanese visitors appreciated an almost replica of Disneyland in Tokyo, European tastes were very different, requiring a long period of adaptation to the local market conditions and causing Euro Disney (later renamed Disneyland Resort Paris) to suffer significant losses during a number of years.

Then, in 1994, Frank Wells was killed in a helicopter crash, Eisner had bypass heart surgery, and a period of boardroom infighting commenced, leading to the high profile departure of the studio head, Katzenberg, who later teamed up with Steven Spielberg and David Geffen to found a new independent film company, DreamWorks SKG. Other executives also left, pointing to Eisner's overbearing presence. 'People get tired of being second guessed and beaten down', a former studio executive remarked. 'When people came out of Michael's office wounded, Frank was the emergency room', another Disney insider reported to *Fortune*, but with Wells gone, no one was there to repair damaged egos and soothe hurt feelings. However, Eisner viewed the situation differently: 'I've never had a problem with anybody who was truly talented … This autonomy crap? That means you're off working alone. If you want autonomy, be a poet.'

In 1996, Eisner made his biggest move yet, acquiring Capital Cities/ABC for US$ 19.6 billion. This deal included the ABC Television Network (distributing to 224 affiliated stations), the ABC Radio Networks (with 3,400 radio outlets) and an 80 per cent share of ESPN, a sports-oriented network, which includes various cable channels and radio stations. Ironically, Eisner had previously worked for ABC as daytime programmer, and felt that he had a lot to add to ABC: 'I would love, every morning, to go over and spend two hours at ABC. Even though my children tell me that I am in the wrong generation and I don't get it any more, I am totally convinced that I could sit with our guys and make ABC No. 1 in two years.' But the opposite happened, as ABC quickly fell to last place, where it lingered for almost ten years.

After Katzenberg's departure, Disney's animation track record also took a turn for the worse – movies such as *Pocahontas* (1995) and *Tarzan* (1999) didn't do too badly, although soaring costs made them only mildly profitable. Other features, such as *Atlantis* (2001), *Treasure Island* (2002) and *Home on the Range* (2004) were box office fiascos. Disney's real animation successes came from their deal with Pixar, an independent studio specializing in computer-generated animations, owned by Apple CEO, Steve Jobs. Such co-productions as *Toy Story* (1995), *Monsters Inc.* (2000) and *Finding Nemo* (2003) were hits in the cinemas and on DVD. In the area of live-action films, Katzenberg's replacement Joe Roth scrapped the policy of setting a 'financial box' within which the creatives had to operate, leading to bigger budgets, big names and big special effects – and just a few too many big disasters. Illustrative were *Pearl Harbor* (2001) and *Gangs of New York* (2002), both with immense production budgets, yet unable to live up to their promise. The result was a high market share for Disney films, but profitability hovering just above zero.

Although Eisner had taken Disney from US$ 1.5 billion in revenues in 1984 to US$ 30 billion 20 years later, a revolt broke out among shareholders, led by Walt's nephew Roy Disney and director Stanley Gold. They lambasted Eisner's perceived arrogance and inability to foster creativity, calling for his resignation. Eventually, Eisner decided to step down, upon which the board appointed Eisner's right hand man and company president since 2000, Bob Iger, to the position of CEO in 2005. Although Gold called Iger 'a modest man with a lot to be modest about', the new CEO was a popular choice among 'Mouseketeers', because of his calm demeanour and team player mentality.

Iger immediately disbanded the strategic planning department at corporate headquarters in Burbank, California, which was held responsible for blocking many of the divisions' strategic initiatives. Instead, Iger gave the heads of the four divisions – Studio Entertainment (films), Parks & Resorts, Media Networks (TV & radio) and Consumer Products (merchandising) – more autonomy to make decisions, while at the same time keeping Eisner's emphasis on leveraging Disney characters across all activities. Iger also mended relationships with Stanley Gold and Roy Disney, asking the latter to join the board of directors as consultant. A surprised Gold remarked: 'He's got the company working like a team again. It's very impressive.'

Relations with Katzenberg and DreamWorks were also restored, leading to further cooperation, but most importantly Iger was able to defuse the tense relationship with Pixar's owner, Steve Jobs. As the six-year co-production agreement with Pixar was about to end, Iger needed to find some way to continue the partnership, since Pixar's films were responsible for more than half of Disney's studio profits. The solution turned out to be a classic win-win, with Disney purchasing Pixar for US$ 7.4 billion in Disney shares, while bringing in Steve Jobs as board member. Part of the deal was also that Pixar's president, Ed Catmull, and its top creative executive, John Lasseter, would take over Disney's struggling animation studios. Furthermore, Disney would work together more closely with Apple in making premium content available through Apple's iTunes stores.

Disney's financial results were further strengthened by a renaissance at ABC, where hit shows like *Lost, Desperate Housewives, Grey's Anatomy* and *Ugly Betty* helped catapult the network to a leading position. Significant growth was also achieved at the Disney Channel, where the traditional focus on the very young was broadened to include 'tweens', nine to 14-year-olds, offering them shows like *Hannah Montana* and *High School Musical*. Not only did these programmes attract a whole new audience, but they led to a wave of new merchandising opportunities. Although Disney once again proved to possess talent for making money by exploiting its franchises, its portfolio was still lacking those that appealed to the male tween audience.

In order to fill this gap, Disney purchased the comic-book publisher Marvel Entertainment for US$ 4.2 billion. Unfortunately, the barrel of the comic-book publisher was not as full as it could have been; various media competitors already had the most famous characters contracted, with Spider-Man, X-Men and the Hulk bound respectively to Sony, News Corporation and Universal. Although Disney received revenue from projects involving these characters, profiting from highly successful movies such as *Iron Man 2* (2010) and *Thor* (2011), for Disney it was only a matter of time before the contracts would run out and it acquired them exclusively. It seems well worth the wait, with *The Avengers* (2012) accumulating impressive box office results of US$ 1.5 billion, making it the third-highest grossing film of all time. In addition, Disney is making good use of the Marvel takeover; television series based on popular Marvel characters debuted on the boy-focused Disney XD channel with the creation of the Marvel Universe block.

Considering *Pirates of the Caribbean* had been the only highly leverageable movie hit Disney had for quite some years, Iger was eagerly looking for new themes around which to build the Disney synergies. He not only found this in Marvel, but also eyeballed Lucasfilm, the company responsible for such hits as *Star Wars* and *Indiana Jones*. Both had a history of collaborating on attractions based on these two franchises for Disney Parks, but the cooperation only went so far. George Lucas, owner of Lucasfilm, considering his retirement, needed someone capable of handling his franchises, while ensuring quality and providing the creators with a certain degree of freedom. He found this in Iger, who had previously handled the acquisition of Pixar well. For a stellar US$ 4.1 billion, Lucasfilm became a subsidiary of Disney and similar to the Pixar deal, George Lucas was welcomed as a board member and future films would be co-branded with both the Disney and Lucasfilm names.

Yet, peace was not restored in the Disney galaxy, as Iger had plenty of strategic issues to deal with. One key strategic challenge for him was to continue to reap the synergies between the divisions, by taking movie characters to television, the Internet, theme parks and Disney stores. Disney now has more than ten of these 'franchises', ranging from *Mickey Mouse* to *Cars*, *Disney Fairies* and *Pirates of the Caribbean*, that it tries to leverage, but the question is how this should be managed, without creating a complex organizational structure and reducing each division's freedom to set its own strategy. Throwing in Marvel and Lucasfilm only reinforced the need for Disney to get this right.

Another issue is internationalization, which Iger has set high on his priority list. If Disney wants to break into non-US markets in a big way, can it do so by leveraging its franchises across borders or must Disney go local, developing local movies and characters? With more or less standardized theme parks in Tokyo, Paris and Hong Kong (2005), and resorts in a variety of locations, there is much to be said for sticking to global franchises. Yet, on the other hand, emerging markets like China, Russia, India and Brazil might be a bit too diverse to cover successfully with globally standardized wares. Yet, the upcoming Shanghai Disney Resort, costumed to serve the taste of China, might be able to better indicate what direction is best for Disney.

Disney's future in interactive media is another issue. So far, its activities in this area have produced a lot of red ink, with a loss in the fiscal year of 2012 of approximately US$ 216 million while previous years had proved to fare hardly any better. A major question facing Iger was how to know where money could be made in the future. Although customers willing to pay for content over the Internet increases, a clear revenue model is lacking. Iger needed to decide whether to keep up the expensive experimentation, or scale back investments until it became clearer where the web-based business was headed.

Probably Iger's biggest challenge, however, was to reinvigorate Disney's heart and soul – its film business. The Parks & Resorts division had done well, growing in revenues from US$ 11.5 in 2008 to 12.9 billion in 2012, while TV and radio had jumped from US$ 16.1 billion to 19.4 billion in the same period, with profitability to match. The merchandising business had also grown a bit, from US$ 2.9 to 3.3 billion, but the core film business had actually dropped from US$ 7.3 to 5.8 billion. With the movie industry suffering from tough times in which people buy less physical copies of movies, be it on DVD or Blu-ray Disc, and cinema success limited to familiar franchises, Disney places fewer bets. But putting only cash cow eggs in one basket, might not guarantee quality can be preserved.

In 2011, Iger's contract was extended through June 2016, making sure that he had enough time to unleash more magic in the Mouse House. He had proven to be able to do so before, a task the company and shareholders now happily entrust him with. But if Iger fails to make the right strategic decisions, the clock might strike 12 and the magic might be over.

Co-authors: Casper van der Veen and Wester Wagenaar

References: http://thewaltdisneycompany.com; *Disney Annual Report 2008–2012; Fortune*, 23 December 2001; *The Economist*, 26 January 2006, 17 April 2008, 3 September 2009 and 3 November 2012; *Business Week*, 5 February 2007, 9 February 2009 and 14 April 2011; *Sunday Times*, 20 February 2005 and 2 October 2005; Bloomberg, 1 September 2009 and 1 November 2012; ABC News, 7 October 2011.

INTRODUCTION TO THE READINGS

Unless a variety of opinions are laid before us, we have no opportunity of selection, but are bound of necessity to adopt the particular view which may have been brought forward. The purity of gold cannot be ascertained by a single specimen; but when we have carefully compared it with others, we are able to fix upon the finest ore.

Herodotus (5th century BC); Greek historian

In the following eleven chapters the readings will represent the different points of view in the debate. The readings will 'lay the variety of opinions before us'. However, in this opening chapter there is no central debate. Therefore, three readings have been selected that provide a stimulating introduction to the topic of strategy, or reinforce some of the arguments made in the preceding pages. Here, each of the readings are briefly introduced and its relevance for the discussion is highlighted.

The opening reading, 'Complexity: The Nature of Real World Problems', is the first chapter of Richard Mason and Ian Mitroff's classic book, *Challenging Strategic Planning Assumptions*. This extract has been selected for this chapter to serve as an introduction to the complex nature of the strategic problems addressed in this book. Mason and Mitroff's main argument is that most strategic problems facing organizations are not 'tame' – that is, they are not simple problems that can be separated and reduced to a few variables and relationships, and then quickly solved. Strategic problems are usually 'wicked': strategists are faced with situations of organized complexity in which problems are complicated and interconnected, there is much uncertainty and ambiguity, and they must deal with opposing views and conflicting interests. Therefore, strategic problems have no clearly identifiable correct solutions, but must be tackled by debating the alternatives and selecting the most promising option. Mason and Mitroff call on strategists to systematically doubt the value of all available solutions and to employ dialectics – which is exactly the approach taken in this book. In the context of this chapter, the most important message that Mason and Mitroff have is that the variety of opinions might make things more complex, but is also a useful resource for finding better quality solutions.

The second reading is a 2005 *Organizational Science* article by Wendy Smith and Michael Tushman: *Managing Strategic Contradictions*. The original article combines insights on several strategy topics in this book, such as strategic innovation, strategizing and strategic leadership; however, its main purpose in this chapter is to discuss why strategists should engage in managing strategic contradictions. The authors, both from Harvard Business School, represent the philosophy of this book well.

The last reading, 'Cultural Constraints in Management Theories' by Geert Hofstede, has been selected to sow seeds of further doubt about the universal validity of strategic management theories. Hofstede is one of the most prominent cross-cultural researchers in the field of management and is known, in particular, for his five dimensions for measuring cultural traits. In this reading he briefly describes the major characteristics of management in Germany, Japan, France, Holland, South-East Asia, Africa, Russia and China, contrasting them all to the United States, to drive home his point that management practices differ from country to country depending on the local culture. Each national style is based on cultural characteristics that differ sharply around the world. Hofstede argues that theories are formulated within these national cultural contexts, and thus reflect the local demands and predispositions. Therefore, he concludes that universal management theories do not exist – each theory is culturally constrained. If Hofstede is right, this re-emphasizes the necessity to view strategic management and strategy theories from an international perspective. Readers must judge which strategy approach is best suited to the national circumstances with which they are confronted.

Complexity: The nature of real world problems

By Richard Mason and Ian Mitroff [1]

Try a little experiment. Make a short list of the major problems or issues facing policymakers in the world today. Now take your list and arrange it as a matrix like the one in Figure 1.1.1. For each element in the matrix ask yourself the following question: Is the solution to one problem (the row problem) in any way related to the solution of the other problem (the column problem)? If the answer is yes, place a check mark at the point where the row and column intersect; otherwise leave it blank. When you have completed the process, review the matrix and count the number of blanks. Are there any?

'Not fair!' you may say. 'There were a lot of check marks in my matrix because many of these world problems are linked together.' World problems involve all nations. One would not expect to get the same result if the focus was, say, on one's company, city, family, or personal life. Really? Try it and see. Recently, several managers at a major corporation tried this little experiment as part of a strategic planning effort.

Among the issues and problem areas they identified were the following:

- Satisfy stockholder dividend and risk requirements.
- Acquire adequate funds for expansion from the capital markets.
- Ensure a stable supply of energy at reasonable prices.
- Train a corps of middle managers to assume more responsibility.
- Develop a marketing force capable of handling new product lines.

The managers found that all of these problems and issues were related to each other. Some were only related weakly, but most were related quite strongly. Repeated attempts in other contexts give the same result: *basically, every real world policy problem is related to every other real world problem*. This is an important finding. It means that every time a policymaker attempts to

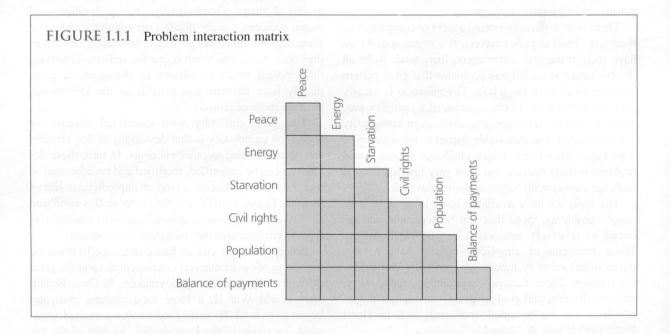

FIGURE 1.1.1   Problem interaction matrix

[1]Source: This article was adapted from Chapter 1 of R. Mason and I. Mitroff, *Challenging Strategic Planning Assumptions*, © John Wiley & Sons, Inc. 1981. This material is used by permission of John Wiley & Sons, Inc.

solve a particular policy problem he or she must consider its potential relationship with all other problems. To do this one must have both a comprehensive set of concepts for dealing with any policy and a rich set of tools for acquiring the holistic information needed to guide policy making.

Characteristics of complexity

There are several characteristics of policy making that the foregoing little experiment is intended to illustrate:

- Any policy-making situation comprises many problems and issues.
- These problems and issues tend to be highly interrelated. Consequently, the solution to one problem requires a solution to all the other problems. At the same time, each solution creates additional dimensions to be incorporated in the solutions to other problems.
- Few, if any, problems can be isolated effectively for separate treatment.

These are the characteristics of complexity. Complexity literally means the condition of being tightly woven or entwined together. Most policymakers find that the problems they face today are complex in this sense. Moreover, almost all of today's problems seem to be getting more plentiful and complex.

There is an especially vexing aspect of complexity as it presents itself to policymakers. It is organized. As we have seen in the little experiment, there tends to be an illusive structure underlying problems that gives pattern and organization to the whole. Organization is usually considered the route to the solution of a complex problem. In reality, however, organization in complexity can become an insurmountable barrier to the solution of a problem. This is the major challenge to real world problem solving because we have very few intellectual tools for coping with 'organized complexity.'

The tools we have available seem to work best on simple problems, those that can be separated and reduced to relatively few variables and relationships. These problems of simplicity usually have a one-dimensional value system or goal structure that guides the solution. Three factors – separability, reducibility, and one-dimensional goal structure – mean that simple problems can be bounded, managed, and, as Horst Rittel (1972) puts it, 'tamed.'

Ironically, problems of the utmost complexity can also be tamed as long as the complexity is 'disorganized.'

That is, whenever the number of variables is very large and the variables are relatively disconnected, the problem can be tamed with the elegant simplicity of statistical mechanics. For example, there is no known way of predicting how a given individual will vote on a political candidate. However, using polling procedures and statistical techniques it is possible to predict with a fair degree of confidence how an entire population of voters will vote. Similarly, it is difficult to predict whether a given customer will purchase a new product or not. However, using market research methods, a fairly good estimate can be made of a new product's potential market share.

Perhaps one of the greatest insights of the 20th century is the discovery that when a problem situation meets the condition for random sampling – many individual elements exhibiting independent, probabilistic behaviour – there is a potential statistical solution to the problem. In short, disorganized complexity can generally be tamed by statistical means.

One place where the assumption of disorganized complexity has proven invaluable in the past is in the actuarial sciences. Today, however, the insurance industry is discovering that many of the risks once assumed to be reasonably independent and hence analysable according to standard actuarial methods are no longer so. People, organizations and facilities have become more tightly woven together over wider geographical areas. Consequently, the probabilities of death, accident, fire, or disaster on which the risks and premiums are based are no longer as straightforward as they once were. The result is that the statistical methods that applied under conditions of disorganized complexity have become less reliable as the system has become more organized.

The great difficulty with connected systems of organized complexity is that deviations in one element can be transmitted to other elements. In turn, these deviations can be magnified, modified and reverberated so that the system takes on a kind of unpredictable life of its own. Emery and Trist (1965) refer to this condition as 'environmental connectedness' and have labelled this type of environment the 'turbulent' environment.

Emery and Trist cite an interesting case to illustrate the nature of environmental connectedness and the great difficulties it presents to policymakers. In Great Britain after World War II, a large food canning company began to expand. Its main product was a canned vegetable – a staple in the English diet. As part of the expansion plan, the company decided to build a new, automated factory, requiring an investment of several million pounds sterling. For over a decade the company had enjoyed a 65 per cent market share for their product line and saw no reason for this strong market position to deteriorate. Given this large volume, the new plant offered the 'experience curve' advantages of economies to scale and made possible the long production runs required to meet the demand from the traditional market.

After ground was broken, but well before the factory was completed, a series of seemingly detached and isolated socioeconomic events occurred. These relatively insignificant events were to change the destiny of the company. Taken collectively, they rendered the factory economically obsolete and threw the corporate board of directors into a state of turmoil. The scenario of events went something like this. Due to the release of wartime controls on steel strip and tin, a number of new small firms that could economically can imported fruit sprang up. Initially, they in no way competed directly with the large vegetable canner. However, since their business was seasonal, they began to look for ways to keep their machinery and labour employed during the winter. Their answer came from a surprising source – the US quick-frozen food industry. The quick-freezing process requires a substantial degree of consistency in the crop. This consistency is very difficult to achieve. However, it turned out that large crops of the vegetable were grown in the United States and a substantial portion of US crops was unsuitable for quick freezing (a big industry in the United States) but quite suitable for canning. Furthermore, American farmers had been selling this surplus crop at a very low price for animal feed and were only too happy to make it available at an attractive price to the small canners in the United Kingdom. The canners jumped at the opportunity and imported the crop. Using off-season production capacity they began to offer a low-cost product in the large canner's market. The small canners' position was further strengthened as underdeveloped countries began to vie with the United States in an effort to become the cheapest source of supply for the crop.

These untimely events in the large canner's supply market were compounded by events in its product market. Prior to the introduction of quick-freezing, the company featured a high quality, higher price premier brand that dominated the market. This market advantage, however, was diminished by the cascading effect of several more unpredictable events. As the scenario unfolded the quick-frozen product captured the high quality strata of the market, a growing dimension due to increased affluence. The smaller canners stripped off the lower price layers of the market, aided in part by

another seemingly unrelated development in retailing – the advent of supermarkets. As supermarkets and large grocery chains developed, they sought to improve their position by establishing their own in-house brand names and by buying in bulk. The small canner filled this need for the supermarket chains. Small canners could undercut the price of the manufacturer's brand product because they had low production costs and almost no marketing expenses. Soon supermarket house brands (which had accounted for less than 1 per cent of the market prior to the war) became the source of 50 per cent of the market sales. The smaller canners were the benefactors of almost all of this growth.

As a result, the company's fancy new automated factory was totally inappropriate for the current market situation. The company's management had failed to appreciate that a number of outside events were becoming connected with each other in a way that was leading up to an inevitable general change. They tried desperately to defend their traditional product lines, but, in the end, this was to no avail. After a series of financial setbacks, the company had to change its mission. It re-emerged several years later with a new product mix and a new identity. Management had learned the hard way that their strategy problems were neither problems of simplicity nor problems of disorganized complexity. They were problems of organized complexity.

Many corporate policy planning and strategy issues exhibit this property of organized complexity. The vegetable canning company's automated plant decision clearly was made under conditions of organized complexity. Pricing problems also frequently display this characteristic. Recently, a large pharmaceutical firm addressed the seemingly simple problem of setting a price for its primary drug line. The company's management soon learned, however, that there was an intricate web of corporate relationships woven around this one decision. Below the surface there was a structure of complex relationships between the firm's drug pricing policy and physicians, pharmacists, patients, competitors, suppliers, the FDA and other parties. These relationships organized the complexity of the firm's pricing decision problem. Purely analytical or statistical methods were rendered inappropriate.

'Wicked' problems

Today, few of the pressing problems are truly problems of simplicity or of disorganized complexity. They are more like the problems described in the illustrative cases above and the ones we uncovered in our little experiment: problems of organized complexity. These problems simply cannot be tamed in the same way that other problems can. For this reason Rittel refers to these problems of organized complexity as 'wicked' problems. Wicked problems are not necessarily wicked in the perverse sense of being evil. Rather, they are wicked like the head of a hydra. They are an ensnarled web of tentacles. The more you attempt to tame them, the more complicated they become.

Rittel (1972) has identified several characteristic properties of wicked problems that distinguish them from tame problems. These properties are:

1 *Ability to formulate the problem*

   a Tame problems can be exhaustively formulated and written down on a piece of paper.

   b Wicked problems have no definitive formulation.

2 *Relationship between problem and solution*

   a Tame problems can be formulated separately from any notion of what their solution might be.

   b Every formulation of a wicked problem corresponds to a statement of solution and vice versa. Understanding the problem is synonymous with solving it.

3 *Testability*

   a The solution to a tame problem can be tested. Either it is correct or it is false. Mistakes and errors can be pinpointed.

   b There is no single criteria system or rule that determines whether the solution to a wicked problem is correct or false. Solutions can only be good or bad relative to one another.

4 *Finality*

   a Tame problems have closure – a clear solution and ending point. The end can be determined by means of a test.

   b There is no stopping rule for wicked problems. Like a Faustian bargain, they require eternal vigilance. There is always room for improvement. Moreover, since there is neither an immediate nor ultimate test for the solution to the problem, one never knows when one's work is done. As a result, the potential consequences of the problem are played out indefinitely.

5 *Tractability*

   a There is an exhaustive list of permissible operations that can be used to solve a tame problem.

   b There is no exhaustive, enumerable list of permissible operations to be used for solving a wicked problem.

6 *Explanatory characteristics*

   a A tame problem may be stated as a 'gap' between what 'is' and what 'ought' to be and there is a clear explanation for every gap.

   b Wicked problems have many possible explanations for the same discrepancy. Depending on which explanation one chooses, the solution takes on a different form.

7 *Level of analysis*

   a Every tame problem has an identifiable, certain, natural form; there is no need to argue about the level of the problem. The proper level of generality can be found for bounding the problem and identifying its root cause.

   b Every wicked problem can be considered as a symptom of another problem. It has no identifiable root cause; since curing symptoms does not cure problems, one is never sure the problem is being attacked at the proper level.

8 *Reproducibility*

   a A tame problem can be abstracted from the real world, and attempts can be made to solve it over and over again until the correct solution is found.

   b Each wicked problem is a one-shot operation. Once a solution is attempted, you can never undo what you have already done. There is no trial and error.

9 *Replicability*

   a The same tame problem may repeat itself many times.

   b Every wicked problem is essentially unique.

10 *Responsibility*

   a No one can be blamed for failing to solve a tame problem, although solving a tame problem may bring someone acclaim.

   b The wicked problem solver has 'no right to be wrong.' He is morally responsible for what he is doing and must share the blame when things go wrong. However, since there is no way of knowing when a wicked problem is solved, very few people are praised for grappling with them.

Characteristics of wicked problems. Most policy planning and strategy problems are wicked problems of organized complexity. These complex wicked problems also exhibit the following characteristics:

1 Interconnectedness. Strong connections link each problem to other problems. As a result, these connections sometimes circle back to form feedback loops. 'Solutions' aimed at the problem seem inevitably to have important opportunity costs and side effects. How they work out depends on events beyond the scope of any one problem.

2 Complicatedness. Wicked problems have numerous important elements with relationships among them, including important 'feedback loops' through which a change tends to multiply itself or perhaps even cancel itself out. Generally, there are various leverage points where analysis and ideas for intervention might focus, as well as many possible approaches and plausible programmes of action. There is also a likelihood that different programmes should be combined to deal with a given problem.

3 Uncertainty. Wicked problems exist in a dynamic and largely uncertain environment, which creates a need to accept risk, perhaps incalculable risk. Contingency planning and also the flexibility to respond to unimagined and perhaps unimaginable contingencies are both necessary.

4 Ambiguity. The problem can be seen in quite different ways, depending on the viewer's personal characteristics, loyalties, past experiences, and even on accidental circumstances of involvement. There is no single 'correct view' of the problem.

5 Conflict. Because of competing claims, there is often a need to trade off 'goods' against 'bads' within the same value system. Conflicts of interest among persons or organizations with different or even antagonistic value systems are to be expected. How things will work out may depend on interaction among powerful interests that are unlikely to enter into fully cooperative arrangements.

6 Societal constraints. Social, organizational and political constraints and capabilities, as well as technological ones, are central both to the feasibility and the desirability of solutions.

These characteristics spell difficulty for the policymaker who seeks to serve a social system by changing it for the better. Policymakers must choose the means for securing improvement for the people they serve. They must design, steer and maintain a stable social system in the context of a complex environment. To do this, they require new methods of real world problem solving to guide their policy-making activities. Otherwise, they run the risk of setting their social systems adrift.

Implications for policy making. The wicked problems of organized complexity have two major implications for designing processes for making policy:

1 There must be a broader participation of affected parties, directly and indirectly, in the policy making process.

2 Policy making must be based on a wider spectrum of information gathered from a larger number of diverse sources.

Let us consider each of these implications in turn. The first implication indicates that policy making is increasingly becoming a political process; political in the sense that it involves individuals forming into groups to pursue common interests. Turn again to the results of the little experiment conducted at the outset of this chapter. You will find that in almost every case there are a variety of individual interests at stake in each problem area cited. Furthermore, one of the major factors creating the linkages between problem areas – organizing their complexity – is the number of diverse individual interests that cut across problem areas. Individuals are part of the problem and hence must be part of the solution.

This means that the raw material for forging solutions to wicked problems is not concentrated in a single head, but rather is widely dispersed among the various parties at stake. For any given wicked problem there is a variety of classes of expertise. Every affected party is an expert on some aspect of the problem and its solution. Furthermore, the disparate parties are bound together in a common venture. Thus some form of collective risk sharing is needed in order to deal effectively with the consequences of wicked problems. This suggests the need for a substantial degree of involvement in the policy-making process by those potentially affected by a policy in its formulation process. Effective policy is made *with*, or if adequate representation is present, *for*, but *not at* people. At least those involved should be able to voice their opinion on the relative goodness or badness of proposed solutions.

The diversity of parties at stake is related to the second implication. Since much of the necessary information for coping with wicked problems resides in the heads of several individuals, methods are needed to obtain this information from them and to communicate it to others. This means that as many of the different sources of information as possible must be identified. The relevant information must be obtained from each and stated in an explicit manner.

Contained in the minds of each participant in a wicked problem are powerful notions as to what is, what ought to be, why things are the way they are, how they can be changed, and how to think about their complexity. This represents a much broader class of information than is commonly used to solve problems of simplicity or of disorganized complexity. Also, this participant-based information is less likely to have been stated and recorded in a communicable form. Consequently, this information must be 'objectified' – explicitly, articulated – so that the basis for each party's judgements may be exchanged with others. Objectification has the advantages of being explicit, providing a memory, controlling the delegation of judgements, and raising pertinent issues that might have been ignored otherwise. It also stimulates *doubt*.

To be in doubt about a piece of information is to withhold assent to it. Given the range of diverse information that characterizes a wicked problem, participants in the policy-making process are well advised to develop a healthy respect for the method of doubt. In dealing with problems of organized complexity one should start with Descartes' rule: 'The first precept was never to accept a thing as true until I knew it was such without a single doubt.' This does not mean that one should be a 'nay sayer' or a permanent sceptic. To do so would impede responsible action that must be taken. What it does imply is that one should withhold judgement on things until they have been tested.

All problem-solving methods presuppose some form of guarantor for the correctness of their solutions. Problems of simplicity can be tested and solutions guaranteed by means of repeated solving, just as a theorem is proven in mathematics. This is because simple problems can be stated in closed form. The solutions to problems of disorganized complexity can be guaranteed within some stated confidence interval or degree of risk because the problems are statistical in nature. However, since there are no clearly identifiable correct solutions to problems of organized complexity, neither analytic nor statistical proofs can guarantee results. For solutions to wicked problems, the method of doubt is the best guarantor available.

Dialectics and argumentation are methods of *systematizing* doubt. They entail the processes of:

1 making information and its underlying assumptions explicit;

2 raising questions and issues toward which different positions can be taken;

3 gathering evidence and building arguments for and against each position;

4 attempting to arrive at some final conclusion.

Being fundamentally an argumentative process, these four processes are inherent to policy making. For every policy decision there are always at least two alternative choices that can be made. There is an argument for and against each alternative. It is by weighing the pros and cons of each argument that an informed decision can be reached. In policy making these processes of dialectics and argumentation are inescapable.

In addition to the need for participation by a variety of parties and the existence of diverse information sources, two other characteristics of wicked problems should be noted. One is that they must be dealt with in a holistic or synthetic way as well as in an analytic way. Two processes are necessary: to subdivide a complex problem into its elements and to determine the nature of the linkages that give organization to its complexity – the task of analysis; and to understand the problem as a *whole* – the task of synthesis. A critical dimension of wicked problems of organized complexity is that they must ultimately be dealt with in their totality. This calls for holistic thinking. Analysis is only an aid toward reaching a synthesis.

A second characteristic of these problems is that there is some form of latent structure within them. They are organized to some extent. Organization is not an all or nothing phenomenon. Consequently, systems thinking and methods can be used to gain better insight into the structural aspects of wicked problems.

Quest for new methods. The nature and implications of organized complexity suggest some new criteria for the design of real world problem-solving methods. These criteria are:

1 Participative. Since the relevant knowledge necessary to solve a complex problem and also the relevant resources necessary to implement the solution are distributed among many individuals, the methods must incorporate the active involvement of groups of people.

2 Adversarial. We believe that the best judgement on the assumptions in a complex problem is rendered in the context of opposition. Doubt is the guarantor.

3 Integrative. A unified set of assumptions and a coherent plan of action are needed to guide effective

policy planning and strategy making. Participation and the adversarial process tend to differentiate and expand the knowledge base. Something else is needed to bring this diverse but relevant knowledge together in the form of a total picture.

4   Managerial mind supporting. Most problem-solving methods and computer aids focus on 'decision support systems,' that is, on systems that provide guidance for choosing a particular course of action to solve a particular decision problem. Problems of

organized complexity, as we have seen, are ongoing, ill structured, and generally 'wicked.' The choice of individual courses of action is only a part of the manager's or policymaker's need. More important is the need to achieve insight into the nature of the complexity and to formulate concepts and world views for coping with it. It is the policymaker's thinking process and his or her mind that needs to be supported.

READING 1.2

Managing strategic contradictions

By Wendy K. Smith and Michael L. Tushmann[1]

It is precisely the function of the executive to facilitate the synthesis in concrete action of the contradictory forces, to reconcile the concrete forces, instincts, interests, conditions, positions, and ideals
(Barnard 1968, p. 21).

The paradox of administration [involves] the dual searches for certainty and flexibility
(Thompson 1967, p. 150).

Even with Thompson's (1967) and Barnard's (1968) early admonitions, effectively managing strategic contradiction has not been at the centre of organizational analysis. While Cameron and Quinn (1988) and Poole and Van de Ven (1989) have explicitly argued that firms must build capabilities to attend to contradictions, the theoretical and empirical work on building teams and architectures to manage these tensions has remained in our field's periphery. However, contradictions abound. Firms are pressed to be both big and small, efficient and effective, and to operate in multiple time frames, as well as to be prospectors and analysers (Gavetti and Levinthal, 2000; Miles and Snow, 1978). Similarly, senior teams are pressed to search both forward and backward, to be both flexible and focused, and to both learn and unlearn (Bunderson and Sutcliffe, 2002; Flynn and Chatman, 2001; Adler et al., 1999). The purpose of this paper is to encourage scholars to bring the dynamics of attending to and dealing with strategic contradiction more to the centre of organization science.

The top management team literature has been particularly silent on teams dealing with contradictions

(e.g., Adner and Helfat, 2003; Finkelstein and Hambrick, 1996). This literature has focused predominantly on overcoming inertia and implementing innovation (Kaplan et al., 2003; Van de Ven et al., 1999). To address this question of balancing inconsistencies, we turn to the organizational literature on paradox, contradiction and conflict (Lewis, 2000; Poole and Van de Ven, 1989). This literature assumes that inconsistent and contradictory agendas coexist and can both succeed simultaneously. By shifting the perspective from choosing between contradictory agendas to embracing the contradictions, this literature provides an important lens through which to understand how to manage contradictions. Building on this literature, we argue that effectively managing contradictions is rooted in paradoxical cognition – managerial frames and processes that recognize and embrace contradiction. We explore how these frames and processes operate in the context of top management teams, and identify aspects of team design and leader behaviours to support these processes.

[1]Source: Reproduced with permission from Wendy K. Smith and Michael L. Tushman (2005) 'Managing Strategic Contradictions', *Organization Science* Vol. 16(5) pp. 522–536.

Top management teams and team outcomes

Top management teams balance short-term performance and long-term adaptability through resource allocation trade-offs and organizational designs decisions (Edmondson *et al.*, 2003; Eisenhardt and Zbaracki, 1992; Hambrick 1994). These strategic decisions require teams to negotiate between the existing product and the innovation, identifying outcomes that will ensure the performance of both agendas. Borrowing from the negotiation and conflict management literature, we define balanced strategic decisions based on two criteria: (1) their distributive nature, which we define as making balanced trade-offs over time; and (2) their integrative nature, which we define as identifying synergies (Bazerman, 1998; Lax and Sebenius, 1986; Walton and McKersie, 1965).

The distributive aspect of a decision involves the division of resources between the existing product and the innovation. Lax and Sebenius (1986) call this "claiming value," as managers identify resources for each individual product. Teams make a number of decisions in which they might preferentially support either the existing product or the innovation. These decisions are balanced when, over time, they support both products. For example, Ciba Vision's top management team balanced the ongoing demands of their conventional hard lenses even as they invested in daily disposables, extended wear and Visudyne (Tushman and O'Reilly, 1997). In allocating scarce resources, this senior team worked to balance the needs of the existing product even as they worked to develop several possible substitutes.

Decisions can also be defined by their integrative nature – the recognition of opportunities, linkages and synergies that might arise. Lax and Sebenius (1986) call this creating value, in which the negotiated value increases when teams identify creative solutions from which both parties benefit. Top management teams might be able to achieve integrative value in their decisions when they identify ways to benefit from shared resources or to benefit from shared selling in the marketplace. For example, Ciba Vision unexpectedly found that introducing soft contact lenses to the market increased the demand for their conventional lenses. Similarly, *USA Today* found that their online business could leverage the newspaper's content and accelerate readership across both platforms (Gilbert, 2005).

While organizations can excel when top management teams effectively balance strategic contradictions, structural, psychological and social psychological barriers often prevent them from doing so (Van de Ven *et al.*, 1999; Bazerman and Watkins, 2004; Virany *et al.*, 1992). Organizations benefit when structural features of the organization (tasks, skills, formal organization and culture) are internally aligned and are aligned with the firm's strategy (Chandler, 1962; Nadler and Tushman, 1992), yet these internally congruent design features are simultaneously associated with structural and social inertia. Thus, when structure, strategies and competencies all reinforce one another, managers are psychologically more resistant to changing them (Henderson and Clark, 1991; Kaplan *et al.*, 2003; Tripsas and Gavetti, 2000). Levinthal and March (1993) suggest that managers are myopic – privileging short term over long term, close rather than far, and certainty of success over risk of failure. More broadly, Bazerman and Watkins (2004) observe that historical success is associated with a set of fundamental individual cognitive biases that drive predictable organizational (and social) pathology.

Finally, distinct from inertial forces rooting organizations and their top management teams to the past, a different impediment to balanced decision making is an individual and team drive for consistency and uncertainty reduction. If individuals privilege consistency over inconsistency, the response to these uncertainties and contradictions is to move toward reducing these inconsistencies and aligning one's own behaviours and cognitions, as well one's multiple activities and social networks, with one another (Lewis, 2000; Denison *et al.*, 1995).

This effort to preserve consistency stems from a fundamental epistemological belief of a unitary truth (Ford and Backoff, 1988; Voorhees, 1986). This belief in a unitary truth means inconsistencies cannot fundamentally coexist. There must be a contingency that mediates between inconsistent ideas. One consequence of consistency-oriented thinking is the need to solve conflicts. As this logic suggests, when two things are in conflict, one of them must be right and the other wrong. In a negotiation, this bias leads to what Bazerman (1998) calls the problem of the mythical fixed pie. By focusing on solving the conflict, negotiators focus on distributing resources between them, rather than finding cooperative means for expanding the value of resources.

However, conflicts and inconsistencies cannot be eliminated. Balancing strategic decisions requires teams to recognize and use these conflicts, rather than try to resolve them. Mary Parker Follett recognized this in her early writings. She observed, "As conflict – difference – is here in the world, as we cannot avoid it, we should, I think, use it" (Follett, 1925/1996, p. 67). Similarly, Eisenhardt *et al.* (1997) found that using conflict improves the quality of managerial strategic decision making. To make balanced strategic decisions, top management teams need to confront and overcome these structural, social psychological and psychological barriers that create tendencies for both inertia and consistency. Top management team conditions must be able to support conflict, despite inertial tendencies, and enable the coexistence of inconsistent agendas, despite forces for consistency.

Managing strategic contradictions: Paradoxical cognition

We develop a model of balancing strategic contradiction. This model takes into account challenges of inertia and consistency that reinforce the existing product and push top management teams to choose one agenda rather than to support multiple agendas. In addressing these biases, we begin with the psychological biases, and identify cognitive frames and processes that can overcome organizational pressures for inertia as well as individual preferences for consistency. We then identify structural features that might facilitate a team's ability to attend to and deal with strategic contradiction.

Cognitive biases define how managers understand a situation, seek information and make decisions (Levinthal and March, 1993; Walsh, 1995). Managers' understanding and processing of tensions and contradictions has an impact on whether they embrace the tensions and benefit from them, or are halted by the

inconsistencies (Ford and Backoff, 1988; Lewis 2000; Smith and Berg, 1987). Paradoxical cognition – paradoxical frames and cognitive processes of differentiating and integrating – enable balanced strategic decisions (see Figure 1.2.1).

Although the distinction between cognitive frames and cognitive processes is latent in the managerial cognition literature (Walsh, 1995; Weick, 1979), we make them explicit here. Cognitive frames are stable constructs that provide a lens to understand a situation. These cognitive frames, in turn, create a context for complex behavioral responses (Walsh, 1995; Denison *et al.*, 1995). Cognitive processes are behavioural routines and ways that managers use to think about and respond to information (Weick *et al.* 1999). These frames create foundations that enable a set of complex cognitive processes. Our explanation and examples of paradoxical cognition move between the individual and team levels. In the following section, we return to explore the grounding of this model at either the individual or team level in more depth.

Cognitive frames

Walsh (1995) defines a cognitive frame as "a mental template that individuals impose on an environment to give it form" (p. 281). These mental templates create a lens through which managers filter knowledge and direct action. More specifically, managerial cognitive frames drive organizational action by directing attention to particular issues (Daft and Weick, 1984; Dutton and Jackson, 1987; Kaplan, 2003), defining the leader's understanding of the issues they face (Dutton and Ashford, 1993; Gilbert, 2005), and assigning socio-emotional information to particular issues (Pinkley, 1990).

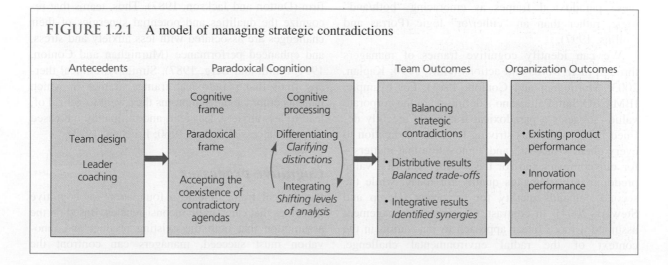

FIGURE 1.2.1 A model of managing strategic contradictions

Balancing strategic contradiction may be associated with paradoxical frames – mental templates in which managers recognize and accept the simultaneous existence of contradictory forces. To more clearly describe paradoxical frames, we explore the nature of paradoxes more generally. Ford and Backoff (1988) define social paradox (paradoxes of thoughts, actions and beliefs, rather than paradoxes of mathematics or rhetoric) as "Some 'thing' that is constructed by individuals when oppositional tendencies are brought into recognizable proximity through reflection or interaction" (p. 89). This definition suggests that paradoxes involve aspects of both a situation (oppositional tendencies) and an actor's cognition (reflection or interaction). Specifically, a paradox is created when (1) tensions in a situation are (2) juxtaposed through actor's cognition.

Organizing inherently involves contradictions. The act of organizing creates distinctions of roles and responsibilities, which must be coordinated and integrated to achieve an overall goal. These distinctions result in contradictions within firms (Poole and Van de Ven, 1989; Weick, 1979). Organizational literature is ripe with the recognition of contradictory relations between, for example, individual and group demands, between focus and flexibility, and between autonomy and democracy (Cameron and Quinn, 1988; Flynn and Chatman, 2001; Nonaka and Toyama, 2002; Rivkin and Siggelkow, 2003). Increasingly, our literature has used the term paradox to define and describe these contradictory contexts. However, this use of paradox often obscures the role of the actor in understanding and then managing these tensions. Paradoxical frames therefore refer to an actor's cognitive juxtaposition of the opposing forces in which actors embrace rather than avoid or deny these tensions. Practitioners refer to these paradoxical frames as embracing "both/and" logic, rather than an "either/or" logic (Porras and Collins, 1997).

We can identify cognitive frames of managers through their words and actions (Huff, 1990; Kaplan, 2003; Murnighan and Conlon, 1991). For example, IBM CEO Sam Palmisano's definition of the corporate values suggests a paradoxical frame. He recently defined IBM's values as striving for both "dedication to every client's success" and "innovation that matters – for our company and for the world." The first value predominantly demands quality for today, while the second demands quality for tomorrow (Hemp and Stewart, 2004). In contrast, Goodyear's management assumed a more linear approach to innovation in the context of the radial environmental challenge.

Confronted by Michelin's introduction of the radial tyre, Goodyear's senior team initially focused on the existing product and avoided the radial challenge. When they finally introduced the radial tyre, Goodyear completely shifted from bias-ply tyres to radials (Sull et al., 1997). This strategic shift at Goodyear was associated with a fundamentally new senior team (see also Virany et al., 1992).

Recognizing and embracing contradictions leads to increased success. At an organizational level, managers of the Toyota Production System, the highly successful just-in-time manufacturing process, framed their organizational goals paradoxically – low costs and high specialization, low (or no) inventory, yet immediate access to parts (Adler et al., 1999, Eisenhardt and Westcott, 1988). The organization then built routines and processes to achieve these goals. At a team level, Murnighan and Conlon (1991) found that the performance among British string quartets was associated with members recognizing contradictions inherent in their group processes – democracy and leadership, conflict and compromise.

How might paradoxical frames increase organizational performance? First, these frames create a context that demands the articulation of distinct goals for the existing product and for the innovation. Creating clear and concise goals motivates the achievement of those goals (Latham and Locke, 1995). By defining distinct goals, managers motivate the success of both the exploitative and the exploratory products. Paradoxical frames are also associated with reduced threat and fear, which enables positive conflict. A paradoxical frame signals that managers expect both frames to succeed. This opportunistic framing helps shift the threat and competition from between the two products to how these products might benefit one another and the larger firm (Dutton and Jackson, 1987). Thus, teams that recognize the dualities and potential synergies of their challenges are associated with less anxiety and stress, and enhanced performance (Murnighan and Conlon, 1991; Smith and Berg, 1987). Similarly, clinical therapy finds that paradoxical frames, frames in which patients embrace the symptoms they want to get rid of, lead to less anxiety, less fear, and ultimately increased clinical success (Frankel, 1960; Linehan, 1993).

Cognitive processes

Paradoxical frames create a foundation for cognitive processes that can handle inconsistencies. Based on the assumption that both the existing product and innovation must succeed, managers can confront the relationship between these two products – both their differences and their similarities. Effectively managing these contradictions is associated with two distinct cognitive processes – differentiating and integrating. Whereas differentiating involves recognizing and articulating distinctions, integrating involves shifting levels of analysis to identify potential linkages. Differentiating helps overcome inertia, both by reinforcing the needs of each product and being vigilant that the innovation is not crowded out by commitments to existing strategies and processes. Integrating, in contrast, is associated with sustained attention to possible synergies between the exploitative and exploratory products. Attention to integration helps the team explicitly look for ways that the contradictory strategies can help each other. By addressing different aspects of paradoxical contexts, differentiating and integrating reinforce one another. This notion of cognitive differentiating and integrating is similar to the Van de Ven *et al.* (1999) notion of innovation processes that involve divergent as well as convergent processes.

Differentiating limits inertia by dampening cognitive commitments to the existing product. Langer's (1989) theory of mindfulness focuses on drawing novel distinctions as a core process to enable learning, creativity and effective decision making. By explicitly drawing distinctions, managers are less committed to existing categories or points of view. Rather, under these conditions, managers generate new categories and classifications. More clearly identifying and articulating the needs of both agendas allows decision makers to more effectively allocate the resources such that each agenda is allowed to evolve. Such differentiating between strategic agendas helps leaders develop the behavioural complexities such that both agendas can succeed (Dutton and Jackson, 1987; Denison *et al.*, 1995).

Cognitive differentiating also encourages managers to explore new markets, new skills and new opportunities for the innovation, unburdened by the context of the existing product. For example, newspaper managers reacted differently to the introduction of online news. In those most successful newspapers, senior managers saw online as a strategic opportunity and were able to creatively differentiate online offerings from their traditional newspaper.

This cognitive differentiation allowed these managers to build firms that excelled both in print and online. In contrast, those less successful teams saw online as a threat and, in turn, focused quickly on leveraging their existing competencies, and in turn restricting the innovation's growth (Gilbert, 2005).

Differentiating helps managers to overcome inertia as they are freed up to seek novelty and opportunity in the innovation (Dutton and Jackson, 1987).

This cognitive differentiating in top management teams generates variation along with abundant information. Such information richness helps make more effective trade-offs and strategic decisions. For example, Eisenhardt and Zbaracki (1992) found that accessing and using more information helped decision makers make decisions more rapidly. Similarly, Weick *et al.* (1999) found that in high-reliability organizations, team members are unwilling to simplify their operations. This ongoing cognitive differentiating leads to the generation of more information and, ultimately, enhanced effectiveness in responding to challenging situations.

While differentiating enables balanced decision making by reducing inertia, it can also lead to increased competition. Noticing distinctions reinforces distributive decision making at the expense of integrative decision making. These distinctions may be associated with group conflict and associated process losses (Steiner, 1972; Edmondson *et al.*, 2003). For example, Firestone's senior team's clarity about the fundamental strategic and organizational differences between radial tyres and their existing bias-ply tyres led them to underfund and undercut their development of an effective radial strategy (Sull, 1999). Similarly, at Polaroid, even with significant resources devoted to digital photography, the senior team's response to this potentially cannibalizing technology was to resist and marginalize senior team members associated with the new technology (Tripsas and Gavetti, 2000).

The potential team conflicts associated with differentiating may be offset by processes of integrating. In their analysis of integrative thinking, Suedfeld *et al.* (1992) define integrating as the "development of conceptual connections among differentiated dimensions or perspectives." Integrating involves shifting levels of analysis from the product level to the organizational level of analysis to identify possible synergies. Where cognitive differentiating at the product level builds in conflict, integrative thinking uses these conflicts to identify synergistic solutions at the organizational level. Shifting to the superordinate level (the organization) and linking to the overarching frame reinforces the cooperation between contradictory agendas and enables teams to better make trade-offs (Langer, 1989; Sherif, 1971). Recognizing conflicts associated with differentiation while also maintaining a belief that both products must succeed leads to creative, synergistic results. Rothenberg (1979) called this process Janusian thinking (after the two-faced Roman god Janus), in which holding inconsistencies simultaneously enabled creative solutions to the conflicts. Rothenberg (1979) found that genius thinking involved embracing inconsistent contradictions simultaneously. For example, at Ciba Vision, the articulation of an overarching aspiration of "Healthy Eyes for Life" as well as active senior team attention to integrative decision making created the context where the senior team was able to make a series of decisions such that both their conventional and disposable lens products flourished (Tushman and O'Reilly, 1997).

Differentiating and integrating are opposing, yet complementary, processes. These processes enable one another. Differentiating results in new categories and dimensions of the products and helps managers find synergies. In turn, as integrating reinforces the investment in each of the distinct products, it reduces the threat and competition that are obstacles to differentiating. It is the engagement in both of these cognitive processes that leads teams to be able to execute balanced decision making.

Team-centric and leader-centric models of embracing paradoxical cognition

How teams embrace paradoxical cognition depends on the locus of integration (Bunderson, 2003; Hambrick, 1994; Perlow *et al.*, 2004). In some top management teams, integration of strategic contradiction occurs at the leader level. In other top management teams, a group of senior managers, typically the CEO/GM and his or her direct reports, share the responsibility for integrating strategic contradictions (Ancona and Nadler, 1989; Bunderson and Sutcliffe, 2003). We label these teams as leader-centric teams and team-centric teams, respectively. Following Amabile (1996), we argue that the nature of the cognitive frames and processes are similar at the individual and the group level of analysis. Where these cognitions occur primarily in the leader in leader-centric teams, they occur through social interactions within team-centric teams. The locus of strategic integration may be contingent on the team's context and the different team types are associated with contrasting antecedent conditions. Following the work of Hackman (2002) and Wageman (2001), we explore team conditions associated with team design and leader coaching. We then explore the impact of team context on the locus of strategic integration (See Figure 1.2.2).

Antecedents of leader-centric teams

In leader-centric teams, the leader integrates the contradictory agendas. Team leaders collect information about each agenda, process that information and make decisions primarily on their own. These leaders recognize the conflicts between the agendas, and they accept and manage those conflicts. These leaders may be able to most successfully embrace paradoxical cognitions and balance strategic decisions with teams that exhibit (1) distinct roles, goals and rewards; (2) a supportive integrator; (3) extensive leader-member interactions, but limited member-member interactions; and (4) leader coaching to focus on the product level and avoid conflict.

Distinct roles, goals, and rewards

Quinn (1984) and Van de Ven *et al.* (1999) both find that teams that successfully manage paradox involve both the roles of an advocate – one who supports a particular agenda – and the role of an integrator – one who creates connections between the disparate parts. In leader-centric teams these roles are allocated to distinct team members. The leader is the integrator and the team members are the advocates. More specifically, leader-centric teams benefit from assigning different individuals to advocate for either the existing product or the innovation. By separating these roles, team members focus on their distinct task, whether exploring or exploiting, unburdened structurally or psychologically by the contradictions associated with the other (Brown and Eisenhardt, 1997; Levinthal and March, 1993). Because the task of exploring and exploiting often requires different skills and leadership styles (Leonard-Barton, 1992; Sutton, 2002; Quinn, 1984), separating these roles allows the team leader to assign appropriate team members to these tasks.

Separating roles also helps the team leaders learn about the different needs of each product. Leaders know who to turn to when seeking information about each product. More importantly, these team members can help the leader hear and understand the needs of their particular agenda. Identifying distinct roles and decision makers for the contrasting strategic agendas may be particularly important for the exploratory product (Adler *et al.*, 1999, Benner and Tushman, 2002). Aligning team members' responsibilities with clear goals and rewards helps motivate these managers

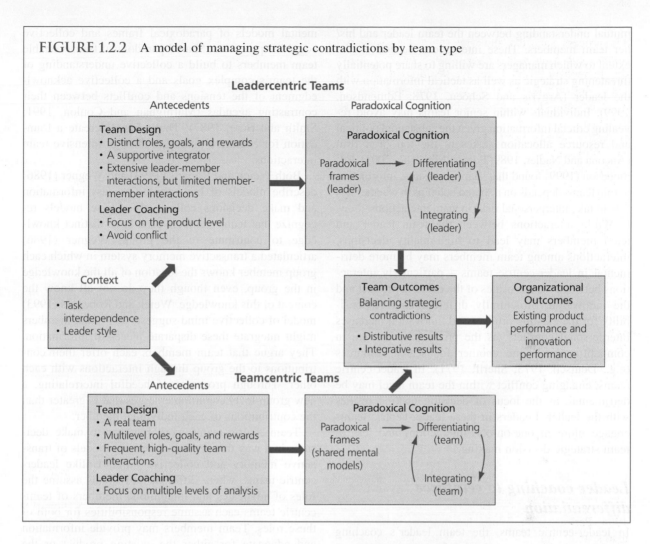

FIGURE 1.2.2   A model of managing strategic contradictions by team type

(Hackman, 2002; Kerr, 1975; Latham and Locke, 1995). Because members have distinct responsibilities for the existing product and innovation, their goals and rewards are quite distinct from one another.

Supportive integrator

In leader-centric teams, the team leader integrates the contradictory agendas. Making these trade-offs is a significant cognitive burden for team leaders (Tetlock et al., 2004) and subjects the team to the leader's decision-making biases (Bazerman and Watkins, 2004). Co-leaders, trusted advisors, or a secondary team member assigned to focus on integration help offset these biases and alleviate some of the leader's cognitive burdens (Eisenhardt et al, 1997). In an assessment of the roles of individuals surrounding American presidents, Porter (1980) found that someone often plays the role of a co-integrator, or "honest broker" to help collect, sort and

assess information. Similarly, Heenan and Bennis (1999) found that in successful co-leadership relationships, each of the partners offers different biases and skills to improve the quality of the leader's decisions. By providing another perspective, these supportive integrators help the team leader make balanced decisions.

High-quality leader-member interactions, but limited member-member interactions

Decision making in leader-centric teams depends on the quality of the interactions between the team members and the team leader. High-quality interactions enable the team leader to seek and process relevant decision-making information and, in turn, to make more balanced decisions (Eisenhardt et al., 1997). High-quality interactions are associated with the amount of information exchanged, the amount of information revealed, and the mutual understanding between the team leader and his/her team members. These interactions depend on the extent to which managers are willing to share potentially threatening strategic as well as tactical information with the leader (Argyris and Schoen, 1978; Edmondson, 1999). Individuals within senior teams may avoid revealing crucial information given the substantial political and resource allocation stakes at the top of a firm (Ancona and Nadler, 1989; Edmondson *et al.*, 2003). Edmondson (1999) found that sharing sensitive information within teams depends on a shared belief as to whether it is safe to take interpersonal risks in team interactions.

While interactions between the team leader and team members may lead to high-quality decisions, interactions among team members may be more detrimental in leader-centric teams – particularly interactions between the advocates of the existing product and the innovation. Structurally differentiating responsibility for the existing product and innovation increases interpersonal conflicts, as the product leaders are in competition with one another for scarce resources (e.g., Deutsch, 1973; Sherif, 1971). In leader-centric teams, engaging conflict within the team level may be detrimental, as the locus of decision making resides with the leader. Leaders in these leader-centric teams engage more in one-on-one interactions and less in team strategic decision making.

Leader coaching to reinforce differentiation

In leader-centric teams, the team leader's coaching provides valuable support that reinforces team processes and team beliefs (Edmondson, 1999; Hackman, 2002; Wageman, 2001). In leader-centric teams, leaders direct and focus strategy at the team level even as they focus team members at their individual product level. Reinforcing differences between the existing product and the innovation encourages the leaders of each product to focus on their particular strategic agenda. Reinforcing the necessity of both products and exhibiting coaching behaviours consistent with the contrasting strategic agendas helps differentially motivate the performance of senior team members (Denison *et al.*, 1995).

Antecedents of team-centric teams

In team-centric teams, the teams themselves integrate the contradictory agendas. Achieving balanced decisions on team-centric teams is associated with shared

mental models of paradoxical frames and collective cognitive processes. Shared paradoxical frames enable team members to build a collective understanding of the team's complex goals and a collective acknowledgment of the tensions and conflicts between their contrasting agendas (Murnighan and Conlon, 1991; Smith and Berg, 1987). These frames create a foundation for cognitive processes through intensive team interactions.

Both Weick and Roberts (1993) and Wegner (1986) describe models of how groups process information and make decisions collectively. These models recognize that team members each have distinct knowledge to contribute to the group. Wegner (1986) articulated a transactive memory system in which each group member knows the location of all the knowledge in the group, even though they do not all know the content of this knowledge. Weick and Roberts's (1993) model of collective mind suggests how team members might integrate these disparate pieces of information. They argue that team members each offer their contributions to the group through interactions with each other. Through processes of heedful interrelating, a new group-level cognition emerges that is greater than the contributions of each individual member.

Team-centric teams work together to make decisions in a way that is similar to these models of transactive memory and collective mind. Unlike leader-centric teams, where different individuals assume the roles of advocates and integrators, members of team-centric teams each assume responsibilities for both of these roles. Team members may provide information and advocate for either the existing product or the innovation. However, through processes of heedful interrelating, these team members are also responsible for integrating across their team.

Effectively embracing both intra- and interpersonal conflict is an important determinant of success for team-centric teams. Whereas leader-centric teams manage conflict by attempting to avoid it, conflict abounds on team-centric teams. Team members may experience intrapersonal conflict in their dual roles of advocates for particular products and as integrators across these products. They may also experience interpersonal conflict with other team members who are competing for scarce resources. Using this conflict to balance contradictions leads to higher quality decisions in team-centric teams. To build shared mental models and collaborative decision making, team-centric teams are associated with teams that are designed as real teams (Hackman, 2002). Further, team-centric teams exhibit (1) roles, goals and rewards at multiple levels of analysis; (2) frequent, high-quality team interactions; and (3) leader coaching to reinforce the organizational level of analysis.

Real teams

Hackman (2002) defines a real team as one with a clear sense of boundaries, an interdependent task and a clear understanding of the team's authority. A real team creates a foundation for groups of individuals to work together to achieve their collective goals. A real team allows team members to allocate clear tasks to one another, know who else has information, and work with the other members to create shared mental models and shared processes. Even as there has been a move toward increasingly using integrated teamwork among senior management, achieving teamwork is often difficult in senior teams because of the political and career issues unique to senior teams (Ancona and Nadler, 1989; Edmondson *et al.*, 2003). However, having the top management team attend to themselves as a real team helps team-centric teams deal with strategic contradiction.

Roles, goals, and rewards at multiple levels of analysis

As with leader-centric teams, team-centric teams benefit from assigning primary existing product and innovation roles to different team members and aligning these roles with product-level goals and rewards. Team members with specific product-level responsibilities focus on seeking product-specific information and ideas (Brown and Eisenhardt, 1997), even as this information is shared with the entire team (Bazerman and Watkins, 2004). These distinct responsibilities are important in overcoming inertia when teams make decisions together. When making group-level decisions, teams often prevent multiple, dissenting opinions from being expressed because team members want to quickly achieve consensus (Eisenhardt *et al.*, 1997; Nemeth and Wachtler, 1983). Often the needs of the minority opinion are not shared in group decision making. In top management teams, this minority opinion is often that of the innovation. Assigning a distinct individual to represent each agenda in team discussions encourages these opinions to be raised in team interactions.

Assigning product-level roles, goals and rewards reinforces the conflict and competition between managers of contradictory agendas. Managers of team-centric teams are able to embrace this conflict and reinforce integrative thinking by identifying a second set of roles,

goals and rewards at the organizational level – dual roles, superordinate and/or opportunistic goals (Dutton and Jackson, 1987; Sherif, 1971) and common fate rewards (Tushman *et al.*, 2003). This second set of organization-level roles, goals and rewards helps motivate team members to consider the organization's overarching and integrative strategic agenda. Creating multilevel roles, goals and rewards helps team members shift from focusing on competition to focusing on individual strategic agendas as well as the firm's overarching strategic agendas (Gilbert, 2005). Team members are asked to engage in multiple leadership roles simultaneously – both integrators as well as advocates (Quinn 1984). As Brown and Eisenhardt (1997) note, these multilevel structures and incentives provide flexibility over time, as team members shift back and forth between each of these levels.

Frequent team interactions

Weick and Roberts (1993) describe a process of integrating across distinct contributions as heedful interrelating, where team members are aware of their own and others' contributions and subordinate their own contributions for the team's benefit. Heedful interrelating involves dynamic learning processes in which team members make contributions to the team and learn from the contributions of others. Heedful interrelating depends on team members' ability to interact. The frequency of their interactions allows for more opportunity to share information with one another. As well, the quality of their interactions ensures that information is actually being shared. As with leader-centric teams, psychological safety on the team (a shared team belief that it is safe to take interpersonal risks) reinforces positive team interactions (Edmondson, 1999).

Leader coaching to facilitate integration

The behaviours of the leader in leader-centric teams reinforce the focus on differentiating products, whereas the behaviours of the leader on team-centric teams reinforce integrative behaviours. In leader-centric teams, the senior leader facilitates his/her team's interaction. These leaders encourage their team members to extend beyond their own product's focus. Team-centric leaders coach their team members to attend to both their products as well as organization-wide issues. As such, team-members in team-centric teams "wear multiple hats" (Ancona and Nadler, 1989). Such team-centric facilitation encourages team members to actively manage conflict rather than allowing it to become an obstacle in team interactions. Under what conditions do leader-centric versus team-centric teams dominate in managing strategic contradictions? It may be that task interdependence and leadership style are important contextual factors affecting the relative effectiveness of these contrasting team types. Innovation streams in which the development of the existing product and innovation are highly interdependent require increased collaborative interaction between members of the team. It may be that such tasks require increased team member interaction to attend to the uncertainty associated with such substantial task interdependence (Rivkin and Siggelkow, 2003; Nadler and Tushman, 1996; Thompson, 1967). Team-centric teams might be more able to deal with substantial interdependence than leader-centric teams. In contrast, under conditions of limited task interdependence, leader-centric teams may have sufficient information-processing capabilities to deal with the more limited coordination requirements.

A second possible moderator is the team leader's preferred leadership style. Leader-centric teams are associated with leadership that is much more authoritative, whereas team-centric teams are associated with more democratic leadership (e.g., Flynn and Chatman, 2001; Perlow et al., 2004). While team leaders may need to express multiple roles and behavioural flexibility in managing contradictory agendas (e.g., Denison et al., 1995), it may be that a leader's preferred leadership style is an important determinant of the differential effectiveness of leader-centric versus team-centric teams.

Conclusion

Competitive pressures make even more salient Thompson's (1967) and Barnard's (1968) admonitions to take contradiction and paradox seriously. We believe that the management of strategic contradiction belongs at the forefront of organizational scholarship. As such, this paper has focused on developing a set of ideas on how top management teams might deal with strategic contradiction. It may be that a root of sustained organizational performance is in the senior team's ability to successfully attend to and deal with the challenges of operating in different timeframes and strategic logics (Adner and Helfat, 2002; Adler et al., 1999; He and Wong, 2004). We argue that sustained performance occurs through attending to and dealing with strategic contradictions – short-term performance and long-term adaptability, exploration and exploitation, focus and flexibility.

The literature on organization design highlights the importance of building organizational forms that can both explore as well as exploit (e.g., Tushman and O'Reilly, 1997; Gibson and Birkinshaw, 2004; Siggelkow and Levinthal, 2003), yet even as this literature highlights the role of the senior team in creating these contradictory contexts, there is little clarity on how these teams might deal with the challenges associated with strategic contradiction. We explore those factors that enable top management teams to achieve balanced strategic decisions in contradictory contexts. We contribute to an emerging body of literature on contradiction and paradox that explores the nature of these challenges and identifies team characteristics associated with managing them. While others have identified the roles of organizational structures, cultures and routines to manage contradictions (Adler et al., 1999; Flynn and Chatman, 2001), we argue that balancing contradiction in decision making is rooted in senior team cognitions. We argue that balanced strategic decision making in the context of contradiction is rooted in paradoxical cognition – cognitive frames and processes that allow teams to effectively embrace, rather than avoid, contradictions. We further argue that, depending on the locus of integration of the inconsistent agendas, these cognitive frames and processes occur either with the senior leader or in the interactions of the entire top management team.

Empirical exploration is necessary to systematically explore the relationships between cognitive frames, cognitive processes, locus of integration, team decisions, and organizational outcomes. Such empirical research must take into account the difficulties of assessing managerial cognition. Empirically exploring such concepts requires multiple methods involving both rich qualitative data to identify and understand the nuances of managerial cognition (Huff, 1997; Kaplan, 2003) and larger sample analysis to validate these ideas (Sundaramurthy and Lewis, 2003).

It might also be important to explore the applicability of these ideas to contradictions at different levels of analysis. While we focus on strategic contradictions between exploration and exploitation for top management teams, organizations face contradictions at multiple levels of analysis. Lorsch and Tierney (2002) and Sundaramurthy and Lewis (2003) raise questions about managing contradictory needs of multiple corporate stakeholders. Adler et al. (1999), Repenning (2002), and Tyre and Von Hippel (1997) describe contradictions between efficiency and effectiveness on the factory floor and in product development. The challenge of balancing financial and social goals has received increased attention in the organizational literature (Margolis and Walsh, 2003; Paine, 2003). It may be that managing contradiction is a window into a range of important and understudied organizational challenges (Cameron and Quinn, 1988;

Poole and Van de Ven, 1989). Bringing the study of contradiction more into the centre of our field may help us rise to the challenge posed so long ago by Thompson (1967) and Barnard (1968).

READING 1.3

Cultural constraints in management theories

By Geert Hofstede[1]

Lewis Carroll's *Alice in Wonderland* contains the famous story of Alice's croquet game with the Queen of Hearts. Alice thought she had never seen such a curious croquet ground in all her life; it was all ridges and furrows; the balls were live hedgehogs, the mallets live flamingoes, and the soldiers had to double themselves up and stand on their hands and feet to make the arches. You probably know how the story goes: Alice's flamingo mallet turns its head whenever she wants to strike with it; her hedgehog ball runs away; and the doubled-up soldier arches walk around all the time. The only rule seems to be that the Queen of Hearts always wins.

Alice's croquet playing problems are good analogies of attempts to build culture-free theories of management. Concepts available for this purpose are themselves alive with culture, having been developed within a particular cultural context. They have a tendency to guide our thinking toward our desired conclusion. As the same reasoning may also be applied to the arguments in this reading, I better tell you my conclusion before I continue – so that the rules of my game are understood. In this reading we take a trip around the world to demonstrate that there are no such things as universal management theories.

Diversity in management *practices* as we go around the world has been recognized in US management literature for more than 30 years. The term 'comparative management' has been used since the 1960s. However, it has taken much longer for the US academic community to accept that not only practices but also the validity of theories may stop at national borders, and I wonder whether even today everybody would agree with this statement.

The idea that the validity of a theory is constrained by national borders is more obvious in Europe, with all its borders, than in a huge borderless country like the US. Already in the 16th century Michel de Montaigne, a Frenchman, wrote a statement which was made famous by Blaise Pascal about a century later: '*Verite en-dega des Pyrenees, erreur au-dela*' – 'There are truths on this side of the Pyrenees which are falsehoods on the other'.

From Don Armado's love to Taylor's science

According to the comprehensive ten-volume *Oxford English Dictionary*, the words 'manage', 'management' and 'manager' appeared in the English language in the 16th century. The oldest recorded use of the word 'manager' is in Shakespeare's *Love's Labour's Lost*, dating from 1588, in which Don Adriano de Armado, 'a fantastical Spaniard', exclaims (Act I, Scene II. 188): 'Adieu, valour! Rust, rapier! Be still, drum! For your manager is in love; yea, he loveth.'

The linguistic origin of the word is from *Latin manus*, hand, via the Italian *maneggiare*, which is the training of horses in the *manege;* subsequently its meaning was extended to skilful handling in general, like of arms and musical instruments, as Don Armado illustrates. However, the word also became associated with the French *menage*, household, as an equivalent of 'husbandry' in its sense of the art of running a household. The theatre of present-day management contains elements of both *manege* and *menage* and

[1]Source: This article was adapted from G. Hofstede, 'Cultural Constraints in Management Theories', *Academy of Management Executive*, Vol. 7, No. 1, 1993, pp. 8–21. © Copyright 1993 by Academy of Management. Reproduced with permission of Academy of Management via Copyright Clearance Center.

different managers and cultures may use different accents.

The founder of the science of economics, the Scot Adam Smith, in his 1776 book *The Wealth of Nations*, used 'manage', 'management' (even 'bad management') and 'manager' when dealing with the process and the persons involved in operating joint stock companies. British economist John Stuart Mill (1806–1873) followed Smith in this use and clearly expressed his distrust of such hired people who were not driven by ownership. Since the 1880s the word 'management' appeared occasionally in writings by American engineers, until it was canonized as a modern science by Frederick W. Taylor in *Shop Management* in 1903 and in *The Principles of Scientific Management* in 1911.

While Smith and Mill used 'management' to describe a process and 'managers' for the persons involved, 'management' in the American sense – which has since been taken back by the British – refers not only to the process but also to the managers as a class of people. This class (1) does not own a business but sells its skills to act on behalf of the owners and (2) does not produce personally but is indispensable for making others produce, through motivation. Members of this class carry a high status and many American boys and girls aspire to the role. In the US, the manager is a cultural hero.

Let us now turn to other parts of the world. We will look at management in its context in other successful modern economies: Germany, Japan, France, Holland and among the overseas Chinese. Then we will examine management in the much larger part of the world that is still poor, especially South-East Asia and Africa, and in the new political configurations of Eastern Europe, and Russia in particular. We will then return to the US via mainland China.

Germany

The manager is not a cultural hero in Germany. If anybody, it is the engineer who fills the hero role. Frederick Taylor's scientific management was conceived in a society of immigrants – where a large number of workers with diverse backgrounds and skills had to work together. In Germany this heterogeneity never existed.

Elements of the medieval guild system have survived in historical continuity in Germany until the present day. In particular, a very effective apprenticeship system exists both on the shop floor and in the office, which alternates practical work and classroom courses. At the end of the apprenticeship the worker receives a certificate, the *Facharbeiterbrief*, which is recognized throughout the country. About two-thirds of the German worker population holds such a certificate and a corresponding occupational pride. In fact, quite a few German company presidents have worked their way up from the ranks through an apprenticeship. In comparison, two thirds of the worker population in Britain have no occupational qualification at all.

The highly skilled and responsible German workers do not necessarily need a manager, American-style, to 'motivate' them. They expect their boss or *Meister* to assign their tasks and to be the expert in resolving technical problems. Comparisons of similar German, British and French organizations show the Germans as having the highest rate of personnel in productive roles and the lowest both in leadership and staff roles.

Japan

The American type of manager is also missing in Japan. In the United States, the core of the enterprise is the managerial class. The core of the Japanese enterprise is the permanent worker group: workers who for all practical purposes are tenured and who aspire to lifelong employment. They are distinct from the non-permanent employees – mostly women and subcontracted teams led by gang bosses, to be laid off in slack periods. University graduates in Japan first join the permanent worker group and subsequently fill various positions, moving from line to staff as the need occurs, while being paid according to seniority rather than position. They take part in Japanese-style group consultation sessions for important decisions, which extend the decision-making period but guarantee fast implementation afterwards. Japanese are to a large extent controlled by their peer group rather than by their manager.

American theories of leadership are ill-suited to the Japanese group-controlled situation. During the past two decades, the Japanese have developed their own 'PM' theory of leadership, in which P stands for performance and M for maintenance. The latter is less a concern for individual employees than for maintaining social stability. In view of the amazing success of the Japanese economy in the past 30 years, many Americans have sought the secrets of Japanese management, hoping to copy them.

France

The manager, US style, does not exist in France either. The French researcher Philippe d'Iribarne (1990) identifies three kinds of basic principles (*logiques*) of management. In the USA, the principle is the *fair contract* between employer and employee, which gives the manager considerable prerogatives, but within its limits. This is really a labour market in which the worker sells his or her labour for a price. In France, the principle is the *honour* of each class in a society which has always been and remains extremely stratified, in which superiors behave as superior beings and subordinates accept and expect this, conscious of their own lower level in the national hierarchy but also of the honour of their own class. The French do not think in terms of managers versus non-managers but in terms of *cadres* versus *noncadres;* one becomes cadre by attending the proper schools and one remains it forever; regardless of their actual task, cadres have the privileges of a higher social class, and it is very rare for a non-cadre to cross the ranks.

The conflict between French and American theories of management became apparent at the beginning of the 20th century, in a criticism by the great French management pioneer Henri Fayol (1841–1925) of his US colleague and contemporary Frederick W. Taylor (1856–1915). Fayol was a French engineer whose career as a *cadre superieur* culminated in the position of *President-Directeur General* of a mining company. After his retirement he formulated his experiences in a pathbreaking text on organization: *Administration industrielle et generale*, in which he focused on the sources of authority. Taylor was an American engineer who started his career in industry as a worker and attained his academic qualifications through evening studies. From chief engineer in a steel company he became one of the first management consultants. Taylor was not really concerned with the issue of authority at all; his focus was on efficiency. He proposed to split the task of the first-line boss into eight specialisms, each exercised by a different person; an idea which eventually led to the idea of a matrix organization.

Taylor's work appeared in a French translation in 1913, and Fayol read it and showed himself generally impressed but shocked by Taylor's 'denial of the principle of the Unity of Command' in the case of the eight-boss-system. Seventy years later Andre Laurent, another of Fayol's compatriots, found that French managers in a survey reacted very strongly against a suggestion that one employee could report to two different bosses, while US managers in the same survey showed fewer misgivings. Matrix organization has never become popular in France as it has in the United States.

Holland

In my own country, Holland, or as it is officially called, the Netherlands, the study by Philippe d'Iribarne found the management principle to be a need for consensus among all parties, neither predetermined by a contractual relationship nor by class distinctions, but based on an open-ended exchange of views and a balancing of interests. In terms of the different origins of the word 'manager', the organization in Holland is more *menage* (household) while in the United States it is more *manege* (horse drill).

At my university, the University of Limburg at Maastricht, we asked both the Americans and a matched group of Dutch students to describe their ideal job after graduation, using a list of 22 job characteristics. The Americans attached significantly more importance than the Dutch to earnings, advancement, benefits, a good working relationship with their boss, and security of employment. The Dutch attached more importance to freedom to adopt their own approach to the job, being consulted by their boss in his or her decisions, training opportunities, contributing to the success of their organization, fully using their skills and abilities, and helping others. This list confirms d'Iribarne's findings of a contractual employment relationship in the United States, based on earnings and career opportunities, against a consensual relationship in Holland. The latter has centuries old roots; the Netherlands was the first republic in Western Europe (1609–1810), and a model for the American republic. The country has been and still is governed by a careful balancing of interests in a multi-party system.

In terms of management theories, both motivation and leadership in Holland are different from what they are in the United States. Leadership in Holland presupposes modesty, as opposed to assertiveness in the United States. No US leadership theory has room for that. Working in Holland is not a constant feast, however. There is a built-in premium on mediocrity and jealousy, as well as time-consuming ritual consultations to maintain the appearance of consensus and the pretence of modesty. There is unfortunately another side to every coin.

The overseas Chinese

Among the champions of economic development in the past 30 years we find three countries mainly populated by Chinese living outside the Chinese mainland: Taiwan, Hong Kong and Singapore. Moreover, overseas Chinese play a very important role in the economies of Indonesia, Malaysia, the Philippines and Thailand, where they form an ethnic minority. If anything, the little dragons – Taiwan, Hong Kong and Singapore – have been more economically successful than Japan, moving from rags to riches and now counted among the world's wealthy industrial countries. Yet very little attention has been paid to the way in which their enterprises have been managed.

Overseas Chinese enterprises lack almost all characteristics of modern management. They tend to be small, cooperating for essential functions with other small organizations through networks based on personal relations. They are family owned, without the separation between ownership and management typical in the West, or even in Japan and Korea. They normally focus on one product or market, with growth by opportunistic diversification; in this, they are extremely flexible. Decision-making is centralized in the hands of one dominant family member, but other family members may be given new ventures to try their skills on. They are low-profile and extremely cost-conscious, applying Confucian virtues of thrift and persistence. Their size is kept small by the assumed lack of loyalty of non-family employees, who, if they are any good, will just wait and save until they can start their own family business.

Overseas Chinese prefer economic activities in which great gains can be made with little manpower, like commodity trading and real estate. They employ few professional managers, except their sons and sometimes daughters who have been sent to prestigious business schools abroad, but who upon return continue to run the family business the Chinese way.

The origin of this system, or – in the Western view – this lack of system, is found in the history of Chinese society, in which there were no formal laws, only formal networks of powerful people guided by general principles of Confucian virtue. The favours of the authorities could change daily, so nobody could be trusted except one's kinfolk – of whom, fortunately, there used to be many, in an extended family structure. The overseas Chinese way of doing business is also very well adapted to their position in the countries in which they form ethnic minorities, often envied and threatened by ethnic violence.

Overseas Chinese businesses following this unprofessional approach command a collective gross national product of some 200 to 300 billion US dollars, exceeding the GNP of Australia. There is no denying that it works.

Management transfer to poor countries

Four-fifths of the world population live in countries that are not rich but poor. After World War II and decolonization, the stated purpose of the United Nations

and the World Bank has been to promote the development of all the world's countries in a war on poverty. After 40 years it looks very much like we are losing this war. If one thing has become clear, it is that the export of Western – mostly American – management practices and theories to poor countries has contributed little or nothing to their development. There has been no lack of effort and money spent for this purpose: students from poor countries have been trained in this country, and teachers and Peace Corps workers have been sent to the poor countries. If nothing else, the general lack of success in economic development of other countries should be sufficient argument to doubt the validity of Western management theories in non-Western environments.

If we examine different parts of the world, the development picture is not equally bleak, and history is often a better predictor than economic factors for what happens today. There is a broad regional pecking order, with East Asia leading. The little dragons have passed into the camp of the wealthy: then follow South-East Asia (with its overseas Chinese minorities), Latin America (in spite of the debt crisis), South Asia, and Africa always trails behind. Several African countries have only become poorer since decolonization.

Russia and China

The crumbling of the former Eastern bloc has left us with a scattering of states and would-be states for which the political and economic future is extremely uncertain. The best predictions are those based on a knowledge of history, because historical trends have taken revenge on the arrogance of the Soviet rulers who believed they could turn them around by brute power. One obvious fact is that the former bloc is extremely heterogeneous, including countries traditionally closely linked with the West by trade and travel, like the Czech Republic, Hungary, Slovenia and the Baltic states, as well as others with a Byzantine or Turkish past: some having been prosperous, others always extremely poor. Let me limit myself to the Russian republic, a huge territory with some 140 million inhabitants, mainly Russians. We know quite a bit about the Russians as their country was a world power for several hundreds of years before communism, and in the 19th century it produced some of the greatest writers in world literature. If I want to understand the Russians – including how they could so long support the Soviet regime – I tend to re-read Lev Nikolayevich Tolstoy. In his most famous novel *Anna Karenina* one of the main characters is a landowner, Levin, whom Tolstoy uses to express his own views and convictions about his people. Russian peasants used to be serfs; serfdom had been abolished in 1861, but the peasants, now tenants, remained as passive as before. Levin wanted to break this passivity by dividing the land among his peasants in exchange for a share of the crops; but the peasants only let the land deteriorate further. Here follows a quote:

[Levin] read political economy and socialistic works … but, as he had expected, found nothing in them related to his undertaking. In the political economy books – in [John Stuart] Mill, for instance, whom he studied first and with great ardour, hoping every minute to find an answer to the questions that were engrossing him – he found only certain laws deduced from the state of agriculture in Europe; but he could not for the life of him see why these laws, which did not apply to Russia, should be considered universal … Political economy told him that the laws by which Europe had developed and was developing her wealth were universal and absolute. Socialist teaching told him that development along those lines leads to ruin. And neither of them offered the smallest enlightenment as to what he, Levin, and all the Russian peasants and landowners were to do with their millions of hands and millions of acres, to make them as productive as possible for the common good.

In the summer of 1991, the Russian lands yielded a record harvest, but a large share of it rotted in the fields because no people were to be found for harvesting. The passivity is still there, and not only among the peasants. And the heirs of John Stuart Mill (whom we met before as one of the early analysts of 'management') again present their universal recipes, which simply do not apply.

Citing Tolstoy, I implicitly suggest that management theorists cannot neglect the great literature of the countries they want their ideas to apply to. The greatest novel in Chinese literature is considered Cao Xueqin's *The Story of the Stone*, also known as *The Dream of the Red Chamber* which appeared around 1760. It describes the rise and fall of two branches of an aristocratic family in Beijing, who live in adjacent plots in the capital. Their plots are joined by a magnificent garden with several pavilions in it, and the young, mostly female members of both families are allowed to live in them. One day the management of the garden is taken over by a young woman, Tan-Chun, who states:

I think we ought to pick out a few experienced trust-worthy old women from among the ones

who work in the Garden – women who know something about gardening already – and put the upkeep of the Garden into their hands. We needn't ask them to pay us rent; all we need ask them for is an annual share of the produce. There would be four advantages in this arrangement. In the first place, if we have people whose sole occupation is to look after trees and flowers and so on, the condition of the Garden will improve gradually year after year and there will be no more of those long periods of neglect followed by bursts of feverish activity when things have been allowed to get out of hand. Secondly, there won't be the spoiling and wastage we get at present. Thirdly, the women themselves will gain a little extra to add to their incomes which will compensate them for the hard work they put in throughout the year. And fourthly, there's no reason why we shouldn't use the money we should otherwise have spent on nurserymen, rockery specialists, horticultural cleaners and so on for other purposes.

As the story goes on, the capitalist privatization – because that is what it is – of the Garden is carried through, and it works. When in the 1980s Deng Xiaoping allowed privatization in the Chinese villages, it also worked. If we remember what Chinese entrepreneurs are able to do once they have become overseas Chinese, we shouldn't be too surprised. But what works in China – and worked two centuries ago – does not have to work in Russia, not in Tolstoy's days and not today. I am not offering a solution: I only protest against a naive universalism that knows only one recipe for development, the one supposed to have worked in the United States.

A theory of culture in management

There is something in all countries called 'management,' but its meaning differs to a larger or smaller extent from one country to another, and it takes considerable historical and cultural insight into local conditions to understand its processes, philosophies and problems. If already the word may mean so many different things, how can we expect one country's theories of management to apply abroad? One should be extremely careful in making this assumption, and test it before considering it proven. Management is not a phenomenon that can be isolated from other processes taking place in a society. It interacts with what happens in the family, at school, in politics and government. It is obviously also related to religion and to beliefs about science. Theories of management always had to be interdisciplinary, but if we cross national borders they should become more interdisciplinary than ever.

As the word culture plays such an important role in my theory, let me give you my definition, which differs from some other very respectable definitions. Culture to me is *the collective programming of the mind which distinguishes one group or category of people from another.* In the part of my work I am referring to now, the category of people is the nation.

Cultural differences between nations can, to some extent, be described using five bipolar dimensions. The position of a country on these dimensions allows us to make some predictions on the way their society operates, including their management processes and the kind of theories applicable to their management.

The first dimension is labelled *power distance*, and it can be defined as the degree of inequality among people which the population of a country considers as normal: from relatively equal (that is, small power distance) to extremely unequal (large power distance). All societies are unequal, but some are more unequal than others.

The second dimension is labelled *individualism*, and it is the degree to which people in a country prefer to act as individuals rather than as members of groups. The opposite of individualism can be called *collectivism*, so collectivism is low individualism. The way I use the word it has no political connotations. In collectivist societies a child learns to respect the group to which it belongs, usually the family, and to differentiate between in-group members and out-group members (that is, all other people). When children grow up they remain members of their group and they expect the group to protect them when they are in trouble. In return, they have to remain loyal to their group throughout life. In individualist societies, a child learns very early to think of itself as 'I' instead of a part of 'we'. It expects one day to have to stand on its own feet and not to get protection from its group anymore; and therefore it also does not feel a need for strong loyalty.

The third dimension is called *masculinity* and its opposite pole *femininity*. It is the degree to which tough values like assertiveness, performance, success and competition, which in nearly all societies are associated with the role of men, prevail over tender values like the quality of life, maintaining warm personal relationships, service, care for the weak and solidarity, which in nearly all societies are more associated with

women's roles. Women's roles differ from men's roles in all countries, but in tough societies, the differences are larger than in tender ones.

The fourth dimension is labelled *uncertainty avoidance*, and it can be defined as the degree to which people in a country prefer structured over unstructured situations. Structured situations are those in which there are clear rules as to how one should behave. These rules can be written down, but they can also be unwritten and imposed by tradition. In countries that score high on uncertainty avoidance, people tend to show more nervous energy, while in countries that score low, people are more easy-going. A (national) society with strong uncertainty avoidance can be called rigid; one with weak uncertainty avoidance, flexible. In countries where uncertainty avoidance is strong a feeling prevails of 'what is different, is dangerous.' In weak uncertainty avoidance societies, the feeling would rather be 'what is different, is curious.'

The fifth dimension is labelled *long-term versus short-term orientation*. On the long-term side one finds values oriented towards the future, like thrift (saving) and persistence. On the short-term side one finds values rather oriented towards the past and present, like respect for tradition and fulfilling social obligations.

Table 1.3.1 lists the scores on all five dimensions for the United States and for the other countries we just discussed. The table shows that each country has its own configuration on the five dimensions. Some of the values in the table have been estimated based on imperfect replications or personal impressions. The different dimension scores do not 'explain' all the differences in management I described earlier. To understand management in a country, one should have both knowledge of and empathy with the entire local scene. However, the scores should make us aware that people in other countries may think, feel and act very differently from us when confronted with basic problems of society.

Idiosyncrasies of American management theories

In comparison to other countries, the US culture profile presents itself as below average on power distance and uncertainty avoidance, highly individualistic, fairly masculine, and short-term oriented. The Germans show a stronger uncertainty avoidance and less extreme individualism; the Japanese are different on all dimensions, least on power distance; the French show larger power distance and uncertainty avoidance, but

TABLE 1.3.1   Culture dimension scores for ten countries

	Power Distance	Individualism	Masculinity	Uncertainty Avoidance	Long-Term Orientation
USA	40 L	91 H	62 H	46 L	29 L
Germany	35 L	67 H	66 H	65 M	31 M
Japan	54 M	46 M	95 H	92 H	80 H
France	68 H	71 H	43 M	86 H	30*L
Netherlands	38 L	80 H	14 L	53 M	44 M
Hong Kong	68 H	25 L	57 H	29 L	96 H
Indonesia	78 H	14 L	46 M	48 L	25*L
West Africa	77 H	20 L	46 M	54 M	16 L
Russia	95*H	50*M	40*L	90*H	10*L
China	80*H	20*L	50*M	60*M	118 H

*Estimated

H = top third, M = medium third, L = bottom third (among 53 countries and regions for the first four dimensions; among 23 countries for the fifth).

are less individualistic and somewhat feminine; the Dutch resemble the Americans on the first three dimensions, but score extremely feminine and relatively long-term oriented; Hong Kong Chinese combine large power distance with weak uncertainty avoidance, collectivism, and are very long-term oriented; and so on. The American culture profile is reflected in American management theories. I will just mention three elements not necessarily present in other countries: the stress on market processes, the stress on the individual, and the focus on managers rather than on workers.

The stress on market processes

During the 1970s and 1980s it has become fashionable in the United States to look at organizations from a 'transaction costs' viewpoint. Economist Oliver Williamson has opposed 'hierarchies' to 'markets.' The reasoning is that human social life consists of economic transactions between individuals. We found the same in d'Iribarne's description of the US principle of the contract between employer and employee, the labour market in which the worker sells his or her labour for a price. These individuals will form hierarchical organizations when the cost of the economic transactions (such as getting information, finding out whom to trust, etc.) is lower in a hierarchy than when all transactions would take place on a free market.

From a cultural perspective the important point is that the 'market' is the point of departure or base

model, and the organization is explained from market failure. A culture that produces such a theory is likely to prefer organizations that internally resemble markets to organizations that internally resemble more structured models, like those in Germany or France. The ideal principle of control in organizations in the market philosophy is competition between individuals. This philosophy fits a society that combines a not-too-large power distance with a not-too-strong uncertainty avoidance and individualism; besides the USA, it will fit all other Anglo countries.

The stress on the individual

I find this constantly in the design of research projects and hypotheses; also in the fact that in the US psychology is clearly a more respectable discipline in management circles than sociology. Culture, however, is a collective phenomenon. Although we may get our information about culture from individuals, we have to interpret it at the level of collectivities. There are snags here known as the 'ecological fallacy' and the 'reverse ecological fallacy'. None of the US college textbooks on methodology I know deal sufficiently with the problem of multilevel analysis.

A striking example is found in the otherwise excellent book *Organizational Culture and Leadership* by Edgar H. Schein (1985). On the basis of his consulting experience he compares two large companies, nicknamed 'Action' and 'Multi'. He explains the difference in cultures between these companies by the group dynamics in their respective boardrooms. Nowhere in the book are any conclusions drawn from the fact that the first company is an American-based computer firm, and the second a Swiss-based pharmaceuticals firm. This information is not even mentioned. A stress on interactions among individuals obviously fits a culture identified as the most individualistic in the world, but it will not be so well understood by the four-fifths of the world population for whom the group prevails over the individual.

One of the conclusions of my own multilevel research has been that culture at the national level and culture at the organizational level – corporate culture – are two very different phenomena and that the use of a common term for both is confusing. If we do use the common term, we should also pay attention to the occupational and the gender level of culture. National cultures differ primarily in the fundamental, invisible values held by a majority of their members, acquired in early childhood, whereas organization cultures are a much more superficial phenomenon residing mainly in the visible practices of the organization, acquired by socialization of the new members who join as young adults. National cultures change only very slowly, if at all; organizational cultures may be consciously changed, although this isn't necessarily easy. This difference between the two types of culture is the secret of the existence of multinational corporations that employ employees with extremely different national cultural values. What keeps them together is a corporate culture based on common practices.

The stress on managers rather than workers

The core element of a work organization around the world is the people who do the work. All the rest is superstructure, and I hope to have demonstrated to you that it may take many different shapes. In the US

literature on work organization, however, the core element, if not explicitly then implicitly, is considered the manager. This may well be the result of the combination of extreme individualism with fairly strong masculinity, which has turned the manager into a cultural hero of almost mythical proportions. For example, he – not really she – is supposed to make decisions all the time. Those of you who are or have been managers must know that this is a fable. Very few management decisions are just 'made' as the myth suggests it. Managers are much more involved in maintaining networks; if anything, it is the rank-and-file worker who can really make decisions on his or her own, albeit on a relatively simple level.

Conclusion

This article started with *Alice in Wonderland*. In fact, the management theorist who ventures outside his or her own country into other parts of the world is like Alice in Wonderland. He or she will meet strange beings, customs, ways of organizing or disorganizing and theories that are clearly stupid, old-fashioned or even immoral – yet they may work, or at least they may not fail more frequently than corresponding theories do at home. Then, after the first culture shock, the traveller to Wonderland will feel enlightened, and may be able to take his or her experiences home and use them advantageously. All great ideas in science, politics and management have travelled from one country to another, and been enriched by foreign influences. The roots of American management theories are mainly in Europe: with Adam Smith, John Stuart Mill, Lev Tolstoy, Max Weber, Henri Fayol, Sigmund Freud, Kurt Lewin and many others. These theories were replanted here and they developed and bore fruit. The same may happen again. The last thing we need is a Monroe doctrine for management.

REFERENCES

Adler, P.S., Goldoftas, B. and Levine, D.I. (1999) 'Flexibility Versus Efficiency? A case study of model changeovers in the Toyota production system', *Organization Science*, 10(1), pp. 43–68.

Adner, R. and Helfat, C.E. (2003) 'Corporate effects and dynamic managerial capabilities', *Strategic Management Journal*, 24(10), pp. 1011–1025.

Amabile, T.M. (1996) *Creativity in Context*, Boulder, CO: Westview Press.

Ancona, D.G. and Nadler, D.A. (1989) 'Top Hats and Executive tales: Designing the senior team', *Sloan Management Review*, 31(1), pp. 19–28.

Argyris, C. and Schon, D. (1978) *Organizational Learning: A Theory of Action Approach*, Reading, MA: Addison Wesley.

Astley, W.G. and Van de Ven, A.H. (1983) 'Central Perspectives and Debates in Organization Theory', *Administrative Science Quarterly*, Vol. 28, pp. 245–273.

Barnard, C.I. (1968) *The Functions of the Executive*, Boston, MA: Harvard University Press, (Vol. 11).

Barrett, D. (1998) *The Paradox Process: Creative Business Solutions Where You Least Expect to Find Them*, New York: Amacom.

Bazerman, M.H. and Watkins, M. (2004) *Predictable Surprises*, Boston, MA: Harvard Business School Press.

Bazerman, M.H. (1998) *Judgement in Managerial Decision Making*, New York: John Wiley, (4th ed.).

Beech, N., Burns, H., de Caestecker, L., Mackintosh, R. and MacLean, D. (2004) 'Paradox as invitation to act in problematic change situations', *Human Relations*, 57, pp. 1313–1332.

Benner, M.J. and Tushman, M. (2002) 'Process Management and Technological Innovation: A longitudinal study of the photography and paint industries', *Administrative Science Quarterly*, 47(4), 676–707.

Benner, M.J. and Tushman, M.L. (2003) 'Exploitation, exploration, and process management: The productivity dilemma revisited', *Academy of Management Review*, 2, pp. 238–256.

Brown, S.L. and Eisenhardt, K.M. (1997) 'The Art of Continuous Change: Linking complexity theory and time-paced evolution in relentlessly shifting organizations', *Administrative Science Quarterly*, 42(1), pp. 1–34.

Bunderson, J.S. (2003) 'Team member functional background and involvement in management teams: Direct effects and the moderating role of power centralization', *Academy of Management Journal*, 46(4), pp. 458–474.

Bunderson, J.S. and Sutcliffe, K.M. (2002) 'Why some teams emphasize learning more than others: Evidence from business unit management teams', in: H. Sondak (ed.) *Towards Phenomenology of Groups and Group Membership*, Vol. 4, Oxford, UK: Elsevier Science, pp. 49–84.

Bunderson, J.S. and Sutcliffe, K.M. (2003) 'Management team learning orientation and business unit performance', *Journal of Applied Psychology*, 88(3), pp. 552–560.

Burgelman, R.A. (1983) 'Corporate Entrepreneurship and Strategic Management: Insights from a Process Study', *Management Science*, Vol. 29, No. 12, pp. 1349–1364.

Burgelman, R.A. (2002) 'Strategy as Vector and the Inertia of Coevolutionary Lock-in', *Administrative Science Quarterly*, 47, pp. 325–357.

Cameron, K.S. and Quinn, R.E. (1988) 'Organizational paradox and transformation', in: R.E. Quinn and K.S. Cameron, *Paradox and Transformation: Towards a Theory of Change in Organization and Management*, Cambridge, MA: Ballinger.

Chandler, A.D. (1962) *Strategy and Structure: Chapters in the History of the Industrial Enterprise*, Cambridge, MA: MIT Press.

D'Iribarne, P. (1990) *La Logique d'Honneur*, Paris: Editions du Seuil.

Daft, R.L. and Weick, K.E. (1984) 'Toward a model of organizations as interpretation systems', *Academy of Management Review*, 9(2), pp. 284–295.

Denison, D., Hooijberg, R. and Quinn, R.E. (1995) 'Paradox and performance: Toward a theory of behavioral complexity in managerial leadership', *Organization Science*, 6(5), pp. 524–540.

Deutsch, M. (1973) *The Resolution of Conflict*, New Haven, CT: Yale University Press.

Duncan, R.B. (1976) 'The Ambidextrous Organization: Designing Dual Structures for Innovation', in: R.H. Kilmann, L.R. Pondy and D.P. Slevin (eds.), *The Management of Organizational Design*, New York: Elsevier North Holland, pp. 167–188.

Dutton, J.E. and Ashford, S.J. (1993) 'Selling issues to top management', *Academy of Management Review*, 18(3), pp. 397–428.

Dutton, J.E. and Jackson, S.E. (1987) 'Categorizing strategic issues: Links to organizational action', *Academy of Management Review*, 12(1), pp. 76–90.

Edmondson, A. (1999) 'Psychological safety and learning behavior in work teams', *Administrative Science Quarterly*, 44(2), pp. 350–383.

Edmondson, A.C., Roberto, M.A. and Watkins, M.D. (2003) 'A dynamic model of top management team effectiveness: Managing unstructured task streams', *Administrative Science Quarterly*, 14(3), pp. 297–325.

Eisenhardt, K.M. and Westcott, B.J. (1988) 'Paradoxical demands and the creation of excellence: The case of just-in-time manufacturing', in: R. Quinn and K. Cameron (eds.) *Paradox and Transformation: Towards a Theory of Change in Organization and Management*, Cambridge, MA: Ballinger, pp. 169–194.

Eisenhardt, K.M. and Zbaracki, M.J. (1992) 'Strategic decision making', *Strategic Management Journal*, 13(S2), pp. 17–37.

Eisenhardt, K.M., Kahwajy, J.L. and Bourgeois L.J. (1997) 'Conflict and strategic choice: How top management teams disagree', *California Management Review*, 39(2), pp. 42–62.

Eisenhardt, K.M. (2000) 'Paradox, Spirals, Ambivalence: The New Language of Change and Pluralism', *Academy of Management Review*, Vol. 25, No. 4, pp. 703–705.

Emery, F.E. and Trist, E.L. (1965) 'The Causal Texture of Organizational Environments', *Human Relations*, Vol. 18, pp. 21–32.

Fayol, H. (1916/1949) *General and Industrial Management*, London: Pitman.

Finkelstein, S. and Hambrick, D.C. (1996) *Strategic leadership: Top Executives and Their Effect on Organizations*, St. Paul, MN: West.

Fletcher, J.L. and Olwyler, K. (1997) *Paradoxical Thinking: How to Profit from Your Contradictions*, San Fransisco: Berrett-Koehler.

Flynn, F.J. and Chatman, J.A. (2001) 'Strong cultures and innovation: Oxymoron and opportunity?' in: C. Cooper, S. Cartwright and C. Early (eds.) *International Handbook of Organizational Culture and Climate*, Chichester, England: J. Wiley, pp. 263–287.

Follett, M.P. (1925/1996) 'Constructive conflict', in: P. Graham (ed.) *Mary Parker Follett: Prophet of Management*, Boston, MA: Harvard Business School Press.

Ford, J.D. and Backoff, R.W. (1988) 'Organizational change in and out of dualities and paradox', in: R. Quinn and K. Cameron (eds.) *Paradox and Transformation*, Cambridge, MA: Ballinger Publishing Company, pp. 81–121.

Frankel, V. (1960) 'Paradoxical intention', *American Journal of Psychotherapy*, 14, pp. 520–535.

Gavetti, G. and Levinthal, D. (2000) 'Looking forward and looking backward: Cognitive and experiential search', *Administrative Science Quarterly*, 45(1), pp. 113–137.

Gibson, C.B. and Birkinshaw, J. (2004) 'The antecedents, consequences, and mediating role of organizational ambidexterity', *Academy of Management Journal*, 47(2), pp. 209–226.

Gilbert, C.G. (2005) 'Unbundling the structure of inertia: Resource versus routine rigidity', *Academy of Management Journal*, 48(5), pp. 741–763.

Hackman, J.R. (2002) *Leading Teams: Setting the Stage for Great Performances*, Boston, MA: Harvard Business School Press.

Hambrick, D.C. (1994) 'Top management groups: A conceptual integration and reconsideration of the "team" label', in: B.M. Staw and L. Cummings (eds.) *Research in Organizational Behavior*, Greenwich, CT: JAI Press.

He, Z.L. and Wong, P.K. (2004) 'Exploration vs. exploitation: An empirical test of the ambidexterity hypothesis', *Organization Science*, 15(4), pp. 481–494.

Heenan, D.A. and Bennis, W.G. (1999) *Co-leaders: The Power of Great Partnerships*, New York: John Wiley & Sons.

Hemp, P. and Stewart, T.A. (2004) 'Leading change when business is good: An interview with Sam Palmisano', *Harvard Business Review*, 82(12), pp. 60–71.

Henderson, R. and Clark, K. (1991) 'Architectural innovation: The reconfiguration of existing product technologies and the failure of established firms', *Administrative Science Quarterly*, 35, pp. 9–30.

Hofstede, G. (1993) 'Cultural constraints in management theories', *Academy of Management Executive*, Vol. 7, No. 1, pp. 8–21.

Huff, A.S. (1990) *Mapping Strategic Thought*, Chichester, NY: John Wiley & Sons.

Huff, A.S. (1997) 'A current and future agenda for cognitive research in organizations', *Journal of Management Studies*, 34(6), pp. 947–952.

Jay, J., (2013) 'Navigating paradox as a mechanism of change and innovation in hybrid organizations', *Academy of Management Journal*, February, Vol. 56, No. 1, pp. 137–159.

Johnson, B. (1996) *Polarity Management*, Amherst, MA: HRD Press Inc.

Kaplan S., Murray A. and Henderson R. (2003) 'Discontinuities and senior management: Assessing the role of recognition in pharmaceutical firm response to biotechnology', *Industrial Corporate Change*, 12(4), pp. 203–233.

Kaplan, S. (2003) 'Framing contests: Strategy-making during a technological discontinuity', working paper, Philadelphia, PA: Wharton School, University of Pennsylvania.

Kerr, S. (1975) 'On the folly of rewarding A, while hoping for B', *Academy of Management Journal*, 18(4), pp. 769–782.

Ketchen, D.J., Thomas, J.B. and McDaniel, R.R. (1996) 'Process, content and context: synergistic effects on organizational performance', *Journal of Management*, Vol. 22, pp. 231–257.

Langer, E. (1989) *Mindfulness*, Boston, MA: Addison-Wesley.

Latham, G.P. and Locke, E.A. (eds) (1995) *Goal Setting: A Motivational Technique That Works*, 2nd edition, Englewood Cliffs, NJ: Prentice Hall.

Lawrence, P.R. and Lorsch, J.W. (1967) *Organization and Environment: Managing Differentiation and Integration*, Boston, MA: Harvard University Press.

Lax, D.A. and Sebenius, J.K. (1986) *The Manager as Negotiator: Bargaining for Cooperative and Competitive Gain*, New York: The Free Press.

Leonard-Barton, D. (1992) 'Core capabilities and core rigidities: A paradox in managing new product development', *Strategic Management Journal*, 13(S1), pp. 111–125.

Levinthal, D.A. and March, J.G. (1993) 'The myopia of learning', *Strategic Management Journal*, 14(S2), pp. 95–112.

Lewis, M. (2000) 'Exploring paradox: toward a more comprehensive guide', *Academy of Management Review*, Vol. 25, No. 4, pp. 760–776.

Linehan, M. (1993) *Cognitive-Behavioral Treatment of Borderline Personality Disorder*, New York: Guilford Press.

Lorsch, J.W. and Tierney, T.J. (2002) *Aligning the Stars: How to Succeed When Professionals Drive Results*, Boston, MA: Harvard Business Press.

Margolis, J.D. and Walsh, J.P. (2003) 'Misery loves companies: Rethinking social initiatives by business', *Administrative Science Quarterly*, 48(2), pp. 268–305.

Mason, R.O. and Mitroff, I.I. (1981) *Challenging Strategic Planning Assumptions*, New York: Wiley.

Miles, R.E. and Snow, C.C., (1978) *Organizational Strategy, Structure, and Process*, New York: McGraw-Hill.

Murnighan, J.K. and Conlon, D.E. (1991) 'The dynamics of intense work groups: A study of British string quartets', *Administrative Science Quarterly*, 36, pp. 165–186.

Nadler, D.A. and Tushman, M.L. (1992) 'Designing organizations that have good fit: A framework for understanding new architectures', in: D. Nadler (ed.), *Organizational Architecture*, San Francisco, CA: Jossey-Bass.

Nadler, D. and Tushman, M. (1996) *Competing By Design: The Power of Organizational Architecture*, New York: Oxford University Press.

Nemeth, C.J. and Wachtler, J. (1983) 'Creative problem solving as a result of majority vs minority influence', *European Journal of Social Psychology*, 13(1), pp. 45–55.

Nonaka, I. and Toyama, R. (2002) 'A firm as a dialectical being: towards a dynamic theory of a firm', *Industrial and Corporate Change*, 11(5), pp. 995–1009.

Paine, L.S. (2003) *Value Shift: Why Companies Must Merge Social and Financial Imperatives to Achieve Superior Performance*, New York: McGraw-Hill.

Perlow, L.A., Gittell, J.H. and Katz, N. (2004) 'Contextualizing patterns of work group interaction: Toward a nested theory of structuration', *Organization Science*, 15(5), pp. 520–536.

Pettigrew, A. (1992) 'The character and significance of strategy process research', *Strategic Management Journal*, Vol. 13, pp. 5–16.

Pettigrew, A. and Whipp, R. (1991) *Managing Change for Competitive Success*, Oxford: Basil Blackwell.

Pinkley, R.L. (1990) 'Dimensions of conflict frame: Disputant interpretations of conflict', *Journal of Applied Psychology*, 75(2), pp. 117–126.

Poole, M.S. and Van de Ven, A.H. (1989) 'Using paradox to build management and organization theories', *Academy of Management Review*, Vol. 14, No. 4, pp. 562–578.

Porras, J.I. and Collins, J.C. (1997) *Built to Last: Successful Habits of Visionary Companies*, New York: Harper Business.

Porter, R. (1980) *Presidential Decision Making: The Economic Policy Board*, Cambridge, UK: Cambridge University Press.

Quinn, R.E. (1984) 'Applying the competing values approach to leadership: Towards an integrative model', in: J.G. Hunt, R. Steward, C. Schriesheim and D. Hosking (eds.) *Leaders and Managers: International perspectives on Managerial Behavior and Leadership*, New York: Paragon, pp. 10–27.

Quinn, R.E. (1988) *Beyond Rational Management: Mastering the Paradoxes and Competing Demands of High Performance*, San Francisco: Jossey-Bass.

Raisch, S., Birkinshaw, J., Probst, G. and Tushman, M.L. (2009) 'Organizational ambidexterity: Balancing exploitation and exploration for sustained performance', *Organization Science*, 20(4), pp. 685–695.

Repenning, N.P. (2002) 'A simulation-based approach to understanding the dynamics of innovation implementation', *Organization Science*, 13(2), pp. 109–127.

Rittel, H. (1972) 'On the planning crisis: systems analysis of the "first and second generations"', *Bedriftsokonomen*, No. 8, pp. 390–396.

Rivkin, J.W. and Siggelkow, N. (2003) 'Balancing search and stability: Interdependencies among elements of organizational design', *Management Science*, 49(3), pp. 290–311.

Rothenberg, A. (1979) *The Emerging Goddess: The Creative Process in Art, Science, and Other Fields* (p. 440). Chicago, IL: University of Chicago Press.

Rothermael, F.T. (2001) 'Incumbent's advantage through exploiting complementary assets via interfirm cooperation', *Strategic Management Journal*, 22(6-7), pp. 687–699.

Rumelt, R.P. (1980) 'The Evaluation of Business Strategy', in: W.F. Glueck (ed.), *Business Policy and Strategic Management*, Third Edition, New York: McGraw-Hill.

Schein, E.H. (1985) *Organizational Culture and Leadership*, San Francisco, CA: Jossey-Bass.

Sherif, M. (1971) 'Superordinate goals in the reduction of intergroup conflict', in: B.L. Hinton and H.J. Reits (eds.) *Groups and Organizations*, Belmont CA: Wadsworth.

Siggelkow, N. and Levinthal, D.A. (2003) 'Temporarily divide to conquer: Centralized, decentralized, and reintegrated organizational approaches to exploration and adaptation', *Organization Science*, 14(6), pp. 650–669.

Smith, A. (1776) *An Inquiry into the Nature and Causes of the Wealth of Nations*, London: printed for W. Strahan and T. Cadell, in the Strand.

Smith, K. and Lewis, M.W. (2011) 'Toward a Theory of Paradox: A Dynamic Equilibrium Model of Organizing', *Academy of Management Review*, Vol. 36, No 2, pp. 381–403.

Smith, K.K. and Berg, D.N. (1987) *Paradoxes of Group Life*, San Francisco, CA: Jossey-Bass.

Smith, W.K. (2009), 'A dynamic approach to managing contradictions', *Industrial and Organizational Psychology: Perspectives on Science and Practice*, 2, pp. 338–343.

Smith, W.K. and Tushman, M.L. (2005) 'Managing strategic contradictions: A top management model for managing innovation streams', *Organization Science*, 16(5), pp. 522–536.

Steiner, I. (1972) *Group Processes and Productivity*, New York: Academic Press.

Suedfeld, P., Tetlock, T. and Streufert, S (1992), 'Conceptual/integrative complexity', in: C. Smith, J. Atkinson, D. McClelland and J. Verof (eds.) *Motivation and Personality: Handbook of Thematic Content Analysis*, Cambridge, England: Cambridge University Press, pp. 393–400.

Sull, D.N. (1999) 'The dynamics of standing still: Firestone tire & rubber and the radial revolution', *Business History Review*, 73(3), pp. 430–464.

Sull, D.N., Tedlow, R.S. and Rosenbloom, R.S. (1997) 'Managerial commitments and technological change in the US tire industry', *Industrial and Corporate Change*, 6(2), pp. 461–500.

Sun Tzu (1983) *The Art of War*, New York: Delacorte Press.

Sundaramurthy, C. and Lewis, M. (2003) 'Control and collaboration: Paradoxes of governance', *Academy of Management Review*, 28(3), pp. 397–415.

Sutton, R. (2002) *Weird Ideas that Work: 11½ Practices for Promoting, Managing, and Sustaining Innovation*, New York: Free Press.

Taylor, F.W (1903) *Shop Management*, New York: Harper.

Taylor, F.W. (1911) *The Principles of Scientific Management*, New York: Harper.

Teece, D.J. (2007) 'Explicating dynamic capabilities: the nature and microfoundations of (sustainable) enterprise performance', *Strategic Management Journal*, 28(13), pp. 1319–1350.

Teece, D.J., Pisano, G. and Shuen, A. (1997) 'Dynamic Capabilities and Strategic Management', *Strategic Management Journal*, Vol. 18, No. 7, August, pp. 509–533.

Tetlock, P.E., McGraw, A.P. and Kristel, O.V. (2004) 'Proscribed forms of social cognition: Taboo trade-offs, blocked exchanges, forbidden base rates, and heretical counterfactuals', in: N. Haslam (ed.) *Relational Models Theory: A Contemporary Overview*, Mahway, NJ: Erlbaum, pp. 247–262.

Thompson, J.D. (1967) *Organizations in Action: Social Science Bases of Administrative,* New York: McGraw-Hill.

Thurbin, P.J. (1998) *The Influential Strategist: Using the Power of Paradox in Strategic Thinking*, London: Financial Times.

Tripsas, M. and Gavetti, G. (2000) 'Capabilities, cognition, and inertia: Evidence from digital imaging', *Strategic Management Journal*, 21(10–11), pp. 1147–1161.

Tushman, M.L. and O'Reilly III, C.A. (1996) 'Ambidextrous organizations: Managing evolutionary and revolutionary change', *California Management Review*, Vol. 38, No. 4, Summer, pp. 8–30.

Tushman, M.L. and O'Reilly III, C.A. (1997) *Winning Through Innovation: A Practical Guide to Leading Organization Change and Renewal*, Boston, MA: Harvard Business School Press.

Tushman, M., Smith, W., Wood, R., Westerman, G. and O'Reilly, C. (2003) *Innovation Streams and Ambidextrous Organizational Forms*, Working paper, Boston, MA: Harvard Business School.

Tyre, M.J. and Von Hippel, E. (1997) 'The situated nature of adaptive learning in organizations', *Organization Science*, 8(1), pp. 71–83.

Van de Ven, A.D., Poley, D.E., Garud, R. and Venkataraman, S. (1999) *The Innovation Journey*, New York: Oxford University Press.

Virany, B., Tushman, M.L. and Romanelli, E. (1992) 'Executive succession and organization outcomes in turbulent environments: An organization learning approach', *Organization Science*, 3(1), pp. 72–91.

Voorhees, B. (1986) 'Towards Duality Theory', *General Systems Bull.*, 16(2), pp. 58–61.

Wageman, R. (2001) 'How leaders foster self-managing team effectiveness: Design choices versus hands-on coaching', *Organization Science*, 12(5), pp. 559–577.

Walsh, J.P. (1995) 'Managerial and organizational cognition: Notes from a trip down memory lane', *Organization Science*, 6(3), pp. 280–321.

Walton, R.E. and McKersie, R.B. (eds.) (1965) *A Behavioral Theory of Labor Negotiations: An Analysis of a Social Interaction System*, New York: McGraw Hill.

Wegner, D. (1986) 'Transactive memory: A contemporary analysis of group mind', in: B. Mullen and G.R. Goethals (eds.) *Theories of Group Behavior*, New York: Springer-Verlag, pp. 185–208.

Weick, K. (1979) *The Social Psychology of Organizing*, Second Edition, Reading, MA: Addison-Wesley.

Weick, K.E. and Roberts, K.H. (1993) 'Collective mind in organizations: Heedful interrelating on flight decks', *Administrative Science Quarterly*, 38(3), pp. 357–381.

Weick, K.E., Sutcliffe, D. and Obstfeld, D. (1999) 'Organizing for high reliability: Processes of collective mindfulness', in: R.I. Sutton and B.M. Staw (eds.) *Research in Organizational Behavior*, Stamford, CT: JAI Press, pp. 81–123.

Whittington, R. (1993) *What Is Strategy and Does It Matter?* London: Routledge.

Wing, R.L. (1988) *The Art of Strategy: A New Translation of Sun Tzu's Classic 'The Art of War'*, New York: Doubleday.

STRATEGIZING

A mind all logic is like a knife all blade. It makes the hand bleed that uses it.

Rabindranath Tagore (1861–1941); Indian philosopher, poet and 1913 Nobel Prize winner

INTRODUCTION

What goes on in the mind of the strategist? A fascinating question that is easy to ask, but difficult to answer. Yet, it is a question that is important in two ways – generally and personally. Generally, knowing what goes on in the minds of managers during strategy processes is essential for understanding their choices and behaviours. Opening up the 'black box' of the strategist's mind to see how decisions are made can help to anticipate or influence this thinking. Grasping how managers shape their strategic views and select their preferred actions can be used to develop more effective strategies. It is due to this importance of strategic thinking that a separate chapter in this book is devoted to the subject. Yet, for each reader personally, the topic of strategizing is also of key importance, as it automatically raises the questions 'what is going on in *my* mind?' and 'how strategic is *my* thinking?' Exploring the subject of strategizing triggers each person to explore their own thought processes and critically reflect on their own strategy preferences. Ideally, wondering about the mind of the strategist should inspire readers to constantly question their own assumptions, thoughts, beliefs and ideas, and to sharpen their strategic thinking, as they move through the following chapters. For this reason, it seems only appropriate to start the book with this topic.

So, what goes on in the mind of the strategist? Well, a lot, but if reduced to its bare essentials it can be said that strategists are engaged in the process of dealing with *strategic problems*. Not problems in the negative sense of troublesome conditions that need to be avoided, but in the neutral sense of challenging situations that need to be resolved – a strategic problem is a set of circumstances requiring a reconsideration of the current course of action, either to profit from observed opportunities or to respond to perceived threats. To deal with these strategic problems, managers must not simply think, but they must go through a *strategic reasoning process,* searching for ways to define and resolve the challenges at hand. Managers must structure their individual thinking steps into a reasoning process that will result in effective strategic behaviour. The question is how managers actually go about defining strategic problems (how do they identify and diagnose what is going on?) and how they go about solving strategic problems (how do they generate, evaluate and decide on potential answers?). It is this issue of strategic reasoning, as a string of strategic thinking activities directed at defining and resolving strategic problems, which will be examined in further detail below.

THE ISSUE OF STRATEGIC REASONING

The mind of the strategist is a complex and fascinating apparatus that never fails to astonish and dazzle on the one hand, and disappoint and frustrate on the other. We are often surprised by the power of the human mind, but equally often stunned by its limitations. For the discussion here it is not necessary to unravel all of the mysteries surrounding the functioning of the human brain, but a short overview of the capabilities and limitations of the human mind will help us to understand the issue of strategic reasoning.

The human ability to know is referred to as 'cognition'. As strategists want to know about the strategic problems facing their organizations, they need to engage in *cognitive activities*. These cognitive activities (or strategic thinking activities) need to be structured into a strategic reasoning process. Hence, the first step towards a better understanding of what goes on in the mind of the strategist is to examine the various cognitive activities making up a strategic reasoning process. The four main cognitive activities will be discussed in the first subsection below. To be able to perform these cognitive activities, people need to command certain mental faculties. While very sophisticated, the human brain is still physically strictly limited in what it can do. These limitations to people's *cognitive abilities* will be reviewed in the second subsection. To deal with its inherent physical shortcomings, the human brain copes by building simplified models of the world, referred to as *cognitive maps*. The functioning of cognitive maps will be addressed in the third subsection.

In Figure 2.1 the relationship between these three topics is visualized, using the metaphor of a computer. The cognitive abilities of our brains can be seen as a hardware level question – what are the physical limits on our mental faculties? The cognitive maps used by our brains can be seen as an operating system level question – what type of platform/language is 'running' in our brain? The cognitive activities carried out by our brains can be seen as an application level question – what type of programme is strategic reasoning?

Cognitive activities

The strategic reasoning process consists of a number of strategic thinking elements or cognitive activities – mental tasks intended to increase the strategist's knowing. A general

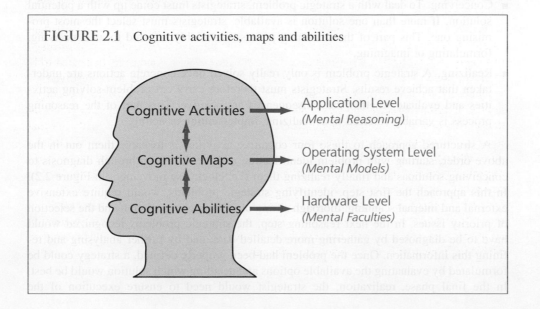

FIGURE 2.1   Cognitive activities, maps and abilities

Cognitive Activities → Application Level
(Mental Reasoning)

Cognitive Maps → Operating System Level
(Mental Models)

Cognitive Abilities → Hardware Level
(Mental Faculties)

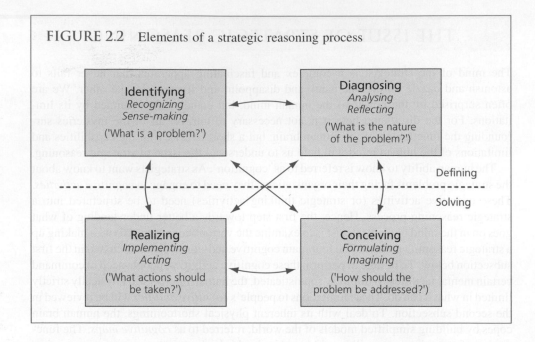

FIGURE 2.2   Elements of a strategic reasoning process

distinction can be made between cognitive activities directed towards *defining* a strategic problem, and cognitive activities directed at *solving* a strategic problem.

Each of these two major categories can be further split in two (see Figure 2.2), leading to the following general elements of a strategic reasoning process:

- Identifying. Before strategists can benefit from opportunities or to counter threats, they must be aware of these challenges and acknowledge their importance. This part of the reasoning process is variably referred to as identifying, recognizing or sense-making.

- Diagnosing. To come to grips with a problem, strategists must try to understand the structure of the problem and its underlying causes. This part of the reasoning process is variably referred to as diagnosing, analysing or reflecting.

- Conceiving. To deal with a strategic problem, strategists must come up with a potential solution. If more than one solution is available, strategists must select the most promising one. This part of the reasoning process is variably referred to as conceiving, formulating or imagining.

- Realizing. A strategic problem is only really solved once concrete actions are undertaken that achieve results. Strategists must therefore carry out problem-solving activities and evaluate whether the consequences are positive. This part of the reasoning process is variably referred to as realizing, implementing or acting.

A structured approach to these four cognitive activities is to carry them out in the above order, starting with problem identification and then moving through diagnosis to conceiving solutions and finally realizing them (i.e. clockwise movement in Figure 2.2). In this approach the first step, identifying strategic problems, would require extensive external and internal scanning, thorough sifting of incoming information and the selection of priority issues. In the next reasoning step, the strategic problems recognized would have to be diagnosed by gathering more detailed data, and by further analysing and refining this information. Once the problem had been properly defined, a strategy could be formulated by evaluating the available options and deciding which solution would be best. In the final phase, realization, the strategist would need to ensure execution of the proposed solution by consciously planning and controlling implementation activities. In this case, the four elements of the strategic reasoning process could actually be labelled recognizing, analysing, formulating and implementing.

However, strategists do not always reason in this step-by-step fashion. Their thinking is often less orderly, with identifying, diagnosing, conceiving and realizing intermingled with one another – even going on at the same time. Nor are the cognitive activities as straightforward as portrayed above. The identification of strategic problems is often not about objective observation, but rather subjective interpretation – by looking at the world from a particular angle, strategists see and value particular strengths, weaknesses, opportunities and threats. Such sense-making activities (Weick, 1979; Gioia and Chittipeddi, 1991) lead to attention being paid to some issues, while others do not make the strategic agenda (Dutton, 1988; Ocasio, 1997). Likewise, diagnosing strategic problems is not always a structured analytical process. Gaining a deeper understanding of strategic problems may involve explicit analysis, but also intuitive reflecting – by employing unconscious reasoning rules strategists often quickly form a general picture of how key aspects of a strategic problem are interrelated.

Conceiving strategic solutions can be equally 'messy' and subjective. Often, strategic options are not chosen from an available repertoire of potential solutions, but they are invented. In other words, new options are often not selected, discovered or figured out, but are envisioned – strategists imagine how things could be done. Such idea generation can involve reasoning by analogy or metaphor, brainstorming or pure fantasizing. New potential solutions may come to the strategist in a flash (Eureka!) or emerge over time, but usually require a period of incubation beforehand and a period of nurturing afterwards. Furthermore, strategists often find it impossible to objectively prove which new idea would be the best solution. Therefore, the process of deciding on the solution to be pursued may involve more judgement than calculation.

Finally, it must be emphasized that action does not always come last, in the form of solution implementation. Often, strategists do not wait for a problem to be precisely defined and for a solution to be fully conceived before starting to act. On the contrary, strategists often feel they must first act – they must have experience with a problem and know that the current strategy will not be able to overcome the problem. To find a suitable solution it is often also necessary to test certain assumptions in practice and to experiment. Hence, acting regularly precedes, or goes hand-in-hand with, all other cognitive activities.

Cognitive abilities

People are not omniscient – they do not have infinite knowledge. To some extent this is due to the nature of reality – many future events are inherently unpredictable, due to factors that are uncertain or unknowable. Yet, humans are also burdened with rather imperfect cognitive abilities. The human brain is severely limited in what it can know (Simon, 1957). The limitation to human's cognitive abilities is largely due to three factors:

■ Limited information sensing ability. Humanity's first 'handicap' is a limited information-sensing ability. While the senses – touch, smell, taste, hearing and seeing – are bombarded with stimuli, much of reality remains unobservable to humans. This is partially due to the physical inability to be everywhere, all the time, noticing everything. However, people's limited ability to register the structure of reality is also due to the inherent superficiality of the senses and the complexity of reality. The human senses cannot directly identify the way the world works and the underlying causal relationships. Only the physical consequences of the complex interactions between elements in reality can be picked up by a person's sensory system. Therefore, the mental representations of the world that individuals build up in their minds are necessarily based on circumstantial evidence.

■ Limited information processing capacity. Unfortunately, a second drawback is that humans do not have unlimited data processing abilities. Thinking through problems with many variables, complex relationships and huge amounts of data is a task that people find extremely difficult to perform. Approaching every activity in this way would totally overload a person's brain. For this reason, humans hardly ever think through a problem with full use of all available data, but necessarily make extensive use of mental shortcuts, referred to as 'cognitive heuristics' (Janis, 1989). Cognitive heuristics are mental 'rules of thumb' that simplify a problem, so that it can be more quickly understood and solved. Cognitive heuristics focus a person's attention on a number of key variables that are believed to be most important, and present a number of simple decision rules to rapidly resolve an issue. The set of possible solutions to be considered is also limited in advance.

■ Limited information storage capacity. Another human cognitive shortcoming is poor memory. People have only a limited capacity for storing information. Remembering all individuals, events, dates, places and circumstances is beyond the ability of the human brain. Therefore, people must store information very selectively and organize this information in a way that it can be easily retrieved when necessary. Here again, cognitive heuristics are at play – 'rules of thumb' make the memorization process manageable in the face of severe capacity limitations. Such heuristics help to simplify complex clusters of data into manageable chunks and help to categorize, label and store this information so that it can be recalled at a later time.

To deal with these severe physical limitations, the brain has come up with more than only simple cognitive heuristics. The human mind has come to work with more holistic cognitive maps.

Cognitive maps

Knowledge that people have is stored in their minds in the form of 'cognitive maps' (e.g. McCaskey, 1982; Weick and Bourgnon, 1986), also referred to as 'cognitive schemata' (e.g. Anderson, 1983; Schwenk, 1988), 'mental models' (e.g. Day and Lord, 1992; Knight *et al.*, 1999), 'knowledge structures' (e.g. Lyles and Schwenk, 1992; Walsh, 1995) and 'construed reality' (Finkelstein and Hambrick, 1996). These cognitive maps are representations in a person's mind of how the world works. A cognitive map of a certain situation reflects a person's beliefs about the importance of the issues and about the cause and effect relationships between them.

Cognitive maps are formed over time through education, experience and interaction with others. Based on the inputs of their senses, people will infer causal relationships between phenomena, making guesses about unobservable factors and resolving inconsistencies between the bits of information received. In turn, people's cognitive maps steer their senses; while cognitive maps are built on past sensory data, they will consequently direct which new information will be sought and perceived. A person's cognitive map will focus attention on particular phenomena, while blocking out other data as noise, and will quickly make clear how a situation should be perceived. In this way, a cognitive map provides an interpretive filter or perceptual screen, aiding the senses in selecting and understanding external stimuli (Starbuck and Milliken, 1988). Furthermore, cognitive maps help to direct behaviour, by providing an existing repertoire of 'problem-solving' responses (also referred to as 'scripts' or 'recipes') from which an appropriate action can be derived.

In building their cognitive maps, people acquire a lot of their knowledge by means of direct experience. By doing, they learn to communicate, play an instrument, drive a vehicle and solve problems. This knowledge is added to people's cognitive maps without being explicitly articulated. In other words, knowledge gained through experiential learning is usually not codified into formal rules, principles, models or theories, but remains tacit (Polanyi, 1966; Nonaka, 1991). People formulate implicit models and draw conclusions, but do so largely unconsciously. In this way, cognitive maps evolve without people themselves being entirely aware of their own cognitive map. Hence, when people use their 'intuition', this is not a mystical or irrational way of reasoning, but thinking guided by the tacit knowledge they have acquired in the past (Behling and Eckel, 1991). Intuitive thinking is the opposite of analytical thinking – informal and holistic (Von Winterfeldt and Edwards, 1986). Informal means that the thinking is largely unconscious and based on assumptions, variables and causal relationships not explicitly identifiable by those doing the thinking. Holistic means that the thinker does not aim at unravelling phenomena into their constituent parts, but rather maintains a more integrated view of reality.

Yet, people's cognitive maps are not developed independently, but rather in interaction with one another. People tend to construct a shared understanding of the world by interacting with each other within a group over an extended period of time. By exchanging interpretations of what they see, it is said that they *enact* a shared reality (Daft and Weick, 1984; Smircich and Stubbart, 1985). The resulting shared cognitive map is variably referred to as the group's dominant logic (Prahalad and Bettis, 1986), common paradigm (Kuhn, 1970) or belief system (Noorderhaven, 1995). Such a shared worldview can exist within small social units, such as a firm or a family, but also within larger units, such as an industry or a nation.

As individuals can belong to different groups, they can be influenced by different belief systems simultaneously. As members of a national culture, their cognitive maps will to a certain extent be influenced by the beliefs dominant within the nation. As employees of a company, their cognitive maps will be affected by the beliefs common within the firm and the industry as well. In the same manner, people can be impacted by the professional community to which they belong, their religious affiliation, their political party and any other groups in which they interact with others (Hambrick *et al.*, 1993; Sutcliffe and Huber, 1998). Due to the mutually inclusive nature of group membership, an individual's cognitive map will be a complex combination of elements taken from different group-level dominant logics. While these paradigms on which an individual draws can be complementary, or overlapping yet consistent, it is quite possible that inconsistencies arise (Schein, 1985; Trice and Beyer, 1993).

As shared beliefs develop over time through interaction and are passed on through socialization, they remain largely tacit. The shared cognitive map of a group is literally 'common sense' – sense shared by a common group of people. However, where members of different groups come into conflict with one another, or where an individual needs to deal with the inconsistencies brought on by multiple group memberships, beliefs can become more articulated (Glynn, 2000). Different behaviours, based on different cognitive maps, will often lead to the identification and codification of beliefs, either to protect them or to engage in debate with people with other views. As paradigms become more articulated, they also become more mobile, making it possible to transfer ideas to people without direct interaction.

The downside of cognitive maps is that they exhibit a high level of rigidity. People are generally not inclined to change their minds. Once people's cognitive maps have formed, and they have a grip on reality, they become resistant to signals that challenge their conceptions. As McCaskey (1982) remarks, the mind 'strives mightily to bring order, simplicity, consistency and stability to the world it encounters', and is therefore reluctant to welcome the ambiguity presented by contradicting data. People tend to significantly overestimate the value of information that confirms their cognitive map, underestimate dis-confirming information, and they actively seek out evidence that supports their current beliefs (Schwenk, 1984). Once an interpretive filter is in place, seeing is not believing, but *believing is seeing*. People might have the impression that they are constantly learning, but they are largely learning within the bounds of a paradigm. When an individual's map is supported by similar beliefs shared within a firm, industry or country, the ability to question key aspects of a paradigm will usually be rather limited. Not only does the individual have no 'intellectual sounding board' for teasing out new ideas, but deviation from the dominant logic might also have adverse social and political ramifications within the group (e.g. DiMaggio and Powell, 1983; Aldrich and Fiol, 1994). Not for nothing the old proverb is: 'old ideas never change; they eventually die out' (Kuhn, 1970).

For strategists, cognitive rigidity is particularly worrying. Strategists should be at the forefront of market developments, identifying changing circumstances and new opportunities before their competitors do. Strategizing is by its very nature focused on understanding and shaping the future, and therefore strategists must have the ability to challenge current beliefs and to change their own mind. They must be able to come up with innovative, yet feasible new strategies that will fit with the unfolding reality. This places extraordinary cognitive demands on strategists – they must be able to overcome the limitations of their own cognitive maps and develop a new understanding.

THE PARADOX OF LOGIC AND INTUITION

Information's pretty thin stuff, unless mixed with experience.
Clarence Day (1874–1935); American essayist

Many management theorists have noted that the opposites of logic and intuition create a tension for managers (e.g. Sadler-Smith, 2004; Hodgkinson and Healey, 2011, Reading 2.2). While some researchers make a strong case for more formal analysis (e.g. Isenberg, 1984; Schoemaker and Russo, 1993), there is a broad understanding that managers need to employ both logical and intuitive thinking, even if they are each other's opposites.

The extensive use of intuitive judgement among managers is understood by most as necessary and beneficial. A manager's intuition is built up through years of experience and contains a vast quantity of tacit knowledge that can only superficially be tapped by formal analysis. Intuition, therefore, can give a richer assessment by blending in qualitative information. Moreover, intuitive thinking is often better at capturing the big picture than logical thinking. And very practically, intuition is needed to cut corners: without the widespread use of cognitive heuristics, management would grind to a halt, overloaded by the sheer complexity of the analyses that would need to be carried out. Such a situation of rationality gone rampant is referred to as 'paralysis by analysis' (Lenz and Lyles, 1985; Langley, 1995).

However, it is equally clear to most that human intuition is often unreliable. Cognitive heuristics are 'quick and dirty' – efficient, but imprecise. They help people to intuitively jump to conclusions without thorough analysis, which increases speed, but also increases the risk of drawing faulty conclusions. The main danger of cognitive heuristics is that they are inherently biased, as they focus attention on only a few variables and interpret them in a particular way, even when this is not appropriate (e.g. Tversky and Kahneman, 1986; Bazerman, 1990). For this reason, many academics urge practitioners to bolster their intuitive judgements with more explicit rational analysis. Especially in the case of strategic decisions, more time and energy should be made available to avoid falling prey to common cognitive biases. Otherwise the ultimate result might be a 'corporate gravestone' with the epitaph *'extinct by instinct'* (Langley, 1995).

For strategists a fundamental question is how they can avoid getting stuck with an outdated cognitive map. How can they avoid the danger of building up a flawed picture of their industry, their markets and themselves? As strategists must be acutely aware of the unfolding opportunities and threats in the environment, and the evolving strengths and weaknesses of the organization, they must be able to constantly re-evaluate their views.

On the one hand, this requires rigorous *logical thinking*. All the key assumptions on which a strategist's cognitive map are based need to be reviewed and tested against developments in the firm and its environment. On the other hand, strategists must have the ability to engage in *intuitive thinking*. To be able to 'feel' new opportunities and strengths, strategists must be able to think beyond their current mental models. Both demands on strategists will now be reviewed in more detail.

The demand for logical thinking

It is clear that if the strategizing managers base their strategic decisions only on heavily biased cognitive maps, unconsciously built up through past experience, this will lead to very poor results. Strategists need to have the ability to critically reflect on the assumptions they hold, to check whether they are based on actual fact, or on organizational folklore and industry recipes. They must be capable of making their tacit beliefs more explicit, so that the validity of these mental models can be evaluated and can be further refined. In short, to be successful strategists, managers need to escape the confines of their own cognitive maps – and those of other stakeholders engaged in the strategy process.

Assessing the validity of a cognitive map requires strong logical thinking. Logical thinking can be characterized as conscious and rigorous, based on formal rules. When employing logic, each step in an argumentation follows from the previous, based on valid principles. In other words, a logical thinker will draw a conclusion only if it is arrived at by a sound succession of arguments.

Logical thinking can be applied to all four cognitive activities outlined in Figure 2.2. When identifying and diagnosing a strategic problem, logical thinking can help to avoid the emotional interpretations that so often colour people's understanding of environmental opportunities and threats, and organizational strengths and weaknesses. Logical thinking can also expose a person's bullish or bearish bias and can be instrumental in discarding old 'theories' of how the firm and its environment function. By analysing the empirical facts and rigorously testing the hypotheses on which the firm's shared cognitive map has been built, the strategist can prevent building a false model of reality.

When conceiving and realizing a strategic solution, logical thinking can help to avoid the danger of following outdated habits and routines. Routines are programmed courses of action that originally were deliberately conceived, but have been subsequently internalized and are used automatically (March and Simon, 1993). Habits are programmed courses of action that have developed unconsciously. By explicitly formulating strategic options and subjecting them to formal evaluation, the strategist can break away from such established behaviour and develop new approaches to gaining and retaining competitive advantage. Moreover, logical thinking can aid in making a distinction between fantasy and feasibility. Sound logic can serve to weed out strategic options that are flights of fancy, by analysing the factors that will determine success or failure.

The demand for intuitive thinking

Intuitive thinking is the opposite of logical thinking. As described above, when employing logic, a thinker bases each step in a train of thought on the previous steps, following formal rules of valid thinking – also coined 'cold cognition' (Bernhein and Rangel, 2004).

However, the intuitive thinker does not follow formal steps in a decision-making process, but instead follows an informal and holistic judgment process. While judging the situation at hand, the intuitive thinker includes multiple inputs, relates the inputs to the unconsciously stored large quantities of information to detect and understand the inputs, and employs his emotions for judging situations – also dubbed 'hot cognition' (Bernhein and Rangel, 2004).

In intuitive thinking a person opens up the unconscious part of his brain. The power of using the unconsciously stored information is that it connects many variables to another into a whole, without a sound explanation of why a correlation is assumed. The power of the unconscious is that – although imprecise – it is both fast and able to combine large numbers of inputs. An understanding boils up and, when it appears to 'make sense', is confronted with supporting evidence. Often logic is used afterwards to justify an understanding that was actually generated by intuitive means.

If a pattern of incidents indicates that there is reason to believe that 'something is going on' which may affect at least some elements of the mental map, common thinking will be challenged. If the intuitive thinker develops a 'gut feeling' in which direction the solution might be, the new idea will be brought forward, even when it challenges orthodoxy and current thinking.

When identifying and diagnosing strategic problems, intuitive thinking is often needed. Old cognitive maps usually have a very compelling logic, locking people into old patterns of thinking. These old cognitive maps are usually tried and tested, and have become immune to external signals that they are no longer fitting. Thinking within the boundaries of a shared cognitive map is generally accepted and people tend to proceed rationally – that is, they try to escape from logical inconsistencies by including dissonant signs in the current thinking. Challenging a cognitive map's fundamental assumptions, however, cannot be done in a way that is logically consistent with the map itself. Contradicting a paradigm is illogical from the point of view of those who accept the paradigm. Therefore, changing a rigid and subjective cognitive map, rooted in a shared paradigm, requires strategists that are not captured by common logic and recognize patterns in a number of seemingly unrelated incidents. Strategic thinkers need to be willing and able to detect signs that may challenge orthodoxy and make leaps of imagination which – although not logically justified – are needed to generate fresh ways of looking at old and new problems.

The same is true when conceiving and realizing strategic solutions. New strategies are not analysed into existence, but need to be generated. Patterns of loosely connected signs need novel solutions that do not follow from the dominant logic, but are the unexpected answers that emerge when the grip of the dominant logic is loosened.

Unfortunately, the conclusion must be that logical thinking and intuitive thinking are not only opposites, but that they are partially incompatible as well. They are based on methods that are at odds with one another. Strategizing managers would probably love to be fully logical and fully intuitive at the same time, but both require such a different mindset and range of cognitive skills that in practice it is very difficult to achieve both simultaneously. The demand for logic and intuition is not only contradictory for each individual, but also within teams, departments and the overall firm: while strategizing groups would like to be fully capable of logical and intuitive thinking, finding ways of incorporating both forms of strategic thinking into a workable strategy process is extremely challenging. Commonly, opposing styles lead to opposing people, and therefore a blend between the two is not that simple. It is for this reason that we speak of the 'paradox of logic and intuition' – the two demands on managers seem to be contradictory, yet both are required at the same time.

EXHIBIT 2.1 SAMSUNG: COSMOPOLITANS ON THE HAN RIVER

While entering the empty boardroom Lee Kun-hee realizes he is a bit early for his first meeting. He looks around and notices the "new car smell" – a residue of the room's recent makeover. The Samsung empire, built by his late father Lee Byung-chul, has achieved recognition around the globe. Together with a few other companies, Samsung helped the South Korean economy expand from near zero to more than a trillion US dollars between the 1960s and 2012. This achievement has become known as the Miracle on the Han River.

The Miracle actually started back in 1938 with his father's small company in the trucking business. Seventy-five years later, the small trading firm has become the largest of South Korea's Chaebols – family business conglomerates – with subsidiaries in apparel, chemicals, electronics, medical equipment, ships, advertising, construction, hospitality, and more. Lee Kun-hee remembers well the moment in 1987 when his father entrusted him with the helm of Samsung Electronics, the most important part of the Chaebol.

Samsung – meaning the "three stars: large, strong and lasting forever" – has strong Japanese roots. South Korea was a Japanese colony when Samsung was founded, and being educated in Japan Lee Byung-chul was highly influenced by the Japanese way of doing business, with its focus on continuous improvement, a hierarchical labour model, unrelated diversification, dependency on the internal capital market, long-term relationships with stakeholders, seniority-based promotions and limited recruitment.

In the aftermath of ending the Japanese ruling in 1945 and the Korean War in 1953, South Korea's economic situation was in terrible shape. Personal conversations with South Korea's first president Syngman Rhee strengthened Lee Byung-chul's belief that he was not just building a company: he was 'engaging in business for national service' – to help create a stronger nation through business prosperity, or "saeobboguk" in Korean. This is illustrated by Samsung's business philosophy – in 1973 coined the 'Samsung Spirit' – which refers to 'the principle of engaging in business for national service', 'man and talent first', and 'pursuit of logic and reality'.

Lee Kun-hee, still in an empty boardroom, remembers a decisive moment for Samsung Electronics' success in the late 1980s, when Samsung Electronics established a position in the white goods business. He had heard of recent developments in semiconductors and decided to personally investigate the situation in Japan. His conclusion after his investigation was that semiconductors were promising enormous opportunities for high-tech products. With a firm position in white goods, the new developments could provide Samsung Electronics with the growth Lee was looking for. He also realized something else: Samsung would be forced to compete in markets dominated by non-Koreans, with new challenges and different competitive rules ahead. Lee was also convinced that Samsung Electronics should not move cautiously, just following the leading Japanese companies Sony and Matsushita. Instead the company should try to claim a leadership role and become an innovative and entrepreneurial industry shaper. But to achieve this, the company's current slow seniority-based HR and focus on operational excellence wasn't going to take Samsung to the top. Lee needed a fresh look on things, which he derived from Western thinking.

Lee launched the 'New Management Initiative', based on introducing the Western way of doing business into the company. He particularly focused on the Western best practices, such as strategy formation, talent management and innovation. This decision introduced analytical Western thinking into the company. For example, employee promotion became merit-based instead of seniority-based. Lee understood that a "cold turkey" method wouldn't do the job as it would certainly result in heavy resistance. Therefore he decided to slowly inject the best practices into the company. But how do you get analysis-based practices into an Eastern firm with holistic DNA? Lee came up with a brilliant idea. He first brought outsiders into his company. Western outsiders, equipped with MBAs and a strong knowhow of the Western ways of doing business, slowly but surely opened up the traditional Korean business mentality. Furthermore, he also did something else. He sent insiders out to the Western world, to experience the Western way of doing business personally and taking Western best practices back into the South Korean context.

The Western best practices were slowly introduced into Samsung. For example, the

▶

merit-based compensation system started with a small differential, increasing annually until it reached 50 per cent. Lee also acquired companies that could help him in entering markets. For example, in 1995 Samsung Electronics acquired a 40 per cent stake in AST Research, a United States-based personal computer maker. Long-term strategic plans were created that would enable Samsung to go beyond supplying simple technology to creating high-tech products, and would finally result in Samsung Electronics becoming a 'Three starred chef' in product and process innovation.

During 1997 and 1998 the industry was hit by a dramatic dip in demand and prices for memory chips. While most competitors became nervous about short-term results, and reduced capital spending and production capacity, Samsung Electronics kept to their strategic long-term planning and continued investing and strengthening its memory chip production operations. When the bust cycle turned into boom again, Samsung was one of the few companies with sufficient manufacturing capacity to reap the benefits. Since then, Samsung has showcased itself to be the world's largest memory chip manufacturer, and the world market leader in LCD screens, monitors, microwave ovens and mobile phones. By 2012 the entire Samsung Electronics had reached an astonishing US$ 201 trillion of revenue, while employing 221,726 people around the world. The unique combination of Eastern and Western ways of thinking has made Samsung Electronics the company it is today.

Lee Kun-hee snapped back into reality, grateful for having been able to follow his late father's footsteps and having guided Samsung Electronics to where it is today. Soon the empty boardroom would be filled with board members and strategy consultants. The agenda for today's meeting consisted of only one topic; creating a long-term company strategy. It would be a tough decision to choose a strategic direction. He was consulted by his advisors to become more of an Asian company with its way of doing business. Furthermore, other advisors told him that it would be much wiser to continue following the West. Lee Kun-hee has not made a final decision. Holistic thinking helped to create the Samsung Chaebol. Analytical thinking helped to enter the non-Korean dominated high-tech electronic markets. And the unique Samsung 'holistic analytical thinking combination' has made Samsung Electronics the market leader in many fields and the South Korean champion on the Han River. Employees are not Koreans or Westerners but cosmopolitans who feel at home all over the globe. 'Well, let's first listen to what the advisors have to say', Lee thinks, 'and then decide what the next route for success will be'. Having heard all arguments, should Lee follow logic or his intuition to being able to live up to what Samsung Electronics stands for: 'large, strong and lasting forever'?

Co-author: Jeroen Brinkhuis

Sources: *Far Eastern Economic Review,* 14 September 2002; Yu, 1999; Haour and Cho, 2000; *The Korea Herald,* 16 January 2009; www.samsung.com; *The Korean Times,* Business Philosophy of Lee Byung-chull, February 2nd, 2010. *Harvard Business Review,* 'The Paradox of Samsung's Rise', July–August 2011.

PERSPECTIVES ON STRATEGIZING

Irrationally held truths may be more harmful than reasoned errors.
T.H. Huxley (1825–1895); English biologist

While the need for both logical and intuitive thinking is clear, this does place strategists in a rather awkward position of needing to bring two partially contradictory forms of thinking together in one strategic reasoning process. Logical thinking helps to make the strategic reasoning process rigorous, precise and consistent, instead of haphazard, fragmentary and *ad hoc*. Intuitive thinking, on the other hand, helps to make the strategic reasoning process comprehensive, informal and fast, instead of rigidly following formal rules and using logic to redefine deviating signs into confirmations of the common.

In finding a balance between these opposite forms of thinking, the main question is whether the strategic reasoning process should actually be a predominantly rational affair, or a much more intuitive process. Is strategizing largely a rational activity, requiring logical thinking to be the dominant modus operandi, with occasional bits of gut feeling needed here and there to generate new ideas? Or is strategizing largely an intuitive activity, requiring integrative thinking as the standard operating procedure, with occasional bits of logical analysis needed here and there to weed out unfeasible ideas?

The answer to this question should be found in the strategic management literature. Yet, upon closer inspection, the opinions outlined in both the academic and popular literature show that views vary widely among researchers and managers alike. A wide spectrum of differing perspectives can be recognized, each giving their own angle on how strategic thinking should use logic and intuition – sometimes explicitly mentioning the need for both, but more commonly making implicit assumptions about the role of logic and intuition in strategy processes.

As was outlined in Chapter 1, it is not the intention here to summarize all of the 'schools of thought' on the topic of strategic thinking. Instead, only the two opposite points of view will be presented in this section. These two poles in the debate form the input for a good debate – a clear-cut thesis and antithesis in a process of dialectical enquiry.

At one end of the spectrum, there are those who argue that strategizing should be a predominantly conscious analytic process, requiring logic to be the main form of thinking in use. This point of view is referred to as the 'analytic reasoning perspective'. At the other pole, there are those who argue that strategizing is mainly an unconscious intuitive process. This point of view will be referred to as the 'holistic reasoning perspective'.

The analytic reasoning perspective

Strategists employing the analytic reasoning perspective argue that strategic reasoning is predominantly a 'logical activity' (Andrews, 1987; Teece, 2007, Reading 2.1). To deal with strategic problems the strategist must first consciously and thoroughly analyse the problem situation. Data must be gathered on all developments external to the organization, and this data must be processed to pinpoint the opportunities and threats in the organization's environment. Furthermore, the organization itself must be appraised, to uncover its strengths and weaknesses and to establish which resources are available. Once the problem has been defined, a number of alternative strategies can be identified by matching external opportunities to internal strengths. Then, the strategic options must be extensively screened, by evaluating them on a number of criteria, such as internal consistency, external consonance, competitive advantage, organizational feasibility, potential return and risks. The best strategy can be selected by comparing the scores of all options and determining the level of risk the strategist is willing to take. The chosen strategy can subsequently be implemented.

This type of intellectual effort requires well-developed analytical skills. Strategists must be able to rigorously, consistently and objectively comb through huge amounts of data, interpreting and combining findings to arrive at a rich picture of the current problem situation. Possible solutions require critical appraisal and all possible contingencies must be logically thought through. Advocates of the analytic reasoning perspective argue that such reasoning strongly resembles the problem-solving approach of chess grandmasters (Simon, 1987). They also thoroughly assess their competitive position, sift through a variety of options and calculate which course of action brings the best chances of success. Therefore, the reasoning processes of chess grandmasters can be used as an analogy for what goes on in the mind of the strategist.

While depicted here as a purely step-by-step process of recognition, analysis, formulation and implementation, proponents of the analytic reasoning perspective note that in reality strategists often have to backtrack and redo some of these steps, as new information becomes available or chosen strategies do not work out. Strategists attempt to be as comprehensive, consistent and rigorous as possible in their analyses and calculations, but of course they cannot know everything and their conclusions are not always perfect: even with the most advanced forecasting techniques, not all developments can be foreseen; even with state of the art market research, some trends can be missed; even with cutting edge test marketing, scenario analyses, competitive simulations and net present value calculations, some selected strategies can turn out to be failures. Strategists are not all knowing, and do make mistakes – their rationality is limited by incomplete information and imperfect cognitive abilities. Yet, strategists try to be as rational as possible. Simon (1957) refers to this as 'bounded rationality' – 'people act intentionally rational, but only limitedly so'.

The (bounded) rational strategist must sometimes improvise to make up for a lack of information, but will try to do this as logically as possible. Inferences and speculation will always be based on the facts as known. By articulating assumptions and explicitly stating the facts and arguments on which conclusions have been based, problem definitions and solutions can be debated within the firm to confirm that they have been arrived at using sound reasoning. This strongly resembles the scientific method, in that hypotheses are formulated and tested as a means for obtaining new knowledge. Only by this consistent alignment of mental models with empirical reality can the strategist avoid the danger of becoming stuck with an outdated cognitive map.

Of course, creativity techniques can be beneficial for escaping from an outdated mental frame. Whether it is by means of brainstorming, six thinking caps or action art, creative thinking can spark some unconventional thoughts. Even a rational scientist like Newton has remarked that 'no great discovery was ever made without a bold guess'. But this is usually where the usefulness of creativity ends, and to which it should be limited. In creative thinking anything goes and that can lead to anything between odd and ludicrous. To be able to sift the sane from the zany, logic is needed. To make sense of the multitude of new ideas the logical thinker must analyse and evaluate them.

The alternative to this rational approach, it is often pointed out, is to be irrational and illogical, which surely cannot be a desirable alternative for the strategist. Non-rational reasoning comes in a variety of forms. For instance, people's thinking can be guided by their emotions. Feelings such as love, hate, guilt, regret, pride, anxiety, frustration and embarrassment can all cloud the strategist's understanding of a problem situation and the possible solutions. Adherents of the analytic reasoning perspective do not dispute the importance of emotions – the purpose of an organization is often based on 'personal values, aspirations and ideals', while the motivation to implement strategies is also rooted in human emotions. However, the actual determination of the optimal strategy is a 'rational undertaking' *par excellence* (Andrews, 1987).

Neither is intuitive thinking an appealing alternative for strategists. Of course, intuition can often be useful: decision rules based on extensive experience (cognitive heuristics) are often correct (even if they have been arrived at unconsciously) and they save time and effort. For example, Simon argues that even chess grandmasters make many decisions intuitively, based on tacit rules of thumb, formulated through years of experience. Yet, intuitive judgements must be viewed with great suspicion, as they are difficult to verify and infamously unreliable (e.g. Hogarth, 1980; Schwenk, 1984). Where possible, intuitive thinking should be made explicit – the strategist's cognitive map should be captured on paper (e.g. Anthony *et al.*, 1993; Eden, 1989), so that the reasoning of the strategist can be checked for logical inconsistencies.

In conclusion, advocates of the analytic reasoning perspective argue that emotions and intuition have a small place in the strategic reasoning process, but that logical thinking should be the dominant ingredient. It could be said that the analytic reasoning process of the strategist strongly resembles that of the scientist. The scientific methods of research, analysis, theorizing and falsification are all directly applicable to the process of strategic reasoning – so much so, that the scientific method can be used as the benchmark for strategy development processes. Consequently, the best preparation for effective strategic reasoning would be to be trained in the scientific tradition.

EXHIBIT 2.2 THE ANALYTIC REASONING PERSPECTIVE

BERKSHIRE HATHAWAY: NOT OUTSIDE THE BOX

At the peak of the dotcom boom in September 1999, few people were derided as much as Warren Buffett (1930), chairman of the insurance and investment conglomerate Berkshire Hathaway. Buffett – admiringly nicknamed the Sage of Omaha – had gained a phenomenal reputation as an investor during the 1980s and 1990s, but to most it was clear that he hadn't grasped the opportunities presented by the Internet. The grand old man might have been the guru of the old economy, but he simply did not understand the new rules of the information age. He was considered a pitiful example of a once brilliant mind that had not been able to make the leap beyond conventional beliefs and comprehend the 'new paradigm'. The investment strategy of Berkshire Hathaway was deemed hopelessly outdated. When almost all funds were rushing into new economy shares, the investment portfolio of Berkshire consisted of companies like Coca-Cola, Walt Disney, Gillette and The Washington Post. The shares of Berkshire traded at the lowest level in years.

The person least perturbed by this new, dubious status was Buffett himself. In his 1999 annual 'Letter to the Berkshire Hathaway Shareholders', he displayed an untouched faith in the fundamentals that had made him one of the richest people in the world: 'If we have a strength, it is in recognizing when we are operating well within our circle of competence and when we are approaching the perimeter. (…) we just stick with what we understand. If we stray, we will have done so inadvertently, not because we got restless and substituted hope for rationality.' He refused to invest in Internet stocks, which he considered 'chain letters', in which early participants get rich at the expense of later ones. As the dotcom bubble eventually burst, Buffett was more than exonerated.

This famous episode was neither Buffet's first provocative stance against lemming behaviour, nor his last. Following his personal mantra that 'when other investors are greedy be fearful, but when other investors are fearful be greedy', Buffett has always stuck to his analysis and gone against the grain. For instance, during the stock market frenzy of 1969 he was widely ridiculed for not participating in the party. To his shareholders he wrote: 'I am out of step with present conditions. When the game is no longer played your way, it is only human to say the new approach is all wrong, bound to lead to trouble, and so on. On one point, however, I am clear. I will not abandon a previous approach whose logic I understand (although I find it difficult to apply) even though it may mean foregoing large, and apparently easy, profits to embrace an approach which I don't fully understand, have not practised successfully, and which possibly could lead to substantial permanent loss of capital.'

Forty years later, during the worst stock market crash since the Great Depression, Warren Buffett was again held to be a fool. With Berkshire Hathaway having lost up to US$ 25 billion of market value within the span of a year, he was arguing that the time was right to boldly buy: 'I don't like to opine on the stock market, and again I emphasize that I have no idea what the market will do in the short term. Nevertheless, I'll follow the lead of a restaurant that opened in an empty bank building and then advertised: "Put your mouth where your money was." Today my money and my mouth both say equities.' True to his words, Buffett invested US$ 5 billion in Goldman Sachs in September 2008, as panic about the American financial system was breaking out all around him. In his 2008 shareholder report, he frankly admitted that he had

▶

done 'some dumb things in investments', but that overall he was satisfied with the new additions to his portfolio: 'Whether we're talking about socks or stocks, I like buying quality merchandise when it is marked down.'

When valuing companies, Buffet's approach has always been based on a thorough analysis of company fundamentals, 'to separate investment from speculation'. Ultimately, share prices will reflect these fundamentals and therefore nothing can substitute for a meticulous diagnosis of the sustainability of the competitive advantage of a firm. As Buffet puts it: 'I try to buy stock in businesses that are so wonderful that an idiot can run them. Because sooner or later, one will.' Following this logic, he stays away from investing in ill-understood businesses and in fast-changing industries, 'in which the long-term winners are hard to identify'. And when he invests, he keeps his shareholdings for years, or even decades. 'Risk', he states, 'comes from not knowing what you're doing.'

His emphasis on rational reasoning and not following the wisdom of crowds ('a public opinion poll is no substitute for thought'), does not mean that he takes a liking to those who pretend to be scientific and rational ('beware of geeks bearing formulas'). He warns of professionals and academicians talking of efficient markets, dynamic hedging and betas: 'Their interest in such matters is understandable, since techniques shrouded in mystery clearly have value to the purveyor of investment advice. After all, what witch doctor has ever achieved fame and fortune by simply advising "Take two aspirins"?'

While still going strong at his advanced age, many commentators have warned that Berkshire Hathaway is vulnerable due to its dependence on its elderly chairman. Buffet's response so far has been totally in character: 'I've reluctantly discarded the notion of my continuing to manage the portfolio after my death – abandoning my hope to give new meaning to the term "thinking outside the box".'

Co-author: Martijn Rademakers

Sources: www.berkshirehathaway.com; *The Economist*, 15 March 2001; 18 December 2008; *The Sunday Times*, 1 March 2009; *The New York Times*, 16 October 2008, 1 March 2009.

The holistic reasoning perspective

Strategists taking a holistic reasoning perspective are strongly at odds with the unassailable position given to logic in the analytic reasoning perspective. They agree that logic is important, but emphasize the 'wicked' nature of strategic problems (Rittel, 1972; Mason and Mitroff, 1981; Reading 1.1). It is argued that strategic problems cannot be rationally and objectively defined, but that they are open to interpretation from a limitless variety of angles. The same is true for the possible solutions – there is no fixed set of problem solutions from which the strategist must select the best one. Defining and solving strategic problems, it is believed, is fundamentally a judgement activity. As such, strategic reasoning has very little in common with the thought processes of the aforementioned chess grand master, as was presumed by the rationalists. Playing chess is a 'tame' problem. The problem definition is clear and all options are known. In the average game of chess, consisting of 40 moves, 10,120 possibilities have to be considered (Simon, 1972). This makes it a difficult game for humans to play, because of their limited computational capacities. Chess grandmasters are better at making these calculations than other people and are particularly good at computational short cuts – recognizing which things to figure out and which not. However, even the best chess grandmasters have been beaten at the game by highly logical computers with a superior number crunching capability. For the poor chess grandmaster, the rules of the game are fixed and there is little room for redefining the problem or introducing innovative approaches.

Engaging in business strategy is an entirely different matter. Strategic problems are wicked. Problem definitions are highly subjective and there are no fixed sets of solutions. It is therefore impossible to 'identify' the problem and 'calculate' an optimal solution. Opportunities and threats do not exist, waiting for the analyst to discover them. A strategist understands that a situation can be 'viewed' as an opportunity and 'believes' that certain factors can be threatening if not approached properly. Neither can strengths and weaknesses be objectively determined – a strategist can employ a company characteristic as a strength but can also turn a unique company quality into a weakness by a lack of vision. Hence, doing a SWOT analysis (strengths, weaknesses, opportunities and threats) actually has little to do with logical analysis, but in reality is nothing less than a creative interpretation of a problem situation. Likewise, it is a fallacy to believe that strategic options follow more or less logically from the characteristics of the firm and its environment. Strategic options are not 'deduced from the facts' or selected from a 2×2 matrix, but are dreamt up. Strategists must be able to use their intuition to imagine previously unknown solutions. If more than one strategic option emerges from the mind of the strategist, these cannot be simply scored and ranked to choose the optimal one. Some analyses can be done, but as the development of many factors is susceptible to fundamental uncertainty, ultimately the strategist will have to intuitively judge which vision for the future has the best chance of being created in reality.

Strategizing is more than just reflecting on the information at hand and having a wild idea every once in a while to escape from an outdated cognitive map. In a holistic reasoning process, strategists need to trust the reflexes of the unconscious mind that combines all sort of unrelated signs into a new and comprehending pattern. This type of holistic thinking is very intense work, as strategists must leave the intellectual safety of generally accepted concepts to explore new ideas, guided by little else than their intuition. They must be willing to operate without the security of a dominant logic; interpreting, testing, arguing, challenging, doubting and living amongst the rubble of demolished certainties, without having proof and new certainties to give them shelter. To proponents of the holistic reasoning perspective, it is essential for strategists to give leeway to the knowing and feelings of the unconscious mind and arrive at the right judgement.

Proponents of the holistic reasoning perspective stress that logic is often more a hindrance than a help. The heavy emphasis placed on rationality can actually frustrate the main objective of strategic reasoning – to generate a novel understanding, based on intuitive judgement of a multitude of factors. Analysis can be a useful tool, but as the aim of strategic reasoning is to tear up outdated cognitive maps and to reinvent the future, intuitive thinking should be the driving force, and logical thinking a supporting means. For this reason, proponents of the holistic reasoning perspective argue that strategists should avoid the false certainty projected by rational approaches to strategic reasoning, but should nurture intuition as their primary cognitive asset.

In conclusion, advocates of the holistic reasoning perspective argue that the essence of strategic reasoning is the ability to generate new and unique ways of understanding and doing things. As such, strategic reasoning closely resembles the frame-breaking behaviour common in the arts. In fields such as painting, music, motion pictures, dancing and architecture, artists are propelled by the drive to challenge convention and to seek out innovative approaches. Many of their methods, such as brainstorming, experimentation, openness to intuition, and the use of metaphors, contradictions and paradoxes, are directly applicable to developing strategy. Consequently, the best preparation for strategic reasoning might actually be to be trained in the artistic tradition of iconoclastic intuition and mental flexibility.

EXHIBIT 2.3   THE HOLISTIC REASONING PERSPECTIVE

Q & A WITH RICHARD BRANSON

He has conquered the most impossible adventure challenges; built over 400 companies by shaking up complacent industries; is on a mission to bring space travel to the man on the street and is committed to building world-class African entrepreneurs. We stalked Richard Branson on a recent trip to the Johannesburg-based Branson Centre of Entrepreneurship and talked intuition vs brainpower and the implausibility of British Airways condoms.

GQ: You and others have said that businesses need to do good in order to stay relevant and in business. Do you think it's easy to get caught out when you are not?

RB: I think the public is no fool and sees through companies that have a corporate-responsibility office at the back of the building and pretend it's at the front of the building. If you are going to do good, it's got to be absolutely genuine. Having said that, I'd rather people tried something than nothing at all.

GQ: The message from many entrepreneurs is to persevere and everything will work out. You have had both experiences – where you have abandoned certain ventures and in other instances hung in there and eventually made money. Is it a gut thing, knowing which way to go?

RB: It is perhaps one of the reasons having mentors is important – someone who can sit young entrepreneurs down and give them advice when they encounter situations like that. I have in the past been known to go on too long with companies because companies are, in the end, people and you don't want to close a company down and have to lose people. I suspect you really do know when the chances of being able to pull a plane out of a nose-dive sound realistic or if the course is too much. Having one or two people you can trust to go to in those situations [is important] because sometimes you get too close to the situation and the people and cannot make a dispassionate decision.

GQ: Your first business was a magazine. Given the climate we are in, if you were to launch a magazine today, what kind of magazine would it be?

RB: I love physical magazines, but I suspect it would have to be an Internet-based magazine. We recently launched a magazine called *Project* on the Internet, which is quite bold and brave because an Internet-only magazine, or on an iPad, has never really existed before. People have kind of been putting *Wired* magazine on the Internet as well as the bookstores, and therefore the advertising market wasn't there for it. But having said that, *Project* has stuck in there and the advertising is coming. I do think there is a good future for advertisers in that space; it can be so much more imaginative than on a flat page.

GQ: You're pretty much a 'gut' man. Can you identify any brain decisions in your career?

RB: Intuition based on experience is perhaps slightly more useful than pure gut. It is the intuition of flying on other people's airlines and finding that the experience was not that good, feeling you can improve on that, and then starting an airline. It's that kind of intuition that works. The intuition that makes you think that if I want to go into space, there are millions of other people like me who would like to go to space. So if we could get the price down to what was affordable then there would be a market and then therefore, screw it, let's go find an engineer who can build a spaceship company. As far as using brainpower, that comes later: finding someone who can build a spaceship and maybe finding someone with the brainpower to mop up after you when your intuition was getting ahead of you.

GQ: You have successfully 'Virginised' many industries and brands. If there was a formula for creating successful brand extensions, what would that be?

RB: Most businesses are focused on one sector. I love challenges and have been able to take Virgin forward into a lot of areas. We have been able to build a reputation that makes going to those businesses that much easier. If you were building another brand to do the same thing, you need a name that can work internationally, that works on any product. British Airways condoms wouldn't work particularly well. Anyway, nothing named British Airways would work that well [laughs]. A brand like Apple, you could stretch that brand, but others you wouldn't. So it is worth keeping in mind the international nature of the brand name.

GQ: You are involved in hundreds of businesses and are in partnership with many. How do young empire-building entrepreneurs learn salient things such as how much to take on themselves, when to get partners or when to employ people?

RB: People spend far too long clinging on and not delegating and dealing with the bigger picture. As early on in the business – as soon as you can afford it – as possible, you should find somebody better than

yourself to run the business so you can push the company forward and make sure the business survives and thrives. It means you can have more time for your family and your friends and have a more decent life. I could not have grown 400 companies if I hadn't learned the art of delegation at a very young age.

Sources: Siphiwe Mpye, GQ Digital Edition; http://www.gq.co.za/report/636702.html. Reproduced by permission of Condé Nast Independent Magazines and Siphiwe Mpye.

MANAGING THE PARADOX OF LOGIC AND INTUITION

Men like the opinions to which they have become accustomed from youth; this prevents them from finding the truth, for they cling to the opinions of habit.
Moses Maimonides (1135–1204); Egyptian physician and philosopher

Opinions differ sharply about whether the rational or the intuitive reasoning perspective is more valuable for understanding strategic thinking. Although they are opposites, and partially contradictory, both perspectives might reveal crucial aspects of strategic thinking that need to be combined to achieve superior results. Of course, the tension is not so pressing for investment managers and art painters, but most strategizing managers struggle with managing the tension. See Table 2.1 for the main differences.

So, how can strategizing managers manage the paradox of logic and intuition? With the taxonomy of the first chapter in mind (Figure 1.8), the following options have been suggested by scholars in the management sciences.

TABLE 2.1 Analytic reasoning versus holistic reasoning perspective

	Analytic reasoning perspective	*Holistic reasoning perspective*
Emphasis on	Logic over creativity	Intuition over logic
Dominant cognitive style	Analytic	Holistic
Thinking follows	Formal, fixed rules	Informal, variable rules
Nature of thinking	Deductive and computational	Inductive and imaginative
Mode of thinking	Structured	Unstructured
Direction of thinking	Vertical	Lateral
System at work	Conscious, reflective	Unconscious, reflexive
Problem solving seen as	Analysing activities	Sensemaking activities
Value placed on	Cold cognition	Hot cognition
Assumption about reality	Objective, (partially) knowable	Subjective, (partially) creatable
Thinking hindered by	Incomplete information	Adherence to current cognitive map
Strategizing speed	Slow	Fast
Strategizing based on	Calculation	Judgement
Metaphor	Strategy as science	Strategy as art

Navigating

Applying logic and intuition at the same time is complex because it requires different thinking modes and procedures. To deal with these contrasting needs, some authors have suggested 'build in mental time-outs' (e.g. Sadler-Smith, 2010) in daily routines to allow creative ideas to incubate. This kind of 'creativity' is accepted by analytical thinkers as a useful contribution to a largely rational process, while intuitive thinkers categorize creativity as an inherent part of the intuitive and holistic thinking mode. When the leadership team separates formal analytic from informal intuitive processes in time, such teams engage in 'temporal separation' or navigating the paradox.

Parallel processing

Not all organizational activities need the same level of logic and intuition. For example, efficient production mainly benefits from analytic reasoning, while new business development leans towards holistic reasoning. Knowing the primary processes within the firm, strategizing managers differentiate not only the activities of the company in separate units, but also the required competences such as different levels of logic and intuition. As the consequence, logical and intuitive thinking are processed in parallel in the organization.

Embracing

Strategists can also deliberately bring analytic and holistic thinkers together in one team, so as to mix 'individuals with analytical and intuitive cognitive styles (Hodgkinson and Clarke, 2007). The intention is not to resolve the tension between logic and intuition, but to capture the advantages of both. Of course, applying different thinking styles in one team is likely to create tensions between team members. Such tensions, however, often actually lead to unexpected solutions and innovations. The option is demanding for the strategizing managers in the team, and therefore requires specific capabilities, such as integrative thinking (Martin, 2007, Reading 2.3) and complexity maturity (Chapter 11).

STRATEGIC THINKING IN INTERNATIONAL PERSPECTIVE

Co-author: Gep Eisenloeffel

When I look carefully I see the dandelion blooming By the hedge
Matsuo Bashō (松尾 芭蕉? (1644–1694), born Matsuo Kinsaku (松尾 金作)), Japanese poet and greatest master of haiku

Flower in the crannied wall, I pluck you out of the crannies; – Hold you here, root and all, in my hand, Little flower – but if I could understand What you are, root and all, and all in all, I should know what God and man is.
Alfred Tennyson, 1st Baron Tennyson, (1809–1892), Poet Laureate of Great Britain and Ireland

In this part of the chapter, strategic thinking is discussed in an international perspective. The explicit question that must be added to the debate on the mind of the strategist is whether there are discernible national differences in approaches to strategic thinking. Are there specific national preferences for the rational or the generative reasoning perspective, or are the differing views spread randomly across the globe? Are each of the perspectives rooted in a particular national context, making it difficult to extend them to other countries, or are they universally applicable? In short, are views on strategic thinking similar all around the world?

Unfortunately, this question is easier asked than answered. Little cross-cultural research has been done in the field of strategic management and hardly any on this specific topic. This may be partially due to the difficulty of international comparative research, but it likely also reflects the implicit assumption by most that theories on strategizing are universally applicable. Few of the authors cited in this chapter suggest that there are international differences or note that their theories might be culturally biased and of limited validity in other national settings.

Yet, the assumption that strategizing is viewed in the same way around the world should be questioned. The human inclination to assume that all others are the same as us is well known – it is a common cognitive bias. In international affairs, however, such an assumption must always be challenged. Strategists operating internationally cannot afford the luxury of assuming that their views are universally accepted and applicable. Therefore, the thought must be entertained that strategists in some countries are more attracted to the rational reasoning perspective, while in other countries the generative reasoning perspective is more pervasive.

As a stimulus to the debate of whether there are such national preferences in perspective on strategizing, a number of factors will be brought forward that might be of influence on how the paradox of logic and creativity is tackled in different countries. It goes almost without saying that more concrete international comparative research is needed to give this debate a firmer footing.

Cultural heritage

In his book *The Social Animal* (2012) Richard Brooks argues that 'the tradition of rationalism in the West tells the story of human history as the story of the logical, conscious mind. It sees human history as the contest between reason and instinct. In the end, reason triumphs over emotion. Science gradually replaces myth. Logic wins out over passion.' The historical narrative usually begins in ancient Greece; the word strategy even derives from the Greek *strategos* (Cummings, 1993), meaning commander of the army, from the verb *agein* (to lead) and the noun *stratos* (army). It is important to notice, however, that strategizing in Ancient Greece, or Rome for that matter, was not yet 'the cognitive process of individual strategists'. Greek philosophers like Plato (427–347 BC) and Aristoteles (384–322) viewed the world as a living organism, assuming that in this perfect state each and everything had its place. The purpose of life was the fulfilment of one's destiny in this great holistic universe. The individual with individual goals and purposeful was not yet recognized. With the great discoveries of New Continents (Columbus 1492), revolutions in science (Copernicus 1514) and the Reformation (Luther 1517) functionalism and rationalism gradually came to dominate philosophy. The first functionalist and rationalist way of strategizing was expressed in the work of Niccolò Machiavelli. His book *The Prince* (printed version 1532) was dedicated to Lorenzo the Magnificent, ruler of Italian city state Florence. Machiavelli advised Lorenzo to take matters in his own hand to hold on to his power and even enlarge it.

In the seventeenth and eighteenth centuries Enlightenment philosophers viewed the universe as a giant clock with God as *the Divine Clockmaker*. According to this rationalist instrumental view the World was a machine that could be taken apart and reconstructed again according to our own wishes and commands. By taking individual action, objectives could be achieved. The Enlightenment philosophers claimed that each problem, from the simplest idea to the most complicated one, had to be separated "into as many parts as may be necessary for an adequate solution." In the realm of physics, chemistry, biology and the other natural sciences, rationalism gained enormous prestige during the eighteenth, nineteenth and twentieth centuries. The rationalist instrumental view also came to dominate other scientific fields such as economics and management, for example in Frederick Taylor's *Scientific Management* (1911). Management became a science with 'toolboxes' as enablers, companies were efficient machines with factory workers as cogs. The ultimate aim was to arrive at universally applicable theories.

As Henry Mintzberg *et al.* point out in their book *Strategy Safari* (1998), pioneering scholars in the strategy field such as Chandler (1962), Ansoff (1965), and Michael Porter (1980) were strongly influenced by the rationalist analytic approach. Strategizing was embedded in the tradition of rationality, including the tools and techniques. Problems were divided into discrete parts and solved on the basis of reliable fact and figures. Conscious cognition (*sensing*) was valued over the unconscious (*intuition*), rational reasoning over generative reasoning. Hampden-Turner and Trompenaars (2000) for example, found that over 70 per cent of managers in the US score highest on Introvert (versus Extrovert), Sensing (as opposed to Intuition), Thinking (instead of Feeling), and Judging (contrary to Perceiving) on the Meyers-Briggs Type Indicator.

Assumptions of the analytic rationalist approach have been heavily criticized by a number of scholars. Economist John Maynard Keynes warned against a predominantly functionalist and rationalist approach for humanitarian studies, arguing that "economics deals with introspection and with values… it deals with motives, expectations, psychological uncertainties. One has to be constantly on guard against treating the material as constant and homogenous." Others were equally critical to the dominating focus of rationalism when human action was involved. Nobel Prize winner Herbert Simon (1957) for instance, coined the terms *cognitive limitations* and *bounded rationality,* arguing that some of the basic assumptions of the rationalist analytic approach are questionable. According to Simon reality is too complex to be boxed into two-by-two matrices; truth cannot be determined by simplistic theories of cause and effect; information is not always correct, complete or presented at the right time. Last but not least, managers are not different from normal acting humans, they also make mistakes, even act non-rationally and are driven by emotions. Charles Lindblom (1959) pointed out that in reality strategy does not manifest itself as a linear process neatly divided in discrete sequential parts but instead, more accurately as 'the fine art of muddling through.' Paul Lawrence and Jay W. Lorsch (1967) coined the term *contingency* arguing that strategy should adapt to the business environment and that there is 'not just one best way'. Richard T. Pascale, co-author of *The Art of Japanese Management* (1981), challenged the Western view of strategizing, considering the rational analytic approach to be "myopic and an oversimplification of reality."

Japanese management practices such as *Kaizen* became a popular research field in the West as from the 1980s, when Japanese companies became immensely successful. For example, Ala and Cordeiro (1999) described the Japanese decision-making process of "ring-iseido", which refers to the opportunity for equal ranking managers or employees of a group within a company to get involved in an individual's idea. This process is embedded in the Japanese cultural desire of "harmony" among people and, more generally, in Asian philosophy. In Asia, thinking is highly influenced by the writings of the best known Chinese philosopher Confucius (the Latin name of K'ong-foe-tzi, which means Master K'ong) who lived around 500 BC. Confucianism, with its emphasis on harmony, group interest and virtue, is important in many Asian countries such as Japan, Korea, Vietnam and, of course, China. In the long and rich history of China many philosophers have been focusing on the problem of how to structure the world, and particularly how to rule the nation. Chinese language uses the same character represents the words structure, order and rule. This started a long time ago when China was divided into competing regions, and philosophers were asked how China could become a unity (which was realized around 200 BC), given all the differences.

Taoism (or Daoism) is a second important philosophy, which emphasizes adapting to nature and living in harmony with Tao. Tao means 'path', 'way' and 'principle', and is both the source and driving force behind everything that exists. Taoism is based on the book *Tao Te Ching* from Master Lao Tse (also: Laozi or Lao Tsu), which together with the writings of Zuangzhi forms the canon of Taoism: the *Daozang*. Equally important in Asia is the influence of Buddhism and Hinduism, which originate from ancient India. Although there are many differences among these traditions, both ways of viewing the world stress that events are more likely to emerge rather than follow a set plan. Both are also object universal laws of truth and reality.

Position of science

Science and scientific method do not play the same role, and are not accorded the same value, in all societies. In some countries, science and scientists are held in high esteem, and scientific enquiry is believed to be the most fruitful way of obtaining new knowledge. Typical for these nations is that the scientific method has come to pervade almost all aspects of life. Objective knowledge and skill in analytical reasoning are widely believed to be the critical success factors in most professions – to become a nurse, a journalist, a sports instructor, an actor or a musician requires a university education. Managers, too, are assumed to be scientifically trained, often specializing in management studies. Much of this education strongly promotes formal, explicit, analytical thinking, and pays little attention to creativity, imagination and intuition. In these nations a more pronounced preference for the rational reasoning perspective might be expected.

In other countries, science holds a less predominant position (Redding, 1980). Scientific methods might shed some light on issues, but other ways of obtaining new insights – such as experience, intuition, philosophizing, fantasizing and drawing analogies – are also valued (Keegan, 1983; Kagono *et al.*, 1985). The bounds of socially acceptable reasoning are less constrictive than in more rationalist nations. Leaps of imagination and logical inconsistencies are tolerated as normal aspects in the messy process of sense-making (Pascale, 1984). In general, thinking is viewed as an art and therefore science has not made deep inroads into most of the professions. Managers, in particular, do not require a specific scientific training, but need to be broadly developed generalists with flexible minds (Nonaka and Johanson, 1985). In these countries, a stronger preference for the holistic reasoning perspective can be expected.

Level of uncertainty avoidance

National cultures also differ with regard to their tolerance for ambiguity. As Hofstede points out in Reading 1.3 in this book, some societies feel uncomfortable with uncertain situations and strive for security. Countries that score high on Hofstede's 'uncertainty avoidance dimension' typically try to suppress deviant ideas and behaviours, and institute rules that everyone must follow. People in these countries exhibit a strong intellectual need to believe in absolute truths and they place great trust in experts (Schneider, 1989). They have a low tolerance for the ambiguity brought on by creative insights, novel interpretations and 'wild ideas' that are not analytically sound. Therefore, it can be expected that strategists in high uncertainty avoidance cultures will be more inclined towards the rational reasoning perspective than in nations with a low score.

Level of individualism

As stated at the beginning of this chapter, strategists with a generative inclination are slightly rebellious. They show little reverence for the status quo, by continuously questioning existing cognitive maps and stimulating creative reinterpretations. Dissenting voices often stand alone and are heavily criticized by the orthodox. This solitary position is difficult to maintain under the best of circumstances, but is especially taxing in highly collectivist cultures. If strategists wish to be accepted within their group, organization and community, they cannot afford to stick out too much. There will be a strong pressure on the strategist to conform. In more individualist cultures, however, there is usually a higher tolerance for individual variety. People find it easier to have their own ideas, independent of their group, organization and community (see Hofstede's individualism dimension, in Reading 1.3). This gives strategists more intellectual and emotional freedom to be the 'odd man out'. Therefore, it can be expected that strategists in more individualist cultures will be more inclined towards the generative reasoning perspective than those in collectivist cultures.

Position of strategists

Countries also differ sharply with regard to the hierarchical position of the managers engaged in strategy. In many countries strategic problems are largely defined and solved by the upper echelons of management. To reach this hierarchical position requires many years of hands-on experience and climbing through the ranks. Therefore, by the time managers are in the position of being a strategist they are middle-aged and thoroughly familiar with their business – with the danger of being set in their ways. They will also have been promoted several times by senior managers who believe that they will function well within the organization. In general, the effect is that the competent and conformist managers are promoted to strategy positions, while innovative dissidents are selected out along the way. In such countries, intuitive strategic reasoning often does not take place within large organizations, but within small start-ups to which the creatively inclined flee.

In cultures that score lower on Hofstede's power distance dimension, managers throughout the organization are often involved in strategy discussions. The responsibility for strategy is spread more widely among the ranks. Younger, less experienced managers are expected to participate in strategy formation processes, together with their senior colleagues. In general, this leads to a more open, messy and lively debate about the organization's strategy and provokes more intuitive strategic thinking. Therefore, it can be expected that in less hierarchical cultures the holistic reasoning perspective will be more popular than in cultures with stronger hierarchical relations.

INTRODUCTION TO THE READINGS

Those who judge by their feelings do not understand reasoning, for they wish to get an insight into a matter at a glance, and are not accustomed to look for principles. Contrarily, others, who are accustomed to argue from principles, do not understand the things of the heart, seeking for principles and not being able to see at a glance.
Blaise Pascal (1623–1662); French scientist and philosopher

So, how should managers engage in strategic reasoning processes and how should they encourage fruitful strategic reasoning within their organizations? Should strategizing managers primarily take an analytic or holistic reasoning perspective? Should strategists train themselves to follow procedural rationality – rigorously analysing problems using scientific methods and calculating the optimal course of action? Or should strategists unleash the unconscious and make judgements based on intuition?

In the strategic management literature the debate has not yet offered a clear-cut answer to the question of which strategic reasoning approach is the optimal one. At the centre of the strategic reasoning issue is the paradox of logic and intuition. Many points of view have been put forward on how to reconcile these opposing demands, but as circumstances differ individual strategists have to find their own way of dealing with the topic of strategizing.

To help strategists to come to grips with the variety of perspectives on this issue, three readings have been selected that each shed their own light on the issue. As outlined in Chapter 1, the first two readings will be representative of the two poles in this debate (see Table 2.1). The third reading addresses a more integrative style of strategizing.

Selecting the first reading to represent the analytical reasoning perspective was not very difficult. In a 2007 *Strategic Management Journal* article, 'Explicating Dynamic Capabilities: The nature and microfoundations of (sustainable) enterprise performance', David Teece explains the microeconomics of the dynamic capabilities perspective, which currently enjoys the attention of most strategy scholars. While in Chapter 4 on business level strategy the contents of this perspective will be discussed, this chapter addresses the microfoundations of dynamic capabilities thinking.

The microfoundations of the dynamic capabilities view are in line with many – but not all – important scholars in the strategy field, as Teece points out. True to the rational reasoning perspective, Teece argues that 'sensing, seizing and reconfiguring' should be conducted consciously, explicitly and rationally. In his view, strategic reasoning is a 'logical activity'.

The second reading in this chapter, highlighting the views of the holistic reasoning perspective, is the 2011 *Strategic Management Journal* article, 'Psychological foundations of dynamic capabilities: Reflexion and reflection in strategic management' by Gerard P. Hodgkinson and Mark P. Healey. The authors build on Teece's 'sensing, seizing and reconfiguring' distinction, but challenge his microfoundations on the basis of academic knowledge in neuroscience and psychology. Hodgkinson and Healey argue that the mind of the strategist is not dominated by linear, logical thinking. On the contrary, a strategist's thought processes are basically intuitive and reflexive rather than rational and reflective. In their view, strategies originate in insights that are beyond the reach of conscious analysis. They do not dismiss logic as unnecessary, but note that it is insufficient for arriving at innovative strategies and for getting organizational members' buy-in.

In contrast to the more theoretical readings 2.1 and 2.2, the author of the third reading, Roger Martin, offers a hands-on approach to using opposing ideas to reach more effective solutions. This recent *Harvard Business Review* article is drawn from his book *The Opposable Mind,* in which he argues that the ability to use opposing ideas is the mental equivalent of having an opposable thumb. Without a thumb opposite to our fingers, we would not be able to create the tension in our hands needed to hold things and perform advanced physical activities. Without the capacity to create a mental tension by holding two opposing ideas in mind, we would not be able to cross-fertilize these ideas to find innovative ways forward. Martin calls this 'integrative thinking' – synthesizing elements from opposing views to find a third way. It is about avoiding 'either/or' thinking in favour of 'both/and' thinking. In this reading Martin explains in more depth the steps that need to be taken to effectively engage in integrative thinking, which will be of particular use in discussing the first two readings, and more in general also throughout the rest of this book.

Explicating dynamic capabilities: The nature and microfoundations of (sustainable) enterprise performance

By David J. Teece[1]

Dynamic capabilities can be disaggregated into the capacity (1) to sense and shape opportunities and threats, (2) to seize opportunities, and (3) to maintain competitiveness through enhancing, combining, protecting, and, when necessary, reconfiguring the business enterprise's intangible and tangible assets. Dynamic capabilities include difficult-to-replicate enterprise capabilities required to adapt to changing customer and technological opportunities. They also embrace the enterprise's capacity to shape the ecosystem it occupies, develop new products and processes, and design and implement viable business models.

Sensing (and shaping) opportunities and threats

Nature of the capability

In fast-paced, globally competitive environments, consumer needs, technological opportunities and competitor activity are constantly in a state of flux. Opportunities open up for both newcomers and incumbents, putting the profit streams of incumbent enterprises at risk. As discussed in Teece, Pisano and Shuen (1997, Reading 4.3), some emerging marketplace trajectories are easily recognized. In microelectronics this might include miniaturization, greater chip density, and compression and digitization in information and communication technology. However, most emerging trajectories are hard to discern. Sensing (and shaping) new opportunities is very much a scanning, creation, learning and interpretive activity. Investment in research and related activities is usually a necessary complement to this activity.

Opportunities get detected by the enterprise because of two classes of factors. First, as stressed by Kirzner (1973), entrepreneurs can have differential access to existing information. Second, new information and new knowledge (exogenous or endogenous) can create opportunities, as emphasized by Schumpeter (1934).

Kirzner stressed how the entrepreneurial function recognizes any disequilibrium and takes advantage of it. The Kirznerian view is that entrepreneurship is the mechanism by which the economy moves back toward equilibrium. Schumpeter, on the other hand, stressed upsetting the equilibrium. As Baumol (2006: 4) notes, 'the job of Schumpeter's entrepreneur is to destroy all equilibria, while Kirzner's works to restore them. This is the mechanism underlying continuous industrial evolution and revolution.' Equilibrium is rarely if ever achieved (Shane, 2003). Both forces are relevant in today's economy.

Microfoundations

The literature on entrepreneurship emphasizes that opportunity discovery and creation can originate from the cognitive and creative ('right brain') capacities of individual(s). However, discovery can also be grounded in organizational processes, such as research and development activity. The ability to create and/or sense opportunities is clearly not uniformly distributed amongst individuals or enterprises. Opportunity creation and/or discovery by individuals require both access to information and the ability to recognize, sense and shape developments. The ability to recognize opportunities depends in part on the individual's capabilities and extant knowledge (or the knowledge and learning capacities of the organization to which the individual belongs), particularly about user needs in relationship to existing as well as novel solutions. This requires specific knowledge, creative activity, the ability to understand user/customer decision making, and practical wisdom (Nonaka and Toyama, 2007). It involves interpreting available information in whatever form it appears – a chart, a picture, a conversation at a trade show, news of scientific and technological breakthroughs, or the angst expressed by a frustrated customer. One must accumulate and then filter information from professional and social contacts to create a conjecture or a hypothesis

[1]Source: Adapted with permission from David Teece (2007) 'Explicating dynamic capabilities: the nature and microfoundations of (sustainable) enterprise performance' *Strategic Management Journal* Vol. 28 (13) pp. 1319–1350. Copyright © John Wiley & Sons, Inc. 2007. Reproduced with permission of John Wiley & Sons, Inc.

about the likely evolution of technologies, customer needs and marketplace responses. This task involves scanning and monitoring internal and external technological developments and assessing customer needs, expressed and latent. It involves learning, interpretation and creative activity.

While certain individuals in the enterprise may have the necessary cognitive and creative skills, the more desirable approach is to embed scanning, interpretative and creative processes inside the enterprise itself. The enterprise will be vulnerable if the sensing, creative and learning functions are left to the cognitive traits of a few individuals. Organizational processes can be put in place inside the enterprise to garner new technical information, tap developments in exogenous science, monitor customer needs and competitor activity, and shape new products and processes opportunities. Information must be filtered, and must flow to those capable of making sense of it. Internal argument and discussion about changing market and technological reality can be both inductive and deductive. Hypothesis development, hypothesis 'testing' and synthesis about the meaning of information obtained via search are critical functions, and must be performed by the top management team. The rigorous assembly of data, facts and anecdotes can help test beliefs. Once a synthesis of the evidence is achieved, recurrent synthesis and updating can be embedded in business processes designed by middle management and/or the planning unit in the business organization (Casson, 1997). If enterprises fail to engage in such activities, they won't be able to assess market and technological developments and spot opportunities. As a consequence, they will likely miss opportunities visible to others.

As noted in Teece, Pisano and Shuen (1997), more decentralized organizations with greater local autonomy are less likely to be blindsided by market and technological developments. Because of the problem of information decay as information moves up (and down) a hierarchy, businesses must devise mechanisms and procedures to keep management informed. Bill Hewlett and David Packard developed 'management by walking about' (Packard, 1995) as a mechanism to prevent top management at Hewlett-Packard from becoming isolated from what was going on at lower levels in the enterprise, and outside the enterprise as well. In other organizations (e.g., professional services) the management ranks can be filled by leading professionals who remain involved with professional work. This protects them from the hazards of managerial isolation.

The search activities that are relevant to 'sensing' include information about what's going on in the business ecosystem. With respect to technologies, R&D activity can itself be thought of as a form of 'search' for new products and processes. However, R&D is too often usually a manifestation of 'local' search. 'Local' search is only one component of relevant search. In fast-paced environments, with a large percentage of new product introductions coming from external sources, search/exploration activity should not just be local. Enterprises must search the core as well as to the periphery of their business ecosystem. Search must embrace potential collaborators – customers, suppliers, complementors – that are active in innovative activity.

Customers are sometimes amongst the first to perceive the potential for applying new technology. Visionary members of customer organizations are often able to anticipate the potential for new technology and possibly even begin rudimentary development activities. Moreover, if the suppliers of new technology do not succeed in properly understanding user/customer needs, it is unlikely that new products they might develop will be successful. Indeed, one of the most consistent findings from empirical research is the probability that an innovation will be successful commercially is highly correlated with the developers' understanding of user/customer needs (Freeman, 1974). Electronic computing and the Internet itself can rightly be viewed as having a significant component of user-led innovations. Business enterprises that are alert and sense the opportunity are often able to leverage customer-led efforts into new products and services, as the users themselves are frequently ill-prepared to carry initial prototypes further forward.

Suppliers can also be drivers of innovation important in the final product. Innovation in microprocessor and DRAMs is a classic case. This upstream or 'component' innovation has impacted competition and competitive outcomes in personal computers, cellular telephony and consumer electronics more generally. Failure to 'design in' new technology/components in a timely fashion will lead to failure; conversely, success can sometimes be achieved by continuous rapid 'design in.' Indeed, continuous and rapid design around new technology/components developed elsewhere can itself be a source of durable competitive advantage. Put differently, with rapid innovation by component suppliers, downstream competitive success can flow from the ability of enterprises to continuously tap into such (external) innovation ahead of the competition. External search and acquisition of technology have been going on for decades, but as Chesbrough (2003) explains, 'Open Innovation' is now a mandate for enterprise success.

The concept and practice of open innovation underscore the importance of broad-based external search and subsequent integration involving customers, suppliers and complementors. Establishing linkages between corporations and universities assists broad-based search, as university programmes are usually unshackled from the near at hand. Indeed, a recent study of patenting in the optical disc industry (Rosenkopf and Nerkar, 2001) seems to suggest that exploration that is more confined generates lower impacts, and that the impact of exploration is highest when exploration spans organizational (but not technological) boundaries. However, it is not just a matter of searching for external inventions/innovations that represent new possibilities. Frequently it is a matter of combining complementary innovations so as to create a solution to a customer problem. The systemic nature (Teece, 2000) of many innovations compounds the need for external search.

Sensing opportunities and threats can also be facilitated if the enterprise and/or the entrepreneur explicitly or implicitly employ some kind of analytical framework, as this can help highlight what is important. Within the dynamic capabilities framework, the 'environmental' context recognized for analytical purposes is not that of the industry, but that of the business 'ecosystem' – the community of organizations, institutions and individuals that impact the enterprise and the enterprise's customers and supplies. The relevant community therefore includes complementors, suppliers, regulatory authorities, standard-setting bodies, the judiciary, and educational and research institutions. It is a framework that recognizes that innovation and its supporting infrastructure have major impacts on competition.

Even when utilizing the ecosystem as the organizing paradigm for assessing developments in the business environment, the full import of particular facts, statistics and developments is rarely obvious. Accordingly, the evaluative and inferential skill possessed by an organization and its management is important. Indeed, much of the information gathered and communicated inside the enterprise has minimal decision relevance. Even if relevant, it often arrives too late. Management must find methods and procedures to peer through the fog of uncertainty and gain insight. This involves gathering and filtering technological, market and competitive information from both inside and outside the enterprise, making sense of it and figuring out implications for action. However, because attention is a scarce resource inside the enterprise (Cyert and March, 1963), management must carefully allocate resources to search and discovery. The enterprise's articulated strategy can become a filter so that attention is not diverted to every opportunity and threat that 'successful' search reveals. Likewise, scenario planning can collapse likely situations into a small number of scenarios that can facilitate cognition, and then action, once uncertainty is resolved.

Seizing opportunities

Nature of the capability

Once a new (technological or market) opportunity is sensed, it must be addressed through new products, processes, or services. This almost always requires investments in development and commercialization activity. Multiple (competing) investment paths are possible, at least early on. The quintessential example is the automobile industry, where in the early days different engine technologies – steam, electric and gasoline – each had their champions. Once a dominant design begins to emerge, strategic choices become much more limited.

Addressing opportunities involves maintaining and improving technological competences and complementary assets and then, when the opportunity is ripe, investing heavily in the particular technologies and designs most likely to achieve marketplace acceptance. When network externalities are present, early entry and commitment are necessary. The presence of increasing returns means that if one network gets ahead, it tends to stay ahead. Getting ahead may require significant upfront investments. Customers will not want an enterprise's products if there are strong network effects and the installed base of users is relatively small. Accordingly, one needs to strategize around investment decisions, getting the timing right, building on increasing return advantages, and leveraging products and services from one application to another. The capacity to make high-quality, unbiased but interrelated investment decisions in the context of network externalities, innovation and change is as rare as decision-making errors and biases are ubiquitous.

However, the issue that the enterprise faces is not just when, where and how much to invest. The enterprise must also select or create a particular business model that defines its commercialization strategy and investment priorities. Indeed, there is considerable evidence that business success depends as much on organizational innovation, e.g., design of business models, as it does on the selection of physical technology. This is true at the enterprise level as well as at the economy-wide level (Nelson, 2005). Indeed, the invention and implementation of business models and associated enterprise boundary choices involve issues as fundamental to business success as the development and adoption of the physical technologies themselves. Business models implicate processes and incentives; their alignment with the physical technology is a much overlooked component of strategic management. The understanding of the institutional/organizational design issues is typically more limited than the understanding of the technologies themselves. This ignorance affords considerable scope for mistakes around the proper design of business models and the institutional structures needed to support innovation in both the private and public sectors.

In theory, one could imagine transactions between entities that scout out and/or develop opportunities, and those that endeavour to execute upon them. In reality, the two functions cannot be cleanly separated, and the activities must be integrated inside a single enterprise, where new insights about markets – particularly those that challenge the conventional wisdom – will likely encounter negative responses. The promoters/visionaries must somehow defeat the naysayers, transform internal views, and facilitate necessary investment. Some level of managerial consensus will be necessary to allow investment decisions to be made. Investment will likely involve committing financial resources behind an informed conjecture about the technological and marketplace future. However, managers of established product lines in large organizations can sometimes have sufficient decision-making authority to starve the new business of financial capital. This posture can be buttressed by capital budgeting techniques that more comfortably support investments for which future cash flow can be confidently projected. In short, the new can lose out to the established unless management is sensitive to the presence of certain biases in accepted investment decision processes. An important class of dynamic capabilities emerges around a manager's ability to override certain 'dysfunctional' features of established decision rules and resource allocation processes.

It helps to begin by recognizing that decision-making processes in hierarchically organized enterprises involve bureaucratic features that are useful for many purposes, but they nevertheless may muzzle innovation proclivities. In particular, a formal expenditure process involving submissions and approvals is characteristic of 'well-managed' companies. Decision making is likely to have a committee structure, with top management requiring reports and written justifications for significant decisions. Moreover, approvals may need to be sought from outside the organizational unit in which the expenditure is to take place. While this may ensure a matching up of expenditures to opportunities across a wider range of economic activity, it unquestionably slows decision making and tends to reinforce the status quo. Committee decision-making structures almost always tend toward balancing and compromise. But innovation is often ill-served by such structures, as the new and the radical will almost always appear threatening to some constituents. Strong leaders can frequently overcome such tendencies, but such leaders are not always present. One consequence is a 'programme persistence bias.' Its corollary is various forms of 'anti-innovation bias,' including the 'anti-cannibalization' basis. Programme persistence refers to the funding of programmes beyond what can be sustained on the merits, and follows from the presence or influence of programme advocates in the resource allocation process. This proclivity almost automatically has the countervailing effect of reducing funds available to new initiatives.

One should not be surprised, therefore, if an enterprise senses a business opportunity but fails to invest. In particular, incumbent enterprises tend to eschew radical competency-destroying innovation in favour of more incremental competency enhancing improvements. The existence of layer upon layer of standard procedures, established capabilities, complementary assets and/or administrative routines can exacerbate decision-making biases against innovation. Incumbent enterprises, relying on (path-dependent) routines, assets and strategies developed to cope with existing technologies, are handicapped in making and/or adopting radical, competency-destroying, non-cumulative innovation (Nelson and Winter, 1982; Tushman and Anderson, 1986; Henderson and Clark, 1990). This is true whether the competence is external to the firm or internal to the firm.

Evidence also shows that decision makers discount outcomes that are merely probable in comparison with outcomes that are certain. This has been called the certainty effect (Kahneman and Lovallo, 1993). It contributes to excessive risk aversion when choices involve possible losses. Further, to simplify choices between alternatives, individuals generally evaluate options in isolation. Viewing each alternative as unique leads decision makers to undervalue possibilities for risk pooling. This approach to decision making may produce inconsistent preferences and decision biases (timid choices) that lead to outcomes that block innovation (Kahneman and Tversky, 1979; Kahneman and Lovallo, 1993). An opposing bias to loss/risk aversion is excessive optimism. This leads to investment in low or negative return projects. As a result, entry decisions often fail.

The existence of established assets and routines exacerbates problems of excessive risk aversion. Specifically, both the isolation effect and the certainty effect can be intensified by the existence of established assets, causing incumbent enterprises to become comparably more risk averse than new entrants. In terms of innovative activity, this excessive risk aversion leads to biased decision making and limits the probability that incumbent enterprises will explore risky radical innovations. In short, success in one period leads to the establishment of 'valid' processes, procedures and incentives to manage the existing business. This can have the unintended effect of handicapping the new business. The proficiency with which such biases are overcome and a new opportunity is embraced is likely to depend importantly on the quality of the enterprise's routines, decision rules, strategies, and leadership around evaluating new investment opportunities. Business historians (e.g., Chandler, 1990a; Lazonick, 2005) and others have reminded us that over the long run the ability of enterprises to commit financing and invest astutely around new technologies is critical to enterprise performance.

Managers need to make unbiased judgments under uncertainty around not just future demand and competitive responses associated with multiple growth trajectories, but also around the pay-offs from making interrelated investments in intangible assets. In the world of tangible assets, this can sometimes be precisely modelled; not so for the world of co-specialized intangibles. In essence, the organizational challenge appears to be that in environments experiencing rapid change, activities are not fully decomposable. Cross-functional activities and associated investments must take place concurrently, rather than sequentially, if enterprises are to cut time-to-market for new products and processes. Managerial judgments (decision-making skills) take on great significance in such contexts. This was also true during prior centuries, as Alfred Chandler's (1990a, 1990b) analysis of successful enterprises from the 1870s through the 1960s makes apparent. No matter how much analytical work is done, tacit investment skills are of great importance. Chandler further argues that success in the late-nineteenth and much of the twentieth century came to those enterprises that pursued his 'three-pronged' strategy: (1) early and large-scale investments behind new technologies; (2) investment in product-specific marketing, distribution and purchasing networks; and

(3) recruiting and organizing the managers needed to supervise and coordinate functional activities. The first and second elements require commitment to investments where irreversibilities and co-specialization are identified. While the nature of required investments may have changed in recent decades (less decomposable/more interrelated), investment decision skills remain important.

Microfoundations

Selecting product architectures and business models. The design and performance specification of products, and the business model employed, all help define the manner by which the enterprise delivers value to customers, entices customers to pay for value, and converts those payments to profit. They reflect management's hypothesis about what customers want and how an enterprise can best meet those needs, and get paid for doing so. They embrace: (1) which technologies and features are to be embedded in the product and service; (2) how the revenue and cost structure of a business is to be 'designed' and if necessary 'redesigned' to meet customer needs; (3) the way in which technologies are to be assembled; (4) the identity of market segments to be targeted; and (5) the mechanisms and manner by which value is to be captured. The function of a business model is to 'articulate' the value proposition, select the appropriate technologies and features, identify targeted market segments, define the structure of the value chain, and estimate the cost structure and profit potential (Chesbrough and Rosenbloom, 2002: 533–534). In short, a business model is a plan for the organizational and financial 'architecture' of a business. This model makes assumptions about the behaviour of revenues and costs, and likely customer and competitor behaviour. It outlines the contours of the solution required to earn a profit, if a profit is available to be earned. Once adopted it defines the way the enterprise 'goes to market.' Success requires that business models be astutely crafted. Otherwise, technological innovation will not result in commercial success for the innovating enterprise. Generally there is a plethora of business models that can be designed and employed, but some will be better adapted to the ecosystem than others. Selecting, adjusting and/or improving the business model is a complex art.

Designing good business models is in part 'art.' However, the chances of success are greater if enterprises (1) analyse multiple alternatives, (2) have a deep understanding of user needs, (3) analyse the value chain thoroughly so as to understand just how to deliver what the customer wants in a cost-effective and timely fashion, and (4) adopt a neutrality or relative efficiency perspective to outsourcing decisions. Useful tools include market research and transaction cost economics. Chesbrough and Rosenbloom (2002) suggest that established enterprises often have blinders with respect to alternative business models and that this prevails even if the technology is spun off into a separate organization, where other (path-dependent constraints) are less likely to exist. In short, designing the business correctly, and figuring out what John Seeley Brown refers to as the 'architecture of the revenues' (and costs), involve processes critical to the formation and success of new and existing businesses. No amount of good governance and leadership is likely to lead to success if the wrong business model is in place. Good business models achieve advantageous cost structures and generate value propositions acceptable to customers. They will enable innovators to capture a large enough portion of the (social) value generated by innovation to permit the enterprise at least to earn its cost of capital.

Avoiding bias, delusion, deception and hubris.
As noted, proclivities toward decision errors are not uncommon in managerial decision making, particularly in large organizations. Investment decision errors already identified include excessive optimism, loss aversion, isolation errors, strategic deception and programme persistence. As Nelson and Winter (2002: 29) note, organizational decision processes often display features that seem to defy basic principles of rationality and sometimes border on the bizarre. These errors can be especially damaging in fast-paced environments with path dependencies and network effects, as there is less opportunity to recover from mistakes. When investments are small and made frequently, there are many opportunities to learn from mistakes. Since large investments are usually occasional, major investment decisions are likely to be (potentially) more vulnerable to error.

Fortunately, biases can be recognized ahead of time. Enterprises can bring discipline to bear to purge bias, delusion, deception and hubris. However, the development of disciplines to do so is still in its infancy. The implementation of procedures to overcome decision-making biases in enterprise settings is, accordingly, not yet a well-distributed skill, and may not be for decades to come. Accordingly, competitive advantage can be gained by early adopters of techniques to overcome decision biases and errors.

Overcoming biases almost always requires a cognitively sophisticated and disciplined approach to decision making. Being alert to the incentives of the decision makers and to possible information asymmetries is a case in point. Obtaining an 'outside view' through the review of external data can help eliminate bias. Testing for errors in logic is also essential. Management also needs to create an environment where the individuals involved in making the decision, at both the management and board level, feel free to offer their honest opinions, and look at objective (historical) data in order to escape from closed thinking. Incentives must also be designed to create neutrality when assessing investments in the old and the new.

Considerable progress in combating biases has been made. Advisors call upon managers to adopt radical, non-formulaic strategies in order to overcome the inertias that inhibit breakthrough innovation (Davidow and Malone, 1992; Handy, 1990). Specifically, corrective strategies encourage change through two basic mechanisms: (1) designing organizational structures, incentives and routines, to catalyse and reward creative action; and (2) developing routines to enable the continual shedding of established assets and routines that no longer yield value. Strategies that provide structures, incentives and processes to catalyse and reward creative action serve to attenuate problems of excessive risk aversion. For example, strategies that call on the enterprise to 'cut overheads' and 'increase divisional authority' can be interpreted as efforts to reduce the number of management layers of the enterprise and to push decision making down to lower levels to minimize the inherent isolation errors associated with multilevel, hierarchical decision-making processes. These recommendations can be viewed as organizational processes and strategic mechanisms to mitigate decision-making biases.

Perhaps most importantly, executives must acknowledge the interaction effect between owning established assets and decision-making biases. Many recommended strategies (such as cannibalizing profitable product lines and licensing your most advanced technology) call for the shedding of established capabilities, complementary assets and/or administrative routines to reduce the intensity of decision-making biases. By jettisoning 'dead' or dying assets, the enterprise is no longer shackled with an asset base that can be a crutch and provide a false sense of security, and sustain groups inside the enterprise that persist in torpedoing new initiatives. In abandoning dead or dying assets, the enterprise frees itself of certain routines, constraints and opportunities for undesirable protective action inside the enterprise.

Sources of the 'anti-cannibalization' bias can also be attacked. Self-serving behaviour inside the enterprise to 'protect' incumbent constituencies undergirds this bias. Flawed investment frameworks may also contribute. Entry into a market by an enterprise with a new and superior technology will cause rapid depreciation of the economic value of an incumbent's plant and equipment. However, the incumbent may well make business decisions based on examining accounting profits that reflect depreciation rates specified by accepted accounting standards. If decision makers confuse depreciation calculated according to generally accepted accounting principles (GAAP) with real economic depreciation, and conclude that the existing business is still profitable when, in fact, it is not, then the business enterprise may eschew profit-enhancing cannibalization of its own products. To guard against this bias, investment decision makers and incumbents must use accounting data cautiously. In particular, they must also consider the opportunity cost associated with not cannibalizing their own products. Capital-budgeting procedures implicitly biased against projects with long-term horizons must be jettisoned or used cautiously. That is not to say that incumbents need to invest on the same schedule as new entrants. As Teece (1986) and Mitchell (1991) demonstrate, incumbents need not be the first movers. Superior positioning in complementary assets may enable incumbents to let the new entrants do the prospecting; investing later once market and technological risk has diminished.

There is an obvious role for leadership in making quality decisions, communicating goals, values and expectations, while also motivating employees and other constituencies. Organizational identification (and commitment, which is the corollary) can dramatically augment enterprise performance, although it is doubtful it can override completely misaligned incentives. Nevertheless, group loyalty is a 'powerful altruistic force' that conditions employee goals and the cognitive models they form of their situation (Simon, 1993: 160). Top management through its action and its communication has a critical role to play in garnering loyalty and commitment and achieving adherence to innovation and efficiency as important goals.

Since there is already an extensive literature on culture, commitment and leadership, these issues are not discussed further. However, it would be a significant oversight in a summary statement of the dynamic capabilities framework to ignore them completely. Their full integration into the framework is left

to others. However, it is recognized that to the extent such properties are not ubiquitously distributed amongst business enterprises, they can be a very important source of superior performance.

Managing threats and reconfiguration

Nature

The successful identification and calibration of technological and market opportunities, the judicious selection of technologies and product attributes, the design of business models, and the commitment of (financial) resources to investment opportunities can lead to enterprise growth and profitability. Profitable growth will lead to the augmentation of enterprise-level resources and assets. Success will cause the enterprise to evolve in a path-dependent way. A key to sustained profitable growth is the ability to recombine and to reconfigure assets and organizational structures as the enterprise grows, and as markets and technologies change, as they surely will. Reconfiguration is needed to maintain evolutionary fitness and, if necessary, to try and escape from unfavourable path dependencies. In short, success will breed some level of routine, as this is necessary for operational efficiency. Routines help sustain continuity until there is a shift in the environment. Changing routines is costly, so change will not be (and should not be) embraced instantaneously. Departure from routines will lead to heightened anxiety within the organization, unless the culture is shaped to accept high levels of internal change. If innovation is incremental, routines and structures can probably be adapted gradually or in (semi-continuous) steps. When it is radical, possibly because it is science-based, then there will be a mandate to completely revamp the organization and create an entirely new 'break out' structure (Teece, 2000) within which an entirely different set of structures and procedures is established.

As discussed earlier, the 'anti-cannibalization' bias is a particular manifestation of incentive and structural problems that can thwart innovation in established enterprises. Incumbent enterprises possessing fixed assets may further tend to limit their new investments to innovations that are 'close-in' to the existing asset base. They tend to narrowly focus search activities to exploit established technological and organizational assets. This effect makes it difficult for these enterprises to see potential radical innovations. In addition, incumbent enterprises tend to frame new problems in a manner consistent with the enterprise's current knowledge base, assets, and/or established problem-solving heuristics and established business model. This second effect means that managers may not successfully address opportunities or potential innovations even when they do recognize them. Managers face and must overcome at least two constraints – cognitive limitations and framing biases – arising from established assets (Teece, 2000).

As the enterprise grows, it has more assets to manage and to protect against malfeasance and mismanagement. Shirking, free riding, the strategic manipulation of information, and internal complacency are all issues that established enterprises will confront continuously. As discussed earlier, over time successful enterprises will develop hierarchies and rules and procedures (routines) that begin to constrain certain interactions and behaviours unnecessarily. Except in very stable environments, such rules and procedures are likely to require constant revamping if superior performance is to be sustained. It is not uncommon to find that a once functional routine becomes dysfunctional, providing inertia and other rigidities that stand in the way of improved performance (Leonard-Barton, 1995; Rumelt, 1995). As a result, less well-resourced enterprises (sometimes established enterprises that have divested certain assets, sometimes new entrants) end up winning in the marketplace.

Traditional management approaches endorse strong hierarchies with at least three levels of management: top, middle and lower. Control is exerted at the top and cascades down through multiple levels. Employees tend to end up beholden to the management and CEO, and not the customer. The existence of independent profit centres can lead to internal boundaries that stand in the way of providing integrated solutions that benefit customers. With centralized structures, strategic decisions made at the top tend to become isolated from marketplace realities. Customer care is relegated to employees who are lower down in the organization. In short, the systems and rules needed to manage many layers of organization tend to create structural rigidities and perversities that in turn handicap customer and technological responsiveness. To sustain dynamic capabilities, decentralization must be favoured because it brings top management closer to new technologies, the customer and the market.

Top management leadership skills are required to sustain dynamic capabilities. An important managerial function is achieving semi-continuous asset orchestration and corporate renewal, including the redesign of routines. This is because the sustained achievement of superior profitability requires semi-continuous and/or continuous efforts to build, maintain and adjust the complementarity of product offerings, systems, routines and structures. Inside the enterprise, the old and the new must complement. If they do not, business units must be disposed of or placed in some type of separate structure. Otherwise, work will not proceed efficiently and conflicts of one kind or another will arise. Put differently, periodic if not sustained asset orchestration – involving achieving asset alignment, co-alignment, realignment, and redeployment – is necessary to minimize internal conflict and to maximize complementarities and productive exchange inside the enterprise.

Redeployment and reconfiguration (Capron, Dussauge and Mitchell, 1998) may also involve business model redesign as well as asset-realignment activities, and the revamping of routines. Redeployment can involve transfer of non-tradeable assets to another organizational or geographic location (Teece, 1977, 1980). It may or may not involve mergers, acquisitions and divestments. Helfat and Peteraf (2003: 1006) suggest that capability redeployment takes one of two forms: the sharing of capability between the old and the new, and the geographic transfer of capability from one market to another. Both are possible, but neither is easy.

Microfoundations

Achieving decentralization and near decomposability.
Every system comprises subsystems (elements) that are to some extent interdependent and independent. However, as discussed earlier, enterprises are unlikely to be continuously responsive to customers and new technologies absent a high degree of decentralization. With decentralized decision making, different managers observe different information and control different decisions, but there is not the need for communication to a single central decision maker, and hence no comprehensive 'rollup' of information is required. Decentralization must be pursued as enterprises expand, otherwise flexibility and responsiveness will erode.

One well-documented restructuring that is widely adopted as enterprises grow is the adoption of the multidivisional form. This involves decomposition and the devolution of decision rights to quasi-independent profit centres. The abandonment of functional structures in favour of the multidivisional form has been analysed by Chandler (1962), Williamson (1975) and many others. The basic rationale of this reconfiguration was to achieve greater accountability of managerial decisions so that the recognition of opportunities and threats could proceed more thoroughly and expeditiously. With functional internal structures, day-to-day problems tend to distract management from long-run strategic issues. Studies showed that decentralization along product or market lines with independent profit centres led to performance improvements in many industries, at least during the period in which these organizational innovations were diffusing (Armour and Teece, 1978; Teece, 1980, 1981). More recent scholarship has suggested that even further decentralization and decomposition in large organizations may be beneficial (Bartlett and Ghoshal, 1993). There is also some evidence that 'modern' human resource management techniques – involving delayering, decentralization of decision rights, teamwork, flexible task responsibilities and performance-based rewards also improve performance (Jantunen, 2005).

Of course, achieving decentralization can compromise the organization's ability to achieve integration. There is little harm and much benefit from decentralization when the customer does not benefit from an integrated product offering, or when sourcing and other inputs do not benefit from integration and/or aggregation. If customer and supply considerations allow decomposability (because the required integration between units is less than within units), then management's ability to identify and implement decomposable sub-units should enhance performance. However, if firm-specific economies of scale and scope are available, they must be captured – otherwise the enterprise is tantamount to a conglomerate. This tension can be managed through a collaborative non-hierarchical management style assisted by establishing councils and other integration forums. Middle management can also play a critical role when such forums are established. They can also design and implement tight financial controls and performance-based reward systems. Since intangibles are key drivers of performance, their enhancement and protection must become a managerial priority.

Managing co-specialization. The field of strategic management and the dynamic capabilities framework recognizes that 'strategic fit' needs to be continuously achieved. However, unless the concept is operationalized it has limited utility. The key dimension of 'fit' emphasized in the dynamic capabilities framework is that of 'co-specialization.' The concept of co-specialization operationalizes at least one

dimension of the otherwise rather vague concept of organizational adaptation and 'fit.' Co-specialization can be of one asset to another, or of strategy to structure, or of strategy to process. It is important to both seizing and reconfiguration. In environments of rapid change, there is a need for continuous or at least semi-continuous realignment.

However, complementary innovation and complementary assets are of great significance, particularly in industries in which innovation might be characterized as cumulative, and/or where industry 'platforms' exist or are needed. Examples of complementary innovation are ubiquitous. In the enterprise software industry, business applications can be especially valuable to users if they can somehow be integrated into a single programme, or into a tightly integrated suite. The development of gyroscopic stabilizers made imaging devices such as video cameras and binoculars easier to use by minimizing the impact of camera shake, and enhanced the product, especially when the new feature was able to be introduced at low cost. Likewise, better high-energy rechargeable batteries enable laptop computers and cellphones to operate for longer times. Situations of complementarities where there is also co-specialization between technologies, and between technologies and other parts of the value chain are common, yet until recently poorly analysed in economic analysis and in strategy formulation.

Co-specialized assets are a particular class of complementary assets where the value of an asset is a function of its use in conjunction with other particular assets. With co-specialization, joint use is value enhancing. Co-specialization results in 'thin' markets; i.e., the assets in question are idiosyncratic and cannot be readily bought and sold in a market. Capturing co-specialization benefits may require integrated operations (Teece, 1980). Co-specialization allows differentiated product offerings or unique cost savings. The inherent 'thin' market environment surrounding specific assets means that competitors are not able to rapidly assemble the same assets by acquisition, and hence cannot offer the same products/services at competing price points.

Management's ability to identify, develop and utilize in combination specialized and co-specialized assets built or bought is an important dynamic capability, but it is not always present in enterprise settings. Special value can be created (and potentially appropriated by another party) through asset combinations, particularly when an asset owner is not cognizant of the value of its assets to another party that owns assets whose value will be enhanced through combination. This arises because the markets for co-specialized assets are necessarily thin or non-existent.

Both innovation and reconfiguration may necessitate co-specialized assets being combined by management in order for (systemic) innovation to proceed. Managers do not always succeed in doing so, sometimes because they do not sense the need or the opportunity, and sometimes because they do but they are unable to effect the integration. If the assets cannot be procured externally, they will need to be built internally.

The ability of management to identify needs and opportunities to 'invest' in co-specialized assets (through its own development or astute purchase) is fundamental to dynamic capabilities. Mere 'horse-trading' skills (which market agents possess) will not suffice to build sustainable competitive advantage, and decisions on when and how to invest – whether and when to build or buy co-specialized assets – will depend upon many factors, including transaction costs. In particular, it will depend on management's entrepreneurial capacities with respect to matching up and integrating relevant co-specialized assets.

It is apparent that co-specialization involves 'lock-in' and is a particular form of complementarity that exists when technologies and other assets need to be part of a tightly integrated system to achieve the performance that customers want. Business success in such circumstances requires the coordination of R&D investment and alliance activity. The manner and timing with which such coordination needs to be accomplished is important to success (Teece, 1986; Mitchell, 1991). Common ownership of the parts facilitates system-wide innovation and economic performance (Teece, 2000) and protects against opportunism (Williamson, 1975).

To summarize, entrepreneurs and managers can create special value by combining co-specialized assets inside the enterprise (Teece, 2007). This may require investments to create the necessary co-specialized technologies – as illustrated by Thomas Edison and the creation of electric power as a system. It is not uncommon in technology-based industries to find that certain technologies are worth more to some market participants than to others, based on the technology they already have, and their technology and product strategy.

Learning, knowledge management and corporate governance. With intangible assets being critical to enterprise success, the governance and incentive structures designed to enable learning and the generation of new knowledge become salient. There are many types of learning – including experiential, vicarious, individual and organizational – and a large literature that explores each type. Also 'sensing' requires learning about the environment and about new technological capabilities. R&D was seen as one way that the enterprise could promote such learning. However, in the context of the dynamic capability discussed in this section, the ability to integrate and combine assets including knowledge is a core skill (Kogut and Zander, 1992; Grant, 1996). The combination of know-how within the enterprise, and between the enterprise and organizations external to it (e.g., other enterprises, universities), is important.

Integrating know-how from outside as well as within the enterprise is especially important to success when 'systems' and 'networks' are present. Good incentive design and the creation of learning, knowledge-sharing and knowledge-integrating procedures are likely to be critical to business performance, and a key (micro-) foundation of dynamic capabilities (Nonaka and Takeuchi, 1995; Chesbrough, 2003). Of equal importance are monitoring and managing the 'leakage,' misappropriation, and misuse of know-how, trade secrets and other intellectual property. Of course, tacit know-how is difficult to imitate and has a certain amount of 'natural' protection. However, much know-how does leak out. Innovating business enterprises with limited experience have been known to inadvertently compromise or lose their intellectual property rights. Failure to proactively monitor and protect know-how and intellectual property is common.

The outsourcing of production and the proliferation of joint development activities likewise create requirements that enterprises develop governance procedures to monitor the transfer of technology and intellectual property. Technology transfer activities, which hitherto took place inside the enterprise, increasingly take place across enterprise boundaries. The development of governance mechanisms to assist the flow of technology, while protecting intellectual property rights from misappropriation and misuse, are foundational to dynamic capabilities in many sectors today.

There are also several other 'governance' issues relevant to dynamic capabilities. At one level there are governance and business model issues associated with an enterprise's ability to achieve asset 'combinations' and reconfiguration. As noted earlier, there is a continuous need to modify product offerings, business models, enterprise boundaries and organizational structures. Decentralized structures that facilitate near decomposability are likely to assist in achieving reconfiguration.

One class of governance issues relates to incentive alignment. The microfoundations of incentive issues are embedded in an understanding of agency and incentive design issues, also discussed earlier. Agency theory has long emphasized that the separation of ownership from control creates interest alignment problems, particularly around management compensation and the allocation of corporate perquisites. The abuse of discretion and the use of corporate assets for private purposes can incur absent appropriate accountability/oversight. These issues become more severe as an enterprise grows and the separation between ownership and management widens. Recent corporate governance scandals in the United States, Europe and Japan indicate the need for continued vigilance. However, increasing the mix of independent and 'inside' directors will not necessarily ameliorate problems associated with strategic 'malfeasance.'

There are likely to be benefits associated with participation at the board level by individuals who can calibrate whether the top management team is sufficiently 'dynamic.' The replacement of the CEO and other members of the top management team, if they demonstrate weak sensing, seizing and reconfiguration capabilities (strategic 'malfeasance'), is important to effect. That is not to say that guarding against financial malfeasance is unimportant. It will always remain as an important corporate governance function; but its significance is likely to pale next to strategic 'malfeasance,' which is harder to detect and evaluate.

A related literature in economics has stressed how poorly designed incentives can produce tensions between the actions of employees and the actions needed to achieve profitable performance. Dysfunctional behaviour, such as activity that generates influence costs, has received considerable attention (Teece, 2003). Also, through use of collective bargaining, employees in industries insulated from global competition have been able to appropriate economic surplus. Above-market wages – which characterized, and to some extent still characterize, certain enterprises in the auto, steel and airline industries in the United States – are a case in point. These conditions can extend to managerial ranks as well. Restructuring may then require the judicious use of bankruptcy laws to rewrite uncompetitive supply contracts that are the product of unrealistic collective bargaining actions in

an earlier period. The ability of some enterprises to craft work specifications, attract and retain more committed talent, design reward systems, develop corporate cultures and blunt the formation of coalitions that extract quasi-rents through threatening to withhold participation, is an important managerial capacity.

The design and creation of mechanisms inside the enterprise to prevent the dissipation of rents by interest groups (both management and employees) would also appear to be very relevant to dynamic capabilities, but has not been high on the agenda of strategy researchers. One exception is Gottschalg and Zollo (2007), who point out that the capacity to continuously achieve incentive alignment is an important performance-enhancing (and rent protecting) dynamic capability.

Many of the issues discussed here have, in the past, fallen under the rubric of human resource management; a closer connection of these issues to strategic management issues would appear to be warranted. The reason is that strategic management is focused not only on how to generate rent streams, but also on how to prevent them from being dissipated or captured by various entities or groups inside and outside the enterprise. For instance, the concepts of the 'appropriability regime' and 'isolating mechanisms' were developed by strategic management scholars to help explain how rents from innovation and other sources of superior performance can be protected and guarded from dissipation by competitors and others. However, the earlier focus on markets or 'external' competition did not address internal appropriation by interest groups.

Dynamic capabilities, 'orchestration' skills and competitive advantage

The general framework advanced here sees dynamic capabilities as the foundation of enterprise-level competitive advantage in regimes of rapid (technological) change. The framework indicates that the extent to which an enterprise develops and employs superior (non-imitable) dynamic capabilities will determine the nature and amount of intangible assets it will create and/or assemble and the level of economic profits it can earn (see Figure 2.1.1). Furthermore, the framework emphasizes that the past will impact current and future performance. However, there is much that management can do to

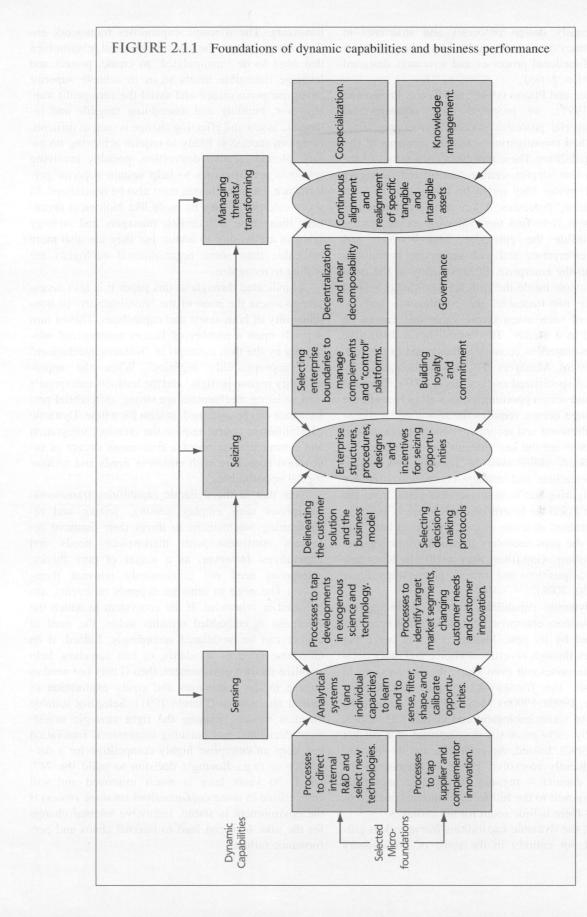

FIGURE 2.1.1 Foundations of dynamic capabilities and business performance

simultaneously design processes and structures to support innovation while unshackling the enterprise from dysfunctional processes and structures designed for an earlier period.

In Teece and Pisano (1994), and Teece, Pisano and Shuen (1997), we proposed three organizational and managerial processes – coordination/integrating, learning, and reconfiguring – as core elements of dynamic capabilities. These processes are a subset of the processes that support sensing, seizing and managing threats. Together they might be thought of as asset 'orchestration' processes. A key strategic function of management is to find new value-enhancing combinations inside the enterprise, and between and amongst enterprises, and with supporting institutions external to the enterprise. Because many of the most valuable assets inside the firm are knowledge related and hence non-tradeable, the coordination and integration of such assets create value that cannot be replicated in a market. This establishes a distinctive role for managers in economic theory and in the economic system. Managers seek new combinations by aligning co-specialized assets (Teece, 2007). The need to sense and seize opportunities, as well as reconfigure when change occurs, requires the allocation, reallocation, combination and recombination of resources and assets. These are the key strategic function of executives. Indeed, skills used to identify and exploit complementarities and manage co-specialization are scarce. Figuring out how to increase value from the use of the assets the enterprise owns involves knowing the fine-grained structure of the firm's asset base, and filling in the gaps necessary to provide superior customer solutions. Gap filling may involve building new assets, or acquisitions and strategic partnerships (Ettlie and Pavlou, 2006).

The dynamic capabilities framework recognizes that the business enterprise is shaped but not necessarily trapped by its past. Management can make big differences through investment choice and other decisions. Enterprises can even shape their ecosystem. In this sense, the framework is quite Chandlerian (Chandler, 1990a, 1990b). Managers really do have the potential to set technological and market trajectories, particularly early on in the development of a market (David, 1992). Indeed, the enterprise and its environment frequently co-evolve. However, because of the assumed context – regimes of rapid technological change exposed to the full force of international competition – there is little room for big mistakes.

Hence, the dynamic capabilities framework is partially but not entirely in the spirit of evolutionary theorizing. The dynamic capabilities framework endeavours to capture the key variables and relationships that need to be 'manipulated' to create, protect and leverage intangible assets so as to achieve superior enterprise performance and avoid the zero-profit trap. However, building and assembling tangible and intangible assets and effecting change is seen as difficult. Long-run success is likely to require achieving necessary internal creative destruction, possibly involving spin-outs and spin-offs to help sustain superior performance. Decision biases must also be neutralized. In short, enterprises may be more like biological organisms than some economists, managers and strategy scholars are willing to admit; but they are also more malleable than some organizational ecologists are willing to recognize.

As indicated throughout this paper it is also necessary to assess the issue of the 'sustainability' or non-imitability of both assets and capabilities. This in turn depends upon a number of factors summarized adequately by the twin concepts of 'isolating mechanism' and 'appropriability regimes.' When the appropriability regime is 'tight' and the business enterprise's own isolating mechanisms are strong, differential performance can be sustained, at least for a time. Dynamic capabilities of course require the creation, integration and commercialization of a continuous stream of innovation consistent with customer needs and technological opportunities.

Note that in the dynamic capabilities framework, enterprises must employ sensing, seizing and reconfiguring mechanisms to direct their financial resources consistent with marketplace needs and imperatives. However, as a matter of pure theory, enterprises need not continuously reinvent themselves. The need to reinvent depends on events, anticipated or otherwise. If the ecosystem in which the enterprise is embedded remains stable, the need to change can be modulated accordingly. Indeed, if an enterprise controls standards, or can somehow help stabilize its own environment, then it may not need to engage in the continuous and costly exploration of radical alternatives (March, 1991). Selecting suitable business models, making the right strategic investment decisions, and pursuing incremental innovation can keep an enterprise highly competitive for a decade or so (e.g., Boeing's decision to build the 747, which 30 years later is much improved and still competitive in some configurations on some routes) if the environment is stable. Excessive internal change for the sake of it can lead to internal chaos and performance failure.

Conclusion

For open economies exposed to rapid technological change, the dynamic capabilities framework highlights organizational and (strategic) managerial competences that can enable an enterprise to achieve competitive advantage, and then semi-continuously morph so as to maintain it. The framework integrates and synthesizes concepts and research findings from the field of strategic management, from business history, industrial economics, law and economics, the organizational sciences, innovation studies, and elsewhere.

Implicit in the dynamic capabilities framework is a recognition that relatively open regimes of free trade and investment, global dispersion in the sources of new knowledge, and the multi-invention or systemic character of such innovation have 'upped the ante' for modern management. Improving quality, controlling costs, lowering inventories and adopting best practices ('technical fitness') will no longer suffice for long-run competitive success. Nor do traditional scale economies in production always have the differentiating power they may once have had. More than scale and scope advantage are needed. Success requires the creation of new products and processes and the implementation of new organizational forms and business models, driven by an intensely entrepreneurial genre of management constantly honing the evolutionary and entrepreneurial fitness of the enterprise. Entrepreneurial managers can sense and even help shape the future, unshackle the enterprise from the past, and stay ahead by augmenting knowledge assets, protecting them with intellectual property rights, establishing new value enhancing asset combinations, and transforming organizational and, if necessary, regulatory and institutional structures. Dynamic capabilities reside in large measure with the enterprise's top management team, but are impacted by the organizational processes, systems and structures that the enterprise has created to manage its business in the past.

Maintaining dynamic capabilities thus requires entrepreneurial management. The entrepreneurial management in question is different, but related to other managerial activity. Entrepreneurship is about sensing and understanding opportunities, getting things started, and finding new and better ways of putting things together. It is about creatively coordinating the assembly of disparate and usually co-specialized elements, getting 'approvals' for non-routine activities, and sensing business opportunities. Entrepreneurial management has little to do with analysing and optimizing. It is more about sensing and seizing – figuring out the next big opportunity and how to address it.

We have come to associate the entrepreneur with the individual who starts a new business providing a new or improved product or service. Such action is clearly entrepreneurial, but the entrepreneurial management function embedded in dynamic capabilities is not confined to startup activities and to individual actors. It is a new hybrid: entrepreneurial managerial capitalism. It involves recognizing problems and trends, directing (and redirecting) resources, and reshaping organizational structures and systems so that they create and address technological opportunities while staying in alignment with customer needs. The implicit thesis advanced here is that in both large and small enterprises entrepreneurial managerial capitalism must reign supreme for enterprises to sustain financial success. Nor is entrepreneurial management merely 'intrapreneurship,' as there is a large role for the entrepreneurial manager in external activities, including shaping the ecosystem.

As discussed, there are obvious tensions and interrelationships between and amongst the three classes of capabilities identified. The managerial skills needed to sense are quite different from those needed to seize and those needed to reconfigure. All functions have a significant 'entrepreneurial' and 'right brain' component. Successful enterprises must build and utilize all three classes of capabilities and employ them, often simultaneously. Since all three classes are unlikely to be found in individual managers, they must be somewhere represented in top management, and the principal executive officer must succeed in getting top management to operate as a team. Of course, if the principal executive officer has depth in all three classes of capabilities, the organization has a better chance of success.

The dynamic capabilities framework goes beyond traditional approaches to understanding competitive advantage in that it not only emphasizes the traits and processes needed to achieve good positioning in a favourable ecosystem, but it also endeavours to explicate new strategic considerations and the decision-making disciplines needed to ensure that opportunities, once sensed, can be seized; and how the business can be reconfigured when the market and/or the technology inevitably is transformed once again. In this sense, dynamic capabilities aspire to be a relatively parsimonious framework for explaining an extremely seminal and complicated issue: how a business enterprise and its management can first spot the opportunity to earn economic profits, make the decisions and institute the disciplines to execute on that opportunity, and then stay agile so as to continuously refresh the foundations of its early success, thereby generating economic surpluses over time. If the framework has

succeeded in some small measure, then we have the beginnings of a general theory of strategic management in an open economy with innovation, outsourcing, and offshoring.

READING 2.2

Psychological foundations of dynamic capabilities: Reflexion and reflection in strategic management

By Gerard P. Hodgkinson and Mark P. Healey[1]

The decision-making paradigm, as it has developed, is the product of a marriage between cognitive psychology and economics. From economics, decision theory inherited, or was socialized into, the language of preferences and beliefs and the religion of utility maximization that provides a unitary perspective for understanding all behaviour. From cognitive psychology, decision theory inherited its descriptive focus, concern with process and many specific theoretical insights. Decision theory is thus the brilliant child of equally brilliant parents. With all its cleverness, however, decision theory is somewhat crippled emotionally, and thus detached from the emotional and visceral richness of life (Loewenstein, 1996: 289).

Introduction

Since its earliest days, the field of strategic management has been preoccupied with developing rational and analytical models and theories (e.g., Ansoff, 1965; Hofer and Schendel, 1978) to understand the nature and causes of sustainable enterprise performance (Teece, Pisano and Shuen, 1997). From Porter's (1980) analysis of competitive positioning informed by the structure-conduct-performance paradigm, to game theoretic analyses of competitive interaction (Brandenburger and Nalebuff, 1996), to the more recent evolutionary (e.g., Nelson and Winter, 1982) and resource-based (e.g., Barney, 1991; Wernerfelt, 1984) perspectives informed by Penrose's writings linking internal resources to rent generation, there is no

question that the dominant perspectives in classic and contemporary strategic management emanate from the field of economics. Over the past two decades, however, a growing body of work has sought to incorporate the insights of human psychology to refine understanding of a wide variety of topics, from the evolution of competitive industry structures (Peteraf and Shanley, 1997; Porac *et al.*, 1995) to the nature and sources of cognitive bias in strategic investment decisions (Bateman and Zeithaml, 1989; Schwenk, 1984).

Reflecting the field's shift away from an analysis of the organization's external environment to a focus on its internal resources and capabilities, strategy scholars have paid increasing attention to the cognitive and behavioural processes underpinning the capabilities that promote organizational learning, adaptation and performance. This body of theory and research has accomplished much. However, this article argues that recent advances in the emerging fields of social cognitive neuroscience (Lieberman, 2007; Ochsner and Lieberman, 2001) and neuroeconomics (Brocas and Carrillo, 2008; Loewenstein, Rick and Cohen, 2008), and indeed the wider organizational sciences (Gavetti, Levinthal and Ocasio, 2007; Hodgkinson and Healey, 2008), call into question its adequacy as a foundation for future theory building and research in the strategy field. We demonstrate that the extant literature on the psychology of strategic management, like its economics-based counterpart, has emphasized the behavioural and cognitive aspects of strategy formulation and implementation at the expense of emotional and affective ones, leading to an inadequate portrayal of strategic management as a series of rational and dispassionate activities. Our analysis provides fresh insights into the origins and development of dynamic capabilities.

[1]Source: Excerpted with permission from Gerard P. Hodgkinson and Mark P. Healey (2011) 'Psychological foundations of dynamic capabilities: Reflexion and reflection in strategic management' *Strategic Management Journal*, 32(13): 1500–1516. Copyright © John Wiley & Sons, Inc. 2011. Reproduced with permission of John Wiley & Sons, Inc.

Teece's (2007) framework is the most comprehensive to date for analysing the psychological foundations of capabilities development. Accordingly, we utilize this framework as a basis for organizing our critique of the wider dynamic capabilities literature as a whole.

Psychological foundations of dynamic capabilities revisited

Teece (2007) posited three generic, behaviourally-based dynamic capabilities as the foundations of the evolutionary and economic fitness of the enterprise, namely: (1) sensing (and shaping) opportunities and threats; (2) seizing opportunities; and (3) reconfiguring assets and structures to maintain competitiveness. Sensing requires searching and exploring markets and technologies both local to and distant from the organization. Seizing, in contrast, necessitates making high-quality, interdependent investment decisions, such as those involved in selecting product architectures and business models. The final capability, reconfiguring, entails continuously transforming the firm in response to market and technological changes, such that it retains evolutionary fitness.

Consistent with most traditional dynamic capability formulations, the microfoundations of Teece's (2007) framework rest on an outmoded conception of the strategist as a cognitive miser. This conception stemmed from several interrelated bodies of theory and research in the cognitive sciences, not least Simon's seminal notion of bounded rationality and classical behavioural decision research, which ultimately reinforced the idea that human cognition operates in two discrete modes of information processing – one relatively automatic, the other more effortful and controlled (e.g., Schneider and Shiffrin, 1977). This core assumption has long underpinned a number of lines of inquiry in strategic management, beyond the dynamic capabilities project *per se,* each of which has privileged effortful forms of reasoning and dispassionate analysis as the means of overcoming cognitive bias and strategic inertia (e.g., Dutton, 1993; Hodgkinson *et al.,* 1999; Louis and Sutton, 1991; Reger and Palmer, 1996). However, contemporary social neuroscience is questioning the veracity of these earlier conceptions of dual-process theory and bounded rationality. Recent developments suggest that the biases and inertial forces that undermine sensing, seizing and transforming capabilities have emotional roots as well as cognitive ones. Building on this fundamental insight, we maintain that although the tools and processes commonly touted for engineering cognitively effortful reasoning and judgment are undoubtedly a *necessary* component of dynamic capabilities, in practice they are rarely a *sufficient* psychological mechanism for ensuring the long-term adaptability of the enterprise. Indeed, as we shall demonstrate, in some circumstances, conventional approaches for augmenting strategic cognition exacerbate the very problems they seek to alleviate.

According to a growing body of work in social cognitive neuroscience, a reflexive system underpins more automatic and basic affective forms of social cognition, such as implicit stereotyping, automatic categorization and empathizing with others, while a reflective system, a more controlled system that developed latterly in evolutionary terms, underpins higher forms of cognition, such as logical reasoning, planning and hypothetical thinking (Lieberman, 2007; Lieberman *et al.,* 2002). Within this view, the two systems operate in a dynamic interplay, reflexion variously facilitating and inhibiting the reflective processes underpinning consciously effortful reasoning and decision making (see also Bechara, Damasio and Damasio, 2000).

While acknowledging the distinction between automatic and controlled processes, neuroeconomics emphasizes the distinction between emotional and analytical processes. Bernheim and Rangel (2004), for example, view the brain as operating in either a 'cold' cognitive mode or a 'hot' emotional mode, while Loewenstein and Small (2007) similarly distinguish between 'emotional' and 'deliberative' systems. One of the key contributions of neuroeconomics has been to shed light on the conditions under which visceral feelings overcome deliberative thinking in judgment and decision making (for an overview, see Loewenstein *et al.,* 2008).

In sum, the left-brain/right-brain cognitive science underpinning Teece's (2007) analysis, which characterizes intuition and heuristic processes as primitive sources of bias, is giving way to the mounting evidence that less deliberative forms of cognition are central to skilled functioning. Rather than acting simply as a disturbance to the reflective system, to be suppressed at every opportunity, affect and emotion are integral to the very nature of cognition, infusing reasoning, learning, decision making and action (LeDoux, 2000). However, as depicted in Figure 2.2.1, the bulk of theory and research on the psychology of strategic management has hitherto focused on but one portion of the available conceptual space (i.e., the lower right-hand quadrant of the circumplex). This myopia has yielded an impoverished portrayal of dynamic capabilities.

FIGURE 2.2.1   The core dimensions of strategic cognition

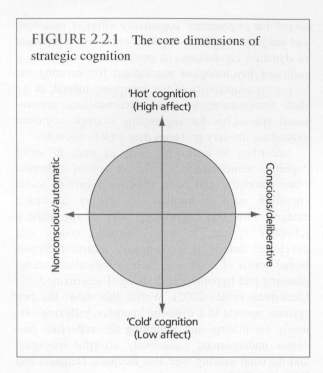

Accordingly, the overarching goal of this article is to open up the wider conceptual space pertaining to the cognitive, affective and behavioural microfoundations of organizational adaptation (cf. Gavetti *et al.*, 2007). To this end, we explicate alternative psychological foundations for the three dynamic capabilities identified by Teece (2007) and consider the implications for theory building, research and practice.

Sensing (and shaping) opportunities and threats

The predominance of the information processing view of the firm has ensured that current conceptions of sensing capabilities are decidedly affect free (Day and Schoemaker, 2006; Gavetti and Levinthal, 2000; Prahalad, 2004; Teece, 2007; Tripsas and Gavetti, 2000). However, to the extent that affect controls attention (Compton, 2003), the moods and emotions of managers likely determine to a significant degree what the firm attends to and how it responds, to say nothing of the emotional significance of the stimuli for the individuals concerned. For instance, high anxiety might narrow attention to a subset of events, whereas an overoptimistic mood might lead to a neglect of certain signals. We postulate that affect is also crucial for effective sensing because it provides the motivation for cognitive adaptation.

Affective mechanisms of cognitive change

The ability to update decision makers' mental representations (variously labelled 'schemas,' 'mental models' and 'cognitive maps') in response to changes in the external environment is a critical sensing capability (Barr, Stimpert and Huff, 1992; Gavetti, 2005; Gavetti and Levinthal, 2000; Levinthal and March, 1993). Current conceptions of adaptive cognitive change assume that the mere effortful processing of schema inconsistent information disconfirms expectations and jolts decision makers into conscious reflection, thereby forcing them to revise their beliefs (e.g., Dutton, 1993; Hodgkinson *et al.*, 1999; Louis and Sutton, 1991; Reger and Palmer, 1996). However, recent research in neuroeconomics shows that people actively try to shield themselves from information that causes psychological discomfort, the so-called 'ostrich effect' of burying one's head in the sand (Karlsson, Loewenstein and Seppi, 2009). In keeping with this observation, studies in social cognitive neuroscience show that conflicting information is not the fundamental mechanism of belief revision, but rather how decision makers handle the affective response to that conflicting information (Lieberman, 2000; Lieberman *et al.*, 2001). Hence, the ability to recognize affective signals and utilize affect as information (Finucane *et al.*, 2000; Slovic *et al.*, 2004) is an essential, but hitherto neglected, component of organizational sensing capabilities. By way of illustration, consider the London Stock Exchange's decision to invest in the Taurus software package to support a transactions settlement IT system (Drummond, 2001). Decision makers experienced deep unease in the early stages of the commissioning process, but unable to articulate the logical basis of their ill feelings, they chose to invest on more reasoned grounds. However, having eventually abandoned the ineffective system, at a cost of £80 million, they then expressed considerable regret at having ignored their initial misgivings. This case demonstrates that when individuals' reasoned reflective responses and visceral reflexive reactions are discordant, effective sensing requires resolution of the disequilibria.

Tensions between reflexive and reflective reactions to opportunities and threats can also occur *between* individuals and groups, as Tripsas and Gavetti's (2000) account of cognitive adaptation at Polaroid illustrates. In this case, senior executives held to a maladaptive belief in an 'instant imaging' business model that discouraged search and development efforts in the growth area of digital imaging, while managers closer to industry changes developed representations that encompassed the emerging digital landscape. Tripsas and Gavetti's (2000) view that the dissonance between the two groups resulted from differences in the industry signals they were receiving construes managers as passive victims of their informational circumstances. The logical extension of this view is that providing the two parties with the same information would have yielded consonant representations. Our analysis suggests an alternative interpretation: because the new information conflicted with executives' assumptions, they likely experienced unease at the mismatch, motivating them to neglect – if not actively reject – the painful information. In contrast, junior managers likely experienced consonance between reflexion and reflection. Put differently, the developments excited one group but troubled the other, leading, respectively, to approach and avoidance. Dissonance between individuals and groups should signal the need to re-evaluate and reconcile competing interpretations of strategic events (cf. Burgelman and Grove, 1996). At Polaroid, such reconciliation was noticeably absent, perhaps due to executives' unwillingness to lose self-esteem by relinquishing their embedded assumptions.

Our re-analysis of the Polaroid case highlights the importance of meta-cognitive capabilities – that is, the ability to develop self-awareness of, and to regulate, cognitive and emotional processes (e.g., Nelson, 1996; Ochsner *et al.*, 2002). Managers need to test the validity of their reflexive reactions to a given strategic issue; if those reactions are warranted, the firm should take whatever course of action is deemed appropriate. In cases where further analysis reveals those reflexive responses are due to managers' underlying beliefs being out of line with the overall attractiveness of the opportunity or threat in question, this likely signals the need to update the executive knowledge base. While recalibrating decision makers is often difficult, because individuals are typically unable to step outside their own framings of the problem at hand (Fischhoff, 1982), group approaches provide a potentially useful means of crosschecking affectively rooted assumptions.

Effective sensing also requires the development of a psychologically secure learning climate – one that takes account of affective signals and intuitive cognitions but also enables, where appropriate, effortful, deliberative processing. Routines that overly focus on planning for the negative consequences of events are likely to heighten negative affect and threat rigidity, and ultimately induce avoidance behaviour (Staw, Sandelands and Dutton, 1981). The converse approach of building routines that mitigate negative affect and create the psychological space for building positive affect around opportunities and threats is conducive to adaptation, because positive affect boosts responsiveness to events by broadening the scope of attention, cognition and action repertoires (Ashby, Isen and Turken, 1999; Fredrickson and Branigan, 2005). The preceding arguments suggest the following proposition:

Proposition 1: Organizations that rely on 'hot cognition' enhancing technologies (i.e., tools and processes aimed at mental model change underpinned by emotionally supportive mechanisms) as an aid to sensing will be significantly less likely to fall prey to cognitive blind spots and strategic inertia than organizations that rely on 'cold cognition' enhancing technologies (i.e., tools and processes aimed at mental model change in the absence of emotionally supportive mechanisms).

To illustrate the practical implications of this proposition, consider the role of scenario planning as an aid to sensing, commonly employed to stretch actors' beliefs regarding future uncertainties (e.g., Schoemaker, 1993). Hodgkinson and Wright's (2002) case analysis illustrates the dangers of designing interventions based solely on a cold cognition logic. The goal in this case was to inculcate mental model change. However, forcing the management team to envisage threatening future scenarios in a vivid manner raised decisional stress and conflict to unacceptably high levels, leading it to adopt dysfunctional coping strategies. In contrast, Doz and Kosonen (2008) observe how organizations such as IBM and Nokia meet the need for psychological security by building a 'culture of care' when seeking to reform the beliefs of actors facing threatening changes. Practical steps include adopting routines that encourage managers to share their emotions and empathize with one another, and the use of techniques that construe strategic change in such a way that those affected do not disconnect the new requirements from enduring sources of pride.

Incorporating intuition into the sensing process

As we have indicated, strategy research has conventionally equated what Teece (2007) outlined as sensing (and shaping) capabilities with explicit, deliberative learning and elaborative formal reasoning and analysis (e.g., Porter, 1980; Zollo and Winter, 2002; for an exception, see Levinthal and Rerup, 2006).

However, this view understates the advantages of non-conscious forms of cognition for navigating the social environment (Bargh and Chartrand, 1999; Bargh and Ferguson, 2000). A particular advantage of reflexive processes is their ability to cut through masses of information about trends in the business environment to reach effective judgments on opportunities and threats. As Sir Martin Sorrell, CEO of WPP recently observed, 'the reality is that leaders must, on the spur of the moment, be able to react rapidly and grasp opportunities' (Sorrell, Komisar and Mulcahy, 2010: 46).

Dane and Pratt's (2007: 40) succinct definition, 'affectively-charged judgments that arise through rapid, non-conscious and holistic associations,' renders abundantly clear why intuition is apposite to the sensing process. While the reflective (i.e., deliberative) system, restricted to the serial processing of small numbers of items, becomes overloaded when faced with complex strategic situations, intuition brings to bear large quantities of implicit knowledge in a focused manner (cf. Dutton, 1993). Moreover, in many strategic situations, executives must operate under time constraints, from the early detection and evaluation of emerging opportunities and threats, to the defence of hostile takeovers, to interventions by regulators. There is a wealth of evidence to suggest that the non-conscious pattern-matching and visceral processes at the heart of intuitive judgment (Lieberman, 2000) likely play a critical role in these circumstances (for overviews see Dane and Pratt, 2007; Hodgkinson, Langan-Fox and Sadler-Smith, 2008; Hodgkinson *et al.*, 2009; Hogarth, 2001; Klein, 2003).

Incorporating intuition into the sensing process demands a reconsideration of the role of information technologies of the sort widely advocated as an aid to organizational responsiveness (cf. Teece, 2007). Knowledge management systems, databases and expert systems designed to externalize knowledge ultimately transfer the tasks of search and sensemaking from the decision maker to the technology. This move precludes the rapid pattern-matching processes that characterize expert decision making, thus undermining true sensing. Mintzberg (1994: 299) illustrated the problems with such architectures in his analysis of elaborate strategic planning systems that 'offered no improved means to deal with the information overload of human brains; indeed, they often made matters worse.... The formal systems could certainly process more information... But they could never internalize it, comprehend it, synthesize it.' Giving due credence to reflexion in sensing requires that supporting analytical technologies be deployed in ways that exploit managers' implicit knowledge and intuitive expertise. The goal is to design search architectures to take advantage of reflexion rather than replace it with technology or effortful reasoning (Jolls, Sunstein and Thaler, 1998). Hence:

Proposition 2: Organizations that incorporate intuition into their repertoire of sensing capabilities will identify and respond to opportunities and threats more effectively than organizations that rely solely on analytic approaches.

One means of incorporating intuition into the repertoire of sensing capabilities is to configure decision making units so as to possess the requisite mixture of individuals with analytical and intuitive cognitive styles (Hodgkinson and Clarke, 2007). Other prescriptions range from recognizing and rewarding those who effectively rely on expert intuition rather than fall back on established procedures (Klein, 2003), to building in 'mental time-outs' to allow creative ideas to incubate (Sadler-Smith, 2010). However, recognizing when to rely on intuition is a vital skill in itself. Kahneman and Klein (2009, 2010) suggest that intuition is appropriate for informing executive action when: (1) there is sufficient environmental regularity to learn the cues that enable the recognition of patterns and irregularities and (2) decision makers have learned those cues. The latter criterion emphasizes the domain-specific nature of intuitive expertise. For example, although a manager with 10 years experience in a particular sector might well provide valid intuitive judgments on developments within that sector, it is unlikely that the validity of those judgments would generalize to other sectors.

Seizing opportunities

It is clear from Teece's (2007) analysis that two major psychological barriers potentially undermine seizing capabilities. First, organizations must be able to evaluate sensed opportunities and threats in a progressive, forward-looking manner and, where appropriate, commit to them in a timely fashion. Second, in order to do so, they must be able to unlock dysfunctional fixations with existing strategies to mitigate or remove decisional bias, inertia and strategic persistence. As indicated in Table 2.2.1, we maintain that developing routines commensurate with the affective mechanisms underpinning decision making provides the ultimate bases for meeting both of these challenges.

TABLE 2.2.1 Psychological foundations of dynamic capabilities revisited

Capability	Extant psychological foundations	Indicative supporting literature(s)[†]	Revised psychological foundations	Indicative supporting literature(s)
Sensing and shaping	Opportunity discovery and creation originate from the cognitive and creative ('right brain') capacities of individuals, requiring access to information and the ability to recognize, sense, and shape developments	Entrepreneurship literature: organizational search (e.g., March and Simon, 1958; Nelson and Winter, 1982)	Identifying and creating opportunities through searching, synthesizing, and filtering information stems from the interaction between reflexive (e.g., intuition, implicit association) and reflective (e.g., explicit reasoning) cognitive and emotional capabilities	Social cognitive neuroscience research on the interaction between reflexive and reflective systems (Lieberman, 2007)
	Recognizing, scanning, and shaping depend on individuals' cognitive capabilities and extant knowledge	Knowledge-based view of the firm (e.g., Grant, 1996); organizational learning (e.g., Levinthal and March, 1993)	Recognizing, scanning, and shaping depend on the capability to harness emotion to update mental representations (e.g., dissonance recognition) and skilled utilization of intuitive processes to synthesize information and form expert judgments	Cognition and capabilities literature (Gavetti, 2005); affective processes in learning (Lieberman, 2000)
Seizing	Seizing innovative investment choices requires managers to override 'dysfunctions of decision making'	Classical behavioural decision theory (e.g., Kahneman and Tversky, 1979)	Seizing opportunities requires the fostering of appropriate emotional reactions to new directions	Neuroeconomics: immediate emotions shape choice (Loewenstein et al., 2008)
	Overcoming biases requires a cognitively sophisticated and disciplined approach to decision making	Classical behavioural decision theory (e.g., Kahneman and Tversky, 1979)	Cognitively effortful processes can exacerbate bias – alleviating bias and inertia requires both cognitive and emotional capabilities	Self-regulation (e.g., Ochsner et al., 2002) and affective routes to de-escalation of commitment (e.g., Sivanathan et al., 2008)
Reconfiguring	Top management ability to coordinate and execute strategic renewal and corporate change	Organizational structure and design and strategy and performance literatures (e.g., Bartlett and Ghoshal, 1993; Chandler, 1962)	Reconfiguration requires management of the transition and repeated redefinition of social identities by alleviating implicit bias and self-regulating emotional responses to identity threats caused by major change	Research on the neural basis of self and social identity processes (e.g., Derks et al., 2008)

[†] *Note*: The references cited in this column are taken from Teece (2007) and Teece, Pisano, and Shuon (1997).

Evaluating and selecting new opportunities

A well-documented tendency is for organizations to shun innovative investment choices in favour of incremental improvements in keeping with their prevailing competencies (Henderson and Clark, 1990; Nelson and Winter, 1982). Drawing on the insights of prospect theory (Kahneman and Lovallo, 1993; Kahneman and Tversky, 1979), Teece (2007) attributes this dysfunction to biases in the computational mechanisms of subjective probability assessment, centred on loss aversion and the certainty effect. From this consequentialist perspective, organizations shun innovative investment choices because their decision makers undervalue new alternatives, based on biased calculations of their likelihood of success. However, more recent evidence that valuation by feeling explains many significant economic behaviours has eroded the long-held assumption that valuation proceeds by calculation and computation alone (Kahneman, Ritov and Schkade, 1999).

Contemporary developments in the decision sciences highlight the critical influence of felt emotions on choice. Loewenstein *et al.*'s (2001) risk-as-feelings model, for example, emphasizes that people typically act based on the emotions they experience at the time of choice in reaction to their mental images of choice outcomes rather than calculations of the probability or expected utility of those outcomes. A welter of evidence demonstrates that when assessments based on affect are at odds with those based on computation, the visceral often overpowers the rational to determine behaviour (Loewenstein, 1996; Loewenstein *et al.*, 2001, 2008; Rottenstreich and Hsee, 2001). The work of Damasio and colleagues (Bechara *et al.*, 2000; Damasio, 1994) shows that the affective consequences of potential courses of action are encoded in somatic markers, which the prefrontal cortex translates for the brain's emotion centres to guide behaviour. Mere activation of a marker provides an immediate basis for action without deliberation, although the marker's visceral information often informs subsequent deliberation. Crucially, whether instigated by cognitive appraisal or the more direct routes emphasized by Damasio (1994) and others, it is the resultant feeling states that determine overt behaviour (see also Finucane *et al.*, 2000; Sanfey *et al.*, 2003; Slovic *et al.*, 2004; Zajonc, 1980). This general point was well appreciated in Janis and Mann's (1977) classic treatise on decision making, but has been overlooked in contemporary strategy research.

The crucial implication of these developments is that harnessing, rather than suppressing, visceral reactions to strategic alternatives is critical to seizing capabilities. In cases where negative affective reactions to new opportunities outweigh the positive feelings invoked, it is unlikely that decision makers will commit fully to pursuing the developments in question – even where more dispassionate, consequentialist analyses are favourable. Because affect arises from salient imagery linked to the experience of choice outcomes, the vividness and valence of such imagery plays a vital role in determining affective valuation and subsequent approach-avoidance behaviour. By way of illustration, consider again the Tripsas and Giavetti (2000) case, in which Polaroid was contemplating a move away from its existing business model to one that prioritized alternative offerings. On one hand, the new model may have brought forth imagery associated with technological developments and rapid market growth, in turn stimulating excitement and hope; such positive emotional reactions are favourable to seizing. On the other hand, the negative mental imagery associated with potential job losses arising from the implementation of the new model might well have stimulated fear and unease. The fact that people tend to overreact emotionally to new risks (Loewenstein *et al.*, 2008) and weigh negative affect more heavily than positive affect in decision making (Ito *et al.*, 1998) compounds such affective barriers to seizing. The foregoing analysis suggests the following proposition:

Proposition 3: The greater the extent to which firms foster emotional commitment to new investment opportunities, the greater the likelihood they will seize those opportunities.

To illustrate the practical implications of this proposition consider again the role of scenario planning. In the light of the foregoing analysis, the next generation of scenario planning techniques could be adapted explicitly for building emotional as well as cognitive commitment to emerging prospects. In the context of seizing, the affect-inducing properties of scenario analysis, when skilfully deployed, could serve as a vehicle to generate and foster strong and vivid positive mental imagery pertaining to new opportunities, in turn stimulating the required visceral reactions to seize the most promising ones (Healey and Hodgkinson, 2008).

Notwithstanding the potency of building emotional commitment as a mechanism for fostering seizing, there are situations when too much emotional commitment can be problematic. Marks and Spencer's (M&S) acquisition of the Brooks Brothers retail chain for $740 million during the late-1980s exemplifies this problem (Finkelstein, Whitehead and Campbell 2008). Despite a welter of analytical evidence that this move was inadvisable, M&S Chairman, Derek Rayner, drove through the purchase, fuelled by the overwhelming positive feelings he experienced in reaction to the long-standing imagery he associated with Brooks Brothers' exclusive clothing products. This decision was to cost more than $1 billion, upon subsequently divesting the poorly performing acquisition for just $225 million. More generally, this case illustrates that when visceral reactions to a low probability/utility but affect-laden alternative outweigh reasoned reactions to a high probability/utility but affect-free alternative, the primacy of the emotional reaction dictates a potentially suboptimal course of action. In all probability, seizing the opportunity in question in such circumstances is ill-advised. Finkelstein *et al.* (2008) outline various safeguards available to help organizations overcome inappropriate emotional attachments to strategic issues and courses of action. These include monitoring processes designed to identify so-called 'red-flag' situations, in which decisions are proceeding based on such attachments, and the separation of decision and governance mechanisms to counter individuals' emotional fixations.

Unlocking fixations with existing strategies

It is important to recognize that although acts of omission (i.e., the failure to pursue fruitful new avenues) can prove more costly than errors of excessive commission (i.e., the tendency to embark on new, ultimately flawed, courses of action), such omission often stems from overcommitment to existing projects (Bazerman and Watkins, 2004). In order to pursue new opportunities, therefore, firms must often shed – or at least lessen – their commitment to existing directions (Eisenhardt and Martin, 2000; Teece, 2007; Teece *et al.*, 1997). One of the most significant biases that militates against this requirement is escalation of commitment, the tendency to 'throw good money after bad' in support of failing investments in an attempt to justify prior choices (Staw, 1976; Staw and Ross, 1987).

Hitherto, and again based on early behavioural decision research that saw biases such as framing and overconfidence as resulting from intuitive processes (e.g., Gilovich, Griffin and Kahneman, 2002), strategy scholars have generally assumed that the means for overcoming escalation of commitment and related dysfunctions is to engage decision makers in more

effortful and analytical information processing (Hodgkinson *et al.*, 1999, 2002; Schwenk, 1986; Wright and Goodwin, 2002). Drawing upon this conventional line of reasoning, Teece (2007: 1333) suggests that, 'overcoming biases almost always requires a cognitively sophisticated and disciplined approach to decision making.' However, merely encouraging rational and effortful information processing *per se* can exacerbate escalation of commitment and related problems. Indeed, individuals with rational thinking styles (who favour effortful, analytical reflection) are particularly prone to escalation because they feel the pressure for vindication more intensely (Wong, Kwong and Ng, 2008). Fortunately, recent work has begun to provide mechanisms for addressing the core emotional roots of escalation and related decision biases. For example, stimulating negative affect when considering whether to reinvest in a failing course of action reduces escalation, because decision makers withdraw their commitment to avoid future regret and the anxiety associated with costs sunk in error (Ku, 2008; Wong, Yik and Kwong, 2006). Hence:

Proposition 4: The greater the strategic decision making unit's tendency to incorporate salient negative affectivity associated with extant courses of action, the lower the likelihood it will fall prey to escalation of commitment and related dysfunctional decision traps.

This analysis highlights the capacity for self regulation as an important means of overcoming dysfunctional fixations. Self-regulation involves controlling internal ego-protective goals (Lord *et al.*, 2010), which are the root cause of the desire to justify specific choices to the self and others in escalation situations. One means of implementing this requirement for self-regulation is to reflect on how new courses of action facilitate the attainment of self-esteem enhancing goals, which essentially transfers the basic drive for self-esteem protection from maintenance of the status quo to the active pursuit of new directions (Henderson, Gollwitzer and Oettinger, 2007; Zhang and Baumeister, 2006). Sivanathan *et al.* (2008) demonstrated the effectiveness of this approach in a study of de-escalation in financial decision making. Giving decision makers the opportunity to affirm their overall self-esteem and personal integrity after they had committed resources to an ineffective strategy made them less inclined to invest further because confidence in the self had alleviated the desire for self-justification that motivates escalation.

Reconfiguring assets to maintain competitiveness

Teece's (2007) explication of the psychological foundations of transforming/reconfiguring is relatively underdeveloped in comparison with his analysis of sensing and seizing, in part because strategy research on the human aspects of the latter capability has been in short supply. However, as noted by Augier and Teece (2009), one of the foremost behavioural challenges associated with the reconfiguration of the enterprise concerns managing the effects of transformation on the core identities and motivations of key individuals and groups. We extend and deepen Teece's framework by explicating how the capacity to reconfigure social identities using reflexive and reflective processes in concert is critical to successful organization transformation.

When change threatens the salient identities and associated self-concepts of managers and employees, considerable resistance can breed at all levels of the organization (Gioia, Schultz and Corley, 2000; Haslam, Eggins and Reynolds, 2003; Hogg and Terry, 2000); actors cling to and defend old directions and ways of thinking intertwined with prevailing identities, and actively resist new strategic initiatives that challenge those identities (Elsbach and Kramer, 1996; Hogg and Terry, 2000; Nag, Corley and Gioia, 2007). In this sense, the fundamental identity of the firm becomes a trap that constrains its adaptive capacity (Bouchikhi and Kimberly, 2003, 2008).

As with earlier work on overcoming dysfunctions in sensing and seizing, the bulk of theory and research concerning the problem of identity inertia during strategic change has focused on cold cognition routes to identity change. Building a common group identity that embraces the extant identities under threat (Hogg and Terry, 2000) and establishing a fluid organizational identity that facilitates adaptation (Gioia, Schultz and Corley, 2000) are the favoured solutions. However, this cold cognition logic overstates the ease of cognitive identity reconstruction and underestimates the emotional difficulties associated with identity threat and the affective processes that mediate the transition to new identities. Given that the social pain caused by identity threat activates the same neural networks as physical pain (Lieberman and Eisenberger, 2009), addressing emotional mechanisms underpinning successful identity change is critical to reconfiguring. As indicated in Table 2.2.1, the emerging evidence in social cognitive neuroscience emphasizes the importance of actors' capabilities to regulate automatic and emotional reactions to self and social identity threats, especially heightened anxiety (Scheepers and Ellemers, 2005), which affect the ability to see new directions without prejudice and embrace changes that impinge upon extant salient identities.

Since much of the bias against the people (e.g., the champions of particular strategic change initiatives) and events (e.g., restructuring to meet the challenges of new opportunities and threats) at the heart of reconfiguring stems from automatic social categorization and stereotyping processes controlled by the reflexive system (Amodio, 2008; Dovidio, Pearson and Orr, 2008), merely encouraging the conscious monitoring and adjustment of prejudices through reflective processes is an insufficient basis for overcoming them. Similar to the alleviation of escalation of commitment, the self-regulation of emotional response is a crucial mechanism for overcoming identity-based resistance to change (Amodio, 2008; Derks, Inzlicht and Kang, 2008; Klein, Rozendal and Cosmides, 2002). However, whereas self-regulation in seizing concerns top managers' ability to regulate their own feelings, self-regulation in transforming concerns the ability of managers at all levels to identify, interpret and respond to the emotions of stakeholders throughout the organization (cf. Huy, 1999, 2002). Because threats to social identities threaten, by extension, the identities and self-concepts of individuals who identify strongly with the entity in question, affirming those aspects of the salient identities unaffected by the required strategic change can help reduce the desire to cling to and defend the extant identity of the organization as a whole. In consequence, actors will be more inclined to embrace the new direction and accompanying work practices. It thus follows that:

Proposition 5: The greater the capacity of the organization to regulate identity-based affective responses to change, the greater the likelihood of successful strategic transformation.

As with sensing and seizing, one of the most significant practical requirements for supporting identity transition during strategic transformation is the creation of a psychologically secure emotional climate. Practices suitable for this purpose include training and coaching in the art of emotional balancing – i.e., attending to feelings expressed during identity threatening change episodes, while building emotional commitment to identity attributes consonant with the new strategic direction (cf. Huy, 1999, 2002).

GE's recent 'ecomagination' project and the ongoing transformation of the Intel Corporation (Heath,

2010) illustrate these principles in action. In high-lighting its own industry-leading green products to its employees, GE is demonstrating that it already has the people and skills needed to succeed in a world focused on sustainability. By appealing on impassioned grounds to a new direction that fits with aspects of the firm's core, the organization is easing the transition to a new identity as an innovator of sustainable solutions in a way that reassures rather than threatens. In similar vein, as PC growth slows, the Intel Corporation is transforming itself into a provider of digital platforms for health, entertainment and mobile applications by using inspiration and motivation rather than in-tellectual justification. One potential barrier to this project is that the senior engineers who built their ca-reers around Intel's identity as a 'chip builder' feel directionless. Sensitized to this danger, Intel's recent national advertising campaign features star engineer Anjay Bhatt, co-inventor of the USB, walking into a canteen cheered on by adoring employees. The mes-sage is that Intel's heart already fits with the new focus on product innovation. As with GE's attempts, this approach seeks to facilitate identity transition using emotionally supportive mechanisms.

Implications

We prefaced this article with Loewenstein's (1996) provocative critique of decision theory because it re-sonates strongly when stepping back to gaze critically upon the behavioural microfoundations of con-temporary strategic management theory. Teece's (2007) framework is not alone in privileging calcula-tion and computation through cold, effortful processes as the primary route to organizational adaptation and performance. Like earlier work that investigated stra-tegic issue diagnosis (Dutton and Jackson, 1987; Jackson and Dutton, 1988) and competitive position-ing strategy (Hodgkinson, 1997; Peteraf and Shanley, 1997; Porac et al., 1995; Reger and Palmer, 1996) from a cognitive standpoint, the dynamic capabilities project as a whole divorces cognition from emotion and affect and affords only a minimal role to auto-matic and non-conscious processes (see, e.g., Adner and Helfat, 2003; Alvarez and Busenitz, 2001; Amit and Schoemaker, 1993; Gavetti, 2005; Kaplan, 2008; Lane et al., 2006; Tripsas and Gavetti, 2000).

Our article has demonstrated how the development and maintenance of dynamic capabilities requires firms to harness managers' reflexive *and* reflective abilities, to utilize implicit and explicit cognitive and emotional processes in harmony, to facilitate sensing, seizing and reconfiguration. In so doing, it responds to Gavetti *et al.*'s (2007) call to render theories of capabilities de-velopment and organizational adaptation consistent with what we know about human functioning from contemporary advances in the psychological sciences. The result of this endeavour is a behaviourally more plausible depiction of organizations: driven by thinking and feeling inhabitants who are fired by affect, and often as reliant on inspiration and the skilful management of emotion and intuition as on calculating cognition.

Implications for practice

Our analysis points to a need for tools and practices that will enhance sensing, seizing and transforming by augmenting the cognitive *and* affective capabilities of individuals and teams. Several commentators have re-cently offered behavioural prescriptions for strategic intervention which, at first glance, appear to be con-sistent with our analysis – for example, sharing diverse perspectives, gathering disconfirmatory evidence, dis-cussing uncertainties, and confronting cognitive biases (for representative examples see Day and Schoemaker, 2006; Kahneman and Klein, 2009, 2010; Lovallo and Sibony, 2010). However, upon closer inspection, many of these prescriptions are predicated on a cold informa-tion processing logic. One reason executives are often reluctant to embrace practices that involve questioning their personal judgements is precisely because these practices raise, rather than assuage, emotional barriers. It is tempting, therefore, to call for a two-step approach for intervening in the strategy process – an initial emotional screening phase followed by the usual gamut of decision-aiding techniques (cf. Elsbach and Barr, 1999). How-ever, such an arrangement runs the risk of perpetuating the error of separating reason from emotion in the strat-egy arena (cf. Damasio, 1994). Accordingly, we have sought to demonstrate throughout how some of the fun-damental tools of strategizing, when suitably embedded in an emotionally supportive climate, can be adapted to integrate cognition and affect.

Our analysis overall signals the need for a new generation of knowledge elicitation and decision-aiding techniques, predicated on hot cognition princi-ples, for both intervention and research purposes. Rather than focusing on the mapping of strategists' conceptual knowledge *per se* (e.g., Eden and Ackermann, 1998; Hodgkinson, Maule and Bown, 2004; Huff, 1990), extant cognitive mapping techni-ques could be modified to elicit and represent feelings and affective reactions to strategic issues and choices, thereby integrating multiple modalities of thought.

Such practices could be particularly valuable in helping managers make sense of how they and others react to particular problems, as an aid to sensing, seizing and transforming.

Techniques commonly used for overcoming decision traps might be similarly adapted to convert them from cold cognition to hot cognition enhancing technologies. By way of illustration, the frame analysis worksheet (Russo and Schoemaker, 1989) might be adapted to assist decision makers in comprehending the emotional tags they and others hold for a given strategic problem, as a basis for recognizing dissonant reactions to the issues at hand. The goal here would be to enhance multiple frame awareness by incorporating affective information into the exercise.

Concluding remarks

In his closing remarks, Teece (2007: 1341) observes that 'enterprises may be more like biological organisms than some economists, managers and strategy scholars are willing to admit.' Our analysis takes this biological metaphor to a new level by illuminating the ways the individuals and groups who manage these entities are governed by thoughts *and* feelings: always boundedly rational, but manifestly driven by emotion. The continued negation of this fundamental insight risks stymieing the field of strategic management from maturing in alignment with economics and psychology, the base disciplines that have hitherto provided its behavioural microfoundations.

READING 2.3

How successful leaders think

By Roger Martin[1]

Brilliant leaders excel at integrative thinking. They can hold two opposing ideas in their minds at once. Then, rather than settling for choice A or B, they forge an innovative 'third way' that contains elements of both but improves on each.

Consider Bob Young, co-founder of Red Hat, the dominant distributor of Linux open-source software. The business model Young created for Red Hat transcended the two prevailing software industry models – winning Red Hat entrée into the lucrative corporate market.

How to become an integrative thinker? Resist the simplicity and certainty that comes with conventional 'either/or' thinking. Embrace the messiness and complexity of conflicting options. And emulate great leaders' decision-making approach – looking beyond obvious considerations.

Your reward? Instead of making unattractive trade-offs, you generate a wealth of profitable solutions for your business.

The idea in practice

What does integrative thinking look like in action? Contrast conventional and integrative thinkers' approaches to the four steps of decision-making:

Step 1. Identifying key factors

Conventional thinkers consider only obviously relevant factors while weighing options. Integrative thinkers seek less obvious but potentially more relevant considerations.

- Example: Bob Young disliked the two prevailing software business models: selling operating software but not source code needed to develop software applications (profitable but anathema to open-source advocates), or selling CD-ROMs containing software and source code (aligned with open-source values but not profitable). Seeking a third choice, he considered the CIOs' reluctance to buy new technology that would be complicated to maintain. Viewing their reluctance as relevant eventually helped Young see that selling software services would be a superior alternative to the existing product-based business models.

Step 2. Analysing causality

Conventional thinkers consider one-way, linear relationships between factors: more of A produces more of B. Integrative thinkers consider multidirectional relationships.

■ Example: Young analysed the complex relationships among pricing, profitability and distribution channels. He recognized that a product based on freely available components would soon become a commodity. Any electronics retailer could assemble its own Linux product and push it through its well-developed distribution channel – leaving Red Hat stranded. Analysis of these causal relationships yielded a nuanced picture of the industry's future.

Step 3. Envisioning the decision's overall structure

Conventional thinkers break a problem into pieces and work on them separately. Integrative thinkers see a problem as a whole – examining how its various aspects affect one another.

■ Example: Young held several issues in his head simultaneously, including the CIOs' concerns, dynamics of individual and corporate markets for system software, and the evolving economics of the free-software business. Each 'piece' could have pushed him toward a separate decision. But by considering the issues as an interrelated whole, Young began to realize only one player would ultimately dominate the corporate market.

Step 4. Achieving resolution

Conventional thinkers make either/or choices. Integrative thinkers refuse to accept conventional options.

■ Example: To pursue market leadership, Young devised an unconventional business model. The model synthesized two seemingly irreconcilable models by combining low product price with profitable service offerings. Red Hat began helping companies manage the software upgrades available almost daily through Linux's open-source platform. It also gave the software away as a free Internet download. Thus, Red Hat acquired the scale and market leadership to attract cautious corporate customers to what became its central offering: service, not software.

We are drawn to the stories of effective leaders in action. Their decisiveness invigorates us. The events that unfold from their bold moves, often culminating in successful outcomes, make for gripping narratives. Perhaps most important, we turn to accounts of their

deeds for lessons that we can apply in our own careers. Books like *Jack: Straight from the Gut* and *Execution: The Discipline of Getting Things Done* are compelling in part because they implicitly promise that we can achieve the success of a Jack Welch or a Larry Bossidy – if only we learn to emulate their actions.

But this focus on what a leader does is misplaced. That's because moves that work in one context often make little sense in another, even at the same company or within the experience of a single leader. Recall that Jack Welch, early in his career at General Electric, insisted that each of GE's businesses be number one or number two in market share in its industry; years later he insisted that those same businesses define their markets so that their share was no greater than 10 per cent, thereby forcing managers to look for opportunities beyond the confines of a narrowly conceived market. Trying to learn from what Jack Welch did invites confusion and incoherence, because he pursued – wisely, I might add – diametrically opposed courses at different points in his career and in GE's history.

So where do we look for lessons? A more productive, though more difficult, approach is to focus on how a leader thinks – that is, to examine the antecedent of doing, or the ways in which leaders' cognitive processes produce their actions.

I have spent the past 15 years, first as a management consultant and now as the dean of a business school, studying leaders with exemplary records. Over the past six years, I have interviewed more than 50 such leaders, some for as long as eight hours, and found that most of them share a somewhat unusual trait: They have the predisposition and the capacity to hold in their heads two opposing ideas at once. And then, without panicking or simply settling for one alternative or the other, they're able to creatively resolve the tension between those two ideas by generating a new one that contains elements of the others but is superior to both. This process of consideration and synthesis can be termed integrative thinking. It is this discipline – not superior strategy or faultless execution – that is a defining characteristic of most exceptional businesses and the people who run them.

I don't claim that this is a new idea. More than 60 years ago, F. Scott Fitzgerald saw 'the ability to hold two opposing ideas in mind at the same time and still retain the ability to function' as the sign of a truly intelligent individual. And certainly not every good leader exhibits this capability, nor is it the sole source of success for those who do. But it is clear to me that integrative thinking tremendously improves people's odds.

This insight is easy to miss, though, since the management conversation in recent years has tilted away from thinking and toward doing (witness the popularity of books like *Execution).* Also, many great integrative thinkers aren't even aware of their particular capability and thus don't consciously exercise it. Take Jack Welch, who is among the executives I have interviewed: he is clearly a consummate integrative thinker – but you'd never know it from reading his books.

Indeed, my aim in this article is to deconstruct and describe a capability that seems to come naturally to many successful leaders. To illustrate the concept, I'll concentrate on an executive I talked with at length: Bob Young, the colourful co-founder and former CEO of Red Hat, the dominant distributor of Linux open-source software. The assumption underlying my examination of his and others' integrative thinking is this: It isn't just an ability you're born with – it's something you can hone.

Opposable thumb, opposable mind

In the mid-1990s, Red Hat faced what seemed like two alternative paths to growth. At the time, the company sold packaged versions of Linux open-source software, mainly to computer geeks, periodically bundling together new versions that included the latest upgrades from countless independent developers. As Red Hat looked to grow beyond its $1 million in annual sales, it could have chosen one of the two basic business models in the software industry.

One was the classic proprietary software model, employed by big players such as Microsoft, Oracle and SAP, which sold customers operating software but not the source code. These companies invested heavily in research and development, guarded their intellectual property jealously, charged high prices, and enjoyed wide profit margins because their customers, lacking access to the source code, were essentially locked into purchasing regular upgrades.

The alternative, employed by numerous small companies, including Red Hat itself, was the so-called free-software model, in which suppliers sold CD-ROMs with both the software and the source code. The software products weren't in fact free, but prices were modest – $15 for a packaged version of the Linux operating system versus more than $200 for Microsoft

Windows. Suppliers made money each time they assembled a new version from the many free updates by independent developers; but profit margins were narrow and revenue was uncertain. Corporate customers, looking for standardization and predictability, were wary not only of the unfamiliar software but also of its small and idiosyncratic suppliers.

Bob Young – a self-deprecating eccentric in an industry full of eccentrics, who signalled his affiliation with his company by regularly sporting red socks and a red hat – didn't like either of these models. The high-margin proprietary model ran counter to the whole philosophy of Linux and the open-source movement, even if there had been a way to create proprietary versions of the software. 'Buying proprietary software is like buying a car with the hood welded shut,' Young told me. 'If something goes wrong, you can't even try to fix it.' But the free software model meant scraping a slim profit from the packaging and distribution of a freely available commodity in a fringe market, which might have offered reasonable returns in the short term but wasn't likely to deliver sustained profitable growth.

Young likes to say that he's not 'one of the smart guys' in the industry, that he's a salesman in a world of technical geniuses. Nonetheless, he managed to synthesize two seemingly irreconcilable business models, placing Red Hat on a path to tremendous success. His response to his strategic dilemma was to combine the free-software model's low product price with the proprietary model's profitable service component, in the process creating something new: a corporate market for the Linux operating system. As is often the case with integrative thinking, Young included some twists on both models that made the synthesis work.

Although inspired by the proprietary model, Red Hat's service offering was quite different. 'If you ran into a bug that caused your systems to crash,' Young said of the service you'd buy from the big proprietary shops, 'you would call up the manufacturer and say, "My systems are crashing." And he'd say, "Oh, dear," while he really meant, "Oh, good." He'd send an engineer over at several hundred dollars an hour to fix his software, which was broken when he delivered it to you, and he'd call that customer service.' Red Hat, by contrast, helped companies manage the upgrades and improvements available almost daily through Linux's open-source platform.

Young also made a crucial change to what had been the somewhat misleadingly dubbed free software model: He actually gave the software away, repackaging it as a free download on the Internet rather than as an inexpensive but cumbersome CD-ROM. This allowed Red Hat to break away from the multitude of small Linux packagers by acquiring the scale and market leadership to generate faith among cautious corporate customers in what would become Red Hat's central offering – service, not software.

In 1999, Red Hat went public, and Young became a billionaire on the first day of trading. By 2000, Linux had captured 25 per cent of the server operating system market, and Red Hat held more than 50 per cent of the global market for Linux systems. Unlike the vast majority of dot-com era start-ups, Red Hat has continued to grow.

What enabled Young to resolve the apparent choice between two unattractive models? It was his use of an innate but underdeveloped human characteristic, something we might call – in a metaphor that echoes another human trait – the opposable mind.

Human beings are distinguished from nearly every other creature by a physical feature: the opposable thumb. Thanks to the tension that we can create by opposing the thumb and fingers, we can do marvellous things – write, thread a needle, guide a catheter through an artery. Although evolution provided human beings with this potential advantage, it would have gone to waste if our species had not exercised it in ever more sophisticated ways. When we engage in something like writing, we train the muscles involved and the brain that controls them. Without exploring the possibilities of opposition, we wouldn't have developed either its physical properties or the cognition that accompanies and animates it.

Analogously, we were born with opposable minds, which allow us to hold two conflicting ideas in constructive, almost dialectic tension. We can use that tension to think our way toward new, superior ideas. Were we able to hold only one thought or idea in our heads at a time, we wouldn't have access to the insights that the opposable mind can produce.

Unfortunately, because people don't exercise this capability much, great integrative thinkers are fairly rare. Why is this potentially powerful but generally latent tool used so infrequently and to less than full advantage? Because putting it to work makes us anxious. Most of us avoid complexity and ambiguity and seek out the comfort of simplicity and clarity. To cope with the dizzying complexity of the world around us, we simplify where we can. We crave the certainty of choosing between well-defined alternatives and the closure that comes when a decision has been made.

For those reasons, we often don't know what to do with fundamentally opposing and seemingly incommensurable models. Our first impulse is usually to determine which of the two models is 'right' and, by the process of elimination, which is 'wrong'. We may even take sides and try to prove that our chosen model is better than the other one. But in rejecting one model out of hand, we miss out on all the value that we could have realized by considering the opposing two at the same time and finding in the tension clues to a superior model. By forcing a choice between the two, we disengage the opposable mind before it can seek a creative resolution.

This nearly universal personal trait is writ large in most organizations. When a colleague admonishes us to 'quit complicating the issue', it's not just an impatient reminder to get on with the damn job – it's also a plea to keep the complexity at a comfortable level.

To take advantage of our opposable minds, we must resist our natural leaning toward simplicity and certainty. Bob Young recognized from the beginning that he wasn't bound to choose one of the two prevailing software business models. He saw the unpleasant trade-offs he'd have to make if he chose between the two as a signal to rethink the problem from the ground up. And he didn't rest until he found a new model that grew out of the tension between them.

Basically, Young refused to settle for an 'either/or' choice. That phrase has come up time and again in my interviews with successful leaders. When asked whether he thought strategy or execution was more important, Jack Welch responded: 'I don't think it's an "either/or".' Similarly, Procter & Gamble CEO A.G. Lafley – when asked how he came up with a turnaround plan that drew on both cost cutting and investment in innovation – said: 'We weren't going to win if it were an "or". Everybody can do "or".'

The four stages of decision-making

So what does the process of integrative thinking look like? How do integrative thinkers consider their options in a way that leads to new possibilities and not merely back to the same inadequate alternatives? They work through four related but distinct stages. The steps themselves aren't particular to integrative thinking: everyone goes through them while thinking through a decision. What's distinctive about integrative thinkers is how they approach the steps (see Exhibit 2.3.1).

question of whether to go to a movie tonight involves deciding, at the very least, which movie to see, which theatre to go to, and which showing to attend. The order in which you make these decisions will affect the outcome. For example, you may not be able to see your preferred movie if you've already decided you need to be back in time to relieve a babysitter who has plans for later in the evening. When you're trying to invent a new business model, the number of decision-making variables explodes. And with that comes the impulse not only to establish a strict sequence in which issues will be considered, but also to dole out pieces of a decision so that various parties – often, different corporate functions – can work on them separately.

What usually happens is that everyone loses sight of the overriding issue, and a mediocre outcome results. Suppose that Bob Young had delegated to different functional heads' questions concerning the pricing, enhancement and distribution of Red Hat's original software product. Would their individual answers, agglomerated into an overall Red Hat strategy, have produced the spectacularly successful new business model that Young came up with? It doesn't seem all that likely.

Integrative thinkers don't break down a problem into independent pieces and work on them separately or in a certain order. They see the entire architecture of the problem: how the various parts of it fit together, how one decision will affect another. Just as important, they hold all of those pieces suspended in their minds at once. They don't parcel out the elements for others to work on piecemeal or let one element temporarily drop out of sight, only to be taken up again for consideration after everything else has been decided. An architect doesn't ask his subordinates to design a perfect bathroom and a perfect living room and a perfect kitchen, and then hope that the pieces of the house will fit nicely together. A business executive doesn't design a product before considering the costs of manufacturing it.

Young held simultaneously in his head a number of issues: the feelings and the challenges of chief information officers and systems administrators, the dynamics of both the individual and the corporate markets for operating system software, the evolving economics of the free-software business, and the motivations behind the major players in the proprietary software business. Each factor could have pushed him toward a separate decision on how to address the challenge. But he delayed making decisions and considered the relationships between these issues as he slowly moved toward the creation of a new business

model, one based on the belief that dominant market share would be critical to Red Hat's success.

Achieving resolution

All of these stages – determining what is salient, analysing the causal relationships between the salient factors, examining the architecture of the problem – lead to an outcome. Too often, we accept an unpleasant trade-off with relatively little complaint, since it appears to be the best alternative. That's because by the time we have reached this stage, our desire for simplicity has led us to ignore opportunities in the previous three steps to discover interesting and novel ways around the trade-off. Instead of rebelling against the meagre and unattractive alternatives, instead of refusing to settle for the best available bad choice, the conventional thinker shrugs and asks, 'What else could we have done?'

'Much else,' the integrative thinker says. A leader who embraces holistic rather than segmented thinking can creatively resolve the tensions that launched the decision-making process. The actions associated with the search for such resolution – creating delays, sending teams back to examine things more deeply, generating new options at the 11th hour – can appear irresolute from the outside. Indeed, the integrative thinker may even be dissatisfied with the fresh batch of options he's come up with, in which case he may go back and start over. When a satisfactory outcome does emerge, though, it is inevitably due to the leader's refusal to accept trade-offs and conventional options.

The outcome in the case of Red Hat was completely unconventional – not many companies suddenly decide to give away their products – and ultimately successful. Young's gradual realization that only one player in his industry would have leverage with and support from corporate customers – and that such leverage and support could reap attractive service revenues from totally free software – shaped the dramatically creative decision he made.

The thinking that he intuitively engaged in is very different from the thinking that produces most managerial decisions. But, he said, his experience was hardly unique: 'People are often faced with difficult choices – for instance, "Do I want to be the high-quality, high-cost supplier or the low-quality, low-cost supplier?" We're trained to examine the pros and cons of such alternatives and then pick one of them. But really successful businesspeople look at choices like these and say, "I don't like either one." Using that recurring phrase, he added: 'They don't accept that it's an "either/or".'

Born and bred

The consequences of integrative thinking and conventional thinking couldn't be more distinct. Integrative thinking generates options and new solutions. It creates a sense of limitless possibility. Conventional thinking glosses over potential solutions and fosters the illusion that creative solutions don't actually exist. With integrative thinking, aspirations rise over time. With conventional thinking, they wear away with every apparent reinforcement of the lesson that life is about accepting unattractive trade-offs. Fundamentally, the conventional thinker prefers to accept the world just as it is, whereas the integrative thinker welcomes the challenge of shaping the world for the better.

Given the benefits of integrative thinking, you have to ask, 'If I'm not an integrative thinker, can I learn to be one?' In F. Scott Fitzgerald's view, only people with 'first-rate intelligence' can continue to function while holding two opposing ideas in their heads. But I refuse to believe that the ability to use our opposable minds is a gift reserved for a small minority of people. I prefer the view suggested by Thomas C. Chamberlin, a 19th century American geologist and former president of the University of Wisconsin. More than 100 years ago, Chamberlin wrote an article in *Science*

magazine proposing the idea of 'multiple working hypotheses' as an improvement over the most commonly employed scientific method of the time: testing the validity of a single hypothesis through trial and error. Chamberlin argued that his approach would provide more accurate explanations of scientific phenomena by taking into account 'the coordination of several agencies, which enter into the combined result in varying proportions'. While acknowledging the cognitive challenges posed by such an approach, Chamberlin wrote that it 'develops a habit of thought analogous to the method itself, which may be designated a habit of parallel or complex thought. Instead of a simple succession of thoughts in linear order … the mind appears to become possessed of the power of simultaneous vision from different standpoints'.

Similarly, I believe that integrative thinking is a 'habit of thought' that all of us can consciously develop to arrive at solutions that would otherwise not be evident. First, there needs to be greater general awareness of integrative thinking as a concept. Then, over time, we can teach it in our business schools – an endeavour that colleagues and I are currently working on. At some point, integrative thinking will no longer be just a tacit skill (cultivated knowingly or not) in the heads of a select few.

REFERENCES

Adner, R. and Helfat, C. (2003) 'Dynamic managerial capabilities and corporate effects', *Strategic Management Journal*, 24(10), pp. 1011–1027.

Ala, M. and Cordeiro, W.P. (1999) 'Can we learn management techniques from the Japanese ringi process?', *Business Forum*, 24(½), pp. 22–24.

Aldrich, H.E. and Fiol, C.M. (1994) 'Fools rush in? the institutional context of industry creation', *Academy of Management Review*, Vol. 19, No. 4, pp. 645–670.

Alvarez, S.A. and Busenitz, L.W. (2001) 'The entrepreneurship of resource-based theory', *Journal of Management*, 27, pp. 755–775.

Amit, R. and Schoemaker, P.J.H. (1993) 'Strategic assets and organization rent', *Strategic Management Journal*, 14(1), pp. 33–46.

Amodio, D.M. (2008) 'The social neuroscience of intergroup relations', *European Review of Social Psychology*, 19, pp. 1–54.

Anderson, J.R. (1983) *The Architecture of Cognition*, Cambridge, MA: Harvard University Press.

Andrews, K. (1987) *The Concept of Corporate Strategy*, Homewood: Irvin.

Ansoff, H.I. (1965) *Corporate Strategy: An Analytic Approach to Business Policy for Growth and Expansion*, New York: McGraw-Hill.

Anthony, W.P., Bennett, R.H., Maddox, E.N. and Wheatley, W.J. (1993) 'Picturing the future: Using mental imagery to enrich strategic environmental assessment', *Academy of Management Executive*, Vol. 7, No. 2, pp. 43–56.

Armour, H. and Teece, D.J. (1978) 'Organizational structure and economic performance: a test of the multidivisional hypothesis', *Bell Journal of Economics*, 9(2), pp. 106–122.

Ashby, F.G., Isen, A.M. and Turken, U. (1999) 'A neuropsychological theory of positive affect and its influence on cognition', *Psychological Review*, 106, pp. 529–550.

Augier, M. and Teece, D.J. (2009) 'Dynamic capabilities and the role of managers in business strategy and economic performance', *Organization Science*, 20, pp. 410–421.

Bargh, J.A. and Chartrand, T.L. (1999) 'The unbearable automaticity of being'. *American Psychologist*, 54(7), pp. 462–479.

Bargh, J.A. and Ferguson, M.J. (2000) 'Beyond behaviorism: on the automaticity of higher mental processes', *Psychological Bulletin*, 126(6), pp. 925–945.

Barney, J.B. (1991) 'Firm resources and sustained competitive advantage', *Journal of Management*, 17(1), pp. 99–120.

Barr, P.S, Stimpert, J.L. and Huff, A.S. (1992) 'Cognitive change, strategic action, and organizational renewal', *Strategic Management Journal*, Summer Special Issue 13, pp. 15–36.

Bartlett, C.A. and Ghoshal, S. (1993) 'Beyond the M-form: toward a managerial theory of the enterprise', *Strategic Management Journal*, Winter Special Issue 14, pp. 23–46.

Bateman, T.S. and Zeithaml, C.P. (1989) 'The psychological context of strategic decisions: a model and convergent experimental findings', *Strategic Management Journal*, 10(1), pp. 59–74.

Baumol, W. (2006) 'Entrepreneurship and invention: toward restoration into microeconomic value theory'. Working paper, Ringberg Castle Presentation, Germany.

Bazerman, M.H. (1990) *Judgment in Managerial Decision Making*, Second Edition, New York: Wiley.

Bazerman, M.H. and Watkins, M.D. (2004) *Predictable Surprises: The Disasters You Should Have Seen Coming, and How to Avoid Them*, Boston, MA: Harvard Business School Press.

Bechara, A., Damasio, H. and Damasio, A.R. (2000) 'Emotion, decision making, and the orbitofrontal cortex', *Cerebral Cortex*, 10(3), pp. 295–307.

Behling, O. and Eckel, N.L. (1991) 'Making Sense Out of Intuition', *Academy of Management Executive*, Vol. 5, No. 1, pp. 46–54.

Bernheim, B.D. and Rangel, A. (2004) 'Addiction and cue triggered decision processes', *American Economic Review*, 94(5), pp. 1558–1590.

Bossidy, L. and Charan, R. with Burck, C. (2002) *Execution: The Discipline of Getting Things Done*, New York: Crown Business.

Bouchikhi, H. and Kimberly, J.R. (2003) 'Escaping the identity trap', *Sloan Management Review*, 44(3), pp. 20–26.

Bouchikhi, H. and Kimberly, J.R. (2008) *The Soul of the Corporation: How to Manage the Identity of Your Company*, Upper Saddle River, NJ: Wharton School Publishing.

Brandenburger, A.M. and Nalebuff, B.J. (1996) *Co-opetition*, New York: Doubleday.

Brocas, I. and Carrillo, J.D. (2008) 'The brain as a hierarchical organization', *American Economic Review*, 98(4), pp. 1312–1346.

Brooks, D. (2012) *The Social Animal*, New York: Random House.

Burgelman, R.A. and Grove, A.S. (1996) 'Strategic dissonance', *California Management Review*, 38, pp. 8–28.

Capron, L., Dussauge, P. and Mitchell, W. (1998) 'Resource redeployment following horizontal mergers and acquisitions in Europe and North America, 1988–1992', *Strategic Management Journal*, 19(7), pp. 631–661.

Casson, M. (1997) *Information and Organization: A New Perspective on the Theory of the Enterprise*, New York: Oxford University Press.

Chandler, A. (1962) *Strategy and Structure: Chapters in the History of Industrial Enterprise*, Cambridge, MA: Harvard University Press.

Chandler, A. (1990a) *Scale and Scope: The Dynamics of Industrial Capitalism*, Cambridge, MA: Harvard University Press.

Chandler, A. (1990b) 'The enduring logic of industrial success', *Harvard Business Review*, 68(2), pp. 130–140.

Chesbrough, H. (2003) *Open Innovation: The New Imperative for Creating and Profiting from Technology*, Boston, MA: Harvard Business School Press.

Chesbrough, H. and Rosenbloom, R.S. (2002) 'The role of the business model in capturing value from innovation: evidence from Xerox Corporation's technology', *Industrial and Corporate Change*, 11(3), pp. 529–555.

Compton, R.J. (2003) 'The interface between emotion and attention: a review of evidence from psychology and neuroscience', *Behavioral and Cognitive Neuroscience Reviews*, 2(2), pp. 115–129.

Cummings, S. (1993) 'Brief case: The first strategists', *Long Range Planning*, 26(3), pp. 133–135.

Cyert, R.M. and March, J.G. (1963) *A Behavioral Theory of the Enterprise*, Englewood Cliffs, NJ: Prentice-Hall.

Daft, R. and Weick, K. (1984) 'Toward a Model of Organizations as Interpretation Systems', *Academy of Management Review*, Vol. 9, pp. 284–295.

Damasio, A.R. (1994) *Descartes' Error: Emotion, Reason, and the Human Brain*, New York: Putnam.

Dane, E. and Pratt, M.G. (2007) 'Exploring intuition and its role in managerial decision making', *Academy of Management Review*, 32(1), pp. 33–54.

David, P. (1992) 'Heroes, herds and hysteresis in technological history: Thomas Edison and the battle of the system reconsidered', *Industrial and Corporate Change*, 1(1), pp. 129–180.

Davidow, W. and Malone, M. (1992) *The Virtual Corporation*, New York: Harper Business.

Day, D.V. and Lord, R.G. (1992) 'Expertise and problem categorization: The role of expert processing in organizational sense-making', *Journal of Management Studies*, Vol. 29, pp. 35–47.

Day, G.S. and Schoemaker, P.J.H. (2006) *Peripheral Vision: Detecting the Weak Signals That Will Make or Break Your Company*, Boston, MA: Harvard Business School Press.

Derks, B., Inzlicht M. and Kang, S. (2008) 'The neuroscience of stigma and stereotype threat', *Group Processes and Intergroup Relations*, 11(2), pp. 163–181.

DiMaggio, P. and Powell, W.W. (1983) 'The iron cage revisited: Institutional isomorphism and collective rationality in organizational fields', *American Sociological Review*, Vol. 48, pp. 147–160.

Dovidio, J.F., Pearson, A.R. and Orr, P. (2008) 'Social psychology and neuroscience: strange bedfellows or a healthy marriage? ', *Group Processes and Intergroup Relations*, 11(2), pp. 247–263.

Doz, Y.L. and Kosonen, M. (2008) *Fast Strategy: How Strategic Agility Will Help You Stay Ahead of the Game*, Harlow: Pearson.

Drummond, H. (2001) *The Art of Decision Making: Mirrors of Imagination, Masks of Fate*, Chichester: Wiley.

Dutton, J.E. (1988) 'Understanding Strategies Agenda Building and its Implications for Managing Change', in: L.R. Pondy, R.J. Boland, Jr. and H. Thomas (eds.) *Managing Ambiguity and Change*, Chichester: Wiley.

Dutton, J.E. (1993) 'Interpretations on automatic: a different view of strategic issue diagnosis', *Journal of Management Studies*, 30(3), pp. 339–357.

Dutton, J.E. and Jackson, S.E. (1987) 'Categorizing strategic issues: links to organizational action', *Academy of Management Review*, 12(1), pp. 76–90.

Eden, C. (1989) 'Using Cognitive Mapping for Strategic Options Development and Analysis (SODA)', in: J. Rosenhead (ed.) *Rational Analysis in a Problematic World*, London: Wiley.

Eden, C. and Ackermann, F. (1998) *Making Strategy: The Journey of Strategic Management*, London: Sage.

Eisenhardt, K. and Martin, J. (2000) 'Dynamic capabilities: what are they?', *Strategic Management Journal*, October–November, Special Issue 21, pp. 1105–1121.

Elsbach, K.D. and Barr, P.S. (1999) 'The effects of mood on individuals' use of structured decision protocols', *Organization Science*, 10(2), pp. 181–198.

Elsbach, K.D. and Kramer, R.M. (1996) 'Members' responses to organizational identity threats: encountering and countering the *Business Week rankings*', *Administrative Science Quarterly*, 41(3), pp. 442–476.

Elster, J. (1999) *Alchemies of the Mind: Rationality and the Emotions*, Cambridge: Cambridge University Press.

Ettlie, J.E. and Pavlou, P.A. (2006) 'echnology-based new product development partnerships', *Decision Sciences*, 37(2), pp. 117–147.

Finkelstein, S. and Hambrick, D.C. (1996) *Strategic Leadership: Top Executives and Their Effects on Organizations*, St. Paul: West.

Finkelstein, S., Whitehead, J. and Campbell, A. (2008) *Think Again: Why Good Leaders Make Bad Decisions and How to Keep it From Happening to You*, Boston, MA: Harvard Business School Press.

Finucane, M.L., Alhakami, A., Slovic, P. and Johnson, S.M. (2000) 'The affect heuristic in judgments of risks and benefits', *Journal of Behavioral Decision Making*, 13(1), pp. 1–17.

Fischhoff, B. (1982) 'Debiasing', in: Kahneman, D., Slovic, P. and Tversky, A. (eds.) *Judgment Under Uncertainty: Heuristics and Biases*, Cambridge: Cambridge University Press, pp. 422–444.

Fredrickson, B.L. and Branigan, C. (2005) 'Positive emotions broaden the scope of attention and thought-action repertoires', *Cognition and Emotion*, 19, pp. 313–332.

Freeman, C. (1974) *The Economics of Industrial Innovation*, Harmondsworth: Penguin.

Gavetti, G. (2005) 'Cognition and hierarchy: rethinking the microfoundations of capabilities development', *Organization Science*, 16(6), pp. 599–617.

Gavetti, G. and Levinthal, D.A. (2000) 'Looking forward and looking backward: cognitive and experiential search', *Administrative Science Quarterly*, 45(1), pp. 113–137.

Gavetti, G., Levinthal, D.A. and Ocasio, W. (2007) 'Neo-Carnegie: the Carnegie School's past, present, and reconstructing for the future', *Organization Science*, 18(3), pp. 523–536.

Gilovich, T., Griffin, D. and Kahneman, D. (eds). (2002) *Heuristics and Biases: The Psychology of Intuitive Judgment*, New York: Cambridge University Press.

Gioia, D.A. and Chittipeddi, K. (1991) 'Sensemaking and Sensegiving in Strategic Change Intuition', *Strategic Management Journal*, Vol. 12, pp. 433–448.

Gioia, D.A., Schultz, M. and Corley, K.G. (2000) 'Organizational identity, image, and adaptive instability', *Academy of Management Review*, 25(1), pp. 63–81.

Glynn, M.A. (2000) 'When cymbals become symbols: Conflict over organizational identity within a symphony orchestra', *Organization Science*, 11(3), pp. 285–298.

Gottschalg, O. and Zollo M. (2007) 'Interest alignment and competitive advantage', *Academy of Management Review*, 32(2), pp. 418–437.

Grant, R.M. (1996) 'Prospering in dynamically-competitive environments: organizational capability as knowledge integration', *Organization Science*, 7(4), pp. 375–387.

Hambrick, D.C., Geletkanycz, M.A. and Fredrickson, J.W. (1993) 'Top executive commitment to the status quo: Some tests of its determinants', *Strategic Management Journal*, Vol. 14, No. 6, pp. 401–418.

Hamel, G. and Prahalad, C.K. (1994) *Competing for the Future*, Boston, MA: Harvard Business School Press.

Hampden-Turner, C. and Trompenaars, F. (2000) *Building Cross-cultural Competence: How to Create Wealth from Conflicting Values*, New Haven: Yale University Press.

Handy, C. (1990) *The Age of Unreason*, Boston, MA: Harvard Business School Press.

Haslam, S.A., Eggins, R.A. and Reynolds, K.J. (2003) 'The ASPIRe model: actualizing social and personal identity resources to enhance organizational outcomes', *Journal of Occupational and Organizational Psychology*, 76, pp. 83–113.

Healey, M.P. and Hodgkinson, G.P. (2008) 'Troubling futures: scenarios and scenario planning for organizational decision making', in: Hodgkinson, G.P. and Starbuck, W.H. (eds.) *The Oxford Handbook of Organizational Decision Making*, Oxford: Oxford University Press, pp. 565–585.

Heath, C. (2010) 'Making the emotional case for change', *McKinsey Quarterly*, March, pp. 88–97.

Helfat, C. and Peteraf, M. (2003) 'The dynamic resource-based view: capability lifecycles', *Strategic Management Journal*, October, Special Issue 24, pp. 997–1010.

Henderson, M.D., Gollwitzer, P.M. and Oettingen, G. (2007) 'Implementation intentions and disengagement from a failing course of action', *Journal of Behavioral Decision Making*, 20(1), pp. 81–102.

Henderson, R.M. and Clark, K.B. (1990) 'Architectural innovation: the reconfiguration of existing product technologies and the failure of established firms', *Administrative Science Quarterly*, 35(1), pp. 9–30.

Hodgkinson, G.P. and Healey, M.P. (2011) 'Psychological foundations of dynamic capabilities: Reflexion and reflection in strategic management', *Strategic Management Journal*, 32(13), pp. 1500–1516.

Hodgkinson, G.P. (1997) 'Cognitive inertia in a turbulent market: the case of U.K. residential estate agents', *Journal of Management Studies*, 34, pp. 921–945.

Hodgkinson, G.P. and Clarke, I. (2007) 'Exploring the cognitive significance of organizational strategizing: a dual process framework and research agenda', *Human Relations*, 60(1), pp. 243–255.

Hodgkinson, G.P. and Healey, M.P. (2008) 'Cognition in organizations', *Annual Review of Psychology*, 59, pp. 387–417.

Hodgkinson, G.P. and Wright, G. (2002) 'Confronting strategic inertia in a top management team: learning from failure', *Organization Studies*, 23, pp. 949–977.

Hodgkinson, G.P., Bown, N.J., Maule, A.J., Glaister, K.W. and Pearman, A.D. (1999) 'Breaking the frame: an analysis of strategic cognition and decision making under uncertainty', *Strategic Management Journal*, 20(10), pp. 977–985.

Hodgkinson, G.P., Langan-Fox, J. and Sadler-Smith, E. (2008) 'Intuition: a fundamental bridging construct in the behavioral sciences', *British Journal of Psychology*, 99(1), pp. 1–27.

Hodgkinson, G.P., Maule, A.J. and Bown, N.J. (2004) 'Causal cognitive mapping in the organizational strategy field: a comparison of alternative elicitation procedures', *Organizational Research Methods*, 7(1), pp. 3–26.

Hodgkinson, G.P., Maule, A.J., Bown, N.J., Pearman, A.D. and Glaister, K.W. (2002) 'Further reflections on the elimination of framing bias in strategic decision making', *Strategic Management Journal*, 23(11), pp. 1069–1076.

Hodgkinson, G.P., Sadler-Smith, G., Burke, L.A., Claxton, G. and Sparrow, P.R. (2009) 'Intuition in organizations: implications for strategic management', *Long Range Planning*, 42, pp. 277–297.

Hofer, C.W. and Schendel, D. (1978) *Strategy Formulation: Analytical Concepts*, St. Paul, MN: West Publishing.

Hogarth, R.M. (1980) *Judgement and Choice: The Psychology of Decision*, Chichester: Wiley.

Hogarth, R.M. (2001) *Educating Intuition*, Chicago, IL: University of Chicago Press.

Hogg, M.A. and Terry, D.J. (2000) 'Social identity and self-categorization processes in organizational contexts', *Academy of Management Review*, 25(1), pp. 121–140.

Huff, A.S. (ed.) (1990) *Mapping Strategic Thought*, Chichester: Wiley.

Huy, Q.N. (1999) 'Emotional capability, emotional intelligence, and radical change', *Academy of Management Review*, 24(2), pp. 325–345.

Huy, Q.N. (2002) 'Emotional balancing of organizational continuity and radical change: the contribution of middle managers', *Administrative Science Quarterly*, 47, pp. 31–69.

Isenberg, D.J. (1984) 'How Senior Managers Think', *Harvard Business Review*, November–December, Vol. 63, No. 6, pp. 81–90.

Ito, T.A., Larsen, J.T., Smith, N.K. and Cacioppo, J.T. (1998) 'Negative information weighs more heavily on the brain: the negativity bias in evaluative categorizations', *Journal of Personality and Social Psychology*, 75(4), pp. 887–900.

Jackson, S.E. and Dutton, J.E. (1988) 'Discerning threats and opportunities', *Administrative Science Quarterly*, 33(3), pp. 370–387.

Janis, I.L. (1989) *Crucial Decisions: Leadership in Policymaking and Crisis Management*, New York: Free Press.

Janis, I.L. and Mann, L. (1977) *Decision Making: A Psychological Analysis of Conflict, Choice, and Commitment*, New York: Free Press.

Jantunen, A. (2005) 'New HRM practices and knowledge utilization', in: *Proceedings of the 5th International Workshop on Human Resource Management,* Seville, Spain.

Jolls, C., Sunstein, C.R. and Thaler, R. (1998) 'A behavioral approach to law and economics', *Stanford Law Review*, 50(5), pp. 1471–1550.

Kagono, T.I., Nonaka, K., Sakakibira, K. and Okumara, A. (1985) *Strategic vs. Evolutionary Management*, Amsterdam: North-Holland.

Kahneman, D. and Klein, G. (2009) 'Conditions for intuitive expertise: a failure to disagree', *American Psychologist*, 64(6), pp. 515–526.

Kahneman, D. and Klein, G. (2010) 'When can you trust your gut?', *McKinsey Quarterly*, March, pp. 58–67.

Kahneman, D. and Lovallo, D. (1993) 'Timid choices and bold forecasts: a cognitive perspective on risk-taking', *Management Science*, 39(1), pp. 17–31.

Kahneman, D. and Tversky, A. (1979) 'Prospect theory: analysis of decision under risk', *Econometrica*, 47(2), pp. 263–291.

Kahneman, D., Ritov, I. and Schkade, D. (1999) 'Economic preferences or attitude expressions? An analysis of dollar responses to public issues', *Journal of Risk and Uncertainty*, 19, pp. 203–235.

Kaplan, S. (2008) 'Cognition, capabilities, and incentives: assessing firm response to the fiber-optic revolution', *Academy of Management Journal*, 51(4), pp. 672–695.

Karlsson, N., Loewenstein, G. and Seppi, D. (2009) 'The ostrich effect: selective attention to information', *Journal of Risk and Uncertainty*, 38, pp. 95–115.

Keegan, W.J. (1983) 'Strategic Market Planning: The Japanese Approach', *International Marketing Review*, Vol. 1, pp. 5–15.

Kirzner, I. (1973) *Competition and Entrepreneurship*, Chicago, IL: University of Chicago Press.

Klein, G.A. (2003) *Intuition at Work*, New York: Doubleday.

Klein, S.B., Rozendal, K. and Cosmides, L. (2002) 'A socialcognitive neuroscience analysis of the self', *Social Cognition*, 20(2), pp. 105–135.

Knight, D., Pearce, C.L., Smith, K.G., Olian, J.D., Sims, H.P, Smith, K.A. and Flood, P. (1999) 'Top Management Team Diversity, Group Process, and Strategic Consensus', *Strategic Management Journal*, Vol. 20, pp. 445–465.

Kogut, B. and Zander, U. (1992) 'Knowledge of the enterprise, combinative capabilities and the replication of technology', *Organizational Science*, 3(3), pp. 383–397.

Ku, G. (2008) 'Learning to de-escalate: the effects of regret in escalation of commitment', *Organizational Behavior and Human Decision Processes*, 105(2), pp. 221–232.

Kuhn, T.S. (1970) *The Structure of Scientific Revolutions,*. Chicago, IL: University of Chicago Press.

Lane, P.J., Koka, B.R. and Pathak, S. (2006) 'The reification of absorptive capacity: a critical review and rejuvenation of the construct', *Academy of Management Review*, 31(4), pp. 833–863.

Langley, A. (1995) 'Between "Paralysis by Analysis" and "Extinction by Instinct"', *Sloan Management Review*, Vol. 36, No. 3, Spring, pp. 63–76.

Lawrence, P.R. and Lorsch, J.W. (1967) *Organization and Environment: Managing Differentiation and Integration*, Boston, MA: Harvard University Press.

Lazonick, W. (2005) 'The innovative firm', in: Fagerberg, J., Mowery, D. and Nelson, R.R. (eds.) *The Oxford Handbook of Innovation*, New York: Oxford University Press, pp. 29–55.

LeDoux, J.E. (2000) 'Emotion circuits in the brain', *Annual Review of Neuroscience*, 23, pp. 155–184.

Lenz, R.T. and Lyles, M. (1985) 'Paralysis by Analysis: Is Your Planning System Becoming Too Rational?', *Long Range Planning*, Vol. 18, No. 4, pp. 64–72.

Leonard-Barton, D. (1995) *Wellsprings of Knowledge-Building and Sustaining the Sources of Innovation*, Boston, MA: Harvard Business School Press.

Levinthal, D.A. and March, J.G. (1993) 'The myopia of learning', *Strategic Management Journal*, 14(4), pp. 95–112.

Levinthal, D.A. and Rerup, C. (2006) 'Crossing an apparent chasm: bridging mindful and less-mindful perspectives on organizational learning', *Organization Science*, 17, pp. 502–513.

Lieberman, M.D. (2000) 'Intuition: a social cognitive neuroscience approach', *Psychological Bulletin*, 126(1), pp. 109–137.

Lieberman, M.D. (2007) 'Social cognitive neuroscience: a review of core processes', *Annual Review of Psychology*, 58, pp. 259–289.

Lieberman, M.D. and Eisenberger, N.I. (2009) 'The pains and pleasures of social life', *Science*, 323, pp. 890–891.

Lieberman, M.D., Gaunt, R., Gilbert, D.T. and Trope, Y. (2002) 'Reflexion and reflection: a social cognitive neuroscience approach to attributional inference', in: *Advances in Experimental Social Psychology* (Vol. 34). San Diego, CA: Academic Press, pp. 199–249.

Lieberman, M.D., Ochsner, K.N., Gilbert, D.T. and Schacter, D.L. (2001) 'Do amnesics exhibit cognitive dissonance reduction? The role of explicit memory and attention in attitude change', *Psychological Science*, 12(2), pp. 135–140.

Lindblom, C.E. (1959) 'The science of "muddling through"', *Public Administration Review*, 19(2), pp. 79–88.

Loewenstein, G. (1996) 'Out of control: visceral influences on behavior', *Organizational Behavior and Human Decision Processes*, 65, pp. 272–292.

Loewenstein, G. and Small, D.A. (2007) 'The Scarecrow and the Tin Man: the vicissitudes of human sympathy and caring', *Review of General Psychology*, 11(2), pp. 112–126.

Loewenstein, G., Rick, S. and Cohen, J.D. (2008) 'Neuroeconomics', *Annual Review of Psychology*, 59, pp. 647–672.

Loewenstein, G., Weber, E.U., Hsee, C.K. and Welch, N. (2001) 'Risk as feelings', *Psychological Bulletin*, 127(2), pp. 267–286.

Lord, R.G., Diefendorff, J.M., Schmidt, A.M. and Hall, R.J. (2010) 'Self-regulation at work', *Annual Review of Psychology*, 61, pp. 543–568.

Louis, M.R. and Sutton, R.I. (1991) 'Switching cognitive gears: from habits of mind to active thinking', *Human Relations*, 44(1), pp. 55–76.

Lovallo, D. and Sibony, O. (2010) 'The case for behavioral strategy', *McKinsey Quarterly*, March, pp. 30–43.

Lyles, M.A. and Schwenk, C.R. (1992) 'Top Management, Strategy and Organizational Knowledge Structures', *Journal of Management Studies*, Vol. 29, pp. 155–174.

Mansfield, E., Rapoport, J., Schnee, J., Wagner, S. and Hamburger, M. (1971) *Research and Innovation in the Modern Corporation*, New York: WW Norton.

March, J.G. (1991) 'Exploration and exploitation in organizational learning', *Organizational Science*, 2(1), pp. 71–87.

March, J.G. and Simon, H.A. (1993) *Organizations*, Second Edition, Cambridge, MA: Blackwell.

Martin, R. (2007) *The Opposable Mind: How Successful Leaders Win through Integrative Thinking*, Cambridge, MA: Harvard Business School Book Press.

Mason, R.O. and Mitroff, I.I. (1981) *Challenging Strategic Planning Assumptions*, New York: Wiley.

McCaskey, M.B. (1982) *The Executive Challenge: Managing Change and Ambiguity*, Boston, MA: Pitman.

Mintzberg, H. (1994) *The Rise and Fall of Strategic Planning*, New York: The Free Press.

Mintzberg, H., Ahlstrand, B. and Lampel, J. (1998) *Strategy Safari: A Guided Tour through the Wilds of Strategic Management*, New York: The Free Press.

Mitchell, W. (1991) 'Dual clocks: entry order influences on industry incumbent and newcomer market share and survival when specialized assets retain their value', *Strategic Management Journal*, 12(2), pp. 85–100.

Nag, R., Corley, K.G. and Gioia, D.A. (2007) 'The intersection of organizational identity, knowledge, and practice: attempting strategic change via knowledge grafting', *Academy of Management Journal*, 50(4), pp. 821–847.

Nelson, R.R. (2005) *Technology, Institutions, and Economic Growth*, Cambridge, MA: Harvard University Press.

Nelson, R.R. and Winter, S.G. (1982) *An Evolutionary Theory of Economic Change*, Cambridge, MA: Harvard University Press.

Nelson, R.R. and Winter, S.G. (2002) 'Evolutionary theorizing in economics', *Journal of Economic Perspectives*, 16(2), pp. 23–46.

Nelson, T.O. (1996) 'Consciousness and metacognition', *American Psychologist*, 51(2), pp. 102–116.

Nonaka, I. (1991) 'The Knowledge-Creating Company', *Harvard Business Review*, Vol. 69, No. 6, November–December, pp. 96–104.

Nonaka, I. and Johanson, J.K. (1985) 'Japanese Management: What about "Hard" Skills?', *Academy of Management Review*, Vol. 10, No. 2, pp. 181–191.

Nonaka, I. and Takeuchi, H. (1995) *The Knowledge Creating Company*, New York: Oxford University Press.

Nonaka, I. and Toyama, R. (2007) 'Strategic management as distributed practical wisdom (phronesis)', *Industrial and Corporate Change*, 16(3), pp. 371–394.

Noorderhaven, N.G. (1995) *Strategic Decision Making*, Wokingham: Addison-Wesley.

Ocasio, W. (1997) 'Towards an Attention-Based View of the Firm', *Strategic Management Journal*, Vol. 18, Special Issue, July, pp. 187–206.

Ochsner, K.N. and Lieberman, M.D. (2001) 'The emergence of social cognitive neuroscience', *American Psychologist*, 56(9), pp. 717–734.

Ochsner, K.N., Bunge, S.A., Gross, J.J. and Gabrieli, J.D.E. (2002) 'Rethinking feelings: an MRI study of the cognitive regulation of emotion', *Journal of Cognitive Neuroscience*, 14(8), pp. 1215–1229.

Packard, D. 1995. *The HP Way: How Bill Hewlett and I Built Our Company*, New York: HarperCollins.

Pascale, R.T. and Athos, A.G. (1981) 'The Art of Japanese Management', *Business Horizons*, 24(6), pp. pp. 83–85.

Pascale, R.T. (1984) 'Perspectives on Strategy: The Real Story Behind Honda's Success', *California Management Review*, Vol. 26, No. 3, Spring, pp. 47–72.

Peteraf, M. and Shanley, M. (1997) 'Getting to know you: a theory of strategic group identity', *Strategic Management Journal*, Summer, Special Issue 18, pp. 165–186.

Polanyi, M. (1966) *The Tacit Dimension*, London: Routledge & Kegan Paul.

Porac, J.F., Thomas, H., Wilson, F., Paton, D. and Kanfer, A. (1995) 'Rivalry and the industry model of Scottish knitwear producers', *Administrative Science Quarterly*, 40(2), pp. 203–227.

Porter, M.E. (1980) *Competitive Strategy: Techniques for Analyzing Industries and Competitors*.

Prahalad, C.K. (2004) 'The blinders of dominant logic', *Long Range Planning*, 37, pp. 171–179.

Prahalad, C.K. and Bettis, R.A. (1986) 'The Dominant Logic: A New Linkage between Diversity and Performance', *Strategic Management Journal*, Vol. 7, No. 6, November–December, pp. 485–601.

Redding, S.G. (1980) 'Cognition as an Aspect of Culture and its Relationship to Management Processes: An Exploratory View of the Chinese Case', *Journal of Management Studies*, Vol. 17, May, pp. 127–148.

Reger, R.K. and Palmer, T.B. (1996) 'Managerial categorization of competitors: using old maps to navigate new environments', *Organization Science*, 7(1), pp. 22–39.

Rittel, H. (1972) 'On the Planning Crisis: Systems Analysis of the "First and Second Generations"', *Bedriftsokonomen*, No. 8, pp. 390–396.

Rosenkopf, L. and Nerkar, A. (2001) 'Beyond local search: boundary-spanning, exploration, and impact in the optical disk industry', *Strategic Management Journal*, 22(4), pp. 287–306.

Rottenstreich, Y. and Hsee, C.K. (2001) 'Money, kisses, and electric shocks: on the affective psychology of risk', *Psychological Science*, 12(3), pp. 185–190.

Rumelt, R. (1995) 'Inertia and transformation', in: Montgomery, C. (ed.) *Resource Based and Evolutionary Theories of the Enterprise*, Boston, MA: Kluwer Academic, pp. 101–132.

Russo, J.E. and Schoemaker, P.J.H. (1989) *Decision Traps*, New York: Doubleday.

Sadler-Smith, E. (2004) 'Cognitive style and the management of small and medium-sized enterprises', *Organization Studies*, 25(2), pp. 155–181.

Sadler-Smith, E. (2010) *The Intuitive Mind: Profiting From the Power of Your Sixth Sense*, Chichester: Wiley.

Sanfey, A.G., Rilling, J.K., Aronson, J.A., Nystrom, L.E. and Cohen, J.D. (2003) 'The neural basis of economic decision-making in the ultimatum game', *Science*, 300(5626), pp. 1755–1758.

Scheepers, D. and Ellemers, N. (2005) 'When the pressure is up: the assessment of social identity threat in low and high status groups', *Journal of Experimental Social Psychology*, 41(2), pp. 192–200.

Schein, E.H. (1985) *Organizational Culture and Leadership*, San Francisco: Jossey-Bass.

Schneider, S.C. (1989) 'Strategy Formulation: The Impact of National Culture', *Organization Studies*, Vol. 10, No. 2, pp. 149–168.

Schneider, W. and Shiffrin, R.M. (1977) 'Controlled and automatic human information processing: 1. detection, search, and attention', *Psychological Review*, 84(1), pp. 1–66.

Schoemaker, P.J.H. (1993) 'Multiple scenario development: its conceptual and behavioral foundation', *Strategic Management Journal*, 14(3), pp. 193–213.

Schoemaker, P.J.H. and Russo, J.E. (1993) 'A Pyramid of Decision Approaches', *California Management Review*, Vol. 36, No. 1, Fall, pp. 9–32.

Schumpeter, J. (1934) *The Theory of Economic Development*, Cambridge, MA: Harvard University Press.

Schwenk, C.R. (1984) 'Cognitive Simplification Processes in Strategic Decision-Making', *Strategic Management Journal*, Vol. 5, No. 2, April–June, pp. 111–128.

Schwenk, C.R. (1986) 'Information, cognitive biases, and commitment to a course of action', *Academy of Management Review*, 11(2), pp. 298–310.

Schwenk, C.R. (1988) *The Essence of Strategic Decision Making*, Lexington, MA: Lexington Books.

Shane, S. (2003) *A General Theory of Entrepreneurship*, Northampton, MA: Edward Elgar.

Simon, H.A. (1957) *Models of Man*, New York: Wiley.

Simon, H.A. (1969) *The Sciences of the Artificial*, Cambridge, MA: MIT Press.

Simon, H.A. (1972) 'Theories of Bounded Rationality', in: C. McGuire and R. Radner (eds.) *Decision and Organization*, Amsterdam, pp. 161–176.

Simon, H.A. (1987) 'Making Management Decisions: The Role of Intuition and Emotion', *Academy of Management Executive*, Vol. 1, No. 1, pp. 57–64.

Simon, H.A. (1993) 'Altruism and economics', *American Economic Review*, 83(2), pp. 156–161.

Sivanathan, N., Molden, D.C., Galinsky, A.D. and Ku, G. (2008) 'The promise and peril of self-affirmation in de-escalation of commitment', *Organizational Behavior and Human Decision Processes*, 107(1), pp. 1–14.

Slovic, P., Finucane, M.L., Peters, E. and MacGregor, D.G. (2004) 'Risk as analysis and risk as feelings: some thoughts about affect, reason, risk, and rationality', *Risk Analysis*, 24(2), pp. 311–322.

Smircich, L. and Stubbart, C. (1985) 'Strategic Management in an Enacted World', *Academy of Management Review*, Vol. 10, No. 4, pp. 724–736.

Sorrell, M., Komisar, R. and Mulcahy, A. (2010) 'How we do it: three executives reflect on strategic decision making', *McKinsey Quarterly*, 2, pp. 46–57.

Starbuck, W. and Milliken, F. (1988) 'Challenger: Fine-Tuning the Odds Until Something Breaks', *Journal of Management Studies*, Vol. 25, No. 4, July.

Staw, B.M. (1976) 'Knee-deep in the big muddy: a study of escalating commitment to a chosen course of action', *Organizational Behavior and Human Performance*, 16(1), pp. 27–44.

Staw, B.M. and Ross, J. (1987) 'Behavior in escalation situations: antecedents, prototypes, and solutions', *Research in Organizational Behavior*, 9, pp. 39–78.

Staw, B.M., Sandelands, L.E. and Dutton, J.E. (1981) 'Threatrigidity effects in organizational behavior: A multilevel analysis', *Administrative Science Quarterly*, 26, pp. 501–524.

Sutcliffe, K.M. and Huber, G.P. (1998) 'Firm and Industry Determinants of Executive Perceptions of the Environment', *Strategic Management Journal*, Vol. 19, pp. 793–807.

Taylor, F.W. (1911) *Principles of Scientific Management*, New York, London: Harper & Brothers.

Teece, D.J. (1977) 'Technology transfer by multinational enterprises: the resource cost of transferring technological know-how', *Economic Journal*, 87, (June), pp. 242–261.

Teece, D.J. (1980) 'Economies of scope and the scope of the enterprise', *Journal of Economic Behavior and Organization*, 1(3), pp. 223–247.

Teece, D.J. (1981) 'Internal organization and economic performance: an empirical analysis of the profitability of principal enterprises', *Journal of Industrial Economics*, 30(2), pp. 173–199.

Teece, D.J. (1986) 'Profiting from technological innovation', *Research Policy*, 15(6), pp. 285–305.

Teece, D.J. (2000) *Managing Intellectual Capital: Organizational, Strategic, and Policy Dimensions*, Oxford: Oxford University Press.

Teece, D.J. (2003) 'Expert talent and the design of (professional services) enterprises', *Industrial and Corporate Change*, 12(4), pp. 895–916.

Teece, D.J. (2007) 'Explicating dynamic capabilities: the nature and microfoundations of (sustainable) enterprise performance', *Strategic Management Journal*, 28(13), pp. 1319–1350.

Teece, D.J. and Pisano, G. (1994) 'The dynamic capabilities of enterprises: an introduction', *Industrial and Corporate Change*, 3(3), pp. 537–556.

Teece, D.J., Pisano, G, and Shuen, A. (1997) 'Dynamic capabilities and strategic management', *Strategic Management Journal*, 18(7), pp. 509–533.

Teece, D.J., Pisano, G. and Shuen, A. (1990a) Enterprise capabilities, resources and the concept of strategy. Consortium on Competitiveness and Cooperation, Working paper CCC 90-8, Institute of Management, Innovation and Organization, University of California, Berkeley, CA.

Teece, D.J., Pisano, G. and Shuen, A. (1990b) 'Firm capabilities, resources and the concept of strategy', *Economic Analysis and Policy Working Paper EAP-38*, Institute of Management, Innovation and Organization, University of California, Berkeley, CA.

Trice, H.M. and Beyer, J.M. (1993) *The Cultures of Work Organizations*, Englewood Cliffs: Prentice Hall.

Tripsas, M. and Gavetti, G. (2000) 'Capabilities, cognition, and inertia: evidence from digital imaging', *Strategic Management Journal*, 21(10/11), pp. 1147–1161.

Tushman, M. and Anderson, P. (1986) 'Technological discontinuities and organizational environments', *Administration Science Quarterly*, 31, pp. 439–465.

Tversky, A. and Kahneman, D. (1986) 'Rational Choice and the Framing of Decisions', *Journal of Business*, Vol. 59, No. 4, pp. 251–278.

Von Winterfeldt, D. and Edwards, W. (1986) *Decision Analysis and Behavioural Research*, Cambridge: Cambridge University Press.

Walsh, J. (1995) 'Managerial and Organizational Cognition: Notes from a Trip Down Memory Lane', *Organization Science*, Vol. 6, pp. 280–321.

Weick, K.E. (1979) *The Social Psychology of Organizing*, New York: Random House.

Weick, K.E. and Bourgnon, M.G. (1986) 'Organizations as Cognitive Maps', in: H.P Sims Jr. and D.A. Gioia (eds.) *The Thinking Organization*, San Francisco, CA: Jossey-Bass.

Welch, J. and Byrne, J.A. (2001) *Jack: Straight from the Gut*, New York: Warner Books.

Wernerfelt, B. (1984) 'A resource-based view of the firm', *Strategic Management Journal*, 5(2), pp. 171–180.

Williamson, O.E. (1975) *Markets and Hierarchies*, New York: Free Press.

Wong, K.F.E., Kwong, J.Y.Y. and Ng, C.K. (2008) 'When thinking rationally increases biases: the role of rational thinking style in escalation of commitment', *Applied Psychology: An International Review*, 57(2), pp. 246–271.

Wong, K.F.E., Yik, M. and Kwong, J.Y.Y. (2006) 'Understanding the emotional aspects of escalation of commitment: the role of negative affect', *Journal of Applied Psychology*, 91(2), pp. 282–297.

Wright, G. and Goodwin, P. (2002) 'Eliminating a framing bias by using simple instructions to "think harder" and respondents with managerial experience: comment on "breaking the frame"', *Strategic Management Journal*, 23(11), pp. 1059–1067.

Zajonc, R.B. (1980) 'Preferences need no inferences', *American Psychologist*, 35, pp. 151–175.

Zhang, L.Q. and Baumeister, R.F. (2006) 'Your money or your self-esteem: threatened egotism promotes costly entrapment in losing endeavors', *Personality and Social Psychology Bulletin*, 32(7), pp. 881–893.

Zollo, M. and Winter, S.G. (2002) 'Deliberate learning and the evolution of dynamic capabilities', *Organization Science*, 13(3), pp. 339–351.

MISSIONING AND VISIONING

I prefer to be a dreamer among the humblest, with visions to be realized, than lord among those without dreams and desires.

Khalil Gibran (1886–1931); Lebanese-American artist, poet and writer

INTRODUCTION

Corporate mission is a rather elusive concept, often used to refer to the woolly platitudes on the first few pages of annual reports. To many people, mission statements are lists of lofty principles that have potential public relations value, but have little bearing on actual business, let alone impact on the process of strategy formation. Yet, while frequently employed in this superficial manner, a corporate mission can be very concrete and play an important role in determining strategic actions.

A good way to explain the term's meaning is to go back to its etymological roots. 'Mission' comes from the Latin word *mittere*, which means 'to send' (Cummings and Davies, 1994). A mission is some task, duty or purpose that 'sends someone on their way' – a motive or driver propelling someone in a certain direction. Hence, 'corporate mission' can be understood as the basic drivers sending the corporation along its way. The corporate mission consists of the fundamental principles that mobilize and propel the firm in a particular direction.

A concept that is often confused with mission is vision. Individuals or organizations have a vision if they picture a future state of affairs they wish to achieve (from the Latin *vide* – to see; Cummings and Davies, 1994). While the corporate mission outlines the fundamental principles guiding strategic choices, a strategic vision outlines the desired future at which the company hopes to arrive. In other words, vision provides a business ambition while mission provides business principles (see Figure 3.1).

Generally, a strategic vision is a type of aim that is less specific than a short-term target or longer-term objective. Vision is usually defined as a broad conception of a desirable future state, of which the details remain to be determined (e.g. Senge, 1990). As such, strategic vision can play a similar role as corporate mission, pointing the firm in a particular direction and motivating individuals to work together towards a shared end.

The corporate mission and strategic vision contribute to 'sending the firm in a particular direction' by influencing the firm's strategy. To understand how mission and vision impact strategy, three topics require closer attention. First, it is necessary to know what types of 'fundamental principles' actually make up a corporate mission. These elements of corporate mission will be described below. Second, it is important to distinguish between different envisioning processes to understand how the vision impacts strategy. Third, it needs to be examined what types of roles are played by a corporate mission and strategic vision in the strategy formation process. These functions of corporate mission and strategic vision will also be described (see Figure 3.2).

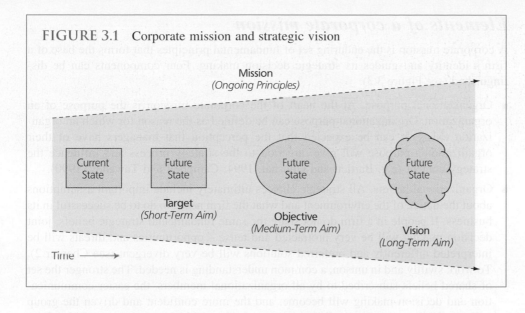

FIGURE 3.1 Corporate mission and strategic vision

Besides the 'what' of corporate mission, it is equally important to explore the 'who' – who should determine a corporate mission. The implicit assumption is often that executives are the primary 'strategic actors' responsible for setting the direction of the firm. But in fact, their actions are formally monitored and controlled by the board of directors. In this way, the direction of the firm must be understood as a result of the interaction between the executives and the board of directors. As the name would imply, directors have an important influence on direction.

The activities of the board of directors are referred to as 'corporate governance' – directors govern the strategic choices and actions of the management of a firm. Due to their importance in setting the corporate mission and strategy, their input will be examined here as well. First, the various functions of corporate governance are reviewed. Then it will be examined what the different forms of corporate governance are, as this can significantly influence the mission, vision and strategy of the organization (see Figure 3.2).

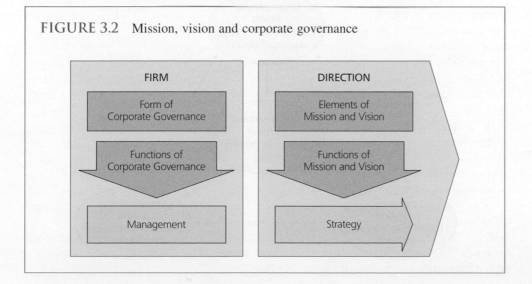

FIGURE 3.2 Mission, vision and corporate governance

Elements of a corporate mission

A corporate mission is the enduring set of fundamental principles that forms the base of a firm's identity and guides its strategic decision making. Four components can be distinguished (see Figure 3.3):

■ Organizational purpose. At the heart of the corporate mission is the purpose of an organization. Organizational purpose can be defined as the reason for which an organization exists. It can be expected that the perception that managers have of their organization's purpose will give direction to the strategy process and influence the strategy content (e.g. Bartlett and Ghoshal, 1994; Campbell and Tawadey, 1990).

■ Organizational beliefs. All strategic choices ultimately include important assumptions about the nature of the environment and what the firm needs to do to be successful in its business. If people in a firm do not share the same fundamental strategic beliefs, joint decision making will be very protracted and tense – opportunities and threats will be interpreted differently and preferred solutions will be very divergent (see Chapter 2). To work swiftly and in unison, a common understanding is needed. The stronger the set of shared beliefs subscribed to by all organizational members, the easier communication and decision making will become, and the more confident and driven the group will be. While researchers refer to the organizational ideology ('system of ideas') as their 'collective cognitive map' (Axelrod, 1976), 'dominant logic' (Prahalad and Bettis, 1986) or 'team mental model' (Klimoski and Mohammed, 1994), companies themselves usually simply speak of their beliefs or philosophy.

■ Organizational values. Each person in an organization can have their own set of values, shaping what they believe to be good and just. Yet, when an organization's members share a common set of values, determining what they see as worthwhile activities, ethical behaviour and moral responsibilities, this can have a strong impact on the strategic direction (e.g. Falsey, 1989; Hoffman, 1989). Such widely embraced organizational values also contribute to a clear sense of organizational identity, attracting

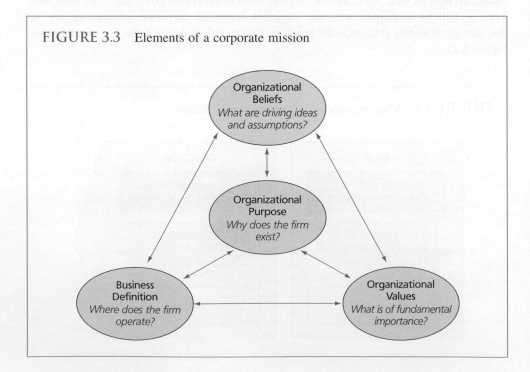

FIGURE 3.3   Elements of a corporate mission

some individuals, while repelling others. Although it can be useful to explicitly state the values guiding the organization, to be influential they must become embodied in the organization's culture (e.g. McCoy, 1985; Collins and Porras, 1996).

- Business definitions. For some firms, any business is good business, as long as they can make a reasonable return on investment. Yet, if any business is fine, the firm will lack a sense of direction. In practice, most firms have a clearer identity, which they derive from being active in a particular line of business. For these firms, having a delimiting definition of the business they wish to be in strongly focuses the direction in which they develop. Their business definition functions as a guiding principle, helping to distinguish opportunities from diversions (e.g. Abell, 1980; Pearce, 1982). Of course, while a clear business definition can focus the organization's attention and efforts, it can likewise lead to short-sightedness and the missing of new business developments (e.g. Ackoff, 1974; Levitt, 1960).

The strength of a corporate mission will depend on whether these four elements fit together and are mutually reinforcing (Campbell and Yeung, 1991). When a consistent and compelling corporate mission is formed, this can infuse the organization with a sense of mission, creating an emotional bond between organizational members and energizing them to work according to the mission.

Elements of a strategic vision

A strategic vision is the desired future state of an organization. Also termed 'strategic intent' (Hamel *et al.*, 1989) and 'envisioned future' (Collins and Porras, 1996), a strategic vision is built on four components (Figure 3.4):

- Envisioned contextual environment. The many contextual factors that influence the future of the company can be roughly split into socio-cultural, economic, political/ regulatory and technological factors. Although developments in the contextual

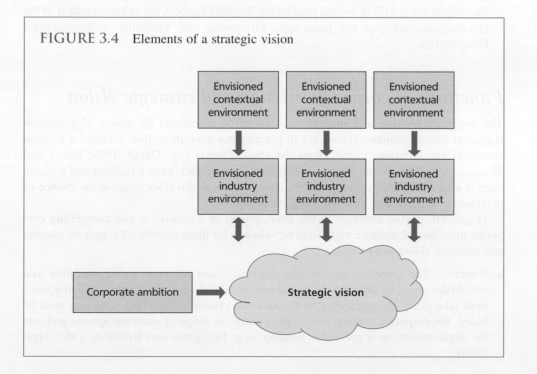

FIGURE 3.4   Elements of a strategic vision

environment cannot be predicted, some factors can be expected to change the company's business. For example, most companies expect an increasing economic importance of emerging countries, and believe that growing environmental awareness will lead to technological innovations. In developing a strategic vision, the contextual developments that are relevant to the company's business are described, and the future state of the contextual factors is envisioned.

■ Envisioned industry environment. The development of contextual factors impact the company's industry environment: suppliers, buyers, incumbent rivals, new entrants, and substitutes and complementors. For example, competitors from emerging countries are expected to enter the industry, and alternative sources of energy are likely to replace fossil fuels in the production process. Some of these developments show up in statistics, strategic intelligence reports, company analyses and other sources of information, while others are based on insider's information. In developing a strategic vision, the relevant industry developments are described, and the future state of the industry environment is envisioned.

■ Desired future organizational position. Based on the envisioned contextual and industry environment, the organization describes its desired position in the future. For example, a company may strive for an industry leadership position by forming an alliance with a strong partner in emerging countries and by implementing new sustainable production technologies. The desired position reflects the company's ambitions, and is translated into long term objectives. In a strategic vision, the desired position of the company in the future is described, and the long term objectives are formulated.

■ Time horizon. When developing a strategic vision, leaders must determine how many years ahead the future position will be envisioned. In fact, the time horizon of company visions differs significantly. For some companies three years is long term, while others develop visions of 30 years or longer. Many factors determine the time horizon of a company's strategic vision, including industry characteristics. For example, the upstream oil industry requires long-term thinking, as it take dozens of years between the first exploratory drilling and oil production. Another factor is the cultural context of the company leaders (see the paragraph 'Missioning and Visioning in International Perspective).

Functions of corporate mission and strategic vision

The corporate mission and strategic vision can be articulated by means of a mission statement and a company vision, but in practice not everything that is called a mission statement and company vision meets the above criteria (e.g. David, 1989; Piercy and Morgan, 1994; Collins and Porras, 1996). Firms can, in fact, have a mission and a vision even if it has not been explicitly written down, although this does increase the chance of divergent interpretations within the organization.

In general, paying attention to the development of a consistent and compelling corporate mission and strategic vision can be valuable for three reasons. A corporate mission and strategic vision can provide:

■ Direction. The corporate mission and strategic vision can point the organization in a certain direction, by defining the boundaries within which strategic choices and actions must take place. By specifying the fundamental principles on which strategies must be based, the corporate mission and strategy limit the scope of strategic options and sets the organization on a particular heading (e.g. Bourgeois and Brodwin, 1983; Hax, 1990).

- Legitimization. The corporate mission and strategic vision can convey to all stakeholders inside and outside the company that the organization is pursuing valuable activities in a proper way. By specifying the business philosophy that will guide the company, the chances can be increased that stakeholders will accept, support and trust the organization (e.g. Klemm, Sanderson and Luffman, 1991; Freeman and Gilbert, 1988).

- Motivation. The corporate mission and strategic vision can go a step further than legitimization, by actually inspiring individuals to work together in a particular way. By specifying the fundamental principles driving organizational actions, an *esprit de corps* can evolve, with the powerful capacity to motivate people over a prolonged period of time (e.g. Campbell and Yeung, 1991; Peters and Waterman, 1982).

Especially these last two functions of a corporate mission and strategic vision divide both management theorists and business practitioners. What is seen as a legitimate and motivating organizational purpose is strongly contested. What the main factors of disagreement are is examined in a later section of this chapter.

Functions of corporate governance

The subject of corporate governance, as opposed to corporate management, deals with the issue of governing the strategic choices and actions of top management. Popularly stated, corporate governance is about managing top management – building in checks and balances to ensure that the senior executives pursue strategies that are in accordance with the corporate mission. Corporate governance encompasses all tasks and activities that are intended to supervise and steer the behaviour of top management.

In the common definition, corporate governance 'addresses the issues facing boards of directors' (Tricker, 1994: xi). In this view, corporate governance is the task of the directors and therefore attention must be paid to their roles and responsibilities (e.g. Cochran and Wartick, 1994; Keasey, Thompson and Wright, 1997). Others have argued that this definition is too narrow, and that in practice there are more forces that govern the activities of top management. In this broader view, boards of directors are only a part of the governance system. For instance, regulation by local and national authorities, as well as pressure from societal groups, can function as checks and balances, limiting top management's discretion (e.g. Mintzberg, 1984; Demb and Neubauer, 1992). Whether employing a narrow or broad definition, three important corporate governance functions can be distinguished (adapted from Tricker, 1994):

- Forming function. The first function of corporate governance is to influence the forming of the corporate mission. The task of corporate governance is shaping, articulating and communicating the fundamental principles that will drive the organization's activities. Determining the purpose of the organization and setting priorities among claimants are part of the forming function. The board of directors can conduct this task by, for example, questioning the basis of strategic choices, influencing the business philosophy, and explicitly weighing the advantages and disadvantages of the firm's strategies for various constituents (e.g. Freeman and Reed, 1983, Reading 3.2).

- Performance function. The second function of corporate governance is to contribute to the strategy process with the intention of improving the future performance of the corporation. The task of corporate governance is to judge strategy initiatives brought forward by top management or to actively participate in strategy development. The board of directors can conduct this task by, for example, engaging in strategy discussions; acting as a sounding board for top management; and networking to secure the support of vital stakeholders (e.g. Baysinger and Hoskisson, 1990; Donaldson and Davis, 1995; Zahra and Pearce, 1989).

■ Conformance function. The third function of corporate governance is to ensure corporate conformance to the stated mission and strategy. The task of corporate governance is to monitor whether the organization is undertaking activities as promised and whether performance is satisfactory. Where management is found lacking, it is a function of corporate governance to press for changes. The board of directors can conduct this task by, for example, auditing the activities of the corporation; questioning and supervising top management; determining remuneration and incentive packages; and even appointing new managers (e.g. Parkinson, 1993; Spencer, 1983).

These functions give the board of directors considerable influence in determining and realizing the corporate mission. As such, they have the ultimate power to decide on the organizational purpose. Therefore, it is not surprising that the question to whom these functions should be given is considered extremely important.

Forms of corporate governance

There is considerable disagreement on how boards of directors should be organized and run. Currently, each country has its own system of corporate governance and the international differences are large. Yet even within many countries, significant disagreements are discernible. In designing a corporate governance regime, three characteristics of boards of directors are of particular importance (adapted from Tricker, 1994):

■ Board structure. Internationally, there are major differences between countries requiring a two-tier board structure (e.g. Austria, China, Germany, the Netherlands and Finland), countries with a one-tier board (e.g. Britain, Canada, Finland, Greece, India, Singapore, Spain, Sweden, Turkey, United States), and countries in which companies are free to choose (e.g. Czech Republic, Denmark, Italy, Japan, France, Slovenia and Switzerland). In a two-tier system there is a formal division of power, with a management board made up of the top executives and a distinct supervisory board made up of non-executives with the task of monitoring and steering the management board. In a one-tier (or unitary) board system, executive and non-executive (outside) directors sit together on one board (see Figure 3.5).

■ Board membership. The composition of boards of directors can vary sharply from company to company and from country to country. Some differences are due to legal requirements that are not the same internationally. For instance, in Germany by law half of the membership of a supervisory board must represent labour, while the other half represents the shareholders. In French companies labour representatives are given observer status on the board. In China, most of the supervisory board members occupy positions in the Chinese Communist Party (Yun and Tan, 2011: 14). In other countries there are no legal imperatives, yet differences have emerged. In some cases outside (non-executive) directors from other companies are common, while in other nations fewer outsiders are involved. Even within countries, differences can be significant, especially with regard to the number, stature and independence of outside (non-executive) directors.

■ Board tasks. The tasks and authority of boards of directors also differ quite significantly between companies. In some cases boards meet infrequently and are merely asked to vote on proposals. Such boards have little formal or informal power to contradict the will of the CEO. In other companies, boards meet regularly and play a more active role in corporate governance, by formulating proposals; proactively selecting new top managers; and determining objectives and incentives. Normally, the power of outside (non-executive) directors to monitor and steer a company only partly depends on their formally defined tasks and authority. To a large degree their impact is determined by how proactive they define their own role.

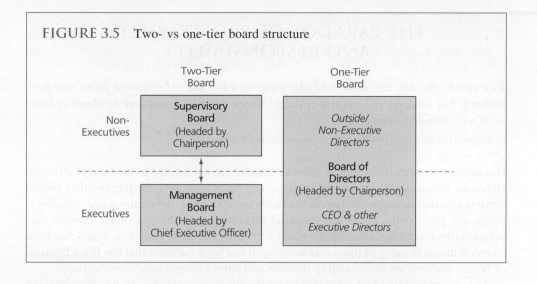

FIGURE 3.5 Two- vs one-tier board structure

The question in the context of this chapter is how a board of directors should be run to ensure that the organization's mission is best achieved. What should be the structure, membership and tasks of the board of directors, to realize the ends for which the organization exists?

THE ISSUE OF ORGANIZATIONAL PURPOSE

For many years there has been a lack of attention to the subject of organizational purpose in the strategic management literature. This might be due to the widespread assumption that it is obvious why business organizations exist. Some writers might have avoided the topic because it is highly value-laden and somehow outside the realm of strategic management. In recent years, however, the subject of organizational purpose has gained increased interest as a result of a number of developments, such as the financial crisis and the increased attention for corporate social responsibility and environmental sustainability.

Managers must constantly make choices and seek solutions based on an understanding of what their organization is intended to achieve. It is hardly possible to avoid taking a stance on what they judge to be the purpose of their organization. They are confronted with many different claimants who believe that the firm exists to serve their interests. Demands are placed on the firm by shareholders, employees, suppliers, customers, governments and communities, forcing managers to weigh whose interests should receive priority over others. Even when explicit demands are not voiced, managers must still determine who will be the main beneficiary of the value-creation activities of the firm.

Determining the organizational purpose is a challenging task, not least because there are so many different views on how it should be done. In this chapter, the issue of organizational purpose will be explored in more detail, with the intention of uncovering the opposite perspectives on the subject of organizational purpose that lie at the heart of the divergent opinions.

THE PARADOX OF PROFITABILITY AND RESPONSIBILITY

The earth, the air, the land and the water are not an inheritance from our fore fathers, but on loan from our children. So we have to handover to them at least as it was handed over to us.
Mahatma Gandhi (1869–1948); Indian politician and lawyer

Discussions on what firms should strive to achieve are not limited to the field of strategy. Given the influential position of business organizations in society, the purpose they should serve is also discussed by theorists in the fields of economics, political science, sociology, ethics and philosophy. Since the industrial revolution, and the rise of the modern corporation, the role of business organizations within the 'political economic order' has been a central theme in many of the social sciences. It has been the topic that has filled libraries of books, inspired society-changing theories and stirred deep-rooted controversies.

The enormous impact of corporations on the functioning of society has also attracted political parties, labour unions, community representatives, environmentalists, the media and the general public to the debate. All take a certain position on the role that business organizations should play within society and the duties that they ought to shoulder. Here, too, the disagreements can be heated, often spilling over from the political arena and negotiating tables into the streets.

In countries with a market economy, it is generally agreed that companies should pursue strategies that ensure economic profitability, but that they have certain social responsibilities that must be fulfilled as well. This is, however, where the consensus ends. Opinions differ sharply with regard to the relative importance of profitability and responsibility. Some people subscribe to the view that profitability is the very purpose of economic organizations and that the only social responsibility of a firm is to pursue profitability within the boundaries of the law. However, other people argue that business corporations are not only economic entities, but also social institutions, embedded in a social environment, which represents significant social responsibilities. In this view, organizations are morally obliged to behave responsibly towards society and all parties with a stake in the activities of the firm, and profitability is only a means to fulfil this duty.

Most executives accept that both economic profitability and social responsibility are valuable goals to pursue. Yet, as organizational purpose, profitability and responsibility are at least partially contradictory. If managers strive towards profit maximization, shareholders might be enamoured, but this will bring executives into conflict with the optimization of benefits for other stakeholders. In other words, to a certain extent there is a tension between profitability and responsibility (e.g. Cannon, 1992; Demb and Neubauer, 1992; Drucker, 1984; Yoshimori, 1995).

The demand for economic profitability

It is clear that business organizations must be profitable to survive. Yet simple profitability, that is having higher income than costs, is not sufficient. To be an attractive investment, a company must earn a higher return on the shareholders' equity than could be realized if the money were deposited in the bank. Put differently, investors must have a financial incentive to run a commercial risk; otherwise they could just as well bring their money to the bank or buy low risk bonds.

Yet, offsetting the risk carried by investors is but a small part of the larger picture. Once a corporation has established a track record of profitability, this inspires trust among financiers. Such trust makes it much easier to raise new capital, either through borrowing (at more attractive rates) or by issuing new shares. And of course, new capital can be used to further the competitive objectives of the organization. Where companies have not been particularly profitable in the past, and cannot authoritatively project an attractive level of profitability in the future, they will find it difficult or virtually impossible to find new financing. This can significantly weaken the position of the firm and undermine its long-term competitiveness.

For publicly traded corporations, strong profitability is usually reflected in higher share prices, which is not only beneficial to the shareholders at that moment, but also makes it easier to acquire other firms and to pay with shares. Moreover, a high share price is the best defence against a hostile takeover and the best negotiating chip for a friendly one. In both publicly and privately held companies, retained profits can also be an important source of funds for new investments.

In short, profitability is not only a *result*, but also a *source*, of competitive power. Profitability provides a company with the financial leeway to improve its competitive position and pursue its ambitions.

The demand for societal responsibility

As economic entities engaging in formalized arrangements with employees, suppliers, buyers and government agencies, corporations have the legal responsibility to abide by the stipulations outlined in their contracts. Equally, they are bound to stay within the 'letter of the law' in each jurisdiction in which they operate. However, being good corporate citizens entails more than just staying out of court.

Companies are more than just 'economic machines' regulated by legal contracts. They are also networks of people, working together towards a common goal. And as members of a social group, people within a company need to develop a sense of 'community' if they are to function properly. One of the most basic needs is to build a level of trust among people – a feeling of security that each individual's interests will be taken into account. Trust evolves where people feel certain that others will behave in a responsible manner, instead of letting their own self-interest prevail without limitation. Once there is enough trust between people, they can engage in productive teamwork and invest in their mutual relationships.

Hence, societal responsibility – that is, acting in the interest of others, even when there is no legal imperative – lies at the basis of trust. And where there is trust, people are generally willing to commit themselves to the organization, both emotionally and practically. Emotionally, they will become involved with, and can become strongly connected to, the organization, which can lead to a sense of pride and loyalty. Practically, they will be willing to invest years acquiring firm-specific knowledge and skills, and in building a career. Such commitments make people dependent on the organization, as they will be less able and inclined to job-hop. It is therefore vital that the organization rewards such commitment by acting responsibly, even where this hurts profitability; otherwise the bond of trust can be seriously damaged.

Acting in the interest of all employees is a limited form of societal responsibility. Just as it is beneficial for trust to evolve within organizations, it is important for trust to develop between the organization and its broader environment of buyers, suppliers, governments, local communities and activist groups. Therefore, it is important that these organizations also come to trust that the organization is willing to act in a societally responsible way, even when this entails sacrificing profitability.

EXHIBIT 3.1   SHORT CASE

FONTERRA: CREAMING THE PROFITS IN DAIRY?

Fonterra is easily one of the world's top six dairy companies – quite an achievement for a firm based in the small, isolated country of New Zealand. An important part of its business is supplying bulk ingredients such as milk powder, butter and cheese to international markets. In 2013, it was the world's largest global processor and trader of milk products. It also owns valuable international brands including Anchor, Anlene and Anmum. Fonterra's strategic position looks highly attractive given that global dairy consumption is forecast to continue outstripping supply growth in India, Africa and much of Asia. On the other hand, size and prominence seldom come without controversy. Fonterra faces conflicting pressures on its strategy, from the farmers who own the business and from other influential stakeholders.

Fonterra, in its present form, was founded in 2001 by a merger of the two largest farmer-owned cooperatives and the Dairy Board, which at that time held a statutory export monopoly. Since then, the dairy industry in New Zealand has continued to expand, growing production volumes from 13 billion litres of milk to 17.3 billion litres by 2010/11. This expansion has been possible because New Zealand's climate allows for a highly efficient model of milk production: the cattle graze almost exclusively on natural pasture, eliminating the expense and energy consumption of heated barns and food concentrate. As a result, milk production is not only cost efficient, but also generates lower carbon emissions than other production methods, even after accounting for shipping. The costs of producing a kilogram of milk solids in New Zealand are lower than in almost any other country, although wider international adoption of industrial-scale dairying threatens this lowest-cost position.

In common with other dairy businesses around the world, Fonterra is a farmer-owned cooperative, with 10,500 owner-suppliers. The principle of the cooperative is that farmers own shares in proportion to the quantity of milk they supply. Fonterra's shares are not traded on any stock exchange, as non-suppliers cannot buy them, and the New Zealand government has no direct involvement with the business. The shares represent a significant financial commitment for the dairy farmers. Many of the farmers are actually highly indebted, due to the cost of land purchases and investment in irrigation, facilities and stock that many have made during the recent expansion.

Fonterra's governance structure reflects its constitution as a cooperative. Not only do the farmers directly elect nine of the thirteen board members, but they also have further oversight of the board via the 35-member elected Shareholders' Council. The Shareholders' Council in turn appoints a Milk Commissioner to mediate in any disputes between Fonterra and individual shareholders. In practice, the farmers indeed have a strong influence on board behaviour. Given the trend towards fewer, larger dairy farms, this influence seems destined to increase.

Another important constraint on Fonterra's strategic freedom to manoeuvre is the reliance many of its shareholders have on dividend payments. This limits the firm's ability to fund growth and investment through retained earnings. When farmers increase the volumes of milk they supply to the cooperative, equity capital flows in and the business can use this capital to fund capacity expansion. However, this dependency on gaining supply volumes biases Fonterra's management towards processing bulk commodity products. In 2012, Fonterra's board introduced a revised capital structure that avoids redemption risk in the event that too many suppliers leave the industry or elect to supply a rival processor. Fonterra suppliers now trade Fonterra shares between them, and can sell economic rights to some of their shares to a separate fund that is open to outside investors. Farmers retain control of the business, as the outside investors do not have voting rights. However, even with the new capital structure, the firm still has fewer options for raising capital than its larger multinational competitors. Tensions remain, too, amongst owner-suppliers, not least because of a rapid rise in share price since trading began.

A recurring strategic issue at Fonterra has been how, and to what extent, to build businesses that add value beyond the efficient processing and trading of commodity dairy products. In 2012, its commodity-focused business generated over two-thirds of corporate revenue. Although New

Zealand's efficient dairy industry means that farmers can profit from the sale of commodities, volatile commodity prices and exchange rates undermine the value of this strategy. So too do trade barriers and farm subsidies in major markets such as the European Union and the United States.

Many of Fonterra's options to develop new sources of value creation draw on its processing and logistics expertise to manage international operations. This often involves partnership agreements with overseas suppliers and customers. The cooperative already sources around 20 per cent of its milk from outside New Zealand. From a shareholder's perspective, this can be problematic because it means that New Zealand farmers' capital helps finance ventures that, by some arguments, compete with their own milk production. The problem is compounded by the fact that many of the opportunities for Fonterra lie in fast-growing but less developed markets such as China and India. This in turn increases the risk involved in such ventures and requires more specialist skills at managing politically complex transnational relationships. Commentators have argued that the skills and preferences of Fonterra's farmer-dominated board are not closely aligned with managing multinational ventures. Furthermore, the higher levels of business risk sit uncomfortably with the financial position of many of Fonterra's owners.

One of Fonterra's international ventures was a joint venture agreement with the Sanlu dairy company in China. This arrangement came to an abrupt end in 2008 when Sanlu was struck by a milk contamination scandal that affected thousands of infants and led to the death of at least six. Because it held a 43 per cent equity stake in the business, Fonterra became embroiled in the scandal. It became clear that Fonterra's oversight of this business was weak at both board and operational levels to the extent that it either did not know about, or was unable to curtail, the contamination scandal for many months after it first came to the attention of Sanlu's management. When Sanlu went bankrupt, Fonterra had to write off over NZ$200 million of its investment in the venture. In response to these events, Fonterra took more control of its supply chain in China, including investing in several farms and managing them to its own standards. At the same time, dairy businesses in China sought the safety of New Zealand-sourced milk. For example, Bright Dairy took a major stake in Synlait, a rival milk processor to Fonterra. This highlights the importance of New Zealand's reputation as a source of pure product: some commentators have questioned the wisdom of part-sourcing Fonterra-owned brands from elsewhere.

As well as dealing with pressures from shareholders, Fonterra must manage its relationship with other influential stakeholders. In lobbying for support, it is not shy to point out that in 2012 it contributed 26 per cent of New Zealand's export revenues. It also makes much of the economic spin-off effects of its activities, which extend beyond dairy farmers to communities, regions and cities. These spin-offs mean that the economic fortunes of the business have a major influence on those of New Zealand as a whole. However, power and importance at this level often does not engender popularity. Fonterra not only controls a very high proportion of the liquid milk supply to the domestic market, but also owns several of the major brands of cheese, butter and yoghurt. When the international commodity milk price is high, dairy prices rise for domestic consumers, which they tend to see as profiteering at their expense.

Another important area of stakeholder interest in Fonterra comes from the environmental impact of its activities. Many of these impacts come from dairy farming itself, and hence Fonterra does not directly control them, but stakeholders still consider them to be inextricably linked to Fonterra. Intensive dairying is both a major consumer of water for irrigation and potentially a polluter of water via runoff of effluent and nitrogen fertilizer. The pollution threatens local ecosystems and threatens to undermine the unusually pure municipal water supply enjoyed by domestic consumers. The high water consumption threatens these same water supplies due to over-extraction of this historically lightly-regulated resource. Fonterra has initiatives and targets to improve the industry's performance in these areas, but critics say these are still not enough. Even in 2011–12, regulators found almost 10 per cent of the country's dairy farms in significant breach of standards for effluent runoff.

Perhaps the most crucial long-term stakeholder challenge for Fonterra and the dairy industry is its contribution to New Zealand's emissions of greenhouse gases. The problem arises principally from methane emissions, a by-product of cows'

▶

digestion. Methane is an especially potent greenhouse gas, such that in 2011, agricultural emissions of methane and nitrous oxide made up 52 per cent of New Zealand's total greenhouse gas output. Because New Zealand has committed to the Kyoto agreement, it must pay directly for above-quota emissions, triggering the government to consider the possibility that farmers should contribute to this expense.

Despite this apparently daunting set of challenges, Fonterra remains a successful, growing firm that is a leader in its industry. The decision Fonterra's board and management face if it is to sustain its performance is whether and to what degree to take into account the diverse set of stakeholder concerns. If it spends heavily to address these concerns, it risks compromising the immediate interests of its owners, hence losing their support. If it does too little, it risks undermining its

operating environment (for example, by stimulating unfavourable legislation), and hence compromising its owners' future interests. The board and management must deal with the latent conflict between competing shareholder interests. They have a delicate path to tread in resolving the tension between respecting the fundamental values perceived by many owners and keeping pace with a dynamic global industry. Quite a few issues to chew over a few times.

Co-author: Paul Knott

Sources: www.fonterra.com; *Sunday Star Times,* September 26, 2008; *The New Zealand Farmers Weekly,* March 16, 2009; Ministry for the Environment (www.mfe.govt.nz), NZ's greenhouse gas inventory 1990–2011; Ministry of Foreign Affairs & Trade (www.mfat.govt.nz), Kyoto Protocol Part II; *New Zealand Herald*, April 14, 2013; *National Business Review*, June 10, 2013; Brook Asset Management News, October 26, 2012.

PERSPECTIVES ON MISSIONING AND VISIONING

Perfection of means and confusion of goals seems, in my opinion,
to characterize our age.
Albert Einstein (1879–1955); German-American physicist

Firms require a certain measure of economic profitability if they want to compete and survive, yet they also need to exhibit a certain amount of social responsibility if they are to retain the trust and support of key stakeholders. In itself, this creates a tension, as the two demands can be at odds with one another. Often, societally responsible behaviour costs money, which can only be partially recouped by the increased 'social dividend' it brings. But if profitability and responsibility are both seen as the ultimate purpose of business firms, the tension becomes even stronger; optimizing the one will be in conflict with maximizing the other. Emphasizing profitability means subjecting all investments to an economic rationale – societally responsible behaviour should only be undertaken if the net present value of such an investment is attractive or there is no legal way of avoiding compliance. Emphasizing responsibility means subjecting all activities to a moral or political rationale – asking who has a legitimate and pressing claim to be included as a beneficiary of the activities being undertaken – which can severely depress profitability.

Hence, it is not surprising to find that the paradox of profitability and responsibility strongly divides people across many walks of life; its relevance reaches far beyond business managers and management theorists. The main point of contention is whether firms should primarily be run for the financial benefit of the legal owners, or for the broader benefit of all parties with a significant interest in the joint endeavour. Should it be the purpose of firms to serve the interests of their shareholders or of their stakeholders? Should profitability be emphasized because economic organizations belong to the providers of risk capital, or should responsibility be emphasized because organizations are joint ventures bringing together various resource providers by means of a social contract?

While there are many points of view on the 'right' organizational purpose in the strategy literature, here the two diametrically opposed positions will be identified and discussed. At the one pole are those who argue that corporations are established to serve the purposes of their owners. Generally, it is in the best interest of a corporation's shareholders to see the value of their stocks increase through the organization's pursuit of profitable business strategies. This point of view is commonly referred to as the 'shareholder value perspective'. At the other end of the spectrum are those who argue that corporations should be seen as joint ventures between shareholders, employees, banks, customers, suppliers, governments and the community. All of these parties hold a stake in the organization and therefore can expect that the corporation will take as its responsibility to develop business strategies that are in accordance with their interests and values. This point of view will be referred to as the 'stakeholder values perspective'.

The shareholder value perspective

 To proponents of the shareholder value perspective it is obvious that companies belong to their owners and therefore should act in accordance with the interests of the owners. Corporations are instruments whose purpose it is to create economic value on behalf of those who invest risk-taking capital in the enterprise. This clear purpose should drive companies, regardless of whether they are privately or publicly held. According to Rappaport (1986, p. xiii), 'the idea that business strategies should be judged by the economic value they create for shareholders is well accepted in the business community. After all, to suggest that companies be operated in the best interests of their owners is hardly controversial.'

There is some disagreement between advocates of this perspective with regard to the best way of advancing the interests of the shareholders, particularly in publicly held companies. Many people taking this point of view argue that the well-being of the shareholders is served if the strategy of a company leads to higher share prices and/or higher dividends (e.g. Hart, 1995; Rappaport, 1986). Others are less certain of the stock markets' ability to correctly value long-term investments, such as R&D spending and capital expenditures. In their view, stock markets are excessively concerned with the short term and therefore share prices myopically overemphasize current results and heavily discount investments for the future. To avoid being pressured into short-termism, these people advocate that strategists must keep only one eye on share prices, while the other is focused on the long-term horizon (e.g. Charkham, 1994; Sykes, 1994).

According to supporters of the shareholder value perspective, one of the major challenges in large corporations is to actually get top management to pursue the shareholders' interests. Where ownership and managerial control over a company have become separated, it is often difficult to get the managers to work on behalf of the shareholders, instead of letting managers' self-interest prevail. This is known as the principal-agent problem (e.g. Jensen and Meckling, 1976; Eisenhardt, 1989) – the managers are agents, working to further the interests of their principals, the shareholders, but are tempted to serve their own interests, even when these are to the detriment of the principals. This has led to a widespread debate in the academic and business communities, especially in Britain and the United States, about the best form of corporate governance. The most important players in corporate governance are the outside, or non-executive, members on the board of directors. It is one of the tasks of these outsiders to check whether the executives are truly running the company in a way that maximizes the shareholders' wealth. For this reason, many proponents of the shareholder value perspective call for a majority of independent-minded outside directors on the board, preferably owning significant amounts of the company's stock themselves.

EXHIBIT 3.2   THE SHAREHOLDER VALUE PERSPECTIVE

MISSION STATEMENT DEAN FOODS

'The Company's primary objective is to maximize long-term stockholder value, while

adhering to the laws of the jurisdiction in which it operates and at all times observing the highest ethical standards.'

Dated: August, 2011

The emphasis placed on profitability as the fundamental purpose of firms does not mean that supporters of the shareholder value perspective are blind to the demands placed on firms by other stakeholders. On the contrary, most exponents of this view argue that it is in the interest of the shareholders to carry out a 'stakeholder analysis' and even to actively manage stakeholder relations. Knowing the force field of stakeholders constraining the freedom of the company is important information for the strategy process. It is never advisable to ignore important external claimants such as labour unions, environmental activists, bankers, governmental agencies and community groups. Few strategists would doubt that proactive engagement is preferable to 'corporate isolationism'. However, recognizing that it is expedient to pay attention to stakeholders does not mean that it is the corporation's purpose to serve them. If parties have a strong bargaining position, a firm might be forced into all types of concessions, sacrificing profitability. This has, however, little to do with any moral responsibility of the firm towards these other powers. The only duty of a company is to maximize shareholder value, within the boundaries of what is legally permissible.

The important conclusion is that in this perspective it might be in the interest of shareholders to treat stakeholders well, but that there is no moral obligation to do so. For instance, it might be a good move for a troubled company not to lay off workers if the resulting loyalty and morale improve the chances of recovery and profitability later on. In this case the decision not to fire workers is based on profit-motivated calculations, not on a sense of moral responsibility towards the employees. Generally, proponents of the shareholder value perspective argue that society is best served by this type of economic rationale. By pursuing enlightened self-interest and maintaining market-based relationships between the firm and all stakeholders, societal wealth will be maximized. Responsibility for employment, local communities, the environment, consumer welfare and social developments are not an organizational matter, but issues for individuals and governments (Friedman, 1970).

The stakeholder values perspective

Advocates of the stakeholder values perspective do not see why the supplier of one ingredient in an economic value-creation process has a stronger moral claim on the organization than the providers of other inputs. They challenge the assumption that individuals with an equity stake in a corporation have the right to demand that the entire organization works on their behalf. In the stakeholder values perspective, a company should not be seen as the instrument of shareholders, but as a coalition between various resource suppliers, with the intention of increasing their common wealth. An organization should be regarded as a joint venture in which the suppliers of equity, loans, labour, management, expertise, parts and service all participate to achieve economic success. As all groups hold a stake in the joint venture and are mutually dependent, it is argued that the purpose of the organization is to serve the interests of all parties involved (e.g. Berle and Means, 1932; Freeman and Reed, 1983, Reading 3.2).

According to endorsers of the stakeholder values perspective, shareholders have a legitimate interest in the firm's profitability. However, the emphasis shareholders place on stock price appreciation and dividends must be balanced against the legitimate demands of the other partners. These demands are not only financial, as in the case of the shareholders, but also qualitative, reflecting different values held by different groups (e.g. Clarke, 1998; Freeman, 1984). For instance, employees might place a high value on job security, occupational safety, holidays and working conditions, while a supplier of parts might prefer secure demand, joint innovation, shared risk-taking and prompt payment. Of course, balancing these interests is a challenging task, requiring an ongoing process of negotiation and compromise. The outcome will in part depend on the bargaining power of each stakeholder – how essential is its input to the economic success of the organization? However, the extent to which a stakeholder's interests are pursued will depend on the perceived legitimacy of their claim as well. For instance, employees usually have a strong moral claim because they are heavily dependent on the organization and have a relatively low mobility, while most shareholders have a spread portfolio and can 'exit the corporation with a phone call' (Stone, 1975).

In this view of organizational purpose, managers must recognize their responsibility towards all constituents (e.g. Clarkson, 1995; Alkhafaji, 1989). Maximizing shareholder value to the detriment of the other stakeholders would be unjust. Managers in the firm have a moral obligation to consider the interests and values of all joint venture partners. Managing stakeholder demands is not merely a pragmatic means of running a profitable business – serving stakeholders is an end in itself. These two interpretations of stakeholder management are often confused. Where it is primarily viewed as an approach or technique for dealing with the essential participants in the value-adding process, stakeholder management is *instrumental*. But if it is based on the fundamental notion that the organization's purpose is to serve the stakeholders, then stakeholder management is *normative* (e.g. Buono and Nichols, 1985; Donaldson and Preston, 1995).

Most proponents of the stakeholder values perspective argue that, ultimately, pursuing the joint interests of all stakeholders it is not only more just, but also more effective for organizations (e.g. Jones, 1995; Solomon, 1992). Few stakeholders are filled with a sense of mission to go out and maximize shareholder value, especially if shareholders bear no responsibility for the other stakeholders' interests (e.g. Campbell and Yeung, 1991; Collins and Porras, 1994). It is difficult to work as a motivated team if it is the purpose of the organization to serve only one group's interests. Furthermore, without a stakeholder values perspective, there will be a deep-rooted lack of trust between all of the parties involved in the enterprise. Each stakeholder will assume that the others are motivated solely by self-interest and are tentatively cooperating in a calculative manner. All parties will perceive a constant risk that the others will use their power to gain a bigger slice of the pie, or even rid themselves of their 'partners'. The consequence is that all stakeholders will vigorously guard their own interests and will interact with one another as adversaries. To advocates of the stakeholder values perspective, this 'every person for themselves' model of organizations is clearly inferior to the partnership model in which sharing, trust and symbiosis are emphasized. Cooperation between stakeholders is much more effective than competition (note the link with the embedded organization perspective in Chapter 6).

Some exponents of the stakeholder values perspective argue that the narrow economic definition of stakeholders given above is too constrictive. In their view, the circle of stakeholders with a legitimate claim on the organization should be drawn more widely. Not only should the organization be responsible to the direct participants in the economic value-creation process (the 'primary stakeholders'), but also to all parties affected by the organization's activities. For example, an organization's behaviour might have an impact on local communities, governments, the environment and society in general, and therefore these groups have a stake in what the organization does as well. Most supporters of the stakeholder values perspective acknowledge that organizations have a moral responsibility towards these 'secondary stakeholders' (e.g. Carroll, 1993; Langtry, 1994). However, opinions differ whether it should actually be a part of business organizations' purpose to serve this broader body of constituents.

The implication of this view for corporate governance is that the board of directors should be able to judge whether the interests of all stakeholders are being justly balanced. This has led some advocates of the stakeholder values perspective to call for representatives of the most important stakeholder groups to be on the board (e.g. Guthrie and Turnbull, 1994). Others argue more narrowly for a stronger influence of employees on the choices made by organizations (e.g. Bucholz, 1986; Blair, 1995). Such co-determination of the corporation's strategy by management and workers can, for instance, be encouraged by establishing work councils (a type of organizational parliament or senate), as is mandatory for larger companies in most countries of the European Union. Yet others emphasize measures to strengthen corporate social responsibility in general. To improve corporate social performance, it is argued, companies should be encouraged to adopt internal policy processes that promote ethical behaviour and responsiveness to societal issues (e.g. Epstein, 1987; Wartick and Wood, 1998). Corporate responsibility should not be, to quote Ambrose Bierce's sarcastic definition, 'a detachable burden easily shifted to the shoulders of God, Fate, Fortune, Luck, or one's neighbour'.

EXHIBIT 3.3   THE STAKEHOLDER VALUES PERSPECTIVE

CREDO JOHNSON & JOHNSON

We believe our first responsibility is to the doctors, nurses and patients, to mothers and fathers and all others who use our products and services. In meeting their needs everything we do must be of high quality. We must constantly strive to reduce our costs in order to maintain reasonable prices. Customers' orders must be serviced promptly and accurately. Our suppliers and distributors must have an opportunity to make a fair profit.

We are responsible to our employees, the men and women who work with us throughout the world. Everyone must be considered as an individual. We must respect their dignity and recognize their merit. They must have a sense of security in their jobs. Compensation must be fair and adequate, and working conditions clean, orderly and safe.

We must be mindful of ways to help our employees fulfil their family responsibilities. Employees must feel free to make suggestions and complaints. There must be equal opportunity for employment, development and advancement for those qualified. We must provide competent management, and their actions must be just and ethical.

We are responsible to the communities in which we live and work and to the world community as well. We must be good citizens – support good works and charities and bear our fair share of taxes. We must encourage civic improvements and better health education. We must maintain in good order the property we are privileged to use, protecting the environment and natural resources.

Our final responsibility is to our stockholders. Business must make a sound profit. We must experiment with new ideas. Research must be carried on, innovative programmes developed and mistakes paid for. New equipment must be purchased, new facilities provided and new products launched. Reserves must be created to provide for adverse times. When we operate according to the principles, the stockholders should realize their fair return.

Source: Johnson & Johnson

MANAGING THE PARADOX OF PROFITABILITY AND RESPONSIBILITY

A business that makes nothing but money is a poor kind of business.
Henry Ford (1863–1947); American industrialist

So, what should be the purpose of a firm? And how should executives manage the tension between profitability and responsibility? Should managers strive to maximize shareholder value or stakeholder values? Or should executives search for a way that combines profitability and responsibility? The proponents of the shareholder value perspective are lobbying for more receptiveness to the interests of the shareholders on the part of the board, to increase top management accountability and to curb perceived executive self-enrichment at the expense of shareholders. The advocates of the stakeholder values perspective are vying for a system that would bring more receptiveness to the interests of stakeholders, to ensure that firms do not become more myopically 'bottom line' oriented. While both sides do agree on one or two points (e.g. corporate governance is generally too weak), on the whole, the question remains how to manage the paradox of profitability and responsibility.

Increased pressure on responsible corporate behaviour

In recent years, several societal stakeholders have increased the pressure on companies to take responsibility for their behaviour and the consequences of their actions. For example, while for many years banks could strive for maximized shareholder value without significant protest of governments, regulators, clients and other stakeholders, the situation changed after the fall of Lehman Brothers in 2008. Since then, the societal role of banks has been emphasized, economic dependency on system banks understood and reduced, new regulations installed, and governments have made system changes. Companies that produce products in low wage countries, such as shoes and smartphones, were publicly accused of using child labour or unsafe working conditions. Oil companies faced increased pressure from environmental groups, Non Government Organizations (NGOs) and governments after a number of accidents and oil spills. Furthermore, the pressure of

TABLE 3.1   Shareholder value versus stakeholder values

	Shareholder value perspective	Stakeholder values perspective
Emphasis on	Profitability over responsibility	Responsibility over profitability
Organizations seen as	Instruments	Joint ventures
Organizational purpose	To serve owner	To serve all parties involved
Measure of success	Share price and dividends (shareholder value)	Satisfaction among stakeholders
Major difficulty	Getting agent to pursue principal's interests	Balancing interests of various stakeholders
Corporate governance through	Independent outside directors with shares	Stakeholder representation
Stakeholder management	Means	End
Social responsibility	Individual, not organizational matter	Both individual and organizational
Society best served by	Pursuing self-interest (economic efficiency)	Pursuing joint-interests (economic symbiosis)

societal stakeholders on companies grows further with the accelerated importance of social media. Societal stakeholders are informed better and quicker, and have more means at their disposal to pressure companies if they deem their conduct questionable.

While the importance of corporate social responsibility increases, shareholders continue to emphasize the need to pursue profitability on behalf of their owners. As a result, executives are constantly trying to balance profitability and responsibility at a higher level. Of course, this does not apply to all companies. For example, the pressure on managers of family-owned firms to enhance profitability is usually less intense, while the attention of governments and NGOs focuses 'only' on a subset of industries and companies.

Resolving the paradox

Managers cannot look to the strategy literature to glean the best practice and apply it to their own company. The situation of each company is unique in the combined set of factors, such as cultural heritage, institutional environment, industry and organizational context. They will need to determine their own point of view on what they believe should be the purpose of the organization, develop a process to manage the tension of profitability and responsibility, and decide on the way the company in its specific context should manage the paradox. Even though just applying best practices is not possible, managers can learn from companies that have showed to be successful, often described in case-studies, books and articles.

In recent years, the number of publications that help managers to deal with the paradox of profitability and responsibility has been growing. While several elements of corporate responsibility, such as social and environmental responsibility, have been widely discussed in academia for many years, the strategy field has picked up the issue recently. This field was pioneered by John Elkington, with a number of publications starting in 1980. With Tom Burke, he published in 1987 *The Green Capitalists: Industry's search for environmental excellence*, in which he blended the emerging green agenda with that of business – a revolutionary idea in these years. His most influential book came in 1997: *Cannibals with Forks: The Triple Bottom Line of 21st Century Business*. In this book, Elkington asked the question whether capitalism itself was sustainable, and he introduced the concept of Triple Bottom Line – a term he had coined in 1984. An other early work in this vein is Jed Emerson's *California Management Review* article 'The Blended Value Proposition: Integrating Social and Financial Returns' (2003). He introduced the concept 'blended value', in which firms seek simultaneously to pursue profit and social and environmental objectives. 'The turning point in the debate about the emerging role and responsibility of business in society is Stuart Hart's book *Capitalism at the Crossroads* (2005)', wrote the late C.K. Prahalad, with whom Hart published his 2002 article 'The Fortune at the Bottom of the Pyramid'. Hart's book stimulated many scholars in the strategy field to reconsider the concepts of value and capitalism.

Yet, it was Michael Porter who guided the issue into the mainstream strategy field. Together with Mark Kramer, he published the 2011 *Harvard Business Review* article 'Creating Shared Value: How to reinvent capitalism and unleash a wave of innovation and growth' (Reading 3.3). In this reading Porter and Kramer argue that 'profits involving a social purpose represent a higher form of capitalism, one that creates a positive cycle of company and community prosperity', and they claim that the shared value concept moves business and society beyond trade-offs. More precisely formulated: the authors strive to achieve a synthesis between firm profitability and societal responsibility. It must be noted that the authors had explored the idea of shared value five years earlier in a 2006 *Harvard Business Review* article, 'Strategy and Society: The Link Between Competitive Advantage and Corporate Social Responsibility'. When considering the timing of both articles and their relative success, it may be argued that the idea behind shared value was in need of a good crisis.

MISSIONING AND VISIONING IN INTERNATIONAL PERSPECTIVE

Co-author: Gep Eisenloeffel

Failure comes only when we forget our ideals and objectives and principles.
Jawaharlal Nehru (1889–1964); First Prime Minister of India

The debate on organizational purpose doesn't take place in a value-free vacuum: institutional and cultural aspects define its context. Although some believe that a 'best practice' solution is at hand or that globalization itself will lead to a convergence of perspectives on organizational purpose, the present day economic reality at least challenges this point of view. Even Fukayama revoked his statement in *The End of History* (1992) that universal liberal and democratic principles would lead to a dominant world order in his later works *State-Building: Governance and World Order in the 21st Century* (2004) and *The Origins of Political Order* (2011).

When analysing similarities and differences in organizational purpose worldwide, two aspects merit further discussion: varieties of capitalism and company norms and values.

Varieties of capitalism

With the fall of the Berlin Wall in 1989, the Cold War division between free market (capitalist) economies and fully state controlled (communist) economies came to an end. Although capitalism appears to be dominant, it is not universally applied in economies around the world. In general terms, this is referred to as *varieties of capitalism*, although this taxonomy is not generally accepted in academia. For example, Coe *et al.* (2007) argue that 'the different historical geographical circumstances from which each nation-state emerged have produced a variety of different states' rather than just varieties of capitalism. Coe *et al.* 'Review six groups of nation-states in relation to their different political-economic governance and power relations: neo-liberal states like the US and the UK; welfare states in Nordic countries and some European countries; developmental states in Asia and South America; transitional states in post-socialist countries in Eastern Europe, the former Soviet Union, China and Southeast Asia; weak and dependent states in Africa, Central/South America, and the Middle East; failed states such as Somalia, Congo, Afghanistan, Iraq and Bosnia.'

The literature offers two leading schools of thought approaching the varieties of capitalism taxonomy. The first school concentrates on similarities and differences in the institutional framework and considers how these affect all or most aspects of organizational purpose. The second school of thoughts focuses on cultural similarities and differences. The simplest and shortest definition of culture in this respect is 'this is the way we do things around here' (Deal and Kennedy, 1982).

Varieties based on institutional differences

When dealing with organizational purpose, institutional aspects play an important role. Michael Porter pointed out in *The Competitive Advantage of Nations* (1990) that the sustainable competitive advantage of industries and individual companies is to a large extent based on the institutional framework within their countries – and regions – of origin.

Institutional forms that have evolved over time in different national contexts have resulted in distinctive models of economic organization. Michel Albert (1993) concentrated on the differences of what he coined as the *Rhineland model* in Germany in comparison with the *Anglo-Saxon model* of the US and (to a lesser extent) the UK. Peter Hall and David Soskice elaborated on this point. In their book *Varieties of Capitalism* (2001), they stress the differences between what they call *Coordinated Market Economies* (CMEs), most commonly associated with such countries as Germany, Sweden and Japan, and *Liberal Market Economies* (LMEs) generally associated with the US and the UK. As Bruno Amable (2003) points out, "the difference between the two is based on one fundamental dimension: coordination. In LMEs coordination is based on market conditions, favouring investments on transferable assets. In CME's, however, it is mainly achieved through non-market means – the so-called strategic coordination – favouring investments in specific assets." Many authors object to this strict dichotomy. Peter Dicken (2011), for instance, identifies four variants of capitalism; neo-liberal market capitalism, social-market capitalism, developmental capitalism and authoritarian capitalism. Dicken shows how differences in coordination take various shapes: States operate as regulators, competitors and collaborators at the same time. In this way, states not only create the context for organizational purpose, they also operate as shareholders and stakeholders. Obviously, the more influential the state, as for instance in Russia and China, the more active its role as shareholder and stakeholder is likely to be. Bruno Amable (2003) on the other hand, posits the existence of five types of capitalism; the market-based model, the social-democratic model, the Continental European model, the Mediterranean model and the Asian model.

Companies have to deal with different institutional contexts in host countries while executing their mission, vision and organizational purpose. This becomes even more relevant in today's shifts in the economic power balance. Economic surveys expect that by 2020 the combined economies of China, India and Brazil will surpass the combined economies of the US, UK, Germany and France. Whether referred to as BRIC (Brazil, Russia, India and China (O'Neill, 2001), BRICS (including South Africa and since 2011 a formal group of countries), BRICM (including Mexico), BRICET (including Eastern Europe and Turkey), or N-11 (next 11), it is clear that the former economic dominance of the traditional countries of *the Triad of Economic Power* (Ohmae, 1985) no longer applies and that the institutional context will further vary.

As Schneider and Barsoux (1999) point out: varieties of capitalism are not only defined by the role of the government and legislation. Media, stakeholders' and shareholders' behaviour also play an important role in creating differences in the context of organizational purpose. For example, concerns over ethics may be due to more aggressive journalism (or as in the case of the US libel suits), 'best company' rankings or greater risk of shareholder activism and consumer boycotts.

Varieties based on differences in cultural values

Institutions are shaped not only by legal systems but also by informal rules or common knowledge acquired through history. Coined by Geert Hofstede (1980) as 'software of the mind', culture plays an important part in analysing differences of organizational purpose. 'It is not to say that culture is the most important influence on varieties of capitalism and organizational purpose, but often it is the most neglected' (Barsoux and Schneider, 1999).

Cultural values are deeply rooted in history and do not change overnight (e.g. Hofstede, 1980; Lewis, 2003). Broadly speaking, there are two approaches to studying culture and its impact on defining organizational purpose. The first is the more or less sociological approach (Kluckhohn and Strodtbeck, 1961; Hofstede, 1980; Schwartz, 1999; House, 2004). Its emphasis is looking at cultural dimensions which are shared throughout the world. Although there is disagreement on which dimensions should be applied and on which criteria these are constructed (see for instance Hofstede, 1996), the strength of this approach is that it is possible to quantify research findings and to compare and even predict differences and similarities in organizational behaviour. This is the *etic approach*, from *phonetic*; sounds that we find in every language in the world. The opposite approach, rooted in anthropology, states that cultural values and behaviour are far too locally specific to be compared. This research focuses on the so-called 'deep levels' of meanings, beliefs and values, which can only be understood from 'the inside.' (Martin, 1992; Schein, 1995; D'Iribarne, 1996). This is the *emic approach,* from *phonemic*; sounds that are specific for a given language.

Whichever approach is taken, there is a wealth of research findings (Hofstede, 1980; Hampden-Turner and Trompenaars, 2000; Adler, 2002; Schein, 2004; Verluyten, 2010) showing how cultural dimensions play an important role in not just *who* is responsible for formulating organizational purpose and on what grounds accountability is conducted, but also *how* and for *whom* the purpose of the company is defined. Hampden-Turner and Trompenaars (2000), for instance, show how in the United States, with its emphasis on individualism and achievement, ethical decisions are considered personal. Likewise moral judgements require individual responsibility and accountability. Universalism is an important 'by-product' of individualism and deeply rooted in US cultural history (Hampden-Turner, 2000; Verluyten, 2010). Ethical standards in the US are considered to apply to everyone in the same way. This results in the US legalistic approach to ethics effecting organizational purpose. In more collectivist countries, however, ethical standards are applied either according to specific circumstances, strongly influenced by the nature of one's social status (*ascription*) like in Brazil, or to social ties (*in-group versus out-group*) like in China.

Traditionally, many Western business schools have preached profit maximization as the ultimate goal. This notion reflects underlying cultural assumptions like task orientation (as opposed to relationship orientation, Hampden-Turner and Trompenaars 2000) and individualism (as opposed to collectivism). Organizations are seen as instrumental and managers as rational economic actors, driven by self-interest. To contrast this approach with defining organization purpose more to promote the well-being of society and organizations as a system of relationships, consider excerpts from the mission statement of Konosuke Matsushita, founder of Matsushita: "Profit comes in compensation for contributing to society." Holden (2002) states how 'Konosuke Matsushita revealed a 250 year plan for the completion of the company mission. These 250 years were divided into ten phases consisting of periods of 'construction' (10 years), 'application' (10 years) and 'fulfilment' (5 years). Matsushita did not just want to contribute to society – the end result called for nothing less than the eradication of poverty from the face of the earth.

Company norms and values

The institutional and cultural framework is an important context variable in defining company norms and values. Should companies impose parent company or home-country norms and values in the host-country environment, or should local customs, rules and regulations be adapted? On the one hand corporate and head-office efforts to insist on 'universal' ethical principles in foreign subsidiaries are often questioned and considered as cultural imperialism or outright self-righteousness. On the other hand, however, adapting to local rules with a *when in Rome do as the Romans* approach and presenting the company as a 'national champion', leads to inconsistently practising corporate norms and values, and tensions with external stakeholders. For example, if company standards are not in line with international rules of conduct, Non Government Organizations (NGOs) and home-country customers are likely to protest. In the words of Cor Herkströter, CEO of Shell in the mid-1990s, 'stakeholders hold the *license to operate* of a company.'

Furthermore, the homogeneity of regulations and cultural norms within nations and of the acclaimed uniformity of organizational purpose can also be questioned (Coe *et al.*, 2007). The regulatory and cultural framework often differs from one region to another and even within regions. In the end this would mean that the firm in its specific circumstances is the proper unit of analysis.

INTRODUCTION TO THE READINGS

As in the previous chapter, the first two readings represent the two perspectives (see Table 3.1) to gain a sharper understanding of the breadth of opinions on this topic, while the third reading aims at bridging the two perspectives. The first reading, representing the shareholder value perspective, is from the 1976 Nobel Prize in Economic Sciences winner Milton Friedman. The title of his 1970 *The New York Times Magazine* article, 'The Social Responsibility of Business is to Increase its Profits', summarizes well the stance of the shareholder value perspective proponents in the debate. Friedman argues that "there is one, and only one, social responsibility of business – to use its resources and engage in activities designed to increase its profits so long as it stays within the rules of the game, which is to say, engages in open and free competition without deception or fraud." In the article, Friedman responds – often in sharp wordings – to a number of critics of his 1962 highly influential book *Capitalism and Freedom*. A main argument in the book is that economic freedom is both necessary and a vital means for political freedom, and that business should not be socially responsible. He argues that 'if there are social responsibilities, they are the social responsibilities of individuals, not of business'. The underlying view on the purpose of a business organization is that the primary purpose of corporations should be to maximize shareholder value.

The opening reading on behalf of the stakeholder values perspective (Reading 3.2) is also a classic – 'Stockholders and Stakeholders: A New Perspective on Corporate Governance', by Edward Freeman and David Reed. This article in *California Management Review* and Freeman's subsequent book *Strategic Management: A Stakeholder Approach* were instrumental in popularizing the stakeholder concept. In their article, Freeman and Reed challenge 'the view that stockholders have a privileged place in the business enterprise'. They deplore the fact that 'it has long been gospel that corporations have obligations to stockholders ... that are sacrosanct and inviolable'. They argue that there has been a long tradition of management thinkers who believe that corporations have a broader responsibility towards stakeholders other than just the suppliers of equity financing. It is their conviction that such a definition of the corporation, as a system serving the interests of multiple stakeholders, is superior to the shareholder perspective. Their strong preference for the stakeholder concept is largely based on the pragmatic argument that, in reality, stakeholders have the power to seriously affect the continuity of the corporation. Stakeholder analysis is needed to understand the actual claims placed by constituents on the firm and to evaluate each stakeholder's power position. Stakeholder management is a practical response to the fact that corporations cannot afford to ignore or downplay the interests of the claimants. Only scarcely do Freeman and Reed hint that corporations have the moral responsibility to work on behalf of all stakeholders (which Freeman does more explicitly in some of his later works, e.g. Freeman and Gilbert, 1988; Freeman and Liedtka, 1991). In their opinion, the consequence of the stakeholder concept for corporate governance is that 'there are times when stakeholders must participate in the decision-making process'. However, they believe that if boards of directors adopt a stakeholder outlook and become more responsive to the demands placed on corporations, structural reforms to give stakeholders a stronger role in corporate governance will not be necessary.

The third reading (Reading 3.3) aims at resolving the paradox of profitability and responsibility: Michael Porter and Mark A. Kramer's 2011 *Harvard Business Review* article 'Creating Shared Value: How to Reinvent Capitalism and Unleash a Wave of Innovation and Growth'. The article has become highly influential in the strategy field, the corporate world and public management. The authors of this article argue that profits involving a social purpose represent a higher form of capitalism, one that creates a positive cycle of company and community prosperity. Consequently, the purpose of the organization must be redefined as shared value, not just the old-fashioned capitalists' purpose of profit. Shared value is defined as 'policies and operating practices that enhance the competitiveness of a company while simultaneously advancing the economic and social conditions in the communities in which it operates'. Shared value creating focuses on 'identifying and expanding the connections between societal and economic progress'. Porter and Kramer claim to reinvent capitalism by combining company profitability and societal responsibility, which will drive the next wave of innovation and productivity growth in the global economy. Re-invented capitalism consists of three elements. The first element is the need to create market ecosystems, especially when selling to the poorest in developing countries. This may require firms to make partnerships with NGOs and governments. The second element is expanding their value chains to include such unconventional partners. And the third element is creating new industrial clusters.

READING

3.1

The social responsibility of business is to increase its profits

By Milton Friedman[1]

When I hear businessmen speak eloquently about the "social responsibilities of business in a free-enterprise system," I am reminded of the wonderful line about the Frenchman who discovered at the age of 70 that he had been speaking prose all his life. The businessmen believe that they are defending free enterprise when they declaim that business is not concerned "merely" with profit but also with promoting desirable "social" ends; that business has a "social conscience" and takes seriously its responsibilities for providing employment, eliminating discrimination, avoiding pollution and whatever else may be the catchwords of the contemporary crop of reformers. In fact they are – or would be if they or anyone else took them seriously – preaching pure and unadulterated socialism. Businessmen who talk this way are unwitting puppets of the intellectual forces that have been undermining the basis of a free society these past decades.

The discussions of the "social responsibilities of business" are notable for their analytical looseness and lack of rigour. What does it mean to say that "business" has responsibilities? Only people can have responsibilities. A corporation is an artificial person and in this sense may have artificial responsibilities, but "business" as a whole cannot be said to have responsibilities, even in this vague sense. The first step toward clarity in examining the doctrine of the social responsibility of business is to ask precisely what it implies for whom.

Presumably, the individuals who are to be responsible are businessmen, which means individual proprietors or corporate executives. Most of the discussion of social responsibility is directed at corporations, so in what follows I shall mostly neglect the individual proprietors and speak of corporate executives.

In a free-enterprise, private-property system, a corporate executive is an employee of the owners of the business. He has direct responsibility to his employers. That responsibility is to conduct the business in accordance with their desires, which generally will be to make as much money as possible while conforming to the basic rules of the society, both those embodied in law and those embodied in ethical custom. Of course, in some cases his employers may have a different objective. A group of persons might establish a corporation for an eleemosynary purpose – for example, a hospital or a school. The manager of such a corporation will not have money profit as his objective but the rendering of certain services.

In either case, the key point is that, in his capacity as a corporate executive, the manager is the agent of the individuals who own the corporation or establish the eleemosynary institution, and his primary responsibility is to them.

Needless to say, this does not mean that it is easy to judge how well he is performing his task. But at least the criterion of performance is straightforward, and the persons among whom a voluntary contractual arrangement exists are clearly defined.

Of course, the corporate executive is also a person in his own right. As a person, he may have many other responsibilities that he recognizes or assumes voluntarily – to his family, his conscience, his feelings of charity, his church, his clubs, his city, his country. He may feel impelled by these responsibilities to devote part of his income to causes he regards as worthy, to refuse to work for particular corporations, even to leave his job, for example, to join his country's armed forces. If we wish, we may refer to some of these responsibilities as "social responsibilities." But in these respects he is acting as a principal, not an agent; he is spending his own money or time or energy, not the money of his employers or the time or energy he has contracted to devote to their purposes. If these are "social responsibilities," they are the social responsibilities of individuals, not of business.

What does it mean to say that the corporate executive has a "social responsibility" in his capacity as businessman? If this statement is not pure rhetoric, it must mean that he is to act in some way that is not in the interest of his employers. For example, that he is to refrain from increasing the price of the product in order to contribute to the social objective of preventing inflation, even though a price increase would be in the best interests of the corporation. Or that he is to make expenditures on reducing pollution beyond the amount that is in the best interests of the corporation or that is required by law in order to contribute to the social objective of improving the environment. Or that, at the expense of corporate profits, he is to hire "hardcore" unemployed instead of better qualified available workmen to contribute to the social objective of reducing poverty.

In each of these cases, the corporate executive would be spending someone else's money for a general social interest. Insofar as his actions in accord with his "social responsibility" reduce returns to stockholders, he is spending their money. Insofar as his actions raise the price to customers, he is spending the customers' money. Insofar as his actions lower the wages of some employees, he is spending their money.

The stockholders or the customers or the employees could separately spend their own money on the particular action if they wished to do so. The executive is exercising a distinct "social responsibility," rather than serving as an agent of the stockholders or the customers or the employees, only if he spends the money in a different way than they would have spent it.

But if he does this, he is in effect imposing taxes, on the one hand, and deciding how the tax proceeds shall be spent, on the other.

This process raises political questions on two levels: principle and consequences. On the level of political principle, the imposition of taxes and the expenditure of tax proceeds are governmental functions. We have established elaborate constitutional, parliamentary and judicial provisions to control these functions, to assure that taxes are imposed so far as possible in accordance with the preferences and desires of the public – after all, "taxation without representation" was one of the battle cries of the American Revolution. We have a system of checks and balances to separate the legislative function of imposing taxes and enacting expenditures from the executive function of collecting taxes and administering expenditure programmes and from the judicial function of mediating disputes and interpreting the law.

Here the businessman – self-selected or appointed directly or indirectly by stockholders – is to be simultaneously legislator, executive and jurist. He is to decide whom to tax, by how much and for what purpose, and he is to spend the proceeds – all this guided only by general exhortations from on high to restrain inflation, improve the environment, fight poverty and so on and on.

The whole justification for permitting the corporate executive to be selected by the stockholders is that the executive is an agent serving the interests of his principal. This justification disappears when the corporate executive imposes taxes and spends the proceeds for "social" purposes. He becomes in effect a public employee, a civil servant, even though he remains in name an employee of a private enterprise. On grounds of political principle, it is intolerable that such civil servants – insofar as their actions in the name of social responsibility are real and not just window-dressing – should be selected as they are now. If they are to be civil servants, then they must be elected through a political process. If they are to impose taxes and make expenditures to foster "social" objectives, then political machinery must be set up to make the assessment of taxes and to determine through a political process the objectives to be served.

This is the basic reason why the doctrine of "social responsibility" involves the acceptance of the socialist view that political mechanisms, not market mechanisms, are the appropriate way to determine the allocation of scarce resources to alternative uses.

On the grounds of consequences, can the corporate executive in fact discharge his alleged "social responsibilities"? On the other hand, suppose he could get away with spending the stockholders' or customers' or employees' money. How is he to know how to spend it? He is told that he must contribute to fighting inflation. How is he to know what action of his will contribute to that end? He is presumably an expert in running his company – in producing a product or selling it or financing it. But nothing about his selection makes him an expert on inflation. Will his holding down the price of his product reduce inflationary pressure? Or, by leaving more spending power in the hands of his customers, simply divert it elsewhere? Or, by forcing him to produce less because of the lower price, will it simply contribute to shortages? Even if he could answer these questions, how much cost is he justified in imposing on his stockholders, customers and employees for this social purpose? What is his appropriate share and what is the appropriate share of others?

And, whether he wants to or not, can he get away with spending his stockholders', customers' or employees' money? Will not the stockholders fire him (either the present ones or those who take over when his actions in the name of social responsibility have reduced the corporation's profits and the price of its stock)? His customers and his employees can desert him for other producers and employers less scrupulous in exercising their social responsibilities.

This facet of "social responsibility" doctrine is brought into sharp relief when the doctrine is used to justify wage restraint by trade unions. The conflict of interest is naked and clear when union officials are asked to subordinate the interest of their members to some more general purpose. If the union officials try to enforce wage restraint, the consequence is likely to be wildcat strikes, rank-and-file revolts and the emergence of strong competitors for their jobs. We thus have the ironic phenomenon that union leaders – at least in the US – have objected to Government interference with the market far more consistently and courageously than have business leaders.

The difficulty of exercising "social responsibility" illustrates, of course, the great virtue of private competitive enterprise – it forces people to be responsible for their own actions and makes it difficult for them to "exploit" other people for either selfish or unselfish purposes. They can do good – but only at their own expense.

Many a reader who has followed the argument this far may be tempted to remonstrate that it is all well and good to speak of Government's having the responsibility to impose taxes and determine expenditures for such "social" purposes as controlling pollution or training the hard-core unemployed, but that the problems are too urgent to wait on the slow course of political processes, that the exercise of social responsibility by businessmen is a quicker and surer way to solve pressing current problems.

Aside from the question of fact – I share Adam Smith's scepticism about the benefits that can be expected from "those who affected to trade for the public good" – this argument must be rejected on grounds of principle. What it amounts to is an assertion that those who favour the taxes and expenditures in question have failed to persuade a majority of their fellow citizens to be of like mind and that they are seeking to attain by undemocratic procedures what they cannot attain by democratic procedures. In a free society, it is hard for "evil" people to do "evil," especially since one man's good is another's evil.

I have, for simplicity, concentrated on the special case of the corporate executive, except only for the brief digression on trade unions. But precisely the same argument applies to the newer phenomenon of calling upon stockholders to require corporations to exercise social responsibility. In most of these cases, what is in effect involved is some stockholders trying to get other stockholders (or customers or employees) to contribute against their will to "social" causes favoured by the activists. Insofar as they succeed, they are again imposing taxes and spending the proceeds.

The situation of the individual proprietor is somewhat different. If he acts to reduce the returns of his enterprise in order to exercise his "social responsibility," he is spending his own money, not someone else's. If he wishes to spend his money on such purposes, that is his right, and I cannot see that there is any objection to his doing so. In the process, he, too, may impose costs on employees and customers. However, because he is far less likely than a large corporation or union to have monopolistic power, any such side effects will tend to be minor.

Of course, in practice the doctrine of social responsibility is frequently a cloak for actions that are justified on other grounds rather than a reason for those actions.

To illustrate, it may well be in the long run interest of a corporation that is a major employer in a small community to devote resources to providing amenities to that community or to improving its government. That may make it easier to attract desirable employees, it may reduce the wage bill or lessen losses from pilferage and sabotage or have other worthwhile effects. Or it may be that, given the laws about the deductibility of corporate charitable contributions, the stockholders can contribute more to charities they favour by having the corporation make the gift than by doing it themselves, since they can in that way contribute an amount that would otherwise have been paid as corporate taxes.

In each of these – and many similar – cases, there is a strong temptation to rationalize these actions as an exercise of "social responsibility." In the present climate of opinion, with its widespread aversion to "capitalism," "profits," the "soulless corporation" and so on, this is one way for a corporation to generate goodwill as a by-product of expenditures that are entirely justified in its own self-interest.

It would be inconsistent of me to call on corporate executives to refrain from this hypocritical window-dressing because it harms the foundations of a free society. That would be to call on them to exercise a "social responsibility"! If our institutions, and the attitudes of the public make it in their self-interest to cloak their actions in this way, I cannot summon much indignation to denounce them. At the same time, I can express admiration for those individual proprietors or owners of closely held corporations, or stockholders of more broadly held corporations, who disdain such tactics as approaching fraud.

Whether blameworthy or not, the use of the cloak of social responsibility, and the nonsense spoken in its name by influential and prestigious businessmen, does clearly harm the foundations of a free society. I have been impressed time and again by the schizophrenic character of many businessmen. They are capable of being extremely farsighted and clearheaded in matters that are internal to their businesses. They are incredibly shortsighted and muddleheaded in matters that are outside their businesses but affect the possible survival of business in general. This shortsightedness is strikingly exemplified in the calls from many businessmen for wage and price guidelines or controls or income policies. There is nothing that could do more in a brief period to destroy a market system and replace it by a centrally controlled system than effective governmental control of prices and wages.

The shortsightedness is also exemplified in speeches by businessmen on social responsibility. This may gain them kudos in the short run. But it helps to strengthen the already too prevalent view that the pursuit of profits is wicked and immoral and must be curbed and controlled by external forces. Once this view is adopted, the external forces that curb the market will not be the social consciences, however highly developed, of the pontificating executives; it will be the iron fist of Government bureaucrats. Here, as with price and wage controls, businessmen seem to me to reveal a suicidal impulse.

The political principle that underlies the market mechanism is unanimity. In an ideal free market resting on private property, no individual can coerce any other, all cooperation is voluntary, all parties to such cooperation benefit or they need not participate. There are no values, no "social" responsibilities in any sense

other than the shared values and responsibilities of individuals. Society is a collection of individuals and of the various groups they voluntarily form.

The political principle that underlies the political mechanism is conformity. The individual must serve a more general social interest – whether that be determined by a church or a dictator or a majority. The individual may have a vote and say in what is to be done, but if he is overruled, he must conform. It is appropriate for some to require others to contribute to a general social purpose whether they wish to or not.

Unfortunately, unanimity is not always feasible. There are some respects in which conformity appears unavoidable, so I do not see how one can avoid the use of the political mechanism altogether.

But the doctrine of "social responsibility" taken seriously would extend the scope of the political mechanism to every human activity. It does not differ in philosophy from the most explicitly collectivist doctrine. It differs only by professing to believe that collectivist ends can be attained without collectivist means. That is why, in my book *Capitalism and Freedom*, I have called it a "fundamentally subversive doctrine" in a free society, and have said that in such a society, "there is one and only one social responsibility of business – to use it resources and engage in activities designed to increase its profits so long as it stays within the rules of the game, which is to say, engages in open and free competition without deception or fraud."

READING 3.2

Stockholders and stakeholders: A new perspective on corporate governance

By Edward Freeman and David Reed[1]

Management thought has changed dramatically in recent years. There have been, and are now underway, both conceptual and practical revolutions in the ways that management theorists and managers think about organizational life. The purpose of this article is to understand the implications of one of these shifts in world view; namely, the shift from 'stockholder' to 'stakeholder'.

The stakeholder concept

It has long been gospel that corporations have obligations to stockholders, holders of the firm's equity that are sacrosanct and inviolable. Corporate action or inaction is to be driven by attention to the needs of its stockholders, usually thought to be measured by stock price, earnings per share, or some other financial measure. It has been argued that the proper relationship of management to its stockholders is similar to that of the fiduciary to the *cestui que trustent*, whereby the interests of the stockholders should be dutifully cared for by management. Thus, any action taken by management must ultimately be justified by whether or not it furthers the interests of the corporation and its stockholders.

There is also a long tradition of departure from the view that stockholders have a privileged place in the business enterprise. Berle and Means (1932) were worried about the 'degree of prominence entitling (the corporation) to be dealt with as a major social institution'. Chester Barnard argued that the purpose of the corporation was to serve society, and that the function of the executive was to instill this sense of moral purpose in the corporation's employees (Barnard, 1938). Public relations and corporate social action have a history too long to be catalogued here. However, a recent development calls for a more far-reaching change in the way that we look at corporate life, and that is the good currency of the idea of 'stakeholders'.

The stakeholder notion is indeed a deceptively simple one. It says that there are other groups to whom the corporation is responsible in addition to stockholders: those groups who have a stake in the actions of the corporation. The word *stakeholder*, coined in an internal memorandum at the Stanford Research Institute in 1963, refers to 'those groups without whose support the organization would cease to exist'. The list of stakeholders originally included shareowners, employees, customers, suppliers, lenders and society. Stemming from the work of Igor Ansoff and Robert Stewart (in the planning department at Lockheed) and, later, Marion Doscher and Stewart (at SRI), stakeholder analysis served and continues to serve an important function in the SRI corporate planning process.

From the original work at SRI, the historical trail diverges in a number of directions. In his now classic *Corporate Strategy: An Analytic Approach to Business Policy for Growth and Expansion*, Igor Ansoff (1965) makes limited use of the theory:

> *While as we shall see later, 'responsibilities' and 'objectives' are not synonymous, they have been made one in a 'stakeholder theory' of objectives. This theory maintains that the objectives of the firm should be derived by balancing the conflicting claims of the various 'stakeholders' in the firm: managers, workers, stockholders, suppliers, vendors.*

Ansoff goes on to reject the stakeholder theory in favour of a view which separates objectives into 'economic' and 'social' with the latter being a 'secondary modifying and constraining influence' on the former.

In the mid-1970s, researchers in systems theory, led by Russell Ackoff (1974) 'rediscovered' stakeholder analysis, or at least took Ansoff's admonition more seriously. Propounding essentially an open systems view of organizations, Ackoff argues that many social problems can be solved by the redesign of fundamental institutions with the support and interaction of stakeholders in the system.

A second trail from Ansoff's original reference is the work of William Dill, who in concert with Ackoff, sought to move the stakeholder concept from the periphery of corporate planning to a central place. In 1975 Dill argued:

> *For a long time, we have assumed that the views and the initiative of stakeholders could be dealt with as externalities to the strategic planning and management process: as data to help management shape decisions, or as legal and social constraints to limit them. We have been reluctant, though, to admit the idea that some of these outside stakeholders might seek and earn active roles with management to make decisions. The move today is from stakeholder influence towards stakeholder participation.*

Dill went on to set out a role for strategic managers as communicators with stakeholders and considered the role of adversary groups such as Nader's Raiders in the strategic process. For the most part, until Dill's paper, stakeholders had been assumed to be non-adversarial, or adversarial only in the sense of labour-management relations. By broadening the notion of stakeholder to 'people outside ... who have ideas about what the economic and social performance of the enterprise should include', Dill set the stage for the use of the stakeholder concept as an umbrella for strategic management.

A related development is primarily responsible for giving the stakeholder concept a boost; namely, the increase in concern with the social involvement of business. The corporate social responsibility movement is too diverse and has spawned too many ideas, concepts and techniques to explain here. Suffice it to say that the social movements of the sixties and seventies – civil rights, the antiwar movement, consumerism, environmentalism and women's rights – served as a catalyst for rethinking the role of the business enterprise in society. From Milton Friedman to John Kenneth Galbraith, there is a diversity of arguments. However, one aspect of the corporate social responsibility debate is particularly relevant to understanding the good currency of the stakeholder concept.

In the early 1970s the Harvard Business School undertook a project on corporate social responsibility. The output of the project was voluminous, and of particular importance was the development of a pragmatic model of social responsibility called 'the corporate social responsiveness model' (Ackerman and Bauer, 1976). It essentially addressed Dill's question with respect to social issues: 'How can the corporation respond proactively to the increased pressure for positive social change?' By concentrating on responsiveness instead of responsibility, the Harvard researchers were able to link the analysis of social issues with the traditional areas of strategy and organization.

By the late 1970s the need for strategic management processes to take account of non-traditional business problems in terms of government, special interest groups, trade associations, foreign competitors, dissident shareholders, and complex issues such as employee rights, equal opportunity, environmental pollution, consumer rights, tariffs, government regulation and reindustrialization had become obvious. To begin to develop these processes, The Wharton School began, in 1977 in its Applied Research Center, a 'stakeholder project'. The objectives of the project were to put together a number of strands of thought and to develop a theory of management which enabled executives to formulate and implement corporate strategy in turbulent environments. Thus, an action research model was used whereby stakeholder theory was generated by actual cases.

To date the project has explored the implications of the stakeholder concept on three levels: as a management theory; as a process for practitioners to use in strategic management; and as an analytical framework.

At the theoretical level the implications of substituting *stakeholder* for *stockholder* needs to be explicated. The first problem at this level is the actual definition of *stakeholder*. SRI's original definition is too general and too exclusive to serve as a means of identifying those external groups who are strategically important. The concentration on generic stakeholders, such as society and customers, rather than specific social interest groups and specific customer segments produces an analysis which can only be used as a background for the planning process. Strategically useful information about the actions, objectives and motivations of specific groups, which is needed if management is to be responsive to stakeholder concerns, requires a more specific and inclusive definition.

We propose two definitions of *stakeholder:* a wide sense, which includes groups who are friendly or hostile, and a narrow sense, which captures the essence of the SRI definition, but is more specific.

- The wide sense of stakeholder. Any identifiable group or individual who can affect the achievement of an organization's objectives or who is affected by the achievement of an organization's objectives. (Public interest groups, protest groups, government agencies, trade associations, competitors, unions, as well as employees, customer segments, shareowners and others are stakeholders, in this sense.)

- The narrow sense of stakeholder. Any identifiable group or individual on which the organization is dependent for its continued survival. (Employees, customer segments, certain suppliers, key government agencies, shareowners, certain financial institutions, as well as others are all stakeholders in the narrow sense of the term.)

While executives are willing to recognize that employees, suppliers and customers have a stake in the corporation, many resist the inclusion of adversary groups. But from the standpoint of corporate strategy, *stakeholder* must be understood in the wide sense: strategies need to account for those groups who can affect the achievement of the firm's objectives. Some may feel happier with other words, such as *influencers, claimants, publics,* or *constituencies.* Semantics aside, if corporations are to formulate and implement strategies in turbulent environments, theories of strategy must have concepts, such as the wide sense of *stakeholder,* which allow the analysis of all external forces and pressures whether they are friendly or hostile. In what follows we will use *stakeholder* in the wide sense, as our primary objective is to elucidate the questions of corporate governance from the perspective of strategic management.

A second issue at the theoretical level is the generation of prescriptive propositions which explain actual cases and articulate regulative principles for future use. Thus, a *post hoc* analysis of the brewing industry and the problem of beverage container legislation, combined with a similar analysis of the regulatory environments of public utilities have led to some simple propositions which serve as a philosophical guideline for strategy formulation. For example:

- Generalize the marketing approach: understand the needs of each stakeholder, in a similar fashion to understanding customer needs, and design products, services and programmes to fulfil those needs.

- Establish negotiation processes: understand the political nature of a number of stakeholders, and the applicability of concepts and techniques of political science, such as coalition analysis, conflict management, and the use and abuse of unilateral action.
- Establish a decision philosophy that is oriented towards seizing the initiative rather than reacting to events as they occur.
- Allocate organizational resources based on the degree of importance of the environmental turbulence (the stakeholders' claims).

Other prescriptive propositions can be put forth, especially with respect to issues of corporate governance. One proposition that has been discussed is to 'involve stakeholder groups in strategic decisions', or 'invite stakeholders to participate in governance decisions'. While propositions like this may have substantial merit, we have not examined enough cases nor marshalled enough evidence to support them in an unqualified manner. There are cases where participation is appropriate. Some public utilities have been quite successful in the use of stakeholder advisory groups in matters of rate setting. However, given the breadth of our concept of stakeholder we believe that cooptation through participation is not always the correct strategic decision.

The second level of analysis is the use of stakeholder concepts in strategy formulation processes. Two processes have been used so far: the *Stakeholder Strategy Process* and the *Stakeholder Audit Process.* The Stakeholder Strategy Process is a systematic method for analysing the relative importance of stakeholders and their cooperative potential (how they can help the corporation achieve its objectives) and their competitive threat (how they can prevent the corporation from achieving its objectives). The process is one which relies on a behavioural analysis (both actual and potential) for input, and an explanatory model of stakeholder objectives and resultant strategic shifts for output. The Stakeholder Audit Process is a systematic method for identifying stakeholders and assessing the effectiveness of current organizational strategies. By itself, each process has a use in the strategic management of an organization. Each analyses the stakeholder environment from the standpoint of organizational mission and objectives and seeks to formulate strategies for meeting stakeholder needs and concerns.

The use of the stakeholder concept at the analytical level means thinking in terms which are broader than current strategic and operational problems. It implies looking at public policy questions in stakeholder terms and trying to understand how the relationships between an organization and its stakeholders would change given the implementation of certain policies.

One analytical device depicts an organization's stakeholders on a two-dimensional grid map. The first dimension is one of 'interest' or 'stake' and ranges from an equity interest to an economic interest or marketplace stake, to an interest or stake as a 'kibitzer' or influencer. Shareowners have an equity stake; customers and suppliers have an economic stake; and single-issue groups have an influencer stake. The second dimension of a stakeholder is its power, which ranges from the formalistic or voting power of stockholders to the economic power of customers, to the political power of special interest groups. By *economic power* we mean 'the ability to influence due to marketplace decisions' and by *political power* we mean 'the ability to influence due to use of the political process'.

Figure 3.2.1 represents this stakeholder grid graphically. It is of course possible that a stakeholder has more than one kind of both stake and power, especially in light of the fact that there are stakeholders who have multiple roles. An employee may be at once shareholder, customer, employee and even kibitzer. Figure 3.2.1 represents the prevailing world view. That is, shareholders and directors have formal or voting power; customers, suppliers and employees have economic power; and government and special interest groups have political power. Moreover, management concepts and principles have evolved to treat this 'diagonal case.' Managers learn how to handle stockholders and boards via their ability to vote on certain key decisions, and conflicts are resolved by the procedures and processes written into the corporate charter or by methods which involve formal legal parameters. Strategic planners, marketers, financial analysts and operations executives base their decisions on marketplace variables, and an entire tradition of management principles is based on the economic analysis of the marketplace. Finally, public relations and public affairs managers and lobbyists learn to deal in the political arena. As long as the real world approximately fits into the diagonal, management processes may be able to deal effectively with them.

A more thoughtful examination, however, reveals that Figure 3.2.1 is either a straw man or that shifts of position have occurred. In the auto industry, for instance, one part of government has acquired economic power in terms of the imposition of import quotas or the trigger price mechanism. The Securities and Exchange

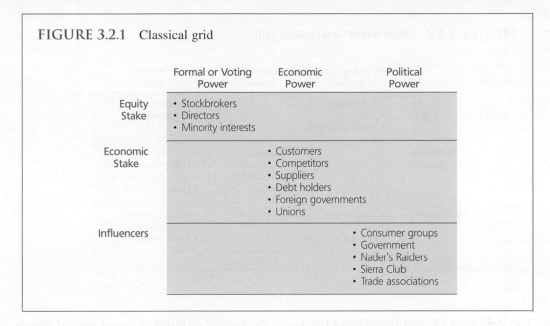

FIGURE 3.2.1 Classical grid

	Formal or Voting Power	Economic Power	Political Power
Equity Stake	• Stockbrokers • Directors • Minority interests		
Economic Stake		• Customers • Competitors • Suppliers • Debt holders • Foreign governments • Unions	
Influencers			• Consumer groups • Government • Nader's Raiders • Sierra Club • Trade associations

Commission might be looked at as a kibitzer with formal power in terms of disclosure and accounting rules. Outside directors do not necessarily have an equity stake, especially those women, minorities and academics who are becoming more and more normal for the boards of large corporations. Some kibitzer groups are buying stock and acquiring an equity stake, and while they also acquire formal power, their main source of power is still political. Witness the marshalling of the political process by church groups in bringing up, at annual meetings, issues such as selling infant formula in the Third World or investing in South Africa. Unions are using their political power as well as their formal clout as managers of large portions of pension funds to influence the company. Customers are being organized by consumer advocates to exercise the voice option and to politicize the marketplace. In short, the real world looks more like Figure 3.2.2. (Of course, each organization will have its own individual grid.) Thus, a search for alternative applications of traditional management processes must begin, and new concepts and techniques are needed to understand the shifts that have occurred and to manage in the new environment.

There is a need to develop new and innovative management processes to deal with the current and future complexities of management issues. At the theoretical level, stakeholder analysis has been developed to enrich the economic approach to corporate strategy by arguing that kibitzers with political power must be included in the strategy process. At the strategic level, stakeholder analysis takes a number of groups into account and analyses their strategic impact on the corporation.

Stakeholder analysis and corporate democracy

The debate on corporate governance and, in particular, corporate democracy has recently intensified. Proposals have been put forth to make the corporation more democratic, to encourage shareholder participation and management responsiveness to shareholder needs, and to make corporations more responsive to other stakeholder needs and, hence, to encourage the participation of stakeholders in the governance process. Reforms from cumulative voting to audit committees have been suggested.

Corporate democracy has come to have at least three meanings over the years, which prescribe that corporations should be made more democratic: by increasing the role of government, either as a watchdog or by having public officials on boards of directors; by allowing citizen or public participation in the managing of its affairs via public interest directors and the like; or by encouraging or mandating the active participation of all or many of its shareholders. The analysis of the preceding section has implications for each of these levels of democratization.

The propositions of stakeholder analysis advocate a thorough understanding of a firm's stakeholders (in the wide sense) and recognize that there are times when stakeholders must participate in the decision-making

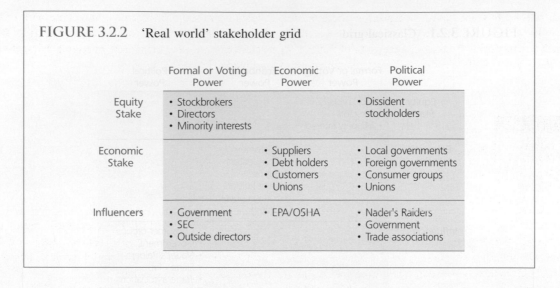

FIGURE 3.2.2   'Real world' stakeholder grid

	Formal or Voting Power	Economic Power	Political Power
Equity Stake	• Stockbrokers • Directors • Minority interests		• Dissident stockholders
Economic Stake		• Suppliers • Debt holders • Customers • Unions	• Local governments • Foreign governments • Consumer groups • Unions
Influencers	• Government • SEC • Outside directors	• EPA/OSHA	• Nader's Raiders • Government • Trade associations

process. The strategic tools and techniques of stakeholder analysis yield a method for determining the timing and degree of such participation. At the absolute minimum this implies that boards of directors must be aware of the impact of their decisions on key stakeholder groups. As stakeholders have begun to exercise more political power and as marketplace decisions become politicized, the need for awareness to grow into responsiveness has become apparent. Thus, the analytical model can be used by boards to map carefully the power and stake of each group. While it is not the proper role of the board to be involved in the implementation of tactical programmes at the operational level of the corporation, it must set the tone for how the company deals with stakeholders, both traditional marketplace ones and those who have political power. The board must decide not only whether management is managing the affairs of the corporation, but indeed, what are to count as the affairs of the corporation. This involves assessing the stake and power of each stakeholder group.

Much has been written about the failure of senior management to think strategically, competitively and globally. Some have argued that American businesspersons are 'managing [their] way to economic decline' (Hayes and Abernathy, 1980). Executives have countered the critics with complaints about the increase in the adversarial role of government and in the number of hostile external interest groups. Yet if the criteria for success for senior executives remain fixated on economic stakeholders with economic power and on short-term performance on Wall Street, the rise of such a turbulent political environment in a free and open society should come as no surprise. If the board sees itself as responsive only to the shareholder in the short term, senior management will continue to manage towards economic decline.[2] We have argued that the problem of governing the corporation in today's world must be viewed in terms of the entire grid of stakeholders and their power base. It is only by setting the direction for positive response and negotiation at the board level that the adversarial nature of the business-government relationship can be overcome.

If this task of stakeholder management is done properly, much of the air is let out of critics who argue that the corporation must be democratized in terms of increased direct citizen participation. Issues which involve both economic and political stakes and power bases must be addressed in an integrated fashion. No longer can public affairs, public relations and corporate philanthropy serve as adequate management tools. The sophistication of interest groups who are beginning to use formal power mechanisms, such as proxy fights, annual meetings, the corporate charter, to focus the attention of management on the affairs of the

[2]It is arguable whether responsiveness to non-market stakeholders is in the long-term interest of the corporation. We believe that there is no need to appeal to utilitarian notions of greatest social good or altruism or social responsibility. Rather, the corporation fulfils its obligations to shareholders in the long term only through proper stakeholder management. In short we believe that enlightened self-interest gives both reasons why (personal motivation) and reasons for (social justification) taking stakeholder concerns into account. The development of this argument is, however, beyond our present scope.

corporation, has increased. Responsive boards will seize these opportunities to learn more about those stakeholders who have chosen the option of voice over the Wall Street Rule. As boards direct management to respond to these concerns, to negotiate with critics, to trade off certain policies in return for positive support, the pressure for mandated citizen participation will subside.

Creating shared value

By Michael E. Porter and Mark R. Kramer[1]

The capitalist system is under siege. In recent years business increasingly has been viewed as a major cause of social, environmental and economic problems. Companies are widely perceived to be prospering at the expense of the broader community. Even worse, the more business has begun to embrace corporate responsibility, the more it has been blamed for society's failures. The legitimacy of business has fallen to levels not seen in recent history. This diminished trust in business leads political leaders to set policies that undermine competitiveness and sap economic growth. Business is caught in a vicious circle.

A big part of the problem lies with companies themselves, which remain trapped in an outdated approach to value creation that has emerged over the past few decades. They continue to view value creation narrowly, optimizing short-term financial performance in a bubble while missing the most important customer needs and ignoring the broader influences that determine their longer-term success. How else could companies overlook the well-being of their customers, the depletion of natural resources vital to their businesses, the viability of key suppliers, or the economic distress of the communities in which they produce and sell? How else could companies think that simply shifting activities to locations with ever lower wages was a sustainable "solution" to competitive challenges? Government and civil society have often exacerbated the problem by attempting to address social weaknesses at the expense of business. The presumed trade-offs between economic efficiency and social progress have been institutionalized in decades of policy choices.

Companies must take the lead in bringing business and society back together. The recognition is there among sophisticated business and thought leaders, and promising elements of a new model are emerging. Yet we still lack an overall framework for guiding these efforts, and most companies remain stuck in a "social responsibility" mind-set in which societal issues are at the periphery, not the core.

The solution lies in the principle of shared value, which involves creating economic value in a way that *also* creates value for society by addressing its needs and challenges. Businesses must reconnect company success with social progress. Shared value is not social responsibility, philanthropy, or even sustainability, but a new way to achieve economic success. It is not on the margin of what companies do but at the centre. We believe that it can give rise to major transformation of business thinking.

A growing number of companies known for their hard-nosed approach to business – such as GE, Google, IBM, Intel, Johnson & Johnson, Nestlé, Unilever and Wal-Mart – have already embarked on important efforts to create shared value by reconceiving the intersection between society and corporate performance. Yet our recognition of the transformative power of shared value is still in its genesis. Realizing it will require leaders and managers to develop new skills and knowledge – such as a far deeper appreciation of societal needs, a greater understanding of the true bases of company productivity, and the ability to collaborate across profit/non-profit boundaries. And government must learn how to regulate in ways that enable shared value rather than work against it.

Capitalism is an unparalleled vehicle for meeting human needs, improving efficiency, creating jobs and building wealth. But a narrow conception of capitalism has prevented business from harnessing its full potential to meet society's broader challenges. The opportunities have been there all along but have been overlooked. Businesses acting as businesses, not as charitable donors, are the most powerful force for addressing the pressing issues we face. The moment for a new conception of capitalism is now; society's needs are large and growing, while customers, employees, and a new generation of young people are asking business to step up.

The purpose of the corporation must be redefined as creating shared value, not just profit *per se*. This will drive the next wave of innovation and productivity growth in the global economy. It will also reshape capitalism and its relationship to society. Perhaps most important of all, learning how to create shared value is our best chance to legitimize business again.

Moving beyond trade-offs

Business and society have been pitted against each other for too long. That is in part because economists have legitimized the idea that to provide societal benefits, companies must temper their economic success. In neoclassical thinking, a requirement for social improvement – such as safety or hiring the disabled – imposes a constraint on the corporation. Adding a constraint to a firm that is already maximizing profits, says the theory, will inevitably raise costs and reduce those profits.

A related concept, with the same conclusion, is the notion of externalities. Externalities arise when firms create social costs that they do not have to bear, such as pollution. Thus, society must impose taxes, regulations and penalties so that firms "internalize" these externalities – a belief influencing many government policy decisions.

This perspective has also shaped the strategies of firms themselves, which have largely excluded social and environmental considerations from their economic thinking. Firms have taken the broader context in which they do business as a given and resisted regulatory standards as invariably contrary to their interests. Solving social problems has been ceded to governments and to NGOs. Corporate responsibility programmes – a reaction to external pressure – have emerged largely to improve firms' reputations and are treated as a necessary expense. Anything more is seen by many as an irresponsible use of shareholders' money. Governments, for their part, have often regulated in a way that makes shared value more difficult to achieve. Implicitly, each side has assumed that the other is an obstacle to pursuing its goals and acted accordingly.

The concept of shared value, in contrast, recognizes that societal needs, not just conventional economic needs, define markets. It also recognizes that social harms or weaknesses frequently create *internal* costs for firms – such as wasted energy or raw materials, costly accidents, and the need for remedial training to compensate for inadequacies in education. And addressing societal harms and constraints does not necessarily raise costs for firms, because they can innovate through using new technologies, operating methods and management approaches – and as a result, increase their productivity and expand their markets.

Shared value, then, is not about personal values. Nor is it about "sharing" the value already created by firms – a redistribution approach. Instead, it is about expanding the total pool of economic and social value. A good example of this difference in perspective is the fair trade movement in purchasing. Fair trade aims to increase the proportion of revenue that goes to poor farmers by paying them higher prices for the same crops. Though this may be a noble sentiment, fair trade is mostly about redistribution rather than expanding the overall amount of value created. A shared value perspective, instead, focuses on improving growing techniques and strengthening the local cluster of supporting suppliers and other institutions in order to increase farmers' efficiency, yields, product quality and sustainability. This leads to a bigger pie of revenue and profits that benefits both farmers and the companies that buy from them. Early studies of cocoa farmers in the Côte d'Ivoire, for instance, suggest that while fair trade can increase farmers' incomes by 10 per cent to 20 per cent, shared value investments can raise their incomes by more than 300 per cent. Initial investment and time may be required to implement new procurement practices and develop the supporting cluster, but the return will be greater economic value and broader strategic benefits for all participants.

The roots of shared value

At a very basic level, the competitiveness of a company and the health of the communities around it are closely intertwined. A business needs a successful community, not only to create demand for its products but also to provide critical public assets and a supportive environment. A community needs successful businesses to provide jobs and wealth creation opportunities for its citizens. This interdependence means that public policies that undermine the productivity and competitiveness of businesses are self-defeating, especially in a global economy where facilities and jobs can easily move elsewhere. NGOs and governments have not always appreciated this connection.

In the old, narrow view of capitalism, business contributes to society by making a profit, which supports employment, wages, purchases, investments and taxes. Conducting business as usual is sufficient social benefit. A firm is largely a self-contained entity, and social or community issues fall outside its proper scope. (This is the argument advanced persuasively by Milton Friedman in his critique of the whole notion of corporate social responsibility.)

This perspective has permeated management thinking for the past two decades. Firms focused on enticing consumers to buy more and more of their products. Facing growing competition and shorter-term performance pressures from shareholders, managers resorted to waves of restructuring, personnel reductions and relocation to lower-cost regions, while leveraging balance sheets to return capital to investors. The results were often commoditization, price competition, little true innovation, slow organic growth, and no clear competitive advantage.

In this kind of competition, the communities in which companies operate perceive little benefit even as profits rise. Instead, they perceive that profits come at their expense, an impression that has become even stronger in the current economic recovery, in which rising earnings have done little to offset high unemployment, local business distress and severe pressures on community services.

It was not always this way. The best companies once took on a broad range of roles in meeting the needs of workers, communities and supporting businesses. As other social institutions appeared on the scene, however, these roles fell away or were delegated. Shortening investor time horizons began to narrow thinking about appropriate investments. As the vertically integrated firm gave way to greater reliance on outside vendors, outsourcing and offshoring weakened the connection between firms and their communities. As firms moved disparate activities to more and more locations, they often lost touch with any location. Indeed, many companies no longer recognize a home – but see themselves as "global" companies.

These transformations drove major progress in economic efficiency. However, something profoundly important was lost in the process, as more fundamental opportunities for value creation were missed. The scope of strategic thinking contracted.

Strategy theory holds that to be successful, a company must create a distinctive value proposition that meets the needs of a chosen set of customers. The firm gains competitive advantage from how it configures the value chain, or the set of activities involved in creating, producing, selling, delivering and supporting its products or services. For decades businesspeople have studied positioning and the best ways to design activities and integrate them. However, companies have overlooked opportunities to meet fundamental societal needs and misunderstood how societal harms and weaknesses affect value chains. Our field of vision has simply been too narrow.

In understanding the business environment, managers have focused most of their attention on the industry, or the particular business in which the firm competes. This is because industry structure has a decisive impact on a firm's profitability. What has been missed, however, is the profound effect that location can have on productivity and innovation. Companies have failed to grasp the importance of the broader business environment surrounding their major operations.

EXHIBIT 3.3.1   WHAT IS "SHARED VALUE"?

The concept of shared value can be defined as policies and operating practices that enhance the competitiveness of a company while simultaneously advancing the economic and social conditions in the communities in which it operates. Shared value creation focuses on identifying and expanding the connections between societal and economic progress.

The concept rests on the premise that both economic and social progress must be addressed using value principles. Value is defined as benefits relative to costs, not just benefits alone. Value creation is an idea that has long been recognized in business, where profit is revenues earned from customers minus the costs incurred. However, businesses have rarely approached societal issues from a value perspective but have treated them as peripheral matters. This has obscured the connections between economic and social concerns.

In the social sector, thinking in value terms is even less common. Social organizations and government entities often see success solely in terms of the benefits achieved or the money expended. As governments and NGOs begin to think more in value terms, their interest in collaborating with business will inevitably grow.

How shared value is created

Companies can create economic value by creating societal value. There are three distinct ways to do this: by reconceiving products and markets, redefining productivity in the value chain, and building supportive industry clusters at the company's locations. Each of these is part of the virtuous circle of shared value; improving value in one area gives rise to opportunities in the others.

The concept of shared value resets the boundaries of capitalism. By better connecting companies' success with societal improvement, it opens up many ways to serve new needs, gain efficiency, create differentiation and expand markets.

The ability to create shared value applies equally to advanced economies and developing countries, though the specific opportunities will differ. The opportunities will also differ markedly across industries and companies – but every company has them. And their range and scope is far broader than has been recognized.

Reconceiving products and markets

Society's needs are huge – health, better housing, improved nutrition, help for the aging, greater financial security, less environmental damage. Arguably, they are the greatest unmet needs in the global economy. In business we have spent decades learning how to parse and manufacture demand while missing the most important demand of all. Too many companies have lost sight of that most basic of questions: Is our product good for our customers? Or for our customers' customers?

In advanced economies, demand for products and services that meet societal needs is rapidly growing. Food companies that traditionally concentrated on taste and quantity to drive more consumption are refocusing on the fundamental need for better nutrition; Intel and IBM are both devising ways to help utilities harness digital intelligence in order to economize on power usage. Wells Fargo has developed a loan of products and tools that help customers budget, manage credit, and pay down debt. Sales of GE's Ecomagination products reached $18 billion in 2009 – the size of a *Fortune* 150 company. GE now predicts that revenues of Ecomagination products will grow at twice the rate of total company revenues over the next five years.

In these and many other ways, whole new avenues for innovation open up and shared value is created. Society's gains are even greater, because businesses will often be far more effective than governments and non-profit organizations are at marketing that motivates customers to embrace products and services that create benefits, like healthier food or environmentally friendly products.

Equal or greater opportunities arise from serving disadvantaged communities and developing countries. Though societal needs are even more pressing there, these communities have not been recognized as viable markets. Today attention is riveted on India, China and, increasingly, Brazil, which offer firms the prospect of reaching billions of new customers at the bottom of the pyramid – a notion persuasively

---

EXHIBIT 3.3.2 BLURRING THE PROFIT/NON-PROFIT BOUNDARY

The concept of shared value blurs the line between for-profit and non-profit organizations. New kinds of hybrid enterprises are rapidly appearing. For example, WaterHealth International, a fast-growing for-profit, uses innovative water purification techniques to distribute clean water at minimal cost to more than one million people in rural India, Ghana and the Philippines. Its investors include not only the socially focused Acumen Fund and the International Finance Corporation of the World Bank but also Dow Chemical's venture fund. Revolution Foods, a four-year-old venture capital-backed US start-up, provides 60,000 fresh, healthful and nutritious meals to students daily – and does so at a higher gross margin than traditional competitors. Waste Concern, a hybrid profit/non-profit enterprise started in Bangladesh 15 years ago, has built the capacity to convert 700 tons of trash, collected daily from neighbourhood slums, into organic fertilizer, thereby increasing crop yields and reducing CO_2 emissions. Seeded with capital from the Lions Club and the United Nations Development Programme, the company improves health conditions while earning a substantial gross margin through fertilizer sales and carbon credits.

The blurring of the boundary between successful for-profits and non-profits is one of the strong signs that creating shared value is possible.

EXHIBIT 3.3.3 THE CONNECTION BETWEEN COMPETITIVE ADVANTAGE AND SOCIAL ISSUES

There are numerous ways in which addressing societal concerns can yield productivity benefits to a firm. Consider, for example, what happens when a firm invests in a wellness programme. Society benefits because employees and their families become healthier, and the firm minimizes employee absences and lost productivity. The graphic below depicts some areas where the connections are strongest.

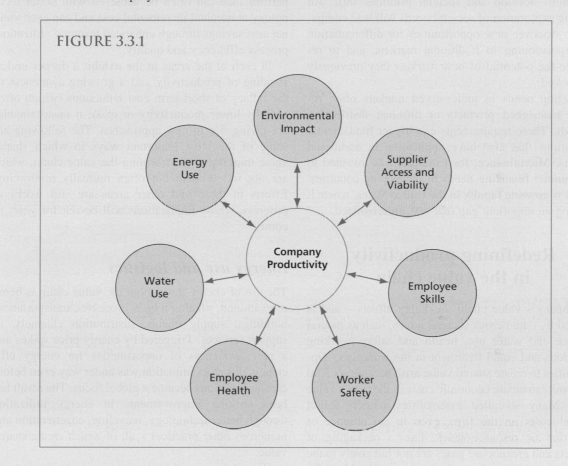

FIGURE 3.3.1

articulated by C.K. Prahalad. Yet these countries have always had huge needs, as do many developing countries.

Similar opportunities await in non-traditional communities in advanced countries. We have learned, for example, that poor urban areas are America's most underserved market; their substantial concentrated purchasing power has often been overlooked.

The societal benefits of providing appropriate products to lower-income and disadvantaged consumers can be profound, while the profits for companies can be substantial. For example, low-priced cellphones that provide mobile banking services are helping the poor save money securely and transforming the ability of small farmers to produce and market their crops. In Kenya, Vodafone's M-PESA mobile banking service signed up 10 million customers in three years; the funds it handles now represent 11 per cent of that country's GDP. In India, Thomson Reuters has developed a promising monthly service for farmers who earn an average of $2,000 a year. For a fee of $5 a quarter, it provides weather and crop-pricing information and agricultural advice. The service reaches an estimated 2 million farmers, and early research indicates that it has helped increase the incomes of more than 60 per cent of them – in some cases even tripling incomes. As capitalism begins to work in poorer communities, new opportunities for economic development and social progress increase exponentially.

For a company, the starting point for creating this kind of shared value is to identify all the societal needs, benefits and harms that are, or could be embodied in the firm's products. The opportunities are not static; they change constantly as technology evolves, economies develop and societal priorities shift. An ongoing exploration of societal needs will lead companies to discover new opportunities for differentiation and repositioning in traditional markets, and to recognize the potential of new markets they previously overlooked.

Meeting needs in underserved markets often requires redesigned products or different distribution methods. These requirements can trigger fundamental innovations that also have application in traditional markets. Microfinance, for example, was invented to serve unmet financing needs in developing countries. Now it is growing rapidly in the United States, where it is filling an important gap that was unrecognized.

Redefining productivity in the value chain

A company's value chain inevitably affects – and is affected by – numerous societal issues, such as natural resource and water use, health and safety, working conditions and equal treatment in the workplace. Opportunities to create shared value arise because societal problems can create economic costs in the firm's value chain. Many so-called externalities actually inflict internal costs on the firm, even in the absence of regulation or resource taxes. Excess packaging of products and greenhouse gases are not just costly to the environment but costly to the business. Wal-Mart, for example, was able to address both issues by reducing its packaging and rerouting its trucks to cut 100 million miles from its delivery routes in 2009, saving $200 million even as it shipped more products. Innovation in disposing of plastic used in stores has saved millions in lower disposal costs to landfills.

The new thinking reveals that the congruence between societal progress and productivity in the value chain is far greater than traditionally believed (see exhibit 3.3.3, "The Connection Between Competitive Advantage and Social Issues"). The synergy increases when firms approach societal issues from a shared value perspective and invent new ways of operating to address them. So far, however, few companies have

reaped the full productivity benefits in areas such as health, safety, environmental performance and employee retention and capability.

But there are unmistakable signs of change. Efforts to minimize pollution were once thought to inevitably increase business costs – and to occur only because of regulation and taxes. Today there is a growing consensus that major improvements in environmental performance can often be achieved with better technology at nominal incremental cost and can even yield net cost savings through enhanced resource utilization, process efficiency and quality.

In each of the areas in the exhibit a deeper understanding of productivity and a growing awareness of the fallacy of short-term cost reductions (which often actually lower productivity or make it unsustainable) are giving rise to new approaches. The following are some of the most important ways in which shared value thinking is transforming the value chain, which are not independent but often mutually reinforcing. Efforts in these and other areas are still works in progress, whose implications will be felt for years to come.

Energy use and logistics

The use of energy throughout the value chain is being re-examined, whether it be in processes, transportation, buildings, supply chains, distribution channels, or support services. Triggered by energy price spikes and a new awareness of opportunities for energy efficiency, this re-examination was under way even before carbon emissions became a global focus. The result has been striking improvements in energy utilization through better technology, recycling, cogeneration and numerous other practices – all of which create shared value.

We are learning that shipping is expensive, not just because of energy costs and emissions, but because it adds time, complexity, inventory costs and management costs. Logistical systems are beginning to be redesigned to reduce shipping distances, streamline handling, improve vehicle routing and the like. All of these steps create shared value. The British retailer Marks & Spencer's ambitious overhaul of its supply chain, for example, which involves steps as simple as stopping the purchase of supplies from one hemisphere to ship to another, is expected to save the retailer £175 million annually by fiscal 2016, while hugely reducing carbon emissions. In the process of re-examining logistics, thinking about outsourcing and location will also be revised (as we will discuss below).

Resource use

Heightened environmental awareness and advances in technology are catalysing new approaches in areas such as utilization of water, raw materials and packaging, as well as expanding recycling and reuse. The opportunities apply to all resources, not just those that have been identified by environmentalists. Better resource utilization – enabled by improving technology – will permeate all parts of the value chain and will spread to suppliers and channels. Landfills will fill more slowly.

For example, Coca-Cola has already reduced its worldwide water consumption by 9 per cent from a 2004 baseline – nearly halfway to its goal of a 20 per cent reduction by 2012. Dow Chemical managed to reduce consumption of fresh water at its largest production site by one billion gallons – enough water to supply nearly 40,000 people in the US for a year – resulting in savings of $4 million. The demand for water-saving technology has allowed India's Jain Irrigation, a leading global manufacturer of complete drip irrigation systems for water conservation, to achieve a 41 per cent compound annual growth rate in revenue over the past five years.

Procurement

The traditional playbook calls for companies to commoditize and exert maximum bargaining power on suppliers to drive down prices – even when purchasing from small businesses or subsistence-level farmers. More recently, firms have been rapidly outsourcing to suppliers in lower-wage locations.

Today some companies are beginning to understand that marginalized suppliers cannot remain productive or sustain, much less improve, their quality. By increasing access to inputs, sharing technology and providing financing, companies can improve supplier quality and productivity while ensuring access to growing volume. Improving productivity will often trump lower prices. As suppliers get stronger, their environmental impact often falls dramatically, which further improves their efficiency.

A good example of such new procurement thinking can be found at Nespresso, one of Nestlé's fastest-growing divisions, which has enjoyed annual growth of 30 per cent since 2000. Nespresso combines a sophisticated espresso machine with single-cup aluminum capsules containing ground coffees from around the world. Offering quality and convenience, Nespresso has expanded the market for premium coffee.

Obtaining a reliable supply of specialized coffees is extremely challenging, however. Most coffees are grown by small farmers in impoverished rural areas of Africa and Latin America, who are trapped in a cycle of low productivity, poor quality and environmental degradation that limits production volume. To address these issues, Nestlé redesigned procurement. It worked intensively with its growers, providing advice on farming practices, guaranteeing bank loans, and helping secure inputs such as plant stock, pesticides and fertilizers. Nestlé established local facilities to measure the quality of the coffee at the point of purchase, which allowed it to pay a premium for better beans directly to the growers and thus improve their incentives. Greater yield per hectare and higher production quality increased growers' incomes, and the environmental impact of farms shrank. Meanwhile, Nestlé's reliable supply of good coffee grew significantly. Shared value was created.

Embedded in the Nestlé example is a far broader insight, which is the advantage of buying from capable local suppliers. Outsourcing to other locations and countries creates transaction costs and inefficiencies that can offset lower wage and input costs. Capable local suppliers help firms avoid these costs and can reduce cycle time, increase flexibility, foster faster

---

EXHIBIT 3.3.4   THE ROLE OF SOCIAL ENTREPRENEURS

Businesses are not the only players in finding profitable solutions to social problems. A whole generation of social entrepreneurs is pioneering new product concepts that meet social needs using viable business models. Because they are not locked into narrow traditional business thinking, social entrepreneurs are often well ahead of established corporations in discovering these opportunities.

Social enterprises that create shared value can scale up far more rapidly than purely social programmes, which often suffer from an inability to grow and become self-sustaining.

Real social entrepreneurship should be measured by its ability to create shared value, not just social benefit.

learning and enable innovation. Buying local includes not only local companies but also local units of national or international companies. When firms buy locally, their suppliers can get stronger, increase their profits, hire more people and pay better wages – all of which will benefit other businesses in the community. Shared value is created.

Distribution

Companies are beginning to re-examine distribution practices from a shared value perspective. As iTunes, Kindle and Google Scholar (which offers texts of scholarly literature online) demonstrate, profitable new distribution models can also dramatically reduce paper and plastic usage. Similarly, microfinance has created a cost-efficient new model of distributing financial services to small businesses.

Opportunities for new distribution models can be even greater in non-traditional markets. For example, Hindustan Unilever is creating a new direct-to-home distribution system, run by underprivileged female entrepreneurs, in Indian villages of fewer than 2,000 people. Unilever provides microcredit and training and now has more than 45,000 entrepreneurs covering some 100,000 villages across 15 Indian states. Project Shakti, as this distribution system is called, benefits communities not only by giving women skills that often double their household income, but also by re-ducing the spread of communicable diseases through increased access to hygiene products. This is a good example of how the unique ability of business to market to hard-to-reach consumers can benefit society by getting life-altering products into the hands of people that need them. Project Shakti now accounts for 5 per cent of Unilever's total revenues in India and has ex-tended the company's reach into rural areas and built its brand in media-dark regions, creating major eco-nomic value for the company.

Employee productivity

The focus on holding down wage levels, reducing benefits, and offshoring is beginning to give way to an awareness of the positive effects that a living wage, safety, wellness, training and opportunities for ad-vancement for employees have on productivity. Many companies, for example, traditionally sought to mini-mize the cost of "expensive" employee health care coverage or even eliminate health coverage altogether. Today leading companies have learned that because of lost workdays and diminished employee productivity,

poor health costs them more than health benefits do. Take Johnson & Johnson. By helping employees stop smoking (a two-thirds reduction in the past 15 years) and implementing numerous other wellness pro-grammes, the company has saved $250 million on health care costs, a return of $2.71 for every dollar spent on wellness from 2002 to 2008. Moreover, Johnson & Johnson has benefited from a more present and productive workforce. If labour unions focused more on shared value too, these kinds of employee approaches would spread even faster.

Location

Business thinking has embraced the myth that location no longer matters, because logistics are inexpensive, information flows rapidly, and markets are global. The cheaper the location, then, the better. Concern about the local communities in which a company operates has faded.

That oversimplified thinking is now being chal-lenged, partly by the rising costs of energy and carbon emissions but also by a greater recognition of the pro-ductivity cost of highly dispersed production systems and the hidden costs of distant procurement discussed earlier. Wal-Mart, for example, is increasingly sourc-ing produce for its food sections from local farms near its warehouses. It has discovered that the savings on transportation costs and the ability to restock in smaller quantities more than offset the lower prices of in-dustrial farms farther away. Nestlé is establishing smaller plants closer to its markets and stepping up efforts to maximize the use of locally available materials.

The calculus of locating activities in developing countries is also changing. Olam International, a lead-ing cashew producer, traditionally shipped its nuts from Africa to Asia for processing at facilities staffed by productive Asian workers. But by opening local processing plants and training workers in Tanzania, Mozambique, Nigeria and Côte d'Ivoire, Olam has cut processing and shipping costs by as much as 25 per cent – not to mention greatly reduced carbon emis-sions. In making this move, Olam also built preferred relationships with local farmers. And it has provided direct employment to 17,000 people – 95 per cent of whom are women – and indirect employment to an equal number of people in rural areas where jobs otherwise were not available.

These trends may well lead companies to remake their value chains by moving some activities closer to home and having fewer major production locations.

Until now, many companies have thought that being global meant moving production to locations with the lowest labour costs and designing their supply chains to achieve the most immediate impact on expenses. In reality, the strongest international competitors will often be those that can establish deeper roots in important communities. Companies that can embrace this new locational thinking will create shared value.

As these examples illustrate, reimagining value chains from the perspective of shared value will offer significant new ways to innovate and unlock new economic value that most businesses have missed.

Enabling local cluster development

No company is self-contained. The success of every company is affected by the supporting companies and infrastructure around it. Productivity and innovation are strongly influenced by "clusters," or geographic concentrations of firms, related businesses, suppliers, service providers and logistical infrastructure in a particular field – such as IT in Silicon Valley, cut flowers in Kenya, and diamond cutting in Surat, India.

Clusters include not only businesses but institutions such as academic programmes, trade associations and standards organizations. They also draw on the broader public assets in the surrounding community, such as schools and universities, clean water, fair-competition laws, quality standards and market transparency.

Clusters are prominent in all successful and growing regional economies and play a crucial role in driving productivity, innovation and competitiveness. Capable local suppliers foster greater logistical efficiency and ease of collaboration, as we have discussed. Stronger local capabilities in such areas as training, transportation services and related industries also boost productivity. Without a supporting cluster, conversely, productivity suffers.

Deficiencies in the framework conditions surrounding the cluster also create internal costs for firms. Poor public education imposes productivity and remedial-training costs. Poor transportation infrastructure drives up the costs of logistics. Gender or racial discrimination reduces the pool of capable employees. Poverty limits the demand for products and leads to environmental degradation, unhealthy workers and high security costs. As companies have increasingly become disconnected from their communities, however, their influence in solving these problems has waned even as their costs have grown.

Firms create shared value by building clusters to improve company productivity, while addressing gaps or failures in the framework conditions surrounding the cluster. Efforts to develop or attract capable suppliers, for example, enable the procurement benefits we discussed earlier. A focus on clusters and location has been all but absent in management thinking. Cluster thinking has also been missing in many economic development initiatives, which have failed because they involved isolated interventions and overlooked critical complementary investments.

A key aspect of cluster building in developing and developed countries alike is the formation of open and transparent markets. In inefficient or monopolized markets where workers are exploited, where suppliers do not receive fair prices, and where price transparency is lacking, productivity suffers. Enabling fair and open markets, which is often best done in conjunction with partners, can allow a company to secure reliable supplies and give suppliers better incentives for quality and efficiency while also substantially improving the incomes and purchasing power of local citizens. A positive cycle of economic and social development results.

When a firm builds clusters in its key locations, it also amplifies the connection between its success and its communities' success. A firm's growth has multiplier effects, as jobs are created in supporting industries, new companies are seeded and demand for ancillary services rises. A company's efforts to improve framework conditions for the cluster spill over to other participants and the local economy. Workforce development initiatives, for example, increase the supply of skilled employees for many other firms as well.

At Nespresso, Nestlé also worked to build clusters, which made its new procurement practices far more effective. It set out to build agricultural, technical, financial and logistical firms and capabilities in each coffee region, to further support efficiency and high-quality local production. Nestlé led efforts to increase access to essential agricultural inputs such as plant stock, fertilizers and irrigation equipment; strengthen regional farmer co-ops by helping them finance shared wet-milling facilities for producing higher-quality beans; and support an extension programme to advise all farmers on growing techniques. It also worked in partnership with the Rainforest Alliance, a leading international NGO, to teach farmers more sustainable practices that make production volumes more reliable. In the process, Nestlé's productivity improved.

A good example of a company working to improve framework conditions in its cluster is Yara, the world's largest mineral fertilizer company. Yara realized that the lack of logistical infrastructure in many parts of Africa was preventing farmers from gaining efficient access to fertilizers and other essential agricultural inputs, and from transporting their crops efficiently to market. Yara is tackling this problem through a $60 million investment in a programme to improve ports and roads, which is designed to create agricultural growth corridors in Mozambique and Tanzania. The company is working on this initiative with local governments and support from the Norwegian government. In Mozambique alone, the corridor is expected to benefit more than 200,000 small farmers and create 350,000 new jobs. The improvements will help Yara grow its business but will support the whole agricultural cluster, creating huge multiplier effects.

The benefits of cluster building apply not only in emerging economies but also in advanced countries. North Carolina's Research Triangle is a notable example of public and private collaboration that has created shared value by developing clusters in such areas as information technology and life sciences. That region, which has benefited from continued investment from both the private sector and local government, has experienced huge growth in employment, incomes and company performance, and has fared better than most during the downturn.

To support cluster development in the communities in which they operate, companies need to identify gaps and deficiencies in areas such as logistics, suppliers, distribution channels, training, market organization and educational institutions. Then the task is to focus on the weaknesses that represent the greatest constraints to the company's own productivity and growth, and distinguish those areas that the company is best equipped to influence directly from those in which collaboration is more cost-effective. Here is where the shared value opportunities will be greatest. Initiatives that address cluster weaknesses that constrain companies will be much more effective than community-focused corporate social responsibility programmes, which often have limited impact because they take on too many areas without focusing on value. But efforts to enhance infrastructure and institutions in a region often require collective action, as the Nestlé, Yara and Research Triangle examples show. Companies should try to enlist partners to share the cost, win support, and assemble the right skills. The most successful cluster development programmes are ones that involve

collaboration within the private sector, as well as trade associations, government agencies and NGOs.

Creating shared value in practice

Not all profit is equal – an idea that has been lost in the narrow, short-term focus of financial markets and in much management thinking. Profits involving a social purpose represent a higher form of capitalism – one that will enable society to advance more rapidly while allowing companies to grow even more. The result is a positive cycle of company and community prosperity, which leads to profits that endure.

Creating shared value presumes compliance with the law and ethical standards, as well as mitigating any harm caused by the business, but goes far beyond that. The opportunity to create economic value through creating societal value will be one of the most powerful forces driving growth in the global economy. This thinking represents a new way of understanding customers, productivity and the external influences on corporate success. It highlights the immense human needs to be met, the large new markets to serve, and the internal costs of social and community deficits – as well as the competitive advantages available from addressing them. Until recently, companies have simply not approached their businesses this way.

Creating shared value will be more effective and far more sustainable than the majority of today's corporate efforts in the social arena. Companies will make real strides on the environment, for example, when they treat it as a productivity driver rather than a feel good response to external pressure. Or consider access to housing. A shared value approach would have led financial services companies to create innovative products that prudently increased access to home ownership. This was recognized by the Mexican construction company Urbi, which pioneered a mortgage-financing "rent-to-own" plan. Major US banks, in contrast, promoted unsustainable financing vehicles that turned out to be socially and economically devastating, while claiming they were socially responsible because they had charitable contribution programmes.

Inevitably, the most fertile opportunities for creating shared value will be closely related to a company's particular business, and in areas most important to the business. Here a company can benefit the most economically and hence sustain its commitment over time. Here is also where a company brings the most resources to bear, and where its scale and market presence equip it to have a meaningful impact on a societal problem.

Ironically, many of the shared value pioneers have been those with more limited resources – social entrepreneurs and companies in developing countries. These outsiders have been able to see the opportunities more clearly. In the process, the distinction between for-profits and non-profits is blurring.

Shared value is defining a whole new set of best practices that all companies must embrace. It will also become an integral part of strategy. The essence of strategy is choosing a unique positioning and a distinctive value chain to deliver on it. Shared value opens up many new needs to meet, new products to offer, new customers to serve, and new ways to configure the value chain. And the competitive advantages that arise from creating shared value will often be more sustainable than conventional cost and quality improvements. The cycle of imitation and zero-sum competition can be broken.

The opportunities to create shared value are widespread and growing. Not every company will have them in every area, but our experience has been that companies discover more and more opportunities over time as their line operating units grasp this concept. It has taken a decade, but GE's Ecomagination initiative, for example, is now producing a stream of fast-growing products and services across the company.

A shared value lens can be applied to every major company decision. Could our product design incorporate greater social benefits? Are we serving all the communities that would benefit from our products? Do our processes and logistical approaches maximize efficiencies in energy and water use? Could our new plant be constructed in a way that achieves greater community impact? How are gaps in our cluster holding back our efficiency and speed of innovation? How could we enhance our community as a business location? If sites are comparable economically, at which one will the local community benefit the most? If a

---

EXHIBIT 3.3.5 HOW SHARED VALUE DIFFERS FROM CORPORATE SOCIAL RESPONSIBILITY

Creating shared value (CSV) should supersede corporate social responsibility (CSR) in guiding the investments of companies in their communities. CSR programmes focus mostly on reputation and have only a limited connection to the business, making them hard to justify and maintain over the long run. In contrast, CSV is integral to a

company's profitability and competitive position. It leverages the unique resources and expertise of the company to create economic value by creating social value.

In both cases, compliance with laws and ethical standards, and reducing harm from corporate activities are assumed.

CSR	CSV
Value: doing good	Value: economic and societal benefits relative to cost
Citizenship, philanthropy, sustainability	Joint company and community value creation
Discretionary or in response to external pressure	Integral to competing
Separate from profit maximization	Integral to profit maximization
Agenda is determined by external reporting and personal preferences	Agenda is company specific and internally generated
Impact limited by corporate footprint and CSR budget	Realigns the entire company budget
Example:	Example:
Fair trade purchasing	Transforming procurement to increase quality and yield

company can improve societal conditions, it will often improve business conditions and thereby trigger positive feedback loops.

The three avenues for creating shared value are mutually reinforcing. Enhancing the cluster, for example, will enable more local procurement and less dispersed supply chains. New products and services that meet social needs or serve overlooked markets will require new value chain choices in areas such as production, marketing and distribution. And new value chain configurations will create demand for equipment and technology that saves energy, conserves resources and supports employees.

Creating shared value will require concrete and tailored metrics for each business unit in each of the three areas. While some companies have begun to track various social impacts, few have yet tied them to their economic interests at the business level.

Shared value creation will involve new and heightened forms of collaboration. While some shared value opportunities are possible for a company to seize on its own, others will benefit from insights, skills and resources that cut across profit/non-profit and private/public boundaries. Here, companies will be less successful if they attempt to tackle societal problems on their own, especially those involving cluster development. Major competitors may also need to work together on precompetitive framework conditions; something that has not been common in reputation-driven CSR initiatives. Successful collaboration will be data driven, clearly linked to defined outcomes, well connected to the goals of all stakeholders, and tracked with clear metrics.

Governments and NGOs can enable and reinforce shared value or work against it.

The next evolution in capitalism

Shared value holds the key to unlocking the next wave of business innovation and growth. It will also reconnect company success and community success in ways that have been lost in an age of narrow management approaches, short-term thinking and deepening divides among society's institutions.

Shared value focuses companies on the right kind of profits – profits that create societal benefits rather than diminish them. Capital markets will undoubtedly continue to pressure companies to generate short-term profits, and some companies will surely continue to reap profits at the expense of societal needs. But such profits will often prove to be shortlived, and far greater opportunities will be missed.

The moment for an expanded view of value creation has come. A host of factors, such as the growing social awareness of employees and citizens and the increased scarcity of natural resources, will drive unprecedented opportunities to create shared value.

We need a more sophisticated form of capitalism, one imbued with a social purpose. But that purpose should arise not out of charity but out of a deeper understanding of competition and economic value creation. This next evolution in the capitalist model recognizes new and better ways to develop products, serve markets and build productive enterprises.

Creating shared value represents a broader conception of Adam Smith's invisible hand. It opens the doors of the pin factory to a wider set of influences. It is not philanthropy but self-interested behaviour to create economic value by creating societal value. If all companies individually pursued shared value connected to their particular businesses, society's overall interests would be served. And companies would acquire legitimacy in the eyes of the communities in which they operated, which would allow democracy to work as governments set policies that fostered and supported business. Survival of the fittest would still prevail, but market competition would benefit society in ways we have lost.

Creating shared value represents a new approach to managing that cuts across disciplines. Because of the traditional divide between economic concerns and social ones, people in the public and private sectors have often followed very different educational and career paths. As a result, few managers have the understanding of social and environmental issues required to move beyond today's CSR approaches, and few social sector leaders have the managerial training and entrepreneurial mind-set needed to design and implement shared value models. Most business schools still teach the narrow view of capitalism, even though more and more of their graduates hunger for a greater sense of purpose and a growing number are drawn to social entrepreneurship. The results have been missed opportunity and public cynicism.

Business school curricula will need to broaden in a number of areas. For example, the efficient use and stewardship of all forms of resources will define the next-generation thinking on value chains. Customer behaviour and marketing courses will have to move beyond persuasion and demand creation to the study of deeper human needs and how to serve non-traditional customer groups. Clusters, and the broader locational influences on company productivity and innovation, will form a new core discipline in business schools;

economic development will no longer be left only to public policy and economics departments. Business and government courses will examine the economic impact of societal factors on enterprises, moving beyond the effects of regulation and macroeconomics. And finance will need to rethink how capital markets can actually support true value creation in companies – their fundamental purpose – not just benefit financial market participants.

There is nothing soft about the concept of shared value. These proposed changes in business school curricula are not qualitative and do not depart from economic value creation. Instead, they represent the next stage in our understanding of markets, competition and business management.

Not all societal problems can be solved through shared value solutions. But shared value offers corporations the opportunity to utilize their skills, resources and management capability to lead social progress in ways that even the best-intentioned governmental and social sector organizations can rarely match. In the process, businesses can earn the respect of society again.

REFERENCES

Abell, D. (1980) *Defining the Business: The Starting Point of Strategic Planning*, Englewood Cliffs, NJ: Prentice Hall.

Ackermann, R.W. and Bauer, R.A. (1976) *Corporate Social Performance: The Modern Dilemma*, Reston, VA: Reston.

Ackoff, R.L. (1974) *Redesigning the Future*, New York: Wiley.

Adler, N.J. (2002) *International Dimensions of Organizational Behavior*, Cincinnati: South-Western/ Thomson Learning.

Albert, M. (1993) *Capitalism Against Capitalism*, London: Whurr Publishers.

Alkhafaji, A.F. (1989) *A Stakeholder Approach to Corporate Governance: Managing a Dynamic Environment*, Westport, CT: Quorum Books.

Amable, B. (2003) *The Diversity of Modern Capitalism*, Oxford: Oxford University Press.

Ansoff, I. (1965) *Corporate Strategy: An Analytic Approach to Business Policy for Growth and Expansion*, New York: McGraw-Hill.

Axelrod, R. (1976) *The Structure of Decision: The Cognitive Maps of Political Elites*, Princeton, NJ: Princeton University Press.

Barnard, C. (1938) The Function of the Executive, Cambridge, MA: Harvard University Press.

Bartlett, C.A. and Ghoshal, S. (1994) 'Changing the Role of Top Management: Beyond Strategy to Purpose', *Harvard Business Review*, November–December, pp. 79–88.

Baysinger, B.D. and Hoskisson, R.E. (1990) 'The Composition of Boards of Directors and Strategic Control: Effects of Corporate Strategy', *Academy of Management Review*, Vol. 15, No. 1, January, pp. 72–81.

Berle, A.A. and Means, G.C. (1932) *The Modern Corporation and Private Property*, New York: Transaction Publishers, McMillan.

Blair, M. (1995) *Ownership and Control: Rethinking Corporate Governance for the Twenty-First Century*, Washington: Brookings Institution.

Bourgeois, L.J. and Brodwin, D.R. (1983) 'Putting Your Strategy into Action', *Strategic Management Planning*, March–May.

Bucholz, R.A. (1986) *Business Environment and Public Policy*, Englewood Cliffs, NJ: Prentice Hall.

Buono, A.F. and Nichols, L.T. (1985) *Corporate Policy, Values and Social Responsibility*, New York: Praeger.

Campbell, A. and Tawadey, K. (1990) *Mission and Business Philosophy*, Oxford: Butterworth-Heinemann.

Campbell, A. and Yeung, S. (1991) 'Creating a Sense of Mission', *Long Range Planning*, Vol. 24, No. 4, August, pp. 10–20.

Cannon, T. (1992) *Corporate Responsibility*, London: Pitman.

Carroll, A.B. (1993) *Business and Society: Ethics and Stakeholder Management*, Second Edition, Cincinnati: South-Western Publishing.

Charkham, J. (1994) *Keeping Good Company: A Study of Corporate Governance in Five Countries*, Oxford: Oxford University Press.

Clarke, T. (1998) 'The Stakeholder Corporation: A Business Philosophy for the Information Age', *Long Range Planning*, Vol. 31, No. 2, April, pp. 182–194.

Clarkson, M.B.E. (1995) 'A Stakeholder Framework For Analyzing and Evaluating Corporate Social Performance', *Academy of Management Review*, Vol. 20, No. 1, January, pp. 92–117.

Cochran, P.L. and Wartick, S.L. (1994) 'Corporate Governance: A Review of the Literature', in: R.I. Tricker (ed.) *International Corporate Governance: Text, Readings and Cases*, Singapore: Prentice-Hall.

Coe, N.M., Kelly, P.F. and Yeung, H.W.C. (2007) *Economic Geography: A Contemporary Introduction*, Malden, MA: Blackwell Publishing.

Collins, J.C. and Porras, J. (1994) *Built To Last: Successful Habits of Visionary Companies*, London: Random House.

Collins, J.C. and Porras, J. (1996) 'Building Your Company's Vision', *Harvard Business Review*, Vol. 75, No. 5, September–October, pp. 65–77.

Cummings, S. and Davies, J. (1994) 'Mission, Vision, Fusion', *Long Range Planning*, Vol. 27, No. 6, December, pp. 147–150.

David, F.R. (1989) 'How Companies Define Their Mission', *Long Range Planning*, Vol. 22, No. 1, February, pp. 90–97.

Deal, T. E. and Kennedy, A. A. (1982) *Corporate Cultures: The Rites and Rituals of Organizational Life*, New York: Addison-Wesley.

Demb, A. and Neubauer, F.F. (1992) *The Corporate Board: Confronting the Paradoxes*, Oxford: Oxford University Press.

Dicken, P. (2011) *Global Shift: Mapping the Changing Contours in the World Economy*, New York: The Guilford Press.

Dill, W.R. (1975) 'Public Participation in Corporate Planning: Strategic Management in a Kibitzer's World', *Long Range Planning*, pp. 57–63.

D'Iribarne, P. (1996) 'The usefulness of an ethnographic approach to the international comparison of organizations', *International Studies of Management & Organization*, 26(4), pp. 30–47.

Donaldson, L. and Davis, J.H. (1995) 'Boards and Company Performance: Research Challenges the Conventional Wisdom', *Corporate Governance*, Vol. 2, pp. 151–160.

Donaldson, T. and Preston, L.E. (1995) 'The Stakeholder Theory of the Corporation: Concepts, Evidence, and Implications', *Academy of Management Review*, Vol. 20, No. 1, January, pp. 65–91.

Drucker, P.F. (1984) 'The New Meaning of Corporate Social Responsibility', *California Management Review*, Vol. 26, No. 2, Winter, pp. 53–63.

Eisenhardt, K.M. (1989) 'Agency Theory: An Assessment and Review', *Academy of Management Review*, Vol. 14, No. 1, January, pp. 57–74.

Elkington, J. (1980) *The Ecology of Tomorrow's World*, London: Associated Press.

Elkington, J. (1997) *Cannibals with Forks: The Triple Bottom Line of 21st Century Business*, Oxford: Capstone Publishing.

Elkington, J., & Burke, T. (1987) *The Green Capitalists: Industry's Search for Environmental Excellence*, Victor Gollancz.

Emerson, J. (2003) 'The Blended Value Proposition: Integrating Social and Financial Returns', *California Management Review*, Summer.

Epstein, E.M. (1987) 'The Corporate Social Policy Process: Beyond Business Ethics, Corporate Social Responsibility, and Corporate Social Responsiveness', *California Management Review*, Vol. 29, No. 3, Spring, pp. 99–114.

Falsey, T.A. (1989) *Corporate Philosophies and Mission Statements*, New York: Quorum Books.

Freeman, R.E. (1984) *Strategic Management: A Stakeholder Approach*, Boston: Pitman/Ballinger.

Freeman, R.E. and Gilbert Jr., D.R. (1988) *Corporate Strategy and the Search for Ethics*, Englewood Cliffs, NJ: Prentice Hall.

Freeman, R.E. and Liedtka, J. (1991) 'Corporate Social Responsibility: A Critical Approach', *Business Horizons*, July–August.

Freeman, R.E. and Reed, D.L. (1983) 'Stockholders and Stakeholders: A New Perspective on Corporate Governance', *California Management Review*, Vol. 25, No. 3, Spring, pp. 88–106.

Friedman, M. (1962) *Capitalism and Freedom*, Chicago, IL: University of Chicago Press.

Friedman, M. (1970) 'The Social Responsibility of Business is to Increase Its Profits', *The New York Times Magazine*, September 13–13.

Fukayama, F. (1992) *The End of History and the Last Man*, New York: The Free Press.

Fukayama, F. (2004) *State-Building: Governance and World Order in the 21st Century*, Ithaca, NY: Cornell University Press.

Fukayama, F. (2011) *The Origins of Political Order*, London: Profile Books.

Guthrie, J. and Turnbull, S. (1994) 'Audit Committees: Is There a Role for Corporate Senates and/or Stakeholder Councils?', *Corporate Governance*, Vol. 3, pp. 78–89.

Hall, P.A. and Soskice D. (ed.) (2001) *Varieties of Capitalism: The Institutional Foundations of Comparative Advantage*, New York: Oxford University Press.

Hamel, G., Doz, Y. L. and Prahalad, C. K. (1989) 'Collaborate with your competitors and win', *Harvard Business Review*, 67(1), pp. 133–139.

Hart, O.D. (1995) *Firms, Contracts and Financial Structure*, Oxford: Clarendon Press.

Hax, A.C. (1990) 'Redefining the Concept of Strategy and the Strategy Formation Process', *Planning Review*, May–June, pp. 34–40.

Hayes, R. and Abernathy, W. (1980) 'Managing Our Way to Economic Decline', *Harvard Business Review*, Vol. 58, No. 4, pp. 66–77.

Hoffman, W.M. (1989) 'The Cost of a Corporate Conscience', *Business and Society Review*, Vol. 94, Spring, pp. 46–47.

Hofstede, G. (1996) 'Riding the waves of commerce: A test of Trompenaars' "model" of national culture differences', *International Journal of Intercultural Relations*, 20(2), pp. 189–198.

Hofstede, G. (1980) *Culture's Consequences: International Differences in Work Related Values*, Beverly Hills, CA: Sage.

Holden, N.J. (2002) *Cross-Cultural Management: A Knowledge Management Perspective*, Harlow: Financial Times/Prentice Hall.

House, R. J., Hanges, P. J., Javidan, M., Dorfman, P. W. and Gupta, V. (2004) *Culture, Leadership, and Organizations*, London: Sage.

Jensen, M.C. and Meckling, W.H. (1976) 'Theory of the Firm, Managerial Behavior, Agency Costs, and Ownership Structure', *Journal of Financial Economics*, Vol. 3, No. 4, October, pp. 305–360.

Jones, T.M. (1995) 'Instrumental Stakeholder Theory: A Synthesis of Ethics and Economics', *Academy of Management Review*, Vol. 20, No. 2, April, pp. 404–437.

Keasey, K., Thompson, S. and Wright, M. (eds.) (1997) *Corporate Governance: Economic, Management, and Financial Issues*, Oxford: Oxford University Press.

Klemm, M., Sanderson, S. and Luffman, G. (1991) 'Mission Statements', *Long Range Planning*, Vol. 24, No. 3, June, pp. 73–78.

Klimoski, R. and Mohammed, S. (1994) 'Team Mental Model: Construct or Metaphor', *Journal of Management*, Vol. 20, pp. 403–437.

Kluckhohn, F.R. and Strodtbeck, F.L. (1961) *Variations in Value Orientations*, New York: Row, Peterson & Company.

Langtry, B. (1994) 'Stakeholders and the Moral Responsibilities of Business', *Business Ethics Quarterly*, Vol. 4, pp. 431–443.

Levitt, T. (1960) 'Marketing Myopia', *Harvard Business Review*, Vol. 38, July–August, pp. 45–56.

Lewis, R.D. (2003) *The Cultural Imperative: Global Trends in the 21st Century*, London: Nicholas Brealey Publishing.

Martin, J. (1992) *Cultures in Organizations: Three Perspectives*, Oxford University Press.

Martin, R. (2010) 'The Age of Customer Capitalism', *Harvard Business Review*, Jan–Feb, pp. 3–9.

McCoy, C.S. (1985) *Management of Values*, Cambridge, MA: Ballinger: Cambridge, MA:.

Mintzberg, H. (1984) 'Who Should Control the Corporation?' *California Management Review*, Vol. 27, No. 1, Fall, pp. 90–115.

Ohmae, K. (1985) *Triad Power: The Coming Shape of Global Competition*, New York: The Free Press.

O'Neill, J. (2001) *Building Better Global Economic BRICs*, Global Economics Paper No. 66, Goldman Sachs & Co.

Pearce, J.A. (1982) 'The Company Mission as a Strategic Tool', *Sloan Management Review*, Spring, pp. 15–24.

Peters, T.J. and Waterman, R.H. (1982) *In Search of Excellence*, New York: Harper & Row.

Piercy, N.F. and Morgan, N.A. (1994) 'Mission Analysis: An Operational Approach', *Journal of General Management*, Vol. 19, No. 3, pp. 1–16.

Porter, M.E. (1990) *The Competitive Advantage of Nations*, New York: The Free Press.

Porter, M.E. and Kramer, M.A. (2006) 'Strategy and Society: The Link Between Competitive Advantage and Corporate Social Responsibility', *Harvard Business Review*, December.

Porter, M.E. and Kramer, M.A. (2011) 'Creating Shared Value: How to reinvent capitalism and unleash a wave of innovation and growth', *Harvard Business Review*, January–February, pp. 3–17.

Prahalad, C.K. and Bettis, R.A. (1986) 'The Dominant Logic: A New Linkage Between Diversity and Performance', *Strategic Management Journal*, November–December, pp. 485–601.

Prahalad, C.K. and Hart S.L. (2002) 'The Fortune ate the Bottom of the Pyramid', *Strategy+Business*, 26–26, First quarter.

Rappaport, A. (1986) *Creating Shareholder Value: The New Standard for Business Performance*, New York: Free Press.

Schein, E. H. (1995) *Organizational Culture*, Frankfurt/New York: Campus Verlag.

Schein, E.H. (2004) *Organizational Culture and Leadership*, San Francisco: John Wiley & Sons.

Schneider, S. and Barsoux, J-L. (1999) *Managing Across Cultures*, London: Pearson Education.

Schwartz, S.H. (1999) 'A theory of cultural values and some implications for work', *Applied Psychology*, 48(1), pp. 23–47.

Senge, P. (1990) *The Fifth Discipline: The Art and Practice of the Learning Organization*, New York: Doubleday.

Solomon, R.C. (1992) *Ethics and Excellence: Cooperation and Integrity in Business*, New York: Oxford University Press.

Spencer, A. (1983) *On the Edge of the Organization: The Role of the Outside Director*, New York: Wiley.

Stone, C.D. (1975) *Where the Law Ends*, New York: Harper & Row.

Sykes, A. (1994) 'Proposals for Internationally Competitive Corporate Governance in Britain and America', *Corporate Governance*, Vol. 2, No. 4, pp. 187–195.

Tricker, R.I. (ed.) (1994) *International Corporate Governance: Text, Readings and Cases*, Singapore: Prentice Hall.

Verluyten, S. (2010) *Intercultural Skills for Business and International Relations: A Practical Introduction with Exercise*, Leuven: Acco.

Wartick, S.L. and Wood, D.J. (1998) *International Business and Society*, Oxford: Blackwell.

Yoshimori, M. (1995) 'Whose Company Is It? The Concept of the Corporation in Japan and the West', *Long Range Planning*, Vol. 28, pp. 33–45.

Zahra, S.A. and Pearce, J.A. (1989) 'Boards of Directors and Corporate Financial Performance: A Review and Integrative Model', *Journal of Management*, Vol. 15, pp. 291–334.

STRATEGY CONTENT

Every generation laughs at the old fashions but religiously follows the new.

Henry David Thoreau (1817–1862); American philosopher

The strategy content section deals with the question of *what* the strategy should be – what should be the course of action the firm should follow to achieve its purpose? In determining what the strategy should be, two types of 'fit' are of central concern to managers. First, there needs to be a fit between the firm and its environment. If the two become misaligned, the firm will be unable to meet the demands of the environment and will start to underperform, which can eventually lead to bankruptcy or takeover. This type of fit is also referred to as 'external consonance'. At the same time, managers are also concerned with achieving an internal fit between the various parts of the firm. If various units become misaligned, the organization will suffer from inefficiency, conflict and poor external performance, which can eventually lead to its demise as well. This type of fit is also referred to as 'internal consistency'.

As external consonance and internal consistency are prerequisites for a successful strategy, they need to be achieved for each organizational unit. Most organizations have various levels, making it necessary to ensure internal and external fit at each level of aggregation within the firm. In Figure II.1 all these possible levels within a corporation have been reduced to just three general categories, to which a fourth, supra-organizational level has been added. At each level the strategy should meet the requirements of external consonance and internal consistency:

- Functional level strategy. For each functional area, such as marketing, operations, finance, logistics, human resources, procurement and R&D, a strategy needs to be developed. At this level, internal consistency means having an overarching functional strategy that integrates various functional sub-strategies (e.g. a marketing strategy that aligns branding, distribution, pricing, product and communication strategies). External consonance is achieved when strategy is aligned with the demands in the relevant external arena (e.g. the logistics or procurement environment).

- Business level strategy. At the business level, an organization can only be effective if it can integrate functional level strategies into an internally consistent whole. To achieve external consonance the business unit must be aligned with the specific demands in the relevant business area.

- Corporate level strategy. When a company operates in two or more business areas, the business level strategies need to be aligned to form an internally consistent corporate level strategy. Between business and corporate levels there can also be divisions, yet for most strategy purposes they can be approached as mini-corporations (both divisional and corporate level strategy are technically speaking 'multi-business level'). Achieving external consonance at this level of aggregation means that a corporation must be able to act as one tightly integrated unit or as many autonomous, differentiated units, depending on the demands of the relevant environment.

- Network level strategy. When various firms work together, it sometimes is deemed necessary to align business and/or corporate level strategies to shape an internally consistent network level strategy. Such a network, or multi-company, level strategy can involve anywhere between two and thousands of companies. Here, too, the group must develop a strategy that fits with the demands in the relevant environment.

As the strategy content issues differ greatly depending on the level of aggregation under discussion, this section has been divided along the following lines. Chapter 4 focuses on business level strategy, Chapter 5 on corporate level strategy and Chapter 6 on

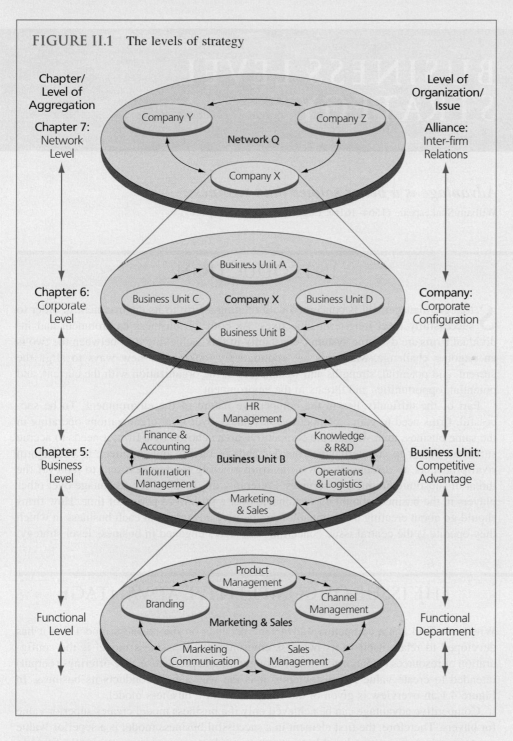

FIGURE II.1   The levels of strategy

Chapter/Level of Aggregation

Chapter 7:
Network Level

Chapter 6:
Corporate Level

Chapter 5:
Business Level

Functional Level

Level of Organization/Issue

Alliance:
Inter-firm Relations

Company:
Corporate Configuration

Business Unit:
Competitive Advantage

Functional Department

Network Q
Company Y
Company Z
Company X

Company X
Business Unit A
Business Unit C
Business Unit D
Business Unit B

Business Unit B
HR Management
Finance & Accounting
Knowledge & R&D
Information Management
Operations & Logistics
Marketing & Sales

Marketing & Sales
Product Management
Branding
Channel Management
Marketing Communication
Sales Management

network level strategy. Only the functional level strategies will be given no extensive coverage, as they are usually explored in great detail in functionally oriented books. It must be noted, however, that the aggregation levels used here are an analytical distinction and not an empirical reality that can always be found in practice – where one level stops and the other starts is more a matter of definition than of thick demarcation lines. Hence, when discussing strategy issues at any level, it is important to understand how they fit with higher and lower level strategy questions.

BUSINESS LEVEL STRATEGY

Advantage is a better soldier than rashness.
William Shakespeare (1564–1616); English dramatist and poet

INTRODUCTION

Strategic management is concerned with relating a firm to its environment in order to successfully meet long-term objectives. As both the business environment and individual firms are dynamic systems, constantly in flux, achieving a fit between the two is an ongoing challenge. Managers are continuously looking for new ways to align the current, and potential, strengths and weaknesses of the organization with the current, and potential, opportunities and threats in the environment.

Part of the difficulty lies in the competitive nature of the environment. To be successful, firms need to gain a competitive advantage over rival organizations operating in the same business area. Within the competitive arena chosen by a firm, it needs to accrue sufficient power to counterbalance the demands of buyers and suppliers, to outperform rival producers, to discourage new firms from entering the business and to fend off the threat of substitute products or services. Preferably this competitive advantage over other players in the business should be sustainable over a prolonged period of time. How firms should go about creating a (sustainable) competitive advantage in each business in which they operate is the central issue concerning managers engaged in business level strategy.

THE ISSUE OF COMPETITIVE ADVANTAGE

Whether a firm has a competitive advantage depends on the business model that it has developed to relate itself to its business environment. A business model is the configuration of resources (inputs), activities (throughput) and product/service offerings (output) intended to create value for customers – it is the way a firm conducts its business. In Figure 4.1 an overview is given of the components of a business model.

Competitive advantage can be achieved only if a business model creates superior value for buyers. Therefore, the first element in a successful business model is a superior 'value proposition'. A firm must be able to supply a product or service more closely fitted to client needs than rival firms. To be attractive, each element of a firm's 'product offering' needs to be targeted at a particular segment of the market and have a superior mix of attributes (e.g. price, availability, reliability, technical specifications, image, colour, taste, ease of use, etc.). Second, a successful company must also have the ability to actually develop and supply the superior product offering. It needs to have the capability to perform the necessary value-adding activities in an effective and efficient manner.

FIGURE 4.1 Components of a business model

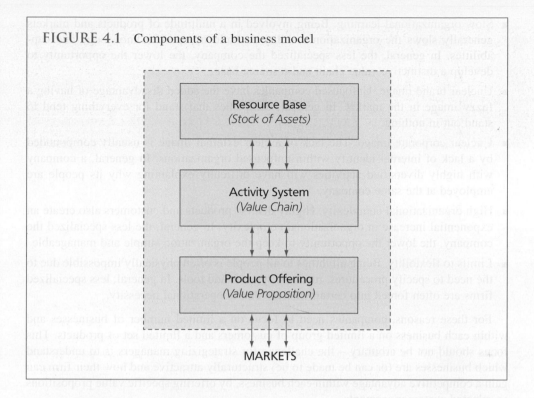

Resource Base
(Stock of Assets)

Activity System
(Value Chain)

Product Offering
(Value Proposition)

MARKETS

These value-adding activities, such as R&D, production, logistics, marketing and sales, are jointly referred to as a firm's value chain. The third component of a business model consists of the resource base required to perform the value-adding activities. Resources such as know-how, patents, facilities, money, brands and relationships make up the stock of assets that can be employed to create the product offering. If these firm-specific assets are distinctive and useful, they can form the basis of a superior value proposition. To create a competitive advantage, alignment must be achieved between all three elements of a business model. In the following pages all three elements will be discussed in more detail.

Product offering

At the intersection between a firm and its environment, transactions take place whereby the firm supplies goods or performs services for clients in the marketplace. It is here that the alignment of the firm and its environment is put to the test. If the products and services offered by the firm are more highly valued by customers than alternatives, a profitable transaction could take place. In other words, for sales to be achieved a firm must have a competitive value proposition – a cluster of physical goods, services or additional attributes with a superior fit to customer needs.

For the strategizing manager the key question is which products should be developed and which markets should be served. In many cases the temptation is to be everything to everybody – making a wide range of products and serving as many clients as possible. However, a number of practical constraints inhibit companies from taking such an unfocused approach to the market. Companies that do not focus on a limited set of product–market combinations run the risk of encountering a number of major problems:

■ Low economies of scale. Being unfocused is expensive, because of the low economies of scale that can be achieved. In general, the less specialized the company, the lower the opportunities to organize the value chain efficiently and leverage its resource base.

- Slow organizational learning. Being involved in a multitude of products and markets generally slows the organization's ability to build up specific knowledge and capabilities. In general, the less specialized the company, the lower the opportunity to develop a distinctive value chain and resource base.

- Unclear brand image. Unfocused companies have the added disadvantage of having a fuzzy image in the market. In general, companies that stand for everything tend to stand out in nothing.

- Unclear corporate image. The lack of a clear external image is usually compounded by a lack of internal identity within unfocused organizations. In general, a company with highly diversified activities will have difficulty explaining why its people are employed at the same company.

- High organizational complexity. Highly diverse products and customers also create an exponential increase in organizational complexity. In general, the less specialized the company, the lower the opportunity to keep the organization simple and manageable.

- Limits to flexibility. Being all things to all people is often physically impossible due to the need to specify procedures, routines, systems and tools. In general, less specialized firms are often forced into certain choices due to operational necessity.

For these reasons, companies need to focus on a limited number of businesses and within each business on a limited group of customers and a limited set of products. This focus should not be arbitrary – the challenge for strategizing managers is to understand which businesses are (or can be made to be) structurally attractive and how their firm can gain a competitive advantage within each business, by offering specific value propositions to selected customer segments.

Determining a focus starts by looking for the 'boundaries' of a business – how can managers draw meaningful delineation lines in the environment, distinguishing one arena of competition from another, so that they can select some and ignore others? Ideally, the environment would be made up of neatly compartmentalized businesses, with clear borders separating them. In reality, however, the picture is much more messy. While there are usually certain clusters of buyers and suppliers interacting more intensely with one another, suggesting that they are operating in the same business, there are often numerous exceptions to any neat classification scheme. To explore how a business can be defined, it is first necessary to specify how a business differs from an 'industry' and a 'market'.

Delineating industries.   An industry is defined as a group of firms making a similar type of product or employing a similar set of value-adding processes or resources. In other words, an industry consists of producers that are much alike – there is *supply side similarity* (Kay, 1993). The simplest way to draw an industry boundary is to use product similarity as the delineation criterion. For instance, British Airways can be said to be in the airline industry, along with many other providers of the same product, such as Singapore Airlines and Ryanair. However, an industry can also be defined on the basis of value chain similarity (e.g. consulting industry and mining industry) or resource similarity (e.g. information technology industry and oil industry).

Economic statisticians tend to favour fixed industry categories based on product similarity and therefore most figures available about industries are product-category based, often making use of Standard Industrial Classification (SIC) codes. Strategists, on the contrary, like to challenge existing definitions of an industry, for instance by regrouping them on the basis of underlying value-adding activities or resources. Take the example of Swatch – how did it conceptualize which industry it was in? If they had focused on the physical product and the production process, then they would have been inclined to situate Swatch in the watch industry. However, Swatch also viewed its products as fashion accessories, placing emphasis on the key value-adding activities of fashion design and

FIGURE 4.2 Alternative industry categorizations

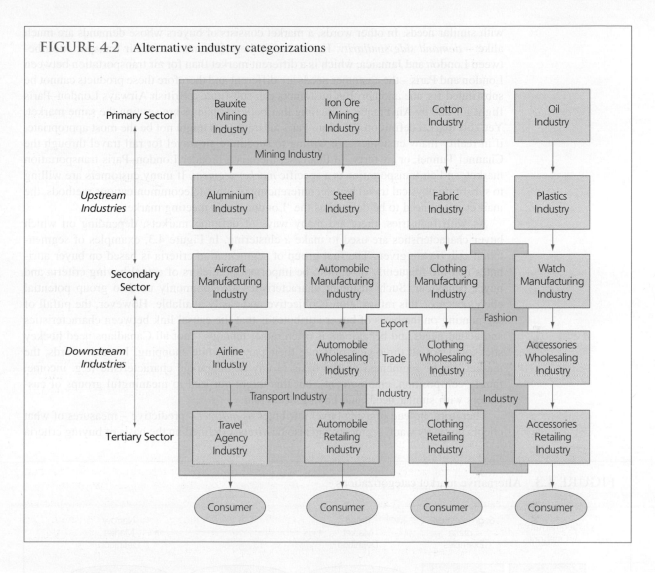

marketing. On this basis, Swatch could just as well be categorized as a member of the fashion industry (Porac, Thomas and Baden-Fuller, 1989). For the strategizing manager, the realization that Swatch can be viewed in both ways is an important insight. As creating a competitive advantage often comes from doing things differently, rethinking the definition of an industry can be a powerful way to develop a unique product offering.

Figure 4.2 gives four examples of traditionally defined 'industry columns', which Porter (1980) draws not top-down, but left-right, using the term 'value system'. These columns start with upstream industries, which are involved in the extraction/growing of raw materials and their conversion into inputs for the manufacturing sector. Downstream industries take the output of manufacturing companies and bring them to clients, often adding a variety of services into the product mix. In practice, industry columns are not as simple as depicted in Figure 4.2, as each industry has many different industries as suppliers and usually many different industries as buyers.

A second limitation of the industry columns shown in Figure 4.2 is that they are materials-flow oriented – industry boundaries are drawn on the basis of product.

Segmenting markets. While economists see the market as a place where supply and demand meet, in the business world a market is usually defined as a group of customers with similar needs. In other words, a market consists of buyers whose demands are much alike – *demand side similarity*. For instance, there is a market for air transportation between London and Jamaica, which is a different market than for air transportation between London and Paris – the customer needs are different and therefore these products cannot be substituted for one another. But customers can substitute a British Airways London–Paris flight for one by Air France, indicating that both companies are serving the same market. Yet, this market definition (London–Paris air transport) might not be the most appropriate, if in reality many customers are willing to substitute air travel for rail travel through the Channel Tunnel, or by ferry. In this case, there is a broader London–Paris transportation market, and air transportation is a specific *market segment*. If many customers are willing to substitute physical travel by teleconferencing or other telecommunications methods, the market might need to be defined as the 'London–Paris meeting market'.

As with industries, there are many ways of defining markets, depending on which buyer characteristics are used to make a clustering. In Figure 4.3, examples of segmentation criteria are given. The first group of segmentation criteria is based on buyer attributes that are frequently thought to be important predictors of actual buying criteria and buyer behaviour. Such customer characteristics are commonly used to group potential clients because this information is objective and easily available. However, the pitfall of segmenting on the basis of buyer attributes is that the causal link between characteristics and actual needs and behaviours is often rather tenuous – not all Canadians need hockey sticks and not all three-year-olds nag their parents while shopping. In other words, the market can be segmented on the basis of any demographic characteristic (e.g. income, family composition, employment), but this might not lead to meaningful groups of customers with similar needs and buying behaviour.

Therefore, instead of using buyer attributes as *indirect* – predictive – measures of what clients probably want, segments can also be *directly* defined on the basis of buying criteria

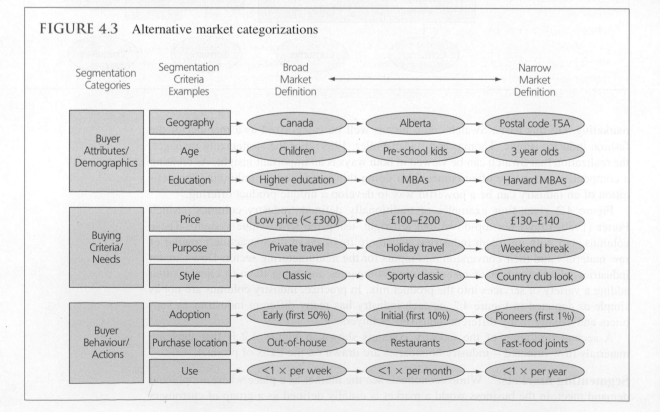

FIGURE 4.3 Alternative market categorizations

employed or buyer behaviours exhibited. The advantage is that segments can then be identified with clearly similar wishes or behaviours. The disadvantage is that it is very difficult to gather and interpret information on what specific people want and how they really act.

For strategists, one of the key challenges is to look at existing categorizations of buyers and to wonder whether a different segmentation would offer new insights and new opportunities for developing a product offering specifically tailored to their needs. As with the redefining of industry boundaries, it is often in the reconceptualization of market segments that a unique approach to the market can be found.

Defining and selecting businesses.   A business is a set of related product–market combinations. The term 'business' refers neither to a set of producers nor a group of customers, but to the domain where the two meet. In other words, a business is a competitive arena where companies offering similar products serving similar needs compete against one another for the favour of the buyers. Hence, a business is delineated in both industry and market terms (see Figure 4.4). Typically, a business is narrower than the entire industry and the set of markets served is also limited. For instance, within the airline industry the charter business is usually recognized as rather distinct. In the charter business, a subset of the airline services is offered to a number of tourist markets. Cheap flights from London to Jamaica and from London to Barcelona fall within this business, while service levels will be different than in other parts of the airline industry. It should be noted, though, that just as with industries and markets, there is no best way to define the boundaries of a business (Abell, 1980).

As stated earlier, companies cannot afford to be unfocused, operating superficially in a whole range of businesses. They must direct their efforts by focusing in two ways:

1 Selecting a limited number of businesses. The first constraint that companies need to impose on themselves is to choose a limited array of businesses within which they wish to be successful. This essential strategic challenge is referred to as the issue of corporate configuration and will be examined in more detail in Chapter 5 (multi-business level strategy). Here it suffices to say that firms need to analyse the structural characteristics of interesting businesses to be able to judge whether they are attractive enough for the firm, or can be made to be attractive. Porter presents the 'five forces analysis' as a framework for mapping the structure of industries and businesses.

FIGURE 4.4   Industries, markets and businesses

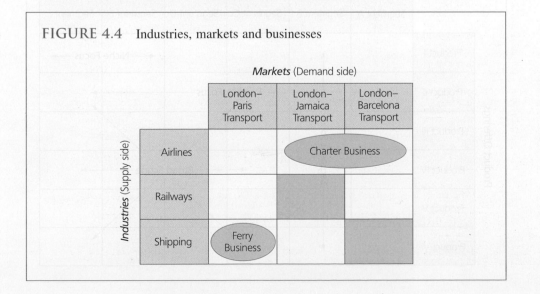

2 Focusing within each selected business. Even within the limited set of businesses selected, firms need to determine what they want to be and what they want to leave aside. To be competitive, it is necessary to choose a number of distinct market segments and to target a few special product offerings to meet these customers' needs. As illustrated in Figure 4.1, these specific product offerings in turn need to be aligned with a focused value chain and resource base.

This act of focusing the overall business model to serve the particular needs of a targeted group of buyers, in a way that distinguishes the firm vis-a-vis rivals, is called positioning. This positioning of the firm in the business requires a clearly tailored product offering (product positioning), but also a value chain and resource base that closely fit with the demands of the specific group of customers and competitors being targeted.

Positioning within a business. Positioning is concerned with both the questions of 'where to compete' and 'how to compete' (Porter, 1980). Determining in which product–market combinations within a business a firm wants to be involved is referred to as the issue of competitive scope. Finding a way to beat rivals and win over customers for a product offering is the issue of competitive advantage. The two questions are tightly linked, because firms need to develop a specific advantage to be competitive within a specific product–market domain. If they try to use the same competitive advantage for too many dissimilar products and customers, they run the risk of becoming unfocused.

In selecting a competitive scope, firms can vary anywhere between being widely oriented and very tightly focused. Firms with a broad scope compete in a large number of segments within a business, with varied product offerings. Firms with a narrow scope target only one, or just a few, customer segments and have a more limited product line (see Figure 4.5). If there is a small part of the business with very specific demands, requiring a distinct approach, firms can narrowly focus on this niche as their competitive scope. In between these two extremes are firms with a segment focus and firms with a product focus, but in practice many other profiles are also possible.

FIGURE 4.5   Determining competitive scope

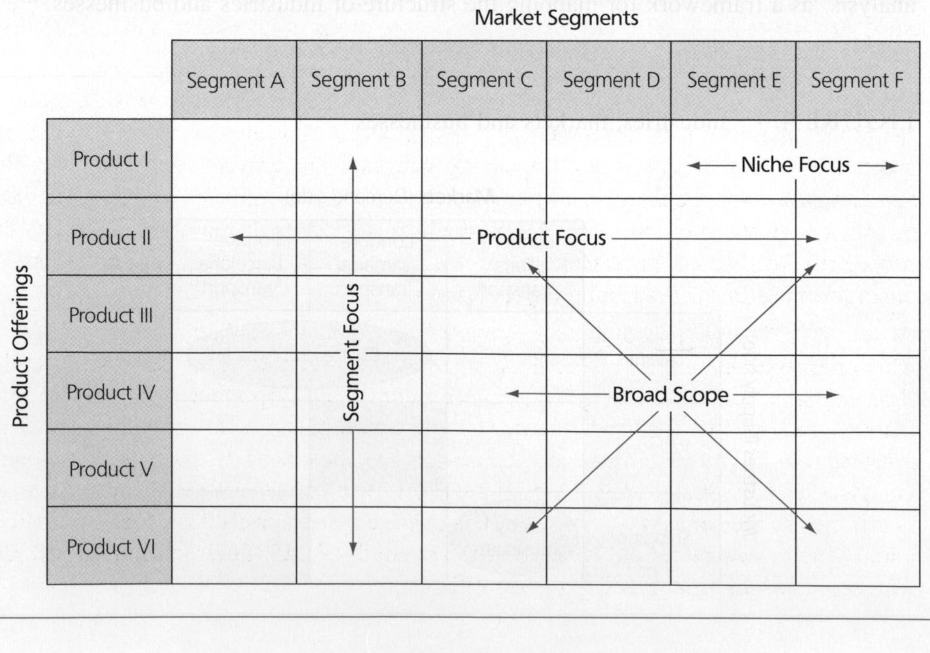

In developing a competitive advantage, firms have many dimensions along which they can attempt to outdo their rivals. Some of the most important bases of competitive advantage are the following:

- Price. The most straightforward advantage a firm can have in a competitive situation is the ability to charge a lower price. All things being equal, buyers generally prefer to pay the lowest amount necessary. Hence, when purchasing a commodity product or service, most customers will be partial to the lowest priced supplier. And even when selecting among differentiated products, many customers will be inclined to buy the cheapest or at least the cheapest within a subgroup of more comparable products. For a firm wanting to compete on price, the essential point is that it should have a *low cost* product offering, value chain and resource base to match the price positioning. After all, in the long run a firm can survive at a lower price level only if it has developed a business model that can sustainably operate at a lower cost level.

- Features. Firms can also distinguish their product offerings by having different intrinsic functional characteristics rather than competing offerings. There are many ways to make a product or service different, for instance by changing its size, smell, taste, colour, functionality, compatibility, content, design or style. An ice cream manufacturer can introduce a new flavour and more chunky texture, a motorcycle producer can design a special low rider model for women, a pay TV company can develop special channels for dog owners and science fiction addicts, and a utility company can offer environmentally friendly electricity. To be able to compete on each of these product features, firms need to command different specialized resources and value chains. In some cases, they require significant technological knowledge and a technically sophisticated value chain, while in other cases design capabilities, marketing prowess or a satellite infrastructure are essential to the functioning of the business model.

- Bundling. Another way to offer a uniquely different value proposition is to sell a package of products or services 'wrapped together'. By bundling a number of separate elements into a package, the customer can have the convenience of 'one stop shopping', while also having a family of related products or services that fit together well. So, for instance, many customers prefer to purchase their software from one supplier because this raises the chance of compatibility. In the chocolate industry, the leading manufacturer of chocolate-making machines, Rademakers, was able to gain a competitive advantage by bundling its machines with various services, such as installation, repair, spare parts and financing.

- Quality. When competing with others, a firm's product offering doesn't necessarily have to be fundamentally different, it can just be better. Customers generally appreciate products and services that exhibit superior performance in terms of usability, reliability and durability, and are often willing to pay a premium price for such quality. Excellent quality can be secured on many fronts, for instance through the materials used, the people involved, the manufacturing process employed, the quality assurance procedures followed or the distribution system used.

- Availability. The method of distribution can in itself be the main competitive edge on which a firm bases its positioning. Having a product available at the right place, at the right moment and in the right way, can be much more important to customers than features and quality. Just ask successful ice cream manufacturers – most of their revenues are from out-of-doors impulse sales, so they need to have their products available in individually wrapped portions at all locations where people have the urge to indulge. In the same way, Avon's cosmetics are not primarily sold because of their uniqueness or low price, but because of the strength of their three million sales force, who can be at the right place at the right time.

■ Image. In the competition for customers' preference, firms can also gain an advantage by having a more appealing image than their rivals. In business-to-consumer markets this is particularly clear when looking at the impact of brands. Consumers often feel attracted to brands that project a certain image of the company or the products it sells. Brands can communicate specific values that consumers want to be associated with (Nike's 'just do it'), or can help to build trust among consumers who have too little information on which to base their product choices (GE's 'we bring good things to life'). But even in business-to-business markets, buyers often suffer from a shortage of information about the available product offerings or lack the time to research all possible suppliers. Therefore, the image of suppliers, mostly in terms of their standing ('a leading global player') and reputation ('high quality service') can be essential to be considered at all (to be 'shortlisted') and to be trusted as a business partner.

■ Relations. Good branding can give customers the impression that they know the supplier, without actually being in direct contact. Yet, having a direct relation with customers can in itself be a potent source of competitive advantage. In general, customers prefer to know their suppliers well, as this gives them more intimate knowledge of the product offering being provided. Having a relationship with a supplier can also give the customer more influence on what is offered. Besides these rational points, customers often value the personal contact, the trust and the convenience of having a longstanding relationship as well. For suppliers this means that they might acquire a competitive edge by managing their customer relationships well. To do so, however, does imply that the value chain and resource base are fit to fulfil this task.

The type of competitive advantage that a firm chooses to pursue will be influenced by what the targeted group of buyers find important. These factors of importance to potential clients are referred to as 'value drivers' – they are the elements responsible for creating value in the eyes of the customer. Which value drivers a firm will want to base its value proposition on is a matter of positioning.

According to Porter (1980) all the specific forms of competitive advantage listed above can be reduced to two broad categories, namely lower cost and differentiation. On the one hand, firms can organize their business models in such a manner that, while their products or services are largely the same as other manufacturers, their overall cost structure is lower, allowing them to compete on price. On the other hand, firms can organize their business models to supply a product or service that has distinctive qualities compared to rival offerings. According to Porter, these two forms of competitive advantage demand fundamentally different types of business models and therefore are next to impossible to combine. Firms that do try to realize both at the same time run the risk of getting 'stuck in the middle' – not being able to do either properly.

Treacy and Wiersema (1995) argue that there are three generic competitive advantages, each requiring a fundamentally different type of business model (they speak of three distinctive 'value disciplines'). They, too, warn firms to develop an internally consistent business model focused on one of these types of competitive advantage, avoiding a 'mix-and-match' approach to business strategy:

■ Operational excellence. Firms striving for operational excellence meet the buyers' need for a reliable, low cost product offering. The value chain required to provide such no-frills, standardized, staple products emphasizes a 'lean and mean' approach to production and distribution, with simple service.

■ Product leadership. Firms taking the route of product leadership meet the buyers' need for special features and advanced product performance. The value chain required to provide such differentiated, state-of-the-art products emphasizes innovation and the creative collaboration between marketing and R&D.

■ Customer intimacy. Firms deciding to focus on customer intimacy meet the buyers' need for a tailored solution to their particular problem. The value chain required to provide such a client-specific, made-to-measure offering emphasizes flexibility and empowerment of the employees close to the customer.

Other strategy researchers, however, argue that there is no such thing as generic competitive strategies that follow from two or three broad categories of competitive advantage (e.g. Baden-Fuller and Stopford, 1992). In their view, there is an endless variety of ways in which companies can develop a competitive advantage, many of which do not fit into the categories outlined by Porter or Treacy and Wiersema – in fact, finding a new type of competitive advantage might be the best way of obtaining a unique position in a business.

Value chain

To be able to actually make what it wants to sell, a firm needs to have a value chain in place. A value chain is an integrated set of value creation processes leading to the supply of product or service offerings. Whether goods are being manufactured or services are being provided, each firm needs to perform a number of activities to successfully satisfy the customers' demands. As these value-adding activities need to be coordinated and linked together, this part of the business model is also frequently referred to as the 'value chain' (Porter, 1985).

Value chains can vary widely from industry to industry. The value chain of a car manufacturer is quite distinct from that of an advertising agency. Yet even within an industry there can be significant differences. Most 'bricks and mortar' bookstores have organized their value chain differently than online book retailers like Amazon.com. The value chains of most 'hub-and-spoke' airline companies hardly resemble that of 'no-frills' carriers such as Southwest in the United States and easyJet in Europe.

While these examples point to radically different value chains, even firms that subscribe to the same basic model can apply it in their own particular way. Fast-food restaurants such as McDonald's and Burger King may employ the same basic model, but their actual value chains differ in quite a few ways. The same goes for the PC manufacturers HP and Lenovo, which share a similar type of value chain, but which still differ on many fronts. 'Online mass-customization' PC manufacturer Dell, on the other hand, has a different model and consequently a more strongly differing value chain than HP and Lenovo.

Having a distinct value chain often provides the basis for a competitive advantage. A unique value chain allows a firm to offer customers a unique value proposition, by doing things better, faster, cheaper, nicer or more tailored than competing firms. Developing the firm's value chain is therefore just as strategically important as developing new products and services.

Although value chains can differ quite significantly, some attempts have been made to develop a general taxonomy of value-adding activities that could be used as an analytical framework (e.g. Day, 1990; Norman and Ramirez, 1993). By far the most influential framework is Porter's value chain, which distinguishes primary activities and support activities (see Figure 4.6). Primary activities 'are the activities involved in the physical creation of the product and its sale and transfer to the buyer, as well as after-sale assistance' (Porter, 1985: 16). Support activities facilitate the primary process, by providing purchased inputs, technology, human resources and various firm-wide functions. The generic categories of primary activities identified by Porter are:

■ Inbound logistics. Activities associated with receiving, storing and disseminating inputs, including material handling, warehousing, inventory control, vehicle scheduling and returns to suppliers.

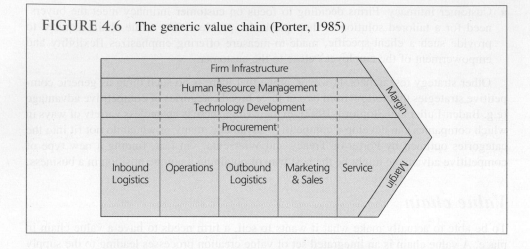

FIGURE 4.6   The generic value chain (Porter, 1985)

- **Operations.** Activities associated with transforming inputs into final products, including machining, packaging, assembly, equipment maintenance, testing, printing and facility operations.
- **Outbound logistics.** Activities associated with collecting, storing and physically distributing products to buyers, including warehousing, material handling, delivery, order processing and scheduling.
- **Marketing and sales.** Activities associated with providing a means by which buyers can purchase the product and inducing them to do so, including advertising, promotion, sales force, quoting, channel selection, channel relations and pricing.
- **Service.** Activities associated with providing service to enhance or maintain the value of products, including installation, repair, training, parts supply and product adjustment.

For service industries Porter argues that the specific activities will be different, and might be performed in a different order, but can still be subdivided into these five generic categories. To ensure that the primary activities can be carried out, each firm also needs to organize four types of support activities:

- **Procurement.** Activities associated with the purchasing of inputs to facilitate all other activities, including vendor selection, negotiations, contracting and invoice administration.
- **Technology development.** Activities associated with the improvement of technologies throughout the firm, including basic research, product and process design, and procedure development.
- **Human resource management.** Activities associated with the management of personnel throughout the organization, including recruiting, hiring, training, development and compensation.
- **Firm infrastructure.** Firm infrastructure consists of all general activities that support the entire value chain, including general management, planning, finance, accounting, legal, government affairs and quality management.

The uniqueness of the value chain, and its strength as the source of competitive advantage, will usually not depend on only a few specialized activities, but on the extraordinary configuration of the entire value chain. An extraordinary configuration multiplies the distinctness of a particular value chain, while often raising the barrier to imitation (Porter, 1996; Amit and Zott, 2001).

Resource base

To carry out activities and to produce goods and services, firms need resources. A firm's resource base includes all means at the disposal of the organization for the performance of value-adding activities. Other authors prefer the term 'assets', to emphasize that the resources belong to the firm (e.g. Dierickx and Cool, 1989; Itami, 1987).

Under the broad umbrella of 'resource-based view of the firm', there has been much research into the importance of resources for the success and even existence of firms (e.g. Penrose, 1959; Wernerfelt, 1984; Barney, 1991, Reading 4.2). No generally accepted classification of firm resources has yet emerged in the field of strategic management, however the following major distinctions (see Figure 4.7) are commonly made:

- Tangible vs intangible resources. Tangible resources are all means available to the firm that can physically be observed (touched), such as buildings, machines, materials, land and money. Tangibles can be referred to as the 'hardware' of the organization. Intangibles, on the other hand, are the 'software' of the organization. Intangible resources cannot be touched, but are largely carried within the people in the organization. In general, tangible resources need to be purchased, while intangibles need to be developed. Therefore, tangible resources are often more readily transferable, easier to price and usually are placed on the balance sheet.

- Relational resources vs competences. Within the category of intangible resources, relational resources and competences can be distinguished. Relational resources are all of the means available to the firm derived from the firm's interaction with its environment (Lowendahl, 1997). The firm can cultivate specific relationships with individuals and organizations in the environment, such as buyers, suppliers, competitors and government agencies, which can be instrumental in achieving the firm's goals. As attested by the old saying, 'it's not what you know, but whom you know', relationships can often be an essential resource (see Chapter 6 for a further discussion). Besides direct relationships, a firm's reputation among other parties in the environment can also be an important resource. Competence, on the other hand, refers to the firm's fitness to perform in a particular field. A firm has a competence if it has the knowledge, capabilities and attitude needed to successfully operate in a specific area.

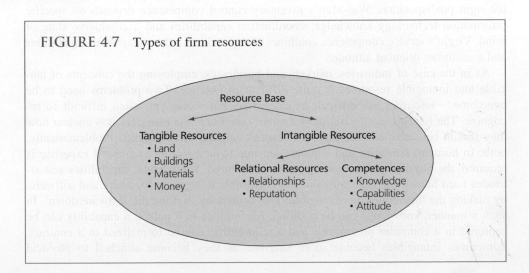

FIGURE 4.7   Types of firm resources

This description of competences is somewhat broad and therefore difficult to employ. However, a distinction between knowledge, capability and attitude (Durand, 1996) can be used to shed more light on the nature of competences:

- Knowledge. Knowledge can be defined as the whole of rules (know-how, know-what, know-where and know-when) and insights (know-why) that can be extracted from, and help make sense of, information. In other words, knowledge flows from, and influences, the interpretation of information (Dretske, 1981). Examples of knowledge that a firm can possess are market insight, competitive intelligence, technological expertise, and understanding of political and economic developments.

- Capability. Capability refers to the organization's potential for carrying out a specific activity or set of activities. Sometimes the term 'skill' is used to refer to the ability to carry out a narrow (functional) task or activity, while the term 'capability' is reserved for the quality of combining a number of skills. For instance, a firm's capability base can include narrower abilities such as market research, advertising and production skills, that if coordinated could result in a capability for new product development (Stalk, Evans and Shulman, 1992).

- Attitude. Attitude refers to the mind-set prevalent within an organization. Sometimes the terms 'disposition' and 'will' are used in the same sense, to indicate how an organization views and relates to the world. Although ignored by some writers, every sports coach will acknowledge the importance of attitude as a resource. A healthy body (tangible resource), insight into the game (knowledge), speed and dexterity (capabilities) – all are important, but without the winning mentality a team will not get to the top. Some attitudes may change rapidly within firms, yet others may be entrenched within the cultural fabric of the organization – these in particular can be important resources for the firm. A company's attitude can, for instance, be characterized as quality-driven, internationally oriented, innovation-minded or competitively aggressive.

It must be noted that the term 'competences' is used in many different ways, partially due to the ambiguous definition given by its early proponents (Prahalad and Hamel, 1990, Reading 5.2 in this book). It is often used as a synonym for capabilities, while Prahalad and Hamel seem to focus more on technologically oriented capabilities ('how to co-ordinate diverse production skills and integrate multiple streams of technologies'). Others (e.g. Durand, 1996) have suggested that a firm has a competence in a certain area, when the firm's underlying knowledge base, capabilities and attitude are all aligned. So, Honda's engine competence is built on specific knowledge, development capabilities and the right predisposition. Wal-Mart's inventory control competence depends on specific information technology knowledge, coordination capabilities and a conducive state of mind. Virgin's service competence combines customer knowledge, adaptation capabilities and a customer-oriented attitude.

As in the case of industries, markets and businesses, employing the concepts of tangible and intangible resources is quite difficult in practice. Two problems need to be overcome – resources are difficult to categorize, but worse yet, often difficult to recognize. The issue of categorization is a minor one. For some resources it is unclear how they should be classified. Are human resources tangible or intangible? Problematically, both. In humans, hardware and software are intertwined – if an engineer's expertise is required, the physical person usually needs to be hired. Knowledge, capabilities and attitudes need human carriers. Sometimes it is possible to separate hardware and software, by making the intangibles more tangible. This is done by 'writing the software down'. In such a manner, knowledge can be codified, for instance in a patent, a capability can be captured in a computer programme and a relationship can be formalized in a contract. Sometimes intangibles become more tangible, as they become attached to physical carriers – for instance, attitude can be embodied by a person or a symbol, while reputation becomes attached to a brand.

More important is the problem of resource identification. Tangible resources, by their very nature, are relatively easy to observe. Accountants keep track of the financial resources, production managers usually know the quality of their machinery and stock levels, while the personnel department will have an overview of all people on the payroll. Intangible resources, on the other hand, are far more difficult to identify (e.g. Grant, 2002; Itami, 1987). With whom does the firm have a relationship and what is the state of this relationship? What is the firm's reputation? These relational resources are hard to pin down. Competences are probably even more difficult to determine. How do you know what you know? Even for an individual it is a formidable task to outline areas of expertise, let alone for a more complex organization. Especially the *tacit* (non-articulated) nature of much organizational knowledge makes it difficult to identify the firm's knowledge base (Polanyi, 1958; Nonaka and Konno, 1998). The same is true for a firm's capabilities, which have developed in the form of organizational routines (Nelson and Winter, 1982). Likewise, the firm's attitudes are difficult to discern, because all people sharing the same disposition will tend to consider themselves normal and will tend to believe that their outlook is 'a matter of common sense' (see Chapter 2). Hence, firms intent on identifying their competences find that this is not an easy task.

While an overview of the firm's resource base is important in itself, a strategizing manager will want to compare the firm's resources to other companies to determine their relative strength. In other words, are the firm's resources unique, superior to or inferior to the resources of (potential) competitors? This type of analysis is particularly difficult, as comparison requires insight into other firms' resource bases. Especially the identification of other firms' intangible resources can be quite arduous.

Sustaining competitive advantage

A firm has a competitive advantage when it has the means to edge out rivals when vying for the favour of customers. In the previous subsections it was argued that competitive advantage is rooted in a unique business model, whereby the resource base, value chain and product–market position are all aligned to provide goods and/or services with a superior fit to customer needs.

A competitive advantage is said to be sustainable if it cannot be copied, substituted or eroded by the actions of rivals, and is not made redundant by developments in the environment (Porter, 1980). In other words, sustainability depends on two main factors, competitive defendability and environmental consonance:

- Competitive defendability. Some competitive advantages are intrinsically easier to defend than others, either because they are difficult for rivals to imitate, or because rivals find it next to impossible to find an alternative route of attack. In general, a firm's competitive advantage is more vulnerable when it is based on only a limited number of distinct elements (e.g. a different packaging technology, a different delivery system or different product colours). For rivals, imitating or substituting a few elements is comparatively easy. If, however, a firm's business model has an entirely different configuration altogether, the barriers to imitation and substitution are much higher. In such a case, it is said that a firm has a 'distinct business model'. So, for instance, in the airline industry the traditional firms have tried to imitate some parts of the low cost service of Southwest in the United States, and Ryanair and easyJet in Europe, but have been largely unsuccessful because their business model as a whole is based on a different logic. Yet, many strategists note that the best defence is not to build walls around a competitive position to 'keep the barbarians out', but to have the ability to run faster than rivals – to be able to upgrade one's resources, value chain and product offering more rapidly than competitors. In this view, a competitive advantage is sustainable due to a company's capacity to stay one step ahead of rivals, *outpacing* them in a race to stay ahead (e.g. Gilbert and Strebel, 1989; Stalk, Evans and Shulman, 1992).

■ Environmental consonance. The sustainability of a firm's competitive advantage is also threatened by developments in the market. Customer needs and wants are in constant flux, distribution channels can change, government regulations can be altered, innovative technologies can be introduced and new entrants can come into the competitive arena. All of these developments can undermine the fit between the firm's competitive advantage and the environment, weakening the firm's position (Rumelt, 1980).

Yet, these two factors for sustaining competitive advantage seem to pose opposite demands on the organization. Building a distinctive business model to fend off competition would suggest that a firm should remain true to its fundamental *strengths,* especially when it comes to unique resources and activities that it has built up over a prolonged period of time. On the other hand, environmental consonance requires a firm to continually adapt its business model to the demands and new *opportunities* in the marketplace. The tension created by these opposite pressures will be discussed in the following section.

THE PARADOX OF MARKETS AND RESOURCES

Instead of being concerned that you have no office, be concerned to think how you may fit yourself for office. Instead of being concerned that you are not known, seek to be worthy of being known.
Confucius (551–479 BC); Chinese philosopher

There must be a fit between an organization and its environment. This point is often expressed in terms of the classic SWOT analysis tool, which suggests that a sound strategy should match a firm's strengths (S) and weaknesses (W) to the opportunities (O) and threats (T) encountered in the firm's environment. The key to success is *alignment* of the two sides (further discussed in Chapter 8). Yet, fitting internal strengths and weaknesses to external opportunities and threats is often frustrated by the fact that the two sides pull in opposite directions – the distinctive resource base and value chain of a firm can point in a totally different direction, as compared to the developments in their current markets. Take the example of Bally, in the 1990s the worldwide market leader in pinball machines. Their strength in the manufacturing of electromechanical games was no longer aligned with developments in the market, where young people were turning to video games produced by companies such as Nintendo, Sega and Sony. As sales of pinball machines were quickly deteriorating, it was clear that Bally had to find a new fit with the market to survive. On the one hand, this meant that there was a strong pressure on Bally to adapt to market developments, for instance by upgrading its technology to also produce video games. On the other hand, Bally felt a strong pressure to exploit its current strength in electromechanical manufacturing, instead of building a new competence base from scratch. It was not self-evident for Bally how the demands for market adaptation and resource leveraging could be met simultaneously, as they seemed to be tugging the firm in diametrically opposite directions.

This tension arising from the partially conflicting demands of market adaptation and resource leveraging is referred to as the paradox of markets and resources. In the following subsections both sides of the paradox will be examined in more detail.

The demand for market adaptation

While adaptation to the environment is a vital requirement for the success of any organization, Bally had been very slow in responding to external developments ever since the introduction of Pac-Man. Bally had not exhibited the ability to shift its product offering to follow changing customer preferences and to respond to new entrants in the gaming market. It had lost its leading position because it no longer fully understood 'the rules of the game' in its own market. As Bally drifted further and further away from developments in the market, the misalignment was threatening the survival of its business. 'Game over' was impending.

To counter this downward trend, Bally needed to identify an attractive market opportunity that it could exploit. Not a short-term sales opportunity, but a market position that could be defended against rival firms and potential new entrants over a longer period. Ideally, this market position would serve buyers willing and able to pay a premium price, and whose loyalty could be won, despite the efforts of the competition. This market position would also need to be largely immune to substitute products and should not make the firm overly dependent on strong suppliers. Once such an opportunity had been identified, it would be essential for Bally to reorganize itself to fully meet the demands of this new positioning.

Adapting to a new market position and subsequently following the many shifts in such factors as customer preferences, competitor moves, government regulations and distribution structures, can have a significant impact on a firm. It requires significant agility in changing the product offering, value chain and resource base to remain in constant alignment with the fluctuating external circumstances. For Bally, adapting to the digital technology and software environment of the current gaming industry would have had far-reaching consequences for its entire business model. Even if Bally decided to stick to electromechanical pinball machines and to target the home market of ageing pinball wizards, the company would need to make significant alterations to its business model, getting to know new distribution channels and developing new marketing competences.

The demand for resource leveraging

Yet, for Bally it was essential to build on the resource base and value chain that it had already developed. It did not want to write off the investments it had made in building up a distinctive profile – it had taken years of acquiring and nurturing resources and fine-tuning the value chain to reach its level of expertise. Its strength in electromechanical manufacturing and the development of large 'moving parts' games was much too valuable to casually throw away just because video games were currently in fashion.

However, building a new area of competence, it was understood, should not be considered lightly. It would take a considerable amount of time, effort and money to shift the resource base and reconfigure the value chain, while there would be many risks associated with this transformation process as well. On the other hand, the danger of attempting to exploit the firm's current resources would be to excel at something of increasing irrelevance. The pinball machine might be joining the buggy whip and the vacuum tube as a museum exhibit, with a real threat that Bally too could become history.

Eventually, the solution found by Bally was to give up on pinball machines altogether and to redirect its existing resources towards a much more attractive market opportunity – slot machines. This move allowed Bally to exploit its electromechanical manufacturing capability and game-making expertise, while building a strong market position in a fast growing market. Even though Bally was able to find a synthesis, reconciling the two conflicting demands, not all companies are as successful. Nor do all managers agree on how the paradox of markets and resources can best be tackled.

EXHIBIT 4.1   SHORT CASE

YAKULT: MESSAGE IN A TINY BOTTLE

The health of the human body is heavily influenced by the food that enters it. Simply eating appropriately can get you quite far, but there seem to be more ways to decrease the risk of getting ill and improve one's body condition. The Japanese pharmaceutical company Yakult first started with the development of functional food, successfully creating a completely new industry segment. It did so in particular by commercializing a certain probiotic milk-like beverage. That size does not matter has been proven well by these 65ml Yakult bottles; they turned out to be filled with blockbuster potential.

When Minoru Shirota finished his medical studies at Kyoto Imperial University in the 1920s, Japan was far from the economic power it is today. Unsanitary conditions caused infectious diseases, which made microorganism research a great opportunity. In his study, Shirota found that certain lactic acid bacteria were useful for improving the state of one's intestines. After he succeeded in culturing and strengthening this *Lactobacillus casei* strain, he decided to capitalize on his discovery in the form of small beverages containing the probiotic preventive medicine.

With the help of volunteers, Shirota managed to manufacture and sell his little drink to the Japanese market from 1935 onwards with the establishment of the Shirota Institute for Research on Protective Bacteria, but it was not until 1955 that he founded Yakult. Although the health condition of Japanese people drastically improved in correlation with Japan's economic rise, Shirota believed that there would still be demand for an illness-preventing beverage. Yet, there was one question that popped up in his mind: how do you sell a 65ml bottle drink to people on a daily basis?

In the hope of providing an appropriate response, the management of Yakult decided to introduce the concept of Yakult Ladies in the 1960s. These women are not your average milkman though. In addition to home-delivering the small bottles – by bicycle, car, cart, motorbike and foot – Yakult Ladies are also able to sell the *Lactobacilli*-fermented milk drink on the spot. The concept of women selling the preventive beverage proved to be successful who can say 'no' to a sweet lady carrying a few bottles of probiotic drinks? This was, however, not limited to marketing the importance of the preventive beverage. Shirota and his team quickly discovered that their special sales organization carries even more benefits.

Since Yakult Ladies are recruited locally, they are able to quickly build an extensive network and herewith help Yakult take root into local communities. By being locally active, by paying periodic visits to retirement homes and organizing crime prevention activities for example, Yakult's special sales women have become familiar in their close environment. As such, Yakult Ladies are able to successfully promote Yakult's products and values.

Although Yakult makes use of special sales ladies, it primarily remains a pharmaceutical company with a focus on microorganism research. In addition to the 65ml bottles filled with lactic acid bacteria and a wide range of varieties on this beverage, Yakult also concerns itself with other types of edible nourishment. In Japan, the company sells guava leaf tea, recommended for diabetic patients anxious about their sugar intake, but also deals with vitamin and mineral drinks, in addition to vegetable, soy and fruit beverages.

By starting out with microbiological research, Yakult's R&D ends up with other projects as well, such as cosmetic products created as a result of the positive effect lactic acid bacteria has on skin. Furthermore, Yakult is occupied with pharmaceuticals. For example, the company verified that *Lacto-bacillus casei* YIT 9018 would inherit an anticancer effect, which resulted in the development of *lactobacilli*-based medical drugs. These business segments have not even come close to the level of profitability of Yakult's food and beverages, which contributed 88 per cent of Yakult's net sales in the fiscal year of 2012. Even though the company is active in over 30 other countries, the Japanese market alone is responsible for 69 per cent of these sales.

These numbers illustrate the problem Yakult is facing. Whereas the company is dominant in Japan and parts of Asia, Yakult is small in the rest of the world, while the competition is fierce. Outside of Japan, only the regular 65ml Yakult bottles and its

Light counterpart have reached firm ground. Where the one Yakult bottle a day concept has been integrated into the daily life of many Japanese, the same can hardly be said about the Western market. Especially Yakult's entrance into the European market was accompanied with issues, since plenty of competitors had already jumped on the functional food bandwagon. In Yakult's case, the French Groupe Danone, owner of Actimel and Activia, is especially apparent.

Since the late 1980s, the European market for functional food has expanded, but most food-products companies have used microorganisms in their products only to expand into the newly created market segment. That these promises of health improvement not necessarily yielded desirable results is highlighted by the European Food Safety Authority (EFSA), which provides scientific advice to the European Commission. Recent legislation demands that promises of health benefits need to be backed up by evidence, as a response to which several companies withdrew their claims precautionary. Danone Group did so too with its probiotic Actimel and Activia products, while the US division of the corporation even had to pay US$ 35 million in a lawsuit as a result of making misleading claims. Even though the functional food branch is perceived with increased scepticism, Danone retained its position largely due to expansive marketing.

But how can Yakult convince people that the positive effects inherited by its own beverages do work? Another problem is its relation with competitor Danone Group. Because the corporation signed a strategic alliance with Yakult in 2004 and became its biggest shareholder, allowing for the representation of three members on Yakult's Board, it effectively exerts influence over the Japanese firm.

The strategic alliance between Yakult and Danone Group, aimed at strengthening the global position of both companies, was terminated in 2013 due to the latter wanting to boost its stake in Yakult. The Japanese company did not regain managerial freedom, however, as Groupe Danone's members remained on its Board. Yet, the clause that ensured Yakult was represented on Danone's Board vanished. Although the corporation declared it had no intention of taking over Yakult, with its history of aggressive takeovers of competitors, Danone's loyalty concerning Yakult's independence can at the very least be called doubtful, putting the need for strategic choices on the Japanese company's even further on the front burner.

Does Yakult need to replicate its competitors in order to successfully compete in the European market? Since the image of functional food has been smudged by negative publicity, it demands a grand marketing campaign in order to alter the negative view shared by many. By putting an emphasis on the positive difference between Yakult and its competitors, the differentiation of the little beverages could be exploited.

On the other hand, one could say that you cannot put new wine in old bottles, although perhaps Yakult is able to put old wine into new containers. In Japan, Yakult has limited competition, but in Europe the situation is quite different. With Yakult's limited assortment in most countries outside of Japan, the expansion of Yakult's probiotic products abroad might be a solution. Yakult's research resulted in a wide range of innovative products, with some of them not having a direct equivalent in the portfolio of competitors, allowing for product differentiation.

Yakult might also emphasize its Yakult Ladies. As of the end of 2012, 41,000 of them are operating globally, a channel from which Europe is excluded, limiting the sales of beverages to stores. With Yakult Ladies accounting for 59 per cent of the sales of dairy products worldwide as of 2011 and the women being able to create long-term loyalty to the company, this channel might be worthwhile to expand, not only towards Europe but also in countries where Yakult already operates.

With a limited budget and equally narrow elbowroom, Yakult's management faces a difficult decision. Due to fierce competition and the current image of functional food in Europe, the message of Yakult's probiotic products may need aggressive marketing. Alternatively, by replicating its successful business model in Japan, Yakult Ladies might tell the probiotics story and sell more products to help swing Yakult on top. Which route will crack the tiny bottle and release Yakult's message?

Co-author: Wester Wagenaar

Sources: www.yakult.co.jp; institute.yakult.co.jp; Yakult Annual Report 2012; Yakult Supplementary Materials for Financial Statements 2005–2013; *Bloomberg,* 15 April 2010 and 26 April 2013; *Business Week,* 25 November 2007; Deguchi and Miyazaki (2010); Heasman and Mellentin (2001); Moloughney (2010); *The Wall Street Journal,* 26 April 2013; World Health Organization (2009).

PERSPECTIVES ON BUSINESS LEVEL STRATEGY

Always to be best, and to be distinguished above the rest.
The Iliad, Homer (8th century BC); Greek poet

Firms need to adapt themselves to market developments and need to build on the strengths of their resource bases and value chains. The main question dividing managers is 'who should be fitted to whom' – should an organization adapt itself to its environment or should it attempt to adapt the environment to itself? What should be the dominant factor driving a firm: its strengths or the opportunities? Should managers take the environment as the starting point, choose an advantageous market position and then build the resource base and value chain necessary to implement this choice? Or should managers take the organization's resource base (and possibly also its value chain) as the starting point, selecting and/or adapting an environment to fit with these strengths?

As before, the strategic management literature comes with strongly differing views on how managers should proceed. The variety of opinions among strategy theorists is dauntingly large, posing many incompatible prescriptions. Here the two diametrically opposed positions will be identified and discussed in order to show the richness of differing opinions. On the one side of the spectrum, there are those managers who argue that the market opportunities should be leading, while implying that the organization should adapt itself to the market position envisioned. This point of view is called the 'outside-in perspective'. At the other end of the spectrum, many managers believe that competition eventually revolves around rival resource bases and that firms must focus their strategies on the development of unique resources and value chains. They argue that product–market positioning is a tactical decision that can be taken later. This view is referred to as the 'inside-out perspective'.

The outside-in perspective

Managers with an outside-in perspective believe that firms should not be self–centred, but should continuously take their environment as the starting point when determining their strategy. Successful companies, it is argued, are externally oriented and market-driven (e.g. Day, 1990; Webster, 1994). They have their sights clearly set on developments in the marketplace and are determined to adapt to the unfolding opportunities and threats encountered. They take their cues from customers and competitors, and use these signals to determine their own game plan (Jaworski and Kohli, 1993). For these successful companies, markets are leading, resources are following.

Therefore, for the outside-in directed manager, developing strategy begins with an analysis of the environment to identify attractive market opportunities. Potential customers must be sought, whose needs can be satisfied more adequately than currently done by other firms. Once these customers have been won over and a market position has been established, the firm must consistently defend or build on this position by adapting itself to changes in the environment. Shifts in customers' demands must be met, challenges from rival firms must be countered, impending market entries by outside firms must be rebuffed and excessive pricing by suppliers must be resisted. In short, to the outside-in manager the game of strategy is about market positioning and understanding, and responding to external developments. For this reason, the outside-in perspective is sometimes also referred to as the 'positioning approach' (Mintzberg, Ahlstrand and Lampel, 1998).

Positioning is not short-term, opportunistic behaviour, but requires a strategic perspective, because superior market positions are difficult to attain. Once conquered, however, can be the source of sustained profitability. Some proponents of the outside-in perspective argue that in each market a number of different positions can yield sustained profitability. For instance, Porter suggests that companies that focus on a particular niche, and companies that strongly differentiate their product offering, can achieve strong and profitable market positions, even if another company has the lowest cost position (Porter, 1980, 1985). Other authors emphasize that the position of being market leader is particularly important (e.g. Buzzell and Gale, 1987). Companies with a high market share profit more from economies of scale, benefit from risk aversion among customers, have more bargaining power towards buyers and suppliers, and can more easily flex their muscles to prevent new entrants and block competitive attacks.

Unsurprisingly, proponents of the outside-in perspective argue that insight into markets and industries is essential. Not only the general structure of markets and industries needs to be analysed, but also the specific demands, strengths, positions and intentions of all major forces need to be determined. For instance, buyers must be understood with regard to their needs, wants, perceptions, decision-making processes and bargaining chips. The same holds true for suppliers, competitors, potential market and/or industry entrants and providers of substitute products (Porter, 1980, 1985). Once a manager knows 'what makes the market tick' – sometimes referred to as the 'rules of the game' – a position can be identified within the market that could give the firm bargaining power vis-a-vis suppliers and buyers, while keeping competitors at bay. Of course, the wise manager will not only emphasize winning under the current rules with the current players, but will attempt to anticipate market and industry developments, and position the firm to benefit from these. Many outside-in advocates even advise firms to initiate market and industry changes, so that they can be the first to benefit from the altered rules of the game (this issue will be discussed further in Chapters 9 and 10).

Proponents of the outside-in perspective readily acknowledge the importance of firm resources and activities for cashing in on market opportunities the firm has identified. If the firm does not have, or is not able to develop or obtain, the necessary resources to implement a particular strategy, then specific opportunities will be unrealizable. Therefore, managers should always keep the firm's strengths and weaknesses in mind when choosing an external position, to ensure that it remains feasible. Yet, to the outside-in strategist, the firm's current resource base should not be the starting point when determining strategy, but should merely be acknowledged as a potentially limiting condition on the firm's ability to implement the best business strategy.

Actually, firms that are market-driven are often the first ones to realize that new resources and/or activities need to be developed and, therefore, are better positioned to build up a 'first mover advantage' (Lieberman and Montgomery, 1988, 1998). Where the firm does not have the ability to catch up with other firms' superior resources, it can always enter into an alliance with a leading organization, offering its partner a crack at a new market opportunity.

EXHIBIT 4.2 THE OUTSIDE-IN PERSPECTIVE

SONY-MICROSOFT BATTLE GOES TO E3 AS TABLETS DENT CONSOLES

Gun-toting fighters take a back seat to Microsoft Corp. and Sony Corp. this week as the console makers' battle to show they've got the best plan for selling pricey machines in the age of cheap play on phones and tablets.

Both present today at E3, the video-game industry's annual conference running through June 13 in Los Angeles, with the $67 billion game market in the grip of a two-year slump. Consumers have cut purchases of consoles and costly packaged games for inexpensive Web-delivered titles like Rovio Entertainment Oy's "Angry Birds," defined as more casual, mobile and social.

Microsoft's Xbox One and Sony's PlayStation 4, set to be in stores for the US holidays, tackle the shift differently. Sony is trying to coax casual and hard-core gamers to line up early for blockbuster titles and smaller exclusives that can develop into hits. Microsoft positioned Xbox One as the centre of living-room entertainment, with programming from director Steven Spielberg, ESPN and

Hollywood studios – leaving gamers to question whether it's their best console choice.

"They're having to resell to their consumer base again," said David Cole, an analyst at industry research firm DFC Intelligence. "It's going to be very much a challenge for both of those companies to capture a casual consumer who is on the fence about replacing their console and buying a new system."

Source: Cliff Edwards, *Business Week*, 9 June, 2013.

The inside-out perspective

Managers adopting an inside-out perspective believe that strategies should not be built around external opportunities, but around a company's strengths. Successful companies, it is argued, build up a strong resource base over an extended period of time, which offers them access to unfolding market opportunities in the medium and short term. For such companies, the starting point of the strategy formation process is the question of which resource base it wants to have. The fundamental strategic issue is which difficult-to-imitate competences and exclusive assets should be acquired and/or further refined. Creating such a resource platform requires major investments and a long breath, and to a large extent will determine the culture and identity of the organization. Hence, it is of the utmost importance and should be the central tenet of a firm's strategy. Once the long-term direction for the building of the resource infrastructure has been set, attention can be turned to identifying market opportunities where these specific strengths can be exploited. To the inside-out oriented manager, the issue of market positioning is essential, as only a strong competitive position in the market will result in above-average profitability. However, market positioning must take place within the context of the broader resource-based strategy and not contradict the main thrust of the firm – selected market positions must leverage the existing resource base, not ignore it. In other words, market positioning is vital, but tactical, taking place within the boundaries set by the resource-driven strategy. For success, resources should be leading, and markets following.

Many managers taking an inside-out perspective tend to emphasize the importance of a firm's competences over its tangible resources (physical assets). Their way of looking at strategy is referred to as the resource-based view (e.g. Wernerfelt, 1984; Barney, 1991, Reading 4.2), competence-based view (e.g. Prahalad and Hamel, 1990, Reading 5.2; Sanchez, Heene and Thomas, 1996) or capabilities-based view (e.g. Stalk, Evans and Shulman, 1992; Teece, Pisano and Shuen, 1997, Reading 4.3). These managers point out that it is especially the development of unique abilities that is such a strenuous and lengthy process, more so than the acquisition of physical resources such as production facilities and computer systems. Some companies might be able to achieve a competitive advantage based on physical assets, but usually such tangible infrastructure is easily copied or purchased. However, competences are not readily for sale on the open market as 'plug-and-play' components, but need to be painstakingly built up by an organization through hard work and experience. Even where a company takes a short cut by buying another organization or engaging in an alliance, it takes significant time and effort to internalize the competences in such a way that they can be put to productive use. Hence, having distinctive competences can be a very attractive basis for competitive advantage, as rival firms generally require a long time to catch up (e.g. Collis and Montgomery, 1995; Barney, 1991, Reading 4.2).

The 'nightmare scenario' for inside-out oriented strategists is where the firm flexibly shifts from one market demand to the next, building up an eclectic collection of unrelated competences, none of which are distinctive compared to competence-focused companies. In this scenario, a firm is fabulously market-driven, adaptively responding to shifts in the environment, but incapable of concentrating itself on forming the distinctive competence base needed for a robust competitive advantage over the longer term.

Most inside-out oriented managers also recognize the 'shadow side' of competences – they are not only difficult to learn, but difficult to unlearn as well. The laborious task of building up competences makes it hard to switch to new competences, even if that is what the market demands (e.g. Christensen, 1997; Rumelt, 1996). Companies far down the route of competence specialization, find themselves locked in by the choices made in the past. In the same way as few concert pianists are able (and willing) to switch to playing saxophone when they are out of a job, few companies are able and willing to scrap their competence base, just because the market is taking a turn for the worse. Becoming a concert pianist not only costs years of practice but is a way of life, with a specific way of working, network and career path, making it very unattractive to make a mid-career shift towards a more marketable trade. Likewise, companies experience that their core competences can simultaneously be their core rigidities, locking them out of new opportunities (Leonard-Barton, 1995). From an inside-out perspective, both companies and concert pianists should therefore first try to build on their unique competences and attempt to find or create a more suitable market, instead of reactively adapting to the unpredictable whims of the current environment (see Figure 4.8).

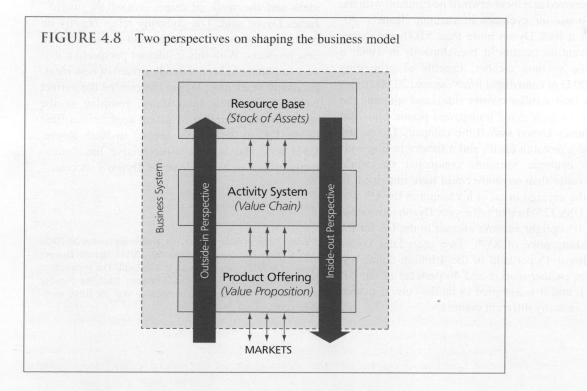

FIGURE 4.8 Two perspectives on shaping the business model

EXHIBIT 4.3   THE INSIDE OUT PERSPECTIVE

DYSON: BLOWN BY THE WIND

Who could have envisioned that the somewhat strange looking invention of the 'Ballbarrow' resulted in a number of innovating game changers in multiple markets, and made its founding father UK's most famous engineer and a billionaire? James Dyson's revolutionary vacuum cleaners, hand-dryers, fans and heaters all changed their marketplace – and at a premium price.

It all started in 1971 with James Dyson renovating his property. The wheel of his wheelbarrow got stuck in the mud, the steel body damaged the paintwork, and the bucket got an unwanted cement coating that could not be removed. A few years later James Dyson came up with the 'Ballbarrow', a wheelbarrow with a spherical wheel and a molded plastic bucket that solved all problems. And while everyone expected the Ballbarrow to flop it became a huge success.

Frustration again triggered the idea for Dyson's next success. When he bought a Hoover vacuum cleaner it got clogged very quickly and lost suction over time. The only option was to change the filters and put in a new bag, resulting in exactly the same problems very quickly. Inspired by the way sawdust was removed at a local sawmill he came up with the idea to use air cyclones in vacuum cleaners. Although it took Dyson more than 5,000 prototypes, his invention became a breakthrough in 1993: a cyclonic vacuum cleaner, capable of generating 100,000 G of centrifugal force (around 20,000 times higher than a roller-coaster ride), and spinning the dirt into a high grade transparent plastic bin. That year James Dyson started the company Dyson and opened a research centre and a factory in England.

His cyclonic vacuums conquered the world much faster than anybody could have imagined. In 2002 the average price of a vacuum in the US was about US$ 125. In that same year Dyson introduced its DC07 upright vacuum cleaner in the US for the astonishing price of $399. Two years later Dyson had almost 15 per cent of the 4 billion dollar US-vacuum cleaner market and 40 per cent of the UK market, and it is assumed to be the current market leader in many different countries.

Profits have been rising rapidly with Dyson's latest inventions added to the product range. The Airblade is an innovative hand dryer that starts with a US$ 1,199 price tag. It uses a HEPA filter to get rid of bacteria in the bathroom air and it then blows a sheet of air onto your hands to scrape off water like a windshield wiper. Because it only takes about 12 seconds to dry your hands, it is not only a design must-have in public lavatories; it is also much more energy and cost efficient than paper towels or standard hand dryers. And then there is the new kid on the block, the Dyson Air Multiplier, an air fan you have never seen before. A fan without fans, drawing up to 33 litres of air per second, and generating a powerful airflow. The airflow passes over the curved outer circle of the Air Multiplier, while air around the machine is also drawn into the airflow amplified up to 18 times. Which – according to the company – is not "chopping the air before it hits you" like conventional fans do. All these innovations have resulted in Dyson creating more than GB £1 billion of revenue in 2011, with more than GB £306 million of profit and more than 4,000 employees.

What is the secret of this company? What is the key to its success? "Our success is down to new ideas and the work of teams around the world," James Dyson said. The company relies heavily on resources, entering new markets and coming up with new products. With this inside-out perspective it is very important to keep a steady stream of new ideas. For many years now, Dyson has created the perfect conditions for new innovations, resulting in the second highest number of patent applications filed in the UK in 2009, only second to Rolls-Royce. Until now, the inside-out-perspective has consistently proven to be the driver of Dyson's success.

Co-author: Jeroen Brinkhuis

Sources: 'How to make it', *The New Yorker*, September 20, 2010; 'Mr. Clean', *Newsweek*, January 13, 2011; 'Inside Dyson', August 13, 2013, www.dyson.com; 'The Inside Out Perspective: Dyson's Profits Rise to £ 190m: Company Doubling Number of Engineers', *The Guardian*, Wednesday May 26, 2010; www.mintel.com.

MANAGING THE PARADOX OF MARKETS AND RESOURCES

One does not gain much by mere cleverness.
Marquis de Vauvenargues (1715–1747); French soldier and moralist

So, how can a sustainable competitive advantage be created? Should generals create a sustainable competitive advantage by first selecting a superior position in the environment (e.g. a mountain pass) and then adapt their military resources to this position, or should generals develop armies with unique resources and then try to let the battle take place where these resources can best be employed? Should football coaches first determine how they want the game to be played on the field and then attract and train players to fit this style, or should coaches develop uniquely talented players and then adapt the team's playing style to make the best use of these resources? Should strategizing managers first understand industry dynamics and then develop resources that fit the environment? Or should they focus on developing unique and difficult-to-imitate resources and compete in industries where these resources fit best? Whether a military, sports or business strategist, an approach to creating competitive advantage must be chosen (see Table 4.1).

While no consensus has yet been developed within the field of strategic management on how to manage the paradox of markets and resources, two options have been suggested by scholars. The first option is *parallel processing,* and the second *juxtaposing* based on dynamic capabilities (see taxonomy in Chapter 1).

Parallel processing

In parallel processing, the company deals with the paradox of markets and resources by separating demands over different organizational units. Some organizational units focus on market demands only – such as sales managers – and others on resource leveraging – such as R&D managers. For example, the sales department analyses client demands, competitive moves and industry dynamics, and then positions the company within the industry environment, while the research and development department leverages company resources to create unique value propositions. In this case, managing the paradox of markets and resources takes place at the next organizational level up. The phenomenon of dual processing companies has also been called 'spatial separation' (see Chapter 1).

TABLE 4.1 Outside-in versus inside-out perspective

	Outside-in perspective	*Inside-out perspective*
Emphasis on	Markets over resources	Resources over markets
Orientation	Opportunity-driven (external potential)	Strength-driven (internal potential)
Starting point	Market demand and industry structure	Resource base and value chain
Fit through	Adaptation to environment	Adaptation of environment
Strategic focus	Attaining advantageous position	Attaining distinctive resources
Strategic moves	External positioning	Building resource base
Tactical moves	Acquiring necessary resources	External positioning
Competitive weapons	Bargaining power and mobility barriers	Superior resources and imitation barriers

Juxtaposing

While some organizational members focus on market demands only – such as sales managers – and others on resource leveraging – such as R&D managers – strategizing managers at different organizational units or with higher hierarchical positions have to juxtapose between both demands, employing dynamic capabilities. Defined as 'the distinct skills, processes, procedures, organizational structures, decision rules and disciplines that form the basis of a company's ability to sensing, seizing and reconfiguring capabilities' (Teece, Pisano and Shuen, 1997, Reading 4.3; Teece, 2007, Reading 2.1), dynamic capabilities propel strategists to accommodate both demands at the same time.

Dynamic capabilities enable strategizing managers to manage the paradox of markets and resources by juxtaposing between the demand for market adaptation and the demand for resource leveraging. Juxtaposing is the continuous process of creating and maintaining a dynamic equilibrium in the paradox of markets and resources. The equilibrium is dynamic, because companies continuously upgrade its competences to protect them against competitors that imitate the firms' competences and to defend their market position. At the same time, it must also actively develop new capabilities in a changing business environment. The paradox is managed either on a project basis; within the same organizational unit; or at a higher organizational level.

BUSINESS LEVEL STRATEGY IN INTERNATIONAL PERSPECTIVE

Co-author: Gep Eisenloeffel

Whoever is winning at the moment will always seem to be invincible.
George Orwell (1903–1950); English novelist

As before, this chapter is concluded by explicitly looking at the issue from an international angle. The difference between this and other chapters, is that comparative management researchers have not reported specific national preferences for an inside-out or an outside-in perspective. This may be due to the fact that there actually are no distinct national inclinations when dealing with this paradox. However, it might also be the case that the late emergence of resource-based theories (starting in the early 1980s) has not yet allowed for cross-national comparisons.

As a stimulus to the debate on whether there are national differences in the approach to business level strategies, several factors will be considered that might influence on how the paradox of markets and resources is tackled in different countries. It goes almost without saying that more international research is needed to give this issue a firmer footing.

Mobility barriers

In general, industry and market positions will be of more value if there are high mobility barriers within the environment (Porter, 1980). Some of these mobility barriers can be specifically national in origin. Government regulation, in particular, can be an important source of mobility barriers. For instance, import quotas and duties, restrictive licensing systems, and fiscal regulations and subsidies, can all – knowingly or unknowingly – result in protection of incumbent firms. Such government intervention enhances the importance of obtained positions. Other national sources of mobility barriers can be unions' resistance to change and high customer loyalty. In some economies high mobility barriers might also be imposed by powerful groups or families.

In such economies, which are more rigid due to high mobility barriers, strategists might have a strong preference to think in terms of market positions first, because these are more difficult to obtain than the necessary resources. The opposite would be true in more dynamic economies, where market positions might easily be challenged by competitors, unless they are based on distinctive and difficult-to-imitate resources.

Resource mobility

A second international difference might be found in the types of resources employed across countries. In nations where the dominant industries are populated by firms using relatively simple and abundant resources, market positions are far more important, since acquisition of the necessary resources is much less of an issue. However, if a national economy is composed of industries using complex bundles of resources, requiring many years of painstaking development, there might be a tendency to emphasize the importance of resources over market positions.

INTRODUCTION TO THE READINGS

Drive thy business; let it not drive thee.
Benjamin Franklin (1706–1790); American writer and statesman

To help strategists to come to grips with the variety of perspectives on this issue, three readings have been selected that each shed their own light on the debate. As in previous chapters, the first two readings will be representatives of the two poles on this issue, while the aim of the third reading is to bridge the two perspectives.

Reading 4.1, 'Strategy from the Outside In', has been taken from the first chapter of George Day and Christine Moorman's 2010 book with the same title. The reading is based on three lessons that the authors claim to have taken from winning companies. The first lesson is that these companies consistently take an outside-in approach to strategy, starting from the market when designing their strategy, not the other way around. The second lesson is that they use market insights, which goes far beyond market data and information, and is based on 'deep and integrated knowledge that reveals patterns and identifies opportunities.' The third lesson is that each and every part of outside-in companies should focus on achieving, sustaining and profiting from customer value. The authors argue that there are many reasons why companies are pushed towards becoming inside-out – including the popularity of the resource-based view of the firm – but company leaders of winning companies resist these forces.

As representative of the inside-out perspective, an often-cited article by Jay Barney has been selected as a thorough introduction to the resource-based view. In Reading 4.2, 'Firm Resources and Sustained Competitive Advantage', Barney differentiates resource-based models of competitive advantage from the Porter-like environmental models. He does not dismiss externally oriented explanations of profitability, but wishes to explore the internally oriented explanation that idiosyncratic firm resources are at the base of superior performance. He sets out on this task by pinpointing the two fundamental assumptions on which the resource-based view rests – that firms have different resources (*resource heterogeneity*) and that these resources cannot be easily transferred to, or copied by, other firms (*resource immobility*). He goes on to argue that these resources can be the basis of competitive advantage if they meet four criteria: they must be valuable and rare, while being difficult to imitate and substitute.

Reading 4.3, 'Dynamic Capabilities and Strategic Management', is an influential and already classic 1997 *Strategic Management Journal* article by David Teece, Gary Pisano and Amy Shuen. The reading addresses the issue of actively managing the paradox of markets and resources by means of dynamic capabilities, maintaining a dynamic equilibrium. Dynamic capabilities are defined as the distinct skills, processes, procedures, organizational structures, decision rules and disciplines that form the basis of a company's ability to sense, seize and reconfigure capabilities. Dynamic capabilities are difficult to develop and deploy, and are the key to competitive advantage in fast-changing business landscapes with rapid innovation.

This reading marked the beginning of the high popularity of the dynamic capabilities concept in the strategy field, and particularly within the 'resource-based view' school of thought. The importance of the dynamic capabilities concept is that it bridges the distinct and theoretically incompatible schools of thought that the outside-in and inside-out perspectives are based on. Even years before official publication as a working paper, this article inspired strategy scholars around the world. In a stream of publications, the nature of dynamic capabilities has been researched and further conceptualized, such as Kathleen Eisenhardt and Jeffrey Martin's *SMJ* article 'Dynamic capabilities: What are they?' (2000). In 2007 David Teece published another influential article in *SMJ:* 'Explicating Dynamic Capabilities: The nature and microfoundations of (sustainable) enterprise performance' (Reading 2.1 in this book). McGrath's 2013 book, provocatively entitled *The End of Competitive Advantage,* stretched the meaning of dynamic capabilities further, and underscores the importance – and confidence – of dynamic capabilities researchers.

Strategy from the outside in

By George S. Day and Christine Moorman[1]

With the wreckage of the Great Recession still smouldering and slow economic growth expected for the foreseeable future, it's not surprising to see that many companies are turning inward and hunkering down. Profits, growth and value creation seem to have become stretch goals rather than baseline expectations. Companies that were praised over the last decade for delivering shareholder value have largely fallen on hard times; buried under debt, they have no clear plan for capitalizing once customers are willing to spend again. The *Fortune* 500's top 25 at the beginning of the century included companies such as General Motors, Ford, Citigroup, Bank of America, AIG, Enron and Compaq. Measured by market value, only 8 of the 25 largest companies in the world in 2000 can claim that distinction today.

Yet a number of companies operating in the same challenging environment have gained market share, grown revenues and profits, and created more value for customers, in contrast to their competitors' intense focus on budget cutting. Indeed, there are companies that have managed market share, profit and customer value growth throughout the vertiginous boom-and-bust business cycles of the last 20 years. These companies may not have been favourite stock picks, nor have all of them topped the lists of the decade's most profitable corporations. But what they have done is found a way to build value over the long term. These are not flash-in-the-pan companies, world-beaters one year and stragglers the next. They are companies like Johnson & Johnson, Procter & Gamble, Fidelity, Cisco, Wal-Mart, Amazon, Apple, IKEA, Texas Instruments, Becton Dickinson and Tesco, among others.

These companies have been successful because they have remained true to the purpose of a business (as stated by Peter Drucker): to create and keep customers. They've kept that purpose not by focusing on shareholders and meeting quarterly numbers, by playing games with their financial statements, or by focusing just on competitive advantages. Instead, they've done it by consistently creating superior customer value – and profiting handsomely from that customer value.

We've spent years looking at these companies – and many not-so-successful ones – looking for patterns and commonalities that explain their stellar results, and we've concluded that they offer three very important lessons for any executive who wants to consistently create superior customer value and generate economic profits over the long term. There is no step-by-step formula, but there are consistencies in how these companies think, how they make strategic decisions, and, most importantly, how they operate to ensure they are maximizing the value they create and the profits they capture.

- These companies approach strategy from the outside in rather than from the inside out. They start with the market when they design their strategy, not the other way around.

- They use deep market insights to inform and guide their outside-in view.

- Their outside-in strategy focuses every part of the organization on achieving, sustaining and profiting from customer value.

Two paths to strategy

The first thing that distinguishes these value- and profit-creating companies is that they drive strategy from the perspective of the market – in other words, from the *outside in*. This may sound trivial, but it is shockingly uncommon. For all the talk about "putting the customer first" and "relentlessly delivering value to customers," most management teams fail to do this. Put most simply, outside-in means standing in the customer's shoes and viewing everything the company does through the customer's eyes.

Far more common than outside-in thinking is inside-out thinking and inside-out strategy. Inside-out companies narrowly frame their strategic thinking by asking, "What can the market do for us?" rather than, "What can we do for the market?" The consequences of inside-out versus outside-in thinking can be seen in the way many business-to-business firms approach

[1]Source: This article was adapted with permission from Chapter 1 of *Strategy From the Outside In, Profiting from customer value*, McGraw Hill, New Jersey, 2010. Copyright © 2010 by George S. Day and Christine Moorman. Reproduced by permission of The McGraw-Hill Companies, Inc.

customer solutions. The inside-out view is that "solutions are bundles of products and services that help us sell more." The outside-in view is that "the purpose of a solution is to help our customers find value and make money-to our mutual benefit."

Inside-out thinking helps explain why a large database company that was looking to grow by leveraging its deep information about the companies' finances spent several million dollars to develop a product for small and medium-sized enterprises without first having in-depth conversations with potential buyers. Management, seduced by the seemingly vast potential of this market, relied on the assurances of the sales force that customers would buy. During the process, no one asked what value the company would be offering customers, or how the company's new product would offer customers more value than the status quo. Instead, managers focused on what customers could do for the company. As a result, the new product flopped and was abandoned in less than a year.

An even more costly example is Ford's unfortunate decision not to add a sliding door on the driver's side of its Windstar minivan. The extra cost of the fifth door was the major factor in this decision, but just to be sure, the designers asked a sample of buyers their opinion. Only one-third of the sample thought it was a good idea, while the rest said no or weren't sure because they couldn't envision the benefits. Meanwhile, Ford's competitors were "living with" prospective buyers at shopping malls, do-it-yourself stores and soccer fields. That fieldwork showed that the fifth door could solve a lot of problems for families and handymen. Based on these benefits to customers, Ford's competitors, including Honda, Chrysler and GM, added the door, which was an immediate hit. Ford's sales suffered so badly because of the lack of this feature that the company was forced to add it later. Doing so meant that Ford had to redesign its van to match competitors' – at an out-of-pocket cost of $560 million (not including the opportunity cost of lost sales).

Winning from the outside in

With an outside-in mindset, top management's strategy dialogue starts with the market. The management team steps outside the boundaries and constraints of the company as it is, and looks first at its market: How and why are customers changing? What new needs do they have? What can we do to solve their problems and help them make more money? What new competitors are lurking around the corner, and how can we derail their efforts? This perspective expands the strategy dialogue

and opens up a richer set of opportunities for competitive advantage and growth.

Jeff Bezos, the founder and chairman of Amazon. com, is a champion of the outside-in approach. He explained how Amazon was able to meet the needs of its customers for Web services by offering access to its cloud computing network and for a more convenient reading experience with the Kindle. He describes it as a "working backward" mentality:

Rather than ask what we are good at and what else can we do with that skill, you ask, who are our customers? What do they need? And then you say we're going to give that to them regardless of whether we have the skills to do so, and we will learn these skills no matter how long it takes.... There is a tendency I think for executives to think that the right course of action is to stick to the knitting-stick with what you are good at. That may be a generally good rule, but the problem is the world changes out from under you if you are not constantly adding to your skill set.

The difficulties faced by Dell Computer over the last four years illustrate the need for outside-in thinking. For several decades, Dell's celebrated mastery of logistics allowed it to deliver leading edge computer hardware at prices and speeds that no rival could match. The whole organization could concentrate on assembling and shipping PCs, laptops and servers as cheaply and quickly as possible. This single-minded emphasis on efficiency made Dell the worldwide market share leader in 2005. Growth came by expanding globally and broadening the range of hardware sold through its direct-to-customer model. Everything was viewed through the prism of this business model and how to leverage it further.

But this inside-out emphasis also kept Dell from seeing and responding to a sea change in its market. More and more customers wanted to buy at retail and own products that conveyed a sense of personal style. Both Apple and Hewlett-Packard (HP) had seen the trend building and were ready to oblige. HP redesigned its machines with a focus on customer experience and distinctive value, beyond price or the latest technology. It advertised, "The Computer Is Personal Again." The market responded, and HP assumed market share leadership in 2006. Dell, on the other hand, faltered and lost sales. Nevertheless, the efficiency focus was so embedded in Dell that manufacturing executives resisted offering distinct designs, even at a premium price.

As one commentator put it, "Dell began to treat consumers and even some business customers like they were passengers on a Greyhound bus". Between 2Q 2008 and 2Q 2009, Dell's share of the US personal computer market dropped from 31.4 per cent to 26.3 per cent. On top of that, many of Dell's advantages were neutralized as HP and other competitors improved their supply-chain management and lowered costs.

Anecdotes aside, there is abundant evidence for the superiority of outside-in thinking. Much of it comes from studying the relative profit performance of market-driven companies. These firms have an inherent advantage over their more self-absorbed rivals because of their superior ability to understand markets, provide superior value over time, and attract and retain customers.

Inside-out myopia

Given both the intuitive and the data-driven appeal of outside-in strategy, why is the inside-out approach to strategy so pervasive? There are many subtle forces that converge to encourage inside-out thinking and slowly disconnect the business from its market.

Positive reinforcement

Inside-out strategic thinking ultimately relies on gaining maximum returns from existing assets – in other words, increasing efficiency. Increasing efficiency usually produces positive results. However, the quest for steady improvement in operations crowds out the question of whether the operations are worth doing in the first place! While the efficiency of the existing assets may be rising, the market is shifting, and customer value is slipping away. By the time companies that are caught in this cozy positive-feedback loop notice they are no longer delivering customer value, it's too late – competitors have seized the initiative.

Competing priorities

For most executives, there are often many stakeholders who are closer at hand than customers. Employees, boards, partners, suppliers and regulators all stand closer to executives than customers do. This proximity means that their concerns can easily become more urgent than those of customers. Meanwhile, within the organization, internal concern about resource allocation, budgeting and turf wars with other functions become the most pressing priorities.

Contemporary strategy theories

The capabilities- or resource-based view of the firm is one culprit. These ideas have inadvertently tilted the

dialogue within firms toward an inside-out view. Their supporters argue that the source of a firm's defensible competitive position lies in its distinctive, hard-to-duplicate resources and capabilities. Excellent service operations, strong supply chains and superior human resource practices are advantages that are cultivated slowly over time. They are hard for competitors to copy, but they also limit the ability of the firm to adapt. In this theory, these resources exist to be used, and the task of management is to improve and fully exploit them. This is certainly a worthwhile goal to be eventually achieved. But as a starting point for strategic thinking, it myopically narrows and anchors the dialogue prematurely.

Darwin in the enterprise

A contributing factor to the lure of inside-out thinking that can't be ignored is employees' inherent drive for self-preservation. Because firms (and business units, departments and teams) are made up of human beings, they are inevitably tempted to put their own survival first. This instinct naturally accords with an inside-out view, since the outside-in view often requires a firm to reinvent itself – to employ creative destruction internally to meet ever-changing customer value expectations.

Going with the flow

Another human trait that also drives inside-out strategy is the tendency to go with the flow and behave like the others around us. Social scientists call this social norming or "groupthink" when they study social dynamics, but companies and organizations are susceptible to social norming, too. Over time, the companies in any industry or sector tend to behave in the same way and to focus on the same issues and strategies – usually inside-out ones. When these industries or sectors are truly shaken up, it is usually because a new entrant makes a breakthrough in delivering customer value that the incumbents have overlooked.

These factors and others continually push executives toward inside-out strategy. Without constant effort and vigilance, inside-out thinking comes to dominate in the firm, and outside-in strategy disappears.

Detecting inside-out thinking

The myopia of inside-out thinking is hard to detect when it becomes embedded in our mental models and

TABLE 4.1.1   Mental models and strategy approaches

Outside-In	Inside-Out
■ All decisions start with the market and opportunities for advantage	■ We'll sell to whoever will buy
■ Profits are gained through a superior value proposition and leveraging the brand and customer assets	■ Profits are gained through cost cutting and efficiency improvements. Six sigma, TQM and replicability of processes take priority
■ Customer knowledge is a valuable asset and channels are value-adding partners	■ Customer data are a control mechanism and channels are conduits
■ We know more than our competitors	■ If competitors do it, it must be good
■ No sacred cows – cannibalize yourself	■ Protect the cash flow stream
■ Customers buy the expectation of benefits	■ Customers buy performance features
■ Superior quality is defined by customers as "fitness for use"	■ Quality is conformance to internal standards
■ The best ideas come from living with customers	■ Customers don't know what they want and they can't tell you if they're asked
■ Customer loyalty is the key to profitability	■ Expanding the customer base is what matters

shapes the way we do business. Mental models are simplifying frameworks that include prevailing assumptions, norms and even the vocabulary used to talk about customers. They help impose order and provide handy rules of thumb. The problem is that these inherent simplifications and untested ideas don't announce themselves. Table 4.1.1 illustrates some that we have encountered in our study of inside-out and outside-in thinking.

Market insight

An outside-in approach to strategy is a clear necessity. However, it will not necessarily lead to a superior customer value proposition or outstanding economic profits unless it is guided by deep market insights. This brings us to the second lesson we've gleaned from the companies we have studied: that it is not sufficient to simply view the firm from the vantage point of the market. It takes smart investments in market intelligence and an organization-wide commitment to sensing and acting on the resulting market insights.

Within inside-out companies, market data usually reside in reports of competitors' moves, unrelated compilations of market research reports, and the occasional analysis of activity in the customer database. But data are not knowledge or insight! Valuable market insights are based on much deeper and more integrated knowledge that reveals patterns and identifies opportunities. Market insights are the difference between simply observing market trends and probing further to explain and exploit those trends.

Casella Wines saw the same trends in the wine market as its rivals did. Its deep dive underneath these trends uncovered a large non-consumption market that was turned off by the myriad of confusing choices, the haughty nature of the category, and the dense vocabulary. Its answer was the Yellow Tail brand, with a simple and fruity taste, few choices, no vintages and an endearing kangaroo symbol, which it parlayed into the most popular imported wine in the United States.

The most valuable market insights are (1) accurate reflections of reality, not just what managers want or expect to see; (2) actionable, with the potential to mobilize and inspire the entire organization to develop new strategies or improve the current strategies; (3) not seen or understood by competitors; and (4) used in novel ways to influence strategy.

When distiller Diageo applied the insight that "Men want to progress in life," the power came not from its inherent novelty, but from its application to Johnnie Walker's label (turning the man so that he is walking forward, not backward) and a mass advertising campaign that used paintings on buildings to show the walking man's progress. The campaign increased sales 50 per cent (to $5 billion) over a nine-year period.

The strategic case for market insights

The case for timely and widely shared market insights has been made persuasively by Anne Mulcahy, chairman and former CEO of Xerox Corporation and *Chief Executive* magazine's 2008 CEO of the Year. Mulcahy believes that marketing and innovation are even more important in an era of demanding customers, information overload and economic recession. To create personalized solutions for data-intensive customers in law firms and health care, Xerox needs new learning capabilities, Mulcahy says.

In Mulcahy's view, learning about the market in which you compete starts at the top, and every senior manager has to be attuned to the voice of the customer, with marketing having overall accountability for what is learned and how it is used. To keep Xerox's management team focused on the market, its top 500 accounts are assigned to senior officers, who take responsibility for fixing customer problems. Mulcahy speaks enthusiastically about "dreaming with customers" by bringing customers into Xerox labs to identify their pain points and guide Xerox's innovation efforts.

Market-leading firms stand out in their ability to continuously sense and act on trends and events in their markets. They are better equipped to anticipate how their markets will respond to actions designed to attract and retain customers and to perceive emerging segment opportunities. In these well-educated firms, every-one from first-line sales and service people to the CEO is sensitized to listen to latent problems and opportunities. They achieve this with market-focused leadership that shapes an open-minded and inquisitive culture and a well-honed market learning capability that infuses the entire strategy development process.

Market insight is difficult for a company to master and for competitors to imitate, making it a basis for a durable competitive advantage. However, like all capabilities, it is vulnerable to creeping complacency and turning inward to focus on cost cutting, and/or an emphasis on short-term results that leads the firm to stop listening to the voice of the customer.

Intuit fell into this trap despite a history of providing superior relational value to customers that earned it the dominant share of the tax preparation market. By May 2000, its products dominated the retail market – Quicken had an 84 per cent share, QuickBooks an 87 per cent share, and TurboTax a high 60 per cent share – and had 83 per cent of the online market! Then Intuit began doing things that irritated loyal customers, such as raising the cost of customer service calls and limiting software licences to one per computer. This caused growth to flatten and made the company vulnerable to attacks from venerable competitors such as H&R Block's TaxCut and easier Web-based financial planning services, such as Mint.com, that also provided storage and better support for customers.

How market insights enable outside-in strategies

Strategically useful insights address such questions as: What are our customers' real needs? Where are competitors likely to attack? Why are valuable customers defecting, and how can we keep them? How far can we stretch our brand? What happens if we selectively cut prices? What social media should we use? Market insights that answer such questions contribute to strategy decisions in four ways.

Making fact-based decisions

Outside-in companies have a superior ability to make decisions based on accurate and up-to-date information rather than relying on gut instincts and familiar heuristics. This means the extensive use of databases that capture what is known about market structures (how are segments evolving and competitive positions changing?), market responses (what are the drivers of customer value?), and market economics (where is the firm making or losing money, and what moves will improve profitability?). The knowledge value in the data is unlocked with statistical analyses and predictive models.

Anticipating competitors' moves and countermoves

We are living in an interdependent world, where the success of strategy depends on the actions of present and potential competitors. The long-run success of the new Boeing 787 Dreamliner commercial jet depends on the way Airbus positions, prices and markets its new A350 and A380 planes. Any intelligence about potential Airbus moves has high value to Boeing, and vice versa.

Deep insights into competitors' strategies can also reveal market opportunities. Nintendo took advantage of the constraints that Sony and Microsoft imposed on themselves with their mutual emphasis on superpowerful video-game consoles that appealed to hard-core gamers. Nintendo, with the Wii console, focused on an enjoyable game experience that appealed to all demographics. Because the console didn't have the expensive digital hub features of its rivals, it was launched at half the price. Best of all, Nintendo learned that because Sony PlayStation and Microsoft's Xbox were so closely associated with hard-core gamers, neither had the consumer's permission to enter the Wii space. This meant that Wii was not likely to suffer attacks from these electronic giants.

Connecting with online and networked customers

The Internet has reshaped markets in many profound ways. Foremost is the shift in power to customers. Many information asymmetries have been wiped away, enabling consumers to ignore traditional push marketing and instead to go online to decide what to buy. This shift began with books and electronics and has steadily expanded to include most products and services. For example, currently almost 60 per cent of baby boomers, not exactly the most tech-savvy demographic, go online to supplement their doctors' advice, and many more do so to search for information about products that they want to buy. The era of the passive consumer has ended.

Proliferating media types and new distribution channels feed and are fed by increased consumer choice. The traditional three television channels and daily print newspapers have been displaced by targeted social media, online magazines, blogs and newsgroups. New media and channels are promising more points of access to customers, but at a cost of fragmented strategies that dilute the efficiency of marketing spending. Traditional communications approaches that rely on one-way broadcast of a brand message over mass media are losing their efficacy. Instead, market insight will come from engaging in two way dialogues with customers to understand what they want, and when and where they want it.

The possibilities can be imagined from Hewlett-Packard's experience with an online contest to design the skin of a new special-edition entertainment laptop. The competition was launched with a low-key announcement via the Web and MTV. But word spread virally, and eventually 8,500 entries were submitted from 112 countries. The contest site got more than 5 million hits, prompting HP to quintuple its forecast of potential sales. These and other stories of new ways to collaborate and interact with customers magnify the need for clear outside-in thinking.

Guiding growth and innovation

Firms that are armed with deep insights into their markets become adept at sensing and acting on growth opportunities ahead of their rivals. Wal-Mart found that its pharmacy customers routinely broke pills in half because they couldn't afford their full prescription. Their solution was $4 prescriptions for a limited list of popular generic medications. This offered a real benefit, especially to the uninsured, and attracted new traffic to Wal-Mart stores.

Deep market insights are essential to the pursuit of new opportunities. By 2001, Toyota (in America) understood that its worthy, reliable brand had little appeal to Gen Y (the generation born between 1980 and 1994) – a group that it knew little about. Ethnographic and clinical research with Gen-Yers of a car-buying age uncovered key differences: these consumers were much more social, time-pressed and able to multi task with technology, and they had a preference for personalizing their possessions with accessories. Toyota designed and then tested different car concepts and mock-ups to ensure that they were in tune with the market. One small, boxy, 10S-hp model tested particularly well and became the basis of the new Scion line of cars. Toyota also learned that Gen-Yers would use only the Internet for initial research and did not want to negotiate price. This meant that dealers offering the Scion brand had to be transparent and accept a fixed price. The ROI on these market insights was impressive. By 2006, sales had reached 175,000 units, and the median age of buyers was 31, compared to 54 for Toyota and Lexus buyers.

Designing strategy from the outside in

The third and final lesson from the companies we've examined is how they operationalize an outside-in strategy and deploy market insight to create customer value and maximize profits. Just as an outside-in perspective doesn't guarantee success without market insight, market insight and an outside-in strategy do not guarantee success without a series of intentional actions to build and reinforce customer value creation and profitability.

These actions are the major focus of this book because we find they are what really distinguish market leaders from other companies that are just muddling through. We call them the four *customer value imperatives,* because they are crucial to success. Moreover, they are imperatives for the top management of the firm. Without constant attention to these imperatives from the very top of the organization, any firm will quickly succumb to the centripetal forces pulling it toward an inside-out approach, and its position in the market will soon erode.

The four customer value imperatives

The first imperative is to *be a customer value leader* with a distinct and compelling customer value proposition. This requires the disciplined choice of where the firm will stake a claim in the market, what value it will offer its target customers, and how the organization will deliver that value.

All firms have to balance the short and the long term. A business strikes the right balance by earning superior economic profits in the short run, by maintaining its customer value leadership, and then by investing in a portfolio of innovations that will deliver results in the medium and long term. This is the second customer value imperative: *innovate new value for customers.*

Customer value and innovation benefit the firm when they are transformed into valuable customer and brand assets. The third imperative is to *capitalize on the customer as an asset.* This requires selecting and developing loyal customers, protecting them from competitive attacks, and then leveraging that customer asset by deepening and broadening relationships with customers.

Strong brands attract and retain customers and hence need to be explicitly managed. Thus, the fourth imperative is to *capitalize on the brand as an asset.* This means strengthening the brand with coherent investments, protecting it against dilution and erosion, and then leveraging it fully to capture new opportunities in both adjacent and international markets.

These imperatives build on each other, just as they build on the outside-in perspective and market insights. Different companies tend to be better at different imperatives, and companies' strengths in these imperatives also tend to vary over time. But the most profitable companies do all four better than their rivals over the long term.

Top-management focus on the four imperatives

The four customer value imperatives are the responsibility of the entire top-management team, or C-suite, and require the engagement and understanding of every part of the organization. The imperatives belong to the C-suite for four reasons.

First, as we've discussed, the pull of inside-out thinking is powerful and can knock even the best companies off course. If the senior management team is not committed to the four imperatives, then inside-out thinking will inevitably take hold, customer value will wane, and profits will erode. There is simply no way that a company can maintain an outside-in perspective if all of the C-suite has not fully bought in and committed to the four imperatives.

Second, executing on the customer value imperatives requires clear strategic choices about the allocation of resources and the capabilities to nurture. If the chief financial officer is attempting to cut working capital to the bone while the chief operations officer is attempting to deliver customer value via best-in-class inventory management, the value proposition is going to collapse. Executing on the imperatives requires every part of the firm's governance and operations to be properly aligned in the pursuit of delivering customer value – rewards and incentives, hiring strategy, risk tolerance, finance and budgeting, and sales. If any of these areas is marching to the beat of a different drummer, the firm's profits will be significantly impaired. Therefore, the C-suite doesn't just need to be familiar with the four imperatives, it needs to deeply understand them and embrace them. Ultimately, strategy is all about choices; the four imperatives crystallize these choices and provide a path toward making better decisions.

Third, these four imperatives have wide-ranging ripple effects throughout the organization. In the best companies, the imperatives resonate with all functions and at every level of the organization. Employees can readily see how their activities contribute to superior customer value. For example, the accounting group creates value when it develops flexible options based on the needs of different customer segments. The logistics/IT group enhances customer value when it works with a major account to coordinate supply chains. Service operations improve customer value by learning to anticipate and solve service problems – even before they happen!

Fourth, the imperatives are fundamental drivers of economic profit. In this reading, we'll show how each imperative contributes in direct and measurable ways to each of the components of economic profit: revenue, margins and asset utilization.

Who should be accountable for the four imperatives?

If everyone in the C-suite is responsible, then no one may be accountable in the sense of being answerable for these actions. The potential cost is lack of strategic consistency, which leads to ambiguous market positions and reactive, not proactive, decisions. Increasingly, firms are recognizing this reality and holding a specific member of the executive team accountable. Someone must be the focal point for orchestrating all the company's activities on behalf of the customer. Many entities within the company come into contact with the customer; but if no one individual is accountable, the total experience will be uneven, the brand will suffer, and customers will defect to rivals.

In many firms, this executive carries the title of chief marketing officer (CMO). But make no mistake – the key issue is the role and *not* the title. A number of

the best companies we've studied do not have a CMO; another executive in the C-suite leads the firm's response to one or more of the customer value imperatives. In fact, in many companies that we've studied, the person holding the title of CMO either does not have the authority, does not have the trust of other C-suite executives, or does not have the ability to succeed in this role. The role of CMO is crucial to the success of an outside-in company, and therefore it must be earned. Executives within a marketing organization should not take it for granted that they will assume this role, nor should C-suite executives simply hand off the imperatives to the marketing function.

READING
4.2

Firm resources and sustained competitive advantage

By Jay Barney[1]

Understanding sources of sustained competitive advantage for firms has become a major area of research in the field of strategic management. Since the 1960s, a single organizing framework has been used to structure much of this research. This framework, summarized in Figure 4.2.1, suggests that firms obtain sustained competitive advantages by implementing strategies that exploit their internal strengths, through

responding to environmental opportunities, while neutralizing external threats and avoiding internal weaknesses. Most research on sources of sustained competitive advantage has focused either on isolating a firm's opportunities and threats (Porter, 1980, 1985), describing its strengths and weaknesses (Hofer and Schendel, 1978; Penrose, 1959), or analysing how these are matched to choose strategies.

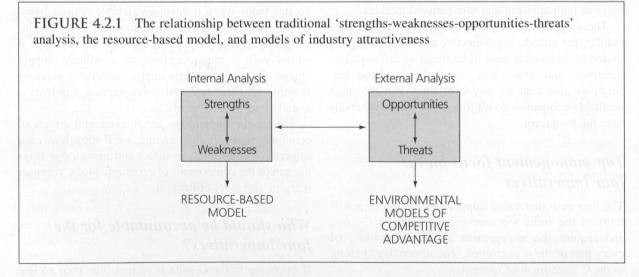

FIGURE 4.2.1   The relationship between traditional 'strengths-weaknesses-opportunities-threats' analysis, the resource-based model, and models of industry attractiveness

[1]Source: This article was adapted from J.B. Barney, 'Firm Resources and Sustained Competitive Advantage', *Journal of Management,* Vol. 17, No. 1, 1991, pp. 99–120. Copyright © 1991 by Sage Publications Ltd, Adapted and reprinted by Permission of SAGE Publications.

Research by Porter and his colleagues (Caves and Porter, 1977; Porter, 1980, 1985) has attempted to describe the environmental conditions that favour high levels of firm performance. Porter's 'five forces model', for example, describes the attributes of an attractive industry and thus suggests that opportunities will be greater, and threats less, in these kinds of industries.

To help focus the analysis of the impact of a firm's environment on its competitive position, much of this type of strategic research has placed little emphasis on the impact of idiosyncratic firm attributes on a firm's competitive position. Implicitly, this work has adopted two simplifying assumptions. First, these environmental models of competitive advantage have assumed that firms within an industry (or firms within a strategic group) are identical in terms of the strategically relevant resources they control and the strategies they pursue. Second, these models assume that should resource heterogeneity develop in an industry or group (perhaps through new entry) that this heterogeneity will be very short lived because the resources that firms use to implement their strategies are highly mobile (i.e. they can be bought and sold in factor markets).

There is little doubt that these two assumptions have been very fruitful in clarifying our understanding of the impact of a firm's environment on performance. However, the resource-based view of competitive advantage, because it examines the link between a firm's internal characteristics and performance, obviously cannot build on these same assumptions. These assumptions effectively eliminate firm resource heterogeneity and immobility as possible sources of competitive advantage. The resource-based view of the firm substitutes two alternate assumptions in analysing sources of competitive advantage. First, this model assumes that firms within an industry (or group) may be heterogeneous with respect to the strategic resources they control. Second, this model assumes that these resources may not be perfectly mobile across firms, and thus heterogeneity can be long lasting. The resource-based model of the firm examines the implications of these two assumptions for the analysis of sources of sustained competitive advantage.

Defining key concepts

To avoid possible confusion, three concepts that are central to the perspective developed in this reading are defined in this section. These concepts are firm resources, competitive advantage, and sustained competitive advantage.

Firm resources

In this reading, firm resources include all assets, capabilities, organizational processes, firm attributes, information, knowledge, etc. controlled by a firm that enable the firm to conceive of and implement strategies that improve its efficiency and effectiveness. In the language of traditional strategic analysis, firm resources are strengths that firms can use to conceive of and implement their strategies.

A variety of authors have generated lists of firm attributes that may enable firms to conceive of and implement value-creating strategies. For purposes of this discussion, these numerous possible firm resources can be conveniently classified into three categories: physical capital resources, human capital resources and organizational capital resources. Those attributes of a firm's physical, human and organizational capital that do enable a firm to conceive of and implement strategies that improve its efficiency and effectiveness are, for purposes of this discussion, firm resources. The purpose of this reading is to specify the conditions under which such firm resources can be a source of sustained competitive advantage for a firm.

Competitive advantage and sustained competitive advantage

A firm is said to have a competitive advantage when it is implementing a value-creating strategy not simultaneously being implemented by any current or potential competitors. It is said to have a sustained competitive advantage when it is implementing a value-creating strategy not simultaneously being implemented by any current or potential competitors and when these other firms are unable to duplicate the benefits of this strategy. That a competitive advantage is sustained does not imply that it will 'last forever'. It only suggests that it will not be competed away through the duplication efforts of other firms. Unanticipated changes in the economic structure of an industry may make what was, at one time, a source of sustained competitive advantage, no longer valuable for a firm, and thus not a source of any competitive advantage. These structural revolutions in an industry redefine which of a firm's attributes are resources and which are not. Some of these resources, in turn, may be sources of sustained competitive advantage in the newly defined industry structure. However, what were resources in a previous industry setting may be weaknesses, or simply irrelevant, in a new industry setting. A firm enjoying a sustained competitive advantage may experience these major shifts in the structure of competition, and may see its competitive advantages nullified by such changes. However, a sustained competitive advantage is not nullified through competing firms duplicating the benefits of that competitive advantage.

Competition with homogeneous and perfectly mobile resources

Armed with these definitions, it is now possible to explore the impact of resource heterogeneity and immobility on sustained competitive advantage. This is done by examining the nature of competition when firm resources are perfectly homogeneous and mobile.

Resource homogeneity and mobility and sustained competitive advantage

Imagine an industry where firms possess exactly the same resources. This condition suggests that firms all have the same amount and kinds of strategically relevant physical, human and organizational capital. Is there a strategy that could be conceived of and implemented by any one of these firms that could not also be conceived of and implemented by all other firms in this industry? The answer to this question must be no. The conception and implementation of strategies employs various firm resources. That one firm in an industry populated by identical firms has the resources to conceive of and implement a strategy means that these other firms, because they possess the same resources, can also conceive of and implement this strategy. Because these firms all implement the same strategies, they all will improve their efficiency and effectiveness in the same way, and to the same extent. Thus, in this kind of industry, it is not possible for firms to enjoy a sustained competitive advantage.

Resource homogeneity and mobility and first-mover advantages

One objection to this conclusion concerns so-called 'first-mover advantages' (Lieberman and Montgomery, 1988). In some circumstances, the first firm in an industry to implement a strategy can obtain a sustained competitive advantage over other firms. These firms may gain access to distribution channels, develop goodwill with customers, or develop a positive reputation, all before firms that implement their strategies later. Thus, first-moving firms may obtain a sustained competitive advantage.

However, upon reflection, it seems clear that if competing firms are identical in the resources they control, it is not possible for any one firm to obtain a competitive advantage from first moving. To be a first mover by implementing a strategy before any competing firms, a particular firm must have insights about the opportunities associated with implementing a strategy that are not possessed by other firms in the industry, or by potentially entering firms (Lieberman and Montgomery, 1988). This unique firm resource (information about an opportunity) makes it possible for the better informed firm to implement its strategy before others. However, by definition, there are no unique firm resources in this kind of industry. If one firm in this type of industry is able to conceive of and implement a strategy, then all other firms will also be able to conceive of and implement that strategy, and these strategies will be conceived of and implemented in parallel, as identical firms become aware of the same opportunities and exploit that opportunity in the same way.

It is not being suggested that there can never be first-mover advantages in industries. It is being suggested that in order for there to be a first-mover advantage, firms in an industry must be heterogeneous in terms of the resources they control.

Resource homogeneity and mobility and entry/mobility barriers

A second objection to the conclusion that sustained competitive advantages cannot exist when firm resources in an industry are perfectly homogeneous and mobile concerns the existence of 'barriers to entry' (Bain, 1956), or more generally, 'mobility barriers' (Caves and Porter, 1977). The argument here is that even if firms within an industry (group) are perfectly homogeneous, if there are strong entry or mobility barriers, these firms may be able to obtain a sustained competitive advantage vis-a-vis firms that are not in their industry (group). This sustained competitive advantage will be reflected in above normal economic performance for those firms protected by the entry or mobility barrier (Porter, 1980).

However, from another point of view, barriers to entry or mobility are only possible if current and potentially competing firms are heterogeneous in terms of the resources they control and if these resources are not perfectly mobile. The heterogeneity requirement is self-evident. For a barrier to entry or mobility to exist, firms protected by these barriers must be implementing different strategies than firms seeking to enter these protected areas of competition. Firms restricted from entry are unable to implement the same strategies as firms within the industry or group. Because the implementation of strategy requires the application of firm resources, the inability of firms seeking to enter an industry or group to implement the same strategies as firms within that industry or group suggests that firms seeking to enter must not have the same strategically relevant resources as firms within the industry or group. Thus, barriers to entry and mobility only exist when competing firms are heterogeneous in terms of the strategically relevant resources they control.

The requirement that firm resources be immobile in order for barriers to entry or mobility to exist is also clear. If firm resources are perfectly mobile, then any resource that allows some firms to implement a strategy protected by entry or mobility barriers can easily be acquired by firms seeking to enter into this industry or group. Once these resources are acquired, the strategy in question can be conceived of and implemented in the same way that other firms have conceived of and implemented their strategies. These strategies are thus not a source of sustained competitive advantage.

Again, it is not being suggested that entry or mobility barriers do not exist. However, it is being suggested that these barriers only become sources of sustained competitive advantage when firm resources are not homogeneously distributed across competing firms and when these resources are not perfectly mobile.

Firm resources and sustained competitive advantage

Thus far, it has been suggested that in order to understand sources of sustained competitive advantage, it is necessary to build a theoretical model that begins with the assumption that firm resources may be heterogeneous and immobile. Of course, not all firm resources hold the potential of sustained competitive advantages. To have this potential, a firm resource must have four attributes:

- it must be valuable, in the sense that it exploits opportunities and/or neutralizes threats in a firm's environment;
- it must be rare among a firm's current and potential competition;
- it must be imperfectly imitable;
- there cannot be strategically equivalent substitutes for this resource that are valuable but neither rare nor imperfectly imitable.

These attributes of firm resources can be thought of as empirical indicators of how heterogeneous and immobile a firm's resources are and thus how useful these resources are for generating sustained competitive advantages. Each of these attributes of a firm's resources is discussed in more detail below.

Valuable resources

Firm resources can only be a source of competitive advantage or sustained competitive advantage when they are valuable. As suggested earlier, resources are valuable when they enable a firm to conceive of or implement strategies that improve its efficiency and effectiveness. The traditional 'strengths-weaknesses-opportunities-threats' model of firm performance suggests that firms are able to improve their performance only when their strategies exploit opportunities or neutralize threats. Firm attributes may have the other characteristics that could qualify them as sources of competitive advantage (e.g. rareness, inimitability, non-substitutability), but these attributes only become resources when they exploit opportunities or neutralize threats in a firm's environment.

That firm attributes must be valuable in order to be considered resources (and thus as possible sources of sustained competitive advantage) points to an important complementarity between environmental models of competitive advantage and the resource-based model. These environmental models help isolate those firm attributes that exploit opportunities or neutralize threats, and thus specify which firm attributes can be considered as resources. The resource-based model then suggests additional characteristics that these resources must possess if they are to generate sustained competitive advantage.

Rare resources

By definition, valuable firm resources possessed by large numbers of competing or potentially competing firms cannot be sources of either a competitive advantage or a sustained competitive advantage. A firm enjoys a competitive advantage when it is implementing a value-creating strategy not simultaneously implemented by large numbers of other firms. If a particular valuable firm resource is possessed by large numbers of firms, then each of these firms have the capability of exploiting that resource in the same way, thereby implementing a common strategy that gives no one firm a competitive advantage.

The same analysis applies to bundles of valuable firm resources used to conceive of and implement strategies. Some strategies require a particular mix of physical capital, human capital and organizational capital resources to implement. One firm resource required in the implementation of almost all strategies is managerial talent (Hambrick, 1987). If this particular bundle of firm resources is not rare, then large numbers of firms will be able to conceive of and implement the strategies in question, and these strategies will not be a source of competitive advantage, even though the resources in question may be valuable.

To observe that competitive advantages (sustained or otherwise) only accrue to firms that have valuable and rare resources is not to dismiss common (i.e. not rare) firm resources as unimportant. Instead, these valuable but common firm resources can help ensure a firm's survival when they are exploited to create competitive parity in an industry. Under conditions of competitive parity, though no one firm obtains a competitive advantage, firms do increase their probability of economic survival.

How rare a valuable firm resource must be in order to have the potential for generating a competitive advantage is a difficult question. It is not difficult to see that if a firm's valuable resources are absolutely unique among a set of competing and potentially competing firms, those resources will generate at least a competitive advantage and may have the potential of generating a sustained competitive advantage. However, it may be possible for a small number of firms in an industry to possess a particular valuable resource and still generate a competitive advantage. In general, as long as the number of firms that possess a particular valuable resource (or a bundle of valuable resources) is less than the number of firms needed to generate perfect competition dynamics in an industry, that resource has the potential of generating a competitive advantage.

Imperfectly imitable resources

It is not difficult to see that valuable and rare organizational resources may be a source of competitive advantage. Indeed, firms with such resources will often be strategic innovators, for they will be able to conceive of and engage in strategies that other firms could either not conceive of, or not implement, or both, because these other firms lacked the relevant firm resources. The observation that valuable and rare organizational resources can be a source of competitive advantage is another way of describing first-mover advantages accruing to firms with resource advantages.

However, valuable and rare organizational resources can only be sources of sustained competitive advantage if firms that do not possess these resources cannot obtain them. These firm resources are imperfectly imitable. Firm resources can be imperfectly imitable for one or a combination of three reasons: (a) the ability of a firm to obtain a resource is dependent upon *unique historical conditions,* (b) the link between the resources possessed by a firm and a firm's sustained competitive advantage is *causally ambiguous,* or (c) the resource generating a firm's advantage is *socially complex.* Each of these sources of the imperfect imitability of firm resources is examined below.

Unique historical conditions and imperfectly imitable resources. Another assumption of most environmental models of firm competitive advantage, besides resource homogeneity and mobility, is that the performance of firms can be understood independently of the particular history and other idiosyncratic attributes of firms. These researchers seldom argue that firms do not vary in terms of their unique histories, but rather that these unique histories are not relevant to understanding a firm's performance (Porter, 1980).

The resource-based view of competitive advantage developed here relaxes this assumption. Indeed, this approach asserts that not only are firms intrinsically historical and social entities, but that their ability to acquire and exploit some resources depends upon their place in time and space. Once this particular unique time in history passes, firms that do not have space- and time-dependent resources cannot obtain them, and thus these resources are imperfectly imitable.

Resource-based theorists are not alone in recognizing the importance of history as a determinant of firm performance and competitive advantage. Traditional strategy researchers often cited the unique historical circumstances of a firm's founding, or the unique circumstances under which a new management team takes over a firm, as important determinants of a firm's long-term performance. More recently, several economists (e.g. Arthur, Ermoliev and Kaniovsky, 1987; David, 1985) have developed models of firm performance that rely heavily on unique historical events as determinants of subsequent actions. Employing path-dependent models of economic performance, these authors suggest that the performance of a firm does not depend simply on the industry structure within which a firm finds itself at a particular point in time, but also on the path a firm followed through history to arrive where it is. If a firm obtains valuable and rare resources because of its unique path through history, it will be able to exploit those resources in implementing value-creating strategies that cannot be duplicated by other firms, for firms without that particular path through history cannot obtain the resources necessary to implement the strategy.

The acquisition of all the types of firm resources examined in this article can depend upon the unique historical position of a firm. A firm that locates its facilities on what turns out to be a much more valuable location than was anticipated when the location was chosen possesses an imperfectly imitable physical capital resource. A firm with scientists who are uniquely positioned to create or exploit a significant scientific breakthrough may obtain an imperfectly imitable resource from the history-dependent nature of these scientists' individual human capital. Finally, a firm with a unique and valuable organizational culture that emerged in the early stages of a firm's history may have an imperfectly imitable advantage over firms founded in another historical period, where different (and perhaps less valuable) organizational values and beliefs come to dominate.

Causal ambiguity and imperfectly imitable resources. Unlike the relationship between a firm's unique history and the imitability of its resources, the relationship between the causal ambiguity of a firm's resources and imperfect imitability has received systematic attention in the literature. In this context, causal ambiguity exists when the link between the resources controlled by a firm and a firm's sustained competitive advantage is not understood or understood only very imperfectly.

When the link between a firm's resources and its sustained competitive advantage is poorly understood, it is difficult for firms that are attempting to duplicate a successful firm's strategies through imitation of its resources to know which resources it should imitate. Imitating firms may be able to describe some of the resources controlled by a successful firm. However, under conditions of causal ambiguity, it is not clear that the resources that can be described are the same resources that generate a sustained competitive advantage, or whether that advantage reflects some other non-described firm resource. Sometimes it is difficult to understand why one firm consistently outperforms other firms. Causal ambiguity is at the heart of this difficulty. In the face of such causal ambiguity, imitating firms cannot know the actions they should take

in order to duplicate the strategies of firms with a sustained competitive advantage.

To be a source of sustained competitive advantage, both the firms that possess resources that generate a competitive advantage and the firms that do not possess these resources but seek to imitate them must be faced with the same level of causal ambiguity (Lippman and Rumelt, 1982). If firms that control these resources have a better understanding of their impact on competitive advantage than firms without these resources, then firms without these resources can engage in activities to reduce their knowledge disadvantage. They can do this, for example, by hiring away well placed knowledgeable managers in a firm with a competitive advantage or by engaging in a careful systematic study of the other firm's success. Although acquiring this knowledge may take some time and effort, once knowledge of the link between a firm's resources and its ability to implement certain strategies is diffused throughout competing firms, causal ambiguity no longer exists, and thus cannot be a source of imperfect imitability. In other words, if a firm with a competitive advantage understands the link between the resources it controls and its advantages, then other firms can also learn about that link, acquire the necessary resources (assuming they are not imperfectly imitable for other reasons), and implement the relevant strategies. In such a setting, a firm's competitive advantages are not sustained because they can be duplicated.

At first, it may seem unlikely that a firm with a sustained competitive advantage will not fully understand the source of that advantage. However, given the very complex relationship between firm resources and competitive advantage, such an incomplete understanding is not implausible. The resources controlled by a firm are very complex and interdependent. Often, they are implicit, taken for granted by managers, rather than being subject to explicit analysis. Numerous resources, taken by themselves or in combination with other resources, may yield sustained competitive advantage. Although managers may have numerous hypotheses about which resources generate their firm's advantages, it is rarely possible to rigorously test these hypotheses. As long as numerous plausible explanations of the sources of sustained competitive advantage exist within a firm, the link between the resources controlled by a firm and sustained competitive advantage remains somewhat ambiguous, and thus which of a firm's resources to imitate remains uncertain.

Social complexity. A final reason that a firm's resources may be imperfectly imitable is that they may be very complex social phenomena, beyond the ability of firms to systematically manage and influence. When competitive advantages are based in such complex social phenomena, the ability of other firms to imitate these resources is significantly constrained.

A wide variety of firm resources may be socially complex. Examples include the interpersonal relations among managers in a firm, a firm's culture (Barney, 1986b), or a firm's reputation among suppliers and customers. Notice that in most of these cases it is possible to specify how these socially complex resources add value to a firm. Thus, there is little or no causal ambiguity surrounding the link between these firm resources and competitive advantage. However, understanding that, say, an organizational culture with certain attributes or quality relations among managers can improve a firm's efficiency and effectiveness does not necessarily imply that firms without these attributes can engage in systematic efforts to create them. Such social engineering may be, for the time being at least, beyond the capabilities of most firms. To the extent that socially complex firm resources are not subject to such direct management, these resources are imperfectly imitable.

Notice that complex physical technology is not included in this category of sources of imperfectly imitable. In general, physical technology, whether it takes the form of machine tools, robots in factories or complex information management systems, is by itself typically imitable. If one firm can purchase these physical tools of production and thereby implement some strategies, then other firms should also be able to purchase these physical tools, and thus such tools should not be a source of sustained competitive advantage.

On the other hand, the exploitation of physical technology in a firm often involves the use of socially complex firm resources. Several firms may all possess the same physical technology, but only one of these firms may possess the social relations, culture, traditions, etc. to fully exploit this technology in implementing strategies. If these complex social resources are not subject to imitation (and assuming they are valuable and rare and no substitutes exist), these firms may obtain a sustained competitive advantage from exploiting their physical technology more completely than other firms, even though competing firms do not vary in terms of the physical technology they possess.

Substitutability

The last requirement for a firm resource to be a source of sustained competitive advantage is that there must be no strategically equivalent valuable resources that are themselves either not rare or imitable. Two valuable firm resources (or two bundles of firm resources) are strategically equivalent when they each can be exploited separately to implement the same strategies. Suppose that one of these valuable firm resources is rare and imperfectly imitable, but the other is not. Firms with this first resource will be able to conceive of and implement certain strategies. If there were no strategically equivalent firm resources, these strategies would generate a sustained competitive advantage (because the resources used to conceive and implement them are valuable, rare and imperfectly imitable). However, that there are strategically equivalent resources suggests that other current or potentially competing firms can implement the same strategies, but in a different way, using different resources. If these alternative resources are either not rare or imitable, then numerous firms will be able to conceive of and implement the strategies in question, and those strategies will not generate a sustained competitive advantage. This will be the case even though one approach to implementing these strategies exploits valuable, rare and imperfectly imitable firm resources.

Substitutability can take at least two forms. First, though it may not be possible for a firm to imitate another firm's resources exactly, it may be able to substitute a similar resource that enables it to conceive of and implement the same strategies. For example, a firm seeking to duplicate the competitive advantages of another firm by imitating that other firm's high quality top management team will often be unable to copy that team exactly. However, it may be possible for this firm to develop its own unique top management team. Though these two teams will be different (different people, different operating practices, a different history, etc.), they may likely be strategically equivalent and thus be substitutes for one another. If different top management teams are strategically equivalent (and if these substitute teams are common or highly imitable), then a high quality top management team is not a source of sustained competitive advantage, even though a particular management team of a particular firm is valuable, rare and imperfectly imitable.

Second, very different firm resources can also be strategic substitutes. For example, managers in one firm may have a very clear vision of the future of their company because of a charismatic leader in their firm. Managers in competing firms may also have a very clear vision of the future of their companies, but this common vision may reflect these firms' systematic, company-wide strategic planning process. From the point of view of managers having a clear vision of the future of their company, the firm resource of a charismatic leader and the firm resource of a formal planning system may be strategically equivalent, and thus substitutes for one another. If large numbers of competing firms have a formal planning system that generates this common vision (or if such a formal planning is highly imitable), then firms with such a vision derived from a charismatic leader will not have a sustained competitive advantage, even though the firm resource of a charismatic leader is probably rare and imperfectly imitable.

Of course, the strategic substitutability of firm resources is always a matter of degree. It is the case, however, that substitute firm resources need not have exactly the same implications for an organization in order for those resources to be equivalent from the point of view of the strategies that firms can conceive of and implement. If enough firms have these valuable substitute resources (i.e. they are not rare), or if enough firms can acquire them (i.e. they are imitable), then none of these firms (including firms whose resources are being substituted for) can expect to obtain a sustained competitive advantage.

The framework

The relationship between resource heterogeneity and immobility; value, rareness, imitability and substitutability; and sustained competitive advantage is summarized in Figure 4.2.2. This framework can be applied in analysing the potential of a broad range of firm resources to be sources of sustained competitive advantage. These analyses not only specify the theoretical conditions under which sustained competitive advantage might exist, they also suggest specific empirical questions that need to be addressed before the relationship between a particular firm resource and sustained competitive advantage can be understood.

That the study of sources of sustained competitive advantage focuses on valuable, rare, imperfectly imitable and non-substitutable resource endowments does not suggest – as some population ecologists would have it (e.g., Hannan and Freeman, 1977) – that managers are irrelevant in the study of such advantages. In fact, managers are important in this model, for it is managers that are able to understand and describe the economic performance potential of a firm's endowments. Without such managerial analyses, sustained competitive advantage is not likely. This is the case even though the skills needed to describe the rare, imperfectly imitable, and non-substitutable resources of a firm may themselves not be rare, imperfectly imitable, or non-substitutable.

Indeed, it may be the case that a manager or a managerial team is a firm resource that has the potential for generating sustained competitive advantages. The conditions under which this will be the case can be outlined using the framework presented in Figure 4.2.2. However, in the end, what becomes clear is that firms cannot expect to 'purchase' sustained competitive advantages on open markets. Rather, such advantages must be found in the rare, imperfectly imitable and non-substitutable resources already controlled by a firm.

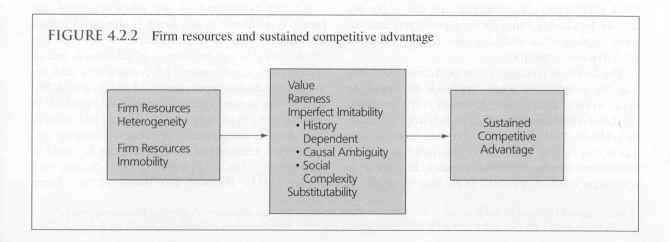

FIGURE 4.2.2   Firm resources and sustained competitive advantage

Dynamic capabilities and strategic management

By David J. Teece, Gary Pisano and Amy Shuen[1]

The fundamental question in the field of strategic management is how firms achieve and sustain competitive advantage. We confront this question here by developing the dynamic capabilities approach, which endeavours to analyse the sources of wealth creation and capture by firms. The development of this framework flows from a recognition by the authors that strategic theory is replete with analyses of firm-level strategies for sustaining and safeguarding extant competitive advantage, but has performed less well with respect to assisting in the understanding of how and why certain firms build competitive advantage in regimes of rapid change. Our approach is especially relevant in a Schumpeterian world of innovation-based competition, price/performance rivalry, increasing returns, and the 'creative destruction' of existing competences. The approach endeavours to explain firm-level success and failure. We are interested in both building a better theory of firm performance, as well as informing managerial practice.

In order to position our analysis in a manner that displays similarities and differences with existing approaches, we begin by briefly reviewing accepted frameworks for strategic management. We endeavour to expose implicit assumptions, and identify competitive circumstances where each paradigm might display some relative advantage as both a useful descriptive and normative theory of competitive strategy. While numerous theories have been advanced over the past two decades about the sources of competitive advantage, many cluster around just a few loosely structured frameworks or paradigms. In this paper we attempt to identify three existing paradigms and describe aspects of an emerging new paradigm that we label dynamic capabilities.

The dominant paradigm in the field during the 1980s was the competitive forces approach developed by Porter (1980). This approach, rooted in the structure-conduct-performance paradigm of industrial organization (Mason, 1949; Bain, 1959), emphasizes the actions a firm can take to create defensible positions against competitive forces. A second approach, referred to as a strategic conflict approach (e.g., Shapiro, 1989), is closely related to the first in its focus on product market imperfections, entry deterrence and strategic interaction. The strategic conflict approach uses the tools of game theory and thus implicitly views competitive outcomes as a function of the effectiveness with which firms keep their rivals off balance through strategic investments, pricing strategies, signalling and the control of information. Both the competitive forces and the strategic conflict approaches appear to share the view that rents flow from privileged product market positions.

Another distinct class of approach emphasizes building competitive advantage through capturing entrepreneurial rents stemming from fundamental firm-level efficiency advantages. These approaches have their roots in a much older discussion of corporate strengths and weaknesses; they have taken on new life as evidence suggests that firms build enduring advantages only through efficiency and effectiveness, and as developments in organizational economics and the study of technological and organizational change become applied to strategy questions. One strand of this literature, often referred to as the 'resource-based perspective,' emphasizes firm-specific capabilities and assets and the existence of isolating mechanisms as the fundamental determinants of firm performance (Penrose, 1959; Rumelt, 1984; Teece, 1984; Wernerfelt, 1984). This perspective recognizes but does not attempt to explain the nature of the isolating mechanisms that enable entrepreneurial rents and competitive advantage to be sustained.

Another component of the efficiency-based approach is developed in this paper. Rudimentary efforts are made to identify the dimensions of firm-specific capabilities that can be sources of advantage, and to explain how combinations of competences and resources can be developed, deployed and protected. We refer to this as the 'dynamic capabilities' approach in order to stress exploiting existing internal and external firm-specific competences to address changing environments. Elements of the approach can be found in Schumpeter (1942), Penrose (1959), Nelson and Winter (1982), Prahalad and Hamel (1990), Teece

[1]Source: Teece, D.J., Pisano, G. and Shuen, A. (1997) 'Dynamic Capabilities and Strategic Management', *Strategic Management Journal*, Vol. 18, No. 7, August, pp. 509–534. Copyright © John Wiley & Sons, Inc. 1997. Reproduced with permission of John Wiley & Sons, Inc.

(1976, 1986a, 1986b, 1988) and in Hayes, Wheel-wright, and Clark (1988). Because this approach emphasizes the development of management capabilities, and difficult-to-imitate combinations of organizational, functional and technological skills, it integrates and draws upon research in such areas as the management of R&D, product and process development, technology transfer, intellectual property, manufacturing, human resources and organizational learning. Because these fields are often viewed as outside the traditional boundaries of strategy, much of this research has not been incorporated into existing economic approaches to strategy issues. As a result, dynamic capabilities can be seen as an emerging and potentially integrative approach to understanding the newer sources of competitive advantage.

We suggest that the dynamic capabilities approach is promising both in terms of future research potential and as an aid to management endeavouring to gain competitive advantage in increasingly demanding environments. To illustrate the essential elements of the dynamic capabilities approach, the sections that follow compare and contrast this approach to other models of strategy. Each section highlights the strategic insights provided by each approach as well as the different competitive circumstances in which it might be most appropriate. Needless to say, these approaches are in many ways complementary and a full understanding of firm-level, competitive advantage requires an appreciation of all four approaches and more.

Models of strategy emphasizing the exploitation of market power

Competitive forces

The dominant paradigm in strategy, at least during the 1980s, was the competitive forces approach. Pioneered by Porter (1980), the competitive forces approach views the essence of competitive strategy formulation as 'relating a company to its environment… [T]he key aspect of the firm's environment is the industry or industries in which it competes.' Industry structure strongly influences the competitive rules of the game as well as the strategies potentially available to firms.

In the competitive forces model, five industry-level forces – entry barriers, threat of substitution, bargaining power of buyers, bargaining power of suppliers, and rivalry among industry incumbents – determine the inherent profit potential of an industry or subsegment of an industry. The approach can be used to help the firm find a position in an industry from which it can best defend itself against competitive forces or influence them in its favour (Porter, 1980: 4).

This 'five-forces' framework provides a systematic way of thinking about how competitive forces work at the industry level and how these forces determine the profitability of different industries and industry segments. The competitive forces framework also contains a number of underlying assumptions about the sources of competition and the nature of the strategy process. To facilitate comparisons with other approaches, we highlight several distinctive characteristics of the framework.

Economic rents in the competitive forces framework are monopoly rents (Teece, 1984). Firms in an industry earn rents when they are somehow able to impede the competitive forces (in either factor markets or product markets) which tend to drive economic returns to zero. Available strategies are described in Porter (1980). Competitive strategies are often aimed at altering the firm's position in the industry vis-à-vis competitors and suppliers. Industry structure plays a central role in determining and limiting strategic action.

Some industries or subsectors of industries become more 'attractive' because they have structural impediments to competitive forces (e.g., entry barriers) that allow firms better opportunities for creating sustainable competitive advantages. Rents are created largely at the industry or subsector level rather than at the firm level. While there is some recognition given to firm-specific assets, differences among firms relate primarily to scale. This approach to strategy reflects its incubation inside the field of industrial organization and in particular the industrial structure school of Mason and Bain (Teece, 1984).

Strategic conflict

The publication of Carl Shapiro's 1989 article, confidently titled 'The Theory of Business Strategy,' announced the emergence of a new approach to business strategy, if not strategic management. This approach utilizes the tools of game theory to analyse the nature of competitive interaction between rival firms. The main thrust of work in this tradition is to reveal how a firm can influence the behaviour and actions of rival firms and thus the market environment. Examples of such moves are investment in capacity (Dixit, 1980), R&D (Gilbert and Newbery, 1982) and advertising (Schmalensee, 1983). To be effective, these strategic moves require irreversible commitment. The moves in question will have no effect if they can be costlessly undone. A key idea is that by manipulating the market environment, a firm may be able to increase its profits.

This literature, together with the contestability literature (Baumol, Panzar and Willig, 1982), has led to a greater appreciation of the role of sunk costs, as opposed to fixed costs, in determining competitive outcomes. Strategic moves can also be designed to influence rivals' behaviour through signalling. Strategic signalling has been examined in a number of contexts, including predatory pricing (Kreps and Wilson, 1982a, 1982b) and limit pricing (Milgrom and Roberts, 1982a, 1982b). More recent treatments have emphasized the role of commitment and reputation (e.g., Ghemawat, 1991) and the benefits of firms simultaneously pursuing competition and cooperation (Nalebuff and Brandenburger, 1995, 1996).

In many instances, game theory formalizes long-standing intuitive arguments about various types of business behaviour (e.g., predatory pricing, patent races), though in some instances it has induced a substantial change in the conventional wisdom. But by rationalizing observed behaviour by reference to suitably designed games, in explaining everything these models also explain nothing, as they do not generate testable predictions (Sutton, 1992). Many specific game-theoretic models admit multiple equilibrium, and a wide range of choice exists as to the design of the appropriate game form to be used. Unfortunately, the results often depend on the precise specification chosen. The equilibrium in models of strategic behaviour crucially depends on what one rival believes another rival will do in a particular situation. Thus the qualitative features of the results may depend on the way price competition is modelled or on the presence or absence of strategic asymmetries such as first-mover advantages. The analysis of strategic moves using game theory can be thought of as 'dynamic' in the sense that multi-period analyses can be pursued both intuitively and formally. However, we use the term 'dynamic' in this paper in a different sense, referring to situations where there is rapid change in technology and market forces, and 'feedback' effects on firms.[2]

We have a particular view of the contexts in which the strategic conflict literature is relevant to strategic management. Firms that have a tremendous cost or other competitive advantage vis-à-vis their rivals ought not be transfixed by the moves and countermoves of their rivals. Their competitive fortunes will swing

more on total demand conditions, not on how competitors deploy and redeploy their competitive assets. Put differently, when there are gross asymmetries in competitive advantage between firms, the results of game-theoretic analysis are likely to be obvious and uninteresting. The stronger competitor will generally advance, even if disadvantaged by certain information asymmetries. To be sure, incumbent firms can be undone by new entrants with a dramatic cost advantage, but no 'gaming' will overturn that outcome. On the other hand, if firms' competitive positions are more delicately balanced, as with Coke and Pepsi, then strategic conflict is of interest to competitive outcomes. Needless to say, there are many such circumstances, but they are rare in industries where there is rapid technological change and fast-shifting market circumstances.

In short, where competitors do not have deep-seated competitive advantages, the moves and countermoves of competitors can often be usefully formulated in game-theoretic terms. However, we doubt that game theory can comprehensively illuminate how Chrysler should compete against Toyota and Honda, or how United Airlines can best respond to Southwest Airlines since Southwest's advantage is built on organizational attributes which United cannot readily replicate. Indeed, the entrepreneurial side of strategy – how significant new rent streams are created and protected – is largely ignored by the game-theoretic approach. Accordingly, we find that the approach, while important, is most relevant when competitors are closely matched and the population of relevant competitors and the identity of their strategic alternatives can be readily ascertained. Nevertheless, coupled with other approaches it can sometimes yield powerful insights.

However, this research has an orientation that we are concerned about in terms of the implicit framing of strategic issues. Rents, from a game-theoretic perspective, are ultimately a result of managers' intellectual ability to 'play the game.' The adage of the strategist steeped in this approach is 'do unto others before they do unto you.' We worry that fascination with strategic moves and Machiavellian tricks will distract managers from seeking to build more enduring sources of competitive advantage. The approach unfortunately ignores competition as a process involving the development, accumulation, combination and protection of unique skills and capabilities. Since strategic interactions are what receive focal attention, the impression one might receive from this literature is that

---

[2]Accordingly, both approaches are dynamic, but in very different senses.

success in the marketplace is the result of sophisticated plays and counterplays, when this is generally not the case at all.

In what follows, we suggest that building a dynamic view of the business enterprise – something missing from the two approaches we have so far identified – enhances the probability of establishing an acceptable descriptive theory of strategy that can assist practitioners in the building of long-run advantage and competitive flexibility. Below, we discuss first the resource-based perspective and then an extension we call the dynamic capabilities approach.

Models of strategy emphasizing efficiency

Resource-based perspective

The resource-based approach sees firms with superior systems and structures being profitable not because they engage in strategic investments that may deter entry and raise prices above long-run costs, but because they have markedly lower costs, or offer markedly higher quality or product performance. This approach focuses on the rents accruing to the owners of scarce firm-specific resources rather than the economic profits from product market positioning. Competitive advantage lies 'upstream' of product markets and rests on the firm's idiosyncratic and difficult-to-imitate resources.

One can find the resources approach suggested by the earlier pre-analytic strategy literature. A leading text of the 1960s (Learned *et al.*, 1969) noted that 'the capability of an organization is its demonstrated and potential ability to accomplish against the opposition of circumstance or competition, whatever it sets out to do. Every organization has actual and potential strengths and weaknesses; it is important to try to determine what they are and to distinguish one from the other.' Thus what a firm can do is not just a function of the opportunities it confronts; it also depends on what resources the organization can muster.

Learned *et al.* proposed that the real key to a company's success or even to its future development lies in its ability to find or create 'a competence that is truly distinctive.' This literature also recognized the constraints on firm behaviour and, in particular, noted that one should not assume that management 'can rise to any occasion.' These insights do appear to keenly anticipate the resource-based approach that has since emerged, but they did not provide a theory or systematic framework for analysing business strategies.

Indeed, Andrews (1987: 46) noted that much of what is intuitive in this process is yet to be identified. Unfortunately, the academic literature on capabilities stalled for a couple of decades.

New impetus has been given to the resource-based approach by recent theoretical developments in organizational economics and in the theory of strategy, as well as by a growing body of anecdotal and empirical literature that highlights the importance of firm-specific factors in explaining firm performance. Cool and Schendel (1988) have shown that there are systematic and significant performance differences among firms which belong to the same strategic group within the US pharmaceutical industry. Rumelt (1991) has shown that intraindustry differences in profits are greater than interindustry differences in profits, strongly suggesting the importance of firm-specific factors and the relative unimportance of industry effects. Jacobsen (1988) and Hansen and Wernerfelt (1989) made similar findings.

A comparison of the resource-based approach and the competitive forces approach (discussed earlier in the paper) in terms of their implications for the strategy process is revealing. From the first perspective, an entry decision looks roughly as follows: (1) pick an industry (based on its 'structural attractiveness'); (2) choose an entry strategy based on conjectures about competitors' rational strategies; (3) if not already possessed, acquire or otherwise obtain the requisite assets to compete in the market. From this perspective, the process of identifying and developing the requisite assets is not particularly problematic. The process involves nothing more than choosing rationally among a well-defined set of investment alternatives. If assets are not already owned, they can be bought. The resource-based perspective is strongly at odds with this conceptualization.

From the resource-based perspective, firms are heterogeneous with respect to their resources capabilities/endowments. Further, resource endowments are 'sticky:' at least in the short run, firms are to some degree stuck with what they have and may have to live with what they lack. This stickiness arises for three reasons. First, business development is viewed as an extremely complex process. Quite simply, firms lack the organizational capacity to develop new competences quickly (Dierickx and Cool, 1989). Secondly, some assets are simply not readily tradable, for example, tacit know-how (Teece, 1976, 1980) and reputation (Dierickx and Cool, 1989). Thus, resource endowments cannot equilibrate through factor input markets. Finally, even when an asset can be purchased, firms may stand to gain little by doing so. As Barney

(1986a) points out, unless a firm is lucky, possesses superior information, or both, the price it pays in a competitive factor market will fully capitalize the rents from the asset.

Given that in the resources perspective firms possess heterogeneous and sticky resource bundles, the entry decision process suggested by this approach is as follows: (1) identify your firm's unique resources; (2) decide in which markets those resources can earn the highest rents; and (3) decide whether the rents from those assets are most effectively utilized by (a) integrating into related market(s); (b) selling the relevant intermediate output to related firms; or (c) selling the assets themselves to a firm in related businesses (Teece, 1980, 1982).

The resource-based perspective puts both vertical integration and diversification into a new strategic light. Both can be viewed as ways of capturing rents on scarce, firm-specific assets whose services are difficult to sell in intermediate markets (Penrose, 1959; Williamson, 1975; Teece, 1980, 1982, 1986a, 1986b; Wernerfelt, 1984). Empirical work on the relationship between performance and diversification by Wernerfelt and Montgomery (1988) provides evidence for this proposition. It is evident that the resource-based perspective focuses on strategies for exploiting existing firm-specific assets.

However, the resource-based perspective also invites consideration of managerial strategies for developing new capabilities (Wernerfelt, 1984). Indeed, if control over scarce resources is the source of economic profits, then it follows that such issues as skill acquisition, the management of knowledge and know-how (Shuen, 1994), and learning become fundamental strategic issues. It is in this second dimension, encompassing skill acquisition, learning, and accumulation of organizational and intangible or 'invisible' assets (Itami and Roehl, 1987), that we believe lies the greatest potential for contributions to strategy.

The dynamic capabilities approach: Overview

The global competitive battles in high-technology industries such as semiconductors, information, services and software have demonstrated the need for an expanded paradigm to understand how competitive advantage is achieved. Well-known companies like IBM, Texas Instruments, Philips and others appear to have followed a 'resource-based strategy' of accumulating valuable technology assets, often guarded by an aggressive intellectual property stance. However, this strategy is often not enough to support a significant competitive advantage. Winners in the global marketplace have been firms that can demonstrate timely responsiveness and rapid and flexible product innovation, coupled with the management capability to effectively coordinate and redeploy internal and external competences. Not surprisingly, industry observers have remarked that companies can accumulate a large stock of valuable technology assets and still not have many useful capabilities.

We refer to this ability to achieve new forms of competitive advantage as 'dynamic capabilities' to emphasize two key aspects that were not the main focus of attention in previous strategy perspectives. The term 'dynamic' refers to the capacity to renew competences so as to achieve congruence with the changing business environment; certain innovative responses are required when time-to-market and timing are critical, the rate of technological change is rapid, and the nature of future competition and markets difficult to determine. The term 'capabilities' emphasizes the key role of strategic management in appropriately adapting, integrating and reconfiguring internal and external organizational skills, resources and functional competences to match the requirements of a changing environment.

One aspect of the strategic problem facing an innovating firm in a world of Schumpeterian competition is to identify difficult-to-imitate internal and external competences most likely to support valuable products and services. Thus, as argued by Dierickx and Cool (1989), choices about how much to spend (invest) on different possible areas are central to the firm's strategy. However, choices about domains of competence are influenced by past choices. At any given point in time, firms must follow a certain trajectory or path of competence development. This path not only defines what choices are open to the firm today, but it also puts bounds around what its internal repertoire is likely to be in the future. Thus, firms, at various points in time, make long-term, quasi-irreversible commitments to certain domains of competence.

The notion that competitive advantage requires both the exploitation of existing internal and external firm-specific capabilities, and developing new ones is partially developed in Penrose (1959), Teece (1982) and Wernerfelt (1984). However, only recently have researchers begun to focus on the specifics of how some organizations first develop firm-specific capabilities and how they renew competences to respond to shifts in the business environment. These issues are intimately tied to the firm's business processes, market positions and expansion paths. Several writers have recently offered insights and evidence on how firms can develop their capability to adapt and even capitalize on rapidly changing environments. The dynamic capabilities approach seeks to provide a coherent framework which can both integrate existing conceptual and empirical knowledge, and facilitate prescription. In doing so, it builds upon the theoretical foundations provided by Schumpeter (1934), Penrose (1959), Williamson (1975, 1985), Barney (1986a), Nelson and Winter (1982), Teece (1988), and Teece *et al.* (1994).

Toward a dynamic capabilities framework

Terminology

In order to facilitate theory development and intellectual dialogue, some acceptable definitions are desirable. We propose the following:

Factors of production.   These are 'undifferentiated' inputs available in disaggregate form in factor markets. By undifferentiated we mean that they lack a firm-specific component. Land, unskilled labour and capital are typical examples. Some factors may be available for the taking, such as public knowledge. In the language of Arrow (1996), such resources must be 'non-fugitive.' Property rights are usually well defined for factors of production.

Resources.   Resources are firm-specific assets that are difficult if not impossible to imitate. Trade secrets and certain specialized production facilities and engineering experience are examples. Such assets are difficult to transfer among firms because of transaction costs and transfer costs, and because the assets may contain tacit knowledge.

Organizational   routines/competences.   When firm-specific assets are assembled in integrated clusters spanning individuals and groups so that they enable distinctive activities to be performed, these activities constitute organizational routines and processes. Examples include quality, miniaturization and systems integration. Such competences are typically viable across multiple product lines, and may extend outside the firm to embrace alliance partners.

Core competences.   We define those competences that define a firm's fundamental business as core. Core competences must accordingly be derived by looking across the range of a firm's (and its competitors') products and services. The value of core competences can be enhanced by combination with the appropriate complementary assets. The degree to which a core competence is distinctive depends on how well endowed the firm is relative to its competitors, and on how difficult it is for competitors to replicate its competences.

Dynamic   capabilities.   We define dynamic capabilities as the firm's ability to integrate, build and reconfigure internal and external competences to address rapidly changing environments. Dynamic capabilities thus reflect an organization's ability to achieve new and innovative forms of competitive advantage given path dependencies and market positions (Leonard-Barton, 1992).

Products.   End products are the final goods and services produced by the firm based on utilizing the competences that it possesses. The performance (price, quality, etc.) of a firm's products relative to its competitors at any point in time will depend upon its competences (which over time depend on its capabilities).

Markets and strategic capabilities

Different approaches to strategy view sources of wealth creation and the essence of the strategic problem faced by firms differently. The competitive forces framework sees the strategic problem in terms of industry structure, entry deterrence and positioning; game-theoretic models view the strategic problem as one of interaction between rivals with certain expectations about how each other will behave; resource-based perspectives have focused on the exploitation of firm-specific assets. Each approach asks different, often complementary questions. A key step in building a conceptual framework related to dynamic capabilities is to identify the foundations upon which distinctive and difficult-to-replicate advantages can be built, maintained and enhanced.

A useful way to vector in on the strategic elements of the business enterprise is first to identify what is not strategic. To be strategic, a capability must be honed to a user need (so there is a source of revenues), unique (so that the products/services produced can be priced without too much regard to competition) and difficult to replicate (so profits will not be competed away). Accordingly, any assets or entity which are homogeneous and can be bought and sold at an established price cannot be all that strategic (Barney, 1986a). What is it, then, about firms which undergirds competitive advantage?

To answer this, one must first make some fundamental distinctions between markets and internal organization (firms). The essence of the firm, as Coase (1937) pointed out, is that it displaces market organization. It does so in the main because inside the firms one can organize certain types of economic activity in ways one cannot using markets. This is not only because of transaction costs, as Williamson (1975, 1985) emphasized, but also because there are many types of arrangements where injecting high-powered (market like) incentives might well be quite destructive of cooperative activity and learning. Inside an organization, exchange cannot take place in the same manner that it can outside an organization, not just because it might be destructive to provide high-powered individual incentives, but because it is difficult if not impossible to tightly calibrate individual contribution to a joint effort. Hence, contrary to Arrow's (1969) view of firms as quasi markets, and the task of management to inject markets into firms, we recognize the inherent limits and possible counterproductive results of attempting to fashion firms into simply clusters of internal markets. In particular, learning and internal technology transfer may well be jeopardized.

Indeed, what is distinctive about firms is that they are domains for organizing activity in a nonmarket-like fashion. Accordingly, as we discuss what is distinctive about firms, we stress competence/capabilities which are ways of organizing and getting things done which cannot be accomplished merely by using the price system to coordinate activity. The very essence of most capabilities/competences is that they cannot be readily assembled through markets (Teece, 1982, 1986a; Zander and Kogut, 1995). If the ability to assemble competences using markets is what is meant by the firm as a nexus of contracts (Fama, 1980), then we unequivocally state that the firm about which we theorize cannot be usefully modelled as a nexus of contracts. By 'contract' we are referring to a transaction undergirded by a legal agreement, or some other arrangement which clearly spells out rights, rewards and responsibilities. Moreover, the firm as a nexus of contracts suggests a series of bilateral contracts orchestrated by a coordinator. Our view of the firm is that the organization takes place in a more multilateral fashion, with patterns of behaviour and learning being orchestrated in a much more decentralized fashion, but with a viable headquarters operation.

The key point, however, is that the properties of internal organization cannot be replicated by a portfolio of business units amalgamated just through formal contracts as many distinctive elements of internal organization simply cannot be replicated in the market. That is, entrepreneurial activity cannot lead to the immediate replication of unique organizational skills through simply entering a market and piecing the parts together overnight. Replication takes time, and the replication of best practice may be illusive. Indeed, firm capabilities need to be understood not in terms of balance sheet items, but mainly in terms of the organizational structures and managerial processes which support productive activity. By construction, the firm's balance sheet contains items that can be valued, at least at original market prices (cost). It is necessarily the case, therefore, that the balance sheet is a poor shadow of a firm's distinctive competences. That which is distinctive cannot be bought and sold short of buying the firm itself, or one or more of its subunits.

There are many dimensions of the business firm that must be understood if one is to grasp firm-level distinctive competences/capabilities. In this paper we merely identify several classes of factors that will help determine a firm's distinctive competence and dynamic capabilities. We organize these in three categories: processes, positions and paths. The essence of competences and capabilities is embedded in organizational processes of one kind or another. But the content of these processes and the opportunities they afford for developing competitive advantage at any point in time are shaped significantly by the assets the firm possesses (internal and market) and by the evolutionary path it has adopted/inherited. Hence organizational processes, shaped by the firm's asset positions and moulded by its evolutionary and co-evolutionary paths, explain the essence of the firm's dynamic capabilities and its competitive advantage.

Processes, positions and paths

We thus advance the argument that the competitive advantage of a firm lies with its managerial and organizational processes, shaped by its (specific) asset position, and the paths available to it. By managerial and organizational processes, we refer to the way things are done in the firm, or what might be referred to as its routines, or patterns of current practice and learning. By position we refer to its current specific endowments of technology, intellectual property, complementary assets, customer base and its external relations with suppliers and complementors. By paths we refer to the strategic alternatives available to the firm, and the presence or absence of increasing returns and attendant path dependencies.

Our focus throughout is on asset structures for which no ready market exists, as these are the only assets of strategic interest. A final section focuses on replication and imitation, as it is these phenomena which determine how readily a competence or capability can be cloned by competitors, and therefore distinctiveness of its competences and the durability of its advantage.

The firm's processes and positions collectively encompass its competences and capabilities. A hierarchy of competences/capabilities ought to be recognized, as some competences may be on the factory floor, some in the R&D labs, some in the executive suites, and some in the way everything is integrated. A difficult-to-replicate or difficult-to-imitate competence was defined earlier as a distinctive competence. As indicated, the key feature of distinctive competence is that there is not a market for it, except possibly through the market for business units. Hence competences and capabilities are intriguing assets, as they typically must be built because they cannot be bought.

Organizational and managerial processes

Organizational processes have three roles: coordination/integration (a static concept); learning (a dynamic concept); and reconfiguration (a transformational concept). We discuss each in turn.

Coordination/integration. While the price system supposedly coordinates the economy, managers coordinate or integrate activity inside the firm. How efficiently and effectively internal coordination or integration is achieved is very important (Aoki, 1990). Likewise for external coordination. Increasingly, strategic advantage requires the integration of external activities and technologies. The growing literature on strategic alliances, the virtual corporation, and buyer-supplier relations and technology collaboration evidences the importance of external integration and sourcing.

There is some field-based empirical research that provides support for the notion that the way production is organized by management inside the firm is the source of differences in firms' competence in various domains. For example, Garvin's (1988) study of 18 room air-conditioning plants reveals that quality performance was not related to either capital investment or the degree of automation of the facilities. Instead,

quality performance was driven by special organizational routines. These included routines for gathering and processing information, for linking customer experiences with engineering design choices, and for coordinating factories and component suppliers. The work of Clark and Fujimoto (1991) on project development in the automobile industry also illustrates the role played by coordinative routines. Their study reveals a significant degree of variation in how different firms coordinate the various activities required to bring a new model from concept to market. These differences in coordinative routines and capabilities seem to have a significant impact on such performance variables as development cost, development lead times and quality. Furthermore, Clark and Fujimoto tended to find significant firm-level differences in coordination routines and these differences seemed to have persisted for a long time. This suggests that routines related to coordination are firm-specific in nature.

Also, the notion that competence/capability is embedded in distinct ways of coordinating and combining helps to explain how and why seemingly minor technological changes can have devastating impacts on incumbent firms' abilities to compete in a market. Henderson and Clark (1990), for example, have shown that incumbents in the photolithographic equipment industry were sequentially devastated by seemingly minor innovations that, nevertheless, had major impacts on how systems had to be configured. They attribute these difficulties to the fact that systems-level or 'architectural' innovations often require new routines to integrate and coordinate engineering tasks. These findings and others suggest that productive systems display high interdependency, and that it may not be possible to change one level without changing others. This appears to be true with respect to the 'lean production' model (Womack *et al.,* 1991) which has now transformed the Taylor or Ford model of manufacturing organization in the automobile industry. Lean production requires distinctive shop floor practices and processes as well as distinctive higher-order managerial processes. Put differently, organizational processes often display high levels of coherence, and when they do, replication may be difficult because it requires systemic changes throughout the organization and also among interorganizational linkages, which might be very hard to effectuate. Put differently, partial imitation or replication of a successful model may yield zero benefits.

The notion that there is a certain rationality or coherence to processes and systems is not quite the same concept as corporate culture, as we understand the latter. Corporate culture refers to the values and beliefs that employees hold; culture can be a de facto governance system as it mediates the behaviour of individuals and economizes on more formal administrative methods. Rationality or coherence notions are more akin to the Nelson and Winter (1982) notion of organizational routines. However, the routines concept is a little too amorphous to properly capture the congruence amongst processes and between processes and incentives that we have in mind. Consider a professional service organization like an accounting firm. If it is to have relatively high-powered incentives that reward individual performance, then it must build organizational processes that channel individual behaviour; if it has weak or low-powered incentives, it must find symbolic ways to recognize the high performers, and it must use alternative methods to build effort and enthusiasm. What one may think of as styles of organization in fact contain necessary, not discretionary, elements to achieve performance.

Recognizing the congruences and complementarities among processes, and between processes and incentives, is critical to the understanding of organizational capabilities. In particular, they can help us explain why architectural and radical innovations are so often introduced into an industry by new entrants. The incumbents develop distinctive organizational processes that cannot support the new technology, despite certain overt similarities between the old and the new. The frequent failure of incumbents to introduce new technologies can thus be seen as a consequence of the mismatch that so often exists between the set of organizational processes needed to support the conventional product/service and the requirements of the new. Radical organizational re-engineering will usually be required to support the new product, which may well do better embedded in a separate subsidiary where a new set of coherent organizational processes can be fashioned (See Abernathy and Clark, 1985).

Learning. Perhaps even more important than integration is learning. Learning is a process by which repetition and experimentation enable tasks to be performed better and quicker. It also enables new production opportunities to be identified (See Levitt and March, 1988). In the context of the firm, if not more generally, learning has several key characteristics. First, learning involves organizational as well as individual skills. While individual skills are of relevance, their value depends upon their employment, in particular organizational settings. Learning

processes are intrinsically social and collective and occur not only through the imitation and emulation of individuals, as with teacher-student or master-apprentice, but also because of joint contributions to the understanding of complex problems. Learning requires common codes of communication and coordinated search procedures. Second, the organizational knowledge generated by such activity resides in new patterns of activity, in 'routines,' or a new logic of organization. As indicated earlier, routines are patterns of interactions that represent successful solutions to particular problems. These patterns of interaction are resident in group behaviour, though certain subroutines may be resident in individual behaviour. The concept of dynamic capabilities as a co-ordinative management process opens the door to the potential for interorganizational learning. Researchers (Doz and Shuen, 1990; Mody, 1993) have pointed out that collaborations and partnerships can be a vehicle for new organizational learning, helping firms to recognize dysfunctional routines, and preventing strategic blindspots.

Reconfiguration and transformation. In rapidly changing environments, there is obviously value in the ability to sense the need to reconfigure the firm's asset structure, and to accomplish the necessary internal and external transformation (Amit and Schoemaker, 1993; Langlois, 1994). This requires constant surveillance of markets and technologies and the willingness to adopt best practice. In this regard, benchmarking is of considerable value as an organized process for accomplishing such ends (Camp, 1989). In dynamic environments, narcissistic organizations are likely to be impaired. The capacity to reconfigure and transform is itself a learned organizational skill. The more frequently practised, the easier accomplished.

Change is costly and so firms must develop processes to minimize low pay-off change. The ability to calibrate the requirements for change and to effect the necessary adjustments would appear to depend on the ability to scan the environment, to evaluate markets and competitors, and to quickly accomplish reconfiguration and transformation ahead of competition. Decentralization and local autonomy assist these processes. Firms that have honed these capabilities are sometimes referred to as 'high-flex'.

Positions. The strategic posture of a firm is determined not only by its learning processes and by the coherence of its internal and external processes and incentives, but also by its specific assets. By specific assets we mean for example its specialized plant and equipment. These include its difficult-to-trade knowledge assets and assets complementary to them, as well as its reputational and relational assets. Such assets determine its competitive advantage at any point in time. We identify several illustrative classes.

Technological assets. While there is an emerging market for know-how (Teece, 1981), much technology does not enter it. This is either because the firm is unwilling to sell it or because of difficulties in transacting in the market for know-how (Teece, 1980). A firm's technological assets may or may not be protected by the standard instruments of intellectual property law. Either way, the ownership protection and utilization of technological assets are clearly key differentiators among firms. Likewise for complementary assets.

Complementary assets. Technological innovations require the use of certain related assets to produce and deliver new products and services. Prior commercialization activities require and enable firms to build such complementarities (Teece, 1986b). Such capabilities and assets, while necessary for the firm's established activities, may have other uses as well. These assets typically lie downstream. New products and processes either can enhance or destroy the value of such assets (Tushman, Newman and Romanelli, 1986). Thus the development of computers enhanced the value of IBM's direct sales force in office products, while disc brakes rendered useless much of the auto industry's investment in drum brakes.

Financial assets. In the short run, a firm's cash position and degree of leverage may have strategic implications. While there is nothing more tangible than cash, it cannot always be raised from external markets without the dissemination of considerable information to potential investors. Accordingly, what a firm can do in short order is often a function of its balance sheet. In the longer run, that ought not to be so, as cash flow ought to be more determinative.

Reputational assets. Firms, like individuals, have reputations. Reputations often summarize a good deal of information about firms and shape the responses of customers, suppliers and competitors. It is sometimes difficult to disentangle reputation from the firm's current asset and market position. However, in our view, reputational assets are best viewed as an intangible asset that enables firms to achieve various goals in the market. Its main value is external, since what is critical about reputation is that it is a kind of summary statistic about the firm's current assets and position, and its

likely future behaviour. Because there is generally a strong asymmetry between what is known inside the firm and what is known externally, reputations may sometimes be more salient than the true state of affairs, in the sense that external actors must respond to what they know rather than what is knowable.

Structural assets. The formal and informal structure of organizations and their external linkages have an important bearing on the rate and direction of innovation, and how competences and capabilities co-evolve (Argyres, 1995; Teece, 1996). The degree of hierarchy and the level of vertical and lateral integration are elements of firm-specific structure. Distinctive governance modes can be recognized (e.g., multi-product, integrated firms; high 'flex' firms; virtual corporations; conglomerates), and these modes support different types of innovation to a greater or lesser degree. For instance, virtual structures work well when innovation is autonomous; integrated structures work better for systemic innovations.

Institutional assets. Environments cannot be defined in terms of markets alone. While public policies are usually recognized as important in constraining what firms can do, there is a tendency, particularly by economists, to see these as acting through markets or through incentives. However, institutions themselves are a critical element of the business environment. Regulatory systems, as well as intellectual property regimes, tort laws and antitrust laws, are also part of the environment. So is the system of higher education and national culture. There are significant national differences here, which is just one of the reasons geographic location matters (Nelson, 1996). Such assets may not be entirely firm specific; firms of different national and regional origin may have quite different institutional assets to call upon because their institutional policy settings are so different.

Market (structure) assets. Product market position matters, but it is often not at all determinative of the fundamental position of the enterprise in its external environment. Part of the problem lies in defining the market in which a firm competes in a way that gives economic meaning. More importantly, market position in regimes of rapid technological change is often extremely fragile. This is in part because time moves on a different clock in such environments. Moreover, the link between market share and innovation has long been broken, if it ever existed (Teece, 1996). All of this is to suggest that product market position, while important, is too often overplayed.

Strategy should be formulated with regard to the more fundamental aspects of firm performance, which we believe are rooted in competences and capabilities and shaped by positions and paths.

Organizational boundaries. An important dimension of 'position' is the location of a firm's boundaries. Put differently, the degree of integration (vertical, lateral and horizontal) is of quite some significance. Boundaries are not only significant with respect to the technological and complementary assets contained within, but also with respect to the nature of the coordination that can be achieved internally as compared to through markets. When specific assets or poorly protected intellectual capital are at issue, pure market arrangements expose the parties to recontracting hazards or appropriability hazards. In such circumstances, hierarchical control structures may work better than pure arms-length contracts.

Paths

Path dependencies. Where a firm can go is a function of its current position and the paths ahead. Its current position is often shaped by the path it has travelled. In standard economics textbooks, firms have an infinite range of technologies from which they can choose and markets they can occupy. Changes in product or factor prices will be responded to instantaneously, with technologies moving in and out according to value maximization criteria. Only in the short run are irreversibilities recognized. Fixed costs – such as equipment and overheads – cause firms to price below fully amortized costs but never constrain future investment choices. 'Bygones are bygones.' Path dependencies are simply not recognized. This is a major limitation of microeconomic theory.

The notion of path dependencies recognizes that 'history matters.' Bygones are rarely bygones, despite the predictions of rational actor theory. Thus a firm's previous investments and its repertoire of routines (its 'history') constrain its future behaviour. This follows because learning tends to be local. That is, opportunities for learning will be 'close in' to previous activities and thus will be transaction and production specific (Teece, 1988). This is because learning is often a process of trial, feedback and evaluation. If too many parameters are changed simultaneously, the ability of firms to conduct meaningful natural quasi experiments is attenuated. If many aspects of a firm's learning environment change simultaneously, the ability to ascertain cause-effect relationships is confounded because cognitive structures will not be formed and rates of learning diminish as a result. One implication is that many investments are much longer term than is commonly thought.

The importance of path dependencies is amplified where conditions of increasing returns to adoption exist. This is a demand-side phenomenon, and it tends to make technologies and products embodying those technologies more attractive the more they are adopted. Attractiveness flows from the greater adoption of the product amongst users, which in turn enables them to become more developed and hence more useful. Increasing returns to adoption has many sources including network externalities (Katz and Shapiro, 1985), the presence of complementary assets (Teece, 1986b) and supporting infrastructure (Nelson, 1996), learning by using Rosenberg, 1982), and scale economies in production and distribution. Competition between and amongst technologies is shaped by increasing returns. Early leads won by good luck or special circumstances (Arthur, 1983) can become amplified by increasing returns. This is not to suggest that first movers necessarily win. Because increasing returns have multiple sources, the prior positioning of firms can affect their capacity to exploit increasing returns. Thus, in Mitchell's (1989) study of medical diagnostic imaging, firms already controlling the relevant complementary assets could in theory start last and finish first.

In the presence of increasing returns, firms can compete passively, or they may compete strategically through technology-sponsoring activities.[3] The first type of competition is not unlike biological competition amongst species, although it can be sharpened by managerial activities that enhance the performance of products and processes. The reality is that companies with the best products will not always win, as chance events may cause 'lock-in' on inferior technologies (Arthur, 1983) and may even in special cases generate switching costs for consumers. However, while switching costs may favour the incumbent, in regimes of rapid technological change switching costs can become quickly swamped by switching benefits. Put differently, new products employing different standards often appear with alacrity in market

---

[3]Because of huge uncertainties, it may be extremely difficult to determine viable strategies early on. Since the rules of the game and the identity of the players will be revealed only after the market has begun to evolve, the pay-off is likely to lie with building and maintaining organizational capabilities that support flexibility.

environments experiencing rapid technological change, and incumbents can be readily challenged by superior products and services that yield switching benefits. Thus the degree to which switching costs cause 'lock-in' is a function of factors such as user learning, rapidity of technological change, and the amount of ferment in the competitive environment.

Technological opportunities. The concept of path dependencies is given forward meaning through the consideration of an industry's technological opportunities. It is well recognized that how far and how fast a particular area of industrial activity can proceed is in part due to the technological opportunities that lie before it. Such opportunities are usually a lagged function of foment and diversity in basic science, and the rapidity with which new scientific breakthroughs are being made.

However, technological opportunities may not be completely exogenous to industry, not only because some firms have the capacity to engage in or at least support basic research, but also because technological opportunities are often fed by innovative activity itself. Moreover, the recognition of such opportunities is affected by the organizational structures that link the institutions engaging in basic research (primarily the university) to the business enterprise. Hence, the existence of technological opportunities can be quite firm specific.

Important for our purposes is the rate and direction in which relevant scientific frontiers are being rolled back. Firms engaging in R&D may find the path dead ahead closed off, though breakthroughs in related areas may be sufficiently close to be attractive. Likewise, if the path dead ahead is extremely attractive, there may be no incentive for firms to shift the allocation of resources away from traditional pursuits. The depth and width of technological opportunities in the neighbourhood of a firm's prior research activities thus are likely to impact a firm's options with respect to both the amount and level of R&D activity that it can justify. In addition, a firm's past experience conditions the alternatives management is able to perceive. Thus, not only do firms in the same industry face 'menus' with different costs associated with particular technological choices, they also are looking at menus containing different choices.

Assessment

The essence of a firm's competence and dynamic capabilities is presented here as being resident in the firm's organizational processes, that are in turn shaped by the firm's assets (positions) and its evolutionary path. Its evolutionary path, despite managerial hubris that might suggest otherwise, is often rather narrow. What the firm can do and where it can go are thus rather constrained by its positions and paths. Its competitors are likewise constrained. Rents (profits) thus tend to flow not just from the asset structure of the firm and, as we shall see, the degree of its imitability, but also by the firm's ability to reconfigure and transform.

The parameters we have identified for determining performance are quite different from those in the standard textbook theory of the firm, and in the competitive forces and strategic conflict approaches to the firm and to strategy. Moreover, the agency theoretic view of the firm as a nexus of contracts would put no weight on processes, positions and paths. While agency approaches to the firm may recognize that opportunism and shirking may limit what a firm can do, they do not recognize the opportunities and constraints imposed by processes, positions and paths.

Moreover, the firm in our conceptualization is much more than the sum of its parts – or a team tied together by contracts. Indeed, to some extent individuals can be moved in and out of organizations and, so long as the internal processes and structures remain in place, performance will not necessarily be impaired. A shift in the environment is a far more serious threat to the firm than is the loss of key individuals, as individuals can be replaced more readily than organizations can be transformed. Furthermore, the dynamic capabilities view of the firm would suggest that the behaviour and performance of particular firms may be quite hard to replicate, even if its coherence and rationality are observable. This matter and related issues involving replication and imitation are taken up in the section that follows.

Replicability and imitability of organizational processes and positions

Thus far, we have argued that the competences and capabilities (and hence competitive advantage) of a firm rest fundamentally on processes, shaped by positions and paths. However, competences can provide competitive advantage and generate rents only if they are based on a collection of routines, skills and complementary assets that are difficult to imitate. We call such competences distinctive. A particular set of routines can lose their value if they support a competence which no longer matters in the marketplace, or if they can be readily replicated or emulated by competitors. Imitation occurs when firms discover and simply copy a firm's organizational routines and procedures. Emulation occurs when firms discover alternative ways of achieving the same functionality.

Replication

To understand imitation, one must first understand replication. Replication involves transferring or redeploying competences from one concrete economic setting to another. Since productive knowledge is embodied, this cannot be accomplished by simply transmitting information. Only in those instances where all relevant knowledge is fully codified and understood can replication be collapsed into a simple problem of information transfer. Too often, the contextual dependence of original performance is poorly appreciated, so unless firms have replicated their systems of productive knowledge on many prior occasions, the act of replication is likely to be difficult (Teece, 1976). Indeed, replication and transfer are often impossible without the transfer of people, though this can be minimized if investments are made to convert tacit knowledge to codified knowledge. Often, however, this is simply not possible.

In short, competences and capabilities, and the routines upon which they rest, are normally rather difficult to replicate. Even understanding what all the relevant routines are that support a particular competence may not be transparent. Indeed, Lippman and Rumelt (1992) have argued that some sources of competitive advantage are so complex that the firm itself, let alone its competitors, does not understand them. As Nelson and Winter (1982) and Teece (1982) have explained, many organizational routines are quite tacit in nature. Imitation can also be hindered by the fact few routines are 'stand-alone'; coherence may require that a change in one set of routines in one part of the firm (e.g., production) requires changes in some other part (e.g., R&D).

Some routines and competences seem to be attributable to local or regional forces that shape firms' capabilities at early stages in their lives. Porter (1990), for example, shows that differences in local product markets, local factor markets and institutions play an important role in shaping competitive capabilities. Differences also exist within populations of firms from the same country. Various studies of the automobile industry, for example, show that not all Japanese automobile companies are top performers in terms of

quality, productivity or product development (see, for example, Clark and Fujimoto, 1991). The role of firm-specific history has been highlighted as a critical factor explaining such firm-level (as opposed to regional or national-level) differences (Nelson and Winter, 1982). Replication in a different context may thus be rather difficult.

At least two types of strategic value flow from replication. One is the ability to support geographic and product line expansion. To the extent that the capabilities in question are relevant to customer needs elsewhere, replication can confer value. Another is that the ability to replicate also indicates that the firm has the foundations in place for learning and improvement. Considerable empirical evidence supports the notion that the understanding of processes, both in production and in management, is the key to process improvement. In short, an organization cannot improve that which it does not understand. Deep process understanding is often required to accomplish codification. Indeed, if knowledge is highly tacit, it indicates that underlying structures are not well understood, which limits learning because scientific and engineering principles cannot be as systematically applied. Instead, learning is confined to proceeding through trial and error, and the leverage that might otherwise come from the application of scientific theory is denied.

Imitation

Imitation is simply replication performed by a competitor. If self-replication is difficult, imitation is likely to be harder. In competitive markets, it is the ease of imitation that determines the sustainability of competitive advantage. Easy imitation implies the rapid dissipation of rents.

Factors that make replication difficult also make imitation difficult. Thus, the more tacit the firm's productive knowledge, the harder it is to replicate by the firm itself or its competitors. When the tacit component is high, imitation may well be impossible, without the hiring away of key individuals and the transfers of key organization processes. However, another set of barriers impedes imitation of certain capabilities in advanced industrial countries. This is the system of intellectual property rights, such as patents, trade secrets and trademarks, and even trade dress. Intellectual property protection is of increasing importance in the United States, as since 1982 the legal system has adopted a more pro-patent posture. Similar trends are evident outside the United States. Besides the patent system, several other factors cause there to be a difference between replication costs and imitation costs. The observability of the technology or the organization is one such important factor. Whereas vistas into product technology can be obtained through strategies such as reverse engineering, this is not the case for process technology, as a firm need not expose its process technology to the outside in order to benefit from it. Firms with product technology, on the other hand, confront the unfortunate circumstances that they must expose what they have got in order to profit from the technology. Secrets are thus more protectable if there is no need to expose them in contexts where competitors can learn about them.

One should not, however, overestimate the overall importance of intellectual property protection; yet it presents a formidable imitation barrier in certain particular contexts. Intellectual property protection is not uniform across products, processes and technologies, and is best thought of as islands in a sea of open competition. If one is not able to place the fruits of one's investment, ingenuity or creativity on one or more of the islands, then one indeed is at sea.

We use the term appropriability regimes to describe the ease of imitation. Appropriability is a function both of the ease of replication and the efficacy of intellectual property rights as a barrier to imitation. Appropriability is strong when a technology is both inherently difficult to replicate and the intellectual property system provides legal barriers to imitation. When it is inherently easy to replicate and intellectual property protection is either unavailable or ineffectual, then appropriability is weak. Intermediate conditions also exist.

Conclusion

The four paradigms discussed above are quite different, though the first two have much in common with each other (strategizing) as do the last two (economizing). But are these paradigms complementary or competitive? According to some authors, 'the resource perspective complements the industry analysis framework' (Amit and Schoemaker, 1993: 35). While this is undoubtedly true, we think that in several important respects the perspectives are also competitive. While this should be recognized, it is not to suggest that there is only one framework that has value. Indeed, complex problems are likely to benefit from insights obtained from all of the paradigms we have identified plus more. The trick is to work out which frameworks are

appropriate for the problem at hand. Slavish adherence to one class to the neglect of all others is likely to generate strategic blindspots. The tools themselves then generate strategic vulnerability. We now explore these issues further.

Efficiency vs market power

The competitive forces and strategic conflict approaches generally see profits as stemming from strategizing – that is, from limitations on competition which firms achieve through raising rivals' costs and exclusionary behaviour (Teece, 1984). The competitive forces approach in particular leads one to see concentrated industries as being attractive – market positions can be shielded behind entry barriers, and rivals costs can be raised. It also suggests that the sources of competitive advantage lie at the level of the industry, or possibly groups within an industry. In text book presentations, there is almost no attention at all devoted to discovering, creating and commercializing new sources of value.

The dynamic capabilities and resources approaches clearly have a different orientation. They see competitive advantage stemming from high-performance routines operating 'inside the firm,' shaped by processes and positions. Path dependencies (including increasing returns) and technological opportunities mark the road ahead. Because of imperfect factor markets, or more precisely the non-tradeability of 'soft' assets like values, culture and organizational experience, distinctive competences and capabilities generally cannot be acquired; they must be built. This sometimes takes years – possibly decades. In some cases, as when the competence is protected by patents, replication by a competitor is ineffectual as a means to access the technology. The capabilities approach accordingly sees definite limits on strategic options, at least in the short run. Competitive success occurs in part because of policies pursued and experience and efficiency obtained in earlier periods.

Competitive success can undoubtedly flow from both strategizing and economizing, but along with Williamson (1991) we believe that 'economizing is more fundamental than strategizing ...' or put differently, that economy is the best strategy.[4] Indeed, we suggest that, except in special circumstances, too much 'strategizing' can lead firms to underinvest in core competences and neglect dynamic capabilities, and thus harm long-term competitiveness.

[4]We concur with Williamson that economizing and strategizing are not mutually exclusive.

Normative implications

The field of strategic management is avowedly normative. It seeks to guide those aspects of general management that have material effects on the survival and success of the business enterprise. Unless these various approaches differ in terms of the framework and heuristics they offer management, then the discourse we have gone through is of limited immediate value. In this paper, we have already alluded to the fact that the capabilities approach tends to steer managers toward creating distinctive and difficult-to-imitate advantages and avoiding games with customers and competitors. We now survey possible differences, recognizing that the paradigms are still in their infancy and cannot confidently support strong normative conclusions.

Unit of analysis and analytic focus

Because in the capabilities and the resources framework business opportunities flow from a firm's unique processes, strategy analysis must be situational. This is also true with the strategic conflict approach. There is no algorithm for creating wealth for the entire industry. Prescriptions they apply to industries or groups of firms at best suggest overall direction, and may indicate errors to be avoided. In contrast, the competitive forces approach is not particularly firm specific; it is industry and group specific.

Strategic change

The competitive forces and the strategic conflict approach, since they pay little attention to skills, know-how and path dependency, tend to see strategic choice occurring with relative facility. The capabilities approach sees value augmenting strategic change as being difficult and costly. Moreover, it can generally only occur incrementally. Capabilities cannot easily be bought; they must be built. From the capabilities perspective, strategy involves choosing among and committing to long-term paths or trajectories of competence development.

In this regard, we speculate that the dominance of competitive forces and the strategic conflict approaches in the United States may have something to do with observed differences in strategic approaches adopted by some US and some foreign firms. Hayes (1985) has noted that American companies tend to favour 'strategic leaps' while, in contrast, Japanese and German companies tend to favour incremental, but rapid, improvements.

Entry strategies

Here the resources and the capabilities approaches suggest that entry decisions must be made with reference to the competences and capabilities which new entrants have, relative to the competition. Whereas the other approaches tell you little about where to look to find likely entrants, the capabilities approach identifies likely entrants. Relatedly, whereas the entry deterrence approach suggests an unconstrained search for new business opportunities, the capabilities approach suggests that such opportunities lie close in to one's existing business. As Richard Rumelt has explained it in conversation, 'the capabilities approach suggests that if a firm looks inside itself, and at its market environment, sooner or later it will find a business opportunity.'

Entry timing

Whereas the strategic conflict approach tells little about where to look to find likely entrants, the resources and the capabilities approach identifies likely entrants and their timing of entry. Brittain and Freeman (1980) using population ecology methodologies, argued that an organization is quick to expand when there is a significant overlap between its core capabilities and those needed to survive in a new market. Recent research (Mitchell, 1989) showed that the more industry-specialized assets or capabilities a firm possesses, the more likely it is to enter an emerging technical subfield in its industry, following a technological discontinuity. Additionally, the interaction between specialized assets such as firm-specific capabilities and rivalry had the greatest influence on entry timing.

Diversification

Related diversification – that is, diversification that builds upon or extends existing capabilities – is about the only form of diversification that a resources/capabilities framework is likely to view as meritorious (Rumelt, 1974; Teece, 1980, 1982; Teece et al., 1994). Such diversification will be justifiable when the firms' traditional markets decline. The strategic conflict approach is likely to be a little more permissive; acquisitions that raise rivals' costs or enable firms to effectuate exclusive arrangements are likely to be seen as efficacious in certain circumstances.

Focus and specialization

Focus needs to be defined in terms of distinctive competences or capability, not products. Products are the manifestation of competences, as competences can be moulded into a variety of products. Product market specialization and decentralization configured around product markets may cause firms to neglect the development of core competences and dynamic capabilities, to the extent to which competences require accessing assets across divisions.

The capabilities approach places emphasis on the internal processes that a firm utilizes, as well as how they are deployed and how they will evolve. The approach has the benefit of indicating that competitive advantage is not just a function of how one plays the game; it is also a function of the 'assets' one has to play with, and how these assets can be deployed and redeployed in a changing market.

REFERENCES

Abell, D. (1980) *Defining the Business: The Starting Point of Strategic Planning*, Englewood Cliffs, NJ: Prentice Hall.

Abernathy, W.J. and Clark, K. (1985) 'Innovation: Mapping the winds of creative destruction', *Research Policy*, 14, pp. 3–22.

Amit, R. and Schoemaker, P. (1993) 'Strategic assets and organizational rent', *Strategic Management Journal*, 14(1), pp. 33–46.

Amit, R. and Zott, C. (2001) 'Value Creation in E-business', *Strategic Management Journal*, Vol. 22, pp. 493–520.

Andrews, K. (1987) *The Concept of Corporate Strategy*, Homewood: Irvin.

Aoki, M. (1990) 'The participatory generation of information rents and the theory of the firm', in: M. Aoki, B. Gustafsson and O.E. Williamson (eds.) *The Firm as a Nexus of Treaties*, London: Sage, pp. 26–52.

Argyres, N. (1995) 'Technology strategy, governance structure and interdivisional coordination', *Journal of Economic Behavior and Organization*, 28, pp. 337–358.

Arrow, K. (1969) 'The organization of economic activity: Issues pertinent to the choice of market vs. nonmarket allocation', in: *The Analysis and Evaluation of Public Expenditures: The PPB System*, 1. US Joint Economic Committee, 91st Session. US Government Printing Office, Washington DC, pp. 59–73.

Arrow, K. (1996) 'Technical information and industrial structure', *Industrial and Corporate Change*, 5(2), pp. 645–652.

Arthur, W.B. (1983) 'Competing technologies and lock-in by historical events: The dynamics of allocation under increasing returns', working paper WP-83-90, International Institute for Applied Systems Analysis, Laxenburg, Austria.

Arthur, W.B., Ermoliev, Y.M. and Kaniovsky, Y.M. (1987) 'Path Dependent Processes and the Emergence of Macro Structure', *European Journal of Operations Research*, Vol. 30, pp. 294–303.

Baden-Fuller, C. and Stopford, J.M. (1992) *Rejuvenating the Mature Business*, London: Routledge.

Bain, J. (1956) *Barriers to New Competition*, Cambridge, MA: Harvard University Press.

Bain, J. (1959) *Industrial Organization*, New York: Wiley.

Barney, J.B. (1986a) 'Strategic factor markets: Expectations, luck and business strategy', *Management Science*, 32(10), pp. 1231–1241.

Barney, J.B. (1986b) 'Organizational Culture: Can It Be a Source of Sustained Competitive Advantage?' *Academy of Management Review*, Vol. 11, pp. 656–665.

Barney, J.B. (1991) 'Firm Resources and Sustained Competitive Advantage', *Journal of Management*, Vol. 17, No. 1, pp. 99–120.

Baumol, W., Panzar, J. and Willig, R. (1982) *Contestable Markets and the Theory of Industry Structure*, New York: Harcourt Brace Jovanovich.

Brittain, J. and Freeman, J. (1980) 'Organizational proliferation and density-dependent selection', in: J.R. Kimberly and R. Miles (eds.) *The Organizational Life Cycle*, San Francisco, CA: Jossey-Bass, pp. 291–338.

Buzzell, R.D. and Gale, B.T. (1987) *The PIMS Principles: Linking Strategy to Performance*, New York: Free Press.

Camp, R. (1989) *Benchmarking: The Search for Industry Best Practices that Lead to Superior Performance*, Milwaukee, WI: Quality Press.

Caves, R.E. and Porter, M.E. (1977) 'From Entry Barriers to Mobility Barriers: Conjectural Decisions and Contrived Deterrence to New Competition', *Quarterly Journal of Economics*, Vol. 91, pp. 241–262.

Christensen, C. (1997) *The Innovator's Dilemma*, New York: HarperBusiness.

Clark, K. and Fujimoto, T. (1991) *Product Development Performance: Strategy, Organization and Management in the World Auto Industries*, Cambridge, MA: Harvard Business School Press.

Coase, R. (1937) 'The nature of the firm', *Economica*, 4, pp. 386–405.

Collis, D.J. and Montgomery, C.A. (1995) 'Competing on Resources: Strategy in the 1990s', *Harvard Business Review*, Vol. 73, No. 4, July–August, pp. 118–128.

Cool, K. and Schendel, D. (1988) 'Performance differences among strategic group members', *Strategic Management Journal*, 9 (3), pp. 207–223.

David, P.A. (1985) 'Clio and the Economics of QWERTY', *American Economic Review Proceedings*, Vol. 75, pp. 332–337.

Day, G. and Moorman, C. (2010) *Strategy from the Outside in: Profiting from Customer Value*, McGraw-Hill Professional.

Day, G.S. (1990) *Market Driven Strategy, Processes for Creating Value*, New York: The Free Press.

Dierickx, I. and Cool, K. (1989) 'Asset Stock Accumulation and Sustainability of Competitive Advantage', *Management Science*, Vol. 35, No. 12, December, pp. 1504–1511.

Dixit, A. (1980) 'The role of investment in entry deterrence', *Economic Journal*, 90, pp. 95–106.

Doz, Y. and Shuen, A. (1990) 'From intent to outcome: A process framework for partnerships', INSEAD working paper.

Dretske, F. (1981) *Knowledge and the Flow of Information*, Cambridge, MA: MIT Press.

Duncan, R. (1976) 'The Ambidextrous Organization: Designing dual structures for innovation', in: R.H. Killman, L.R. Pondy and D. Sleven (eds.) *The Management of Organization*, New York: North Holland, pp. 167–188.

Durand, T. (1996) *Revisiting Key Dimensions of Competence*, Paper presented to the SMS Conference, Phoenix.

Eisenhardt, K.M. and Martin, J.A. (2000) 'Dynamic capabilities: What are they?', *Strategic Management Journal*, 21, pp. 1105–1121.

Fama, E.F. (1980) 'Agency problems and the theory of the firm', *Journal of Political Economy*, 88, pp. 288–307.

Garvin, D. (1988) *Managing Quality*, New York: Free Press.

Ghemawat, P. (1991) *Commitment*, New York: The Free Press.

Gilbert, R.J. and Newbery, D.M. (1982) 'Preemptive patenting and the persistence of monopoly', *The American Economic Review*, 72, pp. 514–526.

Gilbert, X. and Strebel, P. (1989) 'From Innovation to Outpacing', *Business Quarterly*, Summer, pp. 19–22.

Grant, R.M. (2002) *Contemporary Strategy Analysis: Concepts, Techniques, Applications*, Fourth Edition, Oxford: Blackwell Publishers.

Hambrick, D. (1987) 'Top Management Teams: Key to Strategic Success', *California Management Review*, Vol. 30, pp. 88–108.

Hannan, M.T. and Freeman, J. (1977) 'The Population Ecology of Organizations', *American Journal of Sociology*, Vol. 82, No. 5, March, pp. 929–964.

Hansen, G.S. and Wernerfelt, B. (1989) 'Determinants of firm performance: The relative importance of economic and organizational factors', *Strategic Management Journal*, 10(5), pp. 399–411.

Hayes, R. (1985) 'Strategic planning: Forward in reverse', *Harvard Business Review*, 63(6), pp. 111–119.

Hayes, R., Wheelwright, S. and Clark, K. (1988) *Dynamic Manufacturing: Creating the Learning Organization*, New York: The Free Press.

Henderson, R.M. and Clark, K.B. (1990) 'Architectural innovation: the reconfiguration of existing product technologies and the failure of established firms', *Administrative Science Quarterly*, 35(1), pp. 9–30.

Hofer, C. and Schendel, D. (1978) *Strategy Formulation: Analytical Concepts*, St. Paul, MN: West.

Itami, H. (1987) *Mobilizing Invisible Assets*, Cambridge, MA: Harvard University Press.

Itami, H. and Roehl, T.W. (1987) *Mobilizing Invisible Assets*, Cambridge: Harvard University Press.

Jacobson, R. (1988) 'The persistence of abnormal returns', *Strategic Management Journal*, 9(5), pp. 415–430.

Jaworski, B. and Kohli, A.K. (1993) 'Market Orientation: Antecedents and Consequences', *Journal of Marketing*, Vol. 57, No. 3, July, pp. 53–70.

Katz, M.L. and Shapiro, C. (1985) 'Network externalities, competition, and compatibility', *The American Economic Review*, 75(3), pp. 424–440.

Kay, J. (1993) *Foundations of Corporate Success: How Business Strategies Add Value*, Oxford: Oxford University Press.

Kreps, D.M. and Wilson, R. (1982a) 'Reputation and imperfect information', *Journal of Economic Theory*, 27(2), pp. 253–279.

Kreps, D.M. and Wilson, R. (1982b) 'Sequential equilibria', *Econometrica: Journal of the Econometric Society*, 50(4), pp. 863–894.

Langlois, R. (1994) 'Cognition and capabilities: Opportunities seized and missed in the history of the history of the computer industry', working paper, University of Connecticut. Presented at the conference on Technological Oversights and Foresights, Stern School of Business, New York University, 11–12 March 1994.

Learned, E., Christensen, C., Andrews, K. and Guth, W. (1969) *Business Policy: Text and Cases,* Homewood, IL: Irwin.

Leonard-Barton, D. (1992) 'Core capabilities and core rigidities: A paradox in managing new product development', *Strategic Management Journal,* Summer, Special Issue, 13, pp. 111–125.

Leonard-Barton, D. (1995) *Wellsprings of Knowledge*, Boston, MA: Harvard Business School Press.

Levitt, B. and March, J. (1988) 'Organizational learning', *Annual Review of Sociology*, 14, pp. 319–340.

Lieberman, M.B. and Montgomery, D.B. (1988) 'First Mover Adavantages', *Strategic Management Journal,* Vol. 9, No. 1, January February, pp. 41–58.

Lieberman, M.B. and Montgomery, D.B. (1998) 'First-Mover (Dis)Advantages: Retrospective and Link with the Resource-Based View', *Strategic Management Journal*, Vol. 19, No. 12, December, pp. 1111–1126.

Lippman, S. and Rumelt, R. (1992) 'Demand uncertainty and investment in industry-specific capital', *Industrial and Corporate Change*, 1(1), pp. 235–262.

Lowendahl, B.R. (1997) *Strategic Management of Professional Business Service Firms*, Copenhagen: Copenhagen Business School Press.

Mason, E. (1949) 'The current state of the monopoly problem in the US', *Harvard Law Review*, 62, pp. 1265–1285.

McGrath, R.G. (2013) *The End of Competitive Advantage: How to Keep Your Strategy Moving as Fast as Your Business*, Boston, MA: Harvard Business Review Press.

Milgrom, P. and Roberts, J. (1982a) 'Limit pricing and entry under incomplete information: An equilibrium analysis', *Econometrica*, 50, pp. 443–459.

Milgrom, P. and Roberts, J. (1982b) 'Predation, reputation and entry deterrence', *Journal of Economic Theory*, 27, pp. 280–312.

Miller, D., Eisenstat, R. and Foote, N. (2002) 'Strategy from the Inside-Out: Building Capability-Creating Organizations', *California Management Review*, Vol. 44, No. 3, Spring, pp. 37–54.

Mintzberg, H., Ahlstrand, B. and Lampel, J. (1998) *Strategy Safari: A Guided Tour Through the Wilds of Strategic Management*, New York: The Free Press.

Mitchell, W. (1989) 'Whether and when? Probability and timing of incumbents' entry into emerging industrial subfields', *Administrative Science Quarterly*, 34, pp. 208–230.

Mody, A. (1993) 'Learning through alliances', *Journal of Economic Behavior and Organization*, 20(2), pp. 151–170.

Nalebuff, B.J. and Brandenburger, A. (1996) *Co-opetition.* HarperCollinsBusiness.

Nalebuff, B.J. and Brandenburger, A.M. (1995) 'The right game: use game theory to shape strategy', *Harvard Business Review*, 73(4), pp. 57–71.

Nelson, R. (1996) 'The evolution of competitive or comparative advantage: A preliminary report on a study', WP-96-21, International Institute for Applied Systems Analysis, Laxemberg, Austria.

Nelson, R. and Winter, S. (1982) *An Evolutionary Theory of Economic Change*, Cambridge, MA: Harvard University Press.

Nonaka, I. and Konno, N. (1998) 'The Concept of Ba: Building a Foundation for Knowledge Creation', *California Management Review*, Vol. 40, No. 3, Spring, pp. 40–54.

Norman, R. and Ramirez, R. (1993) 'From Value Chain to Value Constellation: Designing Interactive Strategy', *Harvard Business Review,* July–August, pp. 65–77.

Penrose, E.T. (1959) *The Theory of the Growth of the Firm*, New York: Wiley.

Polanyi, M. (1958) *Personal Knowledge*, Chicago, IL: University of Chicago Press.

Porac, J.F., Thomas, H. and Baden-Fuller, C. (1989) 'Competitive Groups as Cognitive Communities: The Case of Scottish Knitwear Manufacturers', *Journal of Management Studies*, Vol. 26, pp. 397–416.

Porter, M.E. (1980) *Competitive Strategy: Techniques for Analyzing Industries and Competitors*, New York: Free Press.

Porter, M.E. (1985) *Competitive Advantage: Creating and Sustaining Superior Performance*, New York: Free Press.

Porter, M.E. (1990) *The Competitive Advantage of Nations*, London: Macmillan.

Porter, M.E. (1996) 'What is Strategy?', *Harvard Business Review*, Vol. 74, No. 6, November–December, pp. 61–78.

Prahalad, C.K. and Hamel, G. (1990) 'The Core Competence of the Corporation', *Harvard Business Review*, Vol. 68, No. 3, May–June, pp. 79–91.

Rosenberg, N. (1982) *Inside the Black Box: Technology and Economics*, Cambridge, MA: Cambridge University Press.

Rumelt, R. (1991) 'How Much Does Industry Matter?', *Strategic Management Journal*, Vol. 12, No. 3, March, pp. 167–186.

Rumelt, R.P. (1974) *Strategy, Structure, and Economic Performance*, Cambridge, MA: Harvard University Press.

Rumelt, R.P. (1980) 'The Evaluation of Business Strategy', in: W.F. Glueck (ed.) *Business Policy and Strategic Management*, Third Edition, New York: McGraw-Hill.

Rumelt, R.P. (1984) 'Towards a strategic theory of the firm', in: Lamb, R.B. (ed.) *Competitive Strategic Management*, Englewood Cliffs, NJ: Prentice-Hall, pp. 556–570.

Rumelt, R.P. (1996) 'Inertia and Transformation', in: C.A. Montgomery (ed.) *Resource-based and Evolutionary Theories of the Firm: Towards a Synthesis*, Boston, MA: Kluwer Academic Publishers, pp. 101–132.

Sanchez, R., Heene, A. and Thomas, H. (eds.) (1996) *Dynamics of Competence-Based Competition*, London: Elsevier.

Schmalensee, R. (1983) 'Advertising and entry deterrence: An exploratory model', *Journal of Political Economy*, 91(4), pp. 636–653.

Schumpeter, J.A. (1934) *Theory of Economic Development*, Cambridge, MA: Harvard University Press.

Schumpeter, J.A. (1942) *Capitalism, Socialism, and Democracy*, New York: Harper.

Shapiro, C. (1989) 'The theory of business strategy', *RAND Journal of Economics*, 20(1), pp. 125–137.

Shuen, A. (1994) 'Technology sourcing and learning strategies in the semiconductor industry', unpublished Ph.D. dissertation, University of California, Berkeley.

Stalk, G., Evans, P. and Schulman, L.E. (1992) 'Competing on Capabilities: The New Rules of Corporate Strategy', *Harvard Business Review*, Vol. 70, No. 2, March–April, pp. 57–69.

Sutton, J. (1992) 'Implementing game theoretical models in industrial economics', in: Del Monte, A. (ed.) *Recent Developments in the Theory of Industrial Organization*, Ann Arbor: University of Michigan Press, pp. 19–33.

Teece, D.J. (1976) *The Multinational Corporation and the Resource Cost of International Technology Transfer*, Cambridge, MA: Ballinger.

Teece, D.J. (1980) 'Economics of scope and the scope of the enterprise', *Journal of Economic Behavior and Organization*, 1, pp. 223–247.

Teece, D.J. (1981) 'The market for know-how and the efficient international transfer of technology', *Annals of the Academy of Political and Social Science*, 458, pp. 81–96.

Teece, D.J. (1982) 'Towards an economic theory of the multiproduct firm', *Journal of Economic Behavior and Organization*, 3, pp. 39–63.

Teece, D.J. (1984) 'Economic analysis and strategic management', *California Management Review*, 26(3), pp. 87–110.

Teece, D.J. (1986a) 'Transaction cost economics and the multinational enterprise', *Journal of Economic Behavior and Organization*, 7, pp. 21–45.

Teece, D.J. (1986b) 'Profiting from technological innovation', *Research Policy*, 15(6), pp. 285–305.

Teece, D.J. (1988) 'Technological change and the nature of the firm', in: Dosi, G., Freeman, C., Nelson, R., Silverberg, G. and Soete, L. (eds.) *Technical Change and Economic Policy*, New York: Pinter Publishers, pp. 256–281.

Teece, D.J. (1996) 'Firm organization, industrial structure, and technological innovation', *Journal of Economic Behavior and Organization*, 31, pp. 193–224.

Teece, D.J. (2007) 'Explicating dynamic capabilities: The nature and microfoundations of (sustainable) enterprise performance', *Strategic Management Journal*, 28, pp. 1319–1350.

Teece, D.J., Pisano, G. and Shuen, A. (1997) 'Dynamic Capabilities and Strategic Management', *Strategic Management Journal*, Vol. 18, No. 7, August, pp. 509–533.

Teece, D.J., Rumelt, R., Dosi, G. and Winter, S. (1994) 'Understanding corporate coherence: Theory and evidence', *Journal of Economic Behavior and Organization*, 23, pp. 1–20.

Treacy, M. and Wiersema, F. (1995) *The Discipline of Market Leaders*, Reading, MA: Addison-Wesley.

Tushman, M.L., Newman, W.H. and Romanelli, E. (1986) 'Convergence and Upheaval: Managing the Unsteady Pace of Organizational Evolution', *California Management Review*, Vol. 29, No. 1, Fall, pp. 29–44.

Webster, F. (1994) *Market Driven Management: Using the New Marketing Concept to Create a Customer-oriented Company*, New York: Wiley.

Wernerfelt, B. (1984) 'A Resource-Based View of the Firm', *Strategic Management Journal*, Vol. 5, No. 2, April–June, pp. 171–180.

Wernerfelt, B. and Montgomery, C. (1988) 'Tobin's Q and the importance of focus in firm performance', *American Economic Review*, 78(1), pp. 246–250.

Williamson, O.E. (1975) *Markets and Hierarchies*, New York: Free Press.

Williamson, O.E. (1985) *The Economic Institutions of Capitalisms*, New York: Free Press.

Williamson, O.E. (1991) 'Strategizing, economizing, and economic organization', *Strategic Management Journal*, Winter, Special Issue, 12, pp. 75–94.

Womack, J., Jones, D. and Roos, D. (1991) *The Machine that Changed the World*, New York: Harper-Perennial.

Zander, U. and Kogut, B. (1995) 'Knowledge and the speed of the transfer and imitation of organizational capabilities: An empirical test', *Organization Science*, 6(1), pp. 76–92.

5

CORPORATE LEVEL STRATEGY

We are not all capable of everything.
Virgil (70–19 BC); Roman philosopher

INTRODUCTION

As firms seek growth, they have a number of directions in which they can expand. The most direct source of increased revenue is to enlarge their market share, selling more of their current product offerings in their current market segments. Besides this growth through focused market penetration, firms can also broaden their scope by extending their product range (product development) or move into neighbouring market segments and geographic areas (market development). All of these growth options can be pursued while staying within the 'boundaries' of a single business (see Figure 5.1). However, firms can broaden their scope even further, venturing into other lines of business, thus becoming multi-business corporations. Some multi-business firms are involved in only two or three businesses, but there are numerous corporations spanning 20, 30, or more, business areas.

This chapter deals with the specific strategic questions facing firms as they work on determining their multi-business scope. At this level, strategists must not only consider how to gain a competitive advantage in each line of business the firm has entered, but also which businesses they should be in at all. Corporate level strategy is about selecting an optimal set of businesses and determining how they should be integrated into the corporate whole. This issue of deciding on the best array of businesses and relating them to one another is referred to as the issue of 'corporate configuration'.

THE ISSUE OF CORPORATE CONFIGURATION

All multi-business firms have a particular configuration, either intentionally designed or as the result of emergent formation. Determining the configuration of a corporation can be disentangled into two main questions: (a) What businesses should the corporation be active in? and (b) How should this group of businesses be managed? This first question of deciding on the business areas that will be covered by the company is called the topic of 'corporate composition'. The second question, of deciding on the organizational system necessary to run the cluster of businesses, is labelled as the issue of 'corporate management'. In the following pages both questions will be explored in more detail.

Corporate composition

A multi-business firm is composed of two or more businesses. When a corporation enters yet another line of business, either by starting up new activities (internal growth) or by

FIGURE 5.1 Corporate growth directions

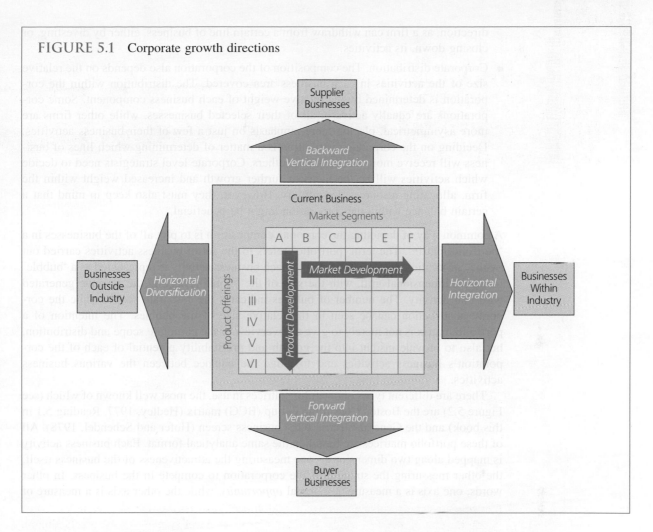

buying another firm (acquisition), this is called diversification. There are two general categories of diversification moves, vertical and horizontal. Vertical diversification, usually called vertical integration, is when a firm enters other businesses upstream or downstream within its own industry column (see Chapter 4) – it can strive for backward integration by getting involved in supplier businesses or it can initiate forward integration by entering the businesses of its buyers. The firm can also integrate related businesses at the same tier in the industry column – an example of such horizontal integration is when a newspaper and magazine publisher moves into educational publishing. If a firm expands outside of its current industry, the term 'integration' is no longer employed, and the step is referred to as straightforward (horizontal) diversification (see Figure 5.1).

The issue of corporate composition deals with the question of where the firm wants to have which level of involvement. Corporate level strategists must decide where to allocate resources, build up activities and try to achieve market sales. The issue of corporate composition can be further subdivided into two parts:

■ Corporate scope. First, the composition of the corporation depends on the business areas selected. The more 'business components' chosen, the broader the scope of the corporation. Deciding on the corporate scope is not only a matter of choosing from the diversification options depicted in Figure 5.1, but can also work in the opposite direction, as a firm can withdraw from a certain line of business, either by divesting, or closing down, its activities.

■ Corporate distribution. The composition of the corporation also depends on the relative size of the activities in each business area covered. The distribution within the corporation is determined by the relative weight of each business component. Some corporations are equally active in all of their selected businesses, while other firms are more asymmetrical, placing more emphasis on just a few of their business activities. Deciding on the corporate distribution is a matter of determining which lines of business will receive more attention than others. Corporate level strategists need to decide which activities will be the focus of further growth and increased weight within the firm, allocating resources accordingly. However, they must also keep in mind that a certain balance within the corporation might be beneficial.

A common way of depicting the corporate composition is to plot all of the businesses in a 'portfolio matrix'. The term 'portfolio' refers to the set of business activities carried out by the corporation. In a portfolio matrix each business activity is represented as a 'bubble' in a two-dimensional grid, with the size of the bubble reflecting the revenue generated with that activity. The number of bubbles indicates the corporate scope, while the corporate distribution can be seen in the relative size of the bubbles. The intention of a portfolio matrix is not merely to give an overview of the corporate scope and distribution, but also to provide insight into the growth and profitability potential of each of the corporation's business activities and to judge the balance between the various business activities.

There are different types of portfolio matrices in use, the most well known of which (see Figure 5.2) are the Boston Consulting Group (BCG) matrix (Hedley, 1977, Reading 5.1 in this book) and the General Electric (GE) business screen (Hofer and Schendel, 1978). All of these portfolio matrices are based on the same analytical format. Each business activity is mapped along two dimensions – one measuring the attractiveness of the business itself, the other measuring the strength of the corporation to compete in the business. In other words, one axis is a measure of external *opportunity,* while the other axis is a measure of

FIGURE 5.2   The BCG matrix and GE business screen

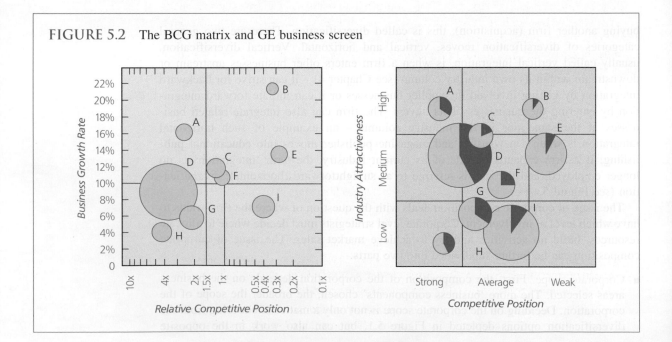

internal *strength* in comparison to rival firms. The major difference between the portfolio matrices is which measures are used along the axes. The BCG matrix employs two simple variables: business growth to determine attractiveness and relative market share to reflect competitive strength. The GE business screen, on the other hand, uses composite measures: both industry attractiveness and competitive position are determined by analysing and weighing a number of different factors. Industry attractiveness will be impacted by such variables as sales growth, demand cyclicality, buyer power, supplier power, the threat of new entrants, the threat of substitutes and competitive intensity. Competitive position often reflects such factors as market share, technological know-how, brand image, customer loyalty, cost structure and distinctive competences. Another difference between the two matrices is that in the BCG portfolio grid the bubbles represent the company's sales in a line of business, while in the GE business screen the bubbles reflect the total business size, with the pie slices indicating the firm's share of the business.

Deciding which portfolio of businesses to pursue, both in terms of corporate scope and corporate distribution, will depend on how the corporate strategist intends to create value – or as Porter (1987) puts it, how the corporate strategist wants to make 'the corporate whole add up to more than the sum of its business unit parts'. After all, there must be some benefit to having the various business activities together in one corporation, otherwise each business activity could just as easily (and with less overhead) be carried out by autonomous firms. This added value of having two or more business activities under one corporate umbrella is called 'multi-business synergy' and it strongly determines the corporate composition the strategist will prefer. But before turning to the topic of synergy, the counterpart of corporate composition, namely corporate management, needs to be reviewed first.

Corporate management

It has become a widespread policy to organize multi-business firms into strategic business units (SBUs). This organizational structure is often referred to as the M-form (Williamson, 1975). Each strategic business unit is given the responsibility to serve the particular demands of one business area. The business units are labelled 'strategic', because each is driven by its own business level strategy.

This dominant approach to structuring multi-business firms does present managers with the issue of how to bring together the separate parts into a cohesive corporate whole. The corporation can be divided into business units with the intent of focusing each on separate business areas, but this *differentiation* must be offset by a certain degree of *integration* to be able to address common issues and realize synergies (Lawrence and Lorsch, 1967). The challenge for managers is to find the most effective and efficient forms of integration between two or more separate business units. Three key integration mechanisms can be distinguished:

- Centralization. The most straightforward form of integration is to bring resources and activities physically together into one organizational unit. In other words, where the 'division of labour' between the business units has not been applied, resources and activities will be kept together in one department. Such a centralized department can be situated at the corporate centre, but can also reside at one of the business units or at another location.

- Coordination. Even where resources, activities and product offerings have been split along business unit lines, integration can be achieved by ensuring that coordination is carried out between business units. Such orchestration of work across business unit boundaries should result in the ability to operate as if the various parts were actually one unit.

- Standardization. Integration can also be realized by standardizing resources, activities and/or product offering characteristics across business unit boundaries. By having

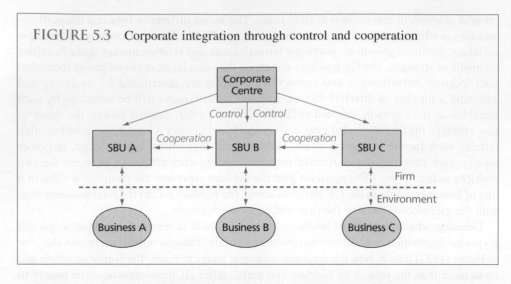

FIGURE 5.3   Corporate integration through control and cooperation

similar resources (e.g. technologies, people), standardized activities (e.g. R&D, human resource management) and common product features (e.g. operating systems, high-tech positioning) such advantages as economies of scale and rapid competence development can be achieved without the need to physically centralize or continuously coordinate.

These three integration mechanisms are the tools available to managers to achieve a certain level of harmonization between the various parts of the corporate whole. Yet often the question is, who should take the initiative to realize integration – where in the management system is the responsibility vested to ensure that centralization, coordination and standardization are considered and carried out? If all business unit managers are looking after their own backyard, who is taking care of the joint issues and cross-business synergies? Basically there are two organizational means available to secure the effective deployment of the integration mechanisms (see Figure 5.3):

■ Control. A straightforward way to manage activities that cross the boundaries of an individual business unit is to give someone the formal power to enforce centralization, coordination and standardization. Such a division level or corporate level manager can exert control in many ways. It can be by direct supervision (telling business units what to do), but often it is indirect, by giving business units objectives that must be met and discussing initiatives. The formal authority to secure integration does not always have to be given to a manager at the corporate centre, but can be assigned to a manager within one of the business units as well. There are also various levels of authority that can be defined, ranging from full final decision-making power to 'coordinator' or 'liaison officer', who have only limited formal means at their disposal.

■ Cooperation. Centralization, coordination and standardization between business units can also be achieved without the use of hierarchical authority. Business units might be willing to cooperate because it is in their interest to do so, or because they recognize the overall corporate interests. If business units believe in the importance of certain joint activities, this can be a powerful impetus to collaborate. Corporate strategists interested in such integration by mutual adjustment will focus on creating the organizational circumstances under which such self-organization can take place (See Chapter 11 for a further discussion). For instance, they might strengthen formal and informal ties between the business units in order to enhance mutual understanding and encourage the exchange of ideas and joint initiatives. They may also support cross-business career paths and try to instil a corporation-wide culture, to facilitate the communication between business units (Eisenhardt and Galunic, 2000).

It is the task of the corporate level strategist to determine the mix of control and cooperation needed to manage the corporation. In their seminal research, Goold and Campbell (1987) distinguish three general corporate control styles, each emphasizing different levels of centralization, coordination and standardization:

- **Financial control style.** In the financial control style the strategic business units are highly autonomous from the corporate centre. Few activities are centralized or standardized (except for the financial reporting system) and the corporate centre does not explicitly attempt to coordinate activities across business unit boundaries. Control is exerted by negotiating, setting and monitoring financial objectives.

- **Strategic control style.** In the strategic control style the strategic business units have a closer relationship with the corporate centre. A number of central services exist, some systems and activities are standardized and the corporate centre explicitly tries to coordinate activities that reach beyond the boundaries of only one business unit. Control is exerted by negotiating, setting and monitoring strategic objectives.

- **Strategic planning style.** In the strategic planning style the strategic business units have relatively little autonomy from the corporate centre. Many key activities are centralized or standardized, and the corporate centre is also heavily involved in securing cross-business coordination. Control is exerted by means of direct supervision.

Which corporate management style is adopted depends strongly on what the corporate strategist wishes to achieve. The preferred corporate management style will be determined by the type of multi-business synergies that the corporate strategist envisages, but also on the level of autonomy that the business units require. On the one hand, strategists will want to encourage integration to reap the benefits of having various business units together under one corporate roof and will therefore have a strong motivation to exert strong corporate centre control and stimulate inter-business cooperation. On the other hand, strategists will be wary of heavy-handed head office intervention, blunt centralization, rigid standardization, paralysing coordination meetings and excessive overhead. Recognizing that the business units need to be highly responsive to the specific demands of their own business area, corporate strategists will also be inclined to give business units the freedom to manoeuvre and to emphasize their own entrepreneurship. Yet, these two demands on the corporate level strategy – *multi-business synergy* and *business responsiveness* – are to a certain extent at odds with one another. How corporate strategists deal with the tension created by these conflicting demands will be examined more closely in the following section.

THE PARADOX OF RESPONSIVENESS AND SYNERGY

None ever got ahead of me except the man of one task.
Azariah Rossi (1513–1578); Italian physician

When Cor Boonstra took over as CEO of Philips Electronics in 1996, after a long career at the fast-moving consumer goods company Sara Lee, one of his first remarks to the business press was that Philips reminded him of 'a plate of spaghetti' – the company's more than 60 business units were intertwined in many different ways, sharing technologies, facilities, sales forces and customers, leading to excessive complexity, abundant bureaucracy, turf wars and a lack of accountability. To Boonstra the pursuit of multi-business synergy had spiralled into an overkill of centralization, coordination and standardization, requiring direct rectification. Thus Boonstra set out to restructure Philips into, in his own words, 'a plate of asparagus', with business units neatly lined up, one next to the other. Over a period of five years he disposed of numerous business units and made sure that the others were independent enough 'to hold up their own pants'. The result was a loss of some valuable synergies, but a significant increase in the business units' responsiveness to the demands in their own business. Then, in 2001, Boonstra handed over the reigns to a Philips insider, Gerard Kleisterlee, who during one of his first media encounters as new CEO stated that the business units within Philips had become too insular and narrowly focused, thereby missing opportunities to capture important synergies. Therefore, he indicated that it would be his priority to get Philips to work more like a team.

What this example of Philips illustrates is that corporate level strategists constantly struggle with the balance between realizing synergies and defending business unit responsiveness. To achieve synergies, a firm must to some extent integrate the activities carried out in its various business units. The autonomy of the business units must be partially limited, in the interest of concerted action. However, integration comes with a price tag. An extra level of management is often required, more meetings, extra complexity, potential conflicts of interest, additional bureaucracy. Harmonization of operations costs money and diminishes a business unit's ability to precisely tailor its strategy to its specific business environment. Hence, for the corporate strategist the challenge is to realize more *value creation* through multi-business synergies than *value destruction* through the loss of business responsiveness (e.g. Campbell, Goold and Alexander, 1995; Prahalad and Doz, 1987).

This tension arising from the partially conflicting demands of business responsiveness and multi-business synergy is called the paradox of responsiveness and synergy. In the following subsections both sides of the paradox will be examined in more detail.

The demand for multi-business synergy

Diversification into new business areas can only be economically justified if it leads to value creation. According to Porter (1987) entering into another business (by acquisition or internal growth) can only result in increased shareholder value if three essential tests are passed:

- The attractiveness test. The business 'must be structurally attractive, or capable of being made attractive'. In other words, firms should only enter businesses where there is a possibility to build up a profitable competitive position (see Chapter 4). Each new business area must be judged in terms of its competitive forces and the opportunities available to the firm to sustain a competitive business model.

- The cost-of-entry test. 'The cost of entry must not capitalize all the future profits.' In other words, firms should only enter new businesses if it is possible to recoup the investments made. This is important for internally generated new business ventures, but even more so for external acquisitions. Many researchers argue that, on average, firms significantly overpay for acquisitions, making it next to impossible to compensate for the value given away during the purchase (e.g. Sirower, 1997).

- The better-off test. 'Either the new unit must gain competitive advantage from its link with the corporation or vice versa.' In other words, firms should only enter new businesses if it is possible to create significant synergies. If not, then the new unit would be better off as an independent firm or with a different parent company, and should be cut loose from the corporation.

It is this last test that reveals one of the key demands of corporate level strategy. Multi-business level firms need to be more than the sum of their parts. They need to create more added value than the extra costs of managing a more complex organization. They need to identify opportunities for synergy between business areas and manage the organization in such a way that the synergies can be realized.

But what are the sources of synergy? For quite some time, strategists have known that potential for synergy has something to do with 'relatedness' (Rumelt, 1974). Diversification moves that were unrelated (or 'conglomerate'), for example a food company's entrance into the bicycle rental business, were deemed to be less profitable, in general, than moves that were related (or 'concentric'), such as a car-maker's diversification into the car rental business (e.g. Chatterjee, 1986; Rumelt, 1982). However, the problem has been to determine the nature of 'relatedness'. Superficial signs of relatedness do not indicate that there is potential for synergy. Drilling for oil and copper mining might seem highly related (both are 'extraction businesses'), but Shell found out the hard way that they were not related, selling the acquired mining company Billiton to Gencor after they were unable to create synergy. Chemicals and pharmaceuticals seem like similar businesses (especially if pharmaceuticals are labelled 'specialty chemicals'), but ICI decided to split itself in two (into ICI and Zeneca), because it could not achieve sufficient synergy between these two business areas.

Strategy researchers have therefore attempted to pin down the exact nature of relatedness (e.g. Prahalad and Bettis, 1986; Ramanujam and Varadarajan, 1989). Following the business model framework outlined in Chapter 4, the areas of relatedness that have the potential for creating synergy can be organized into three categories (see Figure 5.4): resource relatedness, product offering relatedness and activity relatedness.

Synergy by leveraging resources. The first area of relatedness is at the level of the businesses' resource bases. Two or more businesses are related if their resources can be productively shared between them. In principle, all types of resources can be shared, both the tangible and the intangible, although in practice some resources are easier to share

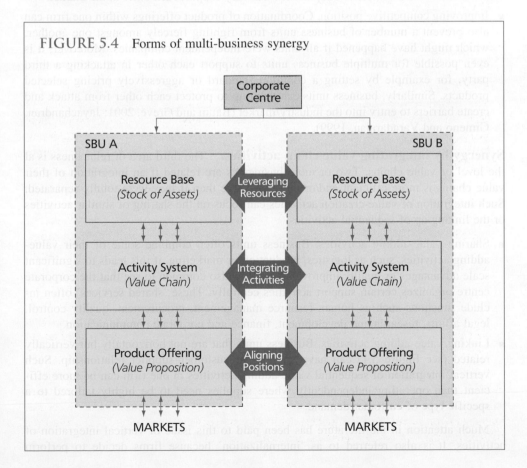

FIGURE 5.4 Forms of multi-business synergy

than others – for example, it is easier to transfer money than knowledge. Such 'resource leveraging' (Hamel and Prahalad, 1993) can be achieved by physically reallocating resources from one business area to another, or by replicating them so they can be used in a variety of businesses simultaneously:

- Achieving resource reallocation. Instead of leaving firm resources in the business unit where they happen to be located, a corporation can create synergy by transferring resources to other business units, where better use can be made of them (Helfat and Eisenhardt, 2004). For instance, money and personnel are often shifted between business units, depending on where they are needed and the potential return is highest.

- Achieving resource replication. While physical resources can only be used in one place at a time, intangible resources can often be copied from one business unit to another, so that the same resource can be used many times over. This happens, for example, when knowledge and capabilities are copied and reused in other business units.

Synergy by aligning positions. A second area of relatedness is at the level of product offerings. Two or more businesses are related if they can help each other by aligning their positioning in the market. Such coordination between product–market combinations can both improve the businesses' bargaining position vis-a-vis buyers, as well as improve the businesses' competitive position vis-a-vis rival firms:

- Improving bargaining position. Business units can improve their bargaining power vis-a-vis buyers by offering a broad package of related products or services to specific customer groups. Especially when the products being offered are complementary, share a common brand and have a comparable reputation, will they support each other in the market.

- Improving competitive position. Coordination of product offerings within one firm can also prevent a number of business units from fighting fiercely amongst one another, which might have happened if all units were independent companies. Moreover, it is even possible for multiple business units to support each other in attacking a third party, for example by setting a common standard or aggressively pricing selected products. Similarly, business units can team up to protect each other from attack and create barriers to entry into the industry/market (Baum and Greve, 2001; Jayachandran, Gimeno and Varadarajan, 1999).

Synergy by integrating value chain activities. The third area of relatedness is at the level of value chains. Two or more businesses are related if an integration of their value chains is more efficient and/or more effective than if they were totally separated. Such integration of value-creation activities can focus on the sharing of similar activities or the linking up of sequential activities:

- Sharing value-adding activities. Business units often combine some of their value-adding activities, such as logistics, production or marketing, if this leads to significant scale advantages or quality improvements. It is also common to see that the corporate centre organizes certain support activities centrally. These 'shared services' often include functions such as human resource management, procurement, quality control, legal affairs, research and development, finance and corporate communication.

- Linking value-adding activities. Business units that are not horizontally but vertically related (see Figure 5.1) can have an internal customer–supplier relationship. Such vertical integration of sequential value-adding activities in one firm can be more efficient than operating independently where supplies need to be highly tailored to a specific type of customer demand.

Much attention in the literature has been paid to this issue of vertical integration of activities. It is also referred to as 'internalization' because firms decide to perform activities inside the firm, instead of dealing with outside suppliers and buyers. In general, companies will strive to integrate upstream or downstream activities where one or more of the following conditions are deemed important (e.g. Harrigan 1985; Mahoney, 1992):

- Operational coordination. It can be necessary for various parts of the value system to be tightly coordinated or even physically integrated, to ensure that the right components, meeting the right specifications, are available in the right quantities, at the right moment, so that high quality, low cost or timely delivery can be achieved. To realize this level of coordination it can be necessary to gain control over a number of key activities in the value system, instead of trying to get suppliers and buyers to cooperate.

- Avoidance of transaction costs. Reaching a deal with a supplier or buyer and transferring the goods or services to the required location may be accompanied by significant direct costs. These contracting costs can include the expenses of negotiations, drawing up a contract, financial transfers, packaging, distribution and insurance. Add to these the search costs required to locate and analyse potential new suppliers or buyers, as well as the policing costs, which are incurred to check whether the contract is being met according to expectations and to take actions against those parties not living up to their contractual responsibilities. If a firm vertically integrates, many of these costs can be avoided, leading to potential savings (Williamson, 1975).

- Increased bargaining power. If a firm is facing a supplier or buyer with a disproportionately high level of bargaining power (for instance, a monopolist), vertical integration can be used to weaken or neutralize such a party. By fully or partially performing the activities inhouse, the firm can lessen its dependence on a strong buyer or supplier. The firm can also strive to acquire the other party, to avoid the bargaining situation altogether.

- Learning curve advantages. Where vertically linked business units work closely together, exchanging knowledge and personnel, they might also learn more quickly and more efficiently than if the business units were independent. Especially where they initiate joint R&D projects and collaborate on business process improvement efforts then significant learning curve advantages can be realized.

- Implementing system-wide changes. Besides continual operational coordination and ongoing learning, there may be a need to coordinate strategic changes throughout the value system. Switching over to new technologies, new production methods and new standards can sometimes only be implemented if there is commitment and a concerted effort in various parts of the value system. Sometimes even neighbouring value systems need to be involved in the changes. Vertical integration and horizontal diversification can give a firm the formal control needed to push through such changes.

Corporate level strategy is about determining the corporate configuration that offers the best opportunities for synergy, and implementing a corporate management system capable of realizing the intended synergies. However, what types of synergies can realistically be achieved without paying a heavier penalty in terms of integration costs? Recognizing the possible benefits of bringing together various businesses under one corporate umbrella is one thing, but developing a corporate management system that does not cost more than it yields is another. Therefore, corporate strategists need to carefully consider the potential downside of resource leveraging, activity integration and position alignment – the loss of business responsiveness.

The demand for business responsiveness

Responsiveness is defined as the ability to respond to the competitive demands of a specific business area in a timely and adequate manner. A business unit is responsive if it has the capability to tightly match its strategic behaviour to the competitive dynamics in its business. If a business unit does not focus its strategy on the conditions in its direct environment and does not organize its value-adding activities and management systems to fit with the business characteristics, it will soon be at a competitive disadvantage compared to more responsive rivals. Business responsiveness is therefore a key demand for successful corporate level strategy.

Yet, in multi-business firms the responsiveness of the business units is constantly under pressure. Various scope disadvantages limit the ability of the corporation to ensure business responsiveness. The major problems encountered by multi-business firms are the following:

- High governance costs. Coordinating activities within a firm requires managers. Layers of management, and the bureaucratic processes that might entail, can lead to escalating costs.

- Slower decision-making. Business units must usually deal with more layers of management, more meetings for coordination purposes, more participants in meetings, more conflicts of interest and more political infighting. This not only increases governance costs, but also slows down decision-making and action.

- Strategy incongruence. The resource leveraging, activity integration and position alignment envisioned in the corporate strategy can be more suited to the conditions in some businesses than to others. Consequently, some business units might need to compromise, adapting their business strategy to fit with the corporate strategy. However, such internal adaptation might lead to a misfit with the business demands.

- Dysfunctional control. The corporate centre might not have the specific business know-how needed to judge business unit strategies, activities and results. However, the corporate centre might feel the need to exert some control over business units, potentially steering them in an inappropriate direction.

- Dulled incentives. Limited autonomy combined with the aforementioned problems can have a significant negative impact on the motivation to perform optimally. This dulled incentive to be entrepreneurial and to excel can be compounded by poorly delineated responsibilities, a lack of clear accountability and the existence of 'captive' internal customers. Together, these factors limit the business units' drive to be responsive.

These threats make clear that multi-business firms must determine their composition and management systems in a way that enables business units to be responsive. Yet, simultaneously, corporate strategists need to strive towards the identification and realization of synergies. The question is how these two conflicting demands can be reconciled – how can corporate level strategists deal with the paradox of responsiveness and synergy?

EXHIBIT 5.1   SHORT CASE

HYUNDAI MOTOR GROUP: DRIVING APART TOGETHER?

Steel, automobiles, construction, finances, logistics, hotels, machine parts and marketing. All of these are businesses in which the Hyundai Motor Group (HMG) is active. HMG's core philosophy is that it aims to provide innovative products able to create a better future for humanity. In other words: it can be

involved in any business it pleases. This has been the way in which Hyundai was formed, and still how HMG approaches industries today. Although old habits die hard, it by no means guarantees that this can be maintained in the upcoming years.

The South Korean economy started to pick up in the 1960s in what was later called the 'miracle on the Han river', characterized by industrialization, better education, an increase in living standards and technological advancement. South Korea's developmental state model was formed principally during the authoritarian regime of Park Chung-hee, the controversial president who seized power in 1961. In order to expand the export of South Korea, his government decided to pursue cooperation with corporations. This helped *chaebol* come into existence: giant Korean financial conglomerates ran by powerful families. Hyundai became one of them.

Yet, this bright future was not apparent when the company was founded in 1947, with the poor Ju-yung Chung establishing a small construction firm. Profiting from the government's drive to rebuild the country in the wake of the Second World War (1939–1945) and the Korean War (1950–1953), his Hyundai Civil Works Company grew at a rapid pace. Chung had the luck to be at the right place at the perfect time, yet fortune does not necessarily have to happen accidentally; it can also be enforced. He actively extorted his luck by entering infant industries, which is how he got involved in manufacturing and selling automobiles.

After establishing the Hyundai Motor Company (HMC) in 1967, Hyundai started with the production of cars. The newly founded company helped out Ford with car manufacturing, and after nine years Hyundai launched its own car: the Hyundai Pony, the first ever mass-produced Korean passenger automobile. This model mostly comprised of parts from overseas partners and Hyundai was still more of an automotive assembler, but there were big plans for the company's future. These were not necessarily Hyundai's however: it was the South Korean government that wanted to drastically improve the domestic automotive industry from the early 1970s onwards. The government allowed three companies to mass produce cars: Hyundai, Daewoo and Kia. In addition, it issued high protectionist tariff barriers to protect the infant industry, on the condition that the car manufacturers would utilize as many locally produced car parts as possible. Chung had hit the mark again.

Chung accumulated an assortment of companies that could benefit from one another, with the steel business functioning as Hyundai's core. For example, he secured a multitude of companies concerned with manufacturing steel, developing of auto parts and producing ships. Chung also entered seemingly unconnected industries by expanding into commercial-banking activities, chemicals, life-insurance businesses and electronics, thus diversifying the portfolio of his company intensely. This expansionist attitude seemed to work well though: what started as a small construction firm eventually became South Korea's biggest *chaebol*. In the mid-1990s, Hyundai had 60 subsidiary companies, comprising 200,000 employees, with total annual revenues of approximately US$ 90 billion. Yet, Chung's luck did not last forever.

His success started to crumble after the 1997 Asian Financial Crisis. At first this did not seem to impact Hyundai that much. While its *chaebol* competitors LG and Samsung backed down and reorganized, Chung continued to expand. He dropped some assets that did not add much to the corporation, but his takeovers were much more abundant: he acquired Kia Motors and 60 per cent of chip-maker LG Semicon. He did so under the premise that the government would save the *chaebols* in case things would get out of hand, as South Korea could not afford such a loss. Chung guessed wrong.

Early in the crisis, five major *chaebols* went bankrupt, while only a few of the largest 30 conglomerates were seen as financially stable. The impact was devastating; several thousands of Koreans lost their source of income. With the South Korean government recording a deficit of US$ 8.7 billion and being in desperate need of a financial bailout, the International Monetary Fund gained the power to act. It decided that South Korea grew too dependent on *chaebols* and put pressure on its government, which in turn forced the family conglomerates to restructure and focus more on their core businesses. Hyundai, with debts of no less than US$ 10.5 billion and which also had to cope with the death of Chung, was not spared. Since Hyundai had multiple core businesses, it was divided into a multitude of companies with the Hyundai name but without an actual corporate connection to a group. While Chung's empire crumbled, not all was lost.

Chung had played the game well. He had positioned relatives in top positions throughout his conglomerate, yet even though his offspring and other family members were fighting for the lucrative parts of the former *chaebol*. The group still lived on, albeit in a disconnected way. The multiple Hyundai companies moved into more businesses and became shareholders of each other, forming complex structures. In this way, even with minority shareholdings the Chung family generally maintained control.

This is illustrated by Hyundai Motor Group, holding company for many of the Hyundai businesses. Hyundai Motor Company, *de facto* representative of the group, possesses some 34 per cent of Kia Motors, which holds 17 per cent of parts supplier Hyundai Mobis. In turn, Mobis owns approximately 21 per cent of HMC. Similar structures are found in the connections between HMG's other subsidiaries, such as finance, logistics and railways. Thanks to good relations with the vast network of the diverse Hyundai businesses and with shares in Hyundai Motor Company and Mobis, Mong-koo Chung, chairman and CEO of HMC and son of the late Ju-yung Chung, retains control of the Motor Group.

Yet, the holding company is not necessarily built to last. The many Hyundai affiliates are not autonomous companies but depend on each other with cross-shareholding and family-based relationships, while integrating compatible resources and activities is a real challenge with minority shareholdings. Hyundai Motor Company may capture synergies with affiliated steel companies and car parts manufacturers by boasting close relationships and leveraging activities, however these may not justify integrating the corporation.

The alternatives are contradictory though. If Chung decided to take apart the current structure of the Hyundai Motor Group and reorganize it into a vertical structure of parent and subsidiaries, this would not only cost approximately US$ 9.6 billion according to research conducted in 2012, but would also result in HMG becoming a true *chaebol* all over again. This would contradict with South Korea's contemporary politics, which are particularly concerned with curtailing the power of family conglomerates. Keeping HMG as it is now is risky as well, since cross-shareholdings are also perceived as a problem in South Korea's political discourse. With the third generation of Chung management dawning, it is imperative that HMG does not suffer the same fate as Hyundai did in the early 2000s.

Should Mong-koo Chung pick one of the alternative routes, or act upon the company's promise: new thinking, new possibilities? Whatever his choice, he will be aware of the situation that Hyundai Motor Group is not driven by only one motor.

Co-author: Wester Wagenaar

Sources: www.fastretailing.com; www.uniqlo.com; *Business Week*, 6 January 2011; *CNN*, 4 February 2008; *Financial Times*, 15 July 2012 and 7 February 2013; *Forbes*, 5 October 2012 and 22 October 2012; *Forrester*, 25 March 2013; *The New York Times*, 22 May 2012; *The Wall Street Journal*, 23 August 2012.

PERSPECTIVES ON CORPORATE LEVEL STRATEGY

We must indeed all hang together, or, most assuredly, we shall all hang separately.

Benjamin Franklin (1706–1790); American politician, inventor and scientist

Corporations need to capture multi-business synergies and they need to ensure each business unit's responsiveness to its competitive environment. In other words, corporations need to be integrated and differentiated at the same time – emphasizing the *whole* and respecting the *part*. Striving towards synergy is a centripetal force, pulling the firm together into an integrated whole, while being responsive to business demands is a centrifugal force, pulling the firm apart into autonomous market-focused units (Ghoshal and Mintzberg, 1994). The main question dividing strategists is whether a corporation should primarily be a collection of parts or an integrated whole. Should corporations be loose federations of business units or tightly knit teams? Should corporations be business groups made up of distinctive parts, where only modest synergies can be realized and business units should be accorded a large measure of leeway to be responsive to their specific market conditions? Or should corporations actually be unitary organizations, with the parts serving the whole, allowing for significant synergies to be achieved, with the challenge of being responsive enough to varied business demands?

As before, the strategic management literature comes with strongly different views on how strategists should proceed. Here the two diametrically opposed positions will be identified and discussed to show the richness of differing opinions. On the one side of the spectrum, there are those strategists who believe that multi-business firms should be viewed as portfolios of autonomous business units in which the corporation has a financial stake. They argue that business responsiveness is crucial and that only a limited set of financial synergies should be pursued. This point of view is referred to as the 'portfolio organization perspective'. At the other end of the spectrum, there are strategists who believe that corporations should be tightly integrated, with a strong central core of shared resources, activities and/or product offerings keeping the firm together. They argue that corporations built up around these strong synergy opportunities can create significantly more value than is lost through limitations to responsiveness. This point of view is referred to as the 'integrated organization perspective'.

The portfolio organization perspective

 In the portfolio organization perspective, responsiveness is strongly emphasized over synergy. Managers taking this perspective usually argue that each business has its own unique characteristics and demands. Firms operating in different businesses must therefore develop a specific strategy for each business and assign the responsibility for each business strategy to a separate strategic business unit. In this manner, the (strategic) business units can be highly responsive to the competitive dynamics in the business, while being a clear unit of accountability towards the corporate centre. High responsiveness, however, requires freedom from corporate centre interference and freedom from cross-business coordination. Hence, a high level of business unit autonomy is required, with the corporate centre's influence limited to arm's length financial control.

In the portfolio organization perspective, the main reason for a number of highly autonomous business units to be in one firm is to leverage financial resources. The only synergies emphasized are financial synergies (e.g. Lubatkin and Chatterjee, 1994; Trautwein, 1990). Actually, the term 'portfolio' entered the business vocabulary via the financial sector, where it refers to an investor's collection of shareholdings in different companies, purchased to spread investment risks. Transferred to corporate strategy, the portfolio organization perspective views the corporate centre as an active investor with financial stakes in a number of stand-alone business units. The role of the centre is one of selecting a promising portfolio of businesses, keeping tight financial control, and allocating available capital – redirecting flows of cash from business units where prospects are dim ('cash cows' or 'dogs'), to other business units where higher returns can be expected ('stars' or 'question marks'). The strategic objective of each business unit is, therefore, also financial in orientation – grow, hold, milk or divest, depending on the business unit's position on the portfolio grid (e.g. Henderson, 1979; Hedley, 1977). A good corporate strategy strives for a balanced portfolio of mature cash producers and high potential ROI cash users, at an acceptable level of overall risk.

The financial synergies can be gained in a number of different ways (e.g. Chatterjee, 1986; Weston, Chung and Hoag, 1990). First, by having various businesses within one firm, the corporate centre can economize on external financing. By internally shifting funds from one business unit to another, the corporation can avoid the transaction costs and taxation associated with external capital markets. Second, the corporation can limit dependence on the whims of external capital providers, who might be less inclined to finance some ventures (e.g. new businesses or high risk turnarounds) at acceptable levels of capital cost. Third, where the corporation does want to secure external financing, the firm's larger size, debt capacity and creditworthiness can improve its bargaining position

As corporate level strategists 'lead from the centre' (Raynor and Bower, 2001) and develop a joint competitive strategy together with business level strategists, they must make very clear which multi-business synergies they intend to foster as the nucleus of the corporation. It is their task to determine what the core of the organization should be and to take the lead in building it. To be successful, it is necessary for them to work closely together with business level managers, whose main task it is to apply the core strengths of the corporation to their specific business area. The consequence of this joint strategy development and synergy realization is that all business units are highly interdependent, requiring continual coordination.

Many different multi-business synergies can form the core of the corporation. In the strategic management literature one specific form has received a large amount of attention – the *core competence* centred corporation (Prahalad and Hamel, 1990, Reading 5.2 in this book). In such an organization a few competences are at the heart of the corporation and are leveraged across various business units. Prahalad and Hamel's metaphor for the corporation is not an investor's portfolio, but a large tree: 'the trunk and major limbs are core products, the smaller branches are business units, the leaves, flowers and fruit are end products; the root system that provides nourishment, sustenance and stability is the core competence.' Business unit branches can be cut off and new ones can grow on, but all spring from the same tree. It is the corporate centre's role to nurture this tree, building up the core competences and ensuring that the firm's competence carriers can easily be redeployed across business unit boundaries. The strategic logic behind leveraging these intangible resources is that high investments in competence development can then be spread over a number of different businesses. Moreover, by using these competences in different business settings they can be further refined, leading to a virtuous circle of rapid learning, profiting the entire corporation. In line with the arguments of the inside-out perspective (see Chapter 4), it is pointed out that in the long run inter-firm rivalries are often won by the corporation who has been able to upgrade its competences fastest – battles in particular markets are only skirmishes in this broader war. From this angle, building the corporation's core competences is strategic, while engaging other corporations in specific business areas is tactical. The corporate centre is therefore at the forefront of competitive strategy, instead of the business units, that are literally divisions in the overall campaign (e.g. Kono, 1999; Stalk, Evans and Schulman, 1992).

As all business units should both tap into, and contribute to, the corporation's core competences, the business units' autonomy is necessarily limited. Unavoidably, the responsiveness to the specific characteristics of each business does suffer from this emphasis on coordination. Yet, to advocates of the core competence model, the loss of business responsiveness is more than compensated for by the strategic benefits gained.

Besides competences as the core of the corporation, other synergies can also be at the heart of a multi-business firm. For instance, corporations can focus on aligning a variety of product offerings for a group of 'core customers'. Many professional service firms, such as PricewaterhouseCoopers and Capgemini, are involved in a broad range of businesses, with the intention of offering an integrated package of services to their selected market segments. Another type of core is where a multi-business firm is built around shared activities. Many of the large airlines, for example, have one 'core process', flying planes, but operate in the very different businesses of passenger travel and cargo transport. Yet another central synergy can be the leveraging of the firm's 'software'. For instance, Disney is such a 'core content' corporation, letting Cinderella work hard selling Disney videos, luring families to Disney theme parks, getting kids to buy Disney merchandise and enticing people to watch the Disney Channel. Whichever synergy is placed centre stage, to the proponents of the integrated organization perspective it should not be trivial, as such minor value-creation efforts do not provide the driving motivation to keep a corporation together. The 'glue' of the corporation must be strong enough to convince all involved that they are much better off as part of the whole than on their own.

The flip side of having a tightly knit group of businesses arranged around a common core is that growth through acquisition is generally much more difficult than in the 'plug and play' set-up of a portfolio organization. To make an acquisition fit into the corporate family and to establish all of the necessary links to let the new recruits profit from, and contribute to, the core synergies, can be very challenging. Taking the previous metaphor a step further, the corporate centre will find it quite difficult to graft oak roots and elm branches on to an existing olive tree. Consequently, acquisitions will be infrequent, as the firm will prefer internal growth.

EXHIBIT 5.3   THE INTEGRATED ORGANIZATION PERSPECTIVE

THE NEW EMPEROR IN MEDIA: FOCUSED BUT NOT SMALL

The way tycoons lead their media empires is starting to change drastically. Whereas the generation of Rupert Murdoch has mainly been after wielding influence and power, their successors take a less flamboyant approach. They trade in "fruit and flower expenses", a well known metaphor in some businesses for, in the words of News Corp CEO Robert Thomson, "*relentless*" cost-cutting. The shift in mindset can be observed in two main areas: increased focus on the core business and creating benefits from scale.

To effectively focus on their core business, media tycoons are shedding their non-core assets. Albeit lagging behind the same trend in other industries, this development is greatly appreciated by investors. In 2013 three major spin-offs occurred. The largest involved Rupert Murdoch's News Corporation splitting its profitable TV and film business from the declining newspaper business. This was a much-contested decision, as it was the latter with which Murdoch had built his media empire. Equally painful decisions had to be made by Time Warner, spinning off its magazine unit and Tribune divesting its newspaper business.

The main rationale behind this focus is the increasingly popular notion, held by external constituents, that TV networks, newspapers, film studios and the music business have very little benefit from sharing a parent. Some even argue that their success can be hindered by their proximity as a result of distracting management. As a result most media empires have decided to divest the shrinking publishing business, and either focus on other more promising markets or devote more attention to their main brand. Whatever the reason, the new way of thinking is very different from what we used to see in the media business.

In addition to shedding non-core assets, a second trend in the media business is to benefit from being very large – which happens to be something quite characteristic of the media industry. In 2009, it made up over two-thirds of the S&P 500 index' value, which comes down to about $200 billion in assets. News Corp, Viacom, Disney and Time Warner deliver double the average S&P return of 6.1 per cent, with the exception of a number of years in which alternative content providers such as Netflix were feared to disrupt the pay TV business model. Combining the ever-growing scale with the newfound desire to focus activities have led to Time Warner having 80 per cent of its revenues coming from cable TV in 2013, as opposed to just 23 per cent in 2008. Viacom has made a comparable leap, leading to 90 per cent of their revenue coming from this source. This allowed both players to benefit greatly from increased efficiencies and strategic clarity.

Not everyone thinks pleasing the investors by becoming more integrated is the right way forward. Comcast bought NBCUniversal and Disney recently acquired Lucasfilm, which increasingly diversified their activities. Who made the right decision can only be speculated about, but the success of firms providing an alternative business model to deliver content, like Netflix and Hulu, might be a detrimental factor. For firms relying on cable TV for a predominant portion of their revenues, lack of diversification might become a liability when a real alternative to pay TV is offered.

Whatever the future might look like, investors are thrilled by the new mindset and subsequent actions. Jeff Bewkes, CEO of Time Warner, states:

Time Inc. will benefit from the flexibility and focus of being a stand-alone public company and will now be able to attract a more natural stockholder base.

In addition, he mentioned that being involved in less categories provided both him and the outside world with greater strategic clarity. Although possibly difficult to accept for those who have built their fortunes in the old fashioned media, the industry will start to focus on its profitable businesses, while leaving behind the less performing counterparts. Whether consolidation is a stroke of genius or a fatal mistake can only be told in hindsight. For now, soaring share prices, continuous growth and happy shareholders make sure the end of this trend is not soon in sight.

Co-author: Jasper de Vries

Sources: 'Time Warner to Offload Magazine Unit in Third Major Spin-off', Bloomberg, March 7, 2013; 'News Corp. Spin-off Forces Publishing Arm to Prove Growth', Bloomberg, June 29, 2013; 'Tribune to Spin Off Newspaper Business', Bloomberg, July 10, 2013; 'Breaking up is not so very hard to do', *The Economist,* June 22, 2013.

MANAGING THE PARADOX OF RESPONSIVENESS AND SYNERGY

Consider the little mouse, how sagacious an animal it is which never entrusts its life to one hole only.
Plautus (254–184 BC); Roman playwright

So, how should the corporate configuration be determined? Should corporate strategists limit themselves to achieving financial synergies, leaving SBU managers to 'mind their own business'? Or should corporate strategists strive to build a multi-business firm around a common core, intricately weaving all business units into a highly integrated whole? As before, the strategic management literature does not offer a clear-cut answer to the question of which corporate level strategies are the most successful (see Table 5.1).

In the management field, a number of options have been put forward on how to manage the opposing demands of responsiveness and synergy. Taking the taxonomy in Chapter 1 the following options are at the strategist's disposal:

Navigating

The common means of managing the paradox of multi-business synergy and business responsiveness is to focus on one demand at a time. Strategists in large firms are often involved in contrary company-wide initiatives. One such initiative aims at strengthening the corporation's advantage of having more than one business unit. Managers at corporate, division and business unit levels, are brought together in groupings to finding potential synergies within the firm. The initiatives usually have an *ad-hoc* character, with more or less defined end dates, and jazzy names such as 'One Firm' and 'All For One'. The initiatives may include capturing and strengthening the firm's core competences, sharing value chain activities such as establishing a shared services centre, and leadership training.

Capturing multi-business synergies usually goes at the expense of reduced market responsiveness. As a result the next corporate initiative will focus on the opposite side of the paradox: improving market responsiveness. Marked with flashy labels such as 'Client First' and 'Agility', strategizing managers need to find avenues to enhance speed and client orientation in the firm's markets. Examples of such initiatives are visiting key clients to find product improvements, reducing overhead and, again, leadership training.

TABLE 5.1   Portfolio organization versus integrated organization perspective

	Portfolio organization perspective	*Integrated organization perspective*
Emphasis on	Responsiveness over synergy	Synergy over responsiveness
Conception of corporation	Collection of business shareholdings	Common core with business applications
Corporate composition	Potentially unrelated (diverse)	Tightly related (focused)
Key success factor	Business unit responsiveness	Multi-business synergy
Focal type of synergy	Cash flow optimization and risk balance	Integrating resources, activities and positions
Corporate management style	Exerting financial control	Joint strategy development
Primary task corporate centre	Capital allocation and performance control	Setting direction and managing synergies
Position of business units	Highly autonomous (independent)	Highly integrated (interdependent)
Coordination between BUs	Low, incidental	High, structural
Growth through acquisitions	Simple to accommodate	Difficult to integrate

After finishing this *ad-hoc* project, the strategizing managers will navigate the firm capturing corporate synergies by 'tacking' to the next initiative.

Balancing

After having navigated the firm to accumulated multi-business synergies or enhanced business responsiveness, the strategists have to manage the new equilibrium. During the phase 'in-between corporate initiatives' managers have to continue balancing demands for multi-business synergies and business responsiveness. As the paradox will never be resolved, strategizing managers are destined to permanently deal will with the tension.

Resolving

While dealing with the opposing demand for multi-business synergy and business responsiveness, strategizing managers notice several frictions within the firm. Most common is the friction between corporate strategists, such as the Executive Board members, and business unit leaders. A key factor in the game between corporate strategists, who are expected to capture synergies, and business unit managers with the main aim to strengthen the business' competitive position, is the firm's reward and compensation scheme. For example, when salaries, bonuses and promotion are related to one demand only, measured by the business unit's revenue and profit, many strategizing managers will not bother too much with corporate level initiatives. This issue is well understood, and so rewards and compensation schemes often include stimuli to capturing corporate synergies.

By managing the tension, opportunities to combine the best-of-both often come across. For example, many firms have discovered the advantages of client relationship software (CRM), which not only has the potential to strengthen the firm's client relationship (at the business unit level) but also to reveal growth options for other business units. Such opportunities often manifest during a company-wide initiative to capture multi-business synergy.

The tension between multi-business synergy and business responsiveness has resulted in arguably the most effective means to combining advantages of synergy and responsiveness: the franchise. While being regarded as a modern organizational form, the franchise is by no means new. The history goes back to the 1840s when German ale brewers granted rights to a selected number of taverns to market their beer. The first person recognized as a franchiser with actual franchise contracts was Albert Singer, an American. This 'business model innovator' started distributing his Singer sewing machines across a large geographic area. The franchise became especially popular in the 'restaurant' business, with Kentucky Fried Chicken in 1930, Dunkin Donuts in 1950, Burger King in 1954 and McDonald's in 1955. Currently there are franchise formulas in many industries, including hotels, manpower companies and retail.

The most well-known franchise, McDonald's, explicates the franchise formula's strength: being close to the market while capturing synergies. McDonald's provides their franchisees with, for example, a strong brand, purchasing power, training (a Hamburger University), restaurant lay-out designs and corporate-wide values (would "Ich Bin Ein Hamburger" be an idea?). Franchisees are close to their local or niche customers with some room to adapt, and while being agile to respond they capitalize on the corporate synergies.

CORPORATE LEVEL STRATEGY IN INTERNATIONAL PERSPECTIVE

Co-author: Gep Eisenloeffel

The key to growth is the introduction of higher dimensions of consciousness into our awareness
Lao Tse (604–507 BC); Chinese philosopher and founder of Taoism

In the strategy field scarce attention has been paid to international differences in multi-business level strategies. Despite the high media profile of major corporations from different countries and despite researchers' fascination with large companies, little comparative research has been done. Yet, it does not seem unlikely that corporate strategy practices and preferences vary across national boundaries. Casual observation of the major corporations around the globe quickly shows that one cannot easily divide the world into portfolio-oriented and integration-oriented countries.

In order to discuss to what extent international differences in corporate strategy perspectives exist, several factors will be put forward that might be of influence on how the paradox of responsiveness and synergy is managed in different countries. It should be noted, however, that these propositions must be viewed as tentative explanations, intended to encourage further discussion and research.

A company's heritage

The importance of a company's heritage can be illustrated by the development of European multinational firms from countries with a colonial history. In the first half of the twentieth century companies like Anglo-Dutch Shell (Yergin, 2011) and Unilever (Fieldhouse, 1978) exploited the natural wealth and market opportunities in their home countries' colonies to the full. Access and control over its own crude oil, as in the case of Shell, or over its palm oil, as in the case of Unilever, resulted in vertical integration of all elements of the supply chain for both companies. Bartlett and Ghoshal (2003) described how after 'expanding their activities in the 1920s and 1930s in a period of rising tariffs and discriminatory legislation, the typical European company was forced to build local production facilities to compete effectively with local competitors. With their own plants, national subsidiaries were able to modify products and demands to meet widely different local market needs. The resulting organizational pattern was a loose federation of independent national subsidiaries, each focused primarily on its local market.'

The situation for European companies *lacking* this sort of outlet was entirely different. Germany, for instance, did not have colonies that could absorb a huge influx of capital. As a result German banks invested in promising new enterprises in their home country. Deutsche Bank for instance, founded in 1870 to facilitate foreign trade and investments, was involved in founding steel conglomerate Krupp and chemical giant Bayer. Today, it still holds a more than 25 per cent stock in car manufacturing power house Daimler Benz. In as early as 1910, were these strong ties between national financial institutions and industrial companies coined *Das Finanzkapital* (Finance Capital) by Austrian born economist and former German Finance Minister, Rudolf Hilferding.

A comparable heritage is visible in what is referred to as the *keiretsu* structure in Japan, consisting of horizontal (or financial) *keiretsu* and vertical (or industrial) *keiretsu* (Miyashita and Russell, 1995). The horizontal *keiretsu* is set up around a Japanese bank. This bank supports its affiliated companies with numerous financial services. The leading, "Big Six", financial *keiretsu* are: Fuyo, Sanwa, Sumitomo, Mitsubishi, Mitsui and Dai-Ichi Kangyo bank groups. Vertical *keiretsu* are linked through ownership of long-term equity and production activities, to suppliers, manufacturers and distributors of one industry. A vertical organizational model is further created to benefit the parent company. This model is divided into different tiers. The second tier constitutes major suppliers, followed by smaller manufacturers, who make up the third and fourth tiers. Bartlett and Ghoshal (2003) describe that Japanese *keiretsu* 'with limited prior overseas exposure chose not to match the well-established local marketing capacities and facilities of their European and US competitors. Indeed, well established Japanese trading companies often provided an easier means of entering foreign markets. A centrally controlled, export-based internalization strategy presented a perfect fit with the external environment and the company's competitive capabilities.' The *keiretsu* model was hit hard by the Japanese recession of the 1990s. Bad loan portfolios forced banks to merge or go out of business. Sumitomo Bank and Mitsui Bank, for instance, became Sumitomo Mitsui Banking Corporation in 2001, while Sanwa Bank became part of Bank of Tokyo-Mitsubishi UFJ. As a result, the *keiretsu* are not as integrated as they were in the era before the 1990s and major companies are no longer easily "bailed out" by their banks.

Although the *keiretsu* corporate model is unique for Japan, there are similarities with South Korean *chaebol* (Steers, Shin and Ungson, 1991). *Chaebol* are giant financial conglomerates run by powerful families, supported by the South Korean government to expand export. The leading South Korean *chaebol* such as the Samsung Group, the LG group and the Hyundai Motor group, expanded their activities in all sorts of businesses.

Keiretsu and *chaebol* are family conglomerates based on strong family ties, hierarchy and loyalty between members of the family or inner circle, characteristics that are found in many Asian countries such as China, India, Indonesia, Malaysia and Thailand. For example, Astra is Indonesia's largest diversified conglomerate and leading in the country's automotive sector. Family conglomerates operating as key players in their respective economies are also dominant in other countries such as Turkey and Mexico. Turkies Haci Ömer Sabanci, for instance, with more than 68 subsidiaries in a variety of industrial sectors like energy, automotive and textiles, is Turkey's second largest holding company. Vitro from Mexico, founded in 1909 and one of the world's leading manufacturers of glass, is another example of such a family conglomerate. In family conglomerates usually 'one person, generally the oldest male head of the family or company, has the final say in any decision that has to be made' (Verluyten, 2000). In Indonesia this is referred to as *Babakism* derived from the word *Bakak,* meaning *father* in the Indonesian language.

Corporate expansion of US firms overseas followed a different trajectory. Some companies, such as United Fruit Company – currently known as Chiquita Brands

International, exploited the US political support for their activities in Latin America. Others, for example Ford, Singer and Gilette, capitalized on their 'advancements in technology that outpaced the growth of the world economy' (Porter, 1986). Internationalization of US companies really took off in the post Second World War (1939–1945) era. US companies not only produced superior products; their production methods were also far more advanced and set a world standard. As Bartlett and Ghoshal (2003) indicate 'reinforcing this strategy, the management approach in most US-based companies was built on a willingness to delegate responsibility, while retaining overall control through sophisticated management systems and specialist corporate staff.' Bartlett and Ghoshal argue that the possible downside of this model is that parent company management often adopted a parochial or even superior attitude towards international operations, coined by Perlmutter (2003) as 'an ethnocentric or home-country approach'.

Functioning of capital and labour markets

One of the arguments levelled against the portfolio organization perspective is that there is no need for corporations that merely act as investors. With efficiently operating capital markets, investing should be left to 'real' investors. Stock markets are an excellent place for investors to spread their risks and for growing firms to raise capital. Start-up companies with viable plans can easily find venture capitalists to assist them. All these capital providers can perform the task of financial control – portfolio-oriented corporations have nothing else to add but overhead costs. Add to this the argument that large corporations no longer have an advantage in terms of professional management skills. While in the past, large firms could add value to smaller units by injecting more sophisticated managers, flexible labour markets now allow small firms to attract the same talent themselves.

Even if this general line of argumentation is true, the extent to which capital and labour markets are 'efficient' varies widely across countries. Porter (1987), an outspoken detractor of the portfolio organization perspective, acknowledges that 'in developing countries, where large companies are few, capital markets are undeveloped and professional management is scarce, portfolio management still works'. However, he quickly adds that portfolio thinking 'is no longer a valid model for corporate strategy in advanced economies'. But are capital and labour markets equally efficient across all so-called advanced economies? Few observers would argue that venture capital markets in Asia and Europe work as well as in the United States, and the terms under which large corporations can raise capital on these continents are usually far better than for smaller companies. Neither does holding shares of a company through the stock markets of Asia and Europe give investors as much influence over the company as in the United States. In short, even in the group of developed economies, various gradations of capital market efficiency seem to exist, suggesting varying degrees to which corporations can create value by adopting the role of investors.

The same argument can be put forward for the efficiency of 'managerial labour' markets. Even if Porter is right when stating that smaller companies can attract excellent professional managers through flexible labour markets, this conclusion is not equally true across advanced economies. Lifetime employment might be a declining phenomenon in most of these countries, but not to the same extent. Job-hopping between larger and smaller companies is far more common in the United States than in many European and Asian countries (e.g., Calori and De Woot, 1994). In many advanced economies large corporations still command a more sophisticated core of professional managers through superior recruiting and training practices, higher compensation and status, and greater perceived career opportunities and job security. Hence, even within this group of countries, different degrees of labour market flexibility exist, suggesting that corporations in some countries might be able to create more value as developers and allocators of management talent than in other countries.

Leveraging of relational resources

With the portfolio organization perspective favouring the leveraging of financial resources and the integrated organization perspective often focusing on the leveraging of competence, the leveraging of relational resources is a topic receiving far less attention within the field of strategic management. It is widely acknowledged that 'umbrella' brands can often be stretched to include more product categories and that the corporation's reputation can commonly be employed to the business units' benefit. However, in the areas of political science and industrial organization, much more attention has been paid to the corporation as leverager of contacts and power. In many circumstances knowing the right people, being able to bring parties together, being able to force compliance and having the power to influence government regulations, are essential aspects of doing business. Often, either by their sheer size or by their involvement in many businesses, corporations will have more clout and essential contacts than can be mustered by individual businesses.

Here the international differences come in. As put forward in Chapter 4, in some countries relational resources are more important than in others. Influence over government policy-making, contacts with the bureaucrats applying the rules, power over local authorities and institutions, connections with the ruling elite, access to informal networks of companies – the importance of these factors differ from country to country. Therefore, it stands to reason that the clustering of businesses around key external relationships and power bases will vary strongly across nations. In some countries 'core contacts' centred corporations are more likely to be encountered than in others.

Costs of coordination

Coordination comes at a cost, it is argued. Individual business units usually have to participate in all types of corporate systems, file reports, ask permission, attend meetings and adapt their strategy to fit with the corporate profile. This can result in time delays, lack of fit with the market, less entrepreneurial action, lack of accountability and a low morale. On top of this, business units have to pay a part of corporate overhead as well. The benefits of coordination should be higher than these costs.

This argument might be suffering from a cultural bias, as it assumes that individuals and businesses are not naturally inclined to coordinate. However, control by the corporate centre and cooperation with other business units is not universally viewed as a negative curtailment of individual autonomy. In many countries coordination is not an unfortunate fact of life, but a natural state of affairs. Coordination within the corporate whole is often welcomed as motivating, as opposed to de-motivating, especially in cultures that are more group-oriented (Hofstede, 1993, Reading 1.3 in this book). If the common form of organization in a country resembles a clan, coordination might not be as difficult and costly as it is in other nations. Therefore, on the basis of this argument, it is reasonable to expect a stronger preference for the portfolio perspective in countries that favour mechanistic organizations.

Preference for control

The last point of international difference ties into the discussion of the next chapter. If the essence of corporate strategy is about realizing synergies between businesses, is it not possible for these businesses to coordinate with one another and achieve synergies without being a part of the same corporation? In other words, is it necessary to be owned and controlled by the same parent in order to leverage resources, integrate activities and align product offerings? Or could individual businesses band together and work as if they were one company – acting as a 'virtual corporation'?

In Chapter 6 it is argued that there are significant international differences on this account. In some countries there is a strong preference to have hierarchical control over two businesses that need to be coordinated. In other countries there is a preference for businesses to use various forms of cooperation to achieve synergies with other businesses, while retaining the flexibility of independent ownership. Preference for control, it will be argued, depends on how managers deal with the paradox of competition and cooperation.

INTRODUCTION TO THE READINGS

To help strategists to come to grips with the variety of perspectives on this issue, three readings have been selected that each shed their own light on the debate. As in previous chapters, the first two readings will be representative of the two poles in this debate (see Table 5.1), while the third reading will bring extra arguments into the discussion.

To open the debate on behalf of the portfolio organization perspective, Barry Hedley's article 'Strategy and the Business Portfolio' has been selected as Reading 5.1. Hedley was an early proponent of the portfolio perspective, together with other consultants from the Boston Consulting Group (BCG), such as Bruce Henderson (1979). In this article, he explains the strategic principles underlying the famed growth–share grid that is commonly known as the BCG matrix. His argument is based on the premise that a complex corporation can be viewed as a portfolio of businesses, which each have their own competitive arena to which they must be responsive. By disaggregating a corporation into its business unit components, separate strategies can be devised for each. The overarching role of the corporate level can then be defined as that of portfolio manager. The major task of the corporate headquarters is to manage the allocation of scarce financial resources over the business units, to achieve the highest returns at an acceptable level of risk. Each business unit can be given a strategic mission to grow, hold or milk, depending on their prospects compared to the businesses in the corporate portfolio. This is where portfolio analysis comes in. Hedley argues that the profit and growth potential of each business unit depends on two key variables: the growth rate of the total business and the relative market share of the business unit within its business. When these two variables are put together in a grid, this forms the BCG matrix. For the discussion in this chapter, the precise details of the BCG portfolio technique are less relevant than the basic corporate strategy perspective that Hedley advocates – running the multi-business firm as a hands-on investor.

Selecting a representative for the integrated organization perspective for Reading 5.2 was a simple choice. In 1990, the late C.K. Prahalad and Gary Hamel published an article in *Harvard Business Review* with the title 'The Core Competence of the Corporation'. This article has had a profound impact on the debate surrounding the topic of corporate level strategy, and has inspired a considerable amount of research and writing investigating resource-based synergies. In this article Hamel and Prahalad (1994) explicitly dismiss the portfolio organization perspective as a viable approach to corporate strategy. Prahalad and Hamel acknowledge that diversified corporations have a portfolio of businesses, but they do not believe that this implies the need for a portfolio organization approach in which the business units are highly autonomous. In their view, 'the primacy of the SBU – an organizational dogma for a generation – is now clearly an anachronism'. Drawing mainly on Japanese examples, they carry on to argue that corporations should be built around a core of shared competences. Business units should use and help to further develop these core competences. The consequence is that the role of corporate level management is much more far-reaching than in the portfolio organization perspective. The corporate centre must 'establish objectives for competence building' and must ensure that this 'strategic architecture' is carried through.

The third reading is 'Seeking Synergies' by Andrew Campbell and Michael Goold. These researchers from the Ashridge Strategic Management Centre have been responsible for a constant stream of insightful work on corporate level strategy. One of their publications has been the book *Synergy: Why Links Between Business Units Often Fail and How to Make Them Work,* from which this is the summary chapter. This reading has been selected for this chapter in order to pay more attention to the issue of realizing synergies. As a large part of the debate revolves around different views on whether synergies can actually be captured or not, it is valuable to get some more input on approaches to synergy creation and a better insight into 'synergy killers'. Campbell and Goold give a structured and practical framework for analysing a corporation's synergy opportunities and synergy approach, followed by an analysis of the most important policies and characteristics that systematically inhibit attempts at reaping synergy advantages. In the context of this debate, it is important to note that Campbell and Goold do not necessarily side with either of the two perspectives. In their view, there are different styles of corporate strategy and different levels of synergy that can be achieved, as long as the 'parent company' develops the matching parenting capabilities and synergy parenting approach.

READING

5.1

Strategy and the business portfolio

By Barry Hedley[1]

All except the smallest and simplest companies comprise more than one business. Even when a company operates within a single broad business area, analysis normally reveals that it is, in practice, involved in a number of product–market segments which are distinct economically. These must be considered separately for purposes of strategy development.

The fundamental determinant of strategy success for each individual business segment is relative competitive position. As a result of the experience curve effect the competitor with high market share in the segment relative to competition should be able to develop the lowest cost position and hence the highest and most stable profits. This will be true regardless of changes in the economic environment. Hence relative competitive position in the appropriately defined business segment forms a simple but sound strategic goal. Almost invariably, any company which reviews its various businesses carefully in this light will discover that they occupy widely differing relative competitive positions. Some businesses will be competitively strong already, and may appear to present no strategic problem; others will be weak, and the company must face the question of whether it would be worthwhile to attempt to improve their position, making whatever investments might be required to achieve this; if this is not done, the company can only expect poor performance from the business and the best option economically will be divestment.

Even in quite small companies, the total number of possible combinations of individual business strategies can be extremely large. The difficulty of making a firm final choice on strategy for each business is normally compounded by the fact that most companies must operate within constraints established by limited resources, particularly cash resources.

The business portfolio concept

At its most basic, the importance of growth in shaping strategy choice is two-fold. First, the growth of a business is a major factor influencing the likely ease –

and hence cost – of gaining market share. In low-growth businesses, any market share gained will tend to require an actual volume reduction in competitors' sales. This will be very obvious to the competitors and they are likely to fight to prevent the throughput in their plants dropping. In high-growth businesses, on the other hand, market share can be gained steadily merely by securing the largest share of the growth in the business: expanding capacity earlier than the competitors, ensuring product availability and effective selling support despite the strains imposed by the *growth,* and so forth. Meanwhile competitors may even be unaware of their share loss because their actual volume of throughput has been well maintained. Even if aware of their loss of share, the competitors may be unconcerned by it given that their plants are still well loaded. This is particularly true of competitors who do not understand the strategic importance of market share for long term profitability resulting from the experience curve effect.

An unfortunate example of this is given by the history of the British motorcycle industry. British market share was allowed to erode in motorcycles worldwide for more than a decade, throughout which the British factories were still fairly full: British motorcycle production volumes held up at around 80,000 units per year throughout the sixties; in sharp contrast, Japanese export volumes leapt from only about 60,000 in 1960 to 2.5 million in 1973; their total production volumes roughly tripled in the same period. The long-term effect was that while Japanese real costs were falling rapidly, British costs were not: somewhat over-simplified, this is why the British motorcycle industry faced bankruptcy in the early seventies.

The second important factor concerning growth is the opportunity it provides for investment. Growth businesses provide the ideal vehicles for investment, for ploughing cash into a business in order to see it compound and return even larger amounts of cash at a later point in time. Of course this opportunity is also a need: the faster a business grows, the more investment it will require just to maintain market share. Yet the

---

[1]Source: This article was adapted from B. Hedley, 'Strategy and the Business Portfolio', *Long Range Planning,* February 1977, Vol. 10, No. 1, pp. 9–15, © 1977. With permission from Elsevier.

experience curve effect means that this is essential if its profitability is not to decline over time.

Whilst these growth considerations affect the rate at which a business will use cash, the relative competitive position of the business will determine the rate at which the business will generate cash: the stronger the company's position relative to its competitors, the higher its margins should be, as a result of the experience curve effect. The simplest measure of relative competitive position is, of course, relative market share. A company's relative market share in a business can be defined as its market share in the business divided by that of the largest other competitor. Thus only the biggest competitor has a relative market share greater than one. All the other competitors should enjoy lower profitability and cash generation than the leader.

The growth–share matrix

Individual businesses can have very different financial characteristics and face different strategic options depending on how they are placed in terms of growth and relative competitive position. Businesses can basically fall into any one of four broad strategic categories, as depicted schematically in the growth–share matrix in Figure 5.1.1.

■ Stars. High growth, high share – are in the upper left quadrant. Growing rapidly, they use large amounts of cash to maintain position. They are also leaders in the business, however, and should generate large amounts of cash. As a result, star businesses are frequently roughly in balance on net cash flow, and can be self-sustaining in growth terms. They represent probably the best profit growth and investment opportunities available to the company, and every effort should therefore be made to maintain and consolidate their competitive position. This will sometimes require heavy investment beyond their own generation capabilities and low margins may be essential at times to deter competition, but this is almost invariably worthwhile for the longer term: when the growth slows, as it ultimately does in all businesses, very large cash returns will be obtained if share has been maintained so that the business drops into the lower left quadrant of the matrix, becoming a cash cow. If star businesses fail to hold share, which frequently happens if the attempt is made to net large amounts of cash from them in the short and medium term (e.g. by cutting back on investment and raising prices, creating an 'umbrella' for competitors), they will ultimately become dogs (lower right quadrant). These are certain losers.

■ Cash cows. Low growth, high share – should have an entrenched superior market position and low costs. Hence profits and cash generation should be high, and because of the low growth reinvestment needs should be light. Thus large cash surpluses should be generated by these businesses. Cash cows pay the dividends and interest, provide the debt capacity, pay for the company overhead and provide

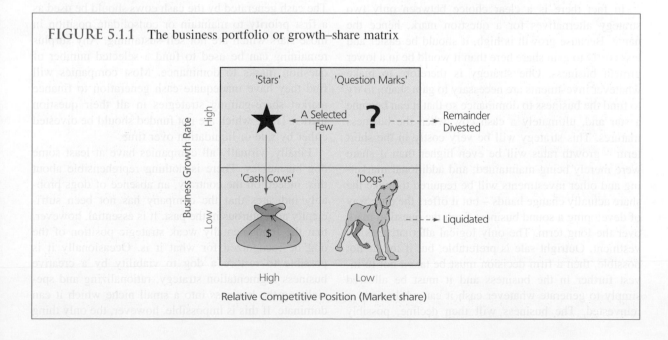

FIGURE 5.1.1 The business portfolio or growth–share matrix

the cash for investment elsewhere in the company's portfolio of businesses. They are the foundation on which the company rests.

- Dogs. Low growth, low share – represent a tremendous contrast. Their poor competitive position condemns them to poor profits. Because the growth is low, there is little potential for gaining sufficient share to achieve a viable cost position at anything approaching a reasonable cost. Unfortunately, the cash required for investment in the business just to maintain competitive position, though low, frequently exceeds that generated, especially under conditions of high inflation. The business therefore becomes a 'cash trap' likely to absorb cash perpetually unless further investment in the business is rigorously avoided. The colloquial term 'dog' describing these businesses, though undoubtedly pejorative, is thus rather apt. A company should take every precaution to minimize the proportion of its assets that remain in this category.

- Question marks. High growth, low share – have the worst cash characteristics of all. In the upper right quadrant, their cash needs are high because of their growth, but their cash generation is small because of their low share. If nothing is done to change its market share, the question mark will simply absorb large amounts of cash in the short term and later, as the growth slows, become a dog. Following this sort of strategy, the question mark is a cash loser throughout its existence. Managed this way, a question mark becomes the ultimate cash trap.

In fact there is a clear choice between only two strategy alternatives for a question mark, hence the name. Because growth is high, it should be easier and less costly to gain share here than it would be in a lower growth business. One strategy is therefore to make whatever investments are necessary to gain share, to try to fund the business to dominance so that it can become a star and, ultimately a cash cow when the business matures. This strategy will be very costly in the short term – growth rates will be even higher than if share were merely being maintained, and additional marketing and other investments will be required to make the share actually change hands – but it offers the only way of developing a sound business from the question mark over the long term. The only logical alternative is divestment. Outright sale is preferable; but if this is not possible, then a firm decision must be taken not to invest further in the business and it must be allowed simply to generate whatever cash it can while none is reinvested. The business will then decline, possibly

quite rapidly if market growth is high, and will have to be shut down at some point. But it will produce cash in the short term and this is greatly preferable to the error of sinking cash into it perpetually without improving its competitive position.

These then, are the four basic categories to which businesses can belong. Some companies tend to fit almost entirely into a single quadrant. General Motors and English China Clays are examples of predominantly cash cow companies. Chrysler, by comparison, is a dog which compounded its fundamental problem of low share in its domestic US market by acquiring further mature low share competitors in other countries (e.g. Rootes which became Chrysler UK). IBM in computers, Xerox in photocopiers, BSR in low cost record autochangers, are all examples of predominantly star businesses. Xerox's computer operation, XDS, was clearly a question mark, however, and it is not surprising that Xerox recently effectively gave it away free to Honeywell, and considered itself lucky to escape at that price! When RCA closed down its computer operation, it had to sustain a write-off of about $490m. Question marks are costly.

Portfolio strategy

Most companies have their portfolio of businesses scattered through all four quadrants of the matrix. It is possible to outline quite briefly and simply what the appropriate overall portfolio strategy for such a company should be. The first goal should be to maintain position in the cash cows, but to guard against the frequent temptation to reinvest in them excessively. The cash generated by the cash cows should be used as a first priority to maintain or consolidate position in those stars which are not self-sustaining. Any surplus remaining can be used to fund a selected number of question marks to dominance. Most companies will find they have inadequate cash generation to finance market share-gaining strategies in all their question marks. Those which are not funded should be divested either by sale or liquidation over time.

Finally, virtually all companies have at least some dog businesses. There is nothing reprehensible about this, indeed on the contrary, an absence of dogs probably indicates that the company has not been sufficiently adventurous in the past. It is essential, however, that the fundamentally weak strategic position of the dog be recognized for what it is. Occasionally it is possible to restore a dog to viability by a creative business segmentation strategy, rationalizing and specializing the business into a small niche which it can dominate. If this is impossible, however, the only thing which could rescue the dog would be an increase in share taking it to a position comparable to the leading competitors in the segment. This is likely to be unreasonably costly in a mature business, and therefore the only prospect for obtaining a return from a dog is to manage it for cash, cutting off all investment in the business. Management should be particularly wary of expensive 'turn around' plans developed for a dog if these do not involve a significant change in fundamental competitive position. Without this, the dog is a sure loser. An indictment of many corporate managements is not the fact that their companies have dogs in the portfolio, but rather that these dogs are not managed according to logical strategies. The decision to liquidate a business is usually even harder to take than that of entering a new business. It is essential, however, for the long-term vitality and performance of the company overall that it be prepared to do both as the need arises.

Thus the appropriate strategy for a multibusiness company involves striking a balance in the portfolio such that the cash generated by the cash cows, and by those question marks and dogs which are being liquidated, is sufficient to support the company's stars and to fund the selected question marks through to dominance. This pattern of strategies is indicated by the arrows in Figure 5.1.1. Understanding this pattern conceptually is, however, a far cry from being able to implement it in practice. What any company should do with its own specific businesses is of course a function of the precise shape of the company's portfolio, and the particular opportunities and problems it presents. But how can a clear picture of the company's portfolio be developed?

The matrix quantified

Based on careful analysis and research it is normally possible to divide a company into its various business segments appropriately defined for purposes of strategy development. Following this critical first step, it is usually relatively straightforward to determine the overall growth rate of each individual business (i.e. the growth of the market, not the growth of the company within the market), and the company's size (in terms of turnover or assets) and relative competitive position (market share) within the business.

Armed with these data it is possible to develop a precise overall picture of the company's portfolio of businesses graphically. This can greatly facilitate the identification and resolution of the key strategic issues facing the company. It is a particularly useful approach where companies are large, comprising many separate

businesses. Such complex portfolios often defy description in more conventional ways.

The nature of the graphical portfolio display is illustrated by the example in Figure 5.1.2. In this chart, growth rate and relative competitive position are plotted on continuous scales. Each circle in the display represents a single business or business segment, appropriately defined. To convey an impression of the relative significance of each business, size is indicated by the area of the circle, which can be made proportional to either turnover or assets employed. Relative competitive position is plotted on a logarithmic scale, in order to be consistent with the experience curve effect, which implies that profit margin or rate of cash generation differences between competitors will tend to be related to the ratio of their relative competitive positions (market shares). A linear axis is used for growth, for which the most generally useful measure is volume growth of the business concerned, as, in general, rates of cash use should be directly proportional to growth.

The lines dividing the portfolio into four quadrants are inevitably somewhat arbitrary. 'High growth', for example, is taken to include all businesses growing in excess of 10 per cent per annum in volume terms. Certainly, above this growth rate market share tends to become fairly fluid and can be made to change hands quite readily. In addition many companies have traditionally employed a figure of 10 per cent for their discount rate in times of low inflation, and so this also tends to be the growth rate above which investment in market share becomes particularly attractive financially.

The line separating areas of high and low relative competitive position is set at 1.5 times. Experience in using this display has been that in high-growth businesses relative strengths of this magnitude or greater are necessary in order to ensure a sufficiently dominant position that the business will have the characteristic of a star in practice. On the other hand, in low-growth businesses acceptable cash generation characteristics are occasionally, but not always, observed at relative strengths as low as 1 times; hence the addition of a second separating line at 1 times in the low growth area, to reflect this. These lines should, of course, be taken only as approximate guides in characterizing businesses in the portfolio as dogs and question marks, cash cows and stars. In actuality, businesses cover a smooth spectrum across both axes of the matrix. There is obviously no 'magic' which transforms a star into a cash cow as its growth declines from 10.5 to 9.5 per cent. It is undeniably useful, however, to have some device for broadly indicating where the transition points occur within the matrix, and the lines suggested

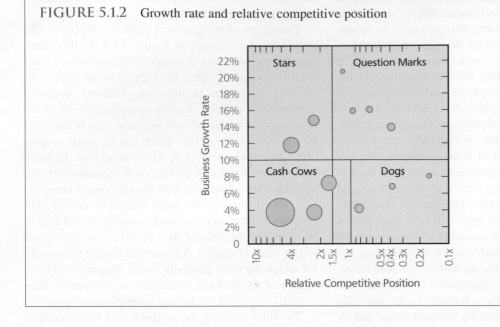

FIGURE 5.1.2   Growth rate and relative competitive position

here have worked well in practical applications of the matrix in a large number of companies.

Portfolio approaches in practice

The company shown in Figure 5.1.2 would be a good example of a potentially well-balanced portfolio. With a firm foundation in the form of two or three substantial cash cows, this company has some well-placed stars to provide growth and to yield high cash returns in the future when they mature. The company also has some question marks, at least two of which are probably sufficiently well placed that they offer a good chance of being funded into star positions at a reasonable cost, not out of proportion to the company's resources. The company is not without dogs, but properly managed there is no reason why these should be a drain on cash.

The sound portfolio, unsoundly managed

Companies with an attractive portfolio of this kind are not rare in practice. In fact Figure 5.1.2 is a disguised version of a representation of an actual UK company analysed in the course of a Boston Consulting Group assignment. What is much rarer, however, is to find that the company has made a clear assessment of the matrix positioning and appropriate strategy for each business in the portfolio.

Ideally, one would hope that the company in Figure 5.1.2 would develop strategy along the following lines. For the stars, the key objectives should be the maintenance of market share; current profitability should be accorded a lower priority. For the cash cows, however, current profitability may well be the primary goal. Dogs would not be expected to be as profitable as the cash cows, but would be expected to yield cash. Some question marks would be set objectives in terms of increased market share; others, where gaining dominance appeared too costly, would be managed instead for cash.

The essence of the portfolio approach is therefore that strategy objectives must vary between businesses. The strategy developed for each business must fit its own matrix position and the needs and capabilities of the company's overall portfolio of businesses. In practice, however, it is much more common to find all businesses within a company being operated with a common overall goal in mind. 'Our target in this company is to grow at 10 per cent per annum and achieve a return of 10 per cent on capital.' This type of overall target is then taken to apply to every business in the company. Cash cows beat the profit target easily, though they frequently miss on growth. Nevertheless, their managements are praised and they are normally rewarded by being allowed to plough back what only too frequently amounts to an excess of cash into their 'obviously attractive' businesses. Attractive businesses, yes: but not for growth investment. Dogs on the other hand rarely meet the profit target. But how often is it accepted that it is in fact unreasonable for them ever to hit the target? On the contrary, the most common strategic mistake is that major investments are made in dogs from time to time in hopeless attempts to turn the business around without actually shifting market share. Unfortunately, only too often question marks are regarded very much as dogs, and get insufficient investment funds ever to bring them to dominance. The question marks usually do receive some investment, however, possibly even enough to maintain share. This is throwing money away into a cash trap. These businesses should either receive enough support to enable them to achieve segment dominance, or none at all.

These are some of the strategic errors which are regularly committed even by companies which have basically sound portfolios. The result is a serious suboptimization of potential performance in which some businesses (e.g. cash cows) are not being called on to produce the full results of which they are actually capable, and resources are being mistakenly squandered on other businesses (dogs, question marks) in an attempt to make them achieve performance of which they are intrinsically incapable without a fundamental improvement in market share. Where mismanagement of this kind becomes positively dangerous, is when it is applied within the context of a basically unbalanced portfolio.

The unbalanced portfolio

The disguised example in Figure 5.1.3 is another actual company. This portfolio is seriously out of balance. As shown in Figure 5.1.3(a), the company has a very high proportion of question marks in its portfolio, and an inadequate base of cash cows. Yet at the time of investigation this company was in fact taking such cash as was being generated by its mature businesses and spreading it out amongst all the high-growth businesses, only one of which was actually receiving sufficient investment to enable it even to maintain share! Thus the overall relative competitive position of the portfolio was on average declining. At the same time, the balance in the portfolio was shifting: as shown in the projected portfolio in Figure 5.1.3(b), because of the higher relative growth of the question marks their overall weight in the portfolio was increasing, making them even harder to fund from the limited resources of the mature businesses.

If the company continued to follow the same strategy of spreading available funds between all the businesses, then the rate of decline could only increase over time leading ultimately to disaster.

This company was caught in a vicious circle of decline. To break out of the circle would require firm discipline and the strength of will to select only one or two of the question marks and finance those, whilst

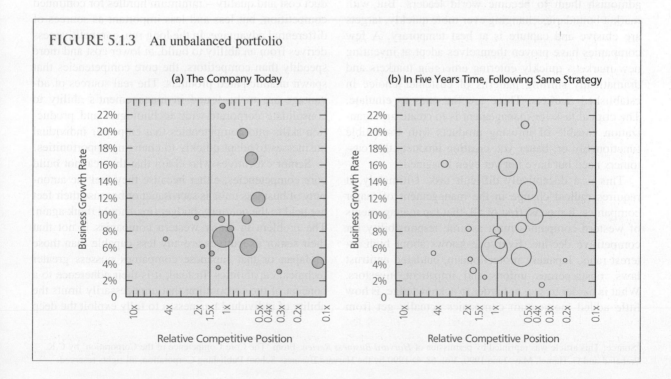

FIGURE 5.1.3   An unbalanced portfolio

(a) The Company Today

(b) In Five Years Time, Following Same Strategy

cutting off investment in the remainder. Obviously the choice of which should receive investment involves rather more than selection at random from the portfolio chart. It requires careful analysis of the actual nature of the businesses concerned and particularly the characteristics and behaviour of the competitors faced in those businesses. However, the nature of the strategic choice facing the company is quite clear, when viewed in portfolio terms. Without the clarity of view provided by the matrix display, which focuses on the real fundamentals of the businesses and their relationships to each other within the portfolio, it is impossible to develop strategy effectively in any multibusiness company.

The core competence of the corporation

By C.K. Prahalad and Gary Hamel[1]

The most powerful way to prevail in global competition is still invisible to many companies. During the 1980s, top executives were judged on their ability to restructure, declutter and delayer their corporations. In the 1990s, they'll be judged on their ability to identify, cultivate and exploit the core competencies that make growth possible – indeed, they'll have to rethink the concept of the corporation itself.

Rethinking the corporation

Once, the diversified corporation could simply point its business units at particular end-product markets and admonish them to become world leaders. But with market boundaries changing ever more quickly, targets are elusive and capture is at best temporary. A few companies have proven themselves adept at inventing new markets, quickly entering emerging markets and dramatically shifting patterns of customer choice in established markets. These are the ones to emulate. The critical task for management is to create an organization capable of infusing products with irresistible functionality or, better yet, creating products that customers need but have not yet even imagined.

This is a deceptively difficult task. Ultimately, it requires radical change in the management of major companies. It means, first of all, that top managements of western companies must assume responsibility for competitive decline. Everyone knows about high interest rates, Japanese protectionism, outdated antitrust laws, obstreperous unions and impatient investors. What is harder to see, or harder to acknowledge, is how little added momentum companies actually get from

political or macroeconomic 'relief'. Both the theory and practice of western management have created a drag on our forward motion. It is the principles of management that are in need of reform.

The roots of competitive advantage

In the short run, a company's competitiveness derives from the price/performance attributes of current products. But the survivors of the first wave of global competition, western and Japanese alike, are all converging on similar and formidable standards for product cost and quality – minimum hurdles for continued competition, but less and less important as sources of differential advantage. In the long run, competitiveness derives from an ability to build, at lower cost and more speedily than competitors, the core competencies that spawn unanticipated products. The real sources of advantage are to be found in management's ability to consolidate corporate-wide technologies and production skills into competencies that empower individual businesses to adapt quickly to changing opportunities.

Senior executives who claim that they cannot build core competencies, either because they feel the autonomy of business units is sacrosanct or because their feet are held to the quarterly budget fire, should think again. The problem in many western companies is not that their senior executives are any less capable than those in Japan or that Japanese companies possess greater technical capabilities. Instead, it is their adherence to a concept of the corporation that unnecessarily limits the ability of individual businesses to fully exploit the deep

[1]Source: This article was reprinted by permission of *Harvard Business Review.* From 'The Core Competence of the Corporation' by C.K. Prahalad and G. Hamel, May–June 1990, Vol. 68. © 1990 by the Harvard Business School Publishing Corporation, all rights reserved.

reservoir of technological capability that many American and European companies possess.

The diversified corporation is a large tree. The trunk and major limbs are core products, the smaller branches are business units; the leaves, flowers and fruit are end products. The root system that provides nourishment, sustenance and stability is the core competence. You can miss the strength of competitors by looking only at their end products, in the same way you miss the strength of a tree if you look only at its leaves (see Figure 5.2.1).

Core competencies are the collective learning in the organization, especially how to coordinate diverse production skills and integrate multiple streams of technologies. Consider Sony's capacity to miniaturize or Philips's optical-media expertise. The theoretical knowledge to put a radio on a chip does not in itself assure a company the skill to produce a miniature radio no bigger than a business card. To bring off this feat, Casio must harmonize know-how in miniaturization, microprocessor design, materials science and ultrathin precision casing – the same skills it applies in its miniature card calculators, pocket TVs and digital watches.

If core competence is about harmonizing streams of technology, it is also about the organization of work and the delivery of value. Among Sony's competencies is miniaturization. To bring miniaturization to its products, Sony must ensure that technologists, engineers and marketers have a shared understanding of customer needs and of technological possibilities. The force of core competence is felt as decisively in services as in manufacturing. Citicorp was ahead of others investing in an operating system that allowed it to participate in world markets 24 hours a day. Its competence in systems has provided the company with the means to differentiate itself from many financial service institutions.

Core competence is communication, involvement and a deep commitment to working across organizational boundaries. It involves many levels of people and all functions. World-class research in, for example, lasers or ceramics can take place in corporate laboratories without having an impact on any of the businesses of the company. The skills that together constitute core competence must coalesce around individuals whose efforts are not so narrowly focused that they cannot recognize the opportunities for blending their functional expertise with those of others in new and interesting ways.

Core competence does not diminish with use. Unlike physical assets, which do deteriorate over time, competencies are enhanced as they are applied and shared. But competencies still need to be nurtured and protected; knowledge fades if it is not used. Competencies are the glue that binds existing businesses. They are also the engine for new business development. Patterns of diversification and market entry may be guided by them, not just by the attractiveness of markets.

Consider 3M's competence with sticky tape. In dreaming up businesses as diverse as 'Post-it' note pads, magnetic tape, photographic film, pressure-sensitive tapes and coated abrasives, the company has brought to

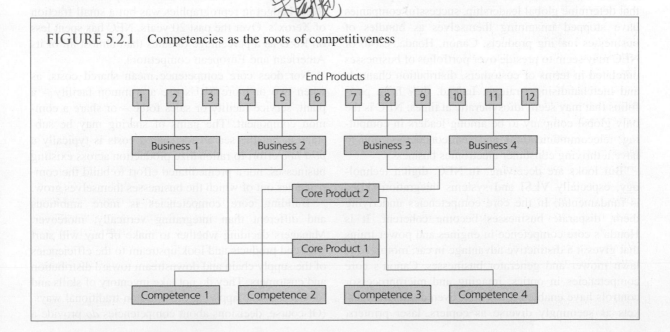

FIGURE 5.2.1   Competencies as the roots of competitiveness

bear widely shared competencies in substrates, coatings and adhesives, and devised various ways to combine them. Indeed, 3M has invested consistently in them. What seems to be an extremely diversified portfolio of businesses belies a few shared core competencies.

In contrast, there are major companies that have had the potential to build core competencies but failed to do so because top management was unable to conceive of the company as anything other than a collection of discrete businesses. General Electric sold much of its consumer electronics business to Thomson of France, arguing that it was becoming increasingly difficult to maintain its competitiveness in this sector. That was undoubtedly so, but it is ironic that it sold several key businesses to competitors who were already competence leaders – Black & Decker in small electrical motors, and Thomson, which was eager to build its competence in microelectronics and had learned from the Japanese that a position in consumer electronics was vital to this challenge.

Management trapped in the strategic business unit (SBU) mind-set almost inevitably finds its individual businesses dependent on external sources for critical components, such as motors or compressors. But these are not just components. They are core products that contribute to the competitiveness of a wide range of end products. They are the physical embodiments of core competencies.

How not to think of competence

Since companies are in a race to build the competencies that determine global leadership, successful companies have stopped imagining themselves as bundles of businesses making products. Canon, Honda, Casio or NEC may seem to preside over portfolios of businesses unrelated in terms of customers, distribution channels and merchandising strategy. Indeed, they have portfolios that may seem idiosyncratic at times: NEC is the only global company to be among leaders in computing, telecommunications and semiconductors, *and* to have a thriving consumer electronics business.

But looks are deceiving. In NEC, digital technology, especially VLSI and systems integration skills, is fundamental. In the core competencies underlying them, disparate businesses become coherent. It is Honda's core competence in engines and power trains that gives it a distinctive advantage in car, motorcycle, lawn mower and generator businesses. Canon's core competencies in optics, imaging and microprocessor controls have enabled it to enter, even dominate, markets as seemingly diverse as copiers, laser printers,

cameras and image scanners. Philips worked for more than 15 years to perfect its optical-media (laser disc) competence, as did JVC in building a leading position in video recording. Other examples of core competencies might include mechantronics (the ability to marry mechanical and electronic engineering), video displays, bioengineering and microelectronics. In the early stages of its competence building, Philips could not have imagined all the products that would be spawned by its optical-media competence, nor could JVC have anticipated miniature camcorders when it first began exploring videotape technologies.

Unlike the battle for global brand dominance, which is visible in the world's broadcast and print media and is aimed at building global 'share of mind', the battle to build world-class competencies is invisible to people who aren't deliberately looking for it. Top management often tracks the cost and quality of competitors' products, yet how many managers untangle the web of alliances their Japanese competitors have constructed to acquire competencies at low cost? In how many western boardrooms is there an explicit, shared understanding of the competencies the company must build for world leadership? Indeed, how many senior executives discuss the crucial distinction between competitive strategy at the level of a business and competitive strategy at the level of an entire company?

Let us be clear. Cultivating core competence does not mean outspending rivals on research and development. In 1983, when Canon surpassed Xerox in worldwide unit market share in the copier business, its R&D budget in reprographics was but a small fraction of Xerox's. Over the past 20 years, NEC has spent less on R&D as a percentage of sales than almost all of its American and European competitors.

Nor does core competence mean shared costs, as when two or more SBUs use a common facility – a plant, service facility or sales force – or share a common component. The gains of sharing may be substantial, but the search for shared costs is typically a *post hoc* effort to rationalize production across existing businesses, not a premeditated effort to build the competencies out of which the businesses themselves grow.

Building core competencies is more ambitious and different than integrating vertically, moreover. Managers deciding whether to make or buy will start with end products and look upstream to the efficiencies of the supply chain and downstream toward distribution and customers. They do not take inventory of skills and look forward to applying them in non-traditional ways. (Of course, decisions about competencies *do* provide a logic for vertical integration. Canon is not particularly integrated in its copier business, except in those aspects of the vertical chain that support the competencies it regards as critical.)

Identifying core competencies – and losing them

At least three tests can be applied to identify core competencies in a company. First, a core competence provides potential access to a wide variety of markets. Competence in display systems, for example, enables a company to participate in such diverse businesses as calculators, miniature TV sets, monitors for laptop computers, and automotive dashboards – which is why Casio's entry into the handheld TV market was predictable. Second, a core competence should make a significant contribution to the perceived customer benefits of the end product. Clearly, Honda's engine expertise fills this bill.

Finally, a core competence should be difficult for competitors to imitate. And it will be difficult if it is a complex harmonization of individual technologies and production skills. A rival might acquire some of the technologies that comprise the core competence, but it will find it more difficult to duplicate the more-or-less comprehensive pattern of internal coordination and learning. JVC's decision in the early 1960s to pursue the development of a videotape competence passed the three tests outlined here. RCA's decision in the late 1970s to develop a stylus-based video turntable system did not.

Few companies are likely to build world leadership in more than five or six fundamental competencies. A company that compiles a list of 20 to 30 capabilities has probably not produced a list of core competencies. Still, it is probably a good discipline to generate a list of this sort and to see aggregate capabilities as building blocks. This tends to prompt the search for licensing deals and alliances through which the company may acquire, at low cost, the missing pieces.

Most western companies hardly think about competitiveness in these terms at all. It is time to take a tough-minded look at the risks they are running. Companies that judge competitiveness, their own and their competitors', primarily in terms of the price/ performance of end products are courting the erosion of core competencies – or making too little effort to enhance them. The embedded skills that give rise to the next generation of competitive products cannot be 'rented in' by outsourcing and original equipment manufacturer (OEM) supply relationships. In our view, too many companies have unwittingly surrendered core competencies when they cut internal investment in what they mistakenly thought were just 'cost centres' in favour of outside suppliers.

Of course, it is perfectly possible for a company to have a competitive product line up but be a laggard in developing core competencies – at least for a while. If a company wanted to enter the copier business today, it would find a dozen Japanese companies more than willing to supply copiers on the basis of an OEM private label. But when fundamental technologies changed or if its supplier decided to enter the market directly and become a competitor, that company's product line, along with all of its investments in marketing and distribution, could be vulnerable. Outsourcing can provide a shortcut to a more competitive product, but it typically contributes little to building the people-embodied skills that are needed to sustain product leadership.

Nor is it possible for a company to have an intelligent alliance or sourcing strategy if it has not made a choice about where it will build competence leadership. Clearly, Japanese companies have benefited from alliances. They've used them to learn from western partners who were not fully committed to preserving core competencies of their own. Learning within an alliance takes a positive commitment of resources– travel, a pool of dedicated people, test-bed facilities, and time to internalize and test what has been learned. A company may not make this effort if it doesn't have clear goals for competence building.

Another way of losing is foregoing opportunities to establish competencies that are evolving in existing businesses. In the 1970s and 1980s, many American and European companies – like General Electric, Motorola, GTE, Thorn and General Electric Company (GEC) – chose to exit the colour television business, which they regarded as mature. If by 'mature' they meant that they had run out of new product ideas at precisely the moment global rivals had targeted the TV business for entry, then yes, the industry was mature. But it certainly wasn't mature in the sense that all opportunities to enhance and apply video-based competencies had been exhausted.

In ridding themselves of their television businesses, these companies failed to distinguish between divesting the business and destroying their video media-based competencies. They not only got out of the TV business but they also closed the door on a whole stream of future opportunities reliant on video-based competencies.

There are two clear lessons here. First, the costs of losing a core competence can be only partly calculated in advance. The baby may be thrown out with the bath water in divestment decisions. Second, since core competencies are built through a process of continuous improvement and enhancement that may span a decade or longer, a company that has failed to invest in core competence building will find it very difficult to enter an emerging market, unless, of course, it will be content simply to serve as a distribution channel.

American semiconductor companies like Motorola learned this painful lesson when they elected to forego direct participation in the 256k generation of DRAM chips. Having skipped this round, Motorola, like most of its American competitors, needed a large infusion of technical help from Japanese partners to rejoin the battle in the 1-megabyte generation. When it comes to core competencies, it is difficult to get off the train, walk to the next station, and then reboard.

From core competencies to core products

The tangible link between identified core competencies and end products is what we call the core products – the physical embodiments of one or more core competencies. Honda's engines, for example, are core products, linchpins between design and development skills that ultimately lead to a proliferation of end products. Core products are the components or sub-assemblies that actually contribute to the value of the end products. Thinking in terms of core products forces a company to distinguish between the brand share it achieves in end product markets (for example, 40 per cent of the US refrigerator market) and the manufacturing share it achieves in any particular core product (for example, 5 per cent of the world share of compressor output).

It is essential to make this distinction between core competencies, core products and end products because global competition is played out by different rules and for different stakes at each level. To build or defend leadership over the long term, a corporation will probably be a winner at each level. At the level of core competence, the goal is to build world leadership in the design and development of a particular class of product functionality – be it compact data storage and retrieval, as with Philips's optical-media competence, or compactness and ease of use, as with Sony's micromotors and microprocessor controls.

To sustain leadership in their chosen core competence areas, these companies *seek to maximize their world manufacturing share in core products*. The manufacture of core products for a wide variety of external (and internal) customers yields the revenue and market feedback that, at least partly, determines the pace at which core competencies can be enhanced and extended. This thinking was behind JVC's decision in the mid-1970s to establish VCR supply relationships with leading national consumer electronics companies in Europe and the United States. In supplying Thomson, Thorn and Telefunken (all independent companies at that time) as well as US partners, JVC was able to gain the cash and the diversity of market experience that ultimately enabled it to outpace Philips and Sony. (Philips developed videotape competencies in parallel with JVC, but it failed to build a worldwide network of OEM relationships that would have allowed it to accelerate the refinement of its videotape competence through the sale of core products.)

JVC's success has not been lost on Korean companies like Goldstar, Samsung, Kia and Daewoo, who are building core product leadership in areas as diverse as displays, semiconductors and automotive engines through their OEM-supply contracts with western companies. Their avowed goal is to capture investment initiative away from potential competitors, often US companies. In doing so, they accelerate their competence-building efforts while 'hollowing out' their competitors. By focusing on competence and embedding it in core products, Asian competitors have built up advantages in component markets first and have then leveraged off their superior products to move downstream to build brand share. And they are not likely to remain the low-cost suppliers forever. As their reputation for brand leadership is consolidated, they may well gain price leadership. Honda has proven this with its Acura line, and other Japanese car makers are following suit.

Control over core products is critical for other reasons. A dominant position in core products allows a company to shape the evolution of applications and end markets. Such compact audio disc-related core products as data drives and lasers have enabled Sony and Philips to influence the evolution of the computer-peripheral business in optical-media storage. As a company multiplies the number of application arenas for its core products, it can consistently reduce the cost, time and risk in new product development. In short, well-targeted core products can lead to economies of scale and scope.

The tyranny of the SBU

The new terms of competitive engagement cannot be understood using analytical tools devised to manage the diversified corporation of 20 years ago, when competition was primarily domestic (GE versus Westinghouse, General Motors versus Ford) and all the key players were speaking the language of the same business schools and consultancies. Old prescriptions have potentially toxic side effects. The need for new principles is most obvious in companies organized exclusively according to the logic of SBUs. The implications of the two alternate concepts of the corporation are summarized in Table 5.2.1.

Obviously, diversified corporations have a portfolio of products and a portfolio of businesses. But we believe in a view of the company as a portfolio of competencies as well. United States companies do not lack the technical resources to build competencies, but their top management often lacks the vision to build them and the administrative means for assembling resources spread across multiple businesses. A shift in commitment will inevitably influence patterns of diversification, skill deployment, resource allocation priorities, and approaches to alliances and outsourcing.

We have described the three different planes on which battles for global leadership are waged: core competence, core products and end products. A corporation has to know whether it is winning or losing on each plane. By sheer weight of investment, a company might be able to beat its rivals to blue-sky technologies yet still lose the race to build core competence leadership. If a company is winning the race to build core competencies (as opposed to building leadership in a few technologies), it will almost certainly outpace rivals in new business development. If a company is winning the race to capture world manufacturing share in core products, it will probably outpace rivals in improving product features and the price/performance ratio.

Determining whether one is winning or losing end-product battles is more difficult because measures of product market share do not necessarily reflect various companies' underlying competitiveness. Indeed, companies that attempt to build market share by relying on the competitiveness of others, rather than investing in core competencies and world core-product leadership, may be treading on quicksand. In the race for global brand dominance, companies like 3M, Black & Decker, Canon, Honda, NEC and Citicorp have built global brand umbrellas by proliferating products out of their core competencies. This has allowed their individual businesses to build image, customer loyalty and access to distribution channels.

When you think about this reconceptualization of the corporation, the primacy of the SBU – an organizational dogma for a generation – is now clearly an anachronism. Where the SBU is an article of faith, resistance to the seductions of decentralization can seem heretical. In many companies, the SBU prism means that only one plane of the global competitive battle, the battle to put competitive products on the shelf *today,* is visible to top management. What are the costs of this distortion?

Underinvestment in developing core competencies and core products

When the organization is conceived of as a multiplicity of SBUs, no single business may feel responsible for maintaining a viable position in core products or be able to justify the investment required to build world leadership in some core competence. In the absence of a more comprehensive view imposed by corporate

TABLE 5.2.1   Two concepts of the corporation

	SBU	Core competence
Basis for competition	Competiveness of today's products	Interfirm competition to build competencies
Corporate structure	Portfolio of businesses related in product–market terms	Portfolio of competencies, core products, and businesses
Status of the business unit	Autonomy is sacrosanct; the SBU 'owns' all resources other than cash	SBU is a potential reservoir of core competencies
Resource allocation	Discrete businesses are the unit of analysis; capital is allocated business by business	Businesses and competencies are the unit of analysis: top management allocates capital and talent
Value added of top management	Optimizing corporate returns through capital allocation trade-offs among businesses	Enunciating strategic architecture and building competencies to secure the future

management, SBU managers will tend to underinvest. Recently, companies such as Kodak and Philips have recognized this as a potential problem and have begun searching for new organizational forms that will allow them to develop and manufacture core products for both internal and external customers.

SBU managers have traditionally conceived of competitors in the same way as they've seen themselves. On the whole, they've failed to note the emphasis Asian competitors were placing on building leadership in core products or to understand the critical linkage between world manufacturing leadership and the ability to sustain development pace in core competence. They've failed to pursue OEM-supply opportunities or to look across their various product divisions in an attempt to identify opportunities for coordinated initiatives.

Imprisoned resources

As an SBU evolves, it often develops unique competencies. Typically, the people who embody this competence are seen as the sole property of the business in which they grew up. The manager of another SBU who asks to borrow talented people is likely to get a cold rebuff. SBU managers are not only unwilling to lend their competence carriers but they may actually hide talent to prevent its redeployment in the pursuit of new opportunities. This may be compared to residents of an underdeveloped country hiding most of their cash under their mattresses. The benefits of competencies, like the benefits of the money supply, depend on the velocity of their circulation as well as on the size of the stock the company holds.

Western companies have traditionally had an advantage in the stock of skills they possess. But have they been able to reconfigure them quickly to respond to new opportunities? Canon, NEC and Honda have had a lesser stock of the people and technologies that compose core competencies but could move them much quicker from one business unit to another. Corporate R&D spending at Canon is not fully indicative of the size of Canon's core competence stock and tells the casual observer nothing about the velocity with which Canon is able to move core competencies to exploit opportunities.

When competencies become imprisoned, the people who carry the competencies do not get assigned to the most exciting opportunities, and their skills begin to atrophy. Only by fully leveraging core competencies can small companies like Canon afford to compete with industry giants like Xerox. How strange that SBU managers, who are perfectly willing to compete for cash in the capital budgeting process, are unwilling to compete for people – the company's most precious asset. We find it ironic that top management devotes so much attention to the capital budgeting process yet typically has no comparable mechanism for allocating the human skills that embody core competencies. Top managers are seldom able to look four or five levels down into the organization, identify the people who embody critical competencies, and move them across organizational boundaries.

Bounded innovation

If core competencies are not recognized, individual SBUs will pursue only those innovation opportunities that are close at hand – marginal product-line extensions or geographic expansions. Hybrid opportunities like fax machines, laptop computers, handheld televisions or portable music keyboards will emerge only when managers take off their SBU blinkers. Remember, Canon appeared to be in the camera business at the time it was preparing to become a world leader in copiers. Conceiving of the corporation in terms of core competencies widens the domain of innovation.

Developing strategic architecture

The fragmentation of core competencies becomes inevitable when a diversified company's information systems, patterns of communication, career paths, managerial rewards and processes of strategy development do not transcend SBU lines. We believe that senior management should spend a significant amount of its time developing a corporate-wide strategic architecture that establishes objectives for competence-building. A strategic architecture is a road map of the future that identifies which core competencies to build and their constituent technologies.

By providing an impetus for learning from alliances and a focus for internal development efforts, a strategic architecture like NEC's C&C (computers and communication) can dramatically reduce the investment needed to secure future market leadership. How can a company make partnerships intelligently without a clear understanding of the core competencies it is trying to build and those it is attempting to prevent from being unintentionally transferred?

Of course, all of this begs the question of what a strategic architecture should look like. The answer will be different for every company. But it is helpful to think again of that tree, of the corporation organized around core products and, ultimately, core competencies. To sink sufficiently strong roots, a company must answer some fundamental questions: How long could we preserve our competitiveness in this business if we did not control this particular core competence? How central is this core competence to perceived customer benefits? What future opportunities would be foreclosed if we were to lose this particular competence?

The architecture provides a logic for product and market diversification, moreover. An SBU manager would be asked: Does the new market opportunity add to the overall goal of becoming the best player in the world? Does it exploit or add to the core competence? At Vickers, for example, diversification options have been judged in the context of becoming the best power and motion control company in the world.

The strategic architecture should make resource allocation priorities transparent to the entire organization. It provides a template for allocation decisions by top management. It helps lower-level managers understand the logic of allocation priorities and disciplines senior management to maintain consistency. In short, it yields a definition of the company and the markets it serves. 3M, Vickers, NEC, Canon and Honda all qualify on this score. Honda knew it was exploiting what it had learned from motorcycles – how to make high-revving, smooth-running, lightweight engines – when it entered the car business. The task of creating a strategic architecture forces the organization to identify and commit to the technical and production linkages across SBUs that will provide a distinct competitive advantage.

It is consistency of resource allocation and the development of an administrative infrastructure appropriate to it that breathes life into a strategic architecture and creates a managerial culture, teamwork, a capacity to change, and a willingness to share resources, to protect proprietary skills and to think long term. That is also the reason the specific architecture cannot be copied easily or overnight by competitors. Strategic architecture is a tool for communicating with customers and other external constituents. It reveals the broad direction without giving away every step.

Redeploying to exploit competencies

If the company's core competencies are its critical resource and if top management must ensure that competence carriers are not held hostage by some particular business, then it follows that SBUs should

bid for core competencies in the same way they bid for capital. We've made this point glancingly. It is important enough to consider more deeply.

Once top management (with the help of divisional and SBU managers) has identified overarching competencies, it must ask businesses to identify the projects and people closely connected with them. Corporate officers should direct an audit of the location, number and quality of the people who embody competence.

This sends an important signal to middle managers: core competencies are corporate resources and may be reallocated by *corporate* management. An individual business doesn't own anybody. SBUs are entitled to the services of individual employees so long as SBU management can demonstrate that the opportunity it is pursuing yields the highest possible payoff on the investment in their skills. This message is further underlined if each year in the strategic planning or budgeting process, unit managers must justify their hold on the people who carry the company's core competencies.

Also, reward systems that focus only on product-line results and career paths that seldom cross SBU boundaries engender patterns of behaviour among unit managers that are destructively competitive. At NEC, divisional managers come together to identify next-generation competencies. Together they decide how much investment needs to be made to build up each future competence and the contribution in capital and staff support that each division will need to make. There is also a sense of equitable exchange. One division may make a disproportionate contribution or may benefit less from the progress made, but such short-term inequalities will balance out over the long term.

Incidentally, the positive contribution of the SBU manager should be made visible across the company. An SBU manager is unlikely to surrender key people if only the other business (or the general manager of that business who may be a competitor for promotion) is going to benefit from the redeployment. Cooperative SBU managers should be celebrated as team players. Where priorities are clear, transfers are less likely to be seen as idiosyncratic and politically motivated.

Transfers for the sake of building core competence must be recorded and appreciated in the corporate memory. It is reasonable to expect a business that has surrendered core skills on behalf of corporate opportunities in other areas to lose, for a time, some of its competitiveness. If these losses in performance bring immediate censure, SBUs will be unlikely to assent to skills transfers next time.

Finally, there are ways to wean key employees off the idea that they belong in perpetuity to any particular business. Early in their careers, people may be exposed to a variety of businesses through a carefully planned rotation programme.

Competence carriers should be regularly brought together from across the corporation to trade notes and ideas. The goal is to build a strong feeling of community among these people. To a great extent, their loyalty should be to the integrity of the core competence area they represent and not just to particular businesses. In travelling regularly, talking frequently to customers and meeting with peers, competence carriers may be encouraged to discover new market opportunities.

Core competencies are the wellspring of new business development. They should constitute the focus for strategy at the corporate level. Managers have to win

manufacturing leadership in core products and capture global share through brand-building programmes aimed at exploiting economies of scope. Only if the company is conceived of as a hierarchy of core competencies, core products and market-focused business units will it be fit to fight.

Nor can top management be just another layer of accounting consolidation, which it often is in a regime of radical decentralization. Top management must add value by enunciating the strategic architecture that guides the competence acquisition process. We believe an obsession with competence building will characterize the global winners of the 1990s. With the decade underway, the time for rethinking the concept of the corporation is already overdue.

Seeking synergies

By Andrew Campbell and Michael Goold[1]

A review of synergy management can be triggered in a number of ways. A parent manager may suspect that co-ordination opportunities are being missed, but may not be sure what is being missed, how important it is, or what to do about it. A new chief executive may sense that his predecessor's emphasis on decentralization has led unit managers to overlook sharing opportunities. A visit to other companies that sing the praises of co-ordination may raise concerns about what is being missed. Critical press comments about the company's failure to achieve synergies across its portfolio may prompt questions about what more could be achieved. Given our concern about 'synergy bias', we counsel caution in following up vague disquiets. But an audit of how well synergy management is working can be a useful step in allaying fears or pinpointing areas that need to be addressed.

A review can also be triggered by grumbles at lower levels in the company that current co-ordination efforts are pointless, damaging or contradictory. Business managers may complain that short-term budget targets prevent them from exploring potentially valuable synergy opportunities or about the pointlessness of corporate-wide conferences at expensive resorts to promote 'family feeling'. Corridor gossip about the

negative influence of the parent may percolate up to the chief executive. More direct complaints may be received from frustrated business managers. Bottom-up pressures to think again about a company's approach to synergies should be taken seriously, and, if there are widespread or deep-seated concerns, a systematic and objective stock-taking may be in order.

Some companies build a periodic review of their cross-company initiatives into their regular planning processes. We are less enthusiastic about this practice, since it can easily lead either to superficial, year-by-year reiteration of what everyone already knows about the areas of overlap between businesses or to vain attempts to come up with new ideas. Unless there is a particular reason to review linkage management, it will probably cause more frustration than enlightenment. On the whole, therefore, we believe that a review should only be undertaken when there are identifiable reasons for doing so.

Good reasons to take stock of the current approach include:

- a belief that a major category of synergies such as international rationalization, sharing technical know-how or joint development of new business opportunities, is being systematically missed;

[1]Source: This article was adapted from Chapter 7 of *Synergy: Why Links Between Business Units Often Fail and How to Make Them Work*. Reproduced with permission from John Wiley & Sons Ltd. Copyright © 1998 Andrew Campbell & Michael Goold.

- visible and costly failures of several recent synergy initiatives;
- evidence that business units are favoring links with third parties in preference to internal links.

While it would be useful to have a way of objectively deciding when a stock take is necessary, our experience suggests that it is best judged subjectively by thinking about how well the current organization is working.

The purpose of a review should be to decide whether changes are needed in the overall corporate approach to synergies; to identify any specific opportunities that merit closer investigations; and to propose possible new linkage mechanisms or interventions.

A framework for a review

Our review framework is shown in Figure 5.3.1. It involves taking stock of both synergy opportunities available and the current corporate approach to cross-company linkages. The effectiveness of the approach can be assessed by testing how well it fits with the opportunities. The assessment can then be used to pinpoint new initiatives that may be worth considering. The framework will bring out aspects of the overall approach that are working well or badly, and lead to proposals for changes.

The value of the framework is that it obliges companies to address some fundamental questions:

- What is our current attitude to co-ordination between our business units, and how do we go about managing it?
- What do we believe are the main synergy opportunities in our portfolio, and how fully are we grasping them?
- How well suited is our current approach, including structures, processes and staff support, to the opportunities we believe are on offer?
- What current synergy initiatives should we drop, what new opportunities should we go for, and what changes in processes and mechanisms should we consider?

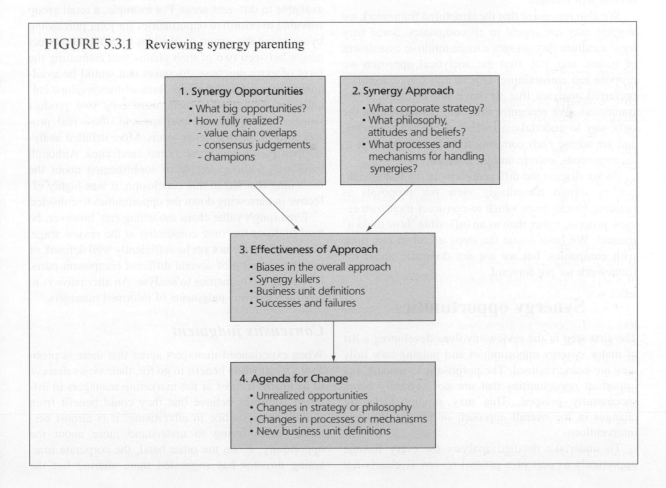

FIGURE 5.3.1 Reviewing synergy parenting

1. Synergy Opportunities
- What big opportunities?
- How fully realized?
  - value chain overlaps
  - consensus judgements
  - champions

2. Synergy Approach
- What corporate strategy?
- What philosophy, attitudes and beliefs?
- What processes and mechanisms for handling synergies?

3. Effectiveness of Approach
- Biases in the overall approach
- Synergy killers
- Business unit definitions
- Successes and failures

4. Agenda for Change
- Unrealized opportunities
- Changes in strategy or philosophy
- Changes in processes or mechanisms
- New business unit definitions

These questions can be asked of the whole company or of a multi-business division within a larger company. The framework is equally applicable when applied to any level above that of the individual business unit. However, when working at a division level, it is valuable to understand some of the broader corporate context in which the division is operating.

Although the framework provides a systematic means of tackling these questions, it should not be treated either as a straitjacket or a panacea. The emphasis of a review should depend on the concerns that prompted it. Is it primarily a matter of fine-tuning the current mechanisms and processes to work more smoothly, or are we more concerned with the underlying philosophy or structure of the company? Did we get into the review to beat the bushes to create a wide agenda of all possible new opportunities, or was it really a means of legitimizing a fresh look at one or two specific issues? With different motivations for the review, the weight given to different areas of analysis will vary, the order in which activities take place will be different, and the level of effort and speed of the review will change.

We also recognize that the structured framework we suggest may not appeal to all companies. Some may have a culture that stresses a more intuitive assessment of issues, and may find the analytical approach we propose too constraining. Others may have their own preferred analyses that we have not included in our framework. We recognize that our approach is not the only way to undertake a review of linkage parenting, and we advise each company to tailor its approach to its own needs, culture and preferences.

As we discuss the different steps in the framework, readers should accordingly view our proposals as building blocks from which to construct their own review process, rather than as an inflexible 'how to do it' manual. We have found the steps useful in our work with companies, but we are not dogmatic about the framework we put forward.

Synergy opportunities

The first step in the review involves developing a list of major synergy opportunities and judging how fully they are being realized. The purpose is to unearth any important opportunities that are not currently being successfully grasped. This may prompt ideas for changes in the overall approach or for specific new interventions.

To undertake detailed analysis for every linkage opportunity as part of a general review is clearly not feasible. It would take too long and cost too much. The challenge is to find efficient ways of homing in quickly on possible areas of high unexploited potential.

In our research, we have identified three useful prompts that can help to reveal neglected potential: rough modelling of value chain overlaps; interviews, focus groups or questionnaires designed to draw out consensus from business unit and parent managers; and identification of pet projects or initiatives that are being strongly championed by individual managers.

Value chain overlaps

Businesses with value chains that overlap, or could overlap, are obvious candidates for linkage opportunities. If two businesses purchase similar components, what benefits might be available by co-coordinating their purchases? If two businesses have overseas offices in the same country, what could be saved by sharing premises, sales forces, or management? We have found that rough modelling of the extent of overlaps and of the economies of scale or utilization available from sharing can rapidly yield a broad sizing of the benefits available in different areas. For example, a retail group was able to prioritize opportunities for joint purchasing by assessing the extent of overlaps in different product ranges between two of their chains, and estimating the level of extra purchase discounts that would be available from combined buying. Back-of-the-envelope calculations showed that there were only two product ranges with significant overlaps and, thus, real prospects for achieving better terms. More detailed analysis then focused on these prime candidates. Although there was nothing precise or sophisticated about the modelling that led to this conclusion, it was highly effective in narrowing down the opportunities to consider.

Even rough value chain modelling can, however, be hard to do or too time consuming at the review stage. The benefits may not yet be sufficiently well defined, or may be made up of several different component parts, or may be too numerous to analyse. An alternative is to rely on consensus judgments of informed managers.

Consensus judgment

When experienced managers agree that there is probably a worthwhile benefit to go for, their views deserve to be heard. If most of the marketing managers in different countries believe that they could benefit from sharing best practice in advertising, it is almost certainly worth trying to understand more about the opportunity. If, on the other hand, the corporate marketing director has suggested more sharing but the national marketing managers are lukewarm, it should probably be put on the backburner – at least unless the corporate director can argue convincingly that the national managers may be misjudging the opportunity. In the difficult field of synergies, the gut-feel and intuitive judgment of experienced managers should carry considerable weight.

In companies where information flows freely and managers are encouraged to express their views, it is comparatively easy for parent managers to discern an emerging consensus. In other companies, it can be much more difficult. Managers from different units may not meet together often enough to share views, or may not feel empowered to express their views to each other. They may also be constrained to follow prevailing corporate policies rather than challenge them. Whatever the reason, a structured approach to eliciting the consensus is frequently needed.

There are a variety of ways to draw out consensus judgments, ranging from questionnaires, through focus groups, to some form of systematic interviewing process. The method chosen needs to be tailored to the circumstances of the company – and we have adopted somewhat different methods in each of the companies we have worked with. In all cases, however, the objective is to discover whether informed managers generally feel that there are important unexplored opportunities going begging, and, if so, what priorities they should receive.

Championing

A third valuable prompt comes from championing. Strong and enthusiastic champions are important for the effective implementation of new interventions. We believe that they can also provide a short cut to identifying priority opportunity areas. If a manager feels so powerfully that an opportunity is worthwhile that he is willing to lobby for it, devote personal sweat equity to it, and risk the displeasure of his colleagues and bosses by repeatedly advocating it, it is usually worth taking notice.

There is little danger that strong champions will not be heard by the corporate parent. The danger is more that they will be too readily discounted. Persistent champions, particularly if their ideas challenge vested interests, can face strong opposition. Their views may be dismissed as unrealistic or irrelevant, or they may be labelled eccentrics or troublemakers. Prudent managers then pipe down, and learn to live with their frustrations. However, frustrated champions welcome any chance to promote their pet projects. A review of linkage parenting is a good opportunity to give them an

objective hearing. Our advice is to listen carefully to what they have to say – even if the rest of the organization has long ago decided not to.

Creativity and realism

In drawing up the short-list of opportunities that merit detailed consideration, we need to balance creativity and open-mindedness with realism. We want managers with new ideas to come forward, we want to encourage brainstorming that will generate fresh thinking, and we want to give a hearing to highly motivated champions. Especially if the purpose of the review is to make sure we're not missing something, we should be positive about new suggestions and supportive of 'thinking the unthinkable'.

We should also be willing to accept that some promising ideas may be clouded by considerable uncertainty. In Consco, for example, there was widespread support for more sharing of best practice in training and management development. But the benefits available were somewhat nebulous. Some managers had fairly specific ideas about how course designs or materials could be shared better. Others were simply reflecting a sense that this was an increasingly important area, in which they did not feel that their units were doing a very good job. Some had anecdotes or examples to support their views. But there was considerable uncertainty about where the real opportunities lay and how they should be pursued. And, in some situations, there is intrinsic uncertainty about the nature of the benefits. In businesses in the middle of rapid technological change, such as media and communications, the benefits of collaborating to develop new businesses to some extent depend on market and technology developments that are simply not predictable. The review should encourage managers to put forward speculative or uncertain opportunities: on closer examination they may turn out to contain real nuggets of gold. But any interventions to pursue them will probably have to be exploratory, designed to find out whether there are solid benefits to be obtained or not.

In creating a short-list of ideas to examine more closely, we should, however, guard against pursuing mirages, and question whether there really are likely to be parenting opportunities to address. When we assess the short-listed ideas, we shall need to be rigorous in applying the mental disciplines to them. In drawing up the short-list, we should therefore reject ideas if there is insufficient logic or evidence to support them. For example, if the champion of a shared salesforce appears to have given little serious consideration to important details, such as salesmen's calling patterns or the purchase criteria of customers, his proposal should receive less weight. Or if, on reflection, no-one can see any possible parenting opportunities associated with the targeted benefit, we should avoid wasting time with further investigation of it. We need to blend support for fresh thinking with the reality checks and tough-mindedness that the mental disciplines provide. It is the ideas that will stand up under closer analysis that we are interested in.

Synergy approach

The next step in the review is to lay out the main features of the company's approach to synergy management. It should cover the role that synergies play within the corporate strategy. It should bring out the company's underlying philosophy, attitudes and beliefs concerning the units' relationships to each other and to the centre. And it should make explicit the mechanisms and processes that the company typically uses to deal with these issues.

Corporate strategy

In our research on corporate strategy, we have found that different companies place very different emphases on the horizontal and vertical linkages that they foster. Some companies, such as Hanson (before the breakup), Emerson, RTZ and BTR (prior to 1995), place much more weight on the value that they add through stand-alone parenting than through linkage parenting. Others, such as Banc One, Unilever, 3M, ABB and Canon, have always seen the management of synergies as a key part of their corporate strategies. Business managers in organizations such as Hanson know that the main focus of the parent's attention will be on opportunities to improve the performance of each business as a stand-alone entity, and that they will receive few brownie points for collaborative efforts with other units. By contrast, business managers in Canon or Unilever know that their bosses expect and require them to seek out and participate in opportunities for working together with other units. Furthermore, they know what sorts of synergies the parent typically promotes most energetically. In Canon, for example, the strongest drive is for new product developments that require cooperation across business unit boundaries, while in Unilever the transfer of product and market information across geographic boundaries is critical.

Exhibit 5.3.1 summarizes the main sources of value creation identified in one international manufacturing and marketing company. This way of summarizing the corporate strategy into a list of parenting tasks helps position the importance of synergy initiatives versus other forms of parenting.

In summary, the review should document the priority given to linkage issues versus other forms of parenting and record the types of linkages that feature most prominently as key sources of added value. The review should also record the direction of movement in the corporate strategy. Is the company looking to build more synergies in the future or unwind some of the links and co-ordinated activities that currently exist? The current corporate strategy and the perceived direction of movement influence the sort of synergies that managers are likely to pursue and the priority they give them.

EXHIBIT 5.3.1   SOURCES OF PARENTING VALUE CREATION

- Transferring know-how about products, markets, marketing, manufacturing and other functions from/to business units around the world.

- Helping businesses (mainly in developed economies) avoid the pitfall of under investment in new product development and consumer understanding.

- Creating a value-based performance culture that has low tolerance of unnecessary costs or weak performance, yet is capable of investing where necessary.

- Orchestrating pools of mobile management talent so that businesses can draw on them in times of need.

- Developing and appointing outstanding managers to lead each business, with skills appropriate to the particular challenges of that business.

- Helping businesses (mainly in emerging markets) to avoid common pitfalls, such as insufficient investment in local management or poor timing of major commitments.

- Developing valuable relationships with potential partners and influential governments, and building the company brand into one of the world's leading corporate brands.

- Providing cost effective central services and corporate governance activities.

Philosophy, attitudes and beliefs

Companies also have different underlying attitudes and beliefs about how best to handle linkages. Often these differences concern the advantages of centralization or decentralization. To achieve benefits from pooled purchasing power, for example, a parent with a belief in the efficacy of central initiatives may set up a central purchasing department and insist that all purchases of certain items are handled by this department. Conversely, a parent that favours decentralized networking may simply circulate data on the purchasing terms and conditions being achieved by each unit, maintaining strong pressure on the businesses to reduce their individual unit costs. Such an intervention leaves the businesses much freer to determine whether and how they wish to work with other businesses to improve their purchasing power, but gives them no direct help

or guidance about what to do. Between these extremes, there are a variety of other possibilities, such as establishing joint purchasing teams with members from different businesses, nominating selected businesses to act as lead units in purchasing for different items, centralizing certain aspects of negotiations on terms and conditions but allowing each business to make its own buying decisions, and hiring a central purchasing expert who is available to the businesses, but need only be used by them if they choose.

For any synergy benefit, a range of possible intervention options can be arrayed along a spectrum of more versus less centralist interventions (see Table 5.3.1). Some companies, such as Mars and Unilever, are philosophically committed to the decentralized, networking end of the spectrum. They believe that it is vital to preserve business-unit autonomy and leave decisions to business-unit managements. Wary of central

TABLE 5.3.1 Differences in linkage philosophy

	Belief in decentralization	Mixed	Belief in central direction
Know-how sharing	■ Network facilitation	■ Some central policies ■ Centres of excellence ■ Lead units ■ Franchise	■ Mandatory central policiesand directives
Tangible resources sharing	■ Internal JVs/contracts ■ Voluntary use of shared resource units ■ Set up as profit centres	■ Limited central functions and resources ■ Service level agreements	■ Mandatory central functions and resources ■ Incomplete SBUs
Pooled negotiating power	■ Information sharing ■ Joint SBU teams and initiatives	■ Lead units	■ Central functions experts
Vertical integration	■ Third party trading relationships, but first refusal in-house	■ Negotiated transfer prices ■ In-house preference ■ Centre influences relationship	■ Centre sets transfer prices and manages relationships for corporate benefit
Co-ordinated strategies	■ Centre arbitrates ■ Minimal constraints on scope/strategy	■ Restrained central role ■ Matrix structure ■ Task forces ■ Franchise	■ Centre directs ■ Low SBU autonomy
New business creation	■ SBU driven	■ Task forces drawn from centre and SBUs	■ Centrally driven

interference, they prefer to rely on the 'enlightened self-interest' of unit managers to guide linkages. Other companies, such as Canon or Rentokil, are more comfortable mandating policies or decisions from the centre on a range of issues. Although they accept the importance of unit motivation and initiative, they believe that there are many important benefits that will not be realized unless the parent makes the decisions.

Differences in attitudes concerning the appropriate degree of centralization affect the range of intervention options that a parent is likely to perceive. Those who favour decentralized solutions will tend to give little or no consideration to more mandatory central interventions. Those who typically mandate central policies and decisions will be less sensitive to how much can be accomplished through a variety of measures that encourage networking. Corporate linkage philosophies represent blinkers that constrain the options that receive attention.

Another important factor is the corporate parent's attitude to central staff resources. Should large, heavyweight staff groups be set up or not? Should the businesses be forced to work with the corporate staff, or should their use by the businesses be voluntary? As with centralization/decentralization choices, companies tend to have a dominant philosophy which governs the role of staff in managing linkages. Companies such as ABB are strenuously opposed to the use of corporate staff, wherever possible relying on decisions and resources in the business units. They fear that, lacking direct profit responsibility, staff can easily lose touch with the needs of the businesses and take on a life of their own, in which power and empire-building take precedence over the benefits delivered to the corporation. Other companies, 3M or Cooper for instance, believe that corporate staff, at least in selected areas, are the best way to ensure that specialist expertise is developed and shared among units. They are therefore a source of valuable linkages. These beliefs will be reflected in the synergy interventions that the parent makes.

Different philosophies therefore influence the sorts of synergies that will be pursued and the means which will be used to pursue them. Take, for example, a new product-development initiative involving joint work between two or more business units. At one extreme, a 'Hanson' approach, suspicious of shared responsibilities of this sort, would likely press for the initiative to be pursued within one of the businesses or else dropped. By contrast, a 'Unilever' approach would be to provide encouragement and, if necessary, expert assistance, while allowing the businesses to pursue the matter in their own way, within a framework of strong corporate cultural norms to guide decision-making. A 'Canon' approach would be different again, entailing willingness to give high corporate priority to the project, including assignment of numbers of both corporate and business staff to work full-time on the project to see it through to commercialization. Some assessment of the underlying corporate attitudes and beliefs about linkages should therefore form part of the review.

Mechanisms and processes

Companies also differ in the nature of the specific mechanisms and processes that they typically use to manage co-ordination. The review should identify the mechanisms and processes that are most frequently used, and should articulate the impact that they have on synergy management. What is the nature and importance of the budget and planning processes and how, if at all, do they affect cross-company initiatives? What sort of cross-business committees are in place and how do they work? What staff groups exist and what role do they play in linkages?

We argue that 'well-grooved' mechanisms are an important factor in gauging the ease with which a company's synergy intervention will be implemented. Equally, ineffective or ill-suited mechanisms and processes can account for failure to realize some opportunities.

'Five lenses analysis'

As a means of describing and analysing the parent's approach to synergy issues, we have found that a display that views the characteristics of the parent through five interlinked lenses is useful (see Goold, Campbell and Alexander, 1994 and Figure 5.3.2). The five lenses are:

■ The beliefs, knowledge or mental maps that guide the behaviour and decisions of senior managers in the parent organization. These mental maps determine the corporate linkage strategy and philosophy, and guide the parent's thinking about the selection and implementation of linkage mechanisms and interventions.

■ The structure of the company, including the way in which the business units are defined and the nature of parenting structures to which they report, and the systems and processes through which parent managers mainly exercise influence, pressure and control. The business-unit definitions determine what links between units need to be managed; the nature of the parenting structure, for example whether there are product divisions, geographical divisions,

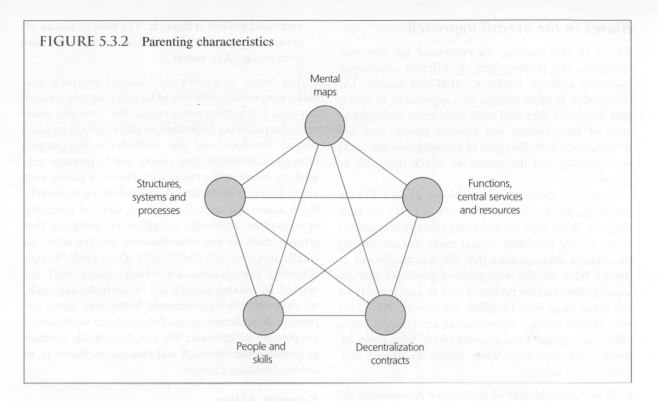

FIGURE 5.3.2 Parenting characteristics

or a matrix structure, influences the parenting opportunities that will be pursued; and the systems and processes that are in place determine how they are most likely to be handled.

- The functional staff, central service groups and corporate resources that are important in synergy management. The size, composition and strengths of the corporate staff and the way in which they operate are key components of the overall approach to cross-company working.

- The people in the parent organization. The experience, skills and biases of key individuals in the parent have a major impact on synergy management.

- The extent to which authority is delegated to business managers, together with the criteria by which their performance is judged and the rewards or sanctions for good or poor performance; we refer to this as the 'decentralization contract' for each business. The manner in which decentralization contracts are defined influences the sorts of linkage intervention that the parent is likely to make and that the businesses are likely to accept.

We have found that these five lenses provide a useful checklist for itemizing those features of the corporate parent's approach to the management of synergies that matter most. By running through each of these headings and taking stock of the key features under each, a picture of the overall approach can be built up and made explicit. The five lenses can also be used to bring out ways in which the approach is changing, giving a direction of movement as well as a static picture.

Effectiveness of approach

The third step is to assess the effectiveness of the current synergy approach. How well does the approach match up with the opportunities? Is it working reasonably well, apart from a few specific problems? Are there any fundamental shortcomings that need to be tackled? Once the approach and the opportunities have been laid out in the first two steps of the review, the answers to these questions may be readily apparent. There are, however, some more structured questions that it may be useful to ask. These include:

- Are there biases in the overall approach that condition which opportunities will be realized?

- Are there any aspects of the approach which are impeding linkages; are there any 'synergy killers'?

- Do any business unit definitions need to be changed?

- What have been the successes and failures of the approach, and what problems need addressing?

Biases in the overall approach

Earlier in this reading, we contrasted the corporate strategies and philosophies of different companies, including Hanson, Unilever, ABB and Canon. The differences in these companies' approaches to synergies mean that they will each steer away from certain sorts of interventions and towards others: their approaches bias both the types of linkages they are likely to emphasize and the means by which they will be pursued.

Nearly all companies have biases in their linkage parenting, and a value of the review is to lay out what they are. What does the corporate strategy emphasize? What are the dominant mental maps that are driving the linkage interventions that the parent chooses to make? What are the well-grooved processes that are usually chosen as the preferred way to intervene? If we can make these biases explicit, we may be able to see why certain synergy opportunities are grasped, while others are systematically overlooked; why some initiatives run smoothly, while others are always contentious and difficult.

- In one manufacturer of automotive components, the corporate strategy stressed the importance of global co-ordination across different national companies. This strategy led to cost savings and superior customer service in many areas. However, it also led to pressure for rationalization of the product range that carried high opportunity costs in some countries. The basic presumption in favour of international coordination made it very difficult for the countries in question to get a fair hearing on these costs. Instead, they were accused of NIH thinking and told to fall into line with global policy. The bias in favour of international co-ordination in the corporate strategy prevented the parent from taking a balanced view of the advantages and disadvantages of product-range rationalization.

- In a building products company, there was a strong commitment to decentralized networking as the best way to capture synergies, based partly on history and partly on a belief in the need to respect differences in each business unit's markets. When the corporate parent wanted to encourage all the businesses to adopt a common MIS system, the networking bias resulted in an endless sequence of project-team meetings, in which it was impossible to reach agreement on a new standard system for all the businesses. It was only after literally years of delay that the parent insisted on a choice being

made and pushed it through. The bias in favour of networking prevented a stronger corporate lead from being taken earlier.

The biases in a company's overall approach will make it especially effective at handling certain sorts of linkages, but ineffective at others. For example, there are some parenting opportunities that require mandated central decisions and are unlikely to be grasped through interventions that simply aim to promote networking between the businesses. Hence, a parent with a bias in favour of decentralized networking is unlikely to be successful at realizing these sorts of parenting opportunities. Similarly, a staff-averse company that always tends to use cross-business project teams to handle linkages will find it difficult to push through parenting opportunities for which central staff are needed. By making explicit any biases in the approach, we may be able to understand better why some opportunities are being successfully realized while others are proving problematic. We can then decide whether to maintain the approach and endorse its biases or to consider making changes.

Synergy killers

Most discussions of synergy concern ways in which the corporate parent can make linkages between business units work better. Unfortunately, the harsh reality is that the corporate parent often inadvertently makes these connections more difficult, not easier. We need to recognize this fact, and can use a review of linkage parenting as a means of rooting out things that are impeding linkages. We refer to policies or characteristics of the parent that are systematically inhibiting linkages as 'synergy killers'.

The effectiveness of the approach to linkages will be compromised if any of the following synergy killers are present:

- Inhibiting corporate strategy. The most common way in which the corporate-level strategy can work against synergy is through lack of clarity. Lack of clarity about corporate priorities leads managers to be excessively cautious about when they collaborate and with whom. If managers in the businesses are unsure whether the corporate parent expects them to be coordinating their technical efforts or looking for cost savings in marketing, the uncertainty can leave them paralysed. A more obvious, if rarer, problem stems from corporate strategies that actively discourage linkages of any sort. In a notorious memorandum written after

GEC's acquisition of English Electric, Lord Weinstock informed the managers of the English Electric businesses that all cross-unit committees and projects were to be disbanded forthwith. In future, they would have only one responsibility: the performance of their own units. Though few companies today take such a radical stance against synergies between businesses, some corporate-level strategies still discourage cooperation. 'In my view', stated one chief executive, 'synergy is always an illusion. What is more, it fatally damages accountability.' Not surprisingly, this attitude had a dampening effect on unit managers' attempts to work together.

■ Infighting between the barons. In some companies, there are battles raging between senior managers. The battles may be about differences in corporate strategy or management philosophy. They may be about competition between managers for the top job. They may be due to personality clashes. They may be due to previous collaborations where one party felt let down. Whatever the reason, these battles have a huge negative impact on cooperation. Managers lower down are often aware of lost opportunities, but the climate of hostility between their bosses means that cooperation to pursue them is stifled. It is simply not acceptable to be seen to be 'working with the enemy'.

■ Culture of secrecy. In secretive companies, people play their cards close to their chests. Information about business unit performance, new product plans, operating issues and organization structures is given out reluctantly. In these circumstances, cooperation is hard, not only because it is difficult to find out what is going on in other units, but also because the free flow of information and communication that is needed to oil the wheels of synergies is inhibited. Why do these cultures occur? Sometimes it is fear of competitor espionage. Sometimes it is a result of resisting corporate information requests and interference. Sometimes it is associated with baronial infighting. Whatever the cause, a culture of secrecy reduces synergy.

■ Misaligned incentives. In many companies, bonus systems and promotion criteria depend largely or exclusively on the results managers achieve in their own businesses, and give no credit for contributions to other businesses or the corporate whole. The personal incentive system then makes it more difficult for business managers to cooperate, unless they can structure a deal that rewards all the units involved.

Where the synergy involves a sacrifice by one unit to help others, and there is no ready process by which to compensate the loser, the incentive system will block progress. Again and again, we encountered situations in which this prevented managers from helping colleagues in other businesses, even though there was a clear net benefit. Where win/lose trade-offs exist, reward systems should aim to make it easier for business managers to cooperate; all too often, they have precisely the reverse effect.

■ Excessive performance pressure. When managers are hounded by close-to-impossible targets, they are apt to become defensive and inward-looking. In companies where business unit performance is paramount and where targets are set too high, managers often concentrate exclusively on things within their own immediate control and cease to be comfortable with situations where they must rely on their colleagues' cooperation. Oppressive targets damp down the spirit of mutuality and collaboration from which synergies flow.

■ Insulation from performance pressure. At the opposite end of the spectrum from excessive performance pressure is insulation from performance pressure. If business units are insulated from performance pressures, the basic drive of enlightened self-interest, on which so many beneficial sharing initiatives depend, will be weakened. In companies where synergies thrive, such as Mars or Canon, senior managers keep up the pressure for constant improvement, knowing that this leads to more energy from working together. In companies where the parent insulates the businesses from such pressures, the businesses are less likely to seek out mutually rewarding synergies.

■ Domineering corporate staff. If corporate staff groups have domineering or insensitive attitudes, business managers will automatically reject their ideas for improving linkages, however sound they may be. In a major chemical company with old-established functional baronies, the heads of the corporate staff departments were inclined to issue policies and guidelines to the businesses with little consultation or recognition of inter-company differences. Over time, the business heads became adept at passive resistance and non-cooperation, spending much more time on the tactics of opposition than on assessing whether the proposed policies were, in fact, beneficial. As a result, genuine synergy opportunities were resisted as strenuously as misguided attempts at standardization.

■ Mistrust. An atmosphere of mistrust undermines cooperation. If the businesses believe that their sister units are out to take advantage of them, or are always unwilling to put themselves out to help, relations are quickly soured to the point where even well-intentioned initiatives are blocked. Equally, if a climate of opinion has grown up where business managers believe that corporate management or staff are incompetent or untrustworthy, synergy interventions are likely to be resisted in principle. Expensive, high profile failures seriously undermine the credibility and prospects of any future proposal. Particular problems arise when the parent is suspected of having a hidden agenda, since all initiatives will be scrutinized for ulterior motives, and interpreted in the worst possible light.

All companies have some synergy killers. Our concern should be with pathological characteristics that may be causing widespread damage, not with minor irritants. Is there a strong sense that some of the parent's characteristics are really preventing collaboration? Can we see evidence from the unrealized opportunities that indicates that these synergy killers are having a real impact? How can the parent adjust the corporate context to make linkages work better?

While synergy killers inhibit linkages, their opposites create the sort of fertile ground in which cooperation flourishes. Clear corporate strategies that support high priority synergies; good personal relationships between senior managers in the businesses; an open culture that promotes sharing; incentive systems that reward attempts to create synergies; corporate pressure to raise performance through sharing best practices; competent staff units that are sensitive in their relationships with the businesses; and an atmosphere of mutual trust and support are all conducive to perceiving synergy opportunities and implementing them successfully. The parent should aim to nurture synergies through creating these fertile ground conditions. Hence, even if no real synergy killers exist, the review may still pinpoint ways in which the corporate context could be made more fertile for synergies.

Business unit definitions

The boundaries established around a group's business units are fundamental for the approach to synergies. By changing the definition of the business units, the parent automatically changes the nature of the potential links between business units. If a new European unit is set up out of previously separate national units, issues of manufacturing co-ordination that used to be handled as linkages between separate units are now managed within a single larger entity. 'Internalizing' the linkages in this way makes a big difference, because there is now a single general manager for the combined business who is in a position to decide on trade-offs between the subunits and who will be held responsible for the results of the integrated entity. This makes certain interventions much easier to push through, although it may involve some reduction in focus on the product–market niches within the larger entity.

The trade-offs between breadth and focus in business-unit definition are complex. There are, however, some business-unit definition issues that should be addressed in a review of synergy management. In particular, it is important to raise the following questions:

■ Are there some important synergies that are never likely to be realized with the current business-unit definitions? If so, are there alternative definitions that should be considered?
■ Are certain synergies harder to achieve because of the manner in which the boundaries around the business units are set up and managed?

There are some circumstances in which coordination between separate businesses is never likely to be achieved, however beneficial it may be for the group. If, for example, the collective net benefits involve costs to one or more units that are hard or impossible to compensate for, the initiative is likely to be blocked. Thus, it may be almost impossible to bring about coordinated production planning between separate units if it involves one or more units shutting their factories and transferring production to another. To avoid the consequent reduction in power and status, the general managers of the units in question will be likely to go to any lengths to block or undermine the initiative. Conclusion: the best way to achieve this synergy benefit will probably be to redefine the business to encompass all the previously separate units, giving responsibility for optimizing performance to a single management team.

Other situations in which managers should consider a redefinition of the businesses to achieve desirable synergies include the following:

■ Deeply embedded hostility and mistrust between senior managers in the different units. If the rivalry between the general managers of the units is intense, they may simply be unwilling to work together, whatever the benefits. The solution may be to redefine the business units and give responsibility for both of them to one or other of the managers.

■ Hard-to-allocate costs and revenues. If shared production facilities or the lack of an open third-party market for products traded between the units make it difficult to agree a split of costs and revenues, any form of cooperation is likely to suffer, since underlying disputes about transfer prices and allocated costs will dominate everything else. In such circumstances, it is often better to expand the business definition to include both units, with a single bottom line. Coordination issues then become a means to maximize aggregate profitability rather than the pretext for haggling over how to divide up the results.

■ Need for speedy and continuous resolution of trade-off judgments. Concerns about contamination and lack of focus have led many companies to create more and more separate profit centres, each with its own management and strategy. This drive for business focus creates major difficulties if the separate businesses need to be in constant touch with each other and have to resolve a series of difficult day-to-day trade-offs. For example, if two petrochemical businesses share a process plant and continuous decisions about output mix are needed to achieve the optimum overall profitability, taking account of the shifting relative prices of different inputs and of different end products, the two businesses will be locked in constant complex negotiations about how to run the plant. A structure in which a single management team is responsible for optimizing both businesses is likely to work more smoothly.

The underlying issue is whether, for whatever reason, co-ordination between the separate businesses' management teams will always be much less effective than co-ordination under a single management team. Managers should therefore examine the current business-unit boundaries to see if they are preventing any important synergies from taking place. If they are, consider altering the boundaries.

Judgments about whether a redefinition of the businesses is necessary should also reflect the nature of the boundaries. If decentralization contracts emphasize the autonomy of the business heads and provide few incentives or opportunities for them to work together, potential problems resulting from separate business definitions will be magnified. If, however, business heads do not expect to have full control over all the functions and resources they need in their businesses, and work in a context that encourages and requires frequent liaison with colleagues from other businesses and from central functions, the boundaries around the separate businesses will be more naturally permeable.

In Canon, for example, business managers are very ready to work on cross-business project teams, to draw on corporate staff support, and to co-ordinate with other businesses: the corporate approach to coordination stresses the connections between the businesses, not the boundaries that separate them. With more permeable boundaries around the businesses, there is more flexibility to make different business definitions work well. With more separation between businesses, there is a greater premium on drawing the boundaries in ways that will internalize linkages that would otherwise become problematic.

Successes and failures

Last, but not least, the effectiveness of the overall approach can be tested in terms of evident successes and failures: well and poorly rated mechanisms and processes, fully and less fully realized synergy opportunities, patterns of success and failure that cast light on organizational strengths and weaknesses.

As part of the audit of the current approach, it is essential to canvas opinion about the effectiveness of the main systems and processes for managing synergies, and of the key staff groups that promote them. Surveys, in-depth discussions or focus groups can bring well-grooved and successful mechanisms into relief and pinpoint areas of friction or dissatisfaction. Poorly rated mechanisms should then be examined more carefully. What are the causes of dissatisfaction? Is it a mechanism for chasing mirages? Are the parenting opportunities on which it is targeted clear, or is it being driven by parenting bias? Is it wasting the time of managers at the centre or in the businesses? Should we consider other ways of intervening to realize the target benefits, or should we simply discontinue our efforts if they are not working?

Another way into the successes and failures analysis is via the synergy opportunities review. Do the unrealized opportunities indicate some underlying gap or shortcoming in our approach? Is there some mismatch between the processes or interventions we use for getting at the opportunities and the nature of the opportunities? If, for example, we are consistently failing to achieve the benefits of better capacity utilization that vertical integration should provide, is this because there is something wrong with our transfer-pricing processes or with our approach to combined investment planning? Or are our business-specific performance measures to blame? Our quest should be to unearth new or different mechanisms for intervening that are better suited for the parenting opportunities open to us, in order to reduce the number of important unrealized opportunities.

We have also found that a retrospective analysis of patterns of success and failure with previous synergy interventions can be useful. Which synergies have we managed well – and probably taken for granted? What notorious initiatives have caused the most trouble and yielded the least benefit? What can we learn from these successes and failures?

By examining the successes, we will be able to see more clearly what mechanisms work best for us. What opportunities have we derived most benefit from? By what means did we realize these opportunities? Answers to these questions will reveal what the organization's well-grooved mechanisms and processes are, and will help to shape thinking about how to tackle new opportunities. By examining the failures, we may discover underlying weaknesses in our skills or processes, or organizational blockages and synergy killers that lie behind our inability to implement certain types of synergies successfully. A sense of these underlying patterns is useful in assessing the effectiveness of the approach.

Agenda for change

The output from the review should be a short-list of possible new initiatives for more detailed consideration. Since the review is a broadly based stock take, the purpose is to create an agenda of possible changes, not to arrive at firm conclusions about how to move forward. Each of the possible initiatives that emerge from the review will then need to be subjected to detailed scrutiny.

The short-list should embrace:

- high priority unrealized synergy opportunities, including ways to address them;
- changes in underlying strategy or philosophy that may increase the effectiveness of the overall approach;
- changes in specific coordination processes or mechanisms, including elements that should be discontinued because they may be having a damaging effect, as well as new initiatives that should be considered;
- possible changes in business unit definitions.

Prioritization of the ideas that emerge from the review is essential. The front-runners normally select themselves, either because of the size of the potential benefits (or disbenefits) or the strength of feeling among managers. But the cut-off on what to take forward is more a matter for judgment. We have four pieces of advice in forming the judgment.

First, be selective. A focused follow-through on three or four key initiatives is much more likely to yield tangible benefits than a long drawn-out survey of a couple of dozen possibly attractive options. And if the review is not seen to lead on fairly quickly to action, its credibility will suffer and managers will lose enthusiasm.

Second, look forward, not back. Give preference to ideas that anticipate breaking trends and build links that will become increasingly valuable in the future. Avoid focusing on initiatives that deal with yesterday's problems or with issues that are likely to become less significant. Concentrate, for example, on putting in place pricing coordination mechanisms to avoid arbitrage in what will become an increasingly integrated European marketplace. Don't struggle to promote common design and manufacturing of components that more and more of the business units are already tending to outsource.

Third, use your rivals and competitors to guide your sense of priorities. If your main competitors are deriving much more benefit from sharing know-how than you are, move it up your priority list, unless there are good reasons why it is always likely to be less important to you than to them. If others have tried and failed with a shared-purchasing initiative, be cautious about pushing ahead with it. The concern should be with the specific achievements of known competitors, not with current general management fads and fashions. Of course, this presumes a certain level of competitive intelligence, which is not always present. However, we believe that efforts to find out about competitors' initiatives can play a valuable role in establishing a final short-list.

Fourth, recognize system effects. The five-lenses analysis brings out the connections between different aspects of the synergy approach. Successes and failures often stem from deeply rooted attitudes that underlie the use of certain mechanisms rather than others. Proposals to make changes in a given process or to address a specific opportunity may therefore entail consequential changes in other areas. Consider whether specific initiatives will work in the whole context in which they will be taken; assess the possibility that a systematic change programme to shift the overall culture may be required as a pre-condition for success in specific areas.

REFERENCES

Amit, R. and Livnat, J. (1988) 'Diversification and the Risk-Return Trade-off', *Academy of Management Journal*, Vol. 31, No. 1, March, pp. 154–165.

Anslinger, P.L. and Copeland, T.E. (1996) 'Growth Through Acquisitions: A Fresh Look', *Harvard Business Review*, Vol. 74, No. 1, January–February, pp. 126–135.

Bartlett, C.A. and Ghoshal, S. (2003) 'What is a Global Manager?', *Harvard Business Review*, 81(8), pp. 101–108.

Baum, J.A.C. and Greve, H.R. (eds.) (2001) *Multiunit Organization and Multimarket Strategy*, Vol. 18, Stamford, CT: JAI Press.

Calori, R. and de Woot, P. (eds.) (1994) *A European Management Model: Beyond Diversity*, Hemel Hempstead: Prentice Hall.

Campbell, A. and Goold, M. (1998) *Synergy: Why Links Between Business Units Often Fail and How to Make Them Work*, Oxford: Capstone Publishing.

Campbell, A., Goold, M. and Alexander, M. (1995) 'The Value of the Parent Company', *California Management Review*, Vol. 38, No. 1, Fall, pp. 79–97.

Chatterjee, S. (1986) 'Types of Synergy and Economic Value: The Impact of Acquisitions on Merging and Rival Firms', *Strategic Management Journal*, Vol. 7, No. 2, March–April, pp. 119–139.

Eisenhardt, K.M. and Galunic, D.C. (2000) 'Coevolving: At Last, a Way to Make Synergies Work', *Harvard Business Review*, Vol. 78, No. 1, January–February, pp. 91–101.

Fieldhouse, D.K. (1978) *Unilever Overseas: The Anatomy of a Multinational 1895–1965*, London: Croom Helm.

Ghoshal, S. and Mintzberg, H. (1994) 'Diversification and Diversifact', *California Management Review*, Vol. 37, No. 1, Fall, pp. 8–27.

Goold, M. and Campbell, A. (1987) *Strategies and Styles: The Role of the Centre in Managing Diverse Corporations*, Oxford: Basil Blackwell.

Goold, M. and Lansdell, S. (1997) *Survey of Corporate Strategy Objectives, Concepts and Tools,* Ashridge Strategic Management Centre.

Goold, M., Campbell, A. and Alexander, M. (1994) *Corporate-Level Strategy: Creating Value in the Multibusiness Company*, New York: Wiley.

Hamel, G. and Prahalad, C.K. (1993) 'Strategy as Stretch and Leverage', *Harvard Business Review*, Vol. 71, No. 2, March–April, pp. 75–84.

Hamel, G. and Prahalad, C.K. (1994) *Competing for the Future: Breakthrough Strategies for Seizing Control of Your Industry and Creating the Markets of Tomorrow*, Harvard Business School Press.

Harrigan, K.R. (1985) 'Vertical Integration and Corporate Strategy', *Academy of Management Journal*, Vol. 28, No. 2, June, pp. 397–425.

Haspeslagh, P. (1982) 'Portfolio Planning: Uses and Limits', *Harvard Business Review*, Vol. 60, No. 1, January–February, pp. 58–73.

Hedley, B. (1977) 'Strategy and the "Business Portfolio"', *Long Range Planning*, Vol. 10, No. 1, February, pp. 9–15.

Helfat, C.E. and Eisenhardt, K.M. (2004) 'Inter-temporal Economies of Scope, Organizational Modularity, and the Dynamics of Diversification', *Strategic Management Journal*, Vol. 25, No. 13, pp. 1217–1296.

Henderson, B.D. (1979) *On Corporate Strategy,* Cambridge, MA: Abt Books.

Hofer, C. and Schendel, D. (1978) *Strategy Formulation: Analytical Concepts*, St. Paul: West.

Hofstede, G. (1993) 'Cultural Constraints in Management Theories', *Academy of Management Executive*, Vol. 7, No. 1, pp. 8–21.

Jayachandran, S., Gimeno, J. and Varadarajan, P.R. (1999) 'Theory of Multimarket Competition: A Synthesis and Implications for Marketing Strategy', *Journal of Marketing*, Vol. 63, No. 3, pp. 49–66.

Kaplan, S. (1989) 'The Effects of Management Buyouts on Operating Performance and Value', *Journal of Financial Economics*, Vol. 24, No. 2, October, pp. 217–254.

Kono, T. (1999) 'A Strong Head Office Makes a Strong Company', *Long Range Planning*, Vol. 32, No. 2, pp. 225–236.

Lawrence, P.R. and Lorsch, J.W. (1967) *Organization and Environment,* Cambridge, MA: Harvard University Press.

Long, W.F. and Ravenscraft, D.J. (1993) 'Decade of Debt: Lessons from LBOs in the 1980s', in: M.M. Blair (ed.) *The Deal Decade: What Takeovers and Leveraged Buyouts Mean for Corporate Governance*, Washington: Brookings Institution.

Lubatkin, M. and Chatterjee, S. (1994) 'Extending Modern Portfolio Theory into the Domain of Corporate Diversification: Does It Apply?', *Academy of Management Journal*, Vol. 37, No. 1, pp. 109–136.

Mahoney, J.T. (1992) 'The Choice of Organizational Form: Vertical Financial Ownership versus Other Methods of Vertical Integration', *Strategic Management Journal*, Vol. 13, No. 8, pp. 559–584.

Miyashita. K. and Russell, D. (1995) *Keiretsu. Inside the Hidden Japanese Conglomerates*, Maidenhead: McGraw Hill.

Perlmutter, H.V. (1969) 'The Tortuous Evolution of Multi-National Enterprises', *Columbia Journal of World Business*, 1, pp. 9–18.

Porter, M.E. (ed.) (1986) *Competition in Global Industries*, Harvard Business Press.

Porter, M.E. (1987) 'From Competitive Advantage to Corporate Strategy', *Harvard Business Review*, Vol. 65, No. 3, May–June, pp. 43–59.

Prahalad, C.K. and Bettis, R.A. (1986) 'The Dominant Logic: A New Linkage Between Diversity and Performance', *Strategic Management Journal*, Vol. 7, No. 6, November–December, pp. 485–601.

Prahalad, C.K. and Doz, Y. (1987) *The Multinational Mission: Balancing Local Demands and Global Vision*, New York: Free Press.

Prahalad, C.K. and Hamel, G. (1990) 'The Core Competence of the Corporation', *Harvard Business Review*, Vol. 68, No. 3, May–June, pp. 79–91.

Ramanujam, V. and Varadarajan, P. (1989) 'Research on Corporate Diversification: A Synthesis', *Strategic Management Journal*, Vol. 10, No. 6, November–December, pp. 523–551.

Raynor, M.E. and Bower, J.L. (2001) 'Lead from the Center: How to Manage Diverse Businesses', *Harvard Business Review*, Vol. 80, No. 5, May, pp. 93–100.

Rumelt, R.P. (1974) *Strategy, Structure, and Economic Performance,* Cambridge, MA: Harvard University Press.

Rumelt, R.P. (1982) 'Diversification Strategy and Profitability', *Strategic Management Journal*, Vol. 3, No. 4, October–December, pp. 359–369.

Seth, A. (1990) 'Value Creation in Acquisitions: A Re-Examination of Performance Issues', *Strategic Management Journal*, Vol. 11, No. 2, February, pp. 99–115.

Sirower, M.L. (1997) *The Synergy Trap: How Companies Lose the Acquisition Game*, New York: Free Press.

Stalk, G., Evans, P. and Schulman, L.E. (1992) 'Competing on Capabilities: The New Rules of Corporate Strategy', *Harvard Business Review*, Vol. 70, No. 2, March–April, pp. 57–69.

Steers, R.M., Shin, Y.K. and Ungson, G.R. (1991) *The Chaebol: Korea's New Industrial Might*, New York: Harper Collins.

Trautwein, F. (1990) 'Merger Motives and Merger Prescriptions', *Strategic Management Journal*, Vol. 11, No. 4, May–June, pp. 283–295.

Verluyten, S.P. (2000) *Intercultural Communication in Business and Organisations*, Leuven: Acco.

Weston, J.F., Chung, K.S. and Hoag, S.E. (1990) *Mergers, Restructuring, and Corporate Control*, Englewood Cliffs, NJ: Prentice Hall.

Williamson, O.E. (1975) *Markets and Hierarchies: Analysis and Antitrust Implications*, New York: Free Press.

Yergin, D. (2011) *The Quest. Energy, Security and the Remaking of the Modern World*, New York: Penguin Books.

NETWORK LEVEL STRATEGY

When bad men combine, the good must associate; else they will fall, one by one, an unpitied sacrifice in a contemptible struggle.

Edmund Burke (1729–1797) British political writer

INTRODUCTION

A business unit can have a strategy, while a group of business units can also have a strategy together – this joint course of action at the divisional or corporate level was discussed in the previous chapter. What has not been examined yet, is whether a group of companies can also have a strategy together. Is it possible that companies do not develop their strategies in 'splendid isolation', but rather coordinate their strategies to operate as a team? And is it a good idea for firms to link up with others for a prolonged period of time to try to achieve shared objectives together?

Where two or more firms move beyond a mere transactional relationship and work jointly towards a common goal, they form an alliance, partnership or network. Their shared strategy is referred to as a network level strategy. In such a case, strategy is not only 'concerned with relating a firm to its environment', as was stated in Chapter 4, but also with relating a network to its broader environment.

The existence of networks does raise a range of questions, not the least of which is whether they make strategic sense or not. Is it beneficial to engage in long-term collaborative relationships with other firms or is it more advantageous for firms to 'keep their distance' and to interact with one another in a more market-like, transactional way? Is it viable to manage a web of partnership relations or is it preferable to keep it simple, by having the firm operate more or less independently? To address these questions is to raise the issue of inter-organizational relationships – what should be the nature of the relationship between a firm and other organizations in its surroundings? This issue will be the focus of further discussion in this chapter.

THE ISSUE OF INTER-ORGANIZATIONAL RELATIONSHIPS

No firm exists that is autarchic. All firms must necessarily interact with other organizations (and individuals) in their environment and therefore they have inter-organizational (or inter-firm) relationships. These relationships can evolve without any clear strategic intent or tactical calculation, but most managers agree that actively determining the nature of their external relations is a significant part of what strategizing is about. Even avoiding relations with some external parties can be an important strategic choice.

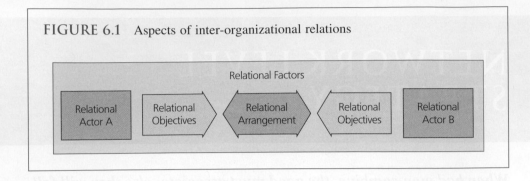

FIGURE 6.1   Aspects of inter-organizational relations

To gain a better understanding of the interaction between firms, four aspects are of particular importance and will be reviewed here – the who, why, what and how of inter-organizational relationships (see Figure 6.1). The first aspect is the question of who – who are the potential counterparts with whom a firm can actually have a relationship? This is referred to as the topic of 'relational actors'. The second aspect is the question of why – why do the parties want to enter into a relationship with one another? This is referred to as the topic of 'relational objectives'. The third aspect is the question of what – what type of influences determine the nature of the relationship? This is referred to as the topic of 'relational factors'. The fourth aspect is the question of how – how can relationships be structured into a particular organizational form to let them function in the manner intended? This is referred to as the topic of 'relational arrangements'.

Relational actors

In Figure 6.2 an overview is given of the eight major groups of external parties with whom the firm can, or must, interact. A distinction has been made between industry and contextual actors. The industry actors are those individuals and organizations that perform value-adding activities or consume the outputs of these activities. The contextual actors are those parties whose behaviour, intentionally or unintentionally, sets the conditions under which the industry actors must operate. The four main categories of relationships between the firm and other industry parties are the following (e.g. Porter, 1980; Reve, 1990):

- Upstream vertical (supplier) relations. Every company has suppliers of some sort. In a narrow definition these include the providers of raw materials, parts, machinery and business services. In a broader definition the providers of all production factors (land, capital, labour, technology, information and entrepreneurship) can be seen as suppliers, if they are not part of the firm itself. All these suppliers can either be the actual producers of the input, or an intermediary (distributor or agent) trading in the product or service. Besides the suppliers with which the firm transacts directly (first-tier suppliers), the firm may also have relationships with suppliers further upstream in the industry. All these relationships are traditionally referred to as upstream vertical relations, because economists commonly draw the industry system as a column.

- Downstream vertical (buyer) relations. On the output side, the firm has relationships with its customers. These clients can either be the actual users of the product or service, or intermediaries trading the output. Besides the buyers with which the firm transacts directly, it may also have relationships with parties further downstream in the industry column.

- Direct horizontal (industry insider) relations. This category includes the relations between the firm and other industry incumbents. Because these competitors produce similar goods or services, they are said to be at the same horizontal level in the industry column.

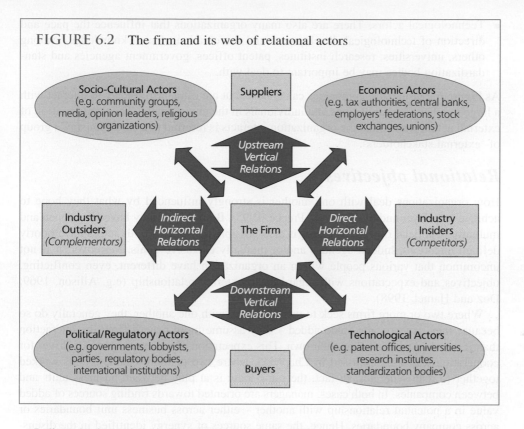

FIGURE 6.2 The firm and its web of relational actors

Indirect horizontal (industry outsider) relations. Where a firm has a relationship with a company outside its industry, this is referred to as an indirect horizontal relation. Commonly, companies will have relationships with the producers of complementary goods and services (e.g. hardware manufacturers with software developers). Such a relationship can develop with the producer of a substitute good or service, either as an adversary or as an ally. A relation can also exist between a firm and a potential industry entrant, whereby the incumbent firm can assist or attempt to block the entry of the industry outsider. Furthermore, a firm can establish a relationship with a firm in another industry, with the intention of diversifying into that, or a third, industry. In reality, where industry boundaries are not clear, the distinction between direct and indirect horizontal relations is equally blurry.

Besides relationships with these industry actors, there can be many contacts with condition-setting parties in the broader environment. Employing the classic SEPTember distinction, the following rough categories of contextual actors can be identified:

Socio-cultural actors. Individuals or organizations that have a significant impact on societal values, norms, beliefs and behaviours may interact with the firm. These could include the media, community groups, charities, religious organizations and opinion leaders.

Economic actors. There can also be organizations influencing the general economic state of affairs, with which the firm interacts. Among others, tax authorities, central banks, employers' federations, stock exchanges and unions may be of importance.

Political/legal actors. The firm may also interact with organizations setting or influencing the regulations under which companies must operate. These could include governments, political parties, special interest groups, regulatory bodies and international institutions.

■ Technological actors. There are also many organizations that influence the pace and direction of technological development and the creation of new knowledge. Among others, universities, research institutes, patent offices, government agencies and standardization bodies may be important to deal with.

As Figure 6.2 visualizes, companies can choose, but are often also forced, to interact with a large number of organizations and individuals in the environment. This configuration of external actors with which the organization interacts is referred to as the company's group of 'external stakeholders'.

Relational objectives

How organizations deal with one another is strongly influenced by what they hope to achieve (e.g. Dyer and Singh, 1998; Preece, 1995). Both parties may have clear, open and mutually beneficial objectives, but it is also possible that one or both actors have poorly defined intentions, hidden agendas and/or mutually exclusive goals. Moreover, it is not uncommon that various people within an organization have different, even conflicting, objectives and expectations with regard to an external relationship (e.g. Allison, 1969; Doz and Hamel, 1998).

Where two or more firms seek to work together with one another, they generally do so because they expect some value added – they assume more benefit from the interaction than if they had proceeded on their own. This expectation of value creation as a driver for cooperation was also discussed in Chapter 5, where two or more business units worked together to reap synergies. In fact, the same logic is at play between business units and between companies. In both cases, managers are oriented towards finding sources of added value in a potential relationship with another – either across business unit boundaries or across company boundaries. Hence, the same sources of synergy identified in the discussion on corporate level strategy are just as relevant when examining the objectives for inter-organizational cooperation (see Figure 6.3).

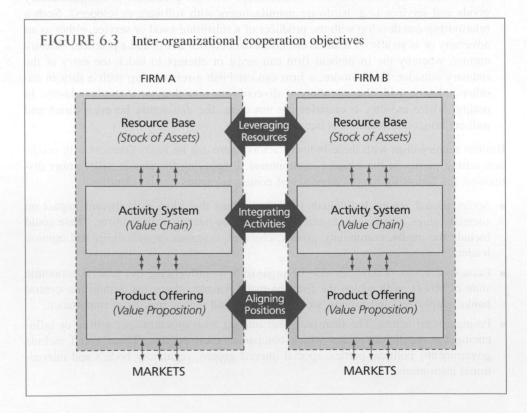

FIGURE 6.3   Inter-organizational cooperation objectives

Relations oriented towards leveraging resources.   The first area where companies can cooperate is at the level of their resource bases. By sharing resources with one another, companies can improve either the quantity or quality of the resources they have at their disposal. There are two general ways for firms to leverage resources to reap mutual benefit:

- Learning. When the objective is to exchange knowledge and skills, or to engage in the joint pursuit of new know-how, the relationship is said to be learning-oriented. Firms can enter into new learning relationships with industry outsiders, but can also team up with industry incumbents, for instance to develop new technologies or standards (e.g. Hamel, Doz and Prahalad, 1989, Reading 6.1; Shapiro and Varian, 1998). However, firms can add a learning objective to an already existing relationship with a buyer or supplier as well.

- Lending. Where one firm owns specific resources that it cannot make full use of, or another firm can make better use of, it can be attractive for both to lend the resource to the other. Lending relationships happen frequently in the areas of technology, copyrights and trademarks, where licensing is commonplace. But physical resources can also be lent, usually in the form of lease contracts. In all cases the benefit to lenders can be financial or they receive other resources in return.

Relations oriented towards integrating activities.   The second area where companies can cooperate is at the level of their activity systems. Few companies can span an entire industry column from top to bottom and excel at every type of activity. Usually, by integrating their value chains with other organizations, firms can be much more efficient and effective than if they were totally separated. There are two general ways for firms to integrate their activities with others:

- Linking. The most common type of relationship in business is the vertical link between a buyer and a seller. All relationships in which products or services are exchanged fall into this category. Most firms have many linking relationships, both upstream and downstream, because they want to focus on only a limited number of value-adding activities, but need a variety of inputs, as well as clients to purchase their finished goods.

- Lumping. Where firms bring together their similar activities to gain economies of scale, the relationship is said to be oriented towards lumping. Sharing operations (e.g. airline alliances), sales infrastructure (e.g. software cross-selling deals), logistics systems (e.g. postal partnerships) or payment facilities (e.g. inter-bank settlement agreements) are examples of where firms can lump their activities together. Because the activities need to be more or less the same to be able to reap scale economies, lumping relationships are usually found between two or more industry insiders.

Relations oriented towards aligning positions.   The third area where companies can cooperate is at the level of their market positions. Even where companies want to keep their value-adding activities separate, they can coordinate their moves in the environment with the intention of strengthening each other's position. Usually, this type of coalition-building is directed at improving the joint bargaining power of the cooperating parties. These position-enhancing relationships can be further subdivided into two categories:

- Leaning. Where two or more firms get together to improve their bargaining position vis-à-vis other industry actors, it is said that they lean on each other to stand stronger. Leaning can be directed at building up a more powerful negotiation position towards suppliers, or to offer a more attractive package of products and services towards buyers. Getting together with other companies to form a consortium to launch a new industry standard can also bolster the position of all companies involved. At the same time, the cooperation can be directed at weakening the position of an alternative group of companies or even heightening the entry barriers for interested industry outsiders.

- Lobbying. Firms can also cooperate with one another with the objective of gaining a stronger position vis-à-vis contextual actors. Such lobbying relationships are often directed at strengthening the firms' voice towards political and regulatory actors, such as governments and regulatory agencies. However, firms can get together to put pressure on various other contextual actors, such as standard setting bodies, universities, tax authorities and stock exchanges as well.

In practice, cooperative relationships between organizations can involve a number of these objectives simultaneously. Moreover, it is not uncommon for objectives to shift over time and for various participants in the relationship to have different objectives.

Relational factors

How inter-organizational relationships develop is strongly influenced by the objectives pursued by the parties involved. However, a number of other factors also have an impact on how relationships unfold. These relational factors can be grouped into four general categories (e.g. Mitchell, Agle and Wood, 1997; Gulati, 1998):

- Legitimacy. Relationships are highly impacted by what is deemed to be legitimate. Written and unwritten codes of conduct give direction to what is viewed as acceptable behaviour. Which topics are allowed on the agenda, who has a valid claim, how interaction should take place and how conflicts should be resolved, are often decided by what both parties accept as 'the rules of engagement'. There is said to be 'trust', where it is expected that the other organization or individual will adhere to these rules. However, organizations do not always agree on 'appropriate behaviour', while what is viewed as legitimate can shift over time as well. It can also be (seen as) advantageous to act opportunistically by not behaving according to the unwritten rules (e.g. Gambetta, 1988; Williamson, 1991).

- Urgency. Inter-organizational relations are also shaped by the factor 'timing'. Relationships develop differently when one or both parties are under time pressure to achieve results, as opposed to a situation where both organizations can interact without experiencing a sense of urgency (e.g. Pfeffer and Salancik, 1978; James, 1985).

- Frequency. Inter-organizational relations also depend on the frequency of interaction and the expectation of future interactions. Where parties expect to engage in a one-off transaction they usually behave differently than when they anticipate a more structural relationship extending over multiple interactions. Moreover, a relationship with a low rate of interaction tends to develop differently than one with a high regularity of interaction (e.g. Axelrod, 1984; Dixit and Nalebuff, 1991).

- Power. Last but not least, relations between organizations are strongly shaped by the power held by both parties. Power is the ability to influence others' behaviour and organizations can have many sources of power. Most importantly for inter-organizational relationships, a firm can derive power from having resources that the other organization requires. In relationships with a very high level of resource dependence, firms tend to behave differently towards each other than when they are interdependent or relatively independent of one another (e.g. Pfeffer and Salancik, 1978; Porter, 1980).

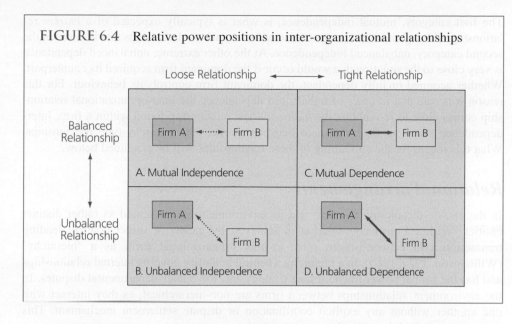

FIGURE 6.4   Relative power positions in inter-organizational relationships

Especially the impact of power differences on inter-organizational relationships is given extensive attention in the strategic management literature. Many authors (e.g. Chandler, 1990; Kay, 1993; Pfeffer and Salancik, 1978; Porter, 1980; Schelling, 1960) stress that for understanding the interaction between firms it is of the utmost importance to gain insight into their relative power positions. One way of measuring relative power in a relationship is portrayed in Figure 6.4, where a distinction is made between the closeness of the relationship (loose vs tight) and the distribution of power between the two parties involved (balanced vs unbalanced). This leads to a categorization of four specific types of inter-firm relationships from the perspective of relative power position. These four categories (adapted from Ruigrok and Van Tulder, 1995) are:

A Mutual independence. Organizations are independent in a relationship if they have full freedom to act according to their own objectives. Independence in an inter-organizational relationship means that organizations will only interact on their own terms and that they have the ability to break off the relationship without any penalty. In a situation of mutual independence, neither organization has significant influence over the other.

B Unbalanced independence. When two organizations work together in a loose relationship, one side (Firm A) can have more power than the other (Firm B). In such a case, it is said that Firm A is more independent than Firm B – Firm A's power gives it more freedom to act, while Firm B can be influenced by the powerful Firm A. This situation is called unbalanced independence, as both sides are independent, but one more so than the other.

C Mutual dependence. Two organizations can have a tight relationship, in which they are mutually dependent, while having an equal amount of sway over their counterpart. This type of situation, where there is a substantial, yet balanced, relationship between two or more parties, is also called interdependence.

D Unbalanced dependence. Where a tight relationship is characterized by asymmetrical dependence, one party will be able to dominate the other. In this situation of unbalanced dependence, the organization with the lower level of dependence will have more freedom to manoeuvre and impose its conditions than its counterpart.

The first category, mutual independence, is what is typically expected of a *market* relationship, although it is not strange to also witness market relationships that fit more in the second category, unbalanced independence. At the other extreme, unbalanced dependence is very close to the situation that would occur if the dominant firm acquired its counterpart. Whether acquired or fully dependent, the dominant firm controls its behaviour. For this reason it is said that in cases of unbalanced dependence the inter-organizational relationship comes close to resembling the *hierarchy-type* relationship found within a firm. Interdependence seems to be somewhere between market and hierarchy-type relationships. What this means for the structuring of these relationships will be examined below.

Relational arrangements

In the classic dichotomy, the firm and its environment are presented as rather distinct entities. Within a firm coordination is achieved by means of direct control, leading transaction cost economists to refer to this organizational form as a 'hierarchy' (Williamson, 1975, 1985). In a hierarchy a central authority governs internal relationships and has the formal power to coordinate strategy and solve inter-departmental disputes. In the environment, relationships between firms are non-hierarchical, as they interact with one another without any explicit coordination or dispute settlement mechanism. This organizational form is referred to as a 'market'.

In Chapter 5 it was argued that there are all types of activities that companies should not want to internalize and run themselves, but should leave up to the marketplace. In many situations, it is much more efficient to buy inputs in the market than to make them yourself – where activities are performed by autonomous parties and outputs are sold in the marketplace, costs will often be lowest. As summarized by Ouchi (1980, p. 130), 'in a market relationship, the transaction takes place between the two parties and is mediated by a price mechanism in which the existence of a competitive market reassures both parties that the terms of exchange are equitable'.

Integration of activities into the firm is only necessary where 'markets do not function properly' – where doing it yourself is cheaper or better. The firm must internalize activities, despite the disadvantages of hierarchy, where the 'invisible hand' of the market cannot be trusted to be equitable and effective. Control over activities by means of formal authority – the 'visible hand' – is needed under these conditions. This is particularly true of all of the synergy advantages mentioned in Chapter 5, that the corporation would not be able to reap if the various business activities were not brought together under one 'corporate roof'.

In reality, however, there are many organizational forms between markets and hierarchies (e.g. Hakansson and Johanson, 1993; Powell, 1990; Thorelli, 1986). These are the networks, partnerships, or alliances introduced at the start of this chapter. In networks, strategies are coordinated and disputes resolved, not through formal top-down power, but by mutual adaptation. To extend the above metaphor, networks rely neither on the visible nor invisible hand to guide relationships, but rather employ the 'continuous handshake' (Gerlach, 1992).

The organizations involved in networks can employ different sorts of collaborative arrangements to structure their ties with one another. In Figure 6.5, an overview of a number of common types of collaborative arrangements is presented. Two major distinctions are made in this overview. First, between bilateral arrangements, which only involve two parties, and multilateral arrangements, which involve three or more. Commonly, only the multilateral arrangements are referred to as networks, although here the term is employed to cover all groupings of two or more cooperating firms. The second distinction is between non-contractual, contractual and equity-based arrangements. Non-contractual arrangements are cooperative agreements that are not binding by law, while

FIGURE 6.5 Examples of collaborative arrangements

	Non-Contractual Arrangements	Contractual Arrangements	Equity-based Arrangements
Multilateral Arrangements	• Lobbying coalition (e.g. European Roundtable of Industrialists) • Joint standard setting (e.g. Linux coalition) • Learning communities (e.g. Strategic Management Society)	• Research consortium (e.g. Symbian in PDAs) • International marketing alliance (e.g. Star Alliance in airlines) • Export partnership (e.g. Netherlands Export Combination)	• Shared payment system (e.g. Visa) • Construction consortium (e.g. Eurotunnel) • Joint reservation system (e.g. Galileo)
Bilateral Arrangements	• Cross-selling deal (e.g. between pharmaceutical firms) • R&D staff exchange (e.g. between IT firms) • Market information sharing agreement (e.g. between hardware and software makers)	• Licensing agreement (e.g. Disney and Coca Cola) • Co-development contract (e.g. Disney and Pixar in movies) • Co-branding alliance (e.g. Coca-Cola and McDonald's)	• New product joint venture (e.g. Sony and Ericsson in cellphones) • Cross-border joint venture (e.g. Daimler Benz and Beijing Automotive) • Local joint venture (e.g. CNN Turk in Turkey)

contractual arrangements do have a clear legal enforceability. Both, however, do not involve taking a financial stake in each other or in a new joint venture, while the equity-based arrangements do.

The intent of these collaborative arrangements is to profit from some of the advantages of vertical and horizontal integration, without incurring their costs. Networks are actually hybrid organizational forms that attempt to combine the benefits of hierarchy with the benefits of the market. The main benefits of hierarchy are those associated with the structural coordination of activities. In non-market relational arrangements, all parties collaborate on a more long-term basis with the intent of realizing a common goal. They will organize procedures, routines and control systems to ensure effective and efficient functioning of their joint activities and a smooth transition at their organizational interfaces. The benefits of the market that these collaborative arrangements retain are flexibility and motivation. By not being entirely locked into a fixed hierarchy, individual firms can flexibly have multiple relationships of varying length and intensity, and can change these relationships more easily where circumstances require adaptation. The market also provides the motivation to be efficient and to optimize the pursuit of the organization's self-interest. This entrepreneurial incentive can be a strong spur for risk-taking, innovation and change.

A significant advantage of collaborative arrangements is that such relationships facilitate the process of 'co-specialization'. Much of humanity's economic progress is based on the principle of specialization by means of a division of labour. As people and firms focus more closely on performing a limited set of value-adding activities, they become more effective and efficient in their work. This division of labour assumes, however, that the value-adding activities that are outsourced by one become the specialization of another, hence co-specialization. Yet, many activities cannot be outsourced to outsiders on the basis of normal market relations, either due to the risk of dependence or because of the need for the structural coordination of activities. Under these conditions, collaborative arrangements can act as a synthesis of hierarchy and market relations, thus catalysing the process of specialization (e.g. Best, 1990; Axelsson and Easton, 1992).

Such co-specialization can progress to such an extent that clusters of firms work together in more or less permanent networks. Such symbiotic groups of collaborating firms can actually function as 'virtual corporations' (e.g. Chesbrough and Teece, 1996; Quinn, 1992). In such networks, the relationships between the participating firms are often very tight and durable, based on a high level of trust and perceived mutual interest. While each organization retains its individual identity, the boundaries between them become fuzzy, blurring the clear distinction between 'the organization' and 'its environment'. When a high level of trust and reciprocity has been achieved, relations can move far beyond simple contractual obligations. The collaborative relations can become more open-ended, with objectives, responsibilities, authority and results not fully determined in advance in a written contract, but evolving over time, given all parties' sincere willingness to 'work on their relationship' (e.g. Jarillo, 1988; Kanter, 1994).

While the intention of collaborative arrangements may be to blend the advantages of hierarchy with the qualities of the market, it is also possible that the weaknesses of both are actually combined. The main weakness of hierarchy is bureaucracy – creating red tape, unnecessary coordination activities and dulling the incentive to perform. In reality, collaborative arrangements might be mechanisms for structuring static relationships and dampening entrepreneurial behaviour. A further danger is that the mutual dependence might become skewed, shifting the balance of power to one of the partners. Under such conditions, one or more organizations can become dependent on a dominant party, without much influence (voice) or the possibility to break off the relationship (exit). Such unbalanced dependency relationships (see Figure 6.4) might be a great benefit for the stronger party, but can easily lead to the predominance of its interests over the interests of the weaker partners (e.g. Oliver and Wilkinson, 1988; Ruigrok and Van Tulder, 1995).

Simultaneously such partnerships are vulnerable to the main disadvantage of the market, namely opportunism. Companies run the risk of opportunism, which is (according to Williamson, 1985: 47):

> *self-interest seeking with guile. This includes but is scarcely limited to more blatant forms, such as lying, stealing and cheating.... More generally, opportunism refers to the incomplete or distorted disclosure of information, especially to calculated efforts to mislead, distort, disguise, obfuscate, or otherwise confuse.*

Such behaviour can be limited by clearly defining objectives, responsibilities, authority and expected results ahead of time, preferably in an explicit contract. Even then collaborative arrangements expose companies to the risk of deception, the abuse of trust and the exploitation of dependence, making their use by no means undisputed.

THE PARADOX OF COMPETITION AND COOPERATION

We have no eternal allies and we have no perpetual enemies. Our interests are eternal and perpetual, and those interests it is our duty to follow.
Lord Palmerston (Henry John Temple) (1784–1865); British prime minister

When former CEO of KLM Royal Dutch Airlines, Pieter Bouw, teamed up with Northwest Airlines in 1989, he was thrilled to have the first major transatlantic strategic alliance in the industry, involving joint flights, marketing and sales activities, catering, ground handling, maintenance and purchasing. Northwest was the fourth largest American carrier at that time, but was in 'Chapter 11', balancing on the verge of bankruptcy, and in dire need of cash. To help their new ally out, KLM gave a US$ 400 million capital injection, in return for 20 per cent of the shares and the option to increase this to a majority stake within a few years. KLM and Northwest were on their way to becoming a virtual transatlantic company – a marriage 'made in the heavens'.

Commercially the deal was a success, but relationally the alliance was a Shakespearean drama. KLM gave up its hopes of an alliance with Swissair, SAS and Delta, to remain loyal to Northwest, but as soon as Northwest emerged from Chapter 11, it blocked KLM's efforts to increase its shareholding. In the resulting two-year legal shooting match between 1995 and 1997, relations deteriorated sharply and the goose laying the golden eggs was threatened to be killed in the cross fire. Disappointed and dismayed, Bouw decided to give in, selling Northwest back its shares, in return for a prolongation of the alliance, after which he immediately resigned. His successor, Leo van Wijk, has managed the alliance since then and it is still 'up in the air', in both senses of the expression. His most important conclusion has been that a collaborative alliance is not only about working together towards a common interest, but equally about being assertive with regard to one's own interests. Alliances are not only *cooperative,* but also have *competitive* aspects.

What this example of KLM and Northwest illustrates is that firms constantly struggle with the tension created by the need to work together with others, while simultaneously needing to pursue their own interests. Firms cannot isolate themselves from their environments, but must actively engage in relationships with suppliers and buyers, while selectively teaming up with other firms inside and outside their industry to attain mutual benefit. But while they are collaborating to create joint value, firms are also each other's rivals when it comes to dividing the benefits. These opposite demands placed on organizations are widely referred to as the pressures for competition and cooperation (e.g. Brandenburger and Nalebuff, 1996; Lado, Boyd and Hanlon, 1997). In the following sections both pressures will be examined in more detail.

The demand for inter-organizational competition

Competition can be defined as the act of working against others, where two or more organizations' goals are mutually exclusive. In other words, competition is the rivalry behaviour exhibited by organizations or individuals where one's win is the other's loss.

Organizations need to be competitive in their relationships with others. As the interests or objectives of different organizations are often mutually exclusive, each organization needs to be determined and assertive in pursuing its own agenda. Each organization needs to be willing to confront others to secure its own interests. Without the will to engage in competitive interaction, the organization will be at the mercy of more aggressive counterparts, e.g. suppliers will charge excessively for products, buyers will express stiff demands for low prices, governments will require special efforts without compensation, and rival firms will poach among existing customers. Taking a competitive posture towards these external parties means that the organization is determined to assert its own interests and fight where necessary.

The resulting competitive relations can vary between open antagonism and conflict on the one hand, and more subtle forms of friction, tension and strain on the other. Blatant competitive behaviour is often exhibited towards organizations whose objectives are fully in conflict – most clearly other producers of the same goods, attempting to serve the same markets (aptly referred to as 'the competition'). Highly competitive behaviour can also be witnessed where a supplier and a buyer confront each other for dominance in the industry value chain (e.g. Porter, 1980; Van Tulder and Junne, 1988). A more restrained competitive stance can be observed where organizations' objectives are less at odds, but assertiveness is still important to protect the organization's interests. Negotiation and bargaining will commonly be employed under these circumstances.

To be competitive an organization must have the power to overcome its rivals and it must have the ability and will to use its power. Many factors shape the power of an organization, but its relative level of resource dependence is one of the most important determining elements. The more independent the organization, and the more others are dependent on it, the more power the organization will wield. In competitive relationships, manoeuvring the other party into a relatively dependent position is a common approach. In general, calculation, bargaining, manoeuvring, building coalitions and outright conflict are all characteristic for the competitive interaction between organizations.

The demand for inter-organizational cooperation

Cooperation can be defined as the act of working together with others, where two or more organizations' goals are mutually beneficial. In other words, cooperation is the collaborative behaviour exhibited by organizations or individuals where both sides need each other to succeed.

Organizations need to be cooperative in their relationships with others. The interests or objectives of different organizations are often complementary and working together can be mutually beneficial. Therefore, organizations must be willing to behave as partners, striving towards their common good. Without the will to engage in cooperative interaction, the organization will miss the opportunity to reap the advantages of joint efforts, e.g. developing new products together with suppliers, creating a better service offering together with buyers, improving the knowledge infrastructure together with government and setting new technical standards together with other firms in the industry. Taking a cooperative posture towards these external parties means that the organization is determined to leverage its abilities through teamwork.

The resulting cooperative relations can vary between occasional alliances on the one hand, to tight-knit, virtual integration on the other. Strongly cooperative behaviour can be witnessed where the long-term interests of all parties are highly intertwined. This type of symbiotic relationship can be found between the producers of complementary goods and services, where success by one organization will positively impact its partners – aptly referred to as the 'network effect' (Arthur, 1994; Shapiro and Varian, 1998). Highly cooperative behaviour can also be observed where suppliers and buyers face a joint challenge (such as government regulation, an innovative technology or a new market entrant) that can only be tackled by significant mutual commitment to a shared objective.

More restrained cooperative behaviour is common where there is potential for a 'positive sum game', but some parties seek to optimize their own returns to the detriment of others. Under such circumstances, exhibiting cooperative behaviour does not mean being naive or weak, but creating conditions under which the long-term shared interests prevail over the short-term temptation by some to cheat their partners. An important ingredient for overcoming the lure of opportunism is to build long-term commitment to one another, not only in words and mentality, but also practically, through a high level of interdependence. Where organizations are tightly linked to one another, the pay-off for cooperative behaviour is usually much more enticing than the possibility to profit from the dependence of one's partner. But to be willing to commit to such a high level of interdependence, people on both sides of a relationship need to trust each other's intentions and actions, while there must be coordination and conflict-resolution mechanisms in place to solve evolving issues (e.g. Dyer, Kale and Singh, 2001; Simonin, 1997).

EXHIBIT 6.1 SHORT CASE

LONDON HEATHROW: THE SKY IS NOT THE LIMIT

From his office in the compass centre of Heathrow Airport London, Colin Matthews overlooks the runways, seeing airplanes landing and taking off every minute. A little smile appears on his face. Before he became CEO of Heathrow Airport Holdings (HAH), he had been managing director of British Airways. He remembers how a pilot once told him: "It's better to be down here wishing you were up there, than to be up there wishing you were down here". He realizes that the answer to the question which of the two situations currently fits Heathrow best remains unanswered. The economic power of Heathrow is so immense that his responsibility to safeguard jobs for the families relying on their source of income is a heavy burden. Across the United Kingdom, Heathrow supports almost 206,000 jobs. The gross value added (GVA) of Heathrow approximates £9.7 billion, which accounts for 2.7 per cent of London's and 0.8 per cent of the entire UK GVA.

The competition is fierce, within the UK as well as with continental Europe. Furthermore, Heathrow faces major capacity problems, as there is little or no room for growth. Consequently, the number of destinations is shrinking and airlines are considering carrying parts of their business elsewhere. Representatives of the London Businesses are pushing towards expansion and claim that every year that deciding on the expansion plan is postponed will cost millions and millions of pounds. Environmental organizations are complaining about increased air and noise pollution due to airplanes is becoming bigger. With the upcoming national elections in 2015, the pressure of national parties is increasing. To make matters worse, local politicians are claiming airtime as well. Boris Johnson, the eccentric mayor of London, wrote an inches thick report called: *Vision 2020 – The Greatest City on Earth: Ambitions for London by Boris Johnson.* And now he has given Heathrow an ultimatum. He has demanded that by the end of the week, Colin Matthews will come up with a durable solution to secure all the Heathrow jobs for the future generation in the London area. If Matthews is unable to come up with a convincing solution, Boris Johnson

will present his own plan to the London City Council. Colin Matthews knows one thing for sure; a politician taking control over one of the biggest private companies in the UK will not satisfy the current owner of HAH and will therefore probably shorten his days as a CEO significantly.

Heathrow is the world's third busiest International hub airport with 70 million passengers per annum (mppa) in 2012. Local passengers – travelling to and from Heathrow – provide a steady revenue basis, while transfer passengers provide the volume. With a total of five passenger terminals and two runways, and after years of passenger growth, Heathrow is bursting at the seams. Located very near London City, there are small villages all around Heathrow. And although the new Terminal 5 has raised the passenger potential capacity to 90 mppa, both runways are at 98 per cent capacity, leaving no space for further expansion. Every 45 seconds a plane takes off or lands at Heathrow and so the tiniest mishap, such as a thunderstorm or high winds, causes delays and cancelled flights. Due to the capacity constraints, the number of destinations served by Heathrow has fallen by 15 per cent from 227 in 1990 to 193 in 2011, as airlines conserved their scarce slots to concentrate on the most profitable routes. Gatwick Airport (Gatwick) and London Stansted Airport (Stansted) profited from this trend: Gatwick became Europe's leading airport for point-to-point flights and Stansted an important base for low-cost carriers like Ryanair and easyJet. However, both are facing capacity problems, similar to those of Heathrow. Gatwick and Stansted were fully owned by HAH, but the Competition Commission report about market dominance forced HAH to sell Gatwick in December 2009 and Stansted in February 2013.

Heathrow's competition is heavy. Amsterdam Schiphol Airport operates five full-size runways with a record breaking 51 million mppa in 2012, Paris Charles de Gaulle (CDG) four runways with 61.5 million mppa in 2012, Madrid–Barajas Airport's four runways with 49 million mppa in 2011, and Frankfurt am Main Airport also four runways with 57.5 million mppa in 2012. While the two Heathrow runways are at 98 per cent capacity, the continental European runways are average just 75 per cent, leaving flexibility for countering delays due to weather conditions. Another major competitor is Dubai Airport which operates six runways and is rapidly becoming a global hub, linking Asia to the rest of the world. Dubai handled 57.7 mppa in 2012 and aims at increasing capacity from the current 70 million to 90 mppa in 2018.

Colin Matthews' time is running out. By the end of the week, he has to present a plan that safeguards the future of Heathrow to London mayor, Boris Johnson. Doing so will be far from easy because the Heathrow's many stakeholders all want to be engaged in the decision-making process. Since many companies benefit from Heathrow, the British Chamber of Commerce, as well as the Confederation of British Industry and the Trades Union Congress are in favour of expanding Heathrow with a third runway and a sixth terminal. In their opinion, this is not only the way to preserve the current business, but to also expand business hovering around Heathrow. However, the expansion plan has triggered fierce resident protests and provoked claims of air pollution by environmental organizations. In order to build a new runway and terminal, the beautiful town of Sipson would have to disappear entirely, forcing hundreds of people out of the homes they've lived in for generations. And then there is severe opposition from environmentalists because of the expected increase of noise and air pollution. Due to this heavy resistance the government cancelled the expansion plan in 2010.

London First, representing many of London's businesses and major employers, is lobbying heavily to put this plan back on the political agenda. A study conducted in collaboration with the British Chambers of Commerce, they estimate economic benefits can amount to £30 billion over the 2020–2080 period. Every year, however, that the plan is delayed will cost the UK between £900 million and £1.1 billion. These projections do not include the estimated 60,000 temporary construction jobs and the 8,000 new Heathrow jobs that will be created with the expansion plan. Furthermore, several stakeholders have mentioned the opportunity for Heathrow to invest in railways. Although this maybe seems a bit odd for an airport holding, at the moment Paris is the top destination from Heathrow with 60 flights a day between the two cities followed by Amsterdam. High-speed railways could be a substitute, replacing about 100,000 flights annually, thus increasing the runway capacity for global flights. But as a CEO, Colin Matthews knows that entering new markets without the know-how of running the business often leads to failure.

Further stakeholders are local and national politics. National politics are especially troublesome as they tend to voice a myriad of different opinions. At the moment the Labour Party favours expansion, while the Conservative Party does not; positions that may well change after the elections. And then there is the popular and eccentric mayor, Boris Johnson. He recently ordered a feasibility study on an entirely newly created airport in the Thames Estuary on an artificial offshore island. Colin Matthews tries to remember a mega project, coordinated by the local government, that wasn't a complete failure due to huge budget and time overhaul, yet at the moment he can't think of one. And then there is also Sir Richard Branson of Virgin Atlantic Airways who has been suggesting that the aviation industry needs to develop a shared solution to climate change.

Time is ticking away and the deadline of Boris Johnson's ultimatum is coming closer. Matthews thinks of all the jobs and families depending on Heathrow, of the stakeholders battering him with their presentations and statistics, of the opponents and the politicians. What could be a durable option to strengthen Heathrow's global position? Cooperating with friendly stakeholders while fighting the opponents is impossible, as it will lead to an unmanageable situation. He knows that the answer lies in finding a mix of cooperation and competition, but what are the options? He has until the end of the week to come up with a strategy that will fly to the sky as smoothly and safely as an airplane.

Co-author: Jeroen Brinkhuis

Sources: www.HeathrowAirport.com; London Municipality, *Vision 2020 – The Greatest City on Earth: Ambitions for London by Boris Johnson* (2012); Heathrow Annual Report and Financial Statements 2012; ICFAI Business School, London Heathrow: The Airport's expansion dilemma, (2008); Eurocontrol Civil Aviation Authority, Eggl – London Heathrow 2012; BBC News, 'Heathrow runway plans scrapped by new government', May 12, 2010; Civil Aviation Authority, www.caa.co.uk; *The Financial Times*, 'Heathrow Ready for U-Turn over more flights', May 12, 2013; *The Independent*, 'Heathrow set for big increase in capacity', June 23, 2012; *Airport International*, 'Third Heathrow Runway Not Needed', David Cameron, June 17, 2008; British Chamber of Commerce, 'Better late than never on infrastructure', July 23, 2012.

PERSPECTIVES ON NETWORK LEVEL STRATEGY

Concordia discors (discordant harmony).

Horace (65–8 BC); Roman poet

Firms need to be able to engage in competition and cooperation simultaneously, even though these demands are each other's opposites. Firms need to exhibit a strongly co-operative posture to reap the benefits of collaboration, and they need to take a strongly competitive stance to ensure that others do not block their interests. Some theorists conclude that what is required is 'co-opetition' (Brandenburger and Nalebuff, 1996). While a catchy word, managers are still left with the difficult question of how to deal with these conflicting demands. To meet the pressure for cooperation, firms must actually become part of a broader 'team', spinning a web of close collaborative relationships. But to meet the pressure for competition, firms must not become too entangled in restrictive relationships, but rather remain free to manoeuvre, bargain and attack, with the intention of securing their own interests. In other words, firms must be *embedded* and *independent* at the same time – embedded in a network of cooperative interactions, while independent enough to wield their power to their own advantage.

The question dividing strategizing managers is whether firms should be more embedded or more independent. Should firms immerse themselves in broader networks to create strong groups, or should they stand on their own? Should firms willingly engage in long-term interdependence relationships or should they strive to remain as independent as possible? Should firms develop network level strategies at all, or should the whole concept of multi-firm strategy-making be directed to the garbage heap?

While strategy writers generally agree about the need to manage the paradox of competition and cooperation, they come to widely differing prescriptions on how to do so. Views within the field of strategic management are strongly at odds with regard to the best approach to inter-organizational relations. As before, here the two diametrically opposed positions will be identified and discussed, to show the scope of differing ideas. On one side of the spectrum, there are strategists who believe that it is best for companies to be primarily competitive in their relationships to all outside forces. They argue that firms should remain independent and interact with other companies under market conditions as much as possible. As these strategists emphasize the discrete boundaries separating the firm from its 'competitive environment', this point of view is called the 'discrete organization perspective'. At the other end of the spectrum, there are strategists who believe that companies should strive to build up more long-term cooperative relationships with key organizations in their environment. They argue that firms can reap significant benefits by surrendering a part of their independence and developing close collaborative arrangements with a group of other organizations. This point of view will be referred to as the 'embedded organization perspective'.

The discrete organization perspective

Managers taking the discrete organization perspective view companies as independent entities competing with other organizations in a hostile market environment. In line with neoclassical economics, this perspective commonly emphasizes that individuals, and the organizations they form, are fundamentally motivated by aggressive self-interest and therefore that competition is the natural state of affairs. Suppliers will try to enhance their bargaining power vis-à-vis buyers with the aim of getting a better price, while conversely buyers will attempt to improve their negotiation position to attain better quality at lower cost. Competing firms will endeavour to gain the upper hand against their rivals if the opportunity arises, while new market entrants and manufacturers of substitute products will consistently strive to displace incumbent firms (e.g. Porter, 1980, 1985).

In such a hostile environment it is a strategic necessity for companies to strengthen their competitive position in relation to the external forces. The best strategy for each organization is to obtain the market power required to get good price/quality deals, ward off competitive threats, limit government demands and even determine the development of the industry. Effective power requires independence and therefore heavy reliance on specific suppliers, buyers, financiers or public organizations should be avoided.

The label 'discrete organization' given to this perspective refers to the fact that each organization is seen as being detached from its environment, with sharp boundaries demarcating where the outside world begins. The competitive situation is believed to be *atomistic,* that is, each self-interested firm strives to satisfy its own objectives, leading to rivalry and conflict with other organizations. Vertical interactions between firms in the industry column tend to be transactional, with an emphasis on getting the best possible deal. It is generally assumed that under such market conditions the interaction will be of a zero-sum nature, that is, a fight for who gets how much of the pie. The firm with the strongest bargaining power will usually be able to appropriate a larger portion of the 'economic rent' than will the less potent party. Therefore, advocates of the discrete organization perspective emphasize that the key to competitive success is the ability to build a powerful position and to wield this power in a calculated and efficient manner. This might sound Machiavellian to the faint-hearted, but it is the reality of the marketplace that is denied at one's own peril.

Essential for organizational power is the avoidance of resource dependence. Where a firm is forced to lean on a handful of suppliers or buyers, this can place the organization in a precariously exposed position. To managers taking a discrete organization perspective, such dependence on a few external parties is extremely risky, as the other firm will be tempted to exploit their position of relative power to their own advantage. Wise firms will therefore not let themselves become overly dependent on any external organization, certainly not for any essential resources. This includes keeping the option open to exit from the relationship at will – with low barriers to exit the negotiating position of the firm is significantly stronger. Therefore the firm must never become so entangled with outsiders that it cannot rid themselves of them at the drop of a hat. The firm must be careful that in a web of relationships it is the spider, not the fly (e.g. Pfeffer & Salancik, 1978; Ruigrok and Van Tulder, 1995).

Keeping other organizations at arm's length also facilitates clear and business-like interactions. Where goods and services are bought or sold, distinct organizational boundaries help to distinguish tasks, responsibilities, authority and accountability. But as other firms will always seek to do as little as possible for the highest possible price, having clear contracts and a believable threat to enforce them will serve as a method to ensure discipline. Arm's-length relations are equally useful in avoiding the danger of vital information leaking to the party with whom the firm must (re)negotiate.

In their relationships with other firms in the industry it becomes even clearer that companies' interests are mutually exclusive. More market share for one company must necessarily come at the expense of another. Coalitions are occasionally formed to create power blocks, if individual companies are not strong enough to compete on their own. Such tactical alliances bring together weaker firms, not capable of doing things independently. But 'competitive collaboration' is usually short lived – either the alliance is unsuccessful and collapses, or it is successful against the common enemy, after which the alliance partners become each other's most important rivals.

Proponents of the discrete organization perspective argue that collaborative arrangements are always second best to doing things independently. Under certain conditions, weakness might force a firm to choose an alliance, but it is always a tactical necessity, never a strategic preference. Collaborative arrangements are inherently risky, fraught with the hazard of opportunism. Due to the ultimately competitive nature of relationships, allies will be tempted to serve their own interests to the detriment of the others, by manoeuvring, manipulating or cheating. The collaboration might even be a useful ploy, to cloak the company's aggressive intentions and moves. Collaboration, it is therefore concluded, is merely 'competition in a different form' (Hamel, Doz and Prahalad, 1989, Reading 6.1). Hence, where collaboration between firms really offers long-term advantages, a merger or acquisition is preferable to the uncertainty of an alliance.

Where collaboration is not the tool of the weak, it is often a conspiracy of the strong to inhibit competition. If two or more formidable companies collaborate, chances are that the alliance is actually ganging up on a third party – for instance on buyers. In such cases the term 'collaboration' is just a euphemism for collusion and not in the interest of the economy at large.

Worse yet, collaboration is usually also bad for a company's long-term health. A highly competitive environment is beneficial for a firm, because it provides the necessary stimulus for companies to continually improve and innovate. Strong adversaries push companies towards competitive fitness. A more benevolent environment, cushioned by competition-inhibiting collaboration, might actually make a firm more content and less eager to implement tough changes. In the long run this will make firms vulnerable to more aggressive companies, battle-hardened by years of rivalry in more competitive environments.

In conclusion, the basic assumption of the discrete organization perspective is that companies should not develop network level strategies, but should strive for 'strategic self-sufficiency'. Collaborative arrangements are a tactical tool, to be selectively employed. The sentiment of this perspective has been clearly summarized by Porter (1990; 224): 'alliances are rarely a solution … no firm can depend on another independent firm for skills and assets that are central to its competitive advantage … Alliances tend to ensure mediocrity, not create world leadership.'

EXHIBIT 6.2   THE DISCRETE ORGANIZATION PERSPECTIVE

WAGING WARS ON THE AFRICAN CONTINENT

Aliko Dangote, born, raised and doing business in Nigeria, was named Africa's richest man the last three years in a row. His empire was founded three decades ago when Mr Dangote started trading in commodities, an enterprise he expanded in the early 2000s to a fully-fledged production business. His take on producing local, value-added products that meet the needs of the African population, is a rather warlike one. Although the subject matter, ranging from cement to pasta, might seem mundane, Mr Dangote's approach to growing his business certainly is not.

Dealing with competitors and governments can be a tiresome business. Whereas most businessmen and women try diplomacy to deal with such issues, Mr Dangote started a full-fledged war campaign in order to gain market dominance. Doing so didn't leave the ability to make good deals up to chance, good arguments or charisma. Instead, he forced the market to bend to his wishes; making sure that failure was no longer an option. His weapon of choice was to siege his competitors by undercutting their prices on major commodities. This forced his adversaries to either give up or sell their goods with negative margins. With a net worth of $75 billion, the Dangote group time and again turned out to have the longest breath, thus taking out many of its rivals and creating a near monopoly in most commodities in Nigeria.

Besides siege tactics, Mr Dangote has developed the ability to make the right allies, but not letting them get too close. Being in good favour with Olugegun Obasanjo by generously funding his presidential campaign would certainly have helped him to take part in the rapid privatization of failing state businesses. Buying these failing businesses cheaply and making them profitable was one of the major early sources of his financial wealth. Another example has to do with the recent collaboration with GE to improve Nigeria's infrastructure. Western companies are anxious to expand into Africa's untapped markets, a dream that Mr Dangote certainly can make reality by using his power, connections and experience in navigating the Nigerian landscape. While GE will make a pretty penny from this building contract, the long term benefits for Mr Dangote's commodity business and the deal's success depending on his ability to navigate Nigeria's upper echelons surely makes clear who calls the shots.

Mr Dangote's current-day empire maintains clear similarities with its early beginnings. As a commodity trader, he was dependent on no one and was able to act as he thought best. Although he certainly made friends as his business expanded, the Dangote group never became dependent on any of them but used them as a lever to reach increasingly greater heights. While his competitors that did make alliances had to take each other's interests into account, without strategic partners Mr Dangote is as free in making business decisions as he ever was. Many wars are waged to retain freedom, a practice the Dangote group managed to successfully convey into the business realm.

Co-author: Jasper de Vries

Sources: '5 Machiavellian Business Lessons From Billionaire Aliko Dangote', Forbes, July 13, 2011; 'Cementing a fortune: The king of concrete has ambitions beyond Nigeria', *The Economist*, June 23, 2012; 'GE partners Dangote on power, transportation, Oil & Gas', *The Sun*, February 4, 2013.

The embedded organization perspective

Strategists taking an embedded organization perspective are fundamentally at odds with the assumption that competition is the predominant factor determining the interaction between organizations. Business isn't war, so to approach all interactions from an antagonistic angle is seen as overly pessimistic, even cynical. On the contrary, it is argued that business is about value creation, which is inherently a positive-sum activity. Creating value brings together organizations towards a common goal, as they can achieve more by working together than by behaving autonomously. In the modern economy, no organization can efficiently perform all activities in-house, as the division of labour has encouraged companies to specialize and outsource as many non-core activities as possible. Companies are necessarily cogs in the larger industrial machine and they can achieve little without working in unison with the other parts of the system. In the embedded organization perspective, atomistic competition is a neoclassical theoretical abstraction that seriously mischaracterizes the nature of relationships between organizations. In reality, cooperation is the predominant factor determining inter-organizational relations. Symbiosis, not aggression, is the fundamental nature of economic functioning (e.g. Jarillo, 1988; Moore, 1996, Reading 6.3).

A company can always find many organizations in its environment with which it shares an interest and whose objectives are largely parallel to its own (Child and Faulkner, 1998). A company might want to develop new products together with its buyers, optimize the logistical system together with its suppliers, expand the industry's potential together with other manufacturers, link technological standards with other industries and improve employment conditions together with the government. In general, most organizations have a stronger interest in increasing the size of the pie, than in deciding who gets what – keeping the focus on making a success of value creation eases the process of finding an equitable solution to the issue of value distribution.

The label 'embedded organization' given to this perspective refers to the fact that firms are becoming increasingly integrated into webs of mutually dependent organizations (e.g. Gnyawali and Madhavan, 2001; Granovetter, 1985). As companies strive to focus on a limited set of core competences and core business processes, they have moved to outsource as many non-core activities as possible. But as firms have attempted to further specialize by outsourcing activities that are close to their core business, they have become more vulnerable to outside suppliers and the need for explicit coordination of activities has often remained high. The outsourcing of such essential and coordination-intensive activities can only take place where the other party can be trusted to closely collaborate with the joint interests in mind. Of course, a company will not quickly move to such dependence on an outside supplier. But as experience and trust build over time, a strategic partnership can develop, where both sides come to accept the value of the close cooperation (e.g. Axelsson and Easton, 1992; Lorenzoni and Baden-Fuller, 1995, Reading 6.2).

For a firm to willingly surrender a part of its independence, it must be certain that its partners are also willing to invest in the relationship and will not behave opportunistically. Ideally, therefore, durable partnerships are based on mutual dependence and reciprocity. Both sides of the relationship must need each other, which gives an important incentive for both to find solutions to the disputes that will inevitably pop up. A balance in the benefits to be gained and the efforts to be exerted will also contribute to the success of a long-term collaborative relationship.

While such close collaborative relationships place a firm in a position of resource dependence, the benefits are well worth it. By specializing in a certain area, the firm can gain scale and experience advantages much faster. Specialization helps the firm to focus on a more limited set of core competences, which can be developed more efficiently and rapidly than if the firm were a 'conglomerate' of activities. At the same time the firm can tap into the complementary resources (Richardson, 1972) developed by its co-specialized partners. These complementary resources will usually be of higher quality and lower price than if the firm had built them up independently.

Specialized firms also use collaborative arrangements to quickly combine their resources with industry outsiders, to create new products and services. As product and business innovation are high paced and usually require the combination of various types of resources, developing everything in isolation is unworkable for most firms. By teaming up with other firms that have complementary resources, a company can make the most of its own resource base, without having to build up other resources from scratch. But again, trust is needed to engage in such a joint venture, as there are significant downside risks that the firm needs to take into account.

So, from the embedded organization perspective, collaboration is not competition in disguise, but a real alternative means of dealing with other organizations (e.g. Contractor and Lorange, 1988; Piore and Sabel, 1984). Successful firms embed themselves in webs of cooperative relationships, developing strategies together with their partners. These networks might compete against other networks (e.g. Gomes-Casseres, 1994; Hamilton and Woolsey Biggart, 1988; Weidenbaum and Hughes, 1996), but even here the relationships need not be fundamentally antagonistic. Proponents of the embedded organization perspective do not believe that firms should become obsessed with 'putting the competition out of business', as this again reduces business to a win–lose, zero-sum game. Firms should be focused on creating value and avoiding direct confrontation with other manufacturers, emphasizing the opportunity for a win–win, positive-sum game (e.g. Kim and Mauborgne, 2004; Moore, 1996, Reading 6.3). With this approach, firms in the same industry will recognize that they often have parallel interests as well. Setting industry standards, lobbying the government, finding solutions to joint environmental problems, improving the image of the industry, investing in fundamental research and negotiating with the unions are just a few of the issues where cooperation can be fruitful.

EXHIBIT 6.3   THE EMBEDDED ORGANIZATION PERSPECTIVE

MAJID AL FUTTAIM ACQUIRES FULL OWNERSHIP OF CARREFOUR FRANCHISE IN THE REGION

Majid Al Futtaim Holding has acquired the remaining 25 per cent stake in Majid Al Futtaim Hypermarkets LLC from its partner, French retailer Carrefour Group for €530 million (Dh2.5 billion), a joint statement said on Wednesday evening. "Carrefour Group announced the sale of its 25 per cent stake in Majid Al Futtaim Hypermarkets for €530 million to its regional partner, Majid Al Futtaim Holding," Carrefour said in a statement. "Carrefour expresses its full confidence in Majid Al Futtaim's ability to continue to develop the brand successfully and consolidate its position in these growing markets."

Majid Al Futtaim (MAF) Holding holds the regional franchise for Carrefour – the world's second biggest retailer after Wal-Mart. Despite Carrefour's stake sale, both partners have agreed to strengthen their partnership by extending the franchise agreement of Carrefour until 2025. "Under the agreement signed, Majid Al Futtaim will own 100 per cent of Majid Al Futtaim Hypermarkets' shares. The exclusive franchise partnership with the Carrefour Group is renewed until 2025 and extended to new formats and new countries," MAF Holding said in a statement. "Majid Al Futtaim sees this as a strategic transaction driving long-term growth, with its demonstrated expertise and track record to develop the brand successfully, and will keep and strengthen the strategic partnership with Carrefour in new countries and new formats." Closing of the transaction is subject to approval by the relevant authorities.

MAF Holding brought Carrefour to the region by acquiring the franchise in 1995 and subsequently opening the first Continent (Carrefour's predecessor) Hypermarket at the Deira City Centre – that had begun to change the face of the UAE's organized retail sector – that used to be dominated by a handful of supermarket chains. It currently operates 50 hypermarkets and 44 supermarkets under the Carrefour brand in several countries in the Middle East, North Africa and Central Asia. The move is a possible reflection of the company's declining sale in its home market – France as well as Europe and China. The company has already discontinued its operations in some of the key markets such as Greece, Singapore, Colombia, Malaysia and Indonesia while it has sold it Portuguese business recently.

Its exit from MAF Hypermarkets stake is part of a strategic move to reduce its €4.3 billion debts and create a leaner and more efficient company. "More generally, the company's international divestment programme is now largely complete – question marks still hang over Turkey and possibly Taiwan – but the business is now leaner and able to invest," Gildas Aitamer, Retail Analyst at Planet Retail, commented recently.

Source: Saifur Rahman, *Gulf News*, 22 May 2013: http://gulfnews.com/business/investment/majid-al-futtaim-acquires-full-ownership-of-carrefour-franchise-in-the-region-1.1187332

MANAGING THE PARADOX OF COMPETITION AND COOPERATION

All for one, one for all.
The Three Musketeers, Alexandre Dumas Jr. (1824–1895); French novelist

So, should managers form network level strategies or not? Should firms consciously embed themselves in a web of durable collaborative relationships, emphasizing the value of cooperative inter-organizational interactions for realizing their long-term aims? Or should firms try to remain as independent as possible, emphasizing the value of competitive power in achieving their strategic objectives? Is it 'all for one, one for all' or must the strong truly stand alone? (see Table 6.1).

TABLE 6.1 Discrete organization versus embedded organization perspective

	Discrete organization perspective	Embedded organization perspective
Emphasis on	Competition over cooperation	Cooperation over competition
Preferred position	Independence	Interdependence
Environment structure	Discrete organizations (atomistic)	Embedded organizations (networked)
Firm boundaries	Distinct and defended	Fuzzy and open
Inter-organizational relations	Arm's-length and transactional	Close and structural
Interaction outcomes	Mainly zero-sum (win/lose)	Mainly positive-sum (win/win)
Interaction based on	Bargaining power and calculation	Trust and reciprocity
Network level strategy	No	Yes
Use of collaboration	Temporary coalitions (tactical alliance)	Durable partnerships (strategic alliance)
Collaborative arrangements	Limited, well-defined, contract-based	Broad, open, relationship-based

The debate on this issue within the field of strategy is far from being concluded. Many perspectives exist on how to reconcile the conflicting demands of competition and cooperation, and many 'best practices' have been put forward. The strategists are in a position to determine their own point of view, with a number of suggestions from the literature in mind. From all the discussed strategy issues in this book, the number of available options to manage the paradox of cooperation and competition is highest. Three options have been brought forward: navigating, parallel processing and juxtaposing.

Navigating

By focusing on one contrary element at a time, the paradox is managed by a series of contrary initiatives. In network level strategy, Gary Hamel, Yves Doz and C.K. Prahalad have suggested the route for strategists to cooperate first and compete later in their *HBR* article: 'Collaborate with your competitor and win' (1989; Reading 6.1). They describe how Japanese strategists collaborate with competitors from the West with the explicit intention to learn, and then beat them as competitors. In this case, vertical (supply chain) relations become horizontal (competitive). But also without this specific change of relationship, navigating vertical partnering is an option. For example, in the retail industry it is common practice that suppliers (A-Brand manufacturers) cooperate with clients (supermarkets) to jointly develop logistical processes and technologies to enhance efficiency. Both parties benefit, but once the new technology and process are in place, parties start negotiating prices and conditions again. This cycle of cooperating and competing is repeated many times.

Other suggestions have also been made. Under the guidance of the Japanese Ministry of International Trade and Industry (MITI) groups of (Japanese) companies have been brought together to jointly develop new technologies, stimulated with government money. The intention was to cooperate in the 'pre-competitive stage', and once the technology was developed to compete in the market place. This industrial policy has been adopted by the European Union with initiative such as ESPRIT and EUREKA to promoting innovation and introducing new standards in the telecommunication sector (Van Tulder and Junne, 1988; Gastells, 2006).

Cooperating first and competing later is not an exclusive industrial policy option. Companies have learned that on some occasions it makes strategic sense to join forces with competitors in the early phase of developing technologies and industry standards. Well-described in the literature is the case of developing an industry standard for video devices (e.g. Bartlett *et al.*, 2008). Three competitors had been competing for the world standard, Philips with V2000, Sony with Betamax, and Matsushita with VCR. The victor was VCR in this winner-takes-all game (Arthur, 1994); the contestants learned the hard way, that competing for standards may be heroic and exciting, but often proves disappointing. For developing a world Wifi standard, several stakeholders have participated in a standardization group, competition started after the new standard had created a level playing field.

Parallel processing

The term co-opetition, an astute portmanteau of cooperation and competition, has become popularized by game theorists (e.g. Brandenburger and Nalebuff, 1996). It is explained as companies interacting with partial congruence of interests. For example, the French car manufacturer PSA Peugeot Citroën and the Japanese firm Toyota share components of city cars, the Peugeot 107, Toyota Aygo and Citroën C1, while competing fiercely for market share. Cooperating to reduce costs while competing for market share are being executed in different organizational units, and hence an example of parallel processing.

Companies can also separate competing and cooperating in different country units. For example, the French company Danone and the Japanese firm Yakult (see also the short case on Yakult in Exhibit 4.1), compete in Europe but cooperate in India. In this case, the arguments in the strategic decision making process to 'make, buy or cooperate' differ over country units, and therefore the decisions vary. Without an overarching corporate policy, the organizational units have the freedom to choose, and so parallel processing is possible.

Juxtaposing

Simultaneously managing competition and cooperation, even with the same network partners, is a next option for strategists. Lord Palmerston's quote earlier in this chapter articulates the position of a strategizing manager quite well: there are no eternal allies and perpetual enemies. Comparable to a cycling race, rival teams can become allies and then turn rivals again, depending on the situation during the race. Managers also keep their options open; rivals can become allies and rivals again, depending on the situation. For example, in the battle for mobile operating model standards some competing providers have a joint interest to defend the chosen platform and join forces, and after a cooperative meeting start competing again.

Juxtaposing is common in business ecosystems, as Moore (1996; Reading 6.3) points out. Moore argues that the pattern of business coevolution consists of 'a complex network of choices, which depend, at least in part, on what participants are aware of'. In other words, managers can not afford to label firms as definite rivals or allies. Positions within the ecosystem can change so fast that allies can turn into rivals within days or vice versa. Ecosystems are often described in innovation contexts, with eroding industry boundaries and companies often unexpectedly finding themselves in fierce competition with the most unlikely of rivals.

NETWORK LEVEL STRATEGY IN INTERNATIONAL PERSPECTIVE

Co-author: Gep Eisenloeffel

Do as adversaries in law, strive mightily, but eat and drink as friends.
William Shakespeare (1564–1616); English dramatist and poet

Of all the debates in the field of strategic management, this one has received the most attention from comparative management researchers. Almost all of them have concluded that firms from different countries display widely divergent propensities to compete and cooperate. Many authors suggest that there are recognizable national inclinations, even national styles, when it comes to establishing inter-firm relationships (e.g. Contractor and Lorange, 1988; Kagono *et al.*, 1985).

While it is difficult to generalize at the national level, since there can be significant variance within a country, it is challenging to debate these observed international dissimilarities. Are there really national inter-organizational relationship styles and what factors might influence their existence? As a stimulus to the international dimension of this debate, a number of country characteristics are put forward as possible influences on how the paradox of competition and cooperation is dealt with in different national settings. As noted before, it is the intention of these propositions to encourage further discussion and cross-cultural research on the topic of inter-organizational relationships.

Cross-border collaborative arrangements

As has been discussed in this chapter, the intentions of companies to become engaged in collaborative arrangements are many. Some of these are cross-border, such as the Dutch company Philips and the German firm Siemens, yet these do not differ significantly from national collaborations. Specific to cross-border arrangements, however, are cooperative agreements intended to overcome entry barriers that exist due to import restrictions. Specific are also cross-border arrangements within trade blocks. For example, faced with Japanese dominance in new core technologies the European Union, in close cooperation with Europe's main major electronic and telecommunication companies, initiated and coordinated programmes like ESPRIT and EUREKA to promote innovation and introduce new standards in the telecommunication sector (Van Tulder and Junne, 1988; Gastells, 2006).

European companies not only cooperated to face Japanese competitors, they also tried to learn lessons from Japanese practices. However, duplication often proved difficult. With suppliers being almost as big as the core network company as in the case of Bosch, the German electric components supplier for car manufacturer Daimler Benz, it is not easy to enforce a 'just in time, zero defect, zero inventories policy', which was the basis of the success of the so-called *Toyotism* production revolution in Japanese car manufacturing.

Type of institutional environment

Of course, the cultural values described above are intertwined with the institutional structures that have developed in each country. Some comparative management researchers focus on these institutional forces, such as governments, banks, universities and unions, to explain the divergent national views on competition and cooperation. It is generally argued that most countries have developed an idiosyncratic economic system – that is, their own distinct brand of capitalism – with a different emphasis on competition and cooperation.

One prominent analysis is that of business historian Chandler (1986, 1990), who has described the historical development of 'personal capitalism' in the United Kingdom, 'managerial capitalism' in the United States, 'cooperative capitalism' in Germany and 'group capitalism' in Japan from 1850 to 1950. The legacy of these separately evolving forms of capitalism is that, to this day, there are significantly different institutional philosophies, roles and behaviours in each of these countries. In the English-speaking nations, governments have generally limited their role to the establishment and maintenance of competitive markets (Hampden-Turner and Trompenaars, 1993). A shared belief in the basic tenets of classical economies has led these governments to be suspicious of competition-undermining collusion masquerading under the term 'cooperation'. For instance, in the United States the Sherman Antitrust Act was passed in 1890 and has been applied with vigour since then to guard the functioning of the market. Many companies that would like to cooperate have been discouraged from doing so (e.g. Teece, 1992; Dyer and Ouchi, 1993).

In the German 'cooperative capitalism' system, the situation has been quite different. The government has major shareholdings in hundreds of companies outside the public services. According to Lessem and Neubauer (1994) 'the attitude to government participation in industry is based not on ideology but on a sense of partnership with the business community. It extends to the local level where local authorities, schools, banks and businesses combine to establish policies of mutual benefit.' Especially the large German banks have played an important role in guiding industrial development, promoting cooperation and defusing potentially damaging conflicts between companies. They have had an intimate knowledge of the business and have had a long-term stake in each relationship, often expressed by a minority shareholding of the bank in the client company and/or a seat on its supervisory board. The offices of the largest bank, Deutsche Bank, hold hundreds of seats on other companies' supervisory boards, although this system has been unravelling since the late 1990s. The trade associations and unions, it should be noted, also employ a long-term, cooperative perspective.

The Japanese 'group capitalism' system is somewhat akin to the German model. In Japan, too, business and social institutions have formed a partnership to promote mutually beneficial developments. However, in Japan, the government has played a more prominent role than in Germany, through its national industrial strategies (Best, 1990). As Thurow (1991) points out, the Japanese government has been actively involved in the indirect protection of some domestic industries, the selection of other sectors as development priorities and the funding of related research and development. Koen (2005, based on research from Teranishi, 1994; Ostrom, 1990; Miyashita and Russell, 1994; and Miwa and Ramseyer, 1996) observed that 'in the postwar years the Japanese Ministry of International Trade and Industry (MITI) decided on the industries to be developed and helped to shape the new bank-led *keiretsu* model, and this primacy remained essentially unchallenged until the late eighties.' Furthermore, the *keiretsu* industry groups, such as Mitsui, Mitsubishi, Sanwa, Hitachi and Sumitomo, have formed long-term networks of cooperating companies. While some consortia have been formed to deal with a particular task at hand, firms within a *keiretsu* are familiar with one another through long historical association and have had durable, open-ended relationships, partially cemented by multilateral minority shareholdings.

In France, the *dirigiste* state planners play an even more prominent role than in Japan. The French model, which could be dubbed 'bureaucratic capitalism', focuses sharply on the state as industrial strategist, coordinating many major developments in the economy. It is the planners' job 'to maintain a constant pressure on industry – as part industrial consultant, part banker, part plain bully – to keep it moving in some desired direction' (Lessem and Neubauer, 1994). This was for instance the case in France's state supported *filière* policy supporting the national communication industry in the mid-1980s (Groenewegen and Beije, 1989). The unions, on the other hand, tend to be more antagonistic, particularly in their relationship to the government. On the work floor, however, a more cooperative attitude prevails.

In the 'familial capitalism' system of Italy, on the contrary, the central government plays a very small role. Instead, local networks of economic, political and social actors cooperate to create a mutually beneficial environment. Trade associations, purchasing cooperatives, educational institutions and cooperative marketing are often created to support a large number of small, specialized firms working together as a loose federation. Trust within the network is often extensive, but institutions outside of these closed communities are mistrusted, especially the central government, tax authorities, bankers and the trade unions.

Market for corporate control

Linked to the general institutional environment is how mergers, acquisitions and take-overs are viewed in each nation. In countries such as the United States and Britain, companies whose shares are traded on the stock exchange are exposed to the threat of a takeover. This relatively open market for corporate control facilitates vertical and horizontal integration. Companies can contemplate acquiring another firm if they believe that internal coordination is preferable to a market-based relationship. In other countries, however, the market for corporate control is less open, if not entirely absent. Where horizontal or vertical integration is difficult to achieve, but working together is still beneficial, potential acquirers often only have collaborative arrangements as an alternative.

Social networks and cultural values

At the most fundamental level, cultural values can place more emphasis on competition or cooperation. Some researchers (e.g. Hofstede, 1993, Reading 1.3; Hampden-Turner and Trompenaars, 1993) point out that this has much to do with a culture's orientation toward individuals or groups. More individualist cultures accentuate the position of each single person as a distinct entity, while more collectivist cultures stress people's group affiliations. In Hofstede's research, the United States surfaced as highest scoring nation in the world on the individualism scale, closely followed by the other English-speaking countries, Australia, Great Britain, Canada and New Zealand respectively. Hofstede argues that 'in the US individualist conception, the relationship between the individual and the organization is essentially calculative, being based on enlightened self-interest', while in more collectivist cultures the relationship 'is not calculative, but moral: It is based not on self interest, but on the individual's loyalty toward the clan, organization, or society – which is supposedly the best guarantee of that individual's ultimate interest'. The willingness of individuals to forego self-interested behaviour for the good of the group is believed to be the same cultural value spurring individual firms to cooperate for the good of an entire network (e.g. Gerlach, 1992). Pascale and Athos (1981) agree that in the highly group-oriented culture of Japan, interdependence is valued, while the 'self' is regarded as an obstacle to joint development. Group members feel indebted and obligated toward one another, and trust results from a shared understanding and acceptance of interdependence.

The strong orientation of the English-speaking ('Anglo-Saxon') cultures toward individualism and the Japanese cultural emphasis on group affiliation is also recognized by Lessem and Neubauer (1994), who place these two cultures at the extreme ends of a continuum. In the socially atomistic Anglo-Saxon nations, individuals are seen as the building blocks of society and each person is inclined to optimize her/his own interests. In the socially symbiotic Japanese culture, the whole is more important than the individual parts, so that individuals are more likely to strive towards a group's common good. Interestingly, Lessem and Neubauer (following Albert, 1991) argue that, on this point, the German and Japanese cultures are strikingly similar. Both cultures exhibit a 'holistic' worldview, in which 'management and banker, employer and employee, government and industry combine forces rather than engage in adversarial relations', to the benefit of the entire system. This collectivist bent can be observed at the multi-company level (industrial networks/*keiretsu*), but also at the industry and national levels of aggregation, leading many analysts to speak of Japan Incorporated and Deutschland AG.

The cultural values of individualism versus collectivism play an important role when it comes to trust and social capital within communities and between business partners. Collectivism, resulting in different modes of group-orientation, correlates with trust and social capital (Fukayama, 1995). Japan, for instance, is such a group-oriented society. Dating back to the era of absolute obedience to the samurai clan chief, group-loyalty is extremely high in Japan. These long established relationships have a positive effect on transaction costs.

Japan is an example of a 'high-context communication culture' whereas the US is a 'low-context communication culture' (Hall, 1976). Simply stated this means that in Japan transaction costs are minimized by long standing relationships. According to Koen (2005) 'one of the most striking characteristics of Japan's industrial organization is the predominance of stable, long-term inter-firm relationships, which are non-exclusive.' Of crucial importance is the element of reciprocity and 'trust' within business-oriented transactional relationships.

China is also a country where longstanding relationships form the basis for business networks functioning, using the Chinese word *guanxi*. Without the proper *guanxi*, for outsiders only to be obtained by investing in long term relationships, doing business is very difficult. Fukayama (1995) defines trust as 'the expectation that arises within a community of regular, honest and cooperative behaviour, based on commonly shared norms, on the part of other members of that community.'

Relational assets based on trust represent the firm's stock of economically beneficial long-term relationships with other business entities. Continued interaction among the partners over a longer period of time helps to form stable relationships. In this way trust transforms into 'social capital'. Fukayama (1995) notes that 'social capital is a capability that arises from the prevalence of trust in a society or in certain parts of it. Social capital differs from other forms of human capital insofar as it is usually created and transmitted through cultural mechanisms like religion, tradition, or historical habits.'

According to Fukayama, in the US 'people who do not trust one another will end up cooperating only under a system of formal rules and regulations, which have to be negotiated, agreed to, litigated and enforced, sometimes by coercive means.' In the same way, Kanter (1994) notes that: 'North American companies, more than others in the world, take a narrow, opportunistic view of relationships, evaluating them strictly in financial terms or seeing them as barely tolerable alternatives to outright acquisition. Preoccupied with the economics of the deal, North American companies frequently neglect the political, cultural, organizational and human aspects of the partnership. Asian companies are the most comfortable with relationships, and therefore they are the most adept at using and exploiting them. European companies fall somewhere in the middle.' Although Kanter's 'classification' is somewhat rough, most strategic management researchers who have done international comparative studies agree with the broad lines of her remark (e.g. Contractor and Lorange, 1988; Kagono *et al.*, 1985).

As a result of the lack of trust, transaction costs tend to be very high. Not surprisingly, Japan has percentage-wise the lowest number of corporate lawyers in the industrialized world. The US, by contrast, has the highest number of corporate lawyers (Schneider and Barsoux, 1999).

Other cultures fall somewhere between these two extremes. Italy, for instance, is often cited for its high number of networked companies (Piore and Sabel, 1984). Besides the well-known example of Benetton, there are many networks in the textile industry of Prato, the ceramics industry of Sassuolo, the farm machine industry of Reggio Emilia and the motorcycle industry of Bologna. Similar to the Germans and Japanese, Italian culture is also characterized by a strong group orientation, but the affiliations valued by Italians tend to be mostly family-like, based on blood-ties, friendships or ideological bonds between individuals. There is often a strong loyalty and trust within these family-like communities, but distrust toward the outside world. Therefore, cooperation tends to be high within these communities, but competition prevails beyond.

In France the situation is again different. In French culture, according to Lessem and Neubauer (1994), there is 'an ingrained mistrust of the natural play of forces of a free economy'. People have a strong sense that cooperation in economic affairs is important, similar to the Japanese, Germans and Italians. However, the French are unwilling to depend on the evolution of cooperation between (semi-) independent firms. Generally, there is a preference to impose cooperation top-down, by integrating companies into efficiently working bureaucracies. Such structuring of the economy usually takes place under influence, or by direct intervention, of the French government. Such *dirigisme* is based on the opposite assumption to Williamson's work (1975, 1985): hierarchical coordination is usually preferable to market transactions. Former prime minister, Edouard Balladur, summarized this assumption far more graciously, when he remarked: 'What is the market? It is the law of the jungle, the law of nature. And what is civilization? It is the struggle against nature' (*The Economist,* March 15, 1997). Based on this view, even relationships with firms not absorbed into the hierarchy are of a bureaucratic nature – that is, formal, rational and depersonalized.

Negative effects of 'groupism'

Social networks, or 'groupism', do not always leads to higher efficiency, as these are based on mutual ineptness and favouring within the group. What applies to members within the group does not apply to outsiders. Trompenaars (2003) refers to this phenomenon as *particularism.* Particularism is the opposite of universalism, where the same rules apply to everyone no matter his status or relationship within a group. Group loyalty also correlates with shame, leading in some cases to stagnation (Verluyten, 2010). In a shame-oriented society individual failing affects not only the person involved but also the prestige of the group, while correcting someone might be a real problem. Bringing a case to court in Japan is terribly shameful and business partners try to avoid this as much as possible. The Japanese prefer paying compensation over having to apologize (Henry, 2003: 237, 238).

Based on Chinese Confucianism and neo-Confucianism, familistic societies such as the People's Republic of China and to a lesser extent Taiwan and South Korea, represent a specific form of groupism, in which family bonds are to be honoured above all other social loyalties. According to Fukayama (1995) a consequence of these familistic in-group ties is the absence of voluntary bonds, or *civil society,* between members of a loosely structured community.

INTRODUCTION TO THE READINGS

To help strategists gain more insight into the variety of perspectives on this issue, three readings have been selected that each takes a different angle on the debate. As in previous chapters, the first two readings will be representative of the two poles in this debate, while the third will combine both perspectives.

To open on behalf of the discrete organization perspective, the classic, 'Collaborate with Your Competitors – and Win', has been selected as Reading 6.1. The authors, Gary Hamel, Yves Doz and C.K. Prahalad, basically take the same stance that inter-firm relations are largely competitive and governed by power and calculation. The authors see collaboration as a useful tool for improving the firm's competitive profile. They argue that alliances with competitors 'can strengthen both companies against outsiders even if it weakens one partner vis-a-vis the other', and therefore that the net result can be positive. Yet they emphasize that companies should not be naive about the real nature of alliances – 'collaboration is competition in a different form'. An alliance is 'a constantly evolving bargain', in which each firm will be fending for itself, trying to learn as much as possible from the other, while attempting to limit the partner's access to its knowledge and skills.

The authors advise firms to procede cautiously with alliances, only when they have clear objectives of what they wish to learn from their allies, a well-developed capacity to learn, and defences against their allies' probing of their skills and technologies. While Hamel, Doz and Prahalad only focus on horizontal relationships in this reading, their message is similar to that of Porter – competition in the environment is paramount and cooperation is merely an opportunistic move in the overall competitive game.

As representative of the embedded organization perspective, an article by Gianni Lorenzoni and Charles Baden-Fuller has been selected for Reading 6.2, entitled 'Creating a Strategic Centre to Manage a Web of Partners'. Lorenzoni and Baden-Fuller are particularly interested in how companies structure their vertical relationships, balancing pressures for competition and cooperation. In their view, where a group of firms works together closely, they can form a 'virtual company'. This type of network can benefit from most of the advantages of being a large vertically integrated company, while avoiding most of the pitfalls of integration. But Lorenzoni and Baden-Fuller articulate that it is necessary for a network of firms to have a strategic centre that can act as builder and coordinator. As builder, the strategic centre can deliberately design and assemble the network components, and as coordinator it can regulate activities and resolve disputes. The authors carry on to specify the conditions under which a network of firms can be an advantageous organizational form and what is required to make them work. Overall, their main message is that durable partnerships between multiple firms are not easy, but if this interdependence can be managed well, it can give the group a strong competitive edge against others.

Reading 6.3, 'Coevolution in Business Ecosystems', by James Moore, describes how both perspectives are combined in business ecosystems. This reading is from Moore's best-selling book *The Death of Competition,* in which he places the paradox of competition and cooperation in the broader context of 'business ecosystems'. He defines a business ecosystem as a part of the business environment where a variety of firms co-exist with one another and co-evolve on the basis of their ongoing interaction. He explains the functioning of a business ecosystem by drawing a parallel with biological ecosystems – plants and animals cannot be understood in isolation, as they co-evolve with one another in an endless cycle of change and selection. So too, the success or failure of companies cannot be understood without understanding how they have been able to nestle into the business ecosystem and how well the entire system is doing. Great companies, like great animal species, will still face extinction if their ecosystem goes into decline. Similarly, companies that want to create a new market must recognize that they actually need to create a new business ecosystem, with a lush variety of suppliers, distributors, service-providers and customers. If a firm only 'plants' its new product without engendering a broader ecosystem, it will be just as successful as a new species of tropical tree in the desert. Moore's point is that you should try to 'understand the economic systems evolving around you and find ways to contribute'. He concludes that 'competitive advantage stems principally from … cooperative, co-evolving relationships with a network of other contributors to the overall economic scene'. In other words, cooperation and systems level thinking are essential to the strategist – however, not to substitute competitive behaviour, but rather to complement it.

READING

6.1

Collaborate with your competitors – and win

By Gary Hamel, Yves Doz and C.K. Prahalad[1]

Collaboration between competitors is in fashion. General Motors and Toyota assemble automobiles, Siemens and Philips develop semiconductors, Canon supplies photocopiers to Kodak, France's Thomson and Japan's JVC manufacture videocassette recorders. But the spread of what we call 'competitive collaboration' – joint ventures, outsourcing agreements, product licensings, cooperative research – has triggered unease about the long-term consequences. A strategic alliance can strengthen both companies against outsiders even as it weakens one partner vis-a-vis the other. In particular, alliances between Asian companies and western rivals seem to work against the western partner. Cooperation becomes a low-cost route for new competitors to gain technology and market access.

Yet the case for collaboration is stronger than ever. It takes so much money to develop new products and to penetrate new markets that few companies can go it alone in every situation. ICL, the British computer company, could not have developed its current generation of mainframes without Fujitsu. Motorola needs Toshiba's distribution capacity to break into the Japanese semiconductor market. Time is another critical factor. Alliances can provide shortcuts for western companies racing to improve their production efficiency and quality control.

We have spent more than five years studying the inner workings of 15 strategic alliances and monitoring scores of others. Our research involves cooperative ventures between competitors from the United States and Japan, Europe and Japan, and the United States and Europe. We did not judge the success or failure of each partnership by its longevity – a common mistake when evaluating strategic alliances – but by the shifts in competitive strength on each side. We focused on how companies use competitive collaboration to enhance their internal skills and technologies while they guard against transferring competitive advantages to ambitious partners.

There is no immutable law that strategic alliances *must* be a windfall for Japanese or Korean partners. Many western companies do give away more than they

gain – but that's because they enter partnerships without knowing what it takes to win. Companies that benefit most from competitive collaboration adhere to a set of simple but powerful principles:

- **Collaboration is competition in a different form.** Successful companies never forget that their new partners may be out to disarm them. They enter alliances with clear strategic objectives, and they also understand how their partners' objectives will affect their success.

- **Harmony is not the most important measure of success.** Indeed, occasional conflict may be the best evidence of mutually beneficial collaboration. Few alliances remain win–win undertakings forever. A partner may be content even as it unknowingly surrenders core skills.

- **Cooperation has limits.** Companies must defend against competitive compromise. A strategic alliance is a constantly evolving bargain whose real terms go beyond the legal agreement or the aims of top management. What information gets traded is determined day to day, often by engineers and operating managers. Successful companies inform employees at all levels about what skills and technologies are off-limits to the partner and monitor what the partner requests and receives.

- **Learning from partners is paramount.** Successful companies view each alliance as a window on their partners' broad capabilities. They use the alliance to build skills in areas outside the formal agreement and systematically diffuse new knowledge throughout their organizations.

Why collaborate?

Using an alliance with a competitor to acquire new technologies or skills is not devious. It reflects the commitment and capacity of each partner to absorb the skills of the other. We found that in every case in which a Japanese company emerged from an alliance

[1]Source: Reprinted by permission of *Harvard Business Review*. From 'Collaborate with your Competitors – and Win' by G. Hamel, Y.L. Doz and C.K. Prahalad, January–February 1989, Vol. 67. © 1989 by the Harvard Business School Publishing Corporation, all rights reserved.

stronger than its western partner, the Japanese company had made a greater effort to learn.

Strategic intent is an essential ingredient in the commitment to learning. The willingness of Asian companies to enter alliances represents a change in competitive tactics, not competitive goals. NEC, for example, has used a series of collaborative ventures to enhance its technology and product competences. NEC is the only company in the world with a leading position in telecommunications, computers and semiconductors – despite its investing less in research and development (R&D) (as a percentage of revenues) than competitors like Texas Instruments, Northern Telecom and L.M. Ericsson. Its string of partnerships, most notably with Honeywell, allowed NEC to leverage its in-house R&D over the last two decades.

Western companies, on the other hand, often enter alliances to avoid investments. They are more interested in reducing the costs and risks of entering new businesses or markets than in acquiring new skills. A senior US manager offered this analysis of his company's venture with a Japanese rival: 'We complement each other well – our distribution capability and their manufacturing skill. I see no reason to invest upstream if we can find a secure source of product. This is a comfortable relationship for us.'

An executive from this company's Japanese partner offered a different perspective: 'When it is necessary to collaborate, I go to my employees and say, "This is bad, I wish we had these skills ourselves. Collaboration is second best. But I will feel worse if after four years we do not know how to do what our partner knows how to do." We must digest their skills.'

The problem here is not that the US company wants to share investment risk (its Japanese partner does too) but that the US company has no ambition beyond avoidance. When the commitment to learning is so one-sided, collaboration invariably leads to competitive compromise.

Many so-called alliances between western companies and their Asian rivals are little more than sophisticated outsourcing arrangements. General Motors buys cars and components from Korea's Daewoo. Siemens buys computers from Fujitsu. Apple buys laser printer engines from Canon. The traffic is almost entirely one way. These original equipment manufacturer (OEM) deals offer Asian partners a way to capture investment initiative from western competitors and displace customer-competitors from value-creating activities. In many cases this goal meshes with that of the western partner: to regain competitiveness quickly and with minimum effort.

Consider the joint venture between Rover, the British automaker, and Honda. Some 25 years ago, Rover's forerunners were world leaders in small car design. Honda had not even entered the automobile business. But in the mid-1970s, after failing to penetrate foreign markets, Rover turned to Honda for technology and product development support. Rover has used the alliance to avoid investments to design and build new cars. Honda has cultivated skills in European styling and marketing as well as multinational manufacturing. There is little doubt which company will emerge stronger over the long term.

Troubled laggards like Rover often strike alliances with surging latecomers like Honda. Having fallen behind in a key skills area (in this case, manufacturing small cars), the laggard attempts to compensate for past failures. The latecomer uses the alliance to close a specific skills gap (in this case, learning to build cars for a regional market). But a laggard that forges a partnership for short-term gain may find itself in a dependency spiral: as it contributes fewer and fewer distinctive skills, it must reveal more and more of its internal operations to keep the partner interested. For the weaker company, the issue shifts from, 'Should we collaborate?' to 'With whom should we collaborate?' to 'How do we keep our partner interested as we lose the advantages that made us attractive to them in the first place?'

There's a certain paradox here. When both partners are equally intent on internalizing the other's skills, distrust and conflict may spoil the alliance and threaten its very survival. That's one reason joint ventures between Korean and Japanese companies have been few and tempestuous. Neither side wants to 'open the kimono'. Alliances seem to run most smoothly when one partner is intent on learning and the other is intent on avoidance – in essence, when one partner is willing to grow dependent on the other. But running smoothly is not the point; the point is for a company to emerge from an alliance more competitive than when it entered it.

One partner does not always have to give up more than it gains to ensure the survival of an alliance. There are certain conditions under which mutual gain is possible, at least for a time:

- The partners' strategic goals converge while their competitive goals diverge. That is, each partner allows for the other's continued prosperity in the shared business. Philips and Du Pont collaborate to develop and manufacture compact discs, but neither side invades the other's market. There is a clear upstream/downstream division of effort.

- The size and market power of both partners is modest compared with industry leaders. This forces each side to accept that mutual dependence may have to continue for many years. Long-term collaboration may be so critical to both partners that neither will risk antagonizing the other by an overtly competitive bid to appropriate skills or competences. Fujitsu's 1 to 5 size disadvantage with IBM means it will be a long time, if ever, before Fujitsu can break away from its foreign partners and go it alone.

- Each partner believes it can learn from the other and at the same time limit access to proprietary skills. JVC and Thomson, both of whom make VCRs, know that they are trading skills. But the two companies are looking for very different things. Thomson needs product technology and manufacturing prowess; JVC needs to learn how to succeed in the fragmented European market. Both sides believe there is an equitable chance for gain.

How to build secure defences

For collaboration to succeed, each partner must contribute something distinctive: basic research, product development skills, manufacturing capacity, access to distribution. The challenge is to share enough skills to create advantage vis-a-vis companies outside the alliance while preventing a wholesale transfer of core skills to the partner. This is a very thin line to walk. Companies must carefully select what skills and technologies they pass to their partners. They must develop safeguards against unintended, informal transfers of information. The goal is to limit the transparency of their operations.

The type of skill a company contributes is an important factor in how easily its partner can internalize the skills. The potential for transfer is greatest when a partner's contribution is easily transported (in engineering drawings, on computer tapes, or in the heads of a few technical experts); easily interpreted (it can be reduced to commonly understood equations or symbols); and easily absorbed (the skill or competence is independent of any particular cultural context).

Western companies face an inherent disadvantage because their skills are generally more vulnerable to transfer. The magnet that attracts so many companies to alliances with Asian competitors is their manufacturing excellence – a competence that is less transferable than most. Just-in-time inventory systems and quality circles can be imitated, but this is like pulling a few threads out of an oriental carpet. Manufacturing excellence is a complex web of employee training, integration with suppliers, statistical process controls, employee involvement, value engineering and design for manufacture. It is difficult to extract such a subtle competence in any way but a piecemeal fashion.

So companies must take steps to limit transparency. One approach is to limit the scope of the formal agreement. It might cover a single technology rather than an entire range of technologies; part of a product line rather than the entire line; distribution in a limited number of markets or for a limited period of time. The objective is to circumscribe a partner's opportunities to learn.

Moreover, agreements should establish specific performance requirements. Motorola, for example, takes an incremental, incentive-based approach to technology transfer in its venture with Toshiba. The agreement calls for Motorola to release its microprocessor technology incrementally as Toshiba delivers on its promise to increase Motorola's penetration in the Japanese semiconductor market. The greater Motorola's market share, the greater Toshiba's access to Motorola's technology.

Many of the skills that migrate between companies are not covered in the formal terms of collaboration. Top management puts together strategic alliances and sets the legal parameters for exchange. But what actually gets traded is determined by day-to-day interactions of engineers, marketers and product developers: who says what to whom, who gets access to what facilities, who sits on what joint committees. The most important deals ('I'll share this with you if you share that with me') may be struck four or five organizational levels below where the deal was signed. Here lurks the greatest risk of unintended transfers of important skills.

Consider one technology-sharing alliance between European and Japanese competitors. The European company valued the partnership as a way to acquire a specific technology. The Japanese company considered it a window on its partner's entire range of competences and interacted with a broad spectrum of its partner's marketing and product development staff. The company mined each contact for as much information as possible.

For example, every time the European company requested a new feature on a product being sourced from its partner, the Japanese company asked for detailed customer and competitor analyses to justify the request. Over time, it developed a sophisticated picture of the European market that would assist its own entry strategy. The technology acquired by the European partner through the formal agreement had a useful life of three to five years. The competitive insights acquired informally by the Japanese company will probably endure longer.

Limiting unintended transfers at the operating level requires careful attention to the role of gatekeepers, the people who control what information flows to a partner. A gatekeeper can be effective only if there are a limited number of gateways through which a partner can access people and facilities. Fujitsu's many partners all go through a single office, the 'collaboration section,' to request information and assistance from different divisions. This way the company can monitor and control access to critical skills and technologies.

We studied one partnership between European and US competitors that involved several divisions of each company. While the US company could only access its partner through a single gateway, its partner had unfettered access to all participating divisions. The European company took advantage of its free rein. If one division refused to provide certain information, the European partner made the same request of another division. No single manager in the US company could tell how much information had been transferred or was in a position to piece together patterns in the requests.

Collegiality is a prerequisite for collaborative success. But *too much* collegiality should set off warning bells to senior managers. CEOs or division presidents should expect occasional complaints from their counterparts about the reluctance of lower level employees to share information. That's a sign that the gatekeepers are doing their jobs. And senior management should regularly debrief operating personnel to find out what information the partner is requesting and what requests are being granted.

Limiting unintended transfers ultimately depends on employee loyalty and self-discipline. This was a real issue for many of the western companies we studied. In their excitement and pride over technical achievements, engineering staff sometimes shared information that top management considered sensitive. Japanese engineers were less likely to share proprietary information.

There are a host of cultural and professional reasons for the relative openness of western technicians. Japanese engineers and scientists are more loyal to their company than to their profession. They are less steeped in the open give-and-take of university research since

they receive much of their training from employers. They consider themselves team members more than individual scientific contributors. As one Japanese manager noted, 'We don't feel any need to reveal what we know. It is not an issue of pride for us. We're glad to sit and listen. If we're patient we usually learn what we want to know.'

Controlling unintended transfers may require restricting access to facilities as well as to people. Companies should declare sensitive laboratories and factories off-limits to their partners. Better yet, they might house the collaborative venture in an entirely new facility. IBM is building a special site in Japan where Fujitsu can review its forthcoming mainframe software before deciding whether to license it. IBM will be able to control exactly what Fujitsu sees and what information leaves the facility.

Finally, which country serves as 'home' to the alliance affects transparency. If the collaborative team is located near one partner's major facilities, the other partner will have more opportunities to learn – but less control over what information gets traded. When the partner houses, feeds and looks after engineers and operating managers, there is a danger they will 'go native'. Expatriate personnel need frequent visits from headquarters as well as regular furloughs home.

Enhance the capacity to learn

Whether collaboration leads to competitive surrender or revitalization depends foremost on what employees believe the purpose of the alliance to be. It is self-evident: to learn, one must want to learn. Western companies won't realize the full benefits of competitive collaboration until they overcome an arrogance borne of decades of leadership. In short, western companies must be more receptive.

We asked a senior executive in a Japanese electronics company about the perception that Japanese companies learn more from their foreign partners than vice versa. 'Our western partners approach us with the attitude of teachers', he told us. 'We are quite happy with this, because we have the attitude of students.'

Learning begins at the top. Senior management must be committed to enhancing their companies' skills as well as to avoiding financial risk. But most learning takes place at the lower levels of an alliance. Operating employees not only represent the front lines in an effective defence but also play a vital role in acquiring knowledge. They must be well briefed on the partner's strengths and weaknesses and understand how acquiring particular skills will bolster their company's competitive position.

This is already standard practice among Asian companies. We accompanied a Japanese development engineer on a tour through a partner's factory. This engineer dutifully took notes on plant layout, the number of production stages, the rate at which the line was running, and the number of employees. He recorded all this despite the fact that he had no manufacturing responsibility in his own company, and that the alliance didn't encompass joint manufacturing. Such dedication greatly enhances learning.

Collaboration doesn't always provide an opportunity to fully internalize a partner's skills. Yet just acquiring new and more precise benchmarks of a partner's performance can be of great value. A new benchmark can provoke a thorough review of internal performance levels and may spur a round of competitive innovation. Asking questions like, 'Why do their semiconductor logic designs have fewer errors than ours?' and 'Why are they investing in this technology and we're not?' may provide the incentive for a vigorous catch-up programme.

Competitive benchmarking is a tradition in most of the Japanese companies we studied. It requires many of the same skills associated with competitor analysis: systematically calibrating performance against external targets; learning to use rough estimates to determine where a competitor (or partner) is better, faster, or cheaper; translating those estimates into new internal targets; and recalibrating to establish the rate of improvement in a competitor's performance. The great advantage of competitive collaboration is that proximity makes benchmarking easier.

Indeed, some analysts argue that one of Toyota's motivations in collaborating with GM in the much-publicized NUMMI venture is to gauge the quality of GM's manufacturing technology. GM's top manufacturing people get a close look at Toyota, but the reverse is true as well. Toyota may be learning whether its giant US competitor is capable of closing the productivity gap with Japan.

Competitive collaboration also provides a way of getting close enough to rivals to predict how they will behave when the alliance unravels or runs its course. How does the partner respond to price changes? How does it measure and reward executives? How does it prepare to launch a new product? By revealing a competitor's management orthodoxies, collaboration can increase the chances of success in future head-to-head battles.

Knowledge acquired from a competitor-partner is only valuable after it is diffused through the organization. Several companies we studied had established internal clearinghouses to collect and disseminate information. The collaborations manager at one Japanese company regularly made the rounds of all employees involved in alliances. He identified what information had been collected by whom and then passed it on to appropriate departments. Another company held regular meetings where employees shared new knowledge and determined who was best positioned to acquire additional information.

Proceed with care – but proceed

After World War II, Japanese and Korean companies entered alliances with western rivals from weak positions. But they worked steadfastly toward independence. In the early 1960s, NEC's computer business was one-quarter the size of Honeywell's, its primary foreign partner. It took only two decades for NEC to grow larger than Honeywell, which eventually sold its computer operations to an alliance between NEC and Group Bull of France. The NEC experience demonstrates that dependence on a foreign partner doesn't automatically condemn a company to also-ran status. Collaboration may sometimes be unavoidable; surrender is not.

Managers are too often obsessed with the ownership structure of an alliance. Whether a company controls 51 per cent or 49 per cent of a joint venture may be much less important than the rate at which each partner learns from the other. Companies that are confident of their ability to learn may even prefer some ambiguity in the alliance's legal structure. Ambiguity creates more potential to acquire skills and technologies. The challenge for western companies is not to write tighter legal agreements but to become better learners.

Running away from collaboration is no answer. Even the largest western companies can no longer outspend their global rivals. With leadership in many industries shifting toward the east, companies in the United States and Europe must become good borrowers – much like Asian companies did in the 1960s and 1970s. Competitive renewal depends on building new process capabilities and winning new product and technology battles. Collaboration can be a low-cost strategy for doing both.

Creating a strategic centre to manage a web of partners

By Gianni Lorenzoni and Charles Baden-Fuller[1]

Strategic alliances and inter-firm networks have been gaining popularity with many firms for their lower overhead costs, increased responsiveness and flexibility, and greater efficiency of operations. Networks that are *strategically guided* are often fast-growing and on the leading edge. In 10 years, Sun Microsystems (founded in 1982) grew to $3.2 billion in sales and $284 million in profits. This remarkable growth has been achieved by Sun's strategic direction of a web of alliances.

Few would expect such rapid growth and technological success in an older and mature industry such as textiles. Yet Benetton, the famous global textile empire, is in many ways like Sun. Founded in 1964, it had by 1991 achieved more than $2 billion in sales and $235 million in profits. Benetton is widely admired in Europe and the Far East for its rapid growth and ability to change the industry's rules of the game through its strategy of 'mass fashion to young people'.

What creates and guides the successful, innovative, leading-edge inter-firm network? Most research into inter-firm networks has emphasized how they can reconcile the flexibility of market relationships with the long-term commitment of hierarchically centralized management. Although all networks reflect the conscious decisions of some managers, it is becoming increasingly apparent that those networks that are not guided strategically by a 'centre' are unable to meet the demanding challenges of today's markets. In this reading, we are concerned with those strategic centres that have had a very significant impact on their sectors, especially as regards innovation. They are not confined to just a few isolated sectors, but have been observed in a wide variety of circumstances, some of which are listed in Table 6.2.1.

In this reading, we examine three dimensions of the strategic centre:

- as a creator of value for its partners;
- as leader, rule setter and capability builder;
- as simultaneously structuring and strategizing.

The role of the strategic centre

The strategic centre (or central firm) plays a critical role as a creator of value. The main features of this role are:

- Strategic outsourcing. Outsource and share with more partners than the normal broker and traditional firm. Require partners to be more than doers, expect them to be problem-solvers and initiators.

- Capability. Develop the core skills and competencies of partners to make them more effective and competitive. Force members of the network to share their expertise with others in the network and with the central firm.

- Technology. Borrow ideas from others which are developed and exploited as a means of creating and mastering new technologies.

- Competition. Explain to partners that the principle dimension of competition is between value chains and networks. The network is only as strong as its weakest link. Encourage rivalry between firms inside the network, in a positive manner.

From subcontracting to strategic outsourcing

All firms that act as brokers or operate networks play only a limited role in undertaking the production and delivery of the good or service to the markets in which the system is involved. What distinguishes central firms is both the extent to which they subcontract, and the way that they collect together partners who contribute to the whole system and whose roles are clearly defined in a positive and creative way.

Many organizations see their subcontractors and partners as passive doers or actors in their quest for competitive advantage. They typically specify exactly what they want the partners to do, and leave little to the creative skills of others. They reserve a special creative role for only a few 'critical' partners. In strategic

TABLE 6.2.1 Some central firms and their activities

Name of company and its industry	Activities of strategic centre	Activities of the network
Apple (computers)	■ Hardware design ■ Software design ■ Distribution	■ Principal subcontractors manufacture ■ 3000 software developers
Benetton (apparel)	■ Designing collections ■ Selected production ■ Developing new technology systems	■ 6000 shops ■ 400 subcontractors in production ■ Principal joint ventures in Japan, Egypt, India and others
Corning (glass, medical products and optical fibres)	■ Technology innovation ■ Production	■ More than 30 joint ventures worldwide
Genentech (biotechnology/DNA)	■ Technology innovation	■ JVs with drug companies for production and distribution, licensing in from universities
McDonald's (fast food) in many foreign countries	■ Marketing ■ Prototyping technology and systems	■ 9000 outlets, joint ventures in many foreign countries
McKesson (drug distribution)	■ Systems ■ Marketing ■ Logistics ■ Consulting advice	■ Thousands of retail drug outlets, and ties with drug companies and government institutions
Nike (shoes and sportswear)	■ Design ■ Marketing	■ Principal subcontractors
Nintendo (video games)	■ Design ■ Prototyping ■ Marketing	■ 30 principal hardware subcontractors ■ 150 software developers
Sun (computers and computer systems)	■ Innovation of technology ■ Software ■ Assembly	■ Licensor/licensees for software and hardware
Toyota (automobiles)	■ Design ■ Assembly ■ Marketing	■ Principal subcontractors for complex components ■ Second tier for other components ■ Network of agents for distribution

networks, it is the norm rather than an exception for partners to be innovators.

Typically each of these partnerships extends beyond a simple subcontracting relationship. Strategic centres expect their partners to do more than follow the rules, they expect them to be creative. For example, Apple worked with Canon and Adobe to design and create a laser jet printer which then gave Apple an important position in its industry. In all the cases we studied, the strategic centre looked to the partners to be creative in solving problems and being proactive in the relationships. They demanded more – and obtained more – from their partners than did their less effective counterparts that used traditional subcontracting.

Developing the competencies of the partners

How should the central firm see its own competencies vis-a-vis its partners? Most writers argue that current competences should guide future decisions. Many have warned of the dangers in allowing the other partners in a joint venture or alliance to exploit the skills of the host organization. For example, Reich and Mankin (1986) noted that joint ventures between Japanese and US firms often result in one side (typically the Japanese) gaining at the expense of the other. Bleeke and Ernst (1991) found similar disappointment in that in only 51 per cent of the cases they studied did both firms gain from alliances. In a study of cross border alliances, Hamel (1991) found that the unwary partner typically found that its competencies were 'hollowed out' and that its collaborator became a more powerful competitor. Badaracco (1991) examined the experiences of GM and IBM, who have signed multiple agreements, and explored the difficulties they face.

Traditional brokers and large integrated firms do not 'hand out' core skills, but the central firms we studied have ignored this advice and won. While keeping a very few skills and assets to themselves, the central firms were remarkable in their desire to transfer skill and knowledge adding value to their partners. Typically, they set out to build up the partners' ability and competencies. At Benetton, site selection and sample selection were skills which Benetton would offer to the new retail partners, either directly or through the agents. Skill transfers were also evident in the machinery networks and at Apple.

Nike brings its partners to its research site at Beaverton to show them the latest developments in materials, product designs, technologies and markets. Sometimes the partners share some of the costs, but the prime benefit is to shorten cycle times and create a more vibrant system. Toyota's subcontractors may receive training from Toyota and are helped in their development of expertise in solving problems pertaining to their particular component. Not only does this encourage them to deliver better quality parts to the Toyota factories, but it also allows the Toyota system to generate an advantage over other car manufacturers.

In contrast to these companies, the less successful organizations we studied did not have groups of specialists to transfer knowledge to partners – nor, it seems, did they appreciate its importance. They did not enlist all their suppliers and customers to fight a common enemy. Moreover, their experiences did not encourage exploration of this approach. They spoke of past difficulties in alliances. Skill transfers between parties did not always result in mutual benefit. One defence contractor explained that their experience of skill transfers nearly always meant that the partner was strengthened and became a stronger rival.

Borrowing–developing–lending new ideas

While all firms bring in new ideas from outside, the central firms we studied have adopted an unusual and aggressive perspective in this sphere. They scan their horizons for all sorts of opportunities and utilize a formula we call *borrow–develop–lend*. 'Borrow' means that the strategic centre deliberately buys or licenses some existing technological ideas from a third party; 'develop' means that it takes these outside ideas and adds value by developing them further in its own organization. This commercialization can then be exploited or 'lent' with great rapidity through its stellar system, creating new adjuncts to leverage to the greatest advantage. Borrowing ideas, which are subsequently developed and exploited, stretches the organization and forces it to grow its capabilities and competencies. It demands a new way of thinking.

In the Italian packaging machinery sector, lead producers follow this strategy. They borrow designs of a new machine from specialist designers or customers. These designs are then prototyped. From these prototypes, small and medium-sized partners or specialists often improve the design in a unique way, such as improving the flows and linkages. The focal firm then re-purchases and exploits the modified design, licensing to producers for the final development and marketing phase. Thus we see a 'to-and-fro' pattern of development between the central firm and its many partners.

Sun also used the borrow-develop-lend approach in their project to build a new workstation delivering 'more power with less cost'. They borrowed existing technology from other parties, re-combined and developed them further inside Sun, and then licensed them to third parties for development and sale under the Sun brand.

The borrow–develop–lend principle helps the central firm reduce the cost of development, make progress more quickly, and, most importantly, undertake projects which would normally lie outside its scope.

This approach contrasts with the procedures used by other large firms. Although these firms may buy ideas from other sources, large firms usually have a slower pace of development and rarely match the speed of exploitation achieved through networking and re-lending the idea to third parties. The strategic centre seems to avoid the *not-invented-here* syndrome, where innovations and ideas are rejected because they are not internally created and developed.

From the view of independent inventors, the strategic centre is an attractive organization with which to do business. The central firms have a track record of rapid commercialization (usually offering large incentives to those with ideas). They emphasize moving quickly from ideas to market by a simultaneous learning process with partners, thereby offering a competitive advantage over other developers. Finally, the willingness to involve others means rapid diffusion with fast payback, thus lessening the risks.

Perceptions of the competitive process

Firms in the same industry experience varying degrees of competitive rivalry. The joint venture, formal agreements, or the use of cross shareholdings are mechanisms used to create common ties, encourage a common view and unite firms against others in the industry. Strategic centres also create this sense of cooperation across competing enterprises.

Competitive success requires the integration of multiple capabilities (e.g. innovation, productivity, quality, responsiveness to customers) across internal and external organizational boundaries. Such integration is a big challenge to most organizations. Strategic centres rise to this challenge and create a sense of common purpose across multiple levels in the value chain and across different sectors. They achieve a combination of specialized capability and large-scale integration at the same time, despite the often destructive rivalry between buyers and customers. Strategic purchasing partnerships are commonly used to moderate this rivalry, but few firms are able to combine both horizontal and vertical linkages.

In building up their partner's capabilities and competencies, strategic centres convey an unusual perspective to their partners on the nature of the competitive process. This perspective permits the partners to take a holistic view of the network, seeing the collective as a unit that can achieve competitive advantage. In this respect, the whole network acts like a complex integrated firm spanning many markets.

Table 6.2.2 illustrates how the actions of the strategic centre differ from other organizations. Chain stores are a good example of organizations that coordinate activities across many actors, yet at a single stage of the value chain. In contrast, the narrowly defined, vertically integrated firm coordinates across many stages but not across many markets or actors. Only the strategic centre and the large multi-market, vertically integrated organization are able to coordinate across many markets and many stages of the value chain.

Beyond the hollow organization

Although the strategic centre outsources more activities than most organizations, it is not hollow. Unlike the traditional broker that is merely a glorified arranger, the central firms we studied understand that they have to develop some critical core competencies. These competencies are, in general, quite different from those stressed by most managers in traditional firms. The agenda for the central firm consists of:

- The idea. Creating a vision in which partners play a critical role.

TABLE 6.2.2 Different kinds of competition across sectors and stages of the value chain

	Single units within the sector	Multiple units within the sector or across related sectors
Multiple stages of the value chain	■ Vertical integration; or ■ Value-added partnerships	■ Strategic centres and their webs of partners; or ■ Large integrated multi-market organizations
Single stages of the value chain	■ Traditional adversarial firm	■ Chain stores; or ■ Simple networks

- The investment. A strong brand image and effective systems and support.
- The climate. Creating an atmosphere of trust and reciprocity.
- The partners. Developing mechanisms for attracting and selecting partners.

Sharing a business idea

Most of the central firms we studied are small, lean and focused operations. They employ comparatively few people and are very selective in what they do. Yet, they have an unusual ability to conceptualize a business idea that can be shared not only internally, but with other partners. In the case of Benetton, this idea has a few key elements such as: mass fashion for young people, and the notion of a strategic network to orchestrate and fulfil this vision. In food-machinery, the key idea of the central firms is to solve the client's problems, rather than selling existing competencies, while new partners are developed in response to customer needs – a novel notion in this sector. These simple ideas are not easy to create or sustain.

These ideas have been able to capture the imagination of the employees and their partners. They also encapsulate strategy and so contain, in the language of Prahalad and Hamel (1990), the features of a clear strategic intent. Common to all the business ideas we studied, there is a notion of partnership which includes the creation of a learning culture and the promotion of systems experiments so as to outpace rival competing organizations. The strategic centres view their role as one of leading and orchestrating their systems. Their distinctive characteristics lie in their ability to perceive the full business idea and understand the role of all the different parties in many different locations across the whole value chain. The managers in the strategic centre have a dream and they orchestrate others to fulfil that dream.

This vision of the organization is not just an idea in the minds of a few managers, it is a feature that is shared throughout the organization. Many of the strategic centres we studied admit that their visions have emerged over time, they are not the work of a moment. Their vision is dynamic, for as their network grows and as the environment changes, the organizational vision also changes. This is not the case in the less successful alliances. They showed the typical characteristics of most organizations, multifaceted views of the world and a less-than-clear expression of their vision.

Clearly, vision is reinforced by success. The ability of central firms to deliver profits and growth for the partners helps cement a vision in their minds and makes their claims credible. It creates a cycle where success breeds clarity, which in turn helps breed more success.

Brand power and other support

To maintain the balance of power in the network, all central firms retain certain activities. The control of the brand names and the development of the systems that integrate the network are two activities that give the organization a pivotal role and allow it to exercise power over the system.

Some of the firms we observed were involved in consumer markets where branding is important. The brand name, owned by the central firm, was promoted by the activities of the partners, who saw the brand as a shared resource. They were encouraged to ensure its success, and quite often these efforts helped the brand become famous in a short period of time. While the brand and marketing are not so vital in producer goods markets, they are still important – and the strategic centre neglects these at its peril. Its importance is highlighted by the experiences of one of the less successful organizations we studied. This aerospace firm had problems as a result of the inability of its members to relinquish many of the aspects of marketing to a single central firm.

To retain its power, the central firm must ensure that the information between partners flows freely and is not filtered. Communication is a costly activity, and developing effective communication systems is always the responsibility of the strategic centre. These systems are not only electronically-based, but include all other methods of communication. Often there is a style for meeting among the partners, which is set and monitored by the central firm. The quality of information is a key requirement if the central firm is to mandate effectively the stream of activities scattered among different firms.

Trust and reciprocity

Leveraging the skills of partners is easy to conceive but hard to implement. The difficulties occur because it takes many partners operating effectively to make the system work, but the negative behaviour of only a few can bring the whole system to a halt. The strategic vision requires all its members to contribute all the time without fail. This is a considerable demand. The typical organizational response to such a need is to circumscribe the contracts with outsiders in a tight legalistic manner. But this is not always wise; contract making and policing can be difficult and expensive. Formal contracts are relatively inflexible and are suitable only where the behaviour is easy to describe and is relatively inflexible. But the relationships are creative and flexible and so very difficult to capture and enforce contractually.

The approach of the central firms we studied is to develop a sense of trust and reciprocity in the system. This trust and reciprocity is a dynamic concept and it can be very tight. The tightness is apparent in each party agreeing to perform its known obligations. This aspect has similarities to contracts in the sense that obligations are precisely understood. But Anglo-Saxon contracts are typically limited in the sense that partners are not expected to go beyond the contract. In contrast, in a network perspective, the behaviour is prescribed for the unknown, each promising to work in a particular manner to resolve future challenges and difficulties as they arise. This means that each partner will promise to deliver what is expected, and that future challenges will also be addressed positively. If there are uncertainties and difficulties in the relationships, these will be resolved after the work is done. If one party goes beyond (in the positive sense) the traditional contract, others will remember and reciprocate at a later date.

Trust and reciprocity are complements, not substitutes, to other obligations. If partners do not subscribe to the trust system, they can hold the whole system hostage whenever they are asked to do something out of the ordinary, or even in the normal course of events. Such behaviour will cause damage to all, and the system will break up. Only with trust can the system work in unison.

The Benetton franchising system is perhaps an extreme version of this trust system. On the continent of Europe, Benetton does not use legal contracts, rather it relies on the unwritten agreement. This, it claims, focuses everyone's attention on making the expectations clear. It also saves a great deal of time and expense. Many other strategic centres also rely on trust, but utilize contracts and formal controls as a complement. Central firms develop rules for settling disputes (for there will be disputes even in a trust system). The central firm also ensures that rewards are distributed in a manner which encourages partners to reinforce the positive circle. Benetton has encountered limits to its approach in the US, where the cultural emphasis on law and contracts has come into conflict with Benetton's strategy.

In sharp contrast are the other less successful systems we studied. There, trust was used on a very limited scale, since most organizations had difficulty in getting partners to deliver even that which was promised. Broken promises and failed expectations were common in the defence systems. Very low anticipated expectations of partner reciprocity were a common feature of the Scottish network and appliance sectors. Most organizations believed that anything crucial had to be undertaken in-house.

Trust is delicate, and it needs fostering and underpinning. One of the ways in which positive behaviour is encouraged is to ensure that the profit-sharing relationships give substantial rewards to the partners. None of the central firms we studied seeks to be the most profitable firm in the system; they are happy for others to take the bulk of the profit. In Benetton, a retailer may find his or her capital investment paid back in three years. In Corning, some partners have seen exceptional returns. This seemingly altruistic behaviour, however, does not mean that the rewards to the central firm are small.

Partner selection

The central firms we studied recognize that creating success and a long-term perspective must begin with the partner selection process. In building a network, partners must be selected with great care. Initially, the central firms followed a pattern of trial and error, but following successful identification of the key points in the selection process, they became more deliberate. The many new styles of operation and new ways of doing things are not easy to grasp, and they are quite difficult to codify – especially at the early stages of the selection process. As time passes, a partner profile emerges together with a selection procedure aimed at creating the correct conditions for the relationships. These relationships require coordination among all the partners, a common long-term perspective, an acceptance of mutual adaptation and incremental innovation. When we looked at the details of the selection procedure, there was a difference between those central firms that had a few large partners and those that had many small-scale partners. In the case of the network composed of a few, large firm alliances, the selection criterion is typically based on careful strategic considerations. There is the question of matching capabilities and resources, as well as considerations of competition. However, most important are the organizational features based on a compatibility of management systems, decision processes and perspectives – in short, a cultural fit.

The selection process must also be tempered by availability. Typically, there are few potential partners to fit the ideal picture. Perhaps it is for this reason that some Japanese and European firms start the process early on by deliberately spinning off some of their internal units to create potential partners. Typically these units will contain some of their best talents. However, these units will have a cultural affinity and a mutual understanding, which makes the partnership easier.

In the case of the large network composed of many small partners, the centre acts as a developer of the community. Its managers must assume a different role. Apple called some of its managers 'evangelists' because they managed the relationships with 3000 third-party developers. So that they could keep constant contact with them, they used images of the 'Figurehead' and the 'Guiding Light'.

Simultaneous structuring and strategizing

Of all the battles firms face, the most difficult is not the battle for position, nor is it even the battle between strong firms and weak firms following the same strategic approaches. Rather, it is the battle between firms adopting different strategies and different approaches to the market. In these battles, the winners are usually those who use fewer and different resources in novel combinations. The central firms we studied fit this category, for they have typically dominated their sectors by stretching and leveraging modest resources to great effect. In trying to understand these battles of stretch and leverage, others have stressed the technical achievements of central firms such as lean production, technical innovation, or flexible manufacturing and service delivery. To be sure, these advances are important and provide partial explanations for the success of Sun, Nintendo, Benetton, Apple and others. Equally important, if not more important, are new ideas on the nature of strategizing and structuring. Strategizing is a shared process between the strategic centre and its partners; structuring of the relationships between the partners goes hand in hand and is seen as a key part of the strategy.

Strategy conception and implementation of ideas is shared between central firms and their webs of partners. Here they differ from most conventional organizations, which neither share their conceptions of strategy with other organizations nor insist that their partners share their ideas with them in a constructive dialogue. While all firms form partnerships with some of their suppliers and customers, these linkages rarely involve sharing ideas systematically. Subcontracting relationships are usually deeper and more complex, and many firms share their notions of strategy with their subcontractors, but the sharing is nearly always limited. Alliances demand even greater levels of commitment and interchange, and it is common for firms involved in alliances to exchange ideas about strategy and to look for strategic fit and even reshaping of strategic directions. Networks can be thought of as a higher stage of alliances, for in the strategic centre there is a conscious desire to influence and shape the strategies of the partners, and to obtain from partners ideas and influences in return.

This conscious desire to share strategy is reflected in the way in which central firms conceive of the boundaries of their operations. Most organizations view their joint ventures and sub-contractors as beyond the boundaries of their firm, and even those involved in alliances do not think of partners as an integral part of the organization. Even firms that are part of a franchise system (and thus have a more holistic perspective) do not view their relationships as a pattern of multilateral contracts. Going beyond the franchise view, central firms and their participants communicate multilaterally across the whole of the value chain. In the words of Johanson and Mattsson (1992), they have a 'network theory,' a perception of governing a whole system.

Strategizing and structuring in the central firms we studied reverses Chandler's famous dictum about structure following strategy. When partner's competencies are so crucial to the developments of the business idea of the strategic centre, the winners are building strategy and structure simultaneously whereas the losers are signing agreements without changing their organizational forms to match them. When each partner's resources and competencies are so essential to the success of the enterprise, new forms must be designed. To achieve this, structuring must come earlier, alongside strategizing, and both require an interaction among partners to create a platform of flexibility and capability. This behaviour challenges much of what is received managerial practice and avoids some of the traps that webs of alliances face.

Like the large integrated cohesive organization, networked firms are able to behave as a single competitive entity which can draw on considerable resources. However, the network form avoids many of the problems of large integrated firms, who typically find themselves paralysed in the struggle between freedom and control. By focusing attention on the matters where commonality is important (e.g. product design) and by allowing each unit to have freedom elsewhere, cooperation is fostered, time and energy spent in monitoring is reduced, and resources are optimized. In this way, the networked organization succeeds in bridging the gap between centralization and decentralization. But cooperation can dull the edge of progress, and the organizations in our study have avoided this trap by fostering a highly competitive spirit.

Marketing and information sharing

The way in which information is collected and shared in the system reveals how structure and strategy go hand in hand. The gathering of information is a central activity in any organization. A strategic feature of a network of alliances is that the firms in the system are closely linked for the sharing of information. Members of the network exchange not only hard data about best practice, but also ideas, feelings and thoughts about customers, other suppliers and general market trends.

The central firm structures the information system so that knowledge is funnelled to the areas that need it the most. Members specializing in a particular function have access to others in the system performing similar tasks, and share their knowledge. This creates a level playing field within the network system. It also provides the opportunity for the members to focus and encourage the development of competitive advantage over rivals.

One of the basic premises in our network view is that new information leading to new ways of doing things emerges in a process of interaction with people and real-life situations. It follows that the 'information ability' of the firm depends critically on a scheme of interactions. The difficulty is that the generation of new information cannot be planned, but has to emerge. Thus, the task of the manager is one of designing a structure which provides an environment favourable for interactions to form, and for new information to be generated. Such a structure is a network.

Our study found, as have others, that the availability of large amounts of high quality information on many aspects of the business facilitated more rapid responses to market opportunities. Information condensed through the network is 'thicker' than that condensed through the brokerage market, but is 'freer' than in the hierarchy.

The need for a sophisticated system was clear when we contrasted the central firms we studied with other firms. In these other firms, we often found that critical information was guarded, not shared. As is so common among organizations, individual players are either afraid of being exploited or they have a desire to exploit the power they have through knowledge. Even in traditional franchise systems, information is typically passed to the centre for filtering before being shared. In the large integrated firm, centralization also causes unnecessary filtering. With centralization, the process of collecting and distributing information can be cumbersome and slow. Moreover, power to manipulate the information can be accidentally or intentionally misused by a small central group.

Some of the 'control group' of firms we studied did share their information, with adverse consequences. For example, defence contractors, unable to create an effective strategic network, found the partners sometimes used the shared information to their own advantage, and then did not reciprocate. The knowledge was exploited by partners to create superior bargaining positions. Opportunities to foster collective interest were missed, and in extreme cases, partners used the information to bolster a rival alliance to the detriment of the original information provider.

Learning races

Whereas identifying opportunities for growth is facilitated by information sharing, responding to the opportunity is more difficult. Here we see some of the clearest evidence that structure and strategy go hand in hand. First and foremost, the central firms we studied reject the idea of doing everything themselves. Instead, they seek help from others to respond to the opportunities they face. When the knowledge and capabilities exist within the network, the role of the centre is to orchestrate the response so that the whole system capitalizes on the opportunity.

It frequently happens that opportunities require an innovative response, and it is common for strategic centres to set up 'learning races'. Here, partners are given a common goal (say a new product or process development) with a prize for the first to achieve the target. The prize may be monetary, but more commonly it is the opportunity to lead off the exploitation of the new development. There is a catch, the development must be shared with others in the network. Learning races create a sense of competition and rivalry, but within an overall common purpose.

Nintendo uses carefully nurtured learning races with its partners to create high quality rapid innovation. Partners are typically restricted in the number of contributions they can make. In the case of software design, the limit may be three ideas a year. These restrictions force a striving for excellence, and the consequence is a formidable pace of progress.

Learning races can be destructive rather than constructive if the partners do not have the skills and resources. The strategic centres we studied get around these difficulties by sharing knowledge and in effect allowing the whole network to 'borrow' skills and competencies from each other.

It is important to understand the role of new members in the process of creating innovations. Many central firms follow the twin strategies of internal and external development. Internal development involves offering existing partners a possibility of sharing in the growth markets. External development involves the finding of new partners to fill the gaps and accelerate the possibilities. New partners typically fit the pattern set by existing partners. These newly found 'look alike' firms allow the strategic centre to truncate development of the necessary capabilities, leveraging off earlier experiences developed by the existing partners. By making growth a race between old and new partners, speed is assured and scale effects exploited. Our strategic centres fostered positive rivalry rather than hostility by ensuring that both old and new partners share in the final gains. When pursuing rapid growth, the twin tracks of internal and external development can lessen tensions. Because they are independent, existing members can respond to the new demands as they wish. But, if they do not respond positively, the central firm can sign up new partners to fill the gaps. The stresses and strains of growth can thus be reduced for each of the members of the network.

Conclusions

The strategically minded central firms in our study view the boundaries of the organization differently because their conception and implementation of strategy are shared with a web of partners. This attitude contrasts sharply with most organizations, which view their joint ventures and sub-contractors as existing beyond the boundaries of their firm. Even those involved in alliances typically do not think of partners as an integral part of their organization; they rarely share their conceptions of strategy and even fewer insist that their partners share their strategy with them in a constructive dialogue. In contrast, strategic centres communicate strategic ideas and intent multilaterally across the whole of the value chain. They have a network view of governing a whole system.

Strategic centres reach out to resolve classic organizational paradoxes. Many sub-contracting and alliance relationships seemed to be mired in the inability to reconcile the advantages of the market with those of the hierarchy. Strategic centres are able to create a system that has the flexibility and freedom of the market coupled with long-term holistic relationships, ensuring the requisite strategic capabilities across the whole system. Another paradox exists between creativity and discipline. Most organizations oscillate between having ample creativity and little discipline, or too much discipline and not enough creativity. Through their unusual attitude to structuring and strategizing, strategic centres attain leading-edge technological and market developments while retaining rapid decision making processes.

All organizations have much to learn from studying strategic centres and their unusual conception of the managerial task. Strategic centres have taken modest resources and won leadership positions in a wide variety of sectors. They have brought a new way of thinking about business and organizing. Much of what they do is at the cutting edge, and they are shining examples of how firms can change the rules of the game by creative and imaginative thinking.

Coevolution in business ecosystems

By James F. Moore[1]

During the past decade, a great deal of insight has been gleaned about complex biological communities – illuminated by biologists poking around in Central American jungles, collecting insects in Asia and observing birds in the Arctic. Much of this work has focused on the intricate and far-reaching

[1]Source: This article © 1996 by James F. Moore. Adapted from Chapter One of James F. Moore, *The Death of Competition: Leadership and Strategy in the Age of Business Ecosystems,* by permission of HarperCollins Publishers Inc.

relationships among species: predator and prey, pollinator and plant, protector and herd. What has become clear is that some ecosystems, notably those besieged by wave after wave of potential settlers, develop a special resiliency, flexibility and resistance to catastrophes. In contrast, those that develop in isolation like Hawaii can become highly vulnerable to ecological disasters, and may even face mass extinctions.

Recent work in community ecology has dwelled on topics like 'keystone' species, the most critical of the species in an ecosystem. When they disappear from an ecosystem, life within the system itself changes radically. One example is the sea otter. Sea otters on the California coast prey on sea urchins. The urchins feast on kelp beds and other seaweeds along the ocean floor. When the otters were hunted almost to extinction during the nineteenth century, urchin populations grew exponentially and consumed much of the kelp beds, diminishing the biodiversity of the ecosystem. The ocean floor became almost barren. Through aggressive efforts, conservationists re-introduced the sea otter to the area. The urchins have now been harvested and the rich complexity along the coast restored.

Biologists have also concentrated on highly aggressive 'exotic' species that can have a particularly disruptive effect when injected into an ecosystem. The hydrilla plant, for instance, was introduced into Florida from Asia in the 1950s. Today hydrilla infests over 40 per cent of the waterways in the state – choking lakes and rivers, killing native fish and other wildlife. The hydrilla is almost impossible to control and seems destined to have a permanently damaging effect on biological diversity and robustness in the region.

Unfortunately, the study of business communities lags well behind the biological. Yet close examination of the history of business innovation and the creation of wealth shows that there are important parallels between these two seemingly dissimilar worlds.

While biological analogies are often applied to the study of business, they are frequently applied much too narrowly. Almost invariably, the recurring focus is on the evolution of species. For example, some argue that in a market economy a Darwinian selection occurs in which the fittest products and companies survive. More recently, as businesses have been dissected into processes through the quality and re-engineering movements, some now maintain that the fittest processes and systems of processes drive out the weak. In either instance, the 'species' are seen to be subject to genetic mutation and selection that gradually transforms them.

I have become convinced that the world is more complicated than that, and that we must think in grander terms. Species-level improvement of business processes is unquestionably crucial for keeping companies successful, and creates unmistakable value for society. But there are complementary forms of evolution that play vital but grossly underrated roles in both biology and business. They encompass the ecological and evolutionary interactions that occur across an entire ecosystem, comprising all the organisms of a particular habitat as well as the physical environment itself. Leaders who learn to understand these dimensions of ecology and evolution will find themselves equipped with a new model for devising strategy, and critical new options for shaping the future of their companies.

In biological ecosystems, changes take place over different time scales: many ecological changes occur within the lifetime of the individual organism, whereas evolutionary changes transpire over numerous generations. In business ecosystems, these two time scales collapse into one, because, unlike biological species, a business can guide its own evolution and effect dramatic evolutionary changes during its lifetime. A leader in a business ecosystem has an important edge over the species in a biological ecosystem: the ability to see the big picture and understand the dynamics of the ecosystem as a whole. This enables a business to alter its traits to better fit its ecosystem. What is more, a business can anticipate future changes in its ecosystem and evolve now so that it is well prepared to face future challenges.

Coevolution: Working together to create the future

The late anthropologist Gregory Bateson, who had a lifelong obsession with the workings of complex systems, greatly influenced my thinking. His thought-provoking theories of coevolution, culture and addiction as they applied to natural and social systems are very intriguing, and I was struck by how he often studied systems in biological terms and then tried to understand how consciousness played its part in those systems.

In his thinking, Bateson focused on patterns. One of his observations was that behaviours within systems – companies, societies, species, families – coevolve. What does 'coevolve' mean in this context? In his book *Mind and Nature*, Bateson (1979) describes coevolution as a process in which interdependent species evolve in an endless reciprocal cycle – 'changes in species A set the stage for the natural selection of changes in species B', and vice versa. Take the caribou and the wolf. The wolf culls the weaker caribou, which strengthens the herd. But with a stronger herd, it is imperative for wolves to evolve and become stronger themselves to succeed. And so the pattern is not simply competition or cooperation, but coevolution. Over time, as coevolution proceeds, the whole system becomes more hardy.

From Bateson's standpoint, coevolution is more important a concept than simply competition or co-operation. The same holds true in business. Too many executives focus their time primarily on day-to-day product and service-level struggles with direct competitors. Over the past few years, more managers have also emphasized cooperation: strengthening key customer and supplier relationships, and in some cases working with direct competitors on initiatives like technical standards and shared research to improve conditions for everyone.

A small number of the most effective firms in the world develop new business advantages by learning to lead economic coevolution. These companies – such as Intel, Hewlett-Packard, Shell, Wal-Mart, Creative Artists Agency and others – recognize that they live in a rich and dynamic environment of opportunities. The job of their top management is to seek out potential centres of innovation where, by orchestrating the contributions of a network of players, they can bring powerful benefits to bear for customers and producers alike. Their executives must not only lead their current competitors and industries – whether by competition or cooperation – but hasten the coming together of disparate business elements into new economic wholes from which new businesses, new rules of competition and cooperation, and new industries can emerge.

Obliterating industry boundaries

There are certain spots on the earth – Amazon rain forests, for instance – where biological evolution proceeds at madcap speed. In these hyperdomains, nature brazenly experiments with new evolutionary loops and wrinkles, as well as new strategies for genetic invention. As a consequence, new organisms are spawned that, in due course, crawl out and populate the rest of the world.

Similar and unprecedented upheaval is astir in the world of business. There are certain identifiable hot spots of rapidly accelerating evolutionary activity in the global economy, places where the speed of business is exceedingly fast and loose. New technologies, deregulation and changes in customer behaviour are the metaphorical equivalent of floods and fires, opening up new competitive landscapes. On such newly cleared and fertile grounds, embryonic or transformed businesses are sprouting.

These new renditions are businesses with an edge. In a sense, they are renegades. In their marauding ways, they do not respect traditional industry paradigms and partitions. Indeed, what they share is a tendency to upend business and industry models and to redraw increasingly porous boundaries.

What we are seeing, in fact, is the end of industry. That's not to say that we now need to mourn the dissolution of the airline industry or the cement industry. Rather, it means the end of industry as a useful concept in contemplating business. The notion of 'industry' is really an artefact of the slowly paced business evolution during the middle of this century. The presumption that there are distinct, immutable businesses within which players scramble for supremacy is a tired idea whose time is past. It has little to do with what is shaping the world. The designation itself is simplistic, describing certain players better than others. But, in truth, the label is not much more than a crude grid used to compare and contrast businesses, a fiction conjured up by policymakers and regulators, investment analysts, and even academic students of business strategy.

There has been a profound change in management thinking of senior executives over recent years. Earlier, many senior managers could rightfully be accused of living in denial about the structural transformations of the world economy and its impact on their businesses. Today, very few senior management teams can really be charged with living in such a state. There is no need to argue that the economic times have shifted – there is widespread agreement that this is true. The traditional industry boundaries that we've all taken for granted throughout our careers are blurring – and in many cases crumbling.

Enter a new logic to guide action

The important question for management today is not whether such changes are upon us but how to make strategy in this new world. Few management teams have been able to put together systematic approaches for dealing with the new business reality. Most find themselves struggling with varying degrees of effectiveness, but with no clear way to think about and communicate, let alone confront, the new strategic issues.

What is most needed is a new language, a logic for strategy, and new methods for implementation. Many of the old ideas simply don't work any more. For instance, diversification strategies that emphasize finding 'attractive' industries often assume the fixedness of industry structure, yet our experience tells us that industry structures evolve very rapidly. Our traditional notions of vertical and horizontal integration fail us in the new world of cooperating communities. Competitive advantage no longer accrues necessarily from economies of scale and scope. Many firms can attain the volume of production to be efficient. Flexible systems are widely available that enable firms to customize their offers, proliferate variety, and do so at little additional cost. In the new world, scale and scope matter, but only as they contribute to a continuing innovation trajectory so that a company continually lowers its costs while increasing its performance.

Companies agitating to be leaders in the volatile new world order must transform themselves profoundly and perpetually so as to defy categorization. Is Wal-Mart a retailer, a wholesaler, or an information services and logistics company? Is Intel governed by the economic realities of the semiconductor industry, or does it lead one of several coevolving, competing personal computer-centred ecosystems? Are its competitors Texas Instruments and NEC or Microsoft and Compaq?

In place of 'industry', I suggest an alternative, more appropriate term: *business ecosystem.* The term circumscribes the microeconomies of intense coevolution coalescing around innovative ideas. Business ecosystems span a variety of industries. The companies within them coevolve capabilities around the innovation and work cooperatively and competitively to support new products, satisfy customer needs, and incorporate the next round of innovation. Microsoft, for example, anchors an ecosystem that traverses at least four major industries: personal computers, consumer electronics, information and communications. Centred on innovation in microprocessing, the Microsoft ecosystem encompasses an extended web of suppliers including Intel and Hewlett-Packard and myriad customers across market segments.

A second new term is 'opportunity environment,' a space of business possibility characterized by unmet customer needs, unharnessed technologies, potential regulatory openings, prominent investors and many other untapped resources. Just as biological ecosystems thrive within a larger environment, so do business ecosystems. As traditional industry boundaries erode around us, companies often unexpectedly find themselves in fierce competition with the most unlikely of rivals. At the same time, the most creative and aggressive companies exploit these wider territories,

transforming the landscape with new ecosystems. Thus, shaping cohesive strategy in the new order starts by defining an opportunity environment. Within such an environment, strategy-making revolves around devising novel ways to seize opportunities and create viable networks with other business ecosystems.

Unfortunately, most prevailing ideas on strategy today begin with the wrong-headed assumption that competition is bounded by clearly defined industries. As a result, these ideas are nearly useless in the current business climate and are sure to be even less valid in the future. Can one understand the economic events of tomorrow relying on these ideas? I very much doubt it. It is more important to see a company within its food web than in competition with superficially similar firms bundled together in an industry.

We compete in a bifurcated world. Executives today really must view strategy from two perspectives: They must pay attention to the wider opportunity environment and strive to lead in establishing the business ecosystems that will best utilize it. The dominant new ecosystems will likely consist of networks of organizations stretching across several different industries, and they will joust with similar networks, spread across still other industries.

At the same time, executives must continue to see their companies in the traditional sense, as members of homogenous industries clawing away at rivals for market share and growth. In terms of strategy, it no longer matters if the industries are old and venerable like banking and automobiles, or frisky new ones like cable television and personal computers. So understanding one's industry will be only the first step to pursuing customers, innovation and the creation of wealth.

Learn from companies investing in the new approach

I believe that this change in conceptualizing is vitally important for three reasons. First, the conditions and challenges prevalent in the fastest-moving sectors of the global economy are spreading inexorably to all the others. The dynamics of these centres, and the challenges confronting their feistiest companies and leaders, are now relevant to us all.

Second, some of the hottest centres of economic competition – computers, communications, media, retailing, health care – are now devising fresh approaches to strategy and leadership. These approaches are not very well understood, even by many of their creators, and they surely are not appreciated by the wider public. Nevertheless, the scope of the strategic ambitions are truly breathtaking. If their creators succeed in their endeavours, their initiatives will have profound implications in our daily lives. What it already means is the end of competition as we know it.

Third, these ideas are already propagating across the general business landscape and thus are guaranteed to have a dramatic and irreversible impact on how we do business from now on. Because of these reasons, business people, no matter what business they conduct, must comprehend at least the broad outlines of what is afoot.

The special task of business leadership: Creating communities of shared imagination

In one significant respect, a strictly biological metaphor does not apply to business. Unlike biological communities of coevolving organisms, business communities are social systems. And social systems are composed of real people who make decisions. A powerful shared imagination, focused on envisioning the future, evolves in a business ecosystem that is unlike anything in biology. Conscious choice does play an important role in ecology. Animals often choose their habitats, their mates and their behaviour. In the economic world, however, strategists, policymakers and investors spend a great deal of time trying to understand the overall game and find fruitful ways to play it or change it. This consciousness is central to economic relationships.

Even more, shared imagination is what holds together economies, societies and companies. Therefore, a great deal of leadership and business strategy relies on creating shared meaning, which in turn shapes the future. For example, during 1995 millions of people from diverse backgrounds became convinced that the Internet would become a major locus for commerce, entertainment and personal communication. They rushed to become involved and, in the act of so doing, established a foundation for the very reality they believed was coming about. While many other factors encouraged the exponential growth of interest in the Internet, Sun Microsystems played a powerful role by introducing a software language called Java. Java made it possible to create appealing animated experiences across the Internet.

Sun makes a wide range of computers. Java was the result of a small research project, outside the company mainstream. Nonetheless, Sun executives saw Java's potential to enliven the community. Sun executives chose not to treat Java as just another product. Instead, they essentially gave away Java to the rest of the world in order to feed the internet frenzy and reinforce Sun's image as a leader of the movement. What mattered was Java the campaign – not Java the product. A widespread perception formed that Sun was prescient and well positioned for the future. Sun's sales rose, its stock appreciated, and it became more able to get other stakeholders to follow its lead.

It is the mind that imparts the harmony and the sense and the syncopation to the business ecosystem. The larger patterns of business coevolution are maintained by a complex network of choices, which depend, at least in part, on what participants are aware of. As Gregory Bateson stressed, if you change the ideas in a social system, you change the system itself. We are seeing the birth of ideas. The very fact that new ideas are coming into existence is changing the conditions. If you don't follow these new ideas, you will be totally lost.

As companies get more sophisticated in creating new ecosystems, become more like the guiding hand of a forester or gardener in an ecological environment, the more this new level of consciousness will become the dominant reality of business strategy. The game of leadership will evolve to new levels. There is a wonderful book of business history by Alfred Chandler (1977) called *The Visible Hand*. It chronicles the rise of the multidivisional organization between 1900 and 1930 and the consciousness of people like Alfred Sloane who made the development of this then new organization possible. We are witnessing the next revolution beyond multidivisional organizations and beyond the visible hand. It is the ability in an environment of immense resources, immense plasticity, and powerful information systems to make and break microeconomic relationships with enormous subtlety and velocity. We are entering an age of imagination.

In an age of imagination, the ultimate struggle among companies is for the souls of customers and the hearts of vast communities of suppliers and other associated companies. Strange things can happen in the new world of virtual organizations. In the new world, strategy based on conventional competition and cooperation gives way to strategy based on coevolution – which in turn defines a new level of competition. At this higher level, competition defines attractive futures and galvanizes concerted action. We can vividly see the tremendous power of a company like Microsoft, which leads and shapes the collective behaviour of thousands of associated suppliers, even though during most of the years of its most powerful influence, Microsoft never had more than $6 billion in sales.

But heightened consciousness of the benefits of ecosystem power and influence can also make prospective partners wary of committing to a leader. Competition to lead coevolution can bring its own peculiar paranoia – and fragment a community of companies. We already see this sort of effect within the PC business, where the heightened consciousness of Microsoft's role in overturning IBM's dominion has put all participants in the computer, communications and even the entertainment business on notice.

Now prospective allies and partners of Microsoft appreciate the costs as well as the benefits of allegiance to the company from Redmond. Many of them have become reluctant co-adventurers. Worries over Microsoft's motives and leadership outweighed the genuine benefits that appeared to be achieved by working together. Such worries also helped Sun Microsystems and Java. Java appealed to some stakeholders in part because it did not originate from Microsoft. The success of Sun and Java was welcomed as a limiter of Microsoft's influence on the future.

The new ecology of business

The heart of strategy is understanding these evolutionary patterns. What is consistent from business to business is the process of coevolution, the complex interplay between competitive and cooperative business strategies.

The immense changes that have taken place in business are minor compared to what is yet to come. When an ecological approach to management becomes more common, and when an increasing number of executives become conscious of coevolution, the pace of business change will accelerate at an exponential rate. Executives whose horizons are bounded by traditional industry perspectives will miss the real challenges and opportunities facing their companies. Shareholders and directors, who perceive the new reality, will eventually oust them. For companies caught up in dynamic business ecosystems, the stakes are considerable, but the rewards are commensurate and the challenges exhilarating as never before.

REFERENCES

Albert, M. (1991) *Capitalisme contre Capitalisme*, Paris: Seuil.

Allison, G.T. (1969) 'Conceptual Models and The Cuban Missile Crisis', *The American Political Science Review*, No. 3, September, pp. 689–718.

Arthur, W.B. (1994) *Increasing Returns and Path Dependence in the Economy*, Ann Arbor, MI: University of Michigan Press.

Axelrod, R. (1984) *The Evolution of Cooperation*, New York: Basic Books.

Axelsson, B. and Easton, G. (1992) *Industrial Networks: A New View of Reality*, New York: Wiley.

Badaracco, J.L. (1991) *The Knowledge Link: How Firms Compete Through Strategic Alliances*, Boston, MA: Harvard Business School Press.

Bartlett, C.A., Ghoshal, S. and Beamish, P. (2008) *Transnational Management: Text, Cases and Readings in Cross Border Management*, Burr Ridge, IL: McGraw-Hill/Irwin, 5th edition.

Bateson, G. (1979) *Mind and Nature: A Necessary Unity*, New York: Dutton.

Best, M.H. (1990) *The New Competition: Institutions of Industrial Restructuring*, Cambridge: Polity.

Bleeke, J. and Ernst, D. (1991) 'The Way to Win in Cross Border Alliances', *Harvard Business Review*, Vol. 69, No. 6, November–December, pp. 127–135.

Brandenburger, A.M. and Nalebuff, B.J. (1996) *Co-opetition*, New York: Currency Doubleday.

Chandler, A.D. (1986) 'The Evolution of Modern Global Competition', in: Porter, M.E. (ed.) *Competition in Global Industries*, Boston, MA: Harvard Business School Press, pp. 405–448.

Chandler, A.D. (1990) *Scale and Scope*, Cambridge, MA: Belknap.

Chandler, A.D. Jr. (1977) *The Visible Hand: The Managerial Revolution in American Business*, Cambridge, MA: Harvard University Press.

Chesbrough, H.W. and Teece, D.J. (1996) 'Organizing for Innovation: When is Virtual Virtuous?', *Harvard Business Review*, Vol. 74, No. 1, January–February, pp. 65–73.

Child, J. and Faulkner, D. (1998) *Strategies for Cooperation: Managing Alliances, Networks, and Joint Ventures*, Oxford: Oxford University Press.

Contractor, F.J. and Lorange, P. (1988) *Cooperative Strategies in International Business*, Lexington, MA: Lexington Books.

Dixit, A.K. and Nalebuff, B.J. (1991) *Thinking Strategically: The Competitive Edge in Business, Politics, and Everyday Life*, New York: WW Norton.

Doz, Y. and Hamel, G. (1998) *The Alliance Advantage: The Art of Creating Value Through Partnering*, Boston, MA: Harvard Business School Press.

Dunning, J.H. (1958) *American Investment in British Manufacturing Industry*, London: George Allen & Unwin.

Dyer, J.H. and Ouchi, W.G. (1993) 'Japanese-Style Partnerships: Giving Companies a Competitive Edge', *Sloan Management Review, Fall*, pp. 51–63.

Dyer, J.H. and Singh, H. (1998) 'The Relational View: Cooperative Strategy and Sources of Inter-organizational Competitive Advantage', *Academy of Management Review*, Vol. 23, No. 4, pp. 660–679.

Dyer, J.H., Kale, P. and Singh, H. (2001) 'How to Make Strategic Alliances Work', *Sloan Management Review*, Vol. 42, No. 4, Summer, pp. 37–43.

Fukuyama, F. (1995) *Trust: Social Virtues and the Creation of Prosperity*, New York: The Free Press.

Gambetta, D. (ed.) (1988) *Trust: Making and Breaking Cooperative Relations*, New York: Blackwell.

Gastells, M. (2006) *The Rise of The Network Society*, Oxford: Blackwell.

Gerlach, M. (1992) *Alliance Capitalism: The Social Organization of Japanese Business*, Berkeley, CA: University of California Press.

Gnyawali, D.R. and Madhavan, R. (2001) 'Cooperative Networks and Competitive Dynamics: A Structural Embeddedness Perspective', *Academy of Management Review*, Vol. 26, No. 3, pp. 431–445.

Gomes-Casseres, B. (1994) 'Group versus Group: How Alliance Networks Compete', *Harvard Business Review*, Vol. 72, No. 4, July–August, pp. 62–74.

Granovetter, M.S. (1985) 'Economic Action and Social Structure: The Problem of Embeddedness', *American Journal of Sociology*, Vol. 91, pp. 481–501.

Greenhalgh, L. (2001) *Managing Strategic Relationships*, New York: The Free Press.

Groenewegen, J. and Beije, P.R. (1989) 'The French Communication Industry Defined and Analyzed through the Social Fabric Matrix, the Filière Approach, and Network Analysis', *Journal of Economic Issues*, Vol. 23, No. 4, December, pp. 1059–1074.

Gulati, R. (1998) 'Alliances and Networks', *Strategic Management Journal*, Vol. 19, No. 4, pp. 293–317.

Hakansson, H. and Johanson, J. (1993) 'The Network as a Governance Structure: Interfirm Cooperation beyond Markets and Hierarchies', in: Grabner, G. (ed.) *The Embedded Firm: On the Socioeconomics of Industrial Networks*, London: Routledge, pp. 35–51.

Hall, E.T. (1976) *Beyond Culture*, New York: Knopf Doubleday Publishing Group.

Hamel, G. (1991) 'Competition for Competence and Inter-Partner Learning Within International Strategic Alliances', *Strategic Management Journal*, Vol. 12, Special Issue, Summer, pp. 83–103.

Hamel, G., Doz, Y.L. and Prahalad, C.K. (1989) 'Collaborate with Your Competitors – and Win', *Harvard Business Review*, Vol. 67, No. 1, January–February, pp. 133–139.

Hamilton, G.G. and Woolsey Biggart, N. (1988) 'Market, Culture and Authority: A Comparative Analysis of Management and Organization in the Far East', *American Journal of Sociology*, Vol. 94, p. 52.

Hampden-Turner, C. and Trompenaars, A. (1993) *The Seven Cultures of Capitalism: Value Systems for Creating Wealth in the United States, Japan, Germany, France, Britain, Sweden and the Netherlands*, New York: Doubleday.

Henry, J. (2003) *Understanding Japanese Society*, London: Routledge.

Hofstede, G. (1993) 'Cultural Constraints in Management Theories', *Academy of Management Executive*, Vol. 7, No. 1, pp. 8–21.

James, B.G. (1985) *Business Wargames*, Harmondsworth: Penguin.

Jarillo, J.C. (1988) 'On Strategic Networks', *Strategic Management Journal*, Vol. 9, No. 1, January–February, pp. 31–41.

Johanson, J. and Mattson, L.G. (1992) 'Network Position and Strategic Action: An Analytical Framework', in: Axelsson, B. and Easton, G. (eds.) *Industrial Networks: A New View of Reality*, London: Routledge.

Kagono, T., Nonaka, I., Sakakibara, K. and Okumara, A. (1985) *Strategic vs. Evolutionary Management*, Amsterdam: North-Holland.

Kanter, R.M. (1994) 'Collaborative Advantage: The Art of Alliances', *Harvard Business Review*, Vol. 72, No. 4, July–August, pp. 96–108.

Kay, J.A. (1993) *Foundations of Corporate Success*, Oxford: Oxford University Press.

Kim, W.C. and Mauborgne, R. (2004) 'Blue Ocean Strategy', *Harvard Business Review, October*, pp. 2–11.

Koen, C. (2005) *Comparative International Management*, Berkshire: McGraw Hill.

Lado, A.A., Boyd, N.G. and Hanlon, S.C. (1997) 'Competition, Cooperation and the Search for Economic Rents: A Syncretic Model', *Academy of Management Review*, Vol. 22, No. 1, January, pp. 110–141.

Lessem, R. and Neubauer, F.F. (1994) *European Management Systems*, London: McGraw-Hill.

Lorenzoni, G. and Baden-Fuller, C. (1995) 'Creating a Strategic Center to Manage a Web of Partners', *California Management Review*, Vol. 37, No. 3, Spring, pp. 146–163.

Mitchell, R.K., Agle, B.R. and Wood, D.J. (1997) 'Toward a Theory of Stakeholder Identification and Salience: Defining the Principle of Who and What Really Counts', *Academy of Management Review*, Vol. 22, No. 4, October, pp. 853–886.

Miwa, Y. and Ramseyer, J.M. (1996) *The Fable of the Keiretsu*, Chicago, IL: Chicago University Press.

Miyashita, K. and Russell, D. (1994) *Keiretsu: Inside the Hidden Japanese Conglomerates*, New York: McGraw-Hill, pp. 21–33.

Moore, J.F. (1996) *The Death of Competition: Leadership and Strategy in the Age of Business Ecosystems*, New York: HarperBusiness.

Oliver, N. and Wilkinson, B. (1988) *The Japanization of British Industry*, London: Basil Blackwell.

Ostrom, E. (1990) *Governing the Commons: The Evolution of Institutions for Collective Action*, Cambridge University Press.

Ouchi, W.G. (1980) 'Markets, Bureaucracies, and Clans', *Administrative Science Quarterly*, Vol. 25, No. 1, pp. 129–142.

Pascale, R.T. and Athos, A.G. (1981) *The Art of Japanese Management*, New York: Simon & Schuster.

Pfeffer, J. and Salancik, G.R. (1978) *The External Control of Organizations: A Resource Dependency Perspective*, New York: Harper & Row.

Piore, M. and Sabel, C.F (1984) *The Second Industrial Divide*, New York: Basic Books.

Porter, M.E. (1980) *Competitive Strategy: Techniques for Analyzing Industries and Competitors*, New York: Free Press.

Porter, M.E. (1985) *Competitive Advantage*, New York: Free Press.

Porter, M.E. (1990) *The Competitive Advantage of Nations*, London: Macmillan.

Powell, W. (1990) 'Neither Market nor Hierarchy: Network Forms of Organization', *Research in Organizational Behavior*, Vol. 12, pp. 295–336.

Prahalad, C.K. and Hamel, G. (1990) 'The Core Competence of the Corporation', *Harvard Business Review*, Vol. 68, No. 3, May–June, pp. 79–91.

Preece, S.B. (1995) 'Incorporating International Strategic Alliances into Overall Firm Strategy: A Typology of Six Managerial Objectives', *The International Executive*, Vol. 37, No. 3, May–June, pp. 261–277.

Quinn, J.B. (1992) *The Intelligent Enterprise: A Knowledge and Service Based Paradigm for Industry*, New York: Free Press.

Reich, R. and Mankin, E. (1986) 'Joint Ventures with Japan Give Away Our Future', *Harvard Business Review*, Vol. 64, No. 2, March–April, pp. 78–86.

Reve, T. (1990) 'The Firm as a Nexus of Internal and External Contracts', in: Aoki, M., Gustafsson, B. and Williamson, O.E. (eds.) *The Firm as a Nexus of Treaties*, London: Sage.

Richardson, G. (1972) 'The Organization of Industry', *Economic Journal*, Vol. 82, pp. 833–896.

Ruigrok, W. and Van Tulder, R. (1995) *The Logic of International Restructuring*, London: Routledge.

Schelling, T. (1960) *The Strategy of Conflict*, Cambridge, MA: Harvard University Press.

Schneider, S. and Barsoux, J. (1999) *Managing Across Cultures*, Pearson Education Limited.

Shapiro, C. and Varian, H. (1998) *Information Rules: A Strategic Guide to the Network Economy*, Cambridge, MA: Harvard Business School Press.

Simonin, B. (1997) 'The Importance of Collaborative Know-How', *Academy of Management Journal*, Vol. 40, No. 5, pp. 1150–1174.

Teece, D.J. (1992) 'Competition, Cooperation, and Innovation: Organizational Arrangements for Regimes of Rapid Technological Progress', *Journal of Economic Behavior and Organization*, Vol. 18, pp. 1–25.

Teranishi, J. (1994) 'Loan syndication in war time Japan and the origins of the main bank system', in: Aoki, N. and Patrick, H. (eds.) *The Japanese Main Bank System*, Oxford: Clarendom Press.

Thorelli, H.B. (1986) 'Networks: Between Markets and Hierarchies', *Strategic Management Journal*, Vol. 7, No. 1, January–February, pp. 37–51.

Thurow, L. (1991) *Head to Head*, Cambridge, MA: MIT Press.

Trompenaars, F. (2003) *Did the Pedestrian Die: Insights from the World's Greatest Culture Guru*, Oxford: Capstone.

Van Tulder, R. and Junne, G. (1988) *European Multinationals and Core Technologies*, London: Wiley.

Verluyten, S.P. (2010) *Intercultural Skills for International Business and International Relations*, Leuven: Acco.

Weidenbaum, M. and Hughes, S. (1996) *The Bamboo Network: How Expatriate Chinese Entrepreneurs Are Creating a New Economic Superpower in Asia*, New York: Free Press.

Williamson, O.E. (1975) *Markets and Hierarchies: Analysis and Antitrust Implications*, New York: Free Press.

Williamson, O.E. (1985) *The Economic Institutions of Capitalism*, New York: Free Press.

Williamson, O.E. (1991) 'Strategizing, Economizing, and Economic Organization', *Strategic Management Journal*, Vol. 12, Winter, Special Issue, pp. 75–94.

STRATEGY PROCESS

Follow the course opposite to custom and you will almost always do well.

Jean Jacques Rousseau (1712–1778); French philosopher

Given the variety of perspectives on strategy, finding a precise definition with which all people agree is probably impossible. Therefore, in this book we will proceed with a very broad conception of strategy as 'a course of action for achieving an organization's purpose'. In this section, it is the intention to gain a better insight into how such a course of action comes about – how is, and should, strategy be made, analysed, dreamt-up, formulated, implemented, changed and controlled; who is involved; and when do the necessary activities take place?

The process by which strategy comes about can be dissected in many ways. Here, the strategy process has been unravelled into three partially overlapping issues, each of which requires managers to make choices, and each of which is (therefore) controversial (see Figure III.1):

■ Strategy formation. This issue focuses on the question of how managers should organize their strategizing activities to achieve a successful strategy formation process.

■ Strategic change. This issue focuses on the question of how managers should organize their strategizing activities to achieve a successful change process.

■ Strategic innovation. This issue focuses on the question of how managers should organize their strategizing activities to achieve a successful strategic innovation process.

The most important term to remember throughout this section is *process*. In each chapter the discussion is not about one-off activities or outcomes – a formed strategy, a strategic change or a strategic innovation – but about the ongoing processes of forming, changing and innovating. These processes need to be organized, structured, stimulated, nurtured and/or facilitated over a prolonged period of time and the question concerns which approach will be successful in the long term, as well as in the short term.

FIGURE III.1   The strategy process chapters

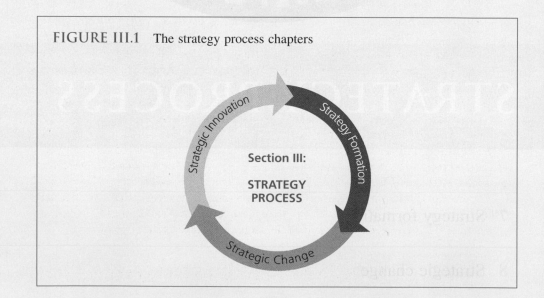

STRATEGY FORMATION

Nothing in progression can rest on its original plan. We may as well think of rocking a grown man in the cradle of an infant.

Edmund Burke (1729–1797); Irish-born politician and man of letters

INTRODUCTION

There are many definitions of strategy and many ideas of how strategies should be made. In the introduction to Section III of this book on 'Strategy Process', our definition of strategy was kept basic to encompass the large majority of these different views – 'strategy is a course of action for achieving an organization's purpose'. Taking this definition as a starting point, a major distinction can be observed between people who see strategy as an *intended* course of action and those who regard strategy as a *realized* course of action. Mintzberg and Waters (1985) have remarked that these two views of strategy are not contradictory, but complementary. Intended strategy is what individuals or organizations formulate prior to action (a *pattern of decisions*), while realized strategy refers to the strategic behaviour exhibited in practice (a *pattern of actions*). Of course, not all behaviour is necessarily strategic – if the actions do not follow a pattern directed at achieving the organization's purpose, it does not qualify as strategy.

The process by which an intended strategy is created is called 'strategy formulation'. Normally strategy formulation is followed by strategy implementation. However, intentions sometimes end up not being put into practice – plans can be changed or cancelled along the way. The process by which a realized strategy is formed is called 'strategy formation'. What is realized might be based on an intended strategy, but it can also be the result of unplanned actions as time goes by. In other words, the process of strategy formation encompasses both formulation and action. Strategy formation is the entire process leading to strategic behaviour in practice.

For managers with the responsibility for getting results, it would be too limited to only look at the process of strategy formulation and to worry about implementation later. Managers must ask themselves how the entire process of strategy formation should be managed to get their organizations to act strategically. Who should be involved, what activities need to be undertaken and to what extent can strategy be formulated in advance? In short, for managers, finding a way to realize a strategic pattern of actions is the key issue.

THE ISSUE OF REALIZED STRATEGY

Getting an organization to exhibit strategic behaviour is what all strategists aim to achieve. Preparing detailed analyses, drawing up plans, making extensive slide presentations and holding long meetings might all be necessary means to achieve this end, but ultimately it is the organization's actions directed at the marketplace that count. The key issue facing managers is, therefore, how this strategic behaviour can be attained. How can a successful course of action be realized in practice?

To answer these questions, it is first necessary to gain a deeper understanding of the 'who' and 'what' of strategy formation – 'what type of strategy formation activities need to be carried out?' and 'what type of strategy formation roles need to be filled by whom?' Both questions will be examined in the following sections.

Strategy formation activities

In Chapter 2 it is argued that the process of strategic reasoning could be divided into four general categories of activities – identifying, diagnosing, conceiving and realizing. These strategic problem-solving activities, taking place in the mind of the strategist, are in essence the same as those encountered in organizations at large. Organizations also need to 'solve strategic problems' and achieve a successful pattern of actions. The difference is that the organizational context – involving many more people, with different experiences, perspectives, personalities, interests and values – leads to different requirements for structuring the process. Getting people within an organization to exhibit strategic behaviour necessitates the exchange of information and ideas, decision-making procedures, communication channels, the allocation of resources and the coordination of actions.

When translated to an organizational environment, the four general elements of the strategic reasoning process can be further divided into the eight basic building blocks of the strategy formation process, as illustrated in Figure 7.1.

Strategic issue identification activities. If a strategy is seen as an answer to a perceived 'problem' or 'issue', managers must have some idea of what the problem is. 'Identifying' refers to all activities contributing to a better understanding of what should be

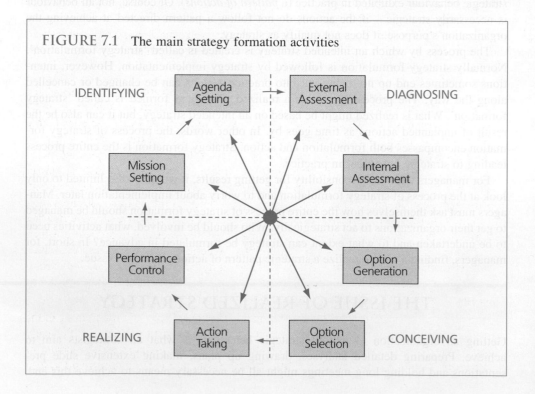

FIGURE 7.1 The main strategy formation activities

IDENTIFYING

DIAGNOSING

REALIZING

CONCEIVING

Agenda Setting

External Assessment

Mission Setting

Internal Assessment

Performance Control

Option Generation

Action Taking

Option Selection

viewed as problematic – what constitutes an important opportunity or threat that must be attended to if the organization's purpose is to be met. The key activities here are:

■ Mission setting. What the organization sees as an issue will in part depend on its mission – the enduring set of fundamental principles outlining what purpose the organization wishes to serve, in what domain and under which conditions. A company's mission, encompassing its core values, beliefs, business definition and purpose, forms the basis of the organization's identity and sets the basic conditions under which the organization wishes to function. Where a company has a clearly developed mission, shared by all key players in the organization, this will strongly colour its filtering of strategic issues. The mission does not necessarily have to be formally captured in a mission statement, but can be informally internalized as a part of the company culture. The topic of mission has been discussed at more length in Chapter 3.

■ Agenda setting. Besides the organizational mission as a screening mechanism, many other factors can contribute to the focusing of organizational attention on specific strategic issues. For instance, the cognitive map of each strategist will influence which environmental and organizational developments are identified as issues. Furthermore, group culture will have an impact on which issues are discussible, which are off-limits to open debate, and under what conditions discussions should take place. Getting people to sit up and take notice will also depend on each actor's communication and political skills, as well as their sources of power, both formal and informal. Together these attention-focusing factors determine which issues are picked up on the 'organizational radar screen', discussed and looked into further. It is said that these issues make it on to the 'organizational agenda', while all other potential problems receive less or no attention. Many of these organizational factors are discussed more extensively in Chapters 8 and 11.

Strategic issue diagnosis activities. To come to grips with a 'problem' or 'issue', managers must try to comprehend its structure and its underlying causes. Especially since most strategic issues are not simple and straightforward, but complex and messy, it is very important to gain a deeper understanding of 'what is going on' – which 'variables' are there and how are they interrelated? This part of the strategy formation processes can be divided into the following activities:

■ External assessment. The activity of investigating the structure and dynamics of the environment surrounding the organization is commonly referred to as an external assessment or analysis. Typically such a diagnosis of the outside world includes both a scan of the direct (market) environment and the broader (contextual) environment. In both cases the analyst wants to move beyond observed behaviour, to understand 'what makes the system tick'. What is the underlying structure of the industry and the market that is conditioning each party's behaviour? And what are the characteristics and strategies of each important actor, including customers, competitors, suppliers, distributors, unions, governments and financiers? Furthermore, only understanding the current state of affairs is generally insufficient; it is also necessary to analyse in which direction external circumstances are developing. Which trends can be discerned, which factors seem to be driving the industry and market dynamics, and can these be used to forecast or estimate future developments? In Chapters 4, 6 and 10, these questions surrounding external assessment are discussed in more detail.

■ Internal assessment. The activity of investigating the capabilities and functioning of the organization is commonly referred to as an internal assessment or analysis. Typically such a diagnosis of the inner workings of the organization includes an assessment of the *business system* with which the firm creates value and the *organizational system* that has been developed to facilitate the business system. When dissecting the business system, attention is directed at understanding the resources and chain of value-adding activities that enable the firm to offer a set of products and services. To gain insight into the functioning of the organizational system, it is necessary to determine the structure of the organization, the processes used to control and coordinate the various people and units, and the organizational culture. In all these analyses a mere snapshot of the firm is generally insufficient – the direction in which the organization is developing must also be examined, including a consideration of the main change drivers and change inhibitors. Furthermore, for strategy making it is important to compare how the organization scores on all aforementioned factors compared to rival firms. In Chapters 4 and 8 these topics are investigated in more depth.

Strategy conception activities.   To deal with a strategic 'problem' or 'issue', managers must come up with a potential solution. A course of action must be found that will allow the organization to relate itself to the environment in such a way that it will be able to achieve its purpose. 'Conceiving' refers to all activities that contribute to determining which course of action should be pursued. In this part of the strategy formation process, the following categories of activities can be discerned:

■ Option generation. Creating potential strategies is what option generation is about. Sometimes managers will immediately jump at one specific course of action, limiting their strategic option generation activities to only one prime candidate. However, many managers will be inclined to explore a number of different avenues for approaching a specific strategic issue, thereby generating multiple strategic options. Each option can range in detail from a general outline of actions to be taken, up to a full-blown strategic plan, specifying goals, actions, tasks, responsibilities, resource allocation, milestones and performance measures. Which questions each strategic option should address is the main focus of discussion in the strategy content section of this book.

■ Option selection. The potential 'solutions' formulated by managers must be evaluated to decide whether they should be acted upon. It must be weighed whether the strategic option generated will actually lead to the results required and then it must be concluded whether to act accordingly. Especially where two or more strategic options have come forward, managers need to judge which one of them is most attractive to act on. This screening of strategic options is done on the basis of evaluation criteria, for instance perceived risk, anticipated benefits, the organization's capacity to execute, expected competitor reactions and follow-up possibilities. Sometimes a number of the evaluation criteria used are formally articulated, but generally the evaluation will at least be partially based on the experience and judgement of the decision-makers involved. Together, these activities of assessing strategic options and arriving at a selected course of action are also referred to as 'strategic decision-making'.

Strategy realization activities.   A strategic 'problem' or 'issue' can only be resolved if concrete actions are undertaken that achieve results. Managers must make adjustments to their business or organizational system, or initiate actions in the market – they must not only think, talk and decide, but also do, to have a tangible impact. 'Realizing' refers to all these practical actions performed by the organization. If there is a clear pattern to these actions, it can be said that there is a realized strategy. In this part of the strategy formation process, the following activities can be distinguished:

■ Action taking. A potential problem solution must be carried out – intended actions must be implemented to become realized actions. This performing of tangible actions encompasses all aspects of a firm's functioning. All hands-on activities, more commonly referred to as 'work', fall into this category – everything from setting up and operating the business system to getting the organizational system to function on a day-to-day basis.

- Performance control. Managers must also measure whether the actions being taken in the organization are in line with the option selected and whether the results are in line with what was anticipated. This reflection on the actions being undertaken can be informal, and even unconscious, but it can be formally structured into a performance monitoring and measuring system as well. Such performance measurement can be employed to assess how well certain people and organizational units are doing vis-a-vis set objectives. Incentives can be linked to achieving targets, and corrective steps can be taken to ensure conformance to an intended course of action. However, deviation from the intended strategy can also be a signal to re-evaluate the original solution or even to re-evaluate the problem definition itself. An important issue when engaging in performance control is to determine which performance indicators will be used – micro-measuring all aspects of the organization's functioning is generally much too unwieldy and time-consuming. Some managers prefer a few simple measures, sometimes quantitative (e.g. financial indicators), sometimes qualitative (e.g. are clients satisfied?), while others prefer more extensive and varied measures, such as a balanced scorecard (Kaplan and Norton, 2001; Simons, 1995).

Note that these strategy formation activities have not been labelled 'steps' or 'phases'. While these eight activities have been presented in an order that seems to suggest a logical sequence of steps, it remains to be seen in which order they should be carried out in practice. In Figure 7.1 the outer arrows represent the logical clockwise sequence, similar to the analytic reasoning process discussed in Chapter 2. The inner arrows represent the possibility to jump back and forth between the strategy formation activities, similar to the irregular pattern exhibited in the holistic reasoning process in Chapter 2.

Strategy formation roles

In all strategy formation processes the activities discussed above need to be carried out. However, there can be significant differences in who carries out which activities. Roles in the strategy formation process can vary as tasks and responsibilities are divided in alternative ways. The main variations are due to a different division of labour along the following dimensions:

- Top vs middle vs bottom roles. Strategy formation activities are rarely the exclusive domain of the CEO. Only in the most extreme cases will a CEO run a 'one-man show', carrying out all activities except realization. Usually some activities will be divided among members of the top management team, while other activities will be pushed further down to divisional managers, business unit managers, and department managers (e.g. Bourgeois and Brodwin, 1983; Floyd and Wooldridge, 2000). Some activities might be delegated or carried out together with people even further down the hierarchy, including employees on the work floor. For activities such as external and internal assessment and option generation it is more common to see participation by people lower in the organization, while top management generally retains the responsibility for selecting, or at least deciding on, which strategic option to follow. The recurrent theme in this question of the vertical division of activities is how far down activities can and should be pushed – how much *empowerment* of middle and lower levels is beneficial for the organization?

- Line vs staff roles. By definition line managers are responsible for realization of strategic options pertaining to the primary process of the organization. Because they are responsible for achieving results, they are often also given the responsibility to participate in conceiving the strategies they will have to realize. Potentially, line managers can carry out all strategy formation activities without staff support. However, many organizations do have staff members involved in the strategy formation process. Important staff input can come from all existing departments, while some organizations institute special strategy departments to take care of strategy formation activities. The responsibilities of such strategy departments can vary from general process facilitation, to process ownership to full responsibility for strategy formulation.

- **Internal vs external roles.** Strategy formation activities are generally seen as an important part of every manager's portfolio of tasks. Yet, not all activities need to be carried out by members of the organization, but can be 'outsourced' to outsiders (e.g. Robinson, 1982). It is not uncommon for firms to hire external agencies to perform diagnosis activities or to facilitate the strategy formation process in general. Some organizations have external consultants engaged in all aspects of the process, even to the extent that the outside agency has the final responsibility for drawing up the strategic options.

In organizing the strategy formation process, a key question is how formalized the assignment of activities to the various potential process participants should be. The advantage of formalization is that it structures and disciplines the strategy formation process (e.g. Chakravarthy and Lorange, 1991, Reading 7.1 in this book; Hax and Maljuf, 1984). Especially in large organizations, where many people are involved, it can be valuable to keep the process tightly organized. Formalization can be achieved by establishing a strategic planning system. In such a system, strategy formation steps can be scheduled, tasks can be specified, responsibilities can be assigned, decision-making authority can be clarified, budgets can be allocated and evaluation mechanisms can be put in place. Generally, having unambiguous responsibilities, clearer accountability and stricter review of performance will lead to a better functioning organization. The added benefit of formalization is that it gives top management more control over the organization, as all major changes must be part of approved plans and the implementation of plans is checked.

Yet, there is a potential danger in using formal planning systems as a means to make strategy. Formalization strongly emphasizes those aspects that can be neatly organized such as meetings, writing reports, giving presentations, making decisions, allocating resources and reviewing progress, while having difficulty with essential strategy-making activities that are difficult to capture in procedures. Important aspects such as creating new insights, learning, innovation, building political support and entrepreneurship can be sidelined or crushed if rote bureaucratic mechanisms are used to produce strategy. Moreover, planning bureaucracies, once established, can come to live a life of their own, creating rules, regulations, procedures, checks, paperwork, schedules, deadlines and double-checks, making the system inflexible, unresponsive, ineffective and demotivating (e.g. Marx, 1991; Mintzberg, 1994a).

THE PARADOX OF DELIBERATENESS AND EMERGENCE

The ability to foretell what is going to happen tomorrow, next week, next month and next year. And to have the ability afterwards to explain why it didn't happen.
Winston Churchill (1874–1965); British prime minister and writer

Strategy has to do with the future. And the future is unknown. This makes strategy a fascinating, yet frustrating, topic. Fascinating because the future can still be shaped and strategy can be used to achieve this aim. Frustrating because the future is unpredictable, undermining the best of intentions, thus demanding flexibility and adaptability. To managers, the idea of creating the future is highly appealing, yet the prospect of sailing for *terra incognita* without a compass is unsettling at best.

This duality of wanting to intentionally design the future, while needing to gradually explore, learn and adapt to an unfolding reality, is the tension central to the topic of strategy formation. It is the conflicting need to figure things out in advance, versus the need to find things out along the way. On the one hand, managers would like to forecast the future and to orchestrate plans to prepare for it. Yet, on the other hand, managers understand that experimentation, learning and flexibility are needed to deal with the fundamental unpredictability of future events.

In their influential article, 'Of Strategies: Deliberate and Emergent', Mintzberg and Waters (1985) were one of the first to explicitly focus on this tension. They argued that a distinction should be made between deliberate and emergent strategy (see Figure 7.2). Where realized strategies were fully intended, one can speak of 'deliberate strategy'. However, realized strategies can also come about 'despite, or in the absence of, intentions', which Mintzberg and Waters labelled 'emergent strategy'. In their view, few strategies were purely deliberate or emergent, but usually a mix between the two.

Hence, in realizing strategic behaviour managers need to blend the conflicting demands for deliberate strategizing and strategy emergence. In the following paragraphs both sides of this paradox of deliberateness and emergence will be examined further.

The demand for deliberate strategizing

Deliberateness refers to the quality of acting intentionally. When people act deliberately, they 'think' before they 'do'. They make a plan and then implement the plan. A plan is an intended course of action, stipulating which measures a person or organization proposes to take. In common usage, plans are assumed to be articulated (made explicit) and documented (written down), although strictly speaking this is not necessary to qualify as a plan.

FIGURE 7.2   Deliberate and emergent strategy

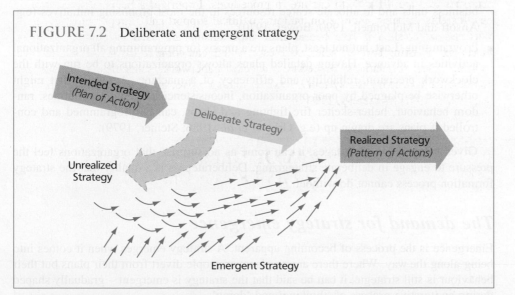

Source: Mintzberg and Waters, 1985; reprinted with permission from Strategic *Management Journal,* © 1985 John Wiley and Sons Ltd.

As an intended course of action, a plan is a means towards an end. A plan details which actions will be undertaken to reach a particular objective. In practice, however, plans can exist without explicit objectives. In such cases, the objectives are implicitly wrapped up in the plan – the plan incorporates both ends and means.

All organizations need to plan. At the operational level, most firms will have some degree of production planning, resource planning, manpower planning and financial planning, to name just a few. When it comes to strategic behaviour, there are also a number of prominent advantages that strongly pressure organizations to engage in deliberate strategizing:

- Direction. Plans give organizations a sense of direction. Without objectives and plans, organizations would be adrift. If organizations did not decide where they wanted to go, any direction and any activity would be fine. People in organizations would not know what they were working towards and therefore would not be able to judge what constitutes effective behaviour (e.g. Ansoff, 1965; Chakravarthy and Lorange, 1991, Reading 7.1).

- Commitment. Plans enable early commitment to a course of action. By setting objectives and drawing up a plan to accomplish them organizations can invest resources, train people, build up production capacity and take a clear position within their environment. Plans allow organizations to mobilize themselves and to dare to take actions that are difficult to reverse and have a long payback period (e.g. Ghemawat, 1991; Marx, 1991).

- Coordination. Plans have the benefit of coordinating all strategic initiatives within an organization into a single cohesive pattern. An organization-wide master plan can ensure that differences of opinion are ironed out and one consistent course of action is followed throughout the entire organization, avoiding overlapping, conflicting and contradictory behaviour (e.g. Ackoff, 1980; Andrews, 1987).

- Optimization. Plans also facilitate optimal resource allocation. Drawing up a plan disciplines strategizing managers to explicitly consider all available information and consciously evaluate all available options. This allows managers to choose the optimal course of action before committing resources. Moreover, documented plans permit corporate level managers to compare the courses of action proposed by their various business units and to allocate scarce resources to the most promising initiatives (e.g. Ansoff and McDonnell, 1990; Bower, 1970).

- Programming. Last, but not least, plans are a means for programming all organizational activities in advance. Having detailed plans allows organizations to be run with the clockwork precision, reliability and efficiency of a machine. Activities that might otherwise be plagued by poor organization, inconsistencies, redundant routines, random behaviour, helter-skelter fire fighting and chaos, can be programmed and controlled if plans are drawn up (e.g. Grinyer et al., 1986; Steiner, 1979).

Given these major advantages, it can come as no surprise that organizations feel the pressure to engage in deliberate strategizing. Deliberateness is a quality that the strategy formation process cannot do without.

The demand for strategy emergence

Emergence is the process of becoming apparent. A strategy emerges when it comes into being along the way. Where there are no plans, or people divert from their plans but their behaviour is still strategic, it can be said that the strategy is emergent – gradually shaped during an iterative process of 'thinking' and 'doing'.

Emergent strategy differs from ad hoc behaviour in that a coherent pattern of action does evolve. While managers may have no prior intentions, they can explore, learn and piece together a consistent set of behaviours over time. Such an approach of letting strategy emerge has a number of major advantages that organizations also need to consider:

- Opportunism. As the future is unknown and therefore unpredictable, organizations must retain enough mental freedom to grab unforeseen opportunities as they emerge. Organizations must keep an open mind to sense where positive and negative circumstances are unfolding, so that they can respond rapidly to these new conditions – proactively riding the wave of opportunity, using the momentum in the environment and/or the organization to their advantage. This ability to 'play the field' is an important factor in effective strategy formation (e.g. Quinn, 2002; Stacey, 2001).

- Flexibility. Not only must managers keep an open mind, they must keep their options open as well, by not unnecessarily committing themselves to irreversible actions and investments. Letting strategy emerge means not prematurely locking the organization into a preset course of action, but keeping alternatives open for as long as practically possible. And where commitments must to be made, managers need to select 'robust' options, which permit a lot of leeway to shift along with unfolding events. This pressure to remain flexible is also an important demand on strategizing managers (e.g. Beinhocker, 1999; Evans, 1991).

- Learning. Often, the best way to find out what works is to give it a try – to act before you know. Letting strategy emerge is based on the same principle, that to learn what will be successful in the market must be discovered by experimentation, pilot projects, trial runs and gradual steps. Through the feedback obtained by hands-on 'doing', a rich insight can grow into what really works. As Thomas Alva Edison is well known for remarking, invention is 5 per cent inspiration and 95 per cent perspiration, and this is probably equally true for 'inventing the corporate future'. Learning is hard work, but it is an essential part of strategy formation (e.g. Pascale, 1984, Mintzberg, 1994b).

- Entrepreneurship. Building on the previous point, often the best way to find out what works is to let various people give it a try – to tap into the entrepreneurial spirits within the organization. Different people in the organization will have different strategic ideas and many of them will feel passionately about proving that their idea 'can fly'. By providing individuals, teams and/or entire units with a measure of autonomy to pursue innovative initiatives, firms can use the energy of 'intrapreneurs' within the organization, instead of forcing them to conform or start on their own (e.g. Amabile, 1998; Pinchot, 1985). As true incubators, firms can facilitate various divergent projects simultaneously, increasing commitment or closing them down as their potential unfolds (e.g. Burgelman, 1983, 1991; Lyon, Lumpkin and Dess, 2000).

- Support. A major shift in strategy generally requires a major shift in the political and cultural landscape of an organization – careers will be affected, vested departmental interests will be impacted and cultural values and beliefs will be challenged. Rarely can such shifts be imposed top-down by decree. Getting things done in organizations includes building coalitions, blocking rivals, convincing wavering parties, confronting opposing ideas and letting things 'sink in', all with the intention of gradually building enough support to move forward. Yet, finding out where enough support can be mustered to move forward, and where side steps or even reversals are needed, is an ongoing process and cannot be predicted in advance. Hence, strategizing managers must understand the internal political and cultural dynamics of their organizations and pragmatically shape strategy depending on what is feasible, not on what is ideal (e.g. Allison, 1971; Quinn, 1980).

Each of these points seems to be the opposite counterpart of the advantages of deliberate strategizing – while deliberateness creates commitment, emergence allows for flexibility; while deliberateness gives direction, emergence allows for opportunism; while deliberateness facilitates fixed programming, emergence allows for ongoing learning. This places managers in a paradoxical position. While both deliberate strategizing and strategy emergence seem to have advantageous characteristics, they are each other's opposites and are to a certain extent contradictory – a firm cannot be fully committed to detailed and coordinated long-term plans, while simultaneously adapting itself flexibly and opportunistically to unfolding circumstances, ongoing learning and unpredictable political and cultural processes. With two conflicting demands placed on the strategy formation process at the same time, managers need to choose one at the expense of the other, trying to strike the best possible balance between deliberateness and emergence.

EXHIBIT 7.1 SHORT CASE

TOMTOM: NAVIGATING THROUGH UNCHARTED WATERS

Few companies can claim to have navigated clients to exactly the right spot, yet TomTom can. Founded in 1991 by CEO Harold Goddijn, TomTom became the world leader in location and navigation products and services but more recently has experienced tough times. It has faced profit warnings, competition by Google's free turn-by-turn navigation on all Android devices with its own maps, and restructurings. The strategy process has become more formalized, yet it remains to be seen whether this will be the right way forward. How can Goddijn combine his emerging entrepreneurial strategy style – which navigated TomTom through the stormy times – with more formal and deliberate routines?

TomTom started as a software development company for mobile devices, such as the then revolutionary clamshell-designed Personal Digital Assistant (PDA) *Psion Organizer* – Goddijn's previous employer. In 2001, when more accurate GPS satellite readings became available, TomTom recognized the opportunity of in-car navigation. The company's first navigation product, the TomTom Navigator, was developed for PDAs, yet the real breakthrough came when the decision was made to put navigation software in a box. An experienced hardware team was recruited to develop an all-in-one Portable Navigation Device (PND), the TomTom GO. The introduction of the TomTom GO was a colossal success; revenues increased from €39 million in 2003 to €720 million in 2005. In May of that year, TomTom was successful in becoming listed on the NYSE Euronext Amsterdam, enabling the firm to fund further growth.

Knowing that products don't have an eternal life – which applies to software, yet equally to PNDs – Goddijn wanted to invest in areas that would broaden its revenue base. From the early days of TomTom as a software company, but also from his previous job as the managing director of Psion, Goddijn had learned that the mobile platform for navigation products is not a stable basis for a sustainable business model. The threat of piracy, a diversity of platforms and various hardware suppliers, together creating a very volatile environment indeed. Supported by a few trusted advisors he was in search of new growth areas to broaden the firm's base, and he did so with a couple of strategic acquisitions.

In August 2005 the German telematics company *Datafactory AG* was acquired, laying the foundation for the business unit 'Business Solutions' which is currently Europe's fastest-growing telematics service provider for fleet management. The acquisition of *Applied Generics,* specializing in using data from mobile networks for advanced routing of vehicles, formed the basis of TomTom's traffic services. Furthermore, in June 2007 TomTom entered the in-dash navigation systems market for automotive manufacturers, as it was expected that within a few years each car would have built-in navigation by default. An automotive engineering team from the Siemens research and development division was attracted. With its specialist knowledge of in-dash navigation systems, it became the core of TomTom's Automotive business unit. TomTom had become a firm with four market-facing business units: Consumer (organized around the PND),

Automotive (built-in navigation devices), Licensing (selling map content), and Business Solutions (offering fleet management solutions); and four centralized R&D units.

One of the key components of a navigation solution is the map. In July 2007 TomTom surprised the industry by making a bid for Tele Atlas (€2.0bn), to which Nokia responded by making a bid for Navteq ($8.1bn) in October 2007. This last development could potentially pose a huge threat to Garmin, the other leading navigation firm, responded with a €2.3 billion bid for Tele Atlas at the end of October. Early in November TomTom raised its offer to €2.9 billion after which Garmin pulled out. It took until May 2008 for the European Commission to approve the acquisition under the EU Merger Regulations – after which the deal was closed in June 2008. Tele Atlas CEO Alain de Taeye became a member of the Management Board, alongside CEO Harold Goddijn and CFO Marina Wyatt.

From a strategic point of view, acquiring Tele Atlas made sense, however in early 2009 it also resulted in difficulties meeting its bank covenants. TomTom went through a financial restructuring and had to raise €430 million of funds, partly via €359 million rights offering, in which Goddijn and the other company founders participated, and via a €71 million private placement. The workforce was reduced by 7 per cent or 115 staff, on top of €35 million annual savings within Tele Atlas.

The storm had not calmed down, though. In October of the same year Google, the firm's largest licensing client, announced they would be offering free turn-by-turn navigation on Android devices based on their own map. By Google entering the mapping market, the scarcity value of the map deteriorated, in conjunction with TomTom's stock value. Even worse, Google's free of charge navigation was based on generating advertising revenues and educating the end-user that they no longer had to pay for navigating services nor for map content. The sales of PNDs, TomTom's main source of revenues, came under direct attack. To make matters even worse, Nokia, owner of Navteq, also announced free turn-by-turn navigation on their devices as from 2010. TomTom's main competitor in the navigation market, Garmin, successfully responded by diversifying into Sport and Fitness products and by entering the aviation and marine markets.

In 2010 Harold Goddijn attracted a new Chief Technology Officer (CTO), Charles Davies. After 20 years of being software director at Psion, Davies had been CTO of Symbian, Nokia's mobile operating system. He was expected to not only understand the future need for mapping and navigation technology, but also bring in a more deliberate strategy mode. The year went relatively well; TomTom managed to show a revenue growth (€1,521 million, +3 per cent). Strong growth of the Automotive business unit (€179 million, +80 per cent) selling in-dash systems, for example to Renault, and Business Solutions (€53 million, +30 per cent), managed to offset the decline of the Consumer business unit (€1,158 million, −4 per cent) which sold more traffic subscriptions to consumers. However, new clouds were forming over the company.

Early 2011, TomTom announced that expected revenue and profitability would be largely in line with 2010 results. Growth in Automotive and Business Solutions was expected to offset the anticipated decline in the PND market. The stock market responded negatively on this outlook though: the share price dropped by 15 per cent. In April and June, TomTom had to give revenue and profit warnings to the market; the economic decline had weakened the consumer electronics markets, a trend that was expected to last. The European PND market was expected to decline by the 10 per cent and for the North American PND market a faster rate of decline of approximately 30 per cent was anticipated. In June, the revenue outlook for 2011 was almost €300 million, or 20 per cent, lower than in February. In four months' time, TomTom's shares lost half its value.

Harold Goddijn and his fellow board members had to do something to act on this negative trend. TomTom was facing strong competition in the PND market, had to compete against 'free' business models and needed to invest in the Automotive business unit. On top of all this, the output of engineering activities had be improved significantly by introducing new innovative products, content and services. In the second half of 2011, TomTom's top management held various steering committee meetings. Tough decisions were needed on the group structure; the firm's activities; reporting lines and review processes; as well as on how to achieve the highly needed savings. The process was top-down driven: only a limited number of key organizational members were involved. The main outcomes of the steering group meetings were a new organization structure, and savings in support activities and marketing expenses. The newly created structure would bring more transparency and accountability, speed up making innovation choices and reduce time to market. The products would continue to be delivered to the market through the existing Consumer, Automotive, Licensing and Business Solutions business units. Furthermore, existing R&D activities would be regrouped into ten product units: Maps, Traffic, Navigation, Automotive Systems, PNDs, Fleet services, Fitness, Mobile, POIs (Points of Interest) and Speedcams. Each product unit was mandated to invest in ongoing development of a well-defined product category to deliver the best products to TomTom's customers.

In the new structure, the product units were imposed to develop a business plan based on a standardized strategy template, including coherent actions, a product roadmap and a financial paragraph. Templates were provided by the Product

Office, a corporate staff organization, headed by CTO Charles Davies. Review sessions were planned three times a year to assess the quality of the plans, while the Product Office informed TomTom's top management. Furthermore, these business plans were to be used as input for the product units that were now required to update their strategic plan annually, and be presented to TomTom's management board and CTO.

Clearly, a much more formal strategy approach had been installed. Will this new strategy process navigate TomTom to renewed growth and stability? Or is the industry way too dynamic for such a structured strategy process and is a more emergent and entrepreneurial approach required? After all, the firm's history has proved that the industry is in constant flux. Perhaps TomTom should invent a brand new navigating device for navigating through unchartered waters.

Co-author: Claudia Janssen

Source: Company information.

PERSPECTIVES ON STRATEGY FORMATION

It is impossible for a man to learn what he thinks he already knows.
Epictetus (c. 60–120); Roman philosopher

In Hollywood, most directors do not start shooting a movie until the script and storyboard are entirely completed – the script details each actor's words, expression and gestures, while the storyboard graphically depicts how each scene will look in terms of camera angles, lighting, backgrounds and stage props. Together they form a master plan, representing the initial intentions of the director. However, it frequently happens that a director has a new insight, and changes are made to the script or storyboard 'on the fly'. Yet, on the whole, most 'realized movies' are fairly close to directors' initial intentions.

For some directors this is madness. They might have a movie idea, but in their mind's eye they cannot yet picture it in its final form. Some elements might have already crystallized in their thoughts, but other parts of the film can only be worked out once the cameras are rolling and the actors start playing their roles. In this way, directors can let movies emerge without having a detailed script or storyboard in advance to guide them. It can be said that such movies are shaped by gradually blending together a number of small intentional steps over a long period of time, instead of taking one big step of making a master plan and implementing it. This approach of taking many small steps is called 'incrementalism'.

The question is how this works for managers making strategy. Is it best to deliberately draw up a storyboard for the film and trust that the 'actors' are flexible enough to adapt to minor changes in the script as time goes by? Or is the idea of a master plan misplaced, and are the best results achieved by developing a strategy incrementally, emergently responding to opportunities and threats as they unfold along the way? In short, how should strategizing managers strike a balance between deliberateness and emergence?

Unfortunately, the strategic management literature does not offer a clear-cut answer to this question. In both the academic journals and the practitioner-oriented literature, a wide spectrum of views can be observed on how managers should engage in strategy formation. While some writers suggest that there might be different styles in balancing deliberateness and emergence (e.g. Chaffee, 1985; Hart, 1992), most seem intent on offering 'the best way' to approach the issue of strategy formation – which often differs significantly from 'the best way' advised by others.

To come to grips with this variety of views, here the two diametrically opposed pole positions will be identified and discussed. On the basis of these two 'points of departure' the debate on how to deal with the paradox of deliberateness and emergence can be further explored. At one pole we find those managers and theorists who strongly emphasize deliberateness over emergence. They argue that organizations should strive to make strategy in a highly deliberate manner, by first explicitly formulating comprehensive plans, and only then implementing them. In accordance with common usage, this point of view will be referred to as the 'strategic planning perspective'. At the other pole are those who strongly emphasize emergence over deliberateness, arguing that in reality most new strategies emerge over time and that organizations should facilitate this messy, fragmented, piecemeal strategy formation process. This point of view will be referred to as the 'strategic incrementalism perspective'.

The strategic planning perspective

Advocates of the strategic planning perspective argue that strategies should be deliberately planned and executed. In their view, anything that emerges unplanned is not really strategy. A successful pattern of action that was not intended cannot be called strategy, but should be seen for what it is – brilliant improvisation or just plain luck (Andrews, 1987). However, managers cannot afford to count on their good fortune or skill at muddling through. They must put time and effort into consciously formulating an explicit plan, making use of all available information and weighing all of the strategic alternatives. Tough decisions need to be made and priorities need to be set, before action is taken. 'Think before you act' is the strategic planning perspective's motto. But once a strategic plan has been adopted, action should be swift, efficient and controlled. Implementation must be secured by detailing the activities to be undertaken, assigning responsibilities to managers and holding them accountable for achieving results (e.g. Ansoff and McDonnell, 1990; Chakravarthy and Lorange, 1991, Reading 7.1).

Hence, in the strategic planning perspective, strategies are intentionally designed, much as an engineer designs a bridge. Building a bridge requires a long formulation phase, including extensive analysis of the situation, the drawing up of a number of rough designs, evaluation of these alternatives, choice of a preferred design, and further detailing in the form of a blueprint. Only after the design phase has been completed do the construction companies take over and build according to plan. Characteristic of such a planning approach to producing bridges and strategies is that the entire process can be disassembled into a number of distinct steps that need to be carried out in a sequential and orderly way. Only by going through these steps in a conscious and structured manner will the best results be obtained (e.g. Armstrong, 1982; Powell, 1992).

For advocates of the strategic planning perspective, the whole purpose of strategizing is to give organizations direction, instead of letting them drift. Organizations cannot act rationally without intentions – if you do not know where you are going, any behaviour is fine, which soon degenerates into 'muddling through' (e.g. Ansoff, 1991; Steiner, 1979). By first setting a goal and then choosing a strategy to get there, organizations can get 'organized'. Managers can select actions that are efficient and effective within the context of the strategy. A structure can be chosen, tasks can be assigned, responsibilities can be divided, budgets can be allotted and targets can be set. Not unimportantly, a control system can be created to measure results in comparison to the plan, so that corrective action can be taken.

Another advantage of the planning approach to strategy formation is that it allows for the *formalization* and *differentiation* of strategy tasks. Because of its highly structured and sequential nature, strategic planning lends itself well to formalization. The steps of the strategic planning approach can be captured in planning systems (e.g. Kukalis, 1991; Lorange and Vancil, 1977), and procedures can be developed to further enhance and organize the strategy formation process. In such strategic planning systems, not all elements of strategy formation need to be carried out by one and the same person, but can be divided among a number of people. The most important division of labour is often between those formulating the plans and those implementing them. In many large companies the managers proposing the plans are also the ones implementing them, but deciding on the plans is passed up to a higher level. Often other tasks are spun off as well, or shared with others, such as diagnosis (strategy department or external consultants), implementation (staff departments) and evaluation (corporate planner and controller). Such task differentiation and specialization, it is argued, can lead to a better use of management talent, much as the division of labour has improved the field of production. At the same time, having a formalized system allows for sufficient coordination and mutual adjustment, to ensure that all specialized elements are integrated back into a consistent organizationwide strategy (e.g. Grinyer *et al.,* 1986; Jelinek, 1979).

Last, but not least, an advantage of strategic planning is that it encourages long-term thinking and commitment. 'Muddling through' is short-term oriented, dealing with issues of strategic importance as they come up or as a crisis develops. Strategic planning, on the other hand, directs attention to the future. Managers making strategic plans have to take a more long-term view and are stimulated to prepare for, or even create, the future (Ackoff, 1980). Instead of just focusing on small steps, planning challenges managers to define a desirable future and to work towards it. Instead of wavering and opportunism, strategic planning commits the organization to a course of action and allows for investments to be made at the present that may only pay off in the long run (e.g. Ansoff, 1991; Miller and Cardinal, 1994).

One of the difficulties of strategic planning, advocates of this perspective will readily admit, is that plans will always be based on assumptions about how future events will unfold. Plans require forecasts. And as the Danish physicist Niels Bohr once joked, 'prediction is very difficult, especially about the future.'. Even enthusiastic planners acknowledge that forecasts will be inaccurate. As Makridakis, the most prolific writer on the topic of forecasting, writes (1990: 66), 'the future can be predicted only by extrapolating from the past, yet it is fairly certain that the future will be different from the past.' Consequently, it is clear that rigid long-range plans based on such unreliable forecasts would amount to nothing less than Russian roulette. Most proponents of the strategic planning perspective therefore caution for overly deterministic plans. Some argue in favour of 'contingency planning', whereby a number of alternative plans are held in reserve in case key variables in the environment suddenly change. These contingency plans are commonly based on different future 'scenarios' (Van der Heijden, 1996; Wilson, 2000; Bodwell and Chermack, 2010, Reading 7.3). Others argue that organizations should stage regular reviews, and realign strategic plans to match the altered circumstances. This is usually accomplished by going through the planning cycle every year, and adapting strategic plans to fit with the new forecasts.

EXHIBIT 7.2   THE STRATEGIC PLANNING PERSPECTIVE

STMICROELECTRONICS PLAN TO UNVEIL NEW STRATEGIC PLAN

STMicroelectronics NV (STM), Europe's largest semiconductor maker, will unveil a new strategic plan on 10 December 2013 after weighing options for a revamp to adjust the company to weakening demand. Chief Executive Officer, Carlo Bozotti, so far has said the new plan will present Geneva-based STMicroelectronics' strategy for the coming years as well as the structure of the company. The group said today it will present a plan before the stock market opens. A company representative declined to provide more details.

Under Bozotti, in his seventh year as CEO, STMicro has pushed to put chips in cars, health and fitness machines to make up for the decline of business from phone-maker Nokia Oyj, one of its biggest customers. The company has also said it plans to cut costs by $150 million a year by the end of 2013, in a move that may affect as many as 500 jobs. The stock today rose as much as 1.2 per cent in Paris intraday trading after STMicroelectronics said it would unveil the plan next month.

Breakup Proposal. Earlier this month, people familiar with the situation said that STMicroelectronics will probably decide against splitting itself into two units after disagreements between French and Italian executives over a breakup proposal. A proposed split between analog and digital businesses hadn't won the full support of the STMicroelectronics Board, and will probably be shelved in favour of smaller asset sales, the people said this month, asking not to be identified discussing private deliberations. French executives including Chairman Didier Lombard and Chief Operating Officer Didier Lamouche had failed to convince Bozotti to support the plan, they said. STMicroelectronics reiterated this month that it has no plans to divide the company. On October 12, STMicroelectronics' shares rose as much as 19 per cent, the biggest intraday gain since it started trading in 1994, after Bloomberg News reported the company was evaluating a breakup.

The semiconductor manufacturer has been dragged down by its digital business, which manufactures chips for handsets and set-top boxes, as key customers like Nokia and BlackBerry maker Research In Motion Ltd. (RIM) see their own sales decline.

More broadly, European semiconductor makers have struggled to cope with the industry's sharp price and demand swings. They are losing market share to Asian and US competitors who have switched to so-called fabless models, dispensing with factories in favour of outsourcing to foundries such as those of Taiwan Semiconductor Manufacturing. That allows semiconductor makers to adjust their designs and production more quickly without the overhead of running their own plants.

Source: Marie Mawad and Matthew Campbell, Bloomberg, Nov 30, 2012; http://www.bloomberg.com/news/2012-11-30/stmicroelectronics-plans-to-unveil-new-strategic-plan.html.

The strategic planning perspective shares many of the assumptions underlying the analytic reasoning perspective discussed in Chapter 2. Both perspectives value systematic, orderly, consistent, logical reasoning and assume that humans are capable of forming a fairly good understanding of reality. And both are based on a calculative and optimizing view of strategy-making. It is, therefore, not surprising that many managers who are rationally inclined also exhibit a distinct preference for the strategic planning perspective.

The strategic incrementalism perspective

To advocates of the strategic incrementalism perspective, the planners' faith in deliberateness is misplaced and counter-productive. In reality, incrementalists argue, new strategies largely emerge over time, as managers proactively piece together a viable course of action or reactively adapt to unfolding circumstances. The strategy formation process is not about rigidly *setting* the course of action in advance, but about flexibly *shaping* the course of action by gradually blending together initiatives into a coherent pattern of actions. Making strategy involves sense-making, reflecting, learning, envisioning, experimenting and changing the organization, which cannot be neatly organized and programmed. Strategy formation is messy, fragmented and piecemeal – much more like the unstructured and unpredictable processes of exploration and invention than like the orderly processes of design and production (e.g. Mintzberg, 1990; Quinn, 1978, Reading 7.2).

Yet proponents of the strategic planning perspective prefer to press strategy formation into an orderly, mechanistic straightjacket. Strategies must be intentionally designed and executed. According to strategic incrementalists, this excessive emphasis on deliberateness is due to planners' obsession with rationality and control (e.g. Wildavsky, 1979; Mintzberg, 1993). Planners are often compulsive in their desire for order, predictability and efficiency. It is the intention of strategic planning to predict, analyse, optimize and programme – to deliberately fine-tune and control the organization's future behaviour. For them, 'to manage' is 'to control' and therefore only deliberate patterns of action constitute good strategic management.

Incrementalists do not question the value of planning and control as a means for managing some organizational processes, but point out that strategy formation is not one of them. In general, planning and control are valuable for routine activities that need to be efficiently organized (e.g. production or finance). But planning is less suitable for non-routine activities – that is, for doing new things. Planning is not appropriate for innovation (e.g. Hamel, 1996; Kanter, 2002). Just as R&D departments cannot plan the invention of new products, managers cannot plan the development of new strategies. Innovation, whether in products or strategies, is not a process that can be neatly structured and controlled. Novel insights and creative ideas cannot be generated on demand, but surface at unexpected moments, often in unexpected places. Nor are new ideas born full-grown, ready to be evaluated and implemented. In reality, innovation requires brooding, tinkering, experimentation, testing and patience, as new ideas grow and take shape. Throughout the innovation process it remains unclear which ideas might evolve into blockbuster strategies and which will turn out to be miserable disappointments. No one can objectively determine ahead of time which strategic initiatives will 'fly' and which will 'crash'. Therefore, managers engaged in the formation of new strategies must move incrementally, letting novel ideas crystallize over time, and increasing commitment as ideas gradually prove their viability in practice. This demands that managers behave not as planners, but as 'inventors' – searching, experimenting, learning, doubting and avoiding premature closure and lock-in to one course of action (e.g. Stacey, 1993, Reading 11.2 in this book; Beinhocker, 1999).

Recognizing that strategy formation is essentially an innovation process has more consequences. Innovation is inherently subversive, rebelling against the status quo and challenging those who are emotionally, intellectually or politically wedded to the current state of affairs. Creating new strategies involves confronting people's cognitive maps, questioning the organizational culture, threatening individuals' current interests and disrupting the distribution of power within the organization (e.g. Hamel, 1996; Johnson, 1988). None of these processes can be conducted in an orderly fashion, let alone be incorporated into a planning system. Changing people's cognitive maps requires complex processes of unlearning and learning. Cultural and political changes are also difficult processes to programme. Even for the most powerful CEO, managing cognitive, cultural and political changes is not a matter of deliberate control, but of incremental shaping. Less powerful managers will have an even weaker grip on the unfolding cognitive, cultural and political reality in their organization, and therefore will be even less able to plan. In short, managers who understand that strategy formation is essentially a disruptive process of organizational change will move incrementally, gradually moulding the organization into a satisfactory form. This demands that managers behave not as commanders, but as 'organizational developers' – questioning assumptions, challenging ideas, getting points on the strategic agenda, encouraging learning, championing new initiatives, supporting change and building political support.

Incrementalists point out that planning is particularly inappropriate when dealing with wicked problems. While solving tame problems can often be planned and controlled, strategizing managers rarely have the luxury of using generic solutions to fix clearly recognizable strategic problems. Strategic problems are inherently wicked – they are essentially unique, highly complex, linked to other problems, can be defined and interpreted in many ways, and have no correct answer, nor a delimited set of possible solutions. The planning approach of recognizing the problem, fully analysing the situation, formulating a comprehensive plan and then implementing the solution, is sure to choke on a wicked problem. A number of weaknesses of planning show up when confronted with a wicked problem:

- Problems cannot be simply recognized and analysed, but can be interpreted and defined in many ways, depending on how the manager looks at it. Therefore, half the work of the strategizing manager is *making sense* out of complex problems. Or, as Rittel and Webber (1973) put it, the definition of a wicked problem is the problem! Managers must search for new ways for understanding old problems and must be aware of how others are reinterpreting what they see (e.g. Liedtka, 2000; Smircich and Stubbart, 1985). This inhibits strategic planning and encourages strategic incrementalism.

- A full analysis of a wicked problem is impossible. Due to a wicked problem's complexity and links to other problems, a full analysis would take, literally, forever. And there would always be more ways of interpreting the problem, requiring more analysis. Strategic planning based on the complete understanding of a problem in advance therefore necessarily leads to paralysis by analysis (e.g. Langley, 1995; Lenz and Lyles, 1985). In reality, however, managers move proactively despite their incomplete understanding of a wicked problem, learning as they go along. By acting and thinking at the same time, strategizing managers can focus their analyses on what seems to be important and realistic in practice, gradually shaping their understanding along the way.

- Developing a comprehensive plan to tackle a wicked problem is asking for trouble. Wicked problems are very complex, consisting of many subproblems. Formulating a master plan to solve all subproblems in one blow would require a very high level of planning sophistication and an organization with the ability to implement plans in a highly coordinated manner – much like the circus performers who can keep ten plates twirling at the ends of poles at the same time. Such organizations are rare at best, and the risk of a grand strategy failing is huge – once one plate falls, the rest usually come crashing down. This is also known as Knagg's law: the more complex a plan, the larger the chance of failure. Incrementalists therefore argue that it is wiser to tackle subproblems individually, and gradually blend these solutions into a cohesive pattern of action.

- Planners who believe that formulation and implementation can be separated underestimate the extent to which wicked problems are interactive. As soon as an organization starts to implement a plan, its actions will induce counteractions. Customers will react, competitors will change behaviour, suppliers will take a different stance, regulatory agencies might come into action, unions will respond, the stock markets will take notice and company employees will draw conclusions. Hence, action by the organization will change the nature of the problem. And since the many counterparties are intelligent players, capable of acting strategically, their responses will not be entirely predictable. Planners will not be able to forecast and incorporate other parties' reactions into the plans. Therefore, plans will be outdated as soon as implementation starts. For this reason, incrementalists argue that action must always be swiftly followed by redefinition of the problem and reconsideration of the course of action being pursued. Over time, this iterative process of action-reaction-reconsideration will lead to the emergence of a pattern of action, which is the best possible result given the interactive nature of wicked problems.

■ This last point, on the unpredictability of external and internal reactions to a plan, leads up to a weakness of strategic planning that is possibly its most obvious one – strategy has to do with the future and the future is inherently *unknown*. Developments cannot be clearly forecast, future opportunities and threats cannot be predicted, nor can future strengths and weaknesses be accurately foreseen. In such unknown terrain, it is foolhardy to commit oneself to a preset course of action unless absolutely necessary. It makes much more sense in new and unpredictable circumstances to remain flexible and adaptive, postponing fixed commitments for as long as possible. An unknown future requires not the mentality of a train conductor, but of an explorer – curious, probing, venturesome and entrepreneurial, yet moving cautiously, step-by-step, ready to shift course when needed.

To proponents of the strategic incrementalism perspective, it is a caricature to call such behaviour ad hoc or muddling through. Rather, it is behaviour that acknowledges the fact that strategy formation is a process of innovation and organizational development in the face of wicked problems in an unknown future. Under these circumstances, strategies must be allowed to emerge and 'strategic planning' must be seen for what it is – a contradiction in terms.

EXHIBIT 7.3   THE STRATEGIC INCREMENTALISM PERSPECTIVE

INSTITUTIONALIZING EMERGENT STRATEGY: PIXAR'S PROCESS FOR "GOING FROM SUCK TO NON-SUCK"

Can Pixar make it an even dozen blockbusters in a row? With the release of *Cars 2,* set for this summer, new attention will be focused on how Pixar is able to pull off such an unblemished record of successful movie innovations.

While many factors contribute to the successful creation of a new product, one of the keys is to follow what we at Innosight refer to as an emergent strategy. A foundational premise of emergent strategy is the assumption that your first product idea is likely wrong or at least incomplete. Therefore, you must identify and test critical assumptions as cheaply and quickly as possible – well before putting a giant flop into production.

Pixar serves as a prime example of how emergent strategy works in practice. Beginning with *Toy Story* in 1995, it has so far produced 11 consecutive mega-hits, an astounding feat that seems almost impossible to mimic. This unparalleled success has

come from following an approach that Pixar co-founder and President Ed Catmull memorably refers to as "going from suck to non-suck."

Following an emergent strategy allows companies to increase their odds of success by addressing the risks and unknowns that are often an inherent part of undertaking a new venture. Quickly investing a little to learn a lot about how you are wrong allows you to remain nimble and thus more easily re-vector your efforts. In the case of Pixar, this is a process that happens before a film's script is even written. As Andrew Stanton, Director of *Finding Nemo* and *WALL-E,* puts it: "My strategy has always been: be wrong as fast as we can, which basically means, we're gonna screw up, let's just admit that. Let's not be afraid of that."

In contrast to this kind of emergent strategy, Hollywood studios typically follow what we would refer to as more of a deliberate strategy, in which their work typically begins with an accepted script. Once a script is optioned or purchased, necessary resources are often devoted to the project and the studio aims to move forward to produce the film. While this process works just fine in some instances, it can be disastrous and often leads to the production of mediocre material or outright flops, such as Disney's recent release of *Mars Needs Moms,* which cost $150 million to make yet only grossed $7 million in its opening weekend.

The big risk that studios take lies in devoting too many resources to an unproven idea that may or may not resonate with audiences. They often fail to hedge risks and when problems arise, more money is thrown at the project in an attempt to solve the problem. Studios then frequently find themselves faced with the obstacle of insufficient time and money, and subsequently produce a mediocre product.

Like all movies studios, Pixar is under pressure to continually produce something new and exciting. Indeed, as Catmull, has noted, Pixar's challenge is that its customers "expect to see something new every time" – a reality that is "downright scary."

While Pixar's record of success may be uniquely unblemished, the challenge it faces is not terribly dissimilar from the challenge many successful companies confront, namely the need to meet shareholder demand by continuing to create new growth businesses. It's not enough to rely upon previous successes – merely pointing at what Nemo has done for you will not drive new growth. New Nemos must be created. But how is this done?

The following three steps of its pre-production process serve to show how emergent strategy works at Pixar:

1 IDENTIFY CRITICAL AREAS OF UN-CERTAINTY: Pixar begins with small "**incubation teams**" that work with directors to identify holes in their story ideas and refine them to the point that they pack emotional power. The material being produced at this stage is still rough and there are several open questions, but the focus is on the potential and whether the team is solving story problems together.

2 EXECUTE SMART EXPERIMENTS: The next stage of pre-production is to create storyboards, which are sketched-out comic book versions of the scenes. The storyboards are reviewed through a highly iterative process. For example, Pixar used an astonishing 27,565 storyboards for

A Bug's Life, 43,536 for *Finding Nemo,* 69,562 for *Ratatouille,* and 98,173 for *WALL-E.* With this kind of "**ongoing prototyping**," experimentation is constant and work is continually revised.

3 ADJUST AND REDIRECT: Storyboards are then converted to story reels, which include the much improved but still rough storyboards along with a voice track. Story reels are also heavily reviewed internally. By making this **feedback and iteration** a normal part of Pixar culture, it creates an environment where individuals feel safe to offer new ideas that can get shot down. Only after passing through extensive iteration and experimentation will a story finally move to the much more costly digital animation phase. Many projects that you never hear about simply don't make it to this phase.

Surrounding it all, Pixar has built a company culture that breeds lifelong learners. For example, it conducts balanced postmortem reviews of films where teams have the opportunity to share what they would and would not do again. To encourage interaction among different departments, it has created a large atrium at its centre with a cafeteria, meeting rooms and mailboxes. The company has even established *Pixar University,* which offers more than 100 courses – from sculpting to belly dancing – and employees are encouraged to devote up to four hours a week on their education.

All told, the process of creating one movie can and does take five years or more. All along, risk is better managed as problems are constantly identified and fixed through multiple mini experiments. As Catmull explains, "We must constantly challenge all of our assumptions and search for the flaws that could destroy our culture."

Your company most likely does not create movies but you may likewise be faced with the challenge of creating new growth and producing the next blockbuster. What can you learn from Pixar?

MANAGING THE PARADOX OF DELIBERATENESS AND EMERGENCE

Those who triumph compute at their headquarters a great number of factors prior to a challenge. Little computation brings defeat. How much more so with no computation at all!
Sun Tzu (5th century BC); Chinese military strategist

So, how should strategies be formed in practice? Should managers strive to formulate and implement strategic plans, supported by a formalized planning and control system? Or should managers move incrementally, behaving as inventors, organizational developers and explorers? (See Table 7.1).

No consensus has yet developed within the field of strategic management on how to manage deliberateness and emergence, which is understandable as it – among other things such as personal and culture differences (see also the next paragraph on the international perspective) – depends on the company's context. For example, strategy formation in hypercompetitive and stable environments will differ significantly. Yet, a number of suggestions have been made by scholars in the strategy and organizational behaviour fields. Taking the taxonomy of Chapter 1, the following options can be considered.

Balancing

In balancing opposite demands, elements of the opposing demands are traded off to find the most appropriate balance. The demand for deliberate strategizing and strategy emergence often differ over departments within the organization; depending on the organizational unit's primary process (see Chapter 4 on Business level strategy). Within business units production departments are generally more planning-oriented, product development units take a more incremental process, and research and development takes a bit of both.

TABLE 7.1   Strategic planning versus strategic incrementalism perspective

	Strategic planning perspective	Strategic incrementalism perspective
Emphasis on	Deliberateness over emergence	Emergence over deliberateness
Nature of strategy	Intentionally designed	Gradually shaped
Nature of formation	Figuring out	Finding out
View of future	Forecast and anticipate	Partially unknown and unpredictable
Posture towards the future	Make commitments, prepare	Postpone commitments, remain flexible
Formation process	Formally structured and comprehensive	Unstructured and fragmented
Formation process steps	First think, then act	Thinking and acting intertwined
Decision-making	Hierarchical	Dispersed
Decision-making focus	Optimal resource allocation and coordination	Experimentation and parallel initiatives
Implementation focused on	Programming (organizational efficiency)	Learning (organizational development)
Strategic change	Implemented top-down	Requires broad cultural and cognitive shifts

In large organizations, the strategy process not only differs over departments but also between the business units. Strategists of business units that are active in stable industries prefer deliberateness over emergence, while in hypercompetitive industries the reverse occurs. The balance between demands in large firms also depends on the firm's perspective on corporate level strategy: in portfolio organizations more variety of strategy processes can be noticed than in integrated organizations (see Chapter 5 on Corporate level strategy).

Balancing the paradox of deliberateness and emergence can also be institutionalized into a formal process. Popular in many organizations is the scenario process (Reading 7.3 by Bodwell and Chermack, 2010). This method, popularized by Royal/Dutch Shell, intentionally combines elements of deliberateness and emergence. It is a formal process, but by developing multiple scenarios and providing opportunity for intuitive and entrepreneurial inputs, it provides a balanced approach to strategy formation.

Juxtaposing

From the perspective of a business level manager the paradox of deliberateness and emergence is managed by balancing the two opposite demands, however a corporate level manager needs to engage in different strategy formation processes. Apart from participating in the corporate strategy process, the strategizing manager is also involved in formation processes in other corporate units – divisions and business units – and company-wide initiatives, international activities and ad hoc projects. Being engaged in such a variety of processes the strategizing manager needs to be juxtaposing, managing opposites or different blends simultaneously. This requires specific dynamic capabilities (Teece, 2007, Reading 2.1; Teece, Pisano and Shuen, 1997, Reading 4.3).

In professional firms the situation for strategists complicates even further. Managing a professional firm is one thing, delivering services is yet another. With multiple clients, professionals need flexibility to juxtapose between clients and their own firm. For example, King (2008) reports that venture capitalists are 'bifurcated strategists', using planning for their portfolio companies, while using emergent strategies on their own behalf.

STRATEGY FORMATION IN INTERNATIONAL PERSPECTIVE

Co-author: Gep Eisenloeffel

What we anticipate seldom occurs; what we least expect generally happens.
Benjamin Disraeli (1804–1881); British prime minister and novelist

The question of whether there are specific national preferences for the strategic planning or the strategic incrementalism perspective seems legitimate, yet with a few exceptions, has been absent in the academic debate. While it has generally been assumed that international differences are a non-issue, a few international comparative studies have been carried out. They show significantly different levels of formal planning across various industrialized countries. For instance, Steiner and Schollhammer (1975) reported that planning was found to be most common and most formalized in the United States, with other English-speaking countries (Britain, Canada and Australia) also exhibiting a high score. At the other extreme were Italy and Japan, where very little formal planning was witnessed. The low propensity to engage in formal planning in Japan has been noted by a number of other authors as well (e.g. Kagono *et al.,* 1985). Hayashi (1978: 221) remarks that Japanese firms 'distrust corporate planning in general', while Ohmae (1982: 225) characterizes Japanese companies as 'less planned, less rigid, but more vision- and mission-driven' than Western companies. Unfortunately, there are no recent cross-cultural studies to confirm that these international dissimilarities still exist. However, many observers have suggested that there remain discernible national differences in approaches to strategy formation (e.g. Gilbert and Lorange, 1995; Mintzberg, 1994a; Schneider, 1989).

Although it is difficult to generalize at the national level, since there can be quite a bit of variance within a country, it is challenging to pursue these observed international dissimilarities. Are there really national strategy formation styles and what factors might influence their existence? As a stimulus to the international dimension of this debate, several country characteristics are put forward as possible influences on how the paradox of deliberateness and emergence is dealt with in different national settings. As noted at the end of Chapter 2, these propositions are intended to encourage discussion, but more concrete international comparative research is needed to give this debate a firmer footing.

Level of professionalism

The popularity of formal planning systems in Australia, Britain, Canada, New Zealand and the United States seems odd, given their high level of individualism and strong preference for a market economy. One might expect that the English-speaking countries' fondness of unplanned markets would be a reflection of a general dislike of planning. Yet, strangely, 'most large US corporations are run like the Soviet economy' of yesteryear, with strong central plans and top-down control, Ohmae concludes (1982: 224).

One explanation might be that formalized planning and control systems are a logical consequence of having professional management (e.g. Mintzberg, 1994a). Nowhere in the industrialized world, with the exception of France, has there been a stronger development of a distinct managerial class than in the English-speaking countries (Hampden-Turner and Trompenaars, 1993; Lessem and Neubauer, 1994). Such professional managers run companies on behalf of the owners, who are usually distant from the operations (i.e. often minority shareholders). In the division of labour, the managers perform the 'thinking' tasks – analysing, planning, coordinating, leading, budgeting, motivating, controlling – while the workforce concentrates on performing the primary activities. This makes it possible for large, complex production processes to be controlled by a hierarchy of professional managers. It is commonly believed that these managers possess general skills that allow them to run a wide variety of different businesses.

In companies with professional management, the split between thinking and doing is made more explicit than in other organizations. The managers are the officers who formulate the strategies and the personnel on the work floor are the troops that must implement them – 'management' has intentions that the 'employees' must realize. This requires formal planning to guide workers' actions and a tight control system to ensure compliance. This mechanism is usually employed all the way up the hierarchy, as higher level managers use a planning and control system to steer and coordinate the behavior of lower level managers. All the way at the top, senior management must also make plans to win the approval of the shareholders.

This stratified organizational model, which Mintzberg dubs the machine bureaucracy (1979), is also prevalent in France, where the distinction between *cadre* employees and *non-cadre* personnel is also very strong (Hofstede, 1993, Reading 1.3 in this book). In many other countries, however, the split between managerial and non-managerial tasks is not as radical. For instance, in Germany and Japan, senior employees are expected to be involved in operational matters, while junior employees are expected to contribute to strategy formation, by coming up with ideas and passing on information to seniors.

In these countries, there is less need to use formal planning and control mechanisms to manage employees since the 'managers' have direct and informal links with those who are 'managed'. Usually these managers have risen through the ranks, giving them the richness of information and contacts needed to manage without highly formalized systems. In these nations, consensus-building and personal control are important management skills, which are not readily transferable to another industry or even another organization.

In yet other countries, the dominant form of organization is that of direct control by one person or a family. This usually means that organizations remain relatively small, although they can compensate by linking up into networks based on personal connections. This organizational model, common in Italy and among the overseas Chinese (see Hofstede, 1993, Reading 1.3; Weidenbaum and Hughes, 1996) is discussed in Chapter 6. Here it is sufficient to conclude that in such organizations there is little need for formalized planning and control systems to manage employees. The top boss, usually also the owner, steers the firm personally with little regard for 'professional' methods.

The conclusion is that the national propensity to engage in formal planning is probably influenced by the level of professionalism of management within the country. In nations where the machine bureaucracy is the predominant organizational model, a stronger inclination towards formal planning systems can be expected.

Preference for internal control

While the previous section discussed different *types* of internal control, and the related organizational models, it should be noted that countries can also differ with regard to the *level* of internal control their citizens prefer. In some cultures, people have a strong desire for order and structure – clear tasks, responsibilities, power rules and procedures. Ambiguous situations and uncertain outcomes are disliked and therefore management strives to control organizational processes. Management can reduce uncertainty in a number of ways. Structure can be offered by strictly following traditions or by imposing top-down paternalistic rule. However, uncertainty can also be reduced by planning (Kagono *et al.,* 1985; Schneider, 1989). By setting direction, coordinating initiatives, committing resources and programming activities, structure can be brought to the organization. In this way, planning can help to alleviate people's anxiety about 'disorganization'. In cultures that are more tolerant towards ambiguity and uncertainty, one can expect a weaker preference for planning.

The importance of planning as a means for structuring and controlling is particularly important in cultures where there is little confidence in self-organization. This holds especially true in individualistic cultures, where organizational members cannot always be counted on to work towards the common good (Hofstede, 1993). In these countries, extensive planning and control systems are often used as a formal means for getting people to cooperate, coordinate and serve the organization's interests. Strategic plans function as internal contracts, to limit dysfunctional opportunistic behaviour (Allaire and Firsirotu, 1990; Bungay and Goold, 1991). In cultures with a stronger group-orientation, there is usually more trust that individuals will be team players, thus making formal control mechanisms redundant (Nonaka and Johansson, 1985). Therefore, in general, one can expect a weaker preference for planning in collectivist cultures.

Preference for external control

Cultures also differ with regard to the level of control that organizational members prefer to have over their environment. At the one extreme are cultures in which people strive to manage or even dominate their surroundings. In these countries, there is a strong desire to create the future and a fear of losing control of one's destiny. George Bernard Shaw's famous remark that 'to be in hell is to drift, to be in heaven is to steer', neatly summarizes these feelings. The consequence is that organizations in these nations are strongly drawn to proactive and deliberate strategy-making, under the motto 'plan or be planned for' (Ackoff, 1980). Drawing up plans to actively engage the outside world meets people's need to determine their own fate. This cultural characteristic is particularly pronounced in Western countries (Trompenaars, 1993).

At the other extreme are cultures in which most people passively accept their destiny. They believe that most external events are out of their hands and that they exert no control over the future. In such fatalistic cultures, people tend to approach opportunities and threats reactively, on a day-to-day basis. Such muddling through behaviour rarely leads to emergent strategy, but more often to disjointed, unpatterned action.

In the middle are cultures in which people believe neither in domination of, or submission to, external circumstances. In these cultures, people accept that events are unpredictable and that the environment cannot be tightly controlled, yet trust that individuals and organizations can proactively seek their own path among these uncertainties. The environment and the firm, it is thought, co-evolve through interaction and mutual adjustment, often in unforeseen ways. This requires firms to 'develop an attitude of receptivity and high adaptability to changing conditions' (Maruyama, 1984). This way of thinking is particularly pronounced in South-East Asia, and leads to a stronger inclination towards the strategic incrementalism perspective (Kagono et al., 1985; Schneider, 1989).

Time orientation

A culture's time orientation can also be expected to influence national preferences for dealing with the paradox of deliberateness and emergence. There are a number of dimensions along which cultures' perception of time can differ. Cultures can be more involved with the past, the present or the future, whereby some make a strong linear separation between these phases, while others emphasize the continuity of time or even its cyclical nature. With regard to the future, a distinction can also be made between cultures with a more short-term or long-term orientation (Hofstede, 1993, Reading 1.3).

In general, it can be expected that people in cultures that heavily accentuate the past, or the present, over the future, will be less inclined to think and act strategically. In cultures that emphasize the near future, however, it is likely that individuals and organizations will exhibit a preference for planning. A focus on the not-too-distant future, which is more predictable than the long-term future, fits well with a strategic planning approach. In these countries, intentions are formulated, courses of action are determined and resources are committed, but with a relatively short planning horizon. Plans will only be adopted if results can be expected in the 'foreseeable' future. As Hofstede (1993) reports, the English-speaking countries belong to this category of short-term oriented cultures (see also Calori, Valla and de Woot, 1994; Kagono et al., 1985).

In cultures with a stronger long-term orientation, strategic incrementalism can be expected to be a more predominant perspective. Since the long-term future is inherently unknown, planning for the future is seen as an inappropriate response. In these countries, it is generally believed that the unpredictability of the long-term future must be accepted and accommodated. This requires an attitude of caution and flexibility, linked to curiosity, learning and persistence. Actions are often taken that are not optimal in the short run, but point in the right long-term direction. As Hofstede (1993) reports, many South-East Asian countries fall into this category, as do some European countries.

INTRODUCTION TO THE READINGS

As an input to the process of assessing the variety of perspectives, three readings have been selected that each shed their own light on this issue. As in the previous chapters, the first two readings will be representative of the two poles in this debate, while the third reading will bring in a middle way to combine perspectives.

As opening reading in this debate, 'Managing the Strategy Process', by Balaji Chakravarthy and Peter Lorange, has been selected to represent the strategic planning perspective. Lorange is one of the most well-known writers on the topic of formal planning systems (Lorange, 1980; Lorange and Vancil, 1977) and this reading is taken from the 1991 textbook he co-authored with Chakravarthy, entitled *Managing the Strategy Process: A Framework for a Multibusiness Firm.* As with most proponents of the strategic planning perspective, Chakravarthy and Lorange do not actively defend their assumption that formal planning is beneficial. Rather, basing themselves on this supposition, they concentrate on outlining a framework for effectively structuring strategic planning activities. Their ideal is an extensive strategic planning system, comprised of a number of distinct steps, procedures, mechanisms and roles. However, they go further than only structuring strategic planning. In their view, a formal planning system will not lead to effective strategy formation if it is not linked to other organizational systems. In particular, the strategic planning system needs to interact with the monitoring, control and learning system, the incentives system and the staffing system. As such, Chakravarthy and Lorange champion a highly comprehensive and structured approach to strategic planning.

As spokesman for the strategic incrementalism perspective, James Brian Quinn has been chosen. Together with Henry Mintzberg, Quinn has been one of the most influential pioneers on the topic of emergent strategy. Quinn's article, 'Logical Incrementalism', which is reprinted here as Reading 7.2, and his subsequent book *Strategies for Change* (1980), are widely accepted as having been instrumental in developing the strategic incrementalism perspective. In his reading, Quinn explains some of the key shortcomings of formal strategic planning and goes on to make a case for strategic incrementalism. Important in his argumentation is that strategic incrementalism is distinguished from muddling through. Incrementalism is a proactive approach to strategy formation – managers can intentionally choose to let unintended strategies emerge. Muddling through is also incremental in nature, but reactive and ad hoc – improvised decisions are made to deal with unplanned and poorly controllable circumstances. To make this distinction more explicit, Quinn refers to the proactive strain of incremental behaviour as 'logical incrementalism'. By 'logical' he means 'reasonable and well-considered'. However, logical incrementalism is not always logical by the definition used in Chapter 2 – incremental behaviour is not necessarily 'dictated by formal logic'. Therefore, for the sake of accuracy and clarity, the term strategic incrementalism will be used in this book instead of logical incrementalism.

Reading 7.3, 'Integrating deliberate and emergent strategy with scenario planning' by Wendy Bodwell and Thomas Chermack has been selected to bring scenario development into the discussion as a means of combining demands for deliberateness and emergence. Both strategic planners and strategic incrementalists agree that strategizing requires managers to think about the future, and scenario development is one of the most often mentioned methods to take a structured approach to such forward thinking. Scenarios are 'plausible descriptions of alternative futures', requiring managers to envision different directions in which the environment and the firm might develop. Much has been written about scenario use in strategy formation processes, although most of the literature comes from business professionals with experience in its application (e.g. Wack, 1985a; Van der Heijden, 1996). Bodwell and Chermack do not go into all of the technical details of scenario development, but focus on scenarios as valuable means of combining deliberate and emergent strategy formation. Using Teece's dynamic capabilities taxonomy – sensing, seizing and reconfiguring (see Reading 4.3) they suggest a new way of development based on Teece's tripartite taxonomy, with the clear intent of realizing what is deliberate about an organization's particular strategy, while leaving room for non-prescribed strategies to emerge.

READING 7.1

Managing the strategy process

By Balaji Chakravarthy and Peter Lorange[1]

There are five distinct steps in the strategy process (see Figure 7.1.1). The first three steps involve the strategic planning system; the final two steps cover the role of the monitoring, control and learning system, and the incentives and staffing systems, respectively.

The strategic planning system

The purpose of the first step in the planning system, objectives setting, is to determine a strategic direction for the firm and each of its divisions and business units. Objectives setting calls for an open-ended reassessment

of the firm's business environments and its strengths in dealing with these environments. At the conclusion of this step, there should be agreement at all levels of the organization on the goals that should be pursued and the strategies that will be needed to meet them. It is worth differentiating here between objectives and goals. Objectives refer to the strategic intent of the firm in the long run. Goals, on the other hand, are more specific statements of the achievements targeted for certain deadlines – goals can be accomplished, and when that happens the firm moves closer to meeting its objectives. Objectives represent a more enduring challenge.

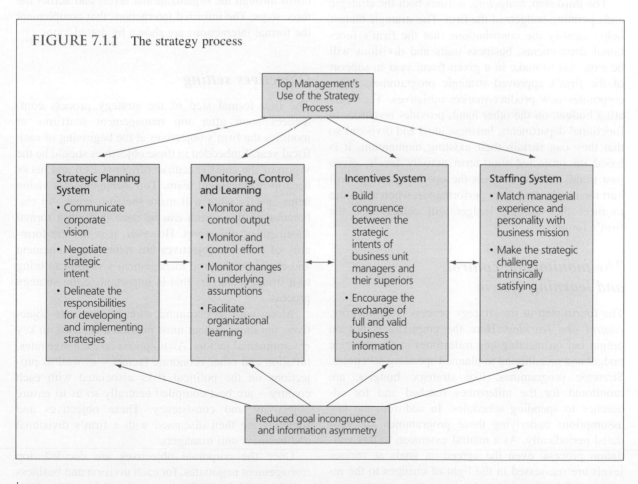

FIGURE 7.1.1   The strategy process

Top Management's Use of the Strategy Process

Strategic Planning System
- Communicate corporate vision
- Negotiate strategic intent
- Delineate the responsibilities for developing and implementing strategies

Monitoring, Control and Learning
- Monitor and control output
- Monitor and control effort
- Monitor changes in underlying assumptions
- Facilitate organizational learning

Incentives System
- Build congruence between the strategic intents of business unit managers and their superiors
- Encourage the exchange of full and valid business information

Staffing System
- Match managerial experience and personality with business mission
- Make the strategic challenge intrinsically satisfying

Reduced goal incongruence and information asymmetry

[1]Source: This article was adapted from Chapter 1 of Chakravarty and Lorange, *Managing the Strategy Process: A Framework for a Multi-business Firm,* 1st Edition. © 1991, reprinted by permission of Pearson Education, Inc., Upper Saddle River, NJ.

The second step, *strategic programming,* develops the strategies identified in the first step and defines the cross-functional programmes that will be needed to implement the chosen strategies. Cross-functional co-operation is essential to this step. At the end of the strategic programming step a long-term financial plan is drawn up for the firm as a whole and each of its divisions, business units and functions. On top of the financial projections from existing operations, the long-term financial plan overlays both the expenditures and revenues associated with the approved strategic programmes of an organizational unit. The time horizon for these financial plans is chosen to cover the typical lead times that are required to implement the firm's strategic programmes. A five-year financial plan is, however, very common. The purpose of the five-year financial plan is to ensure that the approved strategic programmes can be funded through either the firm's internally generated resources or externally financed resources.

The third step, *budgeting,* defines both the strategic and operating budgets of the firm. The strategic budget helps identify the contributions that the firm's functional departments, business units and divisions will be expected to make in a given fiscal year in support of the firm's approved strategic programmes. It incorporates new product–market initiatives. The operating budget, on the other hand, provides resources to functional departments, business units and divisions so that they can sustain their existing momentum. It is based on projected short-term activity levels, given past trends. Failure to meet the operating budget will hurt the firm's short-term performance, whereas failure to meet the strategic budget will compromise the firm's future.

The monitoring, control, and learning system

The fourth step in the strategy process is *monitoring, control and learning.* Here the emphasis is not on output but on meeting key milestones in the strategic budget and on adhering to planned spending schedules. Strategic programmes, like strategic budgets, are monitored for the milestones reached and for adherence to spending schedules. In addition, the key assumptions underlying these programmes are validated periodically. As a natural extension to this validation process, even the agreed-on goals at various levels are reassessed in the light of changes to the resources of the firm and its business environment.

The incentives and staffing systems

The fifth and final step in the strategy process is incentives and staffing. One part of this is the award of incentives as contracted to the firm's managers. If the incentives system is perceived to have failed in inducing the desired performance, redesigning the incentives system and reassessing the staffing of key managerial positions are considered at this step.

Linking organizational levels and steps in strategic planning

An effective strategy process must allow for interactions between the organizational levels and iterations between the process steps. Figure 7.1.2 describes some of the interactions and iterations in the strategic planning steps. The formal interactions in the process are shown in the figure by the solid line that weaves up and down through the organizational levels and across the three steps. The informal interactions that complement the formal interactions are shown by dotted loops.

Objectives setting

The first formal step of the strategy process commences soon after top management reaffirms or modifies the firm's objectives at the beginning of each fiscal year. Embedded in these objectives should be the vision of the chief executive officer (CEO) and his or her top management team. Top management's vision helps specify what will make the firm great. An elaboration of this vision can be done through a formal statement of objectives. However, it is not the formality of a firm's objectives but rather the excitement and challenge that top management's vision can bring to a firm's managers that is important to the strategy process.

Along with its communication of corporate objectives, top management must provide a forecast on key environmental factors. Assumptions on exchange rates, inflation and other economic factors – as well as projections on the political risks associated with each country – are best compiled centrally so as to ensure objectivity and consistency. These objectives and forecasts are then discussed with a firm's divisional and business unit managers.

Once the corporate objectives are decided, top management negotiates, for each division and business unit in the firm, goals that are consistent with these

FIGURE 7.1.2 Steps in the strategy process

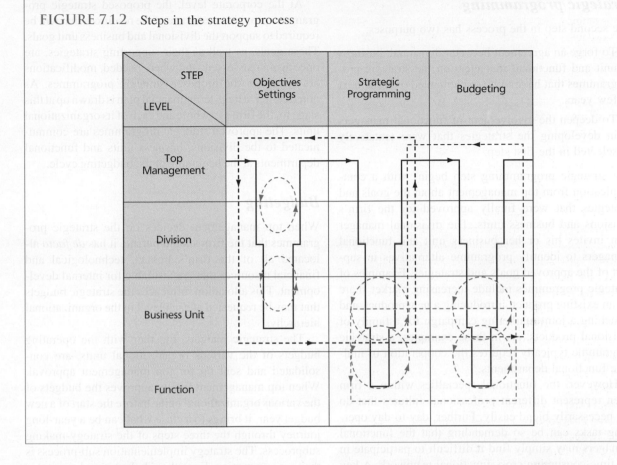

objectives. The nature of these negotiations can vary. In some firms, top management may wish to set goals in a top-down fashion; in others, it may invite subordinate managers to participate in the goal-setting process.

Managers are encouraged to examine new strategies and modify existing ones in order to accomplish their goals. The proposed strategies are approved at each higher level in the organizational hierarchy, then eventually by top management. Top management tries to make certain that the strategies as proposed are consistent with the firm's objectives and can be supported with the resources available to the firm. Modifications, where necessary, are made to the objectives, goals and strategies in order to bring them in alignment. Another important outcome of the objectives-setting step is to build a common understanding across the firm's managerial hierarchy of the goals and strategies that are intended for each organizational unit.

The objectives-setting step in Figure 7.1.2 does not include the functional departments. As we observed

earlier, the primary role of these departments is a supporting one. They do not have a profit or growth responsibility, and their goals cannot be decided until the second step, when strategic programmes in support of approved business unit goals begin to be formed. It is not uncommon, however, for key functional managers to be invited to participate in the objectives-setting step either as experts in a corporate task force or, more informally, as participants in the deliberations that are held at the business unit level.

It is important that divisional proposals be evaluated on an overall basis as elements of a corporate portfolio and not reviewed in a sequential mode. In the latter case, the resulting overall balance in the corporate portfolio would be more or less incidental, representing the accumulated sum of individual approvals. It makes little sense to attempt to judge in isolation whether a particular business family or business strategy is attractive to the corporate portfolio. That will depend on a strategy's fit with the rest of the portfolio and on the competing investment opportunities available to the firm in its business portfolio.

Strategic programming

The second step in the process has two purposes:

1   To forge an agreement between divisional, business unit and functional managers on the strategic programmes that have to be implemented over the next few years.

2   To deepen the involvement of functional managers in developing the strategies that were tentatively selected in the first step.

The strategic programming step begins with a communication from top management about the goals and strategies that were finally approved for the firm's divisions and business units. The divisional manager then invites his or her business unit and functional managers to identify programme alternatives in support of the approved goals and strategies. Examples of strategic programmes include increasing market share for an existing product, introducing a new product, and launching a joint marketing campaign for a family of divisional products. As in these examples, a strategic programme typically requires the cooperation of multiple functional departments.

However, the functional specialties within a firm often represent different professional cultures that do not necessarily blend easily. Further, day-to-day operating tasks can be so demanding that the functional managers may simply find it difficult to participate in the time-consuming cross-functional teamwork. A key challenge for both divisional and business managers is to bring about this interaction.

The proposed strategic programmes travel up the hierarchy for approval at each level. At the division level, the programmes are evaluated not only for how well they support the approved strategies but also for how they promote synergies within the firm. Synergies can come from two sources: through economies of scale or economies of scope. The creation of synergies based on economies of scale calls for a sharing of common functional activities – such as research and development (R&D), raw materials procurement, production and distribution – so as to spread over a larger volume the overhead costs associated with these functions. The creation of economies of scope, on the other hand, requires a common approach to the market. Examples of such an approach include the development of a common trademark, the development of products/services that have a complementary appeal to a customer group, and the ability to offer a common regional service organization for the firm's diverse businesses.

At the corporate level, the proposed strategic programmes provide an estimate of the resources that will be required to support the divisional and business unit goals. These goals, as well as their supporting strategies, are once again reassessed; and where needed, modifications are sought in the proposed strategic programmes. As noted earlier, a long-term financial plan is drawn up at this stage for the firm as a whole and each of its organizational units. The approved strategic programmes are communicated to the divisions, business units and functional departments at the beginning of the budgeting cycle.

Budgeting

When top management decides on the strategic programmes that the firm should pursue, it has *de facto* allocated all of the firm's human, technological and financial resources that are available for internal development. This allocation influences the strategic budgets that may be requested at each level in the organizational hierarchy.

The strategic budgets, together with the operating budgets of the various organizational units, are consolidated and sent up for top management approval. When top management finally approves the budgets of the various organizational units, before the start of a new budget year, it brings to a close what can be a year-long journey through the three steps of the strategy-making subprocess. The strategy implementation sub-process is then set into motion. Even though the two subprocesses are described sequentially here, it is important to mention that even as the budget for a given year is being formed, the one for the prior year will be under implementation. Midcourse corrections to the prior year's budget can have an impact on the formulation of the current budget.

If the actual accomplishments fall short of the strategic budget, in particular, the negative variance may suggest that the firm's managers failed to implement its chosen strategy efficiently. But it can also suggest that the strategic programmes that drive this budget may have been ill-conceived or even that the goals underlying these programmes may have been specified incorrectly. The monitoring, control and learning system provides continuous information on both the appropriateness of a strategic budget and the efficiency with which the budget is implemented. This information, based on the implementation of the prior year's strategic budget, can trigger another set of iterations between the three strategy-making steps, calling into question the goals and strategies on which the current year's budget are based. These iterations are shown by the dotted rectangles in Figure 7.1.2.

Logical incrementalism

By James Quinn[1]

When I was younger I always conceived of a room where all these [strategic] concepts were worked out for the whole company. Later I didn't find any such room ... The strategy [of the company] may not even exist in the mind of one man. I certainly don't know where it is written down. It is simply transmitted in the series of decisions made.
Interview quotation

Introduction

When well-managed major organizations make significant changes in strategy, the approaches they use frequently bear little resemblance to the rational-analytical systems so often touted in the planning literature. The full strategy is rarely written down in any one place. The processes used to arrive at the total strategy are typically fragmented, evolutionary and largely intuitive. Although one can usually find embedded in these fragments some very refined pieces of formal strategic analysis, the real strategy tends to evolve as internal decisions and external events flow together to create a new, widely shared consensus for action among key members of the top management team. Far from being an abrogation of good management practice, the rationale behind this kind of strategy formulation is so powerful that it perhaps provides the normative model for strategic decision-making, rather than the step-by-step 'formal systems planning' approach so often espoused.

The formal systems planning approach

A strong normative literature states what factors should be included in a systematically planned strategy and how to analyse and relate these factors step-by-step. The main elements of this 'formal' planning approach include:

- analysing one's own internal situation: strengths, weaknesses, competencies, problems;
- projecting current product lines, profits, sales, investment needs into the future;
- analysing selected external environments and opponents' actions for opportunities and threats;
- establishing broad goals as targets for subordinate groups' plans;
- identifying the gap between expected and desired results;
- communicating planning assumptions to the divisions;
- requesting proposed plans from subordinate groups with more specific target goals, resource needs and supporting action plans;
- occasionally asking for special studies of alternatives, contingencies, or longer-term opportunities;
- reviewing and approving divisional plans and summing these for corporate needs;
- developing long-term budgets presumably related to plans;
- implementing plans;
- monitoring and evaluating performance (presumably against plans, but usually against budgets).

While this approach is excellent for some purposes, it tends to focus unduly on measurable quantitative factors and to underemphasize the vital qualitative, organizational and power-behavioural factors that so often determine strategic success in one situation versus another. In practice, such planning is just one building block in a continuous stream of events that really determine corporate strategy.

The power-behavioral approach

Other investigators have provided important insights on the crucial psychological, power and behavioural relationships in strategy formulation. Among other

[1]Source: This article was originally published as 'Strategic Change: Logical Incrementalism' in *Sloan Management Review,* Fall, 1978, pp. 7–21. Reproduced by permission. © 1978 from MIT Sloan Management Review/Massachusetts Institute of Technology. All rights reserved. Distributed by Tribune Media Services.

create the broad conceptual consensus, the risk-taking attitudes, the organizational and resource flexibilities, and the adaptive dynamism that determine both the timing and direction of diversification strategies. Most important among these processes are:

- Generating a genuine, top-level psychological commitment to diversification. General Mills, Pillsbury and Xerox all started their major diversification programmes with broad analytical studies and goal-setting exercises designed both to build top-level consensus around the need to diversify and to establish the general directions for diversification. Without such action, top-level bargaining for resources would have continued to support only more familiar (and hence apparently less risky) old lines, and this could delay or undermine the entire diversification endeavour.

- Consciously preparing to move opportunistically. Organizational and fiscal resources must be built up in advance to exploit candidates as they randomly appear. And a 'credible activist' for ventures must be developed and backed by someone with commitment power. All successful acquirers created the potential for profit-centred divisions within their organizational structures, strengthened their financial-controllership capabilities, took action to create low-cost capital access, and maintained the shortest possible communication lines from the acquisitions activist to the resource-committing authority. All these actions integrally determined which diversifications actually could be made, the timing of their accession and the pace at which they could be absorbed.

- Building a 'comfort factor' for risk taking. Perceived risk is largely a function of one's knowledge about a field. Hence well-conceived diversification programmes should anticipate a trial-and-error period during which top managers reject early proposed fields or opportunities until they have analysed enough trial candidates to 'become comfortable' with an initial selection. Early successes tend to be 'sure things' close to the companies' past (real or supposed) expertise. After a few successful diversifications, managements tend to become more confident and accept other candidates – farther from traditional lines – at a faster rate. Again, the way this process is handled affects both the direction and pace of the actual programme.

- Developing a new ethos. If new divisions are more successful than the old – as they should be – they

attract relatively more resources and their political power grows. Their most effective line managers move into corporate positions, and slowly the company's special competency and ethos change. Finally, the concepts and products that once dominated the company's culture may decline in importance or even disappear. Acknowledging these ultimate consequences to the organization at the beginning of a diversification programme would clearly be impolitic, even if the manager both desired and could predict the probable new ethos. These factors must be handled adaptively, as opportunities present themselves and as individual leaders and power centres develop.

Each of the above processes interacts with all others (and with the random appearance of diversification candidates) to affect action sequences, elapsed time and ultimate results in unexpected ways. Complexities are so great that few diversification programmes end up as initially envisioned. Consequently, wise managers recognize the limits to systematic analysis in diversification, and use formal planning to build the 'comfort levels' executives need for risk taking and to guide the programme's early directions and priorities. They then modify these flexibly, step-by-step, as new opportunities, power centres and developed competencies merge to create new potentials.

The divestiture subsystem

Similar practices govern the handling of divestitures. Divisions often drag along in a less-than-desired condition for years before they can be strategically divested. In some cases, ailing divisions might have just enough yield or potential to offer hoped-for viability. In others, they might represent the company's vital core from earlier years, the creations of a powerful person nearing retirement, or the psychological touchstones of the company's past traditions.

Again, in designing divestiture strategies, top executives had to reinforce vaguely felt concerns with detailed data, build up managers' comfort levels about issues, achieve participation in and commitment to decisions, and move opportunistically to make actual changes. In many cases, the precise nature of the decision was not clear at the outset. Executives often made seemingly unrelated personnel shifts or appointments that changed the value set of critical groups, or started a series of staff studies that generated awareness or acceptance of a potential problem. They might then instigate goal assessment, business review, or 'planning' programmes to provide broader forums for discussion and a wider consensus for action. Even then they might wait for a crisis, a crucial retirement, or an attractive sale opportunity to determine the timing and conditions of divestiture. In some cases, decisions could be direct and analytical. But when divestitures involved the psychological centres of the organization, the process had to be much more oblique and carefully orchestrated.

The major reorganization subsystem

It is well recognized that major organizational changes are an integral part of strategy. Sometimes they constitute a strategy themselves, sometimes they precede and/or precipitate a new strategy, and sometimes they help to implement a strategy. However, like many other important strategic decisions, macro-organizational moves are typically handled incrementally and outside of formal planning processes. Their effects on personal or power relationships preclude discussion in open forums and reports of such processes.

In addition, major organizational changes have timing imperatives (or 'process limits') all their own. In making any significant shifts, executives must think through the new roles, capabilities and probable individual reactions of the many principals affected. They may have to wait for the promotion or retirement of a valued colleague before consummating any change. They then frequently have to bring in, train, or test new people for substantial periods before they can staff key posts with confidence. During this testing period they may substantially modify their original concept of the reorganization, as they evaluate individuals' potentials, their performance in specific roles, their personal drives, and their relationships with other team members.

Because this chain of decisions affects the career development, power, affluence and self-image of so many, executives tend to keep close counsel in their discussions, negotiate individually with key people and make final commitments as late as possible in order to obtain the best matches between people's capabilities, personalities and aspirations and their new roles. Typically, all these events do not come together at one convenient time, particularly the moment annual plans are due. Instead executives move opportunistically, step-by-step, selectively moving people toward a broadly conceived organizational goal, which is constantly modified and rarely articulated in detail until the last pieces fit together.

The government-external relations subsystem

Almost all companies cited government and other external activist groups as among the most important forces causing significant changes in their strategic postures during the periods examined. However, when asked 'How did your company arrive at its own strategy vis-a-vis these forces?' it became clear that few companies had cohesive strategies (integrated sets of goals, policies and programmes) for government-external relations, other than lobbying for or against specific legislative actions. To the extent that other strategies did exist, they were piecemeal, ad hoc and had been derived in a very evolutionary manner. Yet there seemed to be very good reasons for such incrementalism. The following are two of the best short explanations of the way these practices develop:

We are a very large company, and we understand that any massive overt action on our part could easily create more public antagonism than support for our viewpoint. It is also hard to say in advance exactly what public response any particular action might create. So we tend to test a number of different approaches on a small scale with only limited or local company identification. If one approach works, we'll'll test it further and amplify its use. If another bombs, we try to keep it from being used again. Slowly we find a series of advertising, public relations, community relations actions that seem to help. Then along comes another issue and we start all over again. Gradually the successful approaches merge into a pattern of actions that becomes our strategy.

I [the president] start conversations with a number of knowledgeable people ... I collect articles and talk to people about how things get done in Washington in this particular field. I collect data from any reasonable source. I begin wide-ranging discussions with people inside and outside the corporation. From these a pattern eventually emerges. It's like fitting together a jigsaw puzzle. At first the vague outline of an approach appears like the sail of a ship in a puzzle. Then suddenly the rest of the puzzle becomes quite clear. You wonder why you didn't see it all along. And once it's crystallized, it's not difficult to explain to others.

In this realm, uncontrollable forces dominate. Data are very soft, often can be only subjectively sensed and may be costly to quantify. The possible responses of individuals and groups to different stimuli are difficult to determine in advance. The number of potential opponents with power is very high, and the diversity in their viewpoints and possible modes of attack is so substantial that it is physically impossible to lay out probabilistic decision diagrams that would have much meaning. Results are unpredictable and error costs extreme. Even the best intended and most rational-seeming strategies can be converted into disasters unless they are thoroughly and interactively tested.

Formal planning in corporate strategy

What role do classical formal planning techniques play in strategy formulation? All companies in the sample do have formal planning procedures embedded in their management direction and control systems. These serve certain essential functions. In a process sense, they:

- provide a discipline forcing managers to take a careful look ahead periodically;
- require rigorous communications about goals, strategic issues and resource allocations;
- stimulate longer-term analyses than would otherwise be made;
- generate a basis for evaluating and integrating short-term plans;
- lengthen time horizons and protect long-term investments such as R&D;
- create a psychological backdrop and an information framework about the future against which managers can calibrate short-term or interim decisions.

In a decision-making sense, they:

- fine-tune annual commitments;
- formalize cost-reduction programmes;
- help implement strategic changes once decided on (for example, coordinating all elements of Exxon's decision to change its corporate name).

Formal plans also 'increment'

Although individual staff planners were often effective in identifying potential problems and bringing them to top management's attention, the annual planning process itself was rarely (if ever) the initiating source of really new key issues or radical departures into new product–market realms. These almost always came from precipitating events, special studies, or conceptions implanted through the kinds of 'logical incremental' processes described above.

In fact, formal planning practices actually institutionalize incrementalism. There are two reasons for this. First, in order to utilize specialized expertise and to obtain executive involvement and commitment, most planning occurs from the bottom up in response to broadly defined assumptions or goals, many of which are longstanding or negotiated well in advance. Of necessity, lower-level groups have only a partial view of the corporation's total strategy, and command only a fragment of its resources. Their power bases, identity, expertise and rewards also usually depend on their existing products or processes. Hence, these products or processes, rather than entirely new departures, should and do receive their primary attention. Second, most managements purposely design their plans to be 'living' or 'evergreen'. They are intended only as frameworks to guide and provide consistency for future decisions made incrementally. To act otherwise would be to deny that further information could have a value. Thus, properly formulated formal plans are also a part of an incremental logic.

Special studies

Formal planning was most successful in stimulating significant change when it was set up as a special study on some important aspect of corporate strategy. For example, when it became apparent that Pilkington's new float glass process would work, the company formed a Directors' Float Glass Committee consisting of all internal directors associated with float glass 'to consider the broad issues of float glass [strategy] in both the present and the future'. The committee did not attempt detailed plans. Instead, it tried to deal in broad concepts, identify alternate routes, and think through the potential consequences of each route some 10 years ahead. Of some of the key strategic decisions it was later remarked, 'It would be difficult to identify an exact moment when the decision was made … Nevertheless, over a period of time a consensus crystallized with great clarity.'

Such special strategic studies represent a subsystem of strategy formulation distinct from both annual planning activities and the other subsystems exemplified above. Each of these develops some important aspect of strategy, incrementally blending its conclusions with those of other subsystems, and it would be virtually impossible to force all these together to crystallize a completely articulated corporate strategy at any one instant.

Total posture planning

Occasionally, however, managements do attempt very broad assessments of their companies' total posture. Shortly after becoming CEO of General Mills, James McFarland decided that his job was 'to take a very good company and move it to greatness', but that it was up to his management group, not himself alone, to decide what a great company was and how to get there. Consequently he took some 35 of the company's topmost managers away for a three-day management retreat. On the first day, after agreeing to broad financial goals, the group broke up into units of six to eight people. Each unit was to answer the question, 'What is a great company?' from the viewpoints of stockholders, employees, suppliers, the public and society. Each unit reported back at the end of the day, and the whole group tried to reach a consensus through discussion.

On the second day the groups, in the same format, assessed the company's strengths and weaknesses relative to the defined posture of 'greatness.' The third day focused on how to overcome the company's weaknesses and move it toward a great company. This broad consensus led, over the next several years, to the surveys of fields for acquisition, the building of management's initial comfort levels with certain fields, and the acquisition-divestiture strategy that characterized the McFarland era at General Mills.

Yet even such a major endeavour is only a portion of a total strategic process. Values that had been built up over decades stimulated or constrained alternatives. Precipitating events, acquisitions, divestitures, external relations and organizational changes developed important segments of each strategy incrementally. Even the strategies articulated left key elements to be defined as new information became available, polities permitted, or particular opportunities appeared. Major product thrusts proved unsuccessful. Actual strategies therefore evolved as each company overextended, consolidated, made errors and rebalanced various thrusts over time. And it was both logical and expected that this would be the case.

Logical incrementalism

All of the above suggest that strategic decisions do not lend themselves to aggregation into a single massive decision matrix where all factors can be treated relatively simultaneously in order to arrive at a holistic optimum. Many have spoken of the cognitive limits that prevent this. Of equal importance are the process limits – that is, the timing and sequencing imperatives necessary to create awareness, build comfort levels, develop consensus, select and train people and so forth – that constrain the system yet ultimately determine the decision itself. Unlike the preparation of a fine banquet, it is virtually impossible for the manager to orchestrate all internal decisions, external environmental events, behavioural and power relationships, technical and informational needs, and actions of intelligent opponents so that they come together at any precise moment.

Can the process be managed?

Instead, executives usually deal with the logic of each subsystem of strategy formulation largely on its own merits and usually with a different subset of people. They try to develop or maintain in their own minds a consistent pattern among the decisions made in each subsystem. Knowing their own limitations and the unknowability of the events they face, they consciously try to tap the minds and psychic drives of others. They often purposely keep questions broad and decisions vague in early stages to avoid creating undue rigidities and to stimulate others' creativity. Logic, of course, dictates that they make final commitments as late as possible consistent with the information they have.

Consequently, many successful executives will initially set only broad goals and policies that can accommodate a variety of specific proposals from below, yet give a sense of guidance to the proposers. As they come forward the proposals automatically and beneficially attract the support and identity of their sponsors. Being only proposals, the executives can treat these at less politically charged levels, as specific projects rather than as larger goal or policy precedents. Therefore, they can encourage, discourage, or kill alternatives with considerably less political exposure. As events and opportunities emerge, they can incrementally guide the pattern of escalated or accepted proposals to suit their own purposes without getting prematurely committed to a rigid solution set that unpredictable events might prove wrong or that opponents find sufficiently threatening to coalesce against.

A strategy emerges

Successful executives link together and bring order to a series of strategic processes and decisions spanning years. At the beginning of the process it is literally impossible to predict all the events and forces that will shape the future of the company. The best executives can do is to forecast the forces most likely to impinge on the company's affairs and the ranges of their possible impact. They then attempt to build a resource base and a corporate posture so strong in selected areas that the enterprise can survive and prosper despite all but the most devastating events. They consciously select market/technological/product segments the concern can dominate given its resource limits, and place some side bets in order to decrease the risk of catastrophic failure or to increase the company's flexibility for future options.

They then proceed incrementally to handle urgent matters, start longer-term sequences whose specific future branches and consequences are perhaps murky, respond to unforeseen events as they occur, build on

successes and brace up or cut losses on failures. They constantly reassess the future, find new congruencies as events unfurl and blend the organization's skills and resources into new balances of dominance and risk aversion as various forces intersect to suggest better – but never perfect – alignments. The process is dynamic, with neither a real beginning nor end.

Strategy deals with the unknowable, not the uncertain. It involves forces of such great number, strength and combinatory powers that one cannot predict events in a probabilistic sense. Hence logic dictates that one proceeds flexibly and experimentally from broad concepts toward specific commitments, making the latter concrete as late as possible in order to narrow the bands of uncertainty and to benefit from the best available information. This is the process of logical incrementalism.

READING 7.3 Organizational ambidexterity: Integrating deliberate and emergent strategy with scenario planning

By Wendy Bodwell and Thomas J. Chermack[1]

The strategy literature has become so diverse, complex and vast, that any review would fall short of covering the entirety of perspectives, views and positions. Strategy generally involves business goals, a vision and usually an explicit plan to get to achieve the vision and accomplish the goals. The notion of starting at point "a" and going to point "b" suggests a metaphor of strategy as either a roadmap to set direction or the link between an organization's present and its future. Roadmap strategists assert that firms need to "understand how they want to compete, where they will make money, and what organizational levers will enhance their performance" (Barber et al., 2002). Eisenhardt et al. (1998) call this a resource roadmap. These strategists spring from a wide variety of "strategy schools" (Mintzberg et al., 1998) and generally do not incorporate a time component into their strategy theories. They note that strategy helps set the organization's direction and ensures that its activities are aligned with the firm's mission. Other authors agree that strategies need not have time components

(present versus future). Eisenhardt et al. (1998) argued that "in high-velocity markets, a strategic plan is an emotional rallying point and a resource roadmap. It is not anything more, and certainly it does not provide insight about the future." Others who define strategy without a time component include Ghemawat (2002), for whom business strategy is the conscious use of formal planning to positively control market forces. Conversely, some strategists emphasize a time component in their conception of strategy and therefore define a strategic plan as the blueprint for a firm's future (Van de Heijden, 2004; Mintzberg and Waters, 1985) which is important because it necessarily allows firms to establish a feedback loop between their present and future status (Olsen and Eoyang, 2001). Brown and Eisenhardt (1997) note that: "successful firms link the present and future together through rhythmic, time-paced transition processes." They state further "successful firms rely on a wide variety of low cost probes into the future, including experimental products, futurists and strategic alliances. Neither

[1]Source: W. Bodwell and T.J. Chermack (2010) 'Organizational ambidexterity: Integrating deliberate and emergent strategy with scenario planning', *Technological Forecasting & Social Change*, 77, 193–202. Copyright 2010, with permission from Elsevier.

planning nor reacting is as effective". Marginson and McAulay (2008) agree and state that "time is significant as a reference point for the strategic decision maker".

Deliberate versus emergent strategy

Despite the wide variation in beliefs, the general discipline of strategy includes ideas of how and why organizations think about, plan, implement, manage and revise their strategies. In this article we use the term "strategic management" since it provides a broad definition of what strategy is and why it is useful. As defined by Nag, Hambrick and Chen (2007), strategic management deals with the "major intended and emergent initiatives taken by general managers on behalf of owners, involving utilization of resources, to enhance the performance of firms in their external environments." This definition is important because it notes that strategy consists of both intended and emergent initiatives. Similarly, Mintzberg *et al.* (1998) distinguish strategy as either deliberate or emergent; and Mintzberg and Waters (1985) note that the more deliberate strategies tend to emphasize central direction and hierarchy, the more emergent ones open the way for collective action and convergent behaviour.

Deliberate strategy is the specification of intended actions the firm plans to take to achieve its goals. It may be successful or unsuccessful, resulting in goals being realized or unrealized and often new goals are developed. It is this aspect of strategy that may be perceived as "slow." Deliberate strategy in organizations was popular in the 1950s through the 1980s, and it is a component of many of the early schools of strategy, including strategy as design, strategy as positioning, strategy as culture and strategy as organizational learning. But deliberate strategy is not about the future and "some management pundits have been sounding the death-knell of planning since the early 1980s" (Veliyath, 1992). Eisenhardt *et al.* (1998) argued that (deliberate) "strategic planning gives managers almost no help in gaining insight about the future. It is a passive approach that does not actively engage the future. And it can even be detrimental to managing the future when the plans are too rigid." Goold and Quinn (1990) agree and suggest that "detailed and precise plans and strategies" don't work very well for today's companies, in view of the fact that decisions are often "messy and political" and firms

need to be flexible enough to take advantage of new opportunities.

Emergent strategy is therefore an absolutely critical element in the current turbulent business environment (King, 2008); it cannot be overlooked and organizations must create space for emergence to occur. Companies cannot sustain any form of competitive advantage without attention to and space for emergent strategy. Emergent strategy happens when companies engage in actions that evolve unplanned from past patterns or newly recognized patterns in the business environment. According to Mintzberg and Waters (1985) "openness to emergent strategy enables management to act before everything is fully understood – to respond to an evolving reality rather than having to focus on a stable fantasy." If an action is explicitly planned, it cannot be emergent. Moncrieff (1999) asserted that emergent strategy "creates deliberate responses to issues emerging within the competitive environment. They are the result of deliberate decisions to marshal and focus resources in order to pursue a new direction, modifying or replacing some aspects of earlier strategic intent". For example, rather than pursuing an explicit integration strategy, a hospital may make a decision to buy a Long Term Care facility. It then buys an Assisted Living facility. It continues to expand and buys some physician practices. These actions were taken one at a time, but they culminated as a pattern in which the hospital became integrated with other healthcare organizations.

Eisenhardt *et al.* (1998) point out that an emergent strategy can arise from an improvisational approach. "It comes from quickly spotting the temporary advantage provided by the confluence of strategy and luck, acting rapidly to take advantage of the competitive opening created, and building from this advantage a platform for combining advantages into a rule-breaking killer strategy." Holland (1998) describes further the notion of emergence: "The hallmark of emergence is this sense of much coming from little. This feature also makes emergence a mysterious, almost paradoxical, phenomenon smacking of 'get rich quick' schemes. Yet emergence is a ubiquitous feature of the world around us. Mundane activities such as farming depend on rules of thumb for emergence – for example, knowing the conditions that influence the germination of seeds. At the same time, human creative activity, ranging from the construction of metaphors through innovation in business and government to the creation of new scientific theories seems to involve a controlled invocation of emergence."

Mintzberg *et al.* (1998) note that: "few, if any strategies are purely deliberate, just as few are purely emergent. One means no learning, the other means no control. All real-world strategies need to mix these in some way: to exercise control while fostering learning." Jett and George's (2005) simulation study found that "superior emergent processes have some elements of deliberate strategy embedded in them … and that decision processes benefit from an ongoing interplay between deliberate and emergent processes". Mintzberg and Waters (1985) explain further that the aforementioned interplay is the best strategic management policy for companies operating in a highly uncertain environment. They called this deliberately emergent strategy, one in which management sets general boundaries but not the details.

Scenario planning

We propose that scenario planning is a critical tool for balancing the ability to "see" new opportunities, while maintaining a focus on current operating advantages. Scenario planning is like organizational radar, allowing decision-makers to develop an early warning system for potentially devastating market conditions, competitor developments and other industry shifts. Much has been written about scenario planning in recent years (e.g. Burt and Van der Heijden, 2003; Chermack, 2007; Korte, 2008). Likely a result of dissatisfaction with outdated planning tools and methods, perhaps organizational leaders have become frustrated to the point that the need for forecasts, concrete answers and other false assurances has finally subsided. To be sure, those men at Shell were onto something back in the 70s, and perhaps we have finally decided to heed their warnings about the nature of planning based on predictions and forecasts – mainly that "sooner or later they will fail – and just when they are needed most" (Wack, 1985).

Scenario planning is an approach that attempts to harness uncertainty, accept it and build it into the planning process. Scenario planning involves intuition, creativity, the ability to wonder about the environment and its possibilities, as well as a deep understanding of industry trends, competitor actions and global forces that drive economic, social and political systems. Most of all, scenario planning allows organizations to balance deliberate and emergent approaches to strategy. Scenario planning evolved from Herman Kahn's methods to "think the unthinkable" (Kahn and Wiener, 1967) in the 1950s. The scenario approach recognizes the inherent weaknesses in forecasts and single-outcome

methods that essentially aim to predict the future. Instead, scenario planning makes use of multiple scenarios or stories of different futures to underscore the fact that the future is unpredictable, unstable and inherently filled with uncertainty. Reframed as tools for learning, scenarios are intended to "shift the thinking inside the organization" (Wack, 1985) and help managers and decision-makers re-perceive the organizational situation and consider numerous ways in which the future might unfold.

Pierre Wack translated Kahn's ideas into a corporate setting in his years as the head of long range planning at Royal Dutch/Shell. Wack spent most of the 1970s experimenting with and refining his methods and he credited Shell's ability to anticipate the oil shocks of the mid 1970s and 80s to this new technique. Wack's work at Shell served as the foundation for the modern scenario planning methods used.

A general scenario planning process

While there are numerous variations on how to conduct a scenario planning exercise, all are variations on a theme. That is, all have certain elements in common. Wilson and Ralston (2006) provide a comprehensive and detailed process for developing and using scenarios. Their process involves 18 steps, which are provided in Table 7.3.1. Each step in this process is a critical point of adding value and exposing mental models and assumptions during the scenario project. These 18 steps are also in four general phases of scenario planning, namely, 1) "getting started, 2) laying the environmental analysis foundation, 3) creating the scenarios, and 4) moving from scenarios to a decision". Steps one to six are all related to starting up the scenario project and these steps are meant to define the scope of the project and assemble the scenario project team. Steps seven to ten are concerned with exploring the internal and external environments and putting these together in a cohesive picture. Steps 11 to 14 focus on developing the scenarios themselves based on all of the work done in the previous steps. The final phase includes steps 15 to 18 and these steps cover the use of the scenarios to examine current strategies and decisions. Wilson and Ralston's (2006) text provides a detailed road map through each of these steps with specific instructions and practitioner tips.

The scenario planning process reflects the tripartite taxonomy of sensing, seizing and reconfiguring as described by Teece (2007, Reading 2.1).

TABLE 7.3.1   A step-by-step approach to developing and using scenarios

Step 1 – Develop the case for scenarios	Step 11 – Assess the importance and uncertainty of forces and drivers
Step 2 – Gain executive understanding, support and participation	Step 12 – Identify key "axes of uncertainty"
Step 3 – Define the decision focus	Step 13 – Select scenario logics to cover the "envelope of uncertainty"
Step 4 – Design the process	
Step 5 – Select the facilitator	Step 14 – Write the story lines for the scenarios
Step 6 – Form the scenario team	Step 15 – Rehearse the future with scenarios
Step 7 – Gather available data, views and projections	Step 16 – Get to the decision recommendations
Step 8 – Identify and assess key decision factors	Step 17 – Identify signposts to monitor
Step 9 – Identify the critical forces and drivers	Step 18 – Communicate the results to the organization
Step 10 – Conduct focused research on key issues, forces and drivers	

Source: Wilson and Ralston (2006).

Sensing

The ability to sense opportunities and threats requires scanning, searching and exploration. The ability to sense new opportunities is based on a balance between centralized and decentralized control such that feedback delays about decision outcomes are necessarily shortened. In other words, sensitive organizations have mechanisms in place to give them quick and constant updates about what is happening in the external environment both as a result of decisions they make, and that occur autonomously. Scenario planning is designed to foster a constant and consistent read of the external environment as well as the internal. Because scenarios explore multiple possible futures rather than a single, most likely future, participants are attuned to possibilities and signals that mark the turning of events toward a variety of options. In short, scenario planning forces decision-makers to adopt a continuous change thinking perspective that demands a consistent level of attention to forces at work in the external and internal environments and what they indicate for strategic business decisions and initiatives currently underway. For example, Shell's well-known scenarios were constantly examining oil prices, and actions and decisions that could affect oil prices. Early scenarios at Shell were concerned with producers, suppliers and consumers of oil, and so the usefulness of scenario planning was explicitly in the ability of decision-makers to use the technique to stay on top of what was happening in the global oil business environment (Wack, 1985). In short, scenario planning was initiated and adopted at Shell specifically because it allowed decision-makers to develop a system for sensing shifts in the external environment, such that opportunities could be exploited more quickly when compared to competitors who had no such sensory system.

Seizing

The ability to seize opportunities comes first from the recognition that they exist. Without sensing, there is no seizing. Seizing opportunities is about executing strategic insight that leads to strategic action. Van der Heijden (1997) discussed a tool he called the business idea, which he likened to Drucker's "theory of the business" or business model. The purpose of this tool in scenario planning projects is to articulate the business model, which can then be tested in a variety of scenarios later in the process. An additional purpose is to share the mental models of the senior management team about precisely what the business model is supposed to be. Once this model is agreed upon, alternatives can be discussed and additional perspectives can be invited into the process to challenge the conventional mindset. To be sure, scenario planning is designed specifically to counter the "groupthink" phenomenon through the use of external experts not related to the content under question. Finally, since scenarios pose multiple plausible future worlds that might actually unfold, strategic decisions can be examined in a variety of contexts prior to implementation. In the scenario literature, this is known as testing the strategic "robustness" which essentially aligns the business model and strategy [64], but takes one additional step in that it does so in a variety of potential environments.

Reconfiguring

"The key to sustained profitably growth is the ability to recombine and reconfigure assets and organizational structures as market and technologies change" (Teece, 2007). While the need, desire and strategic advantage of reconfiguring certain organizational components is brought about by sensing and seizing, reconfiguration is usually a large task, and requires the efficient and effective shifting of resources. We argue that only a highly competent management team with effective communication can carry out this task in strategic contexts. We cannot overstate that this capability is an important one. We also link this capability to scenario planning in that its execution would logically be faster in an organization that has visited multiple varying possible futures, rather than a single one. For example, one key purpose of entertaining multiple futures is specifically that resource allocation can be shifted more quickly due to a) the identification of signals that major shifts are occurring, or are about to occur, and b) the demand of scenario planning that decision-makers have already thought about where, how, and under what provisions, the resources would be re-directed. The ability to reconfigure is precisely what made Shell famous for its scenarios. Because they were able to anticipate oil prices skyrocketing and bottoming out, they were able to react faster than their competitors, and to this day recall the initiation of scenario planning in the 1970s as a major reason for their current market position.

Conclusion

The ability to harness the advantages of both deliberate and emergent forms of strategy would be a useful skill no doubt. Historic cases of scenario planning such as those from Shell clearly highlight the practical utility of being able to "see" ahead into the future, and to consider the implications of present actions well beyond what is practiced as a standard. The process is designed to force participant reflection on their decisions and actions. In a similar way, the process also forces participants to examine what they know, make it clearly conscious and find the hidden opportunities among the shared perceptions of a group of individuals. At a minimum, our proposal suggests a new way of looking at scenario planning and considering Teece's (2007) tripartite taxonomy as another frame for understanding and dealing with uncertainty in the business environment. Facilitators of scenario planning might also consider this frame as an additional basis for their projects. For example, scenario planning workshops could easily be organized into three phases of sensing, seizing and reconfiguring. In fact, the entire scenario planning project could be organized according to these phases, with clear intent of realizing what is deliberate about an organization's particular strategy, and leaving room for non-prescribed strategies to emerge. That is the basis of Mintzberg's (2005) treatise – that there must be room for the "un-thought-ofs" to occur. While some might call scenario planning a faddish idea in management, more than ever, business leaders are struggling with managing uncertainty. For example, a recent article in *The New York Times* presented a "return to scenario planning" in US-based corporations (Tuna, 2009). This trend of returning to scenario planning indicates continued frustration with an inability to manage uncertainty – and repeated judgment failures in an environment growing in complexity.

REFERENCES

Ackoff, R.L. (1980) *Creating the Corporate Future*, Chichester: Wiley.

Allaire, Y. and Firsirotu, M. (1990) 'Strategic Plans as Contracts', *Long Range Planning*, Vol. 23, No. 1, pp. 102–115.

Allison, G.T. (1971) *The Essence of Decision: Explaining the Cuban Missile Crisis*, Boston: Little Brown.

Amabile, T.M. (1998) 'How to Kill Creativity', *Harvard Business Review*, Vol. 76, No. 5, September-October, pp. 76–87.

Andrews, K.R. (1987) *The Concept of Corporate Strategy,* Third Edition, Homewood, IL: Irwin.

Ansoff, H.I. (1965) *Corporate Strategy: An Analytic Approach to Business Policy for Growth and Expansion*, New York: McGraw-Hill.

Ansoff, H.I. (1991) 'Critique of Henry Mintzberg's The "Design School": Reconsidering the Basic Premises of Strategic Management', *Strategic Management Journal*, September, pp. 449–461.

Ansoff, H.I. and McDonnell, E. (1990) *Implanting Strategic Management*, Second Edition, New York: Prentice Hall.

Armstrong, J.S. (1982) 'The Value of Formal Planning for Strategic Decisions: Review of Empirical Research', *Strategic Management Journal*, Vol. 3, pp. 197–211.

Barber, H., Freeland, G. and Brownell, D. (2002) 'A survivor's guide to organization redesign', in: M.S. Deimler (ed.) *The Boston Consulting Group on Strategy, 2nd ed.*, Classic Concepts and New Perspectives, pp. 302–309.

Beinhocker, E.D. (1999) 'Robust Adaptive Strategies', *Sloan Management Review*, Vol. 40, No. 3, Spring, pp. 95–106.

Bodwell, W. and Chermack, T.J. (2010) 'Organizational ambidexterity: Integrating deliberate and emergent strategy with scenario planning', *Technological Forecasting & Social Change*, 77, pp.193–202.

Bourgeois, L.J. and Brodwin, D.R. (1983) 'Putting Your Strategy into Action', *Strategic Management Planning*, March–May.

Bower, J.L. (1970) *Managing the Resource Allocation Process*, Boston: Harvard Business School Press.

Brown, S. and Eisenhardt, K.M. (1997) 'The art of continuous change: linking complexity theory and time-paced evolution in relentlessly shifting organizations', *Adm. Science Quarterly*, 42(1), pp. 1–34.

Bungay, S. and Goold, M. (1991) 'Creating a Strategic Control System', *Long Range Planning*, Vol. 24, No. 6, pp. 32–39.

Burgelman, R.A. (1983) 'Corporate Entrepreneurship and Strategic Management: Insights from a Process Study', *Management Science*, Vol. 29, No. 12, pp. 1349–1364.

Burgelman, R.A. (1991) 'Intraorganizational Ecology of Strategy Making and Organizational Adaptation: Theory and Field Research', *Organization Science*, Vol. 2, No. 3, pp. 239–262.

Burt, G. and Van der Heijden, K. (2003) 'First steps: towards purposeful activities in scenario thinking and future studies', *Futures*, 35(10), pp. 1011–1026.

Calori, R., Valla, J-P. and De Woot, P. (1994) 'Common Characteristics: The Ingredients of European Management', in: R. Calori and P. De Woot (eds.) *A European Management Model: Beyond Diversity*, Hemel Hempstead: Prentice Hall.

Chaffee, E.E. (1985) 'Three Models of Strategy', *Academy of Management Review*, Vol. 10, No. 1, January, pp. 89–98.

Chakravarthy, B.S. and Lorange, P. (1991) *Managing the Strategy Process: A Framework for a Multi-business Firm*, Englewood Cliffs, NJ: Prentice Hall.

Chermack, T.J. (2007) 'Assessing the quality of scenarios in scenario planning', *Futures Res. Q.*, 22(4), pp. 23–35.

Eisenhardt, K.M. and Brown, S.L. (1998) 'Time pacing: competing in markets that won't stand still', *Harvard Business Review*, 76(2), p. 59.

Evans, J.S. (1991) 'Strategic Flexibility for High Technology Manoeuvres: A Conceptual Framework', *Journal of Management Studies*, Vol. 28, January, pp. 69–89.

Floyd, S.W. and Wooldridge, B. (2000) *Building Strategy from the Middle Reconceptualizing Strategy Process*, Thousand Oaks: Sage.

Ghemawat, P. (1991) *Commitment: The Dynamic of Strategies*, New York: Free Press.

Ghemawat, P. (2002) 'Competition and business strategy in historical perspective', *Bus. Hist. Rev.*, 76(1) 37–74.

Gilbert, X. and Lorange, P. (1995) 'National Approaches to Strategic Management: A Resource-based Perspective', *International Business Review*, Vol. 3, No. 4, pp. 411–423.

Goold, M. and J.J. Quinn (1990) 'The paradox of strategic controls', *Strategic Management Journal*, 11, pp. 43–57.

Grinyer, P.H., Al-Bazzaz, S. and Yasai-Ardekani, M. (1986) 'Towards a Contingency Theory of Corporate Planning: Findings in 48 U.K. Companies', *Strategic Management Journal*, Vol. 7, pp. 3–28.

Hamel, G. (1996) 'Strategy as Revolution', *Harvard Business Review*, Vol. 74, No. 4, July–August, pp. 69–82.

Hampden-Turner, C. and Trompenaars, A. (1993) *The Seven Cultures of Capitalism: Value Systems for Creating Wealth in the United States, Japan, Germany, France, Britain, Sweden and the Netherlands*, New York: Doubleday.

Hart, S.L. (1992) 'An Integrative Framework for Strategy-Making Processes', *Academy of Management Review*, Vol. 17, No. 2, pp. 327–351.

Hax, A.C. and Maljuf, N.S. (1984) *Strategic Management: An Integrative Approach*, Englewood Cliffs, NJ: Prentice Hall.

Hayashi, K. (1978) 'Corporate Planning Practices in Japanese Multinationals', *Academy of Management Journal*, Vol. 21, No. 2, pp. 211–226.

Hofstede, G. (1993) 'Cultural Constraints in Management Theories', *Academy of Management Executive*, Vol. 7, No. 1, pp. 81–94.

Holland, J.H. (1998) *Emergence. From Chaos to Order*, Reading, MA: Perseus Books.

Jelinek, M. (1979) *Institutionalizing Innovation*, New York: Praeger.

Jett, Q.R. and George, J.M. (2005) 'Emergent strategies and their consequences: a process study of competition and complex decision making', *Adv. Strategic Management*, 22, pp. 387–411.

Johnson, G. (1988) 'Rethinking Incrementalism', *Strategic Management Journal*, Vol. 9, No. 1, January–February, pp. 75–91.

Kagono, T, Nonaka, I., Sakakibara, K. and Okumara, A. (1985) *Strategic vs. Evolutionary Management*, Amsterdam: North-Holland.

Kahn, H. and Wiener, A.J. (1967) 'The next thirty-three years: a framework for speculation', *Daedalus*, 96(3), pp. 705–732.

Kanter, R.M. (2002) 'Strategy as Improvisational Theater', *Sloan Management Review*, Vol. 43, No. 2, pp. 76–81.

Kaplan, R.S. and Norton, D.P. (2001) *The Strategy-Focused Organization: How Balanced Scorecard Thrive in the New Business Environment*, Boston, MA: Harvard Business School Press.

King, B.L. (2008) 'Strategizing at leading venture capital firms: of planning, opportunism and deliberate emergence', *Long Range Planning*, 41, pp. 345–366.

Korte, R.F. (2008) 'Applying scenario planning across multiple levels of analysis', *Adv. Dev. Human Resources*, 10(2), pp.179–197.

Kukalis, S. (1991) 'Determinants of Strategic Planning Systems in Large Organizations: A Contingency Approach', *Journal of Management Studies*, Vol. 28, pp. 143–160.

Langley, A. (1995) 'Between "Paralysis and Analysis" and "Extinction by Instinct"', *Sloan Management Review*, Vol. 36, No. 3, Spring, pp. 63–76.

Lenz, R.T. and Lyles, M. (1985) 'Paralysis by Analysis: Is Your Planning System Becoming Too Rational?', *Long Range Planning*, Vol. 18, No. 4, pp. 64–72.

Lessem, R. and Neubauer, F.F. (1994) *European Management Systems*, London: McGraw-Hill.

Liedtka, J. (2000) 'In Defense of Strategy as Design', *California Management Review*, Vol. 42, No. 3, pp. 8–30.

Lindblom, C.E. (1959) 'The Science of Muddling Through', *Public Administration Review*, Spring, pp. 79–88.

Lorange, P. (1980) *Corporate Planning: An Executive Viewpoint*, Englewood Cliffs, NJ: Prentice Hall.

Lorange, P. and Vancil, R.F. (1977) *Strategic Planning Systems*, Englewood Cliffs, NJ: Prentice Hall.

Lyon, D.W., Lumpkin, G.T. and Dess, G.G. (2000) 'Enhancing Entrepreneurial Orientation Research: Operationalizing and Measuring a Key Strategic Decision Making Process', *Journal of Management*, Vol. 26, pp. 1055–1085.

Makridakis, S. (1990) *Forecasting, Planning and Strategy for the 21st Century*, New York: Free Press.

Marginson, D. and McAulay, L. (2008) 'Exploring the debate on short-termism: a theoretical and empirical analysis', *Strategic Management Journal*, 29, pp. 273–292.

Maruyama, M. (1984) 'Alternative Concepts of Management: Insights from Asia and Africa', *Asia Pacific Journal of Management*, Vol. 1, January, pp. 100–111.

Marx, T.G. (1991) 'Removing the Obstacles to Effective Strategic Planning', *Long Range Planning*, Vol. 24, No. 4, August, pp. 21–28.

Miller, C.C. and Cardinal, L.B. (1994) 'Strategic Planning and Firm Performance: A Synthesis of more than Two Decades of Research', *Academy of Management Journal*, Vol. 37, No. 6, pp. 1649–1665.

Mintzberg, H. (1979) *The Structuring of Organizations: A Synthesis of the Research*, Englewood Cliffs, NJ: Prentice Hall.

Mintzberg, H. (1990) 'The Design School: Reconsidering the Basic Premises of Strategic Management', *Strategic Management Journal*, Vol. 11, pp. 171–195.

Mintzberg, H. (1993) 'The Pitfalls of Strategic Planning', *California Management Review*, Vol. 36, No. 1, Fall, pp. 32–45.

Mintzberg, H. (1994a) 'The Fall and Rise of Strategic Planning', *Harvard Business Review*, Vol. 73, No. 1, January–February.

Mintzberg, H. (1994b) *The Rise and Fall of Strategic Planning*, Englewood Cliffs, NJ: Prentice Hall.

Mintzberg, H. (2005) *Managers not MBAs: A Hard Look at the Soft Practice of Managing and Management Practice*, San Francisco, CA: Berrett-Koehler.

Mintzberg, H. and Waters, J.A. (1985) 'Of Strategy: Deliberate and Emergent', *Strategic Management Journal*, Vol. 6, No. 3, July–September, pp. 257–272.

Mintzberg, H., Ahlstrand, B. and Lampel, J. (1998) *Strategy Safari: A Guided Tour Through the Wilds of Strategic Management*, New York: The Free Press.

Moncrieff, J. (1999) 'Is strategy making a difference?' *Long Range Planning*, 32(2), pp. 273–276.

Nag, R., Hambrick, D.C. and Chen, M.J. (2007) 'What is strategic management, really? Inductive derivation of a consensus definition of the field', *Strategic Management Journal*, 28, pp. 935–955.

Nonaka, I. and Johansson, J.K. (1985) 'Japanese Management: What about "Hard" Skills?' *Academy of Management Review*, Vol. 10, No. 2, pp. 181–191.

Ohmae, K. (1982) *The Mind of the Strategist*, New York: McGraw-Hill.

Olson, E.E. and Eoyang, G.H. (2001) *Facilitating Organization Change. Lessons from Complexity Science*, San Francisco, CA: Jossey-Bass.

Pascale, R.T. (1984) 'Perspectives on Strategy: The Real Story Behind Honda's Success', *California Management Review*, Vol. 26, No. 3, pp. 47–72.

Pinchot, G., III (1985) *Intrapreneuring: Why You Don't Have to Leave the Company to Become an Entrepreneur*, New York: Harper & Row.

Powell, T.C. (1992) 'Strategic Planning as Competitive Advantage', *Strategic Management Journal*, Vol. 13, pp. 551–558.

Quinn, J.B. (1978) 'Strategic Change: "Logical Incrementalism"', *Sloan Management Review*, Fall, pp. 7–21.

Quinn, J.B. (1980) *Strategies for Change,* Homewood, IL: Irwin.

Quinn, J.B. (2002) 'Strategy, Science and Management', *Sloan Management Review*, Vol. 43, No. 4.

Rittel, H.W. and Webber, M.M. (1973) 'Dilemmas in a General Theory of Planning', *Policy Sciences*, Vol. 4, pp. 155–169.

Schneider, S.C. (1989) 'Strategy Formulation: The Impact of National Culture', *Organization Studies*, Vol. 10, No. 2, pp. 149–168.

Simons, R. (1995) *Levers of Control: How Managers Use Innovative Control Systems to Drive Strategic Renewal*, Boston, MA: HBS Press.

Smircich, L. and Stubbart, C. (1985) 'Strategic Management in an Enacted World', *Academy of Management Review*, Vol. 10, No. 4, pp. 724–736.

Stacey, R.D. (1993) 'Strategy as Order Emerging from Chaos', *Long Range Planning*, Vol. 26, No. 1, pp. 10–17.

Stacey, R.D. (2001) *Complex Responsive Processes in Organizations: Learning and Knowledge Creation*, London: Routledge.

Steiner, G.A. (1979) *Strategic Planning: What Every Manager Must Know*, New York: Free Press.

Steiner, G.A. and Schollhammer, H. (1975) 'Pitfalls in Multi-National Long-Range Planning', *Long Range Planning*, Vol. 8, No. 2, April, pp. 2–12.

Teece, D.J., Pisano, G. and Shuen, A. (1997) 'Dynamic Capabilities and Strategic Management', *Strategic Management Journal*, 18(7), pp. 509–533.

Teece, D.J. (2007) 'Explicating dynamic capabilities: The nature and microfoundations of (sustainable) enterprise performance', *Strategic Management Journal*, 28, pp. 1319–1350.

Trompenaars, A. (1993) *Riding the Waves of Culture: Understanding Cultural Diversity in Business*, London: The Economist Books.

Tuna, C. (2009) 'Pendulum is swinging back on "scenario planning"', July 6, *Wall Street Journal*.

Van der Heijden, K. (1996) *Scenarios: The Art of Strategic Conversation*, New York: Wiley.

Van der Heijden, K. (1997) *Scenarios: Strategies and the Strategy Process*, Nyenrode University Press, The Netherlands.

Van der Heijden, K. (2004) 'Can internally generated futures accelerate organizational learning?', *Futures*, 36, pp.145–159.

Veliyath, R. (1992) 'Strategic planning: balancing short-run performance and longer term prospects', *Long Range Planning*, 25(3), pp. 86–97.

Wack, P. (1985a) 'Scenarios: Unchartered Waters Ahead', *Harvard Business Review*, Vol. 64, No. 5, September–October, pp. 73–89.

Wack, P. (1985b) 'Scenarios: Shooting the Rapids', *Harvard Business Review*, Vol. 64, No. 6, November–December, pp. 139–150.

Weidenbaum, M. and Hughes, S. (1996) *The Bamboo Network: How Expatriate Chinese Entrepreneurs Are Creating a New Economic Superpower in Asia*, New York: Free Press.

Wildavsky, A. (1979) *Speaking Truth to Power: The Art and Craft of Policy Analysis,* Toronto: Little, Brown & Co.

Wilson, I. (2000) 'From Scenario Thinking to Strategic Action', *Technological Forecasting and Social Change*, Vol. 65, No. 1, September, pp. 23–29.

Wilson, I. and Ralston, W. (2006) *Scenario Planning Handbook: Developing Strategies in Uncertain Times,* Belmont, CA: South-Western Educational Publishers.

8

STRATEGIC CHANGE

Alteration, movement without rest,
Flowing through the six empty places,
Rising and sinking without fixed law,
It is only change that is at work here.
I Ching, *Book of Changes*, appr. 2000 BCE

INTRODUCTION

In a world of new technologies, transforming economies, shifting demographics, re-forming governments, fluctuating consumer preferences and dynamic competition, it is not a question of whether firms *should* change, but of where, how and in what direction they *must* change. For 'living' organizations, change is a given. Firms must constantly be aligned with their environments, either by reacting to external events, or by proactively shaping the businesses in which they operate.

While change is pervasive, not all change in firms is strategic in nature. Much of the change witnessed is actually the ongoing operational kind. To remain efficient and effective, firms constantly make 'fine-tuning' alterations, whereby existing procedures are upgraded, activities are improved and people are reassigned. Such operational changes are directed at increasing the performance of the firm within the confines of the existing system – within the current basic set-up used to align the firm with the environment. Strategic changes, on the contrary, are directed at creating a new type of alignment – a new fit between the basic set-up of the firm and the characteristics of the environment. Strategic changes have an impact on the way the firm does business (its 'business model') and on the way the organization has been configured (its 'organizational system').

For managers the challenge is to implement strategic changes on time, to keep the firm in step with the shifting opportunities and threats in the environment. Some parts of the firm's business model and organizational system can be preserved, while others need to be transformed for the firm to stay up-to-date and competitive. This process of constantly enacting strategic changes to remain in harmony with external conditions is called 'strategic alignment'. This chapter examines the issue of the series of strategic change steps required in order to bring about a process of ongoing strategic alignment.

THE ISSUE OF STRATEGIC ALIGNMENT

There are many actions that constitute a strategic change – a reorganization, a diversification move, a shift in core technology, a business process redesign and a product portfolio reshuffle, to name a few. Each one of these changes is fascinating in itself. Yet, here

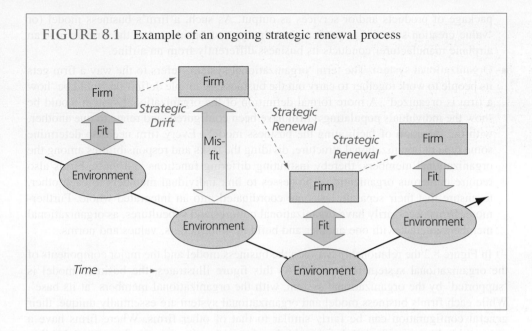

FIGURE 8.1 Example of an ongoing strategic renewal process

the discussion will be broader than just a single strategic change, looking instead at the process of how a series of strategic changes can be used to keep the firm in sync with its surroundings (see Figure 8.1). How can 'a path of strategic changes' be followed to constantly align the firm and avoid a situation whereby the firm 'drifts' too far away from the demands of the environment (Johnson, 1988).

To come to a deeper understanding of the issue of strategic alignment, the first step that must be taken is to examine what is actually being aligned during a process of strategic change. The areas of strategic alignment have been explored in the previous section. After this initial analysis of 'what' is being changed, a distinction will be made between the magnitude and the pace of change. The magnitude of change refers to the size of the steps being undertaken, whereby the question is whether managers should move in bold and dramatic strides, or in moderate and undramatic ones. The pace of change refers to the relative speed at which the steps are being taken, whereby the question is whether managers should move quickly in a short period of time, or more gradually over a longer time span.

Areas of strategic alignment

Firms are complex systems, consisting of many different elements, each of which can be changed. Therefore, to gain more insight into the various areas of potential change, firms need to be analytically disassembled into a number of component parts. The most fundamental distinction that can be made within a firm is between the business model and the organizational system:

■ Business model. The term 'business model' refers to the way a firm conducts its business (for an extensive explanation see Chapter 4). A simple definition would be 'how a firm makes money'. A more formal definition of a business model is 'the specific configuration of resources, value-adding activities and product/service offerings directed at creating value for customers'. Each firm has its own specific system for taking certain resources as inputs (e.g. materials and know-how), adding value to them in some type of manner (e.g. production and branding) and then selling a particular package of products and/or services as output. As such, a firm's business model (or 'value creation system') is particular to the type of business that the firm is in – an airplane manufacturer conducts its business differently from an airline.

■ Organizational system. The term 'organizational system' refers to the way a firm gets its people to work together to carry out the business. A simple definition would be 'how a firm is organized'. A more formal definition of the organizational system would be 'how the individuals populating a firm have been configured, and relate to one another, with the intention of facilitating the business model'. Every firm needs to determine some type of organizational structure, dividing the tasks and responsibilities among the organizational members, thereby instituting differing functions and units. Firms also require numerous organizational processes to link individual members to each other, to ensure that their separate tasks are coordinated into an integrated whole. Furthermore, firms necessarily have organizational cultures and subcultures, as organizational members interact with one another and build up joint beliefs, values and norms.

In Figure 8.2 the relationship between the business model and the major components of the organizational system is depicted. As this figure illustrates, the business model is 'supported' by the organizational system, with the organizational members 'at its base'. While each firm's business model and organizational system are essentially unique, their general configuration can be fairly similar to that of other firms. Where firms have a comparable business 'formula', it is said that they share the same business model. Likewise, where firms have a similar organizational 'form', they are said to subscribe to the same organizational system.

Both the business model and the organizational system can be further disaggregated into component parts and examined in more detail. With this aim in mind, the business model has been at the centre of attention in Chapter 4. In this chapter the organizational system will be further dissected. Actually, the term 'dissection' conjures up images of the organizational system as 'corporate body', which is a useful metaphor for distinguishing the various components of an organizational system (Morgan, 1986).

Following Bartlett and Ghoshal (1995) the organizational system can be divided into its anatomy (structure), physiology (processes) and psychology (culture). Each of these components, summarized in Figure 8.3, will be examined in the following subsection.

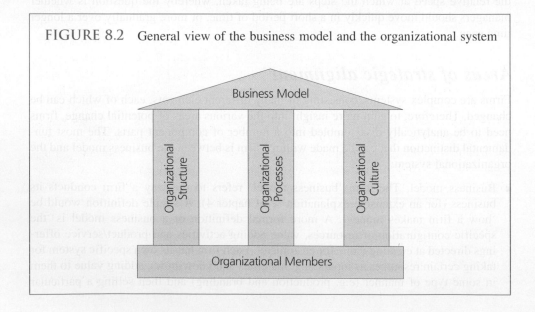

FIGURE 8.2   General view of the business model and the organizational system

Business Model

Organizational Structure

Organizational Processes

Organizational Culture

Organizational Members

FIGURE 8.3 Detailed view of the components of the organizational system

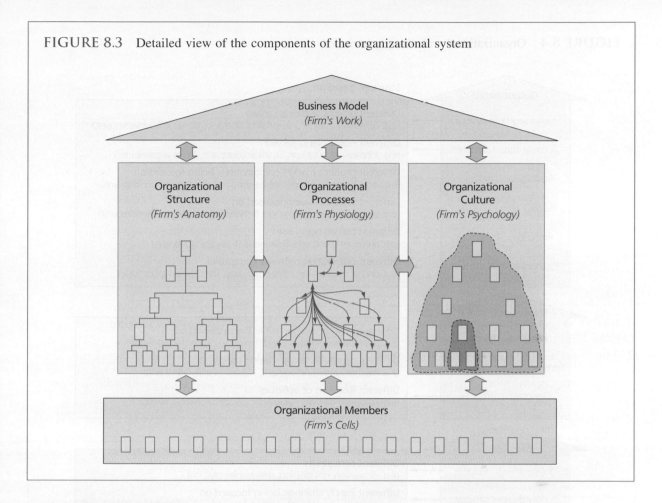

Organizational structure. Organizational structure refers to the clustering of tasks and people into smaller groups. All organizations need at least some division of labour in order to function efficiently and effectively, requiring them to structure the organization into smaller parts. The main question when determining the organizational structure is which criteria will be used to differentiate tasks and to cluster people into particular units. While there are numerous structuring (or decomposition) criteria, the most common ones are summarized in Figure 8.4. In a simple organization tasks might be divided according to just one criterion, but in most organizations multiple criteria are used (either sequentially or simultaneously).

To balance this horizontal differentiation of tasks and responsibilities, all organizations also have integration mechanisms, intended to get the parts to function well within the organizational whole (Lawrence and Lorsch, 1967). While some of these integration mechanisms are found in the categories of organizational processes and culture, the most fundamental mechanism is usually built into the organizational structure – formal authority. In organizations, managers are appointed with the specific task of supervising the activities of various people or units and to report to managers higher up in the hierarchy.

Depending on the span of control of each manager (the number of people or units reporting to him/her), an organizational structure will consist of one or more layers of management. At the apex of this vertical structure is the board of directors, with the ultimate authority to make decisions or ratify decisions made at lower levels in the hierarchy. The most important questions in this context are the number of management layers

FIGURE 8.4 Organizational structuring criteria

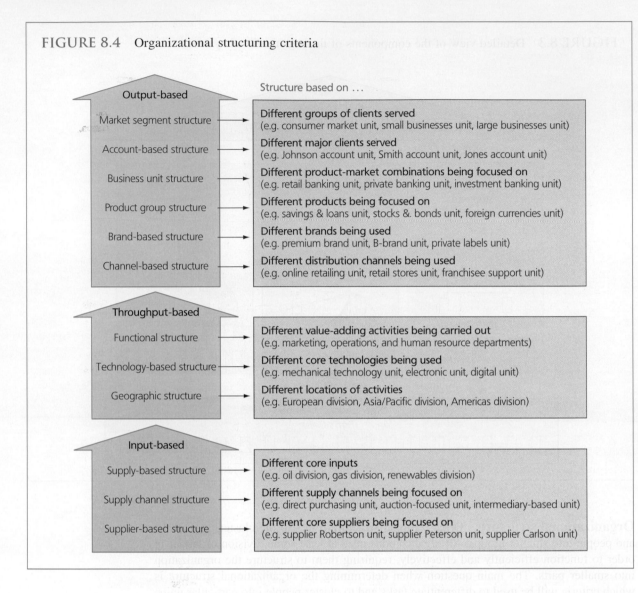

Structure based on …

Output-based

Market segment structure → **Different groups of clients served**
(e.g. consumer market unit, small businesses unit, large businesses unit)

Account-based structure → **Different major clients served**
(e.g. Johnson account unit, Smith account unit, Jones account unit)

Business unit structure → **Different product-market combinations being focused on**
(e.g. retail banking unit, private banking unit, investment banking unit)

Product group structure → **Different products being focused on**
(e.g. savings & loans unit, stocks &. bonds unit, foreign currencies unit)

Brand-based structure → **Different brands being used**
(e.g. premium brand unit, B-brand unit, private labels unit)

Channel-based structure → **Different distribution channels being used**
(e.g. online retailing unit, retail stores unit, franchisee support unit)

Throughput-based

Functional structure → **Different value-adding activities being carried out**
(e.g. marketing, operations, and human resource departments)

Technology-based structure → **Different core technologies being used**
(e.g. mechanical technology unit, electronic unit, digital unit)

Geographic structure → **Different locations of activities**
(e.g. European division, Asia/Pacific division, Americas division)

Input-based

Supply-based structure → **Different core inputs**
(e.g. oil division, gas division, renewables division)

Supply channel structure → **Different supply channels being focused on**
(e.g. direct purchasing unit, auction-focused unit, intermediary-based unit)

Supplier-based structure → **Different core suppliers being focused on**
(e.g. supplier Robertson unit, supplier Peterson unit, supplier Carlson unit)

needed and the amount of authority delegated to lower levels of management. It should be noted that the organizational charts used to represent the formal structure of an organization (see Figure 8.3) need not be an accurate reflection of the informal organizational structure as it operates in reality.

Organizational processes. Organizational processes refer to the arrangements, procedures and routines used to control and coordinate the various people and units within the organization. Some formalized processes span the entire organization, such as business planning and control procedures, and financial budgeting and reporting processes. Other control and coordination processes have a more limited scope, such as new product development meetings, yearly sales conferences, weekly quality circles, web-based expert panels and quarterly meetings with the board of directors. But not all organizational processes are institutionalized as ongoing integration mechanisms. Often, integration across units and departments is needed for a short period, making it useful to employ task forces, committees, working groups, project teams and even joint lunches as means for ensuring coordination.

While all of these processes are formalized to a certain degree, many more informal organizational processes exist, such as communicating via hallway gossip, building support through personal networking, influencing decision-making through informal negotiations and solving conflicts by means of impromptu meetings.

Organizational culture. Organizational culture refers to the worldview and behavioural patterns shared by the members of the same organization (e.g. Schein, 1985; Trice and Beyer, 1993). As people within a group interact and share experiences with one another over an extended period of time, they construct a joint understanding of the world around them. This shared belief system will be emotionally charged, as it encompasses the values and norms of the organizational members and offers them an interpretive filter with which to make sense of the constant stream of uncertain and ambiguous events around them. As this common ideology grows stronger and becomes more engrained, it will channel members' actions into more narrowly defined patterns of behaviour. As such, the organizational culture can strongly influence everything, from how to behave during meetings to what is viewed as ethical behaviour.

As part of the organizational system, culture can act as a strong integration mechanism, controlling and coordinating people's behaviour, by getting them to abide by 'the way we do things around here'. Having a common 'language', frame of reference and set of values also makes it easier to communicate and work together. However, an organizational culture is not always homogeneous – in fact, strongly divergent subcultures might arise in certain units, creating 'psychological' barriers within the organization.

The magnitude of change

Strategic change is by definition far-reaching. We speak of strategic change when fundamental alterations are made to the business model or the organizational system. Adding a lemon-flavoured Coke to the product portfolio is interesting, maybe important, but not a strategic change, while branching out into bottled water was – it was a major departure from Coca-Cola's traditional business model. Hiring a new CEO is also important, but is in itself not a strategic change, while his consequent reorientation towards a new vision is.

Strategic alignment is often even more far-reaching, as a number of strategic changes are executed in a variety of areas to keep the firm aligned with market demands. But while the result of all of these strategic changes is far-reaching, this says nothing about the size of the steps along the way. The strategic alignment process might consist of a few large change steps or numerous small ones. This distinction is illustrated in Figure 8.5. The total amount of strategic changes envisaged is measured along the Y-axis. Change Path A shows the change path taken by a firm that has implemented all changes in two big steps, while Change Path B shows the change path followed by a firm taking numerous smaller steps. Both organizations have completed the same alignment, but via distinctly different routes.

The size of the change steps is referred to as the magnitude of change. This issue of change magnitude can be divided into two component parts:

■ Scope of change. The scope of change in a firm can vary from broad to narrow. Change is broad when many aspects and parts of the firm are aligned at the same time. In the most extreme case the changes might be comprehensive, whereby the business model is entirely revised, and the organizational structure, processes, culture and people are changed in unison. However, change can also be much more narrowly focused on a specific organizational aspect (e.g. new product development processes) or department (e.g. marketing). If many changes are narrowly targeted, the total result will be a more piecemeal change process.

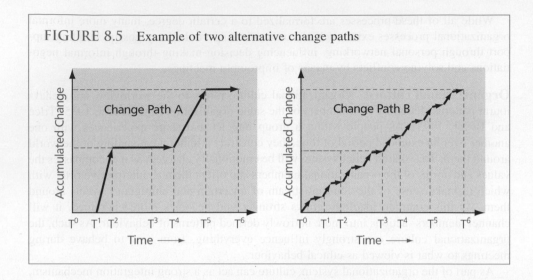

FIGURE 8.5 Example of two alternative change paths

- Amplitude of organizational changes. The amplitude of change in firms can vary from high to low. The amplitude of change is high when the new business model, organizational culture, structure, processes or people are a radical departure from the previous situation. The amplitude of change is low when the step proposed is a moderate adjustment to the previous circumstances.

Where a change is comprehensive and radical, the magnitude of the change step is large. In Figure 8.5 this is represented as a large jump along the Y-axis. Where a change is narrow and moderate, the magnitude of the step is small. However, the above distinction also clarifies that there are two rather different types of medium-sized change steps – a focused radical change (narrow scope, high amplitude) and a comprehensive moderate change (broad scope, low amplitude). Both changes are 'mid-sized', yet significantly different to manage in practice.

The pace of change

Strategic alignment takes time. Yet, there are a variety of ways by which the strategic alignment process can take place over time. Strategic change measures can be evenly spread out over an extended period, allowing the organization to follow a relatively steady pace of strategic alignment. However, it is also possible to cluster all changes into a few short irregular bursts, giving the alignment process an unsteady, stop-and-go pace.

This distinction is seen in Figure 8.5 as well. The total time period needed for achieving a strategic change is measured along the X-axis. Change Path A shows the change path taken by a firm that has had an unsteady pace of change, while Change Path B tracks the path taken by a firm on a more steady change trajectory. Both organizations have completed the same strategic alignment process by T^3 and by T^6, but have distributed their change activities differently during the period.

In Figure 8.5 it also becomes apparent that the pace of organizational changes can be decomposed into two related parts:

- Timing of change. First, the pace of change depends on the moment at which changes are initiated. The timing of change can vary from intermittent to constant. Where change is intermittent, it is important for a firm to determine the right moment for launching a new initiative (for example, T^1 and T^4 in Change Path A). The need to 'wait for the right timing' is often a reason for spreading change activities unevenly over time. On the other hand, change can be constant, so that the exact moment for kicking off any new set of measures is less important, as long as there is no peak at any one moment in time (see Change Path B).

- Speed of change. The pace of change also depends on the time span within which changes take place. The speed of change can vary from high to low. Where a major change needs to be implemented within a short period of time, the speed of change must be high. A short burst of fast action can bring about the intended changes. In Figure 8.5, the speed can be seen by the slope of the arrow (in Change Path A, the speed between T^1 and T^2 is higher than between T^4 and T^5). On the other hand, where the change measures are less formidable and the time span for implementation is longer, the speed of change can be lower.

The variables of timing and speed of change, together with the variables of scope and amplitude of change, create a wide range of possible strategic alignment paths. Firms have many different ways of bringing about strategic change. Unavoidably, this raises the question of which route is best. Why should a firm choose one trajectory over another?

THE PARADOX OF REVOLUTION AND EVOLUTION

It is not the strongest of the species that survive, nor the most intelligent, but the one most responsive to change.
Charles Darwin (1809–1882); English naturalist

In selecting an approach to strategic change, most managers struggle with the question of how bold they should be. On the one hand, they usually realize that to fundamentally transform the organization, a break with the past is needed. To achieve strategic alignment, it is essential to turn away from the firm's heritage and to start with a clean slate. On the other hand, they also recognize the value of continuity, building on past experiences, investments and loyalties. To achieve lasting strategic alignment, people in the organization will need time to learn, adapt and grow into a new organizational reality.

This distinction between disruptive change and gradual change has long been recognized in the strategic management and organizational behaviour literature (e.g. Greiner, 1972; Tushman and O'Reilly, 1996, Reading 8.3 in this book). Disruptive change is variably referred to as 'frame-breaking' (e.g. Baden-Fuller and Stopford, 1992; Grinyer, Mayes and McKiernan, 1987), 'radical' (e.g. Stinchcombe, 1965; Greenwood and Hinings, 1996) and 'revolutionary' (e.g. Gersick, 1991; Tushman, Newman and Romanelli, 1986). Gradual change is variably referred to as 'incremental' (e.g. Quinn, 1980; Johnson, 1987) and 'evolutionary' (e.g. Nelson and Winter, 1982; Tushman and O'Reilly, 1996, Reading 8.3 in this book). Here the labels revolutionary and evolutionary change will be used, in keeping with the terminology used by Greiner (1972) in his classic work.

It is widely accepted among researchers that firms need to balance revolutionary and evolutionary change processes. However, most authors see this as a balancing of strategic (revolutionary) change and operational (evolutionary) change. As strategic change is far-reaching, it is often automatically equated with radical means, while gradual means are reserved for smaller-scale operational changes. Yet, in the previous section it was made clear that a radical result (a strategic change) can be pursued by both revolutionary and evolutionary means (e.g. Hayes, 1985; Krüger, 1996; Nonaka, 1988; Strebel, 1994).

While these two change processes are each other's opposites, and they seem to be at least partially contradictory, both approaches are needed within firms. In practice both change processes have valuable, yet conflicting, qualities. The tension that this creates between revolution and evolution will be explored in the following sections.

The demand for revolutionary change processes

Revolution is a process whereby an abrupt and radical change takes place within a short period of time. Revolutionary change processes are those that do not build on the status quo, but overthrow it. 'Revolutionaries' revolt against the existing business model and organizational system, and attempt to push through changes that will reinvent the firm. Thus, revolution leads to a clear break with the past – a discontinuity in the firm's development path.

Such a 'big bang' approach to strategic change is generally needed when organizational rigidity is so deeply rooted that smaller pushes do not bring the firm into movement. If the firm threatens to become paralysed by these inherited rigidities in the business model and organizational system, the only way to get moving can be to radically break with the past. Typical sources of organizational rigidity include:

- Psychological resistance to change. Many people resist change, because of the un-certainty and ambiguity that unavoidably accompanies any shift in the old way of doing business (e.g. Argyris, 1990; Pondy, Boland and Thomas, 1988). As people become accustomed to fixed organizational routines and established habits, their ability to learn and gradually adapt invariably recedes. New business methods or job de-scriptions are not seen as a challenging opportunity to learn, but as an unwelcome interference in the existing system. It can be necessary to break through this psycho-logical resistance to change by imposing a new business model and/or organizational system on people (e.g. Hammer, 1990, Reading 8.1 in this book; Powell, 1991).

- Cultural resistance to change. As discussed in Chapter 2, people can easily become immune to signals that their cognitive maps are outdated, especially if they are sur-rounded by others with the same flawed belief system. Once an organizational culture develops that perpetuates a number of obsolete assumptions about the market or the organization, it is very difficult for organizational members to challenge and gradually reshape the organizational belief system. It can be necessary to break through this cultural resistance to change by exposing the organization to a shocking crisis or by imposing a new organizational system (e.g. Tushman, Newman and Romanelli, 1986, Senge, 1990a, Reading 8.2).

- Political resistance to change. Change is hardly ever to everyone's advantage. Each organizational change leads to a different constellation of winners and losers. Gen-erally, the potential losers reject a strategic change, although they are likely to think of some seemingly objective reasons for their opposition. Even a situation in which a person or department thinks that it might run the risk of losing power to others can be enough to block a change. Since strategic changes invariably have a significant impact on all people within an organization, there will always be a number of open, and hidden, opponents. It can be necessary to break through this political resistance by imposing a new business model and reshuffling management positions (e.g. Allison, 1969; Krüger, 1996).

- Investment lock-in. Once a firm has committed a large amount of money and time to a certain product portfolio, activity system or technology, it will find that this fixed investment locks the organization in. Any gradual movement away from the past investment will increase the risk of not earning back the sunk cost. Therefore, it can be necessary to break through the lock-in by radically restructuring or disposing of the investment (e.g. Ghemawat, 1991; Bower and Christensen, 1995).

■ Competence lock-in. The better a firm becomes at something, the more a firm becomes focused on becoming even better still – which is also known as the virtuous circle of competence-building. Once a competitive advantage has been built on a particular type of competence, the natural tendency of firms is to favour external opportunities based on these competences. New people are hired that fit the corporate competence profile and R&D spending further hones the firm's skill. But if the firm's competence base threatens to become outdated due to market or technological changes, its former advantage could become its downfall – the firm could become caught in a vicious 'competence trap', unable to gradually shift the organization to an alternative set of competences, because the entire business model and organizational system have been aligned to the old set (e.g. Leonard-Barton, 1995; Teece, Pisano and Shuen, 1997). Changing the core competence of the corporation in a comprehensive and radical manner can be the only way to 'migrate' from one competence profile to another.

■ Systems lock-in. Firms can also become locked into an open standard (e.g. sizes in inches, GAAP accounting rules) or a proprietary system (e.g. Windows operating system, SAP enterprise resource planning software). Once the firm has implemented a standard or system, switching to another platform cannot be done gradually or at low cost. Therefore, the lock-in can usually only be overcome by a big bang transition to another platform (e.g. Arthur, 1996; Shapiro and Varian, 1998).

■ Stakeholder lock-in. Highly restrictive commitments can also be made towards the firm's stakeholders. Long-term contracts with buyers and suppliers, warranties, commitments to governments and local communities and promises to shareholders can all lock firms into a certain strategic direction. To break through the stakeholders' resistance to change, it can be necessary to court a crisis and aim for a radical restructuring of the firm's external relationships (e.g. Freeman, 1984; Oliver, 1991).

Besides the use of revolutionary change to overcome organizational rigidity, such a radical approach to strategic alignment is often also necessary given the short time span available for a large change. The 'window of opportunity' for achieving a strategic change can be small for a number of reasons. Some of the most common triggers for revolutionary strategic change are:

■ Competitive pressure. When a firm is under intense competitive pressure and its market position starts to erode quickly, a rapid and dramatic response might be the only approach possible. Especially when the organization threatens to slip into a downward spiral towards insolvency, a bold turnaround can be the only option left to the firm.

■ Regulatory pressure. Firms can also be put under pressure by the government or regulatory agencies to push through major changes within a short period of time. Such externally imposed revolutions can be witnessed among public sector organizations (e.g. hospitals and schools) and highly regulated industries (e.g. banks and utilities), but in other sectors of the economy as well (e.g. antitrust break-ups, public health regulations).

■ First mover advantage. A more proactive reason for instigating revolutionary change is to be the first firm to introduce a new product, service or technology and to build up barriers to entry for late movers. Especially for know-how that is dissipation-sensitive, or for which the patent period is limited, it can be important to cash in quickly before others arrive on the market (e.g. Kessler and Chakrabarthi, 1996; Lieberman and Montgomery, 1988, 1998).

To some extent all managers recognize that their organizations are prone to inertia, and most will acknowledge that it is often vital to move quickly, either in response to external pressures or to cash in on a potential first mover advantage. It should therefore come as no surprise that most managers would like their organizations to have the ability to successfully pull off revolutionary strategic changes.

The demand for evolutionary change processes

Evolution is a process whereby a constant stream of moderate changes gradually accumulates over a longer period of time. Each change is in itself small, but the cumulative result can be large. Evolutionary change processes take the current firm as a starting point, constantly modifying aspects through extension and adaptation. Some 'mutations' to the firm prove valuable and are retained, while other changes are discarded as dysfunctional. Thus, a new business model and/or organizational system can steadily evolve out of the old, as if the organization were shedding its old skin to grow a new one (e.g. Aldrich, 1999; Kagono *et al.,* 1985).

This 'metamorphosis' approach to strategic change is particularly important where the strategic alignment hinges on widespread organizational learning. Learning is not a process that is easily compressed into a few short bursts of activity (as anyone who has studied knows). Learning is a relatively slow process, whereby know-how is accumulated over an extended period of time. It can take years to learn things, especially if the necessary knowledge is not readily available but must be acquired 'on the job' (e.g. Agryris, 1990; Senge, 1990a, Reading 8.2). This is true for both individuals and firms. When groups of people in a firm need to develop new routines, new competences, new processes, as well as new ways of understanding the world, time is needed to experiment, reflect, discuss, test and internalize. Even in the circumstances where individuals or departments are merely asked to adjust their behaviours to new norms, the learning process is often protracted and difficult (e.g. Nelson and Winter, 1982; Pfeffer and Sutton, 1999).

While the evolutionary nature of learning is a positive factor stimulating gradual change, the organizational reality is often also that power is too dispersed for revolutionary changes to be imposed upon the firm. Where no one has enough sway in the organization to push through radical changes, a more evolutionary approach can be the only viable route forward.

To some extent all managers recognize that their firms need to continuously learn and adapt, while most will acknowledge that they do not have the absolute power to impose revolutionary changes at will. For these reasons, managers generally would like their organizations to have the ability to pursue evolutionary changes.

Yet, engaging in evolutionary change is the opposite of revolutionary change. On the one hand, being opposites might make revolution and evolution complementary. Some authors suggest that organizations should be 'ambidextrous', using both revolution and evolution, contingent upon internal and external conditions (e.g. Duncan, 1976; Krüger, 1996, Tushman and O'Reilly, 1996, Reading 8.3). On the other hand, the above discussion makes clear that the two are, to a certain extent, mutually incompatible. Once the one form of change has been chosen, this will seriously limit the ability of the strategist to simultaneously, or even subsequently, use the other. Hence, managers are once again faced with a paradox, between revolution and evolution.

EXHIBIT 8.1   SHORT CASE

CHINA COSCO: CHANGING SHIPS?

Thanks to the rise of the Internet, distance has rapidly decreased and communication has become easier and faster. There are, however, things the Internet is not capable of sending physical goods. Even now, the primary means of transporting products is still shipping. A lots of goods need to be transported from China particularly, the world's main production site. Large amounts of products, "Made in China", are shipped around the globe. Even though many industries are in flux, there is no alternative for shipping bulk products. This would suggest that shipping is an oasis of stability in a world of change; yet, even giants in seemingly calm waters have no guarantee of stable income. The state-owned China Ocean Shipping Company (COSCO), China's largest corporate group in global shipping, modern logistics and ship building, has encountered restless waters, which its subsidiary China COSCO in particular has to circumnavigate. For China COSCO, this is the final call to choose the right speed and the correct direction.

Founded in 1961, COSCO was China's first international shipping company. What started out as a passenger transportation company, quickly diversified to container shipping. COSCO gathered steam with purchasing and operating ships, financed by long-term bank loans. By the end of 1975, the company proudly announced that the capacity of its fleet had surpassed five million deadweight tons (DWT); the sum of the weights a ship can safely carry. Yet, COSCO's international activities remained limited. It was only during the 1980s that COSCO really gained momentum.

After the death of Mao Zedong in 1976, reformist leader Deng Xiaoping invigorated the Chinese economy by stimulating export-led growth and opening the Chinese market. Also attracted by the country's cheap labour, Western companies started manufacturing products in China, and the demand for shipping started booming. Although COSCO lost its monopoly over China's overseas transport during this time, it retained control over the vast majority of transport to and from China by profiting from new capital influx. Meanwhile, the global economic recession was hitting international shipping hard, creating an overcapacity of ships. COSCO was one

of the few companies seeking to expand the number of ships, and was able to do so cheaply.

With a large share of the Chinese shipping market, COSCO expanded its overseas activities by establishing partnerships and starting transnational business operations. The company created its first overseas joint venture in 1980 in Rotterdam, the Netherlands, and set up a wholly owned subsidiary in London in 1988 by purchasing the remaining shares held by its business partner. Growth continued in the 1990s, and COSCO turned into China Ocean Shipping (Group) Company, or COSCO Group for short. The Group's first overseas-listed subsidiary was COSCO Corporation (Singapore), followed by COSCO Hong Kong, COSCO Korea, COSCO Japan and COSCO Container Lines, among others.

After his successful career at COSCO Corporation (Singapore), Wei Jiafu entered the stage as COSCO Group's CEO in 1998, not abandoning this position ever since. Jiafu decided to further broaden the businesses of COSCO by adding modern logistics, building of vessels and ship maintenance to its activities. Yet, the pursuit of expansion did not necessarily result in better performances, as is highlighted by China COSCO.

This subsidiary, established in 2005, forms the capital platform of the COSCO Group with Jiafu as its chairman, providing such services as dry bulk shipping, terminal operations and the manufacturing, leasing and shipping of containers. As such, the various subsidiaries cover the whole shipping value chain. All seemed to go well for China COSCO, especially profiting from the dry bulk unit that it purchased in 2007 from its parent. With 45 per cent of its 2007 revenues coming from dry bulk shipping, Jiafu and his management believed the future was bright. China COSCO's CEO stated in the annual report of 2007 that 'it is expected that the overall dry bulk shipping market supply and demand conditions will remain favourable'. Unfortunately this was not to be.

In 2008, economies suffered from the global financial crisis and the international shipping industry, a barometer of the global economy, was adversely affected. Still, the COSCO Group was able to keep its head above water, making minor profits during a challenging time for global shipping. However, this cannot be said for China COSCO. Its net profits decreased by 40 per cent in that year, with a record loss of about US$ 1.1 billion in the consecutive year. Yet, a turnaround seemed to dawn during the following year. Due to a modest recovery from the global financial crisis, while also minimizing costs, cancelling new ships and selling a 49 per cent stake in Cosco Logistics to its parent, China COSCO was able to announce an annual profit of US$ 361 million in 2010.

Whereas China COSCO's logistics unit and terminal operations continued to make profits, its dry bulk shipping rebounded to losses. Chairman Jiafu ascribed this to rising fuel prices and over-capacity in the sector, but also pointed to 'over-supply in the market, low freight rate, high cost and [an] imbalanced fleet composition'. Although China COSCO's debts racked up – in 2012 alone it had to endure a loss of US$ 1.54 billion – this was the least of Jiafu's worries. The company's last recorded annual profit stemmed from 2010, and according to the Shanghai stock exchange rules a company could well be de-listed after three consecutive annual losses. As such, the Shanghai Index regulations could make China COSCO sink, fuelling the necessity for strategic change.

In order to regain profitability in 2013, solutions were sought by following an evolutionary path to carefully reforming the company. For instance, China COSCO had to focus on strengthening coordination among internal departments and centralizing procurement. These measures were backed up by downsizing the company's assets in a prudent fashion: one by one. Jiafu was set to sell the lucrative COSCO Logistics to its parent company for US$ 1.1 billion, providing his company with a one-off pretax gain of approximately US$ 316 million for 2013. The options to discard more assets were left open, and by sacrificing other units, dry bulk shipping – China COSCO's core business – could remain intact.

Should China COSCO continue selling its assets and taking other cautious measures? Or should Jiafu boldly get rid of its troublesome core business, thus giving up the company's position as the world's largest bulk cargo fleet operator? Time is running out, and given the difficult situation of the shipping industry the bulk assets are difficult to value, and therefore hard to sell at a reasonable price. Pursuing an evolutionary or revolutionary path: change is eminent at any rate. Jiafu needs to steer China COSCO in a direction that would prevent the company from hitting a record of three consecutive years of losses, and keeping the boat afloat.

Co-author: Wester Wagenaar

Sources: http://en.cosco.co; www.chinacosco.com; China COSCO Annual Reports 2007–2012; *Bloomberg,* 13 March 2013 and 28 March 2013; *Financial Times,* 30 August 2012; Moore (2002); *Reuters,* 29 March 2012; *The Wall Street Journal,* 23 March 2011 and 20 May 2013.

PERSPECTIVES ON STRATEGIC CHANGE

Although the demand for both revolutionary and evolutionary change is clear, this does place managers in the difficult position of having to determine how both must be combined and balanced in a process of ongoing strategic alignment. Revolutionary change is necessary to create *discontinuity* in the alignment process – radical and swift breaks with the past. Evolutionary change is necessary to ensure *continuity* in the alignment process – moderate and gradual metamorphosis from one state into another. In finding a balance between these two demands, the question is which of the two must play a leading role and what type of change path this leads to. Does successful strategic alignment hinge on a few infrequent big bangs, with some minor evolutionary changes in the intervening time span, or is successful strategic alignment essentially a gradual process of mutation and selection, where revolutionary changes are used only in case of emergency?

Yet, as in previous chapters, we see that the strategic management literature comes up with a wide variety of answers to this question. Both among business practitioners and strategy researchers, views differ sharply about the best way of dealing with the paradox of revolution and evolution. To gain insight into the major points of disagreement between people on the issue of strategic alignment, we will again outline the two diametrically opposed perspectives here.

At one end of the virtual continuum of views, are the strategists who argue that real strategic alignment can only be achieved by radical means. Revolutionary change, although difficult to achieve, is at the heart of alignment, while evolutionary changes can only figure in a supporting role. This point of view will be referred to as the 'discontinuous alignment perspective'. At the other end of the spectrum are the strategists who argue that real strategic alignment is not brought about by an 'axe', but must grow out of the existing firm, in a constant stream of small adjustments. Evolutionary change, although difficult to sustain, is at the heart of alignment, while revolutionary changes are a fall-back alternative, if all else fails. This point of view will be referred to as the 'continuous alignment perspective'.

The discontinuous alignment perspective

 According to advocates of the discontinuous alignment perspective, it is a common misconception that firms develop gradually. It is often assumed that organizations move fluidly from one state to the next, encountering minimal friction. In reality, however, strategic change is arduous and encounters significant resistance. Pressure must be exerted, and tension must mount, before a major shift can be accomplished. Movement, therefore, is not steady and constant, as a current in the sea, but abrupt and dramatic, as in an earthquake, where resistance gives way and tension is released in a short shock. In general, the more significant a change is, the more intense the shock will be.

Proponents of this perspective argue that people and organizations exhibit a natural reluctance to change. Humans have a strong preference for stability. Once general policy has been determined, most firms are inclined to settle into a fixed way of working. The organizational structure will solidify, formal processes will be installed, standard operating procedures will be defined, key competence areas will be identified, a distribution of power will emerge and a corporate culture will become established. The stability of an organization will be especially high if all of these elements form a consistent and cohesive configuration (e.g. Mintzberg, 1991; Waterman, Peters and Philips, 1980). Moreover, if a firm experiences a period of success, this usually strongly reinforces the existing way of working (e.g. Markides, 1998; Miller, 1990).

It must be emphasized that stability is not inherently harmful, as it allows people to 'get to work'. A level of stability is required to function efficiently (e.g. March and Simon, 1958; Thompson, 1967). Constant change would only create an organizational mess. There would be prolonged confusion about tasks and authority, poorly structured internal communication and coordination, and a lack of clear standards and routines. The instability brought on by such continuously changing processes and structures would lead to widespread insecurity, political manoeuvring and inter-departmental conflicts.

Advocates of the discontinuous alignment perspective, therefore, argue that long periods of relative stability are necessary for the proper functioning of firms. However, the downside of stability is rigidity – the unwillingness and/or inability to change, even when it is urgently required. To overcome rigidity and get the firm in motion, a series of small nudges will by no means be sufficient. Instead, a big shove will be needed. For strategic changes to really happen, measures must be radical and comprehensive. A coordinated assault is usually required to decisively break through organizational defences and 'shock therapy' is needed to fundamentally change people's cognitive maps. Solving lock-in problems generally also demands a quick, firm-wide switchover to a new system. For instance, business process reengineering must involve all aspects of the value chain at once (e.g. Hammer, 1990, Reading 8.1; Hammer and Champy, 1993). However, proponents of the discontinuous alignment perspective emphasize that the period of turmoil must not take too long. People cannot be indefinitely confronted with high levels of uncertainty and ambiguity, and a new equilibrium is vital for a new period of efficient operations.

Some proponents of the discontinuous change perspective argue that episodes of revolutionary change are generally not chosen freely, but are triggered by crises. A major environmental jolt can be the reason for a sudden crisis (e.g. Meyer, 1982; Meyer, Brooks and Goes, 1990) – for example, the introduction of a new technology, a major economic recession, new government regulations, a novel market entrant or a dramatic event in international political affairs. However, misalignment between the firm and its environment often grows over a longer period of time, causing a mounting sense of impending crisis (e.g. Johnson, 1988; Strebel, 1992). As tension increases, people in the firm become more receptive to submitting to the painful changes that are necessary. This increased willingness to change under crisis circumstances coincides with the physical law that 'under pressure things become fluid'. As long as the pressure persists, revolutionary change is possible, but as soon as the pressure lets up the firm will resolidify in a new form, inhibiting any further major changes (e.g. Lewin, 1947; Miller and Friesen, 1984). For this reason, managers often feel impelled to heighten and prolong the sense of crisis, to keep organization members receptive to the changes being pushed through. Where a crisis is lacking, some managers will induce one, to create the sense of urgency and determination needed to get people in the change mind-set.

It can be concluded that strategic changes, whether proactive or reactive, require an abrupt break with the status quo. Change management demands strong leadership to rapidly push through stressful, discomforting and risky shifts in the business and organizational system. Battling the sources of rigidity and turning crisis into opportunity are the key qualities needed by managers implementing strategic change. Ultimately, strategizing managers should know when to change and when it is wiser to seek stability – they should know when to trigger an 'earthquake' and when to avoid one.

EXHIBIT 8.2   THE DISCONTINUOUS ALIGNMENT PERSPECTIVE

CHANGE BANKING FOR GOOD

In 2012, with the £133 billion financial crisis still echoing, UK citizens again received terrifying news: banks had manipulated their Libor rates (London Inter-Bank Offered Rate) to appear more creditworthy or to profit from trades. The Houses of Parliament responded by installing a "Parliamentary Commission on Banking Standards". The commission was founded to conduct an inquiry into professional standards and culture in the UK banking sector, and to formulate recommendations for future legislation. Those expecting minor measures were in shock. If the commission would find support from the UK treasury, top bankers who had enriched themselves during the financial crisis would have faced colossal penalties or even time in jail: the price the industry had to pay to restore trust in banking.

The commission concluded that too many bankers were not personally accountable, taking shelter in collective decision-making, with sanctions being disproportionate to the severity of the consequences of failure. In addition, many bank staff had been paid too much for doing the wrong things: bonuses provoked short-term personal gain and long-term societal pain. This has led the commission to develop a new framework for individuals working in the industry, the main element being a Senior Persons Regime which would ensure that the key responsibilities within banks are assigned to specific individuals. The bankers would be made fully and unambiguously aware of their responsibilities and held accountable for carrying them out. Regulators would apply the civil powers of fines, restrictions on responsibilities and a ban from the industry.

The new rigorous regime will restore trust in banking – crucial for the UK's dominant position within the global financial services industry. A reformed banking industry with higher standards has the potential, once again, to be a great asset to the United Kingdom. For good.

Co-author: Adriaan de Bruijn

Sources: House of Lords, House of Commons Parliamentary Commission on Banking Standards. June 2013. Volume 1: Summary, and Conclusions and recommendations. http://www.parliament.uk/business/committees/committees-a-z/joint-select/professional-standards-in-the-banking-industry/news/changing-banking-for-good-report/, *The Economist,* 22 June, 2013.

The continuous alignment perspective

According to proponents of the continuous alignment perspective, if firms shift by 'earthquake' it is usually their own 'fault'. The problem with revolution is that it commonly leads to the need for further revolution at a later time – discontinuous change creates its own boom-and-bust cycle. Revolutionary change is generally followed by a strong organizational yearning for stability. The massive, firm-wide efforts to implement agonizing changes can often be sustained for only a short period of time, after which change momentum collapses. Any positive inclination towards change among employees will have totally disappeared by the time the reorganizations are over. Consequently, the firm lapses back into a stable state in which only minor changes occur. This stable situation is maintained until the next round of shock therapy becomes necessary, to jolt the organization out of its ossified state.

To supporters of the continuous alignment perspective, the boom-and-bust approach to strategic change is like running a marathon by sprinting and then standing still to catch one's breath. Yet, marathons are not won by good sprinters, but by runners with endurance and persistence, who can keep a steady pace – runners who are more inspired by the tortoise than by the hare. The same is true for companies in the marathon of competition. Some companies behave like the hare in Aesop's fable, showing off their ability to take great leaps, but burdened by a short span of attention. Other companies behave more like the tortoise, moving gradually and undramatically, but unrelentingly and without interruption, focusing on the long-term goal. In the short run, the hares might dash ahead, suggesting that making big leaps forward is the best way to compete. But in the long run, the most formidable contenders will be the diligent tortoises, whose ability to maintain a constant speed will help them to win the race.

Therefore, the 'big ideas' and 'quantum leaps' that so mesmerize proponents of the discontinuous alignment perspective are viewed with suspicion by supporters of continuous alignment. Revolution not only causes unnecessary disruption and dysfunctional crises, but also is usually the substitute for diligence. If organizations do not have the stamina to continuously improve themselves, quick fix radical change can be used as a short-term remedy. Where firms do not exhibit the drive to permanently upgrade their capabilities, revolutionary alignment can be used as the short cut to improved competitiveness. In other words, the lure of revolutionary change is that of short-term results. By abruptly and dramatically making major changes, managers hope to rapidly book tangible progress – and instantly win recognition and promotion.

To advocates of the continuous alignment perspective, a preference for revolution usually reflects an unhealthy obsession with the short term. Continuous alignment, on the other hand, is more long term in orientation. Development is gradual, piecemeal and undramatic, but as it is constantly maintained over a longer period of time, the aggregate level of change can still be significant.

Everyone in the firm must be motivated to continuously learn. People within the organization must constantly update their knowledge base, which not only means acquiring new information, but challenging accepted company wisdom as well. Learning goes hand in hand with unlearning – changing the cognitive maps shared within the organization. In this respect, it is argued that an atmosphere of crisis actually inhibits continuous alignment. In a situation of crisis, it is not a matter of 'under pressure things become fluid', but 'in the cold everything freezes'. Crisis circumstances might lower people's resistance to imposed change, but it also blunts their motivation for experimenting and learning, as they brace themselves for the imminent shock. Crisis encourages people to seek security and to focus on the short term, instead of opening up and working towards long-term development (e.g. Bate, 1994; Senge, 1990a, Reading 8.2).

Everyone in the firm must not only continuously learn, but also be motivated to continuously adapt. Constant adjustment to external change and fluid internal realignment should be pursued. To this end, the organization must actively avoid inertia, by combating the forces of ossification. Managers should strive to create flexible structures and processes (e.g. Bartlett and Ghoshal, 1995; Eisenhardt and Brown, 1997), to encourage an open and tolerant corporate culture, and to provide sufficient job and career security for employees to accept other forms of ambiguity and uncertainty (e.g. Kagono *et al.,* 1985; Nonaka, 1988).

In an evolutionary firm basically everyone in the organization is involved. Revolutionary change can be initiated by top management, possibly assisted and urged on by a few external consultants, and carried by a handful of change agents or champions (e.g. Maidique, 1980; Day, 1994). Evolutionary change, on the other hand, requires a firm-wide effort. Leaders cannot learn on behalf of their organizations, nor can they orchestrate all of the small adaptations needed for continuous alignment. Managers must realize that evolution can be led from the top, but not be imposed from the top. For strategizing managers to realize change, hands-on guidance of organizational developments is more important than commanding organizational actions.

EXHIBIT 8.3 CONTINUOUS ALIGNMENT PERSPECTIVE

NOKIA FACES TOUGH CHOICES AS SIEMENS SHOPS AROUND NSN

Siemens seems to be increasing its efforts at finding a suitable buyer for its wireless infrastructure joint venture with Nokia, Nokia Siemens Networks. The German company has reportedly approached a number of private equity players, including Blackstone, TPG and KKR, to see if they would like to buy out either the joint venture completely or possibly only its stake in the company. The talks seem to have followed after a recently amended shareholder agreement allowed both Nokia and Siemens the freedom to do as they wish with their stake without the fear of being vetoed by the other party.

Siemens, which has only a non-controlling stake in the JV, has been looking to shed its non-core assets in recent years, and exiting the joint venture fits in well with that strategy. Nokia, on the other hand, faces a tricky situation and may not want to sell out completely given its controlling stake in the venture that is undergoing a successful turnaround in operations currently.

Nokia's dilemma. The joint venture has been the lone bright spot for the handset maker over the past year as its smartphone sales plummeted amid a tough transition to Windows Phone. Due to the ongoing restructuring process as well as the transition to 4G LTE taking place in many parts of the world, the venture has managed to not only return to operating profitability in the last few quarters but has also generated cash for six quarters in a row. At a time when Nokia is conserving cash by suspending dividend payouts and leasing its headquarters instead of owning it, NSN is proving highly valuable with its steady cash flows despite not being a core asset. Last quarter, for example, the company managed to generate cash solely because of NSN's performance. While NSN generated more than €230 million in free cash flow last quarter, Nokia Group, as a whole, could manage less than €90 million.

As a result, we estimate that NSN is Nokia's biggest value contributor currently, accounting for almost 40 per cent of our $5 share price estimate for the company. This essentially means that Nokia won't part with such a valuable asset easily. It would look for an enterprise value of around $6 billion for its half of NSN to cash out or reduce its stake in the company. However, given that NSN hasn't been profitable on an ongoing basis, it might be tough for the JV to command a good valuation right now. And Nokia won't likely settle for anything less considering the ongoing turnaround at NSN and valuable cash flows it is generating. Therefore, while Nokia will eventually look to exit the JV considering it is not its core focus, we don't see this happening until the handset business has sufficiently turned around and NSN has achieved sustained profitability for a few quarters. Until these two conditions are met, we expect Nokia to look for a partner to replace or acquire a part of Siemens' stake in NSN.

NSN's turnaround. The likelihood of NSN sustaining profitability is reasonably good. Over the past year, Nokia Siemens Networks has increasingly shown signs of turning the corner as a result of an ongoing restructuring that has not only helped improve its operating margins but also restored focus on its wireless business. As a result, NSN has fast emerged as the leader in the ongoing 4G LTE transition around the world and is taking share away from competitors. As of the third quarter of last year, NSN had succeeded in increasing its market share to about 20 per cent of the wireless infrastructure industry, only 2 per cent behind No. 2 player, Huawei. It now expects to reclaim its No. 2 spot behind Ericsson by the end of 2013. Most of these gains should come on 4G LTE – a market NSN managed to capture almost 22 per cent of in Q3 2012, up from 13 per cent the previous year.

Apart from revenue share gains, NSN is also benefiting from the streamlining of operations and the ongoing job cuts. By the end of 2013, NSN aims to cut around 17,000 jobs and achieve a total of $1.35 billion in savings as part of the restructuring initiative announced in late 2011. Simultaneously, NSN has been selling off non-core assets and increasing focus on wireless broadband which has strong long-term growth trends as opposed to the relatively stagnant landline market. As a result of the reshuffle, NSN has performed really well recently, returning to operating profitability in Q4 2012 and managing to turn a small profit in a seasonally weak Q1 as well. We estimate NSN's EBITDA margins in 2012 to have doubled over the previous year. This is a big positive sign that the company's cost-cutting initiatives are taking hold – a trend we expect to continue in the coming years as well.

Source: Forbes, 17 June 2013; http://www.forbes.com/sites/greatspeculations/2013/06/17/nokia-faces-tough-choices-as-siemens-shops-around-nsn/. Reproduced by permission of Trefis. www.trefis.com.

MANAGING THE PARADOX OF REVOLUTION AND EVOLUTION

Slow and steady wins the race.
The Hare and the Tortoise, Aesop (c. 620–560 BC); Greek writer

So, how should managers align their organizations? Should managers strive to align abruptly, by emphasizing radical, comprehensive and dramatic changes? Or should they try to align in a more continuous fashion by learning and adaptation? How can strategists best manage the paradox of revolution and evolution (see Table 8.1)?

No consensus has yet been developed within the field of strategic management on how to balance revolution and evolution. In the end, strategic managers have to make up their mind, taking into consideration their specific situation. Fortunately, some researchers have brought forward their view on how to manage the paradox of revolution and evolution. The starting point is the set of arguments put forward in the taxonomy in the first chapter.

Navigating

Strategizing managers have to deal with technological developments, political changes, economic crises and competitive moves, to mention just a few, that differ in their pace and magnitude. Over the long term, the pattern of environmental change is episodic. Periods of relative stability are interrupted by short and dramatic periods of instability, a pattern of development that has been recognized in a variety of other sciences as well (Gersick,

TABLE 8.1 Discontinuous alignment versus continuous alignment perspective

	Discontinuous alignment perspective	Continuous alignment perspective
Emphasis on	Revolution over evolution	Evolution over revolution
Strategic alignment as	Disruptive turnaround	Uninterrupted improvement
Magnitude of change	Radical, comprehensive and dramatic	Moderate, piecemeal and undramatic
Pace of change	Abrupt, unsteady and intermittent	Gradual, steady and constant
Lasting alignment requires	Sudden break with status quo	Permanent learning and flexibility
Reaction to external jolts	Shock therapy	Continuous adjustment
View of organizational crises	Under pressure things becomes fluid	In the cold everything freezes
Long-term alignment dynamics	Stable and unstable states alternate	Persistent transient state
Long-term alignment pattern	Punctuated equilibrium	Gradual development

1991). Following the natural historians Eldredge and Gould, this pattern is often called 'punctuated equilibrium' – stability punctuated by episodes in which many changes take place simultaneously (Tushman and O'Reilly, 1996, Reading 8.3).

When the environment is in flux, organizations must align. Therefore strategizing managers must possess a variety of options in dealing with environmental change. In periods of relative stability, gradual change is the appropriate alignment pattern, while during discontinuous change more drastic measures are needed (Greiner, 1972). Although the strategic alignment process does not precisely mirror environmental developments, it somehow relates to the pace and magnitude of change. Often with a delay and sometimes overly reacting, strategists aim at catching up with the long-term development of the environment.

Management scholars have been looking into this long-term alignment process (Tushman, Newman and Romanelli, 1986; Anderson and Tushman, 1990; Tushman and O'Reilly, 1996). They argue that to be successful during periods of relative stability, the emphasis should be on evolutionary adaptation to the always changing demands in the market. But during discontinuous changes, firms also need to be able to be revolutionary, adapting to whatever external change comes their way. In other words, comparable with a captain of a ship strategists need to navigate the company during sunny weather and occasionally through stormy waters, with one hand on the wheel and one on the throttle.

STRATEGIC CHANGE IN INTERNATIONAL PERSPECTIVE

Co-author: Gep Eisenloeffel

Wisdom lies neither in fixity nor in change, but in the dialectic between the two.
Octavio Paz (1914–1998); Mexican poet and essayist

Authors from different countries, as well as from similar ones, exhibit divergent perspectives on how to deal with the paradox of revolution and evolution. Why do firms in different countries prefer such significantly different approaches to strategic change?

Which factors determine the existence of national strategic change styles? Answers to these questions might assist in defining the most appropriate context for revolutionary change, as opposed to circumstances in which evolutionary change would be more fitting. Understanding international dissimilarities and their roots would clarify whether firms in different countries can borrow practices from one another or are limited by their national context.

As a stimulus to the international dimension in this debate, an overview will be given of the country characteristics mentioned in the literature as the major influencers on how the paradox of revolution and evolution is dealt with in different national settings. It should be noted, however, that cross-cultural research on this topic has not been extensive. Therefore, the propositions brought forward here should be viewed as tentative explanations, intended to encourage further discussion and research.

Prevalence of mechanistic organizations

In Chapter 7, the international differences in organizing work were briefly discussed. It was argued that in some countries the machine bureaucracy is a particularly dominant form of organization, while in other countries organizations can be characterized as more organic. The machine bureaucracy that is more predominant in English-speaking countries and France, is characterized by clear hierarchical authority relationships, strict differentiation of tasks, and highly formalized communication, reporting, budgeting, planning and decision-making processes. In such organizations, there is a relatively clear line separating the officers (management) from the troops, and internal relationships are depersonalized and calculative. In more organic forms of organization, management and production activities are not strictly separated, leading to less emphasis on top-down decision-making, and more on bottom-up initiatives. Job descriptions are less strictly defined and control systems are less sophisticated. Integration within the organization is not achieved by these formal systems, but by extensive informal communication and consultation, both horizontally and vertically, and by a strong common set of beliefs and a shared corporate vision. Internal relationships are based on trust, cooperation and a sense of community, leading Ouchi (1981) to call such organizations 'clans'. This type of organization is more prevalent in Japan, and to a lesser extent in, for example, Germany, the Netherlands and the Nordic countries.

Various researchers have suggested that machine bureaucracies exhibit a high level of inertia (e.g. Kanter, 1989; Mintzberg, 1994). Once formal systems have been created, they become difficult to change. As soon as particular tasks are specified and assigned to a person or group, it becomes their turf, while all else is 'not their business'. Once created, hierarchical positions, giving status and power, are not easily abolished. The consequence, it is argued, is that machine bureaucracies are inherently more resistant to change than clan-like organizations (Kagono *et al.*, 1985). Therefore, revolution is usually the potent mode of change needed to make any significant alterations. It can be expected that in countries where organizations are more strongly mechanistic, the preference for the discontinuous alignment perspective will be more pronounced.

Clan-like organizations, on the other hand, are characterized by a strong capacity for self-organization – the ability to exhibit organized behaviour without a boss being in control (Nonaka, 1988; Stacey, 1993, Reading 11.2). They are better at fluidly and spontaneously reorganizing around new issues because of a lack of rigid structure, the close links between management and production tasks, the high level of group-oriented information-sharing and consensual decision-making, and the strong commitment of individuals to the organization, and vice versa. In countries where organizations are more organic in this way, a stronger preference for continuous alignment can be expected. This issue will be discussed at greater length in Chapter 11.

Position of employees

This second factor is linked to the first. A mechanistic organization, it could be said, is a system into which groups of people have been brought, while an organic organization is a group of people into which some system has been brought. In a machine bureaucracy, people are human resources *for* the organization, while in a clan, people *are* the organization. These two conceptions of organization represent radically different views on the position and roles of employees within organizations.

In mechanistic organizations, employees are seen as valuable, yet expendable resources utilized by the organization. Salaries are determined by prices on the labour market and the value added by the individual employee. In the contractual relationship between employer and employee, it is a shrewd bargaining tactic for employers to minimize their dependence on employees. Organizational learning should, therefore, be captured in formalized systems and procedures, to avoid the irreplaceability of their people. Employees, on the other hand, will strive to make themselves indispensable for the organization, for instance by not sharing their learning. Furthermore, calculating employees will not tie themselves too strongly to the organization, but will keep their options open to job-hop to a better-paying employer. None of these factors contribute to the long-term commitment and receptiveness for ambiguity and uncertainty needed for continuous alignment.

In clan-like organizations the tolerance for ambiguity and uncertainty is higher, because employees' positions within the organization are more secure. Information is more readily shared, as it does not need to be used as a bargaining chip and acceptance within the group demands being a team player. Employers can invest in people instead of systems, since employees are committed and loyal to the organization. These better-trained people can consequently be given more decision-making power and more responsibility to organize their own work to fit with changing circumstances. Therefore, clan-like organizations, with their emphasis on employees as permanent co-producers, instead of temporary contractors, are more conducive to evolutionary change.

A number of factors have been brought forward to explain these international differences in the structuring of work and the position of employees. Some authors emphasize cultural aspects, particularly the level of individualism. It is argued that the mechanistic-organic distinction largely coincides with the individualism-collectivism division (e.g. Ouchi, 1981; Pascale and Athos, 1981). In this view, machine bureaucracies are the logical response to calculative individuals, while clans are more predominant in group-oriented cultures. Other authors point to international differences in labour markets (e.g. Kagono *et al.,* 1985; Calori, Valla and De Woot, 1994). High mobility of personnel is thought to coincide with the existence of mechanistic organizations, while low mobility (e.g. life time employment) fits with organic forms. Yet others suggest that the abundance of skilled workers is important. Machine bureaucracies are suited to deal with narrowly trained individuals, requiring extensive supervision. Clan-like organizations, however, need skilled, self-managing workers, who can handle a wide variety of tasks with relative autonomy. Kogut (1993: 11) reports that the level of workers within a country with these qualifications 'has been found to rest significantly upon the quality of education, the existence of programmes of apprenticeship and worker qualifications, and the elimination of occupational distinctions'.

Role of top management

Various researchers have observed important international differences in leadership styles and the role of top management. In some countries, top management is considered the 'central processing unit' of the company, making the key decisions and commanding the behaviour of the rest of the organizational machine. Visible top-down leadership is the norm, and therefore, strategic change is viewed as a top management responsibility (e.g. Hambrick and Mason, 1984; Hitt *et al.,* 1997). Strategic changes are formulated by top managers and then implemented at lower levels. Top managers are given significant power and discretion to develop bold new initiatives and to overcome organizational resistance to change. If organizational advances are judged to be insufficient or if an organization ends up in a crisis situation, a change of top management is often considered to be necessary measure to transform or turn around the company (e.g. Boeker, 1992; Fredrickson, Hambrick and Baumrin, 1988). In nations where people exhibit a strong preference for this commander type of leadership, an inclination towards the discontinuous alignment perspective can be expected.

In other countries, top managers are viewed as the captains of the team and leadership is less direct and less visible (e.g. Kagono *et al.,* 1985; Hofstede, 1993, Reading 1.3). The role of top managers is to facilitate change among the members of the group. Change comes from within the body of the organization, instead of being imposed upon it by top management. Therefore, change under this type of leadership will usually be more evolutionary than revolutionary. In nations where people exhibit a strong preference for this servant type of leadership, an inclination towards the continuous alignment perspective is more likely.

Time orientation

At the end of Chapter 7, a distinction was made between cultures that are more oriented towards the past, the present and the future. Obviously, it can be expected that cultural inclination to either past or present will perceive change to be much less favourable than future-oriented cultures. Among these future-minded cultures, a further division can be made between those with a long-term and a short-term orientation.

Various researchers have argued that short-term oriented cultures exhibit a much stronger preference for fast, radical change than cultures with a longer time horizon. In short-term oriented cultures, such as most English-speaking countries, there are significant pressures for rapid results, which predispose managers towards revolutionary change. Especially sensitivity to stock prices is often cited as a major factor encouraging firms to focus on short spurts of massive change and pay much less attention to efforts and investments with undramatic long-term benefits. Other contributing factors include short-term oriented bonus systems, stock option plans and frequent job-hopping (e.g. Calori, Valla and De Woot, 1994; Kagono *et al.,* 1985).

In long-term oriented cultures, such as Japan, China and South Korea, there is far less pressure to achieve short-term results. There is broad awareness that firms are running a competitive marathon and that a high, yet steady, pace of motion is needed. Generally, more emphasis is placed on facilitating long-term change processes, instead of intermittently shifting between one short-term change to another. Frequently mentioned factors contributing to this long-term orientation include long-term employment relationships, the lack of short-term bonus systems, and most importantly, the accent on growth as opposed to profit, as firms' prime objective (e.g. Abegglen and Stalk, 1985; Hitt *et al.,* 1997). This topic is discussed at length in Chapter 3.

INTRODUCTION TO THE READINGS

No great thing is created suddenly, any more than a bunch of grapes or a fig. If you tell me that you desire a fig, I answer that there must be time. Let it first blossom, then bear fruit, then ripen.
Epictetus (c. 60–120); Roman philosopher

As an input to the process of assessing the variety of perspectives on this issue, three readings have been selected that each can help readers to make up their own minds. Again, the first two readings will be representative of the two poles in this debate, while the third reading will highlight arguments to find a balance between the opposing demands.

As the opening reading, Michael Hammer's 'Reengineering Work: Don't Automate, Obliterate' has been selected to represent the discontinuous alignment perspective. This paper was published in *Harvard Business Review* in 1990 and was followed in 1993 by the highly influential book *Reengineering the Corporation: A Manifesto for Business Revolution,* that Hammer co-authored with James Champy. In this article, Hammer explains the concept of reengineering in much the same way as in the best-selling book. 'At the heart of reengineering,' he writes, 'is the notion of discontinuous thinking – of recognizing and breaking away from the outdated rules and fundamental assumptions that underlie operations.' In his view, radically redesigning business processes 'cannot be planned meticulously and accomplished in small and cautious steps. It's an all-or-nothing proposition with an uncertain result.' He exhorts managers to 'think big', by setting high goals, taking bold steps and daring to accept a high risk. In short, he preaches business revolution, and the tone of his article is truly that of a manifesto – impassioned, fervent, with here and there 'a touch of fanaticism'.

The second reading, 'Building Learning Organizations' by Peter Senge has been selected to represent the continuous alignment perspective. This reading summarizes many of the major points of Senge's (1990b) acclaimed book *The Fifth Discipline: The Art and Practice of the Learning Organization.* In his view, leaders must facilitate organizational learning – leaders 'are responsible for building organizations where people are continually expanding their capabilities to shape their future'. Creating organizations that want to adapt, learn and evolve means avoiding the traditional sources of inertia. Senge believes that one of the keys to continuous learning is motivation. He suggests that the drive to learn can best be stimulated by establishing a creative tension between the current reality and a compelling vision of the future. But, Senge points out, creating a shared vision and designing the organization in a way that enables learning, instead of impeding it, are clearly leadership tasks. In his opinion, leaders are needed to perform these important formative tasks, as well as to act as organizational teachers. A teacher is not someone with all the right answers, but a leader who can ask challenging questions and can shake up existing cognitive maps. Together, these 'new tasks' of leaders give them plenty of scope to influence the future direction of the firm, while at the same time leaving enough room for organizational members to also contribute to the organization's continuous alignment process.

The articles by Hammer and Senge on the fundamentals of revolution and evolution will be pursued by the third reading, describing how to manage the paradox of revolution and evolution: 'Ambidextrous Organizations: Managing Evolutionary and Revolutionary Change' by Michael Tushman and Charles O'Reilly (1996). While Hammer presents revolution as the radical measure needed to break the shackles of antiquated business models, it is unclear what the corporation must do after it is re-engineered. Tushman and

O'Reilly look beyond a single episode of revolution, to the longer-term pattern of development. In their view, short periods of revolutionary change are usually followed by longer periods of gradual change, similar to the pattern found in nature, which scientists have dubbed 'punctuated equilibrium'. They argue that during periods of relative stability, firms need to commit themselves to a certain strategy, structure and culture, to create a strong fit with the environment, with an emphasis on evolutionary adaptation to the ever changing demands in the market. But as soon as discontinuous changes happen in the environment, firms need to be able to be revolutionary as well. Hence they conclude that the paradox of revolution and evolution needs to be managed by being ambidextrous, i.e. being able to do both, sometimes sequentially, sometimes even at the same time. This can be achieved by stimulating internal diversity, allowing different strategies, structures and cultures to blossom side-by-side, making a firm more robust in adapting to whatever external change comes its way.

READING 8.1

Reengineering work: Don't automate, obliterate

By Michael Hammer[1]

Despite a decade or more of restructuring and downsizing, many US companies are still unprepared to operate in the 1990s. In a time of rapidly changing technologies and ever-shorter product life cycles, product development often proceeds at a glacial pace. In an age of the customer, order fulfilment has high error rates and customer enquiries go unanswered for weeks. In a period when asset utilization is critical, inventory levels exceed many months of demand.

The usual methods for boosting performance – process rationalization and automation – haven't yielded the dramatic improvements companies need. In particular, heavy investments in information technology have delivered disappointing results – largely because companies tend to use technology to mechanize old ways of doing business. They leave the existing processes intact and use computers simply to speed them up.

But speeding up those processes cannot address their fundamental performance deficiencies. Many of our job designs, workflows, control mechanisms and organizational structures came of age in a different competitive environment and before the advent of the computer. They are geared toward efficiency and control. Yet the watchwords of the new decade are innovation and speed, service and quality.

It is time to stop paving the cow paths. Instead of embedding outdated processes in silicon and software, we should obliterate them and start over. We should 'reengineer' our businesses: use the power of modern information technology to radically redesign our business processes in order to achieve dramatic improvements in their performance.

Every company operates according to a great many unarticulated rules. 'Credit decisions are made by the credit department.' 'Local inventory is needed for good customer service.' 'Forms must be filled in completely and in order.' Reengineering strives to break away from the old rules about how we organize and conduct business. It involves recognizing and rejecting some of them and then finding imaginative new ways to accomplish work. From our redesigned processes, new rules will emerge that fit the times. Only

then can we hope to achieve quantum leaps in performance.

Reengineering cannot be planned meticulously and accomplished in small and cautious steps. It's an all-or-nothing proposition with an uncertain result. Still, most companies have no choice but to muster the courage to do it. For many, reengineering is the only hope for breaking away from the antiquated processes that threaten to drag them down. Fortunately, managers are not without help. Enough businesses have successfully reengineered their processes to provide some rules of thumb for others.

What Ford and MBL did

Japanese competitors and young entrepreneurial ventures prove every day that drastically better levels of process performance are possible. They develop products twice as fast, utilize assets eight times more productively and respond to customers ten times faster. Some large, established companies also show what can be done. Businesses like Ford Motor Company and Mutual Benefit Life Insurance have reengineered their processes and achieved competitive leadership as a result. Ford has reengineered its accounts payable processes, and Mutual Benefit Life its processing of applications for insurance.

In the early 1980s, when the American automotive industry was in a depression, Ford's top management put accounts payable – along with many other departments – under the microscope in search of ways to cut costs. Accounts payable in North America alone employed more than 500 people. Management thought that by rationalizing processes and installing new computer systems, it could reduce the head count by some 20 per cent.

Ford was enthusiastic about its plan to tighten accounts payable – until it looked at Mazda. While Ford was aspiring to a 400-person department, Mazda's accounts payable organization consisted of a total of five people. The difference in absolute numbers was astounding, and even after adjusting for Mazda's smaller size, Ford figured that its accounts payable organization was five times the size it should be. The Ford team knew better than to attribute the discrepancy to callisthenics, company songs, or low interest rates.

Ford managers ratcheted up their goal: accounts payable would perform with not just a hundred but many hundreds fewer clerks. It then set out to achieve it. First, managers analysed the existing system. When Ford's purchasing department wrote a purchase order, it sent a copy to accounts payable. Later, when material control received the goods, it sent a copy of the receiving document to accounts payable. Meanwhile, the vendor sent an invoice to accounts payable. It was up to accounts payable, then, to match the purchase order against the receiving document and the invoice. If they matched, the department issued payment.

The department spent most of its time on mismatches, instances where the purchase order, receiving document and invoice disagreed. In these cases, an accounts payable clerk would investigate the discrepancy, hold up payment, generate documents, and all-in-all gum up the works.

One way to improve things might have been to help the accounts payable clerk investigate more efficiently, but a better choice was to prevent the mismatches in the first place. To this end, Ford instituted 'invoiceless processing'. Now when the purchasing department initiates an order, it enters the information into an online database. It doesn't send a copy of the purchase order to anyone. When the goods arrive at the receiving dock, the receiving clerk checks the database to see if they correspond to an outstanding purchase order. If so, he or she accepts them and enters the transaction into the computer system. (If receiving can't find a database entry for the received goods, it simply returns the order.)

Under the old procedures, the accounting department had to match 14 data items between the receipt record, the purchase order and the invoice before it could issue payment to the vendor. The new approach requires matching only three items – part number, unit of measure and supplier code – between the purchase order and the receipt record. The matching is done automatically, and the computer prepares the check, which accounts payable sends to the vendor. There are no invoices to worry about since Ford has asked its vendors not to send them.

Ford didn't settle for the modest increases it first envisioned. It opted for radical change – and achieved dramatic improvement. Where it has instituted this new process, Ford has achieved a 75 per cent reduction in head count, not the 20 per cent it would have gotten with a conventional programme. And since there are no discrepancies between the financial record and the physical record, material control is simpler and financial information is more accurate.

Mutual Benefit Life, the country's eighteenth largest life carrier, has reengineered its processing of insurance applications. Prior to this, MBL handled customers' applications much as its competitors did. The long, multistep process involved credit checking, quoting, rating, underwriting and so on. An application would have to go through as many as 30 discrete steps, spanning five departments and involving 19 people. At the very best, MBL could process an application in 24 hours, but more typical turnarounds ranged from five to 25 days – most of the time spent passing information from one department to the next. (Another insurer estimated that while an application spent 22 days in process, it was actually worked on for just 17 minutes.)

MBL's rigid, sequential process led to many complications. For instance, when a customer wanted to cash in an existing policy and purchase a new one, the old business department first had to authorize the treasury department to issue a check made payable to MBL. The check would then accompany the paperwork to the new business department.

The president of MBL, intent on improving customer service, decided that this nonsense had to stop and demanded a 60 per cent improvement in productivity. It was clear that such an ambitious goal would require more than tinkering with the existing process. Strong measures were in order, and the management team assigned to the task looked to technology as a means of achieving them. The team realized that shared databases and computer networks could make many different kinds of information available to a single person, while expert systems could help people with limited experience make sound decisions. Applying these insights led to a new approach to the application-handling process, one with wide organizational implications and little resemblance to the old way of doing business.

MBL swept away existing job definitions and departmental boundaries and created a new position called a case manager. Case managers have total responsibility for an application from the time it is received to the time a policy is issued. Unlike clerks, who performed a fixed task repeatedly under the watchful gaze of a supervisor, case managers work autonomously. No more hand-offs of files and responsibility, no more shuffling of customer enquiries.

Case managers are able to perform all the tasks associated with an insurance application because they are supported by powerful PC-based workstations that run an expert system and connect to a range of automated systems on a mainframe. In particularly tough cases, the case manager calls for assistance from a senior underwriter or physician, but these specialists work only as consultants and advisers to the case manager, who never relinquishes control.

Empowering individuals to process entire applications has had a tremendous impact on operations. MBL can now complete an application in as little as four hours, and average turnaround takes only two to five days. The company has eliminated 100 field office positions, and case managers can handle more than twice the volume of new applications the company previously could process.

The essence of reengineering

At the heart of reengineering is the notion of discontinuous thinking – of recognizing and breaking away from the outdated rules and fundamental assumptions that underlie operations. Unless we change these rules, we are merely rearranging the deckchairs on the *Titanic*. We cannot achieve breakthroughs in performance by cutting fat or automating existing processes. Rather, we must challenge old assumptions and shed the old rules that made the business underperform in the first place.

Every business is replete with implicit rules left over from earlier decades. 'Customers don't repair their own equipment.' 'Local warehouses are necessary for good service.' 'Merchandising decisions are made at headquarters.' These rules of work design are based on assumptions about technology, people and organizational goals that no longer hold. The contemporary repertoire of available information technologies is vast and quickly expanding. Quality, innovation and service are now more important than cost, growth and control. A large portion of the population is educated and capable of assuming responsibility, and workers cherish their autonomy and expect to have a say in how the business is run.

It should come as no surprise that our business processes and structures are outmoded and obsolete: our work structures and processes have not kept pace with the changes in technology, demographics and business objectives. For the most part, we have organized work as a sequence of separate tasks and employed complex mechanisms to track its progress.

This arrangement can be traced to the Industrial Revolution, when specialization of labour and economies of scale promised to overcome the inefficiencies of cottage industries. Businesses disaggregated work into narrowly defined tasks, reaggregated the people performing those tasks into departments, and installed managers to administer them.

Our elaborate systems for imposing control and discipline on those who actually do the work stem from the post-war period. In that halcyon period of expansion, the main concern was growing fast without going broke, so businesses focused on cost, growth and control. And since literate, entry-level people were abundant but well-educated professionals hard to come by, the control systems funnelled information up the hierarchy to the few who presumably knew what to do with it.

These patterns of organizing work have become so ingrained that, despite their serious drawbacks, it's hard to conceive of work being accomplished any other way. Conventional process structures are fragmented and piecemeal, and they lack the integration necessary to maintain quality and service. They are breeding grounds for tunnel vision, as people tend to substitute the narrow goals of their particular department for the larger goals of the process as a whole. When work is handed off from person to person and unit to unit, delays and errors are inevitable. Accountability blurs, and critical issues fall between the cracks. Moreover, no one sees enough of the big picture to be able to respond quickly to new situations. Managers desperately try, like all the king's horses and all the king's men, to piece together the fragmented pieces of business processes.

Managers have tried to adapt their processes to new circumstances, but usually in ways that just create more problems. If, say, customer service is poor, they create a mechanism to deliver service but overlay it on the existing organization. Bureaucracy thickens, costs rise and enterprising competitors gain market share.

In reengineering, managers break loose from outmoded business processes and the design principles underlying them and create new ones. Ford had operated under the old rule that 'we pay when we receive the invoice.' While no one had ever articulated or recorded it, that rule determined how the accounts payable process was organized. Ford's reengineering effort challenged and ultimately replaced the rule with a new one: 'We pay when we receive the goods.'

Reengineering requires looking at the fundamental processes of the business from a cross-functional perspective. Ford discovered that reengineering only the accounts payable department was futile. The appropriate focus of the effort was what might be called the goods acquisition process, which included purchasing and receiving as well as accounts payable.

One way to ensure that reengineering has a cross-functional perspective is to assemble a team that represents the functional units involved in the process being reengineered and all the units that depend on it. The team must analyse and scrutinize the existing process until it really understands what the process is trying to accomplish. The point is not to learn what happens to form 73B in its peregrinations through the company but to understand the purpose of having form 73B in the first place. Rather than looking for opportunities to improve the current process, the team should determine which of its steps really add value and search for new ways to achieve the result.

The reengineering team must keep asking Why? and What if? Why do we need to get a manager's signature on a requisition? Is it a control mechanism or a decision point? What if the manager reviews only requisitions above $500? What if he or she doesn't see them at all? Raising and resolving heretical questions can separate what is fundamental to the process from what is superficial. The regional offices of an East Coast insurance company had long produced a series of reports that they regularly sent to the home office. No one in the field realized that these reports were simply filed and never used. The process outlasted the circumstances that had created the need for it. The reengineering study team should push to discover situations like this.

In short, a reengineering effort strives for dramatic levels of improvement. It must break away from conventional wisdom and the constraints of organizational boundaries and should be broad and cross-functional in scope. It should use information technology not to automate an existing process but to enable a new one.

Principles of reengineering

Creating new rules tailored to the modern environment ultimately requires a new conceptualization of the business process – which comes down to someone having a great idea. But reengineering need not be haphazard. In fact, some of the principles that companies have already discovered while reengineering their business processes can help jump start the effort for others.

Organize around outcomes, not tasks

This principle says to have one person perform all the steps in a process. Design that person's job around an objective or outcome instead of a single task. The redesign at Mutual Benefit Life, where individual case managers perform the entire application approval process, is the quintessential example of this.

The redesign of an electronics company is another example. It had separate organizations performing each of the five steps between selling and installing the equipment. One group determined customer requirements, another translated those requirements into internal product codes, a third conveyed that information to various plants and warehouses, a fourth received and assembled the components and a fifth delivered and installed the equipment. The process was based on the centuries-old notion of specialized labour and on the limitations inherent in paper files. The departments each possessed a specific set of skills, and only one department at a time could do its work.

The customer order moved systematically from step to step. But this sequential processing caused problems. The people getting the information from the customer in step one had to get all the data anyone would need throughout the process, even if it wasn't needed until step five. In addition, the many hand-offs were responsible for numerous errors and misunderstandings. Finally, any questions about customer requirements that arose late in the process had to be referred back to the people doing step one, resulting in delay and rework.

When the company reengineered, it eliminated the assembly-line approach. It compressed responsibility for the various steps and assigned it to one person, the 'customer service representative'. That person now oversees the whole process – taking the order, translating it into product codes, getting the components assembled, and seeing the product delivered and installed. The customer service rep expedites and coordinates the process, much like a general contractor. And the customer has just one contact, who always knows the status of the order.

Have those who use the output of the process perform the process

In an effort to capitalize on the benefits of specialization and scale, many organizations established specialized departments to handle specialized processes. Each department does only one type of work and is a 'customer' of other groups' processes. Accounting does only accounting. If it needs new pencils, it goes to the purchasing department, the group specially equipped with the information and expertise to perform that role. Purchasing finds vendors, negotiates price, places the order, inspects the goods and pays the invoice – and eventually the accountants get their pencils.

The process works (after a fashion), but it's slow and bureaucratic.

Now that computer-based data and expertise are more readily available, departments, units and individuals can do more for themselves. Opportunities exist to re-engineer processes so that the individuals who need the result of a process can do it themselves. For example, by using expert systems and databases, departments can make their own purchases without sacrificing the benefits of specialized purchasers. One manufacturer has re-engineered its purchasing process along just these lines. The company's old system, whereby the operating departments submitted requisitions and let purchasing do the rest, worked well for controlling expensive and important items like raw materials and capital equipment. But for inexpensive and non-strategic purchases, which constituted some 35 per cent of total orders, the system was slow and cumbersome; it was not uncommon for the cost of the purchasing process to exceed the cost of the goods being purchased.

The new process compresses the purchase of sundry items and pushes it on to the customers of the process. Using a database of approved vendors, an operating unit can directly place an order with a vendor and charge it on a bank credit card. At the end of the month, the bank gives the manufacturer a tape of all credit card transactions, which the company runs against its internal accounting system.

When an electronics equipment manufacturer re-engineered its field service process, it pushed some of the steps of the process on to its customers. The manufacturer's field service had been plagued by the usual problems: technicians were often unable to do a particular repair because the right part wasn't on the van, response to customer calls was slow, and spare parts inventory was excessive.

Now customers make simple repairs themselves. Spare parts are stored at each customer's site and managed through a computerized inventory management system. When a problem arises, the customer calls the manufacturer's field-service hot line and describes the symptoms to a diagnostician, who accesses a diagnosis support system. If the problem appears to be something the customer can fix, the diagnostician tells the customer what part to replace and how to install it. The old part is picked up and a new part left in its place at a later time. Only for complex problems is a service technician dispatched to the site, this time without having to make a stop at the warehouse to pick up parts.

When the people closest to the process perform it, there is little need for the overhead associated with managing it. Interfaces and liaisons can be eliminated, as can the mechanisms used to coordinate those who perform the process with those who use it. Moreover, the problem of capacity planning for the process performers is greatly reduced.

Subsume information-processing work into the real work that produces the information

The previous two principles compress linear processes. This principle suggests moving work from one person or department to another. Why doesn't an organization that produces information also process it? In the past, people didn't have the time or weren't trusted to do both. Most companies established units to do nothing but collect and process information that other departments created. This arrangement reflects the old rule about specialized labour and the belief that people at lower organizational levels are incapable of acting on information they generate. An accounts payable department collects information from purchasing and receiving and reconciles it with data that the vendor provides. Quality assurance gathers and analyses information it gets from production.

Ford's redesigned accounts payable process embodies the new rule. With the new system, receiving, which produces the information about the goods received, processes this information instead of sending it to accounts payable. The new computer system can easily compare the delivery with the order and trigger the appropriate action.

Treat geographically dispersed resources as though they were centralized

The conflict between centralization and decentralization is a classic one. Decentralizing a resource (whether people, equipment, or inventory) gives better service to those who use it, but at the cost of redundancy, bureaucracy and missed economies of scale. Companies no longer have to make such trade-offs. They can use databases, telecommunications networks and standardized processing systems to get the benefits of scale and coordination while maintaining the benefits of flexibility and service.

At Hewlett-Packard, for instance, each of the more than 50 manufacturing units had its own separate purchasing department. While this arrangement provided excellent responsiveness and service to the plants, it prevented H-P from realizing the benefits of its scale, particularly with regard to quantity discounts. H-P's solution was to maintain the divisional purchasing organizations and to introduce a corporate unit to co-ordinate them. Each purchasing unit has access to a shared database on vendors and their performance and issues its own purchase orders. Corporate purchasing maintains this database and uses it to negotiate contracts for the corporation and to monitor the units. The payoffs have come in a 150 per cent improvement in on-time deliveries, 50 per cent reduction in lead times, 75 per cent reduction in failure rates, and a significantly lower cost of goods purchased.

Link parallel activities instead of integrating their results

H-P's decentralized purchasing operations represent one kind of parallel processing in which separate units perform the same function. Another common kind of parallel processing is when separate units perform different activities that must eventually come together. Product development typically operates this way. In the development of a photocopier, for example, independent units develop the various subsystems of the copier. One group works on the optics, another on the mechanical paper-handling device, another on the power supply, and so on. Having people do development work simultaneously saves time, but at the dreaded integration and testing phase, the pieces often fail to work together. Then the costly redesign begins.

Or consider a bank that sells different kinds of credit – loans, letters of credit, asset-based financing – through separate units. These groups may have no way of knowing whether another group has already extended credit to a particular customer. Each unit could extend the full $10 million credit limit.

The new principle says to forge links between parallel functions and to coordinate them while their activities are in process rather than after they are completed. Communications networks, shared databases and teleconferencing can bring the independent groups together so that coordination is ongoing. One large electronics company has cut its product development cycle by more than 50 per cent by implementing this principle.

Put the decision point where the work is performed and build control into the process

In most organizations, those who do the work are distinguished from those who monitor the work and make decisions about it. The tacit assumption is that the people actually doing the work have neither the time nor the inclination to monitor and control it and that they lack the knowledge and scope to make decisions about it. The entire hierarchical management structure is built on this assumption. Accountants, auditors and supervisors check, record and monitor work. Managers handle any exceptions.

The new principle suggests that the people who do the work should make the decisions and that the process itself can have built-in controls. Pyramidal management layers can therefore be compressed and the organization flattened.

Information technology can capture and process data, and expert systems can to some extent supply knowledge, enabling people to make their own decisions. As the doers become self-managing and self-controlling, hierarchy – and the slowness and bureaucracy associated with it – disappears.

When Mutual Benefit Life reengineered the insurance application process, it not only compressed the linear sequence but also eliminated the need for layers of managers. These two kinds of compression – vertical and horizontal – often go together; the very fact that a worker sees only one piece of the process calls for a manager with a broader vision. The case managers at MBL provide end-to-end management of the process, reducing the need for traditional managers. The managerial role is changing from one of controller and supervisor to one of supporter and facilitator.

Capture information once and at the source

This last rule is simple. When information was difficult to transmit, it made sense to collect information repeatedly. Each person, department or unit had its own requirements and forms. Companies simply had to live with the associated delays, entry errors and costly overhead. But why do we have to live with those problems now? Today when we collect a piece of information, we can store it in an online database for all who need it. Bar coding, relational databases and electronic data interchange (EDI) make it easy to collect, store and transmit information. One insurance company found that its application review process required that certain items be entered into 'stovepipe' computer systems supporting different functions as many as five times. By integrating and connecting these systems, the company was able to eliminate this redundant data entry along with the attendant checking functions and inevitable errors.

Think big

Reengineering triggers changes of many kinds, not just of the business process itself. Job designs, organizational structures, management systems – anything associated with the process must be refashioned in an integrated way. In other words, reengineering is a tremendous effort that mandates change in many areas of the organization.

When Ford reengineered its payables, receiving clerks on the dock had to learn to use computer terminals to check shipments, and they had to make decisions about whether to accept the goods. Purchasing agents also had to assume new responsibilities – like making sure the purchase orders they entered into the database had the correct information about where to send the check. Attitudes toward vendors also had to change: vendors could no longer be seen as adversaries; they had to become partners in a shared business process. Vendors too had to adjust. In many cases, invoices formed the basis of their accounting systems. At least one Ford supplier adapted by continuing to print invoices, but instead of sending them to Ford threw them away, reconciling cash received against invoices never sent.

The changes at Mutual Benefit Life were also widespread. The company's job-rating scheme could not accommodate the case manager position, which had a lot of responsibility but no direct reports. MBL had to devise new job-rating schemes and compensation policies. It also had to develop a culture in which people doing work are perceived as more important than those supervising work. Career paths, recruitment and training programmes, promotion policies – these and many other management systems are being revised to support the new process design.

The extent of these changes suggests one factor that is necessary for reengineering to succeed: executive leadership with real vision. No one in an organization wants reengineering. It is confusing and disruptive and affects everything people have grown accustomed to. Only if top-level managers back the effort and outlast the company cynics will people take reengineering seriously. As one wag at an electronics equipment manufacturer has commented, 'Every few months, our senior managers find a new religion. One time it was quality, another it was customer service, another it was flattening the organization. We just hold our breath until they get over it and things get back to normal.' Commitment, consistency – maybe even a touch of fanaticism – are needed to enlist those who would prefer the status quo.

Considering the inertia of old processes and structures, the strain of implementing a reengineering plan can hardly be overestimated. But by the same token, it is hard to overestimate the opportunities, especially for established companies. Big, traditional organizations aren't necessarily dinosaurs doomed to extinction, but they are burdened with layers of unproductive overhead and armies of unproductive workers. Shedding them a layer at a time will not be good enough to stand up against sleek start-ups or streamlined Japanese companies. US companies need fast change and dramatic improvements.

We have the tools to do what we need to do. Information technology offers many options for reorganizing work. But our imaginations must guide our decisions about technology – not the other way around. We must have the boldness to imagine taking 78 days out of an 80-day turnaround time, cutting 75 per cent of overhead, and eliminating 80 per cent of errors. These are not unrealistic goals. If managers have the vision, reengineering will provide a way.

READING 8.2

Building learning organizations

By Peter Senge[1]

Over the past two years, business academics and senior managers have begun talking about the notion of the learning organization. Ray Stata of Ana-

log Devices put the idea succinctly in these pages last spring: 'The rate at which organizations learn may become the only substantial source of competitive

[1]Source: This article was reprinted with permission from Peter Senge (1990) 'The Leader's New Work: Building Learning Organizations', *Sloan Management Review*, Fall, 1990 pp.7–23. © 1990 from MIT Sloan Management Review/Massachusetts Institute of Technology. All rights reserved. Distributed by Tribune Media Services.

advantage.' And in late May of this year, at an MIT-sponsored conference entitled 'Transforming Organizations', two questions arose again and again: How can we build organizations in which continuous learning occurs, and what kind of person can best lead the learning organization? This article, based on Senge's (1990b) book, *The Fifth Discipline: The Art and Practice of the Learning Organization,* begins to chart this new territory, describing new roles, skills and tools for leaders who wish to develop learning organizations.

Human beings are designed for learning. No one has to teach an infant to walk, talk, or master the spatial relationships needed to stack eight building blocks that don't topple. Children come fully equipped with an insatiable drive to explore and experiment. Unfortunately, the primary institutions of our society are oriented predominantly toward controlling rather than learning, rewarding individuals for performing for others rather than for cultivating their natural curiosity and impulse to learn. The young child entering school discovers quickly that the name of the game is getting the right answer and avoiding mistakes – a mandate no less compelling to the aspiring manager.

'Our prevailing system of management has destroyed our people', writes W. Edwards Deming, leader in the quality movement. 'People are born with intrinsic motivation, self-esteem, dignity, curiosity to learn, joy in learning. The forces of destruction begin with toddlers – a prize for the best Halloween costume, grades in school, gold stars, and on up through university. On the job, people, teams, divisions are ranked – reward for the one at the top, punishment at the bottom. Management by Objectives (MBO), quotas, incentive pay, business plans, put together separately, division by division, cause further loss, unknown and unknowable.'

Ironically, by focusing on performing for someone else's approval, corporations create the very conditions that predestine them to mediocre performance. Over the long run, superior performance depends on superior learning.

If anything, the need for understanding how organizations learn and accelerating that learning is greater today than ever before. The old days when a Henry Ford, Alfred Sloan, or Tom Watson learned for the organization are gone. In an increasingly dynamic, interdependent and unpredictable world, it is simply no longer possible for anyone to 'figure it all out at the top'. The old model, 'the top thinks and the local acts', must now give way to integrating thinking and acting at all levels. While the challenge is great, so is the potential payoff.

Adaptive learning and generative learning

The prevailing view of learning organizations emphasizes increased adaptability. Given the accelerating pace of change, or so the standard view goes, 'the most successful corporation of the 1990s', according to *Fortune* magazine, 'will be something called a learning organization, a consummately adaptive enterprise'.

But increasing adaptiveness is only the first stage in moving toward learning organizations. The impulse to learn in children goes deeper than desires to respond and adapt more effectively to environmental change. The impulse to learn, at its heart, is an impulse to be generative, to expand our capability. This is why leading corporations are focusing on *generative* learning, which is about creating, as well as *adaptive* learning, which is about coping.

The total quality movement in Japan illustrates the evolution from adaptive to generative learning. With its emphasis on continuous experimentation and feedback, the total quality movement has been the first wave in building learning organizations. But Japanese firms' view of serving the customer has evolved. In the early years of total quality, the focus was on 'fitness to standard', making a product reliably so that it would do what its designers intended it to do and what the firm told its customers it would do. Then came a focus on 'fitness to need', understanding better what the customer wanted and then providing products that reliably met those needs. Today, leading-edge firms seek to understand and meet the 'latent need' of the customer – what customers might truly value but have never experienced or would never think to ask for.

Generative learning, unlike adaptive learning, requires new ways of looking at the world, whether in understanding customers or in understanding how to better manage a business. For years, US manufacturers sought competitive advantage in aggressive controls on inventories, incentives against overproduction, and rigid adherence to production forecasts. Despite these incentives, their performance was eventually eclipsed by Japanese firms who saw the challenges of manufacturing differently. They realized that eliminating delays in the production process was the key to reducing instability and improving cost, productivity and service. They worked to build networks of relationships with trusted suppliers and to redesign physical production processes to reduce delays in materials procurement, production setup and in-process inventory – a much higher-leverage approach to improving both cost and customer loyalty.

As Boston Consulting Group's George Stalk has observed (Stalk, Evans and Shulman, 1992), the Japanese saw the significance of delays because they saw the process of order entry, production scheduling, materials procurement, production and distribution as an integrated system. 'What distorts the system so badly is time', observes Stalk – the multiple delays between events and responses. 'These distortions reverberate throughout the system, producing disruptions, waste and inefficiency.' Generative learning requires seeing the systems that control events. When we fail to grasp the systemic source of problems, we are left to 'push on' symptoms rather than eliminate underlying causes. The best we can ever do is adaptive learning.

The leader's new work

Our traditional view of leaders – as special people who set the direction, make the key decisions and energize the troops – is deeply rooted in an individualistic and non-systemic worldview. Especially in the West, leaders are heroes – great men (and occasionally women) who rise to the fore in times of crisis. So long as such myths prevail, they reinforce a focus on short-term events and charismatic heroes rather than on systemic forces and collective learning.

Leadership in learning organizations centres on subtler and ultimately more important work. In a learning organization, leaders' roles differ dramatically from that of the charismatic decision maker. Leaders are designers, teachers and stewards. These roles require new skills: the ability to build shared vision, to bring to the surface and challenge prevailing mental models, and to foster more systemic patterns of thinking. In short, leaders in learning organizations are responsible for building organizations where people are continually expanding their capabilities to shape their future – that is, leaders are responsible for learning.

Creative tension: The integrating principle

Leadership in a learning organization starts with the principle of creative tension. Creative tension comes from seeing clearly where we want to be, our 'vision', and telling the truth about where we are, our 'current reality'. The gap between the two generates a natural tension.

Creative tension can be resolved in two basic ways: by raising current reality toward the vision, or by lowering the vision toward current reality. Individuals, groups and organizations who learn how to work with creative tension learn how to use the energy it generates to move reality more reliably toward their visions.

Without vision there is no creative tension. Creative tension cannot be generated from current reality alone. All the analysis in the world will never generate a vision. Many who are otherwise qualified to lead fail to do so because they try to substitute analysis for vision. They believe that, if only people understood current reality, they would surely feel the motivation to change. They are then disappointed to discover that people resist the personal and organizational changes that must be made to alter reality. What they never grasp is that the natural energy for changing reality comes from holding a picture of what might be that is more important to people than what is.

But creative tension cannot be generated from vision alone; it demands an accurate picture of current reality as well. Vision without an understanding of current reality will more likely foster cynicism than creativity. The principle of creative tension teaches that *an accurate picture of current reality is just as important as a compelling picture of a desired future.*

Leading through creative tension is different from solving problems. In problem solving, the energy for change comes from attempting to get away from an aspect of current reality that is undesirable. With creative tension, the energy for change comes from the vision, from what we want to create, juxtaposed with current reality. While the distinction may seem small, the consequences are not. Many people and organizations find themselves motivated to change only when their problems are bad enough to cause them to change. This works for a while, but the change process runs out of steam as soon as the problems driving the change become less pressing. With problem solving, the motivation for change is extrinsic. With creative tension, the motivation is intrinsic. The distinction mirrors the distinction between adaptive and generative learning.

New roles

The traditional authoritarian image of the leader as 'the boss calling the shots' has been recognized as oversimplified and inadequate for some time. According to Edgar Schein (1985), 'Leadership is intertwined with culture formation.' Building an organization's culture and shaping its evolution is the 'unique and essential function' of leadership. In a learning organization, the critical roles of leadership – designer, teacher and steward – have antecedents in the ways leaders have contributed to building organizations in the past. But each role takes on new meaning in the learning organization and, as will be seen in the following sections, demands new skills and tools.

Leader as designer

The functions of design, or what some have called social architecture, are rarely visible; they take place behind the scenes. The consequences that appear today are the result of work done long in the past, and work today will show its benefits far in the future. Those who aspire to lead out of a desire to control, gain fame, or simply to be at the centre of the action will find little to attract them to the quiet design work of leadership.

But what, specifically, is involved in organizational design? 'Organization design is widely misconstrued as moving around boxes and lines', says Hanover's O'Brien. 'The first task of organization design concerns designing the governing ideas of purpose, vision and core values by which people will live.' Few acts of leadership have a more enduring impact on an organization than building a foundation of purpose and core values.

If governing ideas constitute the first design task of leadership, the second design task involves the policies, strategies and structures that translate guiding ideas into business decisions. Leadership theorist Philip Selznick (1957) calls policy and structure the 'institutional embodiment of purpose.' 'Policy making (the rules that guide decisions) ought to be separated from decision making', says Jay Forrester. 'Otherwise, short-term pressures will usurp time from policy creation.'

Traditionally, writers like Selznick and Forrester have tended to see policy-making and implementation as the work of a small number of senior managers. But that view is changing. Both the dynamic business environment and the mandate of the learning organization to engage people at all levels now make it clear that this second design task is more subtle. Henry Mintzberg has argued that strategy is less a rational plan arrived at in the abstract and implemented throughout the organization than an 'emergent phenomenon'. Successful organizations 'craft strategy' according to Mintzberg, as they continually learn about shifting business conditions and balance what is desired and what is possible. The key is not getting the right strategy but fostering strategic thinking.

Behind appropriate policies, strategies and structures are effective learning processes; their creation is the third key design responsibility in learning organizations. This does not absolve senior managers of their strategic responsibilities. Actually, it deepens and extends those responsibilities. Now they are not only responsible for ensuring that an organization has well developed strategies and policies but also for ensuring that processes exist whereby these are continually improved.

In the early 1970s, Shell was the weakest of the big seven oil companies. Today, Shell and Exxon are arguably the strongest, both in size and financial health. Shell's ascendance began with frustration. Around 1971, members of Shell's Group Planning in London began to foresee dramatic change and unpredictability in world oil markets. However, it proved impossible to persuade managers that the stable world of steady growth in oil demand and supply they had known for 20 years was about to change. Despite brilliant analysis and artful presentation, Shell's planners realized, in the words of Pierre Wack (1985), that they 'had failed to change behaviour in much of the Shell organization'. Progress would probably have ended there, had the frustration not given way to a radically new view of corporate planning.

As they pondered this failure, the planners' view of their basic task shifted: 'We no longer saw our task as producing a documented view of the future business environment five or ten years ahead. Our real target was the microcosm (the "mental model") of our decision makers.' Only when the planners reconceptualized their basic task as fostering learning rather than devising plans did their insights begin to have an impact. The initial tool used was 'scenario analysis', through which planners encouraged operating managers to think through how they would manage in the future under different possible scenarios. It mattered not that the managers believed the planners' scenarios absolutely, only that they became engaged in ferreting out the implications. In this way, Shell's planners conditioned managers to be mentally prepared for a shift from low prices to high prices and from stability to instability. The results were significant. When the Organisation of Petroleum Exporting Countries (OPEC) became a reality, Shell quickly responded by increasing local operating company control (to enhance manoeuverability in the new political environment), building buffer stocks, and accelerating development of non-OPEC sources – actions that its competitors took much more slowly or not at all.

Somewhat inadvertently, Shell planners had discovered the leverage of designing institutional learning processes whereby, in the words of former planning director De Geus, 'Management teams change their shared mental models of their company, their markets, and their competitors.' Since then, 'planning as learning' has become a byword at Shell, and Group Planning has continually sought out new learning tools that can be integrated into the planning process. Some of these are described below.

Leader as teacher

Leader as teacher does *not* mean leader as authoritarian expert whose job it is to teach people the 'correct' view of reality. Rather, it is about helping everyone in the organization, oneself included, to gain more insightful views of current reality. This is in line with a popular emerging view of leaders as coaches, guides, or facilitators. In learning organizations, this teaching role is developed further by virtue of explicit attention to people's mental models and by the influence of the systems perspective.

The role of leader as teacher starts with bringing to the surface people's mental models of important issues. No one carries an organization, a market, or a state of technology in his or her head. What we carry in our heads are assumptions. These mental pictures of how the world works have a significant influence on how we perceive problems and opportunities, identify courses of action, and make choices.

One reason that mental models are so deeply entrenched is that they are largely tacit. Ian Mitroff, in his study of General Motors, argues that an assumption that prevailed for years was that, in the United States, 'Cars are status symbols. Styling is therefore more important than quality.' The Detroit automakers didn't say, 'We have a mental model that all people care about is styling.' Few actual managers would even say publicly that all people care about is styling. So long as the view remained unexpressed, there was little possibility of challenging its validity or forming more accurate assumptions.

But working with mental models goes beyond revealing hidden assumptions. Reality, as perceived by most people in most organizations, means pressures that must be borne, crises that must be reacted to, and limitations that must be accepted. Leaders as teachers help people *restructure their views of reality* to see beyond the superficial conditions and events into the underlying causes of problems, and therefore to see new possibilities for shaping the future.

Specifically, leaders can influence people to view reality at three distinct levels: events, patterns of behaviour, and systemic structure.

Systemic Structure (Generative)

↓

Patterns of Behaviour (Responsive)

↓

Events (Reactive)

The key question becomes 'Where do leaders predominantly focus their own and their organization's attention?'

Contemporary society focuses predominantly on events. The media reinforces this perspective, with almost exclusive attention to short-term, dramatic events. This focus leads naturally to explaining what happens in terms of those events: 'The Dow Jones average went up 16 points because high fourth-quarter profits were announced yesterday.'

Pattern-of-behaviour explanations are rarer in contemporary culture than event explanations, but they do occur. Trend analysis is an example of seeing patterns of behaviour. A good editorial that interprets a set of current events in the context of long-term historical changes is another example. Systemic, structural explanations go even further by addressing the question 'What causes the patterns of behaviour?'

In some sense, all three levels of explanation are equally true. But their usefulness is quite different. Event explanations – who did what to whom – doom their holders to a reactive stance toward change. Pattern-of-behaviour explanations focus on identifying long-term trends and assessing their implications. They at least suggest how, over time, we can respond to shifting conditions. Structural explanations are the most powerful. Only they address the underlying causes of behaviour at a level such that patterns of behaviour can be changed.

By and large, leaders of our current institutions focus their attention on events and patterns of behaviour, and under their influence, their organizations do likewise. That is why contemporary organizations are predominantly reactive, or at best responsive – rarely generative. On the other hand, leaders in learning organizations pay attention to all three levels, but focus especially on systemic structure; largely by example, they teach people throughout the organization to do likewise.

Leader as steward

This is the subtlest role of leadership. Unlike the roles of designer and teacher, it is almost solely a matter of attitude. It is an attitude critical to learning organizations.

While stewardship has long been recognized as an aspect of leadership, its source is still not widely understood. I believe Robert Greenleaf (1977) came closest to explaining real stewardship, in his seminal book *Servant Leadership*. There, Greenleaf argues that 'the servant leader *is* servant first … It begins with the natural feeling that one wants to serve, to serve *first*. This conscious choice brings one to aspire to lead. That person is sharply different from one who is leader first, perhaps because of the need to assuage an unusual power drive or to acquire material possessions.'

Leaders' sense of stewardship operates on two levels: stewardship for the people they lead and stewardship for the larger purpose or mission that underlies the enterprise. The first type arises from a keen appreciation of the impact one's leadership can have on others. People can suffer economically, emotionally and spiritually under inept leadership. If anything, people in a learning organization are more vulnerable because of their commitment and sense of shared ownership. Appreciating this naturally instills a sense of responsibility in leaders. The second type of stewardship arises from a leader's sense of personal purpose and commitment to the organization's larger mission. People's natural impulse to learn is unleashed when they are engaged in an endeavour they consider worthy of their fullest commitment. Or, as Lawrence Miller puts it, 'Achieving return on equity does not, as a goal, mobilize the most noble forces of our soul.'

New skills

New leadership roles require new leadership skills. These skills can only be developed, in my judgment, through a lifelong commitment. It is not enough for one or two individuals to develop these skills. They must be distributed widely throughout the organization. This is one reason that understanding the disciplines of a learning organization is so important. These disciplines embody the principles and practices that can widely foster leadership development.

Three critical areas of skills (disciplines) are building shared vision, surfacing and challenging mental models, and engaging in systems thinking.

Building shared vision

The skills involved in building shared vision include the following:

- Encouraging personal vision. Shared visions emerge from personal visions. It is not that people only care about their own self-interest – in fact, people's values usually include dimensions that concern family, organization, community and even the world. Rather, it is that people's capacity for caring is personal.

- Communicating and asking for support. Leaders must be willing to continually share their own vision, rather than being the official representative of the corporate vision. They also must be prepared to ask, 'Is this vision worthy of your commitment?' This can be difficult for a person used to setting goals and presuming compliance.

- Visioning as an ongoing process. Building shared vision is a never-ending process. At any one point there will be a particular image of the future that is predominant, but that image will evolve. Today, too many managers want to dispense with the 'vision business' by going off and writing the Official Vision Statement. Such statements almost always lack the vitality, freshness and excitement of a genuine vision that comes from people asking, 'What do we really want to achieve?'

- Blending extrinsic and intrinsic visions. Many energizing visions are extrinsic – that is, they focus on achieving something relative to an outsider, such as a competitor. But a goal that is limited to defeating an opponent can, once the vision is achieved, easily become a defensive posture. In contrast, intrinsic goals like creating a new type of product, taking an established product to a new level, or setting a new standard for customer satisfaction can call forth a new level of creativity and innovation. Intrinsic and extrinsic visions need to coexist; a vision solely predicated on defeating an adversary will eventually weaken an organization.

- Distinguishing positive from negative visions. Many organizations only truly pull together when their survival is threatened. Similarly, most social movements aim at eliminating what people don't want: for example, anti-drug, anti-smoking, or anti-nuclear arms movements. Negative visions carry a subtle message of powerlessness: people will only pull together when there is sufficient threat. Negative visions also tend to be short term. Two fundamental sources of energy can motivate organizations: fear and aspiration. Fear, the energy source behind negative visions, can produce extraordinary changes in short periods, but aspiration endures as a continuing source of learning and growth.

Surfacing and testing mental models

Many of the best ideas in organizations never get put into practice. One reason is that new insights and initiatives often conflict with established mental models. The leadership task of challenging assumptions without invoking defensiveness requires reflection and inquiry skills possessed by few leaders in traditional controlling organizations.

- Seeing leaps of abstraction. Our minds literally move at lightning speed. Ironically, this often slows our learning, because we leap to generalizations so quickly that we never think to test them. We then confuse our generalizations with the observable data upon which they are based, treating the generalizations as if they were data.

- Balancing enquiry and advocacy. Most managers are skilled at articulating their views and presenting them persuasively. While important, advocacy skills can become counterproductive as managers rise in responsibility and confront increasingly complex issues that require collaborative learning among different, equally knowledgeable people. Leaders in learning organizations need to have both enquiry and advocacy skills.

- Distinguishing espoused theory from theory in use. We all like to think that we hold certain views, but often our actions reveal deeper views. For example, I may proclaim that people are trustworthy, but never lend friends money and jealously guard my possessions. Obviously, my deeper mental model (my theory in use), differs from my espoused theory. Recognizing gaps between espoused views and theories in use (which often requires the help of others) can be pivotal to deeper learning.

- Recognizing and defusing defensive routines. As one CEO (chief executive officer) in our research programme puts it, 'Nobody ever talks about an issue at the eight o'clock business meeting exactly the same way they talk about it at home that evening or over drinks at the end of the day.' The reason is what Chris Argyris calls defensive routines; entrenched habits used to protect ourselves from the embarrassment and threat that come with exposing our thinking. For most of us, such defences began to build early in life in response to pressures to have the right answers in school or at home. Organizations add new levels of performance anxiety and thereby amplify and exacerbate this defensiveness. Ironically, this makes it even more difficult to expose hidden mental models, and thereby lessens learning. The first challenge is to recognize defensive routines, then to enquire into their operation. Those who are best at revealing and defusing defensive routines operate with a high degree of self-disclosure regarding their own defensiveness.

Systems thinking

We all know that leaders should help people see the big picture. But the actual skills whereby leaders are supposed to achieve this are not well understood. In my experience, successful leaders often are 'systems thinkers' to a considerable extent. They focus less on day-to-day events and more on underlying trends and forces of change. But they do this almost completely intuitively. The consequence is that they are often unable to explain their intuitions to others and feel frustrated that others cannot see the world the way they do. One of the most significant developments in management science today is the gradual coalescence of managerial systems thinking as a field of study and practice. This field suggests some key skills for future leaders:

- Seeing interrelationships, not things, and processes, not snapshots. Most of us have been conditioned throughout our lives to focus on things and to see the world in static images. This leads us to linear explanations of systemic phenomenon.

- Moving beyond blame. We tend to blame each other or outside circumstances for our problems. But it is poorly designed systems, not incompetent or unmotivated individuals, that cause most organizational problems. Systems thinking shows us that there is no outside – that you and the cause of your problems are part of a single system.

- Distinguishing detail complexity from dynamic complexity. Some types of complexity are more important strategically than others. Detail complexity arises when there are many variables. Dynamic complexity arises when cause and effect are distant in time and space, and when the consequences over time of interventions are subtle and not obvious to many participants in the system. The leverage in most management situations lies in understanding dynamic complexity, not detail complexity.

- Focusing on areas of high leverage. Some have called systems thinking the 'new dismal science' because it teaches that most obvious solutions don't work – at best, they improve matters in the short run, only to make things worse in the long run. But there is another side to the story. Systems thinking also shows that small, well-focused actions can produce significant, enduring improvements, if they are in the right place. Systems thinkers refer to this idea as the principle of leverage. Tackling a difficult problem is often a matter of seeing where the high leverage lies, where a change – with a minimum of effort – would lead to lasting, significant improvement.

■ Avoiding symptomatic solutions. The pressures to intervene in management systems that are going awry can be overwhelming. Unfortunately, given the linear thinking that predominates in most organizations, interventions usually focus on symptomatic fixes, not underlying causes. This results in only temporary relief, and it tends to create still more pressures later on for further, low-leverage intervention. If leaders acquiesce to these pressures, they can be sucked into an endless spiral of increasing intervention. Sometimes the most difficult leadership acts are to refrain from intervening through popular quick fixes and to keep the pressure on everyone to identify more enduring solutions.

The consequences of leaders who lack systems-thinking skills can be devastating. Many charismatic leaders manage almost exclusively at the level of events. They deal in visions and in crises, and little in between. Under their leadership, an organization hurtles from crisis to crisis. Eventually, the worldview of people in the organization becomes dominated by events and reactiveness. Many, especially those who are deeply committed, become burned out. Eventually, cynicism comes to pervade the organization. People have no control over their time, let alone their destiny.

Similar problems arise with the 'visionary strategist', the leader with vision who sees both patterns of change and events. This leader is better prepared to manage change. He or she can explain strategies in terms of emerging trends, and thereby foster a climate that is less reactive. But such leaders still impart a responsive orientation rather than a generative one.

Many talented leaders have rich, highly systemic intuitions but cannot explain those intuitions to others. Ironically, they often end up being authoritarian leaders, even if they don't want to, because only they see the decisions that need to be made. They are unable to conceptualize their strategic insights so that these can become public knowledge, open to challenge and further improvement.

Developing leaders and learning organizations

In a recently published retrospective on organization development in the 1980s, Marshall Sashkin and N. Warner Burke (1990) observe the return of an emphasis on developing leaders who can develop organizations. They also note Schein's critique that most top executives are not qualified for the task of developing culture. Learning organizations represent a potentially significant evolution of organizational culture. So it should come as no surprise that such organizations will remain a distant vision until the leadership capabilities they demand are developed. 'The 1990s may be the period', suggest Sashkin and Burke, 'during which organization development and (a new sort of) management development are reconnected.'

I believe that this new sort of management development will focus on the roles, skills and tools for leadership in learning organizations. Undoubtedly, the ideas offered above are only a rough approximation of this new territory. The sooner we begin seriously exploring the territory, the sooner the initial map can be improved – and the sooner we will realize an age-old vision of leadership:

The wicked leader is he who the people despise. The good leader is he who the people revere. The great leader is he who the people say, 'We did it ourselves.'

Lao Tsu

READING 8.3

Ambidextrous organizations: Managing evolutionary and revolutionary change

By Michael L. Tushman and Charles A. O'Reilly III[1]

All managers face problems in overcoming inertia and implementing innovation and change. But why is this problem such an enduring one? Organizations are filled with sensible people and usually led by smart managers. Why is anything but incremental change often so difficult for the most successful organizations?

And why are the patterns of success and failure so prevalent across industries and over time? To remain successful over long periods, managers and organizations must be ambidextrous – able to implement both incremental and revolutionary change.

Patterns in organization evolution

Across industries there is a pattern in which success often precedes failure. But industry-level studies aren't very helpful for illustrating what actually went wrong. Why are managers sometimes ineffective in making the transition from strength to strength? To understand this we need to look inside firms and understand the forces impinging on management as they wrestle with managing innovation and change. To do this, let's examine the history of two firms, RCA semiconductors and Seiko watches, as they dealt with the syndrome of success followed by failure.

The stark reality of the challenge of discontinuous change can be seen in Figure 8.3.1. This is a listing of the leading semiconductor firms over a 40-year period. In the mid-1950s, vacuum tubes represented roughly a $700 million market. At this time, the leading firms in the then state-of-the-art technology of vacuum tubes included great technology companies such as RCA, Sylvania, Raytheon and Westinghouse. Yet between 1955 and 1995, there was almost a complete turnover in industry leadership. With the advent of the transistor, a major technological discontinuity, we see the beginnings of a remarkable shake-out. By 1965, new firms such as Motorola and Texas Instruments had become important players while Sylvania and RCA had begun to fade. Over the next 20 years still other upstart companies like Intel, Toshiba and Hitachi became the new leaders while Sylvania and RCA exited the product class.

Why should this pattern emerge? Is it that managers and technologists in 1955 in firms like Westinghouse, RCA and Sylvania didn't understand the technology? This seems implausible. In fact, many vacuum tube producers did enter the transistor market, suggesting that they not only understood the technology, but saw it as important. RCA was initially successful at making the transition. While from the outside it appeared that they had committed themselves to transistors, the inside picture was very different.

Within RCA, there were bitter disputes about whether the company should enter the transistor business and cannibalize their profitable tube business. On one side, there were reasonable arguments that the transistor business was new and the profits uncertain. Others, without knowing whether transistors would be successful, felt that it was too risky not to pursue the new technology. But even if RCA were to enter the solid-state business, there were thorny issues about how to organize it within the company. How could they manage both technologies? Should the solid-state division report to the head of the electronics group, a person steeped in vacuum tube expertise?

FIGURE 8.3.1 Semiconductor industry 1955–1995

	1955 (Vacuum Tubes)	1955 (Transistors)	1965 (Semiconductors)	1975 (Integrated Circuits)	1982 (VLSI)	1995 (Submicron)
1.	RCA	Hughes	TI	TI	Motorola	Intel
2.	Sylvania	Transitron	Fairchild	Fairchild	TI	NEC
3.	General Electric	Philco	Motorola	National	NEC	Toshiba
4.	Raytheon	Sylvania	GI	Intel	Hitachi	Hitachi
5.	Westinghouse	TI	GE	Motorola	National	Motorola
6.	Amperex	GE	RCA	Rockwell	Toshiba	Samsung
7.	National Video	RCA	Sprague	GI	Intel	TI
8.	Rawland	Westinghouse	Philco	RCA	Philips	Fujitsu
9.	Eimac	Motorola	Transitron	Philips	Fujitsu	Mitsubishi
10.	Lansdale	Clevite	Raytheon	AMD	Fairchild	Philips

Source: Adapted from R. Foster, *Innovation: The Attacker's Advantage* (New York, NY 1986).

With its great wealth of marketing, financial and technological resources, RCA decided to enter the business. Historically, it is common for successful firms to experiment with new technologies. Xerox, for example, developed user-interface and software technologies, yet left it to Apple and Microsoft to implement them. Western Union developed the technology for telephony and allowed American Bell (AT&T) to capture the benefits. Almost all relatively wealthy firms can afford to explore new technologies. Like many firms before them, RCA management recognized the problems of trying to play two different technological games but were ultimately unable to resolve them. In the absence of a clear strategy and the cultural differences required to compete in both markets, RCA failed.

In his study of this industry, Richard Foster (then a Director at McKinsey & Company) notes, 'Of the 10 leaders in vacuum tubes in 1955 only two were left in 1975. There were three variants of error in these case histories. First is the decision not to invest in the new technology. The second is to invest but picking the wrong technology. The third variant is cultural. Companies failed because of their inability to play two games at once: To be both effective defenders of what quickly became old technologies and effective attackers with new technologies.' Senior managers in these firms fell victim to their previous success and their inability to play two games simultaneously. New firms, like Intel and Motorola, were not saddled with this internal conflict and inertia. As they grew, they were able to re-create themselves, while other firms remained trapped.

In contrast to RCA, consider Hattori-Seiko's watch business. While Seiko was the dominant Japanese watch producer in the 1960s, they were a small player in global markets. Bolstered by an aspiration to be a global leader in the watch business, and informed by internal experimentation between alternative oscillation technologies (quartz, mechanical and tuning fork), Seiko's senior management team made a bold bet. In the mid-1960s, Seiko transformed itself from being merely a mechanical watch firm into being both a quartz and mechanical watch company. This move into low-cost, high-quality watches triggered wholesale change within Seiko and, in turn, within the worldwide watch industry. As transistors replaced vacuum tubes (to RCA's chagrin), quartz movement watches replaced mechanical watches. Even though the Swiss had invented both the quartz and tuning fork movements, at this juncture in history they moved to re-invest in mechanical movements. As Seiko and other

Japanese firms prospered, the Swiss watch industry drastically suffered. By 1980, SSIH, the largest Swiss watch firm, was less than half the size of Seiko. Eventually, SSIH and Asuag, the two largest Swiss firms, went bankrupt. It would not be until after these firms were taken over by the Swiss banks and transformed by Nicholas Hayek that the Swiss would move to recapture the watch market.

The real test of leadership, then, is to be able to compete successfully by both increasing the alignment or fit among strategy, structure, culture and processes, while simultaneously preparing for the inevitable revolutions required by discontinuous environmental change. This requires organizational and management skills to compete in a mature market (where cost, efficiency and incremental innovation are key) *and* to develop new products and services (where radical innovation, speed and flexibility are critical). A focus on either one of these skill sets is conceptually easy. Unfortunately, focusing on only one guarantees short-term success but long-term failure. Managers need to be able to do both at the same time, that is, they need to be ambidextrous. Juggling provides a metaphor. A juggler who is very good at manipulating a single ball is not interesting. It is only when the juggler can handle multiple balls at one time that his or her skill is respected.

These short examples are only two illustrations of the pattern by which organizations evolve: periods of incremental change punctuated by discontinuous or revolutionary change. Long-term success is marked by increasing alignment among strategy, structure, people and culture through incremental or evolutionary change punctuated by discontinuous or revolutionary change that requires the simultaneous shift in strategy, structure, people and culture. These discontinuous changes are almost always driven either by organizational performance problems or by major shifts in the organization's environment, such as technological or competitive shifts. Where those less successful firms (e.g., SSIH, RCA) react to environmental jolts, those more successful firms proactively initiate innovations that reshape their market (e.g., Seiko).

What's happening? Understanding patterns of organizational evolution

These patterns in organization evolution are not unique. Almost all successful organizations evolve through relatively long periods of incremental change punctuated by environmental shifts and revolutionary change. These discontinuities may be driven by technology, competitors, regulatory events, or significant changes in economic and political conditions. For example, deregulation in the financial services and airline industries led to waves of mergers and failures as firms scrambled to reorient themselves to the new competitive environment. Major political changes in Eastern Europe and South Africa have had a similar impact. The combination of the European Union and the emergence of global competition in the automobile and electronics industries has shifted the basis of competition in these markets. Technological change in microprocessors has altered the face of the computer industry.

The sobering fact is that the cliche about the increasing pace of change seems to be true. Sooner or later, discontinuities upset the congruence that has been a part of the organization's success. Unless their competitive environment remains stable – an increasingly unlikely condition in today's world – firms must confront revolutionary change. The underlying cause of this pattern can be found in an unlikely place: evolutionary biology.

Innovation patterns over time

For many years, biological evolutionary theory proposed that the process of adaptation occurred gradually over long time periods. The process was assumed to be one of variation, selection and retention. Variations occurred naturally within species across generations. Those variations that were most adapted to the environment would, over time, enable a species to survive and reproduce. This form would be selected in that it endured while less adaptable forms reproduced less productively and would diminish over time. For instance, if the world became colder and snowier, animals who were whiter and had heavier coats would be advantaged and more likely to survive. As climatic changes affected vegetation, those species with longer necks or stronger beaks might do better. In this way, variation led to adaptation and fitness, which was subsequently retained across generations. In this early view, the environment changed gradually and species adapted slowly to these changes. There is ample evidence that this view has validity.

But this perspective missed a crucial question: What happened if the environment was characterized, not by gradual change, but periodic discontinuities? What about rapid changes in temperature, or dramatic shifts in the availability of food? Under these conditions, a reliance on gradual change was a one-way ticket to extinction. Instead of slow change, discontinuities required a different version of Darwinian theory – that of punctuated equilibria in which long periods of gradual change were interrupted periodically by massive discontinuities. What then? Under these conditions, survival or selection goes to those species with the characteristics needed to exploit the new environment. Evolution progresses through long periods of incremental change punctuated by brief periods of revolutionary or discontinuous change.

So it seems to be with organizations. An entire subfield of research on organizations has demonstrated many similarities between populations of insects and animals and populations of organizations. This field, known as 'organizational ecology', has successfully applied models of population ecology to the study of sets of organizations in areas as diverse as wineries, newspapers, automobiles, biotech companies and restaurants. The results confirm that populations of organizations are subject to ecological pressures in which they evolve through periods of incremental adaptation punctuated by discontinuities. Variations in organizational strategy and form are more or less suitable for different environmental conditions. Those organizations and managers who are most able to adapt to a given market or competitive environment will prosper. Over time, the fittest survive – until there is a major discontinuity. At that point, managers of firms are faced with the challenge of reconstituting their organizations to adjust to the new environment. Managers who try to adapt to discontinuities through incremental adjustment are unlikely to succeed. The processes of variation, selection and retention that winnow the fittest of animal populations seem to apply to organizations as well.

To understand how this dynamic affects organizations, we need to consider two fundamental ideas; how organizations grow and evolve, and how discontinuities affect this process. Armed with this understanding, we can then show how managers can cope with evolutionary and revolutionary change.

Organizational growth and evolution. There is a pattern that describes organizational growth. All organizations evolve following the familiar S-curve. For instance, consider the history of Apple Computers and how it grew. In its inception, Apple was not so much an organization as a small group of people trying to design, produce and sell a new product, the personal computer. With success, came the beginnings of a formal organization, assigned roles and responsibilities, some rudimentary systems for accounting and payroll, and a culture based on the shared expectations among employees about innovation, commitment and speed. Success at this stage was seen in terms of congruence among the strategy, structure, people and culture. Those who fit the Apple values and subscribed to the cultural norms stayed. Those who found the Jobs and Wozniak vision too cultish left. This early structure was aligned with the strategy and the critical tasks needed to implement it. Success flowed not only from having a new product with desirable features, but also from the ability of the organization to design, manufacture, market and distribute the new PC. The systems in place tracked those outcomes and processes that were important for the implementation of a single product strategy. Congruence among the elements of the organization is a key to high performance across industries.

As the firm continued its successful growth, several inexorable changes occurred. First, it got larger. As this occurred, more structure and systems were added. Although this trend toward professionalization was resisted by Jobs (who referred to professional managers as 'bozos'), the new structures and procedures were required for efficiency and control. Without them, chaos would have reigned. As Apple got older, new norms were developed about what was important and acceptable and what would not be tolerated. The culture changed to reflect the new challenges. Success at Apple and at other firms is based on learning what works and what doesn't.

Inevitably, even Apple's strategy had to change. What used to be a single-product firm (selling the Apple PC and then its successor, the Apple II) now sold a broader range of products in increasingly competitive markets. Instead of a focused strategy, the emphasis shifted to a market-wide emphasis. Not only was Apple selling to personal computer users, but also to the educational and industrial markets. This strategic shift required further adjustment to the structure, people, culture and critical tasks. What worked in a smaller, more focused firm was no longer adequate for the larger, more differentiated Apple. Success at this phase of evolution required management's ability to realign the organization to insure congruence with the strategy. The well-publicized ousting of Steve Jobs by Apple's board of directors reflected the board's judgement that John Sculley had the skills necessary to lead a larger, more diversified company. Jobs's approach was fine for a smaller, more focused firm but inappropriate for the challenges Apple faced in the mid-1980s.

Over an even longer period of success, there are inevitably more changes – sometimes driven by technology, sometimes by competition, customers, or regulation, sometimes by new strategies and ways of competing. As the product class matures, the basis of competition shifts. While in the early stages of a product class, competition is based on product variation, in the later stages competition shifts to features, efficiency, and cost. In the evolution of Apple, this can be seen as the IBM PC and the clones emerged. The Windows operating system loosened the grip Apple had maintained on the easy-to-use graphical interface and triggered a battle between three incompatible operating systems – the Mac, IBM's OS/2, and Microsoft Windows. Once Windows became the industry standard in operating systems, the basis of competition shifted to cost, quality and efficiency. Faced with these realities, Apple managers once again had to re-balance the congruence among strategy, structure, people and culture. Success comes from being able to outdo the competition in this new environment. So the board of directors replaced Sculley as CEO in 1994 with Michael Spindler, who was seen as having the operational skills needed to run the company in a mature market. Spindler's task was to emphasize the efficiencies and lower margins required in today's markets and reshape Apple to compete in this new market. With Apple's performance stagnant, its board chose a turnaround expert, Gil Amelio, to finish what Spindler could not do.

Notice how Apple evolved over a 20-year period. Incremental or evolutionary change was punctuated by discontinuous or revolutionary change as the firm moved through the three stages of growth in the product class; innovation, differentiation and maturity. Each of these stages required different competencies, strategies, structures, cultures and leadership skills. These changes are what drive performance. But while absolutely necessary for short-term success, incremental change is not sufficient for long-term success. It is not by chance that Steve Jobs was successful at Apple until the market became more differentiated and demanded the skills of John Sculley. Nor is it surprising that, as the industry consolidated and competition emphasized costs, operations-oriented managers such as Michael Spindler and, in turn, Gil Amelio were selected to reorient Apple.

To succeed over the long haul, firms have to periodically reorient themselves by adopting new strategies and structures that are necessary to accommodate changing environmental conditions. These shifts often occur through discontinuous changes – simultaneous shifts in strategy, structures, skills and culture. If an environment is stable and changes only gradually, as is the case in industries such as cement, it is possible for an organization to evolve slowly through continuous incremental change. But, many managers have learned (to their stockholders' chagrin) that slow evolutionary change in a fast-changing world is, as it was for the dinosaurs, a path to the boneyard.

Technology cycles. Although organizational growth by itself can lead to a periodic need for discontinuous change, there is another more fundamental process occurring that results in punctuated change. This is a pervasive phenomenon that occurs across industries and is not widely appreciated by managers. Yet it is critical to understanding when and why revolutionary change is necessary: This is the dynamic of product, service and process innovation, dominant designs, and substitution events which together make up technology cycles. Figure 8.3.2 shows the general outline of this process.

In any product or service class (e.g., microprocessors, automobiles, baby diapers, cash management accounts) there is a common pattern of competition that describes the development of the class over time. As shown in Figure 8.3.2, technology cycles begin with a proliferation of innovation in products or services as the new product or service gains acceptance. Think, for example, of the introduction of VCRs. Initially, only a few customers bought them. Over time, as demand increased, there was increasing competition between Beta and VHS. At some point, a design emerged that became the standard preferred by customers (i.e., VHS). Once this occurred, the basis of competition shifted to price and features, not basic product or service design. The emergence of this *dominant design* transforms competition in the product class. Once it is clear that a dominant design has emerged, the basis of competition shifts to process innovation, driving down costs and adding features. Instead of competing through product or service innovation, successful strategies now emphasize compatibility with the standard and productivity improvement. This competition continues until there is a major new product, service or process substitution event and the technology cycle kicks off again as the basis of competition shifts back again to product or service variation (e.g., CDs replacing audio tapes). As technology cycles evolve, bases of competition shift within the market. As organizations change their strategies, they must also realign their organizations to accomplish the new strategic objectives. This usually requires a revolutionary change.

A short illustration from the development of the automobile will help show how dramatic these changes can be for organizations. At the turn of the century, bicycles and horse-driven carriages were threatened by the 'horseless carriage', soon to be called the automobile. Early in this new product class there was

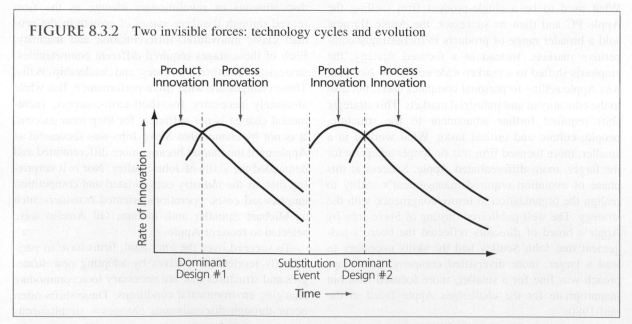

FIGURE 8.3.2 Two invisible forces: technology cycles and evolution

Source: Adapted from J. Utterback, *Mastering the Dynamics of Innovation* (Boston, MA; Harvard Business School Press, 1994).

substantial competition among alternative technologies. For instance, there were several competing alternative energy sources – steam, battery and internal combustion engines. There were also different steering mechanisms and arrangements for passenger compartments. In a fairly short period of time, however, there emerged a consensus that certain features were to be standard – that is, a dominant design emerged. This consisted of an internal combustion engine, steering wheel on the left (in the US), brake pedal on the right, and clutch on the left (this dominant design was epitomized in the Ford Model T). Once this standard emerged, the basis of competition shifted from variations in what an automobile looked like and how it was powered to features and cost. The new competitive arena emphasized lower prices and differentiated market segments, not product variation. The imperative for managers was to change their strategies and organizations to compete in this market. Those that were unable to manage this transition failed. Similar patterns can be seen in almost all product classes (e.g., computers, telephones, fast foods, retail stores).

With a little imagination, it is easy to feel what the managerial challenges are in this environment. Holding aside the pressures of growth and success, managers must continually readjust their strategies and realign their organizations to reflect the underlying dynamics of technological change in their markets. These changes are not driven by fad or fashion but reflect the imperatives of fundamental change in the technology. This dynamic is a powerful cause of punctuated equilibria and can demand revolutionary rather than incremental change. This pattern occurs across industries as diverse as computers and cement, the only issue is the frequency with which these cycles repeat themselves. Faced with a discontinuity, the option of incremental change is not likely to be viable. The danger is that, facing a discontinuous change, firms that have been successful may suffer from life-threatening inertia – inertia that results from the very congruence that made the firm successful in the first place.

The success syndrome: Congruence as a managerial trap

Successful companies learn what works well and incorporate this into their operations. This is what organizational learning is about; using feedback from the market to continually refine the organization to get better and better at accomplishing its mission. A lack of congruence (or internal inconsistency in strategy, structure, culture and people) is usually associated with a firm's current performance problems. Further, since the fit between strategy, structure, people and processes is never perfect, achieving congruence is an ongoing process requiring continuous improvement and incremental change. With evolutionary change, managers are able to incrementally alter their organizations. Given that these changes are comparatively small, the incongruence injected by the change is controllable. The process of making incremental changes is well known and the uncertainty created for people affected by such changes is within tolerable limits. The overall system adapts, but it is not transformed.

When done effectively, evolutionary change of this sort is a crucial part of short-term success. But there is a dark side to this success. As we described with Apple, success resulted in the company becoming larger and older. Older, larger firms develop structural and cultural inertia – the organizational equivalent of high cholesterol. As companies grow, they develop structures and systems to handle the increased complexity of the work. These structures and systems are interlinked so that proposed changes become more difficult, more costly and require more time to implement, especially if they are more than small, incremental modifications. This results in *structural inertia* – a resistance to change rooted in the size, complexity and interdependence in the organization's structures, systems, procedures and processes.

Quite different and significantly more pervasive than structural inertia is the *cultural inertia* that comes from age and success. As organizations get older, part of their learning is embedded in the shared expectations about how things are to be done. These are sometimes seen in the informal norms, values, social networks and in myths, stories and heroes that have evolved over time. The more successful an organization has been, the more institutionalized or ingrained these norms, values and lessons become. The more institutionalized these norms, values and stories are, the greater the cultural inertia – the greater the organizational complacency and arrogance. In relatively stable environments, the firm's culture is a critical component of its success. Culture is an effective way of controlling and coordinating people without elaborate and rigid formal control systems. Yet, when confronted with discontinuous change, the very culture that fostered success can quickly become a significant barrier to change. When Lou Gerstner took over as

CEO at IBM, he recognized that simply crafting a new strategy was not the solution to IBM's predicament. In his view, 'Fixing the culture is the most critical – and the most difficult – part of a corporate transformation.' Cultural inertia, because it is so ephemeral and difficult to attack directly, is a key reason managers often fail to successfully introduce revolutionary change – even when they know that it is needed.

Ambidextrous organizations: Mastering evolutionary and revolutionary change

The dilemma confronting managers and organizations is clear. In the short run they must constantly increase the fit or alignment of strategy, structure and culture. This is the world of evolutionary change. But this is not enough for sustained success. In the long run, managers may be required to destroy the very alignment that has made their organizations successful. For managers, this means operating part of the time in a world characterized by periods of relative stability and incremental innovation, and part of the time in a world characterized by revolutionary change. These contrasting managerial demands require that managers periodically destroy what has been created in order to reconstruct a new organization better suited for the next wave of competition or technology.

Ambidextrous organizations are needed if the success paradox is to be overcome. The ability to simultaneously pursue both incremental and discontinuous innovation and change results from hosting multiple contradictory structures, processes and cultures within the same firm. There are good examples of companies and managers who have succeeded in balancing these tensions. To illustrate more concretely how firms can do this, consider three successful ambidextrous organizations, Hewlett-Packard, Johnson & Johnson and ABB (Asea Brown Boveri). Each of these has been able to compete in mature market segments through incremental innovation and in emerging markets and technologies through discontinuous innovation. Each has been successful at winning by engaging in both evolutionary and revolutionary change.

At one level they are very different companies. HP competes in markets like instruments, computers and networks. J&J is in consumer products, pharmaceuticals and professional medical products ranging from sutures to endoscopic surgical equipment. ABB sells power plants, electrical transmission equipment,

transportation systems and environmental controls. Yet each of them has been able to periodically renew itself and to produce streams of innovation. HP has gone from an instrument company to a minicomputer firm to a personal computer and network company. J&J has moved from consumer products to pharmaceuticals. ABB transformed itself from a slow heavy engineering company based primarily in Sweden and Switzerland to an aggressive global competitor with major investments in Eastern Europe and the Far East. In spite of their differences, each has been ambidextrous in similar ways.

Organizational architectures

Although the combined size of these three companies represents over 350,000 employees, each has found a common way to remain small by emphasizing autonomous groups. For instance, J&J has over 165 separate operating companies that scramble relentlessly for new products and markets. ABB relies on over 5,000 profit centres with an average of 50 people in each. These centres operate like small businesses. HP has over 50 separate divisions and a policy of splitting divisions whenever a unit gets larger than a thousand or so people. The logic in these organizations is to keep units small and autonomous so that employees feel a sense of ownership and are responsible for their own results. This encourages a culture of autonomy and risk taking that could not exist in a large, centralized organization. In the words of Ralph Larsen, CEO of J&J, this approach 'provides a sense of ownership and responsibility for a business you simply cannot get any other way'.

But the reliance on small, autonomous units is not gained at the expense of firm size or speed in execution. These companies also retain the benefits of size, especially in marketing and manufacturing. ABB continually re-evaluates where it locates its worldwide manufacturing sites. J&J uses its brand name and marketing might to leverage new products and technologies. HP uses its relationships with retailers developed from its printer business to market and distribute its new personal computer line. But these firms accomplish this without the top-heavy staffs found at other firms. Barnevik reduced ABB's hierarchy to four levels and a headquarters staff of 150, and purposely keeps the structure fluid. At J&J headquarters, there are roughly a thousand people, but no strategic planning is done by corporate. The role of the centre is to set the vision and review the performance of the 165 operating companies. At HP, the former

CEO, John Young, recognized in the early 1990s that the more centralized structure that HP had adopted in the 1980s to coordinate their minicomputer business had resulted in a suffocating bureaucracy that was no longer appropriate. He wiped it out, flattening the hierarchy and dramatically reducing the role of the centre.

In these companies, size is used to leverage economies of scale and scope, not to become a checker and controller that slows the organization down. The focus is on keeping decisions as close to the customer or the technology as possible. The role of headquarters is to facilitate operations and make them go faster and better. Staff have only the expertise that the field wants and needs. Reward systems are designed to be appropriate to the nature of the business unit and emphasize results and risk taking. Barnevik characterizes this as his 7–3 formula; better to make decisions quickly and be right seven out of ten times than waste time trying to find a perfect solution. At J&J this is expressed as a tolerance for certain types of failure; a tolerance that extends to congratulating managers who take informed risks, even if they fail. There is a delicate balance among size, autonomy, teamwork and speed which these ambidextrous organizations are able to engineer. An important part of the solution is massive decentralization of decision-making, but with consistency attained through individual accountability, information sharing and strong financial control. But why doesn't this result in fragmentation and a loss of synergy? The answer is found in the use of social control.

Multiple cultures

A second commonality across these firms is their reliance on strong social controls. They are simultaneously tight and loose. They are tight in that the corporate culture in each is broadly shared and emphasizes norms critical for innovation such as openness, autonomy, initiative and risk taking. The culture is loose in that the manner in which these common values are expressed varies according to the type of innovation required. At HP, managers value the openness and consensus needed to develop new technologies. Yet, when implementation is critical, managers recognize that this consensus can be fatal. One senior manager in charge of bringing out a new workstation prominently posted a sign saying, 'This is not a democracy.' At J&J, the emphasis on autonomy allows managers to routinely go against the wishes of senior management, sometimes with big successes and

sometimes with failures. Yet, in the changing hospital supply sector of their business, managers recognized that the cherished J&J autonomy was stopping these companies from coordinating the service demanded by their hospital customers. So, in this part of J&J, a decision was made to take away some of the autonomy and centralize services. CEO Larsen refers to this as J&J companies having common standards but unique personalities.

A common overall culture is the glue that holds these companies together. The key in these firms is a reliance on a strong, widely shared corporate culture to promote integration across the company and to encourage identification and sharing of information and resources – something that would never occur without shared values. The culture also provides consistency and promotes trust and predictability. Whether it is the Credo at J&J, the HP Way, or ABB's Policy Bible, these norms and values provide the glue that keeps these organizations together. Yet, at the same time, individual units entertain widely varying subcultures appropriate to their particular businesses. For example, although the HP Way is visible in all HP units worldwide, there are distinct differences between the new video server unit and an old line instrument division. What constitutes risk taking at a mature division is different than the risk taking emphasized at a unit struggling with a brand new technology. At J&J, the Credo's emphasis on customers and employees can be seen as easily in the Philippines as in corporate headquarters in New Brunswick, New Jersey. But the operating culture in the Tylenol division is distinctly more conservative than the culture in a new medical products company.

This tight–loose aspect of the culture is crucial for ambidextrous organizations. It is supported by a common vision and by supportive leaders who both encourage the culture and know enough to allow appropriate variations to occur across business units. These companies promote both local autonomy and risk taking and ensure local responsibility and accountability through strong, consistent financial control systems. Managers aren't second-guessed by headquarters. Strategy flows from the bottom up. Thus, at HP the $7 billion printer business emerged not because of strategic foresight and planning at HP's headquarters, but rather due to the entrepreneurial flair of a small group of managers who had the freedom to pursue what was believed to be a small market. The same approach allows J&J and ABB to enter small niche markets or develop unproven technologies without the burdens of a centralized bureaucratic control system. On the other hand, in return for the autonomy they are granted, there are strong expectations of performance. Managers who don't deliver are replaced.

Ambidextrous managers

Managing units that pursue widely different strategies and that have varied structures and cultures is a juggling act not all managers are comfortable with. At ABB, this role is described as 'preaching and persuading'. At HP, managers are low-key, modest, team players who have learned how to manage this tension over their long tenures with the company. At HP, they also lead by persuasion. 'As CEO my job is to encourage people to work together, to experiment, to try things, but I can't order them to do it', says Lew Platt. Larsen at J&J echoes this theme, emphasizing the need for lower level managers to come up with solutions and encouraging reasonable failures. Larsen claims that the role is one of a symphony conductor rather than a general.

One of the explanations for this special ability is the relatively long tenure managers have in these organizations and the continual reinforcement of the social control system. Often, these leaders are low-keyed but embody the culture and act as visible symbols of it. As a group the senior team continually reinforces the core values of autonomy, teamwork, initiative, accountability and innovation. They ensure that the organization avoids becoming arrogant and remains willing to learn from its competitors. Observers of all three of these companies have commented on their modesty or humility in constantly striving to renew themselves. Rather than becoming complacent, these organizations are guided by leaders who venerate the past but are willing to change continuously to meet the future.

The bottom line is that ambidextrous organizations learn by the same mechanism that sometimes kills successful firms: variation, selection and retention. They promote variation through strong efforts to decentralize, to eliminate bureaucracy, to encourage individual autonomy and accountability, and to experiment and take risks. This promotes wide variations in products, technologies and markets. It is what allows the managers of an old HP instrument division to push their technology and establish a new division dedicated to video servers. These firms also select 'winners' in markets and technologies by staying close to their

customers, by being quick to respond to market signals, and by having clear mechanisms to 'kill' products and projects. This selection process allowed the development of computer printers at HP to move from a venture that was begun without formal approval to the point where it now accounts for almost 40 per cent of HP's profits. Finally, technologies, products, markets, and even senior managers are retained by the market, not by a remote, inwardly focused central staff many hierarchical levels removed from real customers. The corporate vision provides the compass by which senior managers can make decisions about which of the many alternative businesses and technologies to invest in, but the market is the ultimate arbiter of the winners and losers. Just as success or failure in the marketplace is Darwinian, so too is the method by which ambidextrous organizations learn. They have figured out how to harness this power within their comhead panies and organize and manage accordingly.

Summary

Managers must be prepared to cannibalize their own business at times of industry transitions. While this is easy in concept, these organizational transitions are quite difficult in practice. Success brings with it inertia and dynamic conservatism. Four hundred years ago, Niccolo Machiavelli noted, 'There is no more delicate matter to take in hand, nor more dangerous to conduct, nor more doubtful in its success, than to be a leader in the introduction of changes. For he who innovates will have for enemies all those who are well off under the old order of things, and only lukewarm supporters in those who might be better off under the new.'

While there are clear benefits to proactive change, only a small minority of far-sighted firms initiate discontinuous change before a performance decline. Part of this stems from the risks of proactive change. One reason for RCA's failure to compete in the solid-state market or for SSIH's inability to compete in quartz movements came from the divisive internal disputes over the risks of sacrificing a certain revenue stream from vacuum tubes and mechanical watches for the uncertain profits from transistors and quartz watches. However, great managers are willing to take this step. Andy Grove of Intel puts it succinctly, 'There is at least one point in the history of any company when you have to change dramatically to rise to the next performance level. Miss the moment and you start to decline.'

REFERENCES

Abegglen, J.C. and Stalk, G. (1985) *Kaisha, The Japanese Corporation*, New York: Basic Books.

Aldrich, H. (1999) *Organizations Evolving*, London: Sage.

Allison, G.T. (1969) 'Conceptual Models and The Cuban Missile Crisis', *The American Political Science Review*, No. 3, September, pp. 689–718.

Anderson, P. and Tushman, M. (1990) 'Technological discontinuities and dominant designs: A cyclical model of technological change', *Administrative Science Quarterly*, 35, pp. 604–633.

Argyris, C. (1990) *Overcoming Organizational Defenses: Facilitating Organizational Learning*, Boston, MA: Prentice Hall.

Arthur, W.B. (1996) 'Increasing Returns and the New World of Business', *Harvard Business Review*, Vol. 74, No. 4, July–August, pp. 100–109.

Baden-Fuller, C. and Stopford, J.M. (1992) *Rejuvenating the Mature Business*, London: Routledge.

Bartlett, C.A. and Ghoshal, S. (1995) *Transnational Management: Text, Cases, and Readings in Cross-Border Management*, Second Edition, Homewood, IL: R.D. Irwin Inc.

Bate, P. (1994) *Strategies for Cultural Change*, Oxford: Butterworth-Heinemann.

Boeker, W. (1992) 'Power and Managerial Dismissal: Scapegoating at the Top', *Administrative Science Quarterly*, Vol. 37, No. 4, pp. 538–547.

Bower, J.L. and Christensen, C.M. (1995) 'Disruptive Technologies: Catching the Wave', *Harvard Business Review*, Vol. 73, No. 1, January–February, pp. 43–53.

Calori, R., Valla, J-P. and de Woot, P. (1994) 'Common Characteristics: The Ingredients of European Management', in: R. Calori and P. de Woot (eds.) *A European Management Model: Beyond Diversity*, Hemel Hempstead: Prentice Hall.

Day, D.L. (1994) 'Raising Radicals: Different Processes for Championing Innovative Corporate Ventures', *Organization Science*, Vol. 5, No. 2, May, pp. 148–172.

Duncan, R.B. (1976) 'The Ambidextrous Organization: Designing Dual Structures for Innovation', in: R.H. Kilmann, L.R. Pondy and D.P. Slevin (eds.) *The Management of Organizational Design*, New York: Elsevier North Holland, pp. 167–188.

Eisenhardt, K.M. and Brown, S.L. (1997) 'The Art of Continuous Change: Linking Complexity Theory and Time-Paced Evolution in Relentlessly Shifting Organizations', *Administrative Science Quarterly*, Vol. 42, No. 1, March, pp. 1–34.

Forrester, J.W. (2003) 'Dynamic models of economic systems and industrial organizations', *System Dynamics Review*, 19(4), pp. 329–345.

Foster, R. (1986) *Innovation: The Attacker's Advantage*, New York: Summit Books.

Fredrickson, J.W., Hambrick, D.C. and Baumrin, S. (1988) 'A Model of CEO Dismissal', *Academy of Management Review*, Vol. 13, No. 2, April, pp. 255–270.

Freeman, R.E. (1984) *Strategic Management: A Stakeholder Approach*, Boston: Pitman/Ballinger.

Gersick, C.J.G. (1991) 'Revolutionary Change Theories: A Multilevel Exploration of the Punctuated Equilibrium Paradigm', *Academy of Management Review*, Vol. 17, No. 1, January, pp. 10–36.

Ghemawat, P. (1991) *Commitment: The Dynamic of Strategy*, New York: Free Press.

Greenleaf, R.K. (1977) *Servant Leadership: A Journey into the Nature of Legitimate Power and Greatness*, New York: Paulist Press.

Greenwood, R. and Hinings, C.R. (1996) 'Understanding Radical Organizational Change: Bringing Together the Old and the New Institutionalism', *Academy of Management Review*, Vol. 21, No. 4, October, pp. 1022–1054.

Greiner, L.E. (1972) 'Evolution and Revolution as Organizations Grow', *Harvard Business Review*, Vol. 50, No. 4, July–August, pp. 37–46.

Grinyer, P.H., Mayes, D. and McKiernan, P. (1987) *Sharpbenders: The Secrets of Unleashing Corporate Potential*, Oxford: Blackwell.

Hambrick, D.C. and Mason, P. (1984) 'Upper Echelons: The Organization as a Reflection of Its Top Managers', *Academy of Management Review*, Vol. 9, No. 2, April, pp. 193–206.

Hamel, G. (1996) 'Strategy as Revolution', *Harvard Business Review*, Vol. 74, No. 4, July–August, pp. 69–82.

Hammer, M. (1990) 'Reengineering Work: Don't Automate, Obliterate', *Harvard Business Review*, Vol. 68, No. 4, July–August, pp. 104–111.

Hammer, M. and Champy, J. (1993) *Reengineering the Corporation: A Manifesto for Business Revolution*, New York: HarperCollins.

Hannan, M.T. and Freeman, J. (1984) 'Structural Inertia and Organizational Change', *American Sociological Review*, Vol. 49, No. 2, April, pp. 149–164.

Hayes, R.H. (1985) 'Strategic Planning: Forward in Reverse?', *Harvard Business Review*, Vol. 63, No. 6, November–December, pp. 111–119.

Hitt, M.A., Dacin, M.T., Tyler, B.B. and Park, D. (1997) 'Understanding the Differences in Korean and US Executives' Strategic Orientations', *Strategic Management Journal*, Vol. 18, pp. 159–167.

Hofstede, G. (1993) 'Cultural Constraints in Management Theories', *Academy of Management Executive*, Vol. 7, No. 1, pp. 8–21.

Johnson, G. (1987) *Strategic Change and the Management Process*, Oxford: Basil Blackwell.

Johnson, G. (1988) 'Rethinking Incrementalism', *Strategic Management Journal*, Vol. 9, No. 1, January–February, pp. 75–91.

Kagono, T., Nonaka, I., Sakakibara, K. and Okumura, A. (1985) *Strategic vs. Evolutionary Management: A US-Japan Comparison of Strategy and Organization*, Amsterdam: North Holland.

Kanter, R.M. (1989) *When Giants Learn to Dance*, New York: Simon & Schuster.

Kessler, E.H. and Chakrabarthi, A.K. (1996) 'Innovation Speed: A Conceptual Model of Context, Antecedents, and Outcomes', *Academy of Management Review*, Vol. 21, No. 4, October, pp. 1143–1191.

Kogut, B. (ed.) (1993) *Country Competitiveness: Technology and the Organizing of Work*, Oxford: Oxford University Press.

Krüger, W. (1996) 'Implementation: The Core Task of Change Management', *CEMS Business Review*, Vol. 1, pp. 77–96.

Lawrence, P.R. and Lorsch, J.W. (1967) *Organization and the Environment*, Boston, MA: Harvard Business School.

Leonard-Barton, D. (1995) *Wellsprings of Knowledge*, Boston, MA: Harvard Business School Press.

Lewin, K. (1947) 'Frontiers in Group Dynamics: Social Equilbria and Social Change', *Human Relations*, Vol. 1, pp. 5–41.

Lieberman, M.B. and Montgomery, D.B. (1988) 'First Mover Adavantages', *Strategic Management Journal*, Vol. 9, No. 1, January–February, pp. 41–58.

Lieberman, M.B. and Montgomery, D.B. (1998) 'First-Mover (Dis)Advantages: Retrospective and Link with the Resource-Based View', *Strategic Management Journal*, Vol. 19, No. 12, December, pp. 1111–1126.

Maidique, M.A. (1980) 'Entrepreneurs, Champions, and Technological Innovation', *Sloan Management Review*, Vol. 21, pp. 18–31.

March, J.G. and Simon, H.A. (1958) *Organizations*, New York: Wiley.

Markides, C. (1998) 'Strategic Innovation in Established Companies', *Sloan Management Review*, Vol. 39, No. 3, pp. 31–42.

Meyer, A., Brooks, G. and Goes, J. (1990) 'Environmental Jolts and Industry Revolutions: Organizational Responses to Discontinuous Change', *Strategic Management Journal*, Vol. 11, No. 2, February, pp. 93–110.

Meyer, A.D. (1982) 'Adapting to Environmental Jolts', *Administrative Science Quarterly*, Vol. 27, No. 4, December, pp. 515–537.

Miller, D. (1990) *The Icarus Paradox: How Excellent Companies Bring About Their Own Downfall*, New York: Harper Business.

Miller, D. and Friesen, P. (1984) *Organizations: A Quantum View*, Englewood Cliffs, NJ: Prentice Hall.

Mintzberg, H. (1991) 'The Effective Organization: Forces and Forms', *Sloan Management Review*, Vol. 32, No. 2, Winter, pp. 54–67.

Mintzberg, H. (1994) *The Rise and Fall of Strategic Planning*, Englewood Cliffs, NJ: Prentice Hall.

Mintzberg, H. and Norman, R.A. (2001) *Reframing Business: When the Map Changes the Landscape*, New York: Wiley.

Morgan, G. (1986) *Images of Organization*, London: Sage.

Nelson, R.R. and Winter, S.G. (1982) *An Evolutionary Theory of Economic Change*, Cambridge, MA: Harvard University Press.

Nonaka, I. (1988) 'Creating Organizational Order Out of Chaos: Self-Renewal in Japanese Firms', *California Management Review*, Vol. 30, No. 3, Spring, pp. 9–18.

Oliver, C. (1991) 'Strategic Responses to Institutional Processes', *Academy of Management Review*, Vol. 16, No. 1, January, pp. 145–179.

Ouchi, W. (1981) *Theory Z: How American Business Can Meet the Japanese Challenge*, Reading, MA: Addison-Wesley.

Pascale, R.T. and Athos, A.G. (1981) *The Art of Japanese Management*, New York: Simon & Schuster.

Pettigrew, A.M. (1988) *The Management of Strategic Change*, Oxford: Basil Blackwell.

Pfeffer, J. and Sutton, R.I. (1999) 'Knowing "What" to Do is Not Enough: Turning Knowledge Into Action', *California Management Review*, Vol. 42, No. 1, Fall, pp. 83–108.

Pondy, L.R., Boland, J.R. and Thomas, H. (eds.) (1988) *Managing Ambiguity and Change*, New York: Wiley.

Powell, W.W. (1991) 'Expanding the scope of Institutional Analysis', in: W.W. Powell and P.J. DiMaggio (eds.) *The New Institutionalism in Organizational Analysis*, Chicago, IL: University of Chicago Press, pp. 183–123.

Quinn, J.B. (1980) *Strategies for Change*, Homewood, IL: Irwin.

Sashkin, M. and Burke, W.W. (1990) 'Organization development in the 1980s', *Journal of Management*, 13(2), pp. 393–417.

Schein, E.H. (1985) *Organizational Culture and Leadership*, San Francisco, CA: Jossey-Bass.

Schumpeter, J.A. (1950) *Capitalism, Socialism and Democracy*, Third Edition, New York: Harper and Brothers.

Selznick, P. (1957) *Leadership in Administration*, New York: Harper & Row.

Senge, P.M. (1990a) 'The Leader's New Work: Building Learning Organizations', *Sloan Management Review*, Vol. 32, No. 1, Fall, pp. 7–23.

Senge, P. (1990b) *The Fifth Discipline: The Art and Practice of the Learning Organization*, New York: Doubleday/Currency.

Shapiro, C. and Varian, H. (1998) *Information Rules: A Strategic Guide to the Network Economy*, Cambridge, MA: Harvard Business School Press.

Stacey, R.D. (1993) 'Strategy as Order Emerging from Chaos', *Long Range Planning*, Vol. 26, No. 1, pp. 10–17.

Stalk, G., Evans, P. and Shulman, L.E. (1992) 'Competing on Capabilities: The New Rules of Corporate Strategy', *Harvard Business Review*, 70(2), March–April, pp. 57–69.

Stinchcombe, A.L. (1965) 'Social Structure and Organizations', in: J.G. March (ed.) *Handbook of Organizations*, Chicago, IL: Rand McNally, pp. 142–193.

Strebel, P. (1992) *Breakpoints: How Managers Exploit Radical Business Change*, Boston, MA: Harvard Business School Press.

Strebel, P. (1994) 'Choosing the Right Change Path', *California Management Review*, Vol. 36, No. 2, Winter, pp. 29–51.

Teece, D.J., Pisano, G. and Shuen, A. (1997) 'Dynamic Capabilities and Strategic Management', *Strategic Management Journal*, Vol. 18, No. 7, August, pp. 509–533.

Thompson, J.D. (1967) *Organizations in Action*, New York: McGraw-Hill.

Tidd, J., Bessant, J. and Pavitt, K. (1997) *Managing Innovation: Integrating Technological, Market and Organizational Change*, Chichester: Wiley.

Trice, H.M. and Beyer, J.M. (1993) *The Cultures of Work Organizations*, Englewood Cliffs, NJ: Prentice Hall.

Tushman, M.L. and O'Reilly III, C.A. (1996) 'Ambidextrous Organizations: Managing Evolutionary and Revolutionary Change', *California Management Review*, Vol. 38, No. 4, Summer, pp. 8–30.

Tushman, M.L. and O'Reilly III, C.A. (1997) *Winning Through Innovation: A Practical Guide to Leading Organizational Change and Renewal*, Boston, MA: Harvard Business School.

Tushman, M.L., Newman, W.H. and Romanelli, E. (1986) 'Convergence and Upheaval: Managing the Unsteady Pace of Organizational Evolution', *California Management Review*, Vol. 29, No. 1, Fall, pp. 29–44.

Utterback, J. (1994) *Mastering the Dynamics of Innovation*, Boston, MA: Harvard Business School Press.

Wack, P. (1985) 'Scenarios: Uncharted Waters Ahead', *Harvard Business Review,* September–October, 1985.

Waterman, R.H., Peters, T.J. and Phillips, J.R. (1980) 'Structure is Not Organization', *Business Horizons*, Vol. 23, June, pp. 14–26.

9

STRATEGIC INNOVATION

There is nothing more difficult to take in hand, more perilous to conduct, or more uncertain in its success, than to take the lead in the introduction of a new order of things. Because the innovator has for enemies all those who have done well under the old conditions, and lukewarm defenders in those who may do well under the new.

Niccolo Machiavelli (1469–1527); Florentine statesman and political philosopher

INTRODUCTION

In Chapter 8, the magnitude and pace of strategic change in aligning the business model and organizational system to the external environment have been addressed. The distinction has been made between operational change that aims at maintaining the current business model and organizational system, and strategic changes that are directed at aligning them with the firm's environment. Strategizing managers are particularly concerned with business model changes, as this affects the way the company creates value and competes in the business environment (see also Chapter 4).

Changing a firm's business model to defend and create a sustainable advantage over the competition is referred to as strategic innovation. It relates to all technologies, resources, activities and processes by which new ideas are generated and converted into products and services that increase satisfaction of current customers and attract new customers. Strategists innovate to strengthen the firm's competitive position, a process that is both necessary and unending due to the dynamics of the competitive game. Hence this chapter deals with the enduring, and arguably the most challenging, topic for strategizing managers of strategic innovation.

Although a large and increasing number of studies address the topic of strategic innovation, definitions either differ widely or remain implicit. In this chapter, strategic innovation is defined as renewing the firm's business model to create or sustain a competitive advantage (Amit and Zott, 2001, 2012). Ultimately, strategic innovation aims to achieve a successful long-term corporate life.

THE ISSUE OF STRATEGIC RENEWAL

The idea of eternal life has always appealed to people in many parts of the world, including Europe, China and India. For centuries, people have been searching for the golden formula of an elixir of life that would provide eternal life and eternal youth. Indeed, it is a fascinating thought that by just consuming a drink, even if it would only work at a defined moment, in a specific place and from a certain cup, we would live forever. Because the idea is so appealing, there have been blooming markets of supply – the alchemists – and demand – usually rich and powerful people. It is unlikely that an elixir of life has even been found efficacious, however we are quite sure that people have died after consuming an acclaimed elixir. The British historian Joseph Needham (Needham *et al.,* 1976) compiled a list of Chinese emperors whose death was likely caused due to elixir poisoning. Chinese interest in alchemy and the elixir of life vanished with the rise of Buddhism, which claimed to have alternative avenues to eternity.

Although the health industry is working hard on lengthening human life through research and technological innovations, eternal life is most likely not achievable. For organizations the situation is different, but not in the sense that they can exist forever. Yet, organizations have the ability to stay young and vital for hundreds of years. In a study, initiated by Royal Dutch/Shell, on large companies older than 100 years and important in their industry, De Geus (1997) found 40 large and dominant companies over 100 years old. The oldest company that De Geus and his team found was the Swedish paper, pulp and chemical manufacturer Stora (that in 1998 merged with the Finnish company Enzo to form the new entity Stora Enzo), which started as a copper mine in central Sweden over 700 years ago. As second-oldest company, De Geus nominated the Japanese Sumitomo with origins in a copper casting shop founded by Riemon Soga in the year 1590. Furthermore, De Geus estimated the average life expectancy of multi-national Fortune-500 corporations between 40 and 50 years, and speculated that the natural average lifespan of a corporation could be as long as two or three centuries. So firms can potentially become much older than humans, yet the average age of companies turns out to be much lower. The question is thus, why is it so difficult to renew the company?

Characteristics of strategic innovation

Strategic renewal processes are arguably *the* most complex processes to bring to a successful ending. The main reason being that strategic innovation consists of four different processes that are already challenging on their own, and therefore extremely demanding in combination. The following paragraph discusses the constituting elements of strategic innovation: strategizing, entrepreneuring, changing and investing processes (see Figure 9.1).

Strategic innovation as a strategizing process. In strategic renewal processes, strategizing managers must be aware of the unfolding opportunities and threats in the environment, and the evolving strengths and weaknesses of the organization. They must be able to constantly re-evaluate their views and generate a new understanding of the competitive situation, often against the company's dominant logic. For strategists a fundamental question in renewal processes is how to avoid getting stuck with an outdated cognitive map (see also Chapter 2). How can they avoid the danger of building up a flawed picture of their industry, their markets and themselves?

While creative thinking is imperative for generating a new understanding of the current situation, it is at the essence of developing a new business model. Creativity is in every human being, albeit at different levels as not everyone is evenly talented and lives a life that pushes their creative talent to the limit. Everyone can learn to paint, but few will find their paintings displayed in a museum. Likewise the level of creativity that business model innovation requires is quite scarce. Moreover, creativity appears in a variety of modes. While artists have the freedom to choose any kind of material, form and subject with no imposed time constraints, architects are bound by available space, functionality, budget and time. Being engaged in strategic renewal, strategists are like architects,

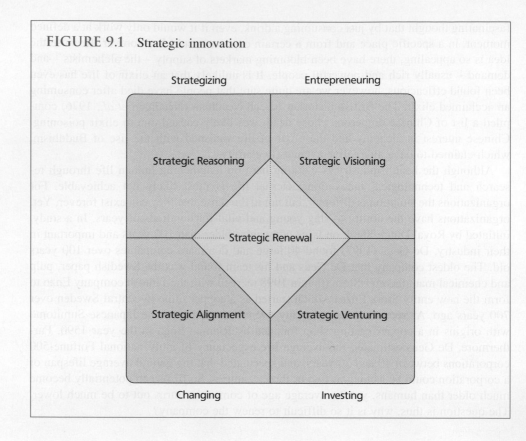

FIGURE 9.1 Strategic innovation

working in a context of 'bounded creativity'. Constrained by, for example, lead time and resource availability, the context of strategic renewal processes is usually framed by more or less articulated input and output criteria.

Strategic innovation as an entrepreneurial process. Each year, thousands of individuals start a new business, expecting to have identified an opportunity that can be exploited. The backgrounds and basic ideas of these entrepreneurs differ widely. For example, some entrepreneurs may have just graduated, others hold many years of experience in an industry they know well; some build their newly established company on the basis of a new technology, others start serving a group of customers that has been overlooked. With all the differences, entrepreneurs share the aim to change the environment and take a personal risk in starting their own business as the vehicle for their dreams. Many, but not all, entrepreneurs succeed and some of their businesses grow large as a family company or public firm. The importance of entrepreneurial activity is widely recognized as the driving force of creating new industries and renewing existing ones.

Not everyone with an entrepreneurial capability likes to take the risks, nor the personal consequences that come with starting a business however. Many prefer a less risky life and start working with an established firm. These people are entrepreneurial but not entrepreneurs, and their entrepreneurial capabilities become a company resource for entrepreneurial initiatives. Entrepreneurial people do not own the company, but they do take ownership over the firm's future. This phenomenon has become known as corporate entrepreneurship.

Established companies make use of entrepreneurial managers for various strategic activities, such as finding new markets for existing products and services, applying new technologies in current markets and setting up new businesses. Entrepreneurial managers realize in established companies what entrepreneurs achieve on their own account: finding growth opportunities. Unique for corporate entrepreneurs, however, is that they often also have to change the company's internal conditions, along with finding avenues for strategic innovation.

Strategic innovation as a change process. Along with changing the company's business model, one or more elements of the company's organizational system (Figure 9.2, see also Chapter 8) also need to be adjusted. The term 'organizational system' refers to how the individuals in the firm have been configured and relate to one another, with the intention of facilitating the business model. The organizational structure divides tasks and responsibilities among the organizational members, by forming different functions and units. The organizational processes link individual members to each other, and coordinate their separate tasks into an integrated whole. Furthermore, firms have organizational cultures and subcultures, as organizational members interact with one another and build up joint beliefs, values and norms.

Some strategic innovation processes require organizational restructuring, for example when new products combine resources that are located in separate units. Also, organizational processes may need to be redesigned, for example as a result of new product offerings. And finally, a change of the firm's culture may be needed to enable strategists renewing the business model, for example when different units are not inclined to share ideas. Strategic change has been discussed at length in Chapter 8.

Strategic innovation as an investing process. Strategic innovation requires resources, such as money, time and management capabilities, and can, therefore, be considered an investment into the company's future. As with all investments, strategic innovation requires a positive return on invested resources. Investments in strategic innovation compete with other investment categories, such as mergers, acquisitions and entering new countries. Consequently, companies engage in decision making routines to decide whether or not to allocate scarce resources for proposed strategic innovation projects.

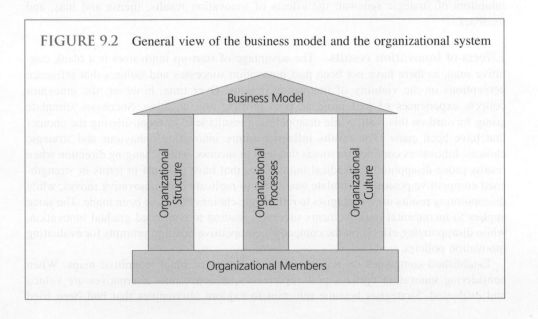

FIGURE 9.2   General view of the business model and the organizational system

Business Model

Organizational Structure

Organizational Processes

Organizational Culture

Organizational Members

Generally, investments that promise to generate returns in the long term are riskier than short term options and therefore harder to take. The same applies to innovation options. In addition, investing in an enhanced long-term competitive position involves more uncertainty about the expected effects as the company environment changes along the way. So, investing in strategic innovation becomes both riskier and more uncertain as the results are to be expected over a longer term.

Managers with the responsibility for innovation processes cannot afford to develop ideas only. They must think of the entire process, from idea generation and managing the renewal process up to the successful implementation of the innovation. Managers must ask themselves upfront how the entire process of strategic innovation should be managed to renew their organizations. Who should be involved, what activities need to be undertaken and to what extent can the results be described in advance? For strategizing managers, strategic innovation encompasses the entire process to arrive at the best possible position to achieve a positive return on the innovation investment.

In sum, strategic innovation is complex for strategizing managers as it combines four processes that separately are, in themselves, challenging to bring to a successful ending: strategizing, entrepreneuring, changing and investing processes. Strategic innovation is equally challenging for management scholars, as the topic crosses and combines several academic disciplines such as Organizational Behaviour, Technology Management, Marketing, Finance and of course Strategy. The multi-disciplinary character of the topic thwarts researchers in understanding strategic innovation in full, with diverse academic contributions as an understandable result. The diverse research findings point to a number of factors that further complicate strategic innovation.

Inhibitors of strategic innovation

As described above, strategic innovation is a difficult process to manage. Although companies may potentially exist for over a century, there are good reasons why only a few companies succeed in surviving for such an extensive period. Some obvious reasons include bad management and unfortunate consequences of wars and natural disasters. But even in the absence of such occasions, strategic renewal is hard to accomplish as strategists face several inhibitors of strategic renewal. The following paragraph discusses such inhibitors of strategic renewal: the effects of innovation results, inertia and bias, and feedback.

Effects of innovation results.   The advantage of start-up innovators is a blank cognitive map, as there have not been past innovation successes and failures that influence perceptions on the viability of innovation options. Over time, however, the innovator collects experiences of past projects, both positive and negative. Successes stimulate going forward on this path, while disappointing results lead to reconsidering the choices that have been made. The results influence future innovating behaviour and strategic choices. Innovators continue on routes that lead to success, while changing direction when results prove disappointing. Radical innovations that have paid off in terms of strengthened competitive position, stimulate strategists to replicate bold innovative moves, while disappointing results urge strategists to rethink the choices that have been made. The same applies to incremental improvements successes leading to continued gradual innovation, while disappointing effects on the company's competitive position prompts for evaluating innovation policies.

Established companies do not have the advantage of blank cognitive maps. When considering innovation options, past experiences influence how alternatives are valued and evaluated. Strategists become reluctant to explore alternatives that had been tried before with disappointing pay-offs. They have learned what works and what doesn't; as a result, they develop perceptions and opinions on the viability of certain options. Past experiences lead to following the proven innovation routines in which they become increasingly more effective – a phenomena that has been commonly termed path dependency (Nelson and Winter, 1982). In other words, positive results of certain innovation routines lead to replicating these routines and building up relevant innovation process competences. Such competences lead to increased chances of success, and ultimately come to define the way the company innovates.

As the organization develops innovation routines and institutionalizes successful practices, the chances of inertia magnify. The organization increasingly comes to rely on patterns of actions it has had sustainable success with in the past (Hannan and Freeman, 1984; Tripsas and Gavetti, 2000), thus becoming less likely to change course (Kelly and Amburgey, 1991). As the organization becomes older, it tends to select innovation routines that have proved to be fruitful (Rahmandad, 2008). Successes lead to bias in evaluating innovation options and outcomes, inertia builds up over time, and the organization loses the ability to value different innovation patterns.

The effects of inertia and bias. Building up inertia and bias over time prohibits organizations from appreciating the potential of innovation options outside the dominant organizational logic and managers' cognitive maps. As a consequence, successful innovations of competitors are hardly noticed, the importance of these innovations is not understood in full, and the organization might miss a crucial industry development. For example, the US retailer Sears Roebuck has missed the advent of discount retailers and home centres (Christensen, 2011, Reading 9.2).

The effects of inertia and bias apply to all innovation routines. Organizations that continuously improve the current business model have a high chance of missing a breakthrough technology, such as Kodak missing the digital imaging revolution, or a revolutionary new business model, as the Sears Roebuck case illustrates. In contrast, companies focusing on the 'next big thing', concentrating key resources on the new breakthrough innovation, build up a blind spot for continuous improvements of competitors. As a result, they may well end up with products that are too expensive or which, when compared with alternatives, lack differentiation value. For example, by continuously improving products, the Japanese electronics firms have come to dominate the market of television sets in the United States, the TV country par excellence.

The effects of feedback. When innovation results are satisfying according to higher level managers, strategists are not challenged to explore innovations that could be even more promising. Innovations are evaluated according to the current dominant logic and based on existing mental models (see also Chapter 2). As long as the results meet the criteria, there is no compelling reason to change course. The company's absorption of innovations that are 'good enough' is reinforced when the full potential of different innovation options is not fully understood or valued.

Continuous feedback of the innovation portfolio complicates business model renewal processes, especially for innovations with a longer development time. During the innovation period, innovations with an extensive lead time are evaluated in multiple intermediate states. Since in each state disappointing progress might be noted, innovations with a long lead time are vulnerable to be discontinued. For example, promising process improvement initiatives can prematurely be abandoned (Repenning and Sterman, 2002), and product development capability can be compromised by reduced investments in concept design activities (Repenning, 2001). The effect of intermediate evaluations is that innovation projects with a relatively short duration, delivering immediate payoffs, become dominant (Rahmandad, 2008). Process improvements in manufacturing pay off relatively fast, while it takes some time before the results of business development become visible.

Of course, strategizing managers do not merely focus on the immediate payback of innovations. The expected future value continues to be a significant factor while evaluating innovations with long lead times. The problem is, however, that in allocating resources priorities may change. For example, some resources may be needed in urgent innovation projects with immediate payoffs and temporal budget cuts may eliminate long term investments. If intermediate moments of evaluation become more frequent, innovations are, thus, more likely to be abandoned.

The key to bringing long-term investment projects to a successful end is to define milestones with clearly described mid-term targets. However, the end state of long-term innovations can usually not be clearly envisioned, making intermediate states are difficult to define. In sum, investment projects with long lead times have the highest chance of being abandoned along the way, especially when intermediate feedback occurs more frequently.

The combination of four challenging processes – strategizing, entrepreneuring, changing and investing – in conjunction with the three main inhibitors may well explain why most companies are unable to approach a century enduring corporate life, which De Geus' study has proven to be possible. The question is, thus, how can strategizing managers extend corporate life? Is there a magic formula for sustained youth, a corporate elixir from magicians in academia or consulting? While this can not be fully excluded, a much more likely answer is that companies should master the ability to renew themselves. This would indicate that strategic renewal is the key strategic issue for a company's long-term success.

Business model renewal

Strategizing managers striving for long-term success are well aware that many factors may change the competitive arena. Although strategists can not predict the future, they know that it will differ from today. Customer needs, competitor's actions and technological advancements are among the many elements that may create a future misfit between the current business model and the company's environment. In order to prepare for a competitive future that is yet unknown, strategizing managers need to renew several elements of the business model. Not only current products and services are to be improved; to create future demands new products and services must also be developed. Strategists are not only *reacting* to changes, they can also *initiate* changes by innovating activities, effectively creating an environmental misfit for competitors.

As strategic innovation is defined as renewing the business model that creates a competitive advantage, the term business model renewal needs to be introduced.

Strategists can renew each element of the company's business model. A business model is the configuration of resources (inputs), activities (throughput) and product/service offerings (output) intended to create value for customers – it is the way a firm conducts its business (See Chapter 4). The first element in a successful business model (*product offering*) is a superior 'value proposition'. A firm must be able to supply a product or service that has a superior mix of attributes (e.g. price, availability, reliability, technical specifications, image, colour, taste, ease of use, etc.). The second element (*value chain*) is the ability to actually develop and supply the superior product offering. It needs to have the capability to perform the necessary value-adding activities in an effective and efficient manner. These value-adding activities, such as R&D, production, logistics, marketing and sales, are jointly referred to as a firm's value chain. The third element of a business model (*resource base*) consists of the resources required to perform the value-adding activities. Resources such as know-how, patents, facilities, money, brands and relationships make up the stock of assets that can be employed to create the product offering. If these firm-specific assets are distinctive and useful, they can form the basis of a superior value proposition.

Strategizing managers can choose between outside-in renewal, inside-out renewal and value chain renewal (see Figure 9.3.).

Outside-in renewal. Strategizing managers can renew their value proposition to customers by increasing the perceived product and service value, and by lowering prices. Reliability, for example, is highly valued by customers in most industries. By continuously improving the reliability of its products, the Korean car maker Hyundai has become known as a company offering high quality yet affordable products (see also the short case of Chapter 5). Another case of outside-in renewal, usually coined marketing innovation or product offering renewal, has to do with the creation of new markets or market segments with existing products. For example, Unilever created new market demand by offering instant soup to the corporate market and by repositioning ice cream to increase adult consumption.

Inside-out renewal. By renewing the company's resource base, new products and services can be created and existing ones can be improved. New technologies are often the prime starting point for inside-out renewal. For example, companies like Philips (medical technology, lighting and household appliances), Merck (pharmaceuticals), and Toyota (motorized vehicles) invest heavily in technological research and development. The know-how and patents add to the firm's resource base, and from there new technologies will create and improve new products and services. Other resources can also be renewed. For example, brands can be renewed by an intensive marketing campaign, and the firm's human resources by training.

Value chain renewal. Along with renewing the firm's value proposition or resource base, strategists can renew some, or even all, elements of the value chain. For example, IKEA has become the world's largest furniture retailer by redesigning the end-to-end value chain, from standardizing production processes to developing flat pack designs and

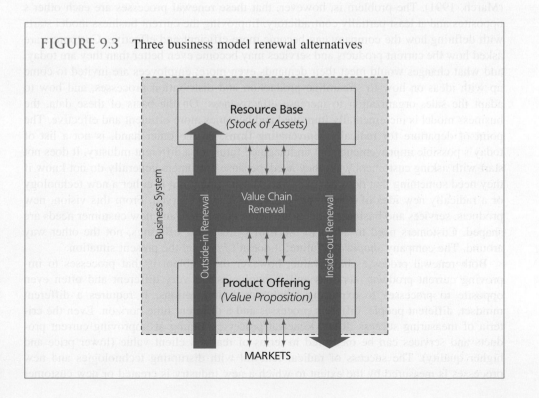

FIGURE 9.3   Three business model renewal alternatives

lowering transportation costs. The value chain innovation of Amazon has prompted competitors and firms in other industries to rethink and renew their chain of value-adding activities.

THE PARADOX OF EXPLOITATION AND EXPLORATION

If you realize that all things change, there is nothing you will try to hold on to. If you are not afraid of dying there is nothing you cannot achieve.
Lao Tsu (6th century BC); Chinese philosopher and author

Many management theorists have addressed the tension between exploitation and exploration (March, 1991, Reading 9.3; Tushman and O'Reilly, 1996; Gupta *et al.*, 2006; Raisch *et al.*, 2009; Zott and Amit, 2013). The question being addressed is whether the company should renew itself by improving the current organization (exploitation) or by radically rejuvenating the organization through disrupting technologies and processes (exploration). On the one hand, they realize that ongoing improvement of products and services will increase customer satisfaction and therefore strengthens the company's competitive position. When ongoing improvement becomes an organizational routine, the company becomes better and faster, which would, in the long run, wear out competitors. On the other hand, they recognize the effects of changing the competitive rules with radically new products, technologies and novel ways of organizing the company. Rule changers leave competitors in the awkward position of catching up with their rules; a feat at which they often fail.

Researchers agree that companies need both exploitative and explorative processes (March, 1991). The problem is, however, that these renewal processes are each other's opposites and at least partially contradictory. Improving the current business model starts with defining how the company can become more efficient and effective. Customers are asked how the current products and services may become even better than they are today, and what changes would meet their demands even more; employees are invited to come up with ideas on how to streamline production and distribution processes, and how to adapt the sales organization to increase effectiveness. On the basis of these data, the business model is incrementally improved and becomes more efficient and effective. The point of departure for radically rejuvenating firms, on the other hand, is not a list of today's possible improvements, but an imagined future of a different industry. It does not start with asking customers what they need, because customers generally do not know if they need something that does not exist yet. The starting point is either a new technology or a radically new idea of how future customers may be served. From this vision, new products, services and business models are being developed, and new customer needs are shaped. Customers need to adapt to the firm's great new offerings, not the other way around. The company *shapes* the future; it doesn't *build* on the present situation.

Both renewal processes have value, however the problem is that processes to improving current products, services and technologies are very different and often even opposite to processes to exploring breakthrough innovations. It requires a different mindset, different people, different processes and a different time horizon. Even the criteria of measuring success differ. Renewal processes aiming at improving current products and services can be measured in terms of realized client value (lower price and higher quality). The success of radical renewal with disrupting technologies and new processes is measured by the extent to which a new industry is created or new customer value is realized. The resulting tension between exploitation and exploration will be explored in the following sections.

The demand for sustained renewal

Sustained renewal refers to the process of permanently improving products and services to strengthen the company's competitive position. It is the never ending quest for raising quality standards and increasing efficiency, achieving ever better and cheaper value propositions – including after-sales, marketing and sales. Each time a higher standard has been reached, the bar is raised to the next level. Quality standards include not only technologies, materials and other physical inputs into the renewal process, but also people – the human resources. People are also developed at ever higher levels.

Sustained renewal is based on factual information, such as customer feedback and market research as well as on ideas from anyone within and outside of the firm. Anything that may bring the current products and services to a higher level is included in the renewal process. The higher level then becomes the new standard both for the company and for competitors and customers. A company needs to improve, even to maintain its current position, because without engaging in this permanent process of improvement, the firm would lag behind competitors and eventually deteriorate. People do not want to read yesterday's newspaper or buy outdated products, and therefore without sustained renewal there is no long-term future for a company.

Ideas for improvement arrive from different internal and external stakeholders. The areas of improvement can widely vary, yet these are usually based on the current understanding of the business the company is in and what kinds of products and services the company relates to the dominant logic (see also Chapter 2). Thinking within the boundaries of a shared paradigm is generally accepted and people tend to proceed accordingly – that is, they renew to sustain the current business model. The downside of a dominant logic is that it usually locks people into shared paradigms that have been tried and tested, and thus becomes immune to external signals that may not fit. This is where the need for disruptive renewal comes in.

The demand for disrupting renewal

Disrupting renewal refers to a process in which current competitive positions are challenged by introducing new technologies and business models. As described above, when improving products and services, a strategist defines each renewing activity on the basis of facts while following the dominant logic. However, when searching for an innovation that will disrupt the industry, a strategist needs to take leaps of imagination. Disruptive innovations do not follow from the facts, but need to be invented. They are not analysed into existence, but need to be generated, if they are to be distinctive and rule-changing.

When generating disrupting solutions, creative thinking is not just important, it is the essence. In disrupting creative thinking, the strategist abandons the rules governing sound argumentation and draws a conclusion that is not justified based on prior arguments. In this way, the strategist generates a new understanding, but without objective proof that the new idea 'makes sense'. Creative thinking takes liberty in following thinking rules. One idea might lead to another idea, without formal logic interfering. One variable might be linked to another, without a sound explanation of why a correlation is assumed. Creativity in effect creates a new understanding, with little attention paid to supporting evidence. Often logic is used afterwards to justify an idea that was actually generated by creative means.

Disruptive renewal does not follow from the dominant logic, but is the unexpected outcome that emerges when the dominant logic is challenged. Changing a shared paradigm requires strategists to imagine new ways of understanding the world that do not follow from current beliefs. Strategic thinkers need to be willing and able to break with orthodoxy and make leaps of imagination, to generate novel ways of looking at old problems.

The conclusion must be that sustained renewal and disruptive renewal are not only opposites, but that they are partially incompatible as well. They are based on methods that are at odds with one another. Strategizing managers would probably love to exploit and explore at the same time, yet both require such a different mindset and range of cognitive skills that in practice it is very difficult to achieve both simultaneously (March, 1991, Reading 9.3). The demand for sustained renewal and disruptive renewal is not only contradictory for each individual, but also within teams, departments and the overall firm. While strategizing groups would like to be fully capable of both exploiting and exploring, finding ways of incorporating both into a workable renewal process is extremely challenging. Conflicting styles often lead to mutual misunderstanding and conflicts among people. Therefore, a blend between the two is not that simple. It is for this reason that we speak of the 'paradox of exploitation and exploration' – the two demands on innovating managers seem to be contradictory, yet both are required at the same time. Inspired by Christensen (2011, Reading 9.2 in this chapter), this can be called *the innovator's paradox.*

EXHIBIT 9.1   SHORT CASE

3M: IN SEARCH OF RENEWAL

If there is one organization that represented innovation and technological breakthroughs in the 20th century, it would be 3M. The company has managed to conquer the world with its innovative culture and well-known products such as Post-it notes. Founded in 1902 by five entrepreneurs, 3M (Minnesota Mining and Manufacturing Company) became the world's most innovative company in 2004. However, when in February 2012 Inge Thulin took the helm as the new CEO, 3M was no longer listed on the Business Week Top 50 most innovative companies.

Shareholders are happy though: with a steady growth and expanding sales in emerging markets such as China and Brazil, 3M gradually climbed in ten years from place 110 to 95 of the best performing companies. But can this be sustained? 3M is facing high competition, increasing environmental regulations and a versatile global market. The current performance is largely the result of past innovations, a capability 3M seems to have lost. Inge Thulin wonders how he can keep shareholders satisfied, while also re-build the innovation capability that made 3M famous by creating future growth.

When Inge Thulin became Chief Executive Officer of 3M in February 2012, he was the first insider after a period of 12 years during which outsiders held the top seat. The stakes for Thulin are high. 3M's revenues have been climbing by 40 per cent in the last 6 years to $29.6 billion, largely due to expanding sales in emerging markets such as China and Brazil. Since 2000, the company has gone through a series of transformations pursuing a balance between fully benefiting from global expansion into new and traditional markets and, in parallel, broadening its product portfolio. The shareholders show confidence and express high expectations, as 3M has shown steady growth in the past years.

The Minnesota Mining and Manufacturing Company was founded in 1902 by five entrepreneurs with the objective to mine and market a relatively rare mineral to be sold as an abrasive. When it appeared that the mine did not contain enough minerals, the company's focus changed. They noted that their customers had great need for better processing materials, to which they responded by developing high-quality sandpaper that caused less dust than hitherto conventional abrasives. From there, 3M developed itself to one of the most successful companies in the world, which it is today in roughly four stages.

Stage 1: Building a company around innovation. The focal point in the first decades of success was 3M CEO, William McKnight, an engineer who stood at the base of developing the first 3M products. He defined 3M's mission as: *solving unsolved problems in innovative ways.* In 1948 he laid the management foundation for 3M's innovative culture:

As our business grows, it becomes increasingly necessary to delegate responsibility and to encourage men and women to exercise their initiative. This requires considerable tolerance. Those men and women, to whom we delegate authority and responsibility, if they are good people, are going to want to do their jobs in their own way.

Mistakes will be made. But if a person is essentially right, the mistakes he or she makes are not as serious in the long run as the mistakes management will make if it undertakes to tell those in authority exactly how they must do their jobs.

Management that is destructively critical when mistakes are made kills initiative. And it's essential that we have many people with initiative if we are to continue to grow.

3M employees gained independence and space to experiment and investigate. Staff were allowed to spend 15 per cent of their working time on self-initiated projects; exploring became part of the job of each employee. An endless array of new products were developed. Examples of breakthrough innovations were the cello tape, magnetic tape, and not to be forgotten: the Post-it. By combining competences, 3M entered different industries such as the pharmaceutical sector with new generation patches, as well as electronics where 3M materials allowed higher resolution for flat screens.

Eight autonomous divisions each had the autonomy to develop new products within their own sector and bring them on the market. From 1914 to 1966, the years that McKnight acted as the CEO, sales exploded from $264,000 to an astonishing $1.15 billion. His internal successors continued this policy. Renewal was central and the bottom-up approach was maintained. In the early 1990s, 3M seemed to lose its grip on financial and intellectual resources. Costly investments were made in both people and products, without the desired market results. Since the launch of the Post-it in 1980, no breakthrough product had been launched; it was time for change. The time to market for new products was too long, managers were insufficiently challenged, and the company that relied heavily on innovative initiatives was characterized as reactive. At the end of the 1990s, 3M lacked focus and was sensitive to all kinds of fads and fashions. Shareholders were murmuring.

Stage 2: Bring focus and accelerate time to market. In early 2000, on the initiative of the shareholders, outsider James McNerney was appointed CEO. Unlike his engineering predecessors, McNerney had a marketing background. His arrival at 3M was the start of a transformation process in search of hidden costs. McNerney had previously worked under the leadership of General Electric's CEO Jack Welch, where he gained credits in creating and transforming lean organizations. In a short period, he managed to bring focus in both the manufacturing and R&D departments. Focusing on the mindset of 3M employees, he imported the GE Six Sigma programme, a series of management techniques aimed at reducing production errors and increasing efficiency. And not without result. Due to these interventions, efficiency and cost awareness at 3M improved significantly.

In parallel, McNerney took some, for 3M, unprecedented steps. He increased competition within the company. The existing plants and research laboratories were downsized and some of their activities were transferred to low-wage countries. In a short time, the workforce was reduced by 8,000 employees (over 10 per cent of the total workforce). Never before in the existence of the organization had job security of workers in the Minnesota plants been threatened. These events had a negative impact on the open and innovative culture of 3M that was built on the strong bond between company and employees. In addition, innovation focused on only those R&D projects that promised the highest and safest return. The time from idea to product was shortened, which resulted in an increased product portfolio in a relatively short time period. Sales increased by 10 per cent annually, making the stockholders happy. In 2005, however, McNerney decided to leave the company and moved to Boeing.

Stage 3: Accelerating growth by acquisitions and strengthening new markets.   George Buckley, a former engineer from Brunswick Company, was appointed at the end of 2005. After a detailed study of the firm, he concluded that 3M was a highly scientific engineering and manufacturing company with conservative values, successfully participating in many niche markets. He wanted to increase collaboration within the company. To further build up and retain competitive advantages, the technology sharing and transfer across products and markets became an important aspect of the company strategy. Buckley decided to bring back the original culture of 3M by restoring the 15 per cent rule, without restrictions for R&D operations. A technology-market architecture was set up in which nine technology platforms, based on the core competences (adhesives, non-woven materials, etc), were distinguished as the fundament for 3M's core assets. Each of the platforms became interconnected with the various markets in which 3M was active (such as aerospace and health care). This way the gap between research and customers had been narrowed.

To assure the expansion of the product portfolio, Buckley chose an acquisition strategy focusing on booming sectors. In 2006, 16 acquisitions were being made, representing at least 24 per cent of the annual company growth. More acquisitions followed. Only 3 per cent of the annual growth had been organic. During the Buckley period, the revenues increased by 40 per cent to $29.6 billion. He retired in 2012.

Stage 4: Restoring organic growth?   Successor Inge Thulin joined 3M in 1979 and rose through the ranks in the company's healthcare business. He had run international operations, for which he helped expand sales to almost $20 billion, about two-thirds of 3M's revenues. When taking the helm in 2012, he had to maintain the sales growth target of 7 to 8 per cent, following the ambitions that were announced in 2009 by his predecessor.

Each of the 3M CEOs emphasized the competitive innovative capabilities of the company in their own way. But do these capabilities still bring the competitive advantage they once did? Between 2004 and 2007, 3M plummeted from being the world's most innovative organization to 7th place in the *Business Week* top 50 of most innovative companies, and as from 2010, 3M is no longer listed. The company that once gave each employee with a "good" idea the space to experiment had changed. Through the interventions of McNerney, only fast promising ideas were given the opportunity to grow. Buckley partly restored the possibilities for bottom up independent R&D projects but focused primarily on growth via Mergers and Acquisitions.

In a rapidly changing environment, the question is whether 3M is currently too much preoccupied with short-term results, focusing on costs and improvements in production processes at the expense of realizing breakthrough innovations that need time and space to grow. On the other hand, the shareholders are visibly satisfied. 3M gradually climbed in ten years from place 110 to place 95 on the Fortune 500 list of best performing companies. For Thulin the biggest challenge is to maintain this market position while simultaneously pursuing the innovative culture that is needed to maintain its competitive position in the future. Future growth comes from invention and innovation; even one single idea may give shape to the company's future, just as it did in the 1960s and 1980s with cello tape and Post-its. But how?

Co-author: Jeroen van der Velden

Sources: www.3m.com; 3M Annual Report 2012; *Business Week* 2007, 'At 3M, a Struggle Between Efficiency and Creativity'; *Business Week* 2012, '3M's Thulin to keep Buckley Focus on Research, Emerging Markets'; www.fortune 500.com; '3M Swot Analysis', Data Monitor 2012; IBS 2012, '3M Cultivating Core Competency'.

PERSPECTIVES ON STRATEGIC INNOVATION

Innovation opportunities do not come with the tempest but with the rustling of the breeze.
Peter Drucker (1909–2005); Austrian – American writer, management thinker and consultant

The demand for both sustained and disruptive renewal puts strategizing managers in the difficult position of having to determine how these two must be combined and balanced in a process of ongoing renewal. Sustained renewal is necessary to ensure ongoing improvement of the current business model – elevating current products and services to ever higher levels of customer satisfaction. Disruptive renewal is necessary to create new business models – imposing competitors to follow the new rules of the competitive game. The question is how strategizing managers go about the demands of renewing the company.

The strategic management literature comes up with a variety of answers to this question. Both among business practitioners and strategy researchers, views differ sharply about the best way of dealing with the paradox of exploitation and exploration. To gain insight into the major points of disagreement on the issue of strategic renewal, the two diametrically opposed perspectives will be outlined here.

At one end of the virtual continuum of views are the strategists who argue that strategic innovation must be achieved by ongoing renewal of the existing firm. Continuous improvement, although difficult to sustain, is at the heart of strategic innovation. This point of view will be referred to as the '*strategic improvement perspective*'. At the other end of the spectrum are the strategists who argue that real strategic innovations are radical departures from the current business model, disrupting the industry in which the firm is active. Not minor improvements are the heart of strategic innovation, but, instead, striving for a significant rejuvenation towards a next state. Disrupting renewal, although difficult to achieve, is at the heart of strategic innovation. This point of view will be referred to as the '*radical rejuvenation perspective*'.

The strategic improvement perspective

 Proponents of the strategic improvement perspective advocate that companies should focus on improving their business model. The point of departure is the permanent battle between rivaling companies that fight for the same customer group. With customers having a choice between comparable products and services that may satisfy their needs, competitive success requires offering the best, cheapest and most novel value propositions. Improved products and services attract more customers, increase market share and generate more returns, and therefore are the key success factor in the competitive game.

The attitude that things can always be advanced is important for the strategic improvement perspective. Everyone within the firm should be driven by constructive dissatisfaction with the status quo. Furthermore, all employees within the firm should be committed to improving all elements of the business model. Company leaders are facilitative in the sustained renewal process; their main role is to coordinate several renewal initiatives. They must also be aware of the danger of the 'success trap': 'sustained renewal often leads to early success, which in turn reinforces further renewal along the same trajectory' (Gupta *et al.*, 2006).

Proponents of the strategic improvement perspective agree that game-changing innovations provide a significant competitive advantage for the innovator. They point out, however, that although the benefits of success can be considerable, it is a risky route with a moderate chance of success at best. In order to increase the chance of a successful breakthrough innovation, the company must allocate the best resources, leaving ample capacity for engaging in continuous improvements that generate immediate competitive success. As the chance of breakthrough success is low, all innovation efforts may well be without results, while the company's rivals have progressed to higher standards. The conclusion must be that radical innovation initiatives absorb the most precious resources for corporate renewal while, due to the high chance of failure, the most likely outcome is that the company loses competitive position or worse: gets kicked out of business by rivals (Imai, 1986, Reading 9.1)

EXHIBIT 9.2   THE STRATEGIC IMPROVEMENT PERSPECTIVE

WEBER GRILLS: MOSTLY MADE IN AMERICA BY PRIVATE EQUITY

Sixty-one years ago, George Stephen got tired of wind and rain messing up his cooking on an open-air grill, the main barbecue tool of the day. He grabbed a buoy made where he worked, Weber Brothers Metal Works in Illinois. He sliced it in half and fashioned a tight-fitting dome lid. It didn't work very well until a neighbour suggested he poke holes in the kettle so air could fuel the fire. The Weber grill was born.

Stephen eventually bought the Weber metal shop, creating Weber-Stephen Products of Palatine, Ill., which is now the world's largest grill manufacturer. The privately held company doesn't disclose financials, but Euromonitor International says Weber-Stephen claims 35 per cent of the $2.5 billion US market, with rival Char-Broil a distant second.

In 1971, Stephen hired Mike Kempster, Weber-Stephen's current chief marketing officer. He calls himself the "godfather of the brand." In a warehouse adjoining a plant in Huntley, Ill., Kempster gestures at thousands of shrink-wrapped boxes of grills and smokers stacked in 20-foot towers. "Looks like a big supply, right?" he asks. "It's probably less than a week." He won't specify how much the factory produces, but around 80 trucks haul stuff away daily. Shipments peak at about 110 semis a day just before July 4. That's a lot of barbecues, but grill sales have flattened over the past few years, partly because of the US housing downturn, Kempster says. While the company sees that turning around, it still faces challenges from Europe's financial struggles, volatile commodity costs, and low-cost overseas manufacturers.

Weber-Stephen has changed more in the past decade than it did in the previous half-century. It contracted to have grills built in China to go with production in Huntley and Palatine. It agreed to stop labelling products "Made in USA" to settle a class-action lawsuit that accused it of buying components from China and Taiwan suppliers. (The company denied wrongdoing.) It also introduced a line of compact grills designed for dense urban areas such as those sprouting up across South-East Asia.

The biggest change was financial: In 2010 the Stephen family sold a majority stake to BDT Capital Partners, the Chicago merchant bank run by Byron Trott, the former Goldman Sachs executive known for his close ties to Warren Buffett. Kempster says BDT's investment will help Weber-Stephen push overseas. The first non-family member to run the company, Thomas Koos, formerly of Jacuzzi Brands and Black & Decker, took over as chief executive officer in April.

The grill maker emulates General Motors' Chevy-to-Caddy range of products, targeting consumers as they climb the income ladder. Weber-Stephen hooks college kids with the $29 Smokey Joe, a miniature kettle, then keeps them buying until they can afford a $799 Genesis gas grill or – if they need a backyard kitchen – a $5,000 Summit Grill Center, a behemoth with six gas burners, a built-in smoker and an infrared rotisserie. There's no fridge, just a cooler. "Consumers told us all they really needed is ice," Kempster says.

When gas grills grew popular in the 1970s, the company offered a kettle fitted with a propane tank. "The shape was so associated with charcoal grilling, it just never caught on," Kempster says. In 1985, Weber-Stephen introduced the rectangular Genesis gas line with triangular "Flavorizer" cooking bars designed to minimize flare-ups while mimicking the mouthwatering effect of meat and fish juices sizzling on hot coals. Today, four of *Consumer Reports'* top seven midsize grills for 2013 are Webers, and the company's new cookbook is an Amazon.com bestseller. Its US call centres handle 500,000 questions a year, from how long to cook a pork tenderloin to the best way to grill a squirrel.

The new Weber-Stephen CEO has asked Kempster, 66, to stay for at least two more years. Kempster has nine Weber grills and smokers in his backyard, including a pair of 36-inch kettles he uses to cook for crowds. His go-to dishes are beef tenderloin and Alaskan king crab legs. He suggests snipping off the thicker ends of the crab legs and cooking them for 10 to 12 minutes before putting the thin ends on the grill.

Meathead Goldwyn, the barbecue impresario (given name: Craig) who runs the website Amazingribs.com, has more than a dozen grills and smokers in his suburban Chicago backyard – and a beat-up Weber kettle he bought for $50 about 20 years ago, Goldwyn says. "For what I do, which is help people learn to cook, you have to have a Weber kettle, because it's ubiquitous."

Source: Bryan Gruley, Bloomberg Businessweek, June 27, 2013.

The radical rejuvenation perspective

According to proponents of the radical rejuvenation perspective, companies should focus on breakthrough innovations that change the rules of the competitive game rather than becoming better at playing by the current rules. Game-changing innovations provide innovators a significant competitive advantage, forcing rivals to follow and play by their rules. The more radical the departure from the industry rules, the more difficult it will be for competitors to follow and the higher the benefits for the innovator are likely to be.

If a firm decides to use a breakthrough technology or a new business model to strengthen its competitive position vis-à-vis rivals, this requires some major changes in a short period of time, as such innovations to the business model are inherently disrupting. Creating novel products and developing a unique business formula requires a sharp break with the past. Old ways must be discarded before new methods can be adopted. This is the essence of what Schumpeter (1950) referred to as the process of 'creative destruction', inherent in the capitalist system. This process is not orderly and protracted, but disruptive and intense. Therefore, it is argued, successful firms must learn to master the skill of radical innovation (e.g. D'Aveni, 1994; Hamel, 1996). Rapid implementation of system-wide change is an essential organizational capability.

In the radical rejuvenation perspective, strong company leadership is essential (Leifer, 2000). Break-through renewal is not only disrupting for rivals, but also for the organization itself. The business model needs to be renewed, usually in conjunction with the organizational system. Such dramatic alterations can only be successful when a strong company leader is in the position to get things done. This is even more prominent as a disruptive renewal project usually takes extensive time to be developed from an idea into an actual product, which makes the continuity of the project vulnerable for feedback sessions along the way. It is crucial that the disruptive renewal project will be a success, because in the absence, there is the danger of the 'failure trap': 'failure promotes the search for even newer ideas and thus more exploration' (Gupta *et al.,* 2006).

Proponents of the radical rejuvenation perspective agree that improvements are useful to help companies defending and strengthening their competitive positions, however, they argue that it comes at a high price. Sustained improvement and allocating key company resources on projects that enhance existing products, services and technologies, goes at the expense of strategically more effective game-changing innovations. Focusing on serving current customers with better propositions at lower costs, leads to maximizing short-term return on innovation budgets, and diminishes the capacity to engage in breakthrough innovations to serve customers in the future. Indeed, many well-managed companies that continuously improve on the basis of customer needs fail *exactly because* they are well managed, a phenomena dubbed by Christensen (1997, 2011, Reading 9.2) as the Innovator's Dilemma.

EXHIBIT 9.3   THE RADICAL REJUVENATION PERSPECTIVE

HAMDI ULUKAYA KEEPS THE YOGHURT MARKET FRESH

Born in Turkey to a Kurdish dairy farmer, Hamdi Ulukaya used his childhood knowledge to build a Greek Yoghurt empire that made him a billionaire in just six years. While his original intent of coming to America was to study business and English, he soon got sidetracked by an ad in the paper offering

an old dairy plant for sale. He dropped out of his studies, a parallel that might have contributed to his officious title, the "Steve Jobs of yoghurt", to buy the 80-year-old plant that he restored himself. He sold his first container of yoghurt just 18 months later and went on to expand at an impressive pace, today employing over 1,000 people.

Until half a decade ago, a very sweet type of yoghurt dominated the American supermarket shelves.

The alternative to this popular breakfast item, Greek yoghurt, containing more protein and less fat, had never been available outside specialty shops. Recession-weary and health-conscious shoppers took very warmly to Mr Ulukaya's efforts to extend their breakfast choices with his traditional Greek product, consequently growing Greek yoghurt sales from 1 to 60 per cent of the total yoghurt business.

One might wonder why yoghurt giants Stark or Danone did not act upon these trends, as retailers certainly welcomed Mr Ulukaya's products with open arms, right from the start. In fact, the Greek yoghurt invasion was not the first time that food and beverage incumbents were caught by surprise. Plum Organics revolutionized baby food packaging, resulting in 20 per cent of American babies now being fed by squirting food out of a container instead of being spoon-fed, while Koppert Cress commoditized decorative foodstuffs to liven up plates in restaurants all over the world; a very profitable niche in which it still maintains a monopoly.

The common practice in the food and beverage industry is that successful start-ups are being acquired by incumbents. Mr Ulukaya, however, has never accepted any of the lucrative offers he got for his Greek yoghurt empire, keeping all shares under his own control. This resulted in him not just disrupting the

market once and then being integrated in a large bureaucracy, but allowed him to keep going. After his first success of introducing Greek yoghurt to the American public, he opened a store in SoHo, one of New York's most fashionable neighbourhoods, selling the most exquisite combinations of Greek yoghurt with peach, dates and much more. With his unique and healthy snacks – nearly as exclusive and expensive as the neighbouring VIP bars' cocktails – Mr Ulukaya tries to vamp up the image of breakfast items. Other savvy moves, in a similar vein, are a new line of healthy products for children and healthy alternatives to Red Bull or coffee.

Mr Ulukaya is an innovator *par excellence*. He has been able to keep surprising the establishment with new and exciting ways to position his products. Whether he can keep momentum once his company has reached a similar size as the yoghurt giants he is competing with remains to be seen, but based on his passion, continuous streak of awards and commitment to being the sole shareholder, we can look forward to many more delicious market disruptions.

Co-author: Jasper de Vries

Sources: 'At Chobani, the Turkish King of Greek Yogurt', Bloomberg, January 31, 2013; 'Cultural revolution: The Greek-yogurt phenomenon in America left big food firms feeling sour. They are trying to get better at innovation', *The Economist*, August 31, 2013.

MANAGING THE PARADOX OF EXPLOITATION AND EXPLORATION

He that will not apply new remedies must expect new evils, for time is the greatest innovator.

Francis Bacon (1561–1626); English philosopher, statesman, scientist, jurist, orator and author

So, how should managers go about renewing their organizations? Should strategizing managers focus on sustained renewal by ongoing improvement of their current business model? Or should they strive for disruptive renewal by focusing on radical, breakthrough innovations? There is no consensus within the field of strategic management on how to balance exploitation and exploration, however a number of scholars have discussed different ways of dealing with the arguments put forward in the debate (see Table 9.1). Depending on the situation, strategizing managers can assess the arguments and develop their own way of dealing with the paradox.

While the general notion of strategy paradoxes and competing demands is often not – or not fully – embraced among scholars, it is one of the key research areas in innovation research. Initiated by March's (1991) pioneering article, the paradox of exploitation and exploration has become highly influential in the fields of organizational learning and

TABLE 9.1 Strategic improvement versus strategic rejuvenation perspective

	Strategic improvement perspective	Radical rejuvenation perspective
Emphasis on	Exploitation over exploration	Exploration over exploitation
Strategic innovation as	Sustained improvements	Disruptive rejuvenation
Innovation effects	Undramatic and long lasting	Dramatic and short-term
Innovation ideas come from	All internal and external company stakeholders	Entrepreneurial company leaders
Innovation investments are	Low risk, small returns	High risk, high returns
Main reinforcement mechanism	Success trap	Failure trap
Strategic renewal process	Organic adaptation	Creative destruction
View on the future	Building the future	Shaping the future
Lasting renewal requires	Continuous learning	Radical breakthrough series
Long-term renewal dynamics	Persistent transient state	Stable and unstable states alternate

organizational behaviour, and currently also enjoys the attention from many strategy researchers. As strategic innovation concerns the future of the company, it is at the core of what strategizing managers are actually doing. The question is thus, how can they best manage the paradox of exploitation and exploration? Taken the taxonomy in Chapter 1 (Figure 1.8) the following options have been discussed in the literature.

Parallel processing

Parallel processing involves separating exploitation and exploration processes in different organizational units (differentiation), while integration takes place at a different – usually higher – organizational level. This option has been coined 'spatial separation' – an academic term still used by organization behaviour scholars. Organizations that employ both exploitation – for example, by improving production processes – and exploration – such as technological research and development – as the means of dealing with the paradox of exploitation and exploration are called ambidextrous organizations (Benner and Tushman, 2003). Ambidextrous organizations separate exploitative and explorative processes in different organizational units. The literature has suggested three distinct parallel processing practices:

Parallel processing internally. A well-known practice is to build a separate research and development (R&D) unit that develop new technologies. The outcomes are then transferred to other organizational units, such as business units or market groups. Some researchers have indicated, however, that differentiating may be easy but integrating often fails. The problems are many, for example when researchers have developed technologies and patents, while managers have difficulties matching the technologies to client demands.

Parallel processing with external partners. Exploitation and exploration can also be separated by outsourcing one of the processes to an external strategic partner. When exploitation is outsourced, partners take responsibility to adopt the firm's exploitative processes, such as manufacturing products, including the ongoing improvement of current processes and products. In this case, the company is able to focus the key organizational resources on exploration processes, creating the new generation of products and services. Conversely, the firm can also outsource exploration to specialized companies, and stay focused on efficient and effective exploitation. Strategizing managers then integrate the partner's deliverables within the company processes. A main advantage of parallel processing with external partners is that it effectively combines the contradicting core capabilities of two firms; a main pitfall is, however, that the partner's strategic objectives may change and become conflicting.

Navigating

Entrepreneurs often separate exploration and exploitation over time in the early start-up phase. When starting a new business on the basis of a new idea for a new technology (such as a new app) or a novel market proposition, the entrepreneur first explores and then exploits – hence navigates over time, also called temporal separation.

In this case, the start-up entrepreneur is not renewing as there is not yet an organization to be renewed, however when this initiative is being taken by a corporate entrepreneur or a business development manager, the entrepreneurial activity may well intend to renew the current company. The new activity is then meant to replace or improve established businesses. This process had become known by the famous CEO from General Electric, Jack Welch, who introduced the 'Destroy your business dot com' programme in the year 2000. The general practice is that the renewing unit stays at a distance from the established company in order to prevent managers from the current business killing the initiative in its infancy. This practice has been advocated by Peters and Waterman (1982), who dubbed these promising corporate start-ups 'skunk works' as the initiative may threaten the current organization and thus 'stinks'.

Balancing

One of the differences between exploitation and exploration is time orientation: sustaining renewal processes (exploitation) has a short-term focus, while disrupting processes (exploration) is long-term oriented. Notwithstanding the differences, it is suggested in the literature that the processes may be combined in the same unit. The strategic agenda then consists of both short-term and long-term innovation projects. The balance between the two is not only company-specific, but also dynamic as priorities can change. Although balancing exploitation and exploration is more complex than parallel processing, some scholars prefer balancing because, although differentiating is relatively easy and fast, the integrating part is usually a problem.

When balancing takes place at the individual level, some strategists are expected to fulfil roles in both sustaining and disrupting renewal processes. For example, knowledge workers both build their professional practice at higher levels and explore radically different ways to serve future clients. Being able to do so requires personal characteristics that not all individuals possess. Smith and Tushman (2005, Reading 1.2) argue that 'the ability to engage in paradoxical thinking may be vital for effectively managing exploitation and exploration.'

The human factor in balancing the paradox, in particular the composition of the company's leadership team, has been explored by Peter Robertson. In a book, provocatively entitled *Always Change a Winning Team* (2005), Robertson combines insights from ethology – a field strongly related to neuroanatomy, ecology and evolution theory – with the dynamics of the well-known S-curve. Robertson argues that the composition of a successful leadership team should differ over the S-curve. In the early phase, the leadership team should mainly be composed of leaders employing visionary feedforward thinking with a passion to explore the unknown, while in the mature phase, the leadership team should mainly consist of analytic feedback thinking leaders (see Figure 9.4). Over the S-curve, the composition of the leadership team should be changed in anticipation of the next phase. According to Robertson, the key role in permanently changing the leadership team is a 'chairperson', the CEO, who connects the feedforward and feedback thinkers and who is in charge of continuously rebalancing the 'winning team'. This individual needs to have what Robertson calls high 'complexity maturity', a term that

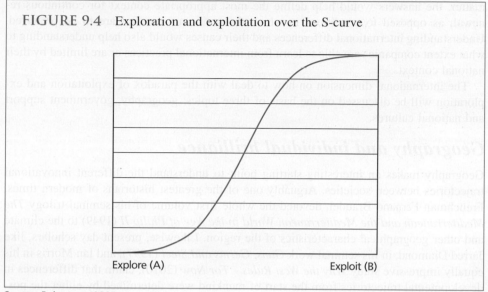

FIGURE 9.4 Exploration and exploitation over the S-curve

Explore (A)   Exploit (B)

Source: Robertson, 2005.

relates to what Smith and Tushman (2005) describe as 'the ability to engage in para-doxical thinking'.

STRATEGIC INNOVATION IN INTERNATIONAL PERSPECTIVE

Co-author: Gep Eisenloeffel

Imagination is more important than knowledge
Albert Einstein (1879–1955) German-American physicist

Again it has become clear that the views on strategic innovation sharply differ within the strategy field. The differences are often explained by international differences. For example, Imai (Reading 9.1) explicitly introduces specific national preferences in his approach to strategic innovation. He argues that 'Japanese companies generally favour the gradualist approach and Western companies the great-leap approach – an approach epitomized by the term innovation. Western management worships at the altar of innovation.' This general, yet fundamental, distinction is supported by other researchers such as Ouchi (1981), Pascale and Athos (1981) and Kagono *et al.* (1985), although all of these international comparative studies concentrate only on US–Japanese differences and are relatively old. The extensive study by Kagono and his colleagues among the top 1000 American and Japanese companies concludes that there are clearly different national change styles: 'The US-style, elite-guided, logical, deductive approach achieves major innovation in strategies geared to surpass other companies. In contrast, the Japanese inductive, step-wise gradual adjustment approach seeks to steadily build upon the existing strengths to *evolve* strategy' (Kagono *et al.*, 1985: 89–90). Other authors suggest that the United States and Japan seem to represent the two extremes, while most other industrialized countries seem to be somewhere in between (e.g. Calori and De Woot, 1994; Krüger, 1996).

Such pronounced international variance raises the question of cause. For what reason do firms in different countries prefer different views on strategic innovation? Are there any country-specific factors that lead to diverse perspectives? If national context would matter, the answers would help define the most appropriate context for continuous renewal, as opposed to conditions in which discontinuous renewal are to be preferred. Understanding international differences and their causes would also help understanding to what extent companies are able to learn from international practices or are limited by their national context.

The international dimension on how to deal with the paradox of exploitation and exploration will be discussed on the basis of three topics: geography, government support and national cultures.

Geography and individual brilliance

Geography makes an interesting starting point to understand the different innovational trajectories between societies. Arguably one of the greatest historians of modern times, Frenchman Fernand Braudel, devoted the whole first volume of his seminal trilogy *The Mediterranean and the Mediterranean World in the Age of Philip II* (1949) to the climate and other geographical characteristics of the region. Likewise, present-day scholars, like Jarred Diamond, in his seminal work *Guns, Germs and Steel* (1997), and Ian Morris in his equally impressive study *Why the West Rules – For Now* (2010), claim that differences in developmental trajectories from the start of mankind were determined by either the possibilities or the impossibilities to foster technologies that enabled progress. Differences in environmental conditions make clear why technological trajectories were – and still are – unevenly distributed.

Throughout history, individuals with great skills and vision invented things to made progress possible; one of them is Thomas Edison. Edison was not only a great inventor; more than anything else he was a great entrepreneur. And he was, as in the words of Hamel and Prahalad, *Competing for the Future* 1994 *avant là lettre*. Edison took immense risks in creating new needs and value for new costumers. In the process he created one of America's greatest enterprises: General Electric Company.

Thomas Edison's success also relates to the favourable context he worked in. For example, all findings and innovations that had to do with the great explorations of Chinese admiral Zheng He in the early fifteenth century were destroyed by order of the emperor. What if great inventions of the Chinese like gunpowder or in the field of astronomy and shipbuilding had resulted in them conquering the world? Freeman and Perez (1988) argue: 'Technological development is not an isolated endogen process. It does not have a life of its own. Specific choices within the realm of technological opportunities are not the product of technological change; they are the product of those who make the choices within the frontier of possibilities. Technology does not drive choice; choice drives technology.'

Governmental support

Proactive governmental support often proves to be crucial. The development of aviation is a good example. From the mere 12 seconds the Wright brothers managed to fly in 1903 to the development of the first commercial airliners operating already in the early 1920s (Royal Dutch Airlines, KLM), the development of this industry cannot be explained without the war of countries involved. Dutch engineer Anthony Fokker, working for the Germans, was one of the first great pioneers in this field exploiting the opportunities presented by him as a result of the war. Many other entrepreneurs, like Howard Hughes, and companies like American Lockheed or French Dassault followed suit. Helicopters were improved and used for the first time in the Korean war and Stealth technology dates back from the late 1950s after earlier attempts in preventing radar tracking of US spy planes during the Cold War by the Soviet Union had been unsuccessful. Furthermore, present-day drones are invented for war and not for commercial purposes. The importance of the relationships between military technological innovations and companies that profit from this relationship was already mentioned by president Eisenhower, who in his farewell address in 1961 warned against the growing power of a so-called 'military-industrial complex.'

Governmental support for the development of technologies played - and still play - also a role in non-military sectors. The immense influence of Japan's Ministry of International Trade and Industry (MITI) has already been mentioned in previous chapters. Likewise, the European Commission in the 1980s supported European companies vis-à-vis Japanese and US competitors with research and technological development programs in the field of information technologies, like ESPRIT and EUREKA (Van Tulder and Junne, 1988). Governmental support and preceding rules and regulations play a decisive role in the transition from one technological platform to another. For instance, since the Second World War, the European Union has been crucial in the transition from coal to an oil- and gas-based energy supply. In China, the government promotes solar power batteries to reduce emissions from two- to four-wheeled motor vehicles.

The absorptive capacity of a region vis-à-vis the implementation of inventions consists of more than governmental support. For one thing, innovations never occur as isolated phenomena. In this respect, Porter's diamond model in his book *The Competitive Advantage of Nations* (1990) is a good starting point. For instance, the ICT sector consists of a cluster of technologies with no company knowing all. Therefore, not just the industry structure is important, but also supporting and relating industries. Moreover, factor endowments, such as infrastructure and knowledge, as well as demand conditions play an important role in the development of separate sectors and the subsequent potential success of individual companies.

Internatiolization of technology

In recent years, there has been a steady expansion in the literature that relates the *internalization* and *international transfer* of technology by MNEs, in combination also termed *Internatiolization*. It is a literature that can be traced back to John Dunning's (1958) study of the effect of American MNEs on technology and productivity in Great Britain, and Raymond Vernon's (1966) product life cycle theory explaining the technological drive accompanying the growth of US foreign direct investment in Europe in the post Second World War era.

Evidence (see Dosi, 1984), however, indicates that technology cannot just be exported. The 'catching up' to narrow existing technological gaps involves more than only foreign direct investment (FDI). Cantwell (1989), for instance, showed 'how inward FDI from the US only proved to be successful when the local industry in a host European country had enough 'absorptive capacity' in indigenous firms, due to an inherited strong technological tradition from the past (such as in the case of the German chemical industry).' The same applies to the success of Japan in the sixties and the so-called Newly Industrializing Countries, like Singapore, Hong Kong, Taiwan and South Korea, of the seventies. Japan already had a pre-war industrial base. Singapore and Hong Kong had a long standing heritage of a highly developed service sector. Taiwan and South Korea had a well-trained working force inherited from their import-substitution policy of the pre Second World War era. Furthermore, it obviously helped that South Korea and Taiwan were financially supported by the US, saving them from the debt crisis many other developing countries faced when trying to make the same transition from import substitution to export orientation.

Two recent developments influence internalizing technologies. First of all, knowledge distribution has become far easier by information technology. Currently, a significant proportion of communication and information transfer is based on digital, rather than analogue, technologies. This means all sorts of information can now be stored, processed, manipulated and transmitted between any two places in the world. This arguably most persuasive and influential development of recent years has led scholars to claim that, due to this globalization of technology, the world will become a 'global village,' a term first coined by Marshall McLuhan (1964) and picked up by other scholars (such as Levitt, 1983, Reading 12.1 in this book).

Freeman and Perez (1988) argue 'that in the latest techno-economic paradigm ICT has become a 'carrier branch' or a 'transmission belt' for the transferral of innovation across sectors.' 'Company evidence now suggests that ICT has become also a core connector of potential fields of technological development within firms or between firms in technology-based alliances that facilitate the technological fusion of a formerly disparate spread of innovative activity. Thus, while in the past the machine-building industry simply passed knowledge of methods from one field of mechanical application to another, ICT potentially combines the variety of technological fields themselves and so increases the scope of wider innovation.'

Secondly, technological development is not only the result of companies exporting their findings on a worldwide scale. Some countries, like the previously mentioned BRIC-countries, have reached the threshold of developing new technologies themselves. Home governments and national capital, often in cooperation with foreign MNEs, stimulate the development of technology. In many cases, like in India, with its huge potential of English speaking Ph.D. students and China, with a whole new generation willing to devote all their time on science-based education, great new findings are just a matter of time.

A good indicator of shifting technological innovations from the traditional industrialized countries in the North West to the upcoming economies in the South East is the number of patents granted per country. This concentration of patents is highly uneven. Between 2000 and 2006, applicants from Japan, the US, the Republic of Korea and Germany received 73 per cent of total patents worldwide. In that same period, the number of patents granted to applicants from China and the Republic of Korea grew with an average annual growth rate of 26.5 per cent and 23.2 per cent respectively. The rapid growth of Chinese patents match the emergence of this country as 'the second largest producer of scientific knowledge' as revealed by an analysis of 10,500 scientific journals worldwide for the period of 1981–2008 (WIPO, 2008).

Culture and technology

Transferring knowledge, and intangible knowledge particularly, is a complex matter. Tangible knowledge can be codified and represented in engineering blueprints and designs, which can be supplemented by formal documents and management guidebooks describing organizational methods. This type of knowledge and resulting technology can be learned and distributed, however it is only one element in the process of learning. Intangible or tacit knowledge, on the other hand, is deeply personalized, which inhibits instructing others by means of official devices.

Most of the literature on cross-cultural management argues that culture plays an important role, from the invention to the implementation of new technologies. And although some scholars, for instance Nigel Holden, explicitly maintain that even culture can be made codifiable, as amplified by the title of Holden's book *Cross Cultural Management a Knowledge Based Perspective* (2002), most scholars claim that cultural values are intangible. In the words of Trompenaars and Hampden-Turner (2000): "we know what the Japanese workers do, and if we could imitate them we would." Or in line with the famous phrase of Geert Hofstede (1980): "culture is a form of mental and physical programming, 'a software of the mind'. It is almost impossible to imitate if you have not been raised to think that way."

An obvious distinction in cultural values is between individualism and collectivism. Many studies (e.g. Trompenaars and Hampden-Turner, 2000) claim the correlation between individualism and innovation. For instance, the two countries considered to be most individualistic, the US and Great Britain, also showed tremendous capacities to realize radical frame-breaking innovations. Furthermore, the US leads the world ranking of Nobel Prizes won, in the practical application of scientific principles.

Strongly correlating with individualism is inner-orientation (Trompenaars and Hampden-Turner, 2000). This cultural dimension is also a great indicator of the willingness and ability to innovate. According to Trompenaars and Hampden-Turner (2000) "the hero of the inner-directed society is the 'great innovator,' the person who began with an idea inside his head, persisted on creating it, and finally established it as a major feature of the external environment."

Trompenaars and Hampden-Turner provide a strong argument claiming that collectivistic and outer-directed cultures have their own merits when it comes to innovations and implementation. Instead of inventing new products or processes, the Japanese, for instance, proved to be masters of improving processes and products initiated by the Americans. Furthermore, outer-oriented cultures are far more adaptable to changes (Schneider and Barsoux, 2003) and often more in tune with demands and value creation for their customers (Trompenaars and Hampden-Turner, 2000). As a result, "during the eighties, America lost several markets it had originated through its inner-directness to outer directed Japanese refinements" (Trompenaars and Hampden-Turner, 2000).

One important element, often overlooked, is the importance of how cultures deal with time. Fordism, for instance, is a production system that is based on a so-called linear and sequential concept of time. Lean production, however, deals with time in a different way. Kaizen deals with time as a circle improving production methods is likewise perceived as a process without beginning or end. The second different way of looking at time relates to a sequential versus a more holistic approach (see also Chapter 2 for a discussion on analytic and holistic strategic reasoning). In lean production, with its emphasis on just-in-time processes, flexibility and synchronization of the production process are crucial.

Culture also plays a role in the way people perceive ownership of inventions. Whereas in Western societies it is obvious that the inventor has the right to pick the fruits from his individual findings, in Eastern societies such as China, influenced by the teachings of Confucius, people have a different attitude towards private intellectual ownership. The teachings of Confucius stress the fact that knowledge is considered to be for the benefit of everybody (Lee, 2010; Chen and Lee, 2008). A great mind (the father), has the obligation to share his wisdom with the people (his children). The father figure is even proud when his children try to make the best of his knowledge. Therefore, people even have to use his knowledge for their own benefits. What in the West is considered to be stealing one's intellectual property rights in the East is seen as copying and improving on the findings of a most honoured father figure.

INTRODUCTION TO THE READINGS

Every act of creation is first of all an act of destruction.
Pablo Picasso (1881–1973); Spanish artist

So, how should managers go about renewing their organizations? The debate will be kicked-off in the first reading (9.1), 'Kaizen', by Masaaki Imai, which has been selected to represent the strategic improvement perspective. This article has been taken from Imai's famous book *Kaizen: The Key to Japan's Competitive Success*. Kaizen (pronounced Ky'zen) is a Japanese term that is best translated as continuous improvement. Imai argues that it is this continuous improvement philosophy that best explains the competitive strength of so many Japanese companies. In his view, Western companies have an unhealthy obsession with one-shot innovations. They are fixated on the great leap forward, while disregarding the power of accumulated small changes. Imai believes that disruptive innovations are also important for competitive success, but that they should be embedded in an organization that is driven to continuously improve.

The radical rejuvenation perspective is represented by Clayton Christensen. In Reading 9.2, adapted from his popular book, *The Innovator's Dilemma, When New Technologies Cause Great Firms to Fail,* Christensen explains why outstanding companies lost their market leadership when confronted with disruptive changes in technology and market structure. This phenomenon applies particularly to excellent firms with an excessive customer focus, Christensen argues, *exactly because* their excessive customer focus prevent them from creating new markets and finding new customers for the products of the future. His argument follows Burgelman, who wrote back in 1991: 'Paradoxically, adaptation to existing environmental demands may reduce the organization's capacity to adapt to future changes in the environment or to seek our new environments (1991: 251). Christensen has termed this strategic innovation paradox 'the innovator's dilemma'.

While the third reading in other chapters predominantly represents recent insights in how to deal with strategy paradoxes, in this chapter the article that actually started the debate on the paradox of exploitation and exploration has been chosen. March's 1991 pioneering and seminal article 'Exploitation and Exploration in Organizational Learning' (Reading 9.3) started a new research stream and stimulated many scholars in several academic fields to understand how companies do and should manage the paradox of exploitation and exploration to achieving long-term success. The first movers were scholars in the field of Organizational Learning and Organizational Behaviour, such as the currently prominent Harvard professor Michael Tushman (e.g. Benner and Tushman (2002; 2003).

March argues that 'companies require both exploitation and exploration to achieve persistent success', and have to manage both by finding a balance, because 'the two are fundamentally incompatible'. These propositions have been – and still are for that matter – subject to scientific debate. However, while alternative avenues have been described and suggested (see for a thorough discussion Gupta *et al.* (2006)), March's proposition still holds. Stronger even: the popular term 'ambidextrous organization' takes March's proposition as a more general characteristic of organizations. From here, the fundamental idea that companies have to manage multiple tensions hallmarks a significant portion of present day research in the organization and strategy sciences.

Kaizen

By Masaaki Imai[1]

B ack in the 1950s, I was working with the Japan Productivity Center in Washington, DC. My job mainly consisted of escorting groups of Japanese businessmen who were visiting American companies to study 'the secret of American industrial productivity'. Toshiro Yamada, now Professor Emeritus of the Faculty of Engineering at Kyoto University, was a member of one such study team visiting the United States to study the industrial vehicle industry. Recently, the members of his team gathered to celebrate the silver anniversary of their trip.

At the banquet table, Yamada said he had recently been back to the United States in a 'sentimental journey' to some of the plants he had visited, among them the River Rouge steelworks in Dearborn, Michigan. Shaking his head in disbelief, he said, 'You know, the plant was exactly the same as it had been 25 years ago.'

These conversations set me to thinking about the great differences in the ways Japanese and Western managers approach their work. It is inconceivable that a Japanese plant would remain virtually unchanged for over a quarter of a century.

I had long been looking for a key concept to explain these two very different management approaches, one that might also help explain why many Japanese companies have come to gain their increasingly conspicuous competitive edge. For instance, how do we explain the fact that while most new ideas come from the West and some of the most advanced plants, institutions and technologies are found there, there are also many plants there that have changed little since the 1950s?

Change is something which everybody takes for granted. Recently, an American executive at a large multinational firm told me his company chairman had said at the start of an executive committee meeting: 'Gentlemen, our job is to manage change. If we fail, we must change management.' The executive smiled and said, 'We all got the message!'

In Japan, change is a way of life, too. But are we talking about the same change when we talk about managing change or else changing management? It dawned on me that there might be different kinds of change: gradual and abrupt. While we can easily observe both gradual and abrupt changes in Japan, gradual change is not so obvious a part of the Western way of life. How are we to explain this difference?

This question led me to consider the question of values. Could it be that differences between the value systems in Japan and the West account for their different attitudes toward gradual change and abrupt change? Abrupt changes are easily grasped by everyone concerned, and people are usually elated to see them. This is generally true in both Japan and the West. Yet what about the gradual changes? My earlier statement that it is inconceivable that a Japanese plant would remain unchanged for years refers to gradual change as well as abrupt change.

Thinking all this over, I came to the conclusion that the key difference between how change is understood in Japan and how it is viewed in the West lies in the Kaizen concept – a concept that is so natural and obvious to many Japanese managers that they often do not even realize that they possess it! The Kaizen concept explains why companies cannot remain the same for long in Japan. Moreover, after many years of studying Western business practices, I have reached the conclusion that this Kaizen concept is non-existent, or at least very weak, in most Western companies today. Worse yet, they reject it without knowing what it really entails. It's the old 'not invented here' syndrome. And this lack of Kaizen helps explain why an American or European factory can remain exactly the same for a quarter of a century.

The essence of Kaizen is simple and straightforward: Kaizen means improvement. Moreover, Kaizen means ongoing improvement involving everyone, including both managers and workers. The Kaizen philosophy assumes that our way of life – be it our working life, our social life, or our home life – deserves to be constantly improved.

In trying to understand Japan's post-war 'economic miracle,' scholars, journalists and businesspeople alike have dutifully studied such factors as the productivity movement, total quality control (TQC), small-group activities, the suggestion system, automation,

---

[1]Source: This article was adapted with permission from Chapters 1 and 2 of *Kaizen: The Key to Japan's Competitive Success,* McGraw-Hill, New York, 1986. Copyright © 1986 by The McGraw-Hill Companies, Inc. Reproduced by permission of The McGraw-Hill Companies, Inc.

industrial robots and labour relations. They have given much attention to some of Japan's unique management practices, among them the lifetime employment system, seniority-based wages and enterprise unions. Yet I feel they have failed to grasp the very simple truth that lies behind the many myths concerning Japanese management.

The essence of most 'uniquely Japanese' management practices – be they productivity improvement, TQC (total quality control) activities, QC (quality control) circles or labour relations – can be reduced to one word: Kaizen. Using the term Kaizen in place of such words as productivity, TQC, ZD (zero defects), *kamban* and the suggestion system paints a far clearer picture of what has been going on in Japanese industry. Kaizen is an umbrella concept covering most of those 'uniquely Japanese' practices that have recently achieved such worldwide fame.

The implications of TQC or CWQC (companywide quality control) in Japan have been that these concepts have helped Japanese companies generate a process-oriented way of thinking and develop strategies that assure continuous improvement involving people at all levels of the organizational hierarchy. The message of the Kaizen strategy is that not a day should go by without some kind of improvement being made somewhere in the company.

The belief that there should be unending improvement is deeply ingrained in the Japanese mentality. As the old Japanese saying goes, 'If a man has not been seen for three days, his friends should take a good look at him to see what changes have befallen him.' The implication is that he must have changed in three days, so his friends should be attentive enough to notice the changes.

After World War II, most Japanese companies had to start literally from the ground up. Every day brought new challenges to managers and workers alike, and every day meant progress. Simply staying in business required unending progress, and Kaizen has become a way of life. It was also fortunate that the various tools that helped elevate this Kaizen concept to new heights were introduced to Japan in the late 1950s and early 1960s by such experts as W.E. Deming and J.M. Juran.

However, most new concepts, systems and tools that are widely used in Japan today have subsequently been developed in Japan and represent qualitative improvements upon the statistical quality control and total quality control of the 1960s.

Kaizen and management

Figure 9.1.1 shows how job functions are perceived in Japan. As indicated, management has two major components: maintenance and improvement. Maintenance refers to activities directed toward maintaining current technological, managerial and operating standards; improvement refers to those directed toward improving current standards.

Under its maintenance functions, management performs its assigned tasks so that everybody in the company can follow the established SOP (Standard Operating Procedure). This means that management must first establish policies, rules, directives and procedures for all major operations and then see to it that everybody follows SOP. If people are able to follow the standard but do not, management must introduce discipline. If people are unable to follow the standard, management must either provide training, or review and revise the standard so that people can follow it.

In any business, an employee's work is based on existing standards, either explicit or implicit, imposed by management. Maintenance refers to maintaining such standards through training and discipline. By contrast, improvement refers to improving the standards. The Japanese perception of management boils down to one precept: maintain and improve standards.

The higher up the manager is, the more he is concerned with improvement. At the bottom level, an unskilled worker working at a machine may spend all his time following instructions. However, as he becomes more proficient at his work, he begins to think about

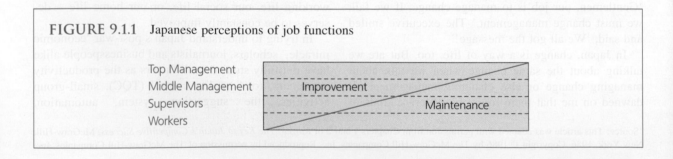

FIGURE 9.1.1 Japanese perceptions of job functions

Top Management
Middle Management
Supervisors
Workers

Improvement

Maintenance

improvement. He begins to contribute to improvements in the way his work is done, either through individual suggestions or through group suggestions.

Ask any manager at a successful Japanese company what top management is pressing for, and the answer will be, 'Kaizen' (improvement). Improving standards means establishing higher standards. Once this is done, it becomes management's maintenance job to see that the new standards are observed. Lasting improvement is achieved only when people work to higher standards. Maintenance and improvement have thus become inseparable for most Japanese managers.

What is improvement? Improvement can be broken down between Kaizen and innovation. Kaizen signifies small improvements made in the status quo as a result of ongoing efforts. Innovation involves a drastic improvement in the status quo as a result of a large investment in new technology or equipment. Figure 9.1.2 shows the breakdown among maintenance, Kaizen and innovation as perceived by Japanese management.

On the other hand, most Western managers' perceptions of job functions are as shown in Figure 9.1.2. There is little room in Western management for the Kaizen concept.

Sometimes, another type of management is found in the high-technology industries. These are the companies that are born running, grow rapidly, and then disappear just as rapidly when their initial success wanes or markets change.

The worst companies are those which do nothing but maintenance, meaning there is no internal drive for Kaizen or innovation, change is forced on management by market conditions and competition and management does not know where it wants to go.

Implications of QC for Kaizen

While management is usually concerned with such issues as productivity and quality, the thrust of this article is to look at the other side of the picture – at Kaizen.

The starting point for improvement is to recognize the need. This comes from recognition of a problem. If no problem is recognized, there is no recognition of the need for improvement. Complacency is the arch enemy of Kaizen. Therefore, Kaizen emphasizes problem-awareness and provides clues for identifying problems.

Once identified, problems must be solved. Thus Kaizen is also a problem-solving process. In fact, Kaizen requires the use of various problem-solving tools. Improvement reaches new heights with every problem that is solved. In order to consolidate the new level, however, the improvement must be standardized. Thus Kaizen also requires standardization.

Such terms as QC (quality control), SQC (statistical quality control), QC circles, and TQC (or CWQC) often appear in connection with Kaizen. To avoid unnecessary confusion, it may be helpful to clarify these terms here. The word *quality* has been interpreted in many different ways, and there is no agreement on what actually constitutes quality. In its broadest sense, quality is anything that can be improved. In this context, quality is associated not only with products and services but also with the way people work, the way machines are operated and the way systems and procedures are dealt with. It includes all aspects of human behaviour. This is why it is more useful to talk about Kaizen than about quality or productivity.

The English term *improvement* as used in the Western context more often than not means improvement in

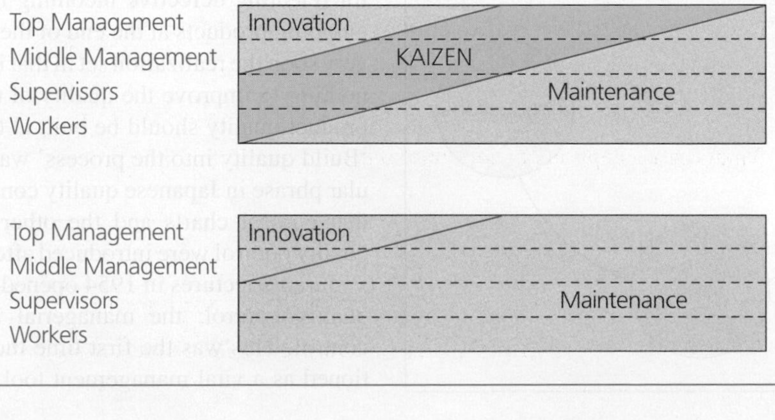

FIGURE 9.1.2   Japanese vs Western perceptions of job functions

equipment, thus excluding the human elements. By contrast, Kaizen is generic and can be applied to every aspect of everybody's activities. This said, however, it must be admitted that such terms as quality and quality control have played a vital role in the development of Kaizen in Japan.

In March 1950, the Union of Japanese Scientists and Engineers (JUSE) started publishing its magazine *Statistical Quality Control*. In July of the same year, W.E. Deming was invited to Japan to teach statistical quality control at an eight-day seminar organized by JUSE. Deming visited Japan several times in the 1950s, and it was during one of those visits that he made his famous prediction that Japan would soon be flooding the world market with quality products.

Deming also introduced the 'Deming cycle', one of the crucial QC tools for assuring continuous improvement, to Japan. The Deming cycle is also called the Deming wheel or the PDCA (Plan-Do-Check-Action) cycle (see Figure 9.1.3.) Deming stressed the importance of constant interaction among research, design, production and sales in order for a company to arrive at better quality that satisfies customers. He taught that this wheel should be rotated on the ground of quality-first perceptions and quality-first responsibility. With this process, he argued, the company could win consumer confidence and acceptance and prosper.

In July 1954, J.M. Juran was invited to Japan to conduct a JUSE seminar on quality-control management. This was the first time QC was dealt with from the overall management perspective.

In 1956, Japan Shortwave Radio included a course on quality control as part of its educational programming. In November 1960, the first national quality month was inaugurated. It was also in 1960 that Q-marks and Q-flags were formally adopted. Then in April 1962 the magazine *Quality Control for the Foreman* was launched by JUSE, and the first QC circle was started that same year.

A QC circle is defined as a small group that *voluntarily* performs quality-control activities within the shop. The small group carries out its work continuously as part of a company-wide programme of quality control, self-development, mutual education, and flow-control and improvement within the workshop. The QC circle is only *part* of a company-wide programme; it is never the whole of TQC or CWQC.

Those who have followed QC circles in Japan know that they often focus on such areas as cost, safety and productivity, and that their activities sometimes relate only indirectly to product-quality improvement. For the most part, these activities are aimed at making improvements in the workshop.

There is no doubt that QC circles have played an important part in improving product quality and productivity in Japan. However, their role has often been blown out of proportion by overseas observers who believe that QC circles are the mainstay of TQC activities in Japan. Nothing could be further from the truth, especially when it comes to Japanese management. Efforts related to QC circles generally account for only 10 per cent to 30 per cent of the overall TQC effort in Japanese companies.

What is less visible behind these developments is the transformation of the term quality control, or QC, in Japan. As is the case in many Western companies, quality control initially meant quality control applied to the manufacturing process, particularly the inspections for rejecting defective incoming material or defective outgoing products at the end of the production line. But very soon the realization set in that inspection alone does nothing to improve the quality of the product, and that product quality should be built at the production stage. 'Build quality into the process' was (and still is) a popular phrase in Japanese quality control. It is at this stage that control charts and the other tools for statistical quality control were introduced after Deming's lectures.

Juran's lectures in 1954 opened up another aspect of quality control: the managerial approach to quality control. This was the first time the term QC was positioned as a vital management tool in Japan. From then

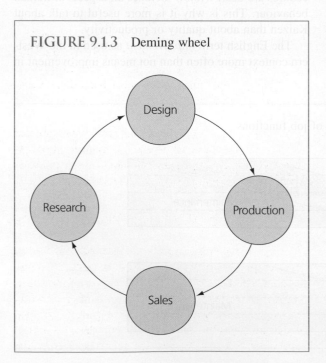

FIGURE 9.1.3　Deming wheel

on, the term QC has been used to mean both quality control and the tools for overall improvement in managerial performance.

At a later stage, other industries started to introduce QC for such products as consumer durables and home appliances. In these industries, the interest was in building quality in at the design stage to meet changing and increasingly stringent customer requirements. Today, management has gone beyond the design stage and has begun to stress the importance of quality product development, which means taking customer-related information and market research into account from the very start.

All this while, QC has grown into a fully-fledged management tool for Kaizen involving everyone in the company. Such company-wide activities are often referred to as TQC (total quality control) or CWQC (company-wide quality control). No matter which name is used, TQC and CWQC mean company-wide Kaizen activities involving everyone in the company, managers and workers alike. Over the years, QC has been elevated to SQC and then to TQC or CWQC, improving managerial performance at every level. Thus it is that such words as QC and TQC have come to be almost synonymous with Kaizen. This is also why I constantly refer to QC, TQC and CWQC in explaining Kaizen.

On the other hand, the function of quality control in its original sense remains valid. Quality assurance remains a vital part of management, and most companies have a QA (quality assurance) department for this.

To confuse matters, TQC or CWQC activities are sometimes administered by the QA department and sometimes by a separate TQC office. Thus it is important that these QC-related words be understood in the context in which they appear.

Kaizen and TQC

Considering the TQC movement in Japan as part of the Kaizen movement gives us a clearer perspective on the Japanese approach. First of all, it should be pointed out that TQC activities in Japan are not concerned solely with quality control. People have been fooled by the term 'quality control' and have often construed it within the narrow discipline of product-quality control. In the West, the term QC is mostly associated with inspection of finished products, and when QC is brought up in discussion, top managers, who generally assume they have very little to do with quality control, lose interest immediately.

It is unfortunate that in the West TQC has been dealt with mainly in technical journals when it is more properly the focus of management journals. Japan has developed an elaborate system of Kaizen strategies as management tools within the TQC movement. These rank among this century's most outstanding management achievements. Yet because of the limited way in which QC is understood in the West, most Western students of Japanese QC activities have failed to grasp their real significance and challenge. At the same time, new TQC methods and tools are constantly being studied and tested.

TQC in Japan is a movement centered on the improvement of managerial performance at all levels. As such, it has typically dealt with:

1 quality assurance;

2 cost reduction;

3 meeting production quotas;

4 meeting delivery schedules;

5 safety;

6 new-product development;

7 productivity improvement;

8 supplier management.

More recently, TQC has come to include marketing, sales and service as well. Furthermore, TQC has dealt with such crucial management concerns as organizational development, cross-functional management, policy deployment and quality deployment. In other words, management has been using TQC as a tool for improving overall performance.

Those who have closely followed QC circles in Japan know that their activities are often focused on such areas as cost, safety and productivity, and that their activities may only indirectly relate to product-quality improvement. For the most part, these activities are aimed at making improvements in the workplace.

Management efforts for TQC have been directed mostly at such areas as education, systems development, policy deployment, cross-functional management and, more recently, quality deployment.

Kaizen and the suggestion system

Japanese management makes a concerted effort to involve employees in Kaizen through suggestions. Thus, the suggestion system is an integral part of the established management system, and the number of workers' suggestions is regarded as an important criterion in reviewing the performance of these workers' supervisor. The manager of the supervisors is in turn expected to assist them so that they can help workers generate more suggestions.

Most Japanese companies active in Kaizen programmes have a quality-control system and a suggestion system working in concert. The role of QC circles may be better understood if we regard them collectively as a group-oriented suggestion system for making improvements.

One of the outstanding features of Japanese management is that it generates a great number of suggestions from workers and that management works hard to consider these suggestions, often incorporating them into the overall Kaizen strategy. It is not uncommon for top management of a leading Japanese company to spend a whole day listening to presentations of activities by QC circles, and giving awards based on predetermined criteria. Management is willing to give recognition to employees' efforts for improvements and makes its concern visible wherever possible. Often, the number of suggestions is posted individually on the wall of the workplace in order to encourage competition among workers and among groups.

Another important aspect of the suggestion system is that each suggestion, once implemented, leads to a revised standard. For instance, when a special foolproof device has been installed on a machine at a worker's suggestion, this may require the worker to work differently and, at times, more attentively.

However, inasmuch as the new standard has been set up by the worker's own volition, he takes pride in the new standard and is willing to follow it. If, on the contrary, he is told to follow a standard imposed by management, he may not be as willing to follow it.

Thus, through suggestions, employees can participate in Kaizen in the workplace and play a vital role in upgrading standards. In a recent interview, Toyota Motor Chairman Eiji Toyoda said, 'One of the features of the Japanese workers is that they use their brains as well as their hands. Our workers provide 1.5 million suggestions a year, and 95 per cent of them are put to practical use. There is an almost tangible concern for improvement in the air at Toyota.'

Kaizen vs innovation

There are two contrasting approaches to progress: the gradualist approach and the great-leap-forward approach. Japanese companies generally favour the gradualist approach and Western companies the great-leap approach – an approach epitomized by the term 'innovation'.

Western management worships at the altar of innovation. This innovation is seen as major change in the wake of technological breakthroughs, or the introduction of the latest management concepts or production techniques. Innovation is dramatic, a real attention-getter. Kaizen, on the other hand, is often undramatic and subtle, and its results are seldom immediately visible. While Kaizen is a continuous process, innovation is generally a one-shot phenomenon.

In the West, for example, a middle manager can usually obtain top management support for such projects as CAD (computer-aided design), CAM (computer-aided manufacture), and MRP (materials requirements planning), since these are innovative projects that have a way of revolutionizing existing systems. As such, they offer ROI (return on investment) benefits that managers can hardly resist.

However, when a factory manager wishes, for example, to make small changes in the way his workers use the machinery, such as working out multiple job assignments or realigning production processes (both of which may require lengthy discussions with the union as well as re-education and retraining of workers), obtaining management support can be difficult indeed.

Table 9.1.1 compares the main features of Kaizen and of innovation. One of the beautiful things about Kaizen is that it does not necessarily require sophisticated technique or state-of-the-art technology. To implement Kaizen, you need only simple, conventional techniques. Often, common sense is all that is needed. On the other hand, innovation usually requires highly sophisticated technology, as well as a huge investment.

Kaizen is like a hotbed that nurtures small and ongoing changes, while innovation is like magma that appears in abrupt eruptions from time to time. One big difference between Kaizen and innovation is that while Kaizen does not necessarily call for a large investment to implement it, it does call for a great deal of continuous effort and commitment. The difference between the two opposing concepts may thus be likened to that of a staircase and a slope. The innovation strategy is supposed to bring about progress in a staircase progression. On the other hand, the Kaizen strategy brings about gradual progress. I say the innovation strategy 'is supposed to' bring about progress in a staircase progression, because it usually does not. Instead of following the staircase pattern, the actual progress achieved through innovation will generally follow the pattern shown in Figure 9.1.4, if it lacks the Kaizen strategy to go along with it. This happens because a system, once it has been installed as a result of

TABLE 9.1.1   Features of Kaizen and innovation

	Kaizen	Innovation
1. Effect	Long-term and long-lasting but undramatic	Short-term but dramatic
2. Pace	Small steps	Big steps
3. Timeframe	Continuous and incremental	Intermittent and non-incremental
4. Change	Gradual and constant	Abrupt and volatile
5. Involvement	Everybody	Select few 'champions'
6. Approach	Collectivism, group efforts, systems approach	Rugged individualism, individual ideas and efforts
7. Mode	Maintenance and improvement	Scrap and rebuild
8. Spark	Conventional know-how and state of the art	Technological breakthroughs, new inventions, new theories
9. Practical requirements	Requires little investment but great effort to maintain it	Requires large investment but little effort to maintain it
10. Effort orientation	People	Technology
11. Evaluation criteria	Process and efforts for better results	Results and profits
12. Advantage	Works well in slow-growth economy	Better suited to fast-growth economy

new innovation, is subject to steady deterioration unless continuing efforts are made first to maintain it and then to improve on it.

In reality, there can be no such thing as a static constant. All systems are destined to deteriorate once they have been established. One of the famous Parkinson's Laws is that an organization, once it has built its edifice, begins its decline. In other words, there must be a continuing effort for improvement to even maintain the status quo.

When such effort is lacking, decline is inevitable (see Figure 9.1.4). Therefore, even when an innovation makes a revolutionary standard of performance attainable, the new performance level will decline unless the standard is constantly challenged and upgraded.

Thus, whenever an innovation is achieved, it must be followed by a series of Kaizen efforts to maintain and improve it (see Figure 9.1.5).

Whereas innovation is a one-shot deal whose effects are gradually eroded by intense competition and deteriorating standards, Kaizen is an ongoing effort with cumulative effects marking a steady rise as the years go by. If standards exist only in order to maintain the status quo, they will not be challenged so long as the level of performance is acceptable. Kaizen, on the other hand, means a constant effort not only to maintain but also to upgrade standards. Kaizen strategists believe that standards are by nature tentative, akin to stepping stones, with one standard leading to another as continuing improvement efforts are made. This is

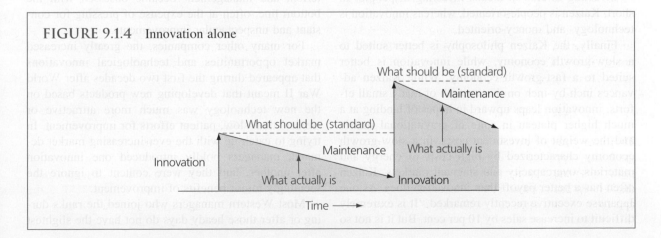

FIGURE 9.1.4   Innovation alone

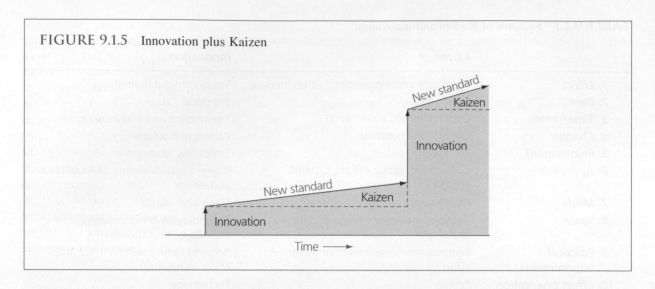

FIGURE 9.1.5 Innovation plus Kaizen

the reason why QC circles no sooner solve one problem than they move on to tackle a new problem. This is also the reason why the so-called PDCA (plan-do-check-action) cycle receives so much emphasis in Japan's TQC movement.

Another feature of Kaizen is that it requires virtually everyone's personal efforts. In order for the Kaizen spirit to survive, management must make a conscious and continuous effort to support it. Such support is quite different from the fanfare recognition that management accords to people who have achieved a striking success or breakthrough. Kaizen is concerned more with the process than with the result. The strength of Japanese management lies in its successful development and implementation of a system that acknowledges the ends while emphasizing the means.

Thus Kaizen calls for a substantial management commitment of time and effort. Infusions of capital are no substitute for this investment in time and effort.

Investing in Kaizen means investing in people. In short, Kaizen is people-oriented, whereas innovation is technology- and money-oriented.

Finally, the Kaizen philosophy is better suited to a slow-growth economy, while innovation is better suited to a fast-growth economy. While Kaizen advances inch-by-inch on the strength of many small efforts, innovation leaps upward in hopes of landing at a much higher plateau in spite of gravitational inertia and the weight of investment costs. In a slow-growth economy characterized by high costs of energy and materials, overcapacity and stagnant markets, Kaizen often has a better payoff than innovation does. As one Japanese executive recently remarked, 'It is extremely difficult to increase sales by 10 per cent. But it is not so difficult to cut manufacturing costs by 10 per cent to even better effect.'

I argued that the concept of Kaizen is non-existent or at best weak in most Western companies today. However, there was a time, not so long ago, when Western management also placed a high priority on Kaizen-like improvement-consciousness. Older executives may recall that before the phenomenal economic growth of the late 1950s and early 1960s, management attended assiduously to improving all aspects of the business, particularly the factory. In those days, every small improvement was counted and was seen as effective in terms of building success.

People who worked with small, privately owned companies may recall with a touch of nostalgia that there was a genuine concern for improvement 'in the air' before the company was bought out or went public. As soon as that happened, the quarterly P/L (profit/loss) figures suddenly became the most important criterion, and management became obsessed with the bottom line, often at the expense of pressing for constant and unspectacular improvements.

For many other companies, the greatly increased market opportunities and technological innovations that appeared during the first two decades after World War II meant that developing new products based on the new technology was much more attractive or 'sexier' than slow, patient efforts for improvement. In trying to catch up with the ever-increasing market demand, managers boldly introduced one innovation after another, and they were content to ignore the seemingly minor benefits of improvement.

Most Western managers who joined the ranks during or after those heady days do not have the slightest concern for improvement. Instead, they take an offensive posture, armed with professional expertise geared toward making big changes in the name of innovation, bringing about immediate gains, and winning instant recognition and promotion. Before they knew it, Western managers had lost sight of improvement and put all their eggs in the innovation basket.

Another factor that has abetted the innovation approach has been the increasing emphasis on financial controls and accounting. By now, the more sophisticated companies have succeeded in establishing elaborate accounting and reporting systems that force managers to account for every action they take and to spell out the precise payout or ROI of every managerial decision. Such a system does not lend itself to building a favourable climate for improvement.

Improvement is by definition slow, gradual and often invisible, with effects that are felt over the long run. In my opinion, the most glaring and significant shortcoming of Western management today is the lack of improvement philosophy. There is no internal system in Western management to reward efforts for improvement; instead, everyone's job performance is reviewed strictly on the basis of results. Thus it is not uncommon for Western managers to chide people with, 'I don't care what you do or how you do it. I want the results – and now!' This emphasis on results has led to the innovation-dominated approach of the West. This is not to say that Japanese management does not care about innovation. But Japanese managers have enthusiastically pursued Kaizen even when they were involved in innovation.

READING **9.2**

The innovator's dilemma

By Clayton M. Christensen[1]

This reading is about the failure of companies to stay atop their industries when they confront certain types of market and technological change. It's not about the failure of simply any company, but of *good* companies – the kinds that many managers have admired and tried to emulate, the companies known for their abilities to innovate and execute. Companies stumble for many reasons, of course, among them bureaucracy, arrogance, tired executive blood, poor planning, short-term investment horizons, inadequate skills and resources, and just plain bad luck. But this reading is not about companies with such weaknesses: It is about well-managed companies that have their competitive antennae up, listen astutely to their customers, invest aggressively in new technologies, and yet still lose market dominance.

Such seemingly unaccountable failures happen in industries that move fast and in those that move slow; in those built on electronics technology and those built on chemical and mechanical technology; in manufacturing and in service industries. Sears Roebuck, for example, was regarded for decades as one of the most astutely managed retailers in the world. At its zenith Sears accounted for more than 2 per cent of all retail

sales in the United States. It pioneered several innovations critical to the success of today's most admired retailers: for example, supply chain management, store brands, catalogue retailing and credit card sales. The esteem in which Sears' management was held shows in this 1964 excerpt from *Fortune:* "How did Sears do it? In a way, the most arresting aspect of its story is that there was no gimmick. Sears opened no big bag of tricks, shot off no skyrockets. Instead, it looked as though everybody in its organization simply did the right thing, easily and naturally. And their cumulative effect was to create an extraordinary powerhouse of a company."

Yet no one speaks about Sears that way today. Somehow, it completely missed the advent of discount retailing and home centres. In the midst of today's catalogue retailing boom, Sears has been driven from that business. Indeed, the very viability of its retailing operations has been questioned. One commentator has noted that "Sears' Merchandise Group lost $1.3 billion (in 1992) even before a $1.7 billion restructuring charge. Sears let arrogance blind it to basic changes taking place in the American marketplace." Another writer has complained:

[1]Source: Reprinted by permission of Harvard Business School Press. From *The Innovator's Dilemma* by Clayton M. Christensen. Boston, MA 1997, pp. ix–xxvi. Copyright © 1997 by the Harvard Business School Publishing Corporation; all rights reserved.

Sears has been a disappointment for investors who have watched its stock sink dismally in the face of unkept promises of a turnaround. Sears' old merchandising approach – a vast, middle-of-the-road array of mid-priced goods and services – is no longer competitive. No question, the constant disappointments, the repeated predictions of a turnaround that never seems to come, have reduced the credibility of Sears' management in both the financial and merchandising communities.

It is striking to note that Sears received its accolades at exactly the time – in the rnid-1960s – when it was ignoring the rise of discount retailing and home centres, the lower-cost formats for marketing name-brand hard goods that ultimately stripped Sears of its core franchise. Sears was praised as one of the best-managed companies in the world at the very time it let Visa and MasterCard usurp the enormous lead it had established in the use of credit cards in retailing.

In some industries this pattern of leadership failure has been repeated more than once. Consider the computer industry. IBM dominated the mainframe market but missed by years the emergence of mini-computers, which were technologically much simpler than mainframes. In fact, no other major manufacturer of mainframe computers became a significant player in the minicomputer business. Digital Equipment Corporation created the minicomputer market and was joined by a set of other aggressively managed companies: Data General, Prime, Wang, Hewlett-Packard and Nixdorf. But each of these companies in turn missed the desktop personal computer market. It was left to Apple Computer, together with Commodore, Tandy and IBM's stand-alone PC division, to create the personal-computing market. Apple, in particular, was uniquely innovative in establishing the standard for user-friendly computing. But Apple and IBM lagged five years behind the leaders in bringing portable computers to market. Similarly, the firms that built the engineering workstation market – Apollo, Sun and Silicon Graphics – were all newcomers to the industry.

As in retailing, many of these leading computer manufacturers were at one time regarded as among the best-managed companies in the world and were held up by journalists and scholars of management as examples for all to follow. Consider this assessment of Digital Equipment, made in 1986: "Taking on Digital Equipment Corp. these days is like standing in front of a moving train. The $7.6 billion computer maker has

been gathering speed while most rivals are stalled in a slump in the computer industry." The author proceeded to warn IBM to watch out, because it was standing on the tracks. Indeed, Digital was one of the most prominently featured companies in the McKinsey study that led to the book *In Search of Excellence* (Peters and Waterman, 1982).

Yet a few years later, writers characterized DEC quite differently:

Digital Equipment Corporation is a company in need of triage. Sales are drying up in its key minicomputer line. A two-year-old restructuring plan has failed miserably. Forecasting and production planning systems have failed miserably. Cost-cutting hasn't come close to restoring profitability.... But the real misfortune may be DEC's lost opportunities. It has squandered two years trying halfway measures to respond to the low-margin personal computers and workstations that have transformed the computer industry.

In Digital's case, as in Sears, the very decisions that led to its decline were made at the time it was so widely regarded as being an astutely managed firm. It was praised as a paragon of managerial excellence at the very time it was ignoring the arrival of the desktop computers that besieged it a few years later.

Sears and Digital are in noteworthy company. Xerox long dominated the market for plain paper photocopiers used in large, high-volume copying centres. Yet it missed huge growth and profit opportunities in the market for small tabletop photocopiers, where it became only a minor player. Although steel mini mills have now captured 40 per cent of the North American steel market, including nearly all of the region's markets for bars, rods and structural steel, not a single integrated steel company – American, Asian, or European – had by 1995 built a plant using mini mill technology. Of the thirty manufacturers of cable-actuated power shovels, only four survived the industry's twenty-five-year transition to hydraulic excavation technology.

The list of leading companies that failed when confronted with disruptive changes in technology and market structure is a long one. At first glance, there seems to be no pattern in the changes that overtook them. In some cases the new technologies swept through quickly; in others, the transition took decades. In some, the new technologies were complex and expensive to develop. In others, the deadly technologies were simple extensions of what the leading companies already did better than anyone else. One theme common to all of these failures, however, is that the decisions that led to failure were made when the leaders in question were widely regarded as among the best companies in the world.

There are two ways to resolve this paradox. One might be to conclude that firms such as Digital, IBM, Apple, Sears, Xerox and Bucyrus Erie must never have been well managed. Maybe they were successful because of good luck and fortuitous timing, rather than good management. Maybe they finally fell on hard times because their good fortune ran out. Maybe. An alternative explanation, however, is that these failed firms were as well-run as one could expect a firm managed by mortals to be – but that there is something about the way decisions get made in successful organizations that sows the seeds of eventual failure.

Our research supports this latter view: It shows that in the cases of well-managed firms such as those cited above, good management was the most powerful reason they failed to stay atop their industries. Precisely because these firms listened to their customers, invested aggressively in new technologies that would provide their customers more and better products of the sort they wanted, and because they carefully studied market trends and systematically allocated investment capital to innovations that promised the best returns, they lost their positions of leadership.

What this implies at a deeper level is that many of what are now widely accepted principles of good management are, in fact, only situationally appropriate. There are times at which it is right not to listen to customers, right to invest in developing lower-performance products that promise lower margins, and right to aggressively pursue small, rather than substantial, markets. This book derives a set of rules, from carefully designed research and analysis of innovative successes and failures in the disk drive and other industries that managers can use to judge when the widely accepted principles of good management should be followed and when alternative principles are appropriate.

These rules, which I call *principles of disruptive innovation,* show that when good companies fail, it often has been because their managers either ignored these principles or chose to fight them. Managers can be extraordinarily effective in managing even the most difficult innovations if they work to understand and harness the principles of disruptive innovation. As in many of life's most challenging endeavours, there is great value in coming to grips with "the way the world works," and in managing innovative efforts in ways that

accommodate such forces. *The Innovator's Dilemma* applies to manufacturing and service businesses – high tech or low – in slowly evolving or rapidly changing environments.

Technology means the processes by which an organization transforms labour, capital, materials and information into products and services of greater value. All firms have technologies. A retailer like Sears employs a particular technology to procure, present, sell and deliver products to its customers, while a discount warehouse retailer like PriceCostco employs a different technology. This concept of technology therefore extends beyond engineering and manufacturing to encompass a range of marketing, investment and managerial processes. *Innovation* refers to a change in one of these technologies.

The failure framework: Why good management can lead to failure

The failure framework is built upon three findings from our study. The first is that there is a strategically important distinction between what I call *sustaining* technologies and those that are *disruptive*. These concepts are very different from the incremental – versus – radical distinction (as described in Chapter 8 of this book) that has characterized many studies of this problem. Second, the pace of technological progress can, and often does, outstrip what markets need. This means that the relevance and competitiveness of different technological approaches can change with respect to different markets over time. And third, customers and financial structures of successful companies colour heavily the sorts of investments that appear to be attractive to them, relative to certain types of entering firms.

Sustaining versus disruptive technologies

Most new technologies foster improved product performance. I call these *sustaining technologies.* Some sustaining technologies can be discontinuous or radical in character, while others are of an incremental nature. What all sustaining technologies have in common is that they improve the performance of established products, along the dimensions of performance that mainstream customers in major markets have historically valued. Most technological advances in a given industry are sustaining in character. An important finding revealed in this book is that rarely have even the most radically difficult sustaining technologies precipitated the failure of leading firms.

Occasionally, however, *disruptive technologies* emerge: innovations that result in worse product performance, at least in the near-term. Ironically, in each of the instances studied in this book, it was disruptive technology that precipitated the leading firms' failure.

Disruptive technologies bring to a market a very different value proposition than had been available previously. Generally, disruptive technologies underperform established products in mainstream markets. But they have other features that a few fringe (and generally new) customers value. Products based on disruptive technologies are typically cheaper, simpler, smaller and, frequently, more convenient to use. There are many examples in addition to the personal desktop computer and discount retailing examples cited above. Small off-road motorcycles introduced in North America and Europe by Honda, Kawasaki and Yamaha were disruptive technologies relative to the powerful, over-the-road cycles made by Harley-Davidson and BMW. Transistors were disruptive technologies relative to vacuum tubes. Health maintenance organizations were disruptive technologies to conventional health insurers.

Trajectories of market need versus technology improvement

The second element of the failure framework, the observation that technologies can progress faster than market demand, illustrated in Figure 9.2.1, means that in their efforts to provide better products than their competitors and earn higher prices and margins, suppliers often "overshoot" their market: They give customers more than they need or ultimately are willing to pay for. And more importantly, it means that disruptive technologies that may underperform today, relative to what users in the market demand, may be fully performance-competitive in that same market tomorrow.

Many who once needed mainframe computers for their data processing requirements, for example, no longer need or buy mainframes. Mainframe performance has surpassed the requirements of many original customers, who today find that much of what they need to do can be done on desktop machines linked to file servers. In other words, the needs of many computer users have increased more slowly than the rate of improvement provided by computer designers. Similarly, many shoppers who in 1965 felt they had to shop at department stores to be assured of quality and selection now satisfy those needs quite well at Target and Wal-Mart.

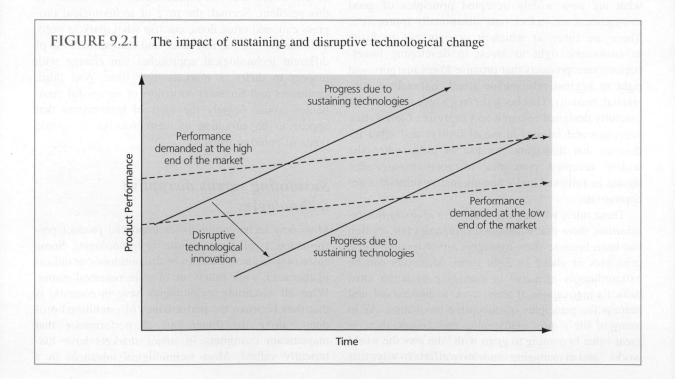

FIGURE 9.2.1   The impact of sustaining and disruptive technological change

Disruptive technologies versus rational investments

The last element of the failure framework, the conclusion by established companies that investing aggressively in disruptive technologies is not a rational financial decision for them to make, has three bases. First, disruptive products are simpler and cheaper; they generally promise lower margins, not greater profits. Second, disruptive technologies typically are first commercialized in emerging or insignificant markets. And third, leading firms' most profitable customers generally don't want, and indeed initially can't use, products based on disruptive technologies. By and large, a disruptive technology is initially embraced by the least profitable customers in a market. Hence, most companies with a practiced discipline of listening to their best customers and identifying new products that promise greater profitability and growth are rarely able to build a case for investing in disruptive technologies until it is too late.

Harnessing the principle of disruptive innovation

Colleagues who have read my academic papers were struck by their near-fatalism. If good management practice drives the failure of successful firms faced with disruptive technological change, then the usual answers to companies' problems – planning better, working harder, becoming more customer-driven and taking a longer-term perspective – all *exacerbate* the problem. Sound execution, speed-to-market, total quality management and process reengineering are similarly ineffective. Needless to say, this is disquieting news to people who teach future managers!

I suggest, however, that although the solution to disruptive technologies cannot be found in the standard tool kit of good management, there are, in fact, sensible ways to deal effectively with this challenge. Every company in every industry works under certain forces – laws of organizational nature – that act powerfully to define what that company can and cannot do. Managers faced with disruptive technologies fail their companies when these forces overpower them.

By analogy, the ancients who attempted to fly by strapping feathered wings to their arms and flapping with all their might as they leapt from high places invariably failed. Despite their dreams and hard work, they were fighting against some very powerful forces of nature. No one could be strong enough to win this fight. Flight became possible only after people came to understand the relevant natural laws and principles that defined how the world worked: the law of gravity, Bernoulli's principle, and the concepts of lift, drag and resistance. When people then designed flying systems that recognized or harnessed the power of these laws and principles, rather than fighting them, they were finally able to fly to heights and distances that were previously unimaginable.

I propose the existence of five laws or principles of disruptive technology. As in the analogy with manned flight, these laws are so strong that managers who ignore or fight them are nearly powerless to pilot their companies through a disruptive technology storm. If managers can understand and harness these forces, rather than fight them, they can in fact succeed spectacularly when confronted with disruptive technological change. I am very confident that great managers will be very capable on their own of finding the answers that best fit their circumstances. But they must first understand what has caused those circumstances and what forces will affect the feasibility of their solutions. The following paragraphs summarize these principles and what managers can do to harness or accommodate them.

Principle #1: Companies depend on customers and investors for resources

The history of the disc drive industry shows that the established firms stayed atop wave after wave of sustaining technologies (technologies that their customers needed), while consistently stumbling over simpler disruptive ones. This evidence supports the *theory of resource dependence* (Pfeffer, 1978) which states that while managers may think they control the flow of resources in their firms, in the end it is really customers and investors who dictate how money will be spent because companies with investment patterns that don't satisfy their customers and investors don't survive. The highest-performing companies, in fact, are those that are the best at this; that is, they have well-developed systems for killing ideas that their customers don't want. As a result, these companies find it very difficult to invest adequate resources in disruptive technologies – lower margin opportunities that their customers don't want – until their customers want them. And by then it is too late.

I suggest a way for managers to align or harness this law with their efforts to confront disruptive technology. With few exceptions, the only instances in which mainstream firms have successfully established a timely position in a disruptive technology were those in which the firms' managers set up an autonomous organization charged with building a new and independent business around the disruptive technology. Such organizations, free of the power of the customers of the mainstream company, ensconce themselves among a different set of customers – those who want the products of the disruptive technology. In other words, companies can succeed in disruptive technologies when their managers align their organizations *with* the forces of resource dependence, rather than ignoring or fighting them.

The implication of this principle for managers is that, when faced with a threatening disruptive technology, people and processes in a mainstream organization cannot be expected to allocate freely the critical financial and human resources needed to carve out a strong position in the small, emerging market. It is very difficult for a company whose cost structure is tailored to compete in high-end markets to be profitable in low-end markets as well. Creating an independent organization, with a cost structure honed to achieve profitability at the low margins characteristic of most disruptive technologies, is the only viable way for established firms to harness this principle.

Principle #2: Small markets don't solve the growth needs of large companies

Disruptive technologies typically enable new markets to emerge. There is strong evidence showing that companies entering these emerging markets early have significant first-mover advantages over later entrants. And yet, as these companies succeed and grow larger, it becomes progressively more difficult for them to enter the even newer small markets destined to become the large ones of the future.

To maintain their share prices and create internal opportunities for employees to extend the scope of their responsibilities, successful companies need to continue to grow. But while a $40 million company needs to find just $8 million in revenues to grow at 20 per cent in the subsequent year, a $4 billion company needs to find $800 million in new sales. No new markets are that large. As a consequence, the larger and more successful an organization becomes, the weaker the argument that emerging markets can remain useful engines for growth.

Many large companies adopt a strategy of waiting until new markets are "large enough to be interesting". But the evidence shows why this is not often a successful strategy. Those large established firms that have successfully seized strong positions in the new markets enabled by disruptive technologies have done so by giving responsibility to commercialize the disruptive technology to an organization whose size matched the size of the targeted market. Small

organizations can most easily respond to the opportunities for growth in a small market. The evidence is strong that formal and informal resource allocation processes make it very difficult for large organizations to focus adequate energy and talent on small markets, even when logic says they might be big someday.

Principle #3: Markets that don't exist can't be analyzed

Sound market research and good planning followed by execution according to plan are hallmarks of good management. When applied to sustaining technological innovation, these practices are invaluable; they are the primary reason, in fact, why established firms led in every single instance of sustaining innovation in the history of the disc drive industry. Such reasoned approaches are feasible in dealing with sustaining technology because the size and growth rates of the markets are generally known, trajectories of technological progress have been established, and the needs of leading customers have usually been well articulated. Because the vast majority of innovations are sustaining in character, most executives have learned to manage innovation in a sustaining context, where analysis and planning were feasible.

In dealing with disruptive technologies leading to new markets, however, market researchers and business planners have consistently dismal records. In fact, based upon the evidence from the disc drive, motorcycle and microprocessor industries, the only thing we may know for sure when we read experts' forecasts about how large emerging markets will become is that they are wrong.

In many instances, leadership in sustaining innovations – about which information is known and for which plans can be made – is not competitively important. In such cases, technology followers do about as well as technology leaders. It is in disruptive innovations, where we know least about the market, that there are such strong first-mover advantages. This is the innovator's dilemma.

Companies whose investment processes demand quantification of market sizes and financial returns before they can enter a market get paralysed or make serious mistakes when faced with disruptive technologies. They demand market data when none exists and make judgments based upon financial projections when neither revenues nor costs can, in fact, be known. Using planning and marketing techniques that were developed to manage sustaining technologies in the very different context of disruptive ones is an exercise in flapping wings.

A different approach to strategy and planning recognizes the law that the right markets, and the right strategy for exploiting them, cannot be known in advance. Called discovery-based planning, it suggests that managers assume that forecasts are wrong, rather than right, and that the strategy they have chosen to pursue may likewise be wrong. Investing and managing under such assumptions drives managers to develop plans for learning what needs to be known, a much more effective way to confront disruptive technologies successfully.

Principle #4: An organization's capabilities define its disabilities

When managers tackle an innovation problem, they instinctively work to assign capable people to the job. But once they've found the right people, too many managers then assume that the organization in which they'll work will also be capable of succeeding at the task. And that is dangerous – because organizations have capabilities that exist independently of the people who work within them. An organization's capabilities reside in two places. The first is in its processes – the methods by which people have learned to transform inputs of labour, energy, materials, information, cash and technology into outputs of higher value. The second is in the organization's values, which are the criteria that managers and employees in the organization use when making prioritization decisions. People are quite flexible, in that they can be trained to succeed at quite different things. An employee of IBM, for example, can quite readily change the way he or she works, in order to work successfully in a small start-up company. But processes and values are not flexible. A process that is effective at managing the design of a minicomputer, for example, would be ineffective at managing the design of a desktop personal computer. Similarly, values that cause employees to prioritize projects to develop high-margin products, cannot simultaneously accord priority to low-margin products. The very processes and values that constitute an organization's capabilities in one context, define its disabilities in another context.

Principle #5: Technology supply may not equal market demand

Disruptive technologies, though they initially can only be used in small markets remote from the mainstream, are disruptive because they subsequently can become fully performance-competitive within the mainstream market against established products. As depicted in Figure 9.2.1, this happens because the pace of technological progress in products frequently exceeds the rate of performance improvement that mainstream customers demand or can absorb. As a consequence, products whose features and functionality closely match market needs today often follow a trajectory of improvement by which they overshoot mainstream market needs tomorrow. And products that seriously underperform today, relative to customer expectations in mainstream markets, may become directly performance-competitive tomorrow.

When this happens, in markets as diverse as disc drives, accounting software and diabetes care, the basis of competition – the criteria by which customers choose one product over another – changes. When the performance of two or more competing products has improved beyond what the market demands, customers can no longer base their choice upon which is the higher performing product. The basis of product choice often evolves from functionality to reliability, then to convenience, and, ultimately, to price.

Many students of business have described phases of the product life cycle in various ways. But the phenomenon in which product performance overshoots market demands is the primary mechanism driving shifts in the phases of the product life cycle.

In their efforts to stay ahead by developing competitively superior products, many companies don't realize the speed at which they are moving up-market, over-satisfying the needs of their original customers as they race the competition toward higher-performance, higher-margin markets. In doing so, they create a vacuum at lower price points into which competitors employing disruptive technologies can enter. Only those companies that carefully measure trends in how their mainstream customers use their products can catch the points at which the basis of competition will change in the markets they serve.

Lessons from spotting disruptive threats and opportunities

Some managers and researchers familiar with these ideas have arrived at this point in the story in an anxious state because the evidence is very strong that even the best managers have stumbled badly when their markets were invaded by disruptive technologies. Most urgently, they want to know whether their own businesses are targets for an attacking disruptive technologist and how they can defend their business against such an attack before it is too late. Others, interested in finding entrepreneurial opportunities, wonder how they can identify potentially disruptive technologies around which new companies and markets can be built.

"Good" companies often begin their descent into failure by aggressively investing in the products and services that their most profitable customers want. No automotive company is currently threatened by electric cars, and none contemplates a wholesale leap into that arena. The automobile industry is healthy. Gasoline engines have never been more reliable. Never before has such high performance and quality been available at such low prices. Indeed, aside from governmental mandates, there is no reason why we should expect the established car makers to pursue electric vehicles.

But the electric car *is* a disruptive technology and potential future threat. The innovator's task is to ensure that this innovation – the disruptive technology that doesn't make sense – is taken seriously within the company without putting at risk the needs of present customers who provide profit and growth. The problem can be resolved only when new markets are considered and carefully developed around new definitions of value – and when responsibility for building the business is placed within a focused organization whose size and interest are carefully aligned with the unique needs of the market's customers.

TABLE 9.2.1

Established technology	Disruptive technology
Silver halide photographic film	Digital photography
Wireline telephony	Mobile telephony
Circuit-switched telecommunications networks	Packet-switched communications network
Notebook computers	Hand-held digital appliances
Desktop personal computers	Sony Playstation II, Internet appliances
Full-service stock brokerage	Online stock brokerage
New York and NASDAQ stock exchanges	Electronic Communications Network (ECNs)
Full-free underwriting of new equity and debt issues	Dutch auctions of new equity and debt issues, conducted on the Internet
Credit decisions based upon the personal judgement of bank lending officers	Automated lending decisions based upon credit scoring systems
Bricks and mortar retailing	Online retailing
Industrial materials distributors	Internet-based sites such as Chemdex and E-steel
Printed greeting cards	Free greeting cards, downloadable over the Internet
Electric utility companies	Distributed power generation (gas turbines, micro-turbines, fuel cells)
Graduate school of management	Corporate universities and in-house management training programmes
Classroom and campus-based instruction	Distance education, typically enabled by the Internet
Standard textbooks	Custom-assembled, modular digital textbooks
Offset printing	Digital printing
Manned fighter and bomber aircraft	Unmanned aircraft
Microsoft Windows operating systems and applications software written in C++	Internet Protocols (IP), and Java software protocols
Medical doctors	Nurse practitioners
General hospitals	Outpatient clinics and in-home patient care
Open surgery	Arthroscopic and endoscopic surgery
Cardiac bypass surgery	Angioplasty
Magnetic resonance imaging (MRI) and Computer Tomography (CT) Scanning	Ultrasound – initially floor - standing machines, ultimately portable machines

Where disruptions are happening today

One of the most gratifying aspects of my life since the first edition of *The Innovators' Dilemma* was published has been the number of people who have called, representing industries that I had never thought about, who have suggested that forces similar to those historical examples I described in these pages are disrupting their industries as well. Some of these are described in Table 9.2.1. Not surprisingly, the Internet looms as an infrastructural technology that is enabling the disruption of many industries.

Each of the innovations in the right column – in the form of a new technology or a new business model – is now in the process of disrupting the established order described in the left column. Will the companies that currently lead their industries using the technologies in the left column survive these attacks? My hope is that the future might be different than the past. I believe that the future can be different, if managers will recognize these disruptions for what they are, and address them in a way that accounts for or harnesses the fundamental principles described in the pages that follow.

READING 9.3

Exploration and exploitation in organizational learning

By James G. March[1]

A central concern of studies of adaptive processes is the relation between the exploration of new possibilities and the exploitation of old certainties (Schumpeter, 1934; Holland, 1975; Kuran, 1988). Exploration includes things captured by terms such as search, variation, risk taking, experimentation, play, flexibility, discovery, innovation. Exploitation includes such things as refinement, choice, production, efficiency, selection, implementation, execution. Adaptive systems that engage in exploration to the exclusion of exploitation are likely to find that they suffer the costs of experimentation without gaining many of its benefits. They exhibit too many undeveloped new ideas and too little distinctive competence. Conversely, systems that engage in exploitation to the exclusion of exploration are likely to find themselves trapped in suboptimal stable equilibria. As a result, maintaining an appropriate balance between exploration and exploitation is a primary factor in system survival and prosperity.

This paper considers some aspects of such problems in the context of organizations. Both exploration and exploitation are essential for organizations, but they compete for scarce resources. As a result, organizations make explicit and implicit choices between the two. The explicit choices are found in calculated decisions about alternative investments and competitive strategies. The implicit choices are buried in many

features of organizational forms and customs, for example, in organizational procedures for accumulating and reducing slack, in search rules and practices, in the ways in which targets are set and changed, and in incentive systems. Understanding the choices and improving the balance between exploration and exploitation are complicated by the fact that returns from the two options vary not only with respect to their expected values, but also with respect to their variability, their timing, and their distribution within and beyond the organization. Processes for allocating resources between them, therefore, embody intertemporal, interinstitutional, and interpersonal comparisons, as well as risk preferences. The difficulties involved in making such comparisons lead to complications in specifying appropriate trade-offs, and in achieving them.

1. The exploration/exploitation trade-off

Exploration and exploitation in theories of organizational action

In rational models of choice, the balance between exploration and exploitation is discussed classically in

[1]Source: This article was adapted with permission of INFORMS. From: 'Exploration and exploitation in organizational learning' by James G. March, *Organization Science*, Vol. 2, No. 1, February 1991.

terms of a theory of rational search (Radner and Rothschild, 1975; Hey, 1982). It is assumed that there are several alternative investment opportunities, each characterized by a probability distribution over returns that is initially unknown. Information about the distribution is accumulated over time, but choices must be made between gaining new information about alternatives and thus improving future returns (which suggests allocating part of the investment to searching among uncertain alternatives), and using the information currently available to improve present returns (which suggests concentrating the investment on the apparently best alternative). The problem is complicated by the possibilities that new investment alternatives may appear, that probability distributions may not be stable, or that they may depend on the choices made by others.

In theories of limited rationality, discussions of the choice between exploration and exploitation emphasize the role of targets or aspiration levels in regulating allocations to search (Cyert and March, 1963). The usual assumption is that search is inhibited if the most preferred alternative is above (but in the neighbourhood of) the target. On the other hand, search is stimulated if the most preferred known alternative is below the target. Such ideas are found both in theories of satisficing (Simon, 1955) and in prospect theory (Kahneman and Tversky, 1979). They have led to attempts to specify conditions under which target-oriented search rules are optimal (Day, 1967). Because of the role of targets, discussions of search in the limited rationality tradition emphasize the significance of the adaptive character of aspirations themselves (March, 1988).

In studies of organizational learning, the problem of balancing exploration and exploitation is exhibited in distinctions made between refinement of an existing technology and invention of a new one (Winter, 1971; Levinthal and March, 1981). It is clear that exploration of new alternatives reduces the speed with which skills at existing ones are improved. It is also clear that improvements in competence at existing procedures make experimentation with others less attractive (Levitt and March, 1988). Finding an appropriate balance is made particularly difficult by the fact that the same issues occur at levels of a nested system – at the individual level, the organizational level and the social system level.

In evolutionary models of organizational forms and technologies, discussions of the choice between exploration and exploitation are framed in terms of balancing the twin processes of variation and selection (Ashby, 1960; Hannan and Freeman, 1987). Effective selection among forms, routines or practices is essential to survival, but so also is the generation of new alternative practices, particularly in a changing environment. Because of the links among environmental turbulence, organizational diversity and competitive advantage, the evolutionary dominance of an organizational practice is sensitive to the relation between the rate of exploratory variation reflected by the practice and the rate of change in the environment. In this spirit, for example, it has been argued that the persistence of garbage-can decision processes in organizations is related to the diversity advantage they provide in a world of relatively unstable environments, when paired with the selective efficiency of conventional rationality (Cohen, 1986).

Vulnerability of exploration

Compared to returns from exploitation, returns from exploration are systematically less certain, more remote in time, and organizationally more distant from the locus of action and adaption. What is good in the long run is not always good in the short run. What is good at a particular historical moment is not always good at another time. What is good for one part of an organization is not always good for another part. What is good for an organization is not always good for a larger social system of which it is a part. As organizations learn from experience how to divide resources between exploitation and exploration, this distribution of consequences across time and space affects the lessons learned. The certainty, speed, proximity and clarity of feedback ties exploitation to its consequences more quickly and more precisely than is the case with exploration. The story is told in many forms. Basic research has less certain outcomes, longer time horizons and more diffuse effects than does product development. The search for new ideas, markets or relations has less certain outcomes, longer time horizons and more diffuse effects than does further development of existing ones.

Because of these differences, adaptive processes characteristically improve exploitation more rapidly than exploration. These advantages for exploitation cumulate. Each increase in competence at an activity increases the likelihood of rewards for engaging in that activity, thereby further increasing the competence and the likelihood (Argyris and Schön, 1978; David, 1985). The effects extend, through network externalities, to others with whom the learning organization interacts (Katz and Shapiro, 1986; David and Bunn, 1988). Reason inhibits foolishness; learning and imitation inhibit experimentation. This is not an accident but is a consequence of the temporal and spatial proximity of the effects of exploitation, as well as their precision and interconnectedness.

Since performance is a joint function of potential return from an activity and present competence of an organization at it, organizations exhibit increasing returns to experience (Arthur, 1996). Positive local feedback produces strong path dependence (David, 1990) and can lead to suboptimal equilibria. It is quite possible for competence in an inferior activity to become great enough to exclude superior activities with which an organization has little experience (Herriott, Levinthal and March, 1985). Since long-run intelligence depends on sustaining a reasonable level of exploration, these tendencies to increase exploitation and reduce exploration make adaptive processes potentially self-destructive.

The social context of organizational learning

The trade-off between exploration and exploitation exhibits some special features in the social context of organizations. The next two sections of the present paper describe two simple models of adaptation, use them to elaborate the relation between exploitation and exploration, and explore some implications of the relation for the accumulation and utilization of knowledge in organizations. The models identify some reasons why organizations may want to control learning and suggest some procedures by which they do so.

Two distinctive features of the social context are considered. The first is the mutual learning of an organization and the individuals in it. Organizations store knowledge in their procedures, norms, rules and forms. They accumulate such knowledge over time, learning from their members. At the same time, individuals in an organization are socialized to organizational beliefs. Such mutual learning has implications for understanding and managing the trade-off between exploration and exploitation in organizations. The second feature of organizational learning considered here is the context of competition for primacy. Organizations often compete with each other under conditions in which relative position matters. The mixed contribution of knowledge to competitive advantage in cases involving competition for primacy creates difficulties for defining and arranging an appropriate balance between exploration and exploitation in an organizational setting.

2. Mutual learning in the development of knowledge

Organizational knowledge and faiths are diffused to individuals through various forms of instruction, indoctrination and exemplification. An organization socializes recruits to the languages, beliefs and practices that comprise the organizational code (Whyte, 1957; Van Maanen, 1973). Simultaneously, the organizational code is adapting to individual beliefs. This form of mutual learning has consequences both for the individuals involved and for an organization as a whole. In particular, the trade-off between exploration and exploitation in mutual learning involves conflicts between short-run and long-run concerns and between gains to individual knowledge and gains to collective knowledge.

A model of mutual learning

Consider a simple model of the development and diffusion of organizational knowledge. There are four key features to the model:

1. There is an external reality that is independent of beliefs about it. Reality is described as having m dimensions, each of which has a value of 1 or −1. The (independent) probability that any one dimension will have a value of 1 is 0.5.

2. At each time period, beliefs about reality are held by each of n individuals in an organization and by an organizational code of received truth. For each of the m dimensions of reality, each belief has a value of 1, 0, or −1. This value may change over time.

3. Individuals modify their beliefs continuously as a consequence of socialization into the organization and education into its code of beliefs. Specifically, if the code is 0 on a particular dimension, individual belief is not affected. In each period in which the code differs on any particular dimension from the belief of an individual, individual belief changes to that of the code with probability, $p1$. Thus, $p1$ is a parameter reflecting the effectiveness of socialization, i.e., learning *from* the code. Changes on the several dimensions are assumed to be independent of each other.

4. At the same time, the organizational code adapts to the beliefs of those individuals whose beliefs correspond with reality on more dimensions than does the code. The probability that the beliefs of the code will be adjusted to conform to the dominant belief within the superior group on any particular dimension

depends on the level of agreement among individuals in the superior group and on $p2$. Thus, $p2$ is a parameter reflecting the effectiveness of learning *by* the code. Changes on the several dimensions are assumed to be independent of each other.

Within this system, initial conditions include: a reality m-tuple (m dimensions, each of which has a value of 1 or -1, with independent equal probability); an organizational code m-tuple (m dimensions, each of which is initially 0); and n individual m-tuples (m dimensions, with values equal 1, 0, or -1, with equal probabilities).

Thus, the process begins with an organizational code characterized by neutral beliefs on all dimensions and a set of individuals with varying beliefs that exhibit, on average, no knowledge. Over time, the organizational code affects the beliefs of individuals, even while it is being affected by those beliefs. The beliefs of individuals do not affect the beliefs of other individuals directly but only through affecting the code. The effects of reality are also indirect. Neither the individuals nor the organizations experience reality. Improvement in knowledge comes by the code mimicking the beliefs (including the false beliefs) of superior individuals and by individuals mimicking the code (including its false beliefs).

Basic properties of the model in a closed system

Consider such a model of mutual learning first within a closed system having fixed organizational membership and a stable reality. Since realizations of the process are subject to stochastic variability, repeated simulations using the same initial conditions and parameters are used to estimate the distribution of outcomes. In all of the results reported here, the number of dimensions of reality (m) is set at 30, the number of individuals (n) is set at 50, and the number of repeated simulations is 80. The quantitative levels of the results and the magnitude of the stochastic fluctuations reported depend on these specifications, but the qualitative results are insensitive to values of m and n.

Since reality is specified, the state of knowledge at any particular time period can be assessed in two ways. First, the proportion of reality that is correctly represented in the organizational code can be calculated for any period. This is the knowledge level of the code for that period. Second, the proportion of reality that is correctly represented in individual beliefs (on average) can be calculated for any period. This is the average knowledge level of the individuals for that period.

Within this closed system, the model yields time paths of organizational and individual beliefs, thus knowledge levels, that depend stochastically on the initial conditions and the parameters affecting learning. The basic features of these histories can be summarized simply: Each of the adjustments in beliefs serves to eliminate differences between the individuals and the code. Consequently, the beliefs of individuals and the code converge over time. As individuals in the organization become more knowledgeable, they also become more homogeneous with respect to knowledge. Equilibrium is reached at which all individuals and the code share the same (not necessarily accurate) belief with respect to each dimension. The equilibrium is stable.

Effects of learning rates. Higher rates of learning lead, on average, to achieving equilibrium earlier. The equilibrium level of knowledge attained by an organization also depends interactively on the two learning parameters. Figure 9.3.1 shows the results when we assume that $p1$ is the same for all individuals. Slower socialization (lower $p1$) leads to greater knowledge at equilibrium than does faster socialization, particularly when the code learns rapidly (high $p2$). When socialization is slow, more rapid learning by the code leads to greater knowledge at equilibrium but when socialization is rapid, greater equilibrium knowledge is achieved through slower learning by the code. By far the highest equilibrium knowledge occurs when the code learns rapidly from individuals whose socialization to the code is slow.

The results pictured in Figure 9.3.1 confirm the observation that rapid learning is not always desirable (Herriott, Levinthal and March, 1985; Lounamaa and March, 1987).

In previous work, it was shown that slower learning allows for greater exploration of possible alternatives and greater balance in the development of specialized competences. In the present model, a different version of the same general phenomenon is observed. The gains to individuals from adapting rapidly to the code (which is consistently closer to reality than the average individual) are offset by second-order losses stemming from the fact that the code can learn only from individuals who deviate from it. Slow learning on the part of individuals maintains diversity longer, thereby providing the exploration that allows the knowledge found in the organizational code to improve.

Effects of learning rate heterogeneity. The fact that fast individual learning from the code tends to have a favourable first-order effect on individual knowledge but an adverse effect on improvement in

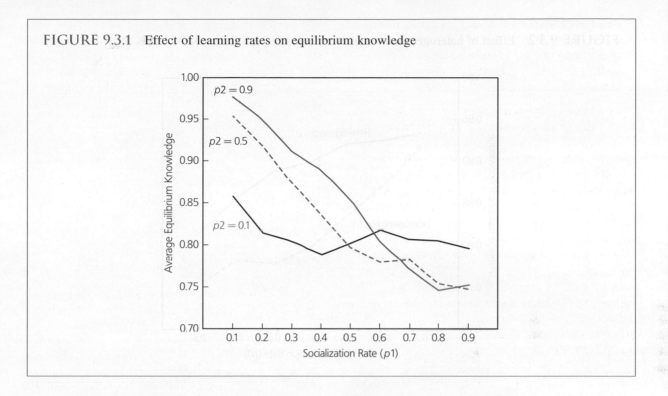

FIGURE 9.3.1   Effect of learning rates on equilibrium knowledge

organizational knowledge and thereby on long-term individual improvement suggests that there might be some advantage to having a mix of fast and slow learners in an organization. Suppose the population of individuals in an organization is divided into two groups, one consisting of individuals who learn rapidly from the code ($p1 = 0.9$) and the other consisting of individuals who learn slowly ($p1 = 0.1$).

If an organization is partitioned into two groups in this way, the mutual learning process achieves an equilibrium in which all individuals and the code share the same beliefs. As would be expected from the results above with respect to homogeneous socialization rates, larger fractions of fast learners result in the process reaching equilibrium faster and in lower levels of knowledge at equilibrium than do smaller fractions of fast learners. However, as Figure 9.3.2 shows, for "any average rate of learning from the code, it is better from the point of view of equilibrium knowledge to have that average reflect a mix of fast and slow learners rather than a homogeneous population." For equivalent average values of the socialization learning parameter ($p1$), the heterogeneous population consistently produces higher equilibrium knowledge.

On the way to equilibrium, the knowledge gains from variability are disproportionate due to contributions by slow learners, but they are disproportionately realized (in their own knowledge) by fast learners.

Figure 9.3.3 shows the effects on period-20 knowledge of varying the fraction of the population of individuals who are fast learners ($p1 = 0.9$) rather than slow learners ($p1 = 0.1$). Prior to reaching equilibrium, individuals with a high value for $p1$ gain from being in an organization in which there are individuals having a low value for $p1$, but the converse is not true.

These results indicate that the fraction of slow learners in an organization is a significant factor in organizational learning. In the model, that fraction is treated as a parameter. Disparities in the returns to the two groups and their interdependence make optimizing with respect to the fraction of slow learners problematic if the rates of individual learning are subject to individual control. Since there are no obvious individual incentives for learning slowly in a population in which others are learning rapidly, it may be difficult to arrive at a fraction of slow learners that is optimal from the point of view of the code if learning rates are voluntarily chosen by individuals.

Basic properties of the model in a more open system

These results can be extended by examining some alternative routes to selective slow learning in a somewhat more open system. Specifically, the role of turnover in the organization and turbulence in the

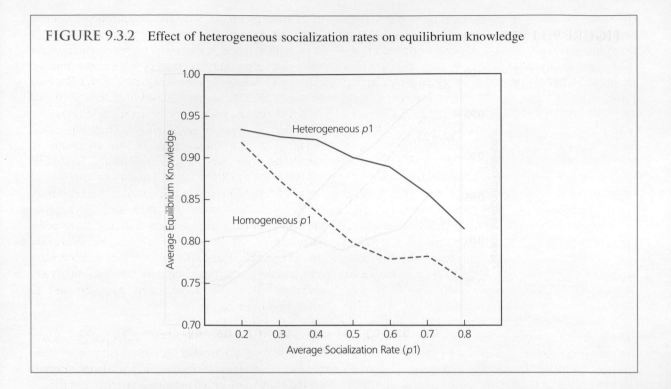

FIGURE 9.3.2   Effect of heterogeneous socialization rates on equilibrium knowledge

environment are considered. In the case of turnover, organizational membership is treated as changing. In the case of turbulence, environmental reality is treated as changing.

Effects of personnel turnover. In the previous section, it was shown that variability is sustained by low values of $p1$. Slow learners stay deviant long enough for the code to learn from them. An alternative way of

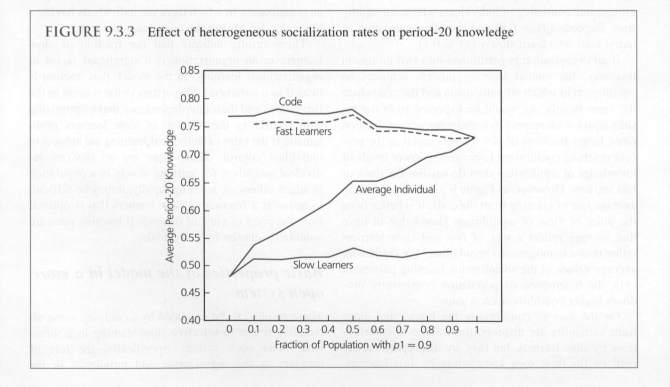

FIGURE 9.3.3   Effect of heterogeneous socialization rates on period-20 knowledge

producing variability in an organization is to introduce personnel turnover. Suppose that each time period each individual has a probability, $p3$, of leaving the organization and being replaced by a new individual with a set of naive beliefs described by an m-tuple, having values equal to 1, 0, or –1, with equal probabilities. As might be expected, there is a consistent negative first-order effect of turnover on average individual knowledge. Since there is a positive relation between lengths of service in the organization and individual knowledge, the greater the turnover, the shorter the average length of service and the lower the average individual knowledge at any point. This effect is strong.

The effect of turnover on the organizational code is more complicated and reflects a trade-off between learning rate and turnover rate. Figure 9.3.4 shows the period-20 results for two different values of the socialization rate ($p1$). If $p1$ is relatively low, period-20 code knowledge declines with increasing turnover. The combination of slow learning and rapid turnover leads to inadequate exploitation. However, if $p1$ is relatively high, moderate amounts of turnover improve the organizational code. Rapid socialization of individuals into the procedures and beliefs of an organization tends to reduce exploration. A modest level of turnover, by introducing less socialized people, increases exploration, and thereby improves aggregate knowledge. The level

of knowledge reflected by the organizational code is increased, as is the average individual knowledge of those individuals who have been in the organization for some time. Note that this effect does not come from the superior knowledge of the average new recruit. Recruits are, on average, less knowledgeable than the individuals they replace. The gains come from their diversity.

Turnover, like heterogeneity in learning rates, produces a distribution problem. Contributions to improving the code (and subsequently individual knowledge) come from the occasional newcomers who deviate from the code in a favourable way. Old-timers, on average, know more, but what they know is redundant with knowledge already reflected in the code. They are less likely to contribute new knowledge on the margin. Novices know less on average, but what they know is less redundant with the code and occasionally better, thus more likely to contribute to improving the code.

Effects of environmental turbulence. Since learning processes involve lags in adjustment to changes, the contribution of learning to knowledge depends on the amount of turbulence in the environment. Suppose that the value of any given dimension of reality shifts (from 1 to –1 or –1 to 1) in a given time period with probability $p4$. This captures in an elementary way

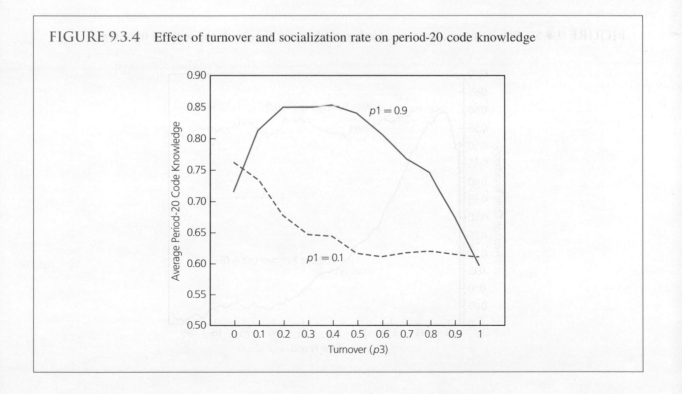

FIGURE 9.3.4 Effect of turnover and socialization rate on period-20 code knowledge

the idea that understanding the world may be complicated by turbulence in the world. Exogenous environmental change makes adaptation essential, but it also makes learning from experience difficult (Weick, 1979). In the model, the level of knowledge achieved in a particular (relatively early) time period decreases with increasing turbulence.

In addition, mutual learning has a dramatic long-run degenerative property under conditions of exogenous turbulence. As the beliefs of individuals and the code converge, the possibilities for improvement in either decline. Once a knowledge equilibrium is achieved, it is sustained indefinitely. The beliefs reflected in the code and those held by all individuals remain identical and unchanging, regardless of changes in reality. Even before equilibrium is achieved, the capabilities for change fall below the rate of change in the environment. As a result, after an initial period of increasing accuracy, the knowledge of the code and individuals is systematically degraded through changes in reality. Ultimately, the accuracy of belief reaches chance (i.e., where a random change in reality is as likely to increase accuracy of beliefs as it is to decrease it). The process becomes a random walk.

The degeneracy is avoided if there is turnover. Figure 9.3.5 plots the average level of code knowledge over time under conditions of turbulence ($p4 = 0.02$).

Two cases of learning are plotted, one without turnover ($p3 = 0$), the other with moderate turnover ($p3 = 0.1$). Where there is turbulence without turnover, code knowledge first rises to a moderate level, and then declines to 0, from which it subsequently wanders randomly. With turnover, the degeneracy is avoided and a moderate level of code knowledge is sustained in the face of environmental change. The positive effects of moderate turnover depend, of course, on the rules for selecting new recruits. In the present case, recruitment is not affected by the code. Replacing departing individuals with recruits closer to the current organizational code would significantly reduce the efficiency of turnover as a source of exploration.

Turnover is useful in the face of turbulence, but it produces a disparity between code knowledge and the average knowledge of individuals in the organization. As a result, the match between turnover rate and level of turbulence that is desirable from the point of view of the organization's knowledge is not necessarily desirable from the point of view of the knowledge of every individual in it, or individuals on average. In particular, where there is turbulence, there is considerable individual advantage to having tenure in an organization that has turnover. This seems likely to produce pressures by individuals to secure tenure for themselves while restricting it for others.

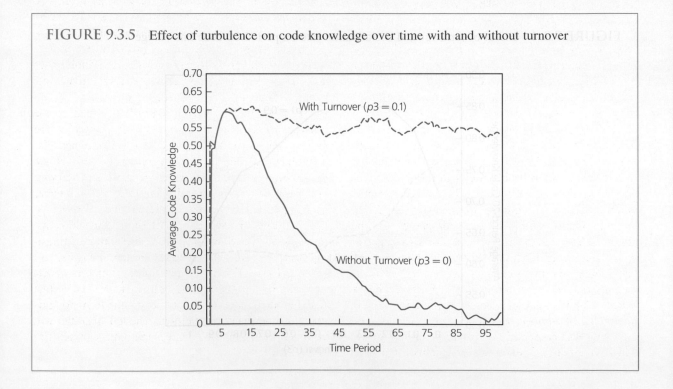

FIGURE 9.3.5   Effect of turbulence on code knowledge over time with and without turnover

3. Knowledge and ecologies of competition

The model in the previous section examines one aspect of the social context of adaptation in organizations, the ways in which individual beliefs and an organizational code draw from each other over time. A second major feature of the social context of organizational learning is the competitive ecology within which learning occurs and knowledge is used. External competitive processes pit organizations against each other in pursuit of scarce environmental resources and opportunities. Examples are competition among business firms for customers and governmental subsidies. Internal competitive processes pit individuals in the organization against each other in competition for scarce organizational resources and opportunities. Examples are competition among managers for internal resources and hierarchical promotion. In these ecologies of competition, the competitive consequences of learning by one organization depend on learning by other organizations. In this section, these links among learning, performance and position in an ecology of competition are discussed by considering some ways in which competitive advantage is affected by the accumulation of knowledge.

Competition and the importance of relative performance

Suppose that an organization's realized performance on a particular occasion is a draw from a probability distribution that can be characterized in terms of some measure of average value and some measure of variability. Knowledge, and the learning process that produces it, can be described in terms of their effects on these two measures. A change in an organization's performance distribution that increases average performance will often be beneficial to an organization, but such a result is not assured when relative position within a group of competing organizations is important. Where returns to one competitor are not strictly determined by that competitor's own performance but depend on the relative standings of the competitors, returns to changes in knowledge depend not only on the magnitude of the changes in the expected value but also on changes in variability and on the number of competitors.

In bilateral competition involving normal performance distributions, learning that increases the mean always pays off, and changes in the variance – whether positive or negative – have no effect. The situation changes as N increases. If N is greater than 1 (but finite), increases in either the mean or the variance have a positive effect on competitive advantage, and sufficiently large increases in either can offset decreases in the other. The trade-off between increases in the mean and increases in the variance is strongly affected by N. As the number of competitors increases, the contribution of the variance to competitive advantage increases until at the limit, as N goes to infinity, the mean becomes irrelevant.

Learning, knowledge, and competitive advantage

The effects of learning are realized in changes in the performance distribution. The analysis indicates that if learning increases both the mean and the variance of a normal performance distribution, it will improve competitive advantage in a competition for primacy. The model also suggests that increases in the variance may compensate for decreases in the mean; decreases in the variance may nullify gains from increases in the mean. These variance effects are particularly significant when the number of competitors is large.

The underlying argument does not depend on competition being only for primacy. Such competition is a special case of competition for relative position. The general principle that relative position is affected by variability, and increasingly so as the number of competitors increases, is true for any position. In competition to achieve relatively high positions, variability has a positive effect. In competition to avoid relatively low positions, variability has a negative effect.

Nor does the underlying argument depend on the assumption of normality or other symmetry in the performance distributions. Normal performance distributions are special cases in which the tails of the distribution are specified when the mean and variance are specified. For general distributions, as the number of competitors increases, the likelihood of finishing first depends increasingly on the right-hand tail of the performance distribution, and the likelihood of finishing last depends increasingly on the left-hand tail (David, 1981). If learning has different effects on the two tails of the distribution, the right-hand tail effect will be such more important in competition for primacy among many competitors. The left-hand tail will be much more important in competition to avoid finishing last.

Some learning processes increase both average performance and variability. A standard example would be the short-run consequences from adoption of a new technology. If a new technology is so clearly superior as to overcome the disadvantages of unfamiliarity with it, it will offer a higher expected value than the old technology. At the same time, the limited experience with the new technology (relative to experience with the old) will lead to an increased variance. A similar result might be expected with the introduction of a new body of knowledge or new elements of cultural diversity to an organization, for example, through the introduction of individuals with untypical skills, attitudes, ethnicity, or gender.

Learning processes do not necessarily lead to increases in both average performance and variation, however. Increased knowledge seems often to reduce the variability of performance rather than to increase it. Knowledge makes performance more reliable. As work is standardized, as techniques are learned, variability, both in the time required to accomplish tasks and in the quality of task performance, is reduced. Insofar as that increase in reliability comes from a reduction in the left-hand tail, the likelihood of finishing last in a competition among many is reduced without changing the likelihood of finishing first. However, if knowledge has the effect of reducing the right-hand tail of the distribution, it may easily decrease the chance of being best among several competitors even though it also increases average performance. The question is whether you can do exceptionally well, as opposed to better than average, without leaving the confines of conventional action. The answer is complicated, for it depends on a more careful specification of the kind of knowledge involved and its precise effects on the right-hand tail of the distribution. But knowledge that simultaneously increases average performance and its reliability is not a guarantee of competitive advantage.

Consider, for example, the case of modern information and decision technology based on computers. In cases where time is particularly important, information technology has a major effect on the mean, less on the variance. Some problems in environmental scanning for surprises, changes or opportunities probably fall into such a category. Under such conditions, appropriate use of information technology seems likely to improve competitive position. On the other hand, in many situations the main effect of information technology is to make outcomes more reliable. For example, additional data, or more detailed analyses, seem likely to increase reliability in decisions more rapidly than they will increase their average returns. In such cases, the effects on the tails are likely to dominate the effects on the mean. The net effect of the improved technology on the chance of avoiding being the worst competitor will be positive, but the effect on the chance of finishing at the head of the pack may well be negative.

Similarly, multiple independent projects may have an advantage over a single, coordinated effort. The average result from independent projects is likely to be lower than that realized from a coordinated one, but their right-hand side variability can compensate for the reduced mean in a competition for primacy. The argument can be extended more generally to the effects of close collaboration or cooperative information exchange. Organizations that develop effective instruments of coordination and communication probably can be expected to do better (on average) than those that are more loosely coupled, and they also probably can be expected to become more reliable, less likely to deviate significantly from the mean of their performance distributions. The price of reliability, however, is a smaller chance of primacy among competitors.

Competition for relative position and strategic action

The arguments above assume that the several individual performances of competitors are independent draws from a distribution of possible performances, and that the distribution cannot be arbitrarily chosen by the competitors. Such a perspective is incomplete. It is possible to see both the mean and the reliability of a performance distribution (at least partially) as choices made strategically. In the long run, they represent the result of organizational choices between investments in learning and in consumption of the fruits of current capabilities, thus the central focus of this paper. In the short run, the choice of mean can be seen as a choice of effort or attention. By varying effort, an organization selects a performance mean between an entitlement (zero-effort) and a capability (maximum-effort) level. Similarly, in the short run, variations in the reliability of performance can be seen as choices of knowledge or risk that can be set wilfully within the range of available alternatives.

These choices, insofar as they are made rationally, will not, in general, be independent of competition. If relative position matters, as the number of competitors increases, strategies for increasing the mean through increased effort or greater knowledge become less attractive relative to strategies for increasing variability. In the more general situation, suppose organizations face competition from numerous competitors who vary in their average capabilities but who can choose their variances. If payoffs and preferences are such that finishing near the top matters a great deal, those organizations with performance distributions characterized by comparatively low means will (if they can) be willing to sacrifice average performance in order to augment the right-hand tails of their performance distributions. In this way, they improve their chances of winning, thus force their more talented competitors to do likewise, and thereby convert the competition into a right-hand tail "race" in which average performance (due to ability and effort) becomes irrelevant. These dynamics comprise powerful countervailing forces to the tendency for experience to eliminate exploration and are a reminder that the learning dominance of exploitation is, under some circumstances, constrained not only by slow learning and turnover but also by reason.

4. Little models and old wisdom

Learning, analysis, imitation, regeneration and technological change are major components of any effort to improve organizational performance and strengthen competitive advantage. Each involves adaptation and a delicate trade-off between exploration and exploitation. The present argument has been that these trade-offs are affected by their contexts of distributed costs and benefits and ecological interaction. The essence of exploitation is the refinement and extension of existing competences, technologies and paradigms. Its returns are positive, proximate and predictable. The essence of exploration is experimentation with new alternatives. Its returns are uncertain, distant and often negative. Thus, the distance in time and space between the locus of learning and the locus for the realization of returns is generally greater in the case of exploration than in the case of exploitation, as is the uncertainty.

Such features of the context of adaptation lead to a tendency to substitute exploitation of known alternatives for the exploration of unknown ones, to increase the reliability of performance rather more than its mean. This property of adaptive processes is potentially self-destructive. As we have seen, it degrades organizational learning in a mutual learning situation. Mutual learning leads to convergence between organizational and individual beliefs. The convergence is generally useful both for individuals and for an organization. However, a major threat to the effectiveness of such learning is the possibility that individuals will adjust to an organizational code before the code can learn from them. Relatively slow socialization of new organizational members and moderate turnover sustains variability in individual beliefs, thereby improving organizational and average individual knowledge in the long run.

An emphasis on exploitation also compromises competitive position where finishing near the top is important. Knowledge-based increases in average performance can be insufficient to overcome the adverse effects produced by reductions in variability. The ambiguous usefulness of learning in a competitive race is not simply an artefact of representing knowledge in terms of the mean and variance of a normal distribution. The key factor is the effect of knowledge on the right-hand tail of the performance distribution. Thus, in the end, the effects stem from the relation between knowledge and discovery. Michael Polanyi, commenting on one of his contributions to physics, observed (Polanyi 1963, p. 1013) that "I would never have conceived my theory, let alone have made a great effort to verify it, if I had been more familiar with major developments in physics that were taking place. Moreover, my initial ignorance of the powerful, false objections that were raised against my ideas protected those ideas from being nipped in the bud."

These observations do not overturn the renaissance. Knowledge, learning and education remain as profoundly important instruments of human well-being. At best, the models presented here suggest some of the considerations involved in thinking about choices between exploration and exploitation and in sustaining exploration in the face of adaptive processes that tend to inhibit it. The complexity of the distribution of costs and returns across time and groups makes an explicit determination of optimality a non-trivial exercise. But it may be instructive to reconfirm some elements of folk wisdom asserting that the returns to fast learning are not all positive, that rapid socialization may hurt the socializers even as it helps the socialized, that the development of knowledge may depend on maintaining an influx of the naive and ignorant, and that competitive victory does not reliably go to the properly educated.

REFERENCES

Amit, R. and Zott, C. (2001) 'Value creation in e-business', *Strategic Management Journal*, 22(6–7), pp. 493–520.

Amit, R. and Zott, C. (2012) 'Creating Value Through Business Model Innovation', *Sloan Management Review*, Spring, Vol. 53, pp. 41–49.

Argyris, C. (1990) *Overcoming Organizational Defenses: Facilitating Organizational Learning*, Boston, MA: Prentice Hall.

Argyris, C. and Schon, D. (1978) *Organizational Learning: A Theory of Action Approach*, Reading, MA: Addison Wesley.

Arthur, W.B. (1996) 'Increasing Returns and the New World of Business', *Harvard Business Review*, Vol. 74, No. 4, July–August, pp. 100–109.

Ashby, W.R. (1960) *Design for a Brain* (2nd edn), New York: Wiley.

Benner, M.J. and Tushman, M.L (2002) 'Process management and technological innovation: A longitudinal study of the photography and paint industries', *Administrative Science Quarterly*, 47, pp. 676–706.

Benner, M.J. and Tushman, M.L. (2003) 'Exploitation, exploration, and process management: The productivity dilemma revisited', *Academy of Management Review*, 2, pp. 238–256.

Braudel, F. (1949) *The Mediterranean and the Mediterranean World in the Age of Philip II*, Scranton, Penn.: HarperCollins.

Burgelman, R. (1991) 'Intraorganizational Ecology of Strategy Making and Organizational Adaptation: Theory and Field Research', *Organization Science*, Vol. 2, No. 3, August, pp. 239–262.

Calori, R. and de Woot, P. (eds.) (1994) *A European Management Model: Beyond Diversity*, Hemel Hempstead: Prentice Hall.

Calori, R., Valla, J.-P. and de Woot, P. (1994) 'Common Characteristics: The Ingredients of European Management', in: R. Calori and P. de Woot (eds.) *A European Management Model: Beyond Diversity*, Hemel Hempstead: Prentice Hall.

Cantwell, J. (1989) *Technological Innovations in Multinational Corporations*, Oxford: Blackwell.

Chen, C.C. and Lee Y.T. (eds.) (2008) *Leadership and Management in China*, Cambridge: Cambridge University Press.

Christensen, C.M. (1997, 2011) *The Innovator's Dilemma, When New Technologies Cause Great Firms to Fail*, New York: Harper Business.

Cohen, E.G. (1986) 'Artificial Intelligence and the Dynamic Performance of Organizational Designs', in: J.G. March and R. Weissinger-Baylon (eds.) *Ambiguity and Command: Organizational Perspectives on Military Decision Making*, Boston, MA: Ballinger.

Cyert, R.M. and March, J. (1963) *A Behavioral Theory of the Firm*, Englewood Cliffs, NJ: Prentice Hall.

D'Aveni, R. (1994) *Hypercompetition: Managing the Dynamics of Strategic Maneuvering*, New York: Free Press.

David, H.A. (1981) *Order Statistics* (2nd edn), New York: John Wiley.

David, P.A. (1985) 'Clio and the Economics of QWERTY', *The American Economic Review*, 75(2), pp. 332–337.

David, P.A. (1990) 'The Hero and the Herd in Technological History: Reflections on Thomas Edison and The Battle of the Systems', in: P. Higgonet and H. Rosovski (eds.) *Economic Development Past and Present: Opportunities and Constraints*, Cambridge, MA: Harvard University Press.

David, P.A. and Bunn, J.A. (1988) 'The Economics of Gateway Technologies and Network Evolution: Lessons from Electricity Supply History', *Information Economics and Policy*, 3(2), pp. 165–202.

Day, R.H. (1967) 'Profits, Learning and the Convergence of Satisficing to Marginalism', *The Quarterly Journal of Economics*, 81, pp. 302–311.

De Geus, A. (1997) 'The Living Company', *Harvard Business Review*, March, pp. 51–59.

Diamond, J.M. (1997) *Guns, Germs and Steel: The Fates of Human Societies*, New York: Norton.

Dosi, G. (1984) *Technical Change and Industrial Transformation*, London, Macmillan.

Dunning, J.H. (1958) *American Investment in British Manufacturing Industry*, London: George Allen & Unwin.

Freeman, C. and Perez, C. (1988) 'Structural Crises of Adjustment, Business Cycles and Investment Behavior', in: G. Dosi, C. Freeman, R. Nelson, G. Silverberg and L. Soete (eds.) *Technical Change And Economic Theory*, London and New York: Pinter Publishers.

Gupta, A.K., Smith, K.G. and Shalley, C.E. (2006) 'The interplay between exploration and exploitation', *Academy of Management Journal*, Vol. 49, No. 4, pp. 693–706.

Hamel, G. (1996) 'Strategy as Revolution', *Harvard Business Review*, Vol. 74, No. 4, July–August, pp. 69–82.

Hamel, G. and Prahalad, C.K. (1994) *Competing for the Future*, Boston, MA: Harvard Business School Press.

Hannan, M.T. and Freeman, J. (1984) 'Structural Inertia and Organizational Change', *American Sociological Review*, Vol. 49, No. 2, April, pp. 149–164.

Hannan, M.T. and Freeman, J. (1987) 'The Ecology of Organizational Foundings: American Labor Unions, 1836–1985', *American Journal of Sociology*, 92, pp. 910–943.

Herriott, S.R., Levinthal, D.A. and March, J.G. (1985) 'Learning from Experience in Organizations', *The American Economic Review*, 75(2), pp. 298–302.

Hey, J.D. (1982) 'Search for Rules for Search', *Journal of Economic Behavior and Organization*, 3(1), pp. 65–81.

Hofstede, G. (1980) *Culture's Consequences*, London: Sage.

Holden, N. (2002) *Cross Cultural Management a Knowledge Based Perspective*, London: Pearson Education.

Holland, J.H. (1995) *Adaptation in Natural and Artificial Systems*, Ann Arbor, MI: University of Michigan Press.

Imai, M. (1986) *Kaizen: The Key to Japan's Competitive Success*, McGraw-Hill, New York.

Kagono, T., Nonaka, I., Sakakibara, K. and Okumura, A. (1985) *Strategic vs. Evolutionary Management: A US-Japan Comparison of Strategy and Organization*, Amsterdam: North Holland.

Kahneman, D. and Tversky, A. (1979) 'Prospect Theory: An Analysis of Decision under Risk', *Econometrica*, pp. 263–291.

Katz, M.L. and Shapiro, C. (1986) 'Technology Adoption in the Presence of Network Externalities', *Journal of Political Economy*, 9, pp. 822–841.

Kelly, D. and Amburgey, T. (1991) 'Organizational inertia and momentum: a dynamic model of strategic change', *Academy of Management Journal*, 34(3), pp. 591–612.

Krüger, W. (1996) 'Implementation: The Core Task of Change Management', *CEMS Business Review*, Vol. 1, pp. 77–96.

Kuran, T. (1998) 'The Tenacious Past: Theories of Personal and Collective Conservatism', *Journal of Economic Behavior and Organization*, 10, pp. 143–171.

Lee, C.C.K. (2010) *Thought and Governance of East Asia: Confucian Humanism, Human Rights and Business Ethics*, Seoul: PerDream.

Leifer, M. (2000) *The Political and Security Outlook for Southeast Asia*, Institute of Southeast Asian Studies.

Levinthal, D. and March, J.G. (1981) 'A Model of Adaptive Organizational Search', *Journal of Economic Behavior & Organization*, 2(4), pp. 307–333.

Levitt, B. and March, J.G. (1988) 'Organizational Learning', *Annual Review of Sociology*, 14, pp. 319–340.

Levitt, T. (1983) 'The Globalization of Markets', *Harvard Business Review*, Vol. 61, No. 3, May–June, pp. 92–102.

Lounamaa, P.H. and March, J.G. (1987) 'Adaptive Coordination of a Learning Team', *Management Science*, 33(1), pp. 107–123.

March, J.G. (1988) 'Variable Risk Preferences and Adaptive Aspirations', *Journal of Economic Behavior and Organization*, 9, pp. 5–24.

March, J.G. (1991) 'Exploitation and Exploration in Organizational Learning', *Organization Science*, 2(1), pp. 71–87.

McLuhan, M. (1964) *Understanding Media: The Extensions of Man*, New York: McGraw-Hill.

Morris, I. (2010), *Why the West Rules – For Now: The Patterns of History, and What They Reveal About the Future*, Farrar, Straus and Giroux.

Needham, J., Ho, P.Y. and Lu, G.D. (1976) *Science and Civilisation in China*, London: Cambridge University Press, Volume V, Part III.

Nelson, R.R. and Winter, S.G. (1982) *An Evolutionary Theory of Economic Change*, Cambridge, MA: Harvard University Press.

Ouchi, W. (1981) *Theory Z: How American Business Can Meet the Japanese Challenge*, Reading, MA: Addison-Wesley.

Pascale, R.T. and Athos, A.G. (1981) *The Art of Japanese Management*, New York: Simon & Schuster.

Peters, T.J. and Waterman, R.H. (1982) *In Search of Excellence*, New York: Warner Books.

Pfeffer, J. and Salancik, G.R. (1978) *The External Control of Organizations: A Resource Dependence Perspective*, New York: Harper and Row.

Polanyi, M. (1963) 'The Potential Theory of Adsorption: Authority in Science Has Its Uses and Its Dangers', *Science*, 141, pp. 1010–1013.

Poole, M.S. and Van de Ven, A.H. (1989) 'Using Paradox to Build Management and Organization Theories', *Academy of Management Review*, Vol. 14, No. 4, pp. 562–578.

Porter, M.E. (1990) *The Competitive Advantage of Nations*, London: Macmillan.

Radner, R. and Rothschild, M. (1975) 'On the Allocation of Effort', *Journal of Economic Theory*, 10(3), pp. 358–376.

Rahmandad, H. (2008) 'Effects of Delays on Complexity of Organizational Learning', *Management Science*, Vol. 54, No. 7, July, pp. 1297–1312.

Raisch, S., Birkinshaw, J., Probst, G. and Tushman, M.L. (2009) 'Organizational Ambidexterity: Balancing Exploitation and Exploration for Sustained Performance', *Organization Science*, Vol. 20, No. 4, pp. 685–695.

Repenning, N.P. (2001) 'Understanding fire fighting in new product development', *Journal of Product Innovation Management*, 18, pp. 285–300.

Repenning, N.P. and Sterman, J.D. (2002) 'Capability traps and self-confirming attribution errors in the dynamics of process improvement', *ASQ*, 47, pp. 265–295.

Robertson, P. (2005) *Always Change a Winning Team, Why Reinvention and Change Are Prerequisite for Business Success,* Singapore: Marshall Cavendish Business.

Schneider, S. and Barsoux, J. (2003) *Managing Across Cultures*, Second edition, Pearson Education Limited.

Schumpeter, J. (1934), *The Theory of Economic Development*, Cambridge, MA: Harvard University Press.

Schumpeter, J.A. (1950) *Capitalism, Socialism and Democracy*, Third Edition, New York: Harper and Brothers.

Simon, H.A. (1955) 'A Behavioral Model of Rational Choice', *Quarterly Journal of Economics*, 69(1), pp. 99–118.

Smith, W.K. and Tushman, M.L. (2005) 'Managing Strategic Contradictions: A Top Management Model for Managing Innovation Streams', *Organization Science*, 16(5), pp. 522–536.

Tellis, G.J. (2013) *Unrelenting Innovation: How to Build a Culture for Market Dominance*, San Francisco, CA: Jossey-Bass.

Tripsas, M. and Gavetti, G. (2000) 'Capabilities, Cognition, and Inertia: Evidence from Digital Imaging', *Strategic Management Journal*, Vol. 21, No. 10/11, Special Issue: The Evolution of Firm Capabilities (October–November), pp. 1147–1161.

Trompenaars, F. and Hampden-Turner, C. (2000) *Building Cross-Cultural Competence*, New Haven: Yale University Press.

Tushman, M.L. and O'Reilly III, C.A. (1996) 'Ambidextrous Organizations: Managing Evolutionary and Revolutionary Change', *California Management Review*, Vol. 38, No. 4, Summer, pp. 8–30.

Van Maanen, J. (1973) 'Observation of the Making of Policemen', *Human Relations*, 32, pp. 407–418.

Van Tulder, R. and Junne, G. (1988) *European Multinationals in Core Technologies*, London: Wiley & Sons.

Vernon, R. (1966) 'International Investment and International Trade in the Product Life Cycle', *Quarterly Journal of Economics*, Vol. 80, No. 2, May, pp. 190–207.

Waterman, R.H., Peters, T.J. and Phillips, J.R. (1980) 'Structure is Not Organization', *Business Horizons*, Vol. 23, June, pp. 14–26.

Weick, K. (1979) *The Social Psychology of Organizing*, 2nd edn, Reading, MA: Addison-Wesley.

Whyte, W.H. Jr. (1957) *The Organization Man*, Garden City, New York: Doubleday.

WIPO (2008) *World Patent Report: A Statistical Review*, World Intellectual Property Organization.

Zott, C. and Amit, R. (2013) 'The Business Model: A Theoretically Anchored Robust Construct for Strategic Analysis', *Strategic Organization*, 11, pp. 403–411.

STRATEGY CONTEXT

Circumstances? I make circumstances!

Napoleon Bonaparte (1769–1821); French emperor

The strategy context is the set of circumstances surrounding strategy-making – the conditions under which both the strategy process and the strategy content are formed. It could be said that strategy context is concerned with the *where* of strategy – where (i.e. in which firm and which environment) the strategy process and strategy content are embedded.

Most strategizing managers have an ambivalent relationship with their strategy context. On the one hand, strategizing is about creating something new, and for this, a healthy level of disregard, or even disrespect, for the present circumstances is required. Much like Napoleon, managers do not want to hear about current conditions limiting their capability to shape the future – they want to create their own circumstances. On the other hand, managers recognize that many contextual limitations are real and that wise strategists must take these circumstances into account. In this section, this fundamental tension between *shaping* the context and *adapting* to it is at the centre of attention.

As visualized in Figure IV.1, the strategy context can be dissected along two different dimensions: industry versus organization, and national versus international. This gives the three key contexts that are explored in Chapters 10, 11 and 12:

- The industry context. The key issue here is how industry development takes place. Can the individual firm influence its industry and to what extent does the industry context dictate particular types of firm behaviour?

- The organizational context. The key issue here is how organizational development takes place. Can strategizing managers influence their own organizational conditions and to what extent does the organizational context determine particular types of firm behaviour?

- The international context. The key issue here is how the international context is developing. Must firms adapt to ongoing global convergence or will international diversity remain a characteristic with which firms will need to cope?

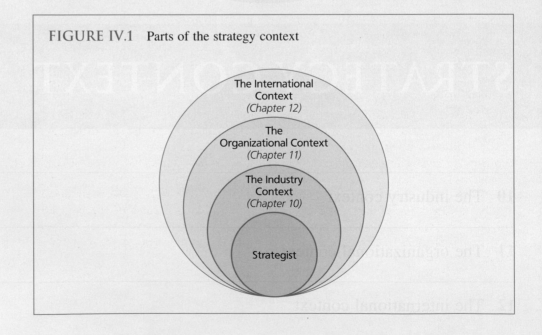

FIGURE IV.1 Parts of the strategy context

THE INDUSTRY CONTEXT

Know the other and know yourself: Triumph without peril.
Know nature and know the situation: Triumph completely.
Sun Tzu (5th century BC); Chinese military strategist

INTRODUCTION

I f strategic management is concerned with relating a firm to its environment, then it is essential to know this environment well. In the previous chapters the factors and actors that shape the external context of the firm have been thoroughly reviewed. While the entire outside world was taken into consideration, emphasis was placed on the direct environment in which a firm needs to compete – its industry context. It has been concluded that an understanding of competitors, buyers, suppliers, substitutes and potential new entrants, as well as the structural factors that influence their behaviour, is invaluable for determining a successful strategy.

A constant theme in the strategy content and strategy process sections was industry change. Knowing the current industry context, it became clear, is not enough to secure an ongoing alignment between a firm and its environment. Strategizing managers need to recognize in which direction the industry is developing to be able to maintain a healthy fit. However, what was not addressed in these discussions is how industry development actually takes place. Important questions such as 'what are the drivers propelling industry development?' and 'what patterns of development do industries exhibit?' have not yet been examined. Nor has it been established whether industries develop in the same way and at the same speed, and whether change is always accompanied by the same opportunities and threats. In this chapter, these questions surrounding the issue of industry development are at the centre of attention.

For strategizing managers, however, the most important question linked to the issue of industry development is how a firm can move beyond *adapting* to *shaping*. How can a firm, or a group of collaborating firms, modify the structure and competitive dynamics in their industry to gain an advantageous position? How can the industry's evolutionary path be proactively diverted into a particular direction? If a firm would be capable of shaping its industry environment instead of following it, this would give them the potential for creating a strong competitive advantage – they could 'set the rules of the competitive game' instead of having to 'play by the rules' set by others. This topic of industry leadership – shaping events as opposed to following them – will be the key focus throughout this chapter.

THE ISSUE OF INDUSTRY DEVELOPMENT

When strategists look at an industry, they are interested in understanding 'the rules of the game' (e.g. Prahalad and Doz, 1987; Hamel, 1996). The industry rules are the demands dictated to the firm by the industry context, limiting the scope of potential strategic behaviours. In other words, industry rules stipulate what must be done to survive and thrive in any chosen line of business – they determine under what conditions the competitive game will be played. For example, an industry rule could be 'must have significant scale economies', 'must have certain technology' or 'must have strong brand'. Failure to adhere to the rules leads to being selected out.

The industry rules arise from the structure of the industry (e.g. Porter, 1980; Tirole, 1988, McGahan, 2000). All of Porter's five forces can impose constraints on a firm's freedom of action. Where the rules are strict, the degrees of freedom available to the strategist are limited. Strict rules imply that only very specific behaviour is allowed – firms must closely follow the rules of the game or face severe consequences. Where the rules are looser, firms have more room to manoeuvre and exhibit distinctive behaviour – the level of managerial discretion is higher (e.g. Hambrick and Abrahamson, 1995; Carpenter and Golden, 1997).

As industries develop, the rules of competition change – vertical integration becomes necessary, certain competences become vital or having a global presence becomes a basic requirement. To be able to play the competitive game well, strategizing managers need to identify which characteristics in the industry structure and which aspects of competitive interaction are changing. This is the topic of 'dimensions of industry development', which is reviewed in more detail below. To determine their response, it is also essential to understand the nature of the change. Are the industry rules gradually shifting or is there a major break with the past? Is the industry development more evolutionary or more revolutionary? A process of slow and moderate industry change demands a different strategic reaction than a process of sudden and dramatic disruption of the industry rules. This topic of 'paths of industry development' is also examined more closely.

As strategists generally like to have the option to shape instead of always being shaped, they need to recognize the determinants of industry development as well. What are the factors that cause the industry rules to change? This subject can be divided into two parts. First, the question of what the drivers of industry development are, pushing the industry in a certain direction. Secondly, the question of what the inhibitors of industry development are, placing a brake on changes. Together, these forces of change and forces for stability will determine the actual path of development that the industry will follow. How these four topics are interrelated is outlined in Figure 10.1.

Dimensions of industry development

Industry development means that the structure of the industry changes. In Chapter 4, the key aspects of the industry structure have already been discussed. Following Porter (1980), five important groups of industry actors were identified (i.e. competitors, buyers, suppliers, new entrants and substitutes) and the underlying factors determining their behaviour were reviewed. Industry development (which Porter calls 'industry evolution'; see also McGahan, 2000, Reading 10.1) is the result of a change in one or more of these underlying factors.

As Porter already indicates, the industry structure can be decomposed into dozens of elements, each of which can change, causing a shift in industry rules. Here it is not the intention to go through all of these elements, but to pick out a number of important

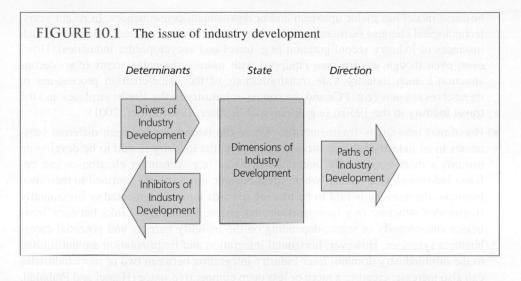

FIGURE 10.1 The issue of industry development

structural characteristics that require special attention. Each of these structural characteristics represents a dimension along which significant industry developments can take place:

- Convergence–divergence. Where the business models that firms employ increasingly start to resemble each other, the industry is said to be moving towards convergence (e.g. insurance and airline industries). In contrast, where many firms introduce new business models, the industry is said to be developing towards more diversity (e.g. car retailing and restaurant industries). Higher diversity can result from the 'mutation' of existing firms, as they strive to compete on a different basis, or the result of new entrants with their own distinct business model. Convergence is the consequence of adaptation by less successful firms to a 'dominant design' in the industry and the selecting out of unfit firms incapable of adequate and timely adaptation (e.g. Hannan and Freeman, 1977; Porter, 1980). Generally, patterns of divergence and convergence can be witnessed in all industries, although the amount of mutation and the pressure for convergence can greatly differ, as can the overall cycle time of an 'evolutionary phase' of mutation and selection (e.g. Aldrich, 1999; Baum and Singh, 1994).

- Concentration–fragmentation. Where an increasing share of the market is in the hands of only a few companies, the industry is said to be developing towards a more concentrated structure (e.g. aircraft and food retailing industries). Conversely, where the average market share of the largest companies starts to decrease, the industry is said to be moving towards a more fragmented structure (e.g. airline and telecom services industries). Concentration can be due to mergers and acquisitions, or result from companies exiting the business. Fragmentation can happen when new companies are formed and grab a part of the market, or through the entry of existing companies into the industry. In a concentrated industry it is much more likely that only one or two firms are dominant than in a fragmented industry, but it is also possible that the industry structure is more balanced.

- Vertical integration–fragmentation. Where firms in the industry are becoming involved in more value-adding activities in the industry column, the industry is said to be developing towards a more vertically integrated structure (e.g. media and IT service providers). Conversely, where firms in the industry are withdrawing from various value-adding activities and 'go back to the core', the industry is said to be moving towards a more disintegrated, layered or vertically fragmented structure (e.g. telecom and automotive industries). It is even possible that the entire vertical structure changes if a new business model has major upstream and/or downstream consequences. In recent years, technological changes surrounding IT and the Internet have triggered a number of such instances of industry reconfiguration (e.g. travel and encyclopaedia industries). However, even though we are now equipped with more fashionable terms (e.g. 'deconstruction'), such industry-wide transformations of the value-creation process are in themselves not new (e.g. PCs and the computer industry in the 1980s; airplanes and the travel industry in the 1950s) (e.g. Evans and Wurster, 1997; Porter, 2001).

■ Horizontal integration–fragmentation. Where the boundaries between different businesses in an industry become increasingly fuzzy, the industry is said to be developing towards a more horizontally integrated structure (e.g. consumer electronics and defence industries). Conversely, where firms become more strictly confined to their own business, the industry is said to be moving towards a more segmented or horizontally fragmented structure (e.g. construction and airline industries). Links between businesses can intensify or wane, depending on the mobility barriers and potential cross-business synergies. However, horizontal integration and fragmentation are not limited to the intra-industry domain. Inter-industry integration between two or more industries can also increase, creating a more or less open competitive space (Hamel and Prahalad, 1994) with few mobility barriers (e.g. the digital industries). Inter-industry integration can also occur where the producers of different products and services are complementary or converge on a common standard or platform (e.g. Android and Linux), making them 'complementers' (e.g. Cusumano and Gawer, 2002; Moore, 1996). Yet, the opposite trend is possible as well, whereby an industry becomes more isolated from neighbouring sectors (e.g. accountancy).

■ International integration–fragmentation. Where the international boundaries separating various geographic segments of an industry become increasingly less important, the industry is said to be developing towards a more internationally integrated structure (e.g. food retailing and business education industries). Conversely, where the competitive interactions in an industry are increasingly confined to a region (e.g. Europe) or country, the industry is said to be moving towards a more internationally fragmented structure (e.g. satellite television and internet retailing). These developments are more thoroughly examined in Chapter 12, which deals with the international context.

■ Expansion–contraction. Industries can also differ with regard to the structural nature of the demand for their products and/or services. Where an industry is experiencing an ongoing increase in demand, the industry is said to be in growth or expansion. Where demand is constantly receding, the industry is said to be in decline or contraction. If periods of expansion are followed by periods of contraction, and vice versa, the industry is said to be cyclical. A prolonged period of expansion is usually linked to the growth phase of the industry life cycle (e.g. Moore, 2000; Porter, 1980; McGahan, 2000, Reading 10.1), while contraction is linked to the decline phase. Often, however, it is rather difficult to apply the 'life cycle' concept to an entire industry (as opposed to a product or technology). As industry growth (expansion) can easily follow a period of industry decline (contraction), the life cycle model has little descriptive value – what does it mean to be mature? – and even less predictive value.

Paths of industry development

The development of an industry can be mapped along any one of the dimensions listed above. The most popular is to track the pattern of expansion and contraction, to gain some indication of the life cycle phase in which the industry might have arrived. Another frequently analysed characteristic is the level of concentration, commonly using a

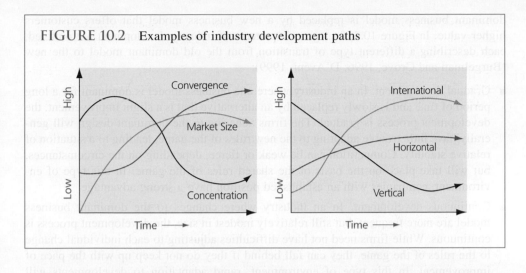

FIGURE 10.2 Examples of industry development paths

concentration index to measure the market share of the four or eight largest companies. But it is equally viable to trace the trajectory of vertical, horizontal or international integration. In Figure 10.2 examples of these paths of industry development are given.

In Figure 10.3 one particular element of the convergence–divergence dimension has been selected for further magnification. As discussed above, in the development of an industry a particular business model can become the dominant design around which the rest of the industry converges. A strategically relevant development occurs when the

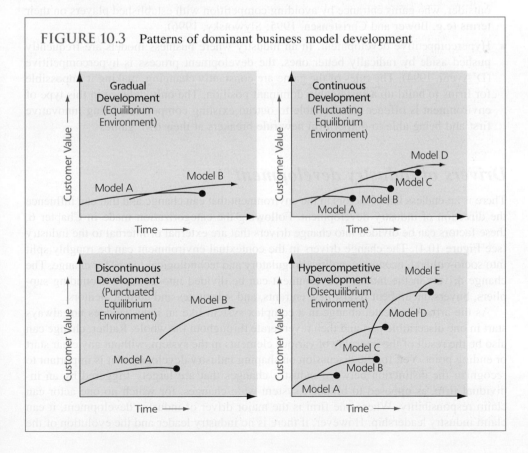

FIGURE 10.3 Patterns of dominant business model development

dominant business model is replaced by a new business model that offers customers higher value. In Figure 10.3, four generic patterns of industry development are outlined, each describing a different type of transition from the old dominant model to the new (Burgelman and Grove, 1996; D'Aveni, 1999):

- Gradual development. In an industry where one business model is dominant for a long period of time and is slowly replaced by an alternative that is a slight improvement, the development process is gradual. The firms adhering to the dominant design will generally have little trouble adapting to the new rules of the game, leading to a situation of relative stability. Competition can be weak or fierce, depending on the circumstances, but will take place on the basis of the shared rules of the game. In this type of environment, companies with an established position have a strong advantage.

- Continuous development. In an industry where changes to the dominant business model are more frequent, but still relatively modest in size, the development process is continuous. While firms need not have difficulties adjusting to each individual change to the rules of the game, they can fall behind if they do not keep up with the pace of improvement. In this type of environment, rapid adaptation to developments will strengthen the competitive position of firms vis-à-vis slow movers.

- Discontinuous development. In an industry where one business model is dominant for a long period of time and is then suddenly displaced by a radically better one, the development process is discontinuous. The firms riding the wave of the new business model will generally have a large advantage over the companies that need to adjust to an entirely different set of industry rules. Where industry incumbents are themselves the 'rule breakers' (Hamel, 1996), they can strongly improve their position vis-à-vis the 'rule takers' in the industry. But the business model innovator can also be an industry outsider, who gains entrance by avoiding competition with established players on their terms (e.g. Bower and Christensen, 1995; Slywotsky, 1996).

- Hypercompetitive development. In an industry where business models are frequently pushed aside by radically better ones, the development process is hypercompetitive (D'Aveni, 1994). The rules of the game are constantly changing, making it impossible for firms to build up a sustainably dominant position. The only defence in this type of environment is offence – being able to outrun existing competitors, being innovative first and being able to outperform new rule breakers at their own game.

Drivers of industry development

There is an endless list of factors in the environment that can change and that can influence the direction of industry development. Following the categorization made in Chapter 6, these factors can be divided into change drivers that are external or internal to the industry (see Figure 10.4). The change drivers in the contextual environment can be roughly split into socio-cultural, economic, political/regulatory and technological forces for change. The change drivers in the industry environment can be divided into groups surrounding suppliers, buyers, incumbent rivals, new entrants, and substitutes and complementors.

As the arrows indicate, change in a complex system like an industry does not always start in one discernible part and then reverberate throughout the whole. Rather, change can also be the result of the interplay of various elements in the system, without any clear start or ending point. Yet, for the discussion on shaping industry development it is important to recognize the distinction between industry changes that are largely triggered by an individual firm, as opposed to broader, system-wide changes, for which no one actor can claim responsibility. Where one firm is the major driver of industry development, it can claim industry leadership. However, if there is no industry leader and the evolution of the

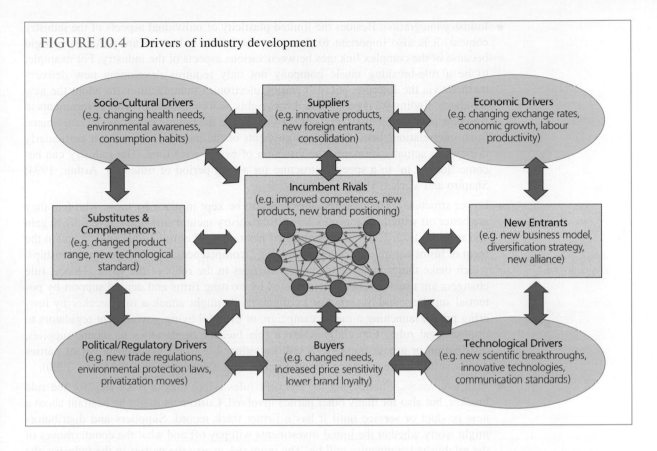

FIGURE 10.4 Drivers of industry development

industry is due to the complex interaction of many different change drivers, it is said that the industry dynamics determine the path of industry development.

Inhibitors of industry development

Forces of change do not always go unopposed. In the discussion on strategic change in Chapter 8, the sources of organizational rigidity have been reviewed, each of which acts as an inhibitor to organizational change. In the same way, there are many sources of industry rigidity, making the industry rules much more difficult to bend or break. Industry rigidity can be defined as the lack of susceptibility to change. If an industry is rigid, the rules of the game cannot be altered and competitive positions are relatively fixed. The opposite term is industry plasticity – an industry's susceptibility to change.

A large number of factors can contribute to rigidity, thereby inhibiting industry development. Some of the most important ones are the following:

■ Underlying conditions. Basically, some rules might be immutable because the underlying industry conditions cannot be changed. In some industries economies of scale are essential (e.g. airplane manufacturing, merchant shipping), while in others economies of scale are not of importance (e.g. wedding services, dentistry services). In some industries buyers are fragmented (e.g. newspapers, moving services), while in others they are highly concentrated (e.g. defence systems, harbour construction). In some industries buyers value product differentiation (e.g. clothing, restaurants), while in others bulk producers must compete on price (e.g. chemicals, general construction). Many of these structural factors are inherent to the industry and defy any attempts to change them (e.g. Bain, 1959; Porter, 1980).

- Industry integration. Besides the limited plasticity of individual aspects of the industry context, it is also important to recognize that some industries are particularly rigid because of the complex linkages between various aspects of the industry. For example, to be a rule-breaking music company not only requires developing new delivery methods via the Internet, but also getting electronics manufacturers to adopt the new standards, finding ways to safeguard copyrights, working together with governments to find new policing methods, and not least to change the buying behaviour of consumers. Such interrelations between various elements of the industry can make it particularly difficult to actually influence the direction of events over time. The industry can become 'locked in' to a specific structure for a long period of time (e.g. Arthur, 1994; Shapiro and Varian, 1998).

- Power structures. The industry rules can also be kept in place by those who feel they are better off with the status quo. Powerful industry incumbents often have little to gain and much to lose. They have established positions and considerable sunk costs, in the form of historical investments in technology, competences, facilities and relationships, which make them reluctant to support changes to the rules of the game. Hence, rule changers are usually vehemently resisted by existing firms and denied support by potential suppliers and buyers. For example, rivals might attack a rule breaker by lowering prices, launching a media campaign, or even lobbying government regulators to impose legal rules. Especially where a rule breaker needs allies to secure supplies, distribution or a new standard, it will be vulnerable to the counter-moves of parties with a vested interest in the current structure (e.g. Ghemawat, 1991; Moore, 2000).

- Risk averseness. Challenging the industry rules is not only a risky step for the rule breaker, but also for many other parties involved. Customers might be hesitant about a new product or service until it has a firmer track record. Suppliers and distributors might worry whether the initial investments will pay off and what the countermoves of the established companies will be. The more risk averse the parties in the industry, the more rigid will be the industry rules (e.g. Christensen, 1997; Parolini, 1999).

- Industry recipes. An industry recipe is a widely held perception among industry incumbents regarding the actual rules of the game in the industry. In other words, an industry recipe is the cognitive map shared by industry incumbents about the structure and demands of an industry. Such a common understanding of the rules of the game can develop over time through shared experiences and interaction – the longer people are in the industry and converse with each other, the greater the chance that a consensus will grow about 'what makes the industry tick'. Thus, the industry recipe can limit people's openness to rule changers who challenge the industry orthodoxy (e.g. Baden-Fuller and Stopford, 1992; Spender, 1989).

- Institutional pressures. While the industry recipe is a shared understanding of how the industry actually functions, industry incumbents usually also share norms of what constitutes socially acceptable economic behaviour. Companies experience strong pressures from governments, professional associations, customers, consultants, trade unions, pressure groups and other industry incumbents prescribing permissible strategies and actions, and generally internalize these behavioural standards. Such conformity to institutional pressures gives companies legitimacy, but makes them less willing to question industry conventions, let alone work together with a maverick rule breaker (e.g. Aldrich and Fiol, 1994; Oliver, 1997).

Taken together, these historically determined factors inhibit developments in the industry. It is said that industry evolution is path dependent – the path that the industry has travelled in the past will strongly limit how and in which direction it can develop in the future. In other words, 'history matters', setting bounds on the freedom to shape the future.

THE PARADOX OF COMPLIANCE AND CHOICE

When people are free to do as they please, they usually imitate each other.
Eric Hoffer (1902–1983); American philosopher

Yet, the question is whether firms should attempt to shape their industries at all, given the required effort and apparent risk of failure. There might be attractive rewards if a firm can lead industry developments, but trying to break industry rules that turn out to be immutable can be a quick way to achieve bankruptcy. Being an industry leader might sound very proactive, and even heroic, but it is potentially suicidal if the industry context defies being shaped.

This duality of wanting to change the industry rules that are malleable, while needing to adapt to the industry rules that are fixed, is the tension central to dealing with the industry context. On the one hand, managers must be willing to irreverently transgress widely acknowledged industry rules, going against what they see as the industry recipe. On the other hand, managers must respectfully accept many characteristics of the industry structure and play according to existing rules of the competitive game. Yet, these conflicting demands of being irreverent and respectful towards the industry rules are difficult for strategists to meet at the same time.

Where firms cannot influence the structure of their industry, *compliance* to the rules of the game is the strategic imperative. Under these circumstances, the strategic demand is for managers to adapt the firm to the industry context. Where firms do have the ability to manipulate the industry structure, they should exercise their freedom of *choice* to break the industry rules. In such a case, the strategic demand is for managers to try to change the terms of competition in their own favour.

This tension between compliance and choice has been widely acknowledged in the strategic management literature (e.g. Porter, 1980; Hrebiniak and Joyce, 1985; McGahan, 2000, Reading 10.1). The pressure for compliance has usually been presented as a form of environmental determinism, as the industry developments force firms to adapt or be selected out (e.g. Astley and Van der Ven, 1983; Wilson, 1992). The freedom of choice has often been labelled as organizational voluntarism, to convey the notion that industry developments can be the result of the wilful actions of individual organizations (e.g. Bettis and Donaldson, 1990; Child, 1972). In the following sections both compliance and choice are further examined.

The demand for firm compliance

It goes almost without saying that organizations must, to a large extent, adapt themselves to their environments. No organization has the ability to shape the entire world to fit its needs. Therefore, to be successful, all organizations need to understand the context in which they operate and need to play by most of the rules of the game.

After all, the alternative of ignoring the rules is fraught with danger. Probably the most common cause of 'corporate death' is misalignment between the organization and its environment (discussed in Chapter 8). And misalignment can happen very quickly, as most industries are constantly in flux. Companies can misinterpret the direction of the changes, can fail to take appropriate corrective action, or can be plainly self-centred, paying insufficient attention to external developments. Most companies have enough difficulty just staying attuned to the current rules of the competitive game, let alone anticipating how the industry context will change in the future.

To achieve compliance with the industry rules, firms must develop structures, processes and a culture in which listening and adapting to the environment becomes engrained. Firms must learn to become customer and market-oriented, reacting to the 'pull' of the market instead of 'pushing' their standard approach and pet projects at an unwilling audience. Firm compliance means avoiding the pitfall of organizational arrogance – knowing better than the market and imposing an approach that no one desires (e.g. Miller, 1990; Whitley, 1999).

The demand for strategic choice

While compliance to the industry rules can be very beneficial, contradicting them can also be strategically valuable. If firms only play by the current rules, it is generally very difficult to gain a significant competitive advantage over their rivals. After all, adapting to the current industry structure means doing business in more or less the same way as competitors, with few possibilities to distinguish the organization. In other words, 'compliance' might be another way of saying 'follow a me-too strategy'.

To be unique and develop a competitive advantage, firms need to do something different, something that does not fit within the current rules of the game. The more innovative the rule breaker, the larger will be the competitive advantage over rivals stuck with outdated business models. The more radical the departure from the old industry recipe, the more difficult it will be for competitors to imitate and catch up. Where companies are capable of constantly leading industry developments, they will have the benefit of capturing attractive industry positions before less proactive competitors eventually follow. In other words, there is a strong pressure for firms to attempt to shape the industry rules.

To achieve organizational choice, firms must find ways of escaping the pitfall of organizational conformity – the strict adherence to current industry rules. Firms must develop structures, processes and a culture in which the current industry recipe is constantly questioned, challenged and changed. Managers must come to see that in the long run the easy path of following the industry rules will be less productive than the rocky road of innovation and change (e.g. Hamel and Prahalad, 1994; Kim and Mauborgne, 2005, reading 10.2).

EXHIBIT 10.1   SHORT CASE

UNIQLO: FAST RETAILING IN SLOW FASHION

Comparing Japanese clothing designer, manufacturer and retailer Uniqlo with its competitors, one might best describe the company as bringing 'slow fashion'. In contrast to the 'fast fashion' approach of Zara or H&M, Uniqlo does little to appeal to the latest fashion trends and nimbly incorporate these in its apparel. Instead, it provides basics clothes for a reasonable price, meant to be combined with more fashionable items to create one's own style. Uniqlo has been quite successful doing this; with the company's 2013 revenues Uniqlo ranks fifth in the world's apparel retailing industry.

Uniqlo was founded in 1984 by the Ogori Shōji Company, which sold relatively cheap and common unisex clothing. Since clothing warehouses were quite uncommon in Japan at the time, Uniqlo gained the opportunity to rapidly expand its formula. Ogori Shōji changed its name into Fast Retailing; and fast it was. In 1992 it possessed some fifty Uniqlo stores in Japan; a number that doubled is just two years.

Keeping up this expansion rate was made feasible by issuing a single formula. Every Uniqlo store is characterized by selling essentially the same kind of apparel. Large quantities of functional clothing, such as Oxford shirts, socks, underwear, V-neck sweaters and polo shirts, are available in any Uniqlo establishment, sporting a simple and clean design with huge piles of aesthetically minimalist clothes stacked up neatly in a wide array of monochrome colours.

Not every piece of clothing by Uniqlo is 'basic' however. The company boasts some innovative fabrics: Heattech, for example, claims to retain warmth and Airism is made of thin fabric that neutralizes body odours. Fast Retailing also differentiates Uniqlo's products by focusing on the production of items made of cashmere, a quite expensive resource. High economies of scale keep production costs low, and as a result Fast Retailing is able to sell high quality products at low prices.

Fast Retailing controls the entire value chain of its products, although it does not own each element: partners take care of manufacturing materials and warehousing. By monitoring, providing guidance and maintaining stable relations with suppliers, the company controls the planning, production and sales phase, enabling the Uniqlo stores to exclusively sell clothes with its own label.

By producing 'basics' for the mass public, products are 'Made for All', as Uniqlo's 2012 slogan reads. Although this might be true, as Uniqlo's clothes are not yet 'Sold to All'; its apparel is hardly available in most countries. As of the end of February 2013, Uniqlo sported over 840 stores in Japan and possessed some 200 establishments in the People's Republic of China. In other words: Uniqlo is a huge player in the East Asian retail market. Yet the Japanese company is of significantly less importance in other parts of the world, with the number of stores in other countries being limited to 165.

But Tadashi Yanai, CEO of Fast Retailing, has a vision. Uniqlo not only needs to become more of a global brand, he also wants his company to become the world's number one seller of apparel. By 2020 the Japanese company is striving to accumulate US$ 50 billion of revenues. With current revenues of US$ 9.45 billion in fiscal year of 2012, it is still nowhere near this goal. In the coming years Uniqlo needs to expand globally in order to overcome this self-imposed hurdle. It is, however, not just ambition that propels the Japanese company into its expansion strategy. Yanai also believes it is merely a matter of time before Japan succumbs to its decline. The country has been in a negative state for twenty years and the share of Uniqlo in the Japanese clothing industry experiences a situation in which it moves ever more closely towards the point of saturation. To ensure that Uniqlo does not sink too, overseas expansion is seen as the only logical solution.

Yanai aims at penetrating the clothing market of the United States in particular. When Uniqlo tried to do so in 2005 by opening a few minor stores in America, this resulted in a downright fiasco. So when Uniqlo recently tried to re-enter the United States' clothing market, it did so in a high-profile manner. By establishing flagship stores in prime locations, Uniqlo tried to become a household name as quickly as possible. Instead of opting for standard-size mall locations – which are about 7,000 square feet – the Uniqlo store on New York's 5th Avenue features 89,000 square feet of shopping space, while the shop on 34th Street is about 64,000 square feet. If a thing is worth doing, it is worth doing well.

Yanai can wear his best bib and tucker, since his current expansion plan seems to be timed quite well. Similar to the sudden popularity boost of Uniqlo after the 1997 Asian Financial Crisis, the aftermath of the 2007 credit crunch provides opportunities for companies such as Uniqlo. In addition, some of the bricks-and-mortar clothing competitors in the United States, like Gap, seem to have had too many stores at too many malls. As a result, hundreds of stores are moved to the chopping block, with mostly foreign companies profiting by expanding existing shops and opening new ones. While the situation seems promising, another challenge arises: e-commerce.

The retail sale of clothes was long thought to resist the rise of online shopping. People were expected to desire actually feeling their clothes and try them to know if they fit well, before deciding to make a purchase. Apparently this is not the case. Although online shopping for clothes has lagged behind other products, Americans now buy over 10 per cent of their clothes via the Internet, while European online sales in key markets – France, Germany, Italy, the Netherlands, Spain, Sweden and the United Kingdom – are expected to witness a rapid growth of about 11 per cent annually until 2017.

Although the increasing importance of e-commerce is apparent, Uniqlo has been rather reluctant in getting involved with selling its clothes via its website. The company got on board late, while it retains an unclear e-commerce strategy. It started with a website tailored towards the American market in October 2012, after re-entering the United States a year earlier. The company knows it lags behind, with Shin Odake, CEO of Uniqlo in the US, expressing concerns that e-commerce is responsible for approximately 20 per cent of the sales of their competitors in America, while not even 4 per cent of Uniqlo's sales can be attributed to its online services.

Even though Uniqlo is currently flourishing, its current expansion strategy is based on the continued implementation of a single business model. Since e-commerce is becoming increasingly important in the apparel industry, the question arises whether Uniqlo should concentrate on this new industry development or continue expanding its current formula. If Yanai wants his company to be world's market leader, does he need to bend the current industry rules to achieve the leading position? E-commerce in the clothing industry is still in its infancy and the rules of the game are not yet entirely clear. For example, an unambiguous solution for the high return rate of clothing bought online (around 40 per cent) has not been found yet. Regardless, it remains to be seen whether Uniqlo's portfolio is actually compatible with e-commerce. Uniqlo is

different from its 'fast fashion' competitors and the last time it shifted more towards the business models of its adversaries – it tried to be more concerned with up-to-date fashion apparel in the fiscal year of 2011 – resulted in negative revenues.

In short, Yanai not only needs to critically analyse his expansion strategy, he also has to look outside his current box. Uniqlo is currently able to differentiate with affordable, high-quality basics, but the company might need a new kind of basic; a business model that can incorporate its ambitious goals in accordance with the future of clothes retailing.

Co-author: Wester Wagenaar

Sources: www.fastretailing.com; www.uniqlo.com; *Business Week,* 6 January 2011; *CNN,* 4 February 2008; *Financial Times,* 15 July 2012 and 7 February 2013; *Forbes,* 5 October 2012 and 22 October 2012; *Forrester,* 25 March 2013; *The New York Times,* 22 May 2012; *The Wall Street Journal,* 23 August 2012.

PERSPECTIVES ON THE INDUSTRY CONTEXT

A wise man will make more opportunity than he finds.
Francis Bacon (1561–1624); Lord Chancellor of England

Once again the strategizing manager seems 'stuck between a rock and a hard place'. The pressures for both compliance and choice are clear, but as opposites they are at least partially incompatible. Developing an organizational culture, structure and processes attuned to compliance will to some extent be at odds with the culture, structure and processes needed to shape an industry. An organization well rehearsed in the art of adaptation and skilful imitation is usually quite different than one geared towards business innovation and contrarian behaviour. How should managers actually deal with the issue of industry development – should they lead or follow?

In the strategic management literature many answers to this question are given – unfortunately, many contradictory ones. The views among management theorists differ sharply, as they emphasize a different balance between the need to comply and the need to choose. To gain a better overview of the range of conflicting opinions, the two diametrically opposed positions will be identified and discussed. On the one hand, there are strategists who argue that industry development is an autonomous process, which individual firms can hardly hope to shape. They believe that compliance to shifting industry characteristics is mandatory – adjust or risk being selected out. This point of view is referred to as the 'industry dynamics perspective'. On the other hand, many strategists believe that the industry context can be shaped in an infinite variety of ways by innovative firms. Therefore, industry development can be driven by firms willing and able to take a leading role. This point of view is referred to as the 'industry leadership perspective'.

The industry dynamics perspective

To those taking an industry dynamics perspective, the popular notion that individual firms have the power to shape their industry is an understandable, but quite misplaced, belief. Of course, the illusion of control is tempting – most people, especially strategists, would like to control their own destiny. Most individuals assume they have a free will and can decide their own future. Many governments suppose that they can shape society and many cultures assume that they control nature. In the same way, it is seductive to believe that the individual firm can matter by influencing the development of its industry.

Unfortunately, this belief is largely a fallacy, brought on by a poor understanding of the underlying industry dynamics. In reality, according to advocates of the industry dynamics perspective, industries are complex systems, with a large number of forces interacting simultaneously, none of which can significantly direct the long-term development of the whole. Firms are relatively small players in a very large game – their behaviours may have some impact on industry development, but none can fundamentally shape the direction of changes. On the contrary, as industries evolve, all firms that do not meet the changing demands of the environment are weeded out. Firms not suited to the new circumstances die, while firms complying with the changing rules prosper. Hence, through selection the industry context determines the group of industry survivors and through the pressures for adaptation, the behaviour of the remaining firms is determined. In short, the industry shapes the firm, not the other way around.

The industry dynamics perspective is often also referred to as the industry evolution perspective, due to the strong parallel with biological evolution. Both evolutionary processes, it is argued, share a number of basic characteristics. In nature, as in business, the survival and growth of entities depends on their fit with the environment. Within each environment variations to a successful theme might come about. These new individuals will thrive, as long as they suit the existing circumstances, but as the environment changes, only those that meet the new demands will perish. Hence, Darwin's well-known principle of 'survival of the fittest' is based on a cycle of variation and environmental selection. Many proponents of the industry dynamics perspective believe that this biological view of evolution is a good model for what happens in industries – new organizations arise as mutations and only the fittest mutations survive. However, it is usually pointed out that in a business environment, organizations do not vary 'at random', but purposefully, and they possess the ability to adapt to selection pressures during the evolution process (e.g. Nelson and Winter, 1982; Baum and Singh, 1994). Therefore, organizations have much more flexibility to evolve along with the unfolding industry dynamics than life forms generally do. This process of mutual adaptation and development between entities in the system is called 'co-evolution' (e.g. Aldrich, 1999; Moore, 1996, Reading 6.3). To proponents of the industry dynamics perspective, the objective of a firm should be to co-evolve with its environment, instead of trying to conquer it.

Supporters of the industry dynamics perspective do not deny that every once in a while a rule breaker comes along, turning an industry upside down and spawning dozens of case studies by admiring business professors and hours of television interviews. But these successes must be put into perspective, just as a lottery winner should not encourage everyone to invest their life savings into buying lottery tickets. Yes, some business innovators are successful, but we have no idea of how many challengers were weeded out along the way – only the most spectacular failures make it into the media, but most go unreported. This is called the 'survivor's bias', and the emphasis on case-based reasoning in the field of strategy makes theorists and practitioners equally susceptible to fall into this trap. But even where a firm has been able to pull off a major industry change once, this does not make them the industry leader of the future. They might have been the right company in the right place at the right time, able to push the industry in a certain direction once, but to assume that they will win the lottery twice is not particularly realistic.

The conclusion drawn by advocates of the industry dynamics perspective is that 'winning big' by changing the rules of the game sounds easy, fast and spectacular – but isn't. If one thing has been learnt from the internet bubble, it is that changing the rules of the game is extremely difficult, slow and hazardous, and should be left up to those 'high rollers' willing to play for 'high stakes' with only a low chance of success (i.e. venture capitalists and entrepreneurs). For regular companies, such an approach cannot be the mainstay of their strategy. Their basic approach must be to stick close to the shifting currents in their industry, which is challenging enough in most cases. Competitive advantage can be sought, but requires hard work within the rules of the game.

The bad news is that this leaves limited freedom to manoeuvre and that the general level of profitability that a firm can achieve is largely predetermined. Once in a poor industry, a firm's growth and profit potential are significantly limited (Porter, 1980). The good news is that this still leaves plenty of room for a firm to score above the industry average, by positioning better than competitors, but also by adapting better to the ongoing industry changes, or even anticipating changes more skilfully and reacting appropriately.

EXHIBIT 10.2   THE INDUSTRY DYNAMICS PERSPECTIVE

A FAIRY WORLD OF PLENTY OPERATING SYSTEMS?

Once upon a time, in a place far away, there was a mobile phone company called Nokia who ruled the market with operating system Symbian as its warhorse. Symbian was by far the most used operating system on mobile phones. Nokia and Symbian OS ruled the mobile phone world and there was peace in the land. But in 2007 everything changed when two rascals entered the stage: iOS from Apple and Android from Google. And in only 3 years time, in 2010, Nokia's Symbian lost its crown of being the biggest, strongest and most used Mobile OS, with Android being the new king.

It almost sounds like a fairy tale how fast the mobile operating system market completely changed with the coming of iOS and Android. As Mapbox.com, the interactive heat map of operating system usage in the world shows, the entire Western world glows with iOS and Android systems, with here and there some BlackBerry pockets. Interestingly, iPhones are more numerous in upper-income parts of cities and Androids in lower-income areas in the United States.

King Symbian has been overthrown by the new ruler Android, yet it is not certain how long the new king will hold the helm. There are more Operating Systems who see chances to claim their share of land. Android and iOS may have the highest penetration rates in the Western world, but that leaves a whole lot of world to gain for these smaller players. Among the many newcomers there are very interesting players, such as Firefox OS, Tizen and Sailfish. Sailfish OS is a project from Jolla, based on the Linux core. It's an open source operating system that can be licensed by any mobile phone manufacturer. Tizen is also an open source operating system, available for a wide range of devices, such as tablets, in-vehicle infotainment devices and smart TVs. Tizen is a project that is driven by the Linux Foundation, the Tizen Association, Samsung and Intel, and therefore a high potential heir to the crown.

And last, but definitely not least, there is Firefox OS, by Mozilla. Mozilla is already well known from the popular Firefox Internet browser and the Thunderbird e-mail application, and now also enters the world of mobile operating systems. The new industry dynamics promise to deliver some fireworks in the near future, with perhaps another fairy tale to come. What about the Fox and the Monkey?

Co-author: Jeroen Brinkhuis

Sources: 'Mobile devices + Twitter use', http://www.mapbox.com/labs/twitter-gnip/brands; www.mozilla.org; www.sailfishos.org; www.android.com; 'Bright-eyed and bushy-tailed', 03-02-2013, *The Economist*; 'Smartphones and Mobile Carriers', 03-13-2013, PCMag.com.

The industry leadership perspective

 Strategists taking an industry leadership perspective fundamentally disagree with the determinism inherent in the industry dynamics perspective. Even in biology, breeders and genetic engineers consistently attempt to shape the natural world. Of course, in industries, as in biology, some rules are immutable. Certain economic, technological, social and political factors have to be accepted as hardly changeable. But the remaining environmental factors that can be manipulated leave strategists with an enormous scope for moulding the industry of the future. This belief is reflected in the remark by the Dutch poet Jules Deelder that 'even within the limits of the possible, the possibilities are limitless'. It is up to the strategist to identify which rules of the game must be respected and which can be ignored in the search for new strategic options. The strategist must recognize both the limits of the possible and the limitless possibilities.

Advocates of the industry leadership perspective do not deny that in many industries the developments are largely an evolutionary result of industry dynamics. For an understanding of the development paths of these 'leaderless' industries, the industry dynamics perspective offers a powerful explanatory 'lens' – many industries do evolve without a clear industry leader. However, these industries have only followed this path because no firm was creative and powerful enough to actively shape the direction of change. A lack of leadership is not the 'natural state of affairs', but simply weakness on behalf of the industry incumbents. Industry developments can be shaped, yet do require innovative companies willing to take on the leadership role (e.g. Baden-Fuller and Stopford, 1992; Hamel and Prahalad, 1994).

A leadership role, supporters of this perspective argue, starts with envisioning what the industry of tomorrow might look like. The firm's strategists must be capable of challenging the existing industry recipe and building a new conception of how the industry could function in the future. They must test their own assumptions about which industry rules can be changed and must, in fact, think of ways of 'destroying their current business'. Hamel and Prahalad (1994) refer to this as intellectual leadership, noting that smart strategists also develop 'industry foresight', anticipating which trends are likely to emerge, so that they can be used to the firm's advantage.

Not only must a firm have the intellectual ability to envision the industry's future, but it must also be able to communicate this vision in a manner that other firms and individuals are willing to buy into. If a vision of the industry of tomorrow is compelling enough, people inside and outside the company will start to anticipate, and will become committed to, that future, making it a self-fulfilling prophecy. This 'inevitablilty' of an industry vision can be important in overcoming risk averseness and resistance from industry incumbents (e.g. Levenhagen, Porac and Thomas, 1993; Moore, 2000, Reading 10.3).

To actually change the rules of the competitive game in an industry, a firm must move beyond a compelling vision, and work out a new competitive business model. If this new business model is put into operation and seems to offer a competitive advantage, this can attract sufficient customers and support to gain 'critical mass' and break through as a viable alternative to the older business models. To shape the industry, the firm will also need to develop new competences and standards required to make the new business model function properly. The better the firm is at building new competences and setting new standards, alone or in cooperation with others, the more power it will have to determine the direction of industry development (e.g. D'Aveni, 1999; Hamel, 1996).

All of the above points together add up to quite a considerable task. But then, industry leadership is not easy and changing the industry rules rarely happens overnight. Rather, it can take years, figuring out which rules can be broken and which cannot. It can be a marathon, trying to get the business model right, while building competences and support. Therefore, organizations require perseverance and commitment if they are to be successful industry shapers (Hamel and Prahalad, 1994).

EXHIBIT 10.3   THE INDUSTRY LEADERSHIP PERSPECTIVE

SPOTIFY: WHO PAYS THE PIPER CALLS THE TUNE

For many years revenues have been declining in the music industry, a trend that actually started when the illegal download site Napster entered the scene in 1999. At first glance, iTunes seemed to be the solution. However this changed people's buying behavior from buying entire albums to buying single songs. Revenues continued to drop, and it became clear that a revolution was needed to save the music industry. Daniel Ek – founder of Spotify – came up with the solution: Give it away for free.

In 1999 the music industry was shocked when the illegal download site Napster reached 80 million users in only two years, all of which had access to free (illegal) music. This fascinated Daniel Ek, who found his two favourite bands on Napster; the Beatles and Led Zeppelin. Daniel wanted to find a legal way to let music inspire people, just the way it inspired him. The question was, how could he come up with a legal service, where music is freely available?

In 2008 Daniel Ek came up with an innovative *freemium* business model for the music industry in Sweden. He launched the music service Spotify, containing a large catalogue of songs, which grew – according to their website – to about 20 million in 2013. The music is offered for free, but with a limit of 20 hours of music streaming per week. Subscribers can make their own playlists of their favourite songs or create a custom radio channel where music they enjoy is automatically selected. Ads are inserted between songs to fund the 'free music'. A second service, *Spotify Unlimited,* offers unlimited streaming music without ads for a monthly fee. Lastly, there is *Spotify Premium* which allows paying subscribers to download their songs of choice to be played back offline.

Daniel Ek started with Spotify in Sweden, and just like "the other Swedish company" IKEA, he

quickly started to conquer the world. Currently the service is available in 34 countries with over 20 million subscribers, more than 5 million of them paying a monthly subscription fee. Yet, Spotify is not an undisputed success. Some musicians their music from the service, as they considered their fee to be too low. The main problem is that Spotify pays revenues to the publishers – about 70 per cent of its turnover – who then distribute to their musicians.

Notwithstanding the restrained succes so far, Spotify is a game changer; a new industry leader with new ideas and new innovations. This is supported by the fact that Apple, Google, Microsoft, Sony and Amazon.com are quickly trying to follow Spotify in its tracks. Although there are some minor differences and availability is limited to a few countries, iTunes Radio, Google Play Music All Access, Amazon Cloud Player, Xbox Music and Sony Music Unlimited are trying to find their way into this new era of experiencing music.

Spotify could well have established the new business model the music industry has been waiting for. Spotify fits perfectly in the current spirit of the age; offering free streaming music to the masses. Therefore, it is likely to set the tone for the years to come. Is there an alternative for the consumer to enjoy music? Maybe the next generation illegal website, the new Napster: The Pirate Bay. Governments in the Western world have been trying to take the illegal Pirate Bay download site down for quite some time, yet until now without success.

Co-author: Jeroen Brinkhuis

Sources: 'Welcome to Nirvana', *The Guardian,* 01-16-2013; 'Spotify's Daniel Ek: The Most Important Man In Music', Forbes, 01-16-2012; 'There's An Awful Lot Of Nonsense Being Talked About Spotify Royalties', Forbes.com, 07-21-2013, Spotify.com; 'Google Play Music All Access vs iTunes vs Spotify vs Amazon Cloud Player vs Xbox Music vs Music Unlimited', Pocket-lint. com, 05-16-2013.

MANAGING THE PARADOX OF COMPLIANCE AND CHOICE

The reasonable man adapts himself to the world; the unreasonable one persists in trying to adapt the world to himself. Therefore, all progress depends on the unreasonable man.
George Bernard Shaw (1856–1950); Irish playwright and critic

So, how should managers deal with the industry context? Should they concentrate on adapting to the dynamics in the industry, honing their ability to respond to changing demands and to adjust their business model to meet new requirements? Or should they take a more proactive role in shaping the future of the industry, changing the rules of the competitive game to suit their own needs? Within the field of strategic management, the views are far apart and no consensus seems to be emerging on how to manage the paradox of compliance and choice (see Table 10.1 for the main arguments).

With so many competing opinions on the nature of the industry context, readers may now want to 'select the fittest one'. Or maybe readers conclude that one view has re-written the rules of competition in the strategy industry. In the international context especially, a much more strategizing stance would be to challenge one's own cognitive map, as perspectives on the industry context are closely related to the well-described and culturally skewed voluntarism versus determinism debate.

Juxtaposing

As described in this chapter, industry characteristics determine which industry rules are malleable by strategists' actions. Attempts to break particular industry rules – such as scale advantages in the steel industry – is outright dangerous, while others may well be successful. Even when the large majority of industry rules cannot be broken, the important attribute of corporate strategists is to know which ones can. So from the perspective of the strategizing manager, the industry dynamics perspective is applicable in some occasions while the industry leadership perspective is preferred in others. The proportion of compliance and choice differs between both perspectives, yet independent from perspectives strategists need to juxtapose between firm compliance and strategic choice.

In the international context, managing the paradox of compliance and choice becomes even more challenging. Not only does the strategist need to find the right combination of

TABLE 10.1   Industry dynamics versus industry leadership perspective

	Industry dynamics perspective	*Industry leadership perspective*
Emphasis on	Compliance over choice	Choice over compliance
Industry development	Uncontrollable evolutionary process	Controllable creation process
Change dynamics	Environment selects fit firms	Firm creates fitting environment
Firm success due to	Fitness to industry demands	Manipulation of industry demands
Ability to shape industry	Low, slow	High, fast
Normative implication	Play by the rules (adapt)	Change the rules (innovate)
Development path	Convergence towards dominant design	Divergence, create new design
Firm profitability	Largely industry-dependent	Largely firm-dependent

rules that need to be followed and can be moulded, the combination often also differs over countries. As will be further explained in the next paragraph 'The industry context in international perspective', in many businesses the industry context is country-specific. For example, industrial policies may influence industry forces, and local or national networks determine the strategic window of opportunities. Hence, the conclusion must be that strategists not only need to juxtapose; in international firms they need to 'country-specifically' juxtapose between demands for firm compliance and strategic choice.

It goes without saying that it takes special capabilities of strategizing managers to juxtapose the paradox. In Chapter 4 on business level strategy it was discussed that strategists need *dynamic capabilities* (Teece, Pisano and Shuen, 1997; Teece, 2007) to juxtapose between demands for firm compliance and strategic choice. We hypothesize that managing the paradox of compliance and choice also needs dynamic capabilities, to be able to juxtapose between following and making industry rules.

In the international context the paradox is even more challenging which would require – following the above reasoning – 'higher-level' dynamic capabilities. In the international human resources field the scarcity of such strategists is well known. In most cases firms choose to manage the paradox by appointing local managers, or expatriates that know the local culture very well.

THE INDUSTRY CONTEXT IN INTERNATIONAL PERSPECTIVE

Co-author: Gep Eisenloeffel

When I hear any man talk of an unalterable law, the only effect it produces on me is to convince me that he is an unalterable fool.
Sydney Smith (1771–1845) English wit, writer and Anglican cleric

In the field of strategy, views differ sharply on whether the industry context can be shaped or not, although these differences of opinion usually remain implicit – few practicing managers or strategy theorists make a point of expounding their assumptions about the nature of the environment. For this reason, it is difficult to identify whether there are national preferences when it comes to industry context perspective. Yet, it seems not unlikely that strategists in different countries have different inclinations regarding this issue. Although it is always difficult to generalize, it seems that strategists in some nations gravitate more towards an industry leadership perspective than in others.

As an input to the debate whether there are international differences in industry context perspective, a number of insights from the field of international economics and international trade are described, followed by comparative culture studies that shed some light on how the paradox of compliance and choice is viewed in different countries. It should be noted, however, that these propositions are intended to encourage discussion and constitute only tentative explanations for cross-country differences in perspective. More specific international research is needed to give this debate a firmer basis.

International economics and trade

For a relatively long time, industry level analysis has been focusing first and for all on understanding the development of a given industrial sector from a national point of view. In the international economics field the central question evolved from understanding countries' location advantage to produce certain goods, to exported and imported products (Rugman and Verbeke, 1993). Interactions between location, the competitiveness of multinational companies and, more specifically, company strategies only entered the debate in the latter part of the twentieth century. From the mid-1960s to the end of the twentieth century onwards, the relative contribution of imperfect market conditions for an industry's potential competitiveness, and thus of home country specific advantages and the role of national governments dominated the debate (Kindleberger, 1962; Krugman, 1985: Porter, 1990).

Comparative advantage and international trade

Before the industrial revolution, the transition period to new manufacturing processes from about 1760 to some time between 1820 and 1840, international trade was either focusing on staple goods, like grain, timber and sugar, or on relatively small quantities of high value added luxury manufactured products, such as porcelain and silk. Only at the end of the eighteenth century did mass production of manufactured products became apparent in the international market. The first two theoretical approaches on the benefits and losses of international trade were *mercantilism* and the theory of *comparative advantage*. Mercantilism started from the assumption that when a country imports more than it exports, it will witness a drain of its gold or silver as standardized modes of payment. The general conclusion, henceforth, was to export more than to import; in this respect, mercantilism can be seen as the beginning of protectionism and import-substitution.

Although politically motivated, the Chinese policy of stopping all international contacts after the 1430s, ending, for instance, its huge international trade exploration programme under admiral Zheng He, is a clear example of a country's policy to concentrate on national inward-oriented autarky instead of exploiting the opportunities of international trade (Morris, 2010). An early sign of mercantilism in Europe is, for instance, England's *Navigation Act* of 1651, which started the fierce battle with the Dutch over the supremacy of Western-European trade. In the mid-seventeenth century French minister Jean-Baptiste Colbert even gave his own name (*colbertism*) to a series of French rules and regulations aimed to protect the French economy vis-à-vis the import of foreign, especially Englishmanufactured, products.

As of the start of the Industrial Revolution and the introduction of mass production, British scholars were the first to articulate the benefits of free trade. In 1776 Adam Smith, generally considered to be the founding father of economics, published *An Inquiry into the Nature and Causes of the Wealth of Nations,* claiming that when two countries devoted their attention to production for which they were uniquely suited, both countries would benefit. Smith's work contributed immensely to the development of economic theories about trade, the location of international production, and the subsequent division of labour. It failed, however, to answer a number of fundamental questions that are relevant up until now. Smith, for one thing, did not address the question of what happens when countries do not have an absolute advantage in any product. Would this mean they are excluded from international trade altogether?

In his book *On the Principles of Political Economy and Taxation* (1817), David Ricardo showed that a country that did not have an absolute advantage in producing one good could still benefit from engaging in international trade. The sole requirement, according to Ricardo, was a *comparative advantage*; a relatively more efficient way to produce a specific good than another country's ability to produce the same good.

Factor endowments

Another shortcoming of the classical theory on trade and production was the assumption that only labour, in terms of hourly input, was responsible for the value of end products. This approach changed drastically from the beginning of the twentieth century onwards. Swedish economist Eli Heckser, his student Bertil Ohlin, and expanded by American Noble Prize winner Paul Samuelson, formulated what came to be known as the so-called Heckser-Ohlin-Samuelson *factor proportion theory*. This theory holds that both labor and capital are, indeed, of equal importance for the value of a product and therefore both factor endowments determine specialization and location of production.

According to this theory, the driving forces behind allocating production and international trade are the costs of a country's endowments of labour and capital. When, for instance, a country such as China possesses cheap labour and a country like the US possesses capital, Chinese companies should specialize in the production of labour-intensive products whereas the US-based firms should concentrate on capital-intensive goods.

Declining terms of trade

Although the assumptions of comparative advantage are still widely supported today by scholars (Friedman; 2005) and decision-makers at the IMF and WTO alike, several complications need to be addressed. A number of critical scholars (e.g., Prebisch, 1950; Frank, 1966; Wallerstein, 1974) have pointed out that it is one thing to claim that the outcome of efficiently allocating international production benefits the world economy at large, but it does not mean every country benefits in the same way. On the contrary: 'countries that had to give up their infant industries because they could not compete with the more efficient ways of production in countries that were better equipped for capital-intensive production did never develop into the industrialized countries like their trading partners' (Frank, 1966). Moreover, so-called *terms of trade,* or what countries paid for imports vis-à-vis what they earned for their exports, deteriorated for countries exporting raw materials and imported end products. According to critical scholars (e.g., Greider, 1997), 'supporting liberalization policies for international trade and investments legitimizes underdevelopment and dependency.'

Leontief paradox

Empirical validation of the factor proportion theory proved to be difficult. A famous test of this theory by Wassily Leontief in 1950 showed that US firms, contrary to the hypothesis, exported relatively more labour-intensive products than capital-intensive products.

In the 1960s and 1970s a number of new studies tried to explain this phenomenon. One of these approaches, the work of Burenstam Linder (1961), elaborated on the empirical fact that most trade took place between countries with almost the same input of production and income levels of consumers. A large part of international trade consisted of buying and selling almost similar end products. Over the years, a number of studies on trade between countries with seemingly comparable levels of income and location advantages (Cox and Harris, 1985, for the US-Canada trade patterns; Smith and Venables, 1988, for the likely impact of a single EU market) tried to explain these intra-industry trade patterns. In explaining why customers would buy an imported identical good, the attention of research shifted from production to preferences of consumers, resulting in studies showing the importance of non-tangible perceived distinctive capacities like branding. This shift from the aggregated nation supply side to the demand side of actual individual buyers marked the rise of international strategic marketing, studying preferences of different market segments (e.g., Kotler, 1967 and later editions; Bradley, 2005).

Market imperfections

The Leontief paradox also made clear that the input of labour and capital in one country were not necessarily comparable to the same inputs in another. The value of a product does not depend on the hourly input of labour or on the amount of money spent on capital, but on the quality or productivity of these endowments. Kindleberger (1962) pointed out that instead of assuming perfect market conditions, the point of departure should be that market conditions are imperfect. Others, like Paul Krugman (1980) and Michael Porter (1985; 1990) elaborated on these assumptions, showing how the structure of a country's industry determines a company's *potential* competitive advantage vis-à-vis competitors from other countries.

From here the strategy field jumped into the discussion (Rumelt, 1991; Baden-Fuller and Stopford, 1992) to explain company success in a given industry context, arguing that the organization's competitive advantage is more important than industry characteristics (Porter, 1980, 1985).

Life cycle and location

Another approach to clarify the outcome of Leontief's findings was taken by Raymond Vernon (1966), who tried to explain why new products were initiated in the highly industrialized countries. Vernon added two premises to the factor endowment theory. The first was that technical innovations lead to new and profitable products. However, technical innovations need, apart from large quantities of capital, especially the input of knowledge, and the costs of an educational infrastructure that go hand in hand with knowledge. Secondly, Vernon showed how technical innovations, both the product itself and, more importantly, the methods for its manufacture, go through different stages. In the first stage, the introduction of a product, R&D requires highly skilled labour and large amounts of capital. During the process of up-scaling to maturation as well as decline, gradually the technical input becomes commercialized and, instead of a unique quality, turns into a standardized commodity, easily to be imitated by other producers. Whereas knowledge and capital are the crucial inputs in the early stages, labour-intensity dominates in the latter ones. This has a large effect on the location of industries as the comparative advantage in production shift across countries (Dicken, 2011). The question how individual companies adjust their strategy and shift attention from producing in their home countries to exploiting possibilities to start production abroad are addressed in Chapter 12 on 'the international context in international perspective'.

Culture and the paradox of compliance and choice

As a further input to the debate whether there are international differences on the issue of industry development, a number of factors are discussed that may influence how the paradox of compliance and choice is being viewed in different countries. It should be noted, however, that these propositions are intended to encourage discussion and constitute only tentative explanations for cross-cultural differences in perspective. More specific international research is needed to give this debate a firmer basis.

Locus of control

Culture researchers have tried to understand differences in how people perceive the power of individuals to shape their environment. In some cultures the view prevails that the individual is at the mercy of external forces, while in other cultures there is a strong belief in the freedom of individuals to act independent of the environment and even to create their own circumstances (Trompenaars and Hampden-Turner, 2000). Psychologists refer to this as the perceived 'locus of control' (e.g. Miller, Kets de Vries and Toulouse, 1982). People with an internal locus of control believe that they largely control their own fate. Their efforts will shape their circumstances – success is earned and failure is one's own fault. People with an external locus of control, on the other hand, believe that their fate is largely the result of circumstances beyond their control. Any effort to improve one's position, if at all possible, should be directed towards complying with external demands – fortune favours those who go with the flow. In the most extreme case, however, people with an external locus of control are deterministic, assuming no efforts will change the inevitable.

Obviously, in countries where the culture is more inclined towards an internal locus of control, it is reasonable to expect that the industry leadership perspective will be more widespread. It is in such nations that one might expect remarks such as Sydney Smith's quote at the beginning of this section. In cultures with a strong emphasis on external locus of control, the industry dynamics perspective is likely to be more predominant.

Time orientation

As was identified in Chapter 8, cultures differ with respect to their time orientation. Some cultures are directed towards the past, while others are more focused on the present or on the future. In countries with a future orientation, the belief is widespread that change is progress. People generally welcome change as an opportunity for advancement. Therefore, in future-oriented cultures, people are even willing to initiate painful change processes expecting they will hold future benefits. In these countries a stronger inclination towards the industry leadership perspective is most likely.

In past-oriented cultures, the belief is widespread that change is decay. People generally actively resist change and protect the status quo. In these cultures, external changes will only be adapted to if strictly necessary. In present-oriented cultures, the commonly held belief is that change is relatively unimportant. People live by the mercy of the day and adapt to changes as they become apparent. In both types of culture, the industry dynamics perspective is likely to be more predominant.

Role of government

Internationally, opinions also differ on the role that governments can play in encouraging the shaping of industries. In some countries the predominant view is that governments should facilitate industry development by creating supportive business circumstances and then staying out of the way of company initiatives. Governments are needed to set basic rules of business conduct, but firms should not be impeded by other governmental intervention in the functioning of industries and markets. Individual companies are seen as the primary drivers of industry development and if companies are given enough leeway, excellent ones can significantly shape their industry context. Such economic liberalism is particularly strong in the English-speaking nations, where governments actually facilitate firms' industry shaping efforts. Unsurprisingly, the industry leadership perspective is rather pronounced in these countries.

In other nations the predominant view is that Adam Smith's free market ideal often proves to be dysfunctional. A fully liberal market, it is believed, can lead to short-termism, negative social consequences, mutually destructive competition and an inability to implement industry-wide changes. Governments must therefore take a more proactive role. They must protect weaker parties, such as workers and the environment, against the negative side effects of the market system, and actively create a shared infrastructure for all companies. Furthermore, the government can develop an industrial policy to encourage the development of new industries, force companies to work together where this is more effective, and push through industry-wide changes, if otherwise a stalemate would occur. Such a 'managed competition' view has been prevalent in Japan and France, and to a lesser extent in Germany (e.g. Hampden-Turner and Trompenaars, 1993; Lessem and Neubauer, 1994). In these countries the industry leadership perspective is not as strongly held as in the English-speaking nations – industries can be shaped, but few companies have the power to do so without a good industrial policy and government backing.

Network of relationships

This factor is linked to the discussion in Chapter 6 on network level strategy. In countries where the discrete organization perspective is predominant, companies often strive to retain their independence and power position vis-à-vis other companies. As these firms are not embedded in complex networks, but operate free from these constraining relationships, they are more at liberty to challenge the existing rules of the game. In other words, where firms are not entangled in a web of long-term relationships, they are better positioned for rule-breaking behaviour – every firm can make a difference. In these countries an industry leadership perspective is more prevalent.

However, in nations where firms are more inclined to operate in networks, each individual firm surrenders a part of its freedom in exchange for long-term relationships. The ability of the individual firm to shape its industry thus declines, as all changes must be discussed and negotiated with its partners. Hence, in these countries, the industry leadership perspective is generally less strongly held than in the countries favouring discrete organizations. It should be noted that a group of firms, once in agreement, is often more powerful than each individual firm and therefore more capable of shaping the industry. However, it is acknowledged that getting network partners to agree is a formidable task and a significant limit on the firm's ability to shape its environment.

INTRODUCTION TO THE READINGS

As an input to the process of assessing the variety of perspectives on this issue, three readings have been selected that each shed their own light on the debate. As in previous chapters, the first two readings will be representative of the two poles in this debate (see Table 10.1), while the third has been chosen to bridge the arguments of both perspectives.

The first reading representing the industry dynamics perspective (Reading 10.1) is 'How Industries Evolve', by Anita McGahan. Building on Michael Porter's seminal works on industry evolution (1980), McGahan argues that firms can improve their performance by riding industry trends rather than trying to fight them. She argues that better corporate performance hinges on understanding how industries evolve and that the main frameworks currently in use (the five forces and the S-curve/product life cycle models) are incomplete for this purpose. The author identifies four basic models of industry evolution which she calls 'receptive', 'blockbuster', 'radical organic' and 'intermediating'. Each kind of evolution involves specific kinds of risks, and each carries different implications for the relevance of established capabilities and investment priorities.

The second article representing the industry leadership perspective (Reading 10.2) is 'Blue Ocean Strategy', by W. Chan Kim and Renée Mauborgne. This *Harvard Business Review* article is a summary of the arguments they put forward in their similarly entitled book. Their core idea is that companies should not focus on competing in existing overcrowded markets, which they call red oceans, bloodied by battle, but should create new uncontested market spaces – blue oceans. Staying in a red ocean means accepting the existing industry conditions and finding a way to survive in this harsh environment, while breaking out into blue oceans means leaving competition behind and having a sea all to yourself. As such, Kim and Mauborgne are fully in line with the industry leadership perspective; rule breaking is superior to rule taking. Looking at a wide range of industries, stretching from automobiles and computers to movie theatres and circuses, Kim and Mauborgne conclude that much of the business innovation comes from fundamentally new and superior ways of creating value for buyers, which they call 'value innovation'. The authors, thus, make an infrequently heard point, namely that industry incumbents can also be rule breakers. The headline grabbing innovators are often new entrants that disrupt the existing industry pecking order, but many of the value innovators reviewed by Kim and Mauborgne are actually industry incumbents who have been able to revolutionize their industries from the inside.

The third reading, 'Living on the Fault Line', has been taken from a book with the same name (note that there are more Moores; Geoffrey's namesake in the previous chapter was James Moore). This reading has been added to introduce an issue of vital importance to industry development – the introduction of new technology. Of all the drivers of industry development, the adoption of disruptive technologies is probably the most prominent. Disruptive technologies are those that do not complement established technologies, but displace them. As such, Moore points out, disruptive technologies can cause dramatic shifts in an industry as 'competitive advantage positions that once seemed secure are abruptly overthrown and management teams … must scramble to recover'. Moore's central thesis is that for the innovators, championing a new technology, creating a mainstream market requires going through a number of phases, each with its own inherent strategic logic. He describes these phases of market development, making use of the widely known technology adoption life cycle. The first phase, or 'early market', is where technology enthusiasts and visionaries adopt the innovation. This phase is generally followed by a 'chasm', which is a period of no adoption, which needs to be bridged to get to the second phase, called the 'bowling alley', where early pragmatists 'knock' others into also adopting the new technology. Once adoption starts picking up speed, the third phase is entered, the 'tornado', where high growth is experienced. Finally, the technology achieves the fourth phase of broad acceptance, called 'Main Street'. Key to success in each phase, Moore concludes, is realizing that the strategy of the previous phase is no longer appropriate and that a new strategy must be developed. In his argumentation Moore focuses his attention on customer acceptance, paying less attention to the reactions of competitors and other industry actors. As such, his contribution is more to understanding market development and less to highlighting overall industry development. However, this reading still provides invaluable insight into the difficult process of changing the rules of the game based on technological innovation, and how the strategist needs to juxtapose over time.

How industries evolve

By Anita M. McGahan[1]

Over the last two decades, the profitability of US firms dropped by nearly a third while stock market values soared to create a huge financial market premium on corporate assets. The absolute level of the financial market premium today puts unprecedented pressure on managers to generate real returns on invested capital. Either fundamental operating performance must improve, or shareholder value will not rise at historic rates.

There is no shortage of theories on how to relieve the pressure. Many of them involve technology. Some optimists believe that the blanket introduction of new technology across the whole economy will somehow result in new value, almost by osmosis. Others look for more specific links between strategy, investment and increased profitability. Building on the five-forces framework (Porter 1980) and on the S-curve framework (Abernathy and Utterback 1978; Foster 1986), the fundamental premise of this article is that you cannot increase profitability without a thorough understanding of the structural changes shaping the industry concerned.

The five-forces framework is essentially static: it provides an approach for determining the financial performance of an industry, and thus its attractiveness for investors, *at a specific point in time.* Although the S-curve framework (Figure 10.1.1) is dynamic – it focuses on how industries evolve over time – it does not deal with how companies move across product generations, i.e. across S-curves. Using a large body of fieldwork and statistical research, this article introduces a new framework that identifies four models of industry evolution. The approach is complementary to the five-forces and S-curve frameworks. How an individual should tackle the problem of increasing profitability in his or her own firm depends largely on which of the four models best characterizes the nature of innovation in the industry.

A major distinction in this new framework is between 'architectural' and non-architectural change. Architectural change (Henderson and Clark 1990) is here defined as any innovation that disrupts the industry's established relationships with *both* suppliers *and* customers. Often this is based on new technology but it can

also involve the redeployment of existing technology (Markides, 1999). For instance, the department store and the supermarket represented architectural changes in retailing, but neither was based on radical technology. Non-architectural change involves innovation through established customer or supplier relationships. Examples include new supermarket layouts or the introduction of a new pharmaceutical product.

Two of the four models of industry evolution identified in this article are non-architectural, with firms innovating within the structure of established relationships. The other two are architectural, with firms innovating outside the structure of the industry's established customer and supplier relationships. Before describing them in detail I first show why we need to go beyond the S-curve.

Beyond the S-curve

The S-curve and the closely-related product life cycle (PLC) frameworks are based on the idea that industries move through periods of emergence, shake-out, maturity and decline. Although the models are appealing, they are hard to use on their own for corporate planning, and may even be misleading in some situations (Foster 1986). Industry leaders may become trapped in a kind of self-fulfilling logic of maturity if they take action based on an oversimplified S-curve; if they believe that an industry has reached the 'mature' phase of the S-curve, they may wrongly assume it is past innovation.

This perspective threatened toy retailers in the early 1990s (Coxe *et al*, 1996). At the time, many studies of toy retailing reported that the industry was mature. Toys-R-Us, Wal-Mart, K-Mart and Kaybee dominated the US mass market. Given the stability in the industry structure, the leading firms invested incrementally to build out their store networks and to improve their information systems. Neighbourhood Mom-and-Pop toy stores exited steadily as the mass marketers grew. A few upstart educational stores – like the Discovery Zone, the Learning Place, and LearningSmith – gained

[1]Source: Anita M. McGahan (2000) 'How Industries Evolve', *Business Strategy Review,* Vol.11(3) pp. 1–16. Copyright © 2000 London Business School. Reproduced with permission of John Wiley & Sons Ltd.

FIGURE 10.1.1   The S-curve

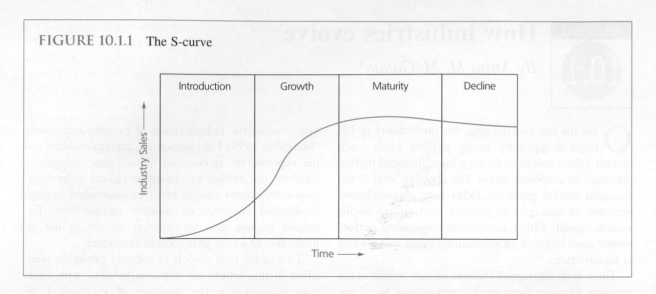

a toehold, but these innovative retail outlets were perceived as too small to threaten the market leaders.

The maturity mindset offered little insight into the impending industry change. By the late 1990s, toy retailing was transformed by new technology, new products and new kinds of customer relationships. Companies like eToys and Amazon.com satisfied customer needs for quick, reliable, convenient and inexpensive access to exciting new products. Old pricing and merchandising formulas no longer reflected competitive conditions. The new systems also affected toy *manufacturing* by making available extensive personalized information about customer preferences. The mass marketers had to preserve their surviving advantages while retrenching to compete effectively against the new retailers. By mid-2000, Toys-R-Us had announced a partnership with Amazon.com to unify convenient access with established distribution capability and manufacturer relationships.

Why the S-curve and product life cycle models are difficult to use

What was wrong with the idea that the industry was in maturity? Conventional wisdom held that maturity was driven by the ageing of the baby boomers and the stability of toy design. The reality of tough price competition at the retail level underscored this perception. Many industry leaders had a sense that new technology might some day support innovation but the possibilities appeared remote and futuristic. Why didn't people foresee that the industry was about to be transformed?

Life cycle phases are difficult to see

First, it was hard to get the timing right on technology and demographic trends. While radical innovation was a theoretical possibility, it was hard to imagine in practice. Upstart entrants that challenged the incumbents typically failed because of high costs and inadequate consumer response. The reality of the industry underscored the hard-edged economics of faddish toys and retail price competition.

Industry boundaries are hard to identify

Second, the S-curve analysis did not capture subtle changes in industry boundaries. Indeed, it reinforced the incumbents' view that toy retailing required storefronts backed by complex distribution networks and tight manufacturer relationships. As toy e-tailing emerged, many incumbents saw it as a separate industry, like catalogue distribution. Catalogues had been limited in their effectiveness mainly because mailing costs were so high and response rates were so low. Unlike traditional retailing, catalogues offered no opportunity for pre-purchase play. Traditional retailers soon learned that the touch-and-feel requirement was not nearly as important to online retailers as they had thought, however.

The S-curve and PLC models offer little help for adapting an organization across generations

Third, the models did not offer toy-retailing executives a point of view on how to survive into the next industry generation when it did finally arrive. Many of the mass merchants kept their core revenue streams even when new entrants like eToys and Amazon began to attract customers. Questions arose about whether the upstarts could fulfil orders. Lingering concerns about the customer's need for touch-and-feel suggested that the traditional bricks-and-mortar retailers should not overreact to the threat. Organizational conflict made it confusing and difficult to go for clicks-and-bricks.

The difficulties are widespread

Across many industries, executives in leading firms have perceived their industries as mature and have later been blindsided by innovative rivals. The problems in applying the S-curve and PLC frameworks in toy retailing are also common in other settings. Challenges of misplaced investment can also arise when executives perceive their industries as emerging or as declining. Field research on industry transitions shows that the most persistent challenges are organizational. Without a better view on how the environment is changing, firms cannot fully commit to organizational adaptation.

Four models of industry evolution

Figure 10.1.2 illustrates the four models of industry evolution: 'receptive', 'blockbuster', 'radical organic' and 'intermediating'. Among the two non-architectural models, the distinction is between those where the customer and supplier markets provide continuous feedback (Model 1, 'Receptive') and those where profitability is mainly determined by the outcome of major projects for which feedback is delayed and unpredictable (Model 2, 'Blockbuster'. When industry evolution involves blockbuster change, firms sustain superior performance if they use long-term relationships to create more value from successful projects than can outsiders. In contrast, firms in receptive industries create value by systematically translating incremental improvements into formulas for success that can be replicated across their businesses. Discount consumer-goods retailing is an industry undergoing 'receptive' change while ethical pharmaceutical manufacture is on a 'blockbuster' path. Within a sector's supply chain, the downstream industries (i.e. pharmacies, movie theatres and gas stations) often evolve receptively even if the upstream industries (i.e. pharmaceuticals, movie production, and oil/gas exploration) undergo blockbuster evolution.

Architectural industry change is less common but may lead to major shifts in the overall character of an industry. It occurs in two ways. The third model, 'radical organic' evolution, encompasses approaches that provide a quantum improvement in customer or supplier value (performance, ease of use, mode of use) big enough to disrupt existing customer and supplier relationships. A classic example is the personal computer, which appealed to a whole new set of customers and engaged a new cadre of components suppliers and employees. The personal computer quickly transformed both the horizontal industry structure (yielding winners and losers among computer manufacturers) and the vertical value chain (including software suppliers, sales and distribution channels, purchasing processes, etc).

The fourth model of industry evolution, 'intermediating' change, describes architectural innovation that originates within established relationships.

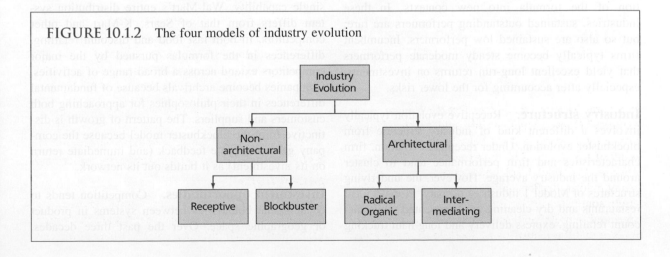

FIGURE 10.1.2   The four models of industry evolution

Intermediating change occurred during the late nineteenth century in consumer-goods retailing, when Sears and Montgomery Ward pioneered mail-order catalogues to create new ways of buying and selling for households. Today, online auctions create intermediating change in the markets for used cars.

Each of the four models has distinctive characteristics in terms of industry structure, historic innovation paths, investment opportunities and performance drivers (Figure 10.1.2). Every industry evolves by one of these models, although industries may move between evolutionary models over time (and especially over long periods of time). An industry may rapidly move from non-architectural change into radical organic change, as in the launch of electronic watches. In most cases, this kind of rapid change is preceded by a long period in which pressure for major change builds in the old industry structure. Similarly, an industry may move from a period of architectural change into a relatively stable period of non-architectural evolution.

Model 1: Receptive evolution

Receptive innovation paths are more stable than other trajectories for industry evolution. Examples of receptive evolution commonly arise in the distribution, transportation and manufacturing sectors. Firms with superior performance in these industries typically grow by expanding their activity systems outward steadily. The characteristic quality of receptive industries is that firms achieve returns on their investments incrementally as the investments are made. Information quickly arrives on whether the firm's approach is viable in the market. In general, investment is less risky than under other evolutionary models. It is as if the industry's leaders have conceived of winning formulas, and their success depends on the steady radiation of the formula into new contexts. In these industries, sustained outstanding performers are rare; but so also are sustained low performers. Incumbent firms typically become steady moderate performers that yield excellent long-run returns on investments, especially after accounting for the lower risks.

Industry structure. Receptive evolution typically involves a different kind of industry structure from blockbuster evolution. Under receptive evolution, firm characteristics and firm performance tend to cluster around the industry average. However, the underlying structures of Model 1 industries do vary. Florists, local restaurants and dry cleaning are fragmented while discount retailing, express delivery and long-haul trucking

are consolidated. In many situations, the attractiveness of the industry depends on whether established firms are being overtaken by the more efficient systems of their rivals. During most of the 1980s, the discount retailing industry in the US was unattractive largely because Wal-Mart was expanding its operations and creating excess capacity in the systems of many of its major rivals. Today, many Mom-and-Pop restauranteurs are exiting for similar reasons. Modern restaurant chains expand into their local markets and offer customers similar experiences at lower prices. As these examples suggest, the profitability of Model 1 industries usually involves shorter and shallower periods of loss than among industries on other evolutionary paths. Under receptive industry evolution, disadvantaged firms normally have trouble surviving unless they can quickly adapt to more efficient approaches.

Historic innovation path. Industries undergoing receptive evolution may have very different histories. Often, however, a long initial period of fragmentation occurs and in some cases industries remain fragmented. (Even fragmentation is not normally associated with substantial losses, however.) Receptive industries tend to consolidate when particularly efficient competitors come to dominate the industry.

Dominating firms often have grown slowly over long periods. Steady radiation from a geographic base is common. Starbucks, Wal-Mart and Federal Express all evolved this way. These successful firms grow by continuously investing in a number of core assets simultaneously. For example, Wal-Mart has added stores, distribution capacity, transportation systems, information-technology features, employee-recognition programmes and merchandise all at the same time. The company innovates by extending its system rather than by looking for a big-hit return on investment in a single capability. Wal-Mart's entire distribution system differs from that of Sears, K-Mart and other competitors. In both fast food and discount retailing, differences in the formulas pursued by the major competitors extend across a broad range of activities. Companies become archrivals because of fundamental differences in their philosophies for approaching both customers and suppliers. The pattern of growth is distinctive from the blockbuster model because the company gets immediate feedback (and immediate return on its investment) as it builds out its network.

Investment opportunities. Competition tends to occur at the boundaries between systems in product or geographic space. Over the past three decades,

McDonald's and Burger King became famous for basic differences in the way they make burgers, with McDonald's adopting a batch process and Burger King cooking to order. (Recent announcements indicate that McDonald's may be moving to a cook-to-order system, which may reflect convergence in strategies as the industry consolidates.)

When industries on a receptive evolutionary path consolidate, they tend to encompass economies of scale and scope based on relationships across specific activities, with continuous feedback from markets. They do not engage in major bets on new technologies in isolation from market forces. Receptive industries are substantially more favourable to mid-course corrections than blockbuster industries, with more market testing of new ideas and less background research and development.

Performance drivers. The highest-performing firms in Model 1 industries continually develop new efficiencies. They are rigorous, disciplined and clear in their willingness to turn away opportunities that may compromise the existing approach. Leading firms also find ways to extend themselves incrementally without directly confronting competitors with equally efficient approaches. High performers avoid price wars as they come into contact with competitors through incremental growth.

Industries on receptive paths are vulnerable to price wars because customers and suppliers tend to be less loyal than in blockbuster industries. Starbucks, Wal-Mart and Federal Express offer more-or-less standardized products and services. The companies generally avoid customizing their approaches to remain efficient and to offer low prices. (Although these firms may be differentiated, the absolute standards for efficiency in their industries are high.) As a result, customers and suppliers (including employees) have low switching costs. When two leaders come into contact, they often face powerful incentives to win customers by cutting price because they cannot rely on customer loyalty. These conditions have plagued the airline industry for years.

Model 2: Blockbuster evolution

Examples of industries on a blockbuster trajectory include pharmaceuticals, applications software, cellular-telephone service, oil-and-gas extraction and movie production. The characteristic quality of a blockbuster industry is that nearly all the costs of developing new products and technologies are incurred before the sponsor learns whether markets will respond favourably.

Critical resources are created through risky investment over long periods before they generate profits. Once the new project is developed, it is commercialized in concert with complementary assets that are already in place.

A film studio cannot truly resolve its uncertainty about a film's market value until the project is finished. However, big box-office hits rarely come from independent film-makers. Established studios use their relationships with key actors and their distribution systems to secure important advantages in bringing their films to market. In this context, the innovation occurs within the framework of these complementary assets. Great new value may be created by innovative film projects like *Titanic*, but the industry is not changed architecturally.

The structural platform for innovation is similar in the pharmaceutical industry, where companies must invest for years in R&D before obtaining reliable estimates of a product's viability. Once a drug passes through the approval process, however, the company may make hundreds of millions. Typically, the innovating company brings the approved drug to market through an established salesforce and distribution system. These complementary assets are critical to the stability of the industry.

Industry structure. What are the structural characteristics of blockbuster industries? It depends on whether incumbents are currently engaged in significant development expenditures or whether dominant designs have emerged. For decades, the cellular-telephone industry was unattractive as firms built out their networks. The payoff is occurring now, as firms begin to achieve above-average returns on their invested capital.

After a dominant design emerges, blockbuster industries typically generate above-average returns. A five-forces analysis normally reveals a low threat of entry, low buyer or supplier power, low rivalry and moderate threats of substitution. What makes buyers and suppliers tolerate high profits on average among industry incumbents? What keeps the industry's rivals from gravitating to similar competitive positions?

First, firms in the industry bear significant operating risk. Film profits are notoriously volatile. Occasionally film companies go out of business by overfunding ill-fated projects. Similarly, the high profits of pharmaceutical leaders may be significantly threatened when drugs go off patent. Buyers and suppliers tolerate the industry's profit as a reward to innovation.

Second, blockbuster industries typically create enormous value for both buyers and suppliers. Firms often adhere to high standards in customer service and in supplier partnering. Successful blockbuster firms create so much value in partnership with buyers and suppliers that all are satisfied with returns on their investments.

Third, the industry's incumbents tend to pursue projects that are distinctive by repeatedly reinvesting in basic technologies. Leading companies generally try to avoid imitating one another because the stakes in blockbuster investment are so high. This taste for distinctiveness in project definition tends to support ongoing differentiation once commercialization occurs.

Blockbuster industries remain stable when the industry's incumbents, its customers and its suppliers earn more from exchange than through the best alternatives that emerge over time. What can jar these industries into architectural change? The underlying technology no longer delivers enough value to keep customers and suppliers interested, or the incremental innovation no longer makes buyers willing to compensate the industry for the risks undertaken in development. For a blockbuster industry to remain stable, customers and suppliers have to perceive more value by continuing to deal with the industry than by pursuing the best alternatives.

Historic innovation path. There are no simple rules for the historical innovation path in blockbuster industries, but many of these industries share common experiences. They tend to have had an early period of extensive development, fragmentation and losses as inventors experiment with new technology. With successful development, firms acquire the complementary assets necessary to realize the commercial potential of their innovations. A shakeout often occurs, and the surviving leaders become positioned for significant returns on their investments.

In the film-production industry during the early decades of the twentieth century, firms experimented with approaches to delivering feature films. Should movies be personalized for individual viewing? How long should they be? Would new documentaries dominate fiction? What production values would be acceptable? After a few big feature-film successes, producers began to develop structural rules that continue to influence the industry today: films are usually between one-and-a-quarter and three hours long; exhibitors pay producers according to a standard formula related to box-office receipts and typically cannot preview a film before committing to show it; all viewers are charged about the same price for admission; previews of forthcoming films are shown before

the featured presentation; and theatre lobbies contain candy stands. Once this basic structure was established, the industry launched a major programme to develop complementary assets in distribution and actor relationships.

Investment opportunities. To find out whether architectural change is imminent, look at the current investments. Are firms continuing to invest in blockbuster technology? Are customers and suppliers renewing the platforms for their interaction with the industry?

The big studios are still developing feature films by decades-old rules. Actors, directors and other talent suppliers continue to hone their skills over long periods and to follow the industry's norms for delivering value to the producers. Despite diminishing financial performance, the exhibitors continue to build multiplex theatres in new locations. Why? By some accounts, the exhibition industry is engaged in a war of attrition. Through consolidation, exhibitors hope to exert countervailing power against the producers in negotiations over film rights. Exhibitors may not be satisfied with their financial returns, but their next-best alternatives still do not swamp their incentives to reinvest. These conditions suggest that film production is likely to remain relatively stable over a five- to ten-year time horizon.

Performance drivers. For blockbuster firms, the most common route to superior returns is by innovating within a specialized niche while also owning the complementary assets necessary for successful commercialization. High-performance film producers develop specialized skills in particular categories (animated features, documentaries, or action films). Leading pharmaceutical firms dominate therapeutic categories. High-performance cellular operators dominate specific geographic regions. Within each of these categories, the leading firms also own and deploy complementary assets critical for quick commercialization of new technology.

While domination of a niche is prevalent, a second blockbuster approach involves the sale of supporting activities to industry incumbents. In some cases, the support may even cover core resources. For example, independent film makers may sell innovative scripts or even finished films to mainstream film producers.

Yet another approach involves partnering with leading firms to maintain and extend complementary assets. Consultants and agents often assist film producers in identifying promising new actors. Lobbyists work with cellular-telephone providers to assure their representation in regulatory hearings that affect their geographic coverage.

What does this mean for a potential entrant that seeks industry leadership? Most established industries resist entry by outsiders. Despite this fact, the potential for massive returns often attracts new entrants anyway. Often, upstart firms begin by trying to innovate within an established niche. Traditional biotechnology firms are a classic example. If an organization beats the odds and is successful at development, it then faces extraordinary challenges of commercialization because it does not hold the complementary assets necessary to bring products to market. At this stage, firms often sell or link up with industry leaders to gain access to critical resources. In cellular-telephone service, for example, entrants with key licences were often bought by larger firms with established customer relationships. Companies tend to perform poorly when they underestimate the power of the established firms' complementary assets.

Model 3: Radical organic evolution

Under radical organic industry evolution, change is driven by radical innovation in the capabilities that support both customer and supplier relationships. The entire system of old capabilities may be dismantled and a new system rebuilt. Although some old capabilities may retain their relevance, major architectural change occurs in the ways that firms interact with both customers and suppliers. What firms do is changing radically, and, as a result, how they interact changes too. Intermediation may be part of the change, but, in Model 3 evolution, intermediation itself is driven by the availability of innovative new technologies for creating value. One consequence is that the new industry's boundaries may be quite different from the old industry's. Indeed, old industry boundaries may be barely distinguishable after the change fully takes hold. As a result, former leaders may lose position and new leaders often emerge.

In high-end leisure travel, for example, old systems for booking traditional vacations are giving way to new options that may make old assets obsolete. New forms and styles of travel that merge leisure with business blur the old boundaries of the industry. Fully integrated provider-agents offer customized packages tailored to the interests of the vacationer. Just enough of the old services may retain their relevance to induce a transition from established incumbents. Even if they make

the transition, though, industry boundaries are likely to be very different over the long run.

At present, the news-services industry is undergoing organic industry evolution. In news services, unprecedented technologies – and especially the Internet – create opportunities to provide more accurate, relevant and timely information to customers. Information is transmitted so quickly to so many people that demand is growing for services to help us cope. Cultural and community organizations are emerging to service this demand. New information-processing vehicles are developing to generate sifted information for news organizations. Some of the news services' old reporting, editing and broadcasting capabilities are relevant in the new environment, but there is no doubt that they must change in character to retain their relevance. Why are news services classified as 'organic' rather than as 'intermediating' (Model 4)? Because this industry's *product* is information. In this case, the core assets, all oriented around information flows, are what is being changed.

Model 3 industries offer significant opportunities for penetration by new entrants. Although CNN was established as a news service in the mid-1970s, it gained attention during the Gulf War as viewers came to value its distributed news-gathering capabilities. Analysis suggests that no dominant design has developed for many of the industry's important capabilities. Continuing component and architectural change will likely reshape the news-services industry for decades.

Industry structure. Industries undergoing architectural change are often less attractive than stable industries. Excess capacity, blurring industry boundaries and races for first-mover advantage all depress profitability. Unlike intermediating industry evolution, however, organic evolution hosts the potential for new approaches that bring together new customers and new suppliers. As a result, pockets of very high profitability may arise, especially among new entrants.

Historic innovation path. Organically-evolving industries are often populated by firms that have resisted the adoption of new technologies for long periods, typically because of strong incentives to preserve established resources. In many cases, the marginal cost of operating from established platforms is lower than the fixed cost of implementing a new approach, giving new entrants a strong advantage over incumbents. These advantages may be partly offset, however, if some of the incumbent's resources can be translated into the new environment. This possibility may create difficult questions about the optimal timing of migration.

Investment opportunities. Firms often announce major new investment programmes that have big implications for the industry. For example, the invention of fibre-optic cable in the 1970s made obsolete copper cable and other technologies for carrying long-distance telephone calls. Current examples include e-mail and express mail, which promise to change the face of the mail-delivery business.

Performance drivers. High performers develop first-mover advantages by bearing the considerable risk of introducing new technologies before they know if customers are going to buy the product which results. Incumbent firms take on massive new investment programmes that may involve interacting with new kinds of customers as well as new suppliers.

Model 4: Intermediating evolution

Under Model 4 evolution, architectural change alters the way transactions occur. Intermediating change describes industries in which there are discontinuities in the value chain itself. This sort of change is topical because information technology is lowering transaction costs in some industries and creating potential for disintermediation/reintermediation.

The characteristic quality of intermediating change is a radical shift in the overall information available in the industry's transactions. These transactions may take place either within established firms or between the industry and its customers or suppliers. Better information tends to reduce transaction costs and diminish the benefits of vertical integration as new layers of intermediate customers and suppliers emerge. In some situations, established firms find new efficiencies through subcontracting. Lower transaction costs can also create incentives to develop new capabilities.

The emergence of eMarketplaces and business-to-business (B2B) commerce on the Web often represents intermediating change. A new B2B exchange in PC devices has emerged to support local resellers and assemblers. No longer do resellers stockpile hard drives, CD-ROM drives and other peripherals: through the B2B exchange, a reseller can obtain a precisely-specified peripheral within 24 hours, often at lower prices than direct from the manufacturer. The new exchange represents architectural change because it shifts the level at which the transaction occurs. The exchange's owner has a chance to build new capabilities

for handling transaction volume and for assuring fair access across buyers and sellers; resellers can build new capabilities that will allow seamless ordering and inventory control; peripheral manufacturers can create value by becoming more efficient. Of course, the PC-peripherals B2B exchange also creates challenges for established customers and firms because it makes many of their old capabilities obsolete. Other industries going through intermediating change at present include retail banking and agricultural supplies.

Industry structure. Again, the characteristics of industry structure may vary widely. In many cases, however, changes in the distribution of information make old capabilities obsolete. As the industry structure shifts, excess capacity arises and firms scramble to dominate new layers of transaction. If transaction efficiency is compromised, then customers and suppliers may turn to new entrants. Eventually, several new industries may emerge to displace an old industry. As these changes take place, industries often are unattractive.

Auto dealing is currently undergoing major changes in the transaction costs that had linked activities. Formerly, auto dealerships performed a broad range of activities that included stocking new cars, preparing cars for sale, advertising, reselling used cars, informing prospective customers, market research, negotiating price and financing. Intermediating change began in auto dealing even before the World Wide Web.

Specialized services emerged for financing, market research and even price negotiations. With the Web, more and more activities that were traditionally performed by dealers are now organized in separate entities. What makes intermediation possible in this context? The exchange of credible information on the Web allows activities to be coordinated in arms-length relationships where once they would have been integrated. As the system evolves, a number of separate new industries are likely to emerge for auto financing, inventory management, credible quality verification and perhaps even price negotiation. During the transition, the traditional auto-dealing industry is likely to continue to be unattractive.

Historic innovation path. Industries on an intermediating evolutionary path typically have accumulated compromises in transactions between the industry's incumbents, their customers and their suppliers. In many cases, these compromises reflect efforts to balance incentives for investment with bargaining strength on either side of the exchange.

FIGURE 10.1.3 The four models: Summary

Evolutionary model	Defining characteristics	Architectural change	Industry structure	Historic innovation path	Investment opportunities	Performance drivers	Examples
1. Receptive	Incremental returns as investments are made	No	Firm performance may cluster around the industry average; firms develop integrated systems of activities	Long initial periods of fragmentation sometimes followed by consolidation around efficient leaders	Incremental at geographic boundaries or at product-attribute boundaries	Constant search for new efficiencies	Retailing before the Web, fast-food
2. Blockbuster	Risky projects with delayed feedback.	No	Firm performance may vary widely; firms seek to dominate riches	Early periods of loss followed by consolidation around leaders that hold complementary assets	Risky and rare over a single specialized asset	Constant risk management on big projects	Film production, pharmaceuticals, oil exploration
3. Radical Organic	Radical innovation in the capabilities that support both customer and supplier relationships	Yes	Often depressed average profitability with attractive pockets	Built-up resistance among incumbents to new technologies; lagging reinvestment by critical customers and suppliers	Risky and rare over many specialized assets	First-mover advantage through commercialization of new product and process technologies	News services, high-end leisure travel
4. Intermediating	Radical shift in the information available when transactions occur	Yes	Often depressed average profitability with attractive layers	Built-up resistance among incumbents in transactions; tough negotiations by critical customers and suppliers	Incremental over both customer and supplier transactions	First-mover advantage through reshaping ways of interacting with customers and suppliers	Auto-dealing, retail banking, agricultural supplies

Companies may have tried to induce their customers to accept low prices by partially integrating forward, for example.

Over time, the accumulation of compromises creates pressure. Customers, suppliers and some dissatisfied incumbents may seek alternative mechanisms for governing how they interact. Old assets that support both customer transactions and supplier relationships become obsolete. In the case of auto dealers, the reputational capital built up between the auto dealers and the auto manufacturers has become obsolete, at least in part. Some manufacturers have sought to break many of their dealer franchise agreements. At the same time, relationships between auto dealers and customers have suffered. Just a few years ago, customers were typically more loyal to dealerships than to car brands. This loyalty is quickly eroding as intermediating change occurs.

Investment opportunities. Under Model 4 change, innovation often starts with experimentation in different mechanisms for organizing transactions. Upstart firms may enter at low scale to test market acceptance for new ways of interacting. Leading firms also may shed activities in an effort to become more efficient, although these efforts may be plagued with difficulty. General Motors' efforts at intermediation led to a major strike in the summer of 1998.

Performance drivers. High performers rely on new technologies to reshape ways of interacting with customers, suppliers and newly-emerging intermediate suppliers. Companies must design mechanisms for decoupling traditional relationships, and especially complex internal transfer-pricing mechanisms that insulate activities from market pressure. The highest performers in this environment find ways to integrate established resources with new transaction mechanisms.

How to analyse industry evolution

Which type of industry are you in? It is worth approaching this question rigorously. Analysis of industry evolution involves taking three different perspectives, and then putting them together. The perspectives are:

■ assessment of the current environment,

■ evaluation of historical trends, and

■ evaluation of prospective returns.

The entire process focuses on the industry's durable, specialized and economically-important investments,

because they shape the incentives of the relevant players (Ghemawat 1991). A comprehensive analysis also assesses investments by the industry's customers and its suppliers. The next step is to take a view on whether the industry is undergoing architectural change. The final step is an assessment of the implications for the firm.

Who should do the analysis? The process within the firm can be as important as the results. Analysing industry evolution can generate compelling insights about emerging opportunities, which may reveal critical weaknesses in the firm's old approaches. This means that the most successful attempts to analyse industry evolution are those which involve full attention over several weeks (or even months) of senior managers from different functions across the company. So the first rule is to assign a senior, cross-functional team which brings together wide-ranging information on customer preferences, supplier technologies and competitive behaviour. The process also requires intellectual flexibility and a capacity to imagine alternative paths of industry evolution, and of the role that the firm might play. Choosing the right team members is a critical preliminary step.

1. Map the existing industry structure and competitive environment

The first analytical step involves taking a snapshot of the current environment. This becomes the foundation for the rest of the study. By looking back from this vantage point, the team later assesses whether accumulated compromises create an incentive for large-scale, punctuated change. By looking forward, the team later evaluates the potential of new kinds of investments.

Begin with an examination of the financial performance of the industry's incumbents. What accounts for current returns on invested capital in the business? Is the industry structurally attractive (Porter, 1980)? What approaches have been used to balance buyer power and supplier power? How do partnerships and strategic alliances influence relationships? Are there significant switching costs for customers, incumbents, or suppliers? Has rivalry generated excess capacity in key activities?

After analysing industry structure, evaluate the competitive position of the firm relative to its direct rivals. Does the firm hold a competitive advantage or disadvantage? Which activities account for differences between the financial performance of the firm and its rivals? Are some competitors saddled with excess capacity? Is the firm locked into specific activities?

In the end, the purpose of this step is to generate a list of strategically-important resources across the industry and within the firm. Each of the resources relies on an underlying technology, and each was acquired to allow a firm to be more efficient at delivering value to customers or suppliers.

2. Look back at how critical resources have developed

Once the team identifies the durable resources created by customers, incumbents and suppliers, the next step is to look historically at how they developed. The relevance of the industry's resources is often revealed through close inspection of customer and supplier behaviour. If customers are making specialized investments that are tailored to specific competitors, then there is evidence that their approaches are still relevant. When customers minimize their exposure to long-term relationships, then they are signaling a desire to lower switching costs. Even if customers (and suppliers) are locked in, the team should assess whether their preferences have shifted since the industry's resources were initially designed and established. Are customers and suppliers seeking fresh approaches?

The team should also assess whether the resources that support scale economies are outdated. When was the technology established? When did scale economies first arise? Have customer tastes and supplier preferences shifted so that the efficiencies are no longer realized in the same way? Has the industry been able to adapt its approach to efficiencies so that established resources are preserved as they are updated? Have some firms in the industry sought trading partnerships that have siphoned volume from firms that pursue efficiency approaches? Mature efficiency approaches may be especially vulnerable to firms that lead with partnership opportunities for customers and suppliers.

In sum, this part of the analysis allows the observer to understand how specific resources developed historically within the industry. Which are most important? Which are mature and vulnerable to radical innovation? Which resources are still in development? Ultimately, the objective is to identify whether customers, incumbents and suppliers have an incentive to transform the underlying business models that shape their interaction.

3. Identify major investment initiatives

After looking historically, the team should look forward to understand the prospective economic impact of newly-formed investments both by incumbents and outsiders. The objective is to look at new investment activity with a clean slate. What major investments in both tangible and intangible assets have been created to meet needs that are currently served within the industry? It is important to consider investments that may originate outside conventional industry boundaries.

The team should also assess the nature of the investment risk associated with innovation. Risks occur whenever the return on investment is deferred. It is risk that creates the prospect of future profitability, however. Without risk, the cost of investment would reflect the entire net-present-value of the return. How much risk are entrepreneurs taking as they pursue major investments? How much investment has to occur before the entrepreneur learns whether the innovation will create value in the marketplace? What early signals are available for assessing market acceptance? Does the investing entrepreneur have contingency plans for redeploying investment if market acceptance is low?

4. Decide whether innovation is architectural

Industries tend to be slow to change. Compromises accumulate because the parties are locked in by their prior commitments. The fourth step involves integrating the historical and prospective points of view to evaluate the accumulated compromises in value-creation strategies. These compromises stimulate innovation because they create incentives for change in the economic relationships between the industry, its customers and its suppliers. When an industry is profitable, and when its customers and its suppliers are also earning high returns on their invested capital, then the incentive for architectural change can be quite low. Occasionally, however, architectural innovation occurs. In this step of the analysis, the team must assess whether the investment activities identified through the analysis amount to architectural change over a five- to ten-year horizon.

It is easy to overestimate the prospective impact of technological change over a moderate time horizon. Technological change is almost certain to create architectural change in an industry over the very long run, but architectural innovation can occur only if the results of the historical analysis point to incentives for change for the industry's customers and its suppliers.

5. Evaluate the implications

The final step is to evaluate the implications for the firm. There are several ways in which the organization may be challenged. The firm may be investing in projects that are either behind or ahead of their time. Invariably, incentives arise to preserve the value of established capital. Executives may be struggling with whether to abandon profitable old approaches in order to develop unprofitable new ones. An organization may find it optimal to invest minimally to preserve old capital at the same time as it invests for the future. Managing the path of innovation requires deep knowledge of economic incentives as well as technology requirements. By looking historically as well as prospectively, the team can assess how quickly customers and suppliers will respond to new opportunity.

The challenges of industry evolution are even more complex if the firm is engaged in close rivalry over the opportunity. A war of attrition may arise over the old approach. These wars are pernicious because they often lead the firm into an unprofitable battle to serve outdated customers. They are also dangerous when they drain capital and keep attention fixed on the old paradigm. A similar kind of war can emerge if the firm competes too closely with a rival for dominance in a new industry structure. Too much competition can rush investment in technologies that may not be optimally suited to long-run opportunities. Worse yet, the rivals may become committed to similar strategies, and may consequently invest inefficiently once the new technologies become established.

Organizational resistance to change can arise regardless of whether innovation is architectural. Companies have devised a broad variety of mechanisms for dealing with this kind of resistance: aligning incentives, making arms-length financial investments and adjusting formal hierarchical structure. By examining how resources and relationships are changing, the team can identify a range of potential approaches for reorganizing, and then recommend which carries appropriate levels of risk and reward.

Implications

What does all this mean? Understanding industry evolution is important because firms are much more likely to survive and to earn high rates of return if their investment strategies are aligned with industry evolution than if they resist it. Extensive analysis on broad patterns of performance suggests that industries evolve on one of the four major models: receptive, blockbuster, radical organic, or intermediating. Companies typically fail when they attempt to jar the path of industry evolution from one model to another.

Evolution is driven by powerful incentives that affect an industry's customers and suppliers as well as its incumbents. When an industry is architecturally stable, change follows either a 'receptive' or 'blockbuster' path. Architecturally unstable industries undergo redefinition, and may offer greater opportunities to displace industry leaders. The risks of pursuing first-mover advantage are also great. Organic and intermediating industries host many more casualties than successes.

Rigorous, disciplined analysis of industry evolution is necessary to anticipate when different kinds of opportunities are likely to emerge over time. Begin with a comprehensive map of existing industry conditions, and then look retrospectively and prospectively to understand how technology may take hold. Assess the accumulated pressure on industry structure that may have emerged as customers, incumbents and suppliers have compromised to preserve the value of established capabilities. Careful analysis frames the viable opportunities for successfully commercializing new technologies. Understanding industry evolution sets the stage for evaluating competitive threats and organizational challenges. Thus, understanding industry evolution is just the first step toward building a comprehensive plan for an organization's development.

READING 10.2

Blue ocean strategy

By W. Chan Kim and Renee Mauborgne[1]

A onetime accordion player, stilt walker and fire-eater, Guy Laliberté is now CEO of one of Canada's largest cultural exports, Cirque du Soleil.

Founded in 1984 by a group of street performers, Cirque has staged dozens of productions seen by some 40 million people in 90 cities around the world. In

20 years, Cirque has achieved revenues that Ringling Bros. and Barnum & Bailey – the world's leading circus – took more than a century to attain.

Cirque's rapid growth occurred in an unlikely setting. The circus business was (and still is) in long-term decline. Alternative forms of entertainment – sporting events, TV and video games – were casting a growing shadow. Children, the mainstay of the circus audience, preferred PlayStations to circus acts. There was also rising sentiment, fuelled by animal rights groups, against the use of animals, traditionally an integral part of the circus. On the supply side, the star performers that Ringling and the other circuses relied on to draw in the crowds could often name their own terms. As a result, the industry was hit by steadily decreasing audiences and increasing costs. What's more, any new entrant to this business would be competing against a formidable incumbent that for most of the last century had set the industry standard.

How did Cirque profitably increase revenues by a factor of 22 over the last ten years in such an unattractive environment? The tagline for one of the first Cirque productions is revealing: 'We reinvent the circus.' Cirque did not make its money by competing within the confines of the existing industry or by stealing customers from Ringling and the others. Instead it created uncontested market space that made the competition irrelevant. It pulled in a whole new group of customers who were traditionally non-customers of the industry – adults and corporate clients who had turned to theatre, opera or ballet and were, therefore, prepared to pay several times more than the price of a conventional circus ticket for an unprecedented entertainment experience.

To understand the nature of Cirque's achievement, you have to realize that the business universe consists of two distinct kinds of space, which we think of as red and blue oceans. Red oceans represent all the industries in existence today – the known market space. In red oceans, industry boundaries are defined and accepted, and the competitive rules of the game are well understood. Here, companies try to outperform their rivals in order to grab a greater share of existing demand. As the space gets more and more crowded, prospects for profits and growth are reduced. Products turn into commodities, and increasing competition turns the water bloody.

Blue oceans denote all the industries *not* in existence today – the unknown market space, untainted by competition. In blue oceans, demand is created rather than fought over. There is ample opportunity for growth that is both profitable and rapid. There are two ways to create blue oceans. In a few cases, companies can give rise to completely new industries, as eBay did with the online auction industry. But in most cases, a blue ocean is created from within a red ocean when a company alters the boundaries of an existing industry. As will become evident later, this is what Cirque did. In breaking through the boundary traditionally separating circus and theatre, it made a new and profitable blue ocean from within the red ocean of the circus industry.

Cirque is just one of more than 150 blue ocean creations that we have studied in over 30 industries, using data stretching back more than 100 years. We analysed companies that created those blue oceans and their less successful competitors, which were caught in red oceans. In studying these data, we have observed a consistent pattern of strategic thinking behind the creation of new markets and industries, what we call blue ocean strategy. The logic behind blue ocean strategy parts with traditional models focused on competing in existing market space. Indeed, it can be argued that managers' failure to realize the differences between red and blue ocean strategy lies behind the difficulties many companies encounter as they try to break from the competition.

In this article, we present the concept of blue ocean strategy and describe its defining characteristics. We assess the profit and growth consequences of blue oceans and discuss why their creation is a rising imperative for companies in the future. We believe that an understanding of blue ocean strategy will help today's companies as they struggle to thrive in an accelerating and expanding business universe.

Blue and red oceans

Although the term may be new, blue oceans have always been with us. Look back 100 years and ask yourself which industries known today were then unknown. The answer: Industries as basic as automobiles, music recording, aviation, petrochemicals, pharmaceuticals and management consulting were unheard-of or had just begun to emerge. Now turn the clock back only 30 years and ask yourself the same question. Again, a plethora of multibillion-dollar industries jump out: mutual funds, cellular telephones, biotechnology, discount retailing, express package delivery, snowboards, coffee bars and home videos, to name a few. Just three decades ago, none of these industries existed in a meaningful way.

This time, put the clock forward 20 years. Ask yourself: How many industries that are unknown today will exist then? If history is any predictor of the future, the answer is many. Companies have a huge capacity to create new industries and re-create existing ones, a fact that is reflected in the deep changes that have been necessary in the way industries are classified. The half-century-old Standard Industrial Classification (SIC) system was replaced in 1997 by the North American Industry Classification System (NAICS). The new system expanded the ten SIC industry sectors into 20 to reflect the emerging realities of new industry territories – blue oceans. The services sector under the old system, for example, is now seven sectors ranging from information to health care and social assistance. Given that these classification systems are designed for standardization and continuity, such a replacement shows how significant a source of economic growth the creation of blue oceans has been.

Looking forward, it seems clear to us that blue oceans will remain the engine of growth. Prospects in most established market spaces – red oceans – are shrinking steadily. Technological advances have substantially improved industrial productivity, permitting suppliers to produce an unprecedented array of products and services. And as trade barriers between nations and regions fall and information on products and prices becomes instantly and globally available, niche markets and monopoly havens are continuing to disappear. At the same time, there is little evidence of any increase in demand, at least in the developed markets, where recent United Nations statistics even point to declining populations. The result is that in more and more industries, supply is overtaking demand.

This situation has inevitably hastened the commoditization of products and services, stoked price wars and shrunk profit margins. According to recent studies, major American brands in a variety of product and service categories have become more and more alike. And as brands become more similar, people increasingly base purchase choices on price. People no longer insist, as in the past, that their laundry detergent be Tide. Nor do they necessarily stick to Colgate when there is a special promotion for Crest, and vice versa. In overcrowded industries, differentiating brands becomes harder both in economic upturns and in downturns.

The paradox of strategy

Unfortunately, most companies seem becalmed in their red oceans. In a study of business launches in 108 companies, we found that 86 per cent of those new ventures were line extensions – incremental improvements to existing industry offerings – and a mere 14 per cent were aimed at creating new markets or industries.

While line extensions did account for 62 per cent of the total revenues, they delivered only 39 per cent of the total profits. By contrast, the 14 per cent invested in creating new markets and industries delivered 38 per cent of total revenues and a startling 61 per cent of total profits.

So why the dramatic imbalance in favour of red oceans? Part of the explanation is that corporate strategy is heavily influenced by its roots in military strategy. The very language of strategy is deeply imbued with military references – chief executive 'officers' in 'headquarters', 'troops' on the 'front lines'. Described this way, strategy is all about red ocean competition. It is about confronting an opponent and driving him off a battlefield of limited territory. Blue ocean strategy, by contrast, is about doing business where there is no competitor. It is about creating new land, not dividing up existing land. Focusing on the red ocean therefore means accepting the key constraining factors of war – limited terrain and the need to beat an enemy to succeed. And it means denying the distinctive strength of the business world – the capacity to create new market space that is uncontested.

The tendency of corporate strategy to focus on winning against rivals was exacerbated by the meteoric rise of Japanese companies in the 1970s and 1980s. For the first time in corporate history, customers were deserting Western companies in droves. As competition mounted in the global marketplace, a slew of red ocean strategies emerged, all arguing that competition was at the core of corporate success and failure. Today, one hardly talks about strategy without using the language of competition. The term that best symbolizes this is 'competitive advantage'. In the competitive-advantage worldview, companies are often driven to outperform rivals and capture greater shares of existing market space.

Of course competition matters. But by focusing on competition, scholars, companies and consultants have ignored two very important – and, we would argue, far more lucrative – aspects of strategy: One is to find and develop markets where there is little or no competition – blue oceans – and the other is to exploit and protect blue oceans. These challenges are very different from those to which strategists have devoted most of their attention.

Toward blue ocean strategy

What kind of strategic logic is needed to guide the creation of blue oceans? To answer that question, we looked back over 100 years of data on blue ocean creation to see what patterns could be discerned. Some

EXHIBIT 10.2.1 A SNAPSHOT OF BLUE OCEAN CREATION

Key blue ocean creations	Was the blue ocean created by a new entrant or an incumbent?	Was it driven by technology pioneering or value pioneering?*	At the time of the blue ocean creation, was the industry attractive or unattractive?
Automobiles			
Ford Model T Unveiled in 1908, the Model T was the first mass-produced car, priced so that many Americans could afford it.	New entrant	Value pioneering (mostly existing technologies)	Unattractive
GM's 'car for every purse and purpose' GM created a blue ocean in 1924 by injecting fun and fashion into the car.	Incumbent	Value pioneering (some new technologies)	Attractive
Japanese fuel-efficient autos Japanese automakers created a blue ocean in the mid-1970s with small, reliable lines of cars.	Incumbent	Value pioneering (some new technologies)	Unattractive
Chrysler minivan With its 1984 minivan, Chrysler created a new class of automobile that was as easy to use as a car but had the passenger space of a van.	Incumbent	Value pioneering (mostly existing technologies)	Unattractive
Computers			
CTR's tabulating machine In 1914, CTR created the business machine industry by simplifying, modularizing and leasing tabulating machines. CTR later changed its name to IBM.	Incumbent	Value pioneering (some new technologies)	Unattractive
IBM 650 electronic computer and System/360 In 1952, IBM created the business computer industry by simplifying and reducing the power and price of existing technology. And it exploded the blue ocean created by the 650 when in 1964 it unveiled the System/360, the first modularized computer system.	Incumbent	Value pioneering (650: mostly existing technologies) Value and technology pioneering (System/360: new and existing technologies)	Non-existent
Apple personal computer Although it was not the first home computer, the all-in-one, simple-to-use Apple II was a blue ocean creation when it appeared in 1978.	New entrant	Value pioneering (mostly existing technologies)	Unattractive
Compaq PC servers Compaq created a blue ocean in 1992 with its ProSignia server, which gave buyers twice the file and print capability of the minicomputer at one-third the price.	Incumbent	Value pioneering (mostly existing technologies)	Non-existent
Dell built to order computers In the mid-1990s, Dell created a blue ocean in a highly competitive industry by creating a new purchase and delivery experience for buyers.	New entrant	Value pioneering (mostly existing technologies)	Unattractive

	Key blue ocean creations	Was the blue ocean created by a new entrant or an incumbent?	Was it driven by technology pioneering or value pioneering?*	At the time of the blue ocean creation, was the industry attractive or unattractive?
Movie Theatres	**Nickelodeon** The first Nickelodeon opened its doors in 1905, showing short films around the clock to working class audiences for five cents.	New entrant	Value pioneering (mostly existing technologies)	Non-existent
	Palace theatres Created by Roxy Rothapfel in 1914, these theatres provided an opera-like environment for cinema viewing at an affordable price.	Incumbent	Value pioneering (mostly existing technologies)	Attractive
	AMC multiplex In the 1960s, the number of multiplexes in America's suburban shopping malls mushroomed. The multiplex gave viewers greater choice while reducing owners' costs.	Incumbent	Value pioneering (mostly existing technologies)	Unattractive
	AMC megaplex Megaplexes, introduced in 1995, offered every current blockbuster and provided spectacular viewing experiences in theatre complexes as big as stadiums, at a lower cost to theatre owners.	Incumbent	Value pioneering (mostly existing technologies)	Unattractive

*Driven by value pioneering does not mean that technologies were not involved. Rather, it means that the defining technologies used had largely been in existence, whether in that industry or elsewhere.

of our data are presented in Exhibit 10.2.1 'A Snapshot of Blue Ocean Creation'. It shows an overview of key blue ocean creations in three industries that closely touch people's lives: autos – how people get to work; computers – what people use at work; and movie theatres – where people go after work for enjoyment. We found that:

■ Blue oceans are not about technology innovation. Leading-edge technology is sometimes involved in the creation of blue oceans, but it is not a defining feature of them. This is often true even in industries that are technology intensive. As the exhibit reveals, across all three representative industries, blue oceans were seldom the result of technological innovation per se; the underlying technology was often already in existence. Even Ford's revolutionary assembly line can be traced to the meat-packing industry in America. Like those within the auto industry, the blue oceans within the computer

industry did not come about through technology innovations alone but by linking technology to what buyers valued. As with the IBM 650 and the Compaq PC server, this often involved simplifying the technology.

■ Incumbents often create blue oceans – and usually within their core businesses. GM, the Japanese automakers, and Chrysler were established players when they created blue oceans in the auto industry. So were CTR and its later incarnation, IBM, and Compaq in the computer industry. And in the cinema industry, the same can be said of Palace Theatres and AMC. Of the companies listed here, only Ford, Apple, Dell and Nickelodeon were new entrants in their industries; the first three were start-ups, and the fourth was an established player entering an industry that was new to it. This suggests that incumbents are not at a disadvantage in creating new market spaces. Moreover, the blue oceans made by incumbents were usually within their core businesses. In fact, as the exhibit shows, most blue oceans are created from within, not beyond, red oceans of existing industries. This challenges the view that new markets are in distant waters. Blue oceans are right next to you in every industry.

■ Company and industry are the wrong units of analysis. The traditional units of strategic analysis – company and industry – have little explanatory power when it comes to analysing how and why blue oceans are created. There is no consistently excellent company; the same company can be brilliant at one time and wrongheaded at another. Every company rises and falls over time. Likewise, there is no perpetually excellent industry; relative attractiveness is driven largely by the creation of blue oceans from within them. The most appropriate unit of analysis for explaining the creation of blue oceans is the strategic move – the set of managerial actions and decisions involved in making a major market-creating business offering. Compaq, for example, is considered by many people to be 'unsuccessful' because it was acquired by Hewlett-Packard in 2001 and ceased to be a company. But the firm's ultimate fate does not invalidate the smart strategic move Compaq made that led to the creation of the multibillion-dollar market in PC servers, a move that was a key cause of the company's powerful comeback in the 1990s.

■ Creating blue oceans builds brands. So powerful is blue ocean strategy that a blue ocean strategic move can create brand equity that lasts for decades. Almost all of the companies listed in the exhibit are remembered in no small part for the blue oceans they created long ago. Very few people alive today were around when the first Model T rolled off Henry Ford's assembly line in 1908, but the company's brand still benefits from that blue ocean move. IBM, too, is often regarded as an 'American institution' largely for the blue oceans it created in computing; the 360 series was its equivalent of the Model T.

Our findings are encouraging for executives at the large, established corporations that are traditionally seen as the victims of new market space creation. For what they reveal is that large R&D budgets are not the key to creating new market space. The key is making the right strategic moves. What's more, companies that understand what drives a good strategic move will be well placed to create multiple blue oceans over time, thereby continuing to deliver high growth and profits over a sustained period. The creation of blue oceans, in other words, is a product of strategy and as such is very much a product of managerial action.

The defining characteristics

Our research shows several common characteristics across strategic moves that create blue oceans. We found that the creators of blue oceans, in sharp contrast to companies playing by traditional rules, never use the competition as a benchmark. Instead they make it irrelevant by creating a leap in value for both buyers and the company itself. (Exhibit 10.2.2 compares the chief characteristics of these two strategy models.)

Perhaps the most important feature of blue ocean strategy is that it rejects the fundamental tenet of conventional strategy: that a trade-off exists between value

---

EXHIBIT 10.2.2 RED OCEAN VERSUS BLUE OCEAN STRATEGY

Red ocean strategy	*Blue ocean strategy*
■ Compete in existing market space.	■ Create uncontested market space.
■ Beat the competition.	■ Make the competition irrelevant.
■ Exploit existing demand.	■ Create and capture new demand.
■ Make the value/cost trade-off.	■ Break the value/cost trade-off.
■ Align the whole system of a company's activities with its strategic choice of differentiation or low cost.	■ Align the whole system of a company's activities in pursuit of differentiation and low cost.

and cost. According to this thesis, companies can either create greater value for customers at a higher cost or create reasonable value at a lower cost. In other words, strategy is essentially a choice between differentiation and low cost. But when it comes to creating blue oceans, the evidence shows that successful companies pursue differentiation and low cost simultaneously.

To see how this is done, let us go back to Cirque du Soleil. At the time of Cirque's debut, circuses focused on benchmarking one another and maximizing their shares of shrinking demand by tweaking traditional circus acts. This included trying to secure more and better-known clowns and lion tamers, efforts that raised circuses' cost structure without substantially altering the circus experience. The result was rising costs without rising revenues and a downward spiral in overall circus demand. Enter Cirque. Instead of following the conventional logic of outpacing the competition by offering a better solution to the given problem – creating a circus with even greater fun and thrills – it redefined the problem itself by offering people the fun and thrill of the circus *and* the intellectual sophistication and artistic richness of the theatre.

In designing performances that landed both these punches, Cirque had to re-evaluate the components of the traditional circus offering. What the company found was that many of the elements considered essential to the fun and thrill of the circus were unnecessary and in many cases costly. For instance, most circuses offer animal acts. These are a heavy economic burden, because circuses have to shell out not only for the animals but also for their training, medical care, housing, insurance and transportation. Yet Cirque found that the appetite for animal shows was rapidly diminishing because of rising public concern about the treatment of circus animals and the ethics of exhibiting them.

Similarly, although traditional circuses promoted their performers as stars, Cirque realized that the public no longer thought of circus artists as stars, at least not in the movie star sense. Cirque did away with traditional three-ring shows, too. Not only did these create confusion among spectators forced to switch their attention from one ring to another, they also increased the number of performers needed, with obvious cost implications. And while aisle concession sales appeared to be a good way to generate revenue, the high prices discouraged parents from making purchases and made them feel they were being taken for a ride.

Cirque found that the lasting allure of the traditional circus came down to just three factors: the clowns, the tent and the classic acrobatic acts. So Cirque kept the clowns, while shifting their humour away from slapstick to a more enchanting, sophisticated style. It glamourized the tent, which many circuses had abandoned in favour of rented venues. Realizing that the tent, more than anything else, captured the magic of the circus, Cirque designed this classic symbol with a glorious external finish and a high level of audience comfort. Gone were the sawdust and hard benches. Acrobats and other thrilling performers were retained, but Cirque reduced their roles and made their acts more elegant by adding artistic flair.

Even as Cirque stripped away some of the traditional circus offerings, it injected new elements drawn from the world of theatre. For instance, unlike traditional circuses featuring a series of unrelated acts, each Cirque creation resembles a theatre performance in that it has a theme and story line. Although the themes are intentionally vague, they bring harmony and an intellectual element to the acts. Cirque also borrows ideas from Broadway. For example, rather than putting on the traditional 'once and for all' show, Cirque mounts multiple productions based on different themes and story lines. As with Broadway productions, too, each Cirque show has an original musical score, which drives the performance, lighting and timing of the acts, rather than the other way around. The productions feature abstract and spiritual dance, an idea derived from theatre and ballet. By introducing these factors, Cirque has created highly sophisticated entertainments. And by staging multiple productions, Cirque gives people reason to come to the circus more often, thereby increasing revenues.

Cirque offers the best of both circus and theatre. And by eliminating many of the most expensive elements of the circus, it has been able to dramatically reduce its cost structure, achieving both differentiation and low cost.

By driving down costs while simultaneously driving up value for buyers, a company can achieve a leap in value for both itself and its customers. Since buyer value comes from the utility and price a company offers, and a company generates value for itself through cost structure and price, blue ocean strategy is achieved only when the whole system of a company's utility, price and cost activities is properly aligned. It is this whole-system approach that makes the creation of blue oceans a sustainable strategy. Blue ocean strategy integrates the range of a firm's functional and operational activities.

A rejection of the trade-off between low cost and differentiation implies a fundamental change in strategic mindset – we cannot emphasize enough how fundamental a shift it is. The red ocean assumption that industry structural conditions are a given and firms are forced to compete within them is based on an intellectual worldview that academics call the *structuralist* view, or *environmental determinism*. According to this view, companies and managers are largely at the mercy of economic forces greater than themselves. Blue ocean strategies, by contrast, are based on a worldview in which market boundaries and industries can be reconstructed by the actions and beliefs of industry players. We call this the *reconstructionist* view.

The founders of Cirque du Soleil clearly did not feel constrained to act within the confines of their industry. Indeed, is Cirque really a circus with all that it has eliminated, reduced, raised and created? Or is it theatre? If it is theatre, then what genre – Broadway show, opera, ballet? The magic of Cirque was created through a reconstruction of elements drawn from all of these alternatives. In the end, Cirque is none of them and a little of all of them. From within the red oceans of theatre and circus, Cirque has created a blue ocean of uncontested market space that has, as yet, no name.

Barriers to imitation

Companies that create blue oceans usually reap the benefits without credible challenges for 10 to 15 years, as was the case with Cirque du Soleil, Home Depot, Federal Express, Southwest Airlines and CNN, to name just a few. The reason is that blue ocean strategy creates considerable economic and cognitive barriers to imitation.

For a start, adopting a blue ocean creator's business model is easier to imagine than to do. Because blue ocean creators immediately attract customers in large volumes, they are able to generate scale economies very rapidly, putting would-be imitators at an immediate and continuing cost disadvantage. The huge economies of scale in purchasing that Wal-Mart enjoys, for example, have significantly discouraged other companies from imitating its business model. The immediate attraction of large numbers of customers can also create network externalities. The more customers eBay has online, the more attractive the auction site becomes for both sellers and buyers of wares, giving users few incentives to go elsewhere.

When imitation requires companies to make changes to their whole system of activities, organizational politics may impede a would-be competitor's ability to switch to the divergent business model of a blue ocean strategy. For instance, airlines trying to follow Southwest's example of offering the speed of air travel with the flexibility and cost of driving would have faced major revisions in routing, training, marketing and pricing, not to mention culture. Few established airlines had the flexibility to make such extensive organizational and operating changes overnight. Imitating a whole-system approach is not an easy feat.

The cognitive barriers can be just as effective. When a company offers a leap in value, it rapidly earns brand buzz and a loyal following in the marketplace. Experience shows that even the most expensive marketing campaigns struggle to unseat a blue ocean creator. Microsoft, for example, has been trying for more than ten years to occupy the centre of the blue ocean that Intuit created with its financial software product Quicken. Despite all of its efforts and all of its investment, Microsoft has not been able to unseat Intuit as the industry leader.

In other situations, attempts to imitate a blue ocean creator conflict with the imitator's existing brand image. The Body Shop, for example, shuns top models and makes no promises of eternal youth and beauty. For the established cosmetic brands like Estée Lauder and L'Oréal, imitation was very difficult, because it would have signalled a complete invalidation of their current images, which are based on promises of eternal youth and beauty.

A consistent pattern

While our conceptual articulation of the pattern may be new, blue ocean strategy has always existed, whether or not companies have been conscious of the fact. Just consider the striking parallels between the Cirque du Soleil theatre-circus experience and Ford's creation of the Model T.

At the end of the nineteenth century, the automobile industry was small and unattractive. More than 500 automakers in America competed in turning out handmade luxury cars that cost around $1,500 and were enormously *un*popular with all but the very rich. Anti-car activists tore up roads, ringed parked cars with barbed wire and organized boycotts of car-driving businessmen and politicians. Woodrow Wilson caught the spirit of the times when he said in 1906 that 'nothing has spread socialistic feeling more than the automobile'. He called it 'a picture of the arrogance of wealth'.

Instead of trying to beat the competition and steal a share of existing demand from other automakers, Ford reconstructed the industry boundaries of cars and horse-drawn carriages to create a blue ocean. At the time, horse-drawn carriages were the primary means of local transportation across America. The carriage had two distinct advantages over cars. Horses could easily negotiate the bumps and mud that stymied cars – especially in rain and snow – on the nation's ubiquitous dirt roads. And horses and carriages were much easier to maintain than the luxurious autos of the time, which frequently broke down, requiring expert repairmen who were expensive and in short supply. It was Henry Ford's understanding of these advantages that showed him how he could break away from the competition and unlock enormous untapped demand.

Ford called the Model T the car 'for the great multitude, constructed of the best materials'. Like Cirque, the Ford Motor Company made the competition irrelevant. Instead of creating fashionable, customized cars for weekends in the countryside, a luxury few could justify, Ford built a car that, like the horse-drawn carriage, was for everyday use. The Model T came in just one colour, black, and there were few optional extras. It was reliable and durable, designed to travel effortlessly over dirt roads in rain, snow, or sunshine. It was easy to use and fix. People could learn to drive it in a day. And like Cirque, Ford went outside the industry for a price point, looking at horse-drawn carriages ($400), not other autos. In 1908, the first Model T cost $850; in 1909, the price dropped to $609, and by

1924 it was down to $290. In this way, Ford converted buyers of horse-drawn carriages into car buyers – just as Cirque turned theatregoers into circusgoers. Sales of the Model T boomed. Ford's market share surged from 9 per cent in 1908 to 61 per cent in 1921, and by 1923, a majority of American households had a car.

Even as Ford offered the mass of buyers a leap in value, the company also achieved the lowest cost structure in the industry, much as Cirque did later. By keeping the cars highly standardized with limited options and interchangeable parts, Ford was able to scrap the prevailing manufacturing system in which cars were constructed by skilled craftsmen who swarmed around one workstation and built a car piece by piece from start to finish. Ford's revolutionary assembly line replaced craftsmen with unskilled labourers, each of whom worked quickly and efficiently on one small task. This allowed Ford to make a car in just four days – 21 days was the industry norm – creating huge cost savings.

Blue and red oceans have always co-existed and always will. Practical reality, therefore, demands that companies understand the strategic logic of both types of oceans. At present, competing in red oceans dominates the field of strategy in theory and in practice, even as businesses' need to create blue oceans intensifies. It is time to even the scales in the field of strategy with a better balance of efforts across both oceans. For although blue ocean strategists have always existed, for the most part their strategies have been largely unconscious. But once corporations realize that the strategies for creating and capturing blue oceans have a different underlying logic from red ocean strategies, they will be able to create many more blue oceans in the future.

READING 10.3
Living on the fault line
By Geoffrey Moore[1]

The technology adoption life cycle models the response of any given population to the offer of a discontinuous innovation, one that forces the abandonment of traditional infrastructure and systems for the promise of a heretofore unavailable set of benefits.

It represents this response as a bell curve, separating out five subpopulations, as illustrated in Figure 10.3.1.

The bell curve represents the total population of people exposed to a new technology offer. The various segments of the curve represent the percentage of

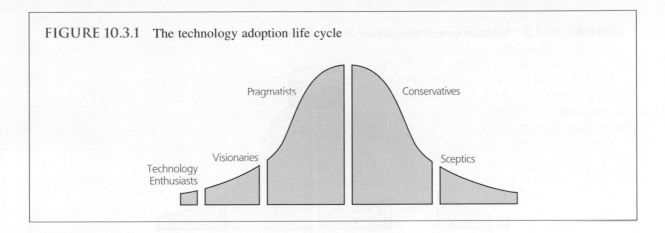

FIGURE 10.3.1   The technology adoption life cycle

people predicted to adopt one or another of the five different strategies for determining when and why to switch allegiance from the old to the new. The five strategies unfold sequentially as follows:

1 The *technology enthusiast strategy* is to adopt the new technology upon its first appearance, in large part just to explore its properties to determine if it is 'cool'. The actual benefits provided may not even be of interest to this constituency, but the mechanism by which they are provided is of great interest. If they are entertained by the mechanism, they often adopt the product just to be able to show it off.

2 The *visionary strategy* is to adopt the new technology as a means for capturing a dramatic advantage over competitors who do not adopt it. The goal here is to be first to deploy an advantaged system and use that head start to leapfrog over the competition, establishing a position so far out in front that the sector realigns around its new leader. Visionaries are mavericks who want to break away from the herd and differentiate themselves dramatically.

3 The *pragmatist strategy* is directly opposed to the visionary. It wants to stay with the herd, adopting the new technology if and only if everyone else does as well. The goal here is to use the wisdom of the marketplace to sort out what's valuable and then to be a fast follower once the new direction has clearly emerged. Pragmatists consult each other frequently about who's adopting what in an effort to stay current but do not commit to any major change without seeing successful implementations elsewhere first.

4 The *conservative strategy* is to stick with the old technology for as long as possible (a) because it works, (b) because it is familiar, and (c) because it is paid for. By putting off the transition to the new

platform, conservatives conserve cash and avoid hitting the learning curve, making themselves more productive in the short run. Long term, when they do switch, the system is more completely debugged, and that works to their advantage as well. The downside of the strategy is that they grow increasingly out of touch for the period they don't adopt and can, if they wait too long, get isolated in old technology that simply will not map to the new world.

5 Finally, the *sceptic strategy* is to debunk the entire technology as a false start and refuse to adopt it at all. This is a winning tactic for those technologies that never do gain mainstream market acceptance. For those that do, however, it creates extreme versions of the isolation problems conservatives face.

Each of these strategies has validity in its own right, and a single individual is perfectly capable of choosing different strategies for different offers. But for any given technology, the market will develop in a characteristic pattern due to the aggregate effects of a population distributing its choices in the proportions outlined by the bell curve. The resulting market development model is shown in Figure 10.3.2.

The model segments the evolution of a technology-based market as follows:

- The first phase, or *early market,* is a time when early adopters (technology enthusiasts and visionaries) take up the innovation while the pragmatic majority holds back. The market development goal at this stage is to gain a few prestigious flagship customers who help publicize the technology and celebrate its potential benefits.

- The early market is followed by a *chasm,* a period of no adoption, when the early adopters have already made their choices, but the pragmatist majority is

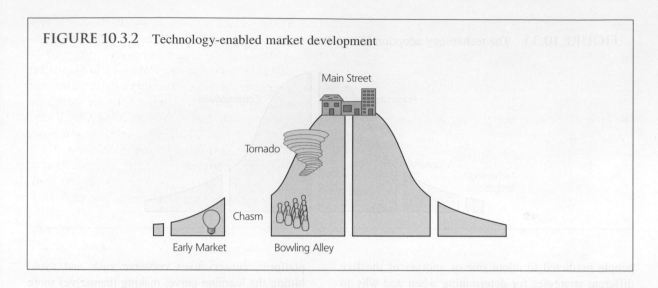

FIGURE 10.3.2 Technology-enabled market development

still holding back. The barrier to further progress is that pragmatists are looking to other pragmatists to be references, but no one wants to go first. The market development goal at this stage is to target an initial beachhead segment of pragmatists who can lead the second wave of adoption.

■ In the development of most technology-enabled markets, specific niches of pragmatic customers adopt the new technology before the general pragmatist population. We call this period the *bowling alley* because the market development goal is to use the first group of adopters as references to help win over the next group, and the next, and so on. Typically the 'head bowling pin' is a niche of pragmatists who have a major business problem that cannot be solved with current technology but that does respond to a solution built around the new innovation. These are the *department managers in charge of a broken, mission-critical process*. Once this first group starts to move it takes much less of a motive to overcome the inertia of the next group.

■ As pragmatist adoption builds in niches, one of two futures emerges. In one, adoption continues to remain localized to niche markets, creating a pattern we call 'bowling alley forever'. In this pattern, each niche's solution is relatively complex and differentiated from every other niche's. As a result, no mass market emerges, and the market development goal is simply to expand existing niches and create new ones as the opportunity arises. In the other pattern, a 'killer app' emerges – a single application of the innovative technology that provides a compelling benefit that can be standardized across

multiple niches. The killer app transforms niche adoption into mass adoption, creating an enormous uptick in demand for the new technology across a wide range of sectors. We call this period the *tornado* because the onrush of mass demand is so swift it creates a vortex that sucks the supply out of the market and puts the category into hypergrowth for a number of years. The market development goal here is to win as much market share as possible during a period when the entire market is choosing its supplier for the new class of technology-enabled offering.

■ Once the supply side of the market finally catches up with the backlog of demand, the tornado phase subsides and the market reaches a state we call *Main Street*. The new technology has been broadly deployed and, with the support of conservatives, now settles down to a (hopefully) long engagement as the incumbent technology. The market development goal here is to continuously improve the value of the offering, decreasing its base costs and recouping margins by increasing the number of value-adding extensions that can supplement it. The ultimate extension in many cases is to convert the offering from a product sale to a services subscription, allowing the customer to gain the benefit of the product without having to take on the responsibility for maintaining it.

It is important to note that the end of the technology adoption life cycle does not represent the end of technology's productive market life. The category of offering can be sustained indefinitely on Main Street, coming to an end only when the next discontinuous innovation renders the prior technology obsolete. Indeed, despite all the emphasis on shortening life cycles, Main Street markets normally last for decades after complete absorption of the enabling technology – witness the car, the telephone, the television, the personal computer and the cell phone. Importantly, however, the marketplace pecking order set by market share that emerges during the bowling alley and tornado phases tends to persist for the life of Main Street. That is, while Main Street represents the final and lasting distribution of competitive advantage, its boundaries get set prior to arrival. Thus success in every prior stage in the life cycle is key to building sustainable Main Street market success.

Stage-one adoption: The early market

The early market begins with the ambitions of two constituencies who live at opposite ends of the value chain (see Figure 10.3.3). On the left is the *technology provider*, the supplier of the discontinuous innovation, with ambitions of constructing an entirely new marketplace based on a new platform. On the right are one or more visionary executives, in the role of *economic buyer*, who also have ambitions of their own. They want to re-architect the marketplaces they participate in to install their company as the new market leader – and they want to do it fast. They see in the new technology an opportunity to disrupt the established order and insert themselves into the lead.

Between these two poles, however, there is at present no existing value chain that can link their ambitions. Indeed, the existing value chain is appalled by them. There is, however, one institution in the market that can bridge the gulf between the two, can transform the technology provider's magic into the economic buyer's dream, and that is the *consulting firm*. Rather than try to incubate a value chain in the marketplace, this consultancy will instead create a temporary value chain to serve a single project's specific needs. That is, they will pull together the products, the applications, the sales and support, the customer service, and in extreme cases even substitute their own people for the customer's technical buyer (and even for the customer's end users), all to make the value chain work *in a single instance for a single customer*.

Needless to say, this is an expensive proposition. But if it pays off, if the sponsoring company really does leapfrog over its competition in a new market order, then the visionary becomes a hero, and whatever money was spent was pocket change by comparison to the appreciation in the customer company's stock price.

Competitive advantage in the early market

The primary competitive advantage strategy for the early market consists of being first to catch the new technology wave. This is often called *first-mover advantage*. Amazon.com, by catching the Web retail wave first, has created a powerful brand that its competitors cannot hope to replicate, regardless of how

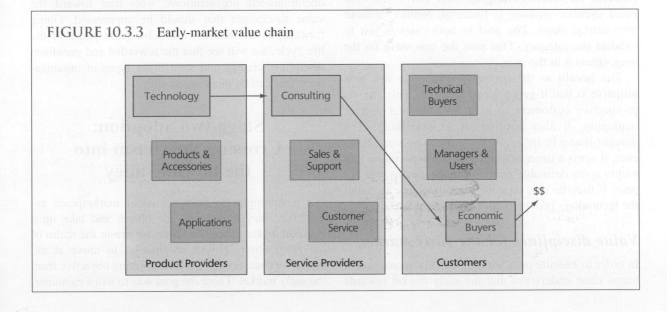

FIGURE 10.3.3   Early-market value chain

much they spend. By being first to introduce auctions onto the Web, eBay gained first-mover advantage also, so that even when assaulted by an alliance of extremely powerful companies – Microsoft, Dell, Lycos, Excite – it has been able to sustain market share. Four years into Web advertising, the top ten sites, with Yahoo! leading the list, garner as much as 85 per cent of the total spending – largely because of first-mover advantage. The Sabre system for airline and other travel-related reservations has had a similar track record, even as Apollo and Galileo and others have entered the market. Same with United Airlines' and American Airlines' frequent-flyer systems.

In every case, first-mover advantage equates to getting the market started around your unique approach and making the others play catch-up. It is a great strategy – when it works. The risk, of course, is that the market never goes forward to adopt the paradigm. At the time when the visionaries make their moves, this is a high probability. Visionaries are always bucking the odds in that most markets, like most mutations, die out before they can reproduce themselves sufficiently to gain persistence. Indeed, market creation is very much like the origin of species in nature, with the early market equating to the emergence of at least a few vital representatives of the new order.

The key metric of competitive advantage at this stage is simply the existence of proof of having one or more such representatives. For the technology provider, the test is one or more major corporate commitments from prestigious customers who champion the new paradigm as a platform for change in their industries. For the customer, the test is whether on top of this new platform an industry-changing offer can be promulgated. Neither measure is financial. Neither measure uses market share. The goal in both cases is just to validate the category. That puts the new wave on the map, enters it in the race.

The benefit to the company sponsoring this new initiative is that it gets a lot of attention. This attracts prospective customers to it at no additional cost of marketing. It also positions it as something of a thought leader in its industry. At the same time, however, it starts a timer ticking, with the expectation that within some definable period dramatic results will appear. If they do not, then the customers lose face and the technology providers lose their company.

Value disciplines for the early market

In order to execute on a winning agenda, management teams must understand that the early market rewards discontinuous innovation and product leadership and penalizes customer intimacy and operational excellence. Thus optimal results are gained by elevating the former and suppressing the latter, as follows:

- Elevate discontinuous innovation and product leadership. The early market is driven by the demands of visionaries for offerings that create dramatic competitive advantages of the sort that would allow them to leapfrog over the other players in their industry. Only discontinuous innovation offers such advantage. In order to field that innovation, however, it must be transformed into a product offering that can be put to work in the real world. Hence the need for product leadership.

- Suppress customer intimacy and operational excellence. When technologies are this new, there are no target markets as yet and thus customer intimacy is not practical. Moreover, discontinuous innovations demand enormous customer tolerance and sacrifice as they get debugged, again not a time for celebrating putting the customer first. At the same time, because everything is so new and so much is yet to be discovered, it is equally impractical to target operational excellence. There is just too much new product, process and procedure to invent and then shake out before pursuing this value discipline would be reasonable. Instead, one has to make peace with the strategy 'Go ugly early.'

Looking at the above, it is not surprising that engineering-led organizations, who resonate with the value disciplines in favour, are much more successful at early-market initiatives than marketing-led or operations-led organizations, who lean toward the value disciplines that should be suppressed. Going forward, as we look at each subsequent phase of the life cycle, we will see that the rewarded and penalized disciplines change and so will the types of organizations that can be most successful.

Stage-two adoption: Crossing the chasm into the bowling alley

For technologies to gain persistent marketplace acceptance, they must cross the chasm and take up a position on the other side. Now we are in the realm of the pragmatists. To get pragmatists to move at all, companies must rethink their marketing objective from the early market. There the goal was to win a customer, and then another and another. To cross the chasm, however, you have to *win a herd*. Here's why:

- Pragmatists only feel comfortable moving in herds. That's why they ask for references and use word of mouth as their primary source of advice on technology purchase decisions. Selling individual pragmatists on acting ahead of the herd is possible but very painful, and the cost of sales more than eats up the margin in the sale itself.
- Pragmatists evaluate the entire value chain, not just the specific product offer, when buying into a new technology. Value chains form around herds, not individual customers. There has to be enough repeatable business in the pipeline to reward an investment in specializing in the new technology. Sporadic deals, regardless of how big they are, do not create persistent value chains.

The visible metric for crossing the chasm, therefore, is to *make a market* and *create a value chain* where there were no market and no value chain before. This is a difficult undertaking. To increase its chances for success, and to decrease the time it takes to achieve, it is best to focus the effort on creating a niche market first before trying to create a mass market. It is simply prudent to minimize the number of variables at risk.

Think of a niche market as a self-contained system of commerce with its own local set of specialized needs and wants. Isolated from the mainstream market, which does not serve these special needs, it offers a *value-chain incubator* for emerging technology-enabled markets. That is, its isolation protects the fragile new chain from direct competitive attacks from the incumbent value chain. The customer community, in effect, nurtures the fledgling enterprise because it hopes to gain great benefit from it.

Value-chain strategy

To visualize the changes in moving from the early market to the bowling alley, let us return to our value-chain diagram, this time focusing on a new set of market makers (see Figure 10.3.4).

At the right-hand end of the chain, the *managers* in the customer domain represent the pre-assembled herd, an aggregation of relatively homogeneous demand. These are the department managers in charge of a broken, mission-critical process, all huddled in a mass. At the other end, the *application provider* in the product domain offers a relatively homogeneous solution to this herd's problem. It will bring its solution to market through a sales and support organization where it is the *support function* that really counts. That is because at the outset of a market the remaining value-chain partners are just getting recruited and cannot be relied upon to assemble the whole product correctly on their own. Later on these same partners will compete to take over the support function – and the enlightened application provider will let them, as it will greatly expand its market and its reach – but for now it is all just too new. So the application provider's support team must take the lead in working through all the glitches until a working whole product is in place, even

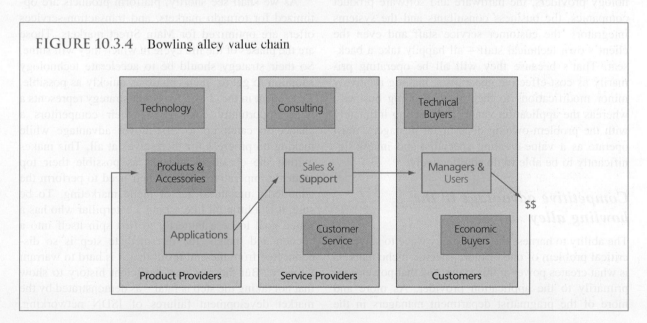

FIGURE 10.3.4   Bowling alley value chain

when the problem is with someone else's part of the offering and not their own.

Note that the money-recycling arrow has now been restored to the diagram. This is the whole point of the niche-market strategy. We are now creating for the first time a self-funding persistent market where the economic gains of the customer lead to increasing and ongoing investment in the products and services that bring them about. Even if no other market ever adopts this technology, it will still be economically viable to maintain this niche. To be sure, the returns will not be all that the investors hoped for, but it will not be a total bust either. That is because niche markets have persistent competitive advantages that allow them to sustain themselves even when the marketplace in general is unsupportive of their efforts. Moreover, if the value chain extends its reach into additional niches, then it can add market growth to its already attractive price margins to produce highly attractive returns indeed.

The major beneficiaries of this strategy are the application providers. It is they who harness the new wave of technology to the specific needs of the target segment, and they who rally the rest of the value chain to support this effort. Because the application provider is the company that really does 'make the market', it gains a dominant market-specific competitive advantage during this market formation period. This advantage will persist indefinitely, even after the technology adoption life cycle goes forward, since once any market falls into a particular pecking order, it is loath to change.

Everyone else in the value chain – the core technology providers, the hardware and software product companies, the business consultants and the systems integrators, the customer service staff and even the client's own technical staff – all happily take a backseat. That's because they will all be operating primarily as cost-effective generalists, making relatively minor modifications to their way of doing business, whereas the application vendor, interacting intimately with the problem-owning department managers, must operate as a value-creating specialist and invest significantly to be able to do so effectively.

Competitive advantage in the bowling alley

The ability to harness the technology wave to solve the critical problem of one or more specific niche markets is what creates power at this stage, and that power goes primarily to the application provider. As more and more of the pragmatist department managers in the niches see their colleagues getting out of the soup, they, too, will come forward and insist on buying this vendor's application. Thus every other company in the value chain becomes dependent on that one vendor's good graces to get into the good deals. In effect, this creates a form of value-chain domination, but it is restricted solely to the niches served, and so it has very different properties – and a very different valuation – from the kind of broad horizontal-market domination we will see develop inside the tornado.

Because they reap the bulk of the rewards, it is relatively easy for application providers to understand and adopt niche marketing, especially if the alternative is to spend another year in the chasm. It is much more problematic, however, for a platform product or a transaction services company to embrace it. Their business plans are normally predicated on either broad horizontal adoption across a multitude of business segments or a broad cross-section of consumers. They are not well positioned to go after niche markets. Vertical industry domain expertise holds little value for them, and voluntarily subordinating themselves to an application vendor just to gain entry into one little niche seems like a huge price to pay. Moreover, even if the tactic proves successful, the resulting order stream will be relatively modest, and worse, may inappropriately cause the rest of the market to misperceive the company as a niche player. For all these very good reasons, platform-products and transaction services vendors tend to shy away from taking the niche approach to crossing the chasm. And yet it is still a mistake. Here's why.

As we shall see shortly, platform products are optimized for tornado markets, and transaction-services offers are optimized for Main Street markets. Those are the phases of the life cycle in which they will shine. So their strategy should be to accelerate technology adoption to get to 'their' phase as quickly as possible. Time spent in the chasm for either strategy represents a huge opportunity cost, giving their competitors a chance to catch up to first-mover advantage while making no progress for themselves at all. This makes exiting the chasm as quickly as possible their top strategic imperative – hence their need to perform the admittedly unnatural act of niche marketing. To be sure, it is a little bit like asking a caterpillar who has a stated goal to be a butterfly to first spin itself into a cocoon and melt – the intermediate step is so disconnected from the end result that it is hard to warrant taking it. But there is now sufficient history to show that not taking the step is fatal – as demonstrated by the market development failures of ISDN networking, object-oriented databases, IBM's OS/2 operating system, pen-based PCs, infrared connectivity protocols and artificial intelligence.

To be sure, once an initial niche market is established, the winning strategy for platform products and transaction services does indeed split off from the application providers. For the latter, the most powerful path forward is to stay in the bowling alley – this is their sweet spot – expanding niche to niche, following a bowling pin strategy. In this manner, such companies can chew their way through multiple markets with a very high probability of securing dominant positions in the majority of their niches. It is a 'bowling alley forever' strategy focused on *preserving complexity* in order to create a source of profit margins for themselves and their service partners. It ends up trading off massive scale in favour of locally dominant roles and eventually makes the transition to Main Street as a leader in a set of mature vertical markets.

By contrast, for platform-product and transaction-services companies, the goal should be to get beyond niches altogether as soon as possible. Their quest instead should be for a single, general-purpose 'killer app' – a word-processing programme, a spreadsheet, e-mail, voice-mail, a Web site, an e-commerce server – something that can be adopted by whole sectors of the economy all at once, thereby leveraging their horizontal business models' strength in being able to scale rapidly. But students of the life cycle should note that in the era prior to pervasive word processing, there were segment-specific solutions for lawyers, doctors, consultants and governmental functions. These were a critical stepping stone toward getting to a mass market.

Value disciplines for the bowling alley

To execute on a niche strategy in an emerging technology-enabled market, companies must realign their value discipline orientation to meet a new set of market priorities, as follows:

- Elevate product leadership and customer intimacy. The bowling alley is driven by the demands of pragmatists for a whole product that will fix a broken mission-critical business process. The fact that the process will not respond to conventional treatment calls out the need for product leadership. The fact that the required whole product will have to integrate elements specific to a particular vertical segment calls out the need for customer intimacy.
- Suppress discontinuous innovation and operational excellence. Pragmatist department managers under

pressure to fix a broken process have neither the time nor the resources to support debugging a discontinuous innovation. At the same time, their need for special attention is incompatible with the kind of standardization needed for operational excellence.

Marketing-led organizations are best at crossing the chasm, specifically those that combine strong domain expertise in the targeted market segment with a solutions orientation. Operations-led organizations struggle with the amount of customization required that cannot be amortized across other segments, all of which offends their sense of efficiency. Engineering-led organizations struggle with the lack of product symmetry resulting from heavily privileging one niche's set of issues over a whole raft of other needed enhancements.

To win with this strategy, the critical success factor is focus – specifically, focus on doing whatever it takes to get that first herd of pragmatist customers to adopt en masse the new technology. Hedging one's bet by sponsoring forays targeted at additional herds at the same time is bad strategy. Both engineering- and operations-oriented organizations, however, are drawn to this approach because they fear that the company is putting all its eggs into one basket. Of course, that is precisely what it *is* doing. The reason it is good strategy to do so is that only by creating critical mass can one move a market and bring into existence a new value chain. Unless they can leverage tornado winds blowing in other markets, alternative initiatives subtract from the needed mass and, ironically, increase rather than decrease market risk.

Stage-three adoption: inside the tornado

A tornado occurs whenever pragmatists across a variety of market sectors all decide simultaneously that it is time to adopt a new paradigm – in other words, when the pragmatist herd stampedes. This creates a dramatic spike in demand, vastly exceeding the currently available supply, calling entire categories of vendors to reconfigure their offerings to meet the needs of a new value chain.

Value-chain strategy

The overriding market force that is shaping the tornado value chain is the desire for everyone in the market, beginning with the customer but quickly passing through to all vendors, to drive the transition to a new paradigm as quickly as possible. That calls to the fore

FIGURE 10.3.5   Tornado value chain

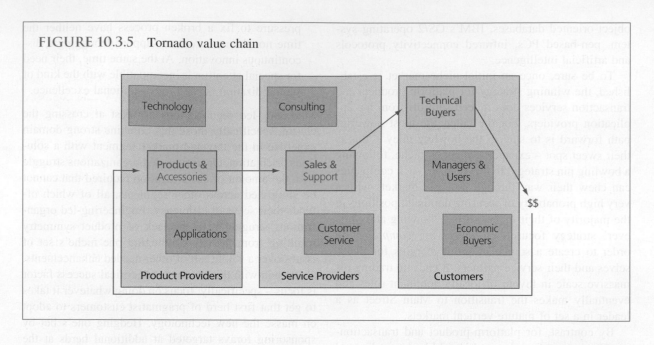

the three constituencies highlighted in Figure 10.3.5. Each of these constituencies is well positioned to benefit from standardization for rapid deployment.

- In the product sphere, it is *products,* not technology and not applications, that get the privileged position. The problem with technology is that it is too malleable to be mass-produced and thus does not lend itself to rapid proliferation of common, standard infrastructure. The problem with applications is that they must be customized to sector-specific processes, and so again they do not deploy as rapidly as desired. By contrast, products, and specifically those that serve as platforms for a broad range of applications, are the ideal engine for paradigm proliferation.

- Now, to be sure, there must be at least one application that warrants the purchase of the platform in the first place, but in a tornado that application must be essentially the same for every sector. Such an application is called 'the killer app', and it becomes the focus for horizontal expansion across multiple sectors of the economy. *Accounting* was the killer app for mainframes, *manufacturing automation* for minicomputers, *word processing* for PCs, *computer-aided design* for workstations and *electronic mail* for local area networks. But in every case, it was the platform product providers, not the killer app vendors, who were ultimately the big tornado winners because as other applications came online, they created still more demand for their platforms.

- In the services sphere, it is the sales and support function, with the emphasis on *sales,* that carries the day. The drawback with consulting is that its projects are too complex, take too long and require resources that are too scarce to ever permit a tornado to go forward. The drawback with customer service is that it is too focused on serving existing customers at a time when the overwhelming emphasis has to be on acquiring new customers.

- Generating sales in the tornado is not a problem of winning over the customer so much as it is of beating the competition. It is critical, therefore, to field the most competitive sales force you can at this time. Because so much wealth is changing hands, and because the long-term consequences of market share are so great, tornado sales tactics are brutal and sales aggressiveness is the core discipline. This is the time when nice guys do finish last.

- On the support side, the key issue is to get new customers up and running on a minimal system as quickly as possible and then move on to the next new customer. The more cookie-cutter the process, the faster it replicates and the more new customers you can absorb. The push is for operational excellence, not customer intimacy. This is not a normal support profile, so once again focusing the team on the right value discipline is a critical executive responsibility.

- On the customer side of the value chain, it is the *technical buyer,* not the end-user departments and not the economic buyer, who becomes the key focus. The problem with end users is that they inevitably seek customization to meet their department-specific needs. Not only is such complexity contrary to the vendor's wishes, it also works against the host institution's imperative to roll out the new infrastructure to everyone in the company as quickly as possible. Such rapid deployment requires a one-size-fits-all approach for the initial rollout, something that the technical buyer understands far better than the end user. It is also not the time to court senior executives in their role as economic buyers. Once the tornado is under way, they sense the need to get over to the new infrastructure and delegate the task, including the selection process, to their technical staff.

- When technical buyers become the target customer, their compelling reason to buy drives sales outcomes. High on their list is conformance to common standards, followed by market leadership status, which initially is signalled by partnerships with other market leaders, and later on confirmed by market share. The technical buyers' biggest challenge is systems integration, and this is where the support function can contribute to faster roll-outs by building standard interfaces to the most prevalent legacy systems.

The tornado, in essence, is one big land grab – a fierce struggle to capture as many new customers as possible during the pragmatist stampede to the new paradigm. Increasing shareholder value revolves entirely around maximizing market share, and to that end there are three sources of competitive-advantage leverage to exploit.

Competitive advantage in the tornado

The primary source of competitive advantage is simply to be riding the new technology wave as it enters into its tornado phase. Mass-market adoption is an awesome market creation force that wreaks havoc on installed bases rooted in old technology. As the incumbents retreat under the impact of this force to protect their increasingly conservative installed bases, your company advances with the new wave of adoption to occupy their lost ground. This is *category advantage* at work, and it alone will enhance your stock price – hence the scramble of every vendor in the sector to position themselves on the bandwagon of whatever this hot new category is.

The second element of competitive advantage derives from the potential institutionalization of key

market-making companies as value-chain leaders or dominators. That is, for each element in the value chain, tornado markets seek out a single market-leading provider to set the de facto standards for that component. That role normally goes to the company that garners the most new customers early in the race. In addition, when a single company can gain power over the rest of the value chain, typically by leveraging the power to withhold its proprietary technology and thereby stymie the entire offer, the market accords even more privilege to it.

The power of market-share leadership is rooted in the pragmatist preference to make the safe buy by going with the market leader. That is, rather than rely on their own judgement, pragmatists prefer to rely on the group's. Once that judgement has been made clear, once one vendor has emerged as the favourite, then pragmatists naturally gravitate to that choice, which of course further increases that company's market share, intensifying its gravitational attraction.

This cycle of positive feedback not only spontaneously generates market leaders, but once they are generated, works to keep them in place. That is, the value chain advantage a market leader gains over its direct competitors is that it has become the default choice for any other company in the chain to round out its offers. Thus the company gains sales that it never initiated and gets invited into deals its competitors never see. Such sales not only add to revenues but to margins, since the absence of competition removes much of the pressure to discount price. In short, winning the market-share prize is a very sweet deal, which, if it is not working for you, is working against you. Hence the need to focus all guns on market share.

Thus the essence of tornado strategy is simply to capture the maximum number of customers in the minimum amount of time and to minimize all other efforts. At each moment the winning strategy is to strike and move on, strike and move on. Anything you can do to slow down a competitor along the way is gravy. What you must not do is voluntarily slow yourself down, not even for a customer. That is, during the tornado *customer acquisition* takes temporary priority over *customer satisfaction*. The entire pragmatist herd is switching from the old to the new – not a frequent event. As customers, in other words, they are temporarily 'up for grabs'. Once they choose their new vendor, they will be highly reluctant to consider changing yet again. So either you win these customers now, or you risk losing them *for the life of the paradigm*.

And then there is the super grand prize bonanza of tornado market development to which we have already alluded, namely, gaining *value-chain power over the other vendors in the value chain*. As noted, this occurs when a single vendor has monopoly control of a crucial element in the value chain, the way Microsoft and Intel each do for the personal computer, the way Cisco does for the Internet, the way Qualcomm appears to do for the future of wireless telephony. In such cases, as the market tornado unfolds, the standard whole product that forms around the killer app incorporates a piece of your proprietary technology. Going forward, for the value-chain offering as a whole to evolve, it must take your technology along with it – and there is no substitute for it. This makes everyone in the chain dependent upon you, which in turn allows you to orchestrate the behaviour of the rest of the chain. This can include pressuring value-chain partners to adopt or support some of your less successful products so that you gain power across a much broader portion of your product line than its actual features and benefits would normally merit.

Value disciplines for the tornado

Elevate product leadership and operational excellence. Whatever position one achieves during the tornado market depends largely on your company's ability to execute a market-share land-grab strategy. To this end, the market rewards a third alignment of value disciplines, as follows:

- Elevate product leadership and operational excellence. The tornado is driven by the demands of infrastructure buyers for standard, reliable offerings suitable for rapid mass deployment. Here product leadership gets translated into shipping the next release with the new set of features ahead of the competition and thereby grabbing additional market share from them. Operational excellence is critical to this effort because if there is any hiccup in the process, the market can still shift to an alternative vendor, with major market-share consequences that will last for the duration of the paradigm.

- Suppress discontinuous innovation and customer intimacy. Any form of discontinuous innovation during a tornado creates opportunity for error, putting rapid mass deployment at risk, and is thus anathema. Customer intimacy is also suppressed for the duration of the roll-out for the same reason, sacrificed to the end of achieving reliable, consistent deployment. Once the infrastructure is set in place, then there will be time to come back and meet customer-specific requests.

Operations-led organizations tend to have the edge in a tornado, where meeting deadlines, shipping in quantity and minimizing returns all take priority over innovation and customer delight. Marketing-led organizations, by contrast, typically flounder because they cannot bear to relinquish their commitment to customer intimacy and customer satisfaction. They need to realize that, in a tornado, just getting the new systems installed and working properly is grounds for customer satisfaction.

Stage-four adoption: On Main Street

Main Street begins as the market-share frenzy that drives tornado winds subsides. The overwhelming bulk of the pragmatists in the market have chosen their vendor, made their initial purchases, and rolled out the first phase of a multiphase deployment. Only a fraction of the total forecastable sales in the segment has actually been made at this point, but from here on out the market-share boundaries are relatively fixed. This has significant implications for the value chain.

Value-chain strategy

Here is the fourth and final mutation in the value chain. This one will endure for the life of the paradigm. In effect, it is the value chain we have been setting up all along (see Figure 10.3.6).

There is a key change underlying this entire value chain, which is that the technology adoption life cycle as a whole has evolved from the pragmatist to the conservative agenda, and every constituency in the value chain is affected by this change. Let's start with the customer.

When companies adopt new paradigms, conservative customers at first hang back, preferring to eke out some last bit of value from the old system. But once it is clear that the new system must supplant the old one, then they seek to put their stamp on the new vendor relationship. They remind all these new arrivals that most of the promises that were made on behalf of their products and services are as yet far from true, and they work to keep everyone focused on making incremental improvements going forward. In effect, they transform what heretofore was a discontinuous innovation into what will from now on be a system of continuous innovation.

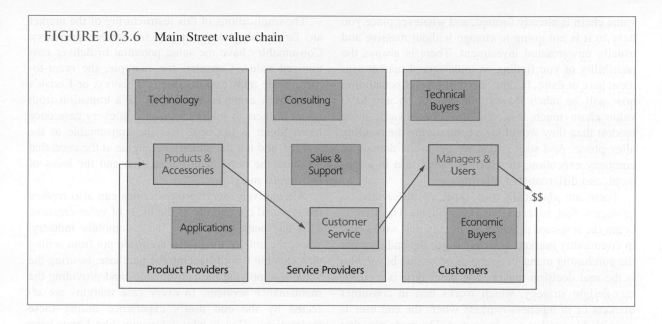

FIGURE 10.3.6 Main Street value chain

In mature – or maturing – markets, both the economic buyer and the technical buyer recede in importance. The economic buyer is no longer looking for competitive advantage or to support a manager in fixing a broken business process; now the issue is simply staying within budget, and that can be delegated. And the technical buyer is no longer concerned about how to either manage or postpone the introduction of a disruptive technology; now the concern is simply to stay compliant with established standards, and that, too, can be delegated. Even within the user community, the managers are now taking the new systems for granted, assuming that it must be doing pretty much what it was bought to do (a naïve, but all too frequent point of view). Thus it is only *end users,* the people who actually interact with the system on a frequent basis, that (a) know anything about how it really works, and (b) have a stake in sponsoring improvements to it.

If these end users do not voice their desires, then the offering becomes a complete commodity, with the purchasing department driving a *supplier relationship* going forward. If they do voice their desires, however, and gain their managers' approval, then end users can drive a *vendor relationship,* a condition that allows a company to earn margins above commodity levels. We are long past the time for customers to embrace you in a *strategic partner relationship,* something that is confined to earlier phases in the life cycle.

To earn preferred margins from end-user sponsorship, focus shifts to those aspects of the value chain that end users can directly experience. On the product side, this suppresses the importance of technology, platform products and even the core of the application. All these are still important, but they are more directly experienced by the technical buyer than the end user. By contrast, any product element that is consumable, is highly user visible. It is here that minor enhancements for a modest increase in price can generate dramatic changes in gross profit margin, the way, for example, the cup holder has done in the automotive industry.

Lucrative as the accessories and consumables business is on Main Street, however, an even bigger opportunity lies in the product-service shift. What customers used to value and buy as products becomes reconceived as service offerings – shifting the burden of system maintenance from the customer back to the vendor. Thus the move from answering machine to voice-mail, from videotapes to pay-per-view, from bar bells to health clubs.

The primary organization tasked with masterminding this shift is *customer service.* Historically this has been a challenge because that organization was not constructed, nor were its personnel recruited with the thought that it would eventually become a lead contributor to the P&L and market valuation of the company. In the age of the Internet, however, investors are now actively pursuing companies that have been founded from day one with just such an agenda in mind.

Competitive advantage on Main Street

The technology wave has crested and broken and no longer provides market development leverage. The value chain is already formed, and whatever place you have in it is not going to change without massive and usually unwarranted investment. There is always the possibility of you finding an underserved market segment here or there, but the speed of market penetration now will be much slower, the impact on any local value chain much less, and thus the rewards more modest than they would have been during the bowling alley phase. And so it is that we get to the domain of company execution, to which we shall turn in a moment, and differentiated offerings.

There are classically two types of differentiation strategies that succeed on Main Street. The first is being the low-cost provider, a strategy that works best in commodity markets where it is not the end user but the purchasing manager acting as economic buyer who is the real decision maker. The other type is a customer-delight strategy, which works best in consumer markets or in business markets where the end user is permitted to behave as a consumer. The more a market matures, the more opportunity your company has to deliver on both of these propositions to be competitive. To do so it must gravitate toward a product or service deployment strategy called *mass customization.*

Mass customization separates any offering into a *surface* and a *substructure.* The surface is what the end user experiences. It is here that changes are made to enhance that experience. This is the *customization* portion of the offer. By contrast, the substructure is the necessary delivery vehicle for the entire performance, but it is not directly experienced by the end user. The goal here is to provide maximum reliability at the lowest possible cost, and the preferred tactic is to reduce variability and increase standardization to achieve high volume. This is the *mass* portion of the offer.

To combine the two without sacrificing the benefits of either, the customizing portion must often be done downstream in the value chain in a separate step from the mass portion. This typically leads to a need to redesign the value chain, creating new opportunities for service providers to create customization value at the point of customer contact. Think of how cell phones are provided, and you get the idea. Everything upstream from the retail outlet is totally standardized; everything downstream is customizable – the phone itself, its accessories, service options, programme pricing, and the like. Prior to retail, everything is sold as a commodity; after retail, it is a value-added offering.

The implications of this restructuring of the market are far-reaching, and not just for service providers. Consumables have the same potential to deliver customized value. Consider, for example, the razor-to-razor-blade transition in Gillette's history, or Kodak's move from cameras to film, or HP's transition from inkjet printers to inkjet cartridges. In every case once Main Street is reached, it is the consumable at the surface, and not the underlying engine at the core, that becomes the basis of differentiation and the locus of high profit margins.

Alternatively, service transactions can also replace the serviced commodity as the locus of value creation. This has been the case in the automobile industry, where the bulk of the profits are made not from selling new cars but from financing the purchase, insuring the vehicle, supplying the consumables and providing the maintenance services. In every case margins are affected by the end user's experience during these transactions. That is why companies like Lexus have been so successful with their customer-care offers. It is also why traditional car dealerships are failing with their customer-unfriendly approach to purchase and financing, driving their customers to brokers and to the Web instead.

In large part the promise of the Internet is based on it being a universal platform for value-adding customization in Main Street value chains. The systems are not yet completely in place to fulfill this proposition today, but forward-thinking executives and enlightened investors can see how with incremental improvements they will be able to generate scaleable, low-cost, high-touch offerings of the sort that create attractive profit margins on Main Street.

Value disciplines

To execute on this strategy of mass customization, companies as elsewhere in the life cycle must learn to elevate one pair of value disciplines and suppress the other:

■ Elevate operational excellence and customer intimacy. Main Street markets are supported by conservative customers seeking incremental gains in value. These can be achieved either through decreasing the costs of the current set of offers – the domain of operational excellence – or by introducing a new set of offers improved through readily absorbed continuous innovations – the domain of customer intimacy.

TABLE 10.3.1 Comparison of market states

	Early market	Bowling alley	Tornado	Main Street
Primary competitive advantage	Catching technology wave	Market-segment domination	Market-share leadership	Differentiated offerings
Product focus	Technology	Applications	Platform products	Consumables
Service focus	Consulting	Support	Sales	Customer service
Customer focus	Economic buyer	Department manager	Technical buyer	End user

■ Suppress discontinuous innovation and product leadership. Discontinuous innovation runs directly contrary to the interests of Main Street customers and is simply not welcome. Even offers based on product leadership are problematic. If they require re-tooling the existing infrastructure, they usually just aren't worth it. What development teams must realize is that now product improvements should be focused either on keeping the core product viable, with operational excellence as a guide, or on making cosmetic changes at the surface, with customer intimacy providing the direction.

Of all the pairings, this particular set should be the most familiar to established companies in mature markets. They should see themselves as the champions of the first pair, and those wretched dotcoms assaulting their marketplace as the purveyors of the second. Note that in this pairing the established company's existing customers are very much on its side, not on the dotcoms'. That's because they, like the company itself, are ruled by conservative interests. It is instead the flock of new customers who are entering the tornado for the next big thing that are undermining this company's stock price going forward.

Implications of living on the fault line

The four market states are set out in a side-by-side comparison in Table 10.3.1. The table maps the working out of the competitive advantage hierarchy over the course of a technology-enabled market's development. The columns lay out the life-cycle phases these markets evolve through. The rows lay out the changes in focus that organizations must make to adapt to this evolution. The first row sets forth the layer in the competitive-advantage hierarchy that has the most impact during each phase. The next three rows highlight the value-chain elements that create the most impact during the phase because they are best suited to leveraging the type of competitive advantage available.

Even a cursory glance shows that the changes companies have to make in order to adapt to these forces are dramatic indeed. Moreover, the time allotted to make them is painfully short. As a result, it should surprise no one that few real-world organizations are very good at actually making them. Indeed, the larger and more successful a company becomes, the less likely it is to attempt making them at all.

REFERENCES

Abernathy, W.J. and Utterback, J.M. (1978) 'Patterns of Industrial Innovation', *Technological Review*, 80(7), June–July, pp. 40–47.

Aldrich, H.E. (1999) *Organizations Evolving*, London: Sage.

Aldrich, H.E. and Fiol, C.M. (1994) 'Fools Rush In? The Institutional Context of Industry Creation', *Academy of Management Review*, Vol. 19, No. 4, pp. 645–670.

Arthur, W.B. (1994) *Increasing Returns and Path Dependence in the Economy*, Ann Arbor, MI: University of Michigan Press.

Astley, W.G. and van der Ven, A.H. (1983) 'Central Perspectives and Debates in Organization Theory', *Administrative Science Quarterly*, Vol. 28, No. 2, June, pp. 245–273.

Baden-Fuller, C.W.F. and Stopford, J.M. (1992) *Rejuvenating the Mature Business*, London: Routledge.

Bain, J.S. (1959) *Industrial Organizations*, New York: Wiley.

Baum, A.C. and Singh, J.V. (eds) (1994) *Evolutionary Dynamics of Organizations*, New York: Oxford University Press.

Bettis, R.A. and Donaldson, L. (1990) 'Market Discipline and the Discipline of Management', *Academy of Management Review*, Vol. 15, No. 3, July, pp. 367–368.

Bower, J.L. and Christensen, C.M. (1995) 'Disruptive Technologies: Catching the Wave', *Harvard Business Review*, Vol. 73, No. 1, January–February, pp. 43–53.

Bradley, F. (2005) *International Marketing Strategy*, Pearson Education.

Burgelman, R.A. and Grove, A.S. (1996) 'Strategic Dissonance', *California Management Review*, Vol. 38, No. 2, pp. 106–131.

Carpenter, M.A. and Golden, B.R. (1997) 'Perceived Managerial Discretion: A Study of Cause and Effect', *Strategic Management Journal*, Vol. 18, No. 3, March, pp. 187–206.

Child, J. (1972) 'Organizational Structure, Environment, and Performance: The Role of Strategic Choice', *Sociology*, January, pp. 2–22.

Christensen, C.M. (1997) *The Innovator's Dilemma*, New York: Harper Business.

Cox, D. and Harris, R. (1985) 'Trade liberalization and industrial organization: Some estimates for Canada', *Journal of Political Economy*, 93, pp. 115–145.

Coxe D.O., Ganot, I., Keller G. and McGahan, A.M. (1996) 'Passion for Learning', HBS 9-796-057.

Cusumano, M.A. and Gawer, A. (2002) 'The Elements of Platform Leadership', *Sloan Management Review*, Vol. 43, No. 3, Spring, pp. 51–58.

D'Aveni, R.A. (1994) *Hypercompetition: Managing the Dynamics of Strategic Maneuvering*, New York: Free Press.

D'Aveni, R.A. (1999) 'Strategic Supremacy through Disruption and Dominance', *Sloan Management Review*, Vol. 40, No. 3, pp. 127–135.

Dicken, P. (2011) *Global Shift, Mapping the Changing Contours of the World Economy*, New York: The Guilford Press.

Evans, P.B. and Wurster, T.S. (1997) 'Strategy and the New Economics of Information', *Harvard Business Review*, Vol. 76, No. 5, September–October, pp. 71–82.

Foster, R. (1986) *Innovation: The Attacker's Advantage*, NY: Summit Books.

Frank, A.G. (1966) *The Development of Underdevelopment*. Monthly Review Press.

Friedman, T.L. (2005) *The World is Flat*, New York: Straus & Giroux.

Ghemawat, P. (1991) *Commitment: The Dynamic of Strategy*, New York: Free Press.

Greider, (1997) *One World, Ready or Not: The Manic Logic of Global Capitalism*, San Francisco: Jossey-Bass.

Hambrick, D.C. and Abrahamson, E. (1995) 'Assessing the Amount of Managerial Discretion in Different Industries: A Multi-Method Approach', *Academy of Management Journal*, Vol. 38, No. 5, October, pp. 1427–1441.

Hamel, G. (1996) 'Strategy as Revolution', *Harvard Business Review*, Vol. 74, No. 4, July–August, pp. 69–82.

Hamel, G. and Prahalad, C.K. (1994) *Competing for the Future*, Boston: Harvard Business School Press.

Hampden-Turner, C. and Trompenaars, A. (1993) *The Seven Cultures of Capitalism: Value Systems for Creating Wealth in the United States, Japan, Germany, France, Britain, Sweden and the Netherlands*, New York: Doubleday.

Hannan, M.T. and Freeman, J. (1977) 'The Population Ecology of Organizations', *American Journal of Sociology*, Vol. 82, No. 5, March, pp. 929–964.

Henderson, R.M. and Clark, K.B. (1990) 'Architectural Innovation: The Reconfiguration of Existing Product Technologies and the Failure of Established Firms', *Administrative Science Quarterly*, 35 (March), pp. 9–30.

Hrebiniak, L.G. and Joyce, W.F. (1985) 'Organizational Adaptation: Strategic Choice and Environmental Determinism', *Administrative Science Quarterly*, Vol. 30, No. 3, September, pp. 336–349.

Kim, W.C. and Mauborgne, R. (2005) 'Blue Ocean Strategy: From Theory to Practice', *California Management Review*, 47(3), pp. 105–121.

Kim, W.C. and Mauborgne, R. (2004) 'Blue Ocean Strategy'. *Harvard Business Review*. October.

Kindleberger, A. (1962) *Foreign Trade and the National Economy*, New Haven: Yale University Press.

Kotler, P. (1967) *Marketing Management: Analysis, Planning and Control*, Englewood Cliffs, NJ: Prentice-Hall.

Krugman, P. (1980) 'Scale Economies, Product Differentiation, and the Pattern of Trade', *The American Economic Review*, Vol. 70, No. 5, Dec. pp. 950–959.

Krugman, P. (1985) 'International debt strategies in an uncertain World', in: G. Smith and J. Cuddington (eds.) *International Debt and the Developing Countries*, Washington: World Bank.

Lessem, R. and Neubauer, F.F. (1994) *European Management Systems*, London: McGraw-Hill.

Levenhagen, M., Porac, J.F. and Thomas, H. (1993) 'Emergent Industry Leadership and the Selling of Technological Visions: A Social Constructionist View', in: J. Hendry, G. Johnson and J. Newton (eds.) *Strategic Thinking: Leadership and the Management of Change*, Chichester: Wiley.

Markides, C. (1999) *All the Right Moves: a Guide to Crafting Breakthrough Strategy*, Harvard Business School Press.

McGahan, A. (2000) How Industries Evolve, *Business Strategy Review*, Vol. 11, No. 3, pp. 1–16.

McGahan, A. and Porter, M.E. (1997) 'How Much Does Industry Matter, Really?', *Strategic Management Journal*, 18(S1), pp. 15–30.

Miller, D. (1990) *The Icarus Paradox: How Excellent Companies Bring About Their Own Downfall*, New York: Harper Business.

Miller, D., Kets de Vries, M. and Toulouse, J.M. (1982) 'Top Executive Locus of Control and its Relationship to Strategy-making, Structure and Environment', *Academy of Management Journal*, Vol. 25, pp. 237–253.

Moore, G.A. (2000) *Living on the Fault Line: Managing for Shareholder Value in the Age of the Internet*, New York: HarperBusiness.

Moore, J.F. (1996) *The Death of Competition: Leadership & Strategy in the Age of Business Ecosystems*, New York: Harper Business.

Morris, I. (2010) *Why The West Rules For Now, The Patterns of History and What They Reveal About the Future*, London: Profile Books.

Nelson, R.R. and Winter, S.G. (1982) *An Evolutionary Theory of Economic Change*, Reading, MA: Harvard University Press.

Oliver, C. (1997) 'Sustainable Competitive Advantage: Combining Institutional and Resource-based Views', *Strategic Management Journal*, Vol. 18, No. 9, October, pp. 697–713.

Parolini, C. (1999) *The Value Net*, Chichester: Wiley.

Porter, M.E. (1980) *Competitive Strategy: Techniques for Analyzing Industries and Competitors*, New York: Free Press.

Porter, M.E. (1985) *Competitive Advantage: Creating and Sustaining Superior Performance*, New York: Free Press.

Porter, M.E. (1990) *The Competitive Advantage of Nations*, New York: The Free Press.

Porter, M.E. (2001) 'Strategy and the Internet', *Harvard Business Review*, Vol. 80, No. 3, March, pp. 62–78.

Prahalad, C.K. and Doz, Y.L. (1987) *The Multinational Mission: Balancing Local Demands and Global Vision*, New York: Free Press.

Prebisch, R. (1950), *The Economic Development of Latin America and Its Principal Problems*, New York: United Nations.

Ricardo, D. (1817) *On the Principles of Political Economy and Taxation*, London: John Murray.

Rugman, A.M. and Verbeke (1993) 'The Double Diamond Model of International Competitiveness: The Canadian Experience', *Management International Review*, Special Issue, 33, pp. 17–39.

Rumelt, R. (1991) 'How Much Does Industry Matter?', *Strategic Management Journal*, Vol. 12, No. 3, March, pp. 167–186.

Shapiro, C.E. and Varian, H.R. (1998) *Information Rules*, Boston, MA: Harvard Business School Press.

Slywotzky, A.J. (1996) *Value Migration*, Boston: Harvard Business School Press.

Smith, A. (1776) *An Inquiry into the Nature and Causes of the Wealth of Nations*, London: printed for W. Strahan and T. Cadell, in the Strand.

Smith, A. and Venables, J. (1988) 'Completing the Internal Market in the European Community: Some Industry Simulations', *European Economic Review*, Vol. 32, No. 7, Sept., pp. 1501–1525.

Spender, J.C. (1989) *Industry Recipe: An Enquiry into the Nature and Sources of Managerial Judgement*, New York: Basil Blackwell.

Teece, D.J. (2007) 'Explicating Dynamic Capabilities: The Nature and Microfoundations of (Sustainable) Enterprise Performance', *Strategic Management Journal*, 28(13), pp. 1319–1350.

Teece, D.J., Pisano, G. and Shuen, A. (1997) 'Dynamic Capabilities and Strategic Management', *Strategic Management Journal*, 18(7), pp. 509–533.

Tirole, J. (1988) *The Theory of Industrial Organization*, MIT Press.

Trompenaars, F. and Hampden-Turner, C. (2000) *Building Cross-Cultural Competence*, New Haven: Yale University Press.

Vernon, R. (1966) 'International Investment and International Trade in the Product Cycle', *The Quarterly Journal of Economics*, Vol. 80, No. 2, pp. 190–207.

Wallerstein, I. (1974) *The Modern World-System, Vol. I: Capitalist Agriculture and the Origins of the European World-Economy in the Sixteenth Century*, New York/London: Academic Press.

Whitley, R.D. (1999) *Divergent Capitalisms: The Social Structuring and Change of Business Systems*, Oxford: Oxford University Press.

Wilson, D.C. (1992) *A Strategy of Change*, London: Routledge.

11 THE ORGANIZATIONAL CONTEXT

We shape our environments, then our environments shape us.
Winston Churchill (1874–1965); British statesman and writer

INTRODUCTION

In organizations, just as in families, each new generation does not start from scratch but inherits properties of their predecessors. In families, a part of this inheritance is in the form of genetic properties, but other attributes are also passed down such as family traditions, myths, habits, connections, feuds, titles and possessions. People might think of themselves as unique individuals, but to some degree they are an extension of the family line, and their behaviour is influenced by this inheritance. In firms the same phenomenon is observable. New top managers may arrive on the scene, but they inherit a great deal from the previous generation. They inherit traditions and myths in the form of an organizational culture. Habits are passed along in the form of established organizational processes, while internal and external relationships and rivalries shape the political constellation in which new managers must function. They are also handed the family jewels – brands, competences and other key resources.

In Chapter 8, it is pointed out that such inheritance is often the source of organizational rigidity and inertia (e.g. Hannan and Freeman, 1977; Rumelt, 1995). Inheritance limits 'organizational plasticity' – the capacity of the organization to change shape. As such, organizational inheritance can partially predetermine a firm's future path of development – which is referred to as path dependency, or sometimes simply summed up as 'history matters' (e.g. Aldrich, 1999; Nelson and Winter, 1982). Therefore, it was concluded that for strategic alignment to take place, some inherited characteristics could be preserved, but others needed to be changed, by either evolutionary or revolutionary means.

What is not discussed in Chapter 8 is *who* should trigger the required strategic changes. Who should initiate adaptations to the firm's business model and who should take steps to reshape the organizational system? Typically, managers have some role to play in all developments in the organizational context, but the question is what role? It is unlikely that any manager will have complete influence over all organizational developments, or would even want to exert absolute control. Inheritance and other organizational factors limit 'organizational malleability' – the capacity of the organization to be shaped by someone. As such, managers need to determine what power they have and where this power should be applied to achieve the best results. At the same time, managers will generally also look for opportunities to tap into the capabilities of other people in the firm to contribute to ongoing organizational adaptation.

So, the question can be summarized as, 'what is the role of managers in achieving a new alignment with the environment and what input can be garnered from other organizational members?' This question is also referred to as the issue of organizational development and is the central topic of further discussion in this chapter.

THE ISSUE OF ORGANIZATIONAL DEVELOPMENT

When it comes to realizing organizational development, managers generally acknowledge that they have some type of leadership role to play. Leadership refers to the act of influencing the views and behaviours of organizational members with the intention of accomplishing a particular organizational aim (e.g. Selznick, 1957; Bass, 1990). Stated differently, leadership is the act of getting organizational members to follow. From this definition it can be concluded that not all managers are necessarily leaders, and not all leaders are necessarily managers. Managers are individuals with a formal position in the organizational hierarchy, with associated authority and responsibilities. Leaders are individuals who have the ability to sway other people in the organization to get something done.

To be able to lead organizational developments, managers need power: the capability to influence. They also need to know how to get power, and how and where to exert it. In the following sections, these three topics are examined in more detail. First, the sources of leadership influence are described, followed by the levers of leadership influence. Finally, the arenas of leadership influence are explored.

Sources of leadership influence

To lead means to use power to influence others. Leaders can derive their potential influence from two general sources – their position and their person (Etzioni, 1961). 'Position power' comes from a leader's formal function in the organization. 'Personal power' is rooted in the specific character, knowledge, skills and relationships of the leader. Managers always have some level of position power, but they do not necessarily have the personal power needed to get organizational members to follow them. These two main types of power can be further subdivided into the following categories (French and Raven, 1959):

- Legitimate power. Legitimate power exists when a person has the formal authority to determine certain organizational behaviours and other employees agree to comply with this situation. Examples of legitimate power are the authority to assign work, spend money and demand information.

- Coercive power. People have coercive power when they have the capability to punish or withhold rewards to achieve compliance. Examples of coercive power include giving a poor performance review, withholding a bonus and dismissing employees.

- Reward power. Reward power is derived from the ability to offer something of value to a person in return for compliance. Examples of reward power include giving praise, awarding wage raises and promoting employees.

- Expert power. Expert power exists when organizational members are willing to comply because of a person's superior knowledge or skills in an important area. Such expert power can be based on specific knowledge of functional areas (e.g. marketing, finance), technologies (e.g. pharmaceuticals, information technology), geographic areas (e.g. South-East Asia, Florida) or businesses (e.g. mining, automotive).

- Referent power. When organizational members let themselves be influenced by a person's charismatic appeal, this is called referent power. This personal attraction can be based on many attributes, such as likeableness, forcefulness, persuasiveness, visionary qualities and image of success.

The first three types of power are largely determined by the organizational position of leaders and their willingness to exert them – coercive and reward capabilities without the credibility of use are not a viable source of power. The last two sources of power, expert and referent power, are largely personal in nature, and therefore more subjective. Whether someone is seen as an expert, and therefore accorded a certain level of respect and influence, depends strongly on the perceptions of the people being led. Expert power can be made more tangible by wearing a white lab coat, putting three pens in your breast pocket or writing a book, but still perceived expertise will be in the eyes of the beholder. The same is true for referent power, as people do not find the same characteristics equally charismatic. What is forceful to one follower might seem pushy to someone else; what is visionary to one person might sound like the murmurings of a madman to others (e.g. Klein and House, 1998; Waldman and Yammarino, 1999).

In practice, leaders will employ a mix of all five types of power to achieve the influence they desire. However, leadership styles can differ greatly depending on the relative weight placed on the various sources of power within the mix.

Levers of leadership influence

The sources of power available to the leader need to be used to have influence. There are three generic ways for leaders to seek influence, each focused on a different point in the activities of the people being influenced. These levers of leadership influence are:

- Throughput control. Leaders can focus their attention directly at the actions being taken by others in the organization. Throughput control implies getting involved hands-on in the activities of others, either by suggesting ways of working, engaging in a discussion on how things should be done, leading by example or simply by telling others what to do. This form of direct influence does require sufficiently detailed knowledge about the activities of others to be able to point out what should be done.

- Output control. Instead of directly supervising how things should be done, leaders can set objectives that should be met. Output control implies reaching agreement on certain performance targets and then monitoring how well they are being lived up to. The targets can be quantitative or qualitative, financial or strategic, simple or complex, realistic or stretch-oriented. And they can be arrived at by mutual consent or imposed by the leader. The very act of setting objectives can have an important influence on people in the organization, but the ability to check ongoing performance and to link results with punishment and rewards can further improve a person's impact.

- Input control. Leaders can also choose to influence the general conditions under which activities are carried out. Input control implies shaping the circumstances preceding and surrounding the actual work. Before activities start a leader can influence who is assigned to a task, which teams are formed, who is hired, where they will work and in what type of environment. During the execution of activities the leader can supply physical and financial resources, mobilize relationships and provide support. Not unimportantly, the leader can also be a source of enthusiasm, inspiration, ambition, vision and mission.

Of these three, throughput control is the most direct in its impact and input control the least. However, throughput control offers the lowest leverage and input control the highest, allowing a leader to influence many people over a longer period of time, while leaving more room for organizational members to take on their own responsibilities as well. In practice, leaders can combine elements of all three of the above, although leadership styles differ greatly with regard to the specific mix.

Arenas of leadership influence

As leaders attempt to guide organizational development, there are three main organizational arenas where they need to direct their influence to achieve strategic changes. These three overlapping arenas are the parts in the organization most resistant to change – they are the subsystems of the firm where organizational inheritance creates its own momentum, resisting a shift into another direction (e.g. Miller and Friesen, 1980; Tushman, Newman and Romanelli, 1986):

- The political arena. While most top managers have considerable position power with which they can try to influence the strategic decision-making process within their organization, very few top managers can impose their strategic agenda on the organization without building widespread political support. Even the most autocratic CEO will need to gain the commitment and compliance of key figures within the organization to be able to successfully push through significant changes. In practice, however, there are not many organizations where the 'officers and the troops' unquestioningly follow the general into battle. Usually, power is more dispersed throughout organizations, with different people and units having different ideas and interests, as well as the assertiveness to pursue their own agenda. Ironically, the more leaders that are developed throughout the organization, the more complex it becomes for any one leader to get the entire organization to follow – broad leadership can easily become fragmented leadership, with a host of strong people all pointing in different directions. For top management to gain control of the organization, they must build coalitions of supporters, not only to get favourable strategic decisions made, but also to ensure acceptance and compliance during the period of implementation. Otherwise strategic plans will be half-heartedly executed, opposed or silently sabotaged. However, gaining the necessary political support in the organization can be very difficult if the strategic views and interests of powerful individuals and departments differ significantly. Cultural and personality clashes can add to the complexity. Yet, top managers cannot recoil from the political arena, for it is here that new strategic directions are set (e.g. Allison, 1969; Pfeffer, 1992).

- The cultural arena. Intertwined with the process of gaining political influence in the organization, there is the process of gaining cultural influence. After all, to be able to change the organization, a leader must be able to change people's beliefs and associated behavioural patterns. Yet, affecting cultural change is far from simple. A leader must be capable of questioning the shared values, ideas and habits prevalent in the organization, even though the leader has usually been immersed in the very same culture for years. Leaders must also offer an alternative worldview and set of behaviours to supercede the old. All of this requires exceptional skills as visionary – to develop a new image of a desired future state for the firm – and as missionary – to develop a new set of beliefs and values to guide the firm. Furthermore, the leader needs to be an excellent teacher to engage the organizational members in a learning process to adapt their beliefs, values and norms to the new circumstances. In practice, this means that leaders often have to 'sell' their view of the new culture, using a mix of rational persuasion, inspirational appeal, symbolic actions, motivational incentives and subtle pressure (e.g. Senge, 1990, Reading 8.2; Ireland and Hitt, 1999).

- The psychological arena. While leaders need to influence the political process and the cultural identity of the organization, attention also needs to be paid to the psychological needs of individuals. To affect organizational change, leaders must win both the hearts and minds of the members of the organization. People must be willing to, literally, 'follow the leader' – preferably not passively, but actively, with commitment, courage and even passion (e.g. Bennis and Nanus, 1985; Kelley, 1988). To achieve such 'followership', leaders must gain the respect and trust of their colleagues. Another important factor in winning people over is the ability to meet their emotional need for certainty, clarity and continuity, to offset the uncertainties, ambiguities and discontinuities surrounding them (e.g. Argyris, 1990; Pfeffer and Sutton, 1999).

Even where political, cultural and psychological processes make the organization difficult to lead, managers might still be able to gain a certain level of control over their organizations. Yet, there will always remain aspects of the organizational system that managers cannot control, and should not even want to control, which is discussed in the following section.

THE PARADOX OF CONTROL AND CHAOS

Of all men's miseries the bitterest is this, to know so much and to have control over nothing.
Herodotus (5th century BC); Greek historian

In general, managers like to be in control. Managers like to be able to shape their own future, and by extension, to shape the future of their firm. Managers do not shy away from power – they build their power base to be able to influence events and steer the development of their organization. In short, to be a manager is to have the desire to be in charge.

Yet, at the same time, most managers understand that their firms do not resemble machines, where one person can sit at the control panel and steer the entire system. Organizations are complex social systems, populated by numerous self-thinking human beings, each with their own feelings, ideas and interests. These people need to decide and act for themselves on a daily basis, without the direct intervention of the manager. They must be empowered to weigh situations, take initiatives, solve problems and grab opportunities. They must be given a certain measure of autonomy to experiment, do things differently and even constructively disagree with the manager. In other words, managers must also be willing to 'let go' of some control for the organization to function at its best.

Moreover, managers must accept that in a complex system, like an organization, trying to control everything would be a futile endeavour. With so many people and so many interactions going on in a firm, any attempt to run the entire system top-down would be an impossible task. Therefore, letting go of some control is a pure necessity for normal organizational functioning.

This duality of wanting to control the development of the organization, while understanding that letting go of control is often beneficial, is the key strategic tension when dealing with the organizational context. On the one hand, managers must be willing to act as benevolent 'philosopher kings', autocratically imposing on the company what they consider to be best. On the other hand, managers must be willing to act as constitutional monarchs, democratically empowering organizational citizens to take their own responsibilities and behave more like entrepreneurs. The strategic paradox arises from the fact that the need for top-down *imposition* and bottom-up *initiative* are conflicting demands that are difficult for managers to meet at the same time.

On one side of this strategy paradox is 'control', which can be defined as the power to direct and impose order. On the other side of the paradox is the need for 'chaos', which can be defined as disorder or the lack of fixed organization. The paradox of control and chaos is a recurrent theme in the literature on strategy, organization, leadership and governance.

In most writings the need for control is presented as a pressure for a directive leadership style or an autocratic governance system (e.g. Tannenbaum and Schmidt, 1958; Vroom and Jago, 1988). The need for chaos is presented as a pressure for a participative leadership style and/or a democratic governance system (e.g. Ackoff, 1980; Stacey, 1992). In the following subsections both control and chaos are further examined.

The demand for top management control

As Herodotus remarked, it would be bitter indeed to have control over nothing. Not only would it be a misery for the frustrated managers, who would be little more than mere administrators or caretakers, it would also be a misery for their organizations, which would need to constantly adjust course without a helmsman to guide the ship. Managers cannot afford to let their organizations drift on the existing momentum. It is a manager's task and responsibility to ensure that the organization changes in accordance to the environment, so that the organizational purpose can still be achieved.

Top management cannot realize this objective without some level of control. They need to be able to direct developments in the organization. They need to have the power to make the necessary changes in the organizational structure, processes and culture, to realign the organization with the demands of the environment. This power, whether positional or personal, needs to be applied towards gaining sufficient support in the political arena, challenging existing beliefs and behaviours in the cultural arena, and winning the hearts and minds of the organizational members in the psychological arena.

The control that top management needs is different from the day-to-day control built in to the organizational structure and processes – they need *strategic control* as opposed to *operational control*. While operational control gives managers influence over activities within the current organizational system, strategic control gives managers influence over changes to the organizational system itself (e.g. Goold and Quinn, 1990; Simons, 1994). It is this power that managers require to be able to steer the development of their organization.

The demand for organizational chaos

To managers the term 'chaos' sounds quite menacing – it carries connotations of rampant anarchy, total pandemonium and a hopeless mess. Yet, chaos only means disorder, coming from the Greek term for the unformed original state of the universe. In the organizational context, chaos refers to situations of disorder, where phenomena have not yet been organized, or where parts of an organizational system have become 'unfreezed'. In other words, something is chaotic if it is unformed or has become 'disorganized'.

While this still does not sound particularly appealing to most managers, it should, because a period of disorganization is often a prerequisite for strategic renewal. Unfreezing existing structures, processes, routines and beliefs, and opening people up to different possibilities might be inefficient in the short run, as well as making people feel uncomfortable, but it is usually necessary to provoke creativity and to invent new ways of seeing and doing things. By allowing experimentation, skunk works, pilot projects and out-of-the-ordinary initiatives, managers accept a certain amount of disorder in the organization, which they hope will pay off in terms of organizational innovations.

But the most appealing effect of chaos is that it encourages 'self-organization'. To illustrate this phenomenon, one should first think back to the old Soviet 'command economy', which was based on the principle of control. It was believed that a rational, centrally planned economic system, with strong top-down leadership, would be the most efficient and effective way to organize industrial development. In the West, on the other hand, the 'market economy' was chaotic – no one was in control and could impose order. Everyone could go ahead and start a company. They could set their own production levels and even set their own prices! As entrepreneurs made use of the freedom offered to them, the economy 'self-organized' bottom-up. Instead of the 'visible hand' of the central planner controlling and regulating the economy, it was the 'invisible hand' of the market that created relative order out of chaos.

As the market economy example illustrates, chaos does not necessarily lead to pandemonium, but can result in a self-regulating interplay of forces. A lack of top-down control frees the way for a rich diversity of bottom-up ventures. Managers who also want to release the energy, creativity and entrepreneurial potential pent up in their organizations must therefore be willing to let go and allow some chaos to exist. In this context, the role of top management is comparable to that of governments in market economies – creating suitable conditions, encouraging activities and enforcing basic rules.

EXHIBIT 11.1   SHORT CASE

GAZPROM: BUILT TO DREAM

Although the slogan *mechty sbyvayutsya* or 'dreams come true' will probably not be familiar to most, the name Gazprom most likely is. The open joint-stock company is Russia's national champion and one of the world's largest energy companies. It has 330,000 employees, 460,000 shareholders and with a length of 153,000 kilometres of pipelines it could wrap the globe almost four times. Its core business consists of geological exploration, production, transportation and storage processing of hydrocarbons, as well as generating heat and electric power. Gazprom equals big business, with the company accounting for about 8 per cent of Russia's GDP and generating 20 per cent of the Russian government's revenues. In others words: if Gazprom suffers, Russia does as well.

Gazprom was an offshoot of the Soviet Gas Ministry, created by Viktor Chernomyrdin, the last Soviet Minister of Gas Industry, in 1989. This young professional made an enterprise association that was granted special privileges, such as favourable taxes and a full monopoly over the foreign trade in piped gas. For years the state-corporate enterprise enjoyed sky-high gas prices with a net profit of US$ 25 billion in 2007. No matter what difficulties came across the company's path, it could always, as Natalia Volchkova of the New Economic School in Moscow phrased it, 'drown it with money'. In May 2008, Gazprom's market capitalization peaked at US$ 350 billion, making it the third most valuable company in the world. Investment banks and energy consultants foresaw a dazzling future and its officials predicted that the giant would become the biggest in the world, worth US$ 1 trillion.

Unfortunately for Gazprom, all good things eventually come to an end. The global financial crisis hit oil prices in 2009, which resulted in Gazprom's production plummeting by about 16 per cent. It was not simply a decline in sales under which the company suffered, since structural problems in its management showed itself as well. With financial crises proven to bring structural weaknesses to light, Russia's national champion seemed no exception to the rule.

Because of these recent events, Gazprom faces several challenges, with its reliability as a supplier being one of them. Whereas Gazprom considers itself a trustworthy gas supplier to Russia and foreign countries, its purchasers tend to see this differently. Few need to be reminded of the trick it pulled with Ukraine by cutting off gas, leaving 16 other European countries, quite literally, in the cold. The somewhat unreliable gas supply makes Gazprom's consumers eager for alternative routes to meet their demands.

And these exist. Normally a warned man counts for two, but CEO Alexei Miller clearly underestimated the development of shale gas in North America by calling it a 'myth' and 'shale fever' in 2010. Shale gas production in Europe is off to a slow start; nevertheless it offers an affordable alternative to Russian gas. In addition, Gazprom not only has to deal with more pressure in the European market, it is challenged by fierce competition in the domestic market as well. Unlike Gazprom, independent producers are capable of selling gas volumes with high profits, making the limited competition it had in the past seem even smaller in comparison.

Gazprom is not only losing ground, but faces more problems with less money at the same time. If it wants to remain a global player, drowning obstacles with money will not be an option any more. An answer seems to lie in one particular area: Gazprom's management. During the last couple of years, its corporate governance has been criticized for being incompetent, bureaucratic, inert and mismanaged. When bearing Russia's history in mind, this summary does not come as a total surprise. During the Soviet regime, Joseph Stalin introduced the concept of the 'command economy', with planned and centralized production replacing a free market. The corporate governance of the current Gazprom illustrates that shaking off the past is easier said than done.

When looking at the enterprise's structure, one might say it resembles an authoritarian system. Gazprom holding group is comprised of the parent company OAO Gazprom and its seven subsidiaries engaged in gas processing, oil, transmission, power industry, ancillary activities, marketing and gas exploration, exploitation and distribution. The Chairman of Gazprom Group forms the broad policy for the CEO and his directors to execute. The CEO is next in line of command, followed by the board of directors that execute the chairman's policy by passing this through to the company's various departments. The responsibility of managers is to ensure the observance of the decisions taken by the board of directors, who can thus be called footsoldiers, rather than leaders.

For Alexei Miller, Gazprom's current head, there was no need to choose between the two top positions; he became Gazprom's chairman as well as its CEO. Although decision-making within Gazprom is controlled and centralized by top-down focused management, he is not in total control of the company. The Russian government possesses over 50 per cent of Gazprom's shares, making it the most powerful shareholder and thus allowing it to exert pressure while also ensuring a certain degree of command.

The idea that a rational and centralized system would be the most efficient and effective way to organize Gazprom did not seem to have proven itself. The Gazprom management did not fully understand the severity of the recent economic changes, with it calling the decline in gas demand a 'temporary inconvenience'. Therefore, the top-down leadership within Gazprom seems to be unfit to adapt to changes on the global stage. Perhaps when managers, as opposed to external shareholders, are given more control, they can allow for more internal organizational freedom to stimulate self-regulating departments.

On the other hand: is it advisable for Gazprom to adapt to the industry and is it realistic to expect Gazprom's customers' stance to change in the upcoming years even if Miller changes his management? Though his top-down focused organization has proven to inherit flaws, one can argue that Gazprom is actually in need of strict control in order to successfully compete in the oil and gas industry. In order to best preserve its monopoly, continue to play it hard seems like a logical option, something that can best be accomplished with a more autocratic company.

Indeed, Gazprom is able to profit from its bureaucratic, state-centred position; state companies are driven not only by commercial gains, but also pursue political imperatives. This provides possibilities to launch grand programmes, such as the Power of Siberia project, a 4,000 km pipeline through east Siberia to the Russian Pacific Coast. No commercial company would ever attempt something like this. Although a project accompanied by a US$ 46 billion bill can be called rather pricey, even for companies Gazprom's size, government support makes it feasible. Power of Siberia is able to create a valuable opportunity for the company as it could lessen the dependence of Gazprom on European markets, especially with talks on connecting the project with the extensive Chinese market in the pipeline.

With a changing oil and gas industry, decreasing revenues and increasing competition, there is a strong need to reform Gazprom's management. Disorganizing the extremely organized company and disconnecting it more from the Russian state might help accomplish strategic renewal and herewith better adapt itself to the industry. Yet, keeping management control exclusive to the top provides Gazprom with merits as well, with a large company demanding a certain level of control. And that is without even considering the difficulty tinkering with Gazprom's management would bring. While both options embody disadvantages as well, making the right decision is challenging, to say the least. It is up to Miller to decide, but what choice can ultimately make Gazprom's dreams come true?

Co-authors: Larissa Kalle and Wester Wagenaar

Sources: www.gazprom.com; Åslund (2010); *Economist*, 23 March 2013; *Financial Times*, 5 June 2013 and 17 June 2013; *Forbes*, 2 June 2005.

strive to overcome organizational inertia and adapt the organization to the strategic direction they intend. This type of controlled strategic behaviour is what Chandler (1962) had in mind when he coined the aphorism 'structure follows strategy' – the organizational structure should be adapted to the strategy intended by the decision-maker. In the organizational leadership perspective it would be more fitting to expand Chandler's maxim to 'organization follows strategy' – all aspects of the company should be matched to the strategist's intentions.

EXHIBIT 11.2   THE ORGANIZATIONAL LEADERSHIP PERSPECTIVE

LEADING BY ITALIAN EXAMPLE AT CHRYSLER

One of the most talked about change-makers in the automobile industry is Sergio Marchionne. After miraculously saving the Italian left-for-dead Fiat in just a couple of years after taking control in 2004, Mr. Marchionne aimed at applying his tried and tested method at Chrysler in which Fiat gained a 20 per cent stake at close to no cost. With Chrysler he chose not the easiest of challenges as the German Daimler – the parent company of Mercedes Benz – had failed in the same job only a couple of years earlier.

Central to the approach employed by Fiat's saviour is a monumental turnaround in leadership. Management should control the strategy process, focusing on dealing quickly with the volatile yet hardly growing industry. To do so, overhead must be cut quickly and old managers that hold on to top-down management need to be replaced by younger executives. This creates an accountable, open, quickly communicating and less politics-ridden ecosystem at the top, capable of steering a firm through the industry's testing challenges.

Mr. Marchionne's 60-day "killing spree", which he initiated after taking over at Chrysler, is a good illustration of the new leadership style. Just as he did with Fiat, he redefined the structure and replaced people himself to become more responsive. This left many of the upper echelons of management being startled with new opportunities or, alternatively, anxiously looking for different jobs. Having forward thinking and flexible leaders at the helm of an organization in an industry as pressured as the car industry is no excessive luxury. The market is expected to become increasingly volatile and the benefits of scale, although necessary for mutual survival, bring about a new class of

challenges. For this reason, a sudden jolt given by renewing the upper echelons of management is not enough. Instead, to be able to continuously benefit from its newfound boons, Mr. Marchionne is visibly leading his senior staff, who in turn need to be visible to the rest of the organization. Only by continuously displaying the right behaviour can a sustainable competitive advantage be maintained.

Leading by example and being visible is surely something Mr. Marchionne does not shy away from. In June 2013, he visited Fiat and Chrysler's headquarters in Turin and Auburn Hills in addition to visiting half a dozen other places around the world. While there he was far from enjoying the tourist locations, but instead visibly busying himself with quenching labour union issues, boosting productivity in Italy as well as his stake in Chrysler and setting up cooperative ventures in China.

According to Mr. Marchionne, faulty leadership is underlying a firm's immediate problems, which one should not hesitate to replace. Saving hundreds of thousands of jobs worldwide surely weighs up to getting rid of a handful of senior executives that are partly responsible for creating the problems in the first place. His second stroke of genius, to make abundantly visible the upper ranks of managers including himself, while showing the desired behaviour, might have been even more impressive. Not fearing structure changes and replacing people while being consistent and visible is what sets him apart. Will Mr. Marchionne succeed where even the renowned carmaker Daimler couldn't? Time will tell.

Co-author: Jasper de Vries

Sources: 'The Italian solution: Fiat chief executive, Sergio Marchionne, has gone merger mad', *The Economist*, May 7, 2009; 'Sergio Marchionne's high-wire act at Fiat-Chrysler', *CNN Money*, July 12, 2013.

The organizational dynamics perspective

To proponents of the organizational dynamics perspective, such an heroic depiction of leadership is understandable, but usually more myth than reality. There might be a few great, wise, charismatic managers that rise to the apex of organizations, but unfortunately, all other organizations have to settle for regular mortals. Strong leaders are an exception, not the norm, and even their ability to mould the organization at will is highly exaggerated – good stories for best-selling autobiographies, but legend nevertheless (e.g. Chen and Meindl, 1991; Kets de Vries, 1994). Yet, the belief in the power of leadership is quite popular, among managers and the managed alike (e.g. Meindl, Ehrlich and Dukerich, 1985; Pfeffer, 1977). Managers like the idea that as leaders of an organization or organizational unit, they can make a difference. To most, 'being in control' is what management is all about. They have a penchant for attributing organizational results to their own efforts (e.g. Hayward, Rindova and Pollock, 2004; Sims and Lorenzi, 1992). As for 'the managed', they too often ascribe organizational success or failure to the figurehead leader, whatever that person's real influence has been – after all, they too like the idea that somebody is in control. In fact, both parties are subscribing to a seductively simple 'great person model' of how organizations work. The implicit assumption is that an individual leader, by the strength of personality, can steer large groups of people, like a present-day Alexander the Great.

However seductive, this view of organizational functioning is rarely satisfactory. A top manager does not resemble a commander leading the troops into battle, but rather a diplomat trying to negotiate peace. The top manager is not like a jockey riding a thoroughbred horse, but more like a cowboy herding mules. Organizations are complex social systems, made up of many 'stubborn individuals' with their own ideas, interests and agendas (e.g. Greenwood and Hinings, 1996; Stacey, 1993). Strategy formation is therefore an inherently political process that leaders can only influence depending on their power base. The more dispersed the political power, the more difficult it is for a leader to control the organization's behaviour. Even if leaders are granted, or acquire, significant political power to push through their favoured measures, there may still be considerable resistance and guerrilla activities. Political processes within organizations do not signify the derailment of strategic decision-making – politics is the normal state of affairs and few leaders have real control over these political dynamics.

Besides such political limitations, a top manager's ability to control the direction of a company is also severely constrained by the organization's culture. Social norms will have evolved, relationships will have been formed, aspirations will have taken root and cognitive maps will have been shaped. A leader cannot ignore the cultural legacy of the organization's history, as this will be deeply etched into the minds of the organization's members. Any top manager attempting to radically alter the direction of a company will find out that changing the underlying values, perceptions, beliefs and expectations is extremely difficult, if not next to impossible. As Weick (1979) puts it, an organization does not have a culture, it is a culture – shared values and norms are what make an organization. And just as it is difficult to change someone's identity, it is difficult to change an organization's culture (e.g. Schein, 1993; Smircich and Stubbart, 1985). Moreover, as most top managers rise through the ranks to the upper echelons, they themselves are a product of the existing organizational culture. Changing your own culture is like pulling yourself up by your own bootstraps – a great trick, too bad that nobody can do it.

In Chapters 4 and 5, a related argument was put forward, as part of the resource-based view of the firm. One of the basic assumptions of the resource-based view is that building up competences is an arduous task, requiring a relatively long period of time. Learning is a slow process under the best of circumstances, but even more difficult if learning one thing means unlearning something else. The stronger the existing cognitive maps (knowledge), routines (capabilities) and disposition (attitude), the more challenging it is to 'teach an old dog new tricks'. The leader's power to direct and speed up such processes, it was argued, is quite limited (e.g. Barney, 1991, Reading 4.2; Leonard-Barton, 1995).

Taken together, the political, cultural and learning dynamics leave top managers with relatively little direct power over the system they want to steer. Generally, they can react to this limited ability to control in one of two basic ways – they can squeeze tighter or let go. Many managers follow the first route, desperately trying to acquire more power, to gain a tighter grip on the organization, in the vain attempt to become the heroic leader of popular legend. Such a move to accumulate more power commonly results in actions to assert control, including stricter reporting structures, more disciplined accountability, harsher punishment for non-conformists and a shakeout among managers. In this manner, control comes to mean restriction, subordination or even subjugation. Yet, such a step towards authoritarian management will still not bring managers very much further towards having a lasting impact on organizational development.

The alternative route is for managers to accept that they cannot, but also should not try to, tightly control the organization. As they cannot really control organizational dynamics, all heavy-handed control approaches will have little more result than making the organization an unpleasant and oppressive place to work. If managers emphasize control, all they will do is run the risk of killing the organization's ability to innovate and learn. Innovation and learning are very difficult to control, especially the business innovation and learning happening outside of R&D labs. Much of this innovation and learning is sparked by organizational members, out in the markets or on the work floor, questioning the status quo. New ideas often start 'in the margins' of the organization and grow due to the room granted to offbeat opinions. Fragile new initiatives often need to be championed by their owners lower down in the hierarchy and only survive if there is a tolerance for unintended 'misfits' in the organization's portfolio of activities. Only if employees have a certain measure of freedom and are willing to act as intrapreneurs, will learning and innovation be an integral part of the organization's functioning (e.g. Amabile, 1998; Quinn, 1985).

In other words, if managers move beyond their instinctive desire for control and recognize the creative and entrepreneurial potential of self-organization, they will not bemoan their lack of control. They will see that a certain level of organizational chaos can create the conditions for development (e.g. Levy, 1994; Stacey, 1993, Reading 11.2). According to the organizational dynamics perspective, the task for managers is to use their limited powers to facilitate self-organization (e.g. Beinhocker, 1999; Wheatley and Kellner-Rogers, 1996). Managers can encourage empowerment, stimulate learning and innovation, bring people together, take away bureaucratic hurdles – all very much like the approach by most governments in market economies, who try to establish conditions conducive to entrepreneurial behaviour instead of trying to control economic activity. Managers' most important task is to ensure that the 'invisible hand of self-organization' functions properly, and does not lead to 'out-of-hand disorganization'.

So, does the manager matter? Yes, but in a different sense than is usually assumed. The manager cannot shape the organization – it shapes itself. Organizational developments are the result of complex internal dynamics, which can be summarized as strategy follows organization, instead of the other way around. Managers can facilitate processes of self-organization and thus indirectly influence the direction of development, but at the same time managers are also shaped by the organization they are in.

EXHIBIT 11.3 ORGANIZATIONAL DYNAMICS PERSPECTIVE

MIGROS: BY AND FOR THE PEOPLE

It is 1925, Zürich, Switzerland. Money is scarce, and healthy yet affordable groceries are hard to find in what has currently become the economic centre of a wealthy country. It was at that time when Gottlieb Duttweiler, a man with a vision and a kind heart, founded Migros, a firm that would later leave a mark on the Swiss retailing industry, as well as on Swiss society. His objective was to meet the demand for low-priced basic food by cutting out the middleman. He would sell a few basic products to households that didn't have easy access to markets, but as demand for his services grew, so did the company. This led to a dilemma for Mr Duttweiler: should he keep control of the growing company and ownership of its potential profits, or become a company "by and for the people"? In 1941 Mr Duttweiler decided to put the customers in charge and transfer the branches into regional cooperatives.

The Migros community organizes itself bounded by a very society oriented way of doing business. There is still a board as well as a Federation of Migros Cooperatives heading the different enterprises, but this governance structure takes more of a facilitating form. The two million strong customer base, amounting to over a quarter of the Swiss population, effectively run the firm, meaning that it is owned by the same people that it serves.

One of the collectively taken decisions is to refrain from selling alcoholic beverages in the Migros flagship supermarkets. Offering products at the lowest price possible has always been a major objective, but when applying this policy to potentially harmful products, the well-being of individuals could be compromised. While a profitability-focused firm may perceive this as an acceptable consequence, for the consumer operated Migros it is not.

In 1996 Migros initiated the M-Budget brand, aimed at individuals with a lower income, which follows tradition. As it turns out, the idealistic philosophy behind this initiative resulted in these items not only appealing to those living on a budget, but also to trendy shoppers sharing this philosophy. Migros followed up on this development by initiating M-budget parties where people were challenged to cook high-end, gastronomic meals using only M-budget products. Naturally, the beverages served at those parties were non-alcoholic.

Co-author: Adriaan de Bruijn

Sources: Migros Annual Report 2012, http://m12.migros.ch/en/migros-group/strategy; Peter Gloor and Scott Cooper, 'The New Principles of a Swarm Business', *Sloan Management Review*, April 2007.

MANAGING THE PARADOX OF CONTROL AND CHAOS

Chaos often breeds life, when order breeds habit.
Henry Brooks Adams (1838–1919); American writer and historian

So, how should organizational development be encouraged? Can the top management of a firm shape the organization to fit with their intended strategy or does the organizational context determine the strategy that is actually followed? And should top management strive to have a tight grip on the organization, or should they leave plenty of room for self-organization? (See Table 11.1.)

As before, views differ strongly, both in business practice and in academia; not only in the field of strategy, but also in neighbouring fields such as organizational behaviour, human resource management and innovation management. And not only in the management sciences, but more broadly in the humanities, including sociology, economics, political science and psychology as well. The economic sociologist Duesenberry once remarked that 'economics is all about how people make choices; sociology is all about

TABLE 11.1 Organizational leadership versus organizational dynamics perspective

	Organizational leadership perspective	*Organizational dynamics perspective*
Emphasis on	Control over chaos	Chaos over control
Organizational development	Controllable creation process	Uncontrollable evolutionary process
Development metaphor	The visible hand	The invisible hand
Development direction	Top-down, imposed organization	Bottom-up, self-organization
Decision-making	Authoritarian (rule of the few)	Democratic (rule of the many)
Change process	Leader shapes new behaviour	New behaviour emerges from interactions
Change determinants	Leader's vision and skill	Political, cultural and learning dynamics
Organizational malleability	High, fast	Low, slow
Development driver	Organization follows strategy	Strategy follows organization
Normative implication	Strategize, then organize	Organize, then strategizing

how they don't have any choices to make'. Although half in jest, his comment does ring true. Much of the literature within the field of economics assumes that people in organizations can freely make choices and have the power to shape their strategy, while possible restraints on their freedom usually come from the environment. Sociological literature, but also psychological and political science work, often features the limitations on individual's freedom. These different disciplinary inclinations are not absolute, but can be clearly recognized in the debate.

With so many conflicting views and incompatible prescriptions on the issue of organizational development, the question is how to manage the paradox of control and chaos. Following the taxonomy in Chapter 1, strategizing managers have the following options at their disposal.

Balancing

Depending on the organization, strategists blend elements of the opposite demands for top management control and organizational chaos into a balance. As has been discussed in Chapter 7 on strategy formation, the primary process of the firm or organizational unit is a key factor. For example, the demand for top management control is higher in production units than in a professional services firm, while the demand for organizational chaos prevails in business development units.

Organizational culture is another factor influencing the blend of opposite demands. For example, the founder's leadership style and the firm's native country are among the factors that create an organization-specific culture (further discussed in the next section on the international perspective on the organizational context).

Juxtaposing

Within the organization, strategists are leading many groups, projects and corporate initiatives. The larger the organization and the higher strategizing managers are ranked in the hierarchy, the more variety of organizational processes they participate in. For example, a manager may be heading a product innovation project, a cost cutting operation and an acquisition process at the same time. These activities require different organizational leadership styles, and thus the strategizing manager needs to juxtapose between different opposites or blends simultaneously. This requires specific dynamic capabilities (Teece, Pisano and Shuen, 1997, Reading 4.3).

Embracing

The tension between the demand for top management control and organizational chaos can also be exploited at the leadership team level, by intentionally bringing together opposite individuals. Diverse leadership teams, bringing together different disciplines and cultures for example, are not the easiest of organizational configurations. Yet, tensions can be exploited as sources of creativity and opportunity.

One specific manifestation of an intentionally designed tension is the phenomenon – or legend – of 'dynamic duos' who have built large firms such as Hewlett and Packard, and Walt and Roy Disney. Actually some authors argue that a large number of new ventures are successful *exactly because* of the combination of two contrary individuals forming the leadership team. They argue that while the attention of academics and journalists is directed to the more outgoing member of the leadership team, the correct level of analysis should be the duo, the yin and yang of success.

One such author was the late David Thomson (2006; Reading 11.3) who analysed the 387 high growth companies that have IPO'd since 1980 and concluded that success often depends on dynamic duos, one of them being the external part and the other the internal of the effort. Together they were able to combine innovation and stability.

THE ORGANIZATIONAL CONTEXT IN INTERNATIONAL PERSPECTIVE

So long as men worship the Caesars and Napoleons, Caesars and Napoleons will duly arise and make them miserable.
Aldous Huxley (1894–1963); English novelist

Again it has become clear that there is little consensus in the field of strategy. Views on the nature of the organizational context vary sharply. Even authors from one and the same country have contrasting opinions on the paradox of control and chaos. However, looking back on the readings in the sections on strategy process and strategy content, it is striking how few of the authors make a point of expounding their outlook on organizational development. The assumptions on which their theories are built are largely left implicit.

For this reason, it is difficult to identify whether there are national preferences when it comes to organizational context perspective. Yet, it seems not unlikely that strategists in different countries have different inclinations on this issue. In large-scale fieldwork carried out by researchers at Cranfield Business School in the United Kingdom (Kakabadse *et al.,* 1995), significantly different 'leadership styles' were recognized among European executives. The predominant approach in Sweden and Finland was typified as the 'consensus' style (low power distance, low masculinity), while executives in Germany and Austria had a style that was labelled 'working towards a common goal' (specialists working together within a rule-bound structure). In France, the most popular style was 'managing from a distance' (focus on planning, high power distance), while executives from the United Kingdom, Ireland and Spain preferred 'leading from the front'. The latter, leadership style according to the researchers, relies 'on the belief that charisma and skills of some particular individuals will lead to either the success or the failure of their organizations'. This finding suggests that the organizational leadership perspective will be more popular in these three countries (as well as in other 'Anglo-Saxon' and 'Latin' cultures), than in the rest of Europe. Other cross-cultural theorists also support this supposition (e.g. Hampden-Turner and Trompenaars, 1993; Lessem and Neubauer, 1994).

As an input to the debate whether there are international differences in perspective, a number of factors will be put forward that might be of influence on how the paradox of control and chaos is viewed in different countries. It should be noted, however, that these propositions are intended to encourage discussion and constitute only tentative explanations for cross-cultural differences in perspective. More specific international research is needed to give this debate a firm footing.

Locus of control

This point is kept short as it is also raised in Chapter 8. People with an internal locus of control believe that they can shape events and have an impact on their environment. People with an external locus of control believe that they are caught up in events that they can hardly influence. Cross-cultural researchers have argued that cultures can differ significantly with regard to the perceived locus of control that is predominant among the population.

Obviously, in countries where the culture is more inclined towards an internal locus of control, it is reasonable to expect that the organizational leadership perspective will be more widespread. Managers in such 'just do it' cultures will be more strongly predisposed to believe that they can shape organizational circumstances. In cultures that are characterized by a predominantly external locus of control, more support for the organizational dynamics perspective can be expected.

Level of uncertainty avoidance

A cultural characteristic related to the previous point is the preference for order and structure that prevails in some countries. Hofstede (1993, Reading 1.3) refers to this issue as uncertainty avoidance. In some cultures, there is a low tolerance for unstructured situations, poorly defined tasks and responsibilities, ambiguous relationships and unclear rules. People in these nations exhibit a distinct preference for order, predictability and security – they need to feel they are 'in control'. In other cultures, however, people are less nervous about uncertain settings. The tolerance for situations that are 'unorganized' or 'self-organizing', is much higher – even in relatively chaotic circumstances, the call for 'law and order' will not be particularly strong. It can be expected that there will be a more pronounced preference for the organizational leadership perspective in countries that score high on uncertainty avoidance, than in nations with a low score.

Prevalence of mechanistic organizations

In Chapters 7 and 9, different international views on the nature of organizations are discussed. A simple distinction was made between mechanistic and organic conceptions of organizations. In the mechanistic view, organizations exist as systems that are staffed with people, while in the organic view organizations exist as groups of people into which some system has been brought.

When it comes to organizational development, people taking a mechanistic view will see leaders as mechanics – the organizational system can be redesigned, reengineered and restructured to pursue another course of action where necessary. Success will depend on leaders' design, engineering and structuring skills, and their ability to overcome resistance to change by the system's inhabitants. If a leader does not function well, a new one can be installed, and if employees are too resistant, then they can be replaced. In countries where the mechanistic view of organizations is more predominant, a leaning towards the organizational leadership perspective can be expected.

People taking an organic view see a leader as the head of the clan, bound by tradition and loyalty, but able to count on the emotional commitment of the members. Success in reshaping the organization will depend on reshaping the people – changing beliefs, ideas, visions, skills and interests. Important in reorienting and rejuvenating the organization is the leader's ability to challenge orthodox ideas, motivate people and manage the political processes. In countries where the organic view of organizations is more predominant, a leaning towards the organizational dynamics perspective can be expected.

INTRODUCTION TO THE READINGS

To help strategists to come to grips with the variety of perspectives on this issue, three readings have been selected that each shed their own light on the topic. As in previous chapters, the first two readings are representative of the two poles in this debate, while the third reading relates the two contrary perspectives.

To open the debate on behalf of the organizational leadership perspective, Reading 11.1 has been selected entitled 'Defining Leadership and Explicating the Process', which is written by one of the 'godfathers' of organizational theory, Richard Cyert. In this article, Cyert starts by summarizing the functions of a leader: determining the organizational structure, selecting managers, setting strategic objectives, controlling internal and external information flows, maintaining morale and making important decisions. But while some authors take an organizational leadership perspective tend to conjure up an image of the leader as an octopus, with many long arms performing all of these tasks at the same time, Cyert has a more human, two-armed individual in mind. His view of the leader is not the control freak who wants to run the organization single-handedly, but a person who can 'heavily influence the process of determining the goals of the organization', and then can 'have the participants in the organization behave in the ways that the leader believes are desirable'. This definition of leadership has two important ingredients. Firstly, Cyert argues that leaders need to take the initiative in determining a vision and organizational goals, although they do this in interaction with other organizational members. Secondly, Cyert argues that leaders need to focus on modifying the people's behaviours. To get people to move in the desired direction, he states that it is not so important what a leader decides or tells people to do. Rather, an effective leader 'controls the allocation of the attention focus of the participants in the organization … so that their attention is allocated to the areas that the leader considers important'. In this way, Cyert believes, organizational members will voluntarily align their behaviours with where the leader wants to go. He admits that 'this conception of leadership might strike some as making the leader a manipulative person', but feels that if leaders have a genuine belief in what they are doing and have an honest dedication to the people in the organization, exerting this type of leadership is justified. Although Cyert is well aware that organizations are complex systems of interacting human beings, his unquestioned supposition throughout the reading is that leadership is *possible* and *necessary*. As many writers taking an organizational leadership perspective, the demand for top management control is an implicit assumption – the main issue discussed is how to get power and how to exert control. Cyert's preference is for more indirect control, implicitly leaving some room for bottom-up self-organization.

As the opening reading to represent the organizational dynamics perspective (Reading 11.2), an article by Ralph Stacey has been selected, entitled 'Strategy as Order Emerging from Chaos'. Stacey argues that top managers cannot, and should not even try, to control the organization and its strategy. In his view, the organizational dynamics involved in strategy formation, learning and change are too complex to simply be controlled by managers. He states that 'sometimes the best thing a manager can do is to let go and allow things to happen'. The resulting chaos, he argues, does not mean that the organization will be a mess – a lack of control, he assures, does not mean that the organization will be adrift. His reasoning is that non-linear feedback systems, such as organizations, have a self-organizing ability, which 'can produce controlled behaviour, even though no one is in control'. In his view, real strategic change requires the chaos of contention and conflict to destroy old recipes and to encourage the quest for new solutions. The 'self-organizing processes of political interaction and complex learning' ensure that chaos does not result in disintegration. Hence, in Stacey's opinion, it is management's task to help create a situation of bounded instability in which strategy can emerge. Managers do have a role in organizations, but it can hardly be called leadership – 'leaders' must direct their efforts at influencing the organizational context in such a way that the right conditions prevail for self-organization to take place. 'Leaders' are largely facilitators, making it possible for new and unexpected strategies to develop spontaneously.

The third Reading (11.3), combining the two perspectives, is adapted from the book *Blueprint to a Billion: 7 essentials to achieve exponential growth* by David Thomson. The late writer has been researching America's 387 highest growth companies, the 5 per cent that have IPO'd since 1980 and grown to $1 billion in revenue. One surprising finding was that dynamic duos – often visible in the company's naming as in Sears and Roebuck, and Hewlett and Packard – as an essential success factor of high growth companies is more than corporate myth. Thomson found that dynamic duos, 'two individuals who worked tightly together to build the firm from dreams to a billion dollars in revenue' drove many of the star-performing companies, including Yahoo!, Microsoft, Tractor Supply, eBay, Siebel Systems, Starbucks and Broadcom. For the duo to be dynamic, one of them had to excel in the *external* part while the other had the *internal* focus. Together, Thomson observes, they 'are the yin and yang, the weave and warp, the bacon and eggs – and without this dynamic of compatibility their companies could not have made it to the top. As a pair, they were the highest of performance teams'. The duos were able to manage tensions such as the creative tension between the flat and somewhat chaotic innovative organization and the more top-down and structured execution of ideas. The importance of this reading is that if dynamic duos are the key to success in an extremely demanding context it may, more generally, also be essential in strategic leadership.

Defining leadership and explicating the process

By Richard M. Cyert[1]

It is true that organizations, whether for-profit or not-for-profit, are in need of leadership. Most people in leadership positions in organizations tend to be managers rather than leaders. They administer, allocate resources, resolve conflicts and go home at night convinced that they have done a good day's work. They may have, but they have not provided the organization with the critical ingredient that every organization needs – leadership (Zalesnik, 1977; Bavelas, 1964).

It is possible to generalize three broad functions that a leader performs. I specify these functions as organizational, interpersonal and decisional. The organizational function involves the development of the organizational structure and the selection of people to manage the various segments of an organization. It involves the determination of the goal structure and the control of the internal and external information flows. This function requires the leader to make certain that the participants in the organization and the relevant groups external to the organization are knowledgeable about the organization.

The interpersonal function involves the maintenance of morale in the organization. It reflects the degree of concern about the humanness of the organization. It requires the leader to pay attention to individual concerns.

The decision function involves the making of decisions that must be made in order for the organization to progress toward the achievement of its goals. This is the function that has traditionally been associated with leadership.

Nature of leadership

Although there is little agreement on the definition of leadership, most students of leadership would agree that the three functions just described are clearly a part of the definition. In a broad sense, the leader is attempting to have the participants in the organization behave in the ways that the leader believes are desirable. A major step in performing the organizational function is to define desirable behaviour.

Desirability is determined by the goals of the organization. The leader should heavily influence the process of determining the goals of the organization. The determination of a goal structure for an organization is the result of a series of interactions among the participants and between the participants and the leader. The goal structure represents the vision of the leader and of the organization's other members. Projecting a vision for the organization is another characteristic that is commonly associated with leadership.

The vision embedded in the goal structure is essentially a map that is used as a guide for the direction of the organization. Clearly, the map is more detailed as one's view shifts to subunits within the organization. At the top leadership position, a number of broad principles are specified to guide the overall construction of the vision.

These principles relate to the process by which the organization's vision can be constantly modified and reshaped. The specification of strategic principles and of the process by which the vision is modified is another characteristic of leadership. The leader is the helmsman, and the goal structure, together with the strategic principle, is the means by which the leader steers the organization. But, an organization is an interactive system of human beings, and its performance depends on the behaviour of individuals. Regardless of the policies that are promulgated, the participants in the organization will determine the destiny of the organization by their productivity.

The goal structure is important in the leading of an organization. However, organizations can have conflicting goals (Cyert and March, 1963), primarily because they tend to goals sequentially. Also, each unit in an organization can focus on different goals. These goals may conflict, but they can all be embraced by the organization (Birnbaum, 1988).

A definition of leadership

The concept of attention focus is one of the most important variables in organization theory (March and

Simon, 1958; Cyert and March, 1963). Participants in an organization allocate their attention to a variety of matters. The amount of attention allocated to each matter has been a subject of study. It can affect the organization in crucial ways. For example, if attention is not given to problems concerned with the future, the organization may flounder from myopia – too much attention to immediate problems. Clearly, the problems, concerns, ideas, concepts and so on to which the participants pay attention will determine the long-run viability of the organization. The control of this allocation of attention is vital to the organization.

In discussing the formation of the organizational coalition, Cyert and March (1963, p. 39) argue that one of the five basic mechanisms for a theory of coalition formation is 'an attention-focus mechanism'; however, 'we know rather little about the actual mechanisms that control this attention factor.' In this paper, I argue that the leadership function is one of the mechanisms that control the attention factor.

In fact, my definition of leadership is that the leader controls the allocation of the attention focus of the participants in the organization. The leader of any organization, no matter how small or large it is, affects the allocation of attention by participants. In a decentralized, structured organization, standard operating procedures determine the allocation of attention if the leader does not intervene. In general, in any organization where managers dominate, structured rules tend to influence the allocation of attention, but the leader will try to capture the attention focus of the participants so that their attention is allocated to the areas that the leader considers important.

The issues or problems on which the leader attempts to focus attention reflect, at least in part, the vision of the organization that exists in the leader's mind. This vision will generally have been developed from discussions with relevant participants, from the leader's experience and knowledge, and from his or her assessment of the organization's future in the light of existing information. This vision will change over time as the leader gets feedback from the organization's performance. As the vision changes, so does the priority of individual issues and problems to which the leader wishes to allocate the attention of participants. Organizations are dynamic, and attention allocation is an ongoing and always necessary process. Leadership, in the sense in which I have defined it here, must also be continuous.

Leadership, as I define it here, must also have substance. A leader cannot succeed in allocating attention without a strong intellectual position for a particular attention focus. This position can only come from a knowledge of the organization and of the area in which it functions. This need for specific knowledge is one of the reasons why it is difficult for executives to move from an organization in one industry to an organization in a different industry. The executive may be able to function as a manager, but he or she will have more difficulty functioning as a leader.

A second definition of leadership

Subgroups develop in every organization. Participants involved in the same department or in similar endeavours form a natural alliance (March and Simon, 1958). Important individuals in an organization can constitute subgroups in and of themselves. The point is that subgroups can develop a goal structure of their own, and this goal structure may conflict with that of the central organization.

The leader must bring about conformity between subgroup goals and the goals of the central organization. In other words, the leader must convince the members of the subgroup to give up or modify their goals and adopt the central organization's goals. In some cases, of course, the leader may decide that the central goals should be changed in the direction of the subgroup's goals. The point is that the leader cannot tolerate conflicting goals in the organization (Vroom and Jago, 1988). There must be a single goal structure, and everyone in the organization must accept it if the organization's goals are to be achieved. The concept of teamwork – of everyone working together – is a necessity for any organization.

Definitions of leadership and the three leadership functions

Having defined leadership, it is now logical for us to discuss the methods that one uses in the act of leadership. However, before we move to that topic, it will be useful to relate our two definitions of leadership – which really are essentially one – to the three functions of leadership discussed earlier.

In order to understand the leader's role, we need to go back to the distinction between managers and leaders. Every leader must perform some managerial functions, even though every manager cannot take a leadership role.

For example, in an effort to change organizational performance, many managers attempt to change the structure of their organizations. Currently, in an effort to reduce costs, many managers are attempting to reduce the number of hierarchical levels. Sometimes, the structure is changed by modifying the reporting relationship among units. The level at which decisions are made can also be changed. The organization can become more centralized or more decentralized with respect to decision making. Yet, changes in organizational structure alone are not likely to have any lasting impact on the organization's performance unless the structure affects the basic desire of participants to improve their performance.

The leader recognizes that it is necessary to focus the attention of participants on factors that will change performance. Thus, the leader makes changes in structure for their effect on attention focus, not because he or she believes that organizational structure alone can change the performance of participants. If the leader wishes to focus attention on costs, he or she looks at changes in the organization's structure that will encourage participants to allocate their attention to costs. Increased decentralization will often accomplish such a shift. The point is that leaders look at organizational tasks with a view to the impact that their actions will have on the attention focus of participants. Attention focus is central to the performance of the organizational function of leadership.

A similar statement can be made about the interpersonal function. The leader's role is to relate to the participants in ways that will affect their attention focus. The interpersonal function of leadership is sometimes viewed as one that holds the leader responsible for making everyone in the organization feel good. Friendliness and openness can be good for an organization if they help participants to focus their attention on the elements that the leader deems to be important. The interpersonal function is extremely important, but the leader must relate his or her actions in this area to the desired impact on attention focus. There is ample evidence that there is a low correlation between high morale and high productivity (Misumi, 1985).

The relation between the decisional function and attention focus is perhaps the most interesting of the three. Bavelas (1964, p. 206) defined leadership in terms of decision-making: 'leadership consists of the continuous choice-making process that permits the organization as a whole to proceed toward its objectives despite all sorts of internal and external perturbations.' More explicitly, he regards leadership as consisting of the reduction of uncertainty; this reduction is achieved by making choices.

This definition, which is close to the commonly accepted view of leadership, is quite different from those propounded here. My definitions focus on the leader's responsibility for modifying the behaviour of participants in the organization. They assume that behaviour is affected by the items to which individuals allocate their attention. The leader is able to capture the attention focus of participants. The leader gets participants to allocate attention to the items that he or she deems to be important. There is no question that the decisions that a leader makes are ways of making the priorities for attention clear. That is the aspect of decision-making that in my view is part of leadership, not the fact that decision-making reduces uncertainty. Nevertheless, it could be argued that influencing the allocation of attention tends to reduce uncertainty.

Studies of decision-making tend to show that decisions are rarely made by a single individual without regard to the views of the members of the organization. Leadership in an organization has to be less individualistic than it is in a combat situation where the leader may single-handedly eliminate a machine gun nest. Decision-making in an organization must take into account the fact that members of the organization are interested in the direction that the organization takes. If the leader has captured the attention focus of the members, then it is possible to demonstrate 'the highest expressions of personal leadership' (Bavelas, 1964) and carry the organization along with those expressions.

Methods of leadership

If leadership is adequately encompassed by my definitions, we may ask how leadership is actually implemented in an organization. How does a person act in an organization when he or she plays a leadership role and wants to exert leadership?

There are at least three general approaches that are taken. They can be classified as communication, role modelling, and reward systems. I will discuss each of these approaches.

Communication

The first action that influences attention focus is oral interaction. These talks are ways of capturing the attention focus of participants. The ultimate aim is to change the behaviour of people in the organization by influencing their focus. The underlying theory is that individuals' behaviour is controlled by their attention focus. Put another way, the leader brings about the behaviour that he or she desires by convincing participants to focus their attention on the ideas and actions that the leader considers important.

The interesting and difficult problem is that the methods of communication in organizations are not well defined (March and Simon, 1958). In general, it is best to use a variety of communication channels. These channels can vary from one-on-one discussions to departmental meetings and meetings of the whole faculty and staff.

The leader also uses written communication. Again, different approaches must be found. Written communications can vary from personal letters to letters to the whole organization and formal reports. Even articles written for newspapers or other publications can be used to explicate the leader's desired priorities for the allocation of attention among participants.

Communication is perhaps the most important mechanism of leadership. The leader must have a clear understanding of the message that he or she is communicating, and he or she must be aware that the goal of communication is to influence the allocation of attention of the organization's members.

Role model

As a way of continuing to communicate with members of the organization, the leader must take into account the impact of his or her behaviour on the attention focus of participants. The actions of the leader clearly represent the ideas that he or she considers to be important. If a university president is trying to emphasize research as an activity of importance, he or she should engage in research activity as well as emphasize research in the direct communications that he or she makes. Role modelling is a case in which actions speak as loudly as words.

The leader's activities are widely known among the members of any organization. Thus, the leader has ample opportunity to affect the attention focus of participants by demonstrating the factors that are important in his or her own behaviour. In other words, role modelling is a form of communication. The leader's behaviour exerts leadership whether the leader intends it or not.

Reward system

The reward system that the leader establishes is another way of reinforcing the attention focus of members. The relationship between particular rewards and performance is not well established. An organization cannot offer a specific monetary award and achieve a particular performance. However, a leader can use rewards to reinforce the priority system for attention allocation that

he or she has established. The reward system can lead to both honour and money for recipients. The reward system is also a means of communicating the leader's priorities to participants. Obviously, a reward system cannot guarantee that performance in teaching will improve, but it can supplement the leader's effort to capture the attention focus of participants and allocate attention to areas that the leader considers important.

Conclusion

The theory of leadership just outlined is essentially a simple one. It assumes that participants in an organization behave in accordance with their focus attention. Behaviour follows from the items on which they focus. From this perspective, leadership is the effort to capture the attention focus of the members of an organization. Three mechanisms help to perform the leadership function: communication between leader and participants, role modelling and reward systems. The three mechanisms are alike in that all are ways of communicating the matters on which the leader wants members to focus their attention. There are other, related mechanisms. My list is not exhaustive. In all cases, the effort is to capture the attention focus of participants.

This conception of leadership might strike some as making the leader a manipulative person (Glassman, 1986). The key is that the leader must believe in what he or she is expressing. Mintzberg (1989) has put it exactly right: 'To my mind, key to the development of an organization ideology, in a new or existing organization, is a leadership with a genuine belief in mission and an honest dedication to the people who must carry it out.'

It is obvious, although I have not emphasized it, that a leader must have the ability and the knowledge needed to select the right items for the attention focus of participants (Mintzberg, 1982). That is, the items singled out for attention must enable the organization to attain its goals. The process of capturing the attention focus is also a dynamic one. The items on which the leader wishes participants to focus will change, and the leader must be perceptive enough to select the new items properly.

Although I have simplified the nature of leadership and the methods by which leadership can be exerted, I do not mean to imply that leadership is anything but complex. In any organization of significant size, the leader uses a system composed of many variables. To attend to the appropriate constituencies and focus their attention on the appropriate items requires thought, planning, energy, conviction and an ability to persuade.

Strategy as order emerging from chaos
By Ralph Stacey[1]

There are four important points to make on the recent discoveries about the complex behaviour of dynamic systems, all of which have direct application to human organizations.

Chaos is a form of instability where the specific long-term future is unknowable

Chaos in its scientific sense is an irregular pattern of behaviour generated by well defined non-linear feedback rules commonly found in nature and human society. When systems driven by such rules operate away from equilibrium, they are highly sensitive to selected tiny changes in their environments, amplifying them into self-reinforcing virtuous and vicious circles that completely alter the behaviour of the system. In other words, the system's future unfolds in a manner dependent upon the precise detail of what it does, what the systems constituting its environments do, and upon chance. As a result of this fundamental property of the system itself, specific links between cause and effect are lost in the history of its development, and the specific path of its long-term future development is completely unpredictable. Over the short term, however, it is possible to predict behaviour because it takes time for the consequences of small changes to build up.

Is there evidence of chaos in business systems? We would conclude that there was if we could point to small changes escalating into large consequences; if we could point to self-reinforcing vicious and virtuous circles; if we could point to feedback that alternates between the amplifying and the damping. It is not difficult to find such evidence.

Creative managers seize on small differences in customer requirements and perceptions to build significant differentiators for their products. Customers may respond to this by switching from other product offerings, leading to a virtuous circle; or they may switch away, causing the kind of vicious circle that Coca-Cola found itself caught up in when it made that famous soft drink slightly sweeter.

Managers create, or at the very least shape, the requirements of their customers through the product offerings they make. Sony created a requirement for personal hi-fi systems through its Walkman offering, and manufacturers and operators have created requirements for portable telephones. Sony and Matsushita created the requirement for video recorders, and when companies supply information systems to their clients, they rarely do so according to a complete specification – instead, the supplier shapes the requirement. When managers intentionally shape customer demands through the offerings they make, this feeds back into customer responses, and managers may increase the impact by intentionally using the copying and spreading effects through which responses to product offerings feed back into other customers' responses. When managers do this, they are deliberately using positive feedback – along with negative feedback controls to meet cost and quality targets, for example – to create business success.

A successful business is also affected by many amplifying feedback processes that are outside the control of its managers and produce effects that they did not intend. Successful businesses are quite clearly characterized by feedback processes that flip between the negative and the positive, the damping and the amplifying; that is, they are characterized by feedback patterns that produce chaos. The long-term future of a creative organization is absolutely unknowable, and no one can intend its future direction over the long term or be in control of it. In such a system long-term plans and visions of future states can be only illusions.

But in chaos there are boundaries around the instability

While chaos means disorder and randomness in the behaviour of a system at the specific level, it also means that there is a qualitative pattern at a general, overall level. The future unfolds unpredictably, but it always does so according to recognizable family-like resemblances. This is what we mean when we say that

[1]Source: This article was reprinted from *Long Range Planning,* Vol. 26, No. 1, R. Stacey, 'Strategy as Order Emerging from Chaos', pp. 3–9, © 1993. With permission from Elsevier.

history repeats itself, but never in the same way. We see this combination of unpredictable specific behaviour within an overall pattern in snowflakes. As two nearby snowflakes fall to the earth, they experience tiny differences in temperature and air impurities. Each snowflake amplifies those differences as they form, and by the time they reach the earth they have different shapes – but they are still clearly snowflakes. We cannot predict the shape of each snowflake, but we can predict that they will be snowflakes. In business, we recognize patterns of boom and recession, but each time they are different in specific terms, defying all attempts to predict them.

Chaos is unpredictable variety within recognizable categories defined by irregular features, that is, an inseparable intertwining of order and disorder. It is this property of being bounded by recognizable qualitative patterns that makes it possible for humans to cope with chaos. Numerous tests have shown that our memories do not normally store information in units representing the precise characteristics of the individual shapes or events we perceive. Instead, we store information about the strength of connection between individual units perceived. We combine information together into categories or concepts using family resemblance-type features. Memory emphasizes general structure, irregular category features, rather than specific content. We remember the irregular patterns rather than the specific features and we design our next actions on the basis of these memorized patterns. And since we design our actions in this manner, chaotic behaviour presents us with no real problem. Furthermore, we are adept at using analogical reasoning and intuition to reflect upon experience and adapt it to new situations, all of which is ideally suited to handling chaos.

Unpredictable new order can emerge from chaos through a process of spontaneous self-organization

When non-linear feedback systems in nature are pushed far from equilibrium into chaos, they are capable of creating a complex new order. For example, at some low temperatures the atoms of a particular gas are arranged in a particular pattern and the gas emits no light. Then, as heat is applied, it agitates the atoms causing them to move, and as this movement is amplified through the gas it emits a dull glow. Small changes in heat are thus amplified, causing instability, or chaos, that breaks the symmetry of the atoms' original behaviour. Then at a critical point, the atoms in

the gas suddenly all point in the same direction to produce a laser beam. Thus, the system uses chaos to shatter old patterns of behaviour, creating the opportunity for the new. And as the system proceeds through chaos, it is confronted with critical points where it, so to speak, makes a choice between different options for further development. Some options represent yet further chaos and others lead to more complex forms of orderly behaviour, but which will occur is inherently unpredictable. The choice itself is made by spontaneous self-organization amongst the components of the system in which they, in effect, communicate with each other, reach a consensus, and commit to a new form of behaviour. If a more complex form of orderly behaviour is reached, it has what scientists call a dissipative structure, because continual attention and energy must be applied if it is to be sustained – for example, heat has to be continually pumped into the gas if the laser beam is to continue. If the system is to develop further, then the dissipative structure must be short-lived; to reach an even more complex state, the system will have to pass through chaos once more.

It is striking how similar the process of dealing with strategic issues in an organization is to the self-organizing phenomenon just outlined. The key to the effectiveness with which organizations change and develop new strategic directions lies in the manner in which managers handle what might be called their strategic issue agenda. That agenda is a dynamic, unwritten list of issues, aspirations and challenges that key groups of managers are attending to. Consider the steps managers can be observed to follow as they handle their strategic issue agenda:

■ Detecting and selecting small disturbances. In open-ended strategic situations, change is typically the result of many small events and actions that are unclear, ambiguous and confusing, with consequences that are unknowable. The key difficulty is to identify what the real issues, problems or opportunities are, and the challenge is to find an appropriate and creative aspiration or objective. In these circumstances the organization has no alternative but to rely on the initiative of individuals to notice and pursue some issue, aspiration or challenge. In order to do this, those individuals have to rely on their experience-based intuition and ability to detect analogies between one set of ambiguous circumstances and another.

■ Amplifying the issues and building political support. Once some individual detects some potential issue, that individual begins to push for organizational attention to it. A complex political process of building special interest groups to support an issue is required before it gains organizational attention and can thus be said to be on the strategic issue agenda.

- Breaking symmetries. As they build and progress strategic issue agendas, managers are in effect altering old mental models, existing company and industry recipes, to come up with new ways of doing things. They are destroying existing perceptions and structures.

- Critical points and unpredictable outcomes. Some issues on the agenda may be dealt with quickly, while others may attract attention, continuous or periodic, for a very long time. How quickly an issue is dealt with depends upon the time required to reach enough consensus and commitment to proceed to action. At some critical point, an external or internal pressure in effect forces a choice. The outcome on whether and how to proceed to action over the issue is unpredictable because it depends upon the context of power, personality and group dynamic within which it is being handled. The result may or may not be action, and action will usually be experimental at first.

- Changing the frame of reference. Managers in a business come to share memories of what worked and what did not work in the past – the organizational memory. In this way they build up a business philosophy or culture, establishing a company recipe and in common with their rivals an industry recipe too. These recipes have a powerful effect on what issues will subsequently be detected and attended to, that is, they constitute a frame of reference within which managers interpret what to do next. The frame of reference has to be continually challenged and changed because it can easily become inappropriate to new circumstances. The dissipative structure of consensus and commitment is therefore necessarily short-lived if an organization is to be innovative.

These phases constitute a political and learning process through which managers deal with strategic issues, and the key point about these processes is that they are spontaneous and self-organizing: no central authority can direct anyone to detect and select an open-ended issue for attention, simply because no one knows what it is until someone has detected it; no one can centrally organize the factions that form around specific issues; nor can anyone intend the destruction of old recipes

and the substitution of new ones since it is impossible to know what the appropriate new ones are until they are discovered. The development of new strategic direction requires the chaos of contention and conflict, and the self-organizing processes of political interaction and complex learning.

Chaos is a fundamental property of non-linear feedback systems, a category that includes human organizations

Feedback simply means that one action or event feeds into another; that is, one action or event determines the next according to some relationship. For example, one firm repackages its product and its rival responds in some way, leading to a further action on the part of the first, provoking in turn yet another response from the second, and so on. The feedback relationship may be linear or proportional, and when this is the case, the first firm will repackage its product and the second will respond by doing much the same. The feedback relationship could be non-linear, or non-proportional, however, so that when the first firm repackages its product, the second introduces a new product at a lower price; this could lead the first to cut prices even further, so touching off a price war. In other words, non-linear systems are those that use amplifying (positive) feedback in some way. To see the significance of positive feedback, compare it with negative feedback.

All effective businesses use negative or damping feedback systems to control and regulate their day-to-day activities. Managers fix short-term targets for profits and then prepare annual plans or budgets, setting out the time path to reach the target. As the business moves through time, outcomes are measured and compared with annual plan projections to yield variances. Frequent monitoring of those variances prompts corrective action to bring performance indicators back onto their planned paths; that is, variances feed back into corrective action and the feedback takes a negative form, so that when profit is below target, for example, offsetting action is taken to restore it. Scheduling, budgetary and planning systems utilize negative feedback to keep an organization close to a predictable, stable equilibrium path in which it is adapted to its environment. While negative feedback controls a system according to prior intention, positive feedback produces explosively unstable equilibrium where changes are amplified, eventually putting intolerable pressure on the system until it runs out of control.

The key discovery about the operation of non-linear feedback systems, however, is that there is a third choice. When a non-linear feedback system is driven away from stable equilibrium toward explosive unstable equilibrium, it passes through a phase of bounded instability – there is a border between stability and instability where feedback flips autonomously between the amplifying and the damping to produce chaotic behaviour; a paradoxical state that combines both stability and instability.

All human interactions take the form of feedback loops simply because the consequences of one action always feed back to affect a subsequent one. Furthermore, all human interactions constitute non-linear feedback loops because people under- and overreact. Since organizations are simply a vast web of feedback loops between people, they must be capable of chaotic, as well as stable and explosively unstable, behaviour. The key question is which of these kinds of behaviours leads an organization to success. We can see the answer to this question if we reflect upon the fundamental forces operating on an organization.

All organizations are powerfully pulled in two fundamentally different directions:

■ Disintegration. Organizations can become more efficient and effective if they divide tasks, segment markets, appeal to individual motivators, empower people, promote informal communication and separate production processes in geographic and other terms. These steps lead to fragmenting cultures and dispersed power that pull an organization toward disintegration, a phenomenon that can be seen in practice as companies split into more and more business units and find it harder and harder to maintain control.

■ Ossification. To avoid this pull to disintegration, and to reap the advantages of synergy and coordination, all organizations are also pulled to a state in which tasks are integrated, overlaps in market segments and production processes managed, group goals stressed above individual ones, power concentrated, communication and procedures formalized, and strongly shared cultures established. As an organization moves in this direction it develops more and more rigid structures, rules, procedures and systems until it eventually ossifies, consequences that are easy to observe as organizations centralize.

Thus, one powerful set of forces pulls every organization toward a stable equilibrium (ossification) and another powerful set of forces pulls it toward an explosively unstable equilibrium (disintegration). Success lies at the border between these states, where managers continually alter systems and structures to avoid attraction either to disintegration or to ossification. For example, organizations typically swing to centralization in one period, to decentralization in another, and back again later on. Success clearly lies in a non-equilibrium state between stable and unstable equilibria; and for a non-linear feedback system, that is chaos.

Eight steps to create order out of chaos

When managers believe that they must pull together harmoniously in pursuit of a shared organizational intention established before they act, they are inevitably confined to the predictable – existing strategic directions will simply be continued or innovations made by others will simply be imitated. When, instead of this, managers create the chaos that flows from challenging existing perceptions and promote the conditions in which spontaneous self-organization can occur, they make it possible for innovation and new strategic direction to emerge. Managers create such conditions when they undertake actions of the following kind.

Develop new perspectives on the meaning of control

The activity of learning in a group is a form of control that managers do not normally recognize as such. It is a self-organizing, self-policing form of control in which the group itself discovers intention and exercises control. Furthermore, we are all perfectly accustomed to the idea that the strategic direction of local communities, nation-states and international communities is developed and controlled through the operation of political systems, but we rarely apply this notion to organizations. When we do, we see that a sequence of choices and actions will continue in a particular direction only while those espousing that direction continue to enjoy sufficient support. This constitutes a form of control that is as applicable to an organization when it faces the conflicts around open-ended change, as it is to a nation. The lesson is that self-organizing processes can produce controlled behaviour even though no one is in control – sometimes the best thing a manager can do is to let go and allow things to happen.

Design the use of power

The distribution of power and the way in which it is used provide very important boundaries around the group learning process from which new strategic directions emerge. The application of power in particular forms has fairly predictable consequences for group dynamics. Where power is applied as force and consented to out of fear, the group dynamic will be one of submission, or where such power is not consented to, the group dynamic will be one of rebellion, either covert or overt. Power may be applied as authority, and the predictable group dynamic here is one in which members of the group suspend their critical faculties and accept instructions from those above them. Groups in states of submission, rebellion or conformity are incapable of complex learning, that is, the development of new perspectives and new mental models.

The kind of group dynamics that are conducive to complex learning occur when highly competitive win/lose polarization is removed and open questioning and public testing of assertions encouraged. When this happens, people use argument and conflict to move toward periodic consensus and commitment to a particular issue. That consensus and commitment cannot, however, be the norm when people are searching for new perspectives – rather, they must alternate between conflict and consensus, between confusion and clarity. This kind of dynamic is likely to occur when they most powerfully alternate the form in which they use their power: sometimes withdrawing and allowing conflict; sometimes intervening with suggestions; sometimes exerting authority.

Encourage self-organizing groups

A group will be self-organizing only if it discovers its own challenges, goals and objectives. Mostly, such groups need to form spontaneously – the role of top managers is simply to create the atmosphere in which this can happen. When top managers do set up a group to deal with strategic issues, however, they must avoid the temptation to write terms of reference, set objectives or prod the group to reach some predetermined view. Instead top managers must present ambiguous challenges and take the chance that the group may produce proposals they do not approve of. For a group of managers to be self-organizing, it has to be free to operate as its members jointly choose, within the boundaries provided by their work together. This means that when they work together in this way, the normal hierarchy must be suspended for most of the time. Members are there because of the contributions they are able to make and the influence they can exert through those contributions and their own personalities. This suspension of the normal hierarchy can take place only if those on higher levels behave in a manner

that indicates that they attach little importance to their position for the duration of the work of the group.

Provoke multiple cultures

One way of developing the conflicting countercultures required to provoke new perspectives is to rotate people between functions and business units. The motive here is to create cultural diversity as opposed to the current practice of using rotation to build a cadre of managers with the same management philosophy. Another effective way of promoting countercultures is that practised by Canon and Honda, where significant numbers of managers are hired at the same time, midway through their careers in other organizations, to create sizeable pockets of different cultures that conflict with the predominant one.

Present ambiguous challenges instead of clear long-term objectives or visions

Agendas of strategic issues evolve out of the clash between different cultures in self-organizing groups. Top managers can provoke this activity by setting ambiguous challenges and presenting half-formed issues for others to develop, instead of trying to set clear long-term objectives. Problems without objectives should be intentionally posed to provoke the emotion and conflict that lead to active search for new ways of doing things. This activity of presenting challenges should also be a two-way activity, where top executives hold themselves open to challenge from subordinates.

Expose the business to challenging situations

Managers who avoid taking chances face the certainty of stagnation and therefore the high probability of collapse in the long term, simply because innovation depends significantly on chance. Running for cover because the future is unknowable is in the long run the riskiest response of all. Instead, managers must intentionally expose themselves to the most challenging of situations. In his study of international companies, Michael Porter concludes that those who position themselves to serve the world's most sophisticated and demanding customers, who seek the challenge of competing with the most imaginative and competent competitors, are the ones who build sustainable competitive advantage on a global scale.

Devote explicit attention to improving group learning skills

New strategic directions emerge when groups of managers learn together in the sense of questioning deeply held beliefs and altering existing mental models rather than simply absorbing existing bodies of knowledge and sets of techniques. Such a learning process may well be personally threatening and so arouse anxiety that leads to bizarre group dynamics – this is perhaps the major obstacle to effective organizational learning. To overcome it, managers must spend time explicitly exploring how they interact and learn together – the route to superior learning is self-reflection in groups.

Create resource slack

New strategic directions emerge when the attitudes and behaviour of managers create an atmosphere favourable to individual initiative and intuition, to political interaction, and to learning in groups. Learning and political interaction are hard work, and they cannot occur without investment in spare management resources. A vital precondition for emergent strategy is

thus investment in management resources to allow it to happen.

Conclusion

Practicing managers and academics have been debating the merits of organizational learning as opposed to the planning conceptualization of strategic management. That debate has not, however, focused clearly on the critical unquestioned assumptions upon which the planning approach is based, namely, the nature of causality. Recent discoveries about the nature of dynamic feedback systems make it clear that cause and effect links disappear in innovative human organizations, making it impossible to envisage or plan their long-term futures. Because of this lack of causal connection between specific actions and specific outcomes, new strategic directions can only emerge through a spontaneous, self-organizing political and learning process. The planning approach can be seen as a specific approach applicable to the short-term management of an organization's existing activities, a task as vital as the development of a new strategic direction.

Dual leadership

By David G. Thomson[1]

In 1994 Jerry Yang and David Filo, two doctoral candidates in Stanford University's electrical engineering programme, spent as much time surfing the newly created World Wide Web as they were pursuing their doctoral studies. They even created their own website, "Jerry's Guide to the World Wide Web," which linked Internet users to their favourite places in cyberspace.

"Jerry's Guide," however, did not make the Yang and Filo site sound very interesting, so one night they changed the name. Teeing off the phrase Yet Another Compiler Compiler (YACC) – a favourite among Unix computer code programmers – they came up with Yet Another Hierarchical Officious Oracle – or YAHOO! for short because Yang and Filo considered themselves

a couple of major yahoos after all, and thus a famous brand name was born.

Then in 1995 Marc Andreessen, cofounder of Netscape Communications, invited Yang and Filo to move Yahoo! from the Stanford University computer system, which Yahoo! had outgrown, to Netscape's big facility. Commercialization soon followed. Advertising revenues began to rise – and Yang and Filo soon realized that they could not manage the business by themselves anymore.

That is when they recruited an experienced technology professional and former Stanford PhD, Tim Koogle, to serve as CEO. Koogle, in turn, recruited Jeff Mallett as COO, who had already cut his teeth at Reference Software and WordPerfect and was Vice

[1]Source: This article was adapted from David G. Thomson (2006) 'Chapter: 7 Dual leadership' *Blueprint To A Billion: 7 essentials to achieve exponential growth,* John Wiley & Sons. Copyright © David G Thomson 2006. Reproduced with permission of John Wiley & Sons, Inc.

President and General Manager of Novell Inc.'s consumer division. Together, Koogle and Mallett began transforming Yahoo!, turning it into one of the most popular stops along the information highway.

While Yang and Filo would arrive at work wearing T-shirts and sneakers, Koogle and Mallett preferred suits. Many viewed the foursome's working relationship as one of children with ideas and their parents who could turn their children's ideas into action. As analyst Andrea Williams of Volpe Brown Whelan & Co. noted, "Americans are captivated by the idea of two college kids like Yang and Filo starting an incredible service. But Mallet and Koogle have turned it into a business that advertisers and investors understand and respect."

Indeed, the relationship between Mallett and Koogle helped turn Yahoo! into a winning High Growth Company for the first five years of its development. Mallett was a strong internal leader and responsible for running operations. Koogle was an ideal outside-facing CEO. In the first 12 months on the job, Koogle took a startup and signed 50 alliances, hired a sales team and several crucial top management team members, and took the company public.

Koogle essentially guided the company through tremendous growth as he contributed to building its management team, creating its adventurous organizational culture and signing up alliance partners. Together the two men made Yahoo! into one of the few profitable, high-growth Internet companies of the late 1990s. After the dot.com meltdown, however, and Yahoo!'s well-chronicled falters, another team turned around the company and got it onto its present track. Current Chairman and CEO Terry Semel and COO Dan Rosensweig have also made a compelling team – with all the requisite external and internal skills needed to get Yahoo! onto the fast lane of the enormous Internet search-and advertising industry.

To pin all the early success of Yahoo! on Koogle and Mallett – and where it is today on Semel and Rosensweig – would oversimplify a complex corporate history. But teams of such effective pairs do, in fact, perform much of the work that catapults their companies to record-breaking success. The following sections explain why.

The importance of dynamic duos

Among High Growth Companies, we found that "dynamic duos" drove many of the star-performing companies. These are two individuals who worked tightly together to build the firm from dreams to a billion dollars in revenue.

Dynamic duos are the stuff of corporate legend: Sears and Roebuck, Roy and Walt Disney, Hewlett and Packard, and the like. What we found is that in High Growth Companies it is more than corporate myth – High Growth Companies *do* spring from such pairings.

More surprises surfaced as we drilled deeper into this finding. We learned that for the duo to be dynamic, one of them had to excel in the *external* part of the effort – in marketing and sales. The other had to be the *internal* – keeping the operations purring or, perhaps, inventing new products. Together, they had to explore and innovate continuously – whether it was in product innovation or marketing innovation. They had to make swift decisions – and often quick and nimble correction of their mistakes. Most important they had to have complete trust in and respect for one another.

The Koogle-Mallett combo at Yahoo! is typical of what we found in the High Growth companies: an Internal–External leadership pair (working in partnership with the founding team) who managed to execute all the essentials simultaneously. This particular pair, like others we have seen repeatedly in High Growth Companies, had a unique chemistry that electrified the evolution of their service. Cisco, eBay, Nike, Starbucks and many others have applied the same pattern, as shown by the list of dynamic duos in Table 11.3.1.

There is one other thing that struck us. These dynamic duos who lead High Growth Companies are not just colleagues or even just friends. They have a remarkable chemistry between them, built on a very high level of respect and trust. They benefit from having

TABLE 11.3.1 Internal–External leadership pairs

Company	Leadership pair examples
Yahoo!	Jeff Mallett and Tim Koogle
Microsoft	Jon Shirley and Bill Gates
Tractor Supply	Jim Wright and Joe Scarlett
eBay	Maynard Webb and Meg Whitman
Siebel Systems	Patricia House and Tom Siebel
Starbucks	Orin Smith and Howard Schultz
Broadcom	Harry Samueli and Henry Nicholas III

Source: Company reports

complementary skills and talents. They are the yin and yang, the weave and warp, the bacon and eggs, and without this dynamic of compatibility their companies could not have made it to the top. Their relationship is dynamic in the way that they use their complementary strengths. Any individual weaknesses or flip-flops went unseen by outside observers because they used each other's strengths in ways that compensated for what the other lacked or could not do. As a pair, they were the highest of performance teams.

The essentials of high growth leadership

To get from an early High Growth to an actual billion dollars in revenue, you need a breakthrough value proposition, Launching Customers, and a powerhouse business model. What about leadership? What kind of management does it take to propel a company from a High Growth to a billion dollars in a few years? What are the roles of the CEO in a High Growth Company, the COO, the engineering team – even the founders themselves?

To answer these questions, we – in collaboration with Peter Robertson of the London-based consulting firm Human Insight – took a closer look at the best High Growth Companies. With Robertson's help we assessed a sample of the top High Growth Companies. There we found patterns in – and answers about – High Growth Companies leadership.

In addition to these assessments, we studied published interviews and articles that featured the leaders of top High Growth Companies. Their statements gave us clues to the best management practices. We conducted our own interviews with numerous founders, CEOs, COOs and investors. These individuals helped identify the elements of management that they believed drove their success. After a year of this kind of exploration, we had a much clearer understanding about this unique set of leadership dimensions.

Three leadership dimensions of the internal-outside leadership duo

High Growth leadership, it turns out, has three dimensions:

1 *Focus on relationships and products.* One member of the dynamic duo is focused on company-shaping relationships – that is, building relationships with Launching Customers, Big Brother alliances, strategic investors, board members and outsiders such as other High Growth CEOs, suppliers and community leaders. The other half of the duo focuses on logical ideas concerned with product development, processes and systems that fuel the company's product or service pipeline.

2 *Drive to innovate and explore.* While one member of the duo manages for internal structure, that is, problem solving for disciplined and predictable responses, the other is forward looking by exploring and shaping opportunities. This is a delicate balance between preserving the past and exploring in order to innovate. That said, there is a useful back-and-forth and, sometimes, even a brief exchange of roles that keeps this chemistry dynamic and replenishing.

3 *The ability to manage simultaneously.* Most important, we learned the importance of management's ability to balance the execution of the essentials. In such a high-powered environment, there are always many balls to juggle and it takes a particularly talented, collegial team to keep those balls in the air. Dropping one can cause a High Growth Company to risk falling off trajectory. Successful High Growth management teams learn how to do it all – how to deal with the simultaneous execution of the essentials and still keep the corporate trajectory heading rapidly toward a billion dollars and more.

The first two leadership dimensions, focus and drive, form the basis for clearly defining the roles of the Internal–External leadership pair (see Figure 11.3.1).

When we started our research for this book, we sensed that High Growth Companies had a unique management style. What we learned was that *High Growth* management is unique. With limited resources these teams execute "1 + 1 = 3" miracles. What can we learn from these impressive leaders?

Breakaway marketing leaders

First, High Growth leaders are superb communicators. They possess the personal chemistry, even charisma, which lets them bridge the gaps between alliance members, Launching Customers, community leaders and important investors. They are accomplished at finding, qualifying and shaping the deals and relationships that ultimately shape the company.

One member of the leadership pair, typically the CEO, fills this role. The CEO could be an external hire,

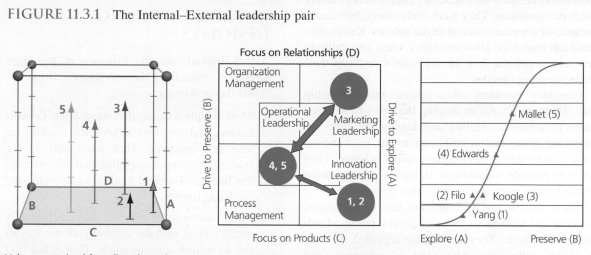

FIGURE 11.3.1 The Internal–External leadership pair

Focus on Relationships (D)

Yahoo: perceived founding dynamics

Focus & Drive: form the basis for defining the roles of the Internal–External leadership pair

Drive is related to the contribution of roles to the standard Growth-curve. This is shown in the right picture, where the explore (A) – Preserve (B) characteristics of the Growth-curve correlate reversely with the role positions in the left and middle picture.

The vertical axis (left picture) relates to the capacity to manage simultaneously. The higher a role scores, the more this role is capable of aligning the contribution of other roles to the Growth-curve. This makes these roles more generalistic, as contrast to roles that score lower, which relates to being more specialist (managing less, but more in depth)

---

typically brought in early – or a founding member. Meg Whitman was brought in early; Bill Gates, Howard Schultz and Phil Knight are founding members.

The role of the leader depends on the value proposition of the company. Nike's Phil Knight was a showcase of breakaway marketing leadership. Knight constantly pushed the boundaries and changed the ground rules. Instead of marketing shoes, he marketed the athletes who wore the shoes and what they achieved in their Nikes.

As new market segments emerged, Knight tried to be the first to spot them. In 1984, when the National Basketball Association (NBA) games began televising in prime time, Knight was instrumental in getting an endorsement from Michael Jordan, then just a promising player. The Air Jordan shoes helped make Nike's basketball shoes into a $500 million business by 1990. No wonder that a recent *Fortune* magazine cover read: "Nike After Knight: The maverick built a company like no other. Can anyone fill his shoes?"

Tom Siebel aggressively shaped Launching Customer relationships with Charles Schwab and General Electric, shaped a Big Brother alliance with Microsoft and Andersen Consulting, and shaped his board by adding Charles Schwab and the head of Andersen as a result of an investment in Siebel.

External-facing CEOs are highly exploratory – particularly with relationships and creating opportunities. This forward-thinking style is critical to proactively developing Launching Customers and Big Brother alliances, securing the right board members and evangelizing the company's vision to employees and the community. This leader affects the forward-thinking approaches of the person whose role is focused more primarily on the Internal, who is usually responsible for innovation leadership.

Breakaway innovation leaders

While the dynamic duo is evangelizing customers, conceiving a brilliant marketing strategy and managing the business, a third critical leader is what we call *Breakaway Innovation Leadership*. These leaders, typically the founders of the company, focus more on the product rather than on External relationships. They are often highly creative, with a broad range of interests, perhaps skipping from mathematics to biology to music in a single thought. They have a need for innovation because they have a passion for extremely creative inventions. They work with others, but mostly because of a mutual interest in the subject. Rather than personal charm or charisma, they often use brilliant new ideas and the lure of exploration to keep their teams working together.

Company founders often assume this leadership role. They are pivotal in shaping the innovation-based value proposition, creating and leading the core engineering team, and contributing to the fundamental principles by which the business model is based. They serve to provide a consistent trajectory of innovation aligned to the company's core value proposition.

These leaders are an important link to customers, partners and markets in terms of getting product feedback from them. They are highly regarded by their specialist colleagues, who exist as customers and partners in the same technical community, and who breathe the same air. As corporations grow with new employees, these product-centred innovators act as a critical adhesive element by spurring the team on to higher levels of innovation.

More key roles in high growth management

If you relied on the covers of the business magazines, you would think that it takes only an individual or two to run a High Growth Company. No single CEO can possibly keep all of the essentials in motion without help. In fact, the more our team debated the unique qualities of High Growth Companies, the more we realized that the successful corporation was much more like an *ecosystem* than a cult of personality or personalities.

High Growth Companies need steady-handed managers who bring stability to the enterprise. These individuals exhibit control, discipline and predictability. With this keel beneath them, High Growth marketing and product innovators can feel secure enough to keep their minds out on the cutting edge.

Process Managers, for instance, typically are the captains of supply chain leadership. They are controlling and process focused. They can either operate within existing boundaries or shape new boundaries within which to operate. They tend to be the key team to support the COO and CEO. Of course, not every High Growth Company needs to invest in its own supply chain to get to the top. Many of them, on the faster four- and six-year trajectory, tended to outsource manufacturing. That allowed them to grow quickly, to minimize capital costs and to achieve lower product

THREE SURPRISING INSIGHTS

As we looked into the histories of the High Growth Companies, three counterintuitive insights dawned on us:

1 Most people assume that most High Growth leaders had previous experience working in smaller companies. That, we found, is not true. Of the top companies that we studied, the Internal–External leaders came from varied backgrounds.

2 There seems to be a belief that the founders rarely stayed with the company all the way to the $1 billion revenue mark. That is not true with these companies. A significant number of the original leaders were still at the helm when the High Growth startup crossed the billion dollar line: Bill Gates, Larry Ellison, Tom Sternberg and Pierre Omidyar to name a few.

3 The third misconception is that High Growth founders are of the same breed, that stereotype of the young, tousle-haired, pizza-gobbling, brilliant college dropout – or some variation of the theme. However, High Growth leaders did not have a common background. They came from all walks of professional life – from college dropouts to college grads, from small company leaders to large company leaders. They came as business professionals or customer advocates with little marketing and sales expertise or with a lot of it.

costs. Cisco, for instance, outsourced its manufacturing early. Broadcom also outsourced its semiconductor manufacturing. Nike moved its manufacturing to several Asian footwear producers.

Organization Managers are another role. These leaders are at home in the caring role. They foster a more congenial atmosphere in the organization and will do their best to maintain it. Especially important in high-growth and services companies, these leaders believe that caring for employees is fundamental for the company to provide a highly differentiated service to customers. This leadership style is typically humble. They are leaders by example, great listeners who pick up on feedback and quickly resolve issues. Typically, they support the CEO and COO.

A third role is *Operational Leadership,* the Chief Operating Officer. This role forms the complementary half of the Dynamic Duo – and is the internal counterpart to the outside-facing CEO. COOs are known as Mr./Ms. Internal and are at the right hand of the outside-facing CEO. Operational leaders are centred and well balanced. Often, they are so far behind the scenes that you hardly hear about them in the business press or notice them when you walk in the door of a company. As shown in Figure 11.3.1, they are highly versatile across all of the leadership styles. They have a trust-based relationship with a very high propensity to effective and efficient problem solving. They are real partners. If you can envision a high performance team of two, this would be it.

The number-one Internal–External pair of the 1990s

Today, people often think of the prototypical Internal–External pair as Bill Gates and Steve Ballmer. But another great example of the Internal–External dynamic pair can be found in the evolution of Microsoft. Back in 1983, when Microsoft was at the inflection point, the company outgrew its small-time style faster than Bill Gates could handle it. Gates had tried to take charge of five product lines. As a result, he paid little attention to tailoring programmes to meet customers' needs. Key planning decisions were often delayed or not made.

Gates recognized his own shortcomings. He tried to hire a president, but that individual did not work out. He tried again in August 1983, and this time he hit gold – Jon Shirley, a 25-year career veteran at Tandy Corp. who had known Gates as a customer.

Shirley recalled, "The company lacked a lot of systems that it needed to grow to become big. It was nothing like an ideal organizational setup and it had no MIS system. They were using a Tandy Model 2 for the general ledger." Shirley also discovered that Microsoft lacked key statistical data about its products, its markets and its sales. "We were totally out of manufacturing space, and we had no one who knew how to run the manufacturing side," he said looking back, adding that he threw himself into developing "a whole lot of structures and systems that would give us the tools we needed."

Shirley had performed many of the same operations for the much larger Tandy and felt comfortable operating within Microsoft's "get-it-done" corporate culture. Shirley viewed his role as one of building up the support side of the business, hiring the chief financial officer (Francis Gaudette, who would later play a critical role in shepherding Microsoft's initial public offering through Wall Street in 1986), and honing the management team, whose members had almost all been hired from within the company.

In August 1984 the management team took serious action. It reorganized around two divisions: (1) systems software, the programmes that control a computer's internal operations; and (2) business applications, programmes that tell a machine to do specific tasks, such as word processing. Four years later, in 1988, Microsoft restructured the Applications Division into five business units. The business units would have profit and loss responsibility for their product lines and would be responsible for marketing and documentation of their products, said Shirley. "It gave them a great deal of control to run as a small business," he noted.

Analysts give Shirley credit for quarterbacking many of the key strategic alliances that helped catapult Microsoft to industry prominence (though Shirley said they naturally evolved from simple customer relationships). In contrast, Gates played the market and standards leadership role, shaping the technologies for various product areas. "Gates and Shirley absolutely occupied different ends of the business," said Arthur Block, Manufacturers Hanover Trust VP in charge of end-user support. "Bill focused on the IBM alliance while Shirley focused on Hewlett-Packard (HP). Gates talked to user groups while Shirley talked to the financial community. Gates linked product/market opportunities to technology, while Jon applied structure and process to the business so that it could scale."

On the day-to-day level, Shirley mirrored a management style that was supportive and didactic, well-suited to Microsoft's campus ambience. "I believe in delegation and teaching," Shirley said. "You've got to give people sufficient authority to make mistakes."

Shirley retired in 1989 – after Microsoft passed $800 million revenue (on the way to $1 billion next year). He had essentially guided the company from the inflection point to $1 billion as Bill Gates' "Mr Internal."

A leading Internal–External pair today

Tractor Supply is a wonderful case study of a similar management pair in today's management world. Tractor Supply is the number one US farm and ranch store, with sales of $1.7 billion and over 7,000 team members. The company is known for its great customer service, which it provides to full- and part-time farmers and ranchers as well as the general public. Tractor Supply carries a complete line of livestock and pet products; maintenance products for agricultural and rural use; hardware and tools; lawn-and-garden power equipment; truck, trailer and towing gear; and work clothing. Despite the wide variety of products that Tractor Supply offers, the most popular item it sells harkens back to the roots of the business: the simple lynchpin, that basic item that connects the farm tractor to what it pulls.

While Joe Scarlett's official title is Chairman, he is more often described by those he works with as coach, cheerleader, company's conscience and chief missionary of the gospel at Tractor Supply. Scarlett provided us with a unique perspective on the dynamic duo leadership paradigm. During his tenure, he worked with an internal counterpart – and without one:

Before I became Chairman and my right hand, Jim Wright, became President and CEO in 2004, we served as the CEO and COO team. Then and today, we are on the same page at all times. We share the same values. We finish each other's sentences. Just the other day someone remarked that we are "like an old married couple." The chemistry started during the interviewing process.

When I hired Jim, we spent hours interviewing. We went to Florida and walked the stores for hours at a time. We attended a manager's meeting in Florida together. We spent two days walking through Wal-Mart, Lowe's, Home Depot and a score of other stores learning from them. In each of these settings, we asked questions of one another, we talked strategy, we discussed values, we discussed the competition, we problem solved. We would ask each other "How would you handle this situation?" in merchandising, operations, logistics, competition, people and training. We got into each others heads so well that when we are in meetings today and look at each other across the room we often know what the other is thinking.

Today, when Jim and I get the same email and I send a follow up I often find that Jim independently sent a similar follow up to the same people. What makes us successful is that we have similar but different backgrounds. We each managed a lot of different parts of the business over the years. We both have merchandising and operations experience, which we believe are

critical factors for leadership success in high growth retailing. We both have run businesses before. Jim was previously the CEO of a smaller company. We are honest with one another. We are quick problem solvers. No problem lingers.

Scarlett explained that Wright is process driven and more inside facing. He can take a problem and determine the right priority, the right person, and the right process to get it solved. In contrast, Scarlett said he is more focused on big picture strategies and people issues. He spends much time preaching the message and interacting with employees – even though he is ostensibly more externally facing. "Of course," said Scarlett, "both of us are committed to our people first. Leadership in each store is our top priority." Scarlett spends 50 per cent of his time coaching, mentoring, career planning and training. Together they just brought in their 22 top high-potential store managers, with whom Scarlett spent two days discussing the business and customers. In fact, Scarlett personally visits about 150 stores a year.

Scarlett continued to elaborate on the differences of style in Tractor Supply's leadership pair:

In contrast there was a time before Jim [was at Tractor Supply] when it was a struggle. I am not process oriented. We found ourselves talking a lot and didn't execute. I would unrealistically expect people to do things based on how I thought it should get done. We would "take three steps forward and two back." He could get things done realistically. He could break down problems into tasks with a process. With Jim on board we take three steps forward and stay there. I found that when I wore both hats, I simply did not have enough time for it all!

There was another aspect of this High Growth winner that impressed me. "We are very close to our suppliers," Scarlett said and continued in some detail:

I am on a first-name basis with our 50 top supplier CEOs. We bring the Presidents and CEOs in each year to share leadership, business strategy, direction, plans, philosophy and values. We share confidential information with them so that they can partner with us to innovate and be first to market. We count on our suppliers to help us offer products that are both key to our target customer and not part of the offering from the big-box retailers such as Wal-Mart and Home Depot. We work with our suppliers to serve as a guide for them so that we are first to market. We become their "Test kitchen." Today we are very proud of the fact that 35 per cent of our business is from new products that weren't in the product line three years earlier. We listen to our customers carefully to offer them higher quality and better lifestyle products.

Finally Scarlett explained that his company espouses some down-home, old-fashioned values and they have paid off. Scarlett said the company mission statement is *"Work hard, have fun, and make money by providing legendary service and great products at everyday low prices"* – and there is not a meeting where he or Jim do not discuss the values of the company in terms of everyday decision making. *"When I visit stores, I am consistently preaching our values,"* he explained. *"For example, we will discuss ethics with the store teams, what are breaches, how not to get in these situations. I preach and repeat our values consistently."*

"Why preach and repeat?" I asked.

"We continually have a lot of new people," he replied with a country man's grin, *"and people naturally only retain a small portion of what they hear!"*

Calm in the midst of the storm

In contrast to the intense stress environment that typically comes with high-energy innovation for both products and marketing, High Growth Companies share another trait: The ability to remain calm in the midst of the storm, to stay consistent and fairly unflappable even under the onslaught of chaos and ever increasing change. The "secret weapon" is having consistent values with the ability to self-correct.

One of the most important tasks of management is ensuring a climate in which people feel safe to explore. Exploration can only be achieved if leadership values are consistent. Leadership values are not one action, but a demonstrated set of actions over time in all kinds of situations that demonstrate consistency of values. There are two equally weighted drivers of consistency.

Consistent behaviours, communications and messaging

Marshall Goldsmith, world-renowned executive coach whose skills are in demand by many major CEOs, shared his perspective on this important leadership

aspect. "What matters in leadership," Goldsmith said, "is not the words hanging on the wall; it is the behaviour demonstrated in the hall." This is the case in High Growth Companies, given the consistent nature of the communications that we found in which CEOs are always "on message."

For Joe Scarlett, Tractor Supply's Mission and Values are integrated into all of his communications and messages. This leads him to be consistent and aligned with communicating corporate values. As already mentioned, Scarlett spends much of his time with employees discussing the application of values to behaviours and customer service.

Consistent values at defining moments

Consistency means that personal values and organizational aims will largely dictate what a manager does. These are best illustrated during defining moments – times when an organization is facing a crisis. All eyes are on the leader. Consistency is tested when there is a worrisome opportunity for the leader to act in *opposition* to stated values – and a broader sense of ethics. If he or she demonstrates consistent values, they are not only proven a good leader, they have reinforced the culture of the company and, hence, the conditions for continued growth.

> Leaders who lay out a consistent communications plan and vision – and act with upright values even in crisis – are critical to mobilizing an organization into consistent behaviours.

We found often that, early in the company's trajectory, many leaders of High Growth Companies are pretty unimpressed by the wealth and fame that might follow. They are focused on the business – or even how it might help the community. eBay's IPO, for example, established a charitable fund. Instead of focusing on themselves, High Growth leaders focus on the company. Mark Leslie, who built Veritas software to over $1 billion in revenue, came to this understanding: "I wasn't a great CEO until I realized it was about everybody *but* me."

High Growth leaders are goal- and results-oriented. They manage for long-term results. They know how to leverage customers and alliance partners to shape products and services, thereby creating exponential revenue growth. In certain sectors, software for example, it was paramount that these companies dominate their markets. These leaders, therefore, placed a high value on beating the competition.

We found that High Growth leaders communicate consistent messages about the company's value proposition. Their passion is aligned to the value proposition and the priorities that they must execute, as in the case of Meg Whitman.

In 1999, when eBay's website crashed for 22 hours, Meg Whitman stepped up. She called this event eBay's "near-death experience" – the young company risked losing its entire trove of customer and transaction data. The outage exposed a glaring weakness for an Internet company – and eBay did not have the in-house talent to fix the site. What saved her, and eBay too, was a new technology chief. "I was like a crazed woman on a mission," she recalled about her meeting with Maynard Webb, then Gateway Computer's tech boss, a few days after the outage. Whitman successfully pleaded with him to come over to eBay and the infrastructure that he built now handles, in a typical day, more transactions than NASDAQ – with no major outages in almost six years.

The defining moment does not stop there. Everyone at eBay was given a list of 100 customers to call and apologize to. It turned into a defining moment of another nature. The customers were genuinely touched and the company reconnected to the community. If you ask any eBay employee, this defining moment is one that is often described as part of the company's lore. In 2005, six years later, when the pricing changes were not understood by the community, the employees again picked up the phone to call the community and Meg Whitman joined the town hall meeting that week to explain the changes to customers.

PASSION OVER PAIN

Although the management world has been taught that pain, crisis and the need to overcome deficiencies motivate change, High Growth Companies reveal a different picture. Top High Growth Companies innovate because they have an inner drive to explore. This exploration is not limited to products. It includes new markets, new alliances, new customers and new business models. Although pain can drive change, it often comes too late to be of much use.

Having your values in place also means that you can move fast to acquire an opportunity. For Tractor Supply, this happened in the summer of 2001. A competitor had gone bankrupt, and Tractor Supply had the chance to buy its stores. The problem was that the investment banker for the creditor said that Tractor Supply would have to buy all of them, not the 40 that Tractor Supply wanted. Tractor Supply could have lost the opportunity, but instead it came up with what CEO Joe Scarlett described as Project 110, in which the company had to open up all 110 stores by the end of 2002, with 87 of them opened in 110 days.

"Project 110 galvanized the whole organization," recalled Scarlett. "We brought the top 20 leaders in Tractor Supply together. Jim Wright ran the project. The teams met every week to read out the status: on target, nearly on target, or screwed up. No one wanted to report screwed up. This lifted the confidence of the management team. We opened 87 stores in 110 days – when the maximum we had ever opened was 30 in a year. Jim and I spent hours in each of the 87 stores talking with the entire team, sitting around in a circle on those five-gallon buckets and talking about the values of our company, relationship with our customers, our value over Wal-Mart, and the things we can do to continue making our culture very special. Since then, we have never looked back."

A change in leadership can also become a defining moment. It may be the need to change senior management or the search for a successor when "the shoes are hard to fill." The spotlight is on the board, founders or CEO at this defining moment. Yahoo!'s founding team was wise to recognize early on that they could not shape the business themselves. Their defining moment – bringing in Koogle as an Outside leader – brought increased talent and structure to the business. Koogle then brought his Internal counterpart, Mallett, into the company. And what would eBay be without Meg Whitman brought in as CEO in 1998? Not nearly as big a success.

The ability to quickly self-correct

When growing to $1 billion, whether you are a four-, six-, or twelve-year trajectory company, at the inflection point you should expect revenues to double every 4, 9, or 24 months, respectively. The speed at which four- and six-year companies double revenues particularly requires that these companies exhibit the ability to not only self-correct, but to do so with speed. Failure to correct quickly increases the likelihood that a company can fall off trajectory.

Joe Scarlett passed this lesson on to other leaders at Tractor Supply. "Drill down if you don't know a lot about a problem or opportunity. Ask a lot of questions," he said, describing his style of self-correction.

"Once I failed to do that when we bought a computer system. We bought too large a system when we could only manage a fraction of it. It wouldn't have happened if I had asked more questions." Scarlett says you have to challenge the status quo, and not "fall in love with your own thinking. "Scarlett offers another homily: "Get close to everyone in the organization – customers and suppliers, too. Any CEO spending over 50 per cent of his or her time in the office is doing a disservice. Go where the action is."

The third leadership dimension: managing simultaneously

We have already noted that High Growth leaders must demonstrate breakaway marketing and breakaway product innovation leadership. Their third challenge is the toughest of them all: Managing simultaneously. Yet the leaders of our top High Growth Companies have proven themselves to be shapers – leaders who can effectively shape their company's destiny in the face of intense uncertainty.

These leaders are problem solvers. But even more, they have a comfort level for problems with a lot of moving parts. Beyond that they have a superior capacity to recognize patterns – the pattern of Launching Customer behaviour, the pattern of Big Brother alliances, patterns of linkages between the essentials, to name a few. As in crewing a racing shell, all oars dip and swing simultaneously. The rowing team is comfortable managing scale, scope and complexity – balanced in a single stroke and aligned.

Second, they are also *collaborators*. They keep the team, employees, customers, partners and investors passionate about the company's direction and execution. They develop a balanced board (as an extension of themselves for execution).

These CEOs shape the company and its opportunity through their exploratory passion, which leads them to new markets, new strategic customer and alliance deals, and new standards. Just as Bill Gates shaped the IBM alliance, Tom Siebel shaped Launching Customers early on with the Andersen alliance and Phil Knight shaped new markets for running shoes, the most notable being the game of basketball with Nike's groundbreaking Air Jordan.

Passion for the company

In truth, passion is present in both High Growth Companies *and* failed start-ups. In all of these cases, founders loved their companies. They were willing to sacrifice for

their success. They poured their heart and souls (and real money) into the enterprise. So what's different?

> The Internal–External team is critical. They determine the cross-functional initiatives. More important, they balance the mix of preservation of the past and exploration for the future as the company experiences exponential growth.

We found three big differences.

First, High Growth Company leaders articulate their passion as one that is also relevant to customers, often in terms that will deliver higher-order benefits. By this we mean that their passion is tightly aligned with the value proposition; a pursuit for higher-order benefits. For Bill Gates it was "conceiving ideas to make personal computers easier to use and to programme." Gates envisioned a computer on every desk and in every home." He was known for having a one-track mind – microcomputers.

For John Morgridge, Cisco's original CEO, it was "realizing Cisco had a solution in anticipation of customer demand." Morgridge passionately drove to be early and dominant in capturing the big advantage. For Howard Schultz, it was about becoming the "third place" for the Starbucks community after home and work. In other words, the passion of the leader could also be viewed as a valued passion of the customer.

Second, such leaders had a consistent strength of will to execute. As Cisco's former VP Sales, Terry Eger said, "In the face of limited resources, you have to have superior strength of will to execute. You have to have superior energy to execute ahead of the growth curve."

Third, these leaders are intensely committed to the company, not to the position they fill. They are hands-on managers. They get involved in shaping deals with partners and customers. They serve as an important link between the engineering team and the customer. They work incredibly hard at the details.

Superior problem solvers

High Growth leaders are superior problem solvers. They can navigate and execute in the context of a growth strategy. They can break problems down in the height of uncertain outcomes. They can best define and lead strategic initiatives enabling teams to link execution to strategy. These might sound like traits of all leaders, but they are not.

High Growth leaders can qualify, shape and execute deals with partners that shape the company. When Starbucks' Howard Schultz entered into a relationship with Pepsi to co-develop their first product together, it failed. So Schultz suggested they try working on another idea together: Frappuccino. It became a $500 million-plus business opportunity. Tenacity, stubborn optimism and the ability to shape markets with their own hands mark High Growth winners. When we interviewed companies that had failed or were on the slippery slope downward, we didn't pick up the same vibes. They just weren't closing in on the big opportunities.

Ever see a "hands-off" leader who focuses only on process with little understanding of the details of the business? Ever find leaders who are focused only on cost reduction at the expense of growth? Ever find leaders who are simply maxed-out with no time to manage all the moving parts? Not the leader of a High Growth Company.

REFERENCES

Ackoff, R.L. (1980) *Creating the Corporate Future*, Chichester: Wiley.

Aldrich, H. (1999) *Organizations Evolving*, London: Sage.

Allison, G. (1969) 'Conceptual Models and The Cuban Missile Crisis', *The American Political Science Review*, Vol. 63, No. 3, September, pp. 689–718.

Amabile, T.M. (1998) 'How to Kill Creativity', *Harvard Business Review*, Vol. 76, No. 5, September–October, pp. 76–87.

Argyris, C. (1990) *Overcoming Organizational Defenses: Facilitating Organizational Learning*, Needham, MA: Allyn & Bacon.

Barney, J.B. (1991) 'Firm Resources and Sustained Competitive Advantage', *Journal of Management*, Vol. 17, No. 1, pp. 99–120.

Bass, B.M. (1990) *Bass and Stogdill's Handbook of Leadership*, Third Edition, New York: The Free Press.

Bavelas, A. (1964) 'Leadership: Man and Function', in: H.H. Leavitt and L.R. Pondy (eds.) *Readings in Managerial Psychology*, Chicago, IL: University of Chicago Press.

Beinhocker, E.D. (1999) 'Strategy at the Edge of Chaos', *The McKinsey Quarterly*, No. 1, pp. 24–39.

Bennis, W. and Nanus, B. (1985) *Leaders: The Strategies for Taking Charge*, New York: Harper & Row.

Birnbaum, R. (1988) *How Colleges Work: The Cybernetics of Academic Organization and Leadership*, San Francisco, CA: Jossey-Bass.

Bourgeois, L.J. and Brodwin, D.R. (1983) 'Putting Your Strategy into Action', *Strategic Management Planning*, March–May.

Cannella, A.A. and Monroe, M.J. (1997) 'Contrasting Perspectives on Strategic Leaders: Toward a More Realistic View of Top Managers', *Journal of Management*, Vol. 23, No. 3, pp. 213–237.

Chandler, A.D. (1962) *Strategy and Structure: Chapters in the History of the American Industrial Enterprise*, Cambridge, MA: MIT Press.

Chen, C.C. and Meindl, J.R. (1991) 'The Construction of Leadership Images in the Popular Press: The Case of Donald Burr and People Express', *Administrative Science Quarterly*, Vol. 36, No. 4, December, pp. 521–551.

Child, J. (1972) 'Organizational Structure, Environment, and Performance: The Role of Strategic Choice', *Sociology*, January, pp. 2–22.

Cyert, R.M. (1990) 'Defining Leadership and Explicating the Process', *Non-Profit Management and Leadership*, Vol. 1, No. 1, Fall, pp. 29–38.

Cyert, R.M. and March, J.G. (1963) *A Behavioral Theory of the Firm*, Englewood Cliffs: Prentice Hall.

Etzioni, A. (1961) *A Comparative Analysis of Complex Organizations*, New York: Free Press.

Finkelstein, S. and Hambrick, D.C. (1996) *Strategic Leadership: Top Executives and Their Effects on Organizations*, St. Paul, MN: West.

French, J. and Raven, B.H. (1959) 'The Bases of Social Power', in: D. Cartwright (ed.) *Studies of Social Power*, Ann Arbor, MI: Institute for Social Research.

Glassman, R.M. (1986) 'Manufactured Charisma and Legitimacy', in: R.M. Glassman and W.H. Swatos, Jr. (eds.) *Charisma, History, and Social Structure*, New York: Glenwood Press.

Goold, M. and Quinn, J.J. (1990) *Strategic Control: Milestones for Long-Term Performance*, London: Hutchinson.

Greenwood, R. and Hinings, C.R. (1996) 'Understanding Radical Organizational Change: Bringing Together the Old and the New Institutionalism', *Academy of Management Review*, Vol. 21, No. 4, October, pp. 1022–1054.

Greiner, L.E. (1972) 'Evolution and Revolution as Organizations Grow', *Harvard Business Review,* July–August, pp. 37–46.

Hambrick, D.C. and Mason, P.A. (1984) 'Upper Echelons: The Organization as a Reflection of Its Top Managers', *Academy of Management Review*, Vol. 9, No. 2, April, pp. 193–206.

Hampden-Turner, C. and Trompenaars, A. (1993) *The Seven Cultures of Capitalism: Value Systems for Creating Wealth in the United States, Japan, Germany, France, Britain, Sweden, and the Netherlands*, New York: Doubleday.

Hannan, M.T. and Freeman, J. (1977) 'The Population Ecology of Organizations', *American Journal of Sociology*, Vol. 82, No. 5, March, pp. 929–964.

Hayward, M.L.A., Rindova, V.P. and Pollock, T.G. (2004) 'Believing One's Own Press: The Causes and Consequences of CEO Celebrity', *Strategic Management Journal*, Vol. 25, No. 7, pp. 637–653.

Hofstede, G. (1993) 'Cultural Constraints in Management Theories', *Academy of Management Executive*, Vol. 7, No. 1, pp. 8–21.

House, R.J. and Aditya, R.N. (1997) 'The Social Science Study of Leadership: Quo Vadis?', *Journal of Management*, Vol. 23, No. 3, May June, pp. 409–474.

Ireland, R.D. and Hitt, M.A. (1999) 'Achieving and Maintaining Strategic Competitiveness in the 21st Century: The Role of Strategic Leadership', *Academy of Management Executive*, Vol. 13, No. 1, February, pp. 43–57.

Kakabadse, A., Myers, A., McMahon, T. and Spony, G. (1995) 'Top Management Styles in Europe: Implications for Business and Cross-National Teams', *European Business Journal*, Vol. 7, No. 1, pp. 17–27.

Kelley, R.E. (1988) 'In Praise of Followers', *Harvard Business Review*, Vol. 66, No. 6, November–December, p. 142.

Kets de Vries, M.F.R. (1994) 'The Leadership Mystique', *Academy of Management Executive*, Vol. 8, No. 3, August, pp. 73–92.

Klein, K.J. and House, R.J. (1998) 'Further Thoughts on Fire: Charismatic Leadership and Levels of Analysis', in: F. Dansereauand and F.J. Yammarino (eds.) *Leadership: The Multi-Level Approaches*, Stamford, CT: JAI Press, Vol. 2, pp. 45–52.

Kotter, J.P. (1990) 'What Leaders Really Do', *Harvard Business Review*, Vol. 68, No. 3, May–June, p. 103.

Leonard-Barton, D. (1995) *Well-Springs of Knowledge: Building and Sustaining the Sources of Innovation,* Boston, MA: Harvard Business School Press.

Lessem, R. and Neubauer, F.F. (1994) *European Management Systems*, London: McGraw-Hill.

Levy, D. (1994) 'Chaos Theory and Strategy: Theory, Application, and Managerial Implications', *Strategic Management Journal*, Vol. 15, pp. 167–178.

March, J.G. and Simon, H.A. (1958) *Organizations*, New York: Wiley.

Meindl, J.R., Ehrlich, S.B. and Dukerich, J.M. (1985) 'The Romance of Leadership', *Administrative Science Quarterly*, Vol. 30, No. 1, March, pp. 78–102.

Miles, R.E. and Snow, C.C. (1978) *Organizational Strategy: Structure and Process*, New York: McGraw-Hill.

Miller, D. and Friesen, P.H. (1980) 'Momentum and Revolution in Organizational Adaptation', *Academy of Management Journal*, Vol. 23, No. 4, December, pp. 591–614.

Mintzberg, H. (1982) 'If You're Not Serving Bill and Barbara, Then You're Not Serving Leadership', in: J.G. Hunt, U. Sekaran, and C.A. Schreisheim (eds.) *Leadership: Beyond Establishment Views*, Carbondale, IL: Southern Illinois University.

Mintzberg, H. (1989) *Mintzberg on Management*, New York: Free Press.

Misumi, J. (1985) *The Behavioral Science of Leadership*, Ann Arbor, MI: University of Michigan Press.

Nanus, B. (1992) *Visionary Leadership: Creating a Compelling Sense of Direction for Your Organization*, San Francisco, CA: Jossey-Bass.

Nelson, R.R. and Winter, S.G. (1982) *An Evolutionary Theory of Economic Change*, Reading, MA: Harvard University Press.

Pfeffer, J. (1977) 'The Ambiguity of Leadership', *Academy of Management Review*, Vol. 2, No. 1, January, pp. 104–112.

Pfeffer, J. (1982) *Organizations and Organization Theory,* Boston, MA: Pitman.

Pfeffer, J. (1992) *Managing With Power: Politics and Influence in Organizations,* Boston, MA: Harvard Business School Press.

Pfeffer, J. and Salancik, G. (1978) *The External Control of Organizations: A Resource Dependency Perspective*, New York: Harper & Row.

Pfeffer, J. and Sutton, R.I. (1999) *The Knowing–Doing Gap: How Smart Companies Turn Knowledge Into Action,* Boston, MA: Harvard Business School Press.

Porter, M.E. (1990) *The Competitive Advantage of Nations*, London: Macmillan.

Quinn, J.B. (1980) 'Managing Strategic Change', *Sloan Management Review*, Summer, pp. 3–20.

Quinn, J.B. (1985) 'Managing Innovation: Controlled Chaos', *Harvard Business Review*, Vol. 63, No. 3, May–June, pp. 73–84.

Rowe, W.G. (2001) 'Creating Wealth in Organizations: The Role of Strategic Leadership', *Academy of Management Executive*, Vol. 15, No. 1, February, pp. 81–94.

Rumelt, R.P. (1995) 'Inertia and Transformation', in: C.A. Montgomery (ed.) *Resource-based and Evolutionary Theories of the Firm: Towards a Synthesis,* Boston, MA: Kluwer Academic Publishers, pp. 101–132.

Schein, E.H. (1985) *Organizational Culture and Leadership*, San Francisco, CA: Jossey-Bass.

Schein, E.H. (1993) 'On Dialogue, Culture, and Organizational Learning', *Organizational Dynamics*, Vol. 22, No. 2, pp. 40–51.

Selznick, P. (1957) *Leadership in Administration: A Sociological Interpretation*, New York: Harper & Row.

Senge, P.M. (1990) 'The Leader's New Work: Building Learning Organizations', *Sloan Management Review*, Vol. 32, No. 1, Fall, pp. 7–23.

Simons, R. (1994) 'How New Top Managers Use Control Systems as Levers of Strategic Renewal', *Strategic Management Journal,* Vol. 15, No. 3, March, pp. 169–189.

Sims, H.P. and Lorenzi, P. (1992) *The New Leadership Paradigm: Social Learning and Cognition in Organizations*, London: Sage.

Smircich, L. and Stubbart, C. (1985) 'Strategic Management in an Enacted World', *Academy of Management Review*, Vol. 10, No. 4, pp. 724–736.

Stacey, R.D. (1992) *Managing Chaos: Dynamic Business Strategies in an Unpredictable World*, London: Kogan Page.

Stacey, R.D. (1993) 'Strategy as Order Emerging from Chaos', *Long Range Planning*, Vol. 26, No. 1, pp. 10–17.

Strebel, P. (1994) 'Choosing the Right Change Path', *California Management Review*, Vol. 36, No. 2, Winter, pp. 29–51.

Tannenbaum, R. and Schmidt, W.H. (1958) 'How to Choose a Leadership Pattern', *Harvard Business Review*, Vol. 36, No. 2, March–April, pp. 95–101.

Teece, D.J., Pisano, G. and Shuen, A. (1997) 'Dynamic Capabilities and Strategic Management', *Strategic Management Journal*, 18(7), pp. 509–533.

Thomson, D.G. (2006) *Blueprint To A Billion: 7 Essentials to Achieve Exponential Growth*, New Jersey: John Wiley & Sons.

Tichy, N. and Cohen, E. (1997) *The Leadership Engine: How Winning Companies Build Leaders at Every Level*, New York: Harper Collins.

Tucker, R.C. (1968) 'The Theory of Charismatic Leadership', *Daedalus*, Vol. 97, No. 3, pp. 731–756.

Tushman, M.L., Newman, W.H. and Romanelli, E. (1986) 'Convergence and Upheaval: Managing the Unsteady Pace of Organizational Evolution', *California Management Review*, Vol. 29, No. 1, Fall, pp. 29–44.

Vroom, V.H., and Jago, A.G. (1988) *The New Leadership: Managing Participation in Organizations*, Englewood Cliffs, NJ: Prentice Hall.

Waldman, D.A. and Yammarino, F.H. (1999) 'CEO Charismatic Leadership: Levels-of-Management and Levels-of-Analysis Effects', *Academy of Management Review*, Vol. 24, No. 2, pp. 266–285.

Weick, K.E. (1979) *The Social Psychology of Organizing*, New York: Random House.

Wheatley, M.J. and Kellner-Rogers, M. (1996) 'Self-Organization: The Irresistible Future of Organizing', *Strategy, and Leadership*, Vol. 24, No. 4, pp. 18–25.

Zalesnik, A. (1977) 'Managers and Leaders: Are They Different?' *Harvard Business Review*, Vol. 55, No. 3, May–June, pp. 67–78.

THE INTERNATIONAL CONTEXT

There never were, since the creation of the world, two cases exactly parallel.

Philip Dormer Stanhope (1694–1773); English Secretary of State

INTRODUCTION

As firms move out of their domestic market on to the international stage, they are faced with differing business arenas. The nations they expand to can vary with regard to consumer behaviour, language, legal system, technological infrastructure, business culture, educational system, labour relations, political ideology, distribution structures and fiscal regime, to name just a few. At face value, the plurality of the international context can seem daunting. Yet, the question is how important the international differences are for firms operating across borders. Do firms need to adapt to the international diversity encountered, or can they find ways of overcoming the constraints imposed by distinct national systems, structures and behaviours? This matter of understanding and dealing with international variety is one of the key topics for managers operating across borders.

A second question with regard to the international context is that of international linkages. To what extent do events in one country have an impact on what happens in other countries? When a number of nations are tightly linked to one another in a particular area, this is referred to as a case of international integration. If, on the other hand, there are very weak links between developments in one country and developments elsewhere, this is referred to as a situation of international fragmentation. The question for managers is how tightly linked nations around the world actually are. Countries might be quite different, yet developments in one nation might significantly influence developments elsewhere. For instance, if interest rates rise in the United States, central bankers in most other countries cannot ignore this. If the price of oil goes down on the spot market in Rotterdam, this will have a 'spill over effect' towards most other nations. And if a breakthrough chip technology is developed in Taiwan, this will send a shockwave through the computer industry around the world. If nations are highly integrated, the manager must view all countries as part of the same system – as squares on a chessboard, not to be judged in isolation.

When looking at the subjects of international variety and linkages, it is also important to know in which direction they have been moving, and will develop further, over time. Where a development towards lower international variety and tighter international linkages on a worldwide scale can be witnessed, a process of globalization is at play. Where a movement towards more international variety and a loosening of international linkages is apparent, a process of localization is taking place.

For managers operating in more than one nation, it is vital to understand the nature of the international context. Have their businesses been globalizing or localizing, and what can be expected in the future? Answers to these questions should guide strategizing managers in choosing which countries to be active in and how to manage their activities across borders. Taken together, these international context questions constitute the issue of international configuration, and are the focus of the further discussion in this chapter.

THE ISSUE OF INTERNATIONAL CONFIGURATION

How a firm configures its activities across borders is largely dependent on how it deals with the fundamental tension between the opposite demands of globalization and localization. To understand these forces, pulling the organization in contrary directions, it is first necessary to further define them. Globalization and localization are terms used by many, but explained by few. This lack of uniform definition often leads to an unfocused debate, as different people employ the same terms, but actually refer to different phenomena. Therefore, this discussion starts with a clarification of the concepts of globalization and localization. Subsequently, attention will turn to the two central questions facing the international manager: which countries should the firm be active in and how should this array of international activities be managed? This first question, of deciding on which geographic areas the organization should be involved in, is the issue of international composition. The second question, of deciding on the organizational structure and systems needed to run the multi-country activities, is the issue of international management.

Dimensions of globalization

Clearly, globalization refers to the process of becoming more global. But what is global? Although there is no agreement on a single definition, most writers use the term to refer to one or more of the following elements (see Figure 12.1):

- Worldwide scope. 'Global' can simply be used as a geographic term. A firm with operations around the world can be labelled a global company, to distinguish it from firms that are local (not international) or regional in scope. In such a case, the term 'global' is primarily intended to describe the spatial dimension – the broadest possible international scope is to be global. When this definition of global is employed, globalization is the process of international expansion on a worldwide scale (e.g. Patel and Pavitt, 1991).

- Worldwide similarity. 'Global' can also refer to homogeneity around the world. For instance, if a company decides to sell the same product in all of its international markets, it is often referred to as a global product, as opposed to a locally tailored product. In such a case, the term 'global' is primarily intended to describe the variance dimension – the ultimate level of worldwide similarity is to be global. When this definition of global is employed, globalization is the process of declining international variety (e.g. Levitt, 1983, Reading 12.1 in this book).

- Worldwide integration. 'Global' can also refer to the world as one tightly linked system. For instance, a global market can be said to exist if events in one country are significantly impacted by events in other geographic markets. This contrasts with local markets, where price levels, competition, demand and fashions are hardly influenced by developments in other nations. In such a case, the term 'global' is primarily intended to describe the linkages dimension – the ultimate level of worldwide integration is to be global. When this definition of global is employed, globalization is the process of increasing international interconnectedness (e.g. Porter, 1986).

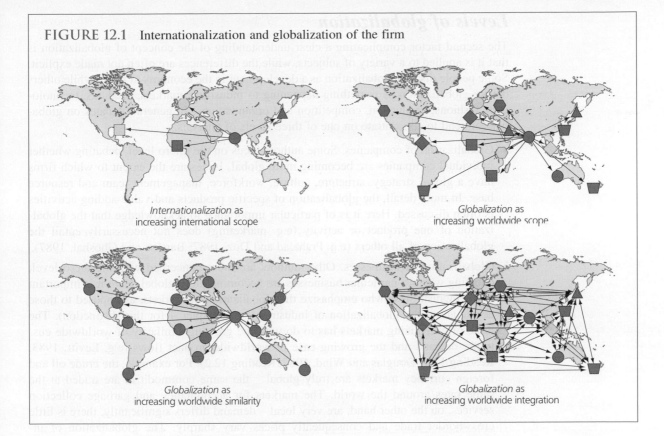

FIGURE 12.1 Internationalization and globalization of the firm

Internationalization as
increasing international scope

Globalization as
increasing worldwide scope

Globalization as
increasing worldwide similarity

Globalization as
increasing worldwide integration

So is, for example, McDonald's a global company? That depends along which of the above three dimensions the company is measured. When judging the international scope of McDonald's, it can be seen that the company is globalizing, but far from global. The company operates in approximately half the countries in the world, but in many of these only in one or a few large cities. Of McDonald's worldwide revenues, more than half is still earned in the United States. This predominance of the home country is even stronger if the composition of the company's top management is looked at (Ruigrok and Van Tulder, 1995). However, when judging McDonald's along the dimension of international similarity, it is simple to observe that the company is relatively global, as it takes a highly standardized approach to most markets around the world. Although, it should be noted that on some aspects as menu and interior design there is leeway for local adaptation. Finally, when judging McDonald's along the dimension of international integration, the company is only slightly global, as it is not very tightly linked around the world. Some activities are centralized or coordinated, but in general there is relatively little need for concerted action.

As for localization – the opposite of the process of globalization – it is characterized by decreasing international scope, similarity and integration. From the angle of international strategy, the most extreme form of localness is when firms operate in one country and there is no similarity or integration between countries (e.g. the hairdressing and driving school businesses). However, this equates local with national, while firms and businesses can be even more local, all the way down to the state/province/department/district and municipal playing fields.

Levels of globalization

The second factor complicating a clear understanding of the concept of globalization is that it is applied to a variety of subjects, while the differences are often not made explicit. Some people discuss globalization as a development in the economy at large, while others debate globalization as something happening to industries, markets, products, technologies, fashions, production, competition and organizations. In general, debates on globalization tend to concentrate on one of three levels of analysis:

■ Globalization of companies. Some authors focus on the micro level, debating whether individual companies are becoming more global. Issues are the extent to which firms have a global strategy, structure, culture, workforce, management team and resource base. In more detail, the globalization of specific products and value-adding activities is often discussed. Here it is of particular importance to acknowledge that the globalization of one product or activity (e.g. marketing) does not necessarily entail the globalization of all others (e.g. Prahalad and Doz, 1987; Bartlett and Ghoshal, 1987).

■ Globalization of businesses. Other authors are more concerned with the meso level, debating whether particular businesses are becoming more global. Here it is important to distinguish those who emphasize the globalization of markets, as opposed to those accentuating the globalization of industries (see Chapter 4 for this distinction). The issue of globalizing markets has to do with the growing similarity of worldwide customer demand and the growing ease of worldwide product flows (e.g. Levitt, 1983, Reading 12.1; Douglas and Wind, 1987, Reading 12.2). For example, the crude oil and foreign currency markets are truly global – the same commodities are traded at the same rates around the world. The markets for accountancy and garbage collection services, on the other hand, are very local – demand differs significantly, there is little cross-border trade and consequently prices vary sharply. The globalization of industries is quite a different issue, as it has to do with the emergence of a set of producers that compete with one another on a worldwide scale (e.g. Prahalad and Doz, 1987; Porter, 1990a, 1990b). So, for instance, the automobile and consumer electronics industries are quite global – the major players in most countries belong to the same set of companies that compete against each other all around the world. Even the accountancy industry is relatively global, even though the markets for accountancy services are very local. On the other hand, the hairdressing and retail banking industries are very local – the competitive scene in each country is relatively uninfluenced by competitive developments elsewhere.

■ Globalization of economies. Yet other authors take a macro level of analysis, arguing whether or not the world's economies in general are experiencing a convergence trend. Many authors are interested in the macroeconomic dynamics of international integration and its consequences in terms of growth, employment, inflation, productivity, trade and foreign direct investment (e.g. Kay, 1989; Krugman, 1990). Others focus more on the political realities constraining and encouraging globalization (e.g. Klein, 2000; McGrew and Lewis, 1992). Yet others are interested in the underlying dynamics of technological, institutional and organizational convergence (e.g. Dunning, 1986; Kogut, 1993).

Ultimately, the question in this chapter is not only whether economies, businesses and companies are actually globalizing, but also whether these developments are a matter of choice. In other words, is global convergence or continued international diversity an uncontrollable evolutionary development to which firms (and governments) must comply, or can managers actively influence the globalization or localization of their environment?

International composition

An international firm operates in two or more countries. When a firm starts up value-adding activities in yet another country, this process is called internationalization. In Figure 12.2 an overview is presented of the most common forms of internationalization. One of the earliest international growth moves undertaken by firms is to sell their products to foreign buyers, either directly (internet or telephone sales), through a travelling sales-person, or via a local agent or distributor. Such types of export activities are generally less taxing for the organization than the establishment of a foreign sales subsidiary (or sales unit). Serving a foreign market by means of a sales subsidiary often requires a higher level of investment in terms of marketing expenditures, sales force development and after-sales service provision. A firm can also set up a foreign production subsidiary (or 'off-shore' production unit), whose activities are focused on manufacturing goods to be exported back to the firm's other markets. Alternatively, a firm can begin an integrated foreign subsidiary that is responsible for a full range of value-adding activities, including pro-duction and sales. In practice, there are many variations to these basic forms of inter-nationalization, depending on the specific value-adding activities carried out in different countries. For example, some subsidiaries have R&D, assembly and marketing their portfolio of activities, while others do not (Birkinshaw and Hood, 1998).

When establishing a foreign subsidiary, the firm must decide whether to purchase an existing local company (entry by acquisition) or to start from scratch (greenfield entry). In both cases the firm can work independently or by means of a joint venture with a local player or foreign partner. It is also possible to dispense with the establishment of a sub-sidiary at all, by networking with local manufacturers, assemblers, sales agents and dis-tributors (as discussed in Chapter 6).

The issue of international composition deals with the question of where the firm wants to have a certain level of involvement. The firm's strategists must decide where to allocate

FIGURE 12.2 International growth options

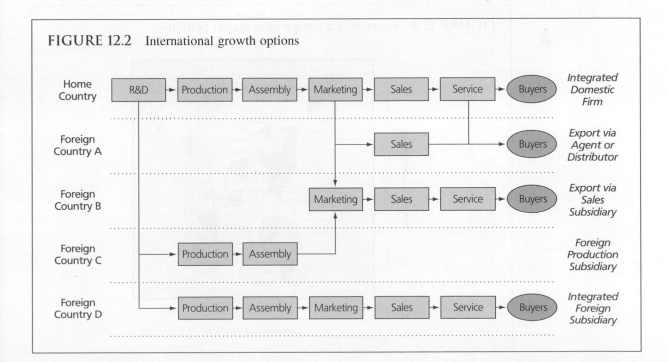

resources, build up activities and try to achieve results. The issue of international composition can be further subdivided into two parts:

■ International scope. The international composition of the firm depends first of all on the countries selected to do business in. The geographic spectrum covered by the firm is referred to as its international scope. The firm's strategists must decide how many countries they want to be active in, and which countries these should be.

■ International distribution. The international composition of the firm also depends on how it has distributed its value-adding activities across the countries selected. In some firms all national subsidiaries carry out similar activities and are of comparable size. However, in many firms activities are distributed less symmetrically, with, for example, production, R&D and marketing concentrated in only a few countries (Porter, 1986). Commonly some countries will also contribute much more revenue and profits than others, but these might not be the countries where new investments can best be made. It is the task of the firm's strategists to determine how activities can best be distributed and how resources can best be allocated across the various countries.

Just as a corporation's portfolio of businesses could be visualized by means of a portfolio grid, so too can a business's portfolio of foreign sales markets be displayed using such a matrix. In Figure 12.3 a fictitious example is given of a firm's international sales portfolio using the GE business screen as analysis tool. Instead of industry attractiveness along the vertical axis, country attractiveness is used, calculating items such as market growth, competitive intensity, buyer power, customer loyalty, government regulation and operating costs. Following a similar logic, firms can also evaluate their international portfolios of, for instance, production locations and R&D facilities.

Deciding which portfolio of countries to be active in, both in terms of international scope and distribution, will largely depend on the strategic motives that have stimulated

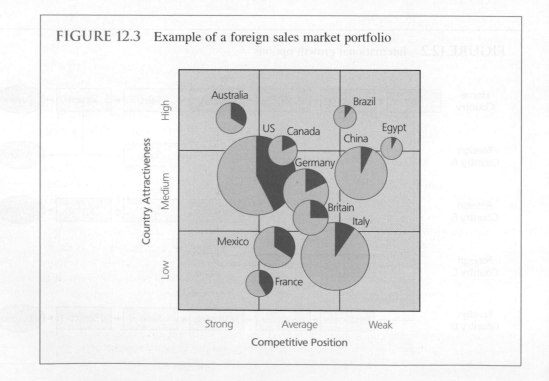

FIGURE 12.3   Example of a foreign sales market portfolio

the firm to enter the international arena in the first place. After all, there must be some good reasons why a firm is willing to disregard the growth opportunities in its home market and to enter into uncertain foreign adventures. There must be some advantages to being international that offset the disadvantages of foreignness and distance. These advantages of having activities in two or more countries – cross-border synergies – are discussed in more detail, after an account of the second international configuration question, the issue of international management.

International management

A firm operating in two or more countries needs to find some way of organizing itself to deal with its border-spanning nature. As managing across borders is difficult and costly, the simplest solution would be to organize all operations on a country-by-country basis, and to leave all country units as autonomous as possible. Yet, internationalization is only economically rational if 'the international whole is more than the sum of the country parts' (see Chapter 5). In other words, internationalization only makes sense if enough cross-border synergies can be reaped to offset the extra cost of foreignness and distance.

Therefore, the firm needs to have international integration mechanisms to facilitate the realization of cross-border synergies. The three most important integration mechanisms used in international management are:

- Standardization. An easy way to reap cross-border synergies is to do the same thing in each country, without any costly adaptation. Such standardization can be applied to all aspects of the business model (see Chapter 4) – the product offerings, value-adding activities and resources employed. Standardization is particularly important for achieving economies of scale (e.g. Hout, Porter and Rudden, 1982; Levitt, 1983), but can be equally valuable for serving border-crossing clients who want to encounter a predictable offering (e.g. Hamel and Prahalad, 1985; Yip, 1993).

- Coordination. Instead of standardizing products or activities, international firms can also align their varied activities in different countries by means of cross-border coordination. Getting the activities in the various countries aligned is often inspired by the need to serve border-crossing clients in a coordinated manner (e.g. global service level agreements), or to counter these clients' policy of playing off the firm's subsidiaries against one another (e.g. cross-border price shopping). International coordination can be valuable when responding to, or attacking, competitors as well. A coordinated assault on a few markets, financed by the profits from many markets (i.e. cross-subsidization), can sometimes lead to competitive success (Prahalad and Doz, 1987).

- Centralization. Of course, activities within the firm can also be integrated at one central location, either in the firm's home country or elsewhere. Such centralization is often motivated by the drive for economies of scale (e.g. Buckley and Casson, 1985; Dunning, 1981), but might be due to the competitive advantage of a particular country as well. For example, production costs might be much lower, or quality much higher, in a certain part of the world, making it a logical location for centralized production. Centralization of knowledge intensive activities is sometimes also needed, to guard quality or to ensure faster learning than could be attained with decentralized activities (e.g. Porter, 1990b; Dunning, 1993).

It is up to the firm's strategists to determine the most appropriate level of standardization, coordination and centralization needed to function efficiently and effectively in an international context. The level chosen for each of these three characteristics will largely determine the organizational model adopted by the international firm.

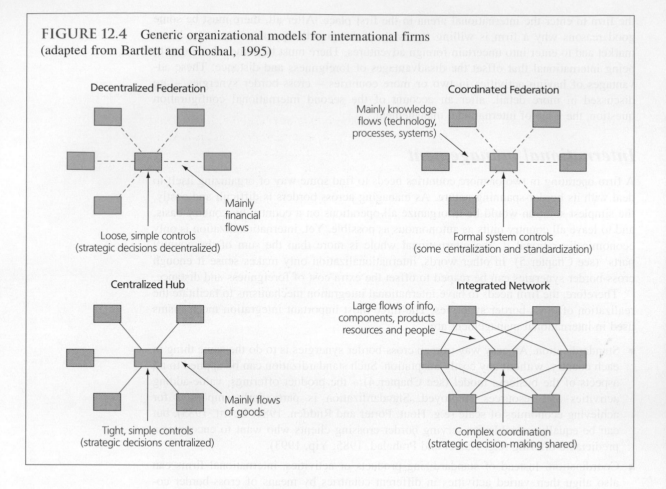

FIGURE 12.4 Generic organizational models for international firms
(adapted from Bartlett and Ghoshal, 1995)

In their seminal research, Bartlett and Ghoshal (1989) distinguish four generic organizational models for international firms, each with its own mix of standardization, coordination and centralization (see Figure 12.4):

- Decentralized federation. In a decentralized federation, the firm is organized along geographic lines, with each full-scale country subsidiary largely self-sufficient and autonomous from international headquarters in the home country. Few activities are centralized and little is coordinated across borders. The level of standardization is also low, as the country unit is free to adapt itself to the specific circumstances in its national environment. Bartlett and Ghoshal refer to this organizational model as 'multinational'. Another common label is 'multi-domestic' (e.g. Prahalad and Doz, 1987; Stopford and Wells, 1972).

- Coordinated federation. In a coordinated federation, the firm is also organized along geographic lines, but the country subsidiaries have a closer relationship with the international headquarters in the home country. Most of the core competences, technologies, processes and products are developed centrally, while other activities are carried out locally. As a consequence, there is some standardization and coordination, requiring some formalized control systems (i.e. planning, budgeting, administration). Another name employed by Bartlett and Ghoshal to refer to this organizational model is 'international'.

- Centralized hub. In a centralized hub, national units are relatively unimportant, as all main activities are carried out in the home country. Generally a highly standardized approach is used towards all foreign markets. As centralization and standardization are high, foreign subsidiaries are limited to implementing headquarters' policies in the local markets. Coordination of activities across countries is made easy by the dominance of headquarters. Bartlett and Ghoshal use the term 'global' to describe this organizational model.

■ Integrated network. In an integrated network, the country subsidiaries have a close relationship with international headquarters, just as in the coordinated federation, but also have a close relationship with each other. Very little is centralized at the international headquarters in the home country, but each national unit can become the worldwide centre for a particular competence, technology, process or product. Thus subsidiaries need to coordinate the flow of components, products, knowledge and people between each other. Such a networked organization requires a certain level of standardization to function effectively. Another name used by Bartlett and Ghoshal for this organizational model is 'transnational'.

Which international organizational model is adopted depends strongly on what the corporate strategist wishes to achieve. The preferred international management structure will be largely determined by the type of cross-border synergies that the strategists envisage. This topic of multi-country synergies is examined more closely in the following section.

THE PARADOX OF GLOBALIZATION AND LOCALIZATION

The axis of the earth sticks out visibly through the center of each and every town or city.

Oliver Wendell Holmes (1809–1894); American physician, poet and essayist

It requires almost no argumentation that internationally operating companies are faced with a tension between treating the world as one market and acknowledging national differences. During the last few decades, achieving a balance between international uniformity and meeting local demands has been the dominant theme in the literature on international management. All researchers have recognized the tension between international standardization and local adaptation. The key question has been whether international firms have the *liberty* to standardize or face the *pressure* to adapt.

However, since the mid-1980s, this standardization-adaptation discussion has progressed significantly as strategy researchers have moved beyond the organizational design question, seeking the underlying strategic motives for standardization and adaptation (e.g. Bartlett and Ghoshal, 1987; Porter, 1986; Prahalad and Doz, 1987). It has been acknowledged that international standardization is not a matter of organizational convenience that companies naturally revert to when the market does not demand local adaptation. Rather, international standardization is a means for achieving cross-border synergies. A firm can achieve cross-border synergies by leveraging resources, integrating activities and aligning product offerings across two or more countries. Creating additional value in this way is the very *raison d'etre* of the international firm. If internationalizing companies would fully adapt to local conditions, without leveraging a homegrown quality, they would have no advantage over local firms, while they would be burdened by the extra costs of international business (e.g. overcoming distance and foreignness). Therefore, international companies need to realize at least enough cross-border synergies to compensate for the additional expenses of operating in multiple countries.

Much of the theoretical discourse has focused on the question of which cross-border synergies can be achieved on the ultimate, global scale. Most researchers identify various potential opportunities for worldwide synergy, yet recognize the simultaneous demands to meet the specific conditions in each local market (e.g. Dicken, 1992; Yip, 1993). These possibilities for reaping global synergy will be examined first, followed by the counter-vailing pressures for local responsiveness.

The demand for global synergy

Striving for cross-border synergies on as large a scale as possible can be an opportunity for an international firm to enhance its competitive advantage. However, realizing global synergies is often less an opportunity than a competitive demand. If rival firms have already successfully implemented a global strategy, there can be a severe pressure to also reap the benefits of globalization through standardization, coordination or centralization.

There are many different types of cross-border synergies. In accordance with the business model framework described in Chapter 4, these synergies can be organized into three categories: aligning product offerings, integrating activities and leveraging resources (see Figure 12.5).

Synergy by aligning positions.   The first way to create cross-border synergies is to align market positions in the various countries in which the firm operates. Taking a coordinated approach to different national markets can be necessary under two

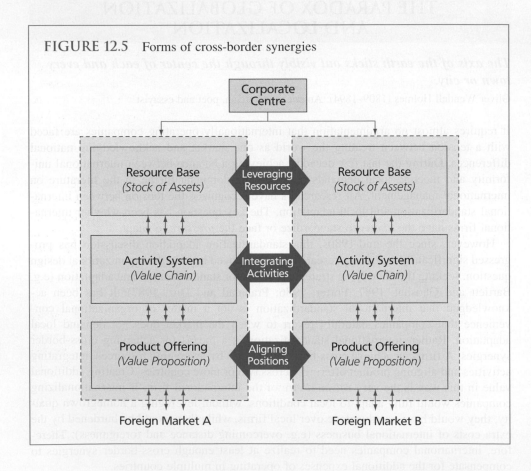

FIGURE 12.5   Forms of cross-border synergies

circumstances – namely to provide a concerted cross-border product offering to customers and to stage a concerted cross-border attack on competitors:

■ Dealing with cross-border customers. An international firm is ideally placed to offer border-crossing customers an internationally coordinated product or service offering. Whether it is for a tourist who wants to have the same hotel arrangements around the world, or for an advertiser who wants to stage a globally coordinated new product introduction, it can be important to have a standardized and coordinated offering across various nations. It might be equally necessary to counter the tactics of customers shopping around various national subsidiaries for the best deals, or to meet the customer's demand to aggregate all global buying via one central account.

■ Dealing with cross-border competition. An international firm is also in an ideal position to successfully attack locally oriented rivals, if it does not spread its resources too thinly around the world, but rather focuses on only a few countries at a time. By coordinating its competitive efforts and bringing its global power to bear on a few national markets, an international firm can push back or even defeat local rivals country-by-country. Of course, an international company must also have the capability of defending itself against such a globally coordinated attack by a rival international firm.

Synergy by integrating activities.   Cross-border synergies can also be achieved by linking the activity systems of the firm in its various national markets. Integrating the value-creation processes across borders can be useful to realize economies of scale and to make use of the specific competitive advantages of each nation:

■ Reaping scale advantages. Instead of organizing the international firm's activity system on a country-by-country basis, certain activities can be pooled to reap economies of scale. Commonly this means that activities must be centralized at one or a few locations, and that a certain level of product and/or process standardization must be accepted. Economies of scale can be realized for many activities, most notably production, logistics, procurement and R&D. However, scale advantages might be possible for all activities of the firm. Although scale advantages are often pursued by means of centralization, it is often possible to achieve economies by standardizing and coordinating activities across borders (e.g. joint procurement, joint marketing campaigns).

■ Reaping location advantages. For some activities certain locations are much more suited than others, making it attractive to centralize these activities in the countries that possess a particular competitive advantage. A national competitive advantage can consist of inexpensive or specialist local inputs, such as raw materials, energy, physical infrastructure or human resources, but can also be due to the presence of attractive buyers and related industries (Porter, 1990a).

Synergy by leveraging resources.   A third manner in which cross-border synergies can be realized is by sharing resources across national markets. Such resource leveraging can be achieved by physically reallocating resources to other countries where they can be used more productively, or by replicating them so they can be used in many national markets simultaneously:

■ Achieving resource reallocation. Instead of leaving resources in countries where they happen to be, international firms have the opportunity to transfer resources to other locations, where they can be used to more benefit. For example, money, machinery and people can be reallocated out of countries where the return on these resources is low, into countries where they can reap a higher return. Managers specializing in market development might be sent to new subsidiaries, while older machinery might be transferred to less advanced markets (Vernon, 1966; Buckley and Casson, 1976).

■ *Achieving resource replication.* While leveraging tangible resources requires physical reallocation or sharing (see reaping scale advantages), intangible resources can be leveraged by means of replication. Intangibles such as knowledge and capabilities can be copied across borders and reused in another country. This allows international companies to leverage their know-how with regard to such aspects as technology, production, marketing, logistics and sales (Kogut and Zander, 1993; Liebeskind, 1996).

For all of these cross-border synergies it holds that the wider the geographic scope, the greater the potential benefit. Where possible, realizing these synergies on a global scale would result in the highest level of value creation.

These opportunities for global synergy represent a strong demand on all companies, both international and domestic. If a company can reap these synergies more quickly and successfully than its competitors, this could result in a strong offensive advantage. If other companies have a head start in capturing these global synergies, the firm must move quickly to catch up. Either way, there is a pressure on companies to seek out opportunities for global synergy and to turn them to their advantage.

The demand for local responsiveness

Yet the pressure to pursue global synergies is only half the equation. Simultaneously, companies must remain attuned to the specific demands of each national market and retain the ability to respond to these particular characteristics in a timely and adequate manner. In other words, firms must have the capability to be responsive to local conditions. If they lose touch with the distinct competitive dynamics in each of their national markets, they might find themselves at a competitive disadvantage compared to more responsive rivals.

While business responsiveness is always important, it becomes all the more pressing when the differences between various national markets are large. The more dissimilar the national markets, the more pressure on the international firm to be attuned to these distinct characteristics. The most important differences between countries include:

■ *Differences in market structure.* Countries can differ significantly with regard to their competitive landscape. For example, in some national markets there are strong local competitors, requiring the international firm to respond differently than in countries where it encounters its 'regular' international rivals. Another difference is that in some countries there are only a few market parties, while in other countries the market is highly fragmented among numerous competitors. There can also be large differences from country to country in the background of competitors – in some countries conglomerates dominate the business scene, while in other countries single business competitors are more frequent.

■ *Differences in customer needs.* Customers in each national market can have needs that are significantly different than the needs exhibited in other countries. The nature of these customer differences can vary from divergent cultural expectations and use circumstances, to incompatible technical systems and languages employed.

■ *Differences in buying behaviour.* Not only the customers' needs can differ across countries, but so can their buying behaviour. For example, customers can be different with regard to the way they structure buying decisions, the types of information they consider and the relationship they wish to have with their suppliers.

■ *Differences in substitutes.* National markets can also differ with regard to the types of indirect competition that needs to be faced. In some countries, for instance, beer brewers have to deal with wine as an important rival product, while in other markets tea or soft drinks might be the most threatening substitutes.

- **Differences in distribution channels.** Countries can exhibit remarkable differences in the way their distribution channels work. For example, countries can vary with regard to the kinds of distribution channels available, the number of layers in the distribution structure, their level of sophistication, their degree of concentration and the negotiating power of each player.

- **Differences in media structure.** National markets can have very different media channels available for marketing communication purposes. In the area of television, for instance, countries vary widely with regard to the number of stations on the air (or on the cable), the types of regulation imposed, the amount of commercial time available, and its cost and effectiveness. In the same way, all other media channels may differ.

- **Differences in infrastructure.** Many products and services are heavily dependent on the type of infrastructure available in a country. For example, some products rely on a digital telephone system, high-speed motorways, 24-hour convenience stores, or a national healthcare system. Some services require an efficient postal service, poor public transport, electronic banking or cable television.

- **Differences in supply structure.** If a company has local operations, the differences between countries with regard to their supply structures can also force the company to be more locally responsive. Not only the availability, quality and price of raw materials and components can vary widely between countries, but the same is true for other inputs such as labour, management, capital, facilities, machinery, research, information and services.

- **Differences in government regulations.** As most government regulations are made on a country-by-country basis, they can differ significantly. Government regulations can affect almost every aspect of a company's operations, as they range from antitrust and product liability legislation, to labour laws and taxation rules.

Responsiveness to these local differences is not only a matter of adaptation. Simple adaptation can be reactive and slow. Being responsive means that the firm has to have the ability to be proactive and fast. As each market develops in a different way and at a different pace, the international firm needs to be able to respond quickly and adequately to remain in tune.

It is clear that international managers cannot afford to neglect being responsive to local conditions. Yet, at the same time, they need to realize cross-border synergies to create additional value. Unfortunately for managers, these two key demands placed on the international firm are, at least to some extent, in conflict with one another. Striving for cross-border synergies on a global scale will interfere with being locally responsive and vice versa. Therefore, the question is how these two conflicting demands can be reconciled – how can the international manager deal with the paradox of globalization and localization?

EXHIBIT 12.1 SHORT CASE

NESPRESSO IN CHINA: WHERE ELSE?

Ever since the Swiss company Nestlé created a new market segment by developing an innovative system for premium portioned coffee under the Nespresso brand, it has seen remarkable growth in the global coffee market. Nespresso launched its products on the international market in 1991 and is currently operating in almost 60 countries worldwide. In pursuit of new growth markets, the company's focus has recently shifted towards the huge

▶

upcoming Chinese market. This seems an obvious choice, but how to become successful is not an easy question for Nespresso's market director South East Asia, Greater China and Korea, Mark Leenders. While coffee is gaining popularity as a hot beverage in China, consumption is still very low and the age-old tradition of tea consumption in China is deeply imbedded in the national culture. The company's question, expressed in several commercials by actor George Clooney: "Nespresso: what else?" is easily answered in China.

Nespresso's journey started in 1976, when the Nespresso System was developed and patented by one of Nestlé's employees. During the following years, the system went through several improvements and the company started selling different varieties of coffee flavours and machine models to the business sector in Switzerland, Japan and Italy. However, due to low sales, the company was forced to reposition Nespresso as a premium quality brand targeted at households, with an emphasis on individuals with high incomes. A new business model was created, based on three important elements: individually portioned aluminum coffee capsules, specially designed coffee machines that are exclusively compatible with the Nespresso capsules, and unique customer service through the Nespresso Club and Nespresso Boutiques. Nespresso products cannot be purchased in ordinary stores or supermarkets; the company uses its own distribution channels (webshop, e-mail, telephone) and transport service to sell and deliver its products with an emphasis on personal attention for the customer. Since 2000, the company has opened several Nespresso Boutiques around the world, situated at carefully selected locations to give consumers the opportunity to 'experience the brand with all their senses'. After purchasing Nespresso products, consumers automatically become members of the Nespresso Club. Club Members receive information and advice on all grand cru coffees, technical problems, special offers and new machine models. With the Nespresso Club, the company aims at building stronger brand loyalty, encouraging repeat purchasing among its consumers. The company's decision to reposition Nespresso resulted in a period of rapid expansion and can be marked as the beginning of developing a strong global brand. Nowadays, Nespresso is the market leader in the single serve portioned coffee market and has seen an annual growth in profits of 30 per cent with revenues exceeding US$ 1.3 billion.

Aware of the growth potential in China, Nespresso decided to enter the Chinese market in 2007. Three Nespresso Boutiques have been established since then, in the cities Shanghai, Beijing and Chengdu. Market director Mark Leenders is convinced there are huge possibilities for Nespresso in China. However, the choice is not as obvious as it seems, considering the preference for tea as a hot and cold beverage in China's domestic market. Tea symbolizes an important cultural element in the Chinese society and has been enjoyed by the Chinese for thousands of years. Originally tea was mainly appreciated for its medical effects, in particular because it helps to digest food. Nowadays, Chinese drink tea at almost any time of the day, especially during and after every meal. Over 1.1 million tons of annually consumed tea make up for approximately 95 per cent of hot drinks in China, while coffee represents only 2 per cent of which only 0.1 per cent in pods. Besides, the majority of the Chinese are not used to the bitter taste of pure coffee.

American coffee house Starbucks entered the Chinese market as one of the first coffee companies in 1998, successfully introduced high-end premium coffee to Chinese consumers, and made them more familiar with drinking and appreciating coffee. The consumption of regular and quality coffee is gaining popularity in China, in accordance with the rising living standards of the growing urban middle class who get increasingly accustomed to Western standards and ways of living. According to market analysts the coffee market in China grew with an average of 18.4 per cent every year between 2007 and 2012. But still, Chinese consumers only drink an average of five cups of coffee per person per year, compared to for example the Americans or Swiss who drink respectively 400 and 1,117 cups of coffee annually. Because of the general lack of knowledge of how to prepare coffee, drinking instant coffee at home and ready-to-drink coffee at coffee houses is much more common in China, while preparing ground coffee at home is a rare habit.

Mark Leenders is facing a difficult challenge. Should Nespresso maintain its way of doing business as the company does in other countries? In the past 27 years, Nespresso has developed itself as one of the most famous brands for premium coffee, with an important focus on its global status, brand image and exclusive customer service. The company's business model and marketing strategy are homogeneous worldwide, which is manifested in, for example, the Nespresso Club and Boutiques. This uniform strategy proved to be a successful formula in Europe and the United States. In addition, the Chinese upcoming urban middle class consumers increasingly attach importance to popular Western brands to boost their image and enhance their social position. Should Nespresso maintain its winning formula?

On the other hand, it could also be a sagacious move for Nespresso to adapt its comprehensive business model to the Chinese market, since the market is not that familiar with Nespresso's core product: high quality ground coffee for individual households. Chinese consumers might have specific preferences compared to other consumers in the global marketplace. Leenders acknowledges the difficulty of selling pricey coffee machines and coffee capsules in a country with an entrenched tea culture. Should Nespresso adjust its products to meet, for example, the dislike of the bitter taste of pure coffee by Chinese consumers? Perhaps Nespresso should change its marketing strategy and put special attention on providing more information about brewing coffee for its Chinese customers.

In attempting to create a higher brand loyalty among its Chinese customers and generate a greater demand for its coffee products, Nespresso has a number of coffee beans to crack. Should the company put effort in making Chinese consumers more accustomed to drinking high quality, pure ground coffee and keep its homogeneous business model? Or should the company offer new varieties of coffee flavours and machine designs, especially developed for Chinese consumer preferences? For example, in 2012 Nespresso collaborated with the Hong Kong-based company *Shanghai Tang* to develop a red coffee machine with a dragon integrated in the design to adapt to the Chinese taste. Red is a very important colour in the Chinese culture and is associated with prosperity, while the dragon is the zodiac sign of the year 2012 and symbolizes good fortune.

Mark Leenders needs to decide which road the company has to follow and how to position in the Chinese market. The Chinese market has huge potential scope in several ways and it is definitely worth the try. Whether he decides to stick to Nespresso's homogeneous business model and brand image, adapt to local differences, or even decide to deviate from its core product and focus on tea instead; each decision will have important implications for the company's future position in the Chinese market.

Co-authors: Laura Kamsma and Qolian Hu

Sources: www.nestle-nespresso.com; Lu Chang, 'Pod People', *China Daily*, Oct 1, 2012; Alice Lau, 'Hot Competition and Coffee Culture with Chinese Characteristics', *Context China*. Oct. 23, 2012; *Financial Times* 2012; Analysis of the China Coffee Market, *SPR coffee*, 2009; Mintel Global Market Navigator, *Coffee in China*, Mintel 2012.

PERSPECTIVES ON THE INTERNATIONAL CONTEXT

You may say I'm a dreamer, but I'm not the only one; I hope some day you'll join us, and the world will live as one.
John Lennon (1940–1980); British musician and songwriter

When doing business in an international context, it is generally accepted that the challenge for firms is to strive for cross-border synergies, while simultaneously being responsive to the local conditions. It is acknowledged that international managers need to weigh the specific characteristics of their business when reconciling the paradox of globalization and localization – some businesses are currently more suited for a global approach than others. Where opinions start to diverge is on the question of which businesses will become more global, or can be made more global, in the near future. To some managers it is evident that countries are rapidly becoming increasingly similar and more closely interrelated. To them globalization is already far advanced and will continue into the future, wiping out the importance of nations as it progresses. Therefore, they argue that it is wise to anticipate, and even encourage, a 'nationless' world, by focusing on global synergies over local responsiveness. Other managers, however, are more sceptical about the speed and impact of globalization. In their view, much so-called globalization is quite superficial, while at a deeper level important international differences are not quickly changing and cross-border integration is moving very slowly. They also note that there are significant counter-currents creating more international variety, with the potential of loosening international linkages. Therefore, wise managers should remain highly responsive to the complex variety and fragmentation that characterizes our world, while only carefully seeking out selected cross-border synergy opportunities.

These differing opinions among international strategists are reflected in differing views in the strategic management literature. While there is a wide spectrum of positions on the question of how the international context will develop, here the two opposite poles in the debate will be identified and discussed. On the one side of the spectrum, there are the managers who believe that globalization is bringing Lennon's dream of the 'world living as one' closer and closer. This point of view is called the 'global convergence perspective'. At the other end of the spectrum are the managers who believe that deep-rooted local differences will continue to force firms to 'do in Rome as the Romans do'. This point of view is referred to as the 'international diversity perspective'.

The global convergence perspective

According to proponents of the global convergence perspective, the growing similarity and integration of the world can be argued by pointing to extensive economic statistics, showing significant rises in foreign direct investment and international trade. Yet, it is simpler to observe things directly around you. For instance, are you wearing clothing unique to your country, or could you mingle in an international crowd without standing out? Is the television you watch, the vehicle you drive, the telephone you use and the timepiece you wear specific to your nation, or based on the same technology and even produced by the same companies as those in other countries? Is the music you listen to made by local bands, unknown outside your country, or is this music equally popular abroad? Is the food you eat unique to your region, or is even this served in other countries? Now compare your answers with what your parents would have answered 30 years ago – the difference is due to global convergence.

Global convergence, it is argued, is largely driven by the ease, low cost and frequency of international communication, transport and travel. This has diminished the importance of distance. In the past world of large distances, interactions between countries were few and international differences could develop in relative isolation. But the victory of technology over distance has created a 'global village', in which goods, services and ideas are easily exchanged, new developments spread quickly and the 'best practices' of one nation are rapidly copied in others. Once individuals and organizations interact with one another as if no geographic distances exist, an unstoppable process towards cultural, political, technological and economic convergence is set in motion – countries will become more closely linked to one another and local differences will be superseded by new global norms.

Of course, in the short run there will still be international differences and nations will not be fully integrated into a 'world without borders'. Managers taking a global convergence perspective acknowledge that such fundamental and wide-ranging changes take time. There are numerous sources of inertia, e.g. vested interests, commitment to existing systems, emotional attachment to current habits and fear of change. The same type of change inhibitors could be witnessed during the industrial revolution, as well. Yet, these change inhibitors can only slow the pace of global convergence, not reverse its direction – the momentum caused by the shrinking of distance can only be braked, but not stopped. Therefore, firms thinking further than the short term should not let themselves be guided too much by current international diversity, but rather by the emerging global reality (Ohmae, 1990).

For individual firms, global convergence is changing the rules of the competitive game. While in the past most countries had their own distinct characteristics, pressuring firms to be locally responsive, now growing similarity offers enormous opportunities for leveraging resources and sharing activities across borders, e.g. production can be standardized to save costs, new product development can be carried out on an international scale to reduce the total investments required, and marketing knowledge can easily be exchanged to avoid reinventing the wheel in each country. Simultaneously, international integration has made it much easier to centralize production in large-scale facilities at the most attractive locations and to supply world markets from there, unrestrained by international borders. In the same manner, all types of activities, such as R&D, marketing, sales and procurement, can be centralized to profit from worldwide economies of scale.

An equally important aspect of international integration is that suppliers, buyers and competitors can also increasingly operate as if there are no borders. The ability of buyers to shop around internationally makes the world one global market, in which global bargaining power is very important. The ability of suppliers and competitors to reap global economies of scale and sell everywhere around the world creates global industries, in which competition takes place on a worldwide stage, instead of in each nation separately. To deal with such global industries and global markets, the firm must be able to align its market activities across nations.

These demands of standardization, centralization and coordination require a global firm, with a strong centre responsible for the global strategy, instead of a federation of autonomous national subsidiaries focused on being responsive to their local circumstances. According to proponents of the global convergence perspective, such global organizations, or 'centralized hubs' (Bartlett and Ghoshal, 1995), will become increasingly predominant over time. And as more companies switch to a global strategy and a global organizational form, this will in turn speed up the general process of globalization. By operating in a global fashion, these firms will actually contribute to a further decrease of international variety and fragmentation. In other words, globalizing companies are both the consequence and a major driver of further global convergence.

EXHIBIT 12.2 GLOBAL CONVERGENCE PERSPECTIVE

QOROS: DRIVING A GLOBAL ORCHESTRA

Over the last few decades, China has positioned itself as an attractive region for all kinds of manufacturing activities. In the car industry, several joint ventures have taken place between Chinese and European, Asian and American car manufacturers. However, production has mainly been focused on serving the rapidly expanding internal market. Despite numerous attempts to enter the international

markets, a real worldwide breakthrough for China as a car manufacturing nation has yet to come.

The numerous failing attempts of Chinese carmakers over the past decades to fight themselves into the heavily crowded global car market will not remain unanswered. Israel's largest long-term investment holding, 'Israel Corp.', and the largest Chinese car manufacturer 'Chery Automobile' joined forces in 2007 to create Qoros Automobile. Derived from the Greek word 'khoros', choir in modern English, Qoros' strategy is to attract the

▶

world's best and brightest from the world's leading companies. Supervised by Chinese CEO, Guo Qian, German Vice President, Volker Steinwascher, and Chinese Executive Vice President and COO, Xingcha Fan, a team of top of the bill European designers and engineers are made responsible for what they do best: Designing, engineering, manufacturing and quality management. At the same time, the roles of finance and IT are devoted to renowned Asian managers. This way, Qoros reaps the benefits of each nation's particular strength and thereby ensures success where other Chinese manufacturers have failed. Especially obtaining a profound comprehension of different product requirements as dictated by the different countries is among the core benefits of this internationally diverse team.

Qoros, being a new entrant, finds itself in a position to more adequately respond on rapidly emerging global trends and up-to-date quality standards. Mass individualization, environmentalism, digitalization and higher quality standards are only a grasp of the challenges car manufacturers face in today's world. Qoros tries to exploit its diversity of acquired knowledge to design and manufacture a globally sellable car that fits all of these trends simultaneously. With its production based in a new, sustainability-driven plant in Changshu, China, Qoros enters the global market following a clear recipe of high quality standards, contemporary design and intelligent infotainment systems that provide substance to the modern, urban lifestyle and the increasing demand for information.

The success of Qoros' strategy of acquiring cross-country knowledge for application to a globally accepted product is still to be proven as sales in both Asia and Eastern Europe only started recently. However, Qoros' approach to act as conductor of its own multicultural orchestra might very well lead to the first major Chinese breakthrough as a global car manufacturer. After all, like in all choruses and orchestras, it is not the sum of individual musicians' qualities that makes or breaks the symphony, but the synergy of all the finest instruments, musicians, singers and the audience.

Co-author: Jeremy Slingerland

Sources: 'Qoros signs first European importer agreement in Slovakia', *Automotive Business Review,* September 9, 2013; http://automobiledistribution.automotive-business-review.com/news/qoros-signs-first-european-importer-agreement-in-slovakia-090913; 'Qoros: A New Business Model', *China Automotive Review,* March 17, 2013; http://www.cbuauto.com/pub/CARArticle.aspx?ID=8612; 'East meets West in Qoros' European car market venture: Have you heard the one about the Israeli billionaire, the German designer and the Chinese automaker?', Reuters, March 6, 2013; http://www.reuters.com/article/2013/03/06/autoshow-geneva-qoros-ofer-idUSL4N0BT4GL20130306; http://www.qorosauto.com/en/aboutqoros/Company.

The international diversity perspective

To managers taking an international diversity perspective, the 'brave new world' outlined in the previous subsection is largely science fiction. People around the world might be sporting a Swatch or a Rolex, munching Big Macs and drinking Coke, while sitting in their Toyota or Nissan, but to conclude that these are symptoms of global convergence is a leap of faith. Of course, there are some brand names and products more or less standardized around the world, and their numbers might actually be increasing. The question is whether these manufacturers are globalizing to meet increasing worldwide similarity, or whether they are actually finally utilizing the similarities between countries that have always existed. The actual level of international variety may really be quite consistent.

It is particularly important to recognize in which respects countries remain different. For instance, the world might be drinking the same soft drinks, but they are probably doing it in different places, at different times, under different circumstances and for different reasons in each country. The product might be standardized worldwide, but the cultural norms and values that influence its purchase and use remain diverse across countries. According to proponents of the international diversity perspective, it is precisely these fundamental aspects of culture that turn out to be extremely stable over time – habits change slowly, but cultural norms and values are outright rigid. Producers might be lucky to find one product that fits in with such cultural diversity, but it would be foolish to interpret this as worldwide cultural convergence.

Other national differences are equally resilient against the tides of globalization. No countries have recently given up their national language in favour of Esperanto or English. On the contrary, there has been renewed emphasis on the local language in many countries (e.g. Ireland and the Baltic countries) and regions (e.g. Catalonia and Quebec). In the same way, political systems have remained internationally diverse, with plenty of examples of localization, even within nations. For instance, in Russia and the United States the shift of power to regional governments has increased policy diversity within the country. Similar arguments can be put forward for legal systems, fiscal regimes, educational systems and technological infrastructure – each is extremely difficult to change due to the lock-in effects, vested interests, psychological commitment and complex decision-making processes.

For each example of increasing similarity, a counter-example of local initiatives and growing diversity could be given. Some proponents of the international diversity perspective argue that it is exactly this interplay of divergence and convergence forces that creates a dynamic balance preserving diversity. While technologies, organizing principles, political trends and social habits disperse across borders, resulting in global convergence, new developments and novel systems in each nation arise causing international divergence (Dosi and Kogut, 1993). Convergence trends are usually easier to spot than divergence – international dispersion can be more simply witnessed than new localized developments. To the casual observer, this might suggest that convergence trends have the upper hand, but after more thorough analysis, this conclusion must be cast aside.

Now add to this enduring international diversity the reality of international economic relations. Since World War II attempts have been made to facilitate the integration of national economies. There have been some regional successes (e.g. the North American Free Trade Association and the European Union) and some advances have been made on a worldwide scale (e.g. the World Trade Organization). However, progress has been slow and important political barriers remain.

The continued existence of international diversity and political obstacles, it is argued, will limit the extent to which nations can become fully integrated into one borderless world. International differences and barriers to trade and investment will frustrate firms' attempts to standardize and centralize, and will place a premium on firms' abilities to adapt and decentralize. Of course, there will be some activities for which global economies of scale can be achieved and for which international coordination is needed, but this will not become true for all activities. Empowering national managers to be responsive to specific local conditions will remain an important ingredient for international success. Balancing globalization and localization of the firm's activities will continue to be a requirement in the future international context.

Ideally, the internationally operating company should neither deny nor regret the existence of international diversity, but regard it as an opportunity that can be exploited. Each country's unique circumstances will pose different challenges, requiring the development of different competences. Different national 'climates' will create opportunities for different innovations. If a company can tap into each country's opportunities and leverage the acquired competences and innovations to other countries, this could offer the company an important source of competitive advantage. Naturally, these locally leveraged competences and innovations would subsequently need to be adapted to the specific circumstances in other countries. This balancing act would require an organization that combined strong local responsiveness with the ability to exchange and coordinate internationally, even on a worldwide scale. International organizations blending these two elements are called 'transnational' (Bartlett and Ghoshal, 1995), or 'heterarchical'

(Hedlund, 1986). However, in some businesses the international differences will remain so large that an even more locally responsive organizational form might be necessary, operating on a federative basis.

EXHIBIT 12.3   THE INTERNATIONAL DIVERSITY PERSPECTIVE

WALKING DOWN SESAME STREET IN AFGHANISTAN

Ever since its creation, *Sesame Street* educates children with colourful puppets. The TV show is broadcast in over 140 countries, yet it is not the same everywhere. Because Sesame Workshop specifically adapts its formula to the countries it operates in, its expansion has been especially successful. In 2011, the non-profit organization started with a new group production, this time aimed towards Afghanistan. With around 45 per cent of the population under 15 and less than two-thirds of Afghan children enrolled in primary school, teaching children numbers, letters and messages of love, tolerance and equal treatment, seems like a logical step.

The series, known locally as *Baghch-e-Simsim,* is a co-production between Sesame Workshop and Moby Media, an Afghan company operating some of the leading television channels in Afghanistan as well as possessing some of the biggest brands in the country. This partner is responsible for making *Sesame Street* palatable to the local audience by picking shots from the vast amount of already puppeteered videos from other international *Sesame Street* productions, which are then dubbed over. The rest consists of locally recorded mini-documentaries, aimed at delivering educational messages.

Due to the probability of cultural misunderstandings, some important changes are made to the *Sesame Street* formula. For example, the Afghan script writers feared parents might frown upon encouraging their young viewers to dance in front of the television, since such activity is often perceived as something sexual in Afghanistan. Instead, children are invited to "exercise".

The producers of *Baghch-e-Simsim* have a certain degree of freedom when deciding what is acceptable, most noticeably with picking the puppet videos with the likes of Bert, Ernie, Elmo and Grover. For example, after testing an episode in which Ernie is barking like a dog and getting Bert to copy this, the producers found out that this could encourage indecent behaviour, since a dog is considered to be an unclean animal by many Afghans. Moby Media is also able to leave out characters which are deemed inappropriate altogether. In this regard, The Count has been omitted, since Afghans were thought to not understand why the vampire figure bears fangs, according to Tania Farzana, the Afghan-American executive producer of the show.

It is not just the local producers of Moby Media deciding what is okay and what is not though, since the Sesame Workshop aims to maintain a tight watch on how its international partners handle its show. When trying to film a scene on a building site, the producers struggled with finding one where workers wore clothes in accordance with the health and safety norms Sesame Workshop was accustomed to. Another shot that had to be dropped involved a car ride, because no one in it was actually wearing a seatbelt.

However, some locals might argue that the series still consists of inappropriate scenes. As is quite common for *Sesame Street,* the Afghan edition also occasionally borders on the line of controversy with the messages it tries to convey. When showing the experience of a first day at school, the producers picked a little girl as the main character – a role model – instead of a boy. In a country in which females attending school is still relatively rare, this can be considered to be daring. Still, as Lilith Dollard, content specialist for the US *Sesame Street,* explains: "We don't want to overload the programme with messages – we want it to be fun."

Since November 2011 the series is broadcast on TOLO and LEMAR television stations. In order to best fit with the country's cultural diversity, the series is broadcast in both the Dari and Pashto languages.

Co-author: Wester Wagenaar

Sources: www.mobygroup.com; www.sesameworkshop.org; *AFP,* 29 March 2013; *The Guardian,* 30 November 2011; *The Huffington Post,* 8 December 2011; *Reuters,* 30 November 2011.

MANAGING THE PARADOX OF GLOBALIZATION AND LOCALIZATION

When I am in Milan, I do as they do in Milan; but when I go to Rome, I do as Rome does.

St. Augustine (354–430); Roman theology's and philosopher

So, what does the paradox of global synergy and local responsiveness mean for the international configuration of firms? Should managers anticipate and encourage global convergence by emphasizing global standardization, centralization and coordination? They would choose to place more emphasis on realizing value creation by means of global synergies, accepting some value destruction due to a loss of local responsiveness. Or should managers acknowledge international diversity by emphasizing local adaptation, decentralization and autonomy? They would then focus on being locally responsive, accepting that this will frustrate the realization of cross-border synergies. See Table 12.1 for the main differences.

Again, the strategic management literature does not provide a uniform answer to the question of which international strategy firms can best pursue, however a number of suggestions have been brought forward to manage the paradox of globalization and localization.

If one would be satisfied with a fast solution for the paradox of globalization and localization, the term *glocalization,* widely used by academics, consultants and journalists, would do well. It would suggest that the paradox can be resolved with a synthesis. After taking a closer look on how the term is usually explained, however, a more likely conclusion would be that the solution is not only fast but also rather superficial: going global while adapting to local conditions. With examples such as Coca Cola that had to adapt to local circumstances as its globally standardized strategy had run its course, and McDonald's introducing local products such as Veggie McNuggets in India and McLobster in Canada, the term glocalization is used for companies going global while to some extent adapting locally. Yet, it is hard if not impossible to find a global company that does not need any local adaptations, and so the new term is close to empty.

Glocalization, the semantic compilation of the words globalization and localization, originates from the Japanese word *dochakuka* which means global localization, and originally referred to adapting farming techniques to local conditions. In the strategy field, the term has been picked up from one of many Japanese presenters in the 1980s on

TABLE 12.1   Global convergence versus international diversity perspective

	Global convergence perspective	International diversity perspective
Emphasis on	Globalization over localization	Localization over globalization
International variety	Growing similarity	Remaining diversity
International linkages	Growing integration	Remaining fragmentation
Major drivers	Technology and communication	Cultural and institutional identity
Diversity and fragmentation	Costly, convergence can be encouraged	Reality, can be exploited
Strategic focus	Global-scale synergies	Local responsiveness
Organizational preference	Standardize/centralize unless	Adapt/decentralize unless
Innovation process	Centre-for-global	Locally leveraged
Organizational structure	Global (centralized hub)	Transnational (integrated network)

Japanese management techniques and globalization. These were two hot topics, particularly in the United States, for two reasons. Firstly, Japanese companies had become extremely successful overseas as from the 1970s with for example cars and electronic products, and American companies and scholars wanted to understand Japanese success. And since demand creates supply, Japanese writers were invited to share some valuable insights. Secondly, globalization was a popular subject as new technological innovations changed the firm's understanding of international expansion dramatically (further explained in the next section 'The international context in international perspective'). The Japanese McKinsey consultant Kenichi Ohmae contributed to this topic with his book *Triad of Economic Power* (1985). Humans need language to exchange and discuss ideas; however, the words' connotations are not always understood, including the Japanese word *dochakuka* which had to be understood as Yin Yang Balancing, and not as a quick solution.

Balancing

The Coca Cola example illustrates well the paradox of globalization and localization: it had to give up advantages of global scale and worldwide standardization to become more locally adapted. There are, of course, many different possibilities to be attuned to local conditions, but they are all achieved at the expense of global advantages. In other words, companies have to trade off their demands for global synergy and local responsiveness to find a balance. However, the tension remains when companies have found a balance, and so strategizing managers will continue to search for a more favourable balance.

It should be kept in mind that while companies are trading off global synergy and local responsiveness, international firms do capture the advantages of global operations in local markets. Market presence in many countries leads to economies of scale in production and higher R&D and branding budgets, for example. So while firms have to trade off global synergy and local responsiveness, they reap the benefits of global presence, which is being used as a source of competitive advantage in local markets.

Navigating

In Chapter 5 on corporate level strategy it has been discussed that companies manage the paradox of multi-business synergy and business responsiveness by means of a series of corporate initiatives that sequentially focus on capturing synergy, responsiveness and then synergy again. In the same vain, international strategists navigate multinational companies with international initiatives. Actually, successfully managing the tension of global synergy and local responsiveness is more difficult, as local differences – such as cultural and institutional varieties – come on top of the complexity of managing the corporate level paradox.

Embracing

Tensions between global synergy and local responsiveness are felt by the employees of the international firms. Not only frictions between head office and business units (see also Chapter 5), but also between people from different countries within the country unit often lead to misunderstandings, while some culture-related values are hardly compatible. For example, while drinking coffee is irrelevant for some, it is crucial for others (never install the company's standard English coffee machine in an Italian branch!). Most international firms provide culture trainings to prepare managers for emerging culture issues to manage the cultural tensions.

Yet, international operations create not only tensions, they can also be exploited. In the next section, 'The international context in international perspective', the so-called *New International Division of Labour* (Fröbel, Heinrichs and Kreye, 1980) is discussed. This paradigm claims that labour intensive production will be concentrated in countries with an abundance of cheap labour, while R&D will be concentrated in countries with superior levels of education, income and infrastructure. For example, the Japanese Uniqlo produces labour-intensive cashmere cloths in China while developing high-tech garments in Japan (see short case 10.1). This new division of labour includes much more than just production and research. International firms settle in Silicon Valley to become part of the next technological revolution, have designer teams in Italy, software engineers in India, media innovators in South Korea, lawyers in London and production facilities in Germany.

The importance of the global division of labour is that companies are not searching for one global standard, but instead combine the countries' relative advantages. By blending country-specific differences, the tensions that arise from the paradox of global synergy and local responsiveness are seen as an opportunity (Beech *et al.,* 2004).

Resolving

As has been discussed in Chapter 5 on corporate level strategy, one prominent synthesis between responsiveness and synergy is the franchise. These can also be – and actually often are – international. Franchises are even more advantageous in the international context, as many complicating issues can be handled in an elegant way, such as specific local characteristics in the local food culture – for example with the above mentioned Veggie McNuggets in India – and import restrictions.

THE INTERNATIONAL CONTEXT IN INTERNATIONAL PERSPECTIVE

Co-author: Gep Eisenloeffel

A truth on this side of the Pyrenees, a falsehood on the other.
Montaigne (1533–1592); French moralist and essayist

What a curious title, one might be inclined to think: 'The international context in international perspective'. Isn't this a case of the snake biting itself on its own tail? Of course, the answer is no. Similar to all previous chapters, an international angle can be used to view the debate between proponents of the global convergence perspective and those of the international diversity perspective. The question of interest is whether strategists in certain countries are more inclined towards a specific perspective. In other words, are there nations where the global convergence perspective is more prevalent, while in other nations the international diversity perspective is more widespread?

This is a tantalizing question, but as before, it must be concluded that little comparative research has been done on the issue. As a stimulus to the debate whether there are national differences in international context perspectives, a number of factors will be introduced that might influence how the paradox of globalization and localization is dealt with in different countries. It goes without saying that more international comparative research is required before a clear picture can be formed about the actual international differences.

The discussion starts with the question of why enterprises start activities abroad, rather than just exporting products or achieving advantages through management contracts and licensing agreements. Second, theories of Foreign Direct Investments (FDI) will be described, and the diverse trajectories of multinational enterprises (MNEs) in their internationalization development. The new reality of international businesses will then be described, especially the emerging position of companies from recently developed countries. Finally some remarks will be made on the future of the firm's perspective on the issue of international configuration.

A short history of internationalization

From the times of the first Sumerian merchants in 2500 BC people were engaged in trans-border activities by trading or selling home-made goods. The foreign assets had to be acquired and then locally controlled and coordinated, which was the beginning of what we currently call Foreign Direct Investment (FDI). The first multinational enterprise (MNE) was either the English East Asian Company or the Dutch East Indian Company, both founded in the beginning of the seventeenth century – a long-standing debate which remains unresolved (Wilkins, 2003). Thus, FDI and MNEs existed way before mass production of manufactured goods took off after the industrial revolution of the late eighteenth century and the subsequent rise of large industrial enterprises. Wilkins (1970), however, observed that 'although there were direct investments abroad by 'parent' enterprises in manufacturing, mining and plantation, until the end of the nineteenth century there was not a single manufacturing company that extended as a firm over borders to sell and/or manufacture its products abroad. Likewise, the parents of mining companies abroad were not mining companies.' This specific kind of Foreign Direct Investment in which a parent company expands its core activities abroad, is associated with the modern post Second World War enterprise.

In the first two decades after the Second World War (1939–1945) FDI accelerated at an unprecedented scale, and gradually outpaced the growth of international trade (Dicken, 2011). Attention from economic and international business scholars followed suit. Until the 1960s FDI was understood as an investment activity, either profiting from interest rate differences or reducing overall risks (Markowitz, 1959). However, Hymer (1960) found this explanation not viable. In the first place these assumptions could not explain why FDI was mainly the domain of firms and not of banks – obviously banks would be far better equipped to exploit interest rate differences. In the second place, spreading risks did not seem to be consistent with ownership patterns. In most cases firms did not spread their investments at all, but took majority stakes in their overseas activities, while an overwhelming proportion of foreign affiliates were in the same industry as their parents instead (Vernon, 1977).

Hymer observed, as had others before him (Bain, 1956; Penrose, 1959), a sharp increase in FDI of US firms in Canada and Western Europe, and presented an alternative hypothesis explaining FDI. He shifted the focus from the nation to a firm's strategy, which is widely acknowledged 'to have triggered a stream of literature' on the fundamental question of why companies expand their activities abroad instead of just exporting goods or licensing their production methods to other companies in a foreign country (Dunning, 2001).

In 1980 John Dunning formulated his so-called *eclectic paradigm* that more or less merged several unique theories of international economics into one model. First of all Dunning's theory focused on real (superior quality) or perceived (branding) *ownership advantages*. Secondly, Dunning's paradigm explored the availability of *location advantages* for a specific company like raw materials or low cost labour. Dunning also focused on specific location incentives, such as tax breaks, infrastructure and facilities. Last but not least, Dunning suggested that when a firm has the capabilities to *internalize* different transactions in its value chain – alone or in alliances with companies abroad – it would exploit cost advantages vis á vis its competitors.

Firms as exploiters of market imperfections

Traditional trade theory was based on the assumption that factor endowments for production, capital and labour were of the same quality everywhere in the world (see also the discussion in Chapter 10). Most Foreign Direct Investment theories however, focused on exactly the opposite assumption. As Steven Hymer (1960), Charles Kindleberger, (1973),

Richard Caves (1971), Paul Krugman (1980) and Michael Porter (1990) pointed out: firms try to exploit market imperfections.

Mass production under oligarchic market conditions was – and still is – one of the fundamental forms of market imperfection (Krugman, 1990). This type of production, based on scale advantages and superior efficiency, was first promoted by Frederic Winslow Taylor (1911), and materialized by industrial genius Henry Ford. Coined as *Fordism* (Gramsci, 1934), mass production was supported by governmental rules and regulations (in the US initiated in the *New Deal Policy* of the Roosevelt administration and also institutionalized in Western Europe's *Welfare State model*), and became the dominant economic and sociopolitical model of the post Second World War era in the Western hemisphere.

Mass production of much wanted new durable consumer goods like cars and consumer electronics reached its peak in the early 1960s. Western Europe, with its rising levels of income after the 1950s, was the next step for US companies to exploit their ownership advantages abroad which explained the flow of FDI from the US to the different countries of Western Europe.

By the mid-sixties, however, there were signs that this *Fordist* mode of production had reached the end of its industrial life cycle. The technology to produce these consumer goods had become a commodity, while gaining cost advantages by increasing scale or lowering labour costs had reached its limits. As for labour costs, exactly the opposite occurred: most Western European countries experienced an explosion of real wages. And as this escalation of real wages was no longer compensated by rising productivity, this led to a so-called *profit squeeze* (Chesnais, 1984).

The economic relationship between the US and Western Europe changed from the mid-sixties onwards. Gradually, Western European firms had mastered the mass production technologies invented in the US. The Frenchman Servan-Schreiber, in his famous 1967 political essay *Le Défi Américain* ("The American Challenge"), even claimed that European companies had to look for ways to secure their own profits in labour intensive sectors like the automotive industry, ship building, the garment industry and consumer electronics vis à vis US competitors. The first route would be to finding protection from national governments or EU regulations, the second to looking for opportunities, starting labour intensive production elsewhere, and making use of host country advantages.

Firms as seekers of host country advantages

In 2000, Rugman and Verbeke (2001) provided a synthesis of the key host country advantages that companies seek to acquire. First, they identified *natural resources seeking FDI*. Obviously this category of FDI occurs when the desired resources are not available in the firm's home country. Furthermore, this type of capital influx occurs when firms identify specific host country locations as an attractive source of natural resources at the lowest real cost. With this kind of FDI the predicted direction of location and trade flows is largely consistent with conventional trade theory.

Second, Rugman and Verbeke determined *market seeking FDI*. In deciding to either produce at home and then export to foreign markets, or to produce abroad, the firm would choose to enter markets in which it could use its competitive advantage. Nonetheless, it would also need to consider the extent of control over its properties, technology, information and operations, and the scale of capital that the firm must risk. The complexity here would be that location advantages may shift over time, as demonstrated by the international product cycle model of Raymond Vernon (1966, see also Chapter 10).

Third, *efficiency seeking FDI* would lead to even higher complexity. Efficiency, as a product of both the quality of labour and capital, may change over time and thus affect the location for production.

The fourth type of Rugman and Verbeke's classification was *strategic asset seeking FDI:* 'assets of foreign firms are secured by new plants and acquisitions or joint ventures, to create synergies with the existing pool of assets through common ownership'.

Locational shift of production

From the 1960s onwards three subsequent developments turned Foreign Direct Investments in labour intensive production industries into losses. The first was the liberalization of world trade initiated by the International Monetary Fund (IMF), the World Bank and the General Agreement on Tariffs and Trade (GATT). Under the guidance of GATT a series of trade liberalization rounds were organized. Until the mid-60s GATT mainly facilitated and affected intra-industry trade between established industrial countries or trading blocs. From the mid-60s onwards, membership of GATT and its successor World Trade Organization (WTO) accelerated. Whereas at its start in 1947, GATT only had 23 founding members, at present the number of member countries in the WTO totals 157, including all leading developing economies such as India, a member since 1995, China, joining the WTO in 2001, and Russia that became a member in 2012. As a result liberalization agreements currently affect almost all nations in the world.

The second development was the rise of FDI in developing countries, especially stimulated by the change of policy in a number of these countries. In the 1970s countries changed their policy from import-substitution to export orientation. Dubbed *Newly Industrializing Countries,* or *NICs,* the most successful of these developing countries, such as Singapore, Hong Kong, Taiwan and South Korea, offered cheap labour. Moreover, these countries created all sorts of incentives to attract FDI, such as *Free Trade Zones* (FTZ) and *Export Processing Zones* (EPZ), supported by seaports, international airports and national frontiers. In these FTZ goods could be landed, handled, manufactured or reconfigured, and re-exported without the intervention of the customs authorities. Moreover, corporations setting up commercial activities in a zone were often given tax breaks and in most cases unions were not allowed.

A third development even speeded up the shift of labour intensive manufacturing to the new production sites abroad. Better communication, transport and new process technology enabled companies to maximize cost efficiency whilst at the same time remain in control over the whole supply chain.

Firms as internalizers

The above mentioned coinciding developments have led scholars to formulate the so-called *New International Division of Labour* (Fröbel, Heinrichs and Kreye, 1980) or *Global Shift* (Dicken, 1986). The new paradigm claimed that in due time most, if not all, labour intensive production would be concentrated in countries with an abundance of cheap labour, whereas R&D and higher technological production and supporting service industries such as banking, would be concentrated in countries with superior levels of education, income and infrastructure.

But when external conditions are equal for all, international companies that are best in *internalizing* the emerging opportunities to a competitive advantage. With this in mind, Dunning (1980) elaborated on the research findings of scholars such as Oliver E. Williamson (1975), Peter Buckley and Mark Casson (1976), and Jean-François Hennart (1977). Known as *transaction cost economics,* the research of these scholars concentrated on the question of 'why MNEs organize their own interdependencies that could also be handled by markets.' The answer to this question was that many of the firms' advantages relate to monopolizing their hands-on knowledge of producing and handling their products and services. By establishing their own international operations, firms hold crucial information that is at the core of their competitive advantage to themselves.

Structural changes

The above mentioned developments illustrate the increasing diversity in MNEs trajectories. Nevertheless, they are in line with the evolutionary development of the production locations as explained by the industry life cycle theory of Raymond Vernon (1966).

From the mid-1980s onwards, however, new technological innovations made it possible to offset labour costs with high level of productivity. Originating in Japan, and often dubbed *Toyotism* after the Japanese car manufacturer Toyota, a new production model of flexible automation had emerged (Womack, Jones and Roos, 1990). According to David Harvey in his seminal work *The Conditions of Postmodernity* (1990) "this new regime rests on flexibility with respect to labour processes, labour markets, products and patterns of consumption. It is characterized by the emergence of entirely new sectors of production, new ways of providing financial services, new markets and, above all, great intensified rates of commercial, technological and organizational innovations."

The new production mode had two consequences. In the first place some firms started relocating production back to their home countries, a development also coined as *rerunaway* (Van Tulder and Junne, 1988), in which the input of new production technology could offset higher – but no longer crucial – labour costs. In the second place, immense R&D costs in high end technical sectors, such as telecom, aircraft industries and the automotive sector, forced companies to concentrate on the developed markets of the US, the EU and Japan. Only in these markets, dubbed by Kenichi Ohmae (1985) as the *Triad of Economic Power*, could firms recoup their rising R&D investments. This triad of economic power as the main markets for the influx of FDI made clear that the much used term *globalization* (Levitt, 1985) should be put into perspective. Alan M. Rugman, in his book *The Regional Multinational* (2005) for instance, pointed out that FDI still mainly took place in a relatively small number of countries, and that only a minority of MNEs had an equal share of their production and sales in all countries of the so-called Triad. Moreover, the more strategic the assets, the less global the activities: R&D, headquarter location and stock ownership were mainly concentrated in the MNEs home countries (Rugman, 2005; Ruigrok and Van Tulder, 1995).

Technological changes, affecting not only production but also all aspects of communication and controlling processes, complicated matters further. From the 1990s onwards internalization of non-transferable information as proclaimed by the transaction cost theory and affirmed by many other scholars (Porter, 1990) was no longer the obvious choice in all circumstances to gain a competitive advantage. As we have seen in Chapter 10 all sorts of information sharing agreements, even between competitors, proved to be a suitable strategy in this new era dominated by the 'network society' (Castells, 1996).

FDI from developing countries

After the turn of the century yet another profound change in the balance of economic power emerged. Labour intensive production found its way from the first generation of newly industrializing countries: Singapore, Hong Kong, Taiwan and South Korea, to second and third tier locations like Indonesia, Thailand, Malaysia and Bangladesh. In addition new economic powerhouses, such as China, India, Russia, Turkey and Brazil made their presence felt. These awakening giants attracted FDI because of cheap labour. The rising middle class in countries like China became very interesting markets for Western consumer products, like cars and luxury goods, especially with shrinking home market demands after the 2007/8 financial crisis.

Rising income levels and technological developments in these countries changed locational conditions while markets matured. Regions within China, like greater Beijing, Shanghai or Hong Kong, currently attract not just cheap labour but also higher end production geared for both export and their own home market. A number of important developments are illustrative: Microsoft sells more Office programes in Mandarin than in English; China has more PhD students than the US; and new technological innovations, such as applying solar batteries as the new source of power for the automotive industry, are far more advanced in China than in the traditional industrial nations of US, Western Europe, and even Japan for that matter.

FDI outflows from developing countries

The above mentioned shift in the economic power balance also resulted in the growing number of internationalizing firms from developing countries, a development that can be described 'as a major characteristic in the current world economic scenario' (UNCTAD 2010). 'Over 70 per cent of the FDI from developing countries originate from Asia, especially China and India. Latin America with Brazil, Mexico and Chile as the main countries is in second position with 24 per cent of the total FDI from developing countries. South Africa alone is the major FDI source within Africa, which as a whole continent accounts for 4 per cent of the developing countries total (UNCTAD, 2010).

Many were surprised how fast some companies from these developing countries have risen on the Financial Times Global 500 list. Between 2006 and 2010 the number of enterprises from the four major developing countries, Brazil, Russia, India and China, also called BRIC-countries, has risen from 15 to 80. Moreover, in the 2010 version of the FT Global 500, PetroChina has overtaken Exxon Mobil as the world's most valuable company. Even more surprising is that major MNEs from these countries not just compete on products at the 'bottom of the pyramid' (Prahalad, 2004) or solemnly exploit their home countries' natural resources, but also engage in higher end commercial activities. For instance, Wipro is an Indian IT giant competing on equal footing with other global players from developed economies. Brazilian airplane manufacturer Embraer has become one of the four key players in the civil aviation industry together with American Boeing, European Airbus and Canadian Bombardier. And Petrobras, the semi-public energy corporation from Brazil is the largest company in the southern hemisphere by market capitalization.

Born Globals

A new phenomenon are entrepreneurial ventures labelled as *Born Globals,* starting out as globally active operations from the very beginning (Dicken, 2011), such as Facebook, Twitter and LinkedIn. 'These new species of TNC are different from traditional multinationals in that they are created globally from inception, seizing the opportunities offered by an increasingly integrated and interconnected global economy' (Mathews and Zander, 2007).

The future of internationalization

Although history matters, it does not entirely determine the future. So the question is which nation-specific factors should also be considered to get an idea of how the issue of international configuration will be dealt with. Of course, if the proponents of the global convergence perspective are entirely right, the factors mentioned below will become less and less important as countries grow more similar. All of the international differences in strategic management preferences discussed in the preceding chapters will also wither away. However, if international diversity remains a characteristic of our world, the way strategy paradoxes are dealt with differently in each country will continue to be an important issue to discuss.

Level of nationalism.   In some countries the belief is widespread that foreign values, norms, habits and behaviours are being imposed, that are undermining the national culture, and that the country's ability to decide its own fate is being compromised. This leads many to argue that global convergence should be, and will be, curtailed. In other countries such nationalism is far less pronounced, and the advantages of globalization are more widely accepted. In general, it can be expected that strategists from countries with a strong streak of nationalism will gravitate more toward the international diversity perspective, while strategists from less nationalist countries will be more inclined towards the global convergence perspective.

Size of country.   In general, smaller countries are more exposed to the international context than larger countries. Smaller countries commonly export more of their gross domestic product than larger countries, and import more as well. Hence, their companies are more used to dealing with, and adapting to, a high number of foreign suppliers, customers and competitors. Moreover, companies from smaller countries, confronted with a limited home market, are forced to seek growth in foreign markets earlier than their counterparts in larger countries. During this early internationalization, these companies do not have the benefit of scale economies in the home market and therefore are usually more inclined to adapt themselves to the demands of foreign markets. Companies in larger markets normally grow to a significant size at home, thereby achieving certain economies of scale through national standardization, while also establishing a domestically oriented management style. When they do move abroad, as a more mature company, their international activities will tend to be modest compared to domestic operations and therefore they will be less inclined to be locally adaptive.

It stands to reason that this difference in exposure to the international context has an influence on how strategists from different countries perceive developments in the international context. Generally, strategists from smaller countries, to whom adaptation to international variety has become second nature, will favour the view that international diversity will remain. Strategists from larger countries will be more inclined to emphasize the growing similarities and to seek opportunities for international standardization.

INTRODUCTION TO THE READINGS

To help strategizing managers to come to grips with the variety of perspectives on this issue, three readings have been selected that each shed their own light on the debate. As in previous chapters, the first two readings are representative of the two poles in this debate (see Table 12.1), while the third reading bridges the perspectives.

Reading 12.1, representing the global convergence perspective, is 'The Globalization of Markets' by Theodore Levitt. This article, published in the early 1980s, has probably been the most influential at starting the debate about globalization in the business literature. Levitt's thesis is that the world is quickly moving towards a converging commonality.

He believes that 'the world's needs and desires have been irrevocably homogenized'. The force driving this process is technology, which has facilitated communication, transport and travel, while allowing for the development of superior products at low prices. His conclusion is that 'the commonality of preference leads inescapably to the standardization of products, manufacturing and the institutions of trade and commerce'. The old-fashioned multinational corporation, that adapted itself to local circumstances is 'obsolete and the global corporation absolute'. While a clear proponent of the global convergence perspective, it should be noted that Levitt's bold prediction of global convergence is focused on the globalization of markets. In particular, he is intent on pointing out that converging consumer demand in international markets facilitates – even necessitates – the reaping of economies of scale through the standardization of products, marketing and production. With this emphasis on the demand side, Levitt pays far less attention to the supply side – the globalization of industries and the competition within industries – that other global convergence proponents tend to accentuate. And although he strongly advises companies to become 'global corporations', he does not further detail what a global company should look like. Overall, Levitt views globalization more as growing international similarity, while paying less attention than some other authors to the possibility of growing international integration.

As a direct response to 'the sweeping and somewhat polemic character' of Levitt's argumentation, Susan Douglas and Yoram Wind's article, 'The Myth of Globalization', has been selected for Reading 12.2 representing the international diversity perspective. Douglas and Wind believe that many of the assumptions underlying Levitt's global standardization philosophy are contradicted by the facts. They argue that the convergence of customer needs is not a one-way street; divergence trends are noticeable as well. Furthermore, they believe that Levitt is mistaken in arguing that economies of scale in production and marketing are an irreversible force driving globalization. According to Douglas and Wind, many new technologies have actually lowered the minimum efficient scale of operation, while there are also plenty of industries where economies of scale are not an important issue. The authors conclude by outlining the specific circumstances under which a strategy of global standardization might be effective. Under all other circumstances, Douglas and Wind reiterate, the international strategist will have to deal with the existence of international diversity and search for the right balance between global standardization and local adaptation.

In the third reading, 'Multinational enterprises and local contexts', Klaus Meyer, Ram Mudambi and Rajneesh Narula argue that global integration as relevant to MNE activity is about *increasing interfaces* between people, nations and cultures that in most instances continue to retain their local distinctiveness. In addition, multinational enterprises (MNEs) face growing challenges in managing the complexity of increased frequency and intensity of interactions across local contexts, because they must manage 'multiple embeddedness' across heterogeneous contexts at two levels. First, at the MNE level, they must organize their networks to exploit effectively both the differences and similarities of their multiple host locations. Second, at the subsidiary level, they must balance 'internal' embeddedness within the MNE network, with their 'external' embeddedness in the host milieu. Balancing the subsidiary's strategic role within the MNE with its local identity and its domestic linkages can sometimes represent a trade-off. Multiple embeddedness thus creates both business opportunities and operational challenges.

READING 12.1

The globalization of markets

By Theodore Levitt[1]

A powerful force drives the world toward a converging commonality, and that force is technology. It has proletarianized communication, transport and travel. It has made isolated places and impoverished peoples eager for modernity's allurements. Almost everyone everywhere wants all the things they have heard about, seen, or experienced via the new technologies.

The result is a new commercial reality – the emergence of global markets for standardized consumer products on a previously unimagined scale of magnitude. Corporations geared to this new reality benefit from enormous economies of scale in production, distribution, marketing and management. By translating these benefits into reduced world prices, they can decimate competitors that still live in the disabling grip of old assumptions about how the world works.

Gone are accustomed differences in national or regional preference. Gone are the days when a company could sell last year's models – or lesser versions of advanced products – in the less developed world. And gone are the days when prices, margins and profits abroad were generally higher than at home.

The globalization of markets is at hand. With that, the multinational commercial world nears its end, and so does the multinational corporation.

The multinational and the global corporation are not the same thing. The multinational corporation operates in a number of countries, and adjusts its products and practices in each – at high relative costs. The global corporation operates with resolute constancy – at low relative cost – as if the entire world (or major regions of it) were a single entity; it sells the same things in the same way everywhere.

Which strategy is better is not a matter of opinion but of necessity. Worldwide communications carry everywhere the constant drumbeat of modern possibilities to lighten and enhance work, raise living standards, divert and entertain. The same countries that ask the world to recognize and respect the individuality of their cultures insist on the wholesale transfer to them of modern goods, services and technologies. Modernity is not just a wish but also a widespread practice among those who cling, with unyielding passion or religious fervour, to ancient attitudes and heritages.

Who can forget the televised scenes during the 1979 Iranian uprisings of young men in fashionable French-cut trousers and silky body shirts thirsting with raised modern weapons for blood in the name of Islamic fundamentalism?

In Brazil, thousands swarm daily from pre-industrial Bahian darkness into exploding coastal cities, there quickly to install television sets in crowded corrugated huts and, next to battered Volkswagens, make sacrificial offerings of fruit and fresh-killed chickens to Macumban spirits by candlelight.

A thousand suggestive ways attest to the ubiquity of the desire for the most advanced things that the world makes and sells – goods of the best quality and reliability at the lowest price. The world's needs and desires have been irrevocably homogenized. This makes the multinational corporation obsolete and the global corporation absolute.

Living in the Republic of Technology

Daniel J. Boorstin, author of the monumental trilogy *The Americans* (1973), characterized our age as driven by 'the Republic of Technology (whose) supreme law is convergence, the tendency for everything to become more like everything else'.

In business, this trend has pushed markets toward global commonality. Corporations sell standardized products in the same way everywhere – autos, steel, chemicals, petroleum, cement, agricultural commodities and equipment, industrial and commercial construction, banking and insurance services, computers, semiconductors, transport, electronic instruments, pharmaceuticals and telecommunications, to mention some of the obvious.

Nor is the sweeping gale of globalization confined to these raw material or high-tech products, where the universal language of customers and users facilitates standardization. The transforming winds whipped up

[1]Source: Reprinted by permission of *Harvard Business Review*. From 'The Globalization of Markets' by T. Levitt, May–June 1983, Vol. 61.

by the proletarianization of communication and travel enter every crevice of life.

Commercially, nothing confirms this as much as the success of McDonald's from the Champs Elysees to the Ginza, of Coca-Cola in Bahrain and Pepsi-Cola in Moscow, and of rock music, Greek salad, Hollywood movies, Revlon cosmetics, Sony televisions and Levi jeans everywhere. 'High-touch' products are as ubiquitous as high-tech.

Starting from opposing sides, the high-tech and the high-touch ends of the commercial spectrum gradually consume the undistributed middle in their cosmopolitan orbit. No one is exempt and nothing can stop the process. Everywhere everything gets more and more like everything else as the world's preference structure is relentlessly homogenized.

Consider the cases of Coca-Cola and Pepsi-Cola, which are globally standardized products sold everywhere and welcomed by everyone. Both successfully cross multitudes of national, regional and ethnic taste buds trained to a variety of deeply ingrained local preferences of taste, flavour, consistency, effervescence and aftertaste. Everywhere both sell well. Cigarettes, too, especially American-made, make year-to-year global inroads in territories previously held in the firm grip of other, mostly local, blends.

These are not exceptional examples. (Indeed their global reach would be even greater were it not for artificial trade barriers.) They exemplify a general drift toward the homogenization of the world and how companies distribute, finance and price products. Nothing is exempt. The products and methods of the industrialized world play a single tune for all the world, and all the world eagerly dances to it.

Ancient differences in national tastes or modes of doing business disappear. The commonality of preference leads inescapably to the standardization of products, manufacturing, and the institutions of trade and commerce. Small nation-based markets transmogrify and expand. Success in world competition turns on efficiency in production, distribution, marketing and management, and inevitably becomes focused on price.

The most effective world competitors incorporate superior quality and reliability into their cost structures. They sell in all national markets the same kind of products sold at home or in their largest export market. They compete on the basis of appropriate value – the best combinations of price, quality, reliability and delivery for products that are globally identical with respect to design, function and even fashion.

That, and little else, explains the surging success of Japanese companies dealing worldwide in a vast variety of products – both tangible products like steel, cars, motorcycles, hi-fi equipment, farm machinery, robots, microprocessors, carbon fibres and now even textiles, and intangibles like banking, shipping, general contracting, and soon computer software. Nor are high-quality and low-cost operations incompatible, as a host of consulting organizations and data engineers argue with vigorous vacuity. The reported data are incomplete, wrongly analysed and contradictory. The truth is that low-cost operations are the hallmark of corporate cultures that require and produce quality in all that they do. High quality and low costs are not opposing postures. They are compatible, twin identities of superior practice.

To say that Japan's companies are not global because they export cars with left-side drives to the United States and the European continent, while those in Japan have right-side drives, or because they sell office machines through distributors in the United States but directly at home, or speak Portuguese in Brazil is to mistake a difference for a distinction. The same is true of Safeway and Southland retail chains operating effectively in the Middle East, and to not only native but also imported populations from Korea, the Philippines, Pakistan, India, Thailand, Britain and the United States. National rules of the road differ, and so do distribution channels and languages. Japan's distinction is its unrelenting push for economy and value enhancement. That translates into a drive for standardization at high quality levels.

Vindication of the Model T

If a company forces costs and prices down and pushes quality and reliability up – while maintaining reasonable concern for suitability – customers will prefer its world-standardized products. The theory holds at this stage in the evolution of globalization, no matter what conventional market research and even common sense may suggest about different national and regional tastes, preferences, needs and institutions. The Japanese have repeatedly vindicated this theory, as did Henry Ford with the Model T. Most important, so have their imitators, including companies from South Korea (television sets and heavy construction), Malaysia (personal calculators and microcomputers), Brazil (auto parts and tools), Colombia (apparel), Singapore (optical equipment) and yes, even from the United States (office copiers, computers, bicycles, castings), Western Europe (automatic washing machines), Romania (housewares), Hungary (apparel), the former Yugoslavia (furniture) and Israel (pagination equipment).

Of course, large companies operating in a single nation or even a single city don't standardize everything they make, sell, or do. They have product lines instead of a single product version, and multiple distribution channels. There are neighbourhood, local, regional, ethnic and institutional differences, even within metropolitan areas. But although companies customize products for particular market segments, they know that success in a world with homogenized demand requires a search for sales opportunities in similar segments across the globe in order to achieve the economies of scale necessary to compete.

Such a search works because a market segment in one country is seldom unique; it has close cousins everywhere precisely because technology has homogenized the globe. Even small local segments have their global equivalents everywhere and become subject to global competition, especially on price.

The global competitor will seek constantly to standardize his offering everywhere. He will digress from this standardization only after exhausting all possibilities to retain it, and he will push for reinstatement of standardization whenever digression and divergence have occurred. He will never assume that the customer is a king who knows his own wishes.

Trouble increasingly stalks companies that lack clarified global focus and remain inattentive to the economics of simplicity and standardization. The most endangered companies in the rapidly evolving world tend to be those that dominate rather small domestic markets with high-value-added products for which there are smaller markets elsewhere. With transportation costs proportionately low, distant competitors will enter the now sheltered markets of those companies with goods produced more cheaply under scale-efficient conditions. Global competition spells the end of domestic territoriality, no matter how diminutive the territory may be.

When the global producer offers his lower costs internationally, his patronage expands exponentially. He not only reaches into distant markets, but also attracts customers who previously held to local preferences and now capitulate to the attractions of lesser prices. The strategy of standardization not only responds to worldwide homogenized markets but also expands those markets with aggressive low pricing.

The new technological juggernaut taps an ancient motivation – to make one's money go as far as possible. This is universal – not simply a motivation but actually a need.

The hedgehog knows

The difference between the hedgehog and the fox, wrote Sir Isaiah Berlin in distinguishing between Dostoevski and Tolstoy, is that the fox knows a lot about a great many things, but the hedgehog knows everything about one great thing. The multinational corporation knows a lot about a great many countries and congenially adapts to supposed differences. It willingly accepts vestigial national differences, not questioning the possibility of their transformation, not recognizing how the world is ready and eager for the benefit of modernity, especially when the price is right. The multinational corporation's accommodating mode to visible national differences is medieval.

By contrast, the global corporation knows everything about one great thing. It knows about the absolute need to be competitive on a worldwide basis as well as nationally and seeks constantly to drive down prices by standardizing what it sells and how it operates. It treats the world as composed of few standardized markets rather than many customized markets. It actively seeks and vigorously works toward global convergence. Its mission is modernity and its mode, price competition, even when it sells top-of-the-line, high-end products. It knows about the one great thing all nations and people have in common: scarcity.

Nobody takes scarcity lying down; everyone wants more. This in part explains division of labour and specialization of production. They enable people and nations to optimize their conditions through trade. The median is usually money.

Experience teaches that money has three special qualities: scarcity, difficulty of acquisition and transience. People understandably treat it with respect. Everyone in the increasingly homogenized world market wants products and features that everybody else wants. If the price is low enough, they will take highly standardized world products, even if these aren't exactly what mother said was suitable, what immemorial custom decreed was right, or what market-research fabulists asserted was preferred.

The implacable truth of all modern production – whether of tangible or intangible goods – is that large-scale production of standardized items is generally cheaper within a wide range of volume than small-scale production. Some argue that CAD/CAM (computer aided design/computer aided manufacturing) will allow companies to manufacture customized products on a small scale – but cheaply. But the argument misses the point. If a company treats the world as one or two distinctive product markets, it can serve the world more economically than if it treats it as three, four, or five product markets.

Different cultural preferences, national tastes and standards, and business institutions are vestiges of the past. Some inheritances die gradually; others prosper and expand into mainstream global preferences. So-called ethnic markets are a good example. Chinese food, pitta bread, country and western music, pizza and jazz are everywhere. They are market segments that exist in worldwide proportions. They don't deny or contradict global homogenization but confirm it.

Many of today's differences among nations as to products and their features actually reflect the respectful accommodation of multinational corporations to what they believe are fixed local preferences. They believe preferences are fixed, not because they are but because of rigid habits of thinking about what actually is. Most executives in multinational corporations are thoughtlessly accommodating. They falsely presume that marketing means giving the customer what he says he wants rather than trying to understand exactly what he'd like. So they persist with high-cost, customized multinational products and practices instead of pressing hard and pressing properly for global standardization.

I do not advocate the systematic disregard of local or national differences. But a company's sensitivity to such differences does not require that it ignore the possibilities of doing things differently or better.

With persistence and appropriate means, barriers against superior technologies and economics have always fallen. There is no recorded exception where reasonable effort has been made to overcome them. It is very much a matter of time and effort.

A failure in global imagination

Many companies have tried to standardize world practice by exporting domestic products and processes without accommodation or change – and have failed miserably. Their deficiencies have been seized on as evidence of bovine stupidity in the face of abject impossibility. Advocates of global standardization see them as examples of failures in execution.

In fact, poor execution is often an important cause. More important, however, is failure of nerve – failure of imagination.

Consider the case for the introduction of fully automatic home laundry equipment in Western Europe at a time when few homes had even semi-automatic machines.

The growing success of small, low-powered, low-speed, low-capacity, low-priced Italian machines, even against the preferred but highly priced and highly promoted brand in West Germany, was significant. It contained a powerful message that was lost on managers confidently wedded to a distorted version of the marketing concept according to which you give the customer what he says he wants. In fact the customers said they wanted certain features, but their behaviour demonstrated they'd take other features provided the price and the promotion were right.

In this case it was obvious that under prevailing conditions, people preferred a low-priced automatic over any kind of manual or semi-automatic machine and certainly over higher priced automatics, even though the low-priced automatics failed to fulfil all their expressed preferences. The supposedly meticulous and demanding German consumers violated all expectations by buying the simple, low-priced Italian machines.

This case illustrates how the perverse practice of the marketing concept and the absence of any kind of marketing imagination let multinational attitudes survive when customers actually want the benefits of global standardization. People were asked what features they wanted in a washing machine rather than what they wanted out of life. Selling a line of products individually tailored to each nation is thoughtless. Managers who took pride in practicing the marketing concept to the fullest did not, in fact, practice it at all. Data do not yield information except with the intervention of the mind. Information does not yield meaning except with the intervention of imagination.

Cracking the code of Western markets

Since the theory of the marketing concept emerged a quarter of a century ago, the more managerially advanced corporations have been eager to offer what customers clearly want rather than what is merely convenient. They have created marketing departments supported by professional market researchers of awesome and often costly proportions. And they have proliferated extraordinary numbers of operations and product lines – highly tailored products and delivery systems for many different markets, market segments and nations.

Significantly, Japanese companies operate almost entirely without marketing departments or market research of the kind so prevalent in the West. Yet, in the colourful words of General Electric's chairman John F. Welch Jr., the Japanese, coming from a small cluster of resource-poor islands, with an entirely alien culture and an almost impenetrably complex language, have cracked the code of Western markets. They have done it not by looking with mechanistic thoroughness at the way markets are different but rather by searching for meaning with a deeper wisdom. They have discovered the one great thing all markets have in common – an overwhelming desire for dependable, world-standard modernity in all things, at aggressively low prices. In response, they deliver irresistible value everywhere, attracting people with products that market-research technocrats described with superficial certainty as being unsuitable and uncompetitive.

The wider a company's global reach, the greater the number of regional and national preferences it will encounter for certain product features, distribution systems, or promotional media. There will always need to be some accommodation to differences.

In its highly successful introduction of Contac 600 (the timed-release decongestant) into Japan, Smith-Kline Corporation used 35 wholesalers instead of the 1000-plus that established practice required. Daily contacts with the wholesalers and key retailers, also in violation of established practice, supplemented the plan, and it worked.

Denied access to established distribution institutions in the United States, Komatsu, the Japanese manufacturer of lightweight farm machinery, entered the market through over-the-road construction equipment dealers in rural areas of the Sunbelt, where farms are smaller, the soil sandier and easier to work. Here inexperienced distributors were able to attract customers on the basis of Komatsu's product and price appropriateness.

In cases of successful challenge to prevailing institutions and practices, a combination of product reliability and quality, strong and sustained support systems, aggressively low prices, and sales-compensation packages, as well as audacity and implacability, circumvented, shattered and transformed very different distribution systems. Instead of resentment, there was admiration.

The differences that persist throughout the world despite its globalization affirm an ancient dictum of economics – that things are driven by what happens at the margin, not at the core. Thus, in ordinary competitive analysis, what's important is not the average price but the marginal price, what happens not in the usual case but at the interface of newly erupting conditions. What counts in commercial affairs is what happens at the cutting edge. What is most striking today is the underlying similarities of what is happening now to national preferences at the margin. These similarities at the cutting edge cumulatively form an overwhelming, predominant commonality everywhere.

To refer to the persistence of economic nationalism (protective and subsidized trade practices, special tax aids, or restrictions for home market producers) as a barrier to the globalization of markets is to make a valid point. Economic nationalism does have a powerful persistence. But, as with the present almost totally smooth internationalization of investment capital, the past alone does not shape or predict the future.

Reality is not a fixed paradigm, dominated by immemorial customs and derived attitudes, heedless of powerful and abundant new forces. The world is becoming increasingly informed about the liberating and enhancing possibilities of modernity. The persistence of the inherited varieties of national preferences rests uneasily on increasing evidence of, and restlessness regarding, their inefficiency, costliness and confinement. The historic past, and the national differences respecting commerce and industry it spawned and fostered everywhere, is now subject to relatively easy transformation.

Cosmopolitanism is no longer the monopoly of the intellectual and leisure classes; it is becoming the established property and defining characteristic of all sectors everywhere in the world. Gradually and irresistibly it breaks down the walls of economic insularity, nationalism and chauvinism. What we see today as escalating commercial nationalism is simply the last violent death rattle of an obsolete institution.

The successful global corporation does not abjure customization or differentiation for the requirements of markets that differ in product preferences, spending patterns, shopping preferences and institutional or legal arrangements. But the global corporation accepts and adjusts to these differences only reluctantly, only after relentlessly testing their immutability, after trying in various ways to circumvent and reshape them.

The myth of globalization

By Susan Douglas and Yoram Wind[1]

In recent years, globalization has become a key theme in every discussion of international strategy. Proponents of the philosophy of 'global' products and brands, such as Professor Theodore Levitt of Harvard, and the highly successful advertising agency, Saatchi & Saatchi, argue that in a world of growing internationalization, the key to success is the development of global products and brands, in other words, a focus on standardized products and brands worldwide. Others, however, point to the numerous barriers to standardization, and suggest that greater returns are to be obtained from adapting products and marketing strategies to the specific characteristics of individual markets.

The growing integration of international markets as well as the growth of competition on a worldwide scale implies that adoption of a global perspective has become increasingly imperative in planning strategy. However, to conclude that this mandates the adoption of a strategy of universal standardization appears naive and over simplistic. In particular, it ignores the inherent complexity of operations in international markets, and the formulation of an effective strategy to penetrate these markets. While global products and brands may be appropriate for certain markets and in targeting certain segments, adopting such an approach as a universal strategy in relation to all markets may not be desirable, and may lead to major strategic blunders. Furthermore, it implies a product orientation, and a product-driven strategy, rather than a strategy grounded in a systematic analysis of customer behaviour and response patterns and market characteristics.

The purpose of this article is thus to examine critically the notion that success in international markets necessitates adoption of a strategy of global products and brands. Given the restrictive characteristic of this philosophy, a somewhat broader perspective in developing global strategy is proposed which views standardization as merely one option in the range of possible strategies which may be effective in global markets.

The traditional perspective on international strategy

Traditionally, discussion of international business strategy has been polarized around the debate concerning the pursuit of a uniform strategy worldwide versus adaptation to specific local market conditions. On the one hand, it has been argued that adoption of a uniform strategy worldwide enables a company to take advantage of the potential synergies arising from multicountry operations, and constitutes the multinational company's key competitive advantage in international markets. Others however, have argued that adaptation of strategy to idiosyncratic national market characteristics is crucial to success in these markets.

Fayerweather (1969), in his seminal work in international business strategy, described the central issue as one of conflict between forces toward unification and those resulting in fragmentation. He pointed out that within a multinational firm, internal forces created pressures toward the integration of strategy across national boundaries. On the other hand, differences in the sociocultural, political and economic characteristics of countries as well as the need for effective relations with the host society, constitute fragmenting influences that favour adaptation to the local environment.

Recent discussion of global competitive strategy echoes the same theme of the dichotomy between the forces that have triggered the globalization of markets and those that constitute barriers to global competition. Factors such as economies of scale in production, purchasing, faster accumulation of learning from operating worldwide, decrease in transportation and distribution costs, reduced costs of product adaptation, and the emergence of global market segments have encouraged competition on a global scale. However, barriers such as governmental and institutional constraints, tariff barriers and duties, preferential treatment of local firms, transportation costs, differences in customer demand and so on, call for nationalistic or 'protected niche' strategies.

[1]Source: This article was published in *Columbia Journal of World Business*, Winter 1987, Susan Douglas and Yoram Wind, 'The myth of globalization', pp. 19–29. Copyright © Elsevier 1987.

Compromise solutions such as 'pattern standardization' have also been proposed. In this case, a global promotional theme or positioning is developed, but execution is adapted to the local market. Similarly, it has been pointed out that even where a standardized product is marketed in a number of countries, its positioning may be adapted in each market. Conversely, the positioning may be uniform across countries, but the product itself adapted or modified.

Although this debate first emerged in the 1960s, it has recently taken on a new vigour with the widely publicized pronouncements of proponents of 'global standardization' such as Professor Levitt and Saatchi & Saatchi.

The sweeping and somewhat polemic character of their argument has sparked a number of counter-arguments as well as discussion of conditions under which such a strategy may be most appropriate. It has, for example, been pointed out that the potential for standardization may be greater for certain types of products such as industrial goods or luxury personal items targeted to upscale consumers, or products with similar penetration rates. Opportunities for standardization are also likely to occur more frequently among industrialized nations, and especially the Triad countries where customer interests as well as market conditions are likely to be more similar than among developing countries.

The role of corporate philosophy and organizational structure in influencing the practicality of implementing a strategy of global standardization has also been recognized. Here, it has been noted that few companies pursue the extreme position of complete standardization with regard to all elements of the marketing mix, and business functions such as R&D, manufacturing and procurement in all countries throughout the world. Rather, some degree of adaptation is likely to occur relative to certain aspects of the firm's operations or in certain geographic areas. In addition, the feasibility of implementing a standardized strategy will depend on the autonomy accorded to local management. If local management has been accustomed to substantial autonomy, considerable opposition may be encountered in attempting to introduce globally standardized strategies.

An examination of such counterarguments suggests that there are a number of dangers in espousing a philosophy of global standardization for all products and services, and in relation to all markets worldwide. Furthermore, there are numerous difficulties and constraints to implementing such a strategy in many markets, stemming from external market conditions (such as government and trade regulation, competition, the marketing infrastructure and so on), as well as from the current structure and organization of the firm's operations.

The global standardization philosophy: The underlying assumptions

An examination of the arguments in favour of a strategy of global products and brands reveals three key underlying assumptions:

- Customer needs and interests are becoming increasingly homogeneous worldwide.

- People around the world are willing to sacrifice preferences in product features, functions, design and the like, for lower prices at high quality.

- Substantial economies of scale in production and marketing can be achieved through supplying global markets.

There are, however, a number of pitfalls associated with each of these assumptions. These are discussed here in more detail.

Homogenization of the world's wants

A key premise of the philosophy of global products is that customers' needs and interests are becoming increasingly homogeneous worldwide. But while global segments with similar interests and response patterns may be identified in some product markets, it is by no means clear that this is a universal trend. Furthermore, there is substantial evidence to suggest an increasing diversity of behaviour within countries, and the emergence of idiosyncratic country-specific segments.

Lack of evidence of homogenization. In a number of product markets ranging from watches, perfume and handbags to soft drinks and fast foods, companies have successfully identified global customer segments, and developed global products and brands targeted to these segments. These include such stars as Rolex, Omega and Le Baume & Mercier watches, Dior, Patou or Yves St Laurent perfume. But while these brands are highly visible and widely publicized, they are often, with a few notable exceptions such as Classic Coke or McDonald's, targeted to a relatively restricted upscale international customer segment.

Numerous other companies, however, adapt lines to idiosyncratic country preferences, and develop local brands or product variants targeted to local market segments. The Findus frozen food division of Nestle, for example, markets fish cakes and fish fingers in the United Kingdom, but beef bourguignon and coq au vin in France, and vitello con funghi and braviola in Italy. Similarly, Coca-Cola in Japan markets Georgia, cold coffee in a can, and Aquarius, a tonic drink, as well as Classic Coke and Hi-C.

Growth of intracountry segmentation price sensitivity.

Furthermore, there is a growing body of evidence that suggests substantial heterogeneity within countries. In the United States, for example, the VALS (Value of American Lifestyles) study has identified nine value segments, while other studies have identified major differences in behaviour between regions and subcultural segments. Many other countries are also characterized by substantial regional differences as well as different lifestyle and value segments.

Similarly, in industrial markets, while some global segments, often consisting of firms with international operations, can be identified, there also is considerable diversity within and between countries. Often local businesses constitute an important market segment and, especially in developing countries, may differ significantly in technological sophistication, business philosophy and strategy, emphasis on product quality, and service and price, from large multinationals.

The evidence thus suggests that the similarities in customer behaviour are restricted to a relatively limited number of target segments or product markets, while for the most part, there are substantial differences between countries. Proponents of standardization counter that the international strategist should focus on similarities among countries rather than differences. This may, however, imply ignoring a major part of a local market, and the potential profits that may be obtained from tapping other market segments.

Universal preference for low price at acceptable quality

Another critical component of the argument for global standardization is that people around the world are willing to sacrifice preferences in product features, functions, design and the like for lower prices, assuming equivalent quality. Aggressive low pricing for quality products that meet the common needs of customers in markets around the world is believed to further expand the global markets facing the firm. Although an appealing argument, this has three major problems.

Lack of evidence of increased price sensitivity.

Evidence to suggest that customers are universally willing to trade off specific product features for a lower price is largely lacking. While in many product markets there is invariably a price-sensitive segment, there is no indication that this is on the increase. On the contrary, in many product and service markets, ranging from watches, personal computers and household appliances to banking and insurance, an interest in multiple product features, product quality and service appears to be growing.

Low price positioning is a highly vulnerable strategy.

Also, from a strategic point of view, emphasis on price positioning may be undesirable, especially in international markets, since it offers no long-term competitive advantage. A price-positioning strategy is always vulnerable to new technological developments that may lower costs, as well as to attack from competitors with lower overhead, and lower operating or labour costs. Government subsidies to local competitors may also undermine the effectiveness of a price-positioning strategy. In addition, price-sensitive customers typically are not brand or source loyal.

Standardized low price can be overpriced in some countries and underpriced in others.

Finally, a strategy based on a combination of a standardized product at a low price, when implemented in countries that vary in their competitive structure as well as the level of economic development, is likely to result in products that are overdesigned and overpriced for some markets and underdesigned and underpriced for others. Cost advantages may also be negated by transportation and distribution costs as well as tariff barriers or price regulation.

Economies of scale of production and marketing

The third assumption underlying the philosophy of global standardization is that a key force driving strategy is product technology, and that substantial economies of scale can be achieved by supplying global markets. This does, however, neglect three critical and interrelated points:

1 Technological developments in flexible factory automation enable economies of scale to be achieved at lower levels of output and do not require production of a single standardized product.

2 Cost of production is only one and often not the critical component in determining the total cost of the product.

3 Strategy should not be solely product-driven but should take into account the other components of a marketing strategy, such as positioning, packaging, brand name, advertising, PR, consumer and trade promotion and distribution.

Developments in flexible factory automation. Recent developments in flexible factory automation methods have lowered the minimum efficient scale of operation and have thus enabled companies to supply smaller local markets efficiently, without requiring operations on a global scale. However, diseconomies may result from such operations due to increased transportation and distribution costs, as well as higher administrative overhead, and additional communication and coordination costs.

Furthermore, decentralization of production and establishment of local manufacturing operations enables diversification of risk arising from political events, fluctuations in foreign exchange rates, or economic instability. Recent swings in foreign exchange rates, coupled with the growth of offshore sourcing have underscored the vulnerability of centralizing production in a single location. Government regulations relating to local component or offset requirements create additional pressures for local manufacturing. Flexible automation not only implies that decentralization of manufacturing and production may be cost efficient but also makes minor modifications in products or models in the latter stages of production feasible, so that a variety of model versions can be produced without major retooling. Adaptations to product design can thus be made to meet differences in preferences from one country to another without loss of economies of scale.

Production costs are often a minor component of total cost. In many consumer and service industries, such as cosmetics, detergents, pharmaceuticals or financial institutions, production costs are a small fraction of total cost. The key to success in these markets is an understanding of the tastes and purchase behaviour of target customers' distribution channels, and tailoring products and strategies to these rather than production efficiency. In the detergent industry, for example, mastery of mass-merchandising techniques and an effective brand management system are typically considered the key elements in the success of the giants in this field, such as Procter & Gamble (P&G) or Colgate-Palmolive.

The standardization philosophy is primarily product driven. The focus on product- and brand-related aspects of strategy in discussions of global standardization is misleading since it ignores the other key strategy variables. Strategy in international markets should also take into consideration other aspects of the marketing mix, and the extent to which these are standardized across country markets rather than adapted to local idiosyncratic characteristics.

Requisite conditions for global standardization

The numerous pitfalls in the rationale underlying the global standardization philosophy suggests that such a strategy is far from universally appropriate for all products, brands or companies. Only under certain conditions is it likely to prove a 'winning' strategy in international markets. These include:

- the existence of a global market segment;
- potential synergies from standardization;
- the availability of a communication and distribution infrastructure to deliver the firm's offering to target customers worldwide.

Existence of global market segments

As noted previously, global segments may be identified in a number of industrial and consumer markets. In consumer markets these segments are typically luxury- or premium-type products. Global segments are, however, not limited to such product markets, but also exist in other types of markets, such as motorcycle, record, stereo equipment and computer, where a segment with similar needs and wants can be identified in many countries.

In industrial markets, companies with multinational operations are particularly likely to have similar needs and requirements worldwide. Where the operations are integrated or coordinated across national boundaries, as in the case of banks or other financial institutions, compatibility of operational systems and equipment may be essential. Consequently, they may seek vendors who can supply and service their operations worldwide, in some cases developing global contrasts for such purchases. Similarly, manufacturing companies with worldwide operations may source globally in order to ensure uniformity in quality, service and price of components and other raw materials throughout their operations.

Marketing of global products and brands to such target segments and global customers enables development of a uniform global image throughout the world. In some markets such as perfume or fashions, association with a specific country of origin or a foreign image in general may carry a prestige connotation. In other cases, for example, Sony electronic equipment, McDonald's hamburgers, Hertz or Avis car rental, IBM computers, or Xerox office equipment, it may help to develop a worldwide reputation for quality and service. Just as multinational corporations may seek uniformity in supply worldwide, some consumers who travel extensively may be interested in finding the same brand of cigarettes and soft drinks or hotels, in foreign countries. This may be particularly relevant in product markets used extensively by international travellers.

While the existence of a potential global segment is a key motivating factor for developing a global product and brand strategy, it is important to note that the desirability of such a strategy depends on the size and economic viability of the segment in question, the strength of the segment's preference for the global brand, as well as the ability to reach the segment effectively and profitably.

Synergies associated with global standardization

Global standardization may also have a number of synergistic effects. In addition to those associated with a global image noted above, opportunities may exist for the transfer of good ideas for products or promotional strategies from one country to another.

The standardization of strategy and operations across a number of countries may also enable the acquisition or exploitation of specific types of expertise that would not be feasible otherwise. Expertise in assessing country risk or foreign exchange risk, or in identifying and interpreting information relating to multiple country markets, for example, may be developed.

Such synergies are not, however, unique to a strategy of global standardization, but may also occur wherever operations and strategy are coordinated or integrated across country markets. In fact, only certain scale economies associated with product and advertising copy standardization, and the development of a global image as discussed earlier, are unique to global standardization.

Availability of an international communication and distribution infrastructure

The effectiveness of global standardization also depends to a large extent on the availability of an international infrastructure of communications and distribution. As many corporations have expanded overseas, service organizations have followed their customers abroad to supply their needs worldwide.

Advertising agencies such as Saatchi & Saatchi, McCann Erickson and Young & Rubicam now have an international network of operations throughout the world, while many research agencies can also supply services in major markets worldwide. With the growing integration of financial markets, banks, investment firms, insurance and other financial institutions are also becoming increasingly international in orientation and are expanding the scope of their operations in world markets. The physical distribution network of shippers, freight forwarding, export and import agents, customs clearing, invoicing and insurance agents is also becoming increasingly integrated to meet demand for international shipment of goods and services.

Improvements in telecommunications and in logistical systems have considerably increased capacity to manage operations on a global scale and hence facilitate adoption of global standardization strategies. The spread of telex and fax systems, as well as satellite linkages and international computer linkages, all contribute to the shrinking of distances and facilitate globalization of operations. Similarly, improvements in transportation systems and physical logistics such as containerization and computerized inventory and handling systems have enabled significant cost savings as well as reducing time required to move goods across major distances.

Operational constraints to effective implementation of a standardization strategy

While adoption of a standardized strategy may be desirable under certain conditions, there are a number of constraints that severely restrict the firm's ability to develop and implement a standardized strategy.

External constraints to effective standardization

The numerous external constraints that impede global standardization are well recognized. Here, four major categories are highlighted, namely:

1 government and trade restrictions;

2 differences in the marketing infrastructure, such as the availability and effectiveness of promotional media;

3 the character of resource markets, and differences in the availability and costs of resources;

4 differences in competition from one country to another.

Government and trade restrictions. Government and trade restrictions, such as tariff and other trade barriers, product, pricing or promotional regulation, frequently hamper standardization of the product line, pricing or promotional strategy. Tariffs or quotas on the import of key materials, components or other resources may, for example, affect production costs and thus hamper uniform pricing or alternatively result in the substitution of other components and modifications in product design. Local content requirements or compensatory export requirements, which specify that products contain a certain proportion of components manufactured locally or that a certain volume of production is exported to offset imports of components or other services, may have a similar impact.

The existence of cartels such as the European steel cartel, or the Swiss chocolate cartel, may also impede or exclude standardized strategies in countries covered by these agreements. In particular, they may affect adoption of a uniform pricing strategy as the cartel sets prices for the industry. Cartel members may also control established distribution channels, thus preventing use of a standardized distribution strategy. Extensive grey markets in countries such as India, Hong Kong and South America may also affect administered pricing systems, and require adjustment of pricing strategies.

The nature of the marketing infrastructure. Differences in the marketing infrastructure from one country to another may hamper use of a standardized strategy. These may, for example, include differences in the availability and reach of various promotional media, the availability of certain distribution channels or retail institutions, or in the existence and efficiency of the communication and transportation network.

Such factors may, therefore, require considerable adaptation of strategy of local market conditions.

Interdependencies with resource markets. Yet another constraint to the development of standardized strategies is the nature of resource markets, and their operation in different countries throughout the world as well as the interdependency of these markets with marketing decisions. Availability and cost of raw materials, as well as labour and other resources in different locations, will affect not only decisions regarding sourcing of and hence the location of manufacturing activities but also marketing strategy decisions such as product design. For example, in the paper industry, availability of cheap local materials such as jute and sugar cane may result in their substitution for wood fibre.

Cost differentials relative to raw materials, labour, management and other inputs may also influence the trade-off relative to alternative strategies. For example, high packaging costs relative to physical distribution may result in use of cheaper packaging with a shorter shelf life and more frequent shipments. Similarly, low labour costs relative to media may encourage a shift from mass media advertising to labour-intensive promotion such as personal selling and product demonstration.

Availability of capital, technology and manufacturing capabilities in different locations will also affect decisions about licensing, contract manufacturing, joint ventures and other 'make-buy' types of decisions for different markets, as well as decisions about countertrade, reciprocity and other long-term relations.

The nature of the competitive structure. Differences in the nature of the competitive situation from one country to another may also suggest the desirability of adaptation strategy. Even in markets characterized by global competition, such as agricultural equipment and motorcycles, the existence of low-cost competition in certain countries may suggest the desirability of marketing stripped-down models or lowering prices to meet such competition. Even where competitors are predominantly other multinationals, preemption of established distribution networks may encourage adoption of innovative distribution methods or direct distribution to short-circuit an entrenched position. Thus, the existence of global competition does not necessarily imply a need for global standardization.

All such aspects thus impose major constraints on the feasibility and effectiveness of a standardized strategy, and suggest the desirability or need to adapt to specific market conditions.

Internal constraints to effective standardization

In addition to such external constraints on the feasibility of a global standardization strategy, there are also a number of internal constraints that may need to be considered. These include compatibility with the existing network of operations overseas, as well as opposition or lack of enthusiasm among local management toward a standardized strategy.

Existing international operations. Proponents of global standardization typically take the position of a novice company with no operations in international markets, and hence fail to take into consideration the fit of the proposed strategy with current international activities. In practice, however, many companies have a number of existing operations in various countries. In some cases, these are joint ventures or licensing operations, or involve some collaboration in purchasing, manufacturing or distribution with other companies. Even where foreign manufacturing and distribution operations are wholly owned, the establishment of a distribution network will typically entail relationships with other organizations, for example, exclusive distributor agreements.

Such commitments may be difficult if not impossible to change in the short run, and may constitute a major impediment to adoption of a standardized strategy. If, for example, a joint venture with a local company has been established to manufacture and market a product line in a specific country or region, resistance from the local partner (or government authorities) may be encountered if the parent company wishes to shift production or import components from another location. Similarly, a licensing contract will impede a firm from supplying the products covered by the agreement from an alternative location for the duration of the contract, even if it becomes more cost efficient to do so.

Conversely, the establishment of an effective dealer or distribution network in a country or region may constitute an important resource to a company. The addition of new products to the product line currently sold or distributed by this network may therefore provide a more efficient utilization of company resources than expanding to new countries or geographic regions with the existing line, as this would require substantial investment in the establishment of a new distribution network.

In addition, overseas subsidiaries may currently be marketing not only core products and brands from the company's domestic business, but may also have added or acquired local or regional products and brands in response to local market demand. In some cases, therefore, introduction of a global product or brand may be likely to cannibalize sales of local or regional brands.

Advocates of standardization thus need to take into consideration the evolutionary character of international involvement, which may render a universal strategy of global products and brands suboptimal. Somewhat ironically, the longer the history of a multinational corporation's involvement in foreign or international markets, and the more diversified and far-flung its operations, the more likely it is that standardization will not lead to optimal results.

Local management motivation and attitudes. Another internal constraint concerns the motivation and attitudes of local management with regard to standardization. Standardized strategies tend to facilitate or result in centralization in the planning and organization of international activities. Especially if input from local management is limited, this may result in a feeling that strategy is 'imposed' by corporate headquarters, and/or not adequately adapted or appropriate in view of specific local market characteristics and conditions. Local management is likely to take the view 'it won't work here – things are different', which will reduce their motivation to implement a standardized strategy effectively.

A framework for classifying global strategy options

The adoption of a global perspective should not be viewed as synonymous with a strategy of global products and brands. Rather, for most companies such a perspective implies consideration of a broad range of strategic options of which standardization is merely one.

In essence, a global perspective implies planning strategy relative to markets worldwide rather than on a country-by-country basis. This may result in the identification of opportunities for global products and brands or integrating and coordinating strategy across national boundaries to exploit potential synergies of operating on an international scale. Such opportunities should, however, be weighed against the benefits of adaptation to idiosyncratic customer characteristics.

The development of an effective global strategy thus requires a careful examination of all international options in terms of standardization versus adaptation open to the firm.

A firm's international operations are likely to be characterized by a mix of strategies, including not only global products and brands, but also some regional

products and brands and some national products and brands. Similarly, some target segments may be global, others regional and others national. Hybrid strategies of this nature thus enable a company to take advantage of the benefits of standardization and potential synergies from operating on an international scale, while at the same time not losing those afforded by adaptation to specific country characteristics and customer preferences.

Multinational enterprises and local contexts: The opportunities and challenges of multiple-embeddedness

By Klaus E. Meyer, Ram Mudambi and Rajneesh Narula[1]

Introduction

Since at least the first industrial revolution, advances of technology and changes in institutional frameworks have, by fits and starts, facilitated commerce (Jones, 2005). These processes have accelerated since the 1950s, and have been identified as the primary drivers of increasing global integration and the rising importance of multinational enterprises (MNEs) in the global economy. Scholars such as Levitt (1983), Ohmae (1989) and Fukuyama (1992) optimistically expected globalization to accelerate the convergence of cultures, consumption patterns and thus of markets. Such convergence implies that MNEs can generate superior performance by implementing highly centralized, truly global strategies.

On the surface, there seems to be some face validity to the notion of global convergence and many lay writers have been carried away by it (e.g., Friedman, 2005). People around the world, especially those who have entered the middle class, use many of the same sets of goods, similar services and communicate and interact with greater frequency using compatible media. However, as a number of scholars have pointed out, differences between, amongst and within regions, countries, cultures and societies have not been greatly attenuated with globalization. Indeed, there is no shortage of evidence that local contexts continue to be critically

important: despite the hype, scale economies are no longer expected to rapidly lead to global homogenization. Knowledge of and embedding in local context remains a key success factor (Ghemawat, 2007). Thus, within the international business literature, there is an appreciation that the writings of Levitt, Ohmae, Fukuyama and Friedman may be a bit too simplistic.

Instead, the international business literature has moved towards recognizing that global integration as relevant to MNE activity is about *increasing interfaces* between people, nations and cultures that in most instances continue to retain their local distinctiveness. Managing MNEs is regarded as not being about creating homogeneity, but about "managing differences" (Ghemawat, 2007). Thus, it is more useful to view globalization as "*a process leading to greater interdependence and mutual awareness (reflexivity) among economic, political and social units in the world, and among actors in general*" (Guillén, 2001).

Globalization impinges on MNEs and their complex interdependencies within and between multiple host locations as well as on their internal hierarchies. This raises the issue of 'multiple embeddedness' a concept that must be analysed on two different levels. First, at the MNE level, the firm has to interact more frequently with other actors who operate in quite different local contexts, and have to devise strategies that exploit such differences without being overwhelmed by the

[1]Source: Reproduced with permission from Klaus E. Meyer, Ram Madambi and Rajneesh Narula (2011) 'Multinational Enterprises and Local Contexts: The Opportunities and Challenges of Multiple Embeddedness' *Journal of Management Studies* Vol. 48(2) pp. 235–252, © 2010 *The Authors. Journal of Management Studies* © 2010 Blackwell Publishing Ltd and Society for the Advancement of Management Studies.

managerial challenges created by this diversity. This implies managing a portfolio of subsidiary level activities in multiple, heterogeneous, local contexts, whilst devising strategies to most efficiently embed themselves in each of these multiple contexts. For MNEs, the importance of managing such interfaces continues to increase, both for the benefit of their global organization and for the success of their operations in any particular local context.

This raises important challenges for extant theory, since local context has traditionally been seen primarily through the lens of the integration-responsiveness framework developed by Bartlett and Ghoshal (1988). Despite various extensions, this simple dichotomy is limited in that it only analyses the degree of local adaptation (versus global integration) but does not provide an analytical framework on how companies adapt to a variety of widely varying local contexts simultaneously. In other words, it does not recognize the full measure of complexity that is associated with adaptation to local contexts.

Second, at the subsidiary level, multiple embeddedness derives from balancing the forces that require local responsiveness of subsidiaries with those that require subsidiaries' global integration within the umbrella of the MNE's overall structure. To phrase this differently, in order to take full advantage of the opportunities in every local context, subsidiaries must be 'externally embedded' within each local context while also being sufficiently 'internally embedded' within the MNE network for the benefits of external embeddedness to be potentially available to the rest of the MNE.

Given that many larger MNEs are a complex aggregation of a large number of constituent subsidiaries, such multiple embeddedness generates trade-offs between external and internal embeddedness, since each subsidiary must reconcile the interests of its parent with those of its local business interests. For instance, a focal subsidiary may resist headquarters' attempts to re-deploy its locally generated rents to other subsidiaries that have more strategic importance.

Local contexts

What is local context, and why does it matter? Local contexts have a central role in international business research. In fact, the interaction across multiple contexts, where the context is defined as the nation state, is the key distinction between international and domestic business. Contextual variation may be particularly relevant for MNEs bridging large psychic, cultural and economic distances, such as West European and North American businesses entering emerging economies, yet they are also of concern within comparatively homogeneous geographic contexts such as the European Union or large countries such as Russia or China. Local contexts vary in particular on two dimensions: institutional frameworks and resource endowments.

International business research in recent years has focused in particular on institutional variations across countries. Early work explored variations in national culture (Hofstede, 1980) aiming to operationalize and measure this very abstract concept. More recently, IB scholars have been inspired by both institutional economics and institutional theory in sociology to explore the influences of institutional frameworks such as legal frameworks and regulatory systems on business practices and strategies of both local firms and of foreign entrants. While firms and some factors of production are increasingly mobile, formal (legal, political and administrative systems) and informal (relationships and social norms) institutions tend to be internationally immobile, and MNEs must adapt their organization and governance in response to these differences. The costs and benefits associated with such adaptations partially determine the international attractiveness of a location.

Formal and informal institutions affect the interactions between firms and therefore affect the relative transaction and coordination costs of production and innovation. To a considerable extent, as local institutions affect the location choices of firms, competition arises between institutional systems. There is mounting evidence that countries with more open and transparent systems have been more successful in achieving growth, and more MNEs are setting up local operations there. Laggard countries are beginning to selectively emulate the institutions of the successful countries, both to attract more foreign direct investment (FDI) and to accelerate economic growth. Even within countries, regions are competing for FDI by offering more attractive institutional frameworks, such as financial investment incentives.

The second dimension of local context is the resource endowment of local firms, individuals and the economy as a whole. Early work on FDI and trade (for a review, see Dunning 1988, 1998), noted that differences in resource endowments across locations played an important role in MNE location. More recent international business research distinguishes "natural" and "created" assets that make up countries' location advantages, and thus form the foundation for the attraction of foreign MNEs.

The essence of FDI is the combination of firm-specific assets (also known as ownership-advantages) with location-specific assets of foreign locations (also known as location advantages) (Dunning, 1988). This combination of resources is particularly evident when MNEs acquire firms in other countries for the purposes of augmenting their existing asset portfolio, and thus their capability to compete both in the local market of the acquired firm and in wider global markets. This need to internalize local resources can determine how MNEs enter unfamiliar contexts: when sought-after local resources are organizationally embedded in local firms, entrants may choose acquisition or JV entry; when they need resources that can be acquired on markets, such as office space, real estate or employees, land, or natural resources they may choose green field entry.

Three perspectives on context

MNEs interact with multiple local contexts in which their headquarters and subsidiaries are embedded. Yet neither the MNE nor the contexts are monolithic, leading to complex network relationships between agents within the MNE and with the pertinent local contexts.

First, firms are shaped by the home context from which they originate. Firms typically build their original resource endowments in their home country and this original resource endowment drives their international growth. At the same time MNEs' embeddedness in their home contexts may act as either inducements or constraints on some types of overseas business activities. Firms of different nationalities have been shown to vary in terms of their preferred organizational practices, entry strategies and brand images. Mature MNEs have considerable experience interacting with multiple contexts, yet the local context of the corporate headquarters continues to exert strong influences on the organizational practices and strategies.

Second, every MNE is also embedded in the local context of the host country through its local subsidiary. The subsidiary is embedded in the MNE network as well as in its local business network. This dual embedding means that the subsidiary is subject to institutional pressures arising respectively from its home context through its parent MNE and from the local context. This provides texture to the integration-responsiveness framework: MNEs adapt their strategies and organizational practices to local contexts, subject to constraints imposed by the resources available in the local context as well as institutional

constraints imposed by their home context. Prior research has explored for example the adaptation of marketing strategies, the transfer of organizational routines and practices and the choice of entry mode.

Third, the interaction of MNEs with their various local contexts depends on how these contexts relate to each other. International business researchers have investigated this notion using the concepts of psychic distance, cultural distance and institutional distance. However, conceptualizing the interaction between these contexts as distance may be too simplistic. Multiple embeddedness presents MNEs with both opportunities and challenges. The next two sections of this paper examine these at length.

Opportunities: multiplicity and diversity of resources

The ability to create, transfer, recombine and exploit resources across multiple contexts is the rationale for the existence of the MNE. MNEs generate value by leveraging tangible and intangible resources across national borders. At the most fundamental level, their value creation is based on international arbitrage. This arbitrage is made possible by the multiple embeddedness of the MNE – it is embedded in both its home and host environments, so it can capture the gains from trade by internalizing market transactions. The benefits of arbitrage are reinforced by aggregation and economies of scale and by adaptation of central value propositions to suit local contexts.

MNEs are in a strong position to tap into resources and capabilities from multiple local contexts and integrate and leverage them to create a range of competitive advantages. Such strategies are likely to involve specialized design and adaptation capabilities and emphasize the importance of both R&D and marketing intangibles in value creation. Moreover, they include global supply chains that integrate geographically dispersed production processes to take advantage of diverse location advantages. Processes of knowledge management have been analysed in the literature.

There is increasing evidence indicating that knowledge and intangibles account for an ever-increasing share of national incomes in both advanced and emerging economies around the world. Such knowledge takes two forms: R&D knowledge and marketing knowledge. There is also accumulating evidence pointing to the rise of increasing numbers of new knowledge clusters and hotspots in emerging market economies and in formerly "peripheral" regions of advanced market economies (Dicken, 2003). These two trends support a third, namely the increasing importance of MNEs in the world economy.

These three trends are symbiotic and mutually reinforcing. MNEs are becoming increasingly knowledge driven; competition forces them to seek and develop knowledge advantages wherever they can find them. This leads them to cultivate knowledge assets in what were considered non-traditional locations. Many of these locations in Asia (e.g., Bangalore in India, Shanghai in China), in Latin America (e.g., Guadalajara in Mexico, Costa Rica) and on the southern flank of Europe (e.g., Barletta in Italy and Valencia in Spain) have evolved into significant knowledge clusters in a variety of industries including electronics, automobiles, information technology and plastics.

The wider dispersion of MNE knowledge activities implies these firms undertake knowledge-intensive activities in a multiplicity of locations. This diversity of local contexts enables the MNE to access knowledge from many different knowledge clusters and hotspots. Once accessed, the MNE subsidiary can do one (or both) of two things:

■ Transfer the accessed knowledge to other units in the MNE network

■ Integrate the accessed knowledge with its own knowledge, and other knowledge bases within the MNE network to create new competencies

This view of the subsidiary strategy is flexible enough to accommodate both the traditional subsidiary roles of exploiting parental competencies as well as the more creative roles undertaken by competence-creating subsidiaries.

Traditional subsidiary roles

A subsidiary in its traditional role is characterized by "conventional" top-down knowledge inflows from its parent firm. At the most basic level, the subsidiary assembles or delivers and maintains products or services supplied by its parent firm, so-called "screwdriver" operations (see Figure 12.3.1). Such subsidiaries often evolve over time to adapt their parent MNEs' products or services for local markets, e.g., they may integrate MNE technical knowledge with local marketing knowledge to implement a market-seeking strategy. This new knowledge is location-bound.

Creative subsidiary roles

However, subsidiaries that undertake more creative tasks are characterized by "reverse" knowledge flows, i.e., knowledge that flows from the subsidiary to the rest of the corporate group. At a basic level they may function as mere "listening posts", receiving, filtering and transmitting knowledge back to the their parents. Over time they may evolve into regional or even worldwide centres of excellence for their parent MNEs. The knowledge in reverse knowledge flows is "non-location-bound".

In order to generate reverse knowledge flows, the MNE subsidiary must be able to access local external knowledge and then transfer it internally within the firm. In order to access local knowledge, it is necessary for the MNE, through its subsidiary, to understand the nexus within which local knowledge resides. The subsidiary must tap into this network of local firms and institutions in order to learn about customers and technologies and thus 'capture' local knowledge. To undertake the second part of this task, the subsidiary must use its connectivity within the MNE's network to transfer the knowledge. In other words, leveraging local knowledge networks requires solving a "dual-network" problem. Subsidiaries need to be sufficiently embedded within the local milieu to generate knowledge access and inflows, while simultaneously being sufficiently embedded within the MNE's internal

FIGURE 12.3.1   MNE subsidiary level knowledge taxonomy

Knowledge activity		Knowledge directional flow	
		Inflow	Outflow
	Transfer	Screwdriver operations	Listening post
	Integration	Competence exploitation	Competence creation

network for the knowledge to be effectively transferred and used through the MNE.

The subsidiary's ability to play this dual role of tapping into local knowledge and engaging in knowledge exchange with other units is influenced by numerous aspects of the specific local context in which it operates. Contributions in this special issue point in particular to three issues, local versus regional context, higher versus lower level clusters, and advanced versus emerging economy *home* context.

Regional versus local contexts

The local context provides both the institutional framework as well as the resource base that it can access. However, local contexts are themselves embedded in broader regional contexts: issues may pertain to, for example, cities, provinces, nation states or even supranational units. In recent years, the supranational regional dimension has been gaining importance in determining national institutional frameworks. In particular, trading blocs like the European Union, the North American Free Trade Agreement, ASEAN and Mercosur have been growing in strength and number, and increasingly supersede local ones.

Higher versus lower level clusters

Clusters vary in terms of the sophistication of the local resources, both tangible and intangible. Older and more established clusters tend to have deeper and more sophisticated resource pools, while younger and emergent clusters tend to have shallower and less advanced ones. Improved logistics and telecommunications including web services have made it possible to undertake even complex activities like R&D with teams that are widely geographically dispersed. This means that subsidiaries may be located in emergent clusters with lower resource costs, yet collaborate with subsidiaries located in established clusters in highly knowledge-intensive activities. This is possible through the "fine-slicing" of even high value-added complex activities into standardized and specialized components.

Advanced versus emerging economy home contexts

Advanced economy MNEs start out with a strong home base knowledge advantage, as well as a historically evolved international network. However, the home based knowledge of emerging market MNEs

also provides them with a set of (different) advantages. Initially, the advantages of emerging market are cost-based and focused on standardized processes. However, as advanced economy MNEs increasingly fine-slice their value chains, these firms have the opportunity to enter into partnerships and trading relationships with them. They can undertake the standardized components associated with high-knowledge activities. Hence, the increasing geographical dispersal of knowledge-intensive activities sets up a symbiotic relationship between these two types of MNEs.

Challenges: control and coordination in diverse contexts

Different lines of work have focused on the challenges faced by MNEs when interacting with multiple contexts. In any specific context, MNEs must find subtle ways to combine their firm-specific capabilities with local knowledge to create value propositions that suit the particular local context. These integration challenges are substantial, requiring adaptation as well as creative competencies and possibly even the development of entirely new business models. In extreme cases, these challenges can become overwhelming, leading the parent MNE to divest subsidiaries and even to exit markets.

In order for MNEs to make optimal use of the opportunities available across their internal network requires the frictionless functioning of external economic and business systems along with perfect incentive compatibility amongst internal agents. In reality, the *raison d'etre* of headquarters operations is to minimize these frictions and coordinate and control subsidiary activities to maximize goal congruency amongst the various internal subsidiaries and constituencies within the firm. In doing so, the MNE is able to exploit and efficiently channel and link resources and capabilities available between locations, i.e., to fully leverage its opportunities. However, the MNE network is a differentiated one, so that managing systemic frictions as well as aligning incentives is often a daunting task.

Challenges to achieving internal embeddedness

Several factors limit the effectiveness of headquarters' coordination and control functions. Intra-MNE knowledge flows may be impeded simply as a result of size, because there are cognitive limits to resources that determine what firms can and cannot do. The greater the number of subsidiaries, the higher the co-ordination challenge of optimally utilizing and dis-seminating the knowledge generated at the subsidiary level. Managing complex networks is not costless; the costs of managing complex and widely distributed spatial activities are not trivial. The larger the organization, the greater the probability that coordination failures occur. Thus, while there are advantages that derive from multinationality (Dunning 1988) there are also *costs* of multinationality. Firms need to manage not just their corporate networks, but also their external networks, whether these are in the form of informal and formal cooperative agreements, or their arms-length relationships with suppliers and customers. The resource constraints that firms face can be managerial, and this limit to growth is described as the 'Penrose effect' (Hutzschenreuter *et al.*, 2010). Limited re-sources mean that firms often experience a trade-off between product diversification and international diversification.

The degree of embeddedness of subsidiaries is an important issue for several reasons. First, the compe-titive advantages of a subsidiary are not necessarily a subset of those of its parent. In addition to those that derive from the parent, the subsidiary also evolves its own set of managerial and technological capabilities. This may happen because the MNE's strategy is based on a 'federal' model of freestanding and largely au-tonomous country subsidiaries each with its own stra-tegic goals and activities. Thus each subsidiary can evolve its own profile of capabilities, which may overlap with that of the headquarters, but the extent of the overlap is a function of country- and subsidiary-specific path dependency. In other words, the sub-sidiary itself may be a source of unique, unit-specific competencies to the rest of the MNE.

The extent to which a subsidiary is embedded in the local context, and is a source of new assets, is re-flected in the extent to which strategic decision making resides with the subsidiary relative to the headquarters (e.g., Doz and Prahalad, 1984; Mudambi and Navarra, 2004). There are competing forces that require local responsiveness of subsidiaries and those that require subsidiaries' global integration with the umbrella of the MNE's overall structure. Reconciling these con-flicting forces often proves to be a serious challenge for headquarters. There is substantial evidence that MNE headquarters itself is influenced by powerful locally embedded subsidiaries that typically control knowledge resources. This evidence indicates that while headquarters has ownership rights, the extent to

which they translate into enforceable property rights depends on the outcome of the bargaining game be-tween the headquarters (as principal) and the sub-sidiary (as agent). Unconditional legal enforcement of ownership rights through headquarters centralization can destroy the valuable knowledge resources at the subsidiary, i.e., key personnel can leave, key contacts can remain unleveraged and so on.

It is clear that subsidiary local embeddedness is a two-edged sword. This is especially true where sub-sidiaries have traditionally competed with each other for resources from headquarters promoting inter-unit rivalry. Such subsidiaries are unlikely to be keen to cooperate and share knowledge. The challenge for MNE headquarters is to shepherd its most valuable subsidiaries towards 'dual embeddedness', i.e., being simultaneously deeply embedded in the MNE corpo-rate, 'internal' network, as well as within the 'ex-ternal', host environment. Designing control structures to implement dual embeddedness is a delicate balan-cing act. Such structures have the potential to create a conflict of interest in the subsidiary, pitting its loyalties to its local network against those to its parent com-pany. Further, increased embeddedness in the MNE corporate network may be detrimental to its position within the host country milieu, and its positioning within social networks.

From an overall MNE perspective, we can speak of 'multiple embeddedness', where different subsidiaries exhibit varying degrees of internal and external em-beddedness. This affects their strategic significance and contribution to the overall MNE's competitive-ness. The integration-responsiveness framework does not allow differentiation across location advantages in different parts of the value chain. MNEs have begun to 'fine-slice' their value adding activities, such that subsidiaries may specialize in very narrow activity sets in the MNE's value chain. This 'unpacking' of the value chain may mean that there are multiple sub-sidiaries in the same location, each engaged in a dif-ferent aspect of value creation, which may or may not be linked together directly, and may indeed report to different HQs, and have different degrees of strategic importance.

Challenges of organizational inertia

The creation of multi-embedded yet well coordinated MNEs has to overcome organizational inertia. En-trepreneurial firms may evolve in a domestic context and gradually internationalize, thus developing organ-izational routines that fit the original scope of the firm. However, at some stage, these original structures hit their limits, and MNEs wish to adapt new structures such as multi-hubs, multiple headquarters and rationalized value adding activities across locations that optimize efficiency and minimize duplication. Implementing such changes systemically through an organization often requires fundamental re-organization, which is more difficult to achieve as the organization becomes more complex. The formal configuration of organizations can be addressed in major restructuring programmes that are fairly frequent in large MNEs. However, the informal routines that underpin the implementation of these structures often prove much more difficult to modify. Moreover, the organizational structures and capabilities required to manage multiple embeddedness are often highly complex, and therefore hard for even the leaders of the organization to understand. In the face of increasing complexity, bounded rationality reinforces organizational inertia because it is more difficult to identify and correct problems. This was vividly illustrated by the 2010 crisis at Toyota, an organization with particularly complex multiple embeddedness. The plasticity of formal organizational configurations coupled with the organizational inertia of informal routines means that the re-structuring necessitated by new local contexts often results in sub-par performance.

Challenges of institutional inertia

Multi-embedded MNEs often develop linkages in specific locations that go beyond the 'direct' and formal associations any business entity has with suppliers, customers and related MNE subsidiaries within the same network. Such networks include universities, public research institutes, competitors and government agencies, which have helped define the activities of the subsidiary in intangible and largely tacit ways. This web of value-creating linkages is 'sticky' in the sense that it is locationally immobile. Such networks may have evolved over long periods of time, and this creates inertia in the kinds of activities an MNE subsidiary is engaged in. These reflect the co-evolution of organizational cultures and local social networks, shaped by the nature of the political, social and economic institutions of the location. These discussions – common across innovation systems, social network theory and economic geography – highlight the importance of informal institutions and the role of 'clubs' for which membership provides specific benefits. However, such institutional inertia has the potential to hinder restructuring changes that may be needed to

enable the MNE to take full advantage of its opportunities for value creation.

Such inertial challenges also face the home country operations. Traditionally, the MNE has been most deeply embedded in its home location. Despite high levels of internationalization of sales and production, the dominance of the home location in strategically important activities remains stubbornly high, even in the case of peripheral home countries. Strategically important activities tend to be last to be internationalized – the so-called internationalization of the third degree – and even where they are, they tend to be relocated to locations that demonstrate shorter institutional distances, thereby making embeddedness in the 'new' location easier. Nevertheless, such internationalization is an increasingly common feature of MNEs from smaller, more peripheral economies.

The MNE's existing location profile implies a set of linkages with local actors and institutions. This portfolio of linkages that constitute the reality of its multiple embedding, impose constraints on its future growth both in terms of activities as well as locations. Another manifestation of institutional inertia is that the MNE's growth path over time is likely to be characterized by hysteresis leading to path dependency. Hence the network of subsidiaries established in the past influences when and where an MNE may enter in the future.

Concluding remarks

Multinational firms create value by internalizing market transactions over geographic borders. This organizational focus of international business research has a significant location aspect (Dunning, 1998). However, the fundamental difference between FDI and portfolio investment is the high level of engagement with the local context involved in the former. The emergent image of multiple-embeddedness is considerably more complex than models in the established literature, such as the integration-responsiveness framework (Bartlett and Ghoshal, 1988). It creates new challenges for both theoretical treatments of the MNE, for practitioners and for policy makers.

Of the numerous ideas for advancing theory that arise from this special issue, we would like to emphasize two in particular. First, as MNEs grapple with managing the complexities of multiple-embeddedness, it is likely that some develop unique capabilities in the management of the issue that enable them to achieve unique, possibly sustainable competitive advantages.

Further research may explore the nature and antecedents of these operational capabilities in coordinating across multiple contexts. Maintaining flexibility in multi-embedded organizations is a dynamic capability that is based on shaping and deliberately designing intra-firm and inter-firm networks. This enables the MNE to effectively harness the potential of its multiplicity of local contexts as well as to add new contexts to its network.

Second, even companies that build on the scanning, integration and exploitation of knowledge worldwide – such as leading consultancy firms – often fail to achieve the desired knowledge exchange and collaboration amongst constituent subsidiaries because of the incentives faced by individual decision makers. Recent lines of research have begun to address this issue, focusing respectively on the microlevel governance mechanisms and on social capital within organizations. Future research may connect these lines of work with the notion of multiple-embeddedness proposed in this paper.

For policy makers, the main challenge is how to induce multi-embedded MNEs, to establish value adding activities in their territory, without causing distortions that reduce the overall efficiency of the economy or that reduce the efficiency of the MNE when placing operations in the local context. This trend fuels home country fears of hollowing out and loss of competencies as the MNE may have only a few headquarters functions in its country of domicile, with most value adding activity taking place elsewhere. Therefore, exactly how governments can promote greater embeddedness in host contexts is fundamental to the MNE-assisted development strategy that many governments pursue.

Taking a cue from Buckley and Casson (1976), we close this essay by conjecturing about the future of MNEs. Local contexts are likely to become more rather than less important, as locations that provide the necessary infrastructure for sophisticated business operations proliferate. In particular, the ranks of emerging economies are growing as countries like Korea, Mexico and Poland have graduated into the ranks of OECD; others like Chile, Estonia and Russia wait in the wings, and China, India and Brazil are in "enhanced engagement". These local contexts are growing more distinct in terms of their resource pools and institutional frameworks. This suggests that the opportunities arising from multiple-embeddedness are likely to increase. At the same time, the challenges of managing ever more complex MNEs are likely to rise as well.

REFERENCES

Bain, J.S. (1956) *Barriers to New Competition: Their Character and Consequences in Manufacturing*, Harvard University Press.

Bartlett, C.A. and Ghoshal, S. (1988) 'Organizing for worldwide effectiveness: the transnational solution', *California Management Review*, 31, pp. 54–74.

Bartlett, C.A. and Ghoshal, S. (1987) 'Managing across borders: new organizational responses', *Sloan Management Review*, Vol. 29, No. 1, Fall, pp. 43–53.

Bartlett, C.A. and Ghoshal, S. (1989) *Managing Across Borders: The Transnational Solution*, New York: Harvard Business School Press.

Bartlett, C.A. and Ghoshal, S. (1995) *Transnational Management: Text, Cases and Readings in Cross-Border Management*, Second Edition, New York: R.D. Irwin Inc.

Beech, N., Burns, H., de Caestecker, L., Mackintosh, R. and MacLean, D. (2004) 'Paradox as invitation to act in problematic change situations', *Human Relations*, 57, pp. 1313–1332.

Birkenshaw, J. and Hood, N. (1998) *Multinational Corporate Evolution and Subsidiary Development*, London: Macmillan.

Boorstin, D.J. (1973) *The Americans: The Democratic Experience*, NJ: Random House.

Buckley, P.J. and Casson, M.C. (1976) *The Future of the Multinational Enterprise*, London: Macmillan.

Buckley, P.J. and Casson, M.C. (1985) *The Economic Theory of the Multinational Enterprise*, London: Macmillan.

Castells, M. (1996) *The Rise of the Network Society*, Oxford: Blackwell Publishers.

Caves, R.E. (1971) 'International corporations: the industrial economics of foreign investment', *Economica*, 38(149), pp. 1–27.

Chesnais, F. (1984) 'Marx's Crisis Theory Today', in: C. Freeman (ed.) *Design, Innovation and Long Cycles in Economic Development*, London: Frances Pinter.

Dicken, P. (1986) *Global Shift: Industrial Change in a Turbulent World*, London: Harper & Row.

Dicken, P. (1992) *Global Shift: The Internationalisation of Economic Activity*, London: Chapman.

Dicken, P. (2003) *Global Shift: Reshaping the Global Economic Map in the 21st Century*, Sage.

Dicken, P. (2011) *Mapping the Changing Contours of the World Economy*, 2nd edn, New York: Guilford Press.

Dosi, G. and Kogut, B. (1993) 'National Specificities and the Context of Change: The Co-evolution of Organization and Technology', in: B. Kogut (ed.) *Country Competitiveness: Technology and the Organizing of Work*, Oxford: Oxford University Press.

Douglas, S.P. and Wind, Y. (1987) 'The Myth of Globalization', *Columbia Journal of World Business*, Vol. 22, Winter, pp. 19–29.

Doz, Y. and Prahalad, C.K. (1984) 'Patterns of strategic control within multinational corporations', *Journal of International Business Studies*, 15(2), pp. 55–72.

Dunning, J. (1986) *Japanese Participation in British Industry: Trojan Horse or Catalyst for Growth?* Dover, NH: Croom Helm.

Dunning, J. (1993) *The Globalization of Business*, London: Routledge.

Dunning, J.H. (1980) 'Toward an eclectic theory of international production: some empirical tests', *Journal of International Business Studies*, 11(1), pp. 9–31.

Dunning, J.H. (1981), *International Production and the Multinational Enterprise*, London: Allen and Unwin.

Dunning, J.H. (1988) *Explaining international production*. London: Unwin Hyman.

Dunning, J.H. (1998) Location and the multinational enterprise: a neglected factor? *Journal of International Business Studies*, 29(1), pp. 45–66.

Dunning, J.H. (2000) 'The eclectic paradigm as an envelope for economic and business theories of MNE activity', *International Business Review*, 9(2), pp.163–190.

Dunning, J.H. (2001) 'The Key Literature on IB activities: 1960–2000', in: A.M. Rugman and Th. L. Brewer, *The Oxford Handbook of International Business*, Oxford: Oxford University Press, pp. 36–68.

Fayerweather, J. (1969) 'International Business Management', *The International Executive*, 11(1), pp. 10–11.

Friedman, T.L. (2005) *The World is Flat: A Brief History of the Twenty-first Century*, New York: Farrar, Straus and Giroux.

Fröbel, F., Heinrichs, J. and Kreye, O. (1980) *The Tendency Towards a New International Division of Labor: The Utilization of a World-Wide Labor Force for Manufacturing Oriented to the World Market*, Cambridge: Cambridge University Press.

Fukuyama, F. (1992) *The End of History and the Last Man*, New York: The Free Press.

Ghemawat, P. (2007) *Redefining Global Strategy*, Boston, MA: Harvard Business School Press.

Gramsci, A. (1934) 'Americanism and Fordism', in: A. Gramsci *The Prison Notebooks*, Columbia University Press.

Guillén, M. (2001) *The Limits of Convergence: Globalization and Organizational Change in Argentina, South Korea and Spain*, Princeton, NJ: Princeton University Press.

Hamel, G. and Prahalad, C.K. (1985) 'Do You Really Have a Global Strategy?', *Harvard Business Review*, Vol. 63, No. 4, July–August, pp. 139–148.

Hedlund, G. (1986) 'The Hypermodern MNC – A Heterarchy?' *Human Resource Management*, Vol. 25, pp. 9–35.

Hennart, J-F. (1977) *A Theory of Foreign Direct Investment*, Ph.D. dissertation, University of Maryland.

Hofstede, G. (1980) *Culture's Consequences: International Differences in Work-Related Values*, Newbury Park, CA: Sage.

Hout, T.M., Porter, M.E. and Rudden, E. (1982) 'How Global Companies Win Out', *Harvard Business Review*, Vol. 60, No. 5, September–October, pp. 98–108.

Hymer, S (1960) *The International Operations of National Firms: A Study of Direct Investment*, PhD dissertation, Cambridge, MA: MIT Press.

Kay, J. (1989) 'Myths and Realities', in: Davis, E. (ed.) *1992: Myths and Realities*, London: Centre for Business Strategy.

Kindleberger, C.P. (1973) *The World in Depression: 1929–1939*, London: Allen Lane.

Klein, N. (2000) *No Logo, Taking Aim at the Brand Bullies*, London: Flamingo.

Kogut, B. (ed.) (1993) *Country Competitiveness: Technology and the Organizing of Work*, Oxford: Oxford University Press.

Kogut, B. and Zander, U. (1993) 'Knowledge of the firm and the Evolutionary Theory of the Mul', *Journal of International Business Studies*, Vol. 24, No. 4; pp. 625–645.

Krugman, P. (1990) *Rethinking International Trade*, Cambridge, MA: MIT Press.

Krugman, P. (1980) 'Scale Economies, Product Differentiation, and the Pattern of Trade', *The American Economic Review*, Vol. 70, No. 5, pp. 950–959.

Levitt, T. (1983) 'The Globalization of Markets', *Harvard Business Review*, Vol. 61, No. 3, May–June, pp. 92–102.

Liebeskind, J. (1996) 'Knowledge, Strategy and the Theory of the Firm', *Strategic Management Journal*, Vol. 17, Special Issue, Winter, pp. 93–107.

Markowitz, H.M. (1959) *Portfolio Selection: Efficient Diversification of Investments*, New York: John Wiley & Sons.

Mathews, J.A. and Zander, I. (2007) 'The International Entrepreneurial Dynamics of Accelerated Internationalisation', *Journal of international Business Studies*, pp. 1–17.

McGrew, A.G. and Lewis, P.G. (eds.) (1992) *Global Politics: Globalisation and the Nation-State*, Cambridge: Polity Press.

Meyer, K.E., Mudambi, R. and Narula, R. (2011) 'Multinational enterprises and local contexts: the opportunities and challenges of multiple embeddedness', *Journal of Management Studies*, 48(2), pp. 235–252.

Mudambi, R. and Navarra, P. (2004) 'Is knowledge power? Knowledge flows, subsidiary power and rent-seeking within MNCs', *Journal of International Business Studies*, 35(5), pp. 385–406.

Ohmae, K. (1989) 'Managing in a Borderless World', *Harvard Business Review*, Vol. 67, No. 3, May–June, pp. 152–161.

Ohmae, K. (1990) *The Borderless World: Power and Strategy in the Interlinked Economy*, London: Fontana.

Ohmae, K. (1985) *The Triad of Economic Power*, New York, The Free Press.

Patel, P. and Pavitt, K. (1991) 'Large Firms in the Production of the World's Technology: An Important Case of "Non-Globalisation"', *Journal of International Business Studies*, Vol. 22, No. 1, pp. 1–21.

Penrose, E. (1959) *The Theory of the Growth of the Firm*, New York: John Wiley and Sons.

Porter, M.E. (1986) *Competition in Global Industries*, New York: Free Press.

Porter, M.E. (1990a) *The Competitive Advantage of Nations*, London: Macmillan.

Porter, M.E. (1990b) 'New Global Strategies for Competitive Advantage', *Planning Review*, Vol. 18, No. 3, May–June, pp. 4–14.

Prahalad, C.K. and Doz, Y. (1987) *The Multinational Mission: Balancing Local Demands and Global Vision*, New York: Free Press.

Prahalad, C.K. (2004) *The Fortune at the Bottom of the Pyramid*, Philadelphia, PA: Wharton School Publishing.

Rugman, A.M. and Verbeke, A. (2001) 'Location, Competitiveness and the Multinational Enterprise', in: A.M. Rugman and Th. L. Brewer, *The Oxford Handbook of International Business*, Oxford: Oxford University Press, pp. 150–177.

Rugman, A.M. (2005) *The Regional Multinational: MNEs and 'Global' Strategic Management*, Cambridge: Cambridge University Press.

Ruigrok, W. and Van Tulder, R. (1995) *The Logic of International Restructuring*, London: Routledge.

Servan-Schreiber, J.J. (1967) *Le Defi Americain*, Paris: Denoel.

Stopford, J.M. and Wells, L.T. (1972) *Strategy and Structure of Multinational Enterprise*, New York: Basic Books.

Taylor, F.W. (1911) *Principles of Scientific Management*, New York, London: Harper & Brothers.

UNCTAD (2010) *World Investment Report*.

Van Tulder, R. and Junne, G. (1988) *European Multinationals in Core Technologies*, London: Wiley & Sons.

Vernon, R. (1966) 'International Investment and International Trade in the Product Life Cycle', *Quarterly Journal of Economics*, Vol. 80, No. 2, May, pp. 190–207.

Vernon, R. (1977) *Storm Over The Multinationals: The Real Issues*, Cambridge, MA: Harvard University Press.

Wilkins, M. (2003) 'The History of the International Enterprise', in: A.L. Rugman, and Th. L. Brewer, *The Oxford Handbook of International Business*, Oxford: Oxford University Press.

Williamson, O.E. (1975) *Markets and Hierarchies*, New York: The Free Press.

Womack, J.P., Jones, D.T. and Roos, D. (1990) *The Machine That Changed The World*, New York: Harper Perennial.

Yip, G.S. (1993) *Total Global Strategy: Managing for Worldwide Competitive Advantage*, London: Prentice Hall.

CASES

ZARA: Staying fast and fresh

By Felipe Caro

In early 2011, despite a successful decade of continued growth, fashion retailer Zara's CFO Miguel Díaz was anything but complacent. When asked about the future, Díaz responded:

> *Challenges abound. At the pace stores are being added in the rest of the world, the inevitable question is whether we should open our first major distribution center outside Spain. Another concern is that the prices of raw materials and labor are not going down, in part because the cost structure in Asia is changing. The old textile model in which each year better garments were produced at lower costs will not hold on forever, and we have to remain alert to these changes.*

Zara, the flagship brand of the Spanish retail conglomerate Inditex, was one of the leading retailers of fast-fashion, churning out frequent in-season assortment changes of knockoffs of popular runway styles and trendy fashions. The company had received a lot of attention for its centralized distribution model. In the past 10 years, Inditex and more specifically Zara had been studied by MBA students, the world over, to understand its success in distribution and supply chain efficiency. Numerous cases had been written by academics to better understand Zara's operations, marketing, information systems, and overall strategy, but the same authors had always questioned Zara's long-term sustainability. (See Exhibit 1 for a brief survey of previous cases.) Nevertheless, Zara's net sales reached €8,088 million in 2010, representing an increase of 14% over the previous year and right in line with the average growth it had shown over the last decade. (See Exhibit 2 for a graphical representation of Zara's growth and significant events.)

Inditex

In 2010, Inditex founder Amancio Ortega Gaona was considered by Forbes Magazine to be the 9th richest man in the world, but his life did not begin that way. Ortega began his career in 1963 as a clothing manufacturer in A Coruña, Spain making garments for wholesalers. The way the story goes, in 1975, after a customer cancelled a large order, Ortega decided to open his own store as an outlet for unsold products. It was to be called Zorba, following the popular film featuring Anthony Quinn, but that name had already been taken by a nearby store. In a quick display of his decision making, Ortega reused the billboard letters and came up with the name Zara. Through his own store, Ortega learned firsthand what customers wanted and realized that it often did not match the styles that wholesalers were ordering. He then made it a rule to have one hand touching the factory and the other touching the store. The importance of handling large amounts of information also became evident, and in 1976 he purchased his first computer.

In the 1980s, Ortega's interest in technology led him to meet Jose Maria Castellano, a professor at the local university who had experience with information systems, sales and finance. In 1985, the Inditex Group was established as the owner of Zara and Castellano joined as Deputy Chairman. Castellano helped to drive growth in the organization and to develop technological support for the vertically integrated business model that Ortega had envisioned. The philosophy of end-to-end control guided local expansion in the 1980s and world wide expansion in the decades that followed.

In parallel with the international expansion, Inditex also expanded its brand concepts. In 1991, Inditex launched Pull & Bear, which had a larger selection of everyday basics, that is, garments with less fashion content and more competitive prices. The same year, Inditex acquired 65% of Massimo Dutti, a brand originally targeted only to men, offering a more sophisticated look with great attention to fit and fabric quality. Inditex later took full ownership of the brand and diversified its assortment to include women's and children's wear. The concept of Bershka was

Professor Felipe Caro prepared this case as the basis for class discussion. The content does not engage the responsibility of the Inditex Group. The case is not intended to serve as primary source of data, endorsement, or a description of adequate/inadequate managerial practice. Special thanks to Katherine Helfet and Paige Hosler who helped in the writing process. This project was supported by the Easton Technology Leadership Program.

EXHIBIT 1   PREVIOUS ZARA CASES (UP TO 2010)

Year	Case	Focus
2002	**ZARA** Kasra Ferdows, Jose AD Machuca & Michael Lewis – Georgetown University	Operations
2002	**ZARA** Nelson Fraiman, Medini Singh, Linda Arrington & Carolyn Paris – Columbia Business	Operations
2002	**Marks & Spencer and ZARA: Process Competition in the Textile Apparel Industry** Nicolas Harle, Michael Pich & Ludo Van der Heyden – INSEAD	Strategy
2003	**ZARA: Fast Fashion** Pankaj Ghemawat & Jose Luis Nueno – Harvard Business School	Strategy
2003	**ZARA** Guillermo D'Andrea & David Arnold – Harvard Business School	Marketing
2005	**ZARA: Responsive, High Speed, Affordable Fashion** Sophie Linguri & Nirmalya Kumar – London Business School	Strategy
2006	**Inditex: Outsourcing in Tangier** Alfred Vernis, Marc Vilanova & Veronic Figueroa – ESADE Business School	Corporate Social Responsibility
2007	**ZARA: IT for Fast Fashion** Andrew McAfee, Vincent Dessain & Anders Sjoman – Harvard Business School	IT
2010	**ZARA: Managing Stores for Fast Fashion** Zeynep Ton, Elena Corsi & Vincent Dessain – Harvard Business School	HR Operations

Source: case writers.

introduced in 1998, aimed at avant-garde female shoppers in their teens. A year later, Inditex acquired Stradivarius, which complemented its portfolio of trendy garments for women in their mid twenties. Outside of common functions such as human resources, information systems and real estate, and a shared focus on cutting-edge designs at affordable prices, each brand operated independently.

When Ortega decided to step down in 1997, Castellano took over as Inditex's CEO. Castellano's ongoing vision for the company led Inditex to an Initial Public Offering (IPO) on May 23, 2001. Ortega agreed to sell 26% of his stake in the company to the public. The IPO was not intended to generate cash for the company as the revenues from the sale went back to Ortega. Instead, it was intended to stabilize management and solidify the company's leading retail position. The IPO was oversubscribed by 22%, signaling that the shares were undervalued. Simultaneously, Inditex agreed to distribute 4.3 million shares to employees through an Employee Stock Participation Plan. Ortega maintained just over 60% of the company's equity.

In 2005, Castellano resigned as CEO of Inditex. With the help of an executive search firm, the Board of Directors proposed the appointment of Pablo Isla as the new CEO. Isla had achieved great success as a state lawyer chairing the Board of Directors of the Altadis Group and serving as general counsel to Banco Popular. In a press release from Inditex, the company cited its choice of Isla as "a step forward in the design and reorganization of the management team of Inditex." Isla oversaw Inditex's continued growth while emphasizing store execution and overhauling internal processes. His frequent visits to the stores not only demonstrated his commitment to Inditex's "bottom up" structure but also allowed him to recognize opportunities for improvement.

In 2008, an economic crisis hit Spain hard. Much like in the U.S., the crisis was generated by long-term loans, but in addition Spain had a large trade deficit. These factors drove the unemployment rate above 20% in the years that followed. The developed world entered into a recession that depressed consumer confidence and affected most market sectors, in particular the retail industry. (See Exhibit 3 for stock prices for Zara and its direct competitors.) Despite the crisis, Inditex closed the decade in 2010 with a Compound Annual Growth Rate (CAGR) of 37% (see Exhibit 4).

EXHIBIT 2 ZARA STORE GROWTH AND SIGNIFICANT EVENTS

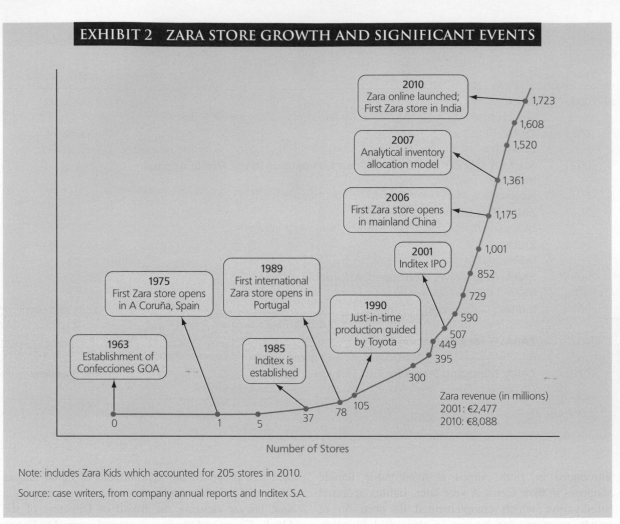

2010
Zara online launched;
First Zara store in India — 1,723

1,608

2007
Analytical inventory
allocation model — 1,520

1,361

2006
First Zara store opens
in mainland China — 1,175

1,001

2001
Inditex IPO

852

729

590

507
449

395

300

1989
First international
Zara store opens in
Portugal

1990
Just-in-time
production guided
by Toyota

1975
First Zara store opens
in A Coruña, Spain

1985
Inditex is
established

1963
Establishment of
Confecciones GOA

0   1   5   37   78   105

Zara revenue (in millions)
2001: €2,477
2010: €8,088

Number of Stores

Note: includes Zara Kids which accounted for 205 stores in 2010.

Source: case writers, from company annual reports and Inditex S.A.

In terms of locations, Inditex had grown from 1,080 stores in 33 countries in 2000 to about 5,000 stores in almost 80 countries ten years later. The number of employees quadrupled over the same period and three more brands were added. Launched in 2001, Oysho offered stylish lingerie and intimate apparel. Zara Home was introduced in 2003, expanding Zara's concept to home decor. Uterqüe opened in 2008 selling high-end accessories and a fashionable selection of leather garments. As for Zara, 2010 crowned a decade during which it consolidated its position as a leading global brand in the apparel market.

Competitive landscape

Among specialty apparel retailers worldwide, Inditex took the lead in annual revenue (see Exhibit 5). Its three most relevant competitors were Gap Inc., H&M and more recently Fast Retailing.

The Gap

Based in San Francisco, CA and originally founded to sell Levi's jeans, The Gap saw great success through the 1980s and 1990s and grew with an expansion of concept stores, including Banana Republic, Old Navy, Gap Outlet and Gap Inc. Direct, the online division. The Gap was known for its unpretentious basics, which included jeans, T-shirts, khakis and regular work clothes. It operated a "buying" model for the manufacturing and production of its garments, and orders to manufacturers in international locations had to be placed 9 months before the season began. Products were manufactured in large quantities and extensive promotions were used to stimulate demand so a 30% markdown off the full price was very common. Led by retail innovator Mickey Drexler, The Gap opened its first international store in the U.K. and reached sales of $1B in 1987. Though global expansion continued, it was hindered by a challenging cost

EXHIBIT 3   COMPETITIVE LANDSCAPE, END-OF-QUARTER STOCK PRICES JAN-07 TO OCT-10

Stock Quarter	INDITEX in EUR	GAP INC in USD	H&M in SEK(*)	FAST RETAILING in JPY	S&P RETAIL (XRT) in USD	S&P 500 (SPY) in USD
Jan-07	€ 43.47	$ 19.17	188.00 €	¥ 11,640	$ 41.96	$ 143.75
Apr-07	€ 45.38	$ 17.95	223.25 €	¥ 9,150	$ 43.09	$ 148.29
Jul-07	€ 44.37	$ 17.20	195.75 €	¥ 8,400	$ 39.55	$ 145.72
Oct-07	€ 51.35	$ 18.90	211.50 €	¥ 6,920	$ 38.51	$ 154.65
Jan-08	€ 33.50	$ 19.09	171.00 €	¥ 7,810	$ 34.00	$ 137.37
Apr-08	€ 34.98	$ 18.62	178.00 €	¥ 9,570	$ 33.00	$ 138.26
Jul -08	€ 31.05	$ 16.12	162.50 €	¥ 9,790	$ 30.39	$ 126.83
Oct-08	€ 26.36	$ 12.94	138.00 €	¥ 12,370	$ 23.11	$ 96.83
Jan-09	€ 29.88	$ 11.28	162.00 €	¥ 12,670	$ 19.67	$ 82.83
Apr-09	€ 32.39	$ 15.54	181.25 €	¥ 11,000	$ 27.70	$ 87.42
Jul -09	€ 37.74	$ 16.32	214.50 €	¥ 12,050	$ 30.50	$ 98.81
Oct-09	€ 40.00	$ 21.34	204.00 €	¥ 11,780	$ 33.76	$ 103.56
Jan-10	€ 45.63	$ 19.08	218.75 €	¥ 16,900	$ 34.62	$ 107.39
Apr-10	€ 46.63	$ 24.73	232.20 €	¥ 16,690	$ 42.76	$ 118.81
Jul-10	€ 50.75	$ 18.11	227.40 €	¥ 13,430	$ 38.12	$ 110.27
Oct-10	€ 60.01	$ 19.01	235.40 €	¥ 11,730	$ 43.61	$ 118.49

(*) On May/31/2010, H&M had a stock split. Prior prices have been halved.

Note: shaded cells denote (i) pre-economic-downturn high; (ii) lowest price during crisis; (iii) post-crisis high up to Oct-10. On July/5/2011, the closing prices were: Inditex 63.61, Gap 18.17, H&M 220.30, Fast Retailing 12,990, XRT 54.50, SPY 133.81.

Source: case writers, from public market data.

structure and adaptations of size and color for different markets. After the departure of Drexler, the consumer trend to more individualized clothing and a failed attempt to make the brand more fashion forward, The Gap saw its revenues decline from a peak of $16.4B in 2004 to $14.2B in 2009. In 2010, The Gap had fully-owned stores in six countries and franchises in another 22 international locations.

Hennes & Mauritz

H&M was founded in 1947 in Sweden and saw good success as a specialty apparel retailer. H&M was seen as Inditex's closest retail competitor on product offerings in specialty apparel, though it operated only one concept with its own name. Although these stores carried a variety of private label brands appealing to different customer segments, H&M delivered large marketplace-like stores with low prices and high variety refreshed daily. Using about 100 in-house designers, H&M designed and purchased its product mix from 700 independent suppliers in Europe and Asia. H&M also depended on a large network of distribution centers located in each country of operation. H&M expanded rapidly in the new century, with revenue growth up to 127 million Swedish kronor in 2010. Its goal was to achieve 10–15% growth in the number of stores each year. In 1998, H&M launched its own online shopping portal in Sweden and then followed in Norway, Denmark, Finland, the Netherlands, Germany and Austria. It was not until September 2010 that H&M launched its online shopping portal in the UK, making it the eighth country with an H&M e-commerce platform.

Fast retailing

Despite revenues equal to only 56% of Inditex's in 2010, Uniqlo and its corporate owner Fast Retailing managed to grow rapidly over the turn of the century. In that time period, CEO Tadashi Yanai doubled the

EXHIBIT 4 INDITEX FINANCIAL DATA 2000–2010

(in millions €)	2000	2006	2007	2008	2009	2010	CAGR
Sales	€ 2,615	€ 8,196	€ 9,435	€ 10,407	€ 11,084	€ 12,527	36.80%
Gross Profit	€ 1,338	€ 4,607	€ 5,349	€ 5,914	€ 6,328	€ 7,422	40.87%
Gross Margin	*51.16%*	*56.21%*	*56.69%*	*56.83%*	*57.09%*	*59.25%*	
EBIT	€ 380	€ 1,356	€ 1,652	€ 1,609	€ 1,728	€ 2,290	43.23%
Operating Margin	*14.53%*	*16.54%*	*17.51%*	*15.46%*	*15.59%*	*18.28%*	
Net Income	€ 259	€ 1,010	€ 1,258	€ 1,262	€ 1,322	€ 1,741	46.36%
Profit Margin	*9.91%*	*12.32%*	*13.33%*	*12.13%*	*11.93%*	*13.90%*	
Assets	€ 2,108	€ 3,448	€ 4,193	€ 4,722	€ 5,329	€ 6,386	
Inventory	€ 245	€ 824	€ 1,007	€ 1,055	€ 993	€ 1,215	
Operating Working Capital	−10.5%	−7.8%	−10.0%	−5.7%	−7.0%	−7.2%	
Number of Stores	1,080	3,131	3,691	4,264	4,607	5,044	
Number of Employees	24,004	69,240	79,517	89,112	92,301	100,138	
% of Sales Attributable to Zara	*78.20%*	*67.52%*	*66.39%*	*65.57%*	*63.85%*	*64.56%*	

Note: operating working capital is presented as percentage of sales.

Source: Inditex S.A.

revenues of Uniqlo and had a big vision for the company going forward. His goal was to expand the company tenfold within ten years to achieve sales of ¥5 trillion by the year 2020. Although Fast Retailing was originally founded in 1963 as a men's apparel retailer, the first Uniqlo store was not opened until 1984. Uniqlo offered inexpensive basic clothes, providing a broad array of colors to its customers. Fast Retailing had pushed its way into foreign markets determined to gain marketshare. In 2009, the company acquired Theory, a New York based apparel design company with a large share of the workplace attire market, providing tailored suits in a high quality stretch textile to young professionals around the world. This expansion of concept further exemplified Fast Retailing's quest to get a foothold in the global apparel market.

Benetton

The Benetton Group was founded in Italy in 1965 and had become a world leader in providing knitwear by the early 1980s, supplying more than 1,900 shops with its sweaters, t-shirts and jeans. Benetton was one of the first major retailers credited with utilizing deferred differentiation in its production of clothing, a strategy that delayed the process of dyeing until after yarn and fabrics were assembled into garments. This strategy gave Benetton a competitive edge, but eventually other retailers followed and deferred differentiation became mainstream. Benetton's operations were highly decentralized and most of its retail stores were owned and operated locally as franchises, limiting its ability to track demand and make changes to product assortment in a timely manner. The Benetton Group was considered a major competitor in this market in the 1980s and 1990s, but it struggled to keep up later on. In fact, Benetton's sales increased less than 2% to €2.05 billion over the period from 2000–2010.[1]

Zara's continuous business cycle

Zara's business depended on the close relationship between manufacturing and retailing. By keeping a pulse on the desires of the customer at retail locations, Zara could quickly manufacture and produce fast fashions and feed them back to the customer, creating a virtuous circle.

[1]Kenna, A. 2011. A Must-Have Becomes a Has-Been. *BusinessWeek* March 10, 2011.

EXHIBIT 5   COMPARABLE REVENUES FOR SPECIALTY APPAREL RETAILERS

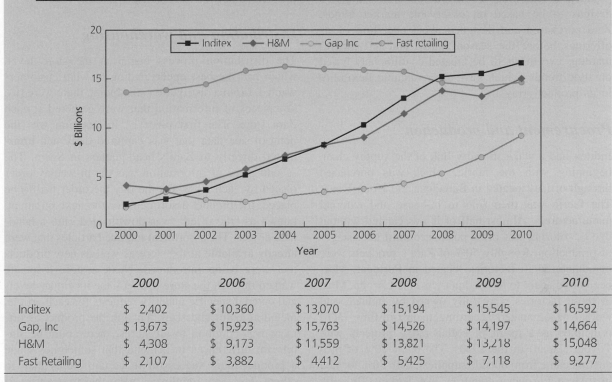

	2000	2006	2007	2008	2009	2010
Inditex	$ 2,402	$ 10,360	$ 13,070	$ 15,194	$ 15,545	$ 16,592
Gap, Inc	$ 13,673	$ 15,923	$ 15,763	$ 14,526	$ 14,197	$ 14,664
H&M	$ 4,308	$ 9,173	$ 11,559	$ 13,821	$ 13,218	$ 15,048
Fast Retailing	$ 2,107	$ 3,882	$ 4,412	$ 5,425	$ 7,118	$ 9,277

Note: millions of US dollars; exchange rates derived using a 365 day average for fiscal year (Feb 1–Jan 31).

Source: annual reports for respective companies.

Customer feedback and fashion trends

The continuous business cycle began with the customer at the store level, and tight communication between store managers and headquarters was vital. Zara designers were constantly listening to advice and comments from store managers who interacted with customers on a daily basis. Market specialists at Zara headquarters, internally known as Commercials, understood the importance of developing deep personal relationships with the store managers for their regions. During their regular contact, the store managers offered suggestions, advice and criticisms on the merchandise, opinions that had been developed through retail experiences with customers. The Commercial then spoke to the designer for that division, for example Women's knitwear, to share the latest market information. After a new design was created and approved, it went to the procurement and production planners to be manufactured.

A Commercial did not have to go very far to talk to the procurement and production planners. Emphasizing

the importance of the communication circle, the layout of Zara's headquarters consisted of large open areas for each section, Women, Men and Children, so that designers, Commercials and procurement and production planners could work next to one another. Communal tables in the area facilitated last-minute meetings. The functional design of the work environment allowed designers to check sketches with co-workers, Commercials to relay feedback from the stores and procurement and production specialists to make initial cost estimates for manufacturing.

Each year designers at Zara came up with approximately 24,000 new products, but only one third were actually produced. This still represented 3–4 times more products than a traditional retailer. A collaborative atmosphere reigned in the design center, and designs were developed from a variety of sources of inspiration, including magazines, catwalks and trend spotters. Large traditional retailers had a nearly 40-week pipeline, meaning buyers had to make calculated guesses of style developments in advance. At Zara, rapid production capabilities and a production lead-time of only a few weeks allowed designs to be based on observable market trends. Zara purchased and designed about one third of its offerings before the season started and left the remaining two thirds to be created continuously based on style trends, which gave Zara valuable flexibility in its product array.

Procurement and production

Inditex had a stake in every link of the supply chain beginning with the fabric, which was purchased through offices located in Barcelona and Hong Kong. The fabric was then sold to in-house and external manufacturers. Almost half of it was carried without dye as coloring was often postponed until later stages of production. Roughly 50% of Zara's products were manufactured in factories located in Portugal, Morocco or adjacent to its headquarters in A Coruña. Most of these factories were fully owned by Inditex, and work was organized according to just-in-time (JIT) principles as a result of collaborative projects with Toyota (Japan) in the 1990s. The other 50% of production came from outside suppliers, with 30% located in eastern European countries like Turkey, Bulgaria and Romania. The remaining 70% were overseas suppliers that had a 15–20% production cost advantage and usually procured Zara's basics. In general, basics were ordered in larger quantities compared to more trendy items that were produced in small batches. Before making any decision regarding procurement or production, Zara made an assessment of speed, expertise, cost-effectiveness and availability. If the company could not produce an item at the price it wanted, Zara would look to outside manufacturers.

For the products manufactured in-house, the next step in the process was cutting the fabric. Operators used CAD systems to check fit and sizing of the cutting pattern in order to minimize waste. After a first cut and approval from the machine operator, several layers of fabric were cut simultaneously following the same pattern. From here, the fabric was sent to a large network of sewing workshops. Zara had developed close relationships with more than 500 sewing subcontractors in the A Coruña vicinity. By outsourcing the labor-intensive work, Zara allowed its own facilities to remain focused and flexible. Finished products were sent back to the factories for ironing and quality control, and then they continued onto the distribution center at the headquarters. An aerial monorail system connected a dozen factories to the distribution center

so that hanging and folded garments could be rapidly transferred between divisions.

Distribution and warehousing

The distribution process began at the store level, which had the best understanding of what customers wanted. From a distribution standpoint, there were two key pieces of information that were gathered at each Zara store. The first piece of information was the point-of-sale data that was captured daily and transmitted directly to Zara's headquarters in Spain. The second piece of information was the bi-weekly order placed by each store. On the day the order had to be placed, the product assortment for the next shipment, known as "the offer", was downloaded onto a handheld device. The assortment included articles that were already available at the store as well as new products that were being introduced. Next, a store associate walked through the store to check the inventory levels and entered specific quantity requests for each article, including color and sizes. Though the product assortment was common to all stores, there could be significant differences in demand that sometimes made a product more successful in certain stores than in others. The store employees were the most aware of these differences and that was reflected in the order quantity that they requested for each article.

Zara had a fixed schedule to place orders and the store manager was responsible for transmitting the information electronically by the cutoff time. The disparity in inventory levels and demand patterns among stores introduced enormous variability in the shipment requests. All of these orders arrived at the headquarters and the distribution team then decided how much to ship to each store. The chosen allocation was transmitted to the warehouse control system, which effectively implemented the physical picking, sorting, packing and freight loading operations. (See Exhibit 6 for a location of Zara's warehouses.) The distribution centers operated far below capacity on average to ensure that they could respond to demand almost immediately. They were divided into two distribution areas, one for the hanging clothes and one for the folded clothes. Picking was done in a *wave picking* fashion. That is, the same article was picked at once for all of the different stores. The second step was sorting so that different items going to the same store were put together in the same shipment. For the hanging clothes, each store had a dedicated rail with a red tag indicating the name of the destination so the warehouse employee knew where to hang each item.

EXHIBIT 6   LOCATION OF INDITEX WAREHOUSES AND LOGISTIC CENTERS (2010)

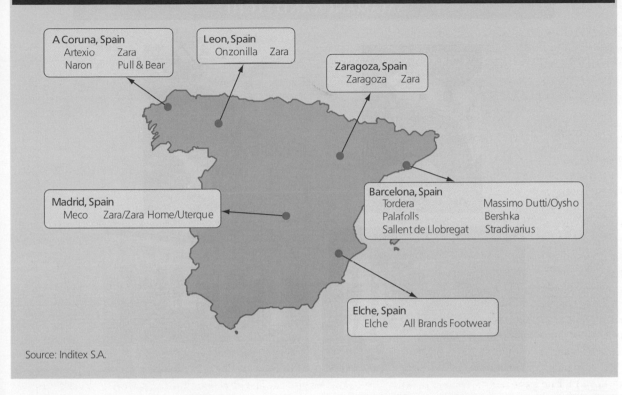

A Coruna, Spain
Artexio   Zara
Naron   Pull & Bear

Leon, Spain
Onzonilla   Zara

Zaragoza, Spain
Zaragoza   Zara

Madrid, Spain
Meco   Zara/Zara Home/Uterque

Barcelona, Spain
Tordera   Massimo Dutti/Oysho
Palafolls   Bershka
Sallent de Llobregat   Stradivarius

Elche, Spain
Elche   All Brands Footwear

Source: Inditex S.A.

For the folded garments, a state-of-the-art sorter was used to place each item in the appropriate shipment.

Shipments were made by truck, or for more remote locations by plane, so that the items reached the destination store within 48–72 hours. In the case of ground transportation, the trucks were loaded directly at the docks attached to the warehouse. In the case of stores reached by plane, an air-cargo container was filled at the warehouse and then transported to the airport and loaded onto the aircraft. Zara divided its worldwide network in four geographical areas, and every day it shipped specifically to one particular area. When the shipment finally arrived at the store, the items were unloaded and the store associates checked the products and quantities that arrived, which could have been different from what they originally ordered depending on the allocation performed by the distribution team. Most of the items were placed immediately on display.

Retailing and closing the circle

At the retail level, special locations were chosen after extensive market research focusing on prestigious locations with a voluminous flow of upscale shoppers. The location of the stores was crucial to the success of the business. Because Zara spent little money on advertising, approximately 10% of competitors' expenditure, brand recognition was dependent upon store visibility.[2] Zara favored landmark buildings, even if they required significant remodeling efforts (see Exhibit 7 for two before-and-after examples). Zara worked hard to create a special store experience. The layout and decor of the stores was managed at headquarters by a designated location team that oversaw the remodel and fixtures in the new openings. The store interior and exterior had to be attractive and give a sense of well being to the customer. The shop floor was designed to be spacious and provide a sense of luxury. The density of a typical Zara store was 28 units of inventory per square meter while traditional retailers usually had between 32 and 43 units/m^2.

The products quickly changed at Zara stores as new items arrived twice a week. Store managers were incentivized to get slower moving inventory off the shelves. Offering fashion forward pieces in small quantities created a sense of urgency among

[2]The industry average for advertising expenditure was 3–4% of revenues.

Source: Inditex S.A.

customers. In fact, when shoppers saw something they liked there was an impulse to buy because the item would likely not be there a week later. Promotions were rare but even so the regular shopper visited Zara stores on a monthly basis. In contrast, the same shopper on average would visit a comparable traditional retailer only a few times a year. Some Zara customers even knew which day inventory arrived and shopped accordingly. Even taking into account clearance sales, the average Zara item sold with half the markdown of a comparable traditional retailer.

In terms of personnel, Zara strived to retain the best store associates. In order to do so, Zara developed a retail sales structure that gave store associates autonomy over their own product lines. In fact, a typical Zara store would have three store managers, one for Zara Women, one for Zara Men and one for Zara Kids. Under Zara Women, for example, each product line (knitwear, suiting, etc.) would have its own product manager. This organizational design meant that almost every store associate had a unique set of products for which they were specifically responsible. Ortega

believed that autonomy and responsibility built company loyalty and dedication. Zara also offered an incentive program that promoted collaboration within each store, as employees were compensated based on salary and overall store sales. Regardless of the rank, everyone at Zara had to have some store experience and promotion from within was strongly encouraged. In an industry with high turnover, employee morale at Zara remained very positive.

International expansion

Zara more than doubled in size over the period from the early 2000s, when it first became known worldwide, to 2010. The majority of that expansion took place outside of Spain. In fact, domestic stores accounted for 22% of total sales in 2010, compared to 37.5% in 2002. Zara considered expansion into a new country after several analyses. First, it did a typical macroeconomic study including the evaluation of tariffs, taxes, legal costs, the labor market and property prices. Second, it did a microeconomic analysis with sector specific demand, channels and available store locations. Finally, headquarters looked at the concentration of key competitors and attempted to understand any region-specific barriers to entry, including political and legal factors and the ability of those factors to resist or inhibit entry. Different from most retailers, Zara determined its product pricing based on market pricing rather than cost forecasting. Instead of using a markup rule, Zara determined what prices the market could handle and then determined product prices accordingly. Such a strategy meant that Zara was positioned differently in each country. In Spain, Zara clothes were seen as inexpensive and meant to be worn only a few times, whereas in the Americas Zara products were positioned to be higher end, leveraging the perception attributed to European designs.

After pricing and positioning were determined, Zara decided how to enter the market operationally. The three options for market entry were wholly owned stores, joint ventures and franchises. Wholly owned stores were common when a country had high growth prospects and low business risk. Joint ventures were usually reserved for larger, more important markets where entry could be challenging. A franchise operation was the most typical strategy for small risky countries with significant cultural barriers. The franchise agreement was usually designed as a 5-year contract with fees of 5–10% of sales, but Zara always maintained the right to either buy out the franchisee or open wholly owned stores during that contract period. This arrangement allowed Zara to test new countries without bearing significant risk. Only 3% of all Zara stores were franchises in 1999 but by 2010 that number grew to 10%.

From 2007–2010, Zara focused its expansion on Asia. In fact, Inditex's growth rate in Asia during that period was double that of the rest of the world. This push was furthered by the economic crisis that hit western countries harder, but that only served as confirmation for a strategic choice that had been made prior to the economic downturn. Zara first entered China in 2006, and only four years later it had opened 71 stores and proven its concept. In contrast, Zara entered the United States in 1987, and by 2010 it had only opened 49 stores. At this rate of growth, China was on track to take over as having Zara's second largest presence outside of Spain, trailing behind only Italy with 84 stores and France with 113 stores. Unlike shipments to Italy and France, however, shipments to Zara's stores in China travelled over 5,000 miles. In 2010, CEO Pablo Isla announced that India would be

EXHIBIT 8   INDITEX'S EXPANSION STRATEGY

Concept	Planned Openings	% Outside Spain	FY 2010 Actual Store Openings
Zara	110–120	98%	123
Zara Home	25–30	65%	23
Pull & Bear	40–50	95%	56
Massimo Dutti	25–35	98%	33
Bershka	45–50	98%	69
Stradivarius	65–75	95%	78
Oysho	30–35	80%	40
Uterque	25–30	65%	23
TOTAL NET OPENINGS	**365–425**	**95%**	**445**

Source: Inditex S.A.

one of Inditex's next top priorities. This statement followed an agreement signed between Inditex and the conglomerate Tata Group for a 50/50 joint venture to introduce Zara stores in India. (See Exhibit 8 for projected store openings in 2010.) Zara's global expansion did have its share of challenges, particularly with operations and store execution. These challenges motivated several initiatives that reflected the company's dynamism.

Internal processes overhaul

One challenge that surfaced was related to the incentive structure and its connection to the inventory allocation process. Given that compensation was based uniquely on total sales, there was an impression that store associates would frequently request quantities exceeding their true weekly needs, particularly when they anticipated that the inventory level of a top-selling article was scarce at the warehouse. Without formal rules for allocating the inventory, the distribution team was constantly struggling to keep store managers and headquarters happy while simultaneously helping to manage the allocation process. Availability of sizes was another key factor in the inventory allocation process. Zara put merchandise out when the set of available sizes was *complete enough*. Zara believed that if there was not enough size availability – in particular, the most popular sizes – it could damage brand perception. Therefore it was important to have a complete enough set of sizes available to the customer at all times. When a store associate realized that there were not enough sizes available for a given product, all remaining inventory of that product was moved from the display area to the backroom, which meant that the product was removed from customers' sight. Therefore, the inventory allocation process had to ensure that a complete enough set of products were in the store at every point in time, making it a complicated rationing problem. Moreover, Zara had to solve this problem for thousands of products in just a few hours.

Zara's leadership viewed the inventory allocation process as an opportunity for improvement. The legacy process of using a few inventory specialists to determine order quantity and size distribution was still functional but there was the feeling that it could be leaving money on the table as the chain expanded beyond its first 1,000 stores. In 2005, Zara teamed up with academics in operations management to develop a new allocation process based on formal forecasting and optimization models. The forecast model used historical sales data and the input of store managers, which was then fed into an optimization model that maximized sales across the entire store network while incorporating inventory availability and the display policy regarding sizes. The use of analytical models, also known as Operations Research, focused on finding the global optimum for the chain rather than many local optima for individual stores and helped to create a scalable process with consistent allocation rules.

Zara was a company that favored vision and judgment for decision-making. Although the use of quantitative tools such as spreadsheets was common, at the time the company had no prior experience using analytical methods. Consequently, the new model-based allocation process was met with natural resistance from the distribution team. The value of the project was severely questioned and threatened to halt on several occasions. Fortunately, the project had the support of CFO Miguel Díaz and it found an internal champion in José Antonio Ramos, who believed in the model's potential from the outset and voluntarily took the lead.

Ramos was the main counterpart for the academics involved and was able to recruit key employees in the Information Technology (IT) department to devote time to the project above and beyond their regular duties.[3]

Overcoming the initial concerns required long sessions and a substantial communication effort, but the tipping point came when the mechanics of the model were understood and the distribution team realized that the new process would shift its responsibilities from repetitive data entry towards exception handling, scenario analysis and process improvement. The breakthrough came in 2007 when a controlled field test was run to ensure that the model accurately forecasted and optimized inventory needs. The live pilot experiment was a success and showed that the new process was able to allocate inventory where it was most needed and was able to ship specific sizes only where it was likely to generate sales. Overall, sales increased by approximately 3–4%. This led to the worldwide rollout of the new process. The estimated realized financial impact was about $233 million and $353 million in additional revenues for 2007 and 2008, respectively.[4]

The success of the inventory allocation model also ignited interest in other applications of analytical methods to support its operations. In the words of Miguel Díaz, "it showed that Operations Research can significantly contribute to Zara's strategic goal of improving the scalability of its operations in order to support its continued growth." In 2008, Zara developed another model to optimize markdowns during clearance sales. In the past, markdowns were determined through a manual process that depended largely on the experience of each country manager. Again, there was an issue of scalability, but most importantly, country managers had a tendency to focus on liquidating stock rather than maximizing revenues, which stemmed from the pressure to open up space for the incoming season. An optimization model proved effective in balancing the forces at play. It gave guidelines on when to markdown aggressively and when it was better to wait.

The markdown project had its own challenges. For one thing, it required country managers to become comfortable with a sales forecast. The average forecast error was less than 24%, which compared favorably to other markdown applications, but this number was still

---

[3] One of the key employees was Jose Manuel "Pepe" Corredoira who at the time of writing was head of an IT team now fully dedicated to analytical model implementations.

[4] Caro, F., J. Gallien, M. Díaz, J. Garcia, J.M. Corredoira, M. Montes, J.A. Ramos, J. Correa. 2010. Zara Uses Operations Research to Reengineer Its Global Distribution Process. *Interfaces* Vol. 40, No. 1, pp. 71–84.

unsettling to several who thought, "How can we trust the model if the forecast is wrong one fourth of the time?" As before, communication proved to be essential and in this case the tipping point came at the recognition that the forecast was only an intermediate step and not the goal itself. For this, several simulated examples were used to show that even with an imperfect forecast the pricing decision could be good enough to achieve near-optimal revenue. (A theoretical justification is that demand curves are downward sloping whereas revenue curves are usually concave and tend to be very flat at the top.) Full validation came again from a controlled field experiment that was conducted in all Belgian and Irish stores during the winter of 2009, and it was estimated that the pricing model increased revenues by 6%. This was equivalent to $90 million in additional sales that went directly to the bottom line since the model did not have a major impact on Zara's costs.[5]

Additional improvements were made under Isla's leadership, including one that moved a time-consuming backroom store process to the factory. Until 2007, store employees were required to attach alarm tags to new merchandise. After evaluation, this process was moved off site to be completed at the factory prior to shipping. In 2010, two other ongoing projects were an optimization model to coordinate inventory and pricing decisions and a pilot to test radio-frequency identification (RFID) technology at the store level. The purpose of this last project was to keep a closer control of the inventory levels during the day in order to re-stock in real time those items that were missing on the shop floor but were available in the backroom. Prior to that technology, store associates had to perform store walks to detect these items, which was a demanding task and therefore happened less frequently on busy days when stock outs were more likely. Zara believed that the reduction in lost sales would compensate for the incremental cost of the RFID tags. This had been confirmed by preliminary results from the pilot, particularly for the larger stores that experienced heavier traffic.

Zara goes online

In 2005, online sales in the United States reached $68.9 billion. Of this amount, $18.3B came from mass merchant and department store sales and another

$7.1B came from online apparel and accessories retailers, together representing 37% of total online sales in the United States. The size of this market was hard to ignore and Zara carefully considered moving into the e-tail space but ultimately decided that online sales were not right for its business model, which relied heavily on the in-store experience. In an effort to build an online presence without losing brick-and-mortar sales, Zara offered an online viewing catalogue of products but customers still had to visit the store to buy the items.

That was 2005. In 2008, The Gap's e-commerce division surpassed $1 billion in sales. In mid-2009, Amazon announced it was purchasing footwear and accessories retailer Zappos.com for $847 million. This acquisition, made by the most successful e-tailer, represented a strong bet on the value of online apparel commerce. Later that year, after almost five years of deliberation, Zara founder Amancio Ortega asked Javier Garcia to spearhead the launch of Zara's online shopping portal. Garcia had built a long career at Inditex, having begun his career at the store level. He continued to grow under the Inditex umbrella and eventually moved into Zara's distribution department, where he assisted with the development and implementation of the model-based inventory allocation system. Garcia was an avid "gadgeteer" – always interested in the latest products and electronics – just like Ortega in the early years. He also knew the company inside out from its customer base to its core processes, which made him a well-suited choice for the job.

Zara's online store officially launched on September 2, 2010 after just one short year of development, a rapid pace that had previously been demonstrated in its manufacturing capabilities. Online shoppers in six countries: France, Germany, Italy, Portugal, Spain and the U.K. were able to shop online for Zara merchandise which was shipped directly to all locations from the warehouse in Madrid. The products sold online carried the same prices as those found in the store, but they were now available from a simple and convenient website. Moreover, customers had the option to ship their purchase to a particular address for a fee or could ship it for free to any Zara store for pickup.

Zara had initially been concerned that the online portal would adversely affect its high urgency/low

[5]Caro, F., J. Gallien. 2011. Clearance Pricing Optimization for a Fast-Fashion Retailer. UCLA Anderson School of Management, working paper.

inventory strategy at the store level. However, there was little evidence that consumer brand perception had changed. In fact, the most notorious change in shopping behavior was that after the launch, Zara customers began walking into stores and asking sales associates to point out items they had found online, showing the pictures on their mobile phones. Another initial concern was the cannibalization effect between the two sales channels, but that also proved to be unsubstantiated since most of the online sales came from locations where there was no Zara store nearby. In November of 2010, online sales were already noticeable, though most of the volume came from countries like the U.K. or Germany that had a previous tradition in catalog commerce.

Corporate social responsibility and the environmental dimension

Zara initially manufactured almost all of its clothing exclusively in Spain, but by 2005 Inditex's supplier network had expanded to include over 1,800 production facilities in Africa, Asia, Europe and the Americas. Inditex joined other clothing suppliers in implementing a combination of offshoring and outsourcing for its labor-intensive garments as a way to drive down costs and stay competitive in the market. As more and more apparel companies joined in this globalization effort, concerns surfaced regarding unfair labor practices and environmental impact issues such as the use of massive amounts of energy and the disposal of toxic chemicals.

Global NGOs and other agencies began reporting large corporations for wrongful labor and environmental practices. Several worldwide campaigns focused on ensuring fair labor practices or denouncing greenwashing received prominent coverage in the press. Inditex, which was becoming the world's largest clothing retailer, was no exception in the attacks. For instance, in 2004, the organization coordinating the Clean Clothes Campaign in Spain – which had purchased Inditex stock to attend the annual meetings – issued a statement labeling Inditex's social responsibility plan as "a deceitful front" and claimed that the company was using it to portray itself in the media as a pioneer in social responsibility issues in Spain. A more balanced assessment was made by

Intermon Oxfam, a development NGO, who gave credit to Inditex's efforts but also acknowledged the difficulty Inditex faced in matching its aggressive marketing strategy with the ethics code expected from its suppliers.[6]

In response to this increasing pressure from the global community and the increasing challenge of monitoring foreign supplier shops, Inditex decided to revamp its Corporate Social Responsibility (CSR) program. The company initiated several programs that not only impacted labor standards and working conditions in the factories but also sought to improve living conditions and social development in local communities (see Exhibit 9). In 2007, Inditex signed an agreement with the global trade union International Textile, Garment and Leather Workers' Federation (ITGLWF). This agreement, the first of its kind to cover a retail supply chain, laid the foundation for ensuring that international labor standards would be observed throughout Inditex's network of supplier factories.

Inditex also made changes to its environmental policies. Starting in 2006, Inditex began publishing its own CO_2 emissions in order to showcase its efforts to remain committed to the environment. Despite significant growth in the number of stores, absolute carbon emissions remained relatively flat and actually decreased when measured per store square meter (see Exhibit 10). One program that helped reduce Inditex's consumption was the creation of the Eco-Efficient Store Manual and training videos to help sensitize and increase awareness among employees on issues such as recycling and the conservation of water and energy (see Exhibit 11 for recent levels of water consumption).

Other large environmental projects included the Pro Kyoto initiative whose aim was to reduce CO_2 waste by 20% and the Terra Project, developed to plant trees and build forests to help offset emissions made by the company. In its 2010 Annual Report, Inditex presented its new 5-year environmental strategic plan. This plan included goals of building new stores and redesigning existing stores to be more environmentally friendly. It also set out a plan to optimize logistical routes and incorporate efficient vehicles with the latest technology. Inditex hoped that these new strategic initiatives would demonstrate its commitment to improving the environment and reducing its carbon footprint.

---

[6]Vernis, Vilanova and Figueroa. 2006. Inditex: Outsourcing in Tangier. ESADE Business School.

EXHIBIT 9   CORPORATE SOCIAL RESPONSIBILITY PROGRAMS

Suppliers

Inditex Internal Code of Conduct	Formal declaration of values which regulate the relations of Inditex with each one of its interest groups (shareholders, employees, customers, business partners, suppliers and society in general).
Code of Conduct for External Manufacturers and Workshops	Formal declaration of values developed from the Internal Code of Conduct which sets the principles which regulate the relationship between Inditex and its suppliers. Modified in 2007, after joining the Ethical Trading Initiative and the incorporation of its Base Code, it includes many ILO agreements.

Institutions

MultiFiber Agreement Forum (MFA)	Multifiber Agreement Forum (MFA) is a dialogue platform which promotes social responsibility of textile industries in countries that are vulnerable.
Ethical Trade Initiative (ETI)	ETI is an organisation which brings together international distribution companies, large suppliers, trade unions and NGOs, and which aims to improve the living conditions of the workers in the supplying companies.
Better Work Program	Better Work Program aims to increase, in a sustainable manner, the competitiveness of certain emerging countries, based on the promotion, respect and encouragement of Basic Human and Employment Rights.

Customers

Clear to Wear	Product health standard created in 2006. Regulates, composition, pH as well as substances that have limited legal uses (e.g. formaldehyde) linked to allergic reactions.
Safe to Wear	A product safety standard which regulates metallic contamination, designs safe laces for children under 14, limits flammability in the clothing, etc.

Society

Programs of Community Development	Supply the tools necessary for the harmonious exercise of a wide concept of development, based on the extension of political, social, training and economic capacities of those communities, institutions and organized groups that are close to our activity.
Monitoring Programs	Programs of social investment which encourage a culture of peace and, as a consequence, the recovery and rehabilitation of the social fabric through the funding of certain health, social and educational projects.
Emergency Programs	Through the Emergency Programmes, Inditex participates in projects of intervention designed to alleviate the negative consequences of natural catastrophes which have occurred in the world.
For & From Programs	Inditex collaborates with the El Moll d'en Puigvert Foundation and the Galician Confederation of the Disabled (COGAMI) in projects for the creation of spaces for giving jobs to persons with physical and/or mental disabilities.

Source: Inditex S.A.

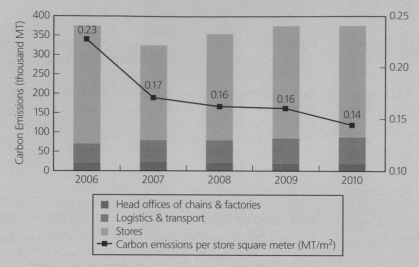

EXHIBIT 10   CARBON FOOTPRINT – GLOBAL CO$_2$ EMISSIONS

Source: Inditex S.A.

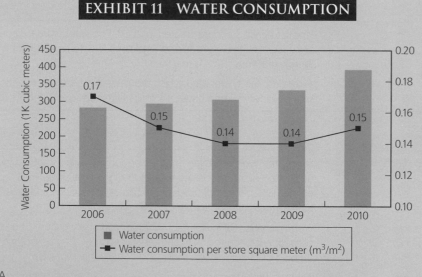

EXHIBIT 11   WATER CONSUMPTION

Source: Inditex S.A.

Challenges continuing forward

Many of the press articles and cases that were written at the beginning of Zara's expansion questioned whether the company's operations could support its continued growth. Several years later, we know that the "Zara way" proved itself resilient even through an adverse economic scenario. Zara successfully sustained ten years of organic growth, but can it do it again? Where should Zara focus its efforts and what should drive its expansion from here? Should Zara localize its operations in China given that it will quickly become its second largest market? Would opening a warehouse in China jeopardize Zara's success with a centralized distribution model? From a competitive standpoint, the success of Inditex, and in particular Zara, pushed H&M and Fast Retailing to expand at a similarly rapid rate. What does this mean for the future of the industry? Several other questions remain open. In globalized world, can Zara continue to price so differently from country to country? If online sales are considerably more profitable, is that the way forward for specialty apparel retailers? Are brick-and-mortar stores becoming obsolete? If environmental regulations become more stringent, would that represent a threat or an opportunity for Zara?

Ndaba Ntsele: Entrepreneurial vision

By Claire Beswick, Mthuli Ncube

On 19 May 2010, Ndaba Ntsele – Ernst & Young World Best Entrepreneur (SA, 2007) and CEO of Pamodzi Investment Holdings (PIH), a diversified investment company – was preparing for the launch of Pamodzi Aviation the next day. The company had secured a licence from the Ukraine-based, government-owned Antonov Aeronautical Scientific Complex to service and sell Antonov planes in Africa. However, he still had to negotiate the terms of the relationship that Pamodzi Aviation would have with Denel Aviation, the organisation providing the necessary technical expertise and infrastructure for the venture. His gut told him that Pamodzi Aviation could make millions – if not billions – of rands, but he was aware that real-world realities might get in the way and he wondered if he had missed anything.

Ntsele's background

I started to fall in love with money. You can't make money unless you love it

– Ntsele[1]

Ntsele was born in Kliptown, Soweto (west of Johannesburg) into a family with a history of entrepreneurial activity: his grandfather was a businessman, his father ran a dry-cleaning business and his aunt sold tea and apples to make a living. He defined an entrepreneur as someone who took risks, thought out of the box, believed in himself and in the team around him, and had the foresight to see opportunities that would work in the real world.[2] These characteristics were evident in the way Ntsele had lived his life.

It started when, as a six-year-old schoolboy, Ntsele would buy apples from his aunt and then sell them himself for a profit. This gave him confidence that he could sell products at a mark-up. The money he earned also gave him a certain amount of independence. When he turned 13, he started pushing trolleys for tips outside a supermarket in Yeoville [just east of the Johannesburg central business district (CBD)]. While doing this, he saw an opportunity to charge a fee for pushing trolleys to the flats of those customers who came on foot. He would charge the fee upfront, to ensure that he actually received the money, and he developed confidence in dealing with white people, who were his predominant customer base.[3]

"I started to fall in love with money," Ntsele explained, adding, "South Africans hate to say that they love money. We think it's an ugly thing to say. But I love money and if you don't love it, you won't have it. Funnily enough, when you have it, they all want some of it! As you accumulate it, they say that you are selfish. But the irony is that you can't be a philanthropist without money."[4] He started to dream big. He decided that, when he grew up, he wanted to be a millionaire.

In his mid-teens, Ntsele started to sell newspapers in Hillbrow, and again saw an opportunity to do things differently and to make more money. "I acquired corners that were doing well and started employing youngsters to sell the papers. Then, when it became too much for me to collect the money from the paper sellers myself, I employed people on scooters to go and collect the money for me," he recounted.[5]

"At that stage, I felt that my world was far bigger than the world others had tried to define for me. The problem was that I am black, and banks were as far from black people as the moon is from the earth. Blacks had

[1]Interview with Ndaba Ntsele, 16 September 2008.
[2]Presentation by Ndaba Ntsele at Wits Business School, 12 August 2008.
[3]Interview with Ndaba Ntsele, 13 October 2008.
[4]Interview with Ndaba Ntsele, 16 September 2008.
[5]Presentation by Ndaba Ntsele at Wits Business School, 12 August 2008.

low self-esteem and it was difficult to find partners to go into business with. We had all been told that money is a root of all evil, so blacks thought that capitalism was not for them; that it was meant for whites."[6]

However, there was another young man in Soweto who had equally big ambitions – Solly Sithole. As a boy, he did not have much time to play soccer with the other children, because over weekends and during school holidays he had gone door-to-door with his grandmother, selling a variety of products. Although his peers had scoffed at him, he found that he was good at sales, and there was the tangible benefit of earning his own money, which he could use to pay for school fees or a new pair of shoes. It was this experience that developed Sithole's spirit of entrepreneurship.[7] After school, Sithole went on to work as a sales representative for Nola, a food company that wanted to establish its products in the townships.

Sithole and Ntsele met through one of Ntsele's cousins, who was impressed by the fact that Sithole had a company car. The meeting spawned a friendship and a highly successful business relationship that was still thriving 30 years later.

Beginning of an empire

I had a goal. I wanted to be a millionaire. If anything got in my way, I found a way around it.

I knew that because of the way blacks and whites were conditioned, I would have to fight for it

– Ntsele[8]

In 1979, with lofty business goals in mind, Ntsele, Sithole and third partner Ncedi Manyoni saw an opportunity to make money – initially by building what became commonly known in the township as 'a two room and a garage'[a] and then by buying serviced stands in Soweto from the Urban Foundation[b] after it partnered with the government to create 99-year lease arrangements for black people. The concept of building and selling houses appealed to Ntsele, because he knew that, if he wanted to be a millionaire, there was

no point in starting small. "In my mind, I had already jumped from being the owner of an SMME," he explained. "I knew that if I looked for small businesses, it would take me my whole life to achieve that dream, so I had to start big. It wouldn't happen just by running a shop."[9] The maths told him that, if a two-room house could fetch R12 000, the company would get to a turnover of R1 million by selling just 100 houses. "You have to think big," he said. 'When you hunt, hunt the Big Five. It feeds a lot of people."[10] For his part, Sithole wanted to be involved in something that would outlive him and be around for 100 years or more. Construction met that criterion.

Thus, Pamodzi was born. The name, which means 'togetherness', was that of a hotel in Lusaka, Zambia, where the partners had stayed while visiting Sithole's brother in exile. (Sithole's brother was later jailed in the same trial as ANC heavyweight, Tokyo Sexwale, in 1977.) Sithole remembered thinking, "This is the kind of name we can build with for many years."[11]

Initially they started small, buying only a few stands at a time, financing the deposit for the stand out of their own funds, and then paying the remaining 90% when the purchaser paid for the house. In 1983/84, the Urban Foundation started looking for organisations with which it could partner in developing 2 500 stands from scratch in Dobsonville Extension 3 (Soweto): thus, the partner would service the stand and sell it, instead of just building on an already-serviced stand. This provided Ntsele with the chance to migrate from building the low-margin 'two rooms and a garage' to building houses for the black middle class. With the prices of the newly built houses ranging from R35 000 to R100 000, this model yielded high margins for the business. However, to finance the deal, Pamodzi needed R6 million upfront, which the partners could not provide themselves. They decided to approach a bank for a loan.

It was here that they encountered the first of many hurdles in trying to raise finance for their business ventures. "The problem was one of attitude," Ntsele related. "You are running a reasonable, small construction company, but you are black. In those days, the maximum you could borrow as a business like that

---

[6]Interview with Ndaba Ntsele, 13 October 2008.

[7]Interview with Solly Sithole, 19 November 2008.

[8]Interview with Ndaba Ntsele, 13 October 2008.

[a]This was an extension that was built onto an existing house and was designed to accommodate a growing family.

[b]The Urban Foundation was a privately funded NGO that aimed to use the power and influence of business to persuade the apartheid government to reform key aspects of its approach to black urbanisation.

[9]Interview with Ndaba Ntsele, 16 September 2008.

[10]*Ibid.*

[11]Interview with Solly Sithole, 19 November 2008.

was R200 000."[12] Pamodzi was banking with Standard Bank at the time but, although the bank provided finance for Pamodzi's next deal, it did not do so for this one. "Our local bank manager didn't even bother to process our application, because it was over the limit," said Ntsele. "He told his secretary to remind him to contact me two days before the deadline to say that we had not been successful." Fortunately, she called straight away to alert Ntsele to the situation, which then gave him enough time to try a different bank.[13]

Unwilling to accept defeat, the Pamodzi partners managed to get an appointment to see the CEO of Barclays Bank,[c] Chris Ball. Sithole remembered: "He asked, 'What are you going to do?' 'How are you going to pay it back?' and then he said, 'Done!'"[14] Pamodzi had its first big break. From there, the company went on to work with the Urban Foundation on a number of other housing development projects. The success evidenced in Soweto was replicated in Mamelodi Gardens and Sluma View in the East Rand.

One of the principles that guided Ntsele and his partners during this early phase and into the future was the belief that, to succeed, they would need to work with people who had the skills and expertise that they did not have. Ntsele saw doing this as a way of bringing together gut feel (his particular strength) and the more scientific information that he would need to run the business. Together, these would aid decision-making. "Great entrepreneurs have a lot of good professionals around them," he noted. "I've always had people around me who will give me information." And he looked to appoint people based on their skills and knowledge, rather than their skin colour. "I must have been the first black guy who appointed a chartered accountant who was white!" he joked.[15]

He was hungry for information that would equip him to succeed, attending numerous courses at Wits University and other institutions in pursuit of knowledge. One of the pieces of information that made a great impact related to the importance of image and personal packaging to securing success. The lecturer had stressed how important it was to present oneself and to dress in such a way as to inspire confidence.

Thus, when seeking funding, it was important to look the part: to look like a serious professional who would be able to pay the bank back. Ntsele had found this to be true in his early days as a businessman, and had carried this philosophy with him since then. It was reflected, among other things, in the design of the PIH offices, where he had ensured that they projected the right image of confidence, reliability and success that he wanted to present to the world.[16]

Diversifying for growth

Having secured the work with the Urban Foundation in Mamelodi Gardens and Sluma View, Ntsele was not happy to stop there. He and his partners were hungry for success and open to any opportunity that came their way, even if it was in a sector in which they had little experience. "As an entrepreneur, you don't have to fear fear," he said. "A medical doctor can run a good truck company."[17] He believed that it was important to have big dreams and to act on them. "Acting on your dream is very, very, very important," he said, "and the size of the dream must not scare you. I like to quote Anton Rupert and say that 'a person who does not believe in miracles is not realistic'." He was also prepared to work very hard to achieve his dreams. "Working 24/7 must not scare you," he said.[18]

Thus, in the early to mid-1980s, Pamodzi started to diversify and expand its focus from just building houses. One activity in which the company became involved early on was that of dealing in Krugerrands. This venture became possible because Pamodzi had opened up an office in the Johannesburg CBD. At that stage, it was illegal for black people – other than doctors and lawyers – to have offices in the CBD, but Pamodzi's one-room office in Soweto was not the right location for the company. The partners decided that their competitors were in the CBD, so their company should be there as well. One of their white business associates was happy to sign a lease agreement for an office in the Carlton Centre on their behalf. So they decided to test the waters, rent the office for a year and see if anyone came to evict them. No-one did.[19]

[12]Interview with Ndaba Ntsele, 16 September 2008.

[13]*Ibid.*

[c]Later in the 1980s, Barclays Bank disinvested from South Africa as part of the movement for sanctions against South Africa. Its South African operations became First National Bank.

[14]Interview with Solly Sithole, 19 November 2008.

[15]Interview with Ndaba Ntsele, 24 March 2010.

[16]*Ibid.*

[17]*Ibid.*

[18]*Ibid.*

[19]Interview with Ndaba Ntsele, 13 October 2008.

"Once we were there," Ntsele recalled, "another guy dealing in Krugerrands introduced us to the Kruger coin business. At that stage, we were building lots of houses, so we had cash flow and were profitable. We bought coins and kept them as an investment."[20] Later, however, they discovered that they could purchase the coins for less themselves, and started to bypass the middleman and buy the coins directly. In the late 1980s, they also started dealing in jewellery and electronic equipment, which they purchased in Hong Kong and sold in South Africa.

In all his dealings, Ntsele recognised the importance of being able to deal well with people. "The most important thing as an entrepreneur is to create relationships, and to create relationships you need a love for people," he said. "You must be comfortable in the company of people from all over the world."[21] To do this, he pointed out, it was important to read and to be educated about what was happening in the world, and about the customs in different cultures. "When you are in the company of a Chinese person, you don't say something stupid about China. So you must be informed, and talk positively to people, because that attracts a positive response," he said.[22]

Ntsele decided early in his career that if he wanted to be rich, he had to be where the rich people were, and one of the things this entailed was to fly only first class. This decision was to stand him in good stead because, on one of his flights to Hong Kong, he met Dr Conrad Strauss, who was CEO of Standard Bank at the time. Strauss, said Ntsele, was fascinated and impressed by "these young black guys" who were flying first class to Hong Kong to do business during the height of apartheid. Ntsele made a contact that would help him with his next big building contract – a school in Fleurhof (a township adjacent to Soweto), being sponsored by the Anglo American Chairman's Fund through the Urban Foundation. This enabled Pamodzi to tender for further involvement in the building of schools and service stations in Soweto.

To secure the tender, Pamodzi needed a guarantee of R600 000 and working capital of between R1.2 million and R1.3 million. Ntsele was still paying off the loan to Barclays, and therefore did not believe that he could go back to that bank for another loan. He

decided, once again, to try Standard Bank – but this time he went directly to Strauss.

"These people are all booked up a year in advance," said Strauss's personal assistant, but Ntsele would not budge. He managed to secure an appointment on the day that the tender had to be submitted, half an hour before the deadline. He and his partners did what they always did: they dressed the part, arrived on time and were very well-prepared. "I told him [Strauss] that I owed Barclays R6 million and that I didn't have enough guts to go to them for another loan," said Ntsele. "Integrity is extremely important. If you lose it, you won't get anywhere." Fifteen minutes after the deadline, Strauss agreed to lend them the money and then phoned the Urban Foundation to explain the delay. Pamodzi won the contract.[23]

At that stage, political upheaval was rife in the townships, and the construction industry in those areas took a turn for the worse. Pamodzi's third partner bowed out of the business, but Ntsele and Sithole remained. They were very glad then that Pamodzi had diversified and was not solely dependent on construction. This solidified their belief that diversification was key to success and they continued with this strategy, winning licences to sell Plascon (paint and other coatings) and PG Bison (wood and chipboard) products in Soweto.[24] The construction side of the business was not wholly dormant, however, and they started to partner with construction company Murray & Roberts on projects, and also to develop petrol stations.[25]

They also built another school in Soweto, which unwittingly provided the impetus for their next big deal. "At that stage, there were sanctions against South Africa, but no sanctions against building schools," noted Ntsele. The Department of Education gave Pamodzi the contract to build the school, and Ntsele went to the United States of America (US) to source the necessary funding from a bank that had a reputation for providing funding to black American businesspeople. He reasoned that the bank might show similar favour to black South Africans. While there, Ntsele was blown away by the different businesses he saw in the US – Nike, McDonald's and Victoria's Secret, in particular. He thought then that, when

[20]*Ibid.*

[21]Interview with Ndaba Ntsele, 24 March 2010.

[22]*Ibid.*

[23]Presentation by Ndaba Ntsele at Wits Business School, 12 August 2008.

[24]Interview with Ndaba Ntsele, 13 October 2008.

[25]W Khuzwayo, 'Pamodzi on the Prowl for R1bn Companies', *Business Report*, 17 November 2008, available *www.busrep.co.za* (accessed 29 January 2009).

sanctions ended, he would bring at least one of them to South Africa.[26]

The Nike deal

He and Sithole got the chance to do this in 1992. They knew that the sanctions era was about to end, and they started to think that there would be opportunities to relaunch a strong international brand in South Africa.[27] In 1993, it became clear that Nike was looking to re-enter South Africa and to appoint a licenced agent in South Africa. Sanctions had not yet been lifted, but Ntsele and Sithole wanted to move early to get an advantage over other bidders. Sithole therefore spoke to his brother, explaining that Pamodzi did not want to break sanctions but needed to move quickly to have a chance of winning the licence, and received the ANC's blessing to pursue the deal.[28]

In the end, Pamodzi was one of more than 200 organisations – including established fashion and sports retail houses – that tendered for the licence. "We won because we were the only truly black-owned company," said Ntsele. "In all the other consortia, the black partners were a front."[29] The R10 million needed to secure the deal was eventually obtained from First National Bank, but no local bank was prepared to provide funding for further expansion as the business started to grow. Eventually, through the intervention of Nike, Pamodzi managed to secure R60 million from CitiBank in the US. Under Ntsele and Sithole's leadership, Nike became a top-selling brand in South Africa and, in 1998, Ntsele and Sithole sold the South African operation back to Nike International.

Pamodzi investment holdings: The empire takes shape

You must find solutions. Our minds must be solutions-oriented

– Ntsele[30]

In the late 1990s, the first wave of BEE deals had just taken place and Ntsele, Sithole and six others saw an opportunity to take advantage of the prospects presented by the BEE phenomenon. Thus, in 1996, Pamodzi Investment Holdings (PIH) was founded. Its eight founding partners – Ntsele, Sithole, Jan Roesch, Kobus du Plooy, Andrew Wheeler, Felicia Mabuza-Suttle, Sifiso Msibi and Peter Vundla – put R1.9 million into the company, with black shareholders owning 65% of the company. "We were starry-eyed, but with only R1.9 million, we were not going to go very far," commented Roesch, executive director of finance at PIH.

Ntsele's aim was to build PIH into a huge conglomerate like an Anglo American, BHP Billiton or Murray & Roberts. He wanted Pamodzi to change the way the world thought of black business. It concerned him that the status quo still remained, and that people still had a sceptical view of black business. "I fought tooth and nail to bring back the money that I borrowed, and I have developed a track record because of this," he noted. "Still, you can't forget that the status quo is still the same. I am still a black businessman. I have a huge track record, but I still can't crack some institutions. Some people still think that all I've achieved is through luck.

"There is a perception that black people can't run big businesses," he added. "Pamodzi proves that to be incorrect. Once we can do that, we will send a strong message globally. It is no longer just Warren Buffett who's the worldwide guru, South Africa can do it too."[31] He saw his as a very important message, because of what it would do for local entrepreneurship. "It will help improve young people and encourage young entrepreneurs," he said. "We must help to kick out the fear, because there's a lot of fear out there. People are scared to go into entrepreneurial ventures. They would prefer to be employed. They study for secure jobs. But you must always think beyond that."[32]

Over the years, PIH made a number of important investments that grew its assets at the end of 2009 to R683 million (down from R800 million in 2008 as a result of the revaluation of investments following the global economic meltdown), although the company registered a net loss to R139 million (down from R84

---

[26]Presentation by Ndaba Ntsele at Wits Business School, 12 August 2008.

[27]Interview with Ndaba Ntsele, 13 October 2008.

[28]Interview with Solly Sithole, 19 November 2008.

[29]Interview with Ndaba Ntsele, 13 October 2008.

[30]Interview with Ndaba Ntsele, 24 March 2010.

[31]Interview with Ndaba Ntsele, 16 September 2008.

[32]Interview with Ndaba Ntsele, 13 October 2008.

million profit in 2008).[33] By May 2010, PIH's portfolio of investments included:

- through **Pamodzi Ukuvikele**, a 26.3% stake in Indwe Risk Services, one of the largest, independent short-term insurance brokers in the country, formed in 2006 as a result of the merger between Thebe Risk Services (the country's oldest black empowered financial institution) and Prestasi Brokers;

- a 32% share in **Pamodzi Industrials** which, in turn, had investments in three operating divisions: Unique Engineering, which produced pantographs, filling and labelling equipment and blast barricades; Relyintracast, which produced investment castings; and Walro Flex, which manufactured automotive cables and had about 60% of the South African auto cable market. Pamodzi also owned 80% of BGG Cable Manufacturers SA (Pty) Ltd;

- a 74.5% share in **Pamodzi Resources**, which held various mining exploration rights;

- a 60% interest in **Rand Uranium** through Pamodzi Resources Fund 1, a private equity fund established to invest in resources and related projects in Africa;

- a 75% interest in **Boxmore (Pty) Ltd**, a company manufacturing PET bottles for the carbonated soft drinks and bottled water markets;

- a 45.5% stake in **Andre Dreyer Motors**, trading as Auto Bavaria Midrand, one of only 10 Mini Cooper and BMW dealerships in the country. Based on sales, this dealership had been one among the top five BMW dealerships in the country since PIH bought a stake in the company;

- a 25% interest in **AltcchIT**, which housed the IT interests of the JSE-listed Altech group of companies. These interests included ISIS (which specialised in system integration software development for telecommunications network operators) and Altech Card Solutions (which operated in the secure electronic transactions industry); and

- an effective 4.54% interest in **Anglo Inyosi Coal**, through Pamodzi Coal's 33% stake in Inyosi, a broad-based empowerment consortium that had partnered with Anglo Coal to form Anglo Inyosi Coal. It operated key Anglo Coal projects, including the Kriel and Sondagsfontein Colliery.

Making and exiting investments

In approaching investment decisions, Ntsele was open to opportunities – even those that looked risky to his advisors. He gave an example of the investment PIH had made in Prestasi insurance brokers in 2001. He had looked at the business, seen that it had more than 200 000 people on its books and decided that it would a be a good business in which to invest. He still sent his executives to perform due diligence investigations, but when they came back reporting serious management flaws that made the company a risky investment in their view, Ntsele was not convinced. Bad management was not a serious enough flaw for him. He knew that if PIH bought the company, it could put in new management who would manage it properly.

His focus was solutions-oriented. "There are two issues in business," he said, "capex and management. If I am going to buy machines that are old and I'm going to have to spend a lot of money and it's going to be difficult to recover that money, then maybe I would not make the investment. But I might look for second-hand machines. Even if the skeletons in the closet at Prestasi were not management, I would have looked for solutions. You must find solutions. Our minds must be solutions-oriented. I would have found a way."[34] By 2010, he felt vindicated in this decision. Prestasi had been incorporated into Indwe Risk Services and had become a very successful company.

Ntsele explained that almost the only thing that would cause him to walk away from a deal was if it did not give PIH real management control and authority, and confined the company to the role of the BEE partner whose skin colour and contacts would bring in business. He had regularly turned his back on a deal in these circumstances. "I don't want to play in business where people play politics. I'm a real businessman. PIH has been around for 13 years and I've been in business for 30 years. I want to play in real business," he said.[35]

Likewise, PIH's philosophy right from the beginning was that traditional, vendor-financed, BEE deals were less than optimal, and to be avoided as far as possible. "BEE is not a normal way of doing business," said Ntsele. "Traditional BEE deals are structured by politicians who have no idea of business."[36] He drew an analogy between playing a game of marbles and making investments, saying that, unless PIH had its own funding ('marbles'), it would not be able

[33]*Ibid.*
[34]Interview with Ndaba Ntsele, 24 March 2010.
[35]*Ibid.*
[36]Presentation by Ndaba Ntsele at Wits Business School, 12 August 2008.

to play. It would merely be a spectator to someone else's game. He argued that traditional BEE deals did not give BEE partners control of their own destiny, and that they consequently did not take responsibility for their own success. Moreover, he did not see the sense in being shackled to a deal for a particular period of time. He wanted to be able to get out when it made financial sense. Likewise, he was scathing of the broad-based BEE transactions that started to take place in the early 2000s. He did not see any advantage to PIH of being bundled together with a range of other non-business, community and NGO partners, who had no business acumen and were not entering into the deal for business purposes.[37]

Having said that, PIH's first investment – into healthcare company Auckland Investments Ltd in 1997 – had a traditional BEE structure. PIH lost money on the Auckland deal, and got out of it in 1999. Fortunately, PIH also invested in two IT firms – Infracomm (Pty) Ltd and Tehnicare (Pty) Ltd – in 1997. Roesch described these as "our saving grace. Sometimes you just need some luck."[38] The company made the deals through the Public Investment Corporation (PIC) and its Isibaya Fund. "Our timing was perfect," said Roesch. "We bought at the beginning of the bubble and sold at the top, when these two companies themselves were sold. That gave us a kitty."

Foodcorp. In 1998, PIH tackled its biggest investment yet: the purchase of a stake in food group Foodcorp. Foodcorp manufactured a range of well-known household brands, including Ouma rusks, Glenryk pilchards and Blue Ribbon bread. To secure the deal, PIH needed a loan of R404 million. Ntsele approached raising the funds with the attitude that "every single game is a new game. You have to start afresh."[39] He knew that he could not rely on his track record, and this proved to be correct. No local banks were prepared to lend PIH the money. "Fortunately, because I had already raised funds internationally, I was liberated globally," said Ntsele.[40] So he and Sithole approached Dutch banking group, ABN AMRO, and managed to secure the necessary funding.

Through the deal, PIH acquired a 50.1% stake in Foodcorp, with Ethos and Foodcorp management acquiring 39.9% and 10% respectively.

During this period, PIH also had to deal with financial dishonesty on the part of some of Foodcorp's managers. Although there was an approval process in place that should have ensured that hedge positions were approved by the board, some managers had been able to bypass this process. In total, R150 million had been lost. Ntsele informed ABN AMRO of the situation, assured them that the money would be recovered and said that the CEO and CFO would have to be fired. ABN AMRO objected, but Ntsele decided that he would fire them anyway.[41]

"You're sitting there with all these white guys," he remembered. "They are shocked to be fired by a black guy. It was no longer a business situation. Even the chairman was asking what we would do without them! "Fifteen months later, the business had recovered. ABN AMRO called me and said that, in future, I mustn't ask their permission."[42] For his part, Ntsele was very pleased that the deal that had allowed PIH to purchase its stake in Foodcorp had not been structured along more traditional BEE lines, and that PIH had a place on Foodcorp's board. "If they could deceive us and we were on the board, imagine what they could have done if we had not been!" he exclaimed.[43]

Come 2004, Ethos decided that it wanted to sell its stake in Foodcorp.[44] This provided PIH with the opportunity to purchase the company entirely, but for this it would need about R2 billion: by far the biggest sum it had raised to date. This time, noted Roesch, PIH was in a position to do a proper leveraged buy-out, because it was able to obtain senior debt (debt secured by assets and repayable at a favourable, fixed rate over a fixed term). The deal was the largest-ever secondary leveraged buy-out in the history of South Africa.[45]

In March 2010, PIH sold its stake in Foodcorp to a consortium that included management, UK fund manager BlueBay Asset Management and a South African private equity investor, Capitaum, for R550 million.[46] Turnover in the company had increased

---

[37]*Ibid.*

[38]Interview with Jan Roesch, 27 October 2008.

[39]Interview with Ndaba Ntsele, 13 October 2008.

[40]*Ibid.*

[41]*Ibid.*

[42]*Ibid.*

[43]*Ibid.*

[44]Available *www.saflii.org.za/cases/ZACT/2004/22.html* (accessed 29 January 2009).

[45]I Mahabane, 'Step in the Right Direction', *Financial Mail,* available *www.financialmail.co.za* (accessed 29 January 2009).

[46]Author not cited, 'BEE', *Business Day,* 18 March 2010, available *www.businessday.co.za* (accessed 30 June 2010).

from R2.8 billion in 2004 to R6.2 billion at the end of 2009.

Pamodzi Gold. In October 2006, PIH made what turned out to be one of its less successful investments when, through is subsidiary Pamodzi Resources (in which it then had a 50.5% share – later increased to 74.5%), it purchased the gold mining assets of Impafa Resources and formed Pamodzi Gold. The aim was to create a black-owned junior gold mining company with a listing on the Johannesburg Stock Exchange Ltd (JSE), and Pamodzi Gold was listed on the JSE at the end of October that year. There were high hopes for the company and PIH believed that it was in a good position – by virtue of its ownership status, access to capital and the quality of its management team – to generate significant deal flow. PIH also saw the possibility of being able to take advantage of the opportunity to purchase other mining assets that might become available as a consequence of the promulgation of the Mineral and Petroleum Resources Development Act (no 28 of 2002), which aimed, among other things, to increase black ownership of the country's mines.[47]

Pamodzi Gold started running into financial difficulty in 2008, however, when it battled to raise the capital necessary to develop to mines that it had acquired early that year. The acquisition of these two mines had tripled the size of Pamodzi Gold and diluted Pamodzi Resources' shareholding in Pamodzi Gold to 38%. In July 2008, the JSE threatened to suspend trade of Pamodzi Gold shares unless it released its annual financial statements. These had been delayed because Pamodzi Gold wanted to raise the necessary funds before it released the report, so that the effect of the acquisitions could be factored into the financial results.[48]

Ntsele and his team fought for more than a year to try to save the Pamodzi Gold business. "I did not want to leave before the final whistle was blown," he said. "As an entrepreneur, you have to see things through to the end."[49] In the end, it was to no avail. Despite securing a loan of R200 million from the IDC, conditional on Pamodzi Gold being able secure the remaining R200 million from elsewhere, they did not manage to raise the necessary capital. Its main mines, with the exception of its operations on the West Rand (west of Johannesburg) were put into provisional liquidation in April 2009,[50] and a final liquidation order was granted in October 2009.[51]

Commenting on this experience, Ntsele said: "I'm glad to have gone though this, because if you don't go through something like this, you'll never be somebody in life." He continued: "These things happen. On paper it looked like a good investment, and when we bought it, gold was trading at about US$500 an ounce, so we bought it at a reasonable price and thought would break even with gold at US$750 an ounce. Since then, gold moved to US$1 000 an ounce. But, in life, you've got a nice spreadsheet – and then you've got the real world." He believed that his mistake had been to take over the new mines before Pamodzi Gold had the necessary money to invest in them. Almost more importantly, though, he had failed to listen to his "belly button". He had drawn a whole team of experts around him to evaluate the purchase of those mines, and their scientific answers had all shown that the deals were good. But instinct should have made him ask, "If this is so good, why is it so cheap? In the end, you can have the spreadsheets, but then you have to make a decision," he said. "I didn't make the right decision. You have to use all of your senses when you make a decision."[52]

He remembered another business venture that had failed, because he and his team had not used all their senses and had failed to take real-world circumstances into consideration. PIH had invested in a public private partnership with government in a paprika plantation and factory in Brits. They had decided to move the plantation and the factory to the Northern Cape in the interests of creating jobs in that area. The Brits factory had been very profitable, and Ntsele had seen no reason why it should not succeed in the Northern Cape too.

"What we failed to do," he said, "was to go and spend some time in the area to see how the people live. If we had, we would have seen that the area has a huge problem with alcoholism, and realised that this would

[47] Available *www.pamodzigold.co.za/profile_corporate.php* (accessed 30 June 2010).

[48] B Mpofu, 'JSE gives Pamodzi Gold a Month's Stay of Execution', *Business Day,* 4 July 2008, available *www.businessday.co.za* (accessed 30 June 2010).

[49] Interview with Ndaba Ntsele, 24 March 2010.

[50] C Mathews, 'New Attempt to Refinance Pamodzi', *Business Day*a, 7 May 2009, available *www.businessday.co.za* (accessed 30 June 2010).

[51] Author not cited, 'Pamodzi Gold Liquidation Order Granted', *Business Day,* 7 October 2009, available *www.businessday.co.za* (accessed 30 June 2010).

[52] Interview with Ndaba Ntsele, 24 March 2010.

have made the people unable to do the work we needed. You can't put people who are hungover into the hot sun to harvest paprika." So the venture had failed. The factory – a state-of-the-art one at that – was still there, but it was a ghost town.[53]

Pamodzi Resources Fund. In October 2007, PIH was involved in another first when it launched the Pamodzi Resources Fund (PRF1) with a commitment from a consortium of investors, including affiliates of American Metals and Coal International,[d] to make available US$1.3 billion (R9.2 billion at that stage) to invest in mining and resources organisations. This made PRF1 the largest private equity fund in South Africa at the time.[54] By May 2010, the fund had invested US$157 million by acquiring a 60% interest in Rand Uranium from Harmony Gold. In May 2010, Rand Uranium was producing and selling gold, but was in the process of establishing a uranium plant. Uranium would be extracted from the existing slime dams and above-ground dumps, with a 34-year life of reserve. Once in production, it was expected to be one of the top 10 uranium producers in the world, with the lowest production risk, given that the uranium did not have to be mined.

The Antonov deal

Based in the Ukraine, Antonov was founded in 1946 by Oleg Antonov by decree of the government of the Union of Soviet Socialist Republics (USSR). It was a government-owned organisation and, since inception, the company had designed and manufactured more than 100 different types of aircraft – including freight planes, passenger planes, military planes, helicopters and special-purpose aircraft. Among its aircraft were the AN225 Mriya, the largest transport aircraft in the world (it had been used to transport oversized building vehicles to help with the clean-up operations after the earthquake in Haiti in January 2010), and the AN-70 heavy transport military aircraft, which competed against planes such as the Airbus A400M. Altogether, Antonov had built more than 20 000 aircraft and,

although its planes were not sold in Europe, they were exported to 70 countries throughout the world.[55]

The *Financial Times* noted that, in the era of the Soviet Union, Antonov's design bureau had been one of the showpieces of the communist world. Since at least the late 1990s, Antonov had been trying to expand the international market for its aircraft. There was nevertheless a lingering perception that Antonov aircraft were not as safe as their European counterparts, which Antonov was working hard to combat – saying that these perceptions were, in fact, unfounded.[56] It marketed the advantages of its aircraft as being "structural reliability, flexibility of transport operations, ability to use unpaved airfields and ease of maintenance",[57] and pointed to the fact that they were far cheaper than the aircraft of their rivals.

Although Antonov aircraft were being widely used on the African continent for humanitarian and cargo operations, the company did not have official representation in Africa. As a consequence, technical and after-sales support had been limited, because they had been provided from the Ukraine.[58] Ntsele and his colleagues had become aware of the opportunity to become the Antonov agent in Africa when they were at the Ukraine embassy and overheard the ambassador talking about it. Further investigation had made Ntsele very interested in securing the deal. There were at least 800 Antonov aircraft in Africa, although the number had to be confirmed. Airlines would have to pay as much as US$2 million upfront for their aircraft to be serviced. This would make it a huge cash generator. The South African Department of Defence was looking to replace its fleet of Lockheed C-130s, and AN-70 could provide an ideal alternative. Ntsele's gut told him it was a really good deal. "Planes fly. They need to be safe. We are in the continent. The price point is good. We can service old planes and we can sell new planes. This could be a huge opportunity," he thought.[59]

Despite this, there were some relatively significant obstacles that Ntsele had to address in pursuing the deal. The first was that PIH would need to be able to provide the necessary infrastructure – hangars,

[53]*Ibid.*

[d]One of the largest privately-owned coal companies in the world.

[54]T Mafu, 'Pamodzi Launches US$1.3bn Fund', *Business Report*, 6 August 2007.

[55]Available *www.antonov.com* (accessed 8 May 2010).

[56]C Clover, 'Ukraine Looks to Extract Commercial Gain from Soviet Military Legacy', *Financial Times*, 12 August 1998.

[57]See *www.antonov.com*, about us link (accessed 8 April 2010).

[58]J Baumann, 'Pamodzi to be African Agent for Antonov', *Business Day*, 20 May 2010, available www.businessday.co.za (accessed 30 June 2010).

[59]Interview with Ndaba Ntsele, 6 April 2010.

technicians and runways, for example – to service the planes, and it would be far too expensive to build and provide this infrastructure from scratch. The second issue of was that of language and culture. The Ukraine was an ex-Soviet nation. As such, its language of business was Russian and its systems were still mired in communist bureaucracy. PIH would therefore need to do business through an interpreter, which was never ideal, and it would have to find a way to manage the bureaucracy. Added to this was the fact that Antonov was a government-owned entity, which would simply deepen the bureaucracy.[60] However, Ntsele reckoned that government bureaucracy was pretty similar to private sector bureaucracy, and he had been faced with his fair share of that in dealing with some of the largest corporations in the world. So this was not enough to put him off the deal.

The deal-breaker would have been the inability to find an infrastructure and technology partner. Ntsele had sought to address this by asking organisations which already had the necessary infrastructure in place to partner with PIH in the deal. He knew that going into partnership would mean that PIH would have to share the profits but, he said, "in a deal like this, if you don't share it with other people and try to do it by yourself, the answer is zero. It will never even get off the ground. In the end, 10% of eight billion is better than 0% of eight billion."[61] There were three organisations with the necessary infrastructure in South Africa: Mafikeng Airport in the North West Province, Denel Aviation [a division of the government-owned defence equipment manufacturer Denel (Pty) Ltd, which serviced military aircraft] and South African Airways (SAA) Technical, which serviced passenger planes for SAA and other international airlines. An initial approach to Mafikeng Airport did not solicit the enthusiasm that Ntsele had anticipated. "They did not see the opportunity as we saw it," he said, "but they did leave the door open, saying that if we did manage to secure the deal, we could come back to them."[62]

Ntsele then decided to go directly to the Department of Trade and Industry (DTI) and ask for its support in acquiring the licence by guaranteeing to Antonov that PIH would be able to secure the necessary infrastructure partner in either Mafikeng, Denel Aviation or SA Technical Services (both of the latter two being government-owned). High-level DTI representatives accompanied PIH to the negotiations with Antonov, and PIH secured the licence.

This then gave Ntsele greater leverage when he approached SA Technical Services and Denel Aviation, because he could tell them that he had a definite deal with potential to bring them huge business into the future. His timing was right with Denel Aviation, which was looking to expand its operations and was therefore interested in partnering with PIH to secure the Antonov business. From Ntsele's perspective, the deal was "made in heaven", because Denel Aviation was already servicing planes from all across Africa, it had the space, it had the technicians and engineers, and it had the necessary training facilities.[63]

Conclusion

As Ntsele prepared to announce the Antonov deal and the launch of Pamodzi Aviation the next day, he still had to formalise PIH's relationship with Denel Aviation. His plan was for PIH to take a stake of between 40% and 50% in Denel Aviation in return for the business that the Antonov licence would bring to Denel. He thought that the deal should take place in the form of a "reasonable share swap, because we are talking about values that are not tangible",[64] and knew that the Antonov licence had given him a way into Denel that would not have been possible otherwise. "If I had just wanted a stake in Denel, without Antonov, I would have paid a fortune. Antonov gives me leverage," he noted.[65]

So he was convinced that the deal made sound business sense, and he believed that Pamodzi Aviation could make billions of rands. There were planes that needed servicing, and there would be a market for new Antonov planes in Africa by virtue of their suitability for the environment. He had just discovered that the entire Angolan fleet of military planes needed to be

[60]*Ibid.*
[61]*Ibid.*
[62]*Ibid.*
[63]*Ibid.*
[64]*Ibid.*
[65]*Ibid.*

replaced. Now Antonov was also prepared to allow Pamodzi Aviation to service and sell its helicopters. For him, this was the "cherry on the top". It had been "mission impossible" when he started out, and now the deal had come to fruition.[66]

Still, he knew that there was no absolute certainty that it would work out, and wondered whether his belly button was correct this time, or whether there were any real-world issues that he had overlooked which could cause Pamodzi Aviation to fail.

[66] *Ibid.*

CASE 3

"Connecting the world through games": Creating shared value in the case of Zynga's corporate social strategy

By Laura P. Hartman, Jenny Mead, Patricia H. Werhane, Danielle Christmas

1. Mark Pincus and Zynga's development

After receiving his M.B.A. from Harvard Business School, Mark Pincus co-founded a series of Internet start-ups, including the social networking site Tribe Networks and the software service-based companies FreeLoader and SupportSoft, the first of which he sold for $38 million in 1995 and the second of which went public in 2000. He was also an early investor in successful Web 2.0 initiatives including Napster and Facebook. When he launched Zynga in January 2007, in an old potato chip factory in San Francisco, Pincus brought his entrepreneurial interest in social networking to bear on his experiences with casual games and Facebook's flexibility, and used the Facebook platform as a foundation for code. He felt that someone needed to answer the question, "What am I going to do while I'm hanging out on Facebook?" Pincus developed his first Zynga game, Texas Hold 'Em (later called Zynga Poker), and soon found that he had 400,000 monthly active users (MAUs) in just four months while, at the same time, he refined and optimized Zynga's potential to actually make money (called "monetization potential" in the industry) (Chaim & Mendelson 2009, p. 3).

By January 2008, Zynga had 27 employees and was known for its innovative social networking approach to classic games such as poker and Risk that allowed people to play games online while also connecting – or reconnecting – with friends (Stone 2008). By November of the same year, the company had grown to 150 employees and had received an infusion of cash from various backers, including venture capital firm Kleiner Perkins. In January 2009 the media started a round of speculations about Zynga's worth that reached estimates of $5 billion by July 2010 (Hopkins 2010,

see also Takahashi 2010) and over $10 billion by April 2011 when rumors of an IPO began to surface (Pepitone 2011).

At the same time Pincus sat down for a lunch with his sister, DePaul University Vincent de Paul Professor of Business Ethics, Laura Hartman. Hartman describes that afternoon as a possible tipping point of a new direction for Zynga, which had by then become one of the most successful and popular social gaming companies in the world. (For a list of names and roles of individuals involved in this case, please see Exhibit 1.)

[I]n January of '09, Mark had reached a point in his career where he was ready ... to move forward with a greater impact on the world, in terms of what role Zynga would play, because Zynga was really a culmination of a lot of his business efforts. So, we had lunch and both of us brainstormed about what that could look like. Mark had been thinking about this for a long time, about what to do and how to place his social vision into practice. Our backgrounds and experiences complimented each other because I had spent years working with corporations, trying to encourage them to do something. So it came together. (Author interview March 19, 2010)

Although these ideas had been germinating with Pincus for some time, that discussion with his sister was the initial step in an effort to build a new brand of corporate social strategy that would avoid the "vicious circle" of unsustainability that has plagued the traditional philanthropy model, and also leverage the unique resources of social media. However, the stakes of this social strategy, tied up as they would be in the non-profit partners with whom Zynga wanted to

This case study has been peer reviewed by the editorial board of the Journal of Business Ethics Education (JBEE). For further information on this journal please visit the JBEE website at www.neilsonjournals.com/JBEE/

EXHIBIT 1   LIST OF NAMED INDIVIDUALS IN CASE

- Mark Pincus, CEO, Zynga
- Laura Pincus Hartman, Vincent de Paul Professor of Business Ethics, DePaul University *and* Director of External Partnerships, Zynga.org
- Virginia McArthur, Director of Operations for Zynga.org and one of Zynga's Executive Producers
- Bim Majekodunmi, Producer of FarmVille, Zynga

- Bill Mooney, was vice president and general manager of FarmVille (has now moved on to another studio)
- Scott Koenigsberg, general manager of Mafia Wars
- Hugh de Loayza, Zynga's vice president of business development

develop relationships, were equally linked to the company's pre-existing corporate strategy. For this young and unabashedly successful company, the new social strategy that Pincus would develop, culminating in the successful launch of Zynga.org, represented an intentional tangent from what Zynga had done overwhelmingly well – develop highly profitable interactive social games.

As Mark Pincus sat in his office at the end of January 2009, weighing his interest in a new kind of social strategy against the arguments of Zynga's studios and vice presidents, he was forced to confront the stakes of making the most wise and effective decision for Zynga's present and future shareholders. Based on the company's success, his corporate strategies had worked thus far. Pincus had an eagle-eye focus on effective productivity and scalability, "you've got to find some way to keep everybody going in productive directions when you're not in the room" (Bryant 2010). His answer was a leadership style that encouraged each of his employees to take responsibility and become decision-makers within their own autonomous units.

> I'd turn people into CEOs. One thing I did at my second company was to put white sticky sheets on the wall, and I put everyone's name on one of the sheets, and I said, "By the end of the week, everybody needs to write what you're CEO of, and it needs to be something really meaningful." And that way, everyone knows who's CEO of what and they know whom to ask instead of me. And it was really effective. People liked it. And there was nowhere to hide.

However, in a firm filled with CEOs, how does the real CEO add a new direction? Pincus needed to make a decision about whether to expand Zynga's fulfilled mission to include a new kind of social engagement and, if so, how to help his game studios to see the bottom-line value in participating in this engagement of their own accord.

2. The evolution of Zynga.org

By June 2009, Mark Pincus's already highly-successful company Zynga, whose employees now numbered over 700, introduced FarmVille, a game that soon reached 70 million users a day and posted the highest monthly active users (MAUs) in the industry (Coelln 2010). FarmVille asked players to build virtual farms, in which they planted and harvested crops, bought and tended to animals, and furnished their farms with buildings and other decorations (Exhibit 2 below). Players invited friends to be their FarmVille neighbors using their Facebook social network and, once connected, could send gifts of animals and other items, fertilize their neighbors' crops, and support award-based farming projects through the co-op feature launched in April 2010. FarmVille, like all of Zynga's social games, was free but players could buy specialty items in the market, or purchase other mechanics that would accelerate their rate of farm growth, allow them to "level up" (access higher levels in the game) or offer them rewards or points. Virginia McArthur, Director of Operations for Zynga.org and one of Zynga's Executive Producers, who played and spent money on FarmVille, described her own motives for spending actual money in the game, or "monetizing".

> [Monetizing] to me is the efficiency when you have two children and you don't have to play all the time. And the unwither tool on FarmVille [which allows you to revive crops that have died for lack of tending] hands down was my saving grace. Because people can come to my farm and

EXHIBIT 2 ZYNGA'S FARMVILLE

Source: Laura P. Hartman. Used with permission.

it always looks happy and healthy. (Author interview, April 1, 2010)

Like other social games, FarmVille's most valuable segment of the market demographic included those players – primarily women and older adults – disinclined to access other gaming platforms. Pincus accounted for the market's shift in virtual gaming development strategy by explaining, "Gaming is a fundamentally social experience, not a single-player experience, and not a technology experience. We are bringing gaming back to its roots" (Bagga 2009). The innovative core of Zynga's corporate strategy consisted of this integration of the essential sociality of gaming with the opportunities for connecting with friends, and making new connections, through social networking platforms.

3. The formalization of a new social strategy: Zynga.org

The ideas that had inspired both Pincus and Hartman as brother and sister for much of their lives, and which they had discussed during their 2009 lunch, evolved over the next few months into concrete plans: a new intra-company sector called Zynga.org. In establishing its vision, Zynga.org had settled on a shared global and domestic focus on supporting the Millennium Development Goals (MDGs) since it was felt that these Goals represented universal values relevant to all players in all countries where Zynga games were played. Because the MDGs embody a significant undertaking, and because Hartman's prior expertise in the area, the Zynga.org team determined that, to begin, contributions would focus on Goals 1, 2 and 3 – the alleviation of global poverty and hunger, universal education and gender equality.

It became a priority that Zynga.org proceed with the highest possible levels of integrity and knowledge. Hartman's preexisting relationships with two grass roots organizations in rural Haiti, among others, were a key consideration in the initial selection of nonprofit partners. The co-directors and Pincus decided to make use of these relationships to focus the nascent project's efforts; an entry-level breadth of knowledge became one of the team's core criteria for Zynga.org (Author interview with Virginia McArthur, April 1, 2010). Zynga.org reflected on what such a partnership might look like, given the organizations' focus on families and self-reliance, and what Zynga franchise would be most compatible with these particular organizations.

Because FarmVille represented Zynga's largest user base, it was the natural platform for Zynga.org's official launch. Although the company had engaged in community partnerships before the creation of Zynga .org, FarmVille would be the first venue in which the company considered using this emerging social strategy on a macro scale while serving Zynga.org's developing mission.

4. Moving forward

With Zynga.org established, and with the specific focus on implementing social changes through the sale of virtual social goods, the social vision that Mark Pincus and his sister Laura Hartman had discussed over lunch in January was on the way to becoming a reality. It was time for implementation, and projects in earthquake-torn Haiti would be Zynga.org's first venture. The plan started to take shape. McArthur and Hartman proposed an innovative strategy to the FarmVille team, whereby the users would be offered a limited time, special edition item within the game: "Sweet Seeds for Haiti". Through FarmVille, Zynga would contribute 50% of all proceeds from each sale ($5.00, in the "Sweet Seeds" case) to two partner organizations: FATEM and Fonkoze. FATEM is a community organization based in both Haiti and Boston dedicated to the education of Haiti's youth. FATEM's central project at this time was its partnership with Zynga in the creation of a K-12 education institution with a focus on quality education, income generation and financial literacy. Starting with the May 2010 Sweet Seeds Zynga.org campaign, all campaign monies raised for FATEM went entirely towards the construction of FATEM's K-12 school L'Ecole de Choix, or "School of Choice" (Zynga, n.d.).[1] Fonkoze is one of Haiti's few truly grassroots microfinance institutions as well as Haiti's largest with more than 40 branches covering every region of the country (Fonkoze 2010c). With a vision "to provide the means for all Haitians, even the poorest, to participate in the economic development of the country", Fonkoze established its target group as women because, "women are the backbone of the Haitian economy and the doorway into the family unit" (Fonkoze 2010b). As of July, 2010, Fonkoze was serving more than 45,000 women borrowers, most of whom lived and worked in the countryside of Haiti, and more than 200,000 savers

(Fonkoze 2010c). Fonkoze's primary function had been to organize solidarity groups, small groups of women who, through shared mentorship and oversight, pursued literacy, healthcare, and business skills as they worked with Fonkoze to apply for small- to medium-sized loans.

As the co-directors introduced the FarmVille team to these partners, Zynga staff took interest in and ownership over the creative possibilities of the campaign. The first Sweet Seeds for Haiti campaign was launched on October 1, 2009, offering players a two-week window to exchange 25 FarmVille Cash in game currency (as mentioned, equivalent to $5.00) to buy and plant the special edition sweet potato seeds. Players were informed through the purchase process that Zynga would contribute 50% from the sale of all Sweet Seeds for Haiti products to support "sustainable and healthy meals for children and their families," with 25% going to FATEM and 25% going to Fonkoze (Exhibit 3 below).

During regular game play, FarmVille players purchase and plant seeds, selling the crops grown for game currency once they could be harvested. The Sweet Seeds sweet potatoes, selected for being indigenous to Haiti (Fonkoze 2009), had special properties. Once players purchased the license, they unlocked the ability to buy the new "high-return" sweet potato crop for nominal in-game currency. The seeds were inexpensive relative to other seeds, grew quickly, and the sweet potatoes sold for much more game currency than comparable FarmVille crops. In addition, Sweet Seeds were the first FarmVille crops to be "unwithering". Usually, once a crop was full grown, players had a limited amount of time to harvest their crop before it withered, wasting the game currency and time spent growing the withered crops. However, the Sweet Seeds sweet potatoes never withered, allowing a player to plant the seeds without the fear that, should they not return to their farm in a timely manner, their investment in the crop would be lost.

These built-in features, designed by the FarmVille franchise to make this limited edition product more attractive, were supported by additional strategies. During the two-week campaign, Sweet Seeds was the top featured marketplace item, prompting players to either buy or renew their license upon signing in, and also appeared as the first and most prominent item in the FarmVille Market. With the Sweet Seeds campaign, Zynga.org made clear its intention to foster and maintain a long-term connection between players and

[1] For a video discussion of this evolution and the resulting project, please see http://www.youtube.com/watch?v=lhNvF1cxEN4

EXHIBIT 3 SWEET SEEDS FOR HAITI

Source: Zynga. Used with permission.

non-profit partners, allowing players to forge a vested interest in specific aid projects. In McArthur's words, "we are [committed] to letting users track where their funding is going and at what point the funding is being used," and the company's website and press releases were designed to make this clear (Author interview, April 1, 2010). A self-sustaining feedback loop between players, non-profit partners, and the communities assisted by the funds was central to the Zynga.org expansion of Zynga's mission to "connect the world through games".

The campaign received an exceptionally positive reception among its user community, and throughout the media (Ashby 2009, Takahashi 2009, Nash 2009, Gunnin 2008). Pincus debriefed the implementation of the fall 2009 Sweet Seeds campaign, which raised more than $1 million.

We experimented with SFSPCA-branded virtual goods. We found that people that wouldn't normally participate would buy them if it went to a cause. We went from a test to full-scale deployment with Sweet Seeds for Haiti. It opened my eyes to the potential of social gaming and how we'll see virtual goods raise amazing amounts of money for great causes in a scalable way. (Cutler 2010)

Subsequent to this first launch, Zynga.org partnered with Zynga's game studios to offer campaigns on a regular basis throughout multiple studios with varying in-game elements in order to find the most effective features for users and results. (Exhibit 4 below)

During this start-up period, the Zynga.org directors began to develop the Zynga.org criteria that would help them in the decision-making that would confront them on a daily basis. These criteria addressed issues such as the organizational focus on worldwide rather than solely domestic challenges in determining the causes or recipients to support, which became particularly important following the success of the original Zynga.org campaign. Reflecting Zynga's user base of socially networked players around the world, Zynga.org would not be identified with a single geographical region or nation, but with nonprofit partners that could have a direct impact on entrenched problems about which most Zynga game players were likely to care. The success of that first campaign in October, 2009 led to an influx of "fifteen to twenty requests a week from organizations about partnering with us and Zynga," as McArthur described it; so having these articulated standards was as much for the directors' peace of mind, in the difficult task of turning away important organizations doing meaningful and urgent work, as it was in providing a satisfactory explanation for the rejected partner (Author interview, April 1, 2010). Other criteria included quality measures such as rankings by Charity Navigator and the Better Business Bureau, transparency, the ability to provide a detailed and accurate accounting of Zynga-specific contributions by program, among other metrics.

Zynga.org made a deliberate choice to differentiate itself as something of its own franchise within the company and McArthur connected this decision to the company's interest in sustainability and core fortification.

EXHIBIT 4 TABLE OF ZYNGA'S EXTERNAL PARTNERSHIPS – ZYNGA.ORG CAMPAIGN DATES

Date	Game	Campaign	Recipient Organization
Mar. 28 2009	YoVille	SFSPCA: Dog/Cat	SFSPCA
Oct. 1	FarmVille	Sweet Seeds 1/Haiti	FATEM/Fonkoze
Nov. 11	Mafia Wars	Dog/Tags	Fisher House
Nov. 13	FarmVille	Sweet Seeds 2/Haiti	FATEM/Fonkoze
Dec. 15	FishVille	Holiday Promotion: Glitter Globe	World Food Programme
Dec. 16	Mafia Wars	Holiday Promotion/Haitian Drum	FATEM
Dec. 16	Poker	Holiday Promotion/Chip Package: Fonkoze	Fonkoze
Dec. 17	YoVille	Holiday Promotion: Cameroon Platter	World Food Programme
Dec. 18	Coaster	Holiday Promotion: Cameroon Cups	World Food Programme
Jan. 14 2010	Mafia Wars	Haiti Relief Fund: Haitian Drum	World Food Programme
Jan. 14	Poker	Haiti Relief Fund: 2$ Chip Package	World Food Programme
Jan. 15	FarmVille	Haiti Relief Fund: White Corn	World Food Programme
Jan. 15	FishVille	Haiti Relief Fund: Haiti Wrasse	World Food Programme
Mar. 10	Mafia Wars	Exploding Teddy Bear	HDSA
Mar. 22	FishVille	Water Week; Water Wrasse	Water.org
May. 4	FarmVille	Sweet Seeds 3/Haiti - New School	FATEM
May. 27	Mafia Wars	Memorial Day Sale - Discounted items	Fisher House
JUNE. 11–20	FishVille	Audubon Sea Turtle and baby turtle	Audubon
April, May, June	YoVille	SFSPCA: Dog/Cat	SFSPCA

Source: Zynga. Used with permission.

I know that we are in our infancy at Zynga and not associat[ing Zynga.org] to a business wouldn't get the attention that I feel like it deserved...I realized that if I did not have metrics to prove the success of the campaign, I would not get the attention or the resources from the teams in which to make that happen....I needed to basically say, "Here are my metrics... to prove that I am a viable entity within this company. (Author interview, April 1, 2010)

This metric assessment along with the other nuances of implementation and back-end evaluation were at the center of McArthur's operations directorship. Hartman's role, as the director of external partnerships, was to establish a rigorous vetting process in connection with due diligence, to manage these relationships once formed, and to participate on the ground once the projects were in the implementation phase in order to ensure that the ultimate fund recipients received a true benefit. The identification of partners who, by virtue of size, could accommodate this kind of

field-level participation and assessment was crucial (Author interview with Virginia McArthur, April 1, 2010). Recalling once again Zynga's mission, "connecting the world through games", it was vital that Zynga.org's organizational partners and all resulting campaigns would have a significant impact on fund recipients.

As Zynga.org evolved and focused on its own sustainability, the directors continued to refine these core criteria – to focus interests and efforts – and to articulate more specific criteria for potential partners. Again referencing scale and its ability to provide users a pipeline to the concrete use of funds raised – e.g. FarmVille players could now receive periodic updates about the application of recent funding – McArthur elaborated on Zynga.org's chosen values.

As Hartman dealt with the external criteria for the selection and validation of partners, McArthur had to negotiate reasonable internal expectations in the selection of franchise partners. With more than twenty game studios active at various times, Zynga ran games that ranged from those in beta mode, to just-launched games that were still struggling to go viral, all the way to industry giant FarmVille, with almost 60 million MAUs in July 2010 (AppData 2010). When assessing how and when to introduce a possible Zynga.org campaign, McArthur noted that the key question for a potential franchise partner was, "Do I even have the resources to support this in my game right now?" (Author interview, April 1, 2010). Together, the directors established a benchmark of games with one million daily active users (DAUs) for the introduction of a Zynga.org campaign; this threshold limited the base of potential Zynga.org franchise partners to FarmVille, YoVille, FrontierVille, Mafia Wars, FishVille, PetVille, Poker, and Café World (Author interview with Virginia McArthur, April 1, 2010). Of those eight, five had already launched their own Zynga.org campaigns by June 2010.

The relationships between franchises and their potential partners developed organically from the implementation of these criteria. For example, following the success of Zynga.org's Sweet Seeds campaign, Pincus forwarded an email to the co-directors introducing Water.org, which seemed precisely appropriate for the FishVille studio. Water.org presented as a potential partner organization that allowed for manageable scale, proved thematically relevant to the franchise, and was also saleable to the user from an operational and content-based perspective. Moreover, the compatibility of the Water.org partnership with the pre-established Haiti partnership supported Zynga.org's evolving goal of establishing "a centralized theme, a centralized effort, such that we could make the biggest impact" possible" (Author interview with Virginia McArthur, April 1, 2010). Their mission was fulfilled, at least in part, by the fact that a user of both FarmVille[2] and FishVille could, by connecting these efforts, be sufficiently confident to monetize in both games with this increased impact in mind.

5. Expectations

Bim Majekodunmi, producer of FarmVille, joined Zynga in September of 2009, less than a month before Zynga.org's first in-game launch. The expectation that Majekodunmi join that studio, maintain its success, and simultaneously sort out the orientation of the

Zynga.org project in the studio's roadmap, raised an important challenge in this synergy: there was no question that Zynga's exponential growth imposed a continuous challenge for both existing staff as well as for new employees to adapt quickly. By integrating the Zynga.org social strategy into the company's mission, Pincus risked distracting these employees from the already arduous and high stakes task of learning and implementing Zynga's standards for success. As Bim reported,

> *[m]y first week, they told me to incorporate the idea for [the first Zynga.org campaign] Sweet Seeds into FarmVille's plan. It was hard to go live [placing the first Zynga.org campaign products online] with that so quickly…because I just got there.[3] I had to incorporate the opinions of people I barely knew and stick to the timing. (Author interview, April 1, 2010)*

Even Pincus questioned whether the Zynga.org strategy would be successful in the long run because of the question of economic sustainability from the studios' perspectives. If any venture, such as a studio, would be measured based on traditional bottom line metrics, Zynga would have to consider the impact of a Zynga.org campaign on those metrics.

> *If you have only a set amount of time and you have to hit your numbers, are you going to work on that item that has money going elsewhere or are you going to give your attention to the item that brings the most money back to your studio? (Author interview with Mark Pincus, April 1, 2010)*

Pincus was concerned not only for questions surrounding employee motivation, but also for perspective of Zynga executives who were responsible for setting company-wide, rather than studio-level, goals. Bill Mooney, the 30th employee of a now 700+ base of workers, was vice president and general manager of FarmVille. Mooney was introduced to Zynga.org while serving as GM of the Mafia Wars studio. His response to Pincus's proposition, though supportive "in theory", was much more critical.

> *I believe in "do-gooder" stuff; I was an organizer before I came to this business. But how often we*

---

[2] FarmVille was the franchise partner for FATEM and Fonkoze during the Fall 2009 Zynga.org campaigns, Sweet Seeds for Haiti I and II. See also, www.zynga.org

[3] Like other social games, FarmVille was in real-time, allowing online users to sign in at their convenience and, through personal avatars, work on their unique simulated farm. Because the game was always available, studios had to "go live" with new features and market items without a lapse in availability, raising the stakes for Majekounmi to understand FarmVille's culture in order to introduce a game-appropriate item the first time around that would launch the brand new company-wide social strategy.

do [a Zynga.org campaign] is the real question.
The most important thing is sustainability. *We*
have to measure sustainability against the risk of
cannibalizing other revenue. (Author interview
with Bill Mooney, April 1, 2010)

Scott Koenigsberg, general manager of Mafia Wars, expressed a similar concern about campaign cadence, saying that it might be "hard to strike the balance of establishing a regular cadence versus getting into a cycle of donating that exhausts [user] goodwill" (Author interview, April 1, 2010). Both additional challenges as well as new opportunities arose in considering how the interaction between the play of the games and the .org campaign would impact on Zynga's financial returns. As with all social games, Zynga's games rely on players' repeated use, which results from a number of in-game elements, ranging from the possibility that one's crops may wither, to missed chances to earn in-game benefits, to a sense that you are disappointing your friends if you do not send gifts that your friends need to level up in the game. A Zynga.org campaign has the potential to increase revenue for the host studio, by offering players an additional level of connection with each other, and with their gaming experience. However, if the campaigns were experienced by players as a call for contributions, this potential could fail to pan out, resulting in revenue sacrifice.

As Majekodunmi told it, however, her team's genuine excitement about the project mitigated any potential conflict or disorientation. "It was a new challenge but it gave us such a good feeling to do it that it didn't matter" (Author interview with Scott Koenigsberg, April 1, 2010).

Pincus concluded that the final measures of a campaign's suitability for Zynga.org were its place in what he called the "virtuous circle" (Author interview, April 1, 2010) as well as its measurable impact. "We have millions of players that raise millions of dollars to reach millions of people. But then again, this makes these people, these millions of people playing our game, happy" (Author interview with Virginia McArthur, April 1, 2010).

6. The original 50/50 profitable partnership model

At its inception, McArthur and Hartman had to determine how to apportion funds raised through Zynga.org campaigns. What should be the percentage split between the recipient organization and the partnering studio? After much consideration by the Zynga.org co-directors, pursuing and analyzing alternative

models of corporate giving, the company originally settled on a fifty-fifty split. For Pincus,

[s]omething feels right about [settling on] fifty-fifty. First of all, it feels more like that's a partnership. It's like, "Okay, we're partnering with Fonkoze or whoever." I think the user can understand that we need to sustain the program. At seventy-five percent, I think the studios are less motivated and it would all of a sudden be a tax again and a more traditional charity. So I think we would be giving away so much of the revenues that our group…would have a hard time justifying it as a business operation. (Author interview, April 1, 2010)

Although they later opted to go well beyond, it was this critical balance that the co-directors initially sought in order to be both intra-organizationally justifiable and externally market-sustainable.

The co-directors examined a variety of corporate social strategy models in connection with many widely known corporate humanitarian campaigns. For instance, some corporations maintained a completely separate foundation for their giving operations, such as Salesforce.org or Google.org. Other corporations partnered with the (RED) initiative, a network organized for the purpose of eliminating AIDS in Africa (Exhibit 5). According to the (RED) fact sheet,

[(RED)] works with the world's best brands to make unique (PRODUCT) RED-branded products and direct up to 50% of their gross profits to the Global Fund to invest in African AIDS programs with a focus on the health of women and children. (RED) was not a charity or "campaign". It was an economic initiative that aims to deliver a sustainable flow of private sector money to the Global Fund. (RED, n.d.)

Most firms would term their orientations in this arena "corporate social responsibility" (CSR) or philanthropy. However, Zynga.org explicitly worked toward a process of creating shared value (CSV), which strives to ensure a return – whether financial or otherwise – to each stakeholder involved. In this way, each participant has a significant stake in the success of the campaign. However, the variability in corporate giving models led to confusion over Zynga.org's original fifty-fifty strategy, particularly following its campaign to raise funds immediately following the January 2010 earthquake, when it shifted permanently to a strategy of 100% contribution to recipient organizations. In an effort to provide disaster relief as

EXHIBIT 5 (RED) INITIATIVE GIVING MODELS

- Bugaboo Strollers: donates 1% of all company proceeds.

- Nike: donates 100% of the proceeds from the sale of (PRODUCT) RED items.

- Gap, Inc.: donates 50% of the proceeds from the sale of (PRODUCT) RED items.

- Armani: donates 40% of the gross profit proceeds from the sale of (PRODUCT) RED items.

- Converse: donates between 5% and 15% of the proceeds from the sale of (PRODUCT) RED items.

- Apple: donates between $10 and 10% of the proceeds from the sale of (PRODUCT) RED items.

- Hallmark: donates 8% of the net wholesale proceeds from the sale of (PRODUCT) RED items.

- Starbucks: donates between 5 cents and $1 of the proceeds from the sale of (PRODUCT) RED items.

Source: http://www.joinred.com/aboutred/about_red__partners

quickly and as significantly as possible to those in desperate need, and because Zynga was already on the ground in Haiti, the firm decided to offer 100% of all proceeds from the five-day launch for that singular purpose. Although well intended, this modification did lead to misunderstandings. In an attempt to place Zynga within the matrix of corporate contributions, Brazilian newspaper *Folha* published a chart comparing Zynga.org's percentage of giving against other high visibility corporations with long-term humanitarian campaigns (Exhibit 6). Because metrics justified its continuation, all subsequent campaigns remained at the 100% level.

7. Monetization, and reputation management

In addition to monetizing through direct payment for in-game virtual goods and virtual social goods, Zynga and other social gaming companies had used "lead generation offers", allowing users to sign up for virtual offers, such as text message subscriptions or video rentals, in exchange for game credits. Players who were not able to or preferred not to spend money on the site for Zynga "cash" had the option of responding to these offers instead, and these lead-generating transactions then monetized players who might otherwise not have provided revenue in the traditional pay-to-play model. This form of monetization came under scrutiny in the fall of 2009, only a few weeks after the October 1st launch of Zynga.org's Sweet Seeds campaign, when *Tech-Crunch*'s Michael Arrington (2009a) published a scathing critique of Zynga's lead generation practices in the much discussed article, "ScamVille: The Social Gaming Ecosystem of Hell". While lead generation

offers in themselves were considered relatively benign, Arrington accused Zynga of accruing as much as one-third of its income, with the tacit support of Facebook, by knowingly working with scam advertisers who would place deceptive offers. Arrington claimed that the offers would manipulate users into downloading software and accepting pricey, recurring mobile subscriptions, both constructed in a way that prevented the average user from removing these features.

As critics and users joined in the criticism, Zynga had a quick turn-around time on its reply; Pincus responded by immediately announcing in his November 2, 2009 blog post that the company would remove all mobile offers of any kind from the site, that it had already terminated its relationship with its principal cell phone subscription offer provider, and that it planned to screen all lead generation offers moving forward before placing any new ones on the site (Pincus 2009). Arrington was not satisfied, though, and on November 6, 2009 he answered Pincus:

> *Zynga CEO Mark Pincus said earlier this week that he intends to make sure his company's games don't include scammy offers in the future...But what he didn't say in that blog post is that Zynga has been scamming users from the beginning quite intentionally as part of their revenue model. (Arrington 2009b)*

Arrington (2009b) was armed with Pincus's own words; he linked his article to a video of the CEO speaking at a StartUp@Berkeley bar mixer in which Pincus explained his early strategy by saying that he "funded [Zynga] myself but did every horrible thing in the book to, just to get revenues right away... We did anything possible just to get revenues so that we could

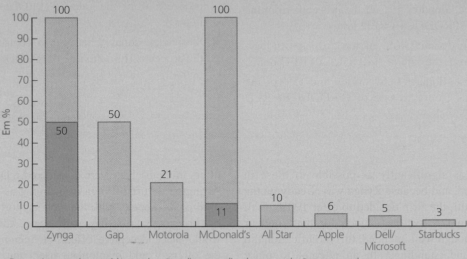

EXHIBIT 6   FOLHA PLEDGE COMPARISON

Donations from sales

How companies pledged in relation to sales of products linked to humanitarian campaigns.

Estes números desconsideram doações diretas realizadas sem relação com vendas

Source: Mauricio Kanno, "Doações não devem depender de lucros, diz especialista sobre 'FarmVille,'" *Folha Online* (Mar. 24, 2010), http://www1.folha.uol.com.br/folha/informatica/ult124u711295.shtml.

grow and be a real business." Pincus was perfectly willing to eat his words. "I didn't mean to be so crass," he said, sighing. "But I was talking in a *bar.*" He later clarified, "I respect companies that build a service that can scale *and* make a lot of money" (Hendrickson 2010).

Under separate circumstances, and long after Arrington's articles and the revival of the Berkeley video, the company's relationship with principal platform, Facebook, became strained. Facebook suspended Zynga's brand-new game FishVille for a few days on claims of advertising violations (Arrington 2009c). Facebook clearly explained that its decision was unrelated to Arrington's article, and all seemed to have been settled since the two companies announced a five-year deal to work together (Ware 2010). Social gaming insiders noted that each organization faced significant challenges at the time: Facebook was confronted by claims of privacy violations, while both Zynga and Facebook were subject to several lawsuits specifically related to shared issues (Swartz 2009, Tate 2009).

In February 2010, Pincus was interviewed by CNN and "acknowledged not being vigilant enough with the automated ads that appeared on Zynga games during the company's early days." Pincus explained, "[w]e were playing Whack-a-Mole. Every time we found one of these or got a complaint, we would take them down. Eventually…we realized we had to take a much more aggressive stance than a normal web site" (Gross 2010). While the simultaneity of the Zynga.org launch with the ScamVille crisis posed strategic challenges during the start of a new and developing social strategy, the overlap was absent from media analyses of the company through November and December 2009. More specifically, as a part of their public relations strategy, the company chose not to capitalize on the Zynga.org venture in support of reputation management.

The special nature of Zynga's social strategy forced Pincus, Hartman and McArthur to consider shareholder accountability, as the company pursued a course that produced measurable benefits in exchange for those resources directed toward extra-corporate purposes. Their decision to avoid engaging Zynga.org during the time when Zynga was taking the greatest public heat over "ScamVille" was not necessarily black and white. Pincus reflected that, "in retrospect, staying away from PR [at that time] may not have been the best strategy" (Piskorski & Chen 2009). Yet, it is highly likely that drawing on the .org campaign for reputation management purposes during the early stages of the campaign's development – before its partnerships with nonprofits and players had taken root – would have backfired, as Zynga.org could have been perceived merely as a short-term reputational fix, rather than a long-term committed corporate social strategy that predated the scandal.

In January 2010, Mark Pincus was voted Crunchies CEO of the Year by a group of Silicon Valley's most influential blogs.[4] As a part of his acceptance speech, Pincus said of Zynga.org's most recent fundraising campaign, "[i]t opened my eyes to the potential of social gaming and how we'll see virtual goods raise amazing amounts of money for great causes in a scalable way" (Cutler 2010). As he further invested Zynga's resources in its evolving social strategy, and the company's growth and reputation could set up the firm for the possibility of increasingly media attention, he would have to determine if and how Zynga.org could intervene in the media discourse before future assaults, and how the project might contribute to the most effective PR strategy once Scamville-like campaigns had already happened.

8. Benefits analysis

8.1. Zynga. Zynga's interests in virtual social goods have been manifold; one of the traditional challenges to encouraging campaigns of this nature has been demonstration of bottom line benefit from historically soft metrics. For instance, the benefit of Hartman's preexisting relationships with the Haiti partners was evident following each of the more than a dozen campaigns. After seven months refining Zynga.org's efficiency, they had a "Zynga speed" precision in turning around detailed progress reports to Zynga's user base. Following the third Sweet Seeds campaign in May 2010, which was the 17th launch for the organization, the funds raised were put directly and immediately into Zynga partner FATEM's L'Ecole du Choix project (the "School of Choice," a school in Mirebalais, Haiti that Zynga has helped to establish); only weeks after purchasing Sweet Seeds, users received pictures and reports on their money at work. McArthur described this feedback loop as a key tenet in the .org's mission, expressing their commitment to show the user how their participation in Sweet Seeds:

> [p]ut food in the hand of someone in Haiti who didn't have it…And [for any given campaign], I can come back and show you exactly where those funds went. I can show you video of food being distributed and then continuing for the next couple months what the [partner] will do with those funds. (Author interview, April 1, 2010)

Hartman's field expertise, due diligence and relationships eliminated the time consuming tasks of locating a focus and cultivating working partnerships with viable community organizations; as director of external partnerships, Hartman's preexisting familiarity with the organizations' missions and projects had, after seven months in operation, permitted a level of precision and transparency that posed a challenge for organizations with longer tenure but without the benefit of this experience. Leveraging Hartman's expertise made the task of constructing a new social strategy in a young company achievable, and brought Zynga.org that much closer to self sustainability following the implementation of this inaugural campaign.

However, these measures translated directly into more conventional metrics, evidencing realized gains for Zynga and providing the business case for the .org. There was an expansion of users who opted to monetize. Users who would not normally monetize would be comfortable purchasing if the funds went to a cause; perhaps they saw a more meaningful purpose to the connections beyond gaming to *gaming for good*.

Further, retention – a measure of whether uses returned to keep playing – was enhanced with an increase in user playing time ("engagement") comparing pre- and post-campaigns, and a high retention rate. Users seemed to have more reasons to come back. Finally, there was an interaction from a communications perspective. Not only was virality enhanced, since the social cause encouraged player sharing across social networks, but Zynga found that those users who opted to participate in the Zynga.org campaigns were already highly social; they had significantly more in-game friends than other players.

Following May 2010's Sweet Seeds campaign, Zynga announced that:

> In just one week, more than 45,000 FarmVille users raised $110,000 through the purchase of virtual social goods…This most recent Sweet

---

[4]Kim-Mai Cutler (2010), a blogger with *VentureBeat,* explains: "Every year, Silicon Valley's biggest blogs (including us) put together the Crunchies, an event where the tech community puts the spotlight on the best entrepreneurs, startups and investors."

Seeds program marks the first of several campaigns Zynga will launch to raise funds for the school...To check products and updates on the school's development, please visit Zynga.org. (Zynga 2010a)

The .org's ability to impact the bottom line in these visible and significant ways, and to conduct, if inadvertently, reputation management through media accounts of this work, joined to Zynga.org's regularly updated web reports, met the interests of shareholders and stakeholders. User access to details on and accounts of the material impact of their original $5 Sweet Seeds investment through the Zynga.org Facebook page and other mechanisms (Exhibit 7) created a "feel good" loop that subverted donor fatigue while the "percent of buyers [go] way up" (Author interview with Mark Pincus, April 1, 2010).

8.2. Partners. The fiscal and extra-fiscal benefits to the partner organizations could be demonstrated through the example of one of its partners, FATEM.

Since November 2009, with Zynga contributions, FATEM continued to establish itself as an agent of change in the Plateau Central region of Haiti. Its outcomes by 2010 included:

- The provision of a daily meal to 225 children and a nutrient-rich snack bar to over 2,500 school children, which made a difference in their ability to concentrate and learn in class. For many of these children, the meal or the snack bar was all they ate for the day.

- Intervention in the week following the 2010 earthquake and assistance to over 200 households with food and hygiene kits. Each of these families was hosting several internally displaced individuals or entire additional families fleeing Port-au-Prince; as many as 25 people in one home, in some cases.

- Partnership with 1000 Jobs/Haiti, through the opening of its Mirebalais office, which made it possible for 53 young men and women to earn an income between February and July 2010.

- A contribution of $15,000 to the construction project of a municipal library and technology center. The library project would raise academic achievement among Mirebalais area's students, extend literacy efforts to include professionals and the community at large, and provide technological opportunities to bridge the digital divide in Mirebalais.

EXHIBIT 7   FACEBOOK PAGE

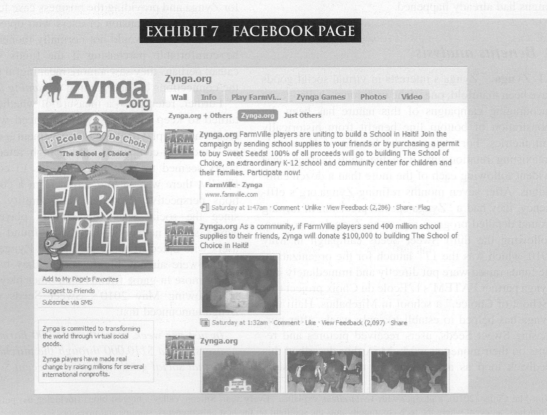

- Fund the development of Ecole de Choix in partnership with Zynga, a K-12 school and community center, intended from its inception to meet the most pressing and critical needs of those living in extreme poverty in Haiti, with a focus on quality education, income generation and financial literacy.

9. The outlook for Zynga.org

As 2010 proceeded, Zynga remained a wildly successful company, with more than 230 million monthly active users (MAUs) as of July 2010, and led the next application developer by more than 400% (AppData 2010). The company certainly saw competition: Playdom, a 2008 start-up that was acquired by Disney in July 2010, led on MySpace with its most popular game, Mobsters, and housed three of the network's four most popular applications; its games Social City and Sorority Life had boasted increasing margins of user growth on Facebook (Playdom 2010). Electronic Arts acquired Playfish in the winter of 2010 and had experienced growing MAUs in games such as Pet Society and Restaurant City (Chang & Mendelson 2009). These companies, joined by a few smaller social gaming firms, had grown so large that the 2009 projection of a market-wide 250 million players was almost satisfied by Zynga's 235 million MAUs, alone (Lacy 2009). By 2010, the market for social gaming was estimated at a potential $5 billion industry (Zacks Equity Research 2010).

In September, 2010, FarmVille ran one of its most successful campaigns ever on behalf of Haiti and Ecole de Choix (the School of Choice), second only to the launch immediately after the earthquake. In a new and novel partnership with Facebook through its Facebook Credits online payment structure, both Facebook and Zynga donated 100% of all player contributions to the school, while Zynga realized inspiring numbers of "likes" on its game and Facebook fan pages, reaching well into the millions.

An otherwise young company, according to traditional measurement standards, not only established itself as successful along conventional objective metrics, but also has placed itself at the sometimes precarious edge of its volatile market through this work. Yet, Mark Pincus and his team at Zynga and Zynga.org had all eyes forward. As market analysts anticipate a possible public offering for Zynga – and certainly its status may change over the next few years – how will this increased pressure on results impact Zynga.org's activities, decisions and metrics?

References

2010 Edelman Trust Barometer: Executive Summary (2010). Retrieved from http://www.edelman.com/trust/2010/

AppData (2010, July 31), App Leaderboard. Retrieved from http://www.appdata.com/leaderboard/apps?metric_select=mau

Arrington, M. (2009a, October 31), "ScamVille: The Social Gaming Ecosystem of Hell", *TechCrunch*. Retrieved from http://techcrunch.com/2009/10/31/scamville-the-social-gaming-ecosystem-of-hell/

Arrington, M. (2009b, November 6), "Zynga CEO Mark Pincus: 'I did every horrible thing in the book just to get revenues'", *TechCrunch*. Retrieved from http://techcrunch.com/2009/11/06/zynga-scamville-mark-pinkus-facebook/

Arrington, M. (2009c, November 8), "Zynga's FishVille Sleeps with the Fishes for Ad Violations", *TechCrunch*. Retrieved from http://techcrunch.com/2009/11/08/zyngas-fishville-swims-with-the-fishes-for-ad-violations/

Arthur, C. (2002, January 18), *Haiti in Focus*, Interlink Publishing Group.

Ashby, A. (2009, October 20), "FarmVille's Sweet Seeds Raise $487K for Charity", *Engage Digital*. Retrieved from http://www.virtualgoodsnews.com/2009/10/farmvilles-sweet-seeds-raise-487k-for-charity.html

Bagga, A. (2009, February 24), "Social Games: Interview with the CEO of Zynga", *Avalon Updates*. Retrieved from http://www.avalon-ventures.com/news/social-games-interview-with-the-ceo-of-zynga

Boyd, D. M. and Ellison, N. B. (2007), "Social Network Sites: Definition, History, and Scholarship", *Journal of Computer-Mediated Communication,* 13 (1), pp. 210–230.

Bryant, A. (2010, Jan. 30), "Are You a CEO of Something?", *New York Times,* BU2. Retrieved from http://www.nytimes.com/2010/01/31/business/31corner.html

Central Intelligence Agency (2010), "The World Factbook: Central America and the Caribbean: Haiti". Retrieved from https://www.cia.gov/library/publications/the-world-factbook/geos/ha.html

Chang, V. and Mendelson, H. (2009, December), "Social Games". HBS no. EC39. Palo Alto: Stanford Graduate School of Business.

Coelln, E. von. (2010, February 19), "How FarmVille Broke Through 30 Million Daily Active Users" [Web log]. Retrieved from http://www.voncoelln.com/eric/2010/02/19/how-farmville-finally-broke-through-30-million-daily-active-users/

Cutler, K. (2010, January 8), "Crunchies: Zynga's Mark Pincus Sees a Future for Socially-Conscious Virtual Goods", *Venture Beat.* Retrieved from http://social.venturebeat.com/2010/01/08/zynga-social-virtual-goods/

Fonkoze. (2010a), "Fonkoze's Fight Against Poverty". Retrieved from http://www.fonkoze.org/aboutfonkoze/whoweare/howworks.html

—. (2010b), "Our History: A Bank the Poor Can Call Their Own: A History of Fonkoze – Haiti's Alternative Bank for the Organized Poor". Retrieved from http://www.fonkoze.org/aboutfonkoze/whoweare/ourhistory.html

—. (2010c), "Who We Are". Retrieved from http://www. fonkoze.org/aboutfonkoze/whoweare.html

—. (2009, October 1), "Zynga Launches Global Social Strategy – Partners with Fonkoze and Others". Retrieved from http://www.fonkoze.org/docs/sweet_seeds_pr.pdf

Freeman, R. E., Harrison, J. S., and Wicks, A. C. (2007), *Managing for Stakeholders: Survival, Reputation, and Success*. New Haven, Conn.: Yale University Press.

Friedman, M. (1970, September 13), "The Social Responsibility of Business Is to Increase Its Profits", *The New York Times Magazine,* pp. 32–33, 122, 126.

Gross, D. (2010, February 23), "The Facebook Games That Millions Love (and Hate)", *CNN Tech.* Retrieved from http://www.cnn.com/2010/TECH/02/23/facebook.games/?hpt=Sbin

Gunnin, L. (2009, October 8), "Farmville's Sweet Seeds for Haiti charity Event Underway". Retrieved from http://www.associatedcontent.com/article/2262915/farmvilles_sweet_seeds_for_haiti_charity. html?cat=19

Hendrickson, M. (2010, May), "Why You Should Love the Most Hated Man on Facebook", *Details.* Retrieved from http://www.details.com/style-advice/tech-and-design/201005/mark-pincus-facebook-mafia-wars-farmville-zynga

Hill, R. P., Ainscough, T., Shank, T., and Manullang, D. (2007), "Corporate Social Responsibility and Socially Responsible Investing: A Global Perspective", *Journal of Business Ethics,* 70(2), pp. 165–174.

Hopkins, C. (2010, July 11), "Google's Stealth Investment in Game Co Zynga exceeds $100 million". Retrieved from http://www.readwriteweb.com/archives/googles_stealth_investment_in_game_co_zynga_exceed.php

Horrigan, B. (2010), *Corporate responsibility in the 21ˢᵗ century: Debates, Models and Practices across Government, Law and Business*. Cheltanham, UK: Edward Elgar Publishing.

Lacy, S. (2009, April 30), "Social Gaming Scores in the Recession", *BusinessWeek.* Retrieved from http://www.businessweek.com/technology/content/apr2009/tc20090429_963394.htm

Nash, A. (2009, October 5), "Farmville Economics" [Web log post]. Retrieved from http://blog.adamnash.com/2009/10/05/farmville-economics-sweet-seeds-are-almost-genius/ (2011, February 1).

Nestle (2010), "Creating Shared Value and Rural Development Summary Report 2010". Retrieved from http://www.nestle.com/Common/NestleDocuments/Documents/Library/Documents/Corporate_Social_Responsibility/Nestle-CSV-Summary-Report-2010-EN.pdf

Nestle (n.d.), "Water and Environmental Sustainability". Retrieved from: http://www.nestle.com/CSV/WaterAndEnvironmental Sustainability/Pages/WaterAndEnvironmentalSustainability. aspx

Nielsen Company (2010, June 15), "Social Networks/Blogs Now Account for One in Every Four and a Half Minutes Online". Retrieved from http://blog.nielsen.com/nielsenwire/online_mobile/social-media-accounts-for-22-percent-of-time-online/

Pepitone, J. (2011, June 3), "Zynga IPO Coming Soon", *CNN Money.* Retrieved from http://money.cnn.com/2011/06/03/technology/zynga_ipo/index.htm

Pincus, M. (2009, November 2), "My Take on Zynga and CPA offers" [Web log post]. Retrieved from http://markpincus.typepad.com/markpincus/2009/11/my-take-on-zynga-and-cpa-offers.html (2010, November 9).

Piskorski, M. J. and Chen, D. (2009), "Zynga". HBS no. 710-464. Boston, MA: Harvard Business School.

playdom (2010), "Until now, PlayDom Has Been the Best Kept Secret in Social Gaming". Retrieved from http://www.playdom.com/about.php

Porter, M. E. and Kramer, M. R. (2006), "Strategy and Society: The Link Between Competitive Advantage and Corporate Social Responsibility", *Harvard Business Review,* 84 (12), pp. 78–92.

Porter, M. and Kramer, M. (2011), "The Big Idea: Creating Shared Value", *Harvard Business Review,* 89 (1/2), pp. 62–77.

Red. (n.d.), "(RED) Fact Sheet". Retrieved from http://www.joinred.com/pdfs/(RED) Fact Sheet.pdf

Stone, B. (2008, January 15), "More Than Games, A Net to Snare Social Networkers", *The New York Times.* Retrieved from http://www.nytimes.com/2008/01/15/technology/15facebook.html#

Swartz, J. (2009, December 7), "Lawsuit Says Ads in Social Games Are Scamming Players", *USA Today.* Retrieved from http://www.usatoday.com/tech/gaming/2009-12-07-games07_ST_N.htm

Takahashi, D. (2010, April 6), "Could Zynga Really Be Worth $5 Billion?", *VentureBeat.* Retrieved from http://games.venturebeat.com/2010/04/06/could-zynga-really-be-worth-5-billion/

Takahashi, D. (2010, October 20), "Zynga's FarmVille Gamers Donate to Haiti's Poor via Virtual Goods", *VentureBeat.* Retrieved from http://venturebeat.com/2009/10/20/zyngas-farmville-gamers-donate-to-haitis-poor-via-virtual-goods/

Tate, R. (2009, November 19), "Facebook Named in Federal Class-action Suit over Scammy Zynga Ads", *Gawker.* Retrieved from http://gawker.com/5408472/facebook-named-in-federal-class+action-suit-over-scammy-zynga-ads

Ware, H. S. (2010, May 19), "Facebook, Zynga Bury the Hatchet", *New York Post.* Retrieved from http://www.nypost.com/p/news/business/facebook_zynga_bury_the_hatchet_7c40mXaPBzAnkJTepwohlN

Zacks Equity Research. (2010, July 9), "Viacom Enters Social Gaming", *Zacks Investment Research.* Retrieved from http://www.zacks.com/stock/news/36677/Viacom+Enters+Social+Gaming

Zynga (2010a, May 12), "FarmVille Players Raise More Than $110,000 to Build School in Haiti". Retrieved from http://www.zynga.com/about/article.php?a=20100512

— (2010b), "The SF/SPCA Is Honored to Have the Support of Zynga Players, Committed to Supporting Our Mission. Your Participation Will Benefit Our Animals!". Retrieved from http://www.zynga.org/initiatives/sfspca.php

— (n.d.), "Sweet Seeds for Haiti Campaign". Retrieved from http://zynga.org/initiatives/sweet-seeds.php

Zynga (2011), *Zynga.org Home Page.* Retrieved from http://www.zynga.org

CASE 4

Turning around a national icon: Yara Branco at Tarbes S.A.

By Ken Mark

Introduction

"We are standing at the edge of a cliff but no one seems to see the danger, no one wants to admit that we are on the precipice of disaster," thought Yara Branco, newly appointed chief executive officer (CEO) of Tarbes S.A. of Sao Paulo, Brazil. Tarbes was South America's largest manufacturer of tablet computers, with a top three share in all major urban markets. It was a warm day on January 28, 2010, and Branco was being driven to one of Tarbes's four assembly plants in San Bernardo, an industrial zone not far from the city centre. Branco continued:

Our employees can see from their own perspective that there is something wrong, but what they do not know is that each of them only sees a small part of the issue. When the pieces of the puzzle are put together, if nothing is changed, I predict that our firm will lose our leadership share in two years and be bankrupt in five years. I need to find a way to communicate with all our stakeholders, including our employees, our shareholders and our customers, to point Tarbes in a different direction.

Traffic was gridlocked as usual, a very common occurrence in bustling Sao Paulo. Sitting in the back of the car, Branco estimated that her trip might take as long as two hours for a total distance of nine kilometres. That said, she enjoyed the opportunity for a quick break from her heavy schedule of meetings these past two weeks. Recently hired as Tarbes's first female CEO, Branco had been a rising star at VBI's South American hardware sales division, where she was being groomed for a senior executive post in the next three years.

Branco was honoured to have been offered the appointment at Tarbes, a well-respected firm in Brazil.

Some would say that it was the closest Brazil had to a national champion, a home-grown entity that had been able to compete with the world's best computer firms. It had developed its own technology and its own operating system, which was based on open-source Linux. Unlike offerings from global giants such as Toshiba and HP, Tarbes's tablets were less expensive, more powerful and slimmer. They had occupied the number one spot on most Brazilian consumer "top picks" lists for at least five years now.

The firm had been expanding into Argentina and Peru, building a direct-to-consumer distribution network and satellite assembly plants that were able to assemble last-minute orders. With 6,000 employees, Tarbes was small by global standards, but it more than made up for its relatively slim employee count by outsourcing production of non-core components to Taiwanese subcontractors. Fully 3,500 employees had an engineering background and were working on every aspect of the Tarbes product from design to production to sales.

But while the company projected an image of efficiency and innovation, on the inside it was shackled by bureaucracy. A publicly traded firm, Tarbes was controlled by the Medeiros family, heirs to a sugar plantation fortune with roots in the country spanning 200 years. The family owned 55 per cent of Tarbes's shares. The rest of the firm's equity was owned by retail investors along with 20 different institutional and private funds. The Medeiros family was not in management, but they held two of five board seats.

Despite its number one ranking, Tarbes's financial situation was showing signs of worsening. Sales were growing, but the rate of growth had dropped to the single digit range. Some managers had argued that this was because consumers were waiting for the next operating system and product upgrades to occur in the latter half of 2010. Others suggested that players such as IBM, Dell and Acer were making inroads, encroaching on Tarbes's share of the market. When net profit continued to hover in the low single digit range despite increases in sales, the board of directors decided to take action. They gave notice to the CEO, a lawyer by training, and initiated a search for a successor.

Yara Branco

The daughter of a postal worker and a high school teacher, Branco had grown up in a Sao Paulo suburb and had attended the University of Sao Paulo. She graduated, magna cum laude, in history and started working for the Rede Ferroviaria Federal, Sociedade Anonima (RFFSA), the state-owned national railway of Brazil. She began as an associate in the planning department and was promoted to district manager within three years. She left RFFSA to join Logitech, working for the Swiss company in Geneva, where she focused on developing Logitech's South American sales strategy. During her time at Logitech, she completed her MBA at IMD, a Swiss business school.

In 1995, Branco left Logitech to join VBI, a large U.S. consulting company, as a consultant in the logistics sector. She stayed with VBI for 15 years before joining Tarbes in 2010. At VBI, Branco had been given various assignments starting up new consulting units (in biotechnology, government and aerospace) and turning around declining programs (in application development and business process outsourcing).

Branco was known to be calm but direct, able to work effectively with employees and colleagues at any level. She did not mince words and did not shy away from conducting difficult conversations on the spot. One of her superiors once mentioned, however, that Branco might have progressed more quickly through the organization had she paid more attention to "politics" instead of "telling it like it is." But another superior had a different opinion: it was rare to find a manager who was willing to put her reputation on the line based on her team's analysis of the situation. "Branco seems to have little concern for whether telling the truth will be a career limiting move," he added. "Strong leaders can see that she is an asset to the organization. But when she identifies and reveals the mistakes that have been made, there are some whose egos are bound to be bruised."

Branco was well-known to corporate recruiters who were eager to recruit her for assignments in other firms.

It was this knowledge that she had marketable skills that afforded her the freedom to operate as she wished. "Branco does not seem to have a hidden agenda," remarked another leader who had worked with her in the past. "She wants to get the job done as quickly as possible and move on to the next assignment. She's never been in a role for more than three years."

Most of her team members enjoyed working with her on their assignments. Branco did not tend to micromanage their work, leaving them to perform the basic analyses but then challenging them – in a constructive manner – on their assumptions and conclusions. There were some associates who preferred to work more closely with their team manager, but Branco preferred to delegate than "hand hold" her employees. She gravitated to the strategic issues – figuring out what needed to be done, when, and by whom – and left the minutiae of execution to her team.

Outside of regular work hours, Branco spent very little time socializing with her co-workers. She often worked late in the office, trying to cram in one evening report reading that others would have allocated a full week to complete. When she was not in the office, she preferred to spend time with her family in Sao Paulo.

Branco at VBI

Branco was working at VBI' hardware sales division, when she was recruited by Tarbes's board of directors to join the firm. In the three years she had been in charge of VBI's hardware sales (from 2007 to 2009), the division had doubled its market share and taken the number two spot in the industry. Looking in from the outside, the hardware sales division seemed to have turned itself around by focusing on customer service, sharpening its prices and producing products that were better than those of their competitors. The regional and national newspapers lauded VBI for its renewed focus on strategy, process and execution.

Branco watched the news coverage of the division's turnaround with curiosity. Although no one asked for her opinion, she would have argued that it was a change in the culture of the organization that set the foundation for the turnaround. The division had been staffed with senior managers who had worked at VBI ever since they graduated from university. They had grown up in the organization when it was unthinkable for corporations not to consider VBI products as the best in the industry. The customers always called VBI's sales hotline; there were very few attempts to conduct outbound business development. This approach of thinking and acting as if it were the incumbent seemed to work for the division for two decades.

However, the division had refused to change course even when less expensive American and Asian competitors entered the market in 2005. By 2006, sales had dropped 20 per cent, and 2007 was looking to be even worse. Branco stepped into the division in early 2007, having never worked in hardware sales before. Her appointment as head of hardware sales was contested by senior managers in the division who felt that they should not be led by someone with no experience in their field, but the country management team still insisted on promoting her. Branco's appointment coincided with the departure of three of the top five hardware sales executives.

Nearly three years later, Branco had succeeded in returning the division to growth. She transformed what had been a hierarchical division to one where employees collaborated across levels and functions. She promoted mid-level managers to senior level positions – unthinkable in the previous regime – assigned them stretch targets and gave them the managerial freedom to make decisions without excessive scrutiny.

Out of a division of 120 employees, one-quarter had left the organization or had been fired by the time Branco was done with her turnaround. Thirty new employees with non-IT backgrounds were hired, mostly in junior positions.

By the end of 2009, Branco was looking for her next assignment. She was informed by senior management that she was on track to become a senior executive in the next three years. Unwilling to wait that long for her next promotion, she decided to take the CEO opportunity at Tarbes.

The Tarbes opportunity

Juan Simien, a corporate recruiter, brought the Tarbes opportunity to Branco. Tarbes's board of directors, including Elan Medeiros and Pascal Medeiros, had insisted on locating an outsider to spearhead a turnaround at the company. In part, they were looking for a different approach to managing and communicating the company's vision. Simien suggested Branco partly due to her direct communication style. Jose Marques, who had been CEO of Tarbes for the past decade, was removed from his post in mid- January 2010.

Branco stepped in the very next day, January 18, 2010. She spent the next 10 days learning about the organization and speaking to as many employees as she could. Her first move was to send a short email introducing herself and inviting employees to voice their opinion on Tarbes's future. The email responses poured in, and Branco attempted to read every single email. She relied on an associate in the strategy department – who was seconded to her as her assistant for the transition into her role – to tabulate the results. He organized employee comments by section and added information gleaned from Tarbes's strategy unit's view of the external and internal issues.

Environment

Tarbes was viewed universally – inside and outside the firm – as a "national champion" in Brazil, an icon of the technology industry. It commanded respect because it had been built from the shell of a furniture manufacturer that had an opportunity to diversify, first, into industrial robotics and, second, into personal computers. Tarbes had achieved significant success from the launch of its tablets but was facing a raft of competitors in the low end of the segment. These tablets were priced at half of Tarbes's cheapest product, yet had 80 to 90 per cent of the same features. These low-end competitors had less than 5 per cent of the market, compared to Tarbes's 55 per cent share, but they were expected to continue attracting consumers looking for an entry level device.

At the higher end, where Tarbes was dominant, Apple Inc. was preparing to launch its iPad tablet. Priced competitively with Tarbes's product, the iPad was expected to be a popular device. Apple had the advantage of very strong brand recognition as a result of its iPod music players, its iTunes music store and its iPhone mobile handsets. Similar to Tarbes, Apple had proprietary software. In the Brazilian market, Tarbes continued to be the only manufacturer with an open source, Linux-based operating system. Virtually all other current competitors were on a Windows or Android-based operating system. Unlike Tarbes, Apple had an "ecosystem" of developers who were launching "apps" – or applications – for its products and that were available to consumers through its iTunes store.

Branco noted that Tarbes employed a group of 30 software engineers dedicated to developing apps for its tablet products. There were about 500 different apps on Tarbes's website for download at a nominal fee. In contrast, the Windows and Android-based competitors – there were four and five of them, respectively – shared a common Windows or Android marketplace for apps. There were approximately 600 apps on each of these marketplaces. In addition, between the two marketplaces, there were 2,000 registered software designers developing apps for sale.

TABLE 1 Tarbes S.A. – Condensed Income Statement.[2]

Income Statement	2005	2006	2007	2008	2009
Revenue	$ 2,355	$ 2,456	$ 2,780	$ 2,500	$ 2,890
Gross Margin	$ 942	$ 860	$ 973	$ 900	$ 954
As a % of sales	*40.0%*	*35.0%*	*35.0%*	*36.0%*	*33.0%*
Total Other Expenses	$ 542	$ 589	$ 751	$ 625	$ 780
As a % of sales	*23.0%*	*24.0%*	*27.0%*	*25.0%*	*27.0%*
EBITDA	$ 400	$ 270	$ 222	$ 275	$ 173
As a % of sales	*17.0%*	*11.0%*	*8.0%*	*11.0%*	*6.0%*
Amortization	$ 50	$ 45	$ 30	$ 35	$ 30
Interest Expense	$ 5	$ 6	$ 6	$ 5	$ 5
EBT	$ 345	$ 219	$ 186	$ 235	$ 138
Tax (38%)	$ 131	$ 83	$ 71	$ 89	$ 53
Net Income	$ 214	$ 136	$ 116	$ 146	$ 86
As a % of sales	*9.1%*	*5.5%*	*4.2%*	*5.8%*	*3.0%*

Strategy

Tarbes had a strong distribution network that delivered products to 1,850 different points of sale throughout the country. It commanded preferential shelf space because it was the number one product in the market. There was a sense within the firm that "if they developed and released their best work, customers will buy" their products. But while Tarbes had enjoyed success, growing sales from $150 million[1] in 2001 to $2.4 billion in 2005, top line growth had slowed since then. Part of the reason was the onset in late 2007 of the global financial crisis, which dampened enthusiasm for new products.

Another reason was a series of high profile product missteps that occurred in 2008 and 2009 as Tarbes attempted to capitalize on the popularity of their "Tab" brand by launching two variants aimed at the industrial market (tougher exterior shell, longer battery life, water resistant) and the entertainment market (stylish designs in various colours, accessories such as leather covers and bags, slimmer profile).

While the strategy of entering new segments seemed prudent, the products were, by many accounts, over priced by 20 per cent. Worse, Tarbes's latest version of its operating system seemed to underperform relative to the current versions of its competitors' Windows and Android platforms. Marques, Tarbes's CEO at that time, promised a new version of its operating system by late 2009. Despite stumbling with the launch of these two products, Tarbes continued to control about one-third of the tablet market at the beginning of 2009. It continued to use its marketing slogan – the same slogan it had used for the past five years – to promote its product. Roughly translated, it read "technologically advanced, at a price you can afford." Tarbes's condensed income statement can be found in Table 1.

Product

Tarbes's engineers were focused on improving current products to reduce cost, improve customer experience and embed new features. The development cycle for typical products was 12 to 18 months, an increase from the six months achieved in the early 2000s. The reason for this increase was the higher attention to detail paid to each step of the process. Tarbes prided itself for its strong, process-oriented engineering culture. Each suggested product change was documented and approved by the supervising engineer and a committee of senior leaders, who often provided helpful suggestions.

A release schedule of the software upgrades was provided to retailers and consumers at the beginning of each year. Tarbes organized itself to be able to deliver each upgrade on time. The management team felt that the increased scrutiny at all levels of product development reduced the risk that poorly thought-out

[1] All figures converted to U.S. dollars.

[2] In millions of U.S. dollars. EBITDA is earnings before interest, taxes, depreciation and amortization. EBT is earnings before taxes.

changes would be incorporated into the next product. Senior engineers working on development had been with the company for, on average, 12 years.

The majority of Tarbes's development efforts focused on improving its Linux operating system to be more power-efficient and quicker on start-up. A secondary focus was on procurement, that is, to locating and purchasing quality parts in bulk. In each of the past three years, the focus on sourcing had reduced component costs by 15 per cent per year. Significant resources had been poured also into redesigning apps from Windows or Android-based environments for use on Tarbes's products. Last, a team of five designers – all with engineering backgrounds – worked on the "look and feel" of Tarbes's products. Tarbes's tablets were designed to look like a sleeker version of a high-end Toshiba or Sony laptop. Its tablet product had 80 per cent brand recognition in Brazil, about twice that of its nearest competitor.

Organization

Branco looked further into the stack of employees' comments for insight into the organization. Tarbes was organized into four units: development, production, sales and marketing. A small top management team of six people – CEO, CFO, CIO, COO, human resources manager and legal counsel – oversaw the units. Each unit was run by an executive director and a team of five directors. Every year, high level strategic development began in October and concluded in late December with the announcement of objectives for the next 12 months. As several senior employees recounted to Branco, crafting strategy at Tarbes required "finesse and diplomatic skills."

Each of the units was run semi-autonomously with control over budgets and hiring. While there seemed to be strong working relationships between the units, there was very little movement of employees between them. Branco noted that turnover rates were extremely low – about 2 per cent per year compared to an industry average of 15 per cent per year. Employees wrote about how proud they were to work for Tarbes, the number one firm in the industry. Here were some other comments from emails sent to Branco:

- We're number one for a reason: we don't get distracted by what's happening outside the firm. We spend all of our precious resources on developing the best product possible.
- I joined Tarbes for a lifelong career in the technology industry. There is no better place to be at this stage of my career.

- It is a typical top-down organization where strategy is decided at the top level and filters down to the bottom. We're most like an industrial operation in that sense.
- Our products are very good, but I find that some of the apps I can get on other sites aren't available on ours.
- We tend to ignore outside criticism of our work. It usually comes from competitors or commentators who are jealous of our success.
- Let's not fix what is not broken: the Tarbes engine has worked very well for more than 10 years, and, while we may have had two or three missteps, there's no ignoring that the system *works*.
- We're the best, and that's the extent of my comments.
- We need to find out how to continue to be number one in the market. There are serious threats to us at the low end.
- We have high expectations for ourselves. But others in the country may have even higher expectations for us, seeing as we're the local solution. I wonder if we can live up to their expectations.
- It's better to work towards perfection – even if it takes a few more days or weeks – rather than release something that's inadequate.
- Our senior managers seem to know best. There are times, however, when we have something to say, but no one asks for our feedback.
- We have the best engineers in the industry, and they tend to receive a lot of attention from recruiters for other jobs. But most of our employees stay with us in spite of this outside attention. Where else would they go to work for a market leader?

Management

Branco reviewed the files of her management team, which included the five other members of the top management team and the various executive directors of each unit. She found that 80 per cent of them had worked for Tarbes since 2000. All engineers, they had grown up in the organization and were well-respected by their employees, according to the emails that included comments on management style and effectiveness.

She had a chance to meet each senior executive in turn and found them polite and respectful, but somewhat cautious. This was normal, she thought: "After all, I'm the outsider who has been hired into the

TABLE 2   Tarbes S.A. – Stock Price, on December 31.

Year	2005	2006	2007	2008	2009
Stock price	$ 55	$ 65	$ 74	$ 46	$ 51

firm to shake things up. They're all wondering what I'm going to do next." Branco also met with her board of directors. Unlike the mood within the firm, the board of directors expressed frustration at Tarbes's inability to grow. One pointed to Tarbes's lackluster stock price over the last five years (see Table 2).

Her board's comments could be summarized as follows:

■ We don't know what we're doing wrong, other than profits are falling. But everyone has had a tough few years.

■ I think the former CEO was holding the organization back, pitting units against each other. But this is just what I heard.

■ We're number one in our industry, but we will be challenged in the next few years. The fact that we had two very weak product launches suggests to me that we have a lot of work to do.

■ How are we preparing ourselves to meet new threats?

■ Are we too insular?

■ Let's not change anything just for change's sake. There has to be some rationale to what we choose to do next.

■ Every move that we make will be scrutinized internally and, because we are the number one in our industry, by the national press.

■ What is our strategy to restore profit growth?

■ If you look at the most recent sales reports for our core products, we're down to 25 per cent share. We no longer own a third of the market, and Apple hasn't even launched the iPad yet.

■ Our operating system upgrade was slated for late 2009, but it's now January 2010 and the upgrade has been pushed back to October 2010.

After 10 days of meeting with 300 employees, reading a few thousand emails, and attending a series of board meetings, Branco came to the conclusion that drastic changes were needed immediately. She learned that the Apple iPad was likely to be the most competitive product that Tarbes had ever faced. She

looked at adoption rates for iPhone and iPod products and concluded that Tarbes would suffer market share losses almost immediately upon the iPad's launch. One recent poll suggested that the iPad, before it had even hit the Brazilian market, commanded awareness levels of 70 per cent among potential consumers.

In addition, the launch of the iPad would likely divide the market into four operating systems: Linux, Windows, Android and Apple. Branco estimated that software engineers aligned with an operating system would likely elect to continue developing products for the most popular systems. Tarbes had no one outside the firm developing apps for its operating system. There was a slight chance that the company would be able to play "catch up" by encouraging others to build apps for its tablets. But Branco was convinced that Tarbes needed to abandon its proprietary operating system and align itself with either the Windows or Android camps.

"We need to 'pivot' the firm to focus on the future, as opposed to resting on the laurels of our past," thought Branco to herself. "But moving to a new operating system will take at least a year, and it will make about 750 people redundant immediately. How can I convey to my new team that this is what needs to be done?"

Communicating a new way forward

Branco's challenge was how she could communicate with maximum effectiveness in a short period of time. She was one of just a few voices calling for change in a company full of loyalists. She wondered how she could communicate her vision for change when she had yet to build a power base of support. The board supported her, which was reassuring, but she still needed to convince the firm that change was needed. She continued:

> *The bigger message is that what we've done thus far will not sustain us in the future. I think we're collectively underestimating the threat that Apple poses to our so-called dominant position. Already, the American news media has commented on the iPad, calling it the tablet that will define the market. And Apple has thousands of developers producing apps for it. We have our*

internal team. We're the market leader, but we've failed to take advantage of our dominant position to build an ecosystem. I fear it may be too late to start.

As she sat in the back of the car, Branco looked outside. Bright sunshine reflected off the steel and glass windows of the industrial park. The driver informed her that they would be arriving in 20 minutes. She pulled out a sheaf of printed email comments from middle management and continued reading them:

- Our firm is strong.
- We may lose our way because we're complacent.
- No one is accountable for mistakes.
- People are afraid to speak up.
- Management is by flavour of the day as opposed to any strategic planning.
- We're too used to winning, we don't know how to fight.
- We have strong brand recognition.

Branco was looking forward to the factory visit. This was the last place she would visit before her presentation to all employees in three days at Morumbi, Sao Paulo's football stadium. Tarbes had rented the stadium for the day to celebrate the fifteenth anniversary of the firm's founding. It would be Branco's first chance to address the employees in one spot. As she stepped out of the car into the heat of the afternoon sun, she thought about her communications strategy for the next few days:

Drastic changes are needed to turn us around before we crash. I have a good sense of what that big picture looks like, but communicating that internally and then externally is going to be a challenge. Many are afraid of and opposed to change. We were successful, and, some would say, we've earned the right to be complacent. But I look on the horizon, at tomorrow's competitors at both ends of our market segment, and I see that unless we reset our perspective, Tarbes, as an entity, will not exist in five years.

Tata Group's growth strategies

By Hadiya Faheem

Introduction

For the fiscal year ended 2010–2011, India's largest multinational conglomerate, the Tata Group, reported that its international operations constituted 58 percent of the group's revenues with US$ 48.3 billion.[1] Analysts opined that while exports from India were the key to the growth of Tata Group's international business, the Tata Group companies' investments in assets overseas through greenfield projects, joint ventures, and acquisitions had also contributed to the group's growth. Of these, inorganic growth was a crucial component of Tata enterprises, according to analysts.

Founded in 1868 by Jamsetji Tata, the Tata Group had pioneered several industries in India: power, steel, airlines, and hospitality. For the FY ended 2011, the group operated in seven broad sectors ranging from automobiles, steel, energy, hotels, chemicals, and consumer goods to communication systems with Tata Steel, Tata Motors, Tata Consultancy Services, and Tata Power accounting for nearly 50 percent of the group's revenue.[2]

In its initial years, the group's growth was largely organic due to the industrial development in India which was not conducive to alliances being formed with international companies. The Tata Group grew majorly through new product developments, technological upgradations, and innovation. The group pioneered the information technology industry in India with the launch of Tata Consultancy Services (TCS) in 1968. In 1998, the group's auto division Tata Motors developed India's first indigenously developed car, the Indica. In 2008, Tata Motors received global attention by unveiling the world's cheapest car, the Nano, by trying out several innovations, different design specifications, and engineering changes, to keep the costs low.

The group had redefined growth after Ratan Tata took over as Chairman of the Tata Group in 1991. He restructured the businesses of the Tata Group and expanded the group globally. The first major instance of inorganic growth was exemplified when the group's Tata Tea (now Tata Global Beverages) division acquired UK-based Tetley in 2000. This was followed by a series of acquisitions by the group. Some of the notable acquisitions were Tata Steel acquiring Corus[3] in 2007 and Tata Motors' acquisition of Jaguar and Land Rover[4] in 2008. Analysts pointed out that though the group had recorded increased revenues due to inorganic growth, it also had to deal with the challenges of integration and proper management of the portfolio of companies.

Going forward, the Tata Group continued to follow its inorganic growth strategy. In March 2012, the group's telecommunication division, Tata Communications, announced its plans to acquire UK-based telecommunication company, Cable & Wireless Worldwide Plc. The deal was expected to strengthen Tata Communication's position as a provider of undersea fiber optic and business communication services provider globally.

Background note

The Tata Group was founded by Jamsetji Tata (Jamsetji) in 1868. In 1874, he began with a textile mill and inaugurated the Empress Mill in 1877. After successfully establishing his business, Jamsetji set up Asia's first iron and steel company, the Tata Iron and Steel Company[5] (TISCO) (now Tata Steel), in Bihar (Refer to Exhibit 1 for a timeline of Tata Group).

In 1904, he started the flagship hotel of India's first luxury chain – the Taj Group of Hotels. On his demise

This case was written by **Hadiya Faheem,** under the direction of **G V Muralidhara,** IBS Hyderabad. It was compiled from published sources, and is intended to be used as a basis for class discussion rather than to illustrate either effective or ineffective handling of a management situation.

© 2012, IBS Center for Management Research. Printed with permission from IBS Center for Management Research and www.thecasecentre.org.

[1]"At Home in the World," www.tata.com, 2012.

[2]"The Tata Group: Challenges in Managing a Large Portfolio," http://tejas-iimb.org.

[3]Corus was formed in October 1999 through the merger of British Steel and Koninklijke Hoogovens. It manufactures, processes, and distributes metal products as well as provides design, technology, and consultancy services. Its plants are spread across the UK, Belgium, the Netherlands, Norway, and France.

[4]Jaguar was founded by William Lyons in Coventry, UK, in 1922. Land Rover, initially the name of a vehicle launched by the Rover Car Company in 1948, became a part of Leyland Motors Ltd. in 1967. As of early 2008, both Jaguar and Land Rover (together with Volvo) were part of the Premier Automotive Group, a company owned by Ford Motor Company.

[5]Tata Iron and Steel Company was established in 1907. As of 2008, it was one of India's largest steel companies with crude steel production capacity of more than 28 million tons.

EXHIBIT 1   TIMELINE OF TATA GROUP

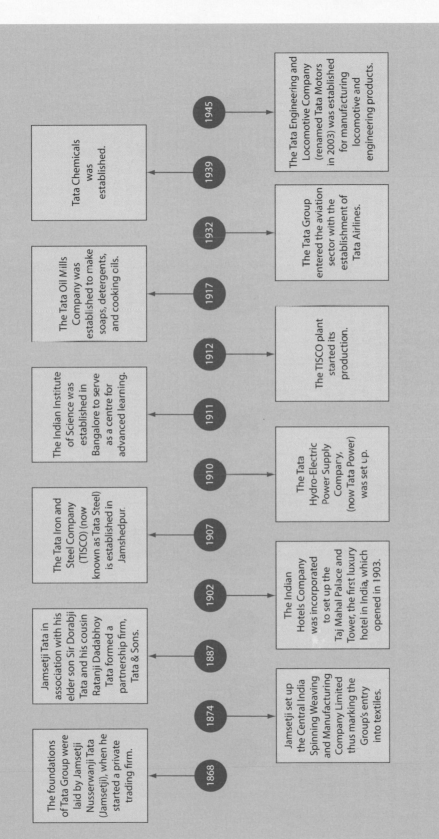

1868 — The foundations of Tata Group were laid by Jamsetji Nusserwanji Tata (Jamsetji), when he started a private trading firm.

1874 — Jamsetji set up the Central India Spinning Weaving and Manufacturing Company Limited thus marking the Group's entry into textiles.

1887 — Jamsetji Tata in association with his elder son Sir Dorabji Tata and his cousin Ratanji Dadabhoy Tata formed a partnership firm, Tata & Sons.

1902 — The Indian Hotels Company was incorporated to set up the Taj Mahal Palace and Tower, the first luxury hotel in India, which opened in 1903.

1907 — The Tata Iron and Steel Company (TISCO) (now known as Tata Steel) is established in Jamshedpur.

1910 — The Tata Hydro-Electric Power Supply Company, (now Tata Power) was set up.

1911 — The Indian Institute of Science was established in Bangalore to serve as a centre for advanced learning.

1912 — The TISCO plant started its production.

1917 — The Tata Oil Mills Company was established to make soaps, detergents, and cooking oils.

1932 — The Tata Group entered the aviation sector with the establishment of Tata Airlines.

1939 — Tata Chemicals was established.

1945 — The Tata Engineering and Locomotive Company (renamed Tata Motors in 2003) was established for manufacturing locomotive and engineering products.

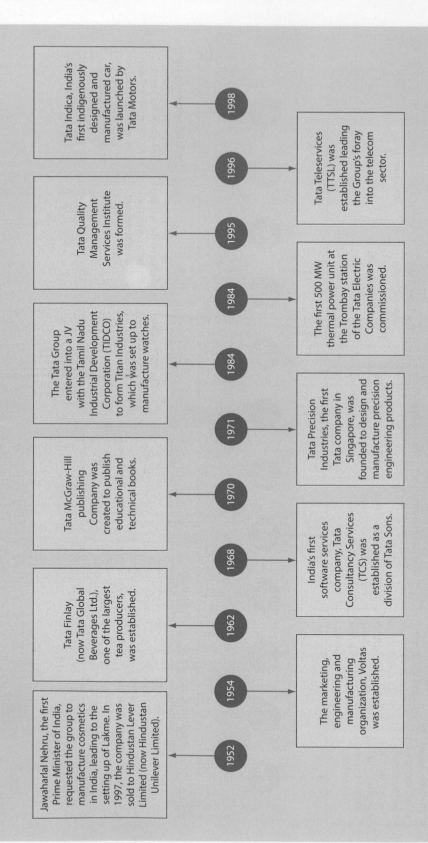

1952 — Jawaharlal Nehru, the first Prime Minister of India, requested the group to manufacture cosmetics in India, leading to the setting up of Lakme. In 1997, the company was sold to Hindustan Lever Limited (now Hindustan Unilever Limited).

1954 — The marketing, engineering and manufacturing organization, Voltas was established.

1962 — Tata Finlay (now Tata Global Beverages Ltd.), one of the largest tea producers, was established.

1968 — India's first software services company, Tata Consultancy Services (TCS) was established as a division of Tata Sons.

1970 — Tata McGraw-Hill publishing Company was created to publish educational and technical books.

1971 — Tata Precision Industries, the first Tata company in Singapore, was founded to design and manufacture precision engineering products.

1984 — The Tata Group entered into a JV with the Tamil Nadu Industrial Development Corporation (TIDCO) to form Titan Industries, which was set up to manufacture watches.

1984 — The first 500 MW thermal power unit at the Trombay station of the Tata Electric Companies was commissioned.

1995 — Tata Quality Management Services Institute was formed.

1996 — Tata Teleservices (TTSL) was established leading the Group's foray into the telecom sector.

1998 — Tata Indica, India's first indigenously designed and manufactured car, was launched by Tata Motors.

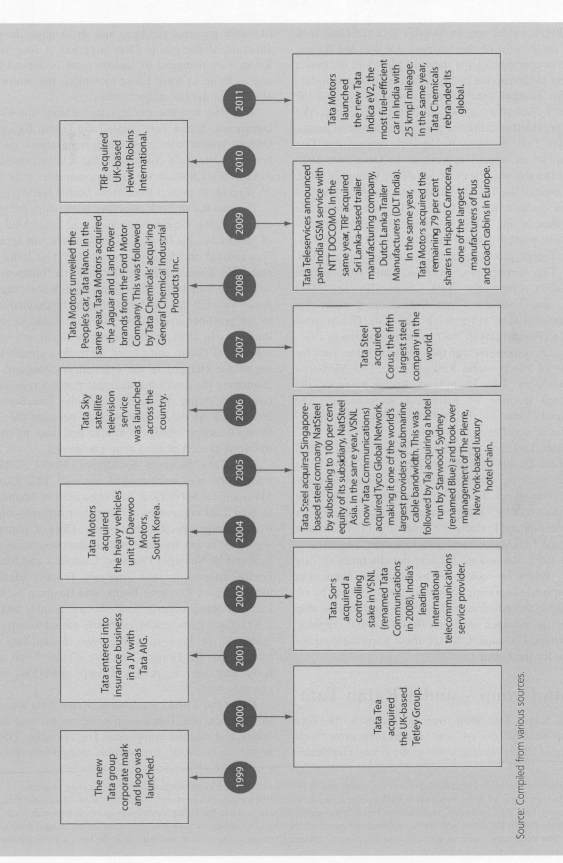

1999
The new Tata group corporate mark and logo was launched.

2000
Tata Tea acquired the UK-based Tetley Group.

2001
Tata entered into insurance business in a JV with Tata AIG.

2002
Tata Sons acquired a controlling stake in VSNL (renamed Tata Communications in 2008), India's leading international telecommunications service provider.

2004
Tata Motors acquired the heavy vehicles unit of Daewoo Motors, South Korea.

2005
Tata Steel acquired Singapore-based steel company NatSteel by subscribing to 100 per cent equity of its subsidiary, NatSteel Asia. In the same year, VSNL (now Tata Communications) acquired Tyco Global Network, making it one of the world's largest providers of submarine cable bandwidth. This was followed by Taj acquiring a hotel run by Starwood, Sydney (renamed Blue) and took over management of The Pierre, New York-based luxury hotel chain.

2006
Tata Sky satellite television service was launched across the country.

2007
Tata Steel acquired Corus, the fifth largest steel company in the world.

2008
Tata Motors unveiled the People's car, Tata Nano. In the same year, Tata Motors acquired the Jaguar and Land Rover brands from the Ford Motor Company. This was followed by Tata Chemicals' acquiring General Chemical Industrial Products Inc.

2009
Tata Teleservices announced pan-India GSM service with NTT DOCOMO. In the same year, TRF acquired Sri Lanka-based trailer manufacturing company, Dutch Lanka Trailer Manufacturers (DLT India). In the same year, Tata Motors acquired the remaining 79 per cent shares in Hispano Carrocera, one of the largest manufacturers of bus and coach cabins in Europe.

2010
TRF acquired UK-based Hewitt Robins International.

2011
Tata Motors launched the new Tata Indica eV2, the most fuel-efficient car in India with 25 kmpl mileage. In the same year, Tata Chemicals rebranded its global.

Source: Compiled from various sources.

in 1904, his elder son Sir Dorabji Tata (Dorabji) took over the control of the business. He was the driving force in operationalizing the steel plant and the power project as envisioned by his father. He also established the Sir Dorabji Tata Trust that was to become the premier charitable endowment of the Tata Group. The trust provided institutional grants and individual grants.

JRD Tata, nephew of Jamsetji, entered the Tata Group as an unpaid apprentice in December 1925 when Dorabji was the chairman of the Group. In 1932, JRD created the Tata Aviation service, which later led to the creation of Air India. JRD Tata became the chairman of the Tata Group in 1938. The Group's business portfolio when JRD took over in 1938 included steel, power, cement, insurance, and aviation. The Tata Group also ventured into Automobiles (TELCO), Chemicals (Tata Chemicals), Tea (Tata Tea), and Software (Tata Consultancy) under his stewardship. The revenues of the Tata Group grew from a few millions in 1947 to Rs.130 billion in 1991. JRD was responsible for the creation of the Tata Institute of Fundamental Research, the Tata Memorial Hospital, the Tata Institute of Social Sciences, the National Institute of Advanced Sciences, and the National Center for the Performing Arts, each an exemplar of excellence in its field.

Ratan Tata, great grandson of Jamsetji Tata, joined the Tata Group in 1962 in TISCO and started his career working on the shop floor, alongside blue-collar employees. In 1977, Ratan Tata was made the chairman of TISCO. He became the chairman of Tata Engineering and Locomotive Company[6] (TELCO, later renamed Tata Motors) and Tata Industries[7] in 1981.

In 1991, Ratan Tata became the chairman of Tata Sons. When he took over as chairman, there was widespread skepticism about whether he would be effective in the position, and whether he would be able to fill the outsized shoes of JRD Tata, the outgoing Chairman. Undaunted, he set about implementing his vision for the Group.

Tata Group – under Ratan Tata

When Ratan Tata took over as chairman, the Tata Group seemed on its way to disintegration, with powerful CEOs running some of the Group companies like their personal fiefdoms and challenging the core structure of the group. Over a period of four years, Ratan Tata managed to replace most of these CEOs and to bring in fresh talent to replace the senior executives in the Group companies.

To bring in greater integration among the Group companies, Ratan Tata created the Group Executive Office, whose members were represented on the boards of the Tata companies. He also increased the stake of Tata Sons in the Group companies to at least 26 percent, to protect them from hostile takeovers.

Prior to Ratan Tata assuming leadership, the work culture at the Group companies had resembled that of the Indian public sector units where job security was assured and lethargy tolerated. While India had embraced liberalization in 1991 and the business environment had been undergoing significant changes, Ratan Tata felt that the Tata Group had remained stuck in the pre-liberalization era. So he decided to shake things up. In 1998, at a gathering of heads and senior officials of Group companies, he made a speech talking of the changes in the external environment and cautioning the senior management that inaction would cost them dearly. He spoke about the Tata Business Excellence Model, which was to become the Tata Group's largest change initiative and was to be introduced in each of the Group companies.

The Tata Business Excellence Model (TBEM) framework was implemented through Tata Quality Management Services, a Tata organization "mandated to help Tata companies achieve their business objectives through specific processes." Once a company signed up, it was annually evaluated on seven criteria – Leadership, Strategic Planning, Customer and Market Focus, Information and Analysis, Process Management, Human Resource Focus, and Business Results. Each of these criteria was allotted points, totaling 1,000. Each participating company aimed to earn 600 points, at the least, over five years. Ratan Tata also established the Group Corporate Center – an apex body that was to review Group operations on a monthly basis.

Using the TBEM framework, Ratan Tata was able to transform the Tata Group's behemoths into much leaner and nimbler companies. For example, TISCO, in the early 1990s, had surplus manpower, obsolete

---

[6]Tata Engineering and Locomotive Company was established in 1945 to manufacture locomotives and other engineering products.

[7]Tata Industries was set up by Tata Sons in 1945 as a managing agency for the businesses it promoted. Following the abolition of the managing agency system, Tata Industries' mandate was recast in the early 1980s to promote the Group's entry into new and high-tech areas. Tata Industries has, in the 1990s and 2000s, initiated and promoted the Group's ventures into several sectors, including control systems, information technology, financial services, auto components, advanced materials, and telecom hardware. It is the key player in the Group's entry into telecommunication services.

equipment and blast furnaces, and quality problems. In fact, the situation was so bad that McKinsey & Co.[8] advised Ratan Tata to dispose of the company. Under the TBEM framework, measures were initiated to enhance productivity at Tata Steel by closing down outdated factories and modernizing mines and steelworks. The size of the workforce was also reduced at Tata Steel.[9] All these measures helped the company record productivity gains; productivity rose from 78 tons of steel per worker per year in 1993 to 264 tons in 2004.

Similarly, TELCO was seeing escalating costs and falling market share. It had quality issues as well. There were far more employees and suppliers than required. Ratan Tata introduced rigorous quality assurance measures in the company's factories and a voluntary retirement scheme to reduce the number of employees. He also took measures to reduce the number of suppliers by half. Ratan Tata tried to shift the focus of the company from manufacturing to marketing. A range of passenger vehicles was launched after the Sierra, an SUV, in 1991, including the Sumo, a multiutility

vehicle, in 1994, the Safari, an SUV, in 1998, and the indigenous passenger car, Indica, also in 1998.

Ratan Tata also noted that while the Tata Group was involved in many businesses – steel, tea, oil mills, cosmetics, chemicals, power, and automobiles, among them, only a few large companies contributed significantly to the Group's revenues and profits. In order to bring in greater focus, Ratan Tata started offloading businesses that he felt did not fit in with his vision for the Group. In 1998, the Group sold its 50 percent stake in Merind (including Tata Pharma), a pharmaceutical company, to Wockhardt.[10] In 1999, it sold its 28 percent stake in Goodlass Nerolac, a paint company, to Kansai.[11] The same year, Lakmé, a cosmetics company, was sold to Hindustan Lever[12] (HLL, now renamed Hindustan Unilever). In 1999–2000, the Group also exited the cement industry by selling its stake in ACC, a cement company, to Gujarat Ambuja Cements (now renamed Ambuja Cements) (Refer to Exhibit 2 for business sectors of Tata Group).

Ratan Tata's plan for the group envisaged two broad directions for growth. One was targeting the

EXHIBIT 2   THE BUSINESS SECTORS OF TATA GROUP

S. No	Industry	Sector	Tata company	Subsidiaries/associates/ joint ventures
1	**ENGINEERING**	**Automotive**	Tata AutoComp Systems	Automotive Composite Systems International, Automotive Stampings and Assemblies, Knorr Bremse Systems for Commercial Vehicles, Tata AutoComp GY Batteries, TACO Engineering, TACO Faurecia Design Center, TACO Hendrickson Suspension Systems, TACO Interiors and Plastics Division, TacoKunststofftechnik, TACO MobiApps Telematics, TACO Supply Chain Management, TACO Tooling, TACO Visteon Engineering Center, Tata Ficosa Automotive Systems, Tata

[8]Founded in 1926 by James O. McKinsey, McKinsey & Co. is a privately owned management consulting firm.

[9]The number of employees at Tata Steel was brought down to 46,350 in 2001–02, from 76,436 in 1993–94.

[10]Wockhardt is a global pharmaceutical and biotechnology company with its headquarters in India.

[11]Kansai Paint Co. Ltd. is a Japanese paint company whose principal activity is to manufacture and sell paints. The company has operations in the UK, USA, Canada, China, Thailand, Taiwan, Singapore, the Philippines, Indonesia, Malaysia, India, Korea, Mexico, and Japan.

[12]Hindustan Unilever Limited is India's largest fast moving consumer products company, with several successful brands such as Lux, Surf, and Rexona.

S. No	Industry	Sector	Tata company	Subsidiaries/associates/ joint ventures
				Johnson Controls Automotive, Tata Toyo Radiator, Tata Yazaki AutoComp, TC Springs, Technical Stampings Automotive
			Tata Motors	Concorde Motors, HV Axels, HV Transmissions, Nita Company, TAL Manufacturing Solutions, Tata Cummins, Tata Daewoo Commercial Vehicles Company, Tata Engineering Services, Tata Precision Industries, Tata Technologies, Telco Construction Equipment
		Engineering Services	Tata Projects Tata Consulting Engineers Voltas	
		Engineering Products	TAL Manufacturing Solutions Telco Construction Equipment Company TRF	
2	MATERIALS	Composites	Tata Advanced Materials	
		Metals	Tata Steel	Hooghly Met Coke and Power Company, Jamshedpur Injection Powder (Jamipol), Jamshedpur Utility and Service Company Limited (JUSCO), Lanka Special Steel, mjunction services, NatSteel, Sila Eastern Company, Tata BlueScope Steel, Tata Metaliks, Tata Pigments, Tata Refractories, Tata Ryerson, Tata Sponge Iron, Tata Steel (Thailand), Tata Steel KZN, Tayo Rolls, The Dhamra Port Company, The Indian Steel and Wire Products, The Tinplate Company of India, TM International Logistics, TRF
3	ENERGY	Power	Tata BP Solar India	
			Tata Power	Tata Ceramics, Tata Power Trading, North Delhi Power Limited
		Oil & Gas	Tata Petrodyne	
4	CHEMICALS	Chemicals	Rallis India	
			Tata Chemicals	
			Tata Pigments	
5	PHARMA		Advinus Therapeutics	

S. No	Industry	Sector	Tata company	Subsidiaries/associates/ joint ventures
6	**HOTELS AND REALTY**	**Hotels**	Indian Hotels	Taj Air, Roots Corporation (Ginger Hotels)
			THDC	
		Realty	Tata Realty and Infrastructure	
7	**FINANCIAL SERVICES**	**Insurance**	Tata AIG General Insurance	
			Tata AIG Life Insurance	
		Other Financial Services	Tata Asset Management	
			Tata Capital	
			Tata Financial Services	
			Tata Investment Corporation	
8	**OTHER SERVICES**		Tata Quality Management Services	
			Tata Services	
			Tata Strategic Management Group	
9	**CONSUMER PRODUCTS**	**Retail**	Infiniti Retail	
			Trent	
		Tea	Tata Tea	Tetley Group, Tata Coffee, Tata Tetley, Tata Tea Inc
		Ceramics	Tata Ceramics	
		Publishing	Tata McGrawHill Publishing Co.	
		Watches, Jewelry, and eyewear	Titan Industries	
10	**INFORMATION SYTEMS AND COMMUNICATIONS**	**Information Systems**	Nelito Systems	
			TCS	APONLINE, Airline Financial Support Services, Aviation Software Development Consultancy, CMC, CMC Americas Inc, Conscripti, HOTV, Tata America International Corporation, WTI Advanced Technology
			Tata Elxsi	
			SerWizSol	
			Tata Interactive Systems	
			Tata Technologies	
		Communi-cation	Tata Teleservices	Tata Teleservices (Maharashtra)
			Tata Sky	
			VSNL	
			Tatanet	
11	**INDUSTRIAL AUTOMATION**		Nelco	

Source: www.tata.com.

emerging mass market in India through product development and innovation. The other was the international route, where the group planned to expand the markets for its existing products.

Organic growth strategies

Ratan Tata strongly believed that to achieve growth at the Tata Group, it was necessary to create technologically superior and exciting products. According to him, the Tata Group would have to distinguish itself from other companies through innovation and low costs.

Under his leadership, the Group companies came up with several new and innovative products. For example, Tata Steel patented several new equipment such as a fuel and reducing gas generator[13], an emulsion atomizer[14], and processes such as the inert gas shrouding process[15] and the corrosion resistant steel production process. More importantly, the company started selling its products, which till then had been sold as commodities, under the Tata brand.

Some businesses such as TCS grew organically through investments in greenfield projects. TCS grew by upgrading its technological capabilities, skill sets, and its infrastructure, and in the process, developed several new innovative software products. In 1981, in a bid to improve its R&D skills, TCS founded the Tata Research, Design and Development Center (TRDDC). The center played a key role in developing world class products.

In the late 1990s, to accelerate its revenue growth, TCS began developing new products with high revenue earning potential and tapping the domestic and other fast growing markets. TCS identified high potential areas in terms of technology and industries on which it would concentrate. For instance, in late 1998, the company decided to concentrate on new revenue opportunities including Y2K and Euro conversion. A major area of focus in the late 1990s was e-business. All TCS products and platforms were web-enabled. It also decided to specialize in e-business consulting. The company offered e-business solutions and consulting in various functional processes.

TCS developed products which addressed different requirements of the industry in areas such as custody, brokerage, stock exchange, clearance, settlement, and depository products. Its products such as Network Custody System (a global custody product), Quartz (a wholesale banking product), and ITBS (an integrated total banking solution) had already gained recognition and finding more customers for these products was a part of TCS' growth strategy.

TCS focused on both the domestic and foreign IT software markets. The company identified the government, insurance, telecom, and manufacturing sectors as key growth areas in India. In the international market, TCS served customers in the BFSI (banking, financial services and insurance), telecom and manufacturing sectors.

The group's Tata Motors division also followed the organic growth strategy. The Indica was a major step forward for Tata Motors, a company that had been known for its bulky trucks. Initially, Ratan Tata had requested the Indian automotive industry to join hands to create a car that would be designed, developed, and produced in India. However, his proposal was met with skepticism. Tata Motors then started work to develop the car on its own. The Indica was launched in December 1998. Although, initially, there were quality issues, it soon became one of the largest selling models in the country.

Tata Motors launched several new products, some of which created new categories in the Indian market. In 2004, it unveiled plans to launch the Indiva, a seven-seater MPV. In September 2004, it launched the Indigo Marina, a station wagon, positioned as a premium car that combined the luxury of a sedan with the convenience of an MPV. The same year, it also launched an improved version of the Indica V2 and the Sumo Victa, an improved version of the Sumo.

At the Geneva Motor Show in March 2005, Tata Motors unveiled the Xover, a concept car which was a fusion of a car and an SUV.

The Nano car project too required Tata Motors to come up with innovative solutions to bring down costs so that the car could be priced at Rs. 100,000 or US$ 2500 – an almost unimaginably low price for other car companies. For example, the company designed a smaller engine for the Nano that would fit snugly under the rear seat, allowing for a compact car while providing extra space for the passengers. The company also used digital validation techniques[16] extensively so

---

[13]An apparatus for heating and mixing industrial tail gases with a reducing gas by burning a mixture of fuel, air, and steam in a combustion chamber.

[14]An emulsion atomizer helps in efficient combustion of liquid fuel for blast furnace operations.

[15]A method for providing a protective gaseous atmosphere around a liquid stream during transfer between containers.

[16]Digital validation techniques unite a number of computer-based tools that rapidly analyze and validate design alternatives. Prior to the use of digital validation techniques, engineers would manually assess the potential impact of every proposed change in an automobile's design. Digital validation techniques have allowed Tata Motors to find the best components or a combination of them even before any parts are actually built, thus drastically reducing the time required to develop the Nano.

as to hasten the product development process. Although the Nano was not a path-breaking product in terms of customer utility, the company brought about small changes in how cars were built that would allow huge cost savings and thus allow for aggressive pricing. Tata Motors announced the commercial launch of the Nano in 2009.

Inorganic growth strategies

Although Jamsetji Tata, the pioneer of the Tata Group, had tried to establish European operations, the Tata Group's overseas ventures had never been large enough to be worth a mention. Ratan Tata, however, was keen on the Group companies entering new markets as he felt that global operations would make them more competitive and efficient. He also believed that a company should be able to take advantage of global opportunities. "The objective of globalization is to move towards becoming globally competitive and to expand your market,"[17] he said.

However, the more compelling reason for going global was risk mitigation. As Ratan Tata said, "Perhaps the most graphic moment came in 1997-1998 or 2000 when we had that economic downturn and when Tata Motors, at that time, produced that Rs. 500 crore [Rs 5 billion] loss. That told me that we had to do something where we would not in the future be dependent on one economic cycle, but we had to have more irons in the fire in different economies and if one economic cycle was down, the chances are that the other might be up. That accelerated the move to go and search, not for acquisitions, but for markets in a serious way."[18]

The route adopted by Ratan Tata to go global was acquisition of foreign companies and he started the process of global acquisitions in the year 2000 when Tata Tea, a Group company, acquired UK-based Tetley Tea in a leveraged buyout for US$ 432 million. The group had previously attempted the inorganic route in 1995. R K Krishna Kumar (Krishna Kumar), director Tata Sons and vice chairman of Tata Tea, commenting on why the group had succeeded with the acquisition of Tetley and why it had failed in 1995, said, "In 1995 we did not succeed because we did not want to go into a high-risk situation. By 2000 we had

become less risk averse. Tetley was three times the size of Tata Tea. In a sense, on paper the risk looked too big, but if you looked beyond the financial and technical to the managerial capability – the real due diligence – it was highly doable. You have to look at it as a partnership not to see it as two entities, but to see the new reality as one entity."[19] The Tetley acquisition gave Tata Tea an international beverage brand.

Though TCS grew mostly through organic growth strategies, it also focused on acquisitions to grow its businesses (Refer to Table 1 for major acquisitions by TCS). Commenting on this strategy, Atul Takle, Vice-President, Corporate Communications, TCS, said, "TCS believes that inorganic growth, such as mergers and acquisitions, would see the company becoming a global leader sooner than later."[20] To consolidate its leadership position in the domestic IT industry, TCS acquired a 51 percent equity stake in a public sector company – CMC Limited – in October 2001 for Rs. 1.52 bn. CMC was a leading infrastructure management, networking, and maintenance company in India. With this, TCS added the business of government and quality consulting into its service offerings. To help the company through the mergers and acquisitions process, TCS created a special M&A cell in December 2001.

TCS also entered into mutually beneficial partnerships with several IT companies for new product and market development. On the international front, TCS set up development centers in several countries across the world to expand its reach beyond the US and emerge as a truly global firm. It set up centers in the UK, Hungary, Australia, China, and Japan. This helped the company to further localize its product/service offerings and strengthen its presence in new markets.

In 2001, Tata acquired a controlling stake in Videsh Sanchar Nigam Ltd. (VSNL), a government company. In 2004, VSNL (now renamed Tata Communications), purchased Tyco International's[21] undersea telecom cables. This made it the world's biggest carrier of international phone calls.

In 2004, the Tata Group made history when Tata Motors acquired Daewoo Commercial Vehicle Company Limited (DWCV) for US$ 102 million, making it the first Indian company to have acquired a major foreign automobile company. The acquisition gave Tata

---

[17]"Driving Global Strategy," www.tata.com.

[18]"I Always Envisaged Tata Could be a Global Group: Ratan Tata," http://markets.moneycontrol.com

[19]Nirmalya Kumar, Pradipta K Mohapatra, and Suj Chandrashekhar, "India's Global Powerhouses," *Harvard Business Press*, 2009.

[20]"TCS Forms Cell to Take Care of Mergers and Acquisitions," www.tcs.com, Financial Express, December 15, 2001.

[21]Tyco International is a highly diversified global company that provides a large range of products and services considered important to residential and commercial customers.

TABLE 1 Major Acquisitions by TCS

Company/Acquired from	Month and year	Description	Value (in US$ million)
CMC Limited from Government of India	October 2001	Government company	33.89
WTI from International Finance Corporation, USA	December 2003	BPO	–
Airline Financial Support Services from Swiss Airlines	January 2004	Airline back office unit, BPO	5.1
Aviation Software Development Consultancy India Ltd (ASDC) from Singapore Airlines	May 2004	Consultancy and solutions in Aviation industry	–
Phoenix Global Solutions (India) Private Limited	July 2004	Insurance-domain consulting and solutions company, BPO	13
Swedish Indian IT Resources AB (SITAR)	May 2005	SITAR was TCS' exclusive partner in Sweden and a non-exclusive partner in Norway	4.8
Pearl Group	October 2005	Life and pension underwriting business	94.7
FNS	October 2005	Core banking product	26
Comicrom	November 2005	Payment processing platform	23.7
TKS-Teknosoft	November 2006	Banking product	80.4
Citi Global Services Limited	October 2008	Business process outsourcing	505

Compiled from various sources.

Motors an opportunity to enter the Korean market, an advanced stage 3 market. Also there were synergies between the two firms in terms of product strategy, R&D, and international marketing. The deal gave Tata Motors access to the medium and heavy commercial markets of China and South East Asia, and also rejuvenated its truck making division through production of bigger vehicles. This acquisition signified a major breakthrough on the globalization front for Tata Motors.

In March 2005, Tata Motors acquired a 21 percent stake in Hispano Carrocera SA, a Spanish bus manufacturing company, giving it controlling rights in the company and an option to buy the remaining stake at a later date.

In September 2005, Tata Motors entered into an agreement with Thai Rung Union Car Plc., Thailand's largest pick-up truck modifier, to set up a manufacturing unit for pick-ups in Thailand. Thailand was the largest manufacturing base for utility vehicles after

the US and a major market for utility vehicles. With this venture, Tata Motors also hoped to gain access to the ASEAN region. Tata Motors also made known its plans to set up a production base for hybrid and low-cost small cars in this region in the future.

Tata Motors also entered into a JV with brazil-based Marcopolo, the largest independent bus-manufacturer in the world, to set up the world's largest bus-manufacturing facility in India, in 2006. In July 2006, a series of alliances with Italian automaker Fiat Auto S.p.A. (Fiat Auto) gave Tata access to a range of technologies.

In 2005, the Tata Group acquired Incat International[22], a major vendor for American auto and aerospace companies. In this period, India Hotels Company, the Group's hotel business, acquired renowned hotels like The Pierre[23], the Ritz-Carlton Boston[24], and Camden Place[25].

In February 2005, Tata Steel acquired the Singapore-based steel manufacturer NatSteel Limited

[22]INCAT is the world's leading independent global professional services company engaged in Engineering & Design Services, Product Lifecycle Management, Enterprise Solutions, and Plant Automation.

[23]The Pierre opened in 1930 as a luxury hotel. Located on Fifth Avenue and opposite to Central Park in New York, this 41-story hotel consists of 201 rooms, 40 suites, and 12 grand suites.

[24]Ritz-Carlton Boston first opened its doors in 1927. Located on Arlington Road and three miles from Logan International Airport, it is one of the leading hotels in the world.

[25]Camden Place is located along Stockton Street in San Francisco and is more than 100 years old.

(NatSteel) for US$ 486.4 million. NatSteel owned steel mills in Australia, China, the Philippines, Thailand, and Vietnam. Thus, with this acquisition, the company gained access to major Asian markets and Australia. To strengthen its position further in the Asian steel industry, Tata Steel acquired the Thailand-based Millennium Steel for US$ 167 million, in December 2005.[26] These two acquisitions not only helped Tata Steel to strengthen its presence in major Asian countries but they also provided it with an additional customer base of two million tons of steel (Refer to Table 2 for Tata Steel's global acquisitions).

In January 2007, Tata Steel achieved a landmark for the Group when it acquired the Anglo-Dutch steel company Corus Group Plc (Corus) for US$ 13.70 billion. The deal made Tata Steel the fifth largest steel producer in the world as of early 2007. B Muthuraman, MD of Tata Steel, speaking on the acquisition said, "Our acquisition of these companies gave us a strong foothold in the growing economies of South East Asia and provided us the base to further consolidate our position in the region. Both these acquisitions proved to be perfect fits in Tata Steel's growth strategy."[27]

In March 2008, Tata Motors acquired Jaguar-Land Rover (JLR) for US$ 2.3 billion. Analysts were of the

view that the acquisition of JLR, which had a global presence and a repertoire of well established brands, would help Tata Motors become one of the major players in the global automobile industry (Refer to Exhibit 3 for the Tata Group's global acquisitions and to Exhibit 4 for a world map depicting the Tata Group's operations worldwide).

TABLE 2   Tata Steel's global acquisitions

Country	Acquired company by Tata Steel
Australia	Tata Steel acquired 5 per cent interest in Carborough Downs Coal
Singapore	NatSteel Asia
South Africa	Tata Steel KZN (Pty)
Sri Lanka	Lanka Special Steel
Thailand	Sila Eastern Company, Tata Steel Thailand
UK	Corus
Vietnam	MoU with Vietnam Steel Corporation

Source: Cynthia Rodrigues, "A Century of Achievements," www.tata.com, October 2007.

EXHIBIT 3   TATA GROUP'S ACQUISITIONS

Year	Tata company	Acquired company	Country	Stake acquired	Value
February 2000	Tata Tea and Tata Sons	Tetley Group	UK	100 percent	GBP 271 million
November 2001	Tata Sons (TCS)	Computer Maintenance Corporation (CMC)	India	51 percent	Not disclosed
2002					
February	Tata Sons	VSNL	India	25 percent	Rs. 14.39 billion
September	Indian Hotels	Regent Hotel (renamed Taj Lands End)	India	100 percent	Rs. 4.50 billion
December	Tata Teleservices	Hughes Telecom (India)	India	50.83 percent	Rs. 8.58 billion
2003					
May	TCS	Airline Financial Support Services India (AFS)	India	75.1 (thereby taking TCS' stake to 100 percent)	Not disclosed
July	VSNL	Gemplex	US	Assets and networks	Not disclosed

---

[26]"Tata Steel: A Decade of Transformation," www.tata.com, September 18, 2008.

[27]Cynthia Rodrigues, "A Century of Achievements," October 2007.

Year	Tata company	Acquired company	Country	Stake acquired	Value
2004					
March	Tata Motors	Daewoo Commercial Vehicle Company	Korea	100 percent	KRW 120 billion (USD102 million)
March	VSNL	Dishnet DSL's ISP division	India	-	Rs. 2.7 billion
March	TCS	Aviation Software Development Consultancy India (ASDC)	India	51 percent (thereby taking Tata Group's stake to 100 percent)	Rs. 140.2 million
June	Tata Chemicals	Hind Chemicals	India	Amalgamation	
July	TCS	Phoenix Global Solutions	India	100 percent	Not disclosed
November	VSNL	Tyco Global Network	US	100 percent	USD 130 million
2005					
February	Tata Steel	NatSteel Asia Pte Ltd	Singapore	100 percent	US$ 468.10 million
February	Tata Motors	Hispano Carrocera	Spain	21 percent	Euro 12 million
March	Tata Chemicals	Indo Maroc Phosphore S.A. (IMACID)	Morocco	33 percent	USD 38 million (Rs. 1.66 billion)
July	Indian Hotels	The Pierre	US	Lease of the property	USD 9 million
July	Tata Industries	Indigene Pharmaceuticals Inc	US	< 30 per cent	Not disclosed
July	VSNL	Teleglobe International	US	100 percent	USD 239 million
August	Tata Tech	INCAT International	UK		
August	Trent	Landmark Ltd	India	76 per cent	USD 24.09 million
September	Tata AutoComp Systems	Wündsch Weidinger	Germany	100 percent	£ 7 million
October	Tata Tea through Tata Tea (GB)	Good Earth Corporation & FMali Herb Inc	US	100 per cent	USD 31 million
October	TCS	Financial Network Services	Australia	100 percent	USD 26 million
October	TCS	Pearl Group	UK	Structured deal	
November	TCS	Comicrom	Chile	10 percent	USD 23 million
December	Indian Hotels	Starwood Group (W Hotel)	Sydney	100 per cent	USD 29 million
December	Tata Chemicals	Brunner Mond	UK	63.5 per cent (December 2005) 36.5 per cent (March 2006)	Rs. 5.08 billion (December 2005) Rs. 2.90 billion (March 2006)
2006					
January	Tata Metaliks	Usha Ispat, Redi Unit	India	100 per cent	Rs. 1.15 billion
January	Tata Interactive	Tertia Edusoft Gmbh	Germany	90 per cent	Not disclosed
		Tertia Edusoft AG	Switzerland	90.38 per cent	
April	Tata Steel	Millenium Steel	Thailand	67.11 per cent	USD 167 million (Baht 6.5 billion)

Year	Tata company	Acquired company	Country	Stake acquired	Value
May	Tata Tea through Tata Tea (GB)	JEMCA	Czech Republic	Assets: intangible and tangible	GBP 11.60 million
June	Tata Coffee	Eight O' Clock Coffee Company	US	100 per cent	USD 220 million
September	Tata Tea through Tata Tea (GB)	Joekels Tea Packers	South Africa	33.3 per cent	GBP 0.91 million
November	Indian Hotels	Ritz Carlton	US		US$ 170 million
2007					
January	Tata Steel	Corus	UK	100 percent	USD 12 billion
March	Tata Steel	Rawmet Industries	India		
April	Indian Hotels	Campton Place Hotel	US		US$ 60 million
April	Tata Power	Coastal Gujarat Power	India		
April	Tata Tea through Tetley group (now Tata Global Beverages)	Vitax and Flosana	Poland		
April	Tata Communications	Transtel Telecoms (TT)	South Africa		
June	Tata Power	PT Kaltim Prima Coal (KPC) (Bumi Resources) and PT Arutmin Indonesia	Indonesia	30 per cent equity stake	US$ 1.1 billion
October	TRF	York Transport Equipment (Asia)	Singapore	51 per cent stake	
2008					
January	Tata Chemicals	Imacid Chemical Company, Morocco			
February		General Chemical Industrial Products			$1 billion
March	Tata Motors	Jaguar-Land Rover	UK	100 percent	USD 2.3 billion
March	Telco Construction Equipment Company (Telcon)	Serviplem SA	Spain	79 per cent	
	Telco Construction Equipment Company (Telcon)	Lebrero SA	Spain	60 per cent	
June	Tata Communications	China Enterprise Communications Limited (CEC)	China	50 per cent equity interest	
August	Voltas	Rohini Industrial Electricals	India	51 per cent	
September	Tata Power	Geodynamics	Australia	10 per cent	
October	Tata Motors European Technical Centre Plc	Miljøbil Grenland/ Innovasjon	Norway	50.3 per cent	
December	TCS	Citigroup Global Services	US	100 per cent	
2009					
January	Tata Communications	Neotel	South Africa	30 per cent	
March	Tata Tea	Grand	Russia	33.2 per cent	

Year	Tata company	Acquired company	Country	Stake acquired	Value
July	TRF Manufacturers	Dutch Lanka Trailer	Sri Lanka	51 percent	
October	Tata Motors	Hispano Carrocera SA	Spain	Remaining 79 per cent	
2010					
January	Tata Communications	BT Group's (BT) Mosaic business	UK	100 per cent	
April	TRF	Hewitt Robins International	UK		
December	Rallis India (through Tata Chemicals)	Metahelix Life Sciences	India	53.5 per cent	
December	Tata Chemicals	British Salt	UK	100 per cent (wholly-owned)	
December	Tata International	Bachi Shoes India	India	76 per cent	
December	Tata International	Euro Shoe Components	India	76 per cent	
2011					
April	Tata Chemicals	Olam International, Republic of Gabon	Republic of Gabon	25.1 per cent	

Compiled from various sources.

EXHIBIT 4 TATA GROUP'S WORLDWIDE OPERATIONS

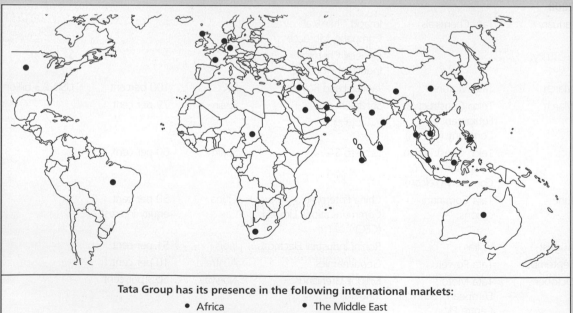

Tata Group has its presence in the following international markets:

- Africa
- Asia Pacific
- China
- Europe
- The Middle East
- North America
- South America
- The UK

Source: www.freeusandworldmaps.com.

The results

The Tata Group operated in several sectors ranging from materials, engineering, energy, consumer products, chemicals, information technology and communications, to services. These sectors contributed significantly to the group's revenues domestically as well as internationally (Refer to Table 3 for the Tata Group's sector-wise financial contribution and to Exhibit 5 for the Tata Group's sector-wise total turnover and sales turnover for FY 2001-2002 to 2010-2011). Industry experts felt that the success of the Tata Group was majorly attributable to its global acquisitions since the group reported international revenues of US\$ 48.3 billion for the FY ended 2011 (Refer to Exhibit 6 for Tata Group's financial highlights).

Many experts opined that the Tata Group had recorded growth through organic as well as inorganic growth strategies. In 2010, Tata Motors won the Indian Car of the Year (ICOTY) Award for its innovative Nano car. In the same year, Tata Motors recorded an increase of 59 percent growth for FY 2010 compared to FY 2009. Commenting on these achievements, Ratan Tata said, "One hundred years from now, I expect the Tatas to be much bigger than it is now. More importantly, I hope the group comes to be regarded as being the best in India – best in the manner in which we operate, best in the products we deliver, and best in our value systems and ethics.

Having said that, I hope that a hundred years from now we will spread our wings far beyond India..."[28]

As in the case of the group's organic growth strategies, the inorganic growth strategies also helped the group gain a stronger presence in the international markets. For instance, Tata Steel's acquisition of Corus gave Tata Steel a significant presence in the value-added steel segment and a strong distribution network in Europe.

Some auto analysts pointed out that Tata Motors' global acquisitions offered it strong synergies like expansion of the product line, good R&D capabilities, and new markets. It also gave Tata Motors the opportunity to de-risk its business by countering domestic market cyclicality through overseas expansion. The acquisitions also helped Tata Motors to accelerate its entry into new markets in China, Western Europe, South Africa, and Latin America.

Some industry observers opined that Tata Motors' alliance with foreign automakers was expected to improve its competitiveness in global automobile markets. For instance, Tata Motors' alliance with Fiat allowed the former to sell its cars in several regions of Europe through Fiat Auto's distribution network. The tie-up between Tata Motors and Fiat also provided better synergy for both the companies in terms of operational efficiency and better utilization of resources.

TABLE 3   Tata Group's sector-wise financial contribution (For FY 2010–2011)

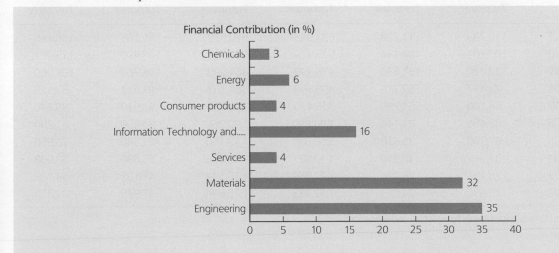

Adapted from "Tata Group Sector-wise Operations, " www.tata.com, 2012.

28"Business Outlook," http://bite.ac.uk, 2010.

EXHIBIT 5A   TATA GROUP'S SECTOR-WISE TOTAL TURNOVER AND SALES TURNOVER FOR FY 2001–2002 TO 2010-2011 (RS. IN MILLIONS)

Year	Materials		Engineering		Energy		Consumer products	
	Total turnover	Sales turnover	Total turnover	Sales turnover	Total turnover	Sales turnover	Total turnover	Sales turnover
2010–2011	1,198,418	1,188,539	1,349,593	1,347,140	200,382	196,173	158,020	155,067
2009–2010	1,036,433	1,024,555	1,059,691	1,039,782	197,107	191,111	126,179	125,485
2008–2009	1,476,470	1,473,780	784,850	774,710	183,760	177,910	96,300	95,310
2007–2008	1,321,361	1,315,609	428,359	424,136	115,552	110,641	84,540	83,727
2006–2007	278,440	274,380	391,310	397,990	74,170	71,450	68,540	67,500
2005–2006	222,400	219,380	3,00,860	2,96,820	71,510	67,610	50,880	49,960
2004–2005	1,66,240	1,64,430	2,47,380	2,44,830	67,480	62,990	48,730	47,880
2003–2004	1,35,443	1,32,043	2,03,116	1,79,042	47,545	45,903	41,894	40,765
2002–2003	1,09,394	1,08,475	1,46,803	1,28,350	47,154	45,645	40,561	39,724
2001–2002	92,543	90,026	1,20,656	1,19,962	43,565	39,926	41,036	40,149

Source: "Tata Group Sector-wise Operations," www.tata.com, 2012.

EXHIBIT 5B   TATA GROUP'S SECTOR-WISE TOTAL TURNOVER AND SALES TURNOVER FOR FY 2001-2002 TO FY 2010-2011 (RS. IN MILLIONS)

Year	Chemicals		Information Technology and Communications		Services	
	Total Turnover	Sales Turnover	Total Turnover	Sales Turnover	Total Turnover	Sales Turnover
2010–2011	112,233	111,228	621,943	610,579	156,165	138,145
2009–2010	107,101	104,134	525,329	510,310	143,499	115,913
2008–2009	132,710	131,630	470,490	464,090	108,760	101,060
2007–2008	73,417	67,718	400,590	388,753	91,612	83,573
2006–2007	66,100	64,290	326,470	318,420	94,910	89,740
2005–2006	42,490	41,140	1,94,650	1,90,960	84,450	81,290
2004–2005	37,260	35,510	1,50,500	1,48,160	81,540	78,950
2003–2004	32,711	30,316	1,37,837	1,34,266	55,696	52,008
2002–2003	28,191	26,476	1,22,984	1,18,544	47,183	54,122
2001–2002	25,996	24,413	1,32,798	1,25,694	37,975	39,830

Source: "Tata Group Sector-wise Operations," www.tata.com, 2012.

Some analysts felt that the global acquisitions gave the group an opportunity to spread its business across different geographies and across different customer segments. For instance, the acquisition of Jaguar and Land Rover provided Tata Motors an opportunity to establish its presence in the high-end premier segment of the global automobile market.

EXHIBIT 6   TATA GROUP'S FINANCIAL HIGHLIGHTS

Particulars	2010–2011 (in US$ billion)	2009–2010 (in US$ billion)	% Change
Total revenue	83.3	67.4	23.6
Sales	82.2	65.6	25.3
Total assets	68.9	52.8	30.5
International revenues	48.3	38.4	25.8
Profit after tax	5.8	1.74	233.3
Net forex earnings	1	–0.16	

Source: "Tata Group Financials," www.tata.com, 2012.

The challenges

Though the conglomerate grew through acquisitions and JVs it had to face the challenge of divesting non-performing firms on a regular basis.

The group also had to deal with the integration challenges since it followed the inorganic route to growth. It had to deal with the challenge of retention of personnel and co-ordination of sales and marketing functions in case of international acquisitions. The group also had to face the worrisome prospect of brand dilution when acquiring global companies.

Critics of Ratan Tata pointed out that he had not been successful in bringing a focus to the business portfolio of the group. The group still had a presence in a wide range of disparate businesses ranging from salt to jewelry, retailing to computer software, trucks to tea, and insurance to steel. Analysts pointed out that Ratan Tata had, in fact, added to the diversity by entering new businesses such as direct-to-home services [Tata Sky] and consumer electronics retail [Croma].

According to analysts, another major challenge for the Tata Group was that it had to face a huge debt. They felt that this was due to aggressive capital expenditure plans and past acquisitions. According to an analyst at Kotak Institutional Equities Research (Kotak), for the FY ended 2009, the Tata Group had an outstanding debt of Rs. 1 trillion.[29] The debt was majorly attributable to two global acquisitions – Tata Steel's acquisition of Corus and Tata Motors' acquisition of JLR. It was reported that the Tata Group had

spent at least two-thirds of Rs. 903.72 billion on acquisitions till 2009.[30]

The analysts estimated that the debt of the Tata Group's five companies – Tata Motors, Tata Steel Ltd, TCS, Tata Power Co. Ltd., and Tata Communications Ltd., – would be Rs. 910 billion in fiscal 2010.[31] In addition to the debt, the Tata Group was expected to face capital expenditure of Rs. 216 billion in 2010. A bulk of this capital expenditure was expected to come from Tata Steel and Tata Power. Tata Motors was also investing heavily on product development and TCS too had aggressive expansion plans. The average cost of debt of all these companies was expected to be in the region of 9 percent.[32] The group planned to revisit its capital expenditure plans if the cost of debt continued to rise like this.

In 2009, the Tata Group's growth was also affected by the sovereign debt crisis in Europe and the slowdown in the US economy, which together accounted for two-thirds of its market, according to industry observers.

Some analysts opined that the funding challenges for Tata Group were manageable and the group would be able to meet its debt obligations through cash flows generated at its various companies and proceeds from a possible sale of stake by Tata Sons. According to Jairam Nathan of Kotak, Tata Sons had the financial flexibility to support group companies in extreme cases such as a "significant drying up of the debt capital markets or deterioration in the domestic and or the globaldemand environment."[33]

---

[29]"Tata Group's Debt to Cross Rs1 Trillion by Apr, but Manageable," www.livemint.com, March 16, 2009.

[30]Satish John, "Tata Group–Scaling that Mountain of Debt," www.livemint.com, May 27, 2009.

[31]"Tata Group's Debt to Cross Rs1 Trillion by Apr, but Manageable," www.livemint.com, March 16, 2009.

[32]"Q&A: Ishaat Hussain, Finance Director, Tata Sons," www.businessstandard.com, September 9, 2011.

[33]Satish John, "Tata Group–Scaling that Mountain of Debt," www.livemint.com, May 27, 2009.

Commenting on how the Tata Group could meet its debt obligation, a Kotak analyst wrote in a report, "We believe the Tata group of companies (represented by five largest listed entities) would generate Rs10,000 crore in free cash flows in fiscal 2010, against Rs11,700 crore in debt coming due for repayment/refinance, implying a funding gap of Rs1,700 crore."[34, 35] Commenting on the Tata Group's position, another industry source opined, "It is not that the Tata group is going through a crisis, however, the high debt burden with companies such as Tata Steel and Tata Motors will have to be trimmed going ahead for the company to cut costs and increase profit margins."[36]

In January 2011, Tata Steel announced its plans to tackle the US$ 10.7 billion debt obligation by charting a three-point strategy that included focusing on internal performance, infusion of external equity, and monitoring the portfolio.[37] In July 2011, Tata Motors announced that its consolidated debt had reduced by 20.7 percent for FY 2010-2011 due to improvement in operations.[38] Despite the group companies announcing their plans of handling their debt obligation, some industry observers felt that it remained to be seen how Cyrus Mistry (Mistry), Ratan Tata's successor and the new deputy chairman of the Tata Group, would deal with the debt obligation of the Tata Group. According to *The Tribune,* a business journal, "The challenge is to rationalise Tata's 98 companies, most of which are loss-making. The total Group profit is modest and the telecom scandal has marred Tata's high ethics image. What is more, after an expensive acquisition spree of companies abroad, the Tata Group is saddled with debts."[39]

Some experts also pointed out the challenge of increasing competition coming from emerging markets such as Brazil, China, the Philippines, and Vietnam for TCS. Commenting on how Mistry would take the group forward, a company insider, said, "Cyrus has been on the board of Tata Sons since 2005 and has been credited with bringing well calibrated and intelligent suggestions to the table."[40]

The road ahead

Despite receiving criticisms for its disparate businesses, the Tata Group continued to grow with its inorganic growth strategies. In January 2012, the Tata Group entered into a JV with international coffee retail chain, Starbucks Corporation to form "Starbucks Coffee – A Tata Alliance". The JV planned to launch 30-50 outlets in India in 2012. According to Krishna Kumar, "The joint venture with Starbucks is in line with Tata Global Beverages' strategy of growing through inorganic growth focusing on strategic alliances in addition to organic growth."[41]

The group's material handling division, TRF Ltd. also announced its plans to follow the organic as well as inorganic growth route in a bid to achieve a turnover of Rs. 25,000 million by 2013.[42]

Going forward, the Tata Group was expected to vigorously pursue the inorganic route to growth. The markets which the group was looking at for inorganic growth included South East Asia, South Africa, the United States, and Europe. Analysts opined that the group should be careful about integrating all these companies under one roof. They felt that when acquiring global companies, the group should devise methods to facilitate easy integration of companies while preserving the Tata culture.

Some industry observers pointed out that the relatively brighter prospects offered by the Indian economy in comparison to developed economies might encourage the group to focus on its organic growth route in sectors such as steel, automobiles, and infrastructure. Jagannadham Thunuguntla (Thunuguntla), head of research at SMC Global, a Delhi-based brokerage, said that Mistry was likely to concentrate on organic growth in future. Thunuguntla said, "Immediate major acquisitions are unlikely under the new leadership. Mr Mistry is known for his conservatism, and the chances are he will prefer to look for organic growth."[43]

[34]"Tata Group's Debt to Cross Rs1 Trillion by Apr, but Manageable," www.livemint.com, March 16, 2009.

[35]Rs. 1 crore = Rs. 10 million.

[36]SPS Pannu and Sanjay Singh, "Challenges Ahead for Ratan Tata's Successor Cyrus Mistry," http://businesstoday.intoday.in, November 25, 2011.

[37]"Tata Steel Charts Three-point Strategy to Tackle Debt," www.telegraphindia.com, January 3, 2011.

[38]"Tata Motors Reduces Net Debt by 21% in FY11," www.financialexpress.com, July 25, 2011.

[39]"The Mystery Man's Work is Cut Out," www.tribuneindia.com, 2011.

[40]SPS Pannu and Sanjay Singh, "Challenges Ahead for Ratan Tata's Successor Cyrus Mistry," http://businesstoday.intoday.in, November 25, 2011.

[41]"Tata Starbucks to Open 30–50 Cafes this Year," January 31, 2012.

[42]Jai Wadia, "Taking the right turns," www.tata.com, January 2010.

[43]James Crabtress, "Corporate Profile: Ratan Tata," www.ft.com, 2012.

TABLE 4 Tata Group under Ratan Tata

Particulars	FY 1992 (Rs. in billion)	FY 2011 (Rs. in billion)	CAGR (in %)
Sales	82.98	3746.87	22.21
PAT	6.29	268.28	21.84
Debt	38.73	1865.65	22.62
Market Capitalization	84.94	4699.64	23.52

Source: Surajeet Dasgupta and Sharmistha Mukherjee, "Ratan Tata's 20-year Tenure: Only a Few Red Marks," www.businessstandard.com, May 8 2012.

Some experts felt that it remained to be seen whether Mistry would follow in Ratan Tata's footsteps in steering the group toward growth. It was reported that under Ratan Tata's leadership, Tata Group sales had registered a compounded annual growth rate of 22 percent between FY 1992 and FY 2011 (Refer to Table 4 for Tata Group under Ratan Tata).

Suggested readings and references

1. **"TCS Forms Cell to Take Care of Mergers and Acquisitions,"** www.tcs.com, *Financial Express,* December 15, 2001.
2. Cynthia Rodrigues, **"A Century of Achievements,"** October 2007.
3. **"Tata Steel: A Decade of Transformation,"** www.tata.com, September 18, 2008.
4. **"Tata Group's Debt to Cross Rs1 Trillion by Apr, but Manageable,"** www.livemint.com, March 16, 2009.
5. Satish John, **"Tata Group–Scaling that Mountain of Debt,"** www.livemint.com, May 27, 2009.
6. Nirmalya Kumar, Pradipta K Mohapatra, and Suj Chandrashekhar, "India's Global Powerhouses," Harvard Business Press, 2009.
7. Jai Wadia, **"Taking the Right Turns,"** www.tata.com, January 2010.
8. **"Business Outlook,"** http://bite.ac.uk, 2010.
9. **"Tata Steel Charts Three-point Strategy to Tackle Debt,"** www.telegraphindia.com, January 3, 2011.
10. **"Tata Motors Reduces Net Debt by 21% in FY11,"** www.financialexpress.com, July 25, 2011.
11. **"Q&A: Ishaat Hussain, Finance Director, Tata Sons,"** www.businessstandard.com, September 9, 2011.
12. **"The Mystery Man's Work is Cut Out,"** www.tribuneindia.com, 2011.
13. **"Tata Starbucks to Open 30–50 Cafes this Year,"** January 31, 2012.
14. SPS Pannu and Sanjay Singh, **"Challenges Ahead for Ratan Tata's Successor Cyrus Mistry,"** http://businesstoday.intoday.in, November 25, 2011.
15. Surajeet Dasgupta and Sharmistha Mukherjee, **"Ratan Tata's 20-year Tenure: Only a Few Red Marks,"** www.businessstandard.com, May 8 2012.
16. **"At Home in the World,"** www.tata.com, 2012.
17. **"Tata Group Financials,"** www.tata.com, 2012.
18. **"Tata Group Sector-wise Operations,"** www.tata.com, 2012.
19. James Crabtress, **"Corporate Profile: Ratan Tata,"** www.ft.com, 2012.
20. **"Driving Global Strategy,"** www.tata.com.
21. **"I Always Envisaged Tata Could be a Global Group: Ratan Tata,"** http://markets.moneycontrol.com.
22. **"The Tata Group: Challenges in Managing a Large Portfolio,"** http://tejas-iimb.org.

CASE 6

Nokia-Microsoft alliance: Joining forces in the smartphone wars

By Adapa Srinivasa Rao

"We are standing on a burning platform."[i]

– Stephen Elop, CEO of Nokia Corporation (Nokia), in February 2011

"There were certain things we needed.... There were certain things Microsoft required. We have found them in each other and we have built something here that together is going to be very successful."[ii]

– Stephen Elop, in February 2011

In October 2011, Nokia announced the launch of its Lumia 800 mobile phone (Refer to Exhibit 1 for Image and Specifications of the Lumia 800).[iii] The Lumia 800 was Nokia's first mobile phone to be released with the Windows Phone mobile Operating System (OS) of Microsoft Corporation (Microsoft). Nokia and Microsoft had entered into a partnership in February 2011 whereby the Windows Phone would become the primary operating system for Nokia's high-end smartphones. Nokia's partnership with Microsoft was intended to help it face up to the heavy competition in the smartphone segment from the newer entrants into the market. Nokia was a pioneer in the smartphone business and held the majority share in the smartphone market till 2007. But it started to face heavy competition from other players like Apple Inc.[1] (Apple) and Google Inc.[2] (Google) which entered the high-end smartphone market after 2007. The new mobile OSs of these companies like Android[3] and iOS[4] captured a large share of the high-end smartphone market. Nokia started to quickly lose market share. With much of the hardware remaining the same,

the OS used in the mobile phones and the number of applications available for a mobile OS were the most important factors which differentiated one smartphone manufacturer from the other. To ensure that there was more of a focus on software, Nokia's board replaced its CEO Olli-Pekka Kallasvuo with Stephen Elop (Elop) in the year 2010. Elop had been the president of Microsoft's business division before being appointed as Nokia's CEO. Soon after taking over as CEO, he wrote a memo to Nokia's employees underlining the need for drastic changes in the company.

Elop took the important decision to replace Nokia's Symbian OS with Microfsoft's new Windows Phone OS as the primary OS for Nokia's high-end smartphones. As per the deal reached, Nokia would pay royalties to Microsoft for using its OS in its smartphones. Microsoft paid Nokia US$1 billion for developing and promoting Windows Phone smartphones. Under the deal, Nokia could continue to develop and use many important applications like Nokia's own mapping software in its phones. News of the alliance received mixed reactions from analysts and industry observers. Some analysts criticized Nokia for its selection of Windows Phone instead of Android. They wondered if Windows Phone had been chosen as Elop was more comfortable with the culture of the company in which he had already worked. Elop responded to the criticism saying that Android would not have permitted Nokia to differentiate itself in the market as many other handset manufacturers used it. Nokia was also criticized for taking a risk in selecting an OS which had not proved itself in the market and which

This case was written by **Adapa Srinivasa Rao,** under the direction of **Debapratim Purkayastha,** IBS Center for Management Research. It was compiled from published sources, and is intended to be used as a basis for class discussion rather than to illustrate either effective or ineffective handling of a management situation. Printed with permission from IBS Center for Management Research and www.thecasecentre.org.

[1]Apple Inc., headquartered in Cupertino, California, USA, is a maker of a number of consumer electronics devices like personal computers, portable music players, mobile phones, etc.

[2]Google Inc., headquartered in Mountain View, California, USA, is an internet and computer software company with a global presence.

[3]Android is a mobile operating system developed and promoted by Google. It is freely distributed to many mobile manufacturing companies in the world.

[4]iOS is the mobile operating system developed by Apple. It is used in a number of its devices like the iPhone, the iPad, and the iPod.

EXHIBIT 1   IMAGE AND SPECIFICATIONS OF NOKIA'S LUMIA 800

Weight	142 grams
Screen	3.7 inches, 480*800 pixels
Camera	8 MP, 3264 × 2448 pixels, Carl Zeiss optics, autofocus, dual-LED flash
Video	720p @ 30 frames per second
OS	Microsoft Windows Phone 7.5 Mango
Processor	1.4 GHz Scorpion processor
Connectivity	Bluetooth, WLAN, HSDPA 14.4 Mbps, HSUPA 5.76 Mbps
Memory	16 GB storage, 512 MB RAM
Battery	Li-Ion 1450 mAh

Source: http://www.gsmarena.com/nokia_lumia_800-4240.php.

came from a company with a poor track record in the mobile phone business. Many industry experts believed that Microsoft was the biggest beneficiary from the alliance. Microsoft had got the biggest mobile phone manufacturer in the world to use its OS as its primary OS without even formally acquiring it. Industry observers said it remained to be seen whether the alliance would pay off and whether Nokia would be able to regain the foothold it had lost in the smartphone business. According to Ben Wood, analyst at CCS Insight,[5] "This is a clear admission that Nokia's own-platform strategy has faltered. Microsoft is the big winner in this deal, but there are no silver bullets for either company given the strength of iPhone and Google's Android."[iv] The challenge before the senior management team at Nokia and Microsoft was how to make the alliance work.

Backgroundnote

Smartphone market

The first decade of the 21st century saw a sudden increase in the market for converged-function smartphones. Convergence of technology refers to the coming together of various technologies to work in a synchronized way and deliver better performance as well as offer several new functions which were till then not available in mobile phones. The turn of the century saw the mobile phone turning into an ultimate device of aspiration for consumers around the world. The advancements in technology also enabled transfer of data at greater speeds on mobile networks. Some of the latest technological advancements like digital photography, music and video players, radios, and

[5]CCS Insight, headquartered in Slough, UK, is an industry analyst firm focusing on the mobile and wireless sector.

even GPS[6] were embedded in mobile phones. The miniaturization of mobile phones facilitated this convergence of various technologies. The mobile phone became a common multi-utility device as many people preferred to buy these converged-function devices instead of standalone electronic devices like digital cameras and music players. All the major mobile phone companies started developing and manufacturing high-end converged-function mobile phones.

Nokia had dominated the market for smartphones since its Symbian OS was released in 1997. Many other technology firms too started to sell high-end smartphones as consumers were increasingly using them for many basic computing functions like browsing the internet. Apple entered the market for smartphones with the launch of its iPhone in 2007. The iPhone was run on Apple's own mobile OS called iOS. The entry of iOS changed the face of the smartphone market. Unlike the older mobile operating systems like Symbian, iOS was custom built to support the touch interface which gaining popularity with consumers. Apple also increased the popularity of small applications (popularly known as apps) which made several tasks like internet browsing on mobile phones much easier for the consumers. Apps were custom built by either the mobile phone manufacturer or by third party developers to suit the requirements of consumers. The entry of Apple made apps the most sought after aspect in high-end smartphones by the consumers. The OS used in the smartphones and the apps along with the devices and operators came to be known as a Mobile Ecosystem. A Mobile OS with a good collection of apps was preferred by consumers. The hardware used in the smartphones from different handset manufacturers was basically the same and did not help differentiate one from the other. The competition between handset manufacturers therefore changed into a war between mobile ecosystems. Google also entered the market for smartphones with its Android mobile OS. Android too had a good collection of apps and was highly successful in the market. Thus, companies like Apple and Google which had the latest mobile OS and a huge collection of apps came to dominate the market for high-end smartphones. As of May 2011, iOS had 500,000 apps followed by Android with 200,000 apps.[v] Nokia's Symbian OS had 50,000 apps.[vi] As of November 2011, Android had a worldwide market share of 52.5 percent in the smartphone market followed by Symbian with a 16.9 percent and

iOS with 15 percent.[vii] By 2011, much of the smartphone market resembled a two-horse race involving Android and iOS.

Nokia

The origins of Nokia can be traced back to 1865, when an engineer called Knut Fredrik Idestam (Idestam) established a wood-pulp mill in southern Finland to manufacture paper. Idestam later named his business as Nokia Ab in 1871. The company also started an electricity business in 1902. Nokia Ab's business grew rapidly thanks to the huge demand for paper and cardboard during those days. The company later merged with two other companies, FCW (Finnish Cable Works) and Finnish Rubber Works (FRW), to create Nokia Corporation (Nokia). FRW was in the business of selling rubber-based products while FCW was involved in the manufacture of cables. The merged entity had five core businesses viz. rubber, cable, forestry, electronics, and power generation. Nokia's mobile phone business had its roots in the electronics section of FCW. This section started to manufacture radio telephones for the armed forces and emergency services. After the merger, the electronics section of FCW was spun off into a separate division and it started manufacturing telecommunication equipment on a full scale. Nokia entered into a joint venture with Salora Oy[7] (Salora) in 1979 to create a radio telephone company called Mobira Oy. Nokia introduced its first car phone called 'Mobira 450' in the year 1982. In 1987, Nokia launched its first handheld mobile phone called the 'Mobira Cityman' which was very successful in the market. The success in the mobile phone business led to Nokia disinvesting from its other businesses and focusing exclusively on the former. Nokia took over Salora in 1989 and the Mobira brand was replaced with the Nokia brand for its mobile phone business. Nokia became a world leader in the mobile phone business in 1998.

Nokia entered the market for high-end smartphones with the launch of mobile phones like the 'Nokia 7650', the 'Nokia 3650', and the 'Nokia 6600' in 2002 and 2003. These found instant success in the market. These smartphones were powered by the Symbian OS launched in 1997. The success of the new generation smartphones from Nokia also made Symbian the top mobile OS in the world. Nokia started two sub brands called the 'NSeries' for high-end multimedia phones

---

[6]The Global Positioning System (GPS) is a satellite-based navigation system which provides information on location and time anywhere on Earth.
[7]Salora Oy was a leading Finnish television manufacturer. It was later taken over by Nokia.

and the 'Eseries' for business phones in 2005. It reached another milestone in 2005 when it sold its billionth phone. For the fiscal year ending December 2010, Nokia's revenues were €42.45 billion.

Microsoft

Microsoft was founded by Bill Gates (Gates) and his friend Paul Allen in 1975. Microsoft was started to develop a programming language called Altair BASIC, an improved version of BASIC.[8] In 1978, Microsoft introduced its own version of COBOL[9] for personal computers (PCs). By the end of the 1970s, the company had emerged as the leader in microcomputer programming languages. Microsoft was awarded a contract by IBM[10] in 1980 to develop an operating system for its first PC, the IBM 5150. Microsoft introduced a new operating system called the Microsoft Disk Operating System (MS-DOS) for IBM PCs. In 1985, Microsoft launched a new operating system called Windows which provided a graphical operating environment for PC users. The company went public in 1986. Microsoft introduced a collection of desktop application software called Microsoft Office in 1986 which became one of its best sellers. It later started to expand its product line into computer networking. To keep pace with the internet era, Microsoft launched several new products like the Internet Explorer, a web browser, and MSN, a suite of internet services.

Microsoft had since then become the undisputed leader of the PC business. It launched a number of successful products like Windows XP and Windows 7. Microsoft also entered the video games industry with the launch of its gaming console, the Xbox. Despite being a market leader in the PC business, Microsoft started to face competition from new portable gadgets like smartphones which consumers were increasingly using for basic computing needs like internet browsing. Microsoft launched a mobile OS called Windows Mobile in the year 2000, to capture the market for smartphones. But Windows Mobile failed to capture a significant market share. Microsoft launched a new mobile OS called Windows Phone which replaced Windows Mobile in the year 2010. The first version of Windows Phone, Windows 7, was officially unveiled in February 2010 and got good reviews from analysts. A major update of Windows Phone called Windows 7.5 was launched in February 2011 with several new features. But Windows Phone still could not capture

a good market share due to heavy competition from established mobile operating systems like iOS and Android. For the fiscal year ending June 2011, Microsoft's revenues were US$ 69.94 billion.

Problems at Nokia

Nokia, considered to be the pioneer in smartphones and a global leader in the mobile phones market, started to face severe challenges to its dominance in the smartphone market in 2007. The problems came mainly in the form of competition from the new mobile operating systems that entered the market like iOS and Android (Refer to Exhibit 2 for competing platforms to Symbian). Nokia had started the smartphone business and had been the leader since the release of its smartphone OS Symbian in 1997. But the release of Apple's revolutionary mobile OS, iOS for mobile phones in 2007 led to a decline in the sales of Nokia. iOS was best suited to touchscreen smartphones which were gaining popularity among the consumers. Analysts said that the main reason for Nokia's declining fortunes was that it took too long to understand consumers' preference for touchscreen phones. Nokia could not come up with a new mobile OS which was more suitable for touchscreen phones and the updates to its existing Symbian OS did not help it in countering the new competition.

EXHIBIT 2   COMPETING MOBILE PLATFORMS TO SYMBIAN

OS	Company
Android	Google
iOS	Apple
Bada	Samsung
web OS	Hewlett-Packard
BlackBerry OS	BlackBerry
Symbian	Symbian Foundation
MeeGo	The Linux Foundation
Brew	Qualcomm
LiMo	LiMo Foundation

Compiled from various sources.

[8]BASIC (Beginners All-Purpose Symbolic Instruction Code) was one of the first programming languages for computers.
[9]COBOL (Common Business Oriented Language) was a programming language for business data processing.
[10]IBM, headquartered in New York, USA, is a multinational computer technology and consulting corporation.

Some analysts said there were some problems with the corporate culture at Nokia. They pointed out that major decisions at Nokia were not based on product vision. Potential ideas were either delayed or ignored by the top management. The management was not innovative and there were too many silos in the company working independently without any communication with other departments, they said. Nokia started to lose market share fast. Its share of the global mobile phone market fell from 34.8 percent in 2006 to 32 percent in 2010.[viii,ix] Nokia's share of the smartphone market too fell from 73 percent in 2006 to 36.6 percent in 2010 and to just 14.4 percent by the third quarter of 2011 (Refer to Exhibit 3 for Nokia's market share figures for 2010 and Exhibit 4 for Nokia's market in third quarter of 2011).[x,xi] By the third quarter of 2011, Symbian's market share had fallen to just 17 percent while Android's had crossed the 50 percent mark (Refer to Exhibit 5 for the market share of various mobile OS for the third quarter of 2011). In order to halt the decline in its market share, Nokia brought down the prices of some of its high-end smartphones, a move that put more pressure on its profits. It still had a significant market share in the low-end feature phones.

EXHIBIT 3   NOKIA'S MARKET SHARE IN 2010

Total mobile phone sales	352.6 million units
Share in total mobile phone sales	32 percent
Smart phone sales	100.3 million units
Share in the smart phone market	36 percent

Source: "Nokia Corporation: Interim Report," http://ncomprod. nokia.com, January 27, 2011.

But the profit margins in that segment were low – which again put the pressure on Nokia's profit numbers. Nokia's profit after tax went down from €4,366 million in 2006 to €1,343 million in 2010 (Refer to Exhibit 6 for the consolidated income statement of Nokia from 2006 to 2010).

What compounded the problems for Nokia, was that some new small players like Micromax[11] had started to target it at the low end of the market in India

EXHIBIT 4   MARKET SHARE OF MOBILE OS FOR 2011 Q3 (IN PERCENTAGES)

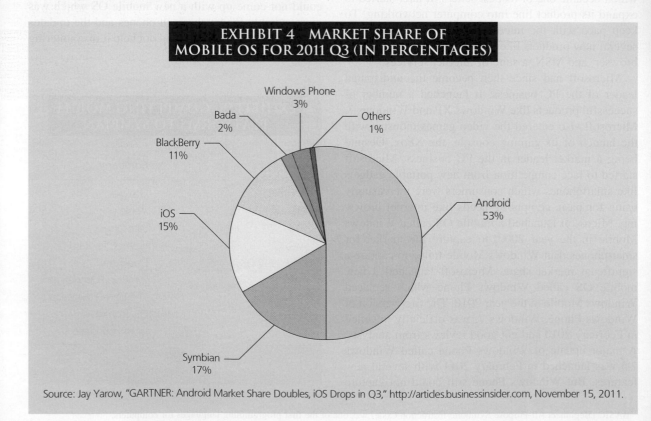

Source: Jay Yarow, "GARTNER: Android Market Share Doubles, iOS Drops in Q3," http://articles.businessinsider.com, November 15, 2011.

[11]Micromax, headquartered in Gurgaon, Haryana, India is a manufacturer of low-end mobile phones.

EXHIBIT 5   GLOBAL SHARE OF SMART PHONE SHIPMENTS FOR 2011 Q3 (IN PERCENTAGES)

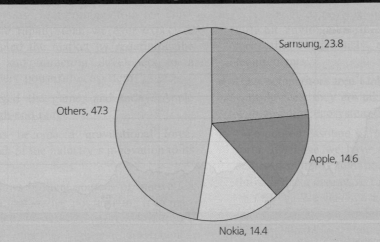

Source: Darren Murph, "Samsung Claims Top Spot in Global Smartphone Shipments for Q3 2011, Apple Slips to Number Two," http://www.engadget.com, October 28, 2011.

EXHIBIT 6   CONSOLIDATED INCOME STATEMENT OF NOKIA FROM 2006 TO 2010

					(figures in Euro (€) million)
	2010	**2009**	**2008**	**2007**	**2006**
Net sales	42,446	40,984	50,710	51,058	41,121
Cost of sales	(29,629)	(27,720)	(33,337)	(33,754)	(27,742)
Gross profit	12,817	13,264	17,373	17,304	13,379
Research and development expenses	(5,863)	(5,909)	(5,968)	(5,647)	(3897)
Selling and marketing expenses	(3,877)	(3,933)	(4,380)	(4,380)	(3,314)
Administrative and general expenses	(1,115)	(1,145)	(1,284)	(1,180)	(666)
Impairment of goodwill	–	(908)	–	–	–
Other income	476	338	420	2,312	522
Other expenses	(368)	(510)	(1,195)	(424)	(536)
Operating profit	2,070	1,197	4,966	7,985	4,639
Profit before tax	1,786	962	4,970	8,268	5,723
Tax	(443)	(702)	(1,081)	(1,522)	(1,357)
Profit	1,343	260	3,889	6,746	4,366

Source: Nokia Form 20-F-2007 and Nokia Form 20-F-2010.

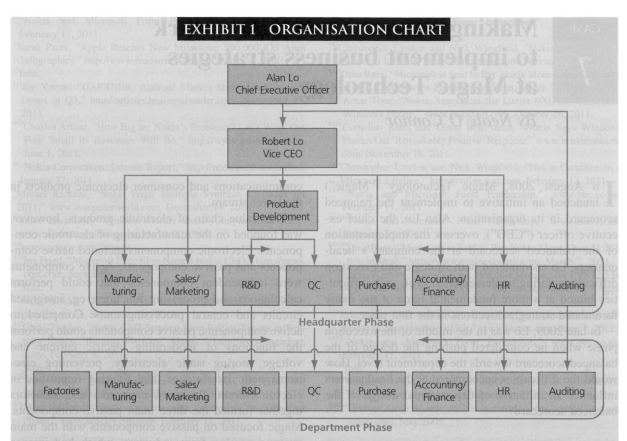

EXHIBIT 1 ORGANISATION CHART

```
                    Alan Lo
              Chief Executive Officer
                        |
                    Robert Lo
                     Vice CEO
                        |
                    Product
                  Development
```

| Manufac-turing | Sales/Marketing | R&D | QC | Purchase | Accounting/Finance | HR | Auditing |

Headquarter Phase

| Factories | Manufac-turing | Sales/Marketing | R&D | QC | Purchase | Accounting/Finance | HR | Auditing |

Department Phase

Source: Lo, P. C. (2009) "The Difficulties Encountered and Suggestions Related to Implementing the Balanced Scorecard: A Case Study of an EMI Components Designer and Manufacturer", EMBA Dissertation, College of Commerce, National Chengchi University, Taiwan; Magic Technology's website: http://www.magictec.com.tw; Company interview on 10 March 2011.

in which strategies were formed through discussions in meetings, using past experience as the basis for decision making, were not obvious. In addition, there was no mechanism to evaluate the strategy execution, so it was difficult to observe the effectiveness of different strategies. Second, the operational execution in the factories was weak. The mainland factories were still constructing the standard operating process, and the stability of production quality was not reliable. Third, the performance checking mechanism had not been completed. The mainland factories had evaluated and tracked the key performance indicators ("KPIs"), but had not connected them to performance. The Taiwan headquarters did not have a system of KPIs at all. Fourth, the management systems needed to be strengthened. There were several management systems implemented at Magic, but Lo felt that these systems had not been fully implemented and the data had not been systematised. Last but not least, the product analysis was insufficient. Product prices had been set by referring to market prices, and there was no data to support the decisions

regarding either internal-made or external-procurement products.

These five business challenges drove Lo to start searching for new management systems for Magic. The balanced scorecard was proposed to deal with the first four of the five business challenges: unclear business strategies, weak execution, difficult performance assessment and weak management systems for Magic.

Preparation phase

To start with, Lo and Magic's management team assessed the current state and the target state of management in three areas: strategy formation, strategy execution and performance management.

First of all, Magic was not equipped with a relevant existing management and operational mechanism for strategy formation. Lo hoped to construct an integrated structure and logic of strategy formation management, in order to build a more comprehensive strategy formation mechanism. Second, there was no

EXHIBIT 2   ELECTRONICS INDUSTRY

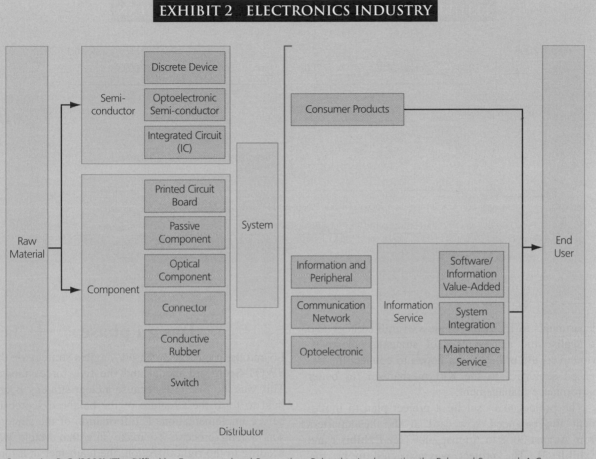

Source: Lo, P. C. (2009) "The Difficulties Encountered and Suggestions Related to Implementing the Balanced Scorecard: A Case Study of an EMI Components Designer and Manufacturer", EMBA Dissertation, College of Commerce, National Chengchi University, Taiwan.

concrete mechanism for strategy execution, causing issues like the miscommunication of strategy, the lack of management for strategy execution and the reduced effectiveness of strategy. Through the discussion about the strategy map, the design of the balanced scorecard and the subsequent implementation, Lo wanted the top management's strategic thinking to be understood more effectively and accurately by the staff. This was meant to help improve execution and management, thereby allowing senior management to spend more time on strategic thinking. Third, Magic had tried to improve the current state of performance management by importing the KPI system, but this KPI system was a bottom-up setting, which could easily lose focus in the long term or when Magic expanded. Lo wanted to integrate the KPI system with the balanced scorecard, in order to increase the visibility of the linkage

between the KPIs of departments and staff and the business strategy. Under this new structure, it would be easier to resolve the problem about the fairness of the incentive mechanism.

With the management objectives borne in mind, Magic set up a project team to oversee the overall project planning, including expected project aims and benefits, project scope and schedule, project team formation, and the related training and communication for change management. The project aimed to turn the intangible strategy into a more concrete one, and accurately execute strategy management. For the project benefits, it was hoped to build up a management and execution mechanism of strategy formation. This helped form a consensus of Magic's strategy among the staff, and build up the specific execution mechanism of the strategy, in order to assist different

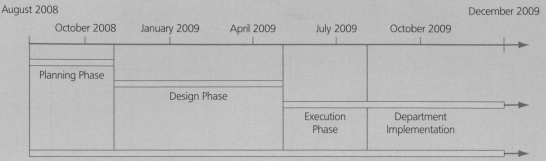

EXHIBIT 3   BALANCED SCORECARD PROJECT PLAN

Source: Lo, P. C. (2009) "The Difficulties Encountered and Suggestions Related to Implementing the Balanced Scorecard: A Case Study of an EMI Components Designer and Manufacturer", EMBA Dissertation, College of Commerce, National Chengchi University, Taiwan.

departments to focus on Magic's overall strategy and to realise the achievement of strategic objectives. Moreover, the project team hoped to connect the balanced scorecard to the KPI mechanism for better performance management.

The project team set up a project plan to implement the balanced scorecard at the headquarters from August 2008 to August 2009 [see **Exhibit 1** and **Exhibit 3**]. The project was expected to be implemented at the headquarters—auditing, sales and marketing, product development (research and development ["R&D"] and quality control), purchasing, accounting and finance, and human resources—in three phases: preparation before implementation, designing the balanced scorecard and executing the balanced scorecard. In late 2009, the implementation would be pushed towards the department level (manufacturing and three factories). Because the project scope involved a number of departments in Magic, its implementation had to cause a great amount of change inside Magic, so the project team member selection and operation were very important. After careful consideration, the project team consisted of an overall project leader, a project manager, project members and external consultants [see **Exhibit 4**]. Moreover, in order to gain the agreement and support from the department managers, the project team scheduled a series of internal learning and training sessions about the conceptual framework of the balanced scorecard, so that the department managers would be more willing to actively participate in and assist with the project implementation.

Design phase

Lo and the project team based Magic's strategy on the SWOT-Scorecard model and the five forces model. This was the first task because a clear strategy is critical to form the structure of the balanced scorecard before implementation. The formation of the strategy was a long process. To make sure that Magic was heading in the right direction, the team met in a long and iterative discussion process to form a detailed strategy and gather the content to structure the balanced scorecard. The formation of strategy underwent six stages, described as follows.

Strategy formation

In the first stage of the discussion process, the project team did an internal and external environment analysis of Magic. This analysis clarified the equipped competencies of Magic to assess the parts that required strengthening and supplementation and to shape the future state of Magic.

Second, the team used the SWOT-Scorecard question set for a strategy discussion. This SWOT-Scorecard question set integrated the SWOT analysis and the four areas of the balanced scorecard to form a matrix, in which each intersected box contained corresponding questions for team members to answer [see **Exhibit 5**]. This question set was used to increase the team's understanding of Magic, but in addition the team found that the less obvious competitors' situation was better observed through this question set. Thus the

EXHIBIT 4   BALANCED SCORECARD PROJECT TEAM

Project team member	Position and responsibility
Overall Project Leader (CEO and vice-CEO)	■ Guide the strategic direction of the project ■ Guiding and ruling the important agendas
Project Manager	■ Assist to exclude the encountered obstacles in the implementation process ■ Provide cross-departmental communication and coordination ■ Command execution staff to complete related operations according to scheduled progress ■ Project detailed planning ■ Coordination and control of productivity and progress ■ Arrange meeting and education training
Project Members	■ Project execution tasks
External Consultants	■ Guiding of project direction ■ Raise suggestions specific to the encountered difficulties in the project implementation ■ Project quality control, and regular productivity inspection

Source: Lo, P. C. (2009) "The Difficulties Encountered and Suggestions Related to Implementing the Balanced Scorecard: A Case Study of an EMI Components Designer and Manufacturer", EMBA Dissertation, College of Commerce, National Chengchi University, Taiwan.

EXHIBIT 5   MAGIC'S SWOT-SCORECARD (STRENGTH)

Perspective	Strength
Financial	■ Own funding is sufficient, with healthy financial structure and relatively low debt ratio ■ Good credit with banks ■ Material procurement advantage in specific markets and vertical integration capability ■ Low-priced raw material for testing and importing
Customer	■ APL product has high share and importing new products is fast ■ High customer segment understanding and good customer interaction ■ High M/B market understanding helps increase the NB market entering advantage ■ Appearance on international renowned brand's vender list can be used to extend to other markets
Process	■ APL semi-automatic manufacturing can reduce costs and increase productivities ■ Strong R&D capability ■ Granted patents ■ Stable and high retention of core personnel ■ Granted patents can hinder competitors
Learning and Growth	■ Importing BSC ■ Strong operation capability can satisfy customer R&D demand that provides a wider range of services than the competitors

Source: Lo, P. C. (2009) "The Difficulties Encountered and Suggestions Related to Implementing the Balanced Scorecard: A Case Study of an EMI Components Designer and Manufacturer", EMBA Dissertation, College of Commerce, National Chengchi University, Taiwan.

strengths insisted on in the beginning did not seem to be unique for Magic in the end. Furthermore, upon the completion of the SWOT-Scorecard, the most important point became how to allocate the existing resources.

To first strengthen the advantages, or to first improve the weaknesses? How to make the decision to allocate the existing resources?

– Alan Lo, CEO of Magic[2]

Thus the discussion turned to exploring the most core issues, what the competitive elements of Magic were, and what the advantages compared with the competitors were, in order to decide the allocation of the existing resources.

Third, the team could see the SWOT-Scorecard from multiple perspectives, which could result in a lot of different strategies, but not all of the strategies were suitable for the current state of Magic. Thus the team needed to have discussions in order to determine the suitable strategic direction. Magic, for example, had the strength of low-priced raw material for testing and importing. On the other hand, it had to respond to the threat of the frequent revisions of labour laws in mainland China, which increased the wage costs, and the threats of products that had low technical entry barriers, high substitutability and high potential to be imitated. Thus the two things together inspired the team to form the strategic direction of automating existing products (Assembly-type plug-in inductor ["APL"] in the motherboard ["M/B"] market, IRON, and the multi-turn loop market).

Fourth, up to this step, the team had formed the strategic directions to pursue operational excellence. But these strategic directions were too broad for different product series, which had different customers, different selling methods, different market shares and different life cycles, in order to guide their required execution plan. Thus, the team used a product matrix of industry attractiveness versus company strength to determine specific product strategies.

Fifth, based on the strategy analysis results, the team formed and summarised specific product strategies and determined the priority of different product strategies. According to the SWOT-Scorecard model with the in-depth analysis of each department, the product strategies were further summarised as three parts. First, because the factories had a problem of insufficient productivity, and a lot of original equipment manufacturers existed in the market and had different automated equipments, the project team hoped to set up an outsourcing department. This outsourcing department would make the product categories of buying and outwork clear, and would set up a clear outsourcing process. Second, besides consolidating the existing printed circuit board market, the team hoped to enter the new notebook board ("NB") market to increase the market share. This was because demand was greater than supply in the NB market, and the team could use existing relationships to enter the market, while there were not many existing Taiwanese factories able to mass produce NB moulding products. This would help push Magic's products into a new market. Third, the team hoped to consolidate and strengthen the existing main product series, and the existing M/B market as well.

Strategy map

Lastly, the team set up the strategy map to formulate Magic's strategic objectives. The strategy map was a standard structure to describe strategy, using a set of consistent and standard strategic language, for the internal staff to align, focus and integrate their ideas with the four perspectives of the balanced scorecard, such that the strategy could be more concrete for the implementation of the balanced scorecard. The strategy map formulated the strategic objectives that would be used in the next stage [see **Exhibit 6**].

Strategic KPI design

The project team considered the previous formulated strategic objectives for the design of strategic KPIs in the balanced scorecard. Strategic KPIs were one or several strategic and representing indicators, which emphasised quantifying the formulated strategic objectives and setting up the estimated target value for management. The project team first thought about and designed the related parts of the strategic KPIs, including the KPIs themselves and their formulae, frequencies and target values. Then the strategic KPIs were discussed with an external consultant during the learning sessions. During the discussions, it was discovered that some KPIs were repetitive, and these were deleted from the balanced scorecard.

---

[2]Lo, P. C. (2009) "The Difficulties Encountered and Suggestions Related to Implementing the Balanced Scorecard: A Case Study of an EMI Components Designer and Manufacturer", EMBA Dissertation, College of Commerce, National Chengchi University, Taiwan.

EXHIBIT 6 STRATEGY MAP

	Customer Value: Operation Excellence Main, Product Leadership Supplement				
Financial	Revenue Increase				Productivities Increase
Customer	Become Customer Trusted Supplier (Brand Advantage)		One Stop Procurement (Existing Market)	Enter New Market (NB Market)	Operation Excellence
Process	Customer Relationship Management	Brand Management	One Stop Procurement Management	New Market Enter Management (NB Market)	Operation Excellence Management
Learning and Growth	Customer Relationship Management Capabilities	Brand Management Capabilities	One Stop Procurement Management Capabilities	New Market Enter Management (NB Market)	Operation Excellence Management Capabilities
	Good Corporate Culture: Trust, System, Execution			Management Leadership Capabilities	IT System Integration Capabilities

Source: Lo, P. C. (2009) "The Difficulties Encountered and Suggestions Related to Implementing the Balanced Scorecard: A Case Study of an EMI Components Designer and Manufacturer", EMBA Dissertation, College of Commerce, National Chengchi University, Taiwan.

Then, the project team connected the formulated strategic objectives and the strategic KPIs together during the design [see **Exhibit 7**]. One example was entering a new NB market, which was prioritised and ordered as one of the very important short-term strategies. In the customer perspective of the balanced scorecard, the strategic objectives included rapid entering of a new market, cost advantages, and quality advantages. The NB products were new products for Magic, so when these strategic objectives were connected to the financial perspective, Magic's financial objective was to "develop new targeted product's revenue". In the process perspective, its objective was "development management in new market". This was to achieve a rapid entering of a new market and a cost advantage, such as the rapid importing of R&D and production, and activity-based cost management ("ABCM"). Towards the downstream of the learning and growth perspective, the objective was "development management capability in new market". Because it had been confirmed that the new product was the SMD Power Choke product series in the new NB market, the learning and growth objective was set to develop the R&D, the production capability and the cost management capability for the SMD Power Choke product series. From this example, it could be seen that, besides the fact that each strategic objective in different perspectives had a casual relationship with each other, each respective KPI in different perspectives had a casual relationship with each other for entering a new NB market too.

Besides, during discussions, the team had difficulty in setting out the calculation formula of KPIs. For the target value, because a lot of KPIs had not been used before, their target values were thus difficult to define.

EXHIBIT 7 STRATEGIC OBJECTIVES AND KPIS (NEW MARKET)

Perspective	Strategic objective	Definition	KPI
Financial	Develop new targeted product's revenue	Targeted products have revenue growth in all markets, including internal-made or external-procure parts.	Revenue growth rate Gross profit
Customer	Rapid entering of new market	To win the first opportunity, competition of timing is the most important element.	R&D progress chart
Customer	Cost advantage	Except the timing is right, the low cost of targeted products is also the need in NB market.	Cost achievement rate No of customers transacted in new market
Customer	Quality advantage	The quality of targeted products is one of the top considering items for customers	Customer complaint rate
Process	Rapid importing of R&D and production	Rapid entering of new market must speed up the R&D and production importing internal process. Besides, to adapt customer needs, the improvement of old products and development of new products are both critical.	Annual R&D and production plan No of old products improved No of new products developed
Process	ABCM	To achieve cost advantage in new market, the right timing of using ABCM is needed for management purpose.	Time to implement ABC
Learning and Growth	R&D and production capability for SMD Power Choke	The understanding and production capability of targeted products must be sufficient, for rapid importing of R&D and production.	No of recruited staff
Learning and Growth	Cost management capability for SMD Power Choke	The capability to manage the cost of targeted products must be equipped, in order to achieve cost management for cost advantage.	Training hours

Source: Lo, P. C. (2009) "The Difficulties Encountered and Suggestions Related to Implementing the Balanced Scorecard: A Case Study of an EMI Components Designer and Manufacturer", EMBA Dissertation, College of Commerce, National Chengchi University, Taiwan.

After the company's headquarters had designed the KPIs, the KPIs were passed on to respective responsible departments for further discussion. The department managers discussed the KPIs' rationale, the difficulty and the method of data collection, in order to understand whether the data tables from the data sources were sufficient, whether the data tables were integral, and whether the KPI's data sources were enough. This could further determine whether the KPIs could be used to evaluate the extent of achievement of strategic objectives, and whether there was a need to revise and add tables in the data sources.

Because Magic had implemented an enterprise resource planning ("ERP") system, to obtain accurate and easily collected content, around 50% of the table sources came from the many direct outputted tables of the ERP system, while the remaining 50% needed hand-made statistics. But, if there were too many KPIs to be concentrated on at the same time, this would cause a diverse focus and a lack of attention

EXHIBIT 8 KPI OPERATIONAL GUIDE TEMPLATE

Process/step	Explanation	Document/system source
1. Collect this quarter's new product number	1. Enter DataSystems ERP, Inventory management system, "Product number creation operation".	DataSystems ERP System
	2. Enter "Product number creation operation". Search for 'Advance Setting'. Set condition to be "Creation date >= This quarter's start date" and "Creation date <= This quarter's end date".	DataSystems ERP System
	3. During collection of results, open the "Management column" in 'Function', in order to see the 'Creation Date' column.	DataSystems ERP System
2. Count this quarter's old series' new part number	1. Export the search results to EXCEL, to count new product numbers.	EXCEL
	2. Add "Count" column. Add "1" in each property, to count new parts. Sum this item to obtain this quarter's valid number of mass produced R&D products.	EXCEL

Source: Lo, P. C. (2009) "The Difficulties Encountered and Suggestions Related to Implementing the Balanced Scorecard: A Case Study of an EMI Components Designer and Manufacturer", EMBA Dissertation, College of Commerce, National Chengchi University, Taiwan.

on the most key strategic KPIs and strategic objectives.

Too many directions meant no direction. We should use the strategic KPIs which needed the most attention and which were immediately implementable as our management emphasis.

– Alan Lo, CEO of Magic[3]

Thus, in order to control and manage the most important strategic KPIs, during the discussions, the project team asked different department managers about which strategic KPIs were the most important and which they were most unwilling to give up. These discussions had produced the strategic KPIs' collection method, and the operational guide to create different strategic KPIs [see **Exhibit 8**].

Execution phase

Lo was aware that a lot of other companies were executing numerous action plans, but those action plans were usually fragmented, in which they had no relationships to the set strategic objectives but competed for limited resources. This inappropriate use of human resources and financial resources could result in a failure to create a competitive advantage, or even a loss to competitors. If Magic could use the balanced scorecard as a foundation for its management system, cohesion could be formed between different action plans to pursue Magic's strategic objectives and measurements all together. The action plans, which aimed to achieve strategic objectives, were called strategic action plans. Strategic action plans had obvious and close connections to Magic's strategies, and could be connected to the budget and the staff's performance as well. Because enterprise resources were limited, to ensure that the strategic objectives reflected on the balanced scorecard could be realised and implemented, there was a need to use the strategic action plans. Therefore, the existing action plans needed to be reviewed, in order to clarify their connections with the strategic objectives. Those action plans that did not have a strategic meaning were deleted, while new strategic action plans had to be created for those strategic objectives that lacked support.

The project team listed out all the action plans in Magic first in the execution phase. Then, the team used the matching table of strategic objectives against action plans to filter out the strategic action plans. New

[3]Ibid.

EXHIBIT 9   PRIORITY AND ORDER TABLE OF STRATEGIC ACTION PLANS

Criteria	Weighting	Explanation	Score (Plan A)	Weighted score (Plan A)
Strategic connection	45%	Have positive influence to the success of strategic objectives or not		
Resource requirement (key personnel)	20%	Required key personnel, investing time and resource		
Demanded completion time	10%	Estimated completion time		
Dependency	10%	The extent of influence from the success of other action plans		
Total costs	15%	Total costs including human resource and material		
Total	100%			

Source: Lo, P. C. (2009) "The Difficulties Encountered and Suggestions Related to Implementing the Balanced Scorecard: A Case Study of an EMI Components Designer and Manufacturer", EMBA Dissertation, College of Commerce, National Chengchi University, Taiwan; Niven, P. R. (2002) *Balanced Scorecard Step by Step: Maximizing Performance and Maintaining Results*, John Wiley & Sons, Inc.: Hoboken, NJ, p. 194.

strategic action plans could be added and existing action plans could be deleted. However, as a result of the discussion, a total of 10 action plans were filtered out, which would require too many resources for Magic.

Are these 10 action plans all required to complete within this year? How to make the decision to prioritize and order the action plans?

– Alan Lo, CEO of Magic[4]

Thus, the filtered strategic action plans were prioritised and ordered [see **Exhibit 9**]. The priority and order of the strategic actions plans were determined using six weighted criteria. The six weighted criteria covered a wide range of areas, including strategic connections, resource requirements (key personnel), demanded completion time, dependency and total costs. In addition, in the matching table, each strategic objective was marked with its importance and completion period, and this could help determine the order of strategic action plans as well.

For each strategic action plan, the team made a strategic action plan proposal, detailing the expected benefits, KPIs, responsible departments, team structure and managers, contents and time schedule, and communication plans. These strategic action plan

proposals could guide the follow-up implementation actions at Magic.

Lastly, the follow-up implementation actions were to integrate the balanced scorecard into the normal operations at Magic. These implementation actions would develop the management system for the balanced scorecard, collect the KPI information, hold the strategy evaluation meetings and push the implementation of the balanced scorecard towards the department level. These implementation actions, however, had not been completed in late 2009.

Departmental design

In late 2009, Lo was in the execution phase when he considered pushing the design of the balanced scorecard towards the department level. As a result, Lo and the project team evaluated the early progress of the process at the company's headquarters to investigate the encountered difficulties and the respective solutions. This evaluation would make the project team better manage the departmental design of the balanced scorecard in the late execution phase.

The evaluation was done for the previous three phases of implementation: preparation before implementation,

[4]Ibid.

design of the balanced scorecard, and the early progress of the execution of the balanced scorecard.

In the preparation phase, the project team encountered several difficulties in understanding Magic's real requirements. In the beginning, Magic's managers could only roughly describe their own challenges, but they did not know what the most urgently required management system was for them. Magic's managers were unfamiliar with the balanced scorecard system, and had difficulty understanding why and how this system could deal with their challenges.

One other preparation issue was related to the project's overall planning. Would the managers need to formulate a strategy, or need to complete some basic foundation and management system, before constructing the balanced scorecard? How to decide the unit level of implementation of the balanced scorecard? Would headquarters need to begin implementation first? Furthermore, the managers did not understand the main difficulties associated with implementing this system, how to overcome them, and how long it would take to import this system into Magic as well.

In the design phase, there were some problems in preparing the SWOT-Scorecard analysis and the quantification of strategic KPIs. For the SWOT-Scorecard analysis, after the completion of the analysis, how should Magic's existing resources be allocated? Should Magic reinforce the strengths first, or should it improve the weaknesses first? For Magic, what would be emphasised when selecting strategies? How to match the strategic position of different product series into Magic's business portfolio? For the quantification of strategic KPIs, if there were some KPIs currently unobtainable, should the balanced scorecard still continue to be implemented, or should the implementation be held until all the KPIs were obtainable? To avoid KPIs being manipulated by employees, it would be better to directly obtain them from the information systems, but should Magic invest in huge costs for setting up information systems for this purpose? Furthermore, would the KPIs fail to achieve their functions or to reach their targets, because of little motivation (eg, the KPIs not connected to incentives) or because of the design of the KPIs themselves?

In the early execution phase, some problems with the strategic action plans had confused the project team as well. How to closely connect the strategic action plans to the strategic objectives, and what could be counted as a close connection to the strategic objectives? These were the difficulties that could hinder the future departmental design of the balanced scorecard.

In late 2009, Lo had to consider some problems with managing the departmental design of the balanced scorecard in the late execution phase. The departmental level often undertook the strategies designed by headquarters, but when the headquarters had set up the strategy map and had designed the strategic KPIs in the balanced scorecard, would the departmental level need to set up the strategy map, or just to undertake the strategic KPIs in the balanced scorecard? The departmental level had some important work items that had not appeared in the headquarters' strategy map. Should these work items be shown on the departmental strategy map, or should just the departmental part of the headquarters' strategy map be shown on the departmental strategy map? How to connect the departmental strategic KPIs to departmental functions that were not strategic?

CASE 8

Sony Corp Japan: Challenges before the new CEO

By Prof. S. Bhaskaran

Abstract

The iconic brand Sony Corp, Japan was a pioneer in the introduction of new innovative electronic gadgets. It had ventured into diverse fields such as Electronics, Games, Entertainment, and Financial Services. Its convergence strategy had placed it in a high pedestal in the consumer electronics industry. But due to stiff competition and other natural disasters, it had suffered losses continually since 2004. The outgoing CEO Howard stringer had taken effective steps to avert these losses, but in vain.

The Sony veteran and the present CEO, Kazuo Hirai was making strategic moves and measures to revive the past glory of the company. These strategic initiatives were expected to bring in more revenue and profits to the ailing electronics major. This case study will analyse the growth of Sony over the years, its fall from glory and if the turnaround initiatives of the present CEO Kazuo Hirai would help in restoring the lost glory of Sony Corporation.

Pedagogical objectives

The case study helps to understand and analyse:

- Growth of Sony Corp, Japan
- Falling Fortunes of Sony
- Challenges Ahead of New CEO Kazuo Hirai.

Case study

"I consider it my job to nurture the creativity of the people I work with, because at Sony we know that a terrific idea is more likely to happen in an open,

free and trusting atmosphere than when everything is calculated, every action analysed and every responsibility assigned by an organisation chart."[1]
– Akio Morita[2]

"It won't be easy for Sony to regain its lost ground under new leadership, as its overall competitiveness has sharply weakened."[3]
– Kim Young-Chan[4]

Sony Corp, Japan was a global leader in Electronics, Pictures, Gaming and Financial services. It had always stood for innovation and quality. The brand Sony was considered iconic. However, in the recent years, it had not kept pace with the rapidly changing global market conditions. The competitors were way ahead of many of Sony's products in terms of pricing and technology. Its convergence strategy had proved costly.

The previous CEO, Howard Stringer (Stringer) was not able to avert its successive losses since 2004. Its TV market was not doing well and the present incumbent CEO Kazuo Hirai (Hirai) had proposed many strategic initiatives to revive the loss making electronics major. The case study traced the growth of Sony Corp, its recurring losses and the initiatives of Hirai to turnaround the company.

Sony Corp, Japan: Ascent as a global brand in electronics

Sony Corp, Japan was founded in 1946[5] by two men Masaru Ibuka, an Engineer and a Physicist Akio Morita (Morita). They had pooled in Yen 190,000 and started the operations with 20 employees. The

---

[1]"On Openness...", http://creatingminds.org/quotes/openness.htm
[2]Chairman, Sony Corporation (1921–1999).
[3]Layne Nathan and Kubota Yoko, "Sony sees $2.9 billion loss, new CEO warns of pain", http://www.msnbc.msn.com/id/46236852/ns/business-world_business/t/sony-sees-billion-loss-new-ceo-warnspain/#.T4Jlnv Ba4W8, February 2nd 2012
[4]An analyst at Shinhan Investment Corp in Seoul.
[5]"About Sony", http://www.sony-europe.com/article/id/1178278971500

company was originally named as Tokyo Tsushin Kogyo K.K.[6] The founders relied on their own intelligence and engineering expertise in developing new products.

Since its inception, the company had stood for innovative products. They had launched 'Soni-Tape', Japan's first magnetite-coated, paper-based recording tape in the year 1950.[7] They also made Japan's first magnetic G-Type tape recorder, which became a popular recording device in government offices.[8] Their innovation streak was made public through the launch of world's first all-transistor radio in 1955.[9] In 1958, they changed the name of the company from Tokyo Tsushin Kogyo K.K. to Sony Corporation.[10] The word Sony was the combination of two words – Sonus, (a Latin word meaning sound) and 'sonny boy' (a young person with free and pioneering spirit).[11] The newly coined word Sony had reflected the energy and passion of the founder members.

Their path breaking innovation was Trinitron Colour Television in 1968. The other new products introduced were colour video cassette player in 1971, Betamax VCR in 1975, Walkman in 1979, the world's first CD player in 1982 and 8mm camcorder based on a universal standard in 1985. In 1991, Sony had brought-in revolution through its gaming systems called PlayStation. A revamped version with CD-ROM-based game was launched as PlayStation X or PSX in 1994. It became a very popular gaming system.[12] They were also the first to introduce digital video camcorder in 1995 for the consumer use. The surveys conducted in early 2000s had revealed that Sony was the most recognised and esteemed brand name in the United States. This was far ahead of brands like Coca Cola, General Motors and General Electric.[13] It was ranked No. 2 globally in consumer electronic goods after Panasonic Company. It was considered as the coolest brand by the American teens after Nike and Tommy Hilfiger.[14] Sony was one of the companies from Japan with international focus, and it had made the tag, "Made In Japan" a reality in quality terms. It had changed the consumer perception of quality electronic products. The compact size of Sony's products with high quality had attracted the customers. Sony continued its innovation streak and launched "Blu-ray Disc" recorder in 2003 and the world's first consumer use digital HD video camera recorder in 2004 that conformed to High Definition Video (HDV) standards.[15] Forbes had ranked Sony as the 72nd largest global company in 2004.[16]

In 2006, it was ranked as the top global brand in Harris poll[17] for the seventh consecutive year. Sony had become an iconic brand and its launch of PlayStation 3 had brought in fresh laurels. Since then, it had grown from strength to strength (Annexure 1). Sony Corp had become a leader in manufacturing audio, video, communications and information technology products for both professional as well as consumer markets.[18] It had emerged as one of the most comprehensive entertainment and technology companies in the world. Sony's consolidated annual sales were $87 billion for the fiscal year ended March 31, 2011. It had employed 168,200 people worldwide.[19]

Sony had used cutting edge technologies in all their innovations such as BRAVIA®TV, BRAVIA®LCD TV, Cyber-shot®, Alpha DSLR and NEX digital cameras, Handycam® camcorder, Walkman® digital music player, Reader Digital Book, and Sony Tablet™.[20] Further, Sony launched personal computers with its VAIO®. And in professional category, it was utilising the XDCAM® HD System, HDCAM® 24-P, Digital Betacam®, DVCAM® VTR and

---

[6]ibid.

[7]"Corporate history", http://www.sony.net/SonyInfo/CorporateInfo/History/history.html

[8]ibid.

[9]"About Sony", op.cit.

[10]"FAQ", http://www.sony.net/SonyInfo/IR/info/faq/history.html#module4

[11]"About Sony", op.cit.

[12]Tyson Jeff, "How PlayStation Works", http://electronics.howstuffworks.com/playstation1.htm

[13]"Sony: Its history and success, Akio Morita, Transistor Radios, the Walkman, Howard Stringer and changes at Sony", http://factsanddetails. com/japan.php?itemid=918&catid=24&subcatid=157,October 2011

[14]ibid.

[15]"About Sony", op.cit.

[16]"Sony: Its history and success, Akio Morita, Transistor Radios, the Walkman, Howard Stringer and changes at Sony", op.cit.

[17]Begun in 1963, The Harris Poll weekly column is one of the longest running; most respected proprietary surveys conducted by Harris Interactive measuring public opinion and is highly regarded throughout the world.

[18]"Sony Companies", http://www.sony.com.au/section/sonycompanies

[19]"Facts & Figures", http://www.stuttgart.sony.de/home/about-us/facts-figures.html

[20]"Sony Corporation of America", http://www.sony.com/SCA/index.shtml

EXHIBIT 1 SONY BRAND CONCEPT

Concept

make.believe The meaning of the dot

The dot that links make and believe is the place where imagination and reality collide. It's the point of ignition that transcends reality. The dot is the role of Sony.

make.believe unites
designers and engineers,
hardware and software,
electronics and entertainment,
Sony and its consumers.

action
do
build
design
make.believe
spirit
think
imagine
dream

Source: "Concept", http://www.sony.net/united/makedotbelieve/

CineAlta™. It also had co-developed the formats for CD, DVD, Super Audio CD and Blu-ray Disc™. Further in the arena of fast emerging gaming field, Sony had developed the latest versions of PlayStation®3, the PlayStation®Move motion controller and the PlayStation®Vita[21], incorporating every aspect of 3D value chain.[22]

Morita had considered the whole world as his market place and he gave prominence to the brand Sony everywhere.[23] Their brand message was 'Make. Believe'[24] (Exhibit 1).

The success story of Sony was attributed to its visionary founders. They had the knack of knowing the consumers preferences and catered to their demands. Their company CEO's invariably reinforced the open-mindedness and the cooperative ideals of Sony's founders. That was popularly called as the Sony Spirit.[25] Sony had become the world's leader in products and content properties across consumer electronics, computing, cameras, film, music, video, gaming and telecommunications.[26] Sony went in for organisational reforms in the year 2009 to boost the sagging sales revenue and profits (Exhibit 2).

Sony had retained its leadership in the LCD TV business and strengthened its profitability in gaming business. It preserved its number one position in the digital imaging brand. It had also integrated the hardware, software and services and provided innovative user experiences. It focused on the 3D-related product businesses and had also reached out to new markets for its expansion activities. It had laid stress on environmentally conscious products and processes.[27] Despite its lofty vision and targets, Sony had faced many problems.

[21]ibid.
[22]ibid.
[23]"Sony's History – Through The Eyes of the Company's Leaders", https://news.sel.sony.com/en/corporate_information/sony_brand
[24]"Concept", http://www.sony.net/united/makedotbelieve/
[25]Shinagawa-ku, "Sony Corporation", http://www.fundinguniverse.com/company-histories/Sony-Corporation-company-History.html
[26]"Sony Companies", op.cit.
[27]"Sony Accelerates Transformation to Drive Innovation and Growth", http://www.sony.net/SonyInfo/News/Press/200911/09-133E/index. html, November 19th 2009

EXHIBIT 2   SONY'S TRANSFORMATIONAL INITIATIVES IN 2009

- Target consistent profitability in core hardware businesses (TV, game and digital imaging)
- Provide new user experiences integrating innovative hardware, software and services
- Reach out to new customers and develop new geographic markets

- Increase Sony's focus on environmentally conscious products and processes

Source: "Sony Accelerates Transformation to Drive Innovation and Growth", http://www.sony.net/SonyInfo/News/Press/200911/09-133E/index.html, November 19th 2009

In the coveted TV segment, Sony was making losses due to stiff competition and the global recessionary trends.[28] Sony had deliberately cut down the TV production and reduced the market share from 20% to 10% in 2011 to keep itself afloat in the competitive consumer electronics market.[29] It had introduced PlayStation Vita in December 2011 and the company had announced that it had sold over 1.2 million Vita units worldwide. It had attainted its iconic brand image over the years and had largely benefitted from its brand equity and loyalty. But it had fallen slowly from its ivory towers since its brand image had depended solely on the PlayStation 3. It could not keep itself in pace with its tough competitors like Samsung, LG and others.[30] Sony was placed at 35th position in the Interbrand[31] Best Global Brands ranking of 2011.[32]

On April 2012, Sony had stated that its projected net loss was Yen 520 billion. This was due to the hefty losses in TV business, a strong yen and natural disasters in Japan and overseas.[33] The Japanese credit ratings agency, R&I had downgraded the ratings of Sony. An analyst commented, "In light of Sony's business portfolio centered on television, the business environment is challenging, and R&I is increasingly concerned that improvement in revenue and expenditure will require further time."[34] Reflecting on the losses made in its TV division, "Sony has not done enough to rescue its TV business"[35], said Jeff Yeh, Chief Investment Officer of Taiwan-based Capital Investment Trust's[36] overseas portfolios. He further added that, " It took them 15 years to become an electronics giant, but it only took them the last five years to plunge to where they are."[37]

Fall of the titan

Considered once as a much-emulated and innovative company, Sony had become a mere shadow of its former glory.[38] Its losses had reflected the downward trend prevalent in the Japanese consumer electronics industry (Annexure 2). Even its close competitor Sharp inc. had also announced a loss of Yen 380 billion for the financial year that ended March 31st 2012.[39] But the losses were more for Sony during the same period, amounting to Yen 520 billion. It was the

[28]Hall Kenji, "Sony Is Still Feeling the Recession's Bite", http://www.businessweek.com/globalbiz/content/jul2009/gb20090730_761001.htm, July 30th 2009

[29]"Japan: Sony announces TV division restructuring, halves sales forecasts, as losses mount", http://www.whathifi.com/news/japan-sony-announces-tv-division-restructuring-halves-sales-forecasts-as-losses-mount, November 2nd 2011

[30]Roll Martin, "Brand Rejuvenation – A case study of Sony", http://www.venturerepublic.com/resources/Brand_Rejuvenation_SONY_brand_brand_leadership.asp

[31]Interbrand is the world's leading brand consultancy, specialized in providing in a wide range of brand services and activities.

[32]"Brand Rejuvenation – A case study of Sony",op.cit.

[33]Tabuchi Hiroko, "Sony Revises Expected Loss to $6.4 Billion", http://www.nytimes.com/2012/04/11/business/global/sony-revises-expected-loss-to-6-4-billion.html, April 10th 2012

[34]"Sony Revises Expected Loss to $6.4 Billion", op.cit.

[35]Reynolds Isabel, "Sony shares sink on massive loss forecast", http://www.reuters.com/article/2011/11/02/us-sony-earnings-idUSTRE7A10UG 20111102, November 2nd 2011

[36]Capital Investment Trust is devoted to the product development, continually increasing new financial goods and establishing new goods development department to promote more fund merchandises.

[37]"Sony shares sink on massive loss forecast", op.cit.

[38]Tabuchi Hiroko, "Incoming Chief Takes On a Sony That Is a Shadow of Its Former Self", http://www.nytimes.com/2012/02/03/technology/incoming-chief-takes-on-a-sony-that-is-a-shadow-of-its-former-self.html, February 2nd 2012

[39]"Sony, Sharp post $11b loss", http://gulfnews.com/business/economy/sony-sharp-post-11b-loss-1.1006972, April 11th 2012

fourth straight year of losses for Sony.[40] It had lost its dominance in portable music players and was also not fruitful in translating its earlier success in innovative products like Walkman to the present digital world.[41] Its TV business was not doing well for many years. This was partly due to its delay in developing flat-panel models and low prices offered by other players in the market.[42] Other extraneous factors were its low sales in its biggest TV market the US, the strong yen and the natural disasters in Japan and Thailand.[43] Its revenue had also fallen in online networks division, as Sony had lagged behind companies like Apple in Internet content offerings.[44]

Further, the brand image of Sony was also on a decline. This was due to many factors. Being a consistent brand in its brand structure and brand management practices, it was not adapting itself to the changing consumers' needs and preferences.[45] There were varied reasons for Sony's fall from its fortunes. The unrelated diversification, dearth in innovation and the lack of brand evolution were the major factors for Sony's debacle.[46]

The level of unrelated diversification had also played a vital role in Sony's fall. Its competitors Samsung, LG and other Asian businesses were largely family controlled businesses. Later they became bloated conglomerates. They learnt to cut down on their size and invariably focused on their core competencies. They left their unrelated businesses for good and focused their resources to very few important core businesses. But, Sony had been retaining its diversified businesses and it in turn had depleted the company's resources. This invariably distracted the focus on main brands.[47] Analysts were of the opinion that the lack of innovation had also paid dearly for Sony.

Inspite of Sony being an innovator in introducing Walkman and other products, it had not furthered its ambitions. The competitors of Sony such as Samsung, Nokia, LG and Apple had launched innovative products and hence established industry standards. This had eroded Sony's brand image. In addition, lack of customer focus was also attributed to Sony's fall.[48] More so, it had not evolved itself with the changing times of the digitalised consumer preferences. Other players in the market like Apple, Samsung have utilised their opportunities and have gained their hold.[49]

In the year 2009, Sony had incurred losses in its four major divisions. It was 17%, for Electronics, 18%, for gaming division, 16.4% for Pictures division and 7.4% in its financial services.[50] In the US, its revenues had plunged by 15.4%, and in Japan it was 15.2%.[51] Another factor as claimed by experts was that the production facilities were in places away from Japan far from its customer base. The pension liabilities of Sony were approximately $3.6 billion which was increasing at the rate of 62% since 2008. This had diverted the much needed cash flow from production to other non productive cash contributions.[52] Further the global economic recession had imparted an adverse effect on Sony's revenues.[53] 74% of its revenues came from the US, Japan and European markets.[54] It also brought into focus the weaknesses and susceptibility of the company. As the Japanese Yen became stronger, Sony's products became expensive in the global market.[55]

Even so, Sony had been hacked many times posing security threats for the company. Hackers had stolen data from more than 77 million accounts from its PlayStation Network in April 2011.[56] Later in May 2011, it also revealed that hackers had stolen data from

[40]"Business News: G-20 Protests, Sony Losses", http://www.npr.org/2011/11/02/141926258/business-news, November 2nd 2011

[41]"Sony Revises Expected Loss to $6.4 Billion", op.cit.

[42]ibid.

[43]ibid.

[44]ibid.

[45]"Brand Rejuvenation - A case study of Sony", op.cit.

[46]Ibid.

[47]Ibid.

[48]ibid.

[49]Ibid.

[50]"SWOT Analysis Sony", http://www.marketing–research.com/marketing/swot-analysis-sony

[51]ibid.

[52]ibid.

[53]"Sony struggles in midst of Japanese Recession", http://www.asiaecon.org/special_articles/read_sp/12095/0/196

[54]"SWOT Analysis Sony", op.cit.

[55]Foster Malcolm, "Weak Sony TV Sales, Strong Yen, Thai Floods Blamed For Company's Huge Projected Loss", http://www.huffingtonpost.com/2012/02/02/sony-tv-sales-net-loss_n_1249620.html, February 2nd 2012

[56]Baker B. Liana and Finkle Jim, "Hackers hit Sony sites raising more security issues", http://www.reuters.com/article/2011/05/20/us-sony-hacker-idUSTRE74J3Z820110520, May 20th 2011

about 25 million user accounts in PC-based games service of Sony Online Entertainment website.[57] This had resulted in the shutting down of its PlayStation Network for a month. It had exposed the vulnerability of Sony's security system. Sony also tried to compensate its users through a series of perks.[58]

Experts were skeptical about the repeated attacks. "Sony is going through a pretty rigorous process and finding the holes to fill, the hackers are going through the same process and they're putting their fingers in the holes faster than Sony can fill them"[59], said Josh Shaul (Shaul), Chief Technology Officer for computer security firm, Application Security Inc.[60] But Sony had to fix its problems thoroughly and Shaul commented further, "I think it's now 'I'm a hacker and I'm bored, let's go after Sony.'"[61]

Sony's high profile TV business was undergoing losses to the tune of $2.2 billion in November 2011.[62] Their pricing strategy came under the scrutiny of many analysts. "When you have competitors like LG (Corp) and Samsung so aggressively attacking the (TV) market, it really does hurt margins"[63], said Michael Yoshikami, Chief Executive of YCMNET[64] Advisors. Further, while commenting on price cuts, he remarked that, "If they can't, they need to get out of the (TV) business... I don't think they are really a brand at this point that can really command a premium price."[65] Sony was expected to revamp its TV business. It was struggling to keep up with the competition posed by Samsung's TV business and Apple's smartphone market.[66] In the TV industry, other competitors like

Panasonic Corp and Philips Electronics were also facing losses.[67] Sony's rescue plans were not yielding results either. In the year 2011, it had cut the sales forecast for its TV business by 9%.[68] While commenting on the importance of their TV businesses, Hirai, its new CEO had opined that, "The TV business is an essential part of Sony's growth strategy. We, as management, feel a great sense of crisis after seven straight years of losses."[69] To tide over the crisis, Sony was proposing to close down some plants, a reduction in its capital spending and to cut jobs.[70]

During the quarter between October and December 2011, Sony had suffered losses of Yen159 billion against its more innovative competitors Apple and Samsung. The reasons were the presence of strong yen, weak economy and the disruption to its supply chains from Thailand due to floods.[71] Sony had predicted an annual loss of Yen 220 billion or £1.8 billion in February 2012.[72] Hirai, the 51-year-old Sony veteran had taken over charge as CEO of Sony from Stringer at this crucial juncture. Hirai was known for turning around the PlayStation business to profitability. He was known for his cost cutting measures. In a market dominated by falling prices, Sony had lagged behind its rivals. Hirai said that he would implement strategies to revive Sony's falling fortunes. "I have a very strong sense of crisis about the environment surrounding us, we cannot be afraid to make painful choices for the future of Sony. Our rivals and the operating environment won't wait for us."[73] But Kim Young-Chan, an Analyst at Shinhan Investment

[57]ibid.

[58]"'Welcome Back': Sony Releases Details Of Compensation Package For PSN Debacle", http://www.huffingtonpost.com/2011/06/03/welcome-back-sony-playstation-network-program_n_871167.html, June 3rd 2011

[59]"Hackers hit Sony sites raising more security issues", op.cit.

[60]Founded in 2001, Application Security, Inc. (AppSecInc) has pioneered database security, risk, and compliance solutions for the enterprise.

[61]"Hackers hit Sony sites raising more security issues", op.cit.

[62]"Sony: sees TV unit posting $2.2 billion operating loss in 2011/12", http://www.reuters.com/article/2011/11/02/us-sony-tv-idUSTRE7A112S20111102, November 2nd 2011

[63]"Sony shares sink on massive loss forecast", op.cit.

[64]The firm based in US provides wealth management services including tax planning, estate planning, retirement planning, and additional planning services to its clients.

[65]"Sony Shares Sink on Massive Loss Forecast", op.cit.

[66]ibid.

[67]ibid.

[68]ibid.

[69]"Sony TV division plunges to $2.2bn loss as customers lose interest in pricey flatscreens", http://www.dailymail.co.uk/sciencetech/article-2056597/Sony-TV-division-loses-2-2bn-customers-lose-flatscreens.html, November 3rd 2011

[70]ibid.

[71]"Sony warns annual loss will be almost twice as bad as forecast", http://www.guardian.co.uk/technology/2012/feb/02/sony-warns-annual-loss, February 2nd 2012

[72]ibid.

[73]ibid.

Corp[74] in Seoul was skeptical about Hirai's attempts in reviving the electronics major. "It's got structural problems that will take years to fix. It's not just Sony – Japanese IT firms have similar problems. They are failing to innovate and produce industry-leading products in almost every major area, from TVs to displays, tablets and Smartphones."[75] Hirai had said that Sony would retain this central and time-honored business of TV segment.[76] Despite the problems faced by Sony, it had endured to regain its lost glory.[77] Sony had wanted to rejuvenate itself under its new CEO to become a top global power brand.[78] On the issue of bloated Sony's product portfolio and the plans for Sony's revamp, Hirai said, "We're going to tell you what you are going to make – not the other way around, this is a complete sea change."[79]

Challenges ahead for the new CEO

The new CEO Kazuo Hirai had proposed many plans to turnaround the ailing company.[80] Dan Ernst, an Analyst for Hudson Square[81] commented on the new CEO as follows, "They've been grooming him for a while, I think he will carry on the plan for Sony – as difficult as it is."[82] Sony had announced a $6.4 billion net loss for March 2012 that was double the forecasts made by the company. It had also proposed 10,000 job cuts representing a 6% of its total workforce[83] and

charge its revenue account by $926 million representing the restructuring costs in the current business year ending March 2013. The company had proposed to make an operating profit of $2.2 billion by end-March 2013.[84] It had planned to cut fixed costs in the TV business by 60% in 2013 and 2014 and reduce 30% of the business' operating costs.[85] Hirai's turnaround plans included selling a part of their chemicals and devices subsidiary, which produced films and adhesives used in televisions, cameras and mobile phones to the state-backed Development Bank of Japan.[86] "We cannot shy away from difficult decisions"[87], opined Hirai. He further stated that he was taking 'painful steps' to revive the company and would scale back or withdraw from non profitable businesses if needed.[88]

Also the flat screen television division was running into losses, which was estimated to be around Yen 480 billion (around £4bn) since 2004[89], while its competitors like Samsung and Apple had performed better than Sony in other sectors. The Sony veteran and new CEO Hirai, on assuming office in April 2012 had indicated to revive the struggling TV business back to track within two years. Defending the losses, the Chief Financial Officer of Sony, Masaru Kato said, "There have been several reasons for our poor results. We are aiming for a rebound and for this we have made management changes."[90] He also stated that all the available options were to be studied before pursuing

---

[74]Shinhan Investment Corp., a securities arm for the Shinhan Financial Group, operates as a securities brokerage and investment banking company in Korea.

[75]"Sony warns annual loss will be almost twice as bad as forecast", op.cit.

[76]"Sony Revises Expected Loss to $6.4 Billion", op.cit.

[77]Reisinger Don, "New CEO Hirai plans to integrate Sony into one", http://www.cnet.com.au/new-ceo-hirai-plans-tointegrate-sony-into-one-339334713.htm, March 28th 2012

[78]"Brand Rejuvenation - A case study of Sony", op.cit.

[79]Wakabayashi Daisuke, "New Sony Chief Executive Reveals Fast-Forward Plans", http://online.wsj.com/article/SB10001424052970204740904577196214261871258.html

[80]Waugh Rob, "Sony plunges to $6.4BN annual loss as Samsung and Apple eat into its businesses – giant cuts 10,000 jobs worldwide", http://www.dailymail.co.uk/sciencetech/article-2127643/Sony-plunges-6-4BN-annual-loss-Samsung-Apple-eat-businesses–giant-cuts-10-000-jobs-worldwide.html, April 10th 2012

[81]Founded in 2004, Hudson Square Research Inc., is a New York-based institutional equity research boutique focused on the technology, media, telecommunications, and consumer sectors.

[82]Kubota Yoko and Baker B. Liana, "Sony names Hirai to replace Stringer as CEO", http://www.reuters.com/article/2012/02/01/us-sony-hirai-idUSTRE8100JS20120201, February 1st 2012

[83]ibid.

[84]Kelly Tim and Gallagher Chris, "Sony will change-CEO", http://www.reuters.com/article/2012/04/12/sonyidUSL3E8FC17620120412, April 12th 2012

[85]ibid.

[86]"Sony plunges to $6.4BN annual loss as Samsung and Apple eat into its businesses – giant cuts 10,000 jobs worldwide", op.cit.

[87]"CEO sketches out strategy to revive Sony", http://arabnews.com/economy/article612214.ece, April 15th 2012

[88]"Sony plunges to $6.4BN annual loss as Samsung and Apple eat into its businesses – giant cuts 10,000 jobs worldwide", op.cit.

[89]"Sony yearly loss for 2011 widens to $2.9bn, new CEO appointed", http://news.idealo.co.uk/news/13155/sony-yearlyloss-for-2011-widens-to-2-9bn-new-ceo-appointed.html, February 2nd 2012

[90]"Sony plunges to $6.4BN annual loss as Samsung and Apple eat into its businesses – giant cuts 10,000 jobs worldwide", op.cit.

the restructuring drive. "We will force through reforms, and there will be no sacred cows, the company management takes these numbers very seriously."[91] The onus had rested on Hirai who had revived the PlayStation division before assuming charge as CEO. Another challenge would be to integrate its entertainment properties[92] which included singers Kelly Clarkson, Michael Jackson, the "Spider-Man" and "Men in Black" film franchises, with Sony's Vaio, Bravia and other electronic brands to stay competitive.[93] This strategy was to differentiate Sony's products from its competitors.[94]

Even during Stringer's tenure, its small LCD panel business had merged with Toshiba and Hitachi to form a new company called Japan Display.[95] In the convergence strategy to lift the TV division from losses, the company was merging its entertainment properties with its Vaio computers, Bravia TVs and other electronics brands to enhance sales.[96] With regard to the consumer demand potential in the TV market, a Sony Engineer had said, "There's still a chance in home electronics and I don't think Sony should quit TVs, but unfortunately I can imagine the day may come when they will pull the plug on the business. This is because when you keep making losses and you have no fresh ideas that become the easy choice."[97] Hirai had said that he would integrate the hardware with content for better efficiency and control. In its 70-year history, the company had been undergoing severe crisis. It had not introduced any new product which was considered as mega-hit.[98]

Industry experts commented that Hirai would divest its loss making TV business. A precedent to this strategy had happened in 2011.[99] Sony Corp, Toshiba Corp and Hitachi Ltd were making losses in small panels and they merged to become the Japan Display company by availing government-backed investment funds from the Innovation Network Corporation of Japan to the tune of $2.6 billion. This was done to stay competitive in the small panel segments against South Korea and Taiwan. This merger also facilitated the merged entities to focus on their core businesses. The Japanese government stepped in to help Sony to tide over the crisis to safeguard the multitude of jobs and enable the growth of home companies. Experts felt that Sony had moved away from making innovative products to content development which had affected the fortunes of Sony[100] and the new CEO had to devise more innovative strategies to restore the Sony brand.[101]

The former CEO, Stringer tried to fix things in Sony. He was not able to forge the rift that had developed between the hardware and the content. He spent most of his time abroad. "For rank-and-file workers, his presence was almost zero"[102] said an R&D engineer at Sony. Stringer passed on his mantle to Hirai in April 2012.[103] He said about his new protégé, "He is a convergence intellect for a convergence world, It's a fast transition that he can accelerate because of his experiences in PlayStation which, for all the complaints some people have about him not being an engineer, is a convergence product that is a model for the future."[104] The problems were persisting even during Stringer's tenure as CEO in Sony. He also did cost cutting to a certain extent. His initiatives included selling off factories in Spain, Slovakia and Mexico. He also outsourced nearly 50% of their production to companies like Hon Hai Precision Industry[105] whose important customer was Apple.[106] More so, Sony had made a strategic decision to exit from a joint venture

[91]"Sony Revises Expected Loss to $6.4 Billion", op.cit.

[92]Nakao Yuriko, "Sony's new chief faces many challenges", http://www.deccanherald.com/content/238754/sonys-chieffaces-many-challenges.html, April 1st 2012

[93]"Sony sees record $6.4bn net loss", http://m.timesofindia.com/PDATOI/articleshow/12609396.cms, April 10th 2012

[94]"Sony Revises Expected Loss to $6.4 Billion", op.cit.

[95]"Sony plunges to $6.4BN annual loss as Samsung and Apple eat into its businesses - giant cuts 10,000 jobs worldwide", op.cit.

[96]"Sony warns annual loss will be almost twice as bad as forecast", op.cit.

[97]ibid.

[98]"Reuters: Sony hardware and content business differences lead to the decline – Xinmin", http://insidechina.onehotspots.com/reuters-sony-hardware-and-content-business-differences-lead-to-the-declinexinmin/21903/, March 27th 2012

[99]Negishi Mayumi, "Japan backs Sony, Toshiba, Hitachi LCD merger", http://www.reuters.com/article/2011/08/31/us-japandisplays-idUSTRE77U0VL20110831, August 31st 2011

[100]"Japan backs Sony, Toshiba, Hitachi LCD merger", http://japan-world.info/archives/1642, September 1st 2011

[101]"Sony warns annual loss will be almost twice as bad as forecast", op.cit.

[102]"Sony's new chief faces many challenges", op.cit.

[103]ibid.

[104]"Special Report: The Sony Schism", http://www.reuters.com/article/2012/03/26/us-sony-idUSBRE82O0HV20120326, March 26th 2012

[105]Hon Hai Precision Industry Co. was ranked as the 156th largest company in the world and the top one in Taiwan.

[106]"Sony names Hirai to replace Stringer as CEO", op.cit.

with Samsung. This move had reduced the price of the screens used in TVs. It had bought 50% of Sony Ericsson smartphone joint venture for $1.47 billion.[107] Stringer had reconfirmed his faith on Sony's revival and commented, "If we hadn't reformed Sony as we did, can you imagine where we would be today? I rest my case."[108]

Hirai was in charge of its PlayStation division since 2006.[109] He was proposing to replicate the model of Apple Inc. and its iTunes in his present job. He wanted a unified content-delivery platform. Industry experts felt that this strategy would not work well. They had foreseen a rift between the old-guard gadget engineers and the new breed of executives. These executives wanted the future of Sony to be in online networks that would deliver entertainment content. Any faulty move would bring down the legendary electronics company down.[110] The predecessors of Hirai were focusing their efforts in the development of contents. Despite not having an engineering background, Hirai was successful in running the gaming division for five years. "Let's not forget, underneath Kaz there are some very strong leaders who have engineering backgrounds"[111] said Phil Molyneux, the CEO of Sony Electronics Inc. in the United States.

The brand value of Sony was worth $9.9 billion as on March 2012.[112] Remarking on the market value of Sony, Jez Frampton, the CEO of Interbrand said, "What it says to me is that if you benchmark them against the likes of Apple and Samsung, that means their market cap should be three or four times what it is now. He (Hirai) has got a big job."[113] Agreeing to this statement Hirai said, "I think that it is a very visible position, both within Japan as well as outside Japan, It's not an easy job, I get that."[114]

The new CEO, as part of its restructuring plans had said that Sony would focus on medical business. Its estimated sales were Yen 50 billion in 2014/15.[115] Further it had aimed for total group sales of $105 billion between in 2014 and 2015.[116] His revival strategy covered the Sony's business operations in mobile electronics – phones, games and cameras – and a medical business with annual sales of $1.2 billion.[117] In the fast-growing medical business, its annual target was 50 billion yen sales between 2014 and 2015. It was looking for acquisitions and other strategic investments in this sector.[118] But the controversy surrounding its links with medical equipment maker Olympus Corp,[119] had to be looked upon, said trade experts.[120] Its expertise in graphics technology was to be beneficial to its focus on medical business field. Michael On, Managing Director at Beyond Asset Management[121] said, "Expanding in medical and electric vehicles is good because these businesses have better margins and they're areas that Japan is good at."[122] In the renewable energy sector, it was looking for partners to produce batteries for its proposed electric vehicles.[123]

Tetsuro Ii, President of Commons Asset Management[124] had commented that, "It doesn't feel like an aggressive makeover, you can't really see the roadmap for how they're going to revive the electronics business, nor how they're going to create new value."[125]

[107]"Sony buys out Ericsson in mobile phone joint venture", http://www.thehindubusinessline.com/industry-andeconomy/info-tech/article2573677.ece, October 27th 2011

[108]"Sony warns annual loss will be almost twice as bad as forecast", op.cit.

[109]"Kazuo Hirai", http://us.playstation.com/corporate/about/management/kazuohirai/

[110]"Special Report: The Sony Schism", op.cit.

[111]ibid.

[112]"Sony's new CEO's 'get well soon' plan", http://articles.timesofindia.indiatimes.com/2012-03-26/strategy/31239874_1_kazuo-hirai-playstation-sony-corp/3, March 26th 2012

[113]"Special Report: The Sony Schism", op.cit.

[114]ibid.

[115]"Sony to expand its mobile and medical technologies", http://www.canhealth.com/News1949.html

[116]Kelly Tim and Gallagher Chris, "'Sony will change,' grow in mobile, medical: CEO", http://www.ibtimes.com/articles/327085/20120412/sony-will-change-grow-in-mobile-medical-ceo.htm, April 12th 2012

[117]ibid.

[118]ibid.

[119]Olympus Corporation is a Japan-based manufacturer of optics and reprography products.

[120]"Sony warns annual loss will be almost twice as bad as forecast", op.cit.

[121]They offered fund management, investment compliance, risk management, MidOffice & BackOffice, Reporting, IT Platform, Standard & Individual Software, Software house, transaction interfaces.

[122]Kelly Tim and Gallagher Chris, "Sony to slash 10,000 jobs as new CEO reveals turnaround strategy", http://www.thestar.com/business/article/1160074–sony-to-slash-10-000-jobs-as-new-ceo-reveals-turnaround-strategy, April 12th 2012

[123]ibid.

[124]Common Asset Management is an investment manager and a leader in global sustainability initiatives.

[125]"Sony to slash 10,000 jobs as new CEO reveals turnaround strategy", op.cit.

"We have heard a multitude of investor voices calling for change" ... Sony will change. Sony has always been an entrepreneurial company. That spirit has not changed"[126], Hirai told at Sony's Tokyo headquarters.[127]

In the light of the new strategic announcements made by Hirai, it remained to be seen if these strategies would restore the Sony's lost reputation.

Annexure 1
About Sony Corp

Company Name ■ Sony Corporation
Founded ■ May 7, 1946
Headquarters ■ 1-7-1 Konan, Minato-ku, Tokyo 108-0075, Japan
Representative Corporate Executive Officers ■ **Chairman** Howard Stringer ■ **President and CEO** Kazuo Hirai ■ **Vice Chairman** Ryoji Chubachi
Major Products ■ **Audio** Home audio, portable audio, etc. ■ **Video** Video cameras, digital still cameras, and DVD-Video players/recorders, and Digital-broadcasting receiving systems ■ **Televisions** LCD televisions ■ **Information and communications** PC, printer system, broadcast and professional use audio/video/monitors and other professional-use equipment ■ **Semiconductors** LCD, CCD and other semiconductors ■ **Electronic components** Optical pickups, batteries, audio/video/data recording media, and data recording systems
Locations Of Major Offices and Research Centers (In Japan) ■ Tokyo, Kanagawa, Miyagi
Headcount (Consolidated) ■ 168,200 (as of March 31, 2011)
Consolidated Sales And Operating Revenue(2010) ■ 7,181,300 million yen

Source: "Sony Corp. info", http://www.sony.net/SonyInfo/CorporateInfo/

[126]"Sony will change," grow in mobile, medical: CEO", op.cit.
[127]"Sony will change," grow in mobile, medical: CEO", op.cit.

Annexure 2
Financials of Sony Corp.

■ Consolidated operating income was significantly higher, 6.3 times the previous fiscal year's amount, despite the large, unfavorable impact of foreign exchange rates.

■ The increase in consolidated operating income was driven primarily by improved results in the Networked Products & Services segment, due principally to the contribution of the game business.

■ A net loss attributable to Sony Corporation's stockholders was recorded, mainly due to a non-cash charge to establish a valuation allowance against certain deferred tax assets in Japan.

Consolidated Financial Results for the Fiscal Year Ended March 31, 2011 (Fiscal Year 2010)	
Sales and Operating revenue	¥7,181.3 billion (−0.5%)
Operating Income	¥199.8 billion (+528.9%)
Income before Income taxes	¥205.0 billion (+661.8%)
Net Income (loss) attributable to Sony Corporation's stockholders	¥259.6 billion (—)

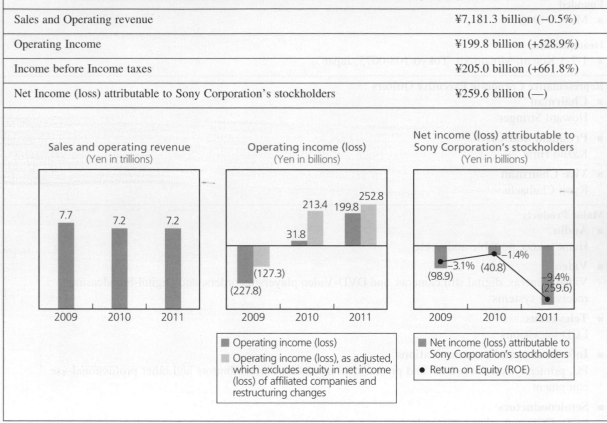

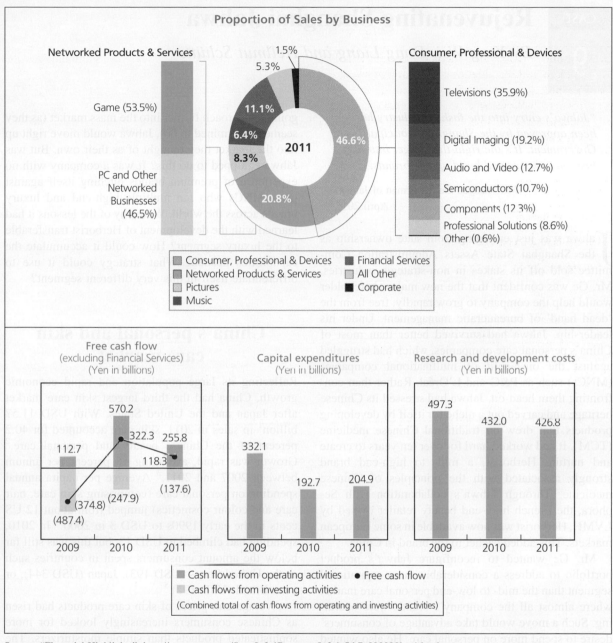

Proportion of Sales by Business

Networked Products & Services

Game (53.5%)

PC and Other Networked Businesses (46.5%)

2011

1.5%
5.3%
11.1%
6.4%
8.3%
20.8%
46.6%

Consumer, Professional & Devices

Televisions (35.9%)
Digital Imaging (19.2%)
Audio and Video (12.7%)
Semiconductors (10.7%)
Components (12.3%)
Professional Solutions (8.6%)
Other (0.6%)

■ Consumer, Professional & Devices   ■ Financial Services
■ Networked Products & Services   ■ All Other
■ Pictures   ■ Corporate
■ Music

Free cash flow
(excluding Financial Services)
(Yen in billions)

570.2
322.3
112.7
255.8
118.3
(374.8)
(247.9)
(137.6)
(487.4)

2009   2010   2011

Capital expenditures
(Yen in billions)

332.1
192.7   204.9

2009   2010   2011

Research and development costs
(Yen in billions)

497.3
432.0   426.8

2009   2010   2011

■ Cash flows from operating activities   ● Free cash flow
■ Cash flows from investing activities
(Combined total of cash flows from operating and investing activities)

Source: "Financial Highlights", http://www.sony.net/SonyInfo/CorporateInfo/qfhh7c000000lpn1.html

Rejuvenating Shanghai Jahwa

By Yang Wei, Dong Liang and Hellmut Schütte

"Jahwa's entry into the fashion industry has been approved by the Shanghai Municipal Government. It's the right time to get into the fashion industry and build up our brands."

–Mr. Wenyao Ge, Chairman of Jahwa,
April 2012

Jahwa was just emerging from state ownership as the Shanghai State Assets Administration Committee sold off its stakes in non-strategic industries. Mr. Ge was confident that the new major shareholder would help the company to grow rapidly, free from the 'dead hand' of bureaucratic management. Under his leadership, Jahwa had survived better than most of China's personal care companies, which had struggled against the onslaught of multinational companies (MNCs) such as P&G and L'Oréal. Rather than confronting them head-on, Jahwa had stressed its Chinese heritage and carved out a niche for itself by developing products that drew on traditional Chinese medicine (TCM). It had worked hard for over ten years to create and nurture Herborist, a mid- to high-end brand strongly associated with the principles of Chinese medicine. Through Jahwa's collaboration with Sephora, the French high-end beauty retailer owned by LVMH, Herborist was now available in some European markets. This added cachet to the brand in China.

Mr. Ge wanted to reconfigure Jahwa's product portfolio to address a considerably more aspirational segment than the mid- to low-end personal care market where almost all the company's brands were operating. Such a move would take advantage of consumers' desire to spend more on personal care. He also wanted to show the big international players that, if they were

going to encroach further into the mass market (as they seemed determined to do), Jahwa would move right up into the market they thought of as their own. But was Jahwa equipped to do this? It was a company with no experience of premium brands pitching itself against giant MNCs who ran multiple high-end and luxury brands across the world. Were any of the lessons it had learned with the development of Herborist transferable to the luxury segment? How could it accumulate the capabilities needed? What strategy could it use to differentiate itself in this very different segment?

China's personal and skin care market

Reflecting its large population and rapid economic growth, China had the third largest skin care market after Japan and the United States. With USD 11.57 billion[1] in sales in 2011, skin care accounted for 40.2 percent of the Chinese beauty and personal care.[2] Growth was rapid, averaging 18 percent per annum between 2007 and 2011.[3] Average per capita annual spending on personal care (comprising skin care, hair care and colour cosmetics) jumped from about 12 US cents in the early 1990s to USD 3 in 2000.[4] In 2010, spending had climbed to USD 13, but this was still far below the amount consumers spent in countries such as the United States (USD 193), Japan (USD 344), or even Brazil (USD 192).[5]

Average unit prices of skin care products had risen as Chinese consumers increasingly looked for more sophisticated products than simple moisturizers. The trend towards more premium products, led by

This case was prepared by Dr. Yang Wei, Case Writer Dong Liang at CEIBS Case Development Center under the supervision of Prof. Hellmut Schütte in collaboration with Jahwa. This case acts as the basis for class discussion rather than illustration of either effective or ineffective management.

[1]The USD: RMB exchange rate as of March 12, 2012 was 1: 6.3246.
[2]Euromonitor, "Beauty and Personal Care in China, 2012", May 2012.
[3]Euromonitor, "Beauty and Personal Care in China, 2012" May 2012.
[4]Li & Fung, "The Booming Cosmetics Market in China", July 2005.
[5]Euromonitor, "Beauty and Personal Care in China, 2010", June 2011.

EXHIBIT A   SKIN CARE COMPANY MARKET SHARES – RETAIL VALUE (PERCENT)

	2007	2008	2009	2010	2011
L'Oréal Group	10.5	10.9	12.4	14.3	14.8
Procter & Gamble Co Ltd	16.7	15.7	14.6	12.4	11.4
Shiseido Co Ltd	6.9	8.6	9.1	9.4	9.6
Mary Kay Inc	5.1	5.2	5.1	5.3	6.2
Amway Corp	7.5	5.7	5.8	6.7	6.2
Avon Products Inc	7.4	6.3	6.5	6.3	5.2
Jiangsu Longliqi Group Co Ltd	3.5	3.6	3.4	3.3	3.2
Beiersdorf AG	1.6	1.9	2.5	3.0	3.1
Jala (Group) Co Ltd	0.6	0.9	1.2	2.0	2.9
Estée Lauder Cos Inc	1.9	2.2	2.4	2.6	2.8
Johnson & Johnson Inc	1.3	1.4	1.5	3.2	2.7
Shanghai Jahwa United Co Ltd	1.6	1.7	1.6	2.2	2.3
Unilever Group	2.3	2.2	2.2	2.2	2
AmorePacific Corp	0.8	1.1	1.2	1.3	1.3
Kosé Corp	1.9	1.9	1.8	1.8	1.7

Source: Euromonitor Report, Beauty and Personal Care in China – Company Shares, May 2012.

international players, was expected to continue and to affect not only the top segments of the market but also mass market brands. Profit margins on high-end products were much greater than in the mass market, suggesting that this segment held good potential for the future. Meanwhile, the enormous scale of the mid- and low-end segments was also attractive to international players, which had extended their product lines further down into these segments in search of new growth.

Competition

As soon as the country opened to foreign businesses, China's skin care market became a magnet for international players. Domestic companies fell behind on their home turf. Only around 3000 Chinese cosmetics manufacturers remained in 2010, 30 percent fewer than eight years earlier. Most were small- and medium-sized enterprises with annual revenues below USD 1.5 million.[6] They offered low-end products, competed on price and spent little, if anything, on product development or brand building. In contrast, foreign MNCs boasted superior company reputation,

brand image, product quality, marketing expertise and financial resources. As a result, they dominated the Chinese market in many product categories, usually in the high- and mid-end segments, and carried a significant price premium. Although domestic personal care brands accounted for 40 percent of the market in volume terms, foreign brands earned 80 percent of the profits.[7]

The sector was highly concentrated, with the top four players accounting for 42 percent of the market in 2011 (Exhibit A). Consolidation accelerated through the acquisition of small local firms by large MNCs. Only three of the top 15 skin care companies were Chinese, including Shanghai Jahwa in twelfth place. The top ten brands took 79.9 percent of skin care product sales in more than 200 major department stores in 2009.[8] (Exhibit B)

All major foreign MNCs – P&G, L'Oréal, Estée Lauder, Unilever, Johnson & Johnson, Amway, Avon, Shiseido and Kosé – had manufacturing operations in China and employed many people. P&G and L'Oréal both had more than 7000 employees in China. Some companies, including L'Oréal and Shiseido, had also established research and development (R&D) centres

[6]"Decline seen in numbers of cosmetics companies", *Cosmetics News,* April 23, 2011.
[7]Euromonitor, "Beauty and Personal Care in China, 2011", June 2011.
[8]Li&Fung, "China?s Cosmetics market, 2010", January 2011.

EXHIBIT B   SKIN CARE BRAND MARKET SHARES – RETAIL VALUE (PERCENT)

	2007	2008	2009	2010	2011
Olay (Procter & Gamble Co)	14.1	12.1	11	10.3	9.5
Shiseido (Shiseido Co Ltd)	1.7	2.1	2.6	3	3
L'Oréal Paris (L'Oréal Group)	5	6.3	6.7	7.6	7.8
Mary Kay (Mary Kay Inc)	5.1	5.3	6.2	6.7	6.7
Artistry (Amway Corp)	5	6	5.5	5.3	5.1
Longliqi (Jiangsu Longliqi Group Co Ltd)	3.4	3.3	3.2	2.9	2.6
Nivea (Beiersdorf AG)	2.3	2.8	2.8	2.8	2.7
Avon (Avon Products Inc)	6.5	6.3	5.2	2.9	1.9
Lancôme (L'Oréal Group)	2.3	2.4	2.6	2.7	3.1
Chcedo (Jala (Group) Co Ltd)	1.2	1.7	2.1	2.3	2.5
Vichy (L'Oréal Group)	2.2	2.2	2.1	2.1	2.1
Estée Lauder (Estée Lauder Cos Inc)	1.4	1.7	2.1	2.4	3
Garnier (L'Oréal Group)	1.4	1.8	1.8	1.8	1.8
Pond's (Unilever Group)	2	2.1	1.9	1.8	1.7
Kosé (Kosé Corp)	1.8	1.8	1.7	1.6	1.5
Fancl (Fancl Corp)	0.7	1.1	1.2	1.2	1.3
MG (Guangzhou Meiji Cosmetics Co Ltd)	0.4	0.6	0.8	1.1	1.1
Yue-sai (L'Oréal Group)	0.6	0.6	0.6	0.6	0.5
DHC (DHC Corp)	0.4	0.7	0.9	1.1	1.2
Dabao (Johnson & Johnson Inc)	–	1.8	1.3	1.1	1
Tjoy (Nanjing Jianong Chemical Co Ltd)	–	–	–	1.1	1.1
Herborist (Shanghai Jahwa United Co Ltd)	0.6	0.8	1	1.1	1.1
Cathy (Arche Group Co Ltd)	1.4	1.3	1.2	1.1	1
Inoherb (Shanghai Inoherb Cosmetics Co Ltd)	0.6	0.9	1.1	1.5	1.9
Meifubao (Huanya Group Co Ltd)	–	0.1	0.4	0.5	0.6
Amore (AmorePacific Corp)	0.7	0.8	0.8	0.8	0.8
Clinique (Estée Lauder Cos Inc)	0.3	0.8	0.9	0.8	0.8
Neutrogena (Johnson & Johnson Inc)	1.1	1.2	1.2	1.3	1.3
Christian Dior (LVMH Louis Vuitton Moët Hennessy SA)	0.7	0.6	0.6	0.6	0.6
Laneíge (AmorePacific Corp)	0.7	0.7	0.7	0.6	0.6
Vitabelle (Lee Kum Kee Co Ltd)	0.6	0.6	0.6	0.6	0.7
Biotherm (L'Oréal Group)	0.3	0.2	0.3	0.5	0.7
SK-II (Procter & Gamble Co)	0.6	0.6	0.5	0.5	0.5
Maxam (Shanghai Jahwa United Co Ltd)	14.1	12.1	11	10.3	9.5

Source: Euromonitor Report, Skin Care in China, 2011 – Brand Shares, May 2012.

in the Asia Pacific region or in China. These R&D centres claimed to study traditional Chinese herbs in order to develop new products specifically suited to Asian/Chinese skins. However, by 2011, no skin care brand launched by any MNC was based on the TCM concept. This part of the market was occupied by domestic names such as the mass-market brand Inoherb,

which by 2011 had captured 1.9 percent of the market despite its limited promotional budget.

Major international players

L'Oréal started exporting to China in 1990, and set up a joint venture (JV) in 1996. Starting from a single product line for basic skin care needs in 1997, it launched many new products catering to more sophisticated demand at higher prices. Its multi-brand strategy tailored products to different types of consumer across the country, at price points ranging from the low- to the high- end. It used a variety of distribution channels. Mininurse (acquired from a Chinese firm in 2003) targeted low-end and rural markets, while Yue-Sai (acquired in 2004) and Garnier served low- to middle-income urban consumers. Lancôme and Biotherm, which were sold through department stores and beauty specialist retailers, addressed the premium segment. The pharma brand Vichy was found in drugstores and pharmacies. In 2010, L'Oreal introduced Kiehl's into China to attract consumers who preferred natural beauty methods. The company overtook P&G in 2008 to become the top player in China's skin care market, capturing a near 15 percent share in value terms in 2011.

The skin care brands under P&G were Olay and SK-II, which targeted the mass and the premium segment respectively. Olay was among the first international brands to enter China in 1989, when consumers had little purchasing power. Although it was a basic skin care range, Olay's two main offerings – a nourishing cream and a moisturizing cream – were quickly perceived by consumers to be of high quality. Since 2003, P&G had introduced several Olay sub brands in the more profitable mid- and high-end segments to dissuade consumers from trading up to competitors' premium brands. But Olay still retained a dozen facial cleansers priced at USD 3, to signal its determination to remain strongly present in the low-end market. The SK-II brand addressed the same high-end market segment as rival Lancôme, but its image in China was damaged in 2006 when products were reported to contain harmful ingredients. From a market share of 1.7 percent in 2005, SK-II crashed to 0.3 percent in 2008, although it gradually recovered in the following two years. Overall, P&G held 11.4 percent of the skin care market in 2011, down from 16.7 percent in 2006.

Seeing China as a key market to drive its growth, the Japanese company Shiseido started operations in 1981, much earlier than other multinational players. In 2011, Shiseido ranked third after L'Oréal and P&G, with a market share of 9.6 percent. It executed a channel-specific marketing strategy centred on brands designed specially for China. For example, department stores sold its premium brands Aupres and Supreme Aupres. Its Urara brand was sold exclusively in cosmetics specialty stores, which were operated by local retailers in lower-tier cities willing to host a Shiseido counter installation. In 2010, Shiseido launched DQ, a premium cosmeceutical brand, via pharmacies, its first venture into this channel.

Marketing and distribution channels

Skin care products were among the most heavily advertised categories in China's mainstream media such as TV, newspapers and magazines. In 2010, Olay and L'Oréal Paris occupied the top slots in TV advertising spending. The MNCs behind these two brands were estimated to have spent close to USD 156.6 thousand each on advertising in China in 2010.[9]

Supermarket and hypermarket chains were the main distribution channel for mass-market brands, and department stores for premium brands. As supermarkets and hypermarkets expanded into areas beyond the big cities, new opportunities arose for further growth. It was very hard for unknown brands to get into department stores, especially the high-end stores in first-tier cities such as Beijing and Shanghai. Department stores often preferred to carry international brands or foreign-acquired brands, and they blocked the entry of domestic brands.

Specialist beauty shops emerged as a new distribution channel in China in the early 2000s. Watsons, a leading health, personal care and beauty retailer in Asia, had by 2011 built a chain of more than 1000 stores in over 100 cities, largely in the south and east of China. Other foreign-owned chains such as Sephora and Sasa, as well as privately owned stand-alone specialty stores, mushroomed. Specialist stores attracted consumers by offering professional personal attention and lower prices than department stores. Shiseido, the first cosmetics giant to try to build a network of specialty stores, expanded its affiliated outlets to 5,000 in 2010,[10] and achieved deep market penetration outside the first- and second-tier cities. In 2009, L'Oréal launched the L'Oréal Paris Glamour Alliance, a plan to co-operate with independent specialty stores in lower-tier cities. Hundreds of specialty stores signed contracts in a short space of time.

Direct selling saw dramatic growth after the government lifted its ban in 2005,[11] accounting for 23.5

[9]"L'Oreal Consolidates China Business With Mindshare", *AdAge,* October 27, 2010.

[10]Shiseido Annual Report, 2010.

[11]From 1998 to 2005, the government banned direct sales to prevent pyramid selling. Direct sales companies are only permitted to tie sales personnel to their own specialty stores, instead of employing the multiple layer model adopted worldwide.

EXHIBIT C   SHANGHAI JAHWA ANNUAL SALES AND PROFITS 2007–2011

USD (million)	2007	2008	2009	2010	2011
Net Sales	357	394	426	489	565
Net Profit Attributed to Parent Company	21.0	29.3	36.8	43.6	57.1

Source: Annual report from Shanghai Jahwa 2007–2011

percent of the market in 2011. Most major direct sales players were foreign-owned enterprises, such as Avon, Mary Kay and Amway. Drug stores and pharmacies, the retail channels for cosmeceutical brands, held a 6.3 percent market share in 2011.[12]

The Shanghai Jahwa heritage

Shanghai Jahwa United was one of China's largest personal care companies, with sales of USD 560 million in 2011 (Exhibit C), giving it a market share of 2.3 percent in 2011.[13] But it was a tiny company compared with the major foreign players. Among its workforce of 1044 employees, 71 percent had at least a college degree. Few staff were involved in production functions, since most manufacturing except for new product introductions was outsourced. Between 2007 and 2011, the company was highly profitable, with a return on assets far in advance of its international competitors (Exhibit D). Its portfolio of beauty and personal care products included skin care, shower products, toilet water (eau de toilette), men's grooming products, and fragrances. Its brands ranged from low-end, mass-market names such as Liushen and

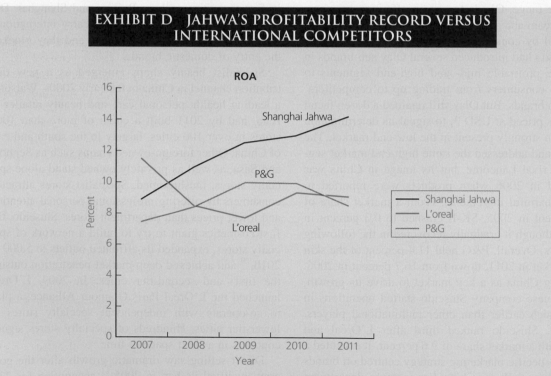

EXHIBIT D   JAHWA'S PROFITABILITY RECORD VERSUS INTERNATIONAL COMPETITORS

Source: Compiled from financial reports of Shanghai Jahwa, P&G and L'Oréal.

[12]Euromonitor, "Beauty and Personal Care – China", May 2012.
[13]Euromonitor, "Beauty and Personal Care in China", May 2012.

Maxam, to mid-market brands such as Herborist and Chinfie, through to the recently launched high-end Shanghai Vive. To differentiate itself from foreign competitors, Jahwa emphasized its Chinese essence and deep understanding of Chinese lifestyles, and often used the principles and ingredients of TCM in its product formulations.

The origins of Jahwa dated back to 1898 and the establishment in Hong Kong of a cosmetics business, Guangsheng Company, which created the famous Shuangmei brand. The cosmetics manufacturing plant that Guangsheng set up in Shanghai in the early 1930s was nationalized in the 1950s and then merged with three other personal care product firms. In the early 1960s, when few consumer products were available to ordinary Chinese people, the company launched Maxam, a personal care brand that quickly became popular. This was the era of state planning, when Chinese factories were assigned production quotas and state monopolies handled all distribution. After the state planning mechanism was abolished in 1978, Shanghai Jahwa[14], – still a state- owned enterprise – opened China's first beauty salon in 1981 under the name Ruby. In 1983, it added a Ruby make-up line to address the high-end personal care segment. When U.S. First Lady Mrs. Nancy Reagan visited China in 1984, the Shanghai government presented her with a set of Ruby products.

The key person responsible for transforming Jahwa was Shanghai-born Mr. Wenyao Ge, now Chairman of Shanghai Jahwa Group. Mr. Ge had been appointed by Jahwa in 1985 as General Manager of a small subsidiary factory which he quickly began to reorganise. He streamlined production by setting up several product-focused plants near Shanghai, in locations that had cheaper labour and offered tax incentives, and he outsourced manufacturing to these partners. This reduced Jahwa's cost base and improved product quality. China was still a seller's market at this time and, like other SOEs, the company lacked modern management structures and processes. Unlike other SOE chiefs, Mr. Ge began hiring university-educated managers in the late 1980s. Dramatic growth between 1985 and 1990 turned the company into the market leader, with a 16 percent share of the Chinese market for personal care products.

In 1991, under pressure from the Shanghai government, Jahwa entered into a JV with U.S. household products specialist S.C. Johnson & Son.[15] Its two strongest brands, Maxam and Ruby, were transferred to the JV. Neglected by foreign management, however, their sales fell from USD 4.7 million in 1990 to USD 0.94 million in 1993.[16] The JV failed, and Maxam and Ruby returned to Jahwa. But by that time major international players had entered China aggressively, leaving Jahwa's brands far behind. Although the Jahwa-Johnson JV was an operational disaster, it taught Mr. Ge about brand management systems and the concept of gross profit. He recognised that Jahwa's ability to compete with global competitors lay in new product development and product quality. For the first time, Jahwa's brand managers were given responsibility for market research, new product launches, design and execution of marketing programmes, and the overall positioning of the brand. They had to work closely with the R&D, market research, and sales departments in order to ensure their brand's overall success. This was a completely new way of operating.

In 1998, the Shanghai government asked Jahwa to rescue Shanghai Chemical Corp. It was a loss-making SOE of 7000 employees and a deficit of USD 28.2 million, compared with Jahwa's then 1300 employees and USD 7.83 million in net profits. Mr. Ge became Chairman of the newly-formed Shanghai Jahwa (Group) Co. Ltd, the umbrella company above Shanghai Jahwa United. In 2001, Shanghai Jahwa United was the first Chinese personal care company to float shares on the Shanghai Stock Exchange. Still it remained in partial state ownership until finally, in 2011, the Shanghai government decided to sell all of its shares as part of China's push for the state to exit non-strategic industries. Pingpu Investment Company, a unit of insurance company Ping An, acquired approximately 30 percent of Jahwa United.

Mr. Wang had returned to Jahwa in 2003 as Vice General Manager, after an MBA and five years of market research experience in the U.S. He saw that one of the company's main problems was the difficulty of attracting and retaining people who had management skills and leadership aptitude. As a state-owned enterprise (SOE), Jahwa had always been more constrained in its ability to hire on the open market

---

[14]Jahwa means 'household chemicals'.

[15]The Shanghai government wanted SC Johnson to invest in Pudong, which at the time was an undeveloped area of farmland on the east side of Shanghai. All foreign firms in those days were required to form JVs with domestic firms. SC Johnson agreed to invest on the condition that its partner was Shanghai Jahwa.

[16]"Jahwa sets its sights higher", *China Daily,* May 2, 2011.

than domestic private firms or MNCs. Young Chinese managers preferred to join MNCs, where they could receive good training and learn systematic management processes, and salaries were perhaps 40 percent higher. Now free from the control of the Shanghai Assets Administration Committee, Jahwa planned to match its managers' salaries with their counterparts' in foreign firms within five years. It also introduced a more competitive incentive programme. In 2008, Jahwa had awarded performance-related stock options to 175 of its middle and top managers. But the maximum income from stock options at SOEs was capped at 30 percent of salary. After the change in ownership, the scope of Jahwa's incentive program would be enlarged to 398 managers and associates. According to Mr. Wang, Jahwa would *"bring some dynamics into the promotion system"*, and function on an *"up or out"* basis, as MNCs did. In the past, poor performance in Jahwa had carried no penalty. Group decision-making had meant that no-one took responsibility for mistakes. Mr. Wang hoped that the change of ownership would *"refresh"* the company and finally eliminate the SOE mindset.

Building and operating brands

Starting in the late 1980s and early 1990s, under Mr. Ge's leadership, Jahwa launched or relaunched several brands in order to target different market segments. Its strategy was to target niche markets and to differentiate itself from competitors through unique positioning and product offerings, rather than by competing on cost. For some brands, Jahwa wanted to build its reputation on the extensive use of traditional Chinese ingredients and medicine. Consumers perceived the Liushen brand, for example, as natural and healthy because the products contained Chinese ingredients and transmitted the feeling of being 'fresh and cool', in contrast to the 'smooth and nourishing' feeling promoted by Unilever's Lux.

Jahwa had also shown an innovative streak. It was the first Chinese company to launch (in 1992) a men's personal care brand called GF; and it entered the cosmeceutical segment in 2009 with the Dr. Richia brand to demonstrate its technology-driven capability. The failure of its Distance perfume brand in 1998 taught Jahwa not simply to copy foreign competitors' brands, because the product had had no distinctive competitive edge.

Jahwa had a history of cooperation with foreign cosmetics and fragrance firms. It was while working with L'Oréal in 1985 to develop its Voila Paris and Chinfie perfumes that Jahwa first became aware of and impressed by the French firm's R&D capabilities. Later, it formed collaborations with other foreign companies, including Kanebo, Lion and Coty.

Since 2002, Jahwa's brands had been run through two separate business divisions. Business Division I handled mass-market brands distributed via supermarkets and hypermarket chains. Business Division II looked after mid- to high-end brands, such as GF and Chinfie, which were sold in department stores and specialty stores. Another independent company, set up later to manage Herborist, shared resources with Business Division II.

The company's extensive distribution network covered more than 530 cities in China, serviced by corporate sub-branches in almost every province. Liushen and Maxam were mostly sold through convenience stores as well as supermarket and hypermarket chains across the country. Chinfie and GF points of sale had become scattered too thinly over a large geographic area and were going to be concentrated in a smaller, more focused region. Herborist was distributed mainly through company-owned and franchised specialist beauty counters. Dr. Richia was sold in drug stores and pharmacies.

For many years Jahwa underestimated the importance of advertising, despite the aggressive inroads made into China by foreign players. The budget for marketing campaigns was tiny and, due to lack of support, brands such as Maxam fell out of fashion. Since 2004, the company had increased spending on media campaigns, and TV advertising in particular had been effective. In 2005, movie star endorsements of Liushen proved very popular, and the GF brand started using Hong Kong pop celebrities in its promotional campaigns. Jahwa expected to commit USD 78.3 million to marketing activities in 2011.

The largest category of expenses after marketing was R&D. Since 1996, the company had spent more than 3 percent of sales annually on R&D. The Jahwa Technical Center employed over 100 researchers into TCM and ingredients to support new product development. They were backed up by collaborations with seven universities and research institutes that specialized in biotechnology and dermatology. Jahwa thought that it could exploit the market potential of TCM better than multinational competitors, due to its fundamental understanding not only of the Chinese consumer mentality but also of the principles of TCM. The use of Chinese medicine and ingredients, in the view of the R&D head, was a clear differentiation strategy for Jahwa. But the company had to ingrain that cultural "essence" more strongly in consumers' minds, if it was going to establish an "unshakable" market position.

Mass-market brands: the foundation for growth

The Maxam brand had gradually recovered after the Jahwa-Johnson JV fiasco. Although brand recognition among consumers was high, its customer profile did not match the target positioning. Younger women did not associate Maxam with modernity, fashion, and high technology. Still, in 2010, Maxam achieved a breakthrough into the hand cream segment, where it became the top selling brand. New ranges were launched in the facial cream segment to stimulate growth, and Maxam's annual sales reached USD 47 million in 2011.

In contrast, the Liushen brand – a name that meant Six Spirits – had quickly captured 25 percent of the market for refreshing toilet waters (eaux de toilette) with the lines it launched in 1990. Foreign competitors were largely absent from this segment, and by 2011 Liushen held more than half of the market. When the Liushen range expanded to include shower cream (in 1992) and soap (in 1997), the brand came into head-to-head competition with market leaders in major product categories. Still, the emphasis on traditional Chinese ingredients and its positioning as a refreshing line for summer use helped Liushen to forge a good reputation and generate high sales in summer.

This strong reputation gave Liushen bargaining power vis-à-vis supermarkets and hypermarkets, including Carrefour and helped it to support other brands in the Jahwa portfolio. With annual sales of USD 204 million in 2009, Liushen accounted for about half of Jahwa's total revenues. Its long running success paved the way for the development of Jahwa's more up-market brand Herborist.

Herborist: A move into the mid-to-high market

The idea for the Herborist brand was born in the early 1990s. A visiting executive from a cosmetics MNC said to Mr. Ge that if he did not build up his own brand, selling products in other countries would be very difficult. Mr. Ge was determined somehow to enter western markets, as his counterpart had done in China. The inspiration for a new natural skin care brand came from a visit Mr. Ge paid to a branch of Body Shop during an overseas business trip. He would

have liked to form a JV for natural/herbal products, but Body Shop had no plans to enter the Chinese market at that time. Instead, he decided Jahwa would create its own brand for the middle-to-high market.

After three years of testing and preparation, in 1998 Jahwa finally launched Herborist. Its niche herbal positioning avoided direct competition with the foreign players that dominated the market. It also differed from domestic competitors, which at the time were simply copying from their foreign rivals. Herborist's selling point was the integration of herbal essences and other TCM ingredients with modern biotechnology. According to a senior Herborist manager, the brand promoted a *"modern interpretation of Chinese traditional culture"* by emphasising the Chinese culture of 'nature and balance'. By 2011, its skin care products addressed the full range of treatments for hydration, dull skin, whitening, pimple treatment, etc. On price, Herborist benchmarked itself against the premium lines of L'Oréal, Aupres (by Shiseido) and Olay (by P&G).

Developing the brand

Brand development went through a three-stage transformation after the launch. In the initial stage, before 2000, the budget for development was a tiny USD 2.35 million. Using Chinese ingredients in skin care products was a new concept. Consumers had difficulty in reconciling their impression of Chinese medicine (often bitter and unpleasant) with Jahwa's attempts to associate Herborist products with nature, freshness and health. Organisationally, Herborist struggled to develop its niche positioning within Jahwa's brand management system. It had to operate alongside mass retail brands like Maxam and Liushen and compete with all the other brands for access to R&D resources. Reflecting Jahwa's SOE heritage, emphasis was placed on maximising production rather than inventory control or meeting sales forecasts.

Redundant feasibility studies slowed new product introductions, and incentive structures did not motivate the sales team. There was no pressure to produce financial results: non-profit budgets were approved for three consecutive years. Annual sales totalled only USD 0.63 million in 2000, from 12 company-owned outlets.

The money raised by the partial listing of Jahwa in 2001 gave the Herborist project team another USD 4.7 million to work with. Finally recognising that Herborist needed different management structures Jahwa established the brand as a separate subsidiary company in charge of its new product development and customer management. The parent company retained control of brand design and marketing. A new team managed the supply chain from forecast through planning to delivery; new product launch procedures were streamlined to a regular quarterly basis; and the sales team received more performance-related incentives. An R&D group working exclusively for Herborist began to research and refine the use of Chinese ingredients and the brand started to emphasize its use of single TCM additives (such as ginseng or rhodiola). But it rapidly discovered that competitors could easily copy this strategy. Then, in 2004, Herborist launched its first product containing a compound created by Jahwa's R&D centre, based on scientific theories underlying TCM. Herborist sales in 2004 reached just under USD 6.26 million.

This product marked the start of the third phase, and heralded the brand's move into profitability. It had taken seven years. The Herborist team realised that the cornerstone of success lay in building a brand culture and lifestyle, rather than simply creating more products. Now every new product line would be based on a TCM formula, and would communicate a balanced lifestyle message. The first big success was the T'ai Chi Clay face mask, which combined Yin-Yang

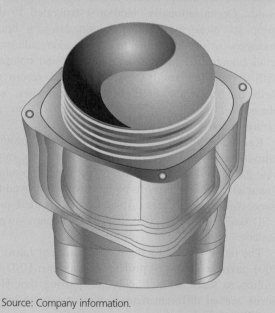

Source: Company information.

ideology in a daring presentation package containing black clay and white moisturizer (Exhibit E): sales reached USD 15.7 million in 2008, its launch year. After 10 years of effort, Herborist had its first star product. Later successful products similarly embodied the deep cultural elements associated with TCM. At last Herborist seemed able to capitalise on its first mover advantage in this niche area. New lines were added: essential oils, herbal teas, and the opening of Herborist Spas to offer customers innovative TCM-inspired herbal beauty-care services. All of this helped to differentiate Herborist from other brands. By this time Herborist had over one million loyalty card members. They were mainly 25-35 year-olds in stable careers, with middle to high levels of education and salary.

Distribution

Herborist regarded department stores as the fitting distribution channel for its products. Rebuffed at first by the refusal of high-end department stores to display a local brand on the first floor, alongside foreign brands, Herborist decided to set up its own free-standing beauty specialty stores. Its flagship store was in the Hong Kong Shopping Plaza on Huai Hai Road, the vanguard of fashion in Shanghai – a very bold choice, according to a senior manager in Herborist, since shopping malls were just appearing as a new retail format in China in the late 1990s. Selling through branded stores allowed Herborist the space and time to present its products and philosophy to every potential consumer. This helped it to build its customer base, but it was a slow and costly strategy.

Starting from 2002, Jahwa decided to speed up expansion by adding counters in department stores in lower-tier cities. The number of points of sale expanded to 100 in 2004. Keeping China's ten largest and strategically most important cities for its own specialty store development, Herborist then turned to franchising. This method would help it to accelerate network expansion to fifty outlets a year, while controlling costs. In 2005, French-owned Sephora chose Jahwa as the JV partner for its entry into China, to satisfy Chinese government rules that required all foreign retailers to have a domestic partner. Brand awareness rose among franchisers and department stores when Herborist products appeared in Sephora's stores in China. The number of outlets selling Herborist rose rapidly, to 500 in 2009 (of which 30 percent were directly owned) and to over 1000 by 2011. Not only did the brand's presence in Sephora stores add 100 points of sale in over 30 Chinese cities, it also enabled Herborist to participate in Sephora's many promotional activities.

Jahwa did not give up on getting Herborist into top-end department stores. A breakthrough came when Zhongyou, one of the most prestigious department stores in Beijing, finally accepted in 2009 that the brand had built a strong consumer following. Annual sales of USD 2.5 million put Herborist into the top ten brands on Zhongyou's elite first floor, and paved the way for entry to department stores in other northern cities. Shanghai top department stores remained an as yet uncracked nut, but would be important for the visibility and availability of the brand.

Brand design and marketing

Herborist brand-building followed a steady course, shifting slowly from channel building to marketing communications. Only in 2008 did Herborist establish its own communications and brand design department. According to a senior manager, *"the challenge for Herborist was not how to grow sales from RMB 100 million (USD 15.8 million) to RMB 1 billion (USD 158 million), but how to reach the first RMB 100 million"* – a hurdle reached only in 2006. The 10 percent of annual sales Herborist had invested in marketing would not even pay for a 15-second commercial on a

provincial TV channel. Rather, Herborist used print advertising and tried to maintain good relationships with the media to win good publicity. Once the brand had broken even, marketing spending was increased to 20 percent. Sales grew rapidly, particularly after 2008 when it started to invest vigorously in TV commercials. The launch of Herborist in France created a media buzz in China and encouraged the company to adopt a more aggressive communications strategy.

International market entry

An attempt in 2000 to expand into the Hong Kong market with a stand-alone store in Causeway Bay proved an expensive failure. The brand concept in those days was still immature and the design of its English language packaging was too westernized, losing any differentiating 'Chineseness'.

Mr. Ge, noting the steady expansion of international manufacturers into the Chinese mass market, was determined that Jahwa should try to sell Herborist on the home turf of foreign competitors: *"if you play in my mass market, I will harass your premium market!"* It was a point of national pride and a dream for Jahwa to sell its products in western markets. Paris seemed an ideal location for Herborist's international debut, because it was the fashion centre of the world and French

---

EXHIBIT F   THE OLD HERBORIST PACKAGING & THE NEW HERBORIST PACKAGING BY CENTDEGRÉS

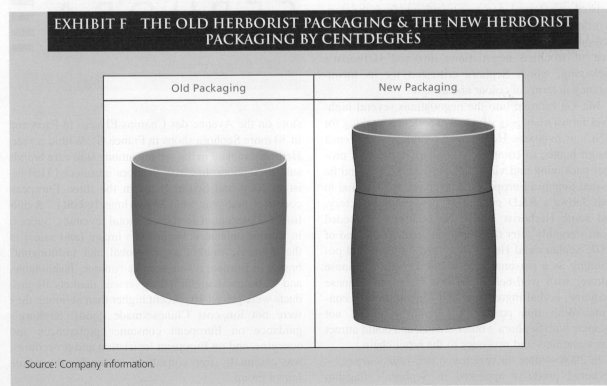

| Old Packaging | New Packaging |

Source: Company information.

consumers were more receptive to products based on herbal ingredients than people in other countries. Mr Ge wanted Herborist to be benchmarked in terms of price and positioning against the organic/herbal L'Occitane brand or L'Oréal's natural beauty business Biotherm.

Finding a reliable sales channel was difficult, since consumers in Europe bought mid- and high-end cosmetics from specialty stores, and the dominant players were different in every country. Sephora was the second-largest cosmetics retailer in France, it carried only first-tier brands, and it targeted young fashion-lovers. Sephora also had a wide presence in other European markets. These were all attractive attributes for Herborist. Although Sephora showed interest in co-operating in Europe, the alliance negotiations that began in 2006 were difficult. Purchasing officers in Sephora were the decision-makers, and they did not trust a 'Made in China' brand. They thought Herborist was not positioned clearly enough and would compete with the herbal brands Sephora already offered. A major disagreement lay in the product categories they proposed Herborist should bring to Europe. Since Herborist was an unknown name outside China and competition among skin care brands was fierce, Sephora recommended Herborist to start with non-skin care categories, such as foot massage products. Skin care products could come later. Jahwa rejected this proposal. It insisted on offering skin care treatments from the start, in order to avoid any perception in Europe of Herborist as a side-line brand of non-skin care products. A second area of troubled negotiations involved Herborist's packaging, which Sephora criticized for its inconsistency in terms of colour and design.

Mr. Ge brought into the negotiations several high-level Jahwa managers who had experience working for MNCs or overseas. He engaged Centdegrés, a French design house, to completely revamp Herborist's product packaging and visual image (Exhibit F). And he invited Sephora Europe's management to Shanghai to visit Jahwa's R&D centre, its new-product factory, and some Herborist stores. Negotiations proceeded more smoothly after the Shanghai visit. At the end of 2007, Sephora and Herborist agreed on the brand positioning as a personal care brand rooted in Chinese culture, with well-being products based on Chinese medicine, herbal ingredients and Chinese beauty concepts. With this positioning Herborist would not compete with Sephora's other brands, and could attract new customers and revenues to the retail chain.

In 2008 – after *"a very tough two-year journey"* – Herborist products appeared in Sephora's flagship

EXHIBIT G HERBORIST ADVERTISEMENT IN SEPHORA FRANCE

En chinois, la beauté se dit équilibre.

Dans la tradition chinoise, équilibre égale harmonie. Harmonie entre l'intérieur et l'extérieur ; le désire et le besoin. Les masques T'ai Chi d'Herborist favorisent la circulation des énergies et révelènt la beauté de la peau, comme venue de l'intérieur.

佰草集
HERBORIST
THE CHINESE BEAUTY REMEDY

Côté yin, le masque noir déstresse votre peau et la purifie.

Côté yang, le masque blanc apaise votre peau et révèle l'éclat.

UNIQUEMENT CHEZ
SEPHORA
AVANCER EN BEAUTÉ

Source: Company information.

store on the Avenue des Champs-Elysées in Paris and in 30 more Sephora shops in France G). Within a year, Herborist ranked in the top ten among skin care brands sold in Sephora. In 2010, Sephora introduced Herborist to Italy and Spain. Sales in the three European countries that year were approximately USD 2.8 million, 1.3 percent of Herborist's total revenues. Success in Europe enhanced Herborist's image (and sales) in the domestic market as a "global and fashionable" brand. In Europe, it was seen as "unique, fashionable, and made in Shanghai". In overseas markets its products were priced 40 percent higher than at home: they were not low-cost Chinese-made goods. Sephora's guidance on European consumer preferences and concerns, and on European legislation and procedures, was essentially free consulting advice for the whole Jahwa group.

EXHIBIT H SHUANGMEI (OLD) AND SHANGHAI VIVE (NEW) ADVERTISEMENTS

Source: Company information.

Herborist today

Herborist recorded more than 60 percent growth in 2009, 50 percent growth in 2010 and reached sales of USD 313 million in 2011. The company forecast 40-50 percent annual growth for the next three years, based on a 20 percent increase in points of sale within China, improved revenues per point of sale, and entry into new European markets through Sephora stores.

Where next for Jahwa?

Mr. Ge observed how foreign personal care companies, with their long domination in the premium segment, had benefited more than domestic players from Chinese consumers' desire for premium brands. For years he had wanted to challenge their position by launching Jahwa's first luxury brand. Rather than delve again into the Chinese medicine chest, as Herborist had done, the next new brand would recall Jahwa's history and memories of Shanghai in the 1930s. The original Shuangmei ("Two Girls" in Chinese) brand would be revived under the name Shanghai Vive. It would target the affluent and the fashionable who were nostalgic for the glory of old Shanghai, and

who were willing to spend a high proportion of their income on personal care.

Shanghai Vive was launched with great fanfare in August 2010 in a flagship boutique inside the recently renovated Peace Hotel, a landmark art deco building on Shanghai's famous Bund. Jahwa invited the great grandson of Chiang Kai-Shek[17] to design the product packaging. Both packaging and presentation were redolent of 1930s Shanghai, when the city was known as the "Paris of the Orient" (Exhibit H). The marketing message suggested the integration of culture, high technology and high quality. The product range included not only skin care products, but also colour cosmetics, body care and hair care products, fragrances, accessories (costume jewellery and scarves), and T-shirts emblazoned with Shuangmei advertisements from the 1930s. Shanghai Vive clearly benchmarked luxury Western brands. A second Vive boutique opened in early 2011 in Shanghai's Tianzifang, a fashionable courtyard of shops and bars popular with foreign visitors and young urban Chinese. Four more boutiques appeared in other parts of Shanghai over the following months. Mr. Ge joked that, since Herborist had taken seven years to earn any money, he could wait six and a half years for Shanghai Vive to become profitable.

[17]Chiang Kai-Shek was the president of China before 1949.

EXHIBIT I SHANGHAI VIVE PRODUCT PACKAGING

Radiance Restorative Cream	Intensive Regenerating Cream	Ye Shanghai Eau De Parfum

Source: Company information.

Did Jahwa have the skills to develop a truly aspirational fashion-lifestyle brand of the type it tried to project with Shanghai Vive? Its experience of developing the Herborist brand had enabled the company to learn what brand management meant, how to build supporting systems and processes, and how to seize market opportunities. Could these capabilities help Jahwa to establish a position in the premium market? MNC players had decades of management expertise in understanding the luxury segment and in building global brands, supported by heavy investment in marketing. Did Jahwa have sufficient financial resouces? And did it have the time to learn?

Rather than the distraction of entering an entirely new market segment, might not Jahwa do better to focus on its existing brands, for example by extending into services through the Herborist Spa chain? Spa business was, after all, still a highly fragmented market in China worth of billions of dollars.

Internally, Jahwa still had much to improve in terms of leadership skills and the professionalization of its management practices. It needed to learn about effective ways of reaching target customers on a limited marketing budget. Would the removal of the Shanghai government from direct ownership allow Jahwa to make bigger investments in marketing and in hiring professionals experienced in the premium segment?

Finally, could Jahwa develop a brand that would overcome consumers' continuing perceptions of cheap, poor quality Chinese-made products?

CASE 10

The evolution of the Bottled Water Industry: Ready for the "Water Wars"?

By Javier Gimeno and Cool

By 2002, the global bottled water industry was at an inflection point. Traditionally, the industry had been fragmented among many local and regional players, but over the last decade four large multinationals (Danone, Nestlé, PepsiCo, and Coca-Cola) had been battling for global market share. These four companies controlled over 30% of the global market, and continued to expand organically and through acquisitions. Yet, in an industry in which many sources of supply existed, with products that were nearly impossible to tell apart by taste, and for which a free substitute existed (tap water), it was not clear whether these global players would be able to create an attractive industry structure that would deliver sustained profits.

In 2002, the U.S. market was one of the main fronts in the battle for market position among these multinationals. In contrast with Western Europe, which had large but mature demand for bottled water, the U.S. market had tripled during the 1990s as health-conscious customers increasingly turned to bottled water. Nestlé, which had acquired the bottled water business of Perrier in 1992, was the clear market leader with many of the strongest regional spring water brands. However, the growing market had attracted new entrants, both small and large. Brands like Fiji and Glaceau sought a premium position. Yet it was the aggressive entry by PepsiCo in 1994, followed by Coca-Cola in 1999 – with new business models based on purified waters and substantially different economics – that had disrupted the industry structure. By 2002, the competitive escalation was starting to produce adverse effects. Since 2001, bottled water prices had dropped by 3%, and some analysts feared that a possible price war could erode industry profitability.

Faced with tougher competitive conditions, Nestlé, PepsiCo, Coca-Cola and Danone had to re-assess their strategic postures and commitments to the US bottled water market. Questions arose about the long-term profitability of the market. Would it ever approach that of the carbonated soft drink industry, which was among the most profitable industries in the world? Or would the competitive escalation and price competition erode industry profits? Questions also arose about the diverse strategies used by the 'big four'. Whose strategy was most appropriate for the future of the market? And how should each adapt their respective strategy to the emerging competitive environment?

The evolution of the bottle water industry

The medicinal properties of mineral water have been valued since antiquity. Visits to natural springs and spas became fashionable among the wealthy elite during the 19th and early 20th centuries. The American bottled water industry got started in 1844 when a Maine inn-keeper, lying on his deathbed, discovered the remarkable therapeutic properties of water from his local spring. As the popularity of the water grew with visitors, the inn turned into a spa resort and the family began to sell the water under the brand of Poland Spring. In France, waters from mineral springs like Evian, Vittel and Perrier were popular in the early 20th century, and patients returning from a "cure" brought back supplies of water to continue their cure at home. A modest demand for bottled mineral waters developed in pharmacies.[1]

The bottled water industry remained small until the 1960s, when the development of large-scale retail surfaces (supermarkets, hypermarkets) boosted

This case was written by Javier Gimeno, Professor of Strategy, Aon Dirk Verbeek Chaired Professor in International Risk and Strategic Management, and Karel Cool, Professor of Strategic Management, BP Chaired Professor of European Competitiveness, both at INSEAD. The case is based on previous reports by INSEAD MBA alumni Manoj Sahasrabudhe, MBA 2002, Alistair Phelps and Vicky Davies, MBA 2003. It is intended to be used as a basis for class discussion rather than to illustrate either effective or ineffective handling of an administrative situation.

[1]Early history of industry from John Sutton's "Sunk Costs and Market Structure" MIT Press (1991).

demand for new categories of groceries. This allowed mineral water to switch from the pharmacy to the grocery category. The introduction of plastic bottles in 1968 enabled a move towards the larger 1.5-litre bottles, which are popular today in many countries.

Another major boost came from the use of mass advertising in the 1970s, when Perrier led the way in developing a new image for mineral water. With its characteristic small green bottle, Perrier had been positioned since the turn of the century mainly as a bar mixer. The "Whisper" (a mix of whisky and Perrier) was fashionable in sophisticated circles outside France. But in the 1960s and 1970s, the company sought to move beyond the older whisky-drinking generation and targeted younger customers. The first major slogan, "Perrier, c'est fou!" ("Perrier, it's crazy!") captured the imagination of a new generation with commercials showing dancing youngsters, creating an image of Perrier as "très 'in", "très 'à la mode". The ad was so effective that future campaigns could play with meaningless variations on the same words ("Ferrier, c'est pou!") and be instantly recognizable.

The success of Perrier sparked imitation. In France, Evian and Vittel reacted by also escalating branding and advertising expenses. Each player emphasized a different image. Perrier focused on a fun and young image. Evian had targeted sales for infants (the baby bottle segment) since the 1960s, and its advertising emphasized its purity, although during the 1970s, as the brand moved to large retail surfaces, it tended to emphasize the idea of everyday use. By the mid-1980s, the top four companies in France accounted for some 80%–85% of sales. The growth of the market, however, had encouraged the opening or reopening of many springs, and some of these producers tended to sell on price with no advertising support, at the bottom end of the price spectrum. By 2001, the top three companies, Nestlé (which owned the Perrier, Vittel, and Contrex brands, among others), Danone (with Evian, Badoit, and Volvic) and Neptune (with low-price brands like Cristaline and Saint-Yorre) controlled 63% of the volume sold in France.

The pattern of consolidation seen in France was not consistently followed around the world, or even in Western Europe. For example, by 2001, the top four companies in each country controlled about 60% of volumes in Italy, 48% of volumes in Spain, 42% in the USA, 35% in the U.K., and only 24% in Germany. These countries exhibited differences in customer preferences, distribution channels, and competitive dynamics that shaped their market structures.

A major change in the industry came with the introduction of purified waters by PepsiCo (Aquafina) in 1994 and Coca-Cola (Dasani) in 1999. In contrast to spring water companies, which typically extracted water from underground aquifers and springs, these companies used municipal tap water filtered through reverse osmosis systems that removed impurities from the water. This move allowed Coke and Pepsi bottlers to use their existing purification equipment (used in the production of soft drinks) and existing distribution channels. Since water did not have to be transported from a single original source, this development allowed the development of strong national (or even global) brands that were produced locally. Aquafina and Dasani were launched with strong advertising campaigns and mid-tier pricing, and quickly gained market share. By 2001, Aquafina and Dasani had gained 4.5% and 4.2% shares of volume in the US market respectively, inching into position behind the volume leader brand Poland Spring (owned by Nestlé). By 2001, Aquafina had become the leading US brand in terms of dollar value.

The market for bottled water

In 2001, about 115 billion litres of bottled water were sold worldwide, for a total retail value (including channel markups) of about $67 billion. Over the last four years, volume had grown 11%, while value had grown by 5.8%. These global statistics masked huge differences in penetration around the world. Western Europe accounted for about 38% of the total global value, North America about 23%, Latin America about 16% and the rest was divided among other regions. Bottled water consumption per capita also varied heavily: about 92 litres in Western Europe versus 60 litres in the US. Within Western Europe, consumption differed markedly, from 159 litres in Italy, 142 in France, 134 in Spain, 104 in Germany, but only 23 litres in the UK. However, markets with greater per capita consumption also experienced lower growth. Annual volume growth from 1998 to 2001 in Western Europe was about 5.5%, versus 9.2% in the US. Within Western Europe, growth rates differed, from 2.3% in Germany to 10.5% in Spain (see Exhibits 7, 8 and 9 for country demand statistics).

The main selling attribute of bottled water was its purity. Many brands emphasized the purity of their springs, which originated typically from underground aquifers in remote locations far from pollution sources. For example, San Pellegrino boasted that: "As it flows underground, protected from sources of pollution, it [water] acquires its mineral salt composition and bacteriological purity." In contrast, tap water mostly came from rivers and lakes and had to travel great distances and pass through routes that were perceived as unclean before reaching the tap. Bottled water gained in popularity as a light, rehydrating alternative to calorie-rich soft drinks or caffeinated drinks that could dehydrate the body (Exhibit 14).

The bottled water market was typically segmented along three dimensions: product characteristics, water sources, and marketing channels. *By product characteristics*, the main water categories were still, sparkling, and flavoured/functional water. Still bottled water was the dominant category, with about 77.6% of global volume and 72.6% of global value. Sparkling water, including natural or added carbonation, was the traditional alternative to still water and took about 21.2% of global volume and 24.4% of value. Because of carbonation pressure, sparkling water was sold in glass or rigid plastic bottles, and at a higher price. For historical reasons, countries differed in their preferences for these types of waters: sparkling water constituted 86% of the retail market in Germany, but only 2% in Spain. Flavoured and functional waters (enriched with calcium, minerals or vitamins) were being introduced in the US. Products like Perrier lemon and lime, and Aquafina FlavorSplash, focused on flavour enhancements, while Quaker Oats' Propel Fitness, or Glaceau's VitaminWater focused on vitamin and mineral enhancing. In 2001, flavoured/functional water took about 1.2% of global volume, and about 3% of value. Since 1998, the volume of still water and flavoured/functional water had grown at about 12% per year, while sparkling water volume grew at about 3.5%.

The market could also be segmented *by water source* (natural springs or purified water sources), although it was not clear whether customers either understood or cared about these distinctions (Exhibit 15). Waters from natural springs could come from a single spring (often called single-spring or mineral water), or from multiple springs (multi-spring waters). Single-spring water brands were typically bottled at source, and had no treatment except filtration. Premium European waters like Perrier, Vittel, Contrex, and San Pellegrino (Nestlé brands) and Evian and Badoit (Danone brands), were single-spring waters, whose transportation costs increased dramatically when sold far from the spring. Multi-spring water brands used a common brand name to market water from multiple springs. A limited number of treatments were permitted, but these had to be listed on the label. The

specific location of the spring source for each bottle also had to be clearly visible on the label. Poland Spring, Arrowhead and Ozarka (Nestlé brands), and Dannon and Sparkletts (Danone brands) in the US, and Aquarel (Nestlé brand) or Cristaline (Neptune brand) in Europe, were examples of multi-spring water brands. Purified (or table) water could be a mixture of spring and tap waters, and could be sourced from above-ground sources like rivers and glaciers. Purified water went through more involved water treatment processes to remove impurities or minerals, or have minerals added to make a kind of artificial mineral water. Pepsi's Aquafina and Coca-Cola's Dasani and BonAqua were examples of purified waters.

Finally, the bottled water market could also be segmented by *marketing channels*. Generally, channels could be divided between the retail (or off-trade) channel, and the on-trade channel, which focused on hospitality, restaurants and catering businesses where consumption occurred on the premises. Worldwide, the retail channel was 84% of volume, but only 57% of total value, since customer prices in the on-trade channel were about four times higher than in the retail channel. Again, countries differed in the share of the different channels. For example, the on-trade channel accounted for 27% of volume sold in the US, but only 4% of volume sold in France. Premium brands tended to perform better in the on-trade channel, since the prestige of the water brands enhanced the image of the outlet, and allowed the outlet to justify high markups. Restaurants were increasingly abandoning the habit of providing free tap water to customers and putting bottled water on their menus. On-trade channels typically stocked one or two brands, and could easily switch brands to get a bargain.

Water retail tended to use three main types of channels: "take home", "cold", and "home and office delivery" (HOD) channels (Exhibit 17). The "take home" channel included grocery stores, supermarkets, hypermarkets, independent food stores, drug stores, discount stores, and mass merchandisers, where purchases were typically planned as part of a shopping trip, intended for home consumption. Typical formats in "take home" channels included jugs and large bottles (over 1 litre), but the biggest growth was in "packs" of 12 or 24 half-litre bottles. The "cold" channel included convenience stores (e.g., 7-Eleven stores), gas stations, and vending machines, where the product was purchased typically in single serve bottles (less than 1 litre) for immediate consumption off-premises. Whereas a 24 pack of half-litre bottles sold in a supermarket for around $5 or $6, the same

24 bottles could sell for about $24 in the cold channel. The HOD channel had emerged for delivery of large 5-gallon (18 litre) bottles for use in home dispensers or office water coolers. Typically, customers would enter into supply contracts with local representatives of water companies or bottlers who would install water coolers and deliver water containers as needed. The US HOD market was highly consolidated, with Nestlé, Suntory, and McKesson (a unit of Danone) jointly controlling 84% of the market (with shares of 35%, 29% and 20% respectively).

Supply chain

The supply chain of bottled water generally involved activities of water sourcing, procurement of packaging, bottling, branding, distribution and retail. Different competitors organized these supply chain activities differently. Nestlé had an integrated production and multi-channel distribution model, while Coca-Cola and PepsiCo relied heavily on exclusive franchised bottlers for production and distribution activities (see Appendix A for a description of the bottler system used in carbonated soft drink production and distribution).

One of the characteristics of bottled water is that the main input (water) is almost free, whether sourced from underground springs, rivers or municipal systems.[2] Spring water could be bought from property owners for between 0.5 and 1.6 cents per litre, depending on volume and market proximity. Water from underground aquifers underwent little treatment beyond filtration, but purified water could undergo more intensive processes, such as distillation, deionization, reverse osmosis, or other purification processes. Water purification involved several steps in which sediment, microbes, and chemicals were eliminated. Reverse osmosis equipment forced water under pressure through semipermeable membranes that filtered out pollutants. By 2002, reverse osmosis technology was mature and equipment was commercially available. Bottlers for Coca-Cola and Pepsi already owned reverse osmosis systems for purifying municipal water used for production of soft drinks, and therefore incurred few additional costs for purification.

The main raw material cost in bottled water was therefore packaging. The industry began to shift from glass to PVC in the 1960s.[?] Nowadays most companies

prefer PET to PVC because of its improved strength, weight, and design options, and its lower environmental impact.[3] PET resin was considered a commodity, and the price varied according to supply and demand, and oil prices (see Exhibit 6). Major brands (including the large Nestlé brands) had bottle and closure moulding equipment on site, and enjoyed some economies of scale in bottle production. Smaller firms bought plastic bottles and caps.

In contrast with other food and drink industries, bottling/filling was relatively simple, since no processing was involved (except when purification or mineral addition was involved). However, the bottling activity involved significant scale economies. Filling costs per litre declined substantially as bottling plant size increased up to 200 million litres per year, and less dramatically thereafter (see Exhibit 5). Large plants also benefited from having filling lines dedicated to specific bottle sizes or different labels. A state-of-the-art bottling facility with a capacity of 200 million litres could be built for around $10 million. Companies could add modules to their existing bottling plants. Coke and Pepsi bottlers could use their existing bottling lines for water bottling but this involved constraints on bottle sizes or shapes, since carbonated soft drinks required thicker PET bottles than was necessary for water.

Efforts to differentiate the brands and grow the category had led to increased spending on new product development, branding and advertising. Advertising was typical among leading brands, representing about 15% of the wholesale price (see Exhibit 4). The introduction in the US of purified waters like Aquafina and Dasani at the national level was accompanied by heavy advertising, with total water advertising expenditures doubling in three years. Advertising expenditures for the major brands in the water sector for 2001 reached $26.4 million for Coca-Cola, $13.2 million for Pepsi, $14.2 million for Nestlé, and $9.5 million for Evian (Danone) (Exhibits 20 and 21). Despite these investments, brand was selected by only 10% of surveyed water customers as a top attribute for product selection (versus 37% for carbonated soft drinks customers), and low price was selected by 38% (versus 26% for carbonated soft drinks). It seemed that water brands had not achieved the level of brand differentiation and loyalty of soft drinks.

Distribution costs varied considerably. They increased with the distance transported from the bottling

---

[2] However, water procurement and transportation systems may involve huge fixed costs.

[3] A remarkable exception to this rule is Germany, where about 97% of water is consumed on returnable glass packaging. Germans drink predominantly sparkling water. Regional water distribution companies handled the distribution and recycling of these bottles. As a consequence, the German market was more regionally fragmented than other similar-size markets.

plant (about one cent per litre for each 100 miles), and decreased with the density of the delivery locations and the size of deliveries: a supplier delivering large volumes to a few nearby warehouses would have much lower costs than one delivering to a large number of restaurants spread out over a large territory. For Coca-Cola and Pepsi, distribution activities were the responsibility of their respective networks of independent or partially-owned bottlers. These bottlers used the "direct store delivery" (DSD) distribution model, which they also used for distributing carbonated soft drinks. According to the DSD model, employees of the bottler managed the brand and stocks directly in the retail store (bypassing the retailer's warehouse) by securing shelf space in the store, stacking products, and setting point-of-purchase displays. Although this method of distribution was very popular with smaller stores and convenience stores, which were happy to outsource the merchandising activities to the bottlers, large chains like Wal-Mart preferred to use their own warehouses and distribution networks. Other water companies, such as Nestlé and Danone relied on independent brokers and wholesalers, which delivered beverages to the supermarkets (either to the warehouse or to the store) as well as to many points of sale, including stands and convenience stores.

The supply chain activities were performed by different actors, depending on the different business models used by the water companies. Coca-Cola and Pepsi used a "bottler model", which relied on franchise bottlers for sourcing, bottling and distribution activities, while product development, branding and advertising remained the responsibility of Coke and Pepsi themselves. Pepsi bottlers would pay a license to Pepsi for their use of the Aquafina brand. For Dasani, Coca-Cola adopted exactly the same model as for soft drinks. Coca-Cola provided a standardized mix of minerals to be added to the purified water, and charged the bottlers for the "concentrate". Bottlers paid $0.10-$0.14 in royalties per litre. In return, Coke and Pepsi invested heavily in advertising and bottler trading support. Despite these charges, bottled water was big business for Coke and Pepsi bottlers, who made higher margins from water sales than from soft drink sales. In soft drink production, concentrate producers (Coca-Cola and PepsiCo) captured the lion's share of margins, and bottlers like Coca-Cola Enterprises (CCE) or Pepsi Bottling Group (PBG) had returns below their cost of capital (Exhibit 23).

The situation was reversed in water. Analysts estimated that while only 2% of Pepsi's and Coke's North American profits came from the water business, Pepsi's and Coke's bottlers (PBG and CCE) derived 7% and 8% of their profits from water respectively, which only accounted for 4% of their volume. Coke and Pepsi saw their bottling and distribution systems as their key strength in the water business. However, the DSD system was not necessarily the most cost-efficient channel to reach some mass-market points of sale.

Nestlé, the market leader, used a business model based on large-scale integrated production (including self-production of bottles and closures) with regional brands (Poland Spring in the North East US, Arrowhead in the West, etc.). Nestlé had over 20 high-speed bottling facilities, and nine PET bottle manufacturing plants strategically located around the country. Focused production and lightweight packaging (more appropriate for water than carbonated beverages) saved on production costs relative to Coke and Pepsi bottlers. Nestlé also had the advantage of a very flexible distribution strategy based on a very dense distribution network and a variety of channels to get its water to market. Said CEO Kim Jeffery of Nestlé Waters North America, "We made Poland Spring PET bottles in New York available to all wholesalers, distributors, produce, candy-tobacco, grocery, dry goods. Poland Spring, not bottled water, became an available commodity." He added: "We have the ability to do warehouse, DSD, direct through club, whatever works. There is no perfect distribution system. People can argue the merits of DSD versus warehouse all day long, but I think that DSD has certain advantages in some classes of trade, and warehouse has advantages in other classes of trade."

In parallel with the four branded bottled water suppliers, some companies pursued a private label strategy. These companies were able to drastically reduce costs by using lower quality packaging, reducing salaries and welfare expenses, avoiding advertising and promotional costs, and cutting distribution costs by delivering to clients' warehouses. Despite these lower costs, private label waters also sold at a low price, and margins for producers were low.

Main competitors

Nestlé

Nestlé was the world's largest packaged food company, with over 8,500 products and operations in over 100 countries. The company's businesses included beverages, milk products, ice cream, prepared food dishes and cooking aids, chocolate and sugar confectionery, and pharmaceutical products. The company had a decentralized structure that allowed the various companies within the group to remain flexible and efficient. The bottled water business represented about 4% of the company's total revenues.

Nestlé had entered the bottled water industry with the acquisition of a stake in Vittel in 1969. By 1992 it had acquired a controlling interest in the Perrier Group, which had undergone in 1990 a worldwide recall of its flagship water after it discovered traces of benzene in some bottles. With that acquisition, Nestlé became the undisputed leader in the US bottled water market, and one of the two global leaders (with Danone). In 1998, it acquired the Italian premium brand San Pellegrino, and in 2002 it bought Blaue Quellen to become the largest player in Germany. By 2001, Nestlé was the market leader in the US, Western Europe, Eastern Europe, and Africa and the Middle East.

Its global water brand portfolio included well-known single-spring water brands like Perrier, Vittel, Contrex, San Pellegrino and Buxton. In the US, its main strategy was based on a set of multi-spring water brands with non-overlapping regional coverage (Poland Spring, Arrowhead, Zephyrhills, Deer Park, Ozarka). These brands allowed Nestlé to occupy a very strong position as the low-cost producer in the market. Nestlé also marketed its European premium waters in the US, at substantial premium prices. It used independent brokers and wholesalers to reach out in multiple retail and on-trade channels. In particular, Nestlé's distribution costs in the supermarket and mass channels were lower than those of Coke and Pepsi bottlers. Although the "take home" market was substantially larger for Nestlé, it had also pushed its regional brands in the home and office delivery (HOD) channel by working with affiliated local distributors, and became the leader in the US HOD market. In Europe, in addition to its premium single-spring water brands, it had launched Aquarel, a multi-spring still water, to develop a low-cost position in the European market.

Danone

In 1969, the Group BSN (which emerged from the merger of two glass companies, and which eventually become Danone) took control of Evian and Badoit, two of the leading brands in France. This was part of a strategy of forward integration from glass containers into contents. The group thus became the leading French producer of beer, mineral waters and baby food. Over the years, it strengthened its position in dairy products, biscuits and bottled water, gaining leading worldwide positions in some categories.

Danone's goal was to be the global water leader. Besides its strong position in Europe, where it was market leader in Spain (FontVella brand) and the UK, Danone engaged in acquisitions, joint ventures and organic growth in North America and Asia. In Asia, Danone acquired several major brands of bottled water, Robust and Wahaha in China, and Aqua in Indonesia, thus making it the leading producer of bottled water in Asia, with a market share of 24%.

Danone had been successful in exporting Evian to the US for many years, and the brand enjoyed a strong presence in the premium segment. However, in 1996, Danone attacked the cheaper spring water segment by creating a national multi-spring water brand called "Dannon". This brand leveraged its nationally recognized brand (Dannon was the leading yogurt brand in the US). By using multiple sources and relying on an independent distribution network, Dannon was able to create a national brand without exploding its distribution costs. It marketed the product at a discount to established regional players, and the brand grew by over 80% in 1998. Meanwhile, Danone was also distributing its Evian brand through the Coke bottling system. In February 2000, Danone purchased McKesson's bottled water business and added the brands Sparkletts, Alhambra and Crystal to its portfolio, becoming the number two player in the US. The acquisition of McKesson also gave Danone a large and profitable HOD business (Exhibit 18). However, this was the time when Aquafina and Dasani started hitting their stride, and Danone's US business began to lose market share at alarming rates.

PepsiCo

During the 1990s, both Coca-Cola and PepsiCo executives claimed that they were no longer cola companies but "total beverage companies" – with one important difference: Pepsi took it seriously. While Coca-Cola pushed the cola wars in developing countries, Pepsi entered the water market in 1994 in cooperation with its bottlers. Entry into this new product category allowed territory-bound bottlers to grow revenues with limited additional investment. The use of a purified water brand was consistent with Pepsi's emphasis on working with its bottlers. The strategy implied a substantial risk, since by 1994 the US bottled water market was dominated by spring water. However, the gamble paid off, and by 2001 Pepsi's Aquafina held 4.5% volume share of the US market and was the second brand in the US in terms of volume and the first in terms of dollar value. Aquafina had gained 13% market share in convenience stores and gas stations, which served about 20% of US demand.

Although Pepsi's bottlers used the DSD delivery method, Pepsi had begun to invest in alternative distribution channels. Pepsi's acquisition of Quaker Oats gave it some synergies in accessing other channels, such as brokers and wholesalers. Quaker Oats commercialized Propel Fitness water, a functional vitamin-enhanced water. Pepsi was rumoured to be preparing the launch of Aquafina Essentials – mineral-enhanced water – in the summer of 2002.

In contrast to the other global players, PepsiCo's bottled water business was relatively weak outside the US, except for an 8% share in Latin America. Its most important presence was the Electropura purified water brand, which was developed in an alliance with its Mexican bottler Gemex, and which was fully acquired by the Pepsi Bottling Group in 2002.

Coca-Cola

Although Coca-Cola had been slow in entering the water business, it had pulled off a remarkable catch up. It launched Dasani in 1999 with a big splash, spending over $20 million in advertising, giving free samples to over 20 million customers, and with a retail price in the mid-tier price range similar to Aquafina. In less than three years, Dasani had registered annual sales of almost 90% those of Aquafina, and become the third brand in the US by volume. Like Pepsi, Coke planned to leverage its DSD distribution system, bottling network and advertising scale to increase national market share for Dasani. Despite that fast growth, sales growth of Dasani in supermarkets started to slow down.

Before the launch of Dasani, Coca-Cola Enterprises (CCE) the largest anchor bottler, had distributed other water brands like Evian and Naya. Soon after the launch of Dasani, CCE ended its distribution agreement with Naya, favouring Dasani. Left without a distribution network overnight, Naya declared bankruptcy soon after, and was eventually acquired by Danone.

In addition to its position in the US, Coca-Cola had tried to expand its bottled water business internationally. It launched a multi-spring still water brand, BonAqua, in Russia and Spain, and the Turkuaz brand in Turkey. However, by 2001, its share in Western Europe was only 0.5%. Coca-Cola had been able to position itself as leader in Latin-America, leveraging its powerful bottler network and its market dominance in the region.

Recent events: A changing competitive landscape

The growth of Aquafina and Dasani during 2001 had a dramatic effect on the market position of the Danone brands. Despite its very successful launch, the volume share of Dannon went down 25% from July 2001 to June 2002. Evian sales also fell 11% in the same period. Sales volume of Volvic and Sparkletts did not fare any better. While Danone maintained good profitability in the HOD market in the US (through its subsidiary McKesson), its Dannon brand was generating losses.

In April 2002, Danone and Coca-Cola announced a strategic alliance whereby Coke would become the master distributor of Evian in the US. While Danone would continue to manage brand positioning and would even keep representatives in Coke's Atlanta headquarters, Coke would become responsible for local promotional spending, merchandising and management of the relationships with the bottlers. Coca-Cola and its bottlers already distributed about 60% of Evian volume in the US, and were expected to bring the remaining 40% in-house when the distribution contracts with other channels expired or were bought out. Danone and Coke had agreed on some volume and sales targets to reverse the slide of Evian sales.

In June 2002, Danone set up an even more far-reaching agreement with Coke. This time, Danone entered into a joint venture with Coca-Cola (49% Danone; 51% Coca-Cola). Coke was to provide its marketing, distribution, and management expertise plus $128 million in cash in return for the assets of Danone's retail bottled waters in the US, ownership of several value brands and production facilities, and the use of the Dannon and Sparkletts brand names. However, Danone remained the owner of the Dannon brand worldwide. The brands going into the venture had estimated 2002 sales of $240 million. The scope of the alliance did not include Coke's Dasani business, which remained fully owned by Coke, and the Evian brand and Danone's HOD operations, which remained fully owned by Danone. For Coke, the alliance offered a multi-tiered approach to the market, with Evian as the premium brand, Dasani in the mid-tier, and Dannon and Sparkletts in the low tier.

These deals marked the end of Danone's direct involvement in the US retail bottled water market. However, since Danone had negotiated volume and profit guarantees, the deals were profit-enhancing. It was expected that Evian would continue to be distributed through the Coke DSD bottler system.

Coca-Cola negotiated with its bottlers the right to distribute the Dannon brand to supermarkets and points of sales through wholesalers and food brokers, similar to Nestlé's waters.

Coke's entry into spring water sent a clear message to Nestlé that it wanted a bigger chunk of the bottled water market. Morgan Stanley estimated that 8% of Nestlé's profits came from US water (5% from retail; 3% from HOD). A Nestlé response was therefore very likely and came swiftly: in August 2002, it announced the launch of a new, national brand, Nestlé Pure. Similar to Dannon, Nestlé Pure was sourced from several springs in the US and would be distributed nationally. It was expected to evolve from Nestlé's budget brand Aberfoyle.

Looking forward, US consumers planned to increase their consumption of bottled water more than any other beverage category (Exhibit 22). This increase was expected to take place partially through category growth and partially at the expense of carbonated soft drinks. Yet it was unclear how competitive dynamics and pricing would play out. While Danone no longer played an active role in the US, it had never really put much pressure on industry prices. When Coke entered the water market, Danone's CEO Riboud stated: "Under no circumstances will we let our margins deteriorate by chasing market share." The JV with Danone had given Coke a position in the single-spring, multi-spring, and purified water categories. On the other hand, PepsiCo was present only in the purified water segment. Nestlé had a very high national market share but this was the result of very strong regional brands (e.g. Poland Spring had more than 50% share in the New York metropolitan area) rather than one national brand.

Now that Nestlé had clearly signalled its commitment to bottled water in the US, all eyes were on Pepsi, Coke and the many other players in the market. In 2001, Pepsi had aggressively priced Aquafina with price cuts of about 10%. The price cuts were partly the result of trade promotions, partly due to an aggressive volume push with ½-litre 12- and 24-unit packs. As large packs tended to have a lower unit price than smaller packs, the Aquafina price level had fallen substantially. This contrasted with Danone, which had continued to raise prices of Dannon and Evian by about 3%. Nestlé had been selective in its price changes; the prices of Poland Spring and Aberfoyle had eroded by 8% (also by selling multi-packs) but the price of Arrowhead had increased by 2%. Coke had sought to maintain its Dasani price and had not pursued the larger multi-packs to the same degree as Pepsi. Media spending had also gone up substantially. During the first half of 2002, Pepsi made a drastic increase in advertising investment for Aquafina, investing $16.2 million during that period (versus $13.3 million for the whole of 2001). Exhibit 19 provides information of retail list prices of major brands.

While Nestlé and Coke were at loggerheads in the bottled water market, they were still 50:50 joint venture partners in the tea business, where they marketed brands such as Nestea, Nescafe, Mad River and Planet Java. In the US, this venture generated about $110 million in revenues and approximately $20 million in profits. The venture had expanded into international markets as well.

While the US water market had seen a spectacular development in just a few years, many observers feared that price reductions would dampen its profitability. Given the reduced profit outlook in the market, should the dominant players reconsider their aggressive commitment to this business? Was a price war scenario inevitable? Was it in the interests of the dominant players to avoid such a scenario? Moreover, a distinctive feature of the US bottled water market was that the four leading firms were deploying different strategies. But, were these strategies still viable in the emerging competitive landscape? Or was it time for incumbents to change strategic direction for their business?

Appendix A

The bottler system in carbonated soft drinks

The structure of the carbonated soft drinks industry involved two major players: concentrate producers (CPs) and bottlers. Concentrate producers, like Coca-Cola, PepsiCo, Cadbury Schweppes, and Cott, developed products, produced a concentrate (a blend of ingredients), and took primary responsibility for brand management. The capital requirements for the production of concentrate were relatively low. CPs developed networks of franchised bottlers. Bottlers added carbonated water and sweeteners, and took primary responsibility for bottling, distribution, sales and merchandising.[4] Bottling was a capital intensive business: bottlers invested in bottling lines, warehouses, trucks and distribution networks. Marketing and promotions were jointly implemented and paid for by CPs and bottlers. CPs also supported bottlers in negotiations with major suppliers, such as sweetener and can producers. In the United States, there were four major concentrate producers, and Coke and Pepsi claimed a combined share of 76% of the market. As capital requirements for bottling increased, the number of US bottlers decreased from over 2,000 in 1970 to less than 300 in 2000. During the 1980s and 1990s, Coke and Pepsi had begun to acquire bottlers, which would then be sold to their "anchor bottlers" Coca-Cola Enterprises (CCE), 49% owned by Coca-Cola, and Pepsi Bottling Group (PBG), 35% owned by PepsiCo. By 2000, CCE and PBG handled respectively about 70% and 55% of the North American volumes of Coke and Pepsi.

The relationship between concentrate producers and bottlers were governed by master franchise contracts. These contracts typically gave exclusive territorial rights to bottlers in perpetuity. CPs negotiated the price of concentrate with bottlers, while bottlers decided on the wholesale price of soft drinks in their territories. During the 1980s and 1990s, the inflation-adjusted price of concentrate went up, even though the price of soft drinks went down. Bottlers had the choice whether or not to adopt new products introduced by the concentrate producers. However, bottlers were not allowed to carry competing brands.

Bottlers used the "direct store door" delivery system to retailers, which involved bottler employees physically managing and maintaining the shelf space, managing inventories in the shelves, and setting point-of-sale displays in the stores. Bottlers and retailers cooperated in setting promotional activities in the store. In contrast, private label soft drinks, like President's Choice, were delivered to the retailer's warehouse for merchandising by the retailer.

Cost per 192 oz. case for Typical US Concentrate Producer and Bottler, 2000

	Concentrate producer		Bottler	
	Dollars per Case	Percent of Sales	Dollars per Case	Percent of Sales
Net Sales	0.71	100%	5.80	100%
Cost of sales	0.12	17	3.77	65
Gross profit	0.59	83	2.03	35
Selling and delivery	0.01	2	1.22	21
Advertising and marketing	0.28	39	0.12	2
General and administration	0.06	8	0.23	4
Pretax profit	0.25	35	0.52	9

Source: Harvard Business School case "Cola Wars Continue: Coke and Pepsi in the Twenty-First Century"

[4]Coca-Cola maintained control of sales for

EXHIBIT 1 MAJOR SOFT DRINKS MANUFACTURERS 2002

Manufacturer	Country of origin	Regional presence	Main area of activity
Coca-Cola Co, The	US	Global	C, F/V, BW, FD, Con, RTD T, RTD C, A
PepsiCo Inc	US	Global	C, F/V, BW, FD, Con, RTD T, RTD C, A
Danone, Groupe	France	Global	F/V, BW, FD
Nestlé SA	Switzerland	Global	C, F/V, BW, FD, Con, RTD T, RTD C, A
Cadbury Schweppes Plc	UK	Global	C, F/V, BW, FD, Con, RTD T, RTD C
Suntory Ltd	Japan	NA, AP, AU	C, F/V, BW, FD, Con, RTD T, RTD C, A
Acqua Minerale San Benedetto SpA	Italy	WE, EE	C, F/V, BW, RTD T
Kirin Brewery Co Ltd	Japan	AP	C, F/V, BW, FD, RTD T, RTD C, A
Castel, Groupe	France	WE, AME	C, BW
Otsuka Pharmaceutical Co Ltd	Japan	AP, NA	BW, C, Con, FD
Unilever Group	UK/NL	Global	F/V, FD, Con, RTD T
AmBev	Brazil	LA, NA, WE	C, BW, FD
Asahi Breweries Ltd	Japan	AP	C, F/V, BW, FD, RTD T, RTD C, A
Uni-President Enterprises Corp	Taiwan	AP, EE	C, F/V, BW, FD, RTD T, RTD C, A
Sunkist Growers Inc	US	All except AME	C, F/V, BW, RTD con, RTD T

Source: Euromonitor from company reports

Key: NA=North America, LA=Latin America, WE=Western Europe, EE=Eastern Europe, AP=Asia-Pacific, AME=Africa and the Middle East, AU=Australasia C – carbonates; F/V – Fruit / vegetable juice, BW – bottled water, FD – functional drinks; Con – concentrates; RTD T – ready-to-drink tea; RTD C – ready-to-drink coffee; A – Asian speciality drinks

EXHIBIT 2 WATER MARKET FUNDAMENTALS – US VERSUS EUROPE

	US market	Europe market
Carbonated Soft Drink (CSD) Penetration	In the US, the non-alcoholic drink category is dominated by CSD. With consumers more and more interested in healthier lifestyles, there is thus substantial room for migration and therefore growth.	Penetration of CSD in Western Europe is a lot lower than in the US and that of bottled water already a lot higher.
Growth	Strong	Limited potential, given that the market is already well developed and quite saturated.
Route to Market	In the US, DSD (direct store delivery) is the prevailing distribution system - acceptable due to high volumes and the key role of convenience stores.	In Europe, the DSD system is not key.
Bottler Relationships	In the US, bottlers are controlled by the large CSD companies.	In Europe, there is a much looser relationship with the bottlers.

	US market	*Europe market*
Competitive Landscape	In the US, the market development is at a very early stage (limited size of competitors with limited national presence).	The main competitors (primarily Nestlé) are already very big, while the rest of the market is quite fragmented. Over the last few years, Coca-Cola has acquired a number of local brands, notably Valser (Switzerland) and Chaudfontaine (Belgium)
Perception of table water	In the US, table water as a business model is accepted by consumers.	In Europe, table water is unlikely to be accepted by the consumer. This is all the more true as brands are key and neither Coca-Cola nor Pepsi have viable strong brands in western Europe.
Pricing	High prices.	In western Europe, prices are already a lot lower than in the North American market.

Source: UBS

EXHIBIT 3 MAJOR SOFT DRINKS MANUFACTURERS: MERGER AND ACQUISITION ACTIVITY 2000–2002

Year	Acquirer	Company acquired	Strategic benefit
2000	Cadbury Schweppes	Snapple Beverage Group (from Triarc Companies Inc)	With brands Royal Crown Cola, Snapple, Mistic and Stewart's, acquisition forms part of strategy to build share through non-sparkling soft drinks
2000	Cadbury Schweppes	Pepsi-Cola Bottlers Australia	Fortifies distribution network
2000	Danone	Robust	Expanding presence in Chinese market
2000	Danone	Aquarius	Gains presence in Chinese home and office delivery market
2000	Danone	McKesson Water	Gains control of leading player in US home and office delivery market
2000	Danone	Naya	Gains control of Canadian water company
2000	Nestlé	Valvita and Schoonspruit (South Africa) and Kekkuti (Hungary)	Gains entry into mineral water markets in South Africa and Hungary
2000	PepsiCo	South Beach Beverage Co	Gains presence in energy drinks through SoBe brand
2001	AmBev	Cympay	Majority stake gives AmBev an 8% share in Uruguayan mineral water market
2001	Cott Corp	Royal Crown Cola's international division (from Cadbury Schweppes)	Cadbury Schweppes retained businesses in US, Canada and Mexico

Year	Acquirer	Company acquired	Strategic benefit
2001	Cadbury Schweppes	La Casera	Secures presence in Iberian peninsula through Spain's third largest soft drinks maker
2001	Cadbury Schweppes	Pernod-Ricard's soft drinks business	Purchase includes brands Orangina and Yoo Hoo in continental Europe, North America and Australasia
2001	Danone	Aqua	Raised stake in Indonesian water company as part of strategy to expand in Asia-Pacific
2001	Danone	Frucor Beverages Group Ltd	Purchase of Australian energy drinks producer, including brands V, H2go and Mizone (bottled water) and gforce (new age beverages, offers chance to expand beyond bottled water sector
2001	Nestlé	Glaciar (Argentina), Sansu (Turkey), Al Manhal (Saudi Arabia), Ava and Fontalia (Pakistan)	Continuing strategic expansion into mineral water sector in developing markets
2001	Nestlé	Aqua Cool (US/Europe), Black Mountain (US), First Choice (UK) and Rossi (France)	Expands presence in home and office delivery market
2001	PepsiCo	Quaker Oats	Control of global leader in sports drinks, Gatorade
2002	AmBev	Quilmes	Stake in Argentine brewer that owns the two largest Pepsi bottlers in Argentina
2002	Cadbury Schweppes	Nantucket Allserve Inc (from Ocean Spray Cranberries Inc)	Expansion in non-carbonated soft drinks
2002	Cadbury Schweppes	Squirt (non-cola carbonate brand from Refremex)	Commitment to fast-growing Mexican carbonates sector
2002	Danone	Patrimoine des Eaux du Quebec	Expanding Danone's presence in Canada, Argentina and Asia
2002	Danone	Sparkling Spring Water Holdings	Consolidating its position in the HOD market in the UK, the US and Canada
2002	Danone	Chateaud'eau International	Control of all water jugs (HOD) businesses of the Suez Group in France. The deal has been made with Ondeo, a subsidiary of the Suez Group
2002	Pepsi Bottling Group	Pepsi-Gemex	Owns the world's No 1 bottled water brand Electropura
2002	Nestlé	Saphir	A 33% stake in Saphir, a major HOD player in France

Source: Euromonitor.

EXHIBIT 4 ESTIMATED COST DIFFERENCES BETWEEN A PREMIUM BRAND AND A PRIVATE LABEL BRAND (PER LITRE) CIRCA 2000

	Premium	Private label
Raw materials	$0.01	$0.01
Packaging	$0.14	$0.10
Salaries	$0.10	$0.05
Depreciation	$0.03	$0.04
Distribution	$0.10	$0.06
Plant operating costs	$0.04	$0.06
Advertising & promotion	$0.09	$0.00
Profit	$0.09	$0.01
Wholesale price	$0.60	$0.32

Source: Company data and BT Alex.Brown International

EXHIBIT 5 ECONOMIES OF SCALE IN BOTTLING

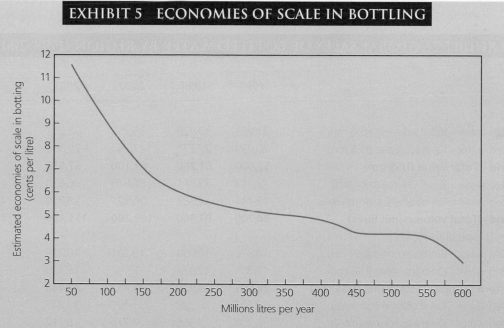

Source: Company data and BT Alex. Brown International/Trade estimates

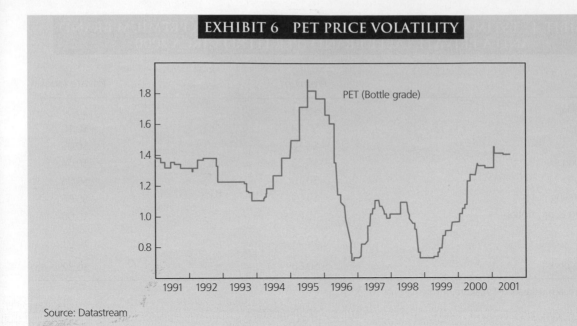

EXHIBIT 6   PET PRICE VOLATILITY

PET (Bottle grade)

Source: Datastream

EXHIBIT 7   GLOBAL SALES OF BOTTLED WATER BY REGION (1998–2001)

	1998	1999	2000	2001	CAGR (98-01)
World (total)					
Bottled water - Retail value rsp (US$ mn)	31,961	33,929	35,356	38,297	6.2%
Bottled water - On-trade value (US$ mn)	25,039	27,271	27,744	29,303	5.4%
World - Total value (US$ mn)	**57,000**	**61,200**	**63,100**	**67,600**	5.8%
Bottled water - Retail volume (mn litres)	72,319	79,311	86,679	96,650	10.1%
Bottled water - On-trade volume (mn litres)	12,381	14,589	16,521	18,750	14.8%
World - Total volume (mn litres)	**84,700**	**93,900**	**103,200**	**115,400**	10.9%
Western Europe (total region)					
Bottled water - Retail value rsp (US$ mn)	10,876	10,954	10,201	10,719	−0.5%
Bottled water - On-trade value (US$ mn)	17,759	17,974	16,552	16,729	−2.0%
Western Europe - Total value (US$ mn)	**28,635**	**28,928**	**26,753**	**27,448**	−1.4%
Bottled water - Retail volume (mn litres)	28,724	30,098	31,497	33,847	5.6%
Bottled water - On-trade volume (mn litres)	6,998	7,368	7,776	8,112	5.0%
Western Europe - Total volume (mn litres)	**35,722**	**37,466**	**39,273**	**41,959**	5.5%
France					
Bottled water - Retail value rsp (US$ mn)	2,307	2,455	2,227	2,262	−0.7%
Bottled water - On-trade value (US$ mn)	1,247	1,354	1,213	1,212	−0.9%
France - Total value (US$ mn)	**3,554**	**3,809**	**3,440**	**3,474**	−0.8%
Bottled water - Retail volume (mn litres)	6,772	7,311	7,664	8,084	6.1%
Bottled water - On-trade volume (mn litres)	291	323	329	334	4.7%
France - Total volume (mn litres)	**7,063**	**7,634**	**7,993**	**8,418**	6.0%

	1998	1999	2000	2001	CAGR (98-01)
Germany					
Bottled water - Retail value rsp (US$ mn)	3,057	2,837	2,489	2,618	−5.0%
Bottled water - On-trade value (US$ mn)	7,658	7,376	6,573	6,352	−6.0%
Germany - Total value (US$ mn)	**10,715**	**10,213**	**9,062**	**8,970**	−5.8%
Bottled water - Retail volume (mn litres)	6,231	6,235	6,152	6,775	2.8%
Bottled water - On-trade volume (mn litres)	1,752	1,783	1,820	1,771	0.4%
Germany - Total volume (mn litres)	**7,983**	**8,018**	**7,972**	**8,546**	2.3%
Italy					
Bottled water - Retail value rsp (US$ mn)	1,638	1,542	1,451	1,494	−3.0%
Bottled water - On-trade value (US$ mn)	2,382	2,356	2,211	2,252	−1.9%
Italy - Total value (US$ mn)	**4,020**	**3,898**	**3,662**	**3,746**	−2.3%
Bottled water - Retail volume (mn litres)	6,741	6,736	7,089	7,306	2.7%
Bottled water - On-trade volume (mn litres)	1,695	1,743	1,865	1,913	4.1%
Italy - Total volume (mn litres)	**8,436**	**8,479**	**8,954**	**9,219**	3.0%
Spain					
Bottled water - Retail value rsp (US$ mn)	588	643	623	679	4.9%
Bottled water - On-trade value (US$ mn)	1,297	1,378	1,335	1,457	4.0%
Spain - Total value (US$ mn)	**1,885**	**2,021**	**1,958**	**2,136**	4.3%
Bottled water - Retail volume (mn litres)	2,870	3,255	3,590	3,946	11.2%
Bottled water - On-trade volume (mn litres)	1,053	1,143	1,237	1,344	8.5%
Spain - Total volume (mn litres)	**3,923**	**4,398**	**4,827**	**5,290**	10.5%
United Kingdom					
Bottled water - Retail value rsp (US$ mn)	914	1,003	1,011	1,064	5.2%
Bottled water - On-trade value (US$ mn)	542	565	595	604	3.7%
UK - Total value (US$ mn)	**1,456**	**1,568**	**1,606**	**1,668**	4.6%
Bottled water - Retail volume (mn litres)	926	1,020	1,126	1,252	10.6%
Bottled water - On-trade volume (mn litres)	109	114	126	132	6.6%
UK - Total volume (mn litres)	**1,035**	**1,134**	**1,252**	**1,384**	10.2%
USA					
Bottled water - Retail value rsp (US$ mn)	6,627	7,151	7,896	8,880	10.2%
Bottled water - On-trade value (US$ mn)	7,799	8,524	9,543	10,597	10.8%
USA - Total value (US$ mn)	**14,426**	**15,675**	**17,439**	**19,477**	10.5%
Bottled water - Retail volume (mn litres)	9,373	10,421	11,182	12,206	9.2%
Bottled water - On-trade volume (mn litres)	3,420	3,739	4,081	4,455	9.2%
USA - Total volume (mn litres)	**12,793**	**14,160**	**15,263**	**16,661**	9.2%
Exchange rate (US$ per Euro)	1.121	1.066	0.924	0.896	−7.2%
Exchange rate (US$ per GBP)	1.656	1.618	1.513	1.439	−4.6%

Source: Euromonitor.

EXHIBIT 8   PER-CAPITA CONSUMPTION OF BOTTLED WATER BY REGION (1998–2001)

	1998	1999	2000	2001	CAGR (98-01)
World (total)					
World - Total value per capita (US$)	9.7	10.3	10.4	11.0	4.3%
World - Total volume per capita (liters)	14.4	15.7	17.1	18.9	9.5%
Western Europe (total region)					
Western Europe - Total value per capita (EUR)	56.7	60.0	63.7	67.3	5.9%
Western Europe - Total volume per capita (liters)	79.3	82.8	86.5	92.1	5.1%
France					
France - Total value per capita (EUR)	54.0	60.6	63.0	65.5	6.7%
France - Total volume per capita (liters)	120.3	129.4	135.3	142.2	5.7%
Germany					
Germany - Total value per capita (EUR)	116.5	116.8	119.7	122.2	1.6%
Germany - Total volume per capita (liters)	97.3	97.7	97.3	104.3	2.3%
Italy					
Italy - Total value per capita (EUR)	62.3	63.5	68.7	72.3	5.1%
Italy - Total volume per capita (liters)	146.6	147.2	155.2	159.6	2.9%
Spain					
Spain - Total value per capita (EUR)	42.7	48.1	53.7	60.4	12.2%
Spain - Total volume per capita (liters)	99.7	111.7	122.4	134.0	10.4%
United Kingdom					
UK - Total value per capita (GBP)	14.9	16.3	17.8	19.5	9.4%
UK - Total volume per capita (liters)	17.5	19.1	21.1	23.3	10.0%
USA					
USA - Total value per capita (US$)	53.6	57.7	63.6	70.4	9.5%
USA - Total volume per capita (liters)	47.6	52.2	55.7	60.2	8.1%
Exchange rate (US$ per Euro)	1.121	1.066	0.924	0.896	−7.2%
Exchange rate (US$ per GBP)	1.656	1.618	1.513	1.439	−4.6%

Source: Euromonitor.

EXHIBIT 9   PER LITRE PRICE OF BOTTLED WATER BY REGION (1998–2001)

	1998	1999	2000	2001	CAGR (98-01)
World (total)					
Bottled water - Retail price/litre (US$)	0.44	0.43	0.41	0.39	−3.4%
Bottled water - On-trade price/litre (US$)	2.02	1.87	1.68	1.56	−8.2%
World - Average price/liter (US$)	0.67	0.65	0.61	0.58	−4.7%
Western Europe (total region)					
Bottled water - Retail price/litre (Euro)	0.34	0.34	0.35	0.35	1.0%
Bottled water - On-trade price/litre (Euro)	2.26	2.29	2.30	2.30	0.6%
Western Europe - Average price/liter (Euro)	0.72	0.72	0.74	0.73	0.5%

	1998	1999	2000	2001	CAGR (98-01)
France					
Bottled water - Retail price/litre (Euro)	0.30	0.32	0.31	0.31	1.1%
Bottled water - On-trade price/litre (Euro)	3.82	3.93	3.99	4.05	2.0%
France - Average price/liter (Euro)	0.45	0.47	0.47	0.46	0.7%
Germany					
Bottled water - Retail price/litre (Euro)	0.44	0.43	0.44	0.43	−0.8%
Bottled water - On-trade price/litre (Euro)	3.90	3.88	3.91	4.00	0.8%
Germany - Average price/liter (Euro)	1.20	1.20	1.23	1.17	−0.8%
Italy					
Bottled water - Retail price/litre (Euro)	0.22	0.21	0.22	0.23	1.5%
Bottled water - On-trade price/litre (Euro)	1.25	1.27	1.28	1.31	1.6%
Italy - Average price/liter (Euro)	0.43	0.43	0.44	0.45	1.5%
Spain					
Bottled water - Retail price/litre (Euro)	0.18	0.19	0.19	0.19	1.8%
Bottled water - On-trade price/litre (Euro)	1.10	1.13	1.17	1.21	3.2%
Spain - Average price/liter (Euro)	0.43	0.43	0.44	0.45	1.5%
United Kingdom					
Bottled water - Retail price/litre (GBP)	0.59	0.61	0.59	0.59	−0.2%
Bottled water - On-trade price/litre (GBP)	3.01	3.06	3.12	3.18	1.9%
UK - Average price/liter (GBP)	0.85	0.86	0.85	0.84	−0.5%
USA					
Bottled water - Retail price/litre (US$)	0.71	0.68	0.70	0.73	0.9%
Bottled water - On-trade price/litre (US$)	2.28	2.28	2.34	2.37	1.4%
USA - Average price/liter (US$)	1.13	1.11	1.15	1.16	1.0%
Exchange rate (US$ per Euro)	1.121	1.066	0.924	0.896	−7.2%
Exchange rate (US$ per GBP)	1.656	1.618	1.513	1.439	−4.6%

Source: Euromonitor.

EXHIBIT 10   SHARES OF THE LEADING PLAYERS IN THE US BOTTLED WATER MARKET (VOLUME)

	1998	1999	2000	2001
Danone	4.3	11.3	10.1	9.9
Nestlé	23.1	23.1	25.4	26.0
Coca-Cola	0.0	0.7	2.3	4.2
PepsiCo	1.9	2.8	3.5	4.5
Suntory	9.3	9.8	10.0	9.3
Crystal Gey.	2.6	3.1	3.4	3.6
Culligan	2.7	2.6	2.7	2.6
Others	56.0	46.4	42.7	40.0
Total	100	100	100	100
Million litres	13,590	15,270	16,350	18,280

Source: Zenith Bottled Water Report

EXHIBIT 11   SHARES OF THE LEADING PLAYERS IN THE US BOTTLED WATER MARKET (WHOLESALE VALUE)

	1998	1999	2000	2001
Danone	7.6	16.1	14.4	13.7
Nestlé	25.6	25.6	27.9	27.8
Coca-Cola	0.0	1.4	4.6	8.2
PepsiCo	4.0	5.9	7.0	8.9
Suntory	6.8	7.4	7.5	6.7
Crystal Gey.	3.2	4.1	4.1	4.2
Culligan	1.5	1.5	1.4	1.4
Others	51.3	38.1	32.9	29.1
Total	100	100	100	100
Million $	4,394	6,006	6,366	7,110

Source: Zenith Bottled Water Report

EXHIBIT 12   GLOBAL MARKET SHARE OF THE LEADING BOTTLED WATER PLAYERS (2001; VOLUMES)

	Danone	Nestlé	Coca-Cola	PepsiCo	Total (million ltr)
N. America	11%	26%	4%	4%	19,200
W. Europe	12%	16%	1%	1%	38,210
E. Europe	3%	6%	5%	5%	6,767
C&L America	8%	2%	11%	8%	25,327
Asia & Australia	24%	3%	6%	1%	22,277
Africa & M.E.	2%	8%	0%	0%	9,204
Total	12%	11%	5%	3%	120,984

Source: Zenith Bottled Water Report

EXHIBIT 13   ESTIMATED REVENUE AND COSTS FOR WATER BOTTLERS IN 2000 (24-PACK CASE OF HALF-LITRE BOTTLES)

	Nestlé	Pepsi	Coke
Retail price (paid by customer)	**$8.44**	**$8.52**	**$8.65**
Retail margin	35%	18%	18%
Wholesale price (paid by channel)	$5.49	$7.03	$7.13
Bottlers			
Support from concentrate producer	$0.00	$0.41	$0.52
Total bottler revenue	$5.49	$7.44	$7.65

	Nestlé	Pepsi	Coke
COGS			
Concentrate / Water	$0.01	$1.67	$1.70
PET bottles	$1.03	$1.16	$1.16
Closures	$0.21	$0.23	$0.23
Secondary packaging	$0.61	$0.68	$0.68
Labor/manufacturing	$0.7	$0.7	$0.77
Depreciation	$0.07	$0.08	$0.08
Total COGS	$2.63	$4.53	$4.63
Gross Profit	$2.85	$2.91	$3.02
SG&A	$2.29	$2.25	$2.53
EBITA	**$0.56**	**$0.66**	**$0.49**

Source: Goldman Sachs Global Equity research

EXIIIBIT 14   TOP ATTRIBUTES WHEN SELECTING WATER AND CARBONATED SOFT DRINK (CSD) BRANDS

	CSD	Water
Great taste	68%	47%
It's cold	48%	39%
It's my favorite brand	37%	10%
Refreshing	35%	44%
Available everywhere	35%	25%
Low price	26%	38%
It rehydrates me	16%	52%

Source: Morgan Stanley Soft Drink Survey. "Water is Water" report, June 7, 2002.

EXHIBIT 15   CUSTOMER PREFERENCES FOR SPRING VERSUS PURIFIED WATERS (% CUSTOMERS)

Do you have a preference between purified and spring water?

	Frequency of use			
I only drink...	Everyday	Several times a week	Occasionally	Total
Spring Water	11%	8%	4%	7%
Purified Water	4%	3%	2%	3%
Prefer one, drink both	25%	24%	13%	19%
No preference	46%	53%	59%	53%
I don't know	15%	12%	22%	17%
Total	100%	100%	100%	100%

Source: Morgan Stanley Soft Drink Survey. "Water is Water" report, June 7, 2002.

EXHIBIT 16   PENETRATION OF BRANDS FOR DIFFERENT RETAIL CHANNELS (YTD 2002 THROUGH OCTOBER 6)

	Share of Volume	Volume growth	Brand volume share by channel					
			Nestle	Aquafina (Pepsi)	Dasani (Coke)	Dannon (Coke)	Crystal geyser	Private label
Mass Merchandisers	27%	45%	38%	9%	6%	3%	0%	39%
Supermarkets	53%	34%	36%	17%	11%	5%	6%	12%
Drugstores	4%	26%	18%	15%	12%	5%	8%	14%
Convenience Stores	16%	14%	25%	26%	20%	0%	1%	6%
4 Major Channels	**100%**	**35%**	**34%**	**16%**	**11%**	**3%**	**4%**	**18%**

Source: USB Soft Drinks report, November 29, 2002.

EXHIBIT 17   THE CHANNEL MIX OF BOTTLED WATER SALES

($ million - value)	1996 Wholesale revenues		2001 Wholesale revenues		2001 Operating profits	
Single Serve Still	$1,480		$4,654		$534	
Take Home		$251		$1,875		$166
Cold-drink		$1,229		$2,779		$368
Single Serve Sparkling	$499		$516		$55	
Jugs	$558		$693		$36	
RETAIL	$2,538		$5,863		$624	
HOD	$1,182		$1,605		$263	
BOTTLED WATER	$3,720		$7,468		$887	

(million litres - volume)	1996 Wholesale volumes		1996 Percent	2001 Wholesale Volumes		2001 Percent
Single Serve Still	1,599		16%	6,010		37%
Take Home		440	5%		3,385	21%
Cold-drink		1,159	11%		2,625	16%
Single Serve Sparkling	703		7%	692		4%
Jugs	3,357		33%	3,884		24%
RETAIL	5,659		56%	10,586		65%
HOD	4,542		44%	5,806		35%
BOTTLED WATER	10,201		100%	16,392		100%

Source: Morgan Stanley, Beverages, August 19 2002.

EXHIBIT 18 DANONE US WATER BUSINESS

	2001 Sales ($m)		2001 EBITA ($m)	
RETAIL	424		18	
Evian		184		22
Dannon		240		−4
HOD (McKesson)	420		60	
TOTAL US WATER	844		78	

Notes: the $ -4m Ebita of Dannon was estimated to be composed of $-10m of Dannon and $6m of Sparkletts
Source: Morgan Stanley, Beverages, June 20 2002

EXHIBIT 19 RETAIL PRICE PER LITRE OF BOTTLED WATER, JUNE 2002

Brand	Type	$/Litre
Sparkling water		
Perrier (Nestlé)	Mineral	2.00
Poland Spring Sparkling (Nestlé)		0.93
La Croix – Sparkling		0.93
Still Water		
Evian (Danone/Coke)	Mineral	1.57
Dasani (Coke)	Purified	1.00
Aquafina (Pepsi)	Purified	0.85
Dannon (Danone)	Multi-spring	0.76
Poland Spring (Nestlé)	Multi-spring	0.75
Ice Mountain (Nestlé)	Multi-spring	0.68
Crystal Spring	Multi-spring	0.67
Zephyrhills (Nestlé)	Multi-spring	0.67
Ozarka (Nestlé)	Multi-spring	0.67
Deer Park (Nestlé)	Multi-spring	0.66
Sparkletts (Danone)	Multi-spring	0.62
Alhambra (Danone)	Multi-spring	0.61
Private Label		0.61
Crystal Geyser (Suntory)	Multi-spring	0.60
Arrowhead (Nestlé)	Multi-spring	0.58
Deja Blue (Cadbury Schweppes)	Purified	0.56
Aberfoyle (Nestlé)	Multi-spring	0.53

Source: Morgan Stanley, Beverages, June 2002.

EXHIBIT 20 SHARE OF MEDIA SPENDING (VOICE), 2001

Share	Share of Volume	Share of Voice
Poland Springs	11%	3%
Other Nestlé	26%	12%
Total Nestlé	37%	16%
PepsiCo- Aquafina	14%	16%
Coca-Cola- Dasani	12%	31%
Evian	3%	11%
Other Danone	8%	11%
Total Danone	11%	23%
Suntori	1%	1%
Cott	3%	0%
Rest	21%	14%
Bottled Water	100%	100%

Source: CMR, Beverage Digest and Morgan Stanley Research

EXHIBIT 21 WATER ADVERTISING EXPENDITURES BY TOP PLAYERS ($000)

	1998	1999	2000	2001	1H 2002
Coca-Cola	0	3,341	23,316	26,406	8,565
PepsiCo	617	304	10,427	13,229	16,279
Nestlé	14,598	5,941	9,700	14,194	9,328
Danone	20,228	13,631	14,382	19,271	6,284
Sum	35,443	23,217	57,825	73,100	40,456

Source: Morgan Stanley Beverage Media Spend Analysis, 9 September 2002, and Beverages analysis report of June 16, 2003.

EXHIBIT 22   CURRENT AND FUTURE CONSUMPTION OF BEVERAGES (% CONSUMERS)

	% consumed	Planned future intake		
		More	Same	Less
Carb. Soft Drinks	84	7	68	25
Bottled water	66	49	48	3
Tap water	60	38	54	8
Fruit juices	53	31	64	5
Hot coffee	53	6	77	18
Iced tea	45	31	62	7
Milk/soy	42	19	78	3
Wine/spirits	29	11	75	14
Beer	26	15	69	15
Hot tea	23	13	67	20
Fruit drinks	17	17	73	10
Sport drinks	17	30	63	6
Mixes	9	24	66	10
Iced coffees	5	29	56	16
Energy drinks	3	26	56	18

Source: Morgan Stanley Beverage Survey, 7 June 2002

EXHIBIT 23   CORPORATE FINANCIALS OF MAJOR ACTORS IN BOTTLED WATER BUSINESS (1997–2001)

Nestle (units: Swiss Francs millions)

	1997	1998	1999	2000	2001
Total Revenue	69,998.0	71,747.0	74,660.0	81,422.0	84,698.0
Earnings Before Interest and Taxes (EBIT)	7,417.0	7,305.0	8,316.0	9,498.0	9,309.0
Net Income	4,182.0	4,205.0	4,724.0	5,763.0	6,681.0
Margin %	6.0%	5.9%	6.3%	7.1%	7.9%
Total Assets	51,581.0	56,703.0	58,939.0	65,524.0	93,786.0
Ratios					
Gross Margin %	48.8%	49.9%	51.9%	53.2%	55.4%
EBIT Margin %	10.6%	10.2%	11.1%	11.7%	11.0%
Return on Assets %	9.0%	8.4%	9.0%	9.5%	7.3%
Return on Equity %	19.7%	19.4%	20.0%	21.2%	21.0%
Total Debt/Equity %	62.6%	64.0%	52.6%	44.0%	105.3%

Nestle Waters Division

	1997	1998	1999	2000	2001
Revenues					7,418.0
Operating Profit Before Tax					622.0
Assets					4,928.0

Coca-Cola Company (units: USD millions)

	1997	1998	1999	2000	2001
Total Revenue	18,868.0	18,813.0	19,284.0	17,354.0	17,545.0
Earnings Before Interest and Taxes (EBIT)	5,001.0	5,040.0	3,982.0	5,134.0	5,352.0
Net Income	4,129.0	3,533.0	2,431.0	2,177.0	3,969.0
Margin %	21.9%	18.8%	12.6%	12.5%	22.6%
Total Assets	16,881.0	19,145.0	21,623.0	20,834.0	22,417.0

Danone (units: EUR millions)

	1997	1998	1999	2000	2001
Total Revenue	13,488.0	12,935.0	13,293.0	14,287.0	14,470.0
Earnings Before Interest and Taxes (EBIT)	1,224.0	1,293.0	1,391.0	1,550.0	1,609.0
Net Income	559.0	598.0	682.0	721.0	132.0
Margin %	4.1%	4.6%	5.1%	5.0%	0.9%
Total Assets	15,029.6	15,042.0	15,015.0	17,233.0	16,900.0
Ratios					
Gross Margin %	43.7%	46.4%	49.9%	51.2%	50.3%
EBIT Margin %	9.1%	10.0%	10.5%	10.8%	11.1%
Return on Assets %	5.1%	5.4%	5.8%	6.0%	5.9%
Return on Equity %	8.9%	9.2%	10.8%	10.8%	2.0%
Total Debt/Equity %	50.4%	57.8%	66.2%	72.1%	99.8%

Waters Division

	1997	1998	1999	2000	2001
Revenues		3,373.0	3,565.0	4,584.0	3,796.0
Operating Profit Before Tax		368.0	440.0	513.0	432.0
Assets		3,178.0	3,901.0	5,423.0	5,494.0

Coca-Cola Enterprises (units: USD millions)

	1997	1998	1999	2000	2001
Total Revenue	11,278.0	13,414.0	14,406.0	14,659.0	14,999.0
Earnings Before Interest and Taxes (EBIT)	720.0	869.0	839.0	1,118.0	679.0
Net Income	171.0	142.0	59.0	236.0	(321.0)
Margin %	1.5%	1.1%	0.4%	1.6%	(2.1%)
Total Assets	17,487.0	21,132.0	22,730.0	22,162.0	23,719.0

Ratios

	Pepsico, Inc (units: USD millions)					Pepsi Bottling Group (units: USD millions)				
Gross Margin %	68.1%	70.4%	68.8%	64.3%	65.6%	37.1%	37.4%	37.4%	38.0%	39.9%
EBIT Margin %	26.5%	26.8%	20.6%	29.6%	30.5%	6.4%	6.5%	5.8%	7.6%	4.5%
Return on Assets %	18.9%	17.5%	12.2%	15.1%	15.5%	3.1%	2.8%	2.4%	3.1%	1.8%
Return on Equity %	61.5%	45.1%	27.1%	23.1%	38.5%	10.3%	6.7%	2.2%	8.2%	(0.7%)
Total Debt/Equity %	53.3%	61.3%	65.5%	50.7%	45.0%	493.4%	440.7%	389.1%	392.4%	431.5%

	Pepsico, Inc (units: USD millions)					Pepsi Bottling Group (units: USD millions)				
Total Revenue	20,917.0	22,348.0	25,093.0	22,337.0	23,512.0	6,592.0	7,041.0	7,505.0	7,982.0	8,443.0
Earnings Before Interest and Taxes (EBIT)	2,952.0	2,872.0	3,556.0	4,002.0	4,023.0	335.0	277.0	351.0	590.0	676.0
Net Income	2,142.0	1,993.0	2,505.0	2,543.0	2,400.0	59.0	(146.0)	118.0	229.0	305.0
Margin %	10.2%	8.9%	10.0%	11.4%	10.2%	0.9%	(2.1%)	1.6%	2.9%	3.6%
Total Assets	20,101.0	22,660.0	17,551.0	20,757.0	21,695.0	-	7,322.0	7,624.0	7,736.0	7,857.0

Ratios

	Pepsico, Inc (units: USD millions)					Pepsi Bottling Group (units: USD millions)				
Gross Margin %	59.2%	58.3%	58.8%	54.2%	54.3%	41.9%	40.6%	42.8%	44.8%	45.8%
EBIT Margin %	14.1%	12.9%	14.2%	17.9%	17.1%	5.1%	3.9%	4.7%	7.4%	8.0%
Return on Assets %	8.7%	8.4%	11.1%	13.1%	11.8%	NA	NA	2.9%	4.8%	5.4%
Return on Equity %	22.0%	29.9%	37.7%	35.1%	29.4%	NA	NA	17.8%	14.3%	18.8%
Total Debt/Equity %	71.3%	124.2%	44.3%	42.1%	34.6%	NM	NA	210.6%	200.3%	210.0%

Source: Capital IQ

IVEY | Publishing

7 Days Inn: Operations strategy

By Gang Chen, Liang Xu

On March 26, 2012, the board of trustees of 7 Days Group Holdings Ltd. (7 Days Inn) appointed the current chief executive officer, Nanyan Zheng, as its co-chair for developing a new hotel chain targeting the high-end market. Yuezhou Lin, the current chief operations officer, would take over as the new CEO after June 30.

Nanyan, Yuezhou and several other young people established 7 Days Inn in 2005. Since then, Yuezhou had been in charge of sales, information systems and customer service. With an innovative business model, 7 Days Inn successfully enrolled more than 30 million customers in its membership system. This made it the largest system in the Chinese economic hotel chain industry. In 2012, 7 Days Inn operated more than 1,000 hotels in 168 major cities and had become one of the top three hotel chains with the most number of hotels in China. Within four years of its founding, the entrepreneurial team of 7 Days Inn had successfully created the first Chinese hotel group listed on the New York Stock Exchange.

Since the start-up, Nanyan had mastered the establishment and growth of 7 Days Inn. (Exhibit 1 shows the growth in hotels from 2005 to 2011.) The expansion of scale gradually influenced operations and resulted in inefficiencies in management and supervision. Yuezhou needed to address problems of how to operate efficiently in the era of 1,000 hotels.

Take marketing as an example. It takes at least two weeks to implement the decision made by Nanyan himself throughout these 1,000 hotels. However, it often happens that 20 per cent of hotel managers probably deny having received the email from headquarters. Among the [remaining] 80 per cent, still 20 per cent claim that they don't understand, 20 per cent comment that there is no sufficient time for preparation

and 20 per cent believe that the decision itself is unreasonable; at the end, probably only 20 per cent of hotel managers would follow the decision. Before 2006, membership cards of 7 Days Inn would be printed out with different themes, such as mid-autumn festival. But right now, this kind of marketing activity is impossible to be spread out, as mid-autumn festival will last one month at most while the preparation of the marketing activity will take one month in total. [Yuezhou sighed.] Previously, decisions made

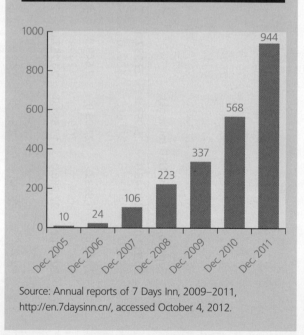

EXHIBIT 1 THE NUMBER OF HOTELS OF 7 DAYS INN THROUGHOUT CHINA, 2005—2011

Source: Annual reports of 7 Days Inn, 2009–2011, http://en.7daysinn.cn/, accessed October 4, 2012.

during Monday routine meetings will be effectively carried out on subsequent Wednesdays; those days will never come back.[1]

Yuezhou also mentioned a recent conversation with Tongmin Su, the vice president for new hotel establishment and pricing. Tongmin pointed out that many hotel managers were not as devoted to the company as before. For example, some did not spend much time on hotel affairs management, nor did they pay attention to the maintenance of the facilities. Some of them did not push sales by themselves nor tried to improve customer service. Under such circumstances, Yuezhou was wondering whether the operations strategy and operating model needed rethinking. Working in the information technology (IT) industry previously, he was convinced that "in a dynamic market environment, the only eternal thing is change. Sometimes, making a change is risky, while remaining unchanged is also risky."

Yuezhou would soon be the new CEO of 7 Days Inn. What should he do to deal with the challenges?

Background

Along with the increase of Chinese per capita income, travel demand (including resort tourism and business trips) has been increasing in China over the last few decades. The National Bureau of Statistics and the National Tourism Administration reported that the number of people traveling reached 1.212 billion in Mainland China in the year 2005[2] when the Chinese hotel industry was still developing. From a traveler's point of view, premium hotels were not economical, while cheap hotels underperformed on service. In addition, there were not enough economic hotels from which to choose: in 2003, there were no more than 100, and by 2004, there were only 166 economic hotels.[3] With the boost in travel demand, there was huge potential for investment in this area.

The 7 Days Inn entrepreneurial team, all in their thirties, recognized that the Chinese economic hotel industry showed a promising outlook. (The entrepreneurial team is portrayed in Exhibit 2.) In March 2005, the first 7 Days Inn hotel was opened on Beijing Road, a walking street in the most bustling area of Guangzhou, the capital city of Guangdong province. The hotel targeted common business travelers with the service concept of "Sleeping Well Every Day" and was devoted to meeting the core demand of accommodation from customers. Since the start-up, 7 Days Inn constantly searched for effective ways to implement its innovative operations strategy and successfully provided higher quality service. From 2006 to 2008, 7 Days Inn obtained the largest amount of investment in the hotel industry, consisting of three investments from globally famous risk investment funds. On November 20, 2009, 7 Days Inn was successfully listed on the New York Stock Exchange (Stock code: SVN). Towards the end of 2011, 7 Days Inn operated more than 900 hotels in 89 main Chinese cities. (Exhibit 3 shows the income statement of 7 Days Inn from 2005 to 2011.)

Entrepreneurship and start-up

In the entrepreneurial team of 7 Days Inn, Nanyan was the only one who had experience in traveling service from Ctrip,[4] while none of the others had any experience in hotel management. Nevertheless, the team expected to design and apply the most effective business model to run economic hotels based on the core value of the customer. In 2005, most premium hotels in Mainland China were equipped with a luxurious lobby, recreation facilities and Chinese/Western restaurants. The team recognized that these services would not bring much value to the customers. Economic hotels should be just like common consumer goods. In a word, most consumers wanted to spend less money for a better sleep.

Vertical cutting

To differentiate from the showy but valueless service provided by premium hotels, 7 Days Inn designed hotel products with the spectacular concept of "vertical cutting," defined as gathering resources for the core value. This would save money by eliminating unnecessary expenses and using it on customers' core demand of "Sleeping Well, Showering Well and Reliable Internet Access."

[1]Interview with the authors at 7 Days Inn headquarters in Guangzhou, China, April 13, 2012. Further quotes from this source in the paper below come from this interview.

[2]"Major Statistics of Domestic Tourism 2005," National Tourism Administration of the People's Republic of China, www.cnta.gov.cn/html/2008-6/2008-6-2-14-52-53-120.html, accessed September 30, 2012.

[3]"The Growth of National Economic Hotels from 2000 to 2006," *China Statistical Yearbook*, 2007.

[4]Ctrip.com International Ltd., www.ctrip.com, accessed September 30, 2012.

EXHIBIT 2 ENTREPRENEURIAL TEAM OF 7 DAYS INN

Member	Background	Contribution to 7 Days Inn
Nanyan Zheng	■ Graduate, School of Information Science & Technology, Sun Yat-sen University, Guangzhou. ■ Founder, Guangzhou Laoye Technologies Ltd. (renamed as Armitage), which was focused on hotel management system. ■ General Manager, Ctrip (South China).	Business model and operations strategy
Yuezhou Lin	■ Graduate, School of Information Science & Technology, Sun Yat-sen University; junior to Nanyan Zheng. ■ Manager, Armitage. ■ CEO, Armitage, after Nanyan left Armitage.	Information infrastructure, information systems and membership system
Chuntian Li	■ Marketing director, Dudu Stationery (founded in 1992, this was once the largest retail chain of office supplies in China).	Marketing strategy of membership program
Qiaofan Han	■ Operations director, 7-11 (China). ■ Operations director, BP (British Petroleum).	Standardization of hotel operations
Ji Huang	■ Chief representative of Asia Pacific for Netherland Merrill Lynch group, in charge of the purchasing unit.	Property development and investment

Source: 7 Days Group Holdings Ltd.

7 Days Inn made many changes to its hotel facilities, taking out conference rooms, bathtubs, mini bars, carpets, luxury decorations and swimming pools and only retaining such core facilities as beds, separate toilets, TVs, telephones, shower rooms, broadband Internet and desks. Rooms were also equipped with small windows and simple lighting. 7 Days Inn also applied innovative practices in services. For example, traditional hotels provided all dining services, while 7 Days Inn hotels only provided breakfast. No free washing supplies (e.g., toothpaste, toothbrush and soap) were provided in the hotels; instead, they provided quality travel wash sets for a low price. Towels were sealed in bags for preservation and re-use. Shampoo and bath gel were provided in a designated location, and hair dryers were put in hallways.

Vertical cutting was not just about excluding several service items but also improving overall quality on products and services to better satisfy customers' core demand. The Business Travelers' Top Concern List of Hotel Facilities issued in 2009[5] showed that,

94.5 per cent were most concerned about a bed; bathrooms came in next with 86.54 per cent. As a consequence, in September 2010, 7 Days Inn partnered with Airland[6] in a plan to spend several million RMB over two years upgrading to the Airland Spinal mattress, which was used in five star hotels.

Practices of vertical cutting allowed 7 Days Inn to be competitive with a very high performance/price ratio in the national economic hotel industry. Many customers were convinced that the price of 7 Days Inn was much more competitive than the other economic hotels. The price of a room in a 7 Days Inn hotel was 150 to 170 RMB per day, while most other hotels at the same level were around 200 RMB per day.

Membership and direct sale

In 2005, room reservations for hotels in China mainly went through agents such as Ctrip.com and conference agents. At that time, direct sale with membership wasn't recognized. 7 Days Inn believed that multiple

[5]Shanghai Inntie Hotel Management Consulting Ltd., Qunar.com and Hostelcn.com, www.inn.net.cn/data/upload/news/09gkwlxq.pdf, accessed September 30, 2012.

[6]Airland Group is a household product manufacturer; www.airland.com, accessed September 30, 2012.

EXHIBIT 3   INCOME STATEMENT OF 7 DAYS INN, 2005–2011

	31/Dec/05 RMB'000	31/Dec/06 RMB'000	31/Dec/07 RMB'000	31/Dec/08 RMB'000	31/Dec/09 RMB'000	31/Dec/10 RMB'000	31/Dec/11 RMB'000
Revenues	14,007	54,852	252,799	721,434	1,141,315	1,498,909	2,003,378
Operating costs and expenses							
Hotel operating costs							
Rental expenses	(7,128)	(26,748)	(130,933)	(295,595)	(351,945)	(441,797)	(571,351)
Staff cost	(2,336)	(10,280)	(49,050)	(164,922)	(203,942)	(233,170)	(317,374)
Depreciation and amortization	(1,461)	(5,585)	(26,808)	(88,939)	(144,417)	(178,279)	(241,020)
Hotel supplies	(1,832)	(5,772)	(21,739)	(49,331)	(59,392)	(64,060)	(97,452)
Utilities	(1,271)	(4,301)	(19,059)	(57,511)	(90,542)	(106,594)	(145,468)
Other	(869)	(6,254)	(25,652)	(73,906)	(121,312)	(159,027)	(220,595)
Sales and marketing expenses	(2,869)	(4,168)	(13,690)	(36,897)	(30,824)	(39,557)	(49,222)
General and administrative expenses	(22,336)	(12,139)	(56,149)	(93,631)	(65,074)	(122,371)	(209,786)
Total operating costs and expenses	(40,162)	(75,247)	(343,080)	(860,732)	(1,067,448)	(1,344,855)	(1,852,268)
Income (loss) from operations	**(26,155)**	**(20,395)**	**(90,281)**	**(139,298)**	**73,867**	**154,054**	**151,110**
Other income(expenses)							
Interest income	74	279	3,185	2,395	3,669	3,127	6,224
Interest expenses		(568)	(31,233)	(84,470)	(81,867)	(2,082)	(7,212)
Loss on debt extinguishment					(26,477)	–	–
Change in fair value of ordinary share purchase warrants			(2,241)	10,484	(76,376)	–	–
Equity in income (loss) of an affiliate		(267)	167	186	23	(18)	120
Income before income tax	(26,081)	(20,951)	(120,403)	(210,703)	(107,161)	155,081	150,242
Income tax expenses	(141)	(535)	(3,262)	781	4,952	(35,833)	(36,259)
Net income	**(26,222)**	**(21,486)**	**(123,665)**	**(209,922)**	**(102,209)**	**119,248**	**113,983**
Net income (loss) attributable to non-controlling interest			933	(608)	(1,745)	(1,557)	14,903
Net income attributable to 7 Days Group Holding Limited	(26,222)	(21,486)	(122,732)	(210,530)	(103,954)	117,691	128,886
Deemed dividends to Series C convertible preferred shareholders					(28,993)	–	
Net Income (loss) attributable to 7 Days Group Holdings Limited ordinary shareholders	(26,222)	(21,486)	(122,732)	(210,530)	(132,947)	117,691	128,886
Basic earnings (losses) per ordinary share	(3483.73)	(0.87)	(2.05)	(3.51)	(1.93)	0.79	0.86
Diluted earnings (losses) per ordinary share	(3483.73)	(0.87)	(2.05)	(3.51)	(1.93)	0.78	0.85

Source: Annual reports of 7 Days Inn, 2009–2011, http://en.7daysinn.cn/, accessed October 4, 2012.

reservation channels would probably disorder the pricing system and were not good for proactive sales. To build up pricing advantages and a customer relationship network, 7 Days Inn started with directed sales by setting up a reservation IT system and a membership system. In April 2005, 7 Days Inn launched its central reservation system (CRS). The company continuously developed and updated the advanced system, making it one of the small number of hotels in China that could support five 24/7 reservation methods, including online, telephone, wireless application protocol, short message service and mobile client reservations.

In the early days of 7 Days Inn, the occupancy rate was below 40 per cent because the advertising budget was not high and the location of hotels was not eye-catching. After establishing the "7 Days Club," the occupancy rate constantly increased with the growth in membership. By the end of 2011, the club had more than 33 million members and had become the largest membership organization in the Chinese economic hotel industry. Through its advanced information platform, 7 Days Inn actively educated the customers of economic hotels in the use of IT. By 2012, 50 per cent of bookings were through Internet reservation, the highest in the industry. At the end of 2008, the visit count to the 7 Days Inn's website was the largest in the hotel industry all over the world, surpassing the French company IBIS, the global founder of the economic hotel.

Chain management

At the end of 2005, 7 Days Inn planned to expand out of Guangdong and build up a hotel chain network. However, the board of trustees and the executive management team could not reach an agreement on how to expand the network. Boquan He, the chairman of the board, believed that Guangdong was the base camp of 7 Days Inn and that the company should not expand out of the province until reaching a higher penetration rate. From his point of view, dispersing hotels in multiple cities was not the way to build brand awareness in an area. He proposed to open as many hotels as possible in a single city, leaving no room for new hotels of competing companies in the industry. This strategy was called "parking the bus."[7] The executive management team was concerned with the mobility of economic hotel customers, noting, in particular, that 7 Days Club members took business trips

frequently. Thus, 7 Days Inn should expand to other provinces to better serve its customers. After intense discussion, the executives reached the agreement that the company would expand out of Guangdong and at the same time apply the parking the bus tactic to open as many hotels as possible in one city. In October 2006, the first hotel out of Guangdong province was opened on Huang-xing Road[8] in Changsha, Hunan province.

Hotel affairs department

In 2005, 7 Days Inn operated five hotels, three of them in Guangzhou and two in Shenzhen, nearly 100 miles apart. During that trial period of the first five hotels, no matter which hotel had a problem, Nanyan would drive there and solve it himself. Since the entrepreneurial team members had little experience in hotel management, they were most concerned with whether the result of vertical cutting met the customers' core demand. To effectively control operations, they decided to manage each hotel directly through departments at headquarters; this would help them obtain experience in operating economic hotels.

As the hotel chain network grew, it became more and more difficult for headquarters to directly manage the hotels. Standardizing operations was put on the agenda. 7 Days Inn aimed to decrease the operational and communication costs that had risen with the establishment of new hotels, all the while improving the service quality and controlling the consistency of service. At the same time, senior executives were freed from concerns with daily hotel affairs.

Qiaofan Han was appointed as operations director in August 2005. She set up many operational regulations, covering procurement, safety management, property assets management, etc. At that time, it was common in the industry to standardize operations by composing operations manuals, and the standardization process of many hotels resulted in dozens of manuals, each of which had hundreds of pages. However, 7 Days Inn described its regulations in only six manuals on hotel rooms, receptions, engineering maintenance, safety (emergency guideline procedures), finance and human resources. The total number of pages in these six manuals was less than one manual of other hotels. In accordance, Qiaofan set up comprehensive and disciplined training programs to ensure that the staff at 7 Days Inn clearly understood the regulations.

[7]Parking the bus refers to a defensive style of playing football. http://uk.eurosport.yahoo.com/blogs/early-doors/parking-busgives-chelsea-chance-075519412.html, assessed September 30, 2012.

[8]Huang-xing Road is the busiest walking street in the downtown area of Changsha, the capital city of Hunan province.

Furthermore, to achieve standardization across the hotel chain, a hotel affairs department was set up under Qiaofan and was vested with the power of managing all hotel operational affairs. For a long period, the department became the only hub connecting headquarters and the hotels. As hotel affairs covered a variety of functional operations, the department set up three functional units, i.e., sales, finance and human resource units. Clear criteria of operational performance, comprehensive training programs and disciplined supervision considerably improved the standardization of daily operations in the hotels.

Matrix structure

7 Days Inn stepped into a growing phase. In the middle of 2006, the company had more than 20 hotels, with many more under construction. Since many hotel affairs required approval from the central hotel affairs department, hotel managers found they were often unable to proceed with daily operations. The department was overloaded with work in setting up new hotels and managing the expansion of the hotel chain, while other departments operated less efficiently than before. Moreover, the communication between departments in headquarters and the hotels became ineffective.

To address these issues, in June 2006, 7 Days Inn decided that the hotel affairs department could no longer be the unique channel through which headquarters communicated with the hotels. The company was reorganized as a matrix structure,[9] as shown in Exhibit 4. A 7 Days Inn hotel would not only report to the hotel affairs department but simultaneously to several other departments. In the vertical dimension, functional departments in headquarters, such as finance and human resources, supervised a hotel. In the horizontal dimension, a hotel manager also managed the hotel. The hotels were like students, while the hotel affairs department was like a head teacher, and the sales department and the finance department were like teachers for mathematics and for physics respectively. This matrix structure not only relieved the stress for the hotel affairs department but also allowed other departments to play their roles appropriately. Functional departments effectively facilitated the operations standardization of hotels. The standardized operating model was quickly replicated to the new hotels. Matrix organizational structure worked well for the expansion in the second half of 2006. However, when the scale of chain network expanded further, it became difficult for functional departments at headquarters to directly manage and support the hotels.

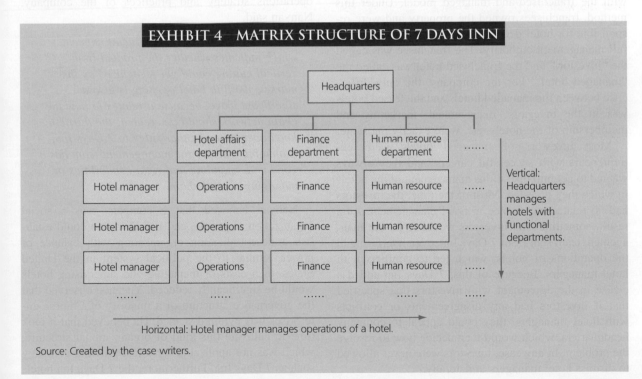

EXHIBIT 4   MATRIX STRUCTURE OF 7 DAYS INN

Source: Created by the case writers.

[9]The hotel affairs department was renamed operations department at the end of 2006.

Franchise and management

In the early stage, 7 Days Inn set up new hotels using a "leased-and-operated" model: headquarters directly invested in or leased the property, then established and managed the hotels. The investment of a leased hotel required 3 to 4 million RMB and the daily operations needed a group of 20 people. As a result, remarkable amounts of human and financial resources were required for the combined rapid expansion strategy and parking the bus tactic.

However, fierce competition and the sudden financial crisis of 2008 made it difficult for 7 Days Inn to get external financing. In early 2008, 7 Days Inn applied an innovative model, namely, "franchised-and-managed." In the traditional franchise model, franchisees own the property and invest on decorations on their own; at the same time, they must pay the franchisor an initial fee along with a royalty fee. Correspondingly, franchisees are allowed to form management teams for operating franchised hotels following the regulations made by the franchisor. However, 7 Days Inn found it difficult to standardize the operations of a franchised hotel. Also, it was not easy to control the service quality, which might spoil the company's image. Therefore, 7 Days Inn came up with the franchised-and-managed model. Under this method, franchisees owned the property and were responsible for hotel decorations, while 7 Days Inn had full management authority. The franchisee was called the "investor," and the franchised hotel was called the "managed hotel." For the company, the only difference between the managed hotels and the leased hotels was in the investors; management, marketing and membership of the hotels, etc. were exactly the same.

Most investors of managed hotels were entrepreneurs with successful careers, and they always wanted to get into operations management of the hotels in which they invested. Most of the time, the investors had no related experience in hotel management. As a result, sometimes the investors would resist the management team sent from 7 Days Inn, even interfering in the operations of hotels, which led to conflicts with hotel managers. Because of this, 7 Days Inn added a clause in the agreement with investors that specified that if investors had any disagreements or conflicts with hotel managers, they could appeal to company headquarters, which would then decide how to resolve the problem. In any case, investors were never allowed to dismiss hotel managers unilaterally.

To enhance the commitment of investors, 7 Days Inn granted them access to the company's internal communications system. Investors could not only receive emails from headquarters but also freely join discussions in the system. Nanyan commented, "We just need to be ourselves with an open internal system to the investors. The investors could make their own decisions. For those who do not fit in, they would be free to walk away."

The access allowed investors to share in the supervision of the management of the hotels, which was not only a good move towards the standardization of operations but would also decrease the principal-agent problems between hotel managers and headquarters. In the meantime, to achieve better operational efficiency, it was necessary for hotel managers to communicate with investors frequently and work proactively with them.

Shepherd management

At the end of 2006, 7 Days Inn operated about 30 hotels and was expanding quickly. Nanyan started to worry not only about the information distortion between headquarters and the hotels but also about inefficiencies of managing and supervising hotels. He gathered senior managers to review and rethink the operations strategy and practices of the company. Nanyan said,

> *The first hotel opening is a crucial moment, which indicates whether the product from vertical cutting could get recognized by the market; the fifth hotel opening is also a significant move, because it relates to how the chain network should be created; the thirtieth hotel opening is another ridge to 7 Days Inn, examining whether the management team has a good understanding and right capabilities in managing a hotel chain.*

Nanyan believed that a company was a social organization of people, and if 7 Days Inn could establish a decentralization organization with balance of power, similar to the political system in the United States, then costs of managing and supervising hotels would be significantly reduced. Yuezhou observed that the governance structure of a majority of Chinese enterprises was pyramid shaped. He believed that it took time to cultivate this kind of organizational structure, which was not applicable for a fast growing company such as 7 Days Inn. Furthermore, the 7 Days Inn hotels were scattered across the country; if the company took a hierarchical or pyramid-shaped structure, it would definitely result in inefficiencies of managing and supervising hotels. In the early days, headquarters managed and operated the hotels strictly by issuing top-down instructions. As such, a large amount of human and financial resources were wasted on formulating, executing and supervising operational regulations, which resulted in low operational efficiency. For such economic hotels as 7 Days Inn in the fast expanding phase, it was necessary to create a new business model and operations strategy so as to release the pressure from the rising costs of managing and supervising hotels.

After intense discussion, senior managers reached an agreement that they should grant more authority to hotel managers, rather than having hotel managers wait for instructions from headquarters on every operation. They redesigned the way of running economic hotels by incorporating market principles in the business. For example, 7 Days Inn instituted the "traffic light principle": a hotel manager could drive anywhere but could not run a red light. Here a red light could be safety regulations; when hotel managers decide on hotel decorations they could not violate the regulations. This would reduce the costs of managing and supervising, which had risen as the firm grew. Therefore, 7 Days Inn kept looking for hotel managers with entrepreneurial spirit who would actively take on the responsibility and risks of managing a hotel. When recruiting hotel managers, the company prepared a series of questions to examine the entrepreneurial spirit of the candidates.

7 Days Inn proposed a new way of managing hotels across the country, namely "shepherd management." Shepherd management was founded on mutual economic benefits, that is, hotel managers agreed with headquarters on the objectives and the direction of 7 Days Inn. Sheep (i.e., hotel managers) would move forward together to lush grass without instructions from a shepherd (i.e., with full authorization and autonomy); if some sheep were willing to go forward (i.e., the hotel managers with entrepreneurial spirit) and a shepherd dog did its duty (i.e., headquarters provides support and supervision), then this would benefit all. (The role orientations of shepherd management are shown in Exhibit 5.) Since January 2007, 7 Days Inn began searching for the best operating model for shepherd management.

Autonomy of hotels

Based on shepherd management, a hotel manager was in charge of the business and operations of a hotel. The manager assistant helped with the administration, while other staff worked as assigned. (Exhibit 6 shows the organizational structure of a typical 7 Days Inn hotel.) The manager was fully authorized to manage and coordinate all the operations related to the hotel; no one would interfere with the decisions the manager made. The manager could, based on personal preference, decide whether the staff would stay or leave and determine the decoration style of the hotel and marketing activities, etc. The manager could also determine personal working time, that is, whether to take specific days off or not charge for overtime. The human resources department at headquarters was only responsible for recruiting hotel managers and the staff for functional departments at headquarters; the recruitment of staff who worked in hotels was outsourced to an independent human resources company.

EXHIBIT 5 ROLE ORIENTATIONS OF SHEPHERD MANAGEMENT

Role in shepherd management	Role in operations management	Position
Shepherd	Senior managers	To formulate strategy and direct the team.
Shepherd dog	Supervision departments and support centres	To inspire leaders to keep the right direction, to deal with people with problems (laggards or inappropriate behaviours), to provide the whole team with professional support.
Led sheep	The outstanding	To lead the team in the right direction.
Lagging sheep	The laggard	Falling behind the team and needs to be supervised to follow the team.
Sick sheep	The incompetent	To be eliminated in case it becomes a drag to the team.
Flock	Most followers	To take the initiative to learn from leaders and follow the shepherd.

Source: 7 Days Inn presentation, 2011.

EXHIBIT 6   ORGANIZATIONAL STRUCTURE OF A TYPICAL 7 DAYS INN HOTEL

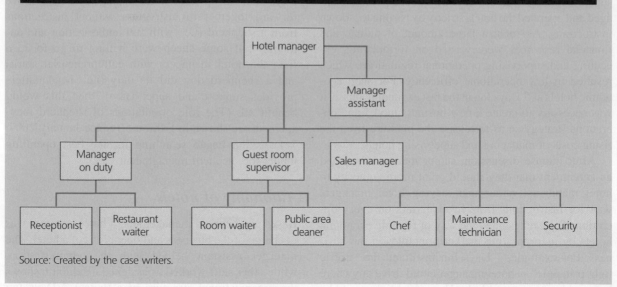

Source: Created by the case writers.

Since 7 Days Inn had a large number of hotels and the outsourcing company provided a limited number of candidates, most staff members were recruited by hotel managers themselves.

Although it did not directly give instructions to hotel managers, headquarters assessed the operational performance of hotels regularly and graded hotel managers on their work. Cash awards were granted to managers who ran their respective hotels with outstanding performance, and an honour award of "star manager" was given to those who continuously ran the business with best outcomes. On the other hand, headquarters would supervise and manage hotels that had poor performance. Headquarters would nominate to eliminate hotel managers with very poor performance, and then senior managers would have a discussion and jointly make a final decision. Moreover, the assessment of performance was no longer for cost control but for gross operating profit (GOP) of a hotel. Some new indicators were incorporated, for example, the number of valid new members and the contribution of new members to the chain network. (Exhibit 7 indicates the assessment indicators of a hotel in operation.)

Support and supervision

Previously, hotel managers could reach all the departments in headquarters. To alleviate communication confusion, 7 Days Inn specified that four functional departments – human resource, operations, sales and finance – would work closely with hotel managers. They were redesigned as four support centres based on

their management responsibilities. Heads of support centres were in charge of the centres' daily work; they had the same rank as hotel managers, which cultivated equality in communication and coordination at work. To support the headquarters' ideology of power, 7 Days Inn authorized that hotel managers could request support from all the support centres, while the support centres could not send any command to the managers. In addition, to better supervise daily hotel operations, the company set up three supervision departments, including quality and safety management, finance auditing and corporate culture. As such, 7 Days Inn established the following operating model: hotel managers controlled hotel operations, while functional departments at headquarters provided support to the managers and supervised the operational performance of hotels as necessary. (Exhibit 8 specifies the four support centres and three supervision departments.) In this way, 7 Days Inn found that hotel managers and staff devoted themselves more to managing the hotels.

At the same time, the advanced information system of 7 Days Inn made operations visible, which strongly supported the practices of the support centres and supervision departments. For example, when customers made reservations, CRS would record the status of rooms and reservations and actively inform the receptionists of respective hotels. Accountants at headquarters, managers on duty and hotel managers could check on the system for the corresponding occupancy and receipt of payment. The central information system of 7 Days Inn included CRS, material requirement planning (MRP), front office (FO), central statistics

EXHIBIT 7   THE ASSESSMENT INDICATORS OF A HOTEL

Before Shepherd Management		Under Shepherd Management	
Indicator	Target	Indicator	Target
Operating cost	No more than 40% of the hotel's revenue.	**Operating cost**	No more than 40% of the average revenue of all the hotels of 7 Days Inn.
Operating profit	No less than 60% of the hotel's revenue.	**Operating profit**	No less than 60% of the average revenue of all the hotels of 7 Days Inn.
Occupancy rate of staying overnight	High than 80%.	**Occupancy rate of staying overnight**	High than 80%.
Amount of new members	More than certain number of people per month.	**Amount of valid new members**	No less than 60% of average number of valid new members of all the hotels of 7 Days Inn.*
		Contribution of new members in a chain network	The amount of consumption of new members at any hotel of 7 Days Inn (except the current hotel).**

*Valid new member refers to a member who spends more than a certain amount within his or her first month of membership
**Note that 40 per cent of this amount will be the bonus to the current hotel.

Source: 7 Days Group Holdings Ltd.

EXHIBIT 8   FOUR SUPPORT CENTRES AND THREE SUPERVISION DEPARTMENTS OF 7 DAYS INN

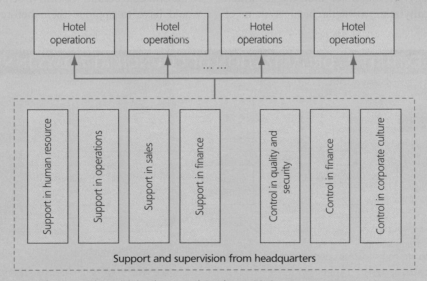

Source: 7 Days Inn, www.7daysinn.cn/about_join.html, accessed October 4, 2012.

report (REPORT) and enterprise internal portal (EIP) systems. It was the first company in the industry to integrate online reservation, back-end membership database, confirmation platform, calling centre, short message service platform and hotel affairs management. Furthermore, the system was able to show to relevant staff the real-time status of rooms, operational indicators of hotels (especially those indicators directly related to cash awards) and the rankings of hotels across the country, which were made based on real-time operational indicators.

In 2009, 7 Days Inn operated almost 300 hotels with around 350 staff members at headquarters. From the company's perspective, shepherd management worked well. The number of staff for 300 hotels was almost the same as for 100 hotels in the past; costs of managing and supervising the hotels were effectively controlled.

Archon and council

To implement shepherd management, the first thing was to keep the interests of the hotels consistent with those of the company. If hotel managers only concentrated on the revenues of their own hotels, they could not cooperate well. When a client at a hotel needed to be transferred to another hotel, the manager of the hotel where the client was currently staying should ensure a smooth transfer, which could improve overall profit of the region and the whole network.

In 2009, 7 Days Inn grouped hotels sited in the same region and launched an "archon" system. This was an unheard-of strategy in the hotel industry in which companies typically ran a hierarchical system of regional managers. All the hotel managers in the region voted for one of them to become the archon of that region for one year with the possibility of being re-elected. The archon was the chair of all the hotels in the region and was not required to report to headquarters. The archon's main tasks were to improve service quality, increase turnover, set up new hotels and co-ordinate hotel managers for finance and performance assessment, etc. An archon needed to not only manage his or her own hotel but also spend more time at other hotels in the region. As all the managers in the region elected an archon, he or she needed to help with the hotel performance of the region while having no authority to directly manage the hotel managers.

At the same time, 7 Days Inn created a "council" system to facilitate communication between hotel managers and headquarters. The council selected representatives of hotel managers all over China and authorized them to participate in formulating operations strategy with headquarters. (Exhibit 9 shows the organization of the council.) In the council's quarterly conferences, the representatives played a significant role, ensuring that hotel managers had a voice in solving strategic problems that the company was facing. The representatives could hand in a variety of proposals; the council would discuss them. If the council could reach an agreement, the whole company would follow unconditionally; if not, it would need to explain why proposals were denied. The council was not only the bridge of communication between managers and headquarters but also had the power to contend against headquarters. The agreed proposals would be delivered to the strategic committee of five senior officers, which would have to approve them before implementation.

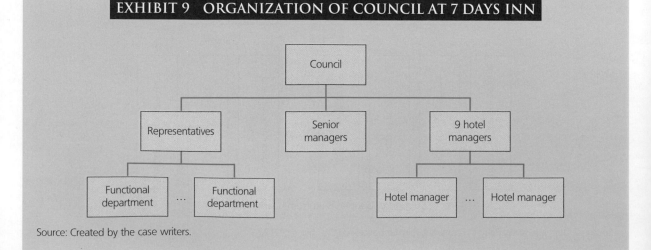

EXHIBIT 9   ORGANIZATION OF COUNCIL AT 7 DAYS INN

Source: Created by the case writers.

Through the council, hotel managers made many proposals that helped 7 Days Inn move forward.

Mergers and acquisitions

At the end of 2011, 7 Days Inn began a new move, that is, mergers and acquisitions of hotels. Considering that many hotel managers dreamed of being an entrepreneur, the company allowed good managers to acquire or merge with hotels of managers with bad operational performance. The acquisitions were done through bidding. With this policy, a hotel manager with a good record could place a bid on target hotels in the same region. A hotel manager who managed a hotel with few rooms was also qualified to place a bid on other hotels. In the bidding process, the base unit was 1 per cent of the profit that the hotel made in the previous year; the maximum bidding price was 9 per cent. The hotel manager who won a bid would take over the target hotel. As human resources were limited, normally the manager would retain all the staff of the target hotel and would not make considerable changes to their positions.

How to operate the target hotel was a serious challenge for the winning manager, who would need to think over post-merger integration and standardization of services. It was observed that the capability and working experience of the manager, as well as the location of the hotel, influenced the performance of the hotel. The cooperation of hotels within a region was also affected by mergers and acquisitions.

By 2011, shepherd management had been carried out for more than four years. Motivated by the management philosophy, many hotel managers ran the hotels as their own business and were devoted to working actively. In the review of employee engagement by Aon Hewitt,[10] 7 Days Inn received a score of 75. A score of 60 or higher indicated a best employer, and the average score of hotels in the industry was 55.

However, shepherd management had its ups and downs in practice. In an executive meeting of operations management, Tongmin discussed his serious concerns. He was worried about the misunderstanding of the shepherd management philosophy by many staff, including some hotel managers and middle and senior managers, who often reverted to the traditional operating model. For example, for a short period, the sales department went back to the traditional model of hierarchical management. It assigned a sales task to a regional archon; the archon then separated the task into sub-tasks and assigned them to hotels in the region. At the same time, the archon set up an administration organization to push the hotel managers to work on the sales target. Similar situations occurred in other departments. For example, some departments gave orders to archons about budget, quota and so on. This is the opposite of what 7 Days Inn expected from hotel managers. Hotel managers should proactively work on their hotels' affairs rather than taking orders from headquarters. Because the shepherd management philosophy was not deeply rooted in everyone's mind, its measures were harder to achieve. More importantly, when hotel managers could not reach the expected outcomes by implementing the measures, they started to waver in their faith in the philosophy.

The future

Until now, Nanyan had been guiding how and where 7 Days Inn would proceed in the future. What would happen to the growth of 7 Days Inn when he began focusing instead on the initiation and operations of the new high-end hotel chain? Could Yuezhou, newly appointed as the CEO of 7 Days Inn, keep the company growing as much as Nanyan had done and come up with solutions for the problems with a different order of priority?

In the past few years, the resignation of hotel managers had gone up to 30 per cent, resulting in a growing pressure on daily operations as the company continued to expand. Yuezhou had many concerns: was the resignation rate within the normal range? Was it related to the mergers and acquisitions policy? Did the policy bring too much pressure to bear on hotel managers? While one objective of shepherd management was to eliminate some sick sheep (i.e., incompetent hotel managers), was the resignation rate a normal consequence of this policy?

Currently, the authorization system included hotel managers only, which meant that headquarters did not directly control hotel managers, while an individual hotel was still managed through bureaucracy. 7 Days Inn called this "aristocratic democracy." Yuezhou wondered whether the staff of a hotel should be included in the authorization system. If so, what would be the benefits and the obstacles?

When the rental cost of property rose after the 2008 financial crisis, the company had difficulty keeping its high profit margin. Many investors were complaining

---

[10]Aon Hewitt is a leading global provider of human capital consulting; www.aon.com, accessed September 30, 2012.

that 7 Days Inn didn't fulfill the promise it made when they became franchisees. As the CEO of a Chinese company that went public overseas, Yuezhou should thoroughly think about how to keep the stability of the stock price and how to attract more investment while at the same time meeting higher expectations from investors.

In the era of 1,000 hotels, Yuezhou noticed the obvious inefficiency of management and supervision. Was it necessary to make some changes to the

shepherd management philosophy? After all, when 7 Days Inn came up with the idea of shepherd management, there were only 30 hotels in operation, not more than 1,000. No model works forever. Did this mean that the company had to break the rules again and make innovations to its business model, operations strategy and operating model – or to all of them? It would be a huge challenge for Yuezhou and 7 Days Inn, no matter what decision was made.

Bel: Inventing new horizons for the family firm

By Anne-Catrin Glemser

PARIS, JUNE 2012. For Antoine Fiévet, CEO of Groupe Bel, the times were, to say the least, challenging. As one of the world leaders in branded cheese, with sales in excess of €2.5 billion and a presence in more than 120 countries, Groupe Bel had been hard-hit by the global financial crisis and a dramatic increase in its raw material prices. Now was the time for creative answers, even possibly the time to revisit some fundamental principles on which the family fortune had been built. For years, the Group had strived to push its limits geographically, becoming a dominant market player in many emerging and frontier economies. But a recent product introduction in Vietnam was even more radical. The strategy team there had just introduced GOODI, a new rice-and-milk nutritional bar targeting consumers at the bottom of the pyramid. Everything about this opportunity was new for Bel: It was the first product in the company's history that was not made mainly out of milk, it targeted unconventional market segments, carried a strong corporate social responsibility (CSR) message and was launched through novel distribution channels. And although Bel had been selling cheese in Vietnam since the 1950s, it only launched its first Asian production facility there in 2011.

The nutritional milk snack was a revolution. But was this new product in line with Bel's biggest asset, its core brand "La vache qui rit" ("The Laughing Cow")? Pursuing "growth with purpose" was certainly important, but was this bottom-of-the-pyramid approach sustainable? How much would Bel learn from this initiative, and how much would translate to other markets and products? Was GOODI the sign of things to come for Bel, the catalyst the firm was looking for to prod

employees and shareholders to "think differently" about the business model that had served it well for almost 150 years? Or was it too far from the company's core value proposition, exposing the brand to unjustifiable risk? How would this play out in an environment in which the Group already had to cope with some of the highest milk prices ever seen and political trouble in some of its key emerging markets, like Egypt, Libya and Syria? Was it time to take more risk or to adopt a more conservative approach?

How can you govern a nation that has 246 varieties of cheese?

— Charles de Gaulle, 1962

For the French, cheese – or *fromage* as they call it – has always occupied a special place in people's lives, in both urban and rural areas, and across all levels of society. Cheese goes beyond nutrition: It embodies a philosophy of life, combining regionalism with deeply held traditions. In 2009, with consumption in excess of 26 kg per year per inhabitant (second only to Greece with 31 kg), cheese was the most prominent dairy product consumed in France, representing close to 7% of a family's typical food budget and more than 40% of its dairy budget.[1]

By 2012, France produced at least 300 different varieties of cheese, 43 of which had received official AOP[2] status. Local cheese specialties were regarded as highly as wines, both of which were much in demand throughout the world.

The origins of fromageries bel

Jules Bel (1842–1904) founded the family business in 1865, in the Jura region of France, near the Swiss

Research Associate Anne-Catrin Glemser prepared this case under the supervision of Professor Benoît Leleux, S. Schmidheiny Professor of Entrepreneurship and Finance, as a basis for class discussion rather than to illustrate either effective or ineffective handling of a business situation.

Bel was the winner of the 2012 IMD-Lombard Odier Global Family Business Award, presented at the 2012 FBN Summit in London.

[1]Source: CNIL and www.statisticbrain.com/cheese-statistics/
[2]Appellation d'Origine Protégée.

border. As a refiner, he took care of the aging of the local cooperative's cheeses and, once they were mature, managed the sales process. His son Léon Bel (1878–1957, 2nd gen.) developed a melted soft cheese by blending comté and emmental with other cheese varieties. The result was a soft, easy-to-mold cheese which, since it had been cooked, also offered a long shelf life outside the cold chain. Until the 20th century cheese production was mainly artisanal, local and imbued with tradition. The raw materials and ingredients – such as the type of milk, the bacteria used and the flavorings added – along with the aging time would determine the texture, taste and color of a cheese. The introduction of a new cheese was a momentous event. When Léon Bel launched his first manufactured product in 1921, he also pioneered new marketing approaches and new ways of consuming cheese, which revolutionized the industry. Not only was it the first branded cheese product registered in the French market, marketed under the evocative La vache qui rit brand but it was also, from 1924, sold in innovative small triangular portions, or wedges.

It all started with The Laughing Cow

In the early days the cow was not red and did not wear any earrings (*refer to* **Exhibit 1**). But in 1923, Benjamin Rabier, a famous French illustrator, used the distinguishing elements that Léon Bel had invented to load the brand with personality and add to its uniqueness. Distinctive packaging and memorable advertising campaigns contributed to building brand equity. The original illustration continued to be gently modified and modernized, evolving into a simplified graphic symbol yet still maintaining consistency in the brand building. The creative and at times unconventional advertising campaigns were always in touch with consumer trends and kept the brand "top of mind" for consumers. In 2011 the red lady celebrated her 90th anniversary. She had become an instantly recognizable, iconic brand translated into many languages and marketed in 120 countries, finding her way to the hearts of children and mothers around the world. About 10 million portions were consumed every day, or some 4,600 triangles every minute.

Growing up and going places

In 1929 Léon Bel started exporting cheese products to the UK and opened Bel's first foreign production plant. In 1936 Léon's son-in-law Robert Fiévet (1908–2002, 3rd gen.) joined the company and a year later became its CEO. Robert led the Group through the next 60 years of successful growth and expansion into new geographies and markets, as well as steering the launch of a series of new brands to make the company one of the leading cheese producers worldwide and the global leader in branded cheese. The company successfully introduced new brands such as Babybel in 1952, Apericube in the late 1950s and Kiri in the 1960s. It also set up production facilities in Germany and Spain. The expansion continued outside Western Europe, with entries into the US and Moroccan markets as early as the 1970s.

By 2011 Bel had an exceptional global footprint, in particular in frontier regions[3] such as the Middle East and Africa. To serve the region it established production sites in Morocco, Algeria, Egypt, Syria, Turkey and Iran. Since 2003 it had enjoyed double digit increases in sales each year on the African continent, while volumes in the Middle East had doubled, confirming the validity of Bel's pioneering engagement in these markets for over 45 years.

Not as mild as you might think:[4] Growth in emerging and frontier markets

It took courage and entrepreneurial vision for Bel to shift from an export model to one of "localization," i.e. adapting products to suit local tastes and producing locally. In Algeria, the shift happened as early as 2003. Following a failed attempt to partner with a local contract manufacturer, Bel established a production facility there in 2005 with an adapted local offer. The safety (thanks to UHT technology[5]), freshness, high quality, differentiated taste, neutral smell and pleasant texture of the product, coupled with the development of a reliable distribution network, caused turnover to quadruple and market share to double between 2005 and 2011. In Algiers, a fairly cosmopolitan city, Bel went a step further and introduced a direct sales delivery service.

In Syria, Bel built its first factory in 2005, becoming the country's first non-oil European investor.

---

[3]Also known as pre-emerging markets, frontier markets are less advanced capital markets in the developing world.
[4]Advertising slogan of the Dutch Leerdammer semi-hard cheese business acquired by Bel in 2002.
[5]Ultra-high temperature processing (UHT) is the sterilization of food by heating it for a short period, around 1 or 2 seconds, at a temperature exceeding 135°C (275°F), which is the temperature required to kill spores in milk. UHT milk has a typical shelf life of six to nine months.

EXHIBIT 1 THE LAUGHING COW PACKAGING AND BRAND 1921–2011

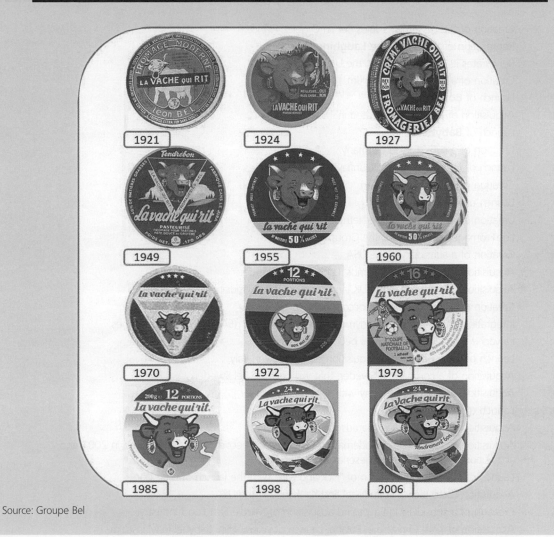

Source: Groupe Bel

When the uprising against President Assad began in March 2011, Bel's biggest concern was to ensure its employees' safety. When the situation deteriorated further in the summer of 2012, the factory in Damascus was temporarily shut down. Bel also closed its factory in Egypt for a couple of weeks in 2011. The company's growth rate in the Arab countries was challenged not only by the "Arab Spring" but also by emerging local competitors like Almarai,[6] the largest integrated dairy food company in the Gulf region, which began offering cream cheese alongside the Middle Eastern favorites of feta and mozzarella.

Through international development, Bel aimed to grow sales outside Western Europe to 50% of overall sales and to combine organic growth, i.e. the expansion of core portfolio brands into new geographies, with a series of strategic acquisitions in either new cheese category markets or new geographies (*refer to Exhibit 2*). Among the most recent acquisitions was, for example, the €190 million purchase of the Dutch Leerdammer business in 2002, which allowed Bel to enter the semi-hard cheese segment. Another was the acquisition in 2007 of Unilever's Boursin – a fresh, spreadable cream cheese – in a deal worth €400 million.

[6]Almarai was established in the Kingdom of Saudi Arabia in 1976 as a partnership between the Irish agri-foods pioneer Alastair McGuckian, along with his brother Paddy, and HH Prince Sultan bin Mohammed bin Saud Al Kabeer. Numerous agricultural projects were launched, including one with fresh milk production from over 70,000 cows. In 2011, the product portfolio included yogurts and desserts, cheese, butter and cream, as well as juices and bakery and poultry products. www.almarai.com.

EXHIBIT 2   BEL GROWTH AND ACQUISITION MILESTONES, TIMELINE 1921–2011

1865:	Creation of "Etablissements Jules Bel" in Orgelet, France.
1921:	Registration of the brand **The Laughing Cow**®.
1929:	Bel creates its first subsidiary in the UK.
1933:	Creation of a subsidiary in Belgium.
1947:	Launch of **Bonbel**.
1950:	Acquisition of **Port Salut**, created in 1816.
1952:	Launch of **Babybel**®.
1959:	Creation of a subsidiary in Germany.
1960:	Launch of **La vache qui rit**® unflavored cocktail cubes.
1965:	Creation of a subsidiary in Spain.
1966:	Launch of **Kiri**®.
1967:	Creation of a subsidiary in the Netherlands.
1968:	Les Fromageries Picon joins the Group.
1970:	Creation of a subsidiary in the USA.
1972:	Acquisition of the company Samos. Launch of **Sylphide**.
1973:	Acquisition of Crowson in the UK, and creation of a subsidiary in Switzerland.
1974:	Creation of a subsidiary in Morocco.
1976:	Integration of the "Société anonyme des fermiers réunis" (SAFR) and its subsidiaries.
1976:	La vache qui rit® cocktail cubes become **Apéricube**®.
1977:	Launch of **Mini Babybel**®, acquisition of company in Italy.
1978:	Acquisition of a company in Sweden that will become Bel Sweden.
1989:	Acquisition of Adler in Germany with becomes Bel Adler.
1990:	Launch of **Mini Bonbel**.
1991:	Acquisition of the company Maredsous in Belgium.
1994:	Acquisition of the company Cademartori in Italy which becomes Bel Cademartori in 2001 and acquisition of the company Queserías Ibéricas in Spain.
1995:	Launch of **Pik & Croq**. Creation of "Pick and Mix" with the launch of 6 au Choix.
1996:	Acquisition Lacto Ibérica in Portugal and Kaukauna in the USA.
1998:	Creation of a subsidiary in Egypt and acquisition of Middle East Food Industry.
	Acquisition of Kraft Chorzele in Poland. Launch of yellow Mini Babybel in Maasdam.
2000:	Acquisition of Zeletavska Syrarna in the Czech Republic and of Zempmilk in Slovakia.
2001:	Creation of a subsidiary in Algeria.
2002:	Acquisition of the assets Merkts and Owl's Nest by Bel Kaukauna in the USA.
	Acquisition of Syrokrem in Slovakia. Creation of subsidiaries in Greece and in Tunisia.
	Termination of SAFR's soft cheese production. Acquisition of the companies in the Dutch **Leerdammer**® Group and its European subsidiaries based in Germany, France, Italy, the United Kingdom, Belgium and the Czech Republic.
2003:	Termination of activities of Manchego of the Bel subsidiary Queserías Ibéricas.
2005:	Termination of activities carried out under the Cademartori brand. Creation of a subsidiary in Syria.
2006:	Creation of a subsidiary in Canada and creation of a subsidiary in Turkey.
2007:	Acquisition of **Boursin**® from Unilever – Creation of the subsidiary in Ukraine – Acquisition of Gervais in Czech Republic – Acquisition of Rouzaneh® in Iran
2010:	Introduction of new corporate design and logo.
2011:	€90 million investment in Mini Babybel production in Dakota, USA. First Bel production site established in SEA, Vietnam; launch of the GOODI test pilot.

Source: Groupe Bel

The US as an emerging market

The acquisition of a few local US brands (notably from Nestlé) in the late 1990s allowed Bel to build a solid platform for growth. The US market was something of a paradox for Bel, offering both enormous growth opportunities and phenomenal challenges. Americans consumed mostly cheddar and mozzarella cheese, not Bel specialties. But cheese consumption and product variety were steadily increasing as a result of new consumption habits, which saw people enjoying more ready-meals and ethnic cooking.

For Bel, the country was an "emerging market"[7] with enormous growth potential. But adapting the brands to local tastes and consumption habits was key to ensuring strong penetration of its core brands. For example, a light version of The Laughing Cow cheese was introduced in the US market in the late 1990s. This new version suited the convenience lifestyle and individualism of the American consumer, as well as catering to a new awareness of healthy eating. Demand for the triangular wedge ultimately exploded when the famous South Beach Diet recommended that it be consumed daily.[8]

Market leadership

By 2011 Bel employed more than 11,400 people and generated sales in excess of $3.07 billion,[9] an increase of 4.5% on 2010 figures (*refer to Exhibit 3*). Bel's main asset was its exceptional portfolio of leading cheese brands, including five global leaders, namely Boursin, Leerdammer, Mini Babybel, Kiri and La vache qui rit. Each of these umbrella brands branched out in many line extensions. With an additional 8 international and 17 national brands (*refer to Exhibit 4*), Fromageries Bel was world leader with its branded cheese portfolio and ranked third in branded cheese sales worldwide. Its international brands accounted for 75% of the company's sales. Bel products were manufactured in 27 production plants, located on all five continents, and reached nearly 400 million consumers

in 120 countries. In France the company was the third-largest cheese producer, after Lactalis[10] and Bongrain, which concentrated on pressed and molded cheese varieties. All three firms were family-owned and controlled and accounted for over half of the total cheese sales in the country. Bel had captured over 75% of the melted cheese segment.

In addition, the Bel Foodservices division offered a wide range of cheese portions for social catering, a line of cheese ingredients for ready-cooked dishes, and a line aimed at commercial catering.[11] Jean-Thierry Dufort (1965, 5th gen.), who had been responsible for this business in Western Europe since 2005, turned it into a substantial and profitable activity, growing it by 60% to reach a turnover of about $125 million[12] in 2011, with double digit percentage increases in three key countries: France, Belgium and Germany.[13] Another business division of strategic relevance for the Group was Bel Industries, which produced dairy proteins that were sold to food manufacturers of, for example, ice cream and yogurt products. Bel Industries exported 60% of its production to 50 different countries, and its leading brand "Nollibel" had become the world leader in this market segment.

Family ownership and leadership

Fromageries Bel became a public company, listed on the Paris stock exchange, in the 1940s. The owners also established a holding company in 1921, an entity that was also publicly listed in the 1940s; since 1970 it had operated under the name Unibel. In 2011 Unibel held 67.4% of Fromageries Bel SA, the main operating entity, with another 3.84% held directly by the family. Effectively family ownership thus stood at 71.24% (*refer to Exhibit 5*). The family owners behind Unibel counted 21 shareholders from the fourth, fifth and sixth generations of the original Bel family, belonging to the three branches – the Sauvin, Fiévet and Dufort families – which each owned one-third of the Unibel capital and voting shares.

[7]Interview Antoine Fiévet, CEO Fromageries Bel, 17.07.2012, Paris.

[8]In the 1980s cardiologist Arthur Agatston designed the South Beach Diet plan as an alternative to low-fat approaches to weight loss. The original purpose of the diet was to prevent heart disease; in the early 2000s, word of the diet spread and it quickly gained popularity as a way of losing weight.

[9]€2.53 billion.

[10]In 2011 Lactalis employed 52,000 people and owned 198 industrial sites worldwide. After the acquisition of 83.3% of the Italian dairy leader Parmalat in the same year, it had become the world's 1st dairy group, the 15th largest agri-food group worldwide and claimed to be Europe's leading milk collector. http://www.lactalis.com.

[11]http://www.belfoodservice.com/bel-foodservice-out-of-home-activity.php.

[12]About €100 million.

[13]Correspondence Francis Le Cam, Vice-President Fromageries Bel, 23.07.2012, Paris.

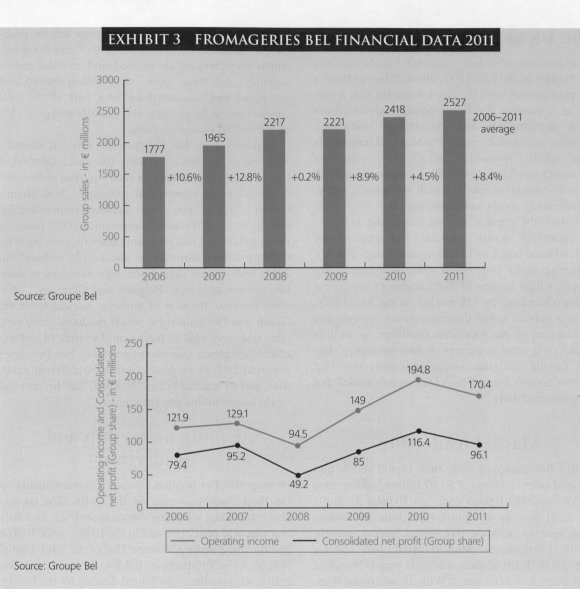

EXHIBIT 3   FROMAGERIES BEL FINANCIAL DATA 2011

Source: Groupe Bel

Source: Groupe Bel

The fourth generation entered the family-owned company in the 1960s and began working alongside Robert's right-hand man Philippe Deloffre,[14] general manager between 1963 and 1986. Robert's son Claude (1935–1977, 4th gen.) and his son-in-law Bertrand Dufort (1940, 4th gen.) entered the operative business at the same time. Both were groomed to take over the leadership of the firm and were formally appointed as vice-presidents. Tragically, Claude died in an accident in 1977 at the age of 41, leaving Bertrand as the successor in-the-making. Robert, however, remained Bel's president for another 20 years. From 1996 to 2001, Bertrand led the operating company as CEO but Robert stayed involved with the business, even into his 90s. Somehow, he felt that his long-prepared succession plan did not take into

[14]Philippe Deloffre has served as a permanent representative of Unibel SA on the board of directors of Fromageries Bel SA since June 27, 2001 and is also chairman of the company's Audit Committee. He worked as a director of sales [OR sales director] for 13 years and then as managing director of various Groupe Bel subsidiaries for around 21 years. At age 92, he was still, in his role of nonexecutive board member, a "discreet and trusted advisor to Antoine Fiévet." Gille de Bure. *C'est une vache, Elle rit....* Edition Nicolas Chaudun, Paris 2008.

EXHIBIT 4   BEL BRAND PORTFOLIO 2011

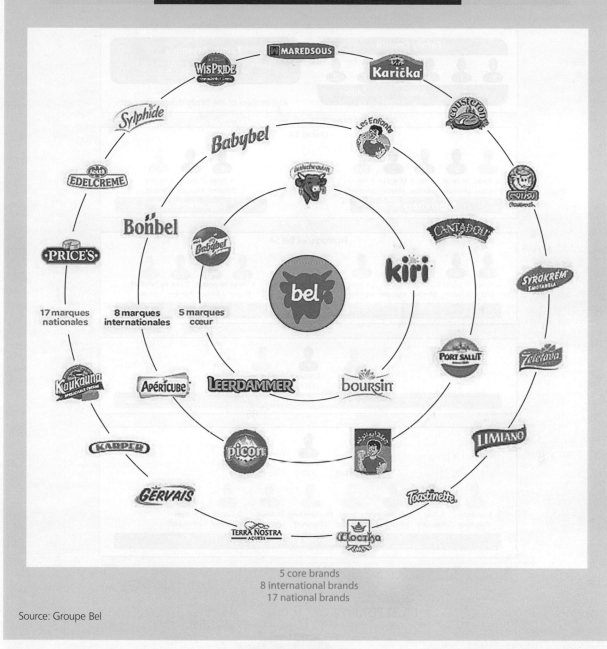

17 marques
nationales

8 marques
internationales

5 marques
coeur

5 core brands
8 international brands
17 national brands

Source: Groupe Bel

account the speed with which the economic landscape was changing or reflect the impact globalization would have on the Group. In 2001 Robert aligned the shareholding families behind the idea of professionalizing the executive leadership by assigning the CEO role to a non-family executive, Gérard Boivin. Bertrand stepped down for the greater good of the company, but the decision left a deep crack in the trust of his family branch.

The industry

The food industry was complex and highly competitive. Bel faced strong players in all segments, from big multinationals like Kraft Foods, Bongrain and Lactalis as well as from many local and regional champions. The market shares of the European cheese manufacturers had been relatively stable since the turn of the century (*refer to Exhibit 6*), but the industry had

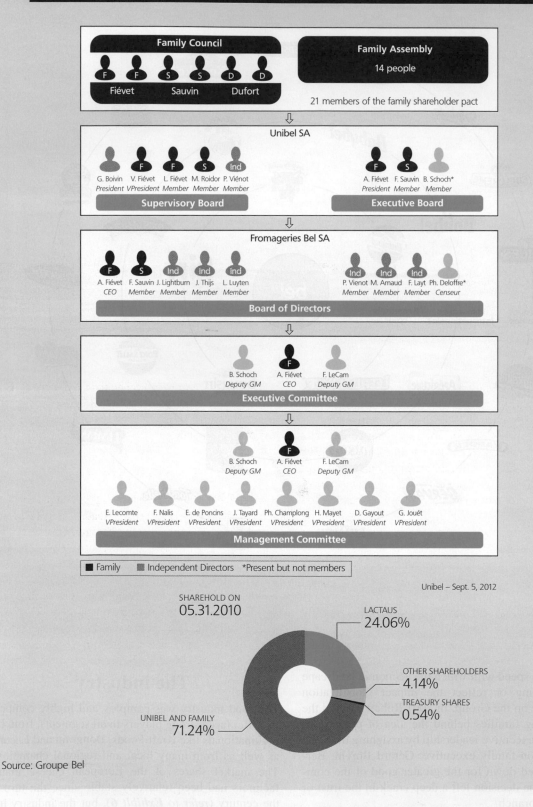

EXHIBIT 5   BEL FAMILY GOVERNANCE AND OWNERSHIP STRUCTURE

Family Council
F F S S D D
Fiévet   Sauvin   Dufort

Family Assembly
14 people

21 members of the family shareholder pact

Unibel SA

G. Boivin — *President*
V. Fiévet — *VPresident* (F)
L. Fiévet — *Member* (F)
M. Roidor — *Member* (S)
P. Viénot — *Member* (Ind)

Supervisory Board

A. Fiévet — *President* (F)
F. Sauvin — *Member* (S)
B. Schoch* — *Member*

Executive Board

Fromageries Bel SA

A. Fiévet — *CEO* (F)
F. Sauvin — *Member* (S)
J. Lightburn — *Member* (Ind)
J. Thijs — *Member* (Ind)
L. Luyten — *Member* (Ind)

P. Vienot — *Member* (Ind)
M. Amaud — *Member* (Ind)
F. Layt — *Member* (Ind)
Ph. Deloffre* — *Censeur*

Board of Directors

B. Schoch — *Deputy GM*
A. Fiévet — *CEO* (F)
F. LeCam — *Deputy GM*

Executive Committee

B. Schoch — *Deputy GM*
A. Fiévet — *CEO* (F)
F. LeCam — *Deputy GM*

E. Lecomte — *VPresident*
F. Nalis — *VPresident*
E. de Poncins — *VPresident*
J. Tayard — *VPresident*
Ph. Champlong — *VPresident*
H. Mayet — *VPresident*
D. Gayout — *VPresident*
G. Jouét — *VPresident*

Management Committee

■ Family   ■ Independent Directors   *Present but not members

Unibel – Sept. 5, 2012

SHAREHOLD ON
05.31.2010

LACTAUS **24.06%**
OTHER SHAREHOLDERS **4.14%**
TREASURY SHARES **0.54%**
UNIBEL AND FAMILY **71.24%**

Source: Groupe Bel

EXHIBIT 6   TOP 10 CHEESE COMPETITORS – 2011 CHEESE ONLY – VOLUMES (KT)

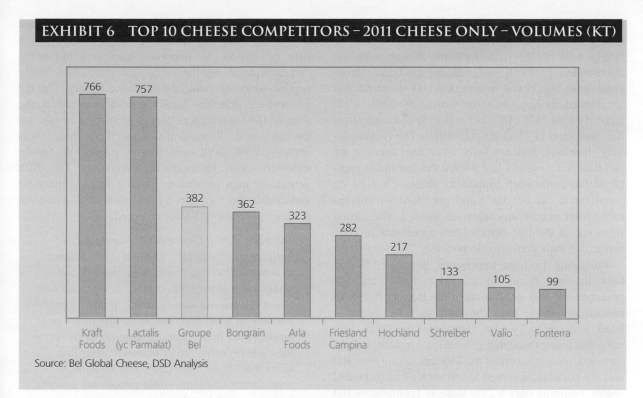

Source: Bel Global Cheese, DSD Analysis

experienced significant shifts. In particular, the manufacturing, processing and distribution of food products were subject to increasingly stringent food regulations.[15] This had an impact on ingredients and composition as well as on the labeling and packaging of cheese products. The competitive landscape was made even more treacherous by the increasing power wielded by international food retailers as they moved into private labels,[16] putting additional pressure on margins and shelf space. By 2011 the global cheese market was mature, competitive and increasingly exposed to volatile raw material markets. The margins had come under pressure due to higher milk prices, the result of higher demand for milk powder from fast-growing markets such as China which increasingly complemented its local milk supply with imported product. Higher raw material prices, combined with growing but more uncertain demand, resulted in greater volatility and exploding costs for milk in 2011,

with prices three times higher than expected.[17] Even with aggressive measures, Bel's operating profits were impacted (*refer to* **Exhibit 3**), which called for innovative solutions.

The "Affaire Bel"

Back in the early '90s, Bel's biggest competitor, Lactalis, had become the market leader in pressed and molded cheese segments in the French market. The company was fully owned and controlled by the Besnier family. In 1992 – as part of an aggressive strategy to grow through acquisitions – Michel Besnier (1928–2000, 2nd gen.) began accumulating shares in Unibel and Fromageries Bel, shares he acquired either from investment funds or directly on the stock market. By 1996 Besnier had collected 16% of Fromageries Bel shares and 25% of Unibel shares. Concerned by the possibility of a hostile takeover, Robert Fiévet and

[15] Regulatory Agencies such as the US Food and Drug Administration (FDA) define standards that require all food businesses to implement food safety systems to ensure food is safe to consume.

[16] Private labels throughout the EU account for about 18% market share on average. The cheese categories of cheddar, gouda and emmental have the highest level of private labels. Unlike most of its competitors, Bel had decided back in the 1980s not to enter this business but to focus on its own brands.

[17] The margins for fresh cheese and yogurt products were much higher than for processed cheese, which needed between 10 and 11 liters of milk to produce 1 kg of cheese, compared with 3 or 4 liters needed to produce 1 kg of fresh cheese. At Bel the cost of milk as the main raw material ingredient represented over 55% of overall production costs.

Bertrand Dufort started working on designing a new family shareholders agreement that would secure the family hold on the firm. In 2000, though, with the shareholders pact still unsigned and the family struggling with succession issues, Lactalis pounced and accelerated its acquisition of shares; by 2001, it effectively held 28% of Unibel and 23% of Fromageries Bel, just short of blocking minorities. The Besnier family, however, had not fully taken into account the fact that Bel's owners had pooled the remaining capital of the partnership limited by shares ("société en commandite par actions") and presented an impregnable front against any takeover attempt. The formal signature of the Bel shareholders agreement in 2001 confirmed their unassailable position.[18]

Following this tense experience, Bel started buying back its own shares on the open market and approached the next generation of the Besnier family to investigate buying back the stake they had accumulated. It was a lucky coincidence that the Besnier family was going through a generational transition of its own and, once it accepted the fact that taking over Bel was not possible, it agreed to sell back all of its Unibel shares, retaining only a 24% stake in Fromageries Bel as a non-controlling long-term investment.

Looking forward: The fifth generation's approach

The family had always been passionate about the business. The early accidental death of Claude Fiévet, one of the potential fourth generation leaders, had taught the family the importance of a well-structured governance model and early succession planning. Valentine Fiévet (1962, 5th gen.) was only 15 years old when her father died. As the oldest child of the fifth generation, she remembered vividly how unprepared she and her mother felt, despite support provided by grandparents, aunts and uncles. At the time information was scarce, ownership education limited, and structures and processes were lacking. With the help of François Bel (1931–2007, 3rd gen.) and Catherine Sauvin (1944, 4th gen.) in their roles as partners or board members, a clear governance model was established, with extensive seminars for family members to learn about the business, the ownership and the family heritage. Antoine pointed out:

> Getting out of the branch spirit and thinking as ONE family is an important challenge for the next generations.

In 2009 the fourth generation decided to proactively step back and hand over responsibility to the fifth generation, an important step to avoid being "taken hostage" by the succession issue. The family needed unity to grow the business further. On the governance side, the family council, created at the time of the shareholders pact, was revised to take on the spirit of a "Wise Men's" council. At first, it was composed of third and fourth generation family members, with balanced representation. The fifth generation then pleaded to make it more democratic and double the members by including representatives from its generation. Valentine noted:

> The main rule – Business 1st, Family 2nd, Individual 3rd – helped us build a governance structure without a "branch mentality" and transform it slowly into a more democratic one. Given the natural demographic, it would not be possible to have everyone at the top in the near future, so we had to build a structure and choose the right representatives whatever their last name was. More objectivity, less emotion, competence and time would smooth the process from one model to the next.

In the operating company, the fifth generation was very present: Antoine Fiévet assumed the CEO position in 2009, his cousin Jean-Thierry Dufort (1965, 5th gen.) ran the Bel Foodservice division, and Florian Sauvin (1979, 5th gen.) at Unibel headed the Bel Access division, which focused on researching and promoting tomorrow's business models.

Succession

When, in 2008, the board began reflecting on the corporate governance and global organization of the Group, they decided to appoint Antoine as non-executive chairman. They also asked the HR committee to begin the search for an external CEO and decided that Antoine would be interim CEO if a suitable candidate had not been found by the end of Gérard Boivin's mandate in May 2009. Antoine suggested to the board and then to the family that he take on the CEO role, but for the family this was an unexpected move and they did not agree, since some family shareholders thought they were being rushed into a decision.

Just before Gérard stepped down, the external CEO candidate who had been identified unexpectedly declined the offer, so Antoine became the interim CEO. He then asked the board and the family to turn this into

---

[18]The shareholders pact, which pooled all the family shares, was renewed in 2006, confirming family unity behind the business.

a full CEO mandate, at least for some time, so he would become a better chairman later, equipped with an in-depth knowledge of the business. The family agreed to a two-year mandate, which was extended for an additional three years in 2011, but with a clear requirement that alternative external candidates would be proposed after this.

As chairman and CEO, Antoine was committed to being as transparent as possible; he was also keen on building trust and strengthening relationships within the family.

*It is important for us to offer possibilities to all family members to be in touch with the Bel heritage and to get them involved in different ways, even outside the formal business roles. We regularly hold family meetings on family matters for example about the family mansion in the south of France which is managed by my cousin Marion.[19] And between 2008 and 2010, we have created opportunities for the current and the still very young next generation shareholders and family members to stay close to the heritage and identity of Groupe Bel by setting up the Bel Foundation; The Home of the Laughing Cow, run by 4th generation member Catherine Sauvin; and the Lab'Bel Art Laboratory, led by Laurent Fiévet (5th gen.) (refer to **Exhibit 7**). We also regularly visit company production sites and affiliates in order to learn about the business or participate to events like the sailing ones.[20]*

EXHIBIT 7   HOME OF THE LAUGHING COW, BEL FOUNDATION AND LAB'BEL ART

La Maison de La vache qui rit® (The Laughing Cow® House) opened its doors on May 21, 2009, in Lons-le-Saunier, France. The idea was initiated by Catherine Sauvin (4th gen.) who wanted to share the rich heritage of the family business with the wider public. Visitors can learn about the brand and its values of conviviality, humor and innovation, which characterize the many advertising campaigns that have contributed to its popularity.
http://www.lamaisondelavachequirit.com

Lab'Bel is Bel's Art Laboratory, inaugurated in the spring of 2010, and sponsored by the Group and its main shareholder, Unibel. Heading up Lab'Bel was the visual artist Laurent Fiévet, (5th gen.) a member of the Bel family whose video works have been the subject of numerous exhibitions and events, and Silvia Guerra, an art critic and exhibition curator.

Lab'Bel, Bel's art laboratory was initiated by the family shareholders in the early 2000s. Whereas in the past, family members were raised with the concept that only one person per branch could work for the group, preferably at its head, the family now wanted to included and use the skills of more talented family members. The idea of the Lab conciliated the desire to build a contemporary art collection and set up exhibitions and art events (that could be held or not at the Maison de la vache qui rit) blending together the story of the company, which has always been open to talented artists since its origins, and the values defended inside and outside the Bel Group of being a humorous, differentiating, unconventional, surprising, daring and audacious entity.
http://www.lab-bel.com

Bel's Corporate Foundation was created in May 2008 by the Bel Group and its reference shareholder, Unibel.

---

[19]Marion Roidor (1975, 5th gen.) belongs to the Sauvin branch.
[20]Interview Antoine Fiévet, CEO Fromageries Bel, 17.07.2012, Paris. Since 2005, Bel has sponsored skipper Kito de Pavant in yacht races. The Group also uses its boat as a vessel for strengthening bonds and promoting team work among employees around the world, and has welcomed over 700 Bel apprentice sailors on board to sail alongside the skipper. For more information see www.sharingsmilestour.com/

The Bel Foundation acts on behalf of children and their well-being around the world by promoting a balanced diet and preserving the environment, as far as it is required for a healthy diet. Rather than supporting big initiatives, the Foundation has chosen to support a number of projects around the world.

How the foundation works

The Bel Corporate Foundation is led by two committees: the Board of Directors and the Selection and Project Follow-up Committee. The Board of Directors defines and guides the Foundation's strategy and examines funding applications twice a year. It is made up of representatives of the fifth generation of Bel and Unibel founders, employees and external experts. The Selection and Project Follow-up Committee, made up of employees and outside people, such as Antoine Fiévet's wife, analyses and selects projects that meet the Foundation's criteria throughout the year. The Selection and Project Follow-up Committee presents these projects to the Board of Directors, follows up on the projects that have been approved by the Board of Directors and ensures that they are implemented.

Source: http://www.fondation-bel.orghttp://www.fondation-bel.org

Say "Cheese": Working with brands

Four generations of passionate marketers and communicators from the owning families ensured that 4 Bel brands were among the top 12 global cheese brands in 2011.[21] The company continuously strived to balance product innovations and creative campaigns while preserving the strong brand equity and heritage of the laughing cow. A particularly telling example was the introduction of Mini Babybel's round, red wax packaging, which stimulated the consumption of cheese as a snack.

Although in the past the Group had drawn on M&A activities to acquire international brands, the focus was now on organic growth, driven by innovation and product development in existing markets. Bel's innovation relied on a deep understanding of emerging consumer trends, such as increasing health awareness which led to the development of reduced fat versions of its product lines. Bel also continuously invested in developing proprietary technologies such as sensory quality perception and assessment, food processing, and other techniques to enhance product quality. A pioneer in miniaturization, Bel aimed to make its brands "immediately recognizable thanks to their packaging, advertising, smile-eliciting flavors and taste for innovation." Bel brands built an emotional connection to consumers, who often remained loyal throughout their lives. For example, many adults still enjoyed Kiri, one of the first cheeses for children.

Other keys to success were the humorous and at times unconventional ad campaigns.

The Laughing Cow speaks Vietnamese: Bel's hub in Asia

Bel constantly pushed the limits on both products and markets, even in countries where it had long had a presence. In Vietnam, for example, a country with a strong French heritage dating from its colonial days, The Laughing Cow had been introduced to the country via the expat community. For the average consumer it was considered an expensive treat.

Processed and reconstituted cheese was the most popular type of cheese sold in Vietnam, and by 2011 it represented about 96% of sales.[22] The Laughing Cow had a market share of about 75% and achieved a compound annual growth rate (CAGR) in sales of 28% from 2006 to 2011. This type of cheese was enjoyed by customers from diverse social classes and backgrounds who frequently consumed it with the Vietnamese version of baguette bread.

Although Bel had strong brand awareness, consumers were not yet very "cheese minded" and not curious about trying other brands and products. The company needed to educate consumers on the health benefits of cheese consumption to sustain the momentum of the double-digit growth achieved in 2010/11.

Vietnam was an interesting market for other reasons, too. Its economy was growing fast – China was

[21]Company Profile: Fromageries Bel, 2.12.2011, www.marketline.com.
[22]"Passport: Cheese in Vietnam." Euromonitor, October 2011.

EXHIBIT 8   THE WORLD BANK: VIETNAM OVERVIEW

Vietnam is a development success story. Political and economic reforms (Doi Moi) launched in 1986 have transformed Vietnam from one of the poorest countries in the world, with per capita income below $100, to a lower middle income country within a quarter of a century with per capita income of $1,130 by the end of 2010. The ratio of population in poverty has fallen from 58% in 1993 to 14.5% in 2008, and most indicators of welfare have improved. Vietnam has already attained five of its ten original Millennium Development Goal targets and is well on the way to attaining two more by 2015.

Vietnam has been applauded for the equity of its development, which has been better than most other countries in similar situations. The country is playing a more visible role on the regional and global stage, having successfully chaired the 2009 Annual Meetings of the Boards of Governors of the World Bank Group and the IMF, and carried out the Chairmanship of the Association of South East Asian Nations (ASEAN) in 2010.

The Eleventh Congress of the Communist Party of Vietnam in January 2011 called for a more comprehensive approach to the country's renovation, decided to promote greater citizens' participation and unity within Vietnam, and to engage proactively in international integration. The Congress re-affirmed Vietnam's approach to state-led development, but also revised key policy documents to place greater emphasis on market processes and non-state ownership of economic assets.

The Socio-Economic Development Strategy (SEDS) 2011-2020 gives attention to structural reforms, environmental sustainability, social equity, and emerging issues of macroeconomic stability. It defines three "breakthrough areas": (i) promoting human resources/skills development (particularly skills for modern industry and innovation), (ii) improving market institutions, and (iii) infrastructure development. The overall goal is for Vietnam to lay the foundations for a modern, industrialized society by 2020.

Over the last quarter of a century, Vietnam's politics and society have gradually evolved towards greater openness and space for civil participation. The ability of the National Assembly to perform the role of a check and balance on the executive has strengthened. Despite this progress, greater openness and opportunity for citizens to participate in governance is needed to support Vietnam's long-term vision of becoming a modern industrialized society.

More recently, the conclusions of the October 2011 Communist Party Plenum recognized the need for economic restructuring and identified restructuring of public investment, of SOEs and the financial sector, as priorities for the next five years.

Source: http://www.worldbank.org/en/country/vietnam/overview

---

the only Asian economy that had grown faster since 2000.[23] Vietnam also had a relatively young and highly literate population of 90 million people, 32% of them under the age of 15.[24] A stable political environment made the country an attractive market for investors looking for emerging markets (*refer to* **Exhibit 8**). Bel's leadership team (*refer to* **Exhibit 9**) had picked up on these factors and had started working out how the company could grow its "foodprint" in Asia. The result was a two-pronged strategy. First, Bel opened its first cheese factory for Asia-Pacific in Vietnam in December 2011. Localizing production allowed the company to sell "con bô cuoi" ("laughing cow" in

Vietnamese) at a locally affordable price of less than $0.12 per piece. The country's geographic position also made it convenient for Bel to export products to other countries in the region, making Bel Vietnam the future hub for Southeast Asia and exports to Japan.

We aimed to turn the Vietnamese market into Bel's cradle in Asia![25]

Second, Bel began to stretch the product boundaries and explore different ways of doing business. Perhaps Vietnam could also provide an opportunity for the company to redefine its prime purpose. Enter the "GOODI Project"...

[23]www.mckinsey.com/insights/mgi/research/asia/sustaining_growth_in_vietnam.
[24]www.hsbc.com/1/2/emerging-markets/gbm/stories/vietnam-growth-rate.
[25]Interview Antoine Fiévet, CEO Fromageries Bel, 17.07.2012, Paris

EXHIBIT 9 FROMAGERIES BEL LEADERSHIP TEAM, 2012

Name	Age	Since	Current Position
Antoine Fiévet	48	2009	Chairman of the Board, Chief Executive Officer, Member of the Management Committee
Bruno Schoch	47	2008	Deputy CEO – Finance and Legal Affairs, Information Systems, Group Development and Bel Eastern Europe, Member of the Management Committee
Francis Le Cam		2012	Deputy Chief Executive Officer – Group Operations, Member of the Management Committee
Eric de Poncins			Vice President – Bel Americas and Asia Pacific, Member of the Management Committee
Denis Gayout		2012	Vice President – Marketing, Member of the Management Committee
Guillaume Jouet		2012	Vice President – Human Resources, Communication and CSR, Member of the Management Committee
Hubert Mayet		2006	Vice President – Group Industrial Operations, Member of the Management Committee
Frederic Nalis		2011	Vice President – Bel Great Africa, Member of the Management Committee
Joe Tayard		2011	Vice President – Beal Near and Middle East, Member of the Management Committee
Philippe Champlong		2012	Vice President Central Europe, Member of Management Committee
Etienne Lecomte		2012	Vice President Western Europe, Member of Management
Philippe Deloffre	92	2001	Director – Permanent Representative of Unibel SA
Pascal Viénot	64	2012	Independent Director Permanent Representative of Unibel SA
Florian Sauvin	33	2009	Director
Michel Arnaud	66	2009	Independent Director
James Lightburn	69	2007	Independent Director
Luc Luyten	67	2002	Independent Director
Johnny Thijs	60	2001	Independent Director
Fatine Layt		2012	Independent Director

Source: Groupe Bel

Daring to enter new dairy territories

Antoine had encouraged the strategy team to think differently, out of the box, developing business ideas that would pursue "growth with purpose." He was excited when he heard that the GOODI project, which he had initiated, was progressing and gaining momentum within the organization. Social responsibility was starting to make companies and individuals reconsider their attitude to the environment in general.

"Growth with a purpose" became a new aspiration for the company, which went beyond merely launching another product or brand. Antoine wanted Bel to become a more active player in emerging and developing countries in Asia and Africa to explore new business opportunities at the bottom of the pyramid, targeting the lower income consumer segments, while making a social impact. When the strategy team presented the fully developed opportunity to him in 2009, it fit the vision perfectly. The idea was to launch a snack product for children that would help combat malnutrition, still a serious problem in Vietnam.[26] From a strategic perspective, this project would become a pilot for other emerging markets and had the potential to increase the brand equity in many countries. This project went way beyond CSR – it was truly business development with a purpose.

GOODI was an affordable, nutritionally sound dairy-based product targeting low and middle income consumers. It would be produced locally and contain the daily dose of essential nutrients. Bel was committed to making a sustainable business out of it – the project would provide income and "well-being" for local communities and might also generate goodwill with local authorities. The Group would partner with GAIN, the Global Alliance for Improved Nutrition, which was already working alongside more than 600 companies in over 30 countries, to reach over 600 million people with nutritionally enhanced food products.[27] GAIN would provide technical assistance on the design, implementation and evaluation of nutrition programs in general and food fortification in particular.

"This project will challenge the way we do business across our value chain," noted Florian Sauvin when discussing it with other board members. It took the company three years from approval in 2008 to the launch of the test pilot in 2011, including product testing and industrialization of the production in leased factories. "We worked a bit like Steve Jobs when he started his business in a garage," smiled Pedro Fernandes.[28] Hosting this new endeavor under the umbrella brand of The Laughing Cow, which in 2011 still represented one quarter of overall Bel sales, also carried some risk. What if the project was a flop? Would it damage the image of The Laughing Cow? Antoine's response was simple:

We just have to make it right. The trust in our brand is such a big asset, we cannot play around with our DNA.

For the pilot, Bel planned to introduce the GOODI stick in three cities – in the south, the center and the north of the country. It was an affordable milk bar, with a retail price of VND 4,500 ($0.18 or €0.15) per unit. As Antoine explained:

GOODI is a hybrid product composed of rice, milk proteins and vitamins, enriched with micronutrients[29] providing Vietnamese children with optimal growth.

A number of issues had to be solved in the process, such as finding the right taste, controlling the cost of the final product and dealing with the tropical heat in the production and distribution chain. Distribution would be local, city-based and rely on traditional channels, supported by door-to-door sales and promotions, which would give Bel the opportunity to learn about the "sachet market" and the consumption habits of consumers at the lower end of the pyramid.

Beyond GOODI: Bel's new challenges

The first feedback after the GOODI test pilot in 2011 was promising but indicated more work was required to improve the product's taste to suit local palates, to extend the door-to-door sales system and to keep the costs in check. At the Group level, this project validated out-of-the-box thinking and new knowledge generation. In a way, GOODI went beyond pushing the limits in a frontier market: It embodied what it would take to reach Bel's ambitious goal of serving 1 billion customers by 2020. Implementation would be key. What did Bel need to do to respond to early pilot feedback? How could it ensure that GOODI could be rolled out nationwide and brought to other countries with similar profiles?

As Antoine pointed out, the owning families were standing strongly behind this vision and would continue "managing by horizons" not by quarterly results... convinced and passionate about sharing smiles with consumers around the world, who would keep wondering "Why is the Laughing Cow laughing?"

---

[26]www.wpro.who.int/vietnam/topics/nutrition/nutritionprojectvietnamwho/en/

[27]http://www.gainhealth.org/about-gain.

[28]Head of Bel Asia-Pacific and former Vice-President Marketing.

[29]Micronutrients, although only needed in minuscule amounts, are essential in order for the body to produce enzymes, hormones and other substances essential for proper growth and development. www.who.int/nutrition/topics/micronutrients/en/.

INDEX

3M, 444–6
Abegglen, J.C. and Stalk, G., 405
Abell, D., 121
Abernathy, W.J.
  and Clark, K., 220
  Utterback, J.M., 515
Ackoff, R., 121, 146, 346, 362, 554
Adler, N.J., 139
Adler, P.S. *et al*, 31, 34, 36
Adner, R. and Helfat, C.E., 31, 40, 101
Afghanistan, 610
African wars, 303–4
agenda setting, 341
Ala, M. and Cordeiro, W.P., 74
Albert, M., 137, 311
Aldrich, H.E., 394, 493, 503, 550
  and Fiol, C.M., 60, 498
Alkhafaji, A.F., 133
Allaire, Y. and Firsirotu, M., 361
Allison, G.T., 290, 347, 392, 553
Alvarez, S.A. and Busenitz, L.W., 101
Amabile, T.M., 347, 563
Amable, B., 138
ambidextrous organizations, 421–2
  managers, 430
  mastering evolutionary/revolutionary
      change, 428–30
  patterns in organization evolution, 422–3
  success syndrome/congruence as managerial
      trap, 427–8
  understanding patterns in organization
      evolution, 423–7
AMC, 530
Amit, R.
  and Livnat, 246
  and Schoemaker, P.J.H., 101, 220, 225
  and Zott, C., 180, 434
Amodio, D.M., 100
Ancona, D.G. and Nadler, D.A., 38, 39
Anderson, P. and Tushman, M.L., 402
Andrews, K.R., 346
Anslinger, P.L. and Copeland, T.E., 246
Ansoff, H.I., 92, 146, 346, 352
  and McDonnell, E., 346, 351
Anthony, W.P. *et al*, 66
Antonov, 668–9
Aoki, M., 219

Apple, 529
  activities, 321
  change strategy, 425
Argyris, C., 221, 392, 394, 553
  and Schön, D., 38, 476
Aristotle, 73
Armour, H. and Teece, D.J., 86
Armstrong, J.S., 351
Arrow, K., 217
Arthur, W.B., 222, 298, 308, 393, 477, 498
  et al, 208
Ashby, F.G. *et al*, 95
assessment, 223–4, 341
  external, 341
  internal, 341–2
assets
  complementary, 221
  financial, 221
  institutional, 221
  market/structure, 221–2
  reconfiguring, 100–1
  reputational, 221
  structural, 221
  technological, 221
Astley, W.G. and Van der Ven, A.H., 499
Augier, M. and Teece, D.J., 100
Axelrod, R., 120, 292
Axelsson, B. and Easton, G., 296, 305

Baden-Fuller, C. and Stopford, J.M., 179, 391, 498, 505
Bain, J., 212, 497
Barber, H. *et al*, 376
Bargh, J.A.
  and Chartrand, T.L., 96
  and Ferguson, M.J., 96
Barnard, C.I., 31, 40, 41, 146
Barney, J.B., 92, 181, 190, 191, 215, 217, 563
Barr, P.S. *et al*, 94
Bartlett, C.A.
  et al, 307
  and Ghoshal, S., 86, 120, 386, 400, 594, 598,
      609, 634
Bass, B.M., 551
Bate, P., 399
Bateman, T.S. and Zeithaml, C.P., 92
Bateson, G., 329
Baum, A.C., and Singh, 493, 503